Fodor's 04

GREAT BRITAIN

D1508312

Where to Stay and Eat
for All Budgets

Must-See Sights
and Local Secrets

Ratings You Can Trust

Fodor's Travel Publications   New York, Toronto, London, Sydney, Auckland
www.fodors.com

FODOR'S GREAT BRITAIN 2004

Editor: Linda Cabasin

Editorial Production: Kristin Milavec
Editorial Contributors: Robert Andrews, Catherine Belonogoff, Jacqueline Brown, James Gracie, Satu Hummasti, Julius Honnor, Kate Hughes, Beth Ingpen, Shona Main, Roger Thomas, Alex Wijeratna
Maps: David Lindroth *cartographer;* Bob Blake and Rebecca Baer, *map editors*
Design: Fabrizio La Rocca, *creative director;* Guido Caroti, *art director;* Melanie Marin, *senior picture editor*
Production/Manufacturing: Lisa Montebello and Angela McLean
Cover Photo (Bakewell, Derbyshire): Catherine Karnow

COPYRIGHT

ISBN 1–4000–1261–9

ISSN 0071–6405

SPECIAL SALES

Fodor's Travel Publications are available at special discounts for bulk purchases for sales promotions or premiums. Special editions, including personalized covers, excerpts of existing guides, and corporate imprints, can be created in large quantities for special needs. For more information, contact your local bookseller or write to Special Markets, Fodor's Travel Publications, 1745 Broadway, New York, NY 10019. Inquiries from Canada should be directed to your local Canadian bookseller or sent to Random House of Canada, Ltd., Marketing Department, 2775 Matheson Boulevard East, Mississauga, Ontario L4W 4P7. Inquiries from the United Kingdom should be sent to Fodor's Travel Publications, 20 Vauxhall Bridge Road, London SW1V 2SA, England.

AN IMPORTANT TIP & AN INVITATION

Although all prices, opening times, and other details in this book are based on information supplied to us at press time, changes occur all the time in the travel world, and Fodor's cannot accept responsibility for facts that become outdated or for inadvertent errors or omissions. So **always confirm information when it matters,** especially if you're making a detour to visit a specific place. Your experiences—positive and negative—matter to us. If we have missed or misstated something, **please write to us.** We follow up on all suggestions. Contact the Great Britain editor at editors@fodors.com or c/o Fodor's at 1745 Broadway, New York, New York 10019.

PRINTED IN THE UNITED STATES OF AMERICA

10 9 8 7 6 5 4 3 2 1

DESTINATION GREAT BRITAIN

To many people, Britain means London, a vibrantly modern metropolis that still preserves its quintessentially British brew of history, royalty, dignity, and civility. Even before you arrive, its images are imprinted on your consciousness. The dome of St. Paul's is iconically familiar, as are Big Ben and the Thames. Beyond London, an afternoon at any stately home, whether in Yorkshire or Kent, reveals Britain at its most appealing. The house is so splendid it must be a mirage, the gardens headily perfumed by flowers. A spot of sun emerges, and you half expect to encounter a character out of English literature. The experience is all the finer because you know that wherever you find yourself on this island, you may come upon some other grace note around the next bend. It may be an enchanted castle or a village whose clocks seem to have stopped two centuries ago, a brooding moor or a glittering loch rimmed by craggy peaks, a half-timber Tudor house or a long-distance footpath where you can tramp for miles with a view of the sea. Little wonder the atlas marks this realm as *Great* Britain. Wherever you go, have a wonderful trip!

Karen Cure, Editorial Director

CONTENTS

ON THE ROAD WITH FODOR'S

A trip takes you out of yourself. Concerns of life at home completely disappear, driven away by more immediate thoughts—about, say, what marvels will beguile the next day, or where you'll have dinner. That's where Fodor's comes in. We make sure that you know all your options, so that you don't miss something that's around the bend just because you didn't know it was there. Because the best memories of your trip might well have nothing to do with what you came to Great Britain to see, we guide you to sights large and small all over the country. You might set out to see the Tower of London, but back at home you find yourself unable to forget sharing beer and conversation at an ancient pub deep in the Yorkshire countryside. With Fodor's at your side, serendipitous discoveries are never far away.

Our success in showing you every corner of Great Britain is a credit to our extraordinary writers. Although there's no substitute for travel advice from a good friend who knows your style, our contributors are the next best thing—the kind of people you would poll for travel advice if you knew them.

Longtime Fodor's contributor Robert Andrews loves warm beer and soggy moors, but hates shopping malls and the sort of weather when you're not sure if it's raining—all of which he found in abundance while updating the South, the West Country, the Heart of England, and the Welsh Borders. He writes and revises other guidebooks and has also found time to pen his own guide to Devon and Cornwall.

San Francisco–born travel writer Catherine Belonogoff moved to London in 2000. She has worked on several Fodor's guides, including *Europe*. Catherine updated London lodging and Smart Travel Tips as well as the Thames Valley, Shakespeare Country, and East Anglia, adding a wealth of new discoveries.

Writer and editor Jacqueline Brown, a London resident for more than 20 years, has found the best and the quirkiest places around the city, some of which she revealed in *Fodor's Around London with Kids*. Jacqueline also updates *Fodor's London*, and she shares her insights in the Exploring and Shopping sections of the London chapter.

James Gracie, who updated the Edinburgh and Borders section of Scotland, has worked as a travel writer for 11 years. His articles have appeared in the *Sunday Herald*, the *Daily Record*, and Scottish magazines.

Julius Honnor, who revised Nightlife & the Arts and Sports & the Outdoors in the London chapter, lives in the city. His Fodor's assignment also covered the Southeast and the Lake District. His work for other guidebooks has taken him to places that include Italy.

Writer and editor Kate Hughes spent her formative years in Yorkshire and studied classical literature in Liverpool. She enjoyed traveling the Northeast coast, in particular her trip to the Farne Islands, but she also checked out the urban pleasures of Manchester in updating the Lancashire & the Peaks, Yorkshire, and Northeast chapters.

Beth Ingpen helped revise the chapter on Scotland as the longtime area editor for *Fodor's Scotland*. She was publishing manager with the Royal Society of Edinburgh and is now a freelance editor and writer.

Shona Main, the Glasgow updater, gave up law to be a journalist, and she now writes about travel, culture, social affairs, and politics for publications such as the *Press and Journal*, the *Scottish Sunday Express*, and the *Sunday Post Magazine*.

Always hoping to entertain—and surprise—his readers, longtime Fodor's contributor Roger Thomas spends almost every minute tracking down the latest and the best of Wales. He has to: he's editor of *A View of Wales* magazine.

A Londoner born and bred, Alex Wijeratna updated the London dining section. With his English/Sri Lankan roots, Alex knows that the real flavor of London is found in its ethnic diversity. He has written for newspapers, including the *Times*.

ABOUT THIS BOOK

There's no doubt that the best source for travel advice is a like-minded friend who's just been where you're headed. But with or without that friend, you'll have a better trip with a Fodor's guide in hand. Once you've learned to find your way around its pages, you'll be in great shape to find your way around your destination.

SELECTION

Our goal is to cover the best properties, sights, and activities in their category, as well as the most interesting communities to visit. We make a point of including local food-lovers' hot spots as well as neighborhood options, and we avoid all that's touristy unless it's really worth your time. You can go on the assumption that everything you read about in this book is recommended wholeheartedly by our writers and editors. Flip to On the Road with Fodor's to learn more about who they are. It goes without saying that no property mentioned in the book has paid to be included.

RATINGS

Orange stars ★ denote sights and properties that our editors and writers consider the very best in the area covered by the entire book. These, the best of the best, are listed in the Fodor's Choice section in the front of the book. Black stars ★ highlight the sights and properties we deem Highly Recommended, the don't-miss sights within any region. Fodor's Choice and Highly Recommended options in each region are usually listed on the title page of the chapter covering that region. Use the index to find complete descriptions. In cities, sights pinpointed with numbered map bullets ❶ in the margins tend to be more important than those without bullets.

SPECIAL SPOTS

Pleasures & Pastimes focuses on types of experiences that reveal the spirit of the destination. Watch for Off the Beaten Path sights. Some are out of the way, some are quirky, and all are worth your while. If the munchies hit while you're exploring, look for Need a Break? suggestions.

TIME IT RIGHT

Wondering when to go? Check On the Calendar up front and the chapters' Timing sections for weather and crowd overviews and best days and times to visit.

SEE IT ALL

Use Fodor's exclusive Great Itineraries as a model for your trip. (For a good overview of the entire destination, follow those that begin the book, or mix regional itineraries from several chapters.) In cities, Good Walks guide you to important sights in each neighborhood; ▶ indicates the starting points of walks and itineraries in the text and on the map.

BUDGET WELL

Hotel and restaurant price categories from £ to £££££ are defined in the opening pages of each chapter—expect to find a balanced selection for every budget. For attractions, we always give standard adult admission fees; reductions are usually available for children, students, and senior citizens. Look in Discounts & Deals in Smart Travel Tips for information on destination-wide ticket plans.

BASIC INFO

Smart Travel Tips lists travel essentials for the entire area covered by the book; city- and region-specific basics end each chapter. To find the best way to get around, see the transportation section; see individual modes of travel ("By Car," "By Train") for details. We assume you'll check Web sites or call for particulars.

ON THE MAPS	Maps throughout the book show you what's where and help you find your way around. Black and orange numbered bullets ❶ ❶ in the text correlate to bullets on maps.
BACKGROUND	In general, we give background information within the chapters in the course of explaining sights as well as in CloseUp boxes and in Understanding Great Britain at the end of the book. To get in the mood, review the suggestions in Books & Movies. The chronology can be invaluable.
FIND IT FAST	Within the book, chapters are arranged in a roughly south to north direction, starting with London. Chapters are divided into small regions, within which towns are covered in logical geographical order; attractive routes and interesting places between towns are flagged as En Route. Heads at the top of each page help you find what you need within a chapter.
DON'T FORGET	Restaurants are open for lunch and dinner daily unless we state otherwise; we mention dress only when there's a specific requirement and reservations only when they're essential or not accepted—it's always best to book ahead. Hotels have private baths, phone, TVs, and air-conditioning and operate on the European Plan (a.k.a. EP, meaning without meals) or, if indicated in the service information after the review, CP (Continental Plan, with Continental breakfast), BP (Breakfast Plan, with full breakfast), or MAP (Modified American Plan, with breakfast and dinner). We always list facilities but not whether you'll be charged extra to use them, so when pricing accommodations, find out what's included.

SYMBOLS

Many Listings

- ★ Fodor's Choice
- ★ Highly recommended
- ✉ Physical address
- ✛ Directions
- ✉ Mailing address
- ☎ Telephone
- 🖷 Fax
- ⊕ On the Web
- ✉ E-mail
- 🎟 Admission fee
- ☉ Open/closed times
- ▶ Start of walk/itinerary
- Ⓤ Underground Tube stations
- 🖃 Credit cards

Hotels & Restaurants

- 🏨 Hotel
- ↩ Number of rooms
- ♨ Facilities
- ❐ Meal plans
- ✕ Restaurant
- ✍ Reservations
- 👔 Dress code
- ⤫ Smoking
- 🍷 BYOB
- ✕🏨 Hotel with restaurant that warrants a visit

Other

- ♨ Family-friendly
- 🛈 Contact information
- ⇨ See also
- ✉ Branch address
- ☞ Take note

Great Britain

SHETLAND ISLANDS
Unst
Yell
Mainland
Lerwick

ORKNEY ISLANDS
Mainland
Kirkwall
Hoy

North Sea

ORKNEY ISLANDS
Thurso
John O'Groats
Wick
Dornoch
Inverness
Aviemore
Loch Ness
Kyle of Lochalsh
Portree
Skye
Ullapool
Stornoway
Lewis
Harris
North Uist
South Uist
OUTER HEBRIDES

Peterhead
Aberdeen
Banff
Montrose
Braemar
Dundee
Firth of Tay
St. Andrew's
Firth of Forth
HIGHLANDS
SCOTLAND
Perth
Dunfermline
Edinburgh
Fort William
Oban
Callander
Stirling
Lanark
Glasgow
Greenock
Kilmarnock
Arran
Ayr
Dumfries
Campbeltown
Islay
Mull
Coll
Tiree
INNER HEBRIDES

Berwick-on-Tweed
Newcastle
Sunderland
Middlesbrough
Whitby
Durham
Carlisle
Keswick
Kirkcudbright

NORTHERN IRELAND
Stranraer
Bangor
Belfast
Londonderry

ATLANTIC OCEAN

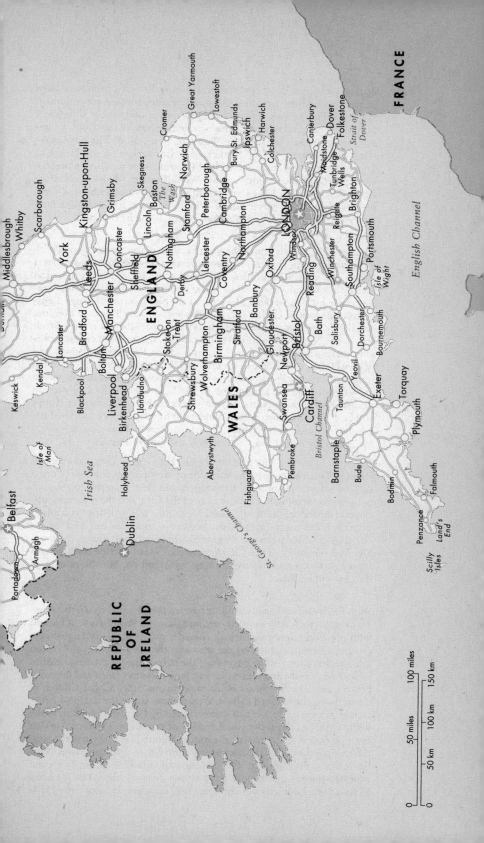

Britain isn't large, but it contains great scenic diversity, from the downs of the South to the fjordlike lochs and heather-covered mountains of Scotland. This section reflects the order of the chapters in this guide. London, the capital of Great Britain, is first; regions to the south of London, from the Southeast to the West Country, follow. The next chapters—the Thames Valley, Shakespeare Country, and the Heart of England—are west and northwest of London. Moving north along the western side of the country are the Welsh Borders, Wales, Lancashire & the Peaks, and the Lake District. Other chapters deal with areas north of London on the eastern side of Britain: East Anglia, Yorkshire, and the Northeast. Scotland, the farthest north, is the final region.

1 London

The city of Big Ben is one of the most exciting places on the planet, with its glittering arts scene, outrageous restaurants created by superstar chefs, and stylish boutiques. Yet despite the buzz, Europe's largest metropolis remains the bastion of just about everything the British traditionally hold most dear. Have tea at the Savoy, stroll through Kensington Gardens or Hyde Park, ogle the jewels in the Tower of London, or take in the British Museum, the Victoria & Albert, the Tate Modern, or the National Gallery. As you explore, the national character begins to reveal itself. Treasure troves such as Kensington Palace and Apsley House, once home to the duke of Wellington, exhibit the national fondness for heroes—after all, this was the duke who defeated Napoléon at Waterloo and gave his name to Wellies, essential foot protection against British downpours. Sacred places such as Westminster Abbey and St. Paul's are laden with reminders of hundreds of years of history. Landmarks such as the Globe Theatre, a copy of Shakespeare's original, recall the British way with words and gift for theater.

The trick to taming this vast metropolis is to regard it as a number of villages. There is the heraldic splendor of Westminster, the chic of artistic Chelsea, the glamour of Kensington and Belgravia, the cosmopolitan charms of Soho, the ancient core of the City, and the museums and cultural centers of the South Bank. No matter which district you adopt as your home-away-from-home, London's contrasts can best be savored by strolling from one neighborhood to another. And as the time-honored ceremony of the Changing of the Guard outside Buckingham Palace proves, London's trends may come and go, but the essence of the city will endure.

2 The Southeast

With fields and orchards unrolling toward the Channel coast, this compact region, including Kent, Surrey, and East and West Sussex, is blessed with places that even the British consider quintessentially English: eccentric, vibrant Brighton by the sea, with the fairy-tale Royal Pavilion and the diversions of Brighton Pier; the extraordinary medieval castles of Bodiam, Leeds, and Hever; Lewes, with its secret lanes and immense beech trees. The Southeast holds major icons, from Christ Church in Canterbury, the beloved cathedral made famous by the death of Archbishop Thomas à Becket and immortalized by Geoffrey Chaucer, to the white cliffs of Dover, cherished symbol of the realm. Here, too, is that triumph of British civilization, the stately country house, often with splendid gardens that equal the treasures within: Knole, Ightham Mote, Penshurst Place, Sissinghurst. The closeness of this area to the European continent means that history has a strong presence here. The Romans, Saxons, and Normans left their mark as invaders, in sites from Hastings to Chichester; this is where William the Conqueror landed in 1066. Castles and fortifications, from medieval to World War II vintage, line the coast. Because of the Southeast's closeness to London, you can make easy excursions and round up a delightful choice of day trips.

③ The South

If Jane Austen's countryside "sweet to the eye and mind" seems familiar, it may be because so much of British history has been played out in this area southwest of London. Thousands of years ago, stone monuments such as Avebury and Stonehenge, and earth-and-stone hill forts such as Maiden Castle, rose on the plains, and these evocative, mysterious prehistoric sites continue to attract speculation. Winchester was England's capital until the 11th century, its cathedral huge and imposing. Salisbury, too, has its cathedral, with its famous spire, captured in the paintings of artists such as John Constable. Stourhead and other grand, stately homes, such as Wilton House and Longleat House, evoke the traditions of past eras. Make a pilgrimage to Jane Austen Country or travel to Dorset—immortalized by Thomas Hardy as his part-fact, part-fiction county of Wessex—to get away from the madding crowd. During Britain's seafaring heyday, the coast here was essential to both commercial and military concerns, with Portsmouth leading the way; today the Portsmouth Historic Dockyard interprets this past, displaying a vessel from the Tudor navy and Nelson's flagship, HMS *Victory*. Other destinations in the South remain highly popular, from the peaceful shores of the Isle of Wight, with its essential Victorian flavor, to the wild scenery of the New Forest.

④ The West Country

The southwestern peninsula made up of the counties of Somerset, Devon, and Cornwall is one of the most beautiful places in Britain. Outside the cathedral towns such as Wells and Exeter, maritime centers such as Plymouth, and tourist-laden fishing villages, however, the region can resemble an ancient ghost town. Scattered throughout the countryside are eroded castles and enigmatic prehistoric stone structures such as the Stanton Drew Circles. The brooding heaths and moors of Exmoor and Dartmoor add to this sense of separateness. To some, the area's mystery is embodied by the legend of King Arthur, who is thought to have been born in Tintagel, to have battled at Bodmin Moor, and to be buried in Glastonbury (now a New Age center). Begin with Bristol—gateway to the West Country and historic shipping port. You'll find that on your way down to Land's End, at the southernmost point of the peninsula, every zig and zag of the road reveals rugged moorlands, lush river valleys, and festive coastal resorts. The engaging towns of St. Ives and Newlyn have attracted artists and writers for generations; the galleries of the Tate St. Ives celebrate this legacy. The impressive Eden Project, with its vast conservatories, shelters more than 70,000 plants. You may have to remind yourself that you're in Britain as you gaze at the palm trees, white beaches, and turquoise waters of Cornwall. Although crowds do arrive in summer, it's still a treat to explore the coastal towns and bays—if you stray far enough, you'll find countryside where the sense of isolation can be exciting.

⑤ The Thames Valley

The rose-cloaked countryside that flanks this stretch of old father Thames west and north of London has become something of a weekend destination for sophisticated urbanites. Rarefied social occasions persist: the annual meeting at Ascot, the world's most famous horse race, and the Henley Royal Regatta, rowing's toniest competition. Windsor, the largest inhabited castle in the world and home to eight successive royal houses, is a popular retreat for Queen Elizabeth. Year-round, the top magnet remains spired-and-turreted Oxford—seat of England's oldest university. Lewis Carroll invented Alice along Oxford's River Cherwell. The duke of Marlborough's Blenheim Palace, close to Oxford, epitomizes baroque splendor. Many other great houses are nearby, from Woburn Abbey to Althorp, where Diana, the late Princess of Wales, is buried. Close to London, St. Albans has a notable cathedral and reminders of the Roman past. But before you assume that these well-groomed riverbanks belong only to the titled and entitled, remember that Western Europe took a bold step toward democracy here when King John signed the Magna Carta at Runnymede in 1215.

6 Shakespeare Country

Admirers of Shakespeare, and even those with only a passing acquaintance with the Bard, cannot resist the lure of the country in which he grew up, worked, and—after a career in London—died. The center is Stratford-upon-Avon, 100 mi northwest of the capital. The man dominates this town, and Elizabethan-era sites bear witness to his days here—Shakespeare's Birthplace and Anne Hathaway's Cottage, to name two highlights. The Royal Shakespeare Theatre presents the master's works by the River Avon, and attending a play is an experience not to be missed. Warwickshire, the ancient county of which Stratford is the southern nexus, is a gentle countryside of thatch-roof cottages, sleepy villages, and sundappled meadows. Heaping doses of history await: Warwick Castle, with its towers and turbulent history, has been called "medieval England in stone," and Kenilworth Castle, although in ruins, is equally evocative. The regal manor houses of Charlecote Park and Baddesley Clinton, and other time-hallowed stately piles, are other landmarks.

7 The Heart of England

This area is the center of *tourist* England, and enormously popular because of its many attractions, but that shouldn't deter you from visiting. Begin with the golden-stone city of Bath—where you can see, as the eminent writer Nigel Nicolson put it, "18th-century England in all its urban glory." After following in the footsteps of social organizer Beau Nash and novelist Jane Austen through Bath's splendid terraces and crescents (or taking in the pleasures of the modern Thermae Bath Spa), head northward to Regency-era Cheltenham, another spa town, to embark on a tour of the Cotswolds. In the peaceful hamlets, stone cottages, old coaching inns, tidy gardens, and tile-roof farmsteads add up to pure rural delight; the many stone churches are a legacy of the age when Cotswold wool made merchants here rich. The finest Cotswold towns include Chipping Campden, Upper Slaughter, and Bourton-on-the-Water, but let the back roads lead you to your own discoveries. Stow-on-the-Wold has antiques shops, although you can't expect bargains: these heavenly tracts are as refined as they are pastoral. Be sure to explore such beauty spots as Hidcote Manor Gardens and Owlpen, and treasure houses such as Sudeley Castle and Chastleton House. Near urban Gloucester is the sylvan Forest of Dean, ideal for hikers and nature lovers.

8 The Welsh Borders

Some of England's loveliest countryside rises and drops over the hills and valleys of Shropshire, Herefordshire, and Cheshire. The border with Wales stretches from the town of Chepstow on the Severn estuary in the south to the well-preserved medieval city of Chester in the north.

Brooding fortresses such as Goodrich Castle loom over the landscape, a reminder that the border was not always tranquil. Herefordshire, in the south, has rich, rolling countryside and river valleys, gradually opening out to Shropshire's high hills and plateaus. Half-timber buildings line elegant avenues in Ludlow, a center of fine dining. A visit to Shrewsbury, with its fine churches and medieval buildings, is a bit of time travel. In the north, the gentler Cheshire plain is dairy country, dotted with small villages and market towns, full of ancient black-and-white, half-timber buildings. A highlight for some is the Black Country, named for the environmental damage, now mostly erased, from 19th-century industry. From Shrewsbury to Chester, you'll find monuments of the Industrial Revolution, including the museums at Ironbridge Gorge. Gateway to the region from the British heartland is the industrial city of Birmingham, now undergoing a cultural renaissance.

9 Wales

On the western border of England, Wales is a country of outstanding natural beauty, with mountain scenery in its interior and long stretches of magnificent coastline. With the exception of the engaging capital, Cardiff, and Swansea, Wales's second-largest city, the country has few large urban areas. What it does have, from north to south, are pretty villages, attractive market towns, traffic-free roads, and fine countryside. Few other regions are as free of modern encroachment, and many people head for the open spaces of the three national parks: Snowdonia with its footpath-beribboned heights, Pembrokeshire Coast, and Brecon Beacons. Beyond the parks, other discoveries beckon: numerous medieval castles such as Conwy and Caernarfon, the slate caverns at Blaenau Ffestiniog, seaside resorts, restored 19th-century mining villages, the glorious Bodnant Garden, the Victorian spa of Llandrindod Wells, and steam train rides through Snowdonia and central Wales.

10 Lancashire & the Peaks

This northwest region of Britain witnessed the birth of Industrial Revolution, when Manchester and Liverpool flourished as major industrial centers. Today Manchester is cleaning up a faded industrial landscape and polishing its Victorian treasures as the city experiences renewed cultural energy. The restored warehouses at Liverpool's Albert Dock now hold shops and restaurants that interpret the port city's maritime history, and the Tate Liverpool displays cutting-edge art. Fans of the Beatles can check out special Liverpool tours tracing the Beatles' earliest days and visit 20 Forthlin Road and Mendips, home of the young Paul McCartney and John Lennon, respectively. As a respite from the urban scene, escape to the emerald tranquillity of the Peak District and Derbyshire's Wye Valley—home to pretty towns such as Bakewell and three supremely regal houses, Chatsworth, Haddon Hall, and Hardwick Hall. The Peak District draws many hikers who delight in the area's rocky outcrops and meadowland.

11 The Lake District

Bordered by Scotland and the waters of Solway Firth, Morecambe Bay, and the Irish Sea, this is a startlingly beautiful area of craggy hills, wild moorland, stone-built villages, and, of course, glittering silvery lakes—more than 100 of them. The Lake District, now a national park, has been one of the most popular tourist destinations in Britain since the beginning of the 19th century, when poets and painters—William Wordsworth, who was born and lived here, and J. M. W. Turner foremost among them—extolled the region's allure. High points of any tour of Cumbria include Wordsworth's homes at Rydal, Grasmere, and Cockermouth, John Ruskin's abode at Coniston, Beatrix Potter's tiny house near Hawkshead, and boating on Derwentwater and Windermere. Some 250 days of rain a year ensure that such noted spots as Keswick, on the shores of Derwentwater, are pleasingly verdant. Follow in the footsteps of Samuel Taylor Coleridge, John Ruskin, and Thomas De Quincey and go for a ramble. Everywhere you'll find specific locations that inspired great poems about subjects as humble as daffodils.

12 East Anglia

A large knob of land jutting out into the North Sea, East Anglia has charms that are endearing for their subtlety. Its flat, arable lands and gentle forests have been spared urbanization by the simple fact that the region is not on the way to anywhere but itself. The region's gateway is Cambridge, one of the world's leading centers of learning. Take a stroll among its medieval colleges or go punting on the placid River Cam. Then there are the magnificent cathedrals of Ely and Norwich and time-warp towns such as 18th-century King's Lynn or medieval Lavenham, unchanged since it boomed with the wool trade five centuries ago. Some great families built magnificent houses here, including Norfolk's stunning Holkham Hall, Blickling, Houghton Hall, and the Royal Family's country retreat, Sandringham. Norfolk has its glorious north coast, with golden, sandy beaches and dark fir trees guarding the shore; you can also go boating in the canals and fens of the reed-bordered Broads. Increasing numbers of Londoners are heading to this area not for nature, however, but for the antiques shops and gastro-pubs. In the Suffolk countryside, rich farmlands are dotted with villages of thatched, pink-washed cottages. Immortalized in paintings by Thomas Gainsborough and Constable, the sylvan countryside all around is splendid.

13 Yorkshire

A wilder, grander part of England in the north, the heather-covered Yorkshire Moors—full of open spaces, wide horizons, and hills that appear to rear violently out of the plain—were inspiration for the Brontë sisters, who, in the little hamlet of Haworth, wrote *Jane Eyre* and *Wuthering Heights*. The moors are linked to the contrasting landscape of the Yorkshire Dales, with their luxuriant green valleys, burgeoning rivers, waterfalls, and sights such as the ruins of Bolton Priory and the castles at Skipton and Richmond. It would be almost unthinkable to journey here without paying a call on the ancient city of York—a must-see for those interested in impressive medieval monuments, including York Minster, the largest Gothic church in the country. Northward lie the seaside resort of Scarborough, the beautiful harbor at Whitby, and the scenically splendid sights of the North York Moors, including picture-perfect Hutton-le-Hole, the soaring, evocative ruins of Rievaulx Abbey, and Castle Howard, one of Britain's most famous treasure houses.

14 The Northeast

The gateway to Scotland, this remote corner of England is the climax to all that is grand and wild in the nation's footpath-crossed northerly reaches. For centuries, Northeasterners struggled to keep outsiders out. Barbarian attacks from the north were repelled by mammoth fortifications such as Hadrian's Wall, the Roman Empire's northernmost boundary; you can now walk along the wall and explore its ancient forts. On the starkly beautiful Northumberland coastline, towering castles such as Bamburgh and Dunstanburgh held marauders at bay; the one at Lindisfarne, also known as Holy Island, sheltered one of England's earliest Christian communities as well. Elaborate Alnwick Castle, with its resplendent interior and gardens, grew up around a Norman keep. Durham Cathedral, the stone centerpiece of one of England's most memorable medieval cities, was described as "half church of God, half castle 'gainst the Scot." Newcastle, the region's liveliest city and one being reinvigorated with ambitious cultural centers, holds reminders of the Industrial Revolution, another force that shaped the Northeast. Both inland and by the sea, the landscape is generously blessed with wide-open space—a precious commodity on this densely populated isle.

15 Scotland

North Sea to Irish Sea, Highlands to Lowlands, the landscapes of Scotland—lush woodlands, windswept moors, lochs as deep as the imagination—may take your breath away. In the southeast, Edinburgh is a gloriously dignified city, with its own castle providing spectacular views. The Old Town district carries all the evidence of its colorful medieval history, and the many elegant, 18th-century classical buildings add to the city's appeal. An excursion to St. Andrews is a pilgrimage for golf aficionados. To the west lies exciting Glasgow, a Victorian powerhouse whose full-fledged urban renaissance crackles with energy. The Borders area—immortalized in the tales of Sir Walter Scott—takes in the hills, moors, and farmland that stretch south from Lothian, the region crowned by Edinburgh, to England. In the north, heath-clad slopes, salmon-filled streams, and the great castles of baronial pride stand hard among the hills. To enjoy the Highlands, head for Royal Deeside, the burg that Queen Victoria made her own. Her Majesty's Balmoral—and numerous other castles—polka-dot northeast Scotland. Northward lie Inverness and shimmering Loch Ness.

GREAT ITINERARIES

Highlights of Britain
16 days

It's no wonder that many people see Great Britain as a giant patchwork quilt thickly studded with must-see sights. This roundup introduces you to the best of them. After two days doing the town in London, head out to Windsor.

WINDSOR
1 day. Windsor Castle is the main reason to be here, resplendent in its finery, but a respite for the riches within is found in its tranquil Great Park. If you want to live like a duke for a day, head up the valley to Lord Astor's Cliveden, the Thames Valley's most spectacular hotel. ⇨ *Windsor & Environs in Chapter 5.*

SALISBURY
1 day. Visible for miles around, Salisbury Cathedral's soaring spire is one of the quintessential images of rural England, immortalized in paint by John Constable (you can still find the exact spot the artist set up his easel on the town path). Pay an afternoon call on either awe-inspiring Stonehenge or Stourhead, the finest garden of England's neoclassical era. ⇨ *Salisbury to the New Forest in Chapter 3.*

BATH & THE COTSWOLDS
2 days. Once upon a time Bath was *the* place to be, and this elegant small city has never forgotten it. Its popularity today is understandable, as Bath is an immaculately preserved gem of Georgian architecture. Key spots to see are the Royal Crescent, the Circus, and the Pump Room; stop by the Roman Baths Museum to see the town's beginnings. The next day head via car or guided-tour bus to the Cotswolds, whose storybook villages will tempt you to stay forever. Antique-shop in Stow-on-the-Wold, visit historic Chastleton House, and then feed the ducks at the brook in

Lower Slaughter. ⇨ *Bath & Environs and The Cotswolds in Chapter 7.*

OXFORD
1 day. The "dreaming spires" of Oxford's weathered old buildings bear witness to the transience of countless generations of students. Tour the town's largest quad at Christ Church College, then don't miss the short trip to Blenheim Palace, England's grandest house. ⇨ *Oxford and Blenheim Palace to Althorp in Chapter 5.*

STRATFORD-UPON-AVON
1 day. If you don't chime with the Bard, skip this stop, because this is Shakespeare's town, end of story; if you dig, then you won't be disappointed. See Shakespeare's Birthplace and Anne Hathaway's Cottage, and catch a once-in-a-lifetime performance at the Royal Shakespeare Theatre. ⇨ *Stratford-upon-Avon in Chapter 6.*

WORCESTER
2 days. On the banks of the River Severn, Worcester Cathedral is a majestic apparition that contains one of the finest chantry chapels in the country. The town's 15th-century Commandery brings alive the days of England's Civil War. Spend your second day here roaming the spa towns of the Malvern Hills, then head north to see the half-timber houses of Shrewsbury and Chester. ⇨ *From Worcester to Dudley and From Shrewsbury to Chester in Chapter 8.*

THE LAKE DISTRICT
2 days. In the area surrounding Windermere and Kendal, you get your chance to expose yourself to the English lakes and mountains and do some real walking. Check out the local Wordsworth industry at Dove Cottage and Grasmere, where you can pay your respects to the Wordsworth family's graves. Bring your sketch pad for your cruise on Windermere. ⇨ *The Southern Lakes in Chapter 11.*

YORK
2 days. The principal city of northern England since Roman times, York is crammed with 15th- and 16th-century buildings in varying degrees of sag, but don't miss York Minster, England's largest Gothic church, and the medieval streets of the Shambles. Save half a day for visiting Castle Howard, where eye-popping baroque grandeur is the keynote. ⇨ *York and The North York Moors in Chapter 13.*

LINCOLN & CAMBRIDGE
2 days. Heading south, make a lunchtime stop at Lincoln, whose stunning Cathedral of St. Mary demands a slow wander. Bed down in Cambridge for your last stop. After touring King's College Chapel, leave an hour or two to hone your punting skills on the River Cam before heading back to London. ⇨ *Lincoln, Boston & Stamford and Cambridge in Chapter 12.*

By Public Transportation
For Windsor, take a train from either London's Waterloo or Paddington station. For Salisbury, head back to London's Clapham Junction to catch a train on the Portsmouth line. Trains leave twice hourly from Salisbury to Bath, itself connected by hourly trains to Oxford. From Oxford there are direct trains to Stratford-upon-Avon, or opt for more frequent Stagecoach bus service. For Worcester change trains at Oxford or Birmingham's New Street station, which is the place to catch trains to Windermere and Oxenholme. Take a train via either station to York (changes required). From York to Lincoln transfer at Doncaster or Retford. For Cambridge change at Doncaster or Newark and again at Peterborough. Trains leave Cambridge for London frequently.

The Literary Trail
12 days

After the Beatles, perhaps the greatest contribution that Britain has made to Western culture has been its literary achievements. The legacy of many centuries of literature has insinuated itself into every aspect of life. You'll have glimpsed many of these landscapes as romantic backdrops in movies, too.

LONDON
2 days. One author strongly associated with London is Charles Dickens, and Dickens House, where he wrote *Oliver Twist* and *Nicholas Nickleby*, sits appropriately in literary Bloomsbury. Dr. Johnson's House lies a short walk south of here, and Shakespeare beckons across the Thames in Southwark at the reconstruction of the Bard's Globe Theatre. ⇨ *Exploring London in Chapter 1.*

WINCHESTER & CHAWTON
1 day. Stop in the lovely old city of Winchester; Jane Austen is buried in Winchester Cathedral. Sixteen miles northeast lies Chawton and Jane Austen's House, where the atmosphere still reverberates with the tinkle of teacups lofted by the likes of Emma and the dashing Mr. Darcy. ⇨ *From Winchester to Southampton in Chapter 3.*

DORCHESTER & LYME REGIS
2 days. Thomas Hardy immortalized this region in *Far from the Madding Crowd* and other novels. The town of Dorchester was the 19th-century author's Casterbridge. The Dorset County Museum has a re-creation of his study, and Hardy walking tours lead to Hardy's Cottage at Higher Bockhampton. To the west is Lyme Regis, a setting in John Fowles's *The French Lieutenant's Woman* and Jane Austen's *Persuasion.* ⇨ *Bournemouth to Lyme Regis in Chapter 3.*

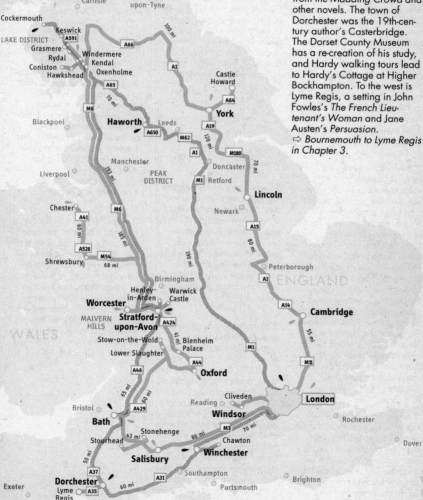

BATH

1 day. Head north to honey-toned Bath, identified with a host of Georgian-era literati, chief among them Jane Austen, who set parts of *Northanger Abbey* and *Persuasion* here. Check out the Jane Austen Centre, look into guided theme walks, and visit the Holburne Museum, where genteel Jane promenaded in the gardens. ⇨ *Bath & Environs in Chapter 7.*

STRATFORD-UPON-AVON

2 days. Scholars rub shoulders with sightseers here. Everyone visits Shakespeare's Birthplace, though you may feel closer to him at his simple tomb in Holy Trinity Church. Take in a play at the Royal Shakespeare Theatre. Escape the tour buses in town by exploring Master Will's country haunts, from Henley-in-Arden to Warwick Castle. ⇨ *Stratford-upon-Avon and Around Shakespeare Country in Chapter 6.*

THE LAKE DISTRICT

2 days. The countryside around Keswick and Windermere is the cradle of English romanticism: its mountains and lakes attracted Wordsworth and other inspired men and women of letters. Visit the poet's homes, Dove Cottage in Grasmere and Rydal Mount in Rydal, young William's school in Hawkshead, and his and sister Dorothy's birthplace at Cockermouth. Brantwood, the home of John Ruskin, is near Coniston and Hawkshead. Beatrix Potter lived at Hill Top, near Hawkshead. ⇨ *The Southern Lakes and Penrith & the Northern Lakes in Chapter 11.*

HAWORTH

2 days. Fans of the Brontë canon will appreciate this literary shrine. Unfortunately that can create some crowds on cobbled Main Street in summer. Still, the Brontë Parsonage Museum casts a spell, as do the paths to the moors and the Brontë Waterfall. Overnight here and head back to London the next day. ⇨ *West Yorkshire & Brontë Country in Chapter 13.*

By Public Transportation

Take the train from Waterloo station to Winchester. For Dorchester change trains at Southampton. To reach Bath from Dorchester change at Yeovil. For Stratford change at Bristol and Birmingham. Catch connections for Keswick or Windermere at Birmingham's New Street Station. From the Lake District to reach Haworth take a train for Keighley from Windermere or Oxenholme, changing at Lancaster, sometimes at Leeds. From Keighley there are frequent Keighley and District buses, which also head to Bradford, from which frequent trains depart for London.

A Stately Homes Grand Tour
9 days

Though occasionally changing hands and even dynasties, Britain's stately houses as a rule have retained the priceless furniture and—sometimes—the wallpaper of generations past. These bastions of privilege contain some of the finest architecture and landscape gardening in the country.

SALISBURY

2 days. Base yourself in this graceful Wiltshire town for trips to a trio of superb stately homes. Wilton House, rebuilt in 1647, contains magnificent state rooms, including the classically proportioned Double Cube Room with its gigantic Sir Anthony Van Dyck family portrait. On the western edge of Wiltshire, Palladian Stourhead is most loved for its parkland. Nearby Longleat House is an Italian Renaissance structure complete with safari park. ⇨ *Salisbury to the New Forest in Chapter 3.*

OXFORD

2 days. Blenheim Palace, home of the dukes of Marlborough and birthplace of Winston Churchill, is one of the most ornate baroque concoctions anywhere. Nine miles southwest of Oxford is medieval Stanton Harcourt Manor; Kelmscott Manor, home of William Morris and a famed Arts and Crafts landmark, is nearby. To the south you can visit Elizabethan Mapledurham House, model for Toad Hall in *Wind in the Willows.* ⇨ *To Henley & Beyond and Blenheim Palace to Althorp in Chapter 5.*

BROADWAY

2 days. Stay in this lovely Cotswold town to explore Sudeley Castle, home of Catherine Parr, Henry VIII's last wife. Stanway House, a short drive away, is a Jacobean manor perfectly in keeping with its setting. Nearby Snowshill Manor, a 17th-century house in pretty Snowshill, has a pretty garden; the house is closed until 2005. Farther west, tiny Owlpen is a Cotswold classic. ⇨ *The Cotswolds in Chapter 7.*

BAKEWELL

2 days. Within hailing distance of this town are three of England's most fabulous historic homes: one of them, Chatsworth House, displays the art treasures of the dukes of Devonshire. Medieval in style, nearby 15th-century Haddon Hall is among the most English of great houses. Hardwick Hall is an Elizabethan treasure. ⇨ *The Peak District in Chapter 10.*

YORK

1 day. Doing the tedious crawl up the M1 motorway is worthwhile so that you can see Yorkshire's spectacular Castle Howard. Twenty-five miles away are Harewood House, which has a cornucopia of Chippendale furniture, and Studley Royal, with its exquisite water gardens. Overnight in York and head back to London the next morning. ⇨ *West Yorkshire & Brontë Country, York Environs, and The North York Moors in Chapter 13.*

By Public Transportation

This tour often leads to backwaters and byways, so public transport can be sketchy. Buses can get you close to many stately homes, but a taxi is sometimes required for the last leg of the journey. From London's Waterloo Station take a train to Salisbury, then a bus to Wilton House or Warminster, for Longleat; for Stourhead, continue on the train to Gillingham. From Salisbury, change at Bath or Basingstoke for Oxford, then catch a bus to Blenheim, Stanton Harcourt, and, for Kelmscott Manor, Faringdon.

Take a train from Oxford to Moreton-in-Marsh for Broadway, then walk to Snowshill Manor; for Sudeley Castle, take a bus from Broadway to Winchcombe, then walk. Take a train back to Oxford and then up to Manchester for the connection to Buxton, then a bus to Bakewell. Take a train from Manchester to York, then a bus to Castle Howard; take a train to Leeds, then a bus over to Harewood House; for Studley Royal, take a train to Harrowgate, then a bus to Ripon. Express trains connect York with London.

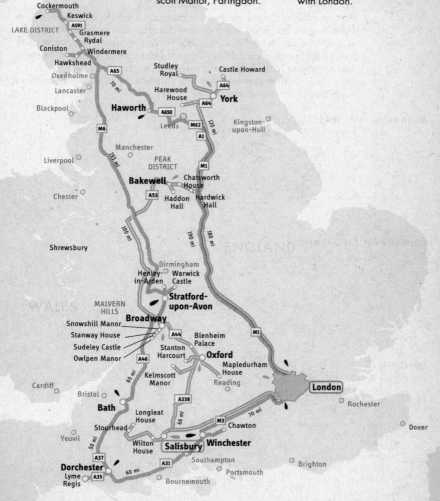

WHEN TO GO

°C		°F
100		212
40		105
37		98.6
30		90
25		80
20		70
15		60
10		50
5		40
0		32
-5		20
-10		10
-15		0
-20		

The British tourist season is year-round—with short lulls. It peaks from mid-April to mid-October, with another burst at Christmas (although most historic houses are closed from October to Easter). Spring is the time to see the countryside at its greenest, whereas in fall the northern moorlands and Scottish Highlands are at their most colorful. June is a good month to visit Wales and the Lake District. During July and August, when most of the British take their vacations, accommodations in popular resorts and areas are in high demand and at their most expensive. The winter season in London is lively with the opera, ballet, and West End theater among the prime attractions; you'll find lower hotel rates and temperatures in the city then, too, making up for the often gray skies. Museums and sights can be busy during school vacations called half-terms: these are generally the third week in October, the last week of December and first week of January, the third week of February, the last week of March, and the first week of June.

Climate

In the main, the climate in Britain is mild, although the weather has been volatile in recent years. Summer temperatures can reach the 90s and the atmosphere can be humid. In winter there can be heavy frost, snow, thick fog, and, of course, rain. What follows are the average daily maximum and minimum temperatures for three major cities in Britain.

📱 Forecasts **Weather Channel Connection** ☎ 900/932-8437, 95¢ per minute from a Touch-Tone phone ⊕ www.weather.com.

ABERYSTWYTH (WALES)

Jan.	44F	7C	May	58F	15C	Sept.	62F	16C
	36	2		45	7		51	11
Feb.	44F	7C	June	62F	16C	Oct.	56F	13C
	35	2		50	10		46	8
Mar.	49F	9C	July	64F	18C	Nov.	50F	10C
	38	4		54	12		41	5
Apr.	52F	11C	Aug.	65F	18C	Dec.	47F	8C
	41	5		54	12		38	4

EDINBURGH (SCOTLAND)

Jan.	42F	6C	May	56F	14C	Sept.	60F	16C
	34	1		43	6		49	9
Feb.	43F	6C	June	62F	17C	Oct.	54F	12C
	34	1		49	9		44	7
Mar.	46F	8C	July	65F	18C	Nov.	48F	9C
	36	2		52	11		39	4
Apr.	51F	11C	Aug.	64F	18C	Dec.	44F	7C
	39	4		52	11		36	2

LONDON

Jan.	43F	6C	May	62F	17C	Sept.	65F	19C
	36	2		47	8		52	11
Feb.	44F	7C	June	69F	20C	Oct.	58F	14C
	36	2		53	12		46	8
Mar.	50F	10C	July	71F	22C	Nov.	50F	10C
	38	3		56	14		42	5
Apr.	56F	13C	Aug.	71F	21C	Dec.	45F	7C
	42	6		56	13		38	4

ON THE CALENDAR

Great Britain's top seasonal events are listed below, and any one of them could provide the stuff of lasting memories. Tickets for popular sporting events must be obtained months in advance; your travel agent may be able to help. Contact information is listed below. VisitBritain's Web site, ⊕ www.visitbritain.com, also has information about events.

ONGOING

Mid-Mar. & Mid-Sept.	Chelsea Antiques Fair is a twice-yearly fair with pre-1830 pieces for sale. ⊠ Old Town Hall, King's Rd., London SW3 ☎ 01444/482514 ⊕ www.penman-fairs.co.uk.
Late May–Aug.	Glyndebourne Opera presents high-quality performances in a lovely rural setting; booking opens in April. ⊠ Glyndebourne, Lewes, East Sussex ☎ 01273/813813 ⊕ www.glyndebourne.com.
Late May–Late Aug.	Shakespeare Under the Stars gives you the chance to see the Bard's plays at Regent's Park Open Air Theatre. Performances are usually Monday through Saturday at 8, with matinees on Wednesday, Thursday, and Saturday. ⊠ Inner Circle, London NW1 ☎ 020/7486–2431 ⊕ www.openairtheatre.org.
Mid-July–Mid-Sept.	Henry Wood Promenade Concerts is a celebrated series of concerts. ⊠ Royal Albert Hall, Kensington Gore, London SW7 ☎ 020/7589–8212 ⊕ www.bbc.co.uk/proms.

WINTER

Mid-Dec.	Olympia International Show Jumping Championships is London's main international equestrian competition, held in Olympia's Grand Hall. Tickets go on sale in June. ⊠ London ☎ 0870/905–0600 ⊕ www.olympiashowjumping.com.
Dec. 27–Jan. 2	Hogmanay, an energetic, Scottish-style celebration of the new year, includes candlelight processions, concerts, and fireworks. ☎ 0131/473–2056 ⊕ www.edinburghshogmanay.org.
Dec. 31	New Year's Eve at Trafalgar Square in London is a huge, freezing, sometimes drunken slosh through the fountains to celebrate the new year. Unorganized by any official body, it is held in the ceremonial heart of London under an enormous Christmas tree.
Jan. 1	London Parade, an extravaganza with floats and marching bands, starts on the south side of Westminster Bridge at noon and finishes in Berkeley Square around 3 PM. No tickets are required. ⊠ London ⊕ www.londonparade.co.uk.
Last Sun. in Jan.	Charles I Commemoration, held on the anniversary of the monarch's execution, brings out Londoners dressed in 17th-century garb to trace his last walk to the Banqueting House in Whitehall.

SPRING

Mid-Mar.	British Antique Dealers' Association Fair is large and prestigious, with many affordable pieces. ⊠ Duke of York's Headquarters, King's Rd., London SW3 ☎ 020/7589–6108; 877/872–0778 in U.S. ⊕ www.bada-antiques-fair.co.uk.

Mid-Mar.	**Crufts Dog Show** brings together more than 8,000 championship dogs for Britain's top canine event. ⊠ *National Exhibition Centre, Birmingham* ☎ *0121/780–4141* ⊕ *www.crufts.org.uk.*
Early Apr.	**Chaucer Festival** allows participants to don medieval garb and parade from Southwark Cathedral to the Tower of London, where strolling minstrels party the day away. ⊠ *London* ☎ *01227/470379.*
Mid-Apr.	**Flora London Marathon** runners start in Greenwich and Blackheath at 9–9:30 AM and run via the Docklands, the Tower of London, and Parliament Square to the Mall. ⊕ *www.london-marathon.co.uk.*
Mid-Apr.	**Head of the River Boat Race** offers the spectacle of 420 eight-man crews from Oxford and Cambridge universities dipping their 6,720 oars in the Thames as they race from Mortlake to Putney. The best view is from Surrey Bank above Chiswick Bridge (tube to Chiswick).
Apr. 21	The **Queen's Birthday** earns a showy 41-gun salute at Hyde Park in London. In June, Elizabeth II's ceremonial birthday is celebrated by Trooping the Colour.
Mid-May	**Royal Windsor Horse Show**, a major five-day show-jumping event, is attended by some members of the Royal Family. ⊠ *Show Office, Royal Mews, Windsor* ☎ *01753/860633* ⊕ *www.royal-windsor-horse-show.co.uk.*
Mid–Late May	The **Chelsea Flower Show**, a prestigious four-day floral extravaganza, covers 22 acres. ⊠ *Royal Horticultural Society, Royal Hospital Rd., London SW3* ☎ *0870/906–3781* ⊕ *www.rhs.org.uk/chelsea.*
Late May	The **Hay Festival** in the Welsh border town of Hay-on-Wye gathers authors and readers from all over Britain for a weeklong celebration of the town's status as the used-book capital of the world. Expect plenty of readings of fiction, nonfiction, and poetry. ⊠ *Hay-on-Wye* ☎ *01497/821–299* ⊕ *www.hayfestival.co.uk.*
SUMMER	
Early June	**Derby Day** is the world-renowned horse-racing event, at Epsom Downs Racecourse. ⊠ *Epsom Downs, Surrey* ☎ *01372/463072* ⊕ *www.epsomderby.com.*
Early June	**Grosvenor House Antiques Fair** is one of the most prestigious antiques fairs in Britain. ⊠ *Grosvenor House Hotel, Park La., London W1* ☎ *020/7399–8100* ⊕ *www.grosvenor-antiquesfair.co.uk.*
Early June	**Trooping the Colour** is Queen Elizabeth's colorful official birthday show at Horse Guards Parade, Whitehall, London. (Her actual birthday is in April.) Note that on the two previous Saturdays, there are two Queenless rehearsals—the Colonel's Review and the Major General's Review. *Write for tickets from January to February 28 (enclose SASE or International Reply Coupon):* ⊠ *Ticket Office, Headquarters Household Division, Horse Guards, London SW1 2AX* ☎ *020/7414–2479.*
Mid-June	**Royal Ascot** is the most glamorous date in British horse racing. Usually held during the third week of June, the four-day event is graced by the Queen and other celebrities. Reserve months in advance for

	tickets. ✉ *Ascot Racecourse, Ascot, Berkshire* ☎ *01344/876876* ⊕ *www.ascot-authority.co.uk.*
Late June–Early July	**Wimbledon Lawn Tennis Championships** get bigger every year. Applications for the ticket lottery for the two-week tournament are available October–December. ✉ *All-England Lawn Tennis & Croquet Club, Church Rd., Wimbledon, London SW19 5AE* ☎ *020/8946–2244* ⊕ *www.wimbledon.org.*
Late June–Early July	**Royal Henley Regatta** attracts premier rowers from around the world on the first weekend in July. High society lines the banks of the Thames during this four-day event. ✉ *Henley-on-Thames, Oxfordshire* ☎ *01491/572153* ⊕ *www.hrr.co.uk.*
Late June–Late July	**City of London Festival** fills the City with theater, poetry, classical music, and dance performed by international artists. ☎ *020/7377–0540.*
Early July	**Hampton Court Palace Flower Show,** a five-day event, nearly rivals the Chelsea Flower Show for glamour. ✉ *Hampton Court, East Molesey, Surrey* ☎ *0870/906–3791* ⊕ *www.rhs.org.uk/hamptoncourt.*
Early–Mid-July	**Llangollen International Musical Eisteddfod** sees the little Welsh town of Llangollen overflow with music. ✉ *Musical Eisteddfod Office, Llangollen* ☎ *01978/860000* ⊕ *www.llangollen.org.uk.*
Early Aug.	**Cowes Regatta** draws high flyers, top yachtsmen, and the occasional royal to this grand weeklong boating festival held off the Isle of Wight. ☎ *01983/291914* ⊕ *www.cowesweek.co.uk.*
Mid–Late Aug.	**Edinburgh Festival Fringe,** one of the world's largest theater and music festivals focusing on fringe art, takes place over three weeks, during the Edinburgh International Festival. It's a great chance to see up-and-comers. ☎ *0131/226–0026* ⊕ *www.edfringe.com.*
Mid-Aug.–Early Sept.	**Edinburgh International Festival,** the world's largest festival of the arts, coincides with the nighttime Edinburgh Military Tattoo. ✉ *Castlehill, EH1 2NE* ☎ *0131/473–2020 information; 0131/473–2000 tickets* ⊕ *www.eif.co.uk.*
Late Aug.	**International Beatles Festival** sees hundreds of Beatles tribute bands descend on Liverpool for a week to play to an international crowd of fans. ✉ *Liverpool* ☎ *0151/236–9091.*
Late Aug.	**Notting Hill Carnival,** one of the liveliest street festivals in London, includes Caribbean foods, reggae music, and street parades. ✉ *London* ☎ *020/8964–0544.*
FALL	
Mid-Oct.	**Cheltenham Festival of Literature** draws world-renowned authors, actors, and critics to the elegant, Regency-era town. ☎ *01242/522878* ⊕ *www.cheltenhamfestivals.co.uk.*
Nov. 5	**Guy Fawkes Day** celebrates a foiled 1605 attempt to blow up Parliament. Fireworks are held throughout London, but the place to be is the bonfire festivity on Primrose Hill near Camden Town.

PLEASURES & PASTIMES

English Gardens What is it with the English and gardens? Is it the inroads of urban and suburban living, transforming green fields into gray concrete, that have made this a nation of gardeners? Or is it the love of nature that compels this wet-weather people to attempt to colonize their own patch of it? Despite the frenzied assaults of frosts, slugs, and plentiful rain, the English will grit their teeth, retrieve their gardening forks, and get down on their knees for the sake of an immaculate floral border or weed-free shrubbery. In fact, this is no recent obsession. The Tudors were the first to produce gardens that were more than strictly utilitarian, and since then French, Italian, Dutch, and even Japanese ideas have been imported and adapted to suit the English aesthetic. As a result, a pilgrimage to an English garden is an essential part of any visit. You'll discover some superb gardens that may be just as (or even more) celebrated than the stately home they adorn. Don't think only colorful flowers: ponds exuberantly carpeted with lilies, monumental box hedges, weird topiary, conservatories with exotic plants of all kinds, and manicured swaths of lawn all play a role in the national pastime. Naturally, spring and summer are the best seasons to view these English Edens. Some places have very limited opening times, most close in winter, and some require no small effort to reach. But beware: what started as a casual jaunt may grow into an all-consuming passion, come rain or shine, whatever the weather.

The Performing Arts There's no better antidote to a surfeit of history, pageantry, and assorted heaps of stones—however evocative—than a face-to-face encounter with another British specialty, the performing arts. After all, the past really resonates only when plugged into the present, and the arts in Britain, fueled by a seemingly bottomless well of talent, provide a direct link. Nowhere is this more true than in the dramatic arts, a field in which Britain can still claim to reign supreme. Every provincial town has its own venue, with offerings that can range from the sublime to the absurd, and there is more guarantee of consistently superb productions at the theatrical meccas of Stratford-upon-Avon and London's West End. All the same, don't dismiss the rest of the pack: you can find yourself surprised and delighted by productions in places from York to Chichester, or by a night out at the open-air cliff-top Minack Theatre, on the tip of Cornwall. For other areas of the performing arts—ballet and opera—choose from among the tried and trusted companies of London and Birmingham, though even here some of the remoter places can be quite fine. In summer, look out for festivals, which encompass everything from classical music concerts to poetry readings. These gatherings have a buzz and atmosphere that more formal events cannot match.

The Pub Experience The British could no more live without their "local" than they could forgo dinner. The pub—or public house, to give it its full title—is ingrained in the British psyche as social center, refuge, second home. Pub culture—revolving around pints, pool, darts, and sports—is still male-dominated. However, as a result of the gentrification trend that was launched in the late '80s by the major breweries (which own most pubs), transforming many ancient, smoke-stained dives into fantasy Edwardian drawing rooms, women have been entering their welcoming doors in unstoppable numbers. The trend, in London and other big cities, is toward the bar, superficially identified by its cocktail list, creative paintwork, bare floorboards, and chrome fittings, and to the gastro-pub, where a good kitchen fuels the relaxed ambience. The social function remains the same, however.

In London, some of the best pubs are Victorian-themed miniparks. Etched glass, chandeliers, wood paneling, art nouveau sculptures—all these elements make up some of the city's most distinctive interiors. Of course, many pubs in London (and throughout the country) have been modernized in dubious taste, with too much chrome, plush, and plastic. But some can be a real joy. They will often be called by the name of the local landed family—*The Bath Arms,* or *Lord Crewe's Arms,* "arms" meaning the family coat of heraldic arms on the inn sign—and very possibly they will have old beams and inglenooks, and a blazing log fire in winter. If you sit at a table in the corner, you can have privacy of a sort; but at the bar, conversation is general, and new acquaintances are quickly made. Locals congregate at lunch and in the evening—either right after work, for a sundowner pint, or right after dinner. In areas popular with walkers and hikers, such as the Lake District, people gather at pubs at the end of the day to share experiences as well as to enjoy a pint. At these times, there's no easier way to meet the locals. Whichever brew you order, just remember the locals drink their beer *warm.*

Sports & the Outdoors

Britain has endless opportunities for golf, tennis, and other outdoor activities, but if you really want to savor the landscape while escaping the crowds, it can't offer any better physical pursuit than walking. Footpaths, usually well out of sight of roads, interweave through every part of the country to give access to some of the most alluring spots. More ambitious hikers can set out on one of the long-distance trails, such as the South West Coast Path and the Cotswold Way. Obviously, you can join and leave these paths at any stage (with some planning, you can coordinate a hike's beginning or end with public transportation routes), and most local tourist offices have details of fun circular walks within one area. In all cases, take a good map as well as provisions for the worst eventualities—usually connected with sudden storms or fogs. Most of Britain's footpaths are scrupulously maintained, and liberally supplied with refreshment stops as well as bed-and-breakfasts along the way. Other outdoor pursuits include swimming or surfing from some surprisingly large, sandy beaches (expect cold water and check on the state of the sea beforehand), relaxed cruising on the extensive network of inland waterways, and horseback riding, for which numerous stables exist close to moors and downs.

Stately Homes

A recipe for a half day of bliss: take a generous pinch of history, blend in plenty of art and beauty, wrap it in anecdote, and serve it in the rural heart of Britain. An Englishman's home is his castle, the saying goes, but very often the reverse is true. If it's not a castle, it may be a country pad of palatial proportions, surrounded by ornamental gardens and endless vistas of parkland. Alternatively, it could be a relatively modest, bijou affair, more likely to inspire affection than awe. Indeed, the sheer diversity and ubiquity of Britain's stately homes—every county has its share—are what impel some to devote whole vacations to tracking down the most remote of these historic piles. Whether predominantly Tudor, Jacobean, baroque, Georgian, or Victorian in character, each is steeped in its own idiosyncratic style, and each has volumes of tales to tell, sometimes touching on pivotal moments in the nation's history and other times (equally absorbing) illustrating the arcane routines of domestic life. Until recently, few outsiders ever came past the gates, and the houses were, in effect, private museums. In the best aristocratic tradition, prestige was reflected in the use of the finest crafts-people, architects, and gardeners from the ranks of those previously recruited to work on great religious buildings, and in the rooms full of *objets* and rich furnishings, much of this booty acquired on extended European tours. You've glimpsed these glamorous backdrops in the movies and on television, but the reality is far better.

And a Word About Harry Potter

J. K. Rowling's five novels about Harry Potter, a young British wizard-in-training, have won the hearts of fans of all ages around the world. The release of film versions of the books—as of this writing, *Harry Potter and the Sorcerer's Stone* (in Britain, *Harry Potter and the Philosopher's Stone*) and *Harry Potter and the Chamber of Secrets*—has brought a surge of interest in the British locations used to depict Harry's adventures, from the Reptile House in the London Zoo to the train station in Goathland, North Yorkshire. VisitBritain has created a Harry Potter map, "Discovering the Magic of Britain," that describes key locations in the movies and related sights, and some tour operators (contact VisitBritain for information) have created Potter-themed tours. In this book, key sights linked with the movies are indexed together under Harry Potter sights.

FODOR'S CHOICE

The sights, restaurants, hotels, and other travel experiences on these pages are our editors' top picks—our Fodor's Choices. They're the best of their type in the area covered by the book—not to be missed and always worth your time. In the destination chapters that follow, you will find all the details.

LODGING

£££££	**Cliveden**, Thames Valley. Want to live like Lord Astor for a night? He once called this mansion home, and today lucky you can enjoy his palatial parlors and breathtaking river parterres.
£££££	**Covent Garden Hotel**, London. Relentlessly stylish, this vintage-1880 abode, a former hospital in artsy Covent Garden, shimmers with painted silks, 19th-century oils, and off-duty celebrities.
£££££	**The Dorchester**, London. Off-the-scale opulence *and* charm come with 1,500 square yards of gold leaf and 1,100 square yards of marble at this gem in the heart of Mayfair.
£££££	**Middlethorpe Hall**, York, Yorkshire. This handsome, superbly restored 18th-century mansion looks like a Gainsborough painting come to life, with stunning grounds to match.
£££££	**The Scotsman**, Edinburgh, Scotland. In a previous incarnation this majestic sandstone building housed the offices of the *Scotsman* newspaper; now it's a model of chic, contemporary hotel design.
££££–£££££	**The Lowry Hotel**, Manchester, Lancashire & the Peaks. The sleekness and Italian-inspired modernity of this glass building, a change from British chintz and dark wood, reflect the new energy of this old industrial city.
££££–£££££	**Lumley Castle Hotel**, Chester-le-Street, near Durham, Northeast. Antiques and rich fabrics, dungeons and flagstone corridors—you can take yourself back to medieval times but still stay in modern luxury at this sumptuously baronial Norman castle.
££££–£££££	**Queensberry Hotel**, Bath, Heart of England. Beau Nash would feel right at home. This intimate hotel near the Circus is in three 1772 town houses built for the marquis of Queensberry.
££££–£££££	**Victoria at Holkham**, Wells-next-the-Sea, East Anglia. In the shadow of stately Holkham Hall, this exotic Eastern-inspired hideaway provides a colorful place for a peaceful rest by the seashore.
££££	**myhotel bloomsbury**, London. List your preferences (music, film) and get exactly the room you expect, and a personal assistant to boot. The spa at this karma-filled hotel for individualists offers a honey-and-ginger body wrap.
££–£££	**Cardynham House**, Painswick, Heart of England. Laying on the luxury in a typically understated English manner, this delightful Cotswold retreat both pampers and soothes.

BUDGET LODGING

££   Ambassador Hotel, Glasgow, Scotland. Sophisticated rooms and faultless service are the trademarks of this superior hotel in a terraced town house across from the Botanic Gardens.

££   County Hall Travel Inn Capital, London. What this South Bank chain offering lacks in trendy decor, it makes up for with an enviable Thames-side location (no river views, though) and a low price.

££   Express by Holiday Inn, Liverpool, Lancashire & the Peaks. You're close to all the action and the amenities of Albert Dock and the waterfront at this up-to-date, thoughtfully decorated hotel.

££   Morgan Hotel, London. This cheerful, Georgian row-house hotel near the British Museum is run with panache; larger, self-contained "apartments" cost a bit more but are great for families.

££   New England Hotel, London. The plaid-and-floral furnishings aren't the height of chic, but this very central guest house has power showers, comfortable beds, and a welcoming staff.

££   Ocean House, Aldeburgh, East Anglia. You're close to the beach at this simple 19th-century B&B pleasantly filled with bric-a-brac and antiques.

££   The Old Rectory, Boscastle, West Country. This Victorian B&B is a must for all Thomas Hardy fans—he stayed here when he was courting his future wife—but it makes an alluring stop whatever your literary tastes.

£–££   Dairy Guest House, York, Yorkshire. Although no one comes to this former dairy to buy milk anymore, all the period features of this Victorian house remain, as well as the peaceful courtyard full of rambling plants.

£   Lamperts Cottage, near Cerne Abbas, South. Thatch-roofed and wood-beamed, this rural hideaway a short drive from Dorchester makes a perfect base for jaunts around the leafy lanes of Dorset.

£   T'Gallants, Charlestown, West Country. Everything is ship-shape and spruce aboard this Georgian B&B within a stone's throw of the fascinating harbor of this tiny Cornwall port.

RESTAURANTS

£££££   Gordon Ramsay at Claridge's, London. Nobody does it better than this hot spot's eponymous French-inspired chef, so people book months in advance for his incomparable creations. (If you're heading to Scotland, check out his Amaryllis in Glasgow.)

£££££   Le Manoir aux Quat' Saisons, Great Milton, Thames Valley. Owner-chef Raymond Blanc's 15th-century manor house has held its position as one of Britain's most patrician restaurants for years because of the creative French cuisine.

££££–£££££   Miller Howe, Windermere, Lake District. At this Edwardian hotel you find some of the best food in England, served with idyllic views across Windermere. Warm rabbit salad with apple chutney and guinea fowl with foie gras on onion compote are perfect after hiking.

£££–£££££	**Locanda Locatelli**, London. The food at this elegant Italian restaurant is confident and polished—superb risottos, silky handmade pastas, beautiful desserts.
£££–£££££	**Rogano**, Glasgow, Scotland. Its dramatic art deco style is the initial lure, but the oyster bar and impeccable seafood and meat dishes keep people coming back.
£££–£££££	**Rules**, London. The capital's answer to Maxim's in Paris has entertained everyone from Dickens to the Prince of Wales in its sublimely beautiful Regency salons. It's the perfect escape from the present.
£££–£££££	**The Seafood Restaurant**, Padstow, West Country. Celebrity chef Rick Stein rules his gastronomic empire from this lively Cornwall fishing port, and seafood fans should make every effort to secure a reservation for an unforgettable repast.
££££	**The Merchant House**, Ludlow, Welsh Borders. Foodies flock to this pretty town, a culinary hot spot. In a Jacobean building you can savor both the best of modern British cuisine and more eclectic fare.
££–£££	**Magpie Café**, Whitby, Yorkshire. All kinds of fish are treated well at this old-fashioned favorite in a glorious coastal town.

BUDGET RESTAURANTS

£–£££	**The Eagle**, London. This superior gastro-pub, with wooden floors, a few sofas, and art on the walls, serves amazingly good-value Portuguese-Spanish food.
££	**The Lighthouse**, Aldeburgh, East Anglia. Look for fresh local produce and creatively prepared oysters, crabs, and other seafood at this easy-going brasserie on the coast.
£–££	**busabe eathai**, London. This Thai canteen with hardwood tables is one of Londoners' favorite cheap spots in Soho; everything from the curries to the stir-fries is delicious.
£–££	**Grand Café**, Oxford, Thames Valley. Try this gracious spot with columns and marble tables for coffee and dessert or excellent sandwiches and salads.
£–££	**Kalpna**, Edinburgh, Scotland. Behind the plain exterior of this South Side eatery, extraordinary vegetarian Indian food is served.
£–££	**Milecastle Inn**, near Greenhead, Northeast. The cook has no difficulty satisfying her customers with meat pies and duck with dumplings at this sturdy 17th-century pub close to Hadrian's Wall.
£–££	**The Social**, London. Come here for some old-school English grub—fish sandwiches or beans on toast—against the backdrop of a DJ spinning cool tunes.
£	**City Fish Bar**, Canterbury, Southeast. People line up for classic, crisply fried fish-and-chips at this popular spot in the center of town.
£	**Herbie's**, Exeter, West Country. Simple vegetarian dishes served with a smile—and exquisite organic ice cream—refresh body and spirit in this pleasant eatery near the town center.

PARKS & GARDENS

Bodnant Garden, near Conwy, Wales. Mountains create a magnificent backdrop for Italianate terraces, rock and rose gardens, and plant collections that include magnolias and camellias; the colors here are dramatic.

Eden Project, near St. Austell, West Country. More than anything, it's the imaginative power of this ambitious gallery of plants that really impresses. The outsize geodesic greenhouses at its heart contain specimens from around the world.

Hidcote Manor Gardens, Hidcote Bartrim, Heart of England. The individually themed "rooms" that make up these gardens in the Arts and Crafts style are a succession of delights and represent the pinnacle of horticultural art in England.

Kew Gardens, near London. The spectacular, 300-acre Royal Botanic Gardens at Kew contains more than 30,000 species of plants, and the 19th-century greenhouses are particular treasures.

Sissinghurst Castle Garden, Cranbrook, Southeast. Vita Sackville-West designed this intimate garden around the striking remains of an Elizabethan house; the White Garden is especially celebrated.

Stourhead, Stourton, South. In a nation of noteworthy house-and-garden combinations, this Palladian mansion and 18th-century masterwork of naturalistic landscaping is one of the most impressive.

Stowe Landscape Garden, near Aylesbury, Thames Valley. The greatest gardeners of the 18th century worked on this influential, 980-acre example of large-scale landscaping; artfully placed statues, arches, and temples grace the valleys and rivers.

Wisley, near Guildford, Southeast. The Royal Horticultural Society's garden splendidly blends the pretty and the practical, with innovative gardens that will inspire anyone with a green thumb.

QUINTESSENTIAL BRITAIN

Changing of the Guard, London. Adding a dash of red to the gloomiest of London days, the colorful regiments of guards march with regal pomp as the band plays.

Conwy Castle, Conwy, Wales. Built by Edward I to control the Welsh, this well-preserved fortress with eight large towers captures the spirit of the medieval age.

Durham Cathedral, Durham, Northeast. The impressive view of the cathedral perched above this small university city is matched by its stunning Norman interior; it's a metaphor for English solidity.

Houses of Parliament at sunset, London. Cross the Thames to Jubilee Gardens to see this view of the capital at its storybook best.

Punting on the river, Oxford, Thames Valley. From the river, perspectives change and Oxford becomes an idyllic landscape, complete with weeping willows on the shore and medieval spires in the background.

A ramble around Windermere, Lake District. Have a colored-pencil kit handy to capture the sublime scenery that once inspired Wordsworth and the great romantic poets.

Shakespeare at the Royal Shakespeare Theatre, Stratford-upon-Avon, Shakespeare Country. Seeing the Bard performed in his hometown is an unforgettable theatrical experience, whatever the play.

Stonehenge early in the morning, near Amesbury, South. Crowds can detract from the magic, so arrive early to appreciate the timeless power of this ancient stone circle on the wide Salisbury plan.

Tintagel Castle, Tintagel, West Country. Despite its popularity, this fabled ruin, supposedly King Arthur's birthplace, retains its mystique. The black, forsaken remains are poised dramatically over the swirling sea.

View of Salisbury Cathedral from the town path, Salisbury, South. Dramatically poised over the town for more than 600 years, this mighty stone confection has one of the most famous profiles in the country. Constable captured the classic view of its soaring spire.

A walk along Hadrian's Wall, Northeast. There's no better way to fire up your imagination to appreciate the legacy of the Romans in Britain than a walk along this wall and a visit to its forts.

Westminster Abbey, London. The majestic abbey exudes history. Nearly all of England's monarchs have been crowned here, amid great heraldic splendor; many are buried here, too.

STATELY HOMES

Blenheim Palace, Woodstock, Thames Valley. "Magnificent" is the adjective to describe this early-18th-century house, seat of the dukes of Marlborough and England's only rival to Versailles.

Castle Howard, Coneysthorpe, Yorkshire. The masterpiece of English baroque architecture, this birthday cake of a house was used to memorable effect as Lord Marchmain's residence in TV's *Brideshead Revisited*. The landscaping is equally extravagant.

Cawdor Castle, near Nairn, Scotland. Shakespeare's Macbeth was Thane (clan chief) of Cawdor, but this 14th-century castle exudes centuries of real, not fictional, history.

Floors Castle, near Kelso, Scotland. The largest inhabited house in Scotland, this 18th-century pile has been the home of the dukes of Roxburghe since it was built. Today you can wander through glorious formal rooms as well as the billiard room.

Haddon Hall, near Bakewell, Lancashire & the Peaks. A medieval book illumination come to life, this castellated 15th-century manor bristles with slate roofs and towers and is surrounded by famous rose gardens.

Holkham Hall, Wells-next-the-Sea, East Anglia. A splendid 60-foot-tall marble entryway modeled after the Roman Baths of Diocletian and salons filled with old masters distinguish this splendid Palladian palace, near an expanse of sandy beaches and a salt marsh.

Ightham Mote, near Sevenoaks, Southeast. This 14th-century manor house with a moat and a lovely garden will transport you back to the Middle Ages.

Knole, Sevenoaks, Southeast. A vast deer park surrounds this sprawling Elizabethan mansion, which counts a remarkable set of silver furniture, impressive tapestries, and family portraits of the Sackvilles among its many highlights.

Lanhydrock, near Bodmin, West Country. It's a stunning ensemble: formal gardens, expansive parkland, and a house that presents the spectrum of life in a Victorian country home from the kitchen to the drawing room.

Petworth House, Petworth, Southeast. Grounds landscaped by Capability Brown, superb paintings, and wood carvings by Grinling Gibbons make this one of the National Trust's treasures.

TOWNS & VILLAGES

Castle Combe, Heart of England. Once a stand-in Puddleby-on-the-Marsh in the Rex Harrison film *Doctor Dolittle*, this village with simple stone cottages and a graceful church has a toylike, once-upon-a-time magic.

Clovelly, West Country. The sheer prettiness of this village perched on a cliff edge above the sea will beguile the most cynical heart.

Dedham, East Anglia. Good restaurants and lodgings add to the pleasure of a visit to this tiny, picture-book town in the heart of Constable country.

Lacock, Heart of England. This slumbering Wiltshire village has it all (including too many summer visitors): an abbey that is now a stately home, some choice inns and tearooms, and a scattering of antiques shops.

Lavenham, East Anglia. Sweet and small, this village is chock-full of well-preserved Tudor half-timber buildings, the former homes of wool merchants and weavers.

Lower Slaughter, Heart of England. One of the Cotswold's "water villages," this is built around Slaughter Brook, home to a gaggle of geese, which can often be seen paddling under the footbridges.

Ludlow, Welsh Borders. Even without its unique concentration of superb restaurants, this town clustered below the ruins of a medieval castle would merit a visit for its fine medieval, Georgian, and Victorian buildings.

Portmeirion, Wales. This fantasy-Italianate village, complete with town hall, shops, and grand hotel, is quite un-Welsh but totally charming.

Whitby, Yorkshire. A ruined abbey and a striking harbor lined with cliffs combine with a rich legacy of fishing and whaling lore to enhance this scenic coastal town.

SMART TRAVEL TIPS

Finding out about your destination before you leave home means you won't squander time organizing everyday minutiae once you've arrived. You'll be more streetwise when you hit the ground as well, better prepared to explore the aspects of Great Britain that drew you here in the first place. The organizations in this section can provide information to supplement this guide; contact them for up-to-the-minute details, and consult the A to Z sections that end each chapter for facts on the various topics as they relate to the region's countries. Happy landings!

AIR TRAVEL

BOOKING

When you book, **look for nonstop flights** and **remember that "direct" flights stop at least once.** Try to avoid connecting flights, which require a change of plane. Two airlines may operate a connecting flight jointly, so ask whether your airline operates every segment of the trip; you may find that the carrier you prefer flies you only part of the way. To find more booking tips and to check prices and make online flight reservations, log on to www.fodors.com.

CARRIERS

British Airways is the national flag carrier and offers mostly nonstop flights from 18 U.S. cities to Heathrow and Gatwick airports outside London, along with flights to Manchester, Birmingham, and Glasgow. It offers myriad add-on options that help bring down ticket costs. In addition, it has a vast program of discount airfare-hotel packages. Britain-based Virgin Atlantic is a strong competitor in terms of packages.

Because Britain is such a small country, internal air travel is much less important there than in the United States. For trips of less than 200 mi, the train is often quicker, with rail stations more centrally located. Flying tends to cost more, but for longer trips—for example, between London and Glasgow or Edinburgh—or where a sea crossing is involved, to places such as the Scottish islands, air travel has a considerable time advantage.

British Airways operates shuttle services between Heathrow or Gatwick and Edinburgh, Glasgow, and Manchester. Passengers can simply turn up and get a flight (usually hourly) without booking. British Midland operates from Heathrow to Aberdeen, Belfast, Dublin, Edinburgh, Glasgow, Leeds, Manchester, and Teesside, as well as to Washington, D.C., and Chicago; it also serves a number of U.S. cities from Manchester.

Low-cost airlines such as Easyjet, BMI Baby, and Ryanair offer flights within the United Kingdom as well as to cities in Ireland and continental Europe. Prices are low, but don't expect to fly into a major destination. These airlines usually use satellite cities and fly out of smaller British airports such as Stansted and Luton (both near London).

🛫 To & from Great Britain **Aer Lingus** ☎ 800/474–7424; 0845/084–4444 in London ⊕ www.aerlingus. com to Heathrow, Gatwick. **American Airlines** ☎ 800/433–7300; 020/8572–5555 in London; 1300/130–757 in Australia; 09/309–9159 in New Zealand ⊕ www.aa.com to Heathrow, Gatwick, Glasgow. **British Airways** ☎ 800/247–9297; 0845/773–3377 in London; 1300/767–177 in Australia; 09/356–8690 in New Zealand ⊕ www.britishairways.com to Heathrow, Gatwick. **British Midland** ☎ 800/788/0555; 020/8745–7321 in London ⊕ www.flybmi.com. **Continental** ☎ 800/231–0856; 0800/776464 in London; 1300/361–400 in Australia; 09/308–3350 in New Zealand ⊕ www.continentalairlines.com to Heathrow, Gatwick, Glasgow. **Delta** ☎ 800/241–4141; 0800/414767 in London; 02/9251–3211 in Australia; 09/379–3370 in New Zealand ⊕ www.delta.com to Gatwick. **Northwest Airlines** ☎ 800/225–2525; 0870/507–4074 in London; 008/221–714 in Australia ⊕ www.nwa.com to Gatwick. **United** ☎ 800/538–2929; 0845/844–4777 in London; 008/131–777 in Australia; 09/379–3800 in New Zealand ⊕ www.ual.com to Heathrow. **US Airways** ☎ 800/622–1015; 0845/600–3300 in London; 02/9959–3922 in Australia; 09/623–4294 in New Zealand ⊕ www.usairways.com to Gatwick. **Virgin Atlantic** ☎ 800/862–8621; 01293/747747 in London; 02/9244–2747 in Australia ⊕ www.virgin-atlantic.com to Heathrow, Gatwick, Glasgow. 🛫 Within Great Britain & to Europe **BMI Baby** ☎ 0870/264–2229 in London ⊕ www.bmibaby.com. **Easyjet** ☎ 0870/600–0000 in London ⊕ www.easyjet.com. **Ryanair** ☎ 0870/246–0000 in London ⊕ www.ryanair.com.

CHECK-IN & BOARDING

Always find out your carrier's check-in policy. Plan to arrive at the airport about two hours before your scheduled departure time for domestic flights and 2½ to 3 hours before international flights. You may need to arrive earlier if you're flying from one of the busier airports or during peak air-traffic times. If you're flying to Europe from Great Britain, arrive at the airport at least two hours in advance.

To avoid delays at airport-security checkpoints, try not to wear any metal. Jewelry, belt and other buckles, steel-toe shoes, barrettes, and underwire bras are among the items that can set off detectors.

Assuming that not everyone with a ticket will show up, airlines routinely overbook planes. When everyone does, airlines ask for volunteers to give up their seats. In return, these volunteers usually get a several-hundred-dollar flight voucher, which can be used toward the purchase of another ticket, and are rebooked on the next flight out. If there are not enough volunteers, the airline must choose who will be denied boarding. The first to get bumped are passengers who checked in late and those flying on discounted tickets, so **get to the gate and check in as early as possible**, especially during peak periods.

Always **bring a government-issued photo I.D. to the airport;** even when it's not required, a passport is best.

CUTTING COSTS

The least expensive airfares to Great Britain are priced for round-trip travel and must usually be purchased in advance. Airlines generally allow you to change your return date for a fee; most low-fare tickets, however, are nonrefundable. It's smart to **call a number of airlines and check the Internet;** when you are quoted a good price, **book it on the spot**—the same fare may not be available the next day, or even the next hour. Always **check different routings** and look into using alternate airports. Also, price off-peak flights, which may be significantly less expensive than others. Travel agents, especially low-fare specialists (⇨ Discounts & Deals), are helpful.

Consolidators are another good source. They buy tickets for scheduled flights at reduced rates from the airlines, then sell them at prices that beat the best fare available directly from the airlines. Sometimes you can even get your money back if you need to return the ticket. Carefully read the fine print detailing penalties for changes and cancellations, purchase the ticket with a credit card, and **confirm your consolidator reservation with the airline. In**

Britain, the best place to **search for consolidator, or so-called bucket shop, tickets** is through Cheap Flights, a Web site that pools all flights available and then directs you to a phone number or site to purchase tickets.

If you plan to fly within Britain or Europe, **look into airline discount passes,** which you must purchase before you leave home. The Discover Europe Airpass from British Midland is available on the airline's British and European flights. The pass is valid for up to 90 days and starts at $109 for shorter routes and $159 for longer flights. The Europe Pass from British Airways offers travelers a way to choose from the airline's and its partners' networks in Great Britain and Europe; prices vary. It can be hard to find pass information on Web sites: try typing the name of the pass into a search engine, or search for "pass" within the carrier's Web site.

🔲 Consolidators **AirlineConsolidator.com** ☎ 888/468-5385 ⊕ www.airlineconsolidator.com, for international tickets. **Best Fares** ☎ 800/576-8255 or 800/576-1600 ⊕ www.bestfares.com; $59.90 annual membership. **Cheap Flights** ⊕ www.cheapflights. com. **Cheap Tickets** ☎ 800/377-1000 or 888/922-8849 ⊕ www.cheaptickets.com. **Expedia** ☎ 800/397-3342 or 404/728-8787 ⊕ www.expedia.com. **Hotwire** ☎ 866/468-9473 or 920/330-9418 ⊕ www. hotwire.com. **Now Voyager Travel** ✉ 45 W. 21st St., 5th floor, New York, NY 10010 ☎ 212/459-1616 🖷 212/243-2711 ⊕ www.nowvoyagertravel.com. **Onetravel.com** ⊕ www.onetravel.com. **Orbitz** ☎ 888/656-4546 ⊕ www.orbitz.com. **Priceline.com** ⊕ www.priceline.com. **Travelocity** ☎ 888/709-5983; 877/282-2925 in Canada; 0870/876-3876 in U.K. ⊕ www.travelocity.com.
🔲 Discount Airfares & Passes **British Airways** ☎ 800/247-9297; 0845/773-3377 in London; 1300/767-177 in Australia; 09/356-8690 in New Zealand ⊕ www.britishairways.com. **British Midland** ☎ 800/788/0555; 020/8745-7321 in London ⊕ www.flybmi.com. **DER Travel Services** ✉ 9501 W. Devon Ave., Rosemont, IL 60018 ☎ 800/782-2424 🖷 800/282-7474 for information; 800/860-9944 for brochures ⊕ www.der.com.

ENJOYING THE FLIGHT

State your seat preference when purchasing your ticket, and then repeat it when you confirm and when you check in. For more legroom, you can request one of the few emergency-aisle seats at check-in, if you are capable of lifting at least 50 pounds—a Federal Aviation Administration requirement of passengers in these seats. Seats behind a bulkhead also offer more legroom, but they don't have underseat storage. Don't sit in the row in front of the emergency aisle or in front of a bulkhead, where seats may not recline.

Ask the airline whether a snack or meal is served on the flight. If you have dietary concerns, **request special meals when booking.** These can be vegetarian, low-cholesterol, or kosher, for example. It's a good idea to pack some healthful snacks and a small (plastic) bottle of water in your carry-on bag. On long flights, try to maintain a normal routine, to help fight jet lag. At night, **get some sleep.** By day, **eat light meals, drink water** (not alcohol), and **move around the cabin** to stretch your legs. For additional jet-lag tips consult *Fodor's FYI: Travel Fit & Healthy* (available at bookstores everywhere).

Smoking policies vary from carrier to carrier. Many airlines prohibit smoking on all of their flights; others allow smoking only on certain routes or certain departures. Ask your carrier about its policy.

FLYING TIMES

Flying time is about 6½ hours from New York, 7½ hours from Chicago, 9½ hours from Dallas, 10 hours from Los Angeles, and 21½ hours from Sydney.

HOW TO COMPLAIN

If your baggage goes astray or your flight goes awry, complain right away. Most carriers require that you **file a claim immediately.** The Aviation Consumer Protection Division of the Department of Transportation publishes *Fly-Rights,* which discusses airlines and consumer issues and is available on-line. You can also find articles and information on mytravelrights.com, the Web site of the nonprofit Consumer Travel Rights Center.
🔲 Airline Complaints **Aviation Consumer Protection Division** ✉ U.S. Department of Transportation, C-75, Room 4107, 400 7th St. SW, Washington, DC 20590 ☎ 202/366-2220 ⊕ airconsumer.ost.dot.gov. **Federal Aviation Administration Consumer Hotline** ✉ For inquiries: FAA, 800 Independence Ave. SW, Washington, DC 20591 ☎ 800/322-7873 ⊕ www.faa.gov.

RECONFIRMING

Check the status of your flight before you leave for the airport. You can do this on your carrier's Web site, by linking to a flight-status checker (many Web booking services offer these), or by calling your carrier or travel agent. Always confirm international flights at least 72 hours ahead of the scheduled departure time.

AIRPORTS

Most international flights to London arrive at either Heathrow Airport (LHR), 15 mi west of London, or at Gatwick Airport (LGW), 27 mi south of the capital. Most flights from the United States go to Heathrow, which is divided into four terminals, with Terminals 3 and 4 handling transatlantic flights (British Airways uses Terminal 4). Gatwick is London's second gateway, serving 21 U.S. destinations. A third, newer airport, Stansted (STN), is 35 mi northeast of the city. It handles mainly European and domestic traffic, although there is a scheduled service from New York. Luton Airport (LLA), just 30 mi north of the city, serves British and European destinations. Luton is the hub for the low-cost Easyjet airline. There are fast connections from all the London airports into the capital. Manchester in the north of England is the hub for British Midland's flights from the United States. Birmingham, in the Midlands, handles mainly European and British flights as well as flights from Chicago, Denver, Newark, New York, and Orlando. All international flights to Scotland arrive at Glasgow airport (➪ Scotland A to Z *in* Chapter 15).

📌 Airport Information **Birmingham Airport** ☎ 0121/767-5511 ⊕ www.bhx.co.uk.**Heathrow Airport** ☎ 0870/000-0123 ⊕ www.baa.co.uk/heathrow. **Gatwick Airport** ☎ 0870/000-2468 ⊕ www.baa.co.uk/gatwick. **Luton Airport** ☎ 01582/405100 ⊕ www.london-luton.co.uk. **Manchester Airport** ☎ 0161/489-3000 ⊕ www.manairport.co.uk. **Stansted Airport** ☎ 0870/000-0303 ⊕ www.baa.co.uk/stansted.

DUTY-FREE SHOPPING

As of July 1999, duty-free shopping allowances between Britain and other European Union member countries were abolished, although there are still numerous merchandise offers for those traveling between EU countries by boat, plane, and via the Channel Tunnel. Duty-free sales for travel outside the EU remain business as usual (➪ Customs & Duties).

AIRPORTS & CITY TRANSFERS TO LONDON

See London A to Z *in* Chapter 1 for information on transportation between the airports and London.

BIKE TRAVEL

Bikes are banned from freeways and most divided highways or main trunk roads, but on side roads and country lanes, the bike is one of the best ways to explore Britain. The National Cycle Network, a work in progress, covers about 7,000 mi of cycling and walking routes. Some routes are in towns and parts of the countryside; for example, in the Peak District National Park, bikes can be rented by the day for use on special traffic-free trails. Cyclists can legally use public bridleways—green, unsurfaced tracks reserved for horses, walkers, and cyclists. Some former railway lines have become popular bike paths, such as the Tarka Trail in North Devon and the Camel Trail in Cornwall. Bikes, from racing to mountain, are usually available for rental, and prices vary by area, anywhere from £3–£5 an hour to £7–£20 for a full day. A deposit of £25 or more is often required. For night cycling, the law requires a full set of reflectors on the wheels and pedals, and lights at the back and front.

Sustrans (a nonprofit organization concerned with sustainable transportation) and the Cyclists' Touring Club (CTC, a national organization; ➪ Sports & Outdoors) can provide route guides and information on cycling in Britain. For maps, the Landranger by Ordnance Survey series costs £5.50 a map and covers the country in scale 1:50,000 in more than 30 editions. Stanfords bookshop stocks the world's largest selection of maps and has a telephone and Internet ordering service. The Highway Code booklet (£1.50), available at a service station, newsstand, or bookstore, contains information for cyclists.

Call ahead to tourist information offices for lists of local rental outlets, or contact the Britain Visitor Centre. The Yellow Pages classified telephone directory lists cycle rentals.

📌 Bike Maps & Travel Information **Cyclists' Touring Club** ✉ Cotterell House, 69 Meadow, Godalm-

ing, GU7 3HS ☎ 01483/417217 ⊕ www.ctc.org.uk.
Landranger by Ordnance Survey ⊠ Order Processing, Romsey Rd., Southampton, SO16 4GU ☎ 02380/792439 ⊕ www.ordnancesurvey.co.uk. **National Cycle Network (Sustrans)** ⊠ 35 King St., Bristol, BS1 4DZ ☎ 0117/926-8893 ⊕ www.sustrans.org.uk. **Stanfords** ⊠ 12-14 Long Acre, London, WC2E 9LP ☎ 020/7836-1321 ⊕ www.stanfords.co.uk.
🚲 Bike Rentals **Britain Visitor Centre** ⊠ 1 Regent St., London, SW1Y 4NX ☎ No phone ⊕ www. visitbritain.com. **Yellow Pages** ⊕ www.yell.co.uk.

BIKES IN FLIGHT

Most airlines accommodate bikes as luggage, provided they are dismantled and boxed; check with individual airlines about packing requirements. Some airlines sell bike boxes, which are often free at bike shops, for about $15 (bike bags can be considerably more expensive). International travelers often can substitute a bike for a piece of checked luggage at no charge; otherwise, the cost is about $100 U.S. and Canadian airlines charge $40–$80 each way.

BIKES ON TRAINS

Most trains allow bicycles on board for free or for up to £3 per journey. Bicycles are generally not allowed during commuter hours; folding bikes are almost always allowed, however. Check with the railway before bringing your bike.

BOAT & FERRY TRAVEL

Ferries, hovercraft, and Seacats (a kind of ferry) travel regular routes to France, Spain, Ireland, and Scandinavia. There are also numerous canal ways through the countryside and to the coast (⇨ Sports & Outdoors).

Hoverspeed provides fast travel to France and Belgium. P&O runs ferries between Belgium, Great Britain, Ireland, France, the Netherlands, and Spain. DFDS Seaways covers Denmark, Holland, Germany, Norway, Poland, and Sweden. Stena Line covers Ireland and the Netherlands.

FARES & SCHEDULES

For fares and schedules, contact ferry companies directly. Travelers checks (in pounds), cash, and major credit cards are accepted for payments. Prices vary; booking early ensures cheaper fares, but also ask about special deals. The Ferry Infor-

mation Service can help with questions about routes and overviews of ferry companies. Seaview is a comprehensive on-line ferry and cruise booking portal for Great Britain and continental Europe.
🚤 Boat & Ferry Information **DFDS Seaways** ☎ 01255/240240 ⊕ www.dfdsseaways.co.uk. **Ferry Information Service** ☎ 020/7436-2449 ⊕ www. ferryinformationservice.co.uk. **Hoverspeed** ☎ 0870/524-0241 ⊕ www.hoverspeed.com. **P&O Irish Sea** ☎ 0870/242-4666 ⊕ www.poirishsea.com. **P&O North Sea** ☎ 0870/129-6002 ⊕ www.ponsf.com. **P&O Portsmouth** ☎ 0870/242-4999 ⊕ www. poportsmouth.com. **P&O Stena Line** ☎ 0870/600-0600 ⊕ www.posl.com. **P&O Ireland and Holland** ☎ 0870/5707070 ⊕ www.poirishsea.com. **Seaview** ⊕ www.seaview.co.uk. **Stena Line** ☎ 0870/570-7070 ⊕ www.stenaline.co.uk.

BUS TRAVEL

Britain has a comprehensive bus (short-haul) and coach (long-distance) network that offers an inexpensive way of seeing the country. National Express is the major coach operator, and Victoria Coach Station in London is the hub of the National Express network, serving around 1,200 destinations within Great Britain and, via Eurolines, continental Europe. Tickets (payable by most major credit cards, reservations are advisable) and information are available from any of the company's 2,500 agents nationwide, including offices at London's Heathrow and Gatwick airport coach stations. Green Line is the next-largest national service; although it serves fewer destinations, airports and major tourist towns are covered. In Scotland, Scottish Citylink runs a similar operation.

Coach tickets can be as low as half the price of a train ticket, and buses are just as comfortable as trains. However, most bus services will double the travel time of trains. Nearly all bus services have a no-smoking policy, and both National Express and Scottish Citylink have on-board refreshments and toilets. There is only one class of service.

Double-decker buses make up many of the extensive networks of local bus services, run by private companies. Check with the local bus station or tourist information center for bus schedules. Most companies offer day or week Explorer or Rover unlimited-travel tickets, and those in popular tourist areas invariably operate special scenic tours in summer. The top deck of a stately double-decker bus is a great place from which to view the countryside.

CUTTING COSTS

National Express's Tourist Trail Pass costs £49 for 2 days of travel within a 3-day period; £85 for 5 days of travel within 30 days; £135 for 8 travel days within 30 days; £190 for 15 travel days within 30 days; and £205 for 15 travel days within 60 days. A Discount Coach Card for students, 16–25s, and over-50s, which costs £9 and is good for one year, qualifies you for 20%–30% discounts off many fares. You can buy your National Express Tourist Trail Pass in advance from the U.S.-based British Travel International travel agency. Most companies offer a discount for children under 15. Scottish Citylink offers the Smart Card for students, 16–25s, and over-50s, which costs £6 for one year and qualifies you for up to 30% off standard fares. Discount cards usually require a passport-size photo upon application. The Scottish Citylink Explorer Pass covering Scotland costs £33 for 3 consecutive days of travel; £55 for 5 consecutive days of travel out of 10; £85 for 8 consecutive days of travel out of 16. The Explorer Pass includes discounts on some Scottish ferries as well as at independent hostels.

FARES & SCHEDULES

🚌 Bus Information **British Travel International** 🏠 Box 299, Elkton, VA 22827 🕾 800/327-6097 🌐 www.britishtravel.com. **Green Line** ✉ Green Line Travel Office, 4a Fountain Sq., 123-151 Buckingham Palace Rd., London, SW1 🕾 0870 /608-7261 🌐 www.greenline.co.uk. **National Express** 🕾 0870/ 580-8080 🌐 www.nationalexpress.com. **Scottish Citylink** ✉ Buchanan Bus Station, Killermont St., Glasgow, G2 3NP 🕾 0870/550-5050 🌐 www. citylink.co.uk. **Victoria Coach Station** ✉ 164 Buckingham Palace Rd., London, SW1W 9TP 🕾 020/ 7730-3466 🌐 www.victoriacoachstation.com.

BUSINESS HOURS

BANKS & OFFICES

Most banks are open weekdays 9:30–3:30 or 4:30. Some have Thursday evening hours, and a few are open Saturday morning. Many offices are open weekdays 9:30–5:30.

GAS STATIONS

Most gas stations in central London are open seven days, 24 hours. Farther out of London or off the major roads, hours vary considerably but are usually daily 8–8.

MUSEUMS & SIGHTS

The major national museums and galleries are open daily, including lunchtime, but with shorter hours on Sunday. Regional museums are usually closed Monday and have shorter hours in winter. In London, many museums are open late one evening a week.

PHARMACIES

British pharmacies are called chemists. Independent chemist shops are generally open Monday–Saturday 9:30–5:30, although in larger cities some stay open until 10 PM; the local newspaper lists which pharmacies are open late. In London, the leading chain drugstore, Boots, is open until 6; the Oxford Street and Piccadilly Circus branches are also open Sunday, and until 8 PM Thursday.

SHOPS

Usual business hours are Monday–Saturday 9–5:30; on Sunday, small grocery stores stay open all day, as do larger food markets, superstores, and shopping malls. Outside the main centers, most shops close at 1 PM once a week, often Wednesday or Thursday. In small villages, many also close for lunch. In large cities—especially London—department stores stay open late (usually until 7:30 or 8) one night a week. On national holidays, most stores are closed, and over the Christmas holidays, most restaurants are closed as well (⇨ Holidays).

CAMERAS & PHOTOGRAPHY

Don't be surprised if you are asked to refrain from taking pictures during theater, ballet, or opera productions, and in galleries. In most museums and stately homes, you need to get permission, and you usually cannot use a flash. Locals are generally happy to feature in your photos, but it's polite to ask. There are many must-photograph sights in Britain, but London's Big Ben and the guards on horseback in Whitehall are top of the list. In the countryside, try for a thatched- or slate-roof cottage or a typical English garden.The *Kodak Guide to Shooting Great Travel Pictures* (available at bookstores everywhere) is loaded with tips.

🔲 Photo Help **Kodak Information Center** ☎ 800/242-2424 ⊕ www.kodak.com.

EQUIPMENT PRECAUTIONS

Don't pack film and equipment in checked luggage, where it is much more susceptible to damage. X-ray machines used to view checked luggage are extremely powerful and therefore are likely to ruin your film. Try to **ask for hand inspection of film,** which becomes clouded after repeated exposure to airport X-ray machines, and **keep videotapes and computer disks away from metal detectors.** Always **keep film, tape, and computer disks out of the sun.** Carry an extra supply of batteries, and **be prepared to turn on your camera, camcorder, or laptop** to prove to airport security personnel that the device is real.

FILM & DEVELOPING

Film is available from chemists, news dealers, and supermarkets, as well as photography stores. Kodak, followed by Agfa and Fuji, are the most common brands, and prices range from £2 to £4 for a roll of 36-exposure color print film. Chain drugstores, such as Boots or Superdrug, and supermarkets run cost-cutting deals and offer one-hour photo developing.

VIDEOS

Remember that most video cartridges sold in Britain (marked PAL) do not interface with American video players (NTSC). The top tourist attractions that have videos also market versions specially made for the American and overseas market. If you're bringing your own video camcorder, bring a supply of cassettes as well.

CAR RENTAL

Rental rates vary widely but are generally expensive, beginning at £50 ($80) a day and £200 ($320) a week for a small economy car, usually with manual transmission. Air-conditioning and unlimited mileage generally come with larger automatic transmission cars.

🔲 Major Agencies **Alamo** ☎ 800/522-9696 ⊕ www.alamo.com. **Avis** ☎ 800/331-1084; 800/879-2847 in Canada; 0870/606-0100 in U.K.; 02/

9353-9000 in Australia; 09/526-2847 in New Zealand ⊕ www.avis.com. **Budget** ☎ 800/527-0700; 0870/156-5656 in U.K. ⊕ www.budget.com. **Dollar** ☎ 800/800-6000; 0124/622-0111 in U.K., where it's affiliated with Sixt; 02/9223-1444 in Australia ⊕ www.dollar.com. **Hertz** ☎ 800/654-3001; 800/263-0600 in Canada; 0870/844-8844 in U.K.; 02/9669-2444 in Australia; 09/256-8690 in New Zealand ⊕ www.hertz.com. **National Car Rental** ☎ 800/227-7368; 0870/600-6666 in U.K. ⊕ www.nationalcar.com.

CUTTING COSTS

For a good deal, **book through a travel agent who will shop around.**

Do **look into wholesalers,** companies that do not own fleets but rent in bulk from those that do and often offer better rates than traditional car-rental operations. Prices are best during off-peak periods. Rentals booked through wholesalers often must be paid for before you leave home.

Easy Car rents stick-shift Mercedes A-class minivans for as little as £9 ($12) a day. You must book early via the Web site. Phoning costs 60p ($1) per minute. Costs are kept low by not offering extras, by using advertising on the vehicles, and by having rental outlets in a limited number of cities: London, Birmingham, Glasgow, Liverpool, and Manchester.

🔲 Local Agencies **Dimple Car Hire** ✉ 19 Varley Parade, London, NW9 6RR ☎ 020/8205-1200 🖷 020/7243-4408 ⊕ www.dimple-selfdrive.co.uk. **Easy Car** ☎ 0906/333-3333, 60p per minute within the U.K. ⊕ www.easycar.com. **Enterprise** ✉ 466-480 Edgeware Rd., London, W2 1EL ☎ 020/7723-4800 🖷 020/7723-4368. **Europcar** ✉ 30 Woburn Pl., London, WC1H 0JR ☎ 020/7637-0514 🖷 020/7323-2189 ⊕ www.europcar.com. **1car1** ✉ 140 Druid St., London, SE1 2HH ☎ 020/7394-8383 🖷 020/7237-6459 ⊕ www.1car1.com.

🔲 Wholesalers **Auto Europe** ☎ 207/842-2000 or 800/223-5555 🖷 207/842-2222 ⊕ www.autoeurope.com. **Europe by Car** ☎ 212/581-3040 or 800/223-1516 🖷 212/246-1458 ⊕ www.europebycar.com. **Destination Europe Resources** (DER) ✉ 9501 W. Devon Ave., Rosemont, IL 60018 ☎ 800/782-2424 ⊕ www.der.com. **Kemwel** ☎ 800/678-0678 🖷 207/842-2124 ⊕ www.kemwel.com.

INSURANCE

When driving a rented car, you are generally responsible for any damage to or loss of the vehicle. Collision policies that car-rental companies sell for European rentals typically do not cover stolen vehicles. Before you rent—and purchase collision or theft coverage—see what coverage you already have under the terms of your personal auto-insurance policy and credit cards.

REQUIREMENTS & RESTRICTIONS

In Britain your own driver's license is acceptable. An International Driver's Permit is a good idea; it's available from the American or Canadian automobile association, and, in the United Kingdom, from the Automobile Association or Royal Automobile Club. These international permits, valid only in conjunction with your regular driver's license, are universally recognized, and having one in your wallet may save you a problem with the local authorities. Companies frequently restrict rentals to people over age 23 or under age 75.

SURCHARGES

Before you pick up a car in one city and leave it in another, **ask about drop-off charges or one-way service fees,** which can be substantial. Note, too, that some rental agencies charge extra if you return the car before the time specified in your contract. To avoid a hefty refueling fee, **fill the tank just before you turn in the car,** but be aware that gas stations near the rental outlet may overcharge. It's almost never a deal to buy the tank of gas that's in the car when you rent it; the understanding is that you'll return it empty, but some fuel usually remains. Car seats usually cost about £20 extra. Adding one extra driver is usually included in the original rental price.

CAR TRAVEL

With close to 60 million inhabitants in a country about the size of California, Britain has some of the most crowded roads in the world. In London, it's best to rely on the excellent public transport network—with the city's tediously slow traffic and restrictive parking rules, a car is a proverbial noose. But away from the towns and cities, you can find miles of little-used roads and lanes where driving can be a real pleasure.

EMERGENCY SERVICES

If your car breaks down, position the red hazard triangle (which should be in the trunk) a few paces away from the rear of the car. Leave the hazard warning lights on. On major highways, emergency roadside telephone booths are positioned within walking-distance intervals. Contact your car rental company or call the Automobile Association toll-free. You can join and receive assistance from the AA on the spot, but the charge is higher—around £75—than a simple membership fee. If you are a member of the AAA (American Automobile Association) or another association, check your membership details before you travel; reciprocal agreements may give you free roadside aid.

⛟ Ambulance, fire, police ☎ 999. **Automobile Association** ☎ 0800/085-2721 ⊕ www.theaa.co.uk.

GASOLINE

Gasoline is called petrol in the United Kingdom and is sold by the liter. Most large stations are open 24 hours a day, seven days a week, except in rural areas, where hours can vary. Service stations generally accept all major credit cards. Service is self-serve; only in small villages are you likely to find a friendly attendant (tips aren't expected). Petrol is becoming increasingly expensive, at 80p per liter at press time. Supermarket pumps just outside the city centers frequently offer the best prices. Unleaded petrol is predominant, denoted by green stickers on fuel pumps and pump lines. Premium and super premium are the two varieties, and most cars run on regular premium.

PARKING

Parking regulations are strictly enforced. In London, meters have an insatiable hunger—£1 buys almost 15 minutes—and some will permit only a two-hour stay. Do check the regulations on the meter, as most meters do not require feeding at night or on weekends. Do not park within 15 yards of an intersection. Within central London parking is permitted on single yellow lines during certain hours (check the signs on the sidewalk), usually after 6 or 7 PM and on weekends. Do not park on double yellow lines or in bus lanes. On "Red Routes"—busy roads with red lines painted in the street—you may not stop even to let out a passenger. At night, you can park in 30-mph zones, but only if you are within 25 yards of a lighted streetlight.

ROAD CONDITIONS

There's a very good network of superhighways (motorways) and divided highways (dual carriageways) throughout most of Britain, although in more remote areas, especially in parts of Wales and Scotland, where unclassified roads join village to village and are little more than glorified agricultural cart tracks, travel is noticeably slower. Motorways (with the prefix *M*), shown in blue on most maps and road signs, are mainly two or three lanes in each direction. Other fast major roads (with the prefix *A*) are shown on maps in green and red. Sections of fast dual carriageway (with black-edged, thick outlines on maps) have both traffic lights and traffic circles, and right turns are sometimes permitted. Turnoffs are often marked by highway numbers, rather than place names, so know the road numbers.

The vast network of lesser roads, for the most part old coach and turnpike roads, might make your trip take twice the time but show you twice as much. Minor roads drawn in yellow or white, the former prefixed by *B*, the latter unlettered and unnumbered, are the ancient lanes and byways, a superb way of discovering the real Britain. Some of these (the white roads, in the main) are pothole-filled switchbacks, littered with blind corners and barely wide enough for one car. Be prepared to reverse into a passing place if you meet an oncoming car or truck.

ROAD MAPS

You can purchase maps and atlases (Michelin is one brand) in advance from bookstores, or buy them in Britain. Good planning maps are available from Britain's Automobile Association or the Royal Automobile Club. The excellent Ordnance Survey or Collins maps, available from newsstands and bookstores in Britain, cost about £3.95 for a paper foldout to £6.99 for a spiral-bound paperback.

⊞ In the U.K. **Automobile Association** ☎ 0870/600-0371 ⊕ www.theaa.co.uk. **Royal Automobile Club** ☎ 0800/731-1104 ⊕ www.rac.co.uk.

RULES OF THE ROAD

Always remember to **drive on the left in Britain**; this takes a bit of getting used to, and it's much easier if you're driving a British car where the steering and mirrors are designed for U.K. conditions. Study your map before leaving the airport, and be sure to give yourself plenty of time to adjust. The use of seat belts is obligatory in the front seat and in the back seat where they exist (except for particularly old models, all cars should have both front and rear seat belts). You can still talk on a hand-held cell phone while you drive, but legislation is being considered that would ban this practice.

If you plan to drive in Britain, **pick up a copy of the official Highway Code** (£1.50) at a service station, newsstand, or bookstore. Besides driving rules and illustrations of signs and road markings, this booklet contains information for motorcyclists, cyclists, and pedestrians.

Speed limits are complicated, and traffic police can be hard on speeders, especially in urban areas. In those areas, the limit (shown on circular red signs) is generally 30 mph, but 40 mph on some main roads. In rural areas the limit is 60 mph on ordinary roads and 70 mph on motorways. At traffic circles ("roundabouts" in Britain), circulation is clockwise, and entering motorists must yield to cars coming from their right. The use of horns is prohibited between 11:30 PM and 7 AM.

Pedestrians have the right-of-way on "zebra" crossings (black and white stripes that stretch across the street between two Belisha beacons—orange-flashing globe lights on posts). The curb on each side of the zebra crossing has zigzag markings. It is illegal to park within the zigzag area or to pass another vehicle at a zebra crossing. At other crossings, pedestrians must yield to traffic, but they do have the right-of-way over traffic turning left—if they dare.

Drunk-driving laws are strictly enforced. The legal limit is 80 milligrams of alcohol, which means roughly two units of alcohol—two glasses of wine, one pint of beer, or one glass of whisky—but these amounts vary, depending on your body weight or the amount you have eaten that day. It's far safer to avoid alcohol if you're driving.

THE CHANNEL TUNNEL

Short of flying, taking the "Chunnel" is the fastest way to cross the English Channel: 35 minutes from Folkestone to Calais, 60 minutes from motorway to motorway, or 3 hours from London's Waterloo Station to

Paris's Gare du Nord. The Eurostar train also has service to Brussels.

⚐ Car Transport Eurotunnel ☎ 0870/535-3535 in U.K.; 070/223210 in Belgium; 03-21-00-61-00 in France ⊕ www.eurotunnel.com. **French Motorail/Rail Europe** ☎ 0870/241-5415 ⊕ www.frenchmotorail.com.

⚐ Passenger Service Eurostar ☎ 1233/617575; 0870/518-6186 in U.K. ⊕ www.eurostar.co.uk. **Rail Europe** ☎ 800/942-4866 or 800/274-8724; 0870/584-8848 U.K. inquiries and credit-card bookings ⊕ www.raileurope.com.

CHILDREN IN GREAT BRITAIN

Plan your itinerary to include places and activities that will keep your children happy, and **involve your youngsters** as you outline your trip. Many museums and major attractions offer special interactive features that appeal to kids; for example, some stately homes and castles have added children's "fun trails," where kids can play detective as they explore the property. Cinemas, concert halls, and theaters have plenty of kid-friendly entertainment, particularly during school holidays. And even the more chic restaurants are learning to welcome well-behaved children.

If you are renting a car, don't forget to **arrange for a car seat** when you reserve. For general advice about traveling with children, consult *Fodor's FYI: Travel with Your Baby* (available in bookstores everywhere).

For information on events for kids in and around London, look for *Kids Out!*, a monthly magazine available from newsstands and bookstores. London Line, the London Tourist Board's information line, offers two options: What's On for Children and Places for Children to Go, both 60p per minute from a U.K. phone. The tourist board publishes *Where to Take Children. Fodor's Around London with Kids* (available in bookstores everywhere) can help you plan your days.

⚐ Local Information London Line ☎ 09068/663344.

FLYING

If your children are two or older, **ask about children's airfares.** As a general rule, infants under two not occupying a seat fly at greatly reduced fares or even for free. But if you want to guarantee a seat for an infant, you have to pay full fare. Consider flying during off-peak days and times; most airlines will grant an infant a seat without a ticket if there are available seats. When booking, **confirm carry-on allowances** if you're traveling with infants. In general, for babies charged 10% to 50% of the adult fare you are allowed one carry-on bag and a collapsible stroller; if the flight is full, the stroller may have to be checked or you may be limited to less.

Experts agree that it's a good idea to use safety seats aloft for children weighing less than 40 pounds. Airlines set their own policies: if you use a safety seat, U.S. carriers usually require that the child be ticketed, even if he or she is young enough to ride free, because the seats must be strapped into regular seats. And even if you pay the full adult fare for the seat, it may be worth it, especially on longer trips. Do **check your airline's policy about using safety seats during takeoff and landing.** Safety seats are not allowed everywhere in the plane, so get your seat assignments as early as possible.

When reserving, **request children's meals or a freestanding bassinet** (not available at all airlines) if you need them. But note that bulkhead seats, where you must sit to use the bassinet, may lack an overhead bin or storage space on the floor.

FOOD

You'll find the usual gamut of burger and fast-food chains (Burger King, McDonald's, Kentucky Fried Chicken) in Britain. Pizza chains, such as Pizza Hut and Pizza Express, are family-friendly—with foods to please parents, too; London has one on nearly every corner, and they also crop up in larger cities nationwide. Many families find that ethnic restaurants offer the best combination of moderate prices and interesting food. Almost every town has its share of Asian eateries and Italian pasta joints. If your children have a taste for spices, try Indian restaurants, which are particularly common in London and in the northern cities of Birmingham and Manchester. Most pubs and small country hotels are becoming more family oriented and have family eating rooms (although these can lack character). Unless your children's behavior is impeccable, avoid the high-class, terribly British establishments.

LODGING

Most hotels in Great Britain allow children under a certain age to stay in their parents' room at no extra charge, but others charge for them as extra adults; be sure to **find out the cutoff age for children's discounts**, which is usually about 12 years old.

PUBS

Most pubs tend to be child-friendly, but many have restricted hours for children. At some pubs, children between the ages of 14 and 17 can enter bar areas; children younger than 14 can be admitted, with an adult, only if the pub has a Children's Certificate. At others, anyone younger than 21 is not allowed in a bar after 6 PM. The Web site www.pubs.com, which covers London pubs, sorts out restrictions and lists child-friendly pubs.

SIGHTS & ATTRACTIONS

Places that are especially appealing to children are indicated by a rubber-duckie icon (☺) in the margin.

SUPPLIES & EQUIPMENT

You'll find everything you need for babies and children in supermarkets such as Sainsbury's and Tesco's and in the Boots and Superdrug pharmacies. American brands are widely available.

TRANSPORTATION

For air transportation, *see* Flying. On trains and buses, children between the ages of 5 and 15 pay half or reduced fares, and kids under 5 travel free. When riding in a car, children are required by law to use seat belts. Children under 5 must ride in a child seat. Many car rental companies rent car seats for younger children; ask in advance.

COMPUTERS ON THE ROAD

If you're traveling with a laptop, carry a spare battery and adapter. Never plug your computer into any socket before asking about surge protection. Some hotels do not have built-in current stabilizers, and extreme electrical fluctuations and surges can short your adapter or even destroy your computer. Before connecting your computer to a phone line, you may want to test the line as well. IBM sells an invaluable pen-size modem tester that plugs into a telephone jack to check whether the line is safe to use.

CONSUMER PROTECTION

Whether you're shopping for gifts or purchasing travel services, **pay with a major credit card** whenever possible, so you can cancel payment or get reimbursed if there's a problem (and you can provide documentation). If you're doing business with a particular company for the first time, **contact your local Better Business Bureau and the attorney general's offices** in your state and (for U.S. businesses) the company's home state as well. Have any complaints been filed? Finally, if you're buying a package or tour, always **consider travel insurance** that includes default coverage (⇨ Insurance).

🔲 BBBs **Council of Better Business Bureaus** ✉ 4200 Wilson Blvd., Suite 800, Arlington, VA 22203 ☎ 703/276-0100 🖨 703/525-8277 ⊕ www.bbb.org.

CRUISE TRAVEL

In 2004 the Cunard Line's new *Queen Mary 2* will replace the *Queen Elizabeth 2* on regular crossings, April–December, between Southampton, England, and Baltimore, Boston, and New York City; arrangements can include one-way airfare. Check the travel pages of your Sunday newspaper for other cruise ships that sail to Britain, or consult a travel agent. For information about cruising waterways in Great Britain, *see* Sports & Outdoors. To learn how to plan, choose, and book a cruise-ship voyage, consult *Fodor's FYI: Plan & Enjoy Your Cruise* (available in bookstores everywhere).

🔲 Cruise Lines **Cunard Line** ☎ 800/728-6273 ⊕ www.cunard.com.

CUSTOMS & DUTIES

When shopping abroad, **keep receipts** for all purchases. Upon reentering the country, **be ready to show customs officials what you've bought.** Pack purchases together in an easily accessible place. If you think a duty is incorrect, appeal the assessment. If you object to the way your clearance was handled, note the inspector's badge number. In either case, first ask to see a supervisor. If the problem isn't resolved, write to the appropriate authorities, beginning with the port director at your point of entry.

IN AUSTRALIA

Australian residents who are 18 or older may bring home A$400 worth of souvenirs and gifts (including jewelry), 250 cigarettes or 250 grams of cigars or other tobacco products, and 1,125 ml of alcohol (including wine, beer, and spirits). Residents under 18 may bring back A$200 worth of goods. Members of the same family traveling together may pool their allowances. Prohibited items include meat products. Seeds, plants, and fruits need to be declared upon arrival.

🛂 **Australian Customs Service** ⚐ Regional Director, Box 8, Sydney, NSW 2001 ☎ 02/9213-2000 or 1300/363263; 02/9364-7222 or 1800/803-006 quarantine-inquiry line 🖷 02/9213-4043 ⊕ www.customs.gov.au.

IN CANADA

Canadian residents who have been out of Canada for at least seven days may bring in C$750 worth of goods duty-free. If you've been away fewer than seven days but more than 48 hours, the duty-free allowance drops to C$200. If your trip lasts 24 to 48 hours, the allowance is C$50. You may not pool allowances with family members. Goods claimed under the C$750 exemption may follow you by mail; those claimed under the lesser exemptions must accompany you. Alcohol and tobacco products may be included in the seven-day and 48-hour exemptions but not in the 24-hour exemption. If you meet the age requirements of the province or territory through which you reenter Canada, you may bring in, duty-free, 1.5 liters of wine or 1.14 liters (40 imperial ounces) of liquor or 24 12-ounce cans or bottles of beer or ale. Also, if you meet the local age requirement for tobacco products, you may bring in, duty-free, 200 cigarettes and 50 cigars. Check ahead of time with the Canada Customs and Revenue Agency or the Department of Agriculture for policies regarding meat products, seeds, plants, and fruits.

You may send an unlimited number of gifts (only one gift per recipient, however) worth up to C$60 each duty-free to Canada. Label the package UNSOLICITED GIFT—VALUE UNDER $60. Alcohol and tobacco are excluded.

🛂 **Canada Customs and Revenue Agency** ✉ 2265 St. Laurent Blvd., Ottawa, Ontario, K1G 4K3 ☎ 800/461-9999, 204/983-3500, or 506/636-5064 ⊕ www.ccra.gc.ca.

IN NEW ZEALAND

All homeward-bound residents may bring back NZ$700 worth of souvenirs and gifts; passengers may not pool their allowances, and children can claim only the concession on goods intended for their own use. For those 17 or older, the duty-free allowance also includes 4.5 liters of wine or beer; one 1,125-ml bottle of spirits; and either 200 cigarettes, 250 grams of tobacco, 50 cigars, or a combination of the three up to 250 grams. Meat products, seeds, plants, and fruits must be declared upon arrival to the Agricultural Services Department.

🛂 **New Zealand Customs** ✉ Head office: The Customhouse, 17-21 Whitmore St., Box 2218, Wellington ☎ 09/300-5399 or 0800/428-786 ⊕ www.customs.govt.nz.

IN THE U.K.

Fresh meats, plants and vegetables, controlled drugs, and firearms and ammunition may not be brought into the United Kingdom. Pets from the United States or Canada with the proper documentation may be brought into the country without quarantine under the U.K. Pet Travel Scheme (PETS). The process takes about six months to complete and involves detailed steps.

You will face no customs formalities if you enter Scotland or Wales from any other part of the United Kingdom.

🛂 **HM Customs and Excise** ✉ Portcullis House, 21 Cowbridge Rd. E, Cardiff, CF11 9SS ☎ 029/2038-6423 or 0845/010-9000 ⊕ www.hmce.gov.uk. **Pet Travel Scheme** ✉ Department for Environment, Food and Rural Affairs, Area 201, 1a Page St., London, SW1P 4PQ ☎ 0870/241-1710 ⊕ www.defra.gov.uk/animalh/quarantine/index.htm.

IN THE U.S.

U.S. residents who have been out of the country for at least 48 hours may bring home, for personal use, $800 worth of foreign goods duty-free, as long as they haven't used the $800 allowance or any part of it in the past 30 days. This exemption may include 1 liter of alcohol (for travelers 21 and older), 200 cigarettes, and 100 non-Cuban cigars. Family members from the same household who are traveling together may pool their $800 personal exemptions. For fewer than 48 hours, the duty-free allowance drops to $200, which may include 50 cigarettes, 10 non-Cuban cigars, and 150 ml of alcohol (or 150 ml of perfume containing alcohol). The $200 allowance cannot be combined with other individuals' exemptions, and if you exceed it, the full value of all the goods will be taxed. Antiques, which the U.S. Bureau of Customs and Border Protection defines as objects more than 100 years old, enter duty-free, as do original works of art done entirely by hand, including paintings, drawings, and sculptures. This doesn't apply to folk art or handicrafts, which are in general dutiable.

You may also send packages home duty-free, with a limit of one parcel per ad-dressee per day (except alcohol or tobacco products or perfume worth more than $5). You can mail up to $200 worth of goods for personal use; label the package PERSONAL USE and attach a list of its contents and their retail value. If the package contains your used personal belongings, mark it AMERICAN GOODS RETURNED to avoid paying duties. You may send up to $100 worth of goods as a gift; mark the package UNSOLICITED GIFT. Mailed items do not affect your duty-free allowance on your return.

To avoid paying duty on foreign-made high-ticket items you already own and will take on your trip, register them with Customs before you leave the country. Consider filing a Certificate of Registration for laptops, cameras, watches, and other digital devices identified with serial numbers or other permanent markings; you can keep the certificate for other trips. Otherwise, bring a sales receipt or insurance form to show that you owned the item before you left the United States.

U.S. Bureau of Customs and Border Protection ⊠ For inquiries and equipment registration, 1300 Pennsylvania Ave. NW, Washington, DC 20229 ⊕ www.customs.gov ☎ 202/354-1000 or 877/287-8667 ⊠ For complaints, Customer Satisfaction Unit, 1300 Pennsylvania Ave. NW, Room 5.5D, Washington, DC 20229.

DISABILITIES & ACCESSIBILITY

Compared with the United States, Great Britain has a ways to go in helping people with disabilities, but it is making strides in making its major cities more accessible. In London, for instance, most Underground (subway) stations have vast escalators and steps, but contact the London Transport

information line for their booklet "Access to the Underground," which gives facts about elevators and ramps at individual tube stations as well as information about buses and Braille maps. The spacious, regal London Black Cabs are perfectly accommodating for people in wheelchairs, and further good news is that many London hotels have wheelchair ramps. More buses are now equipped to deal with wheelchairs, too. The London Tourist Board produces an updated newsletter, *London for All,* available from Tourist Information Centres. Note that VisitBritain and the London Tourist Board will provide lists of London hotels for people with disabilities; these hotels often post the sign H at their door to welcome such travelers.

Artsline provides information on the accessibility of arts venues (theaters and cinemas) and events. For vacation bookings and special deals on equipped hotel rooms, contact Holiday Care or Can Be Done travel agency. RADAR, or the Royal Association for Disability and Rehabilitation, has travel information and advice on accommodations throughout the British Isles and Europe. DIAL, or the Disablement Information and Advice Line, offers information on local groups in Britain that can provide advice. Tripscope covers the ground on all transport questions. Wheelchair Travel & Access Mini Buses advise on where to find converted cars to rent, including chauffeured minibuses and cars with hand controls.

Local Resources **Artsline** ⊠ 54 Chalton St., London, NW11HS ☎ 020/7388-2227 ⊕ www.artsline.org.uk. **Can Be Done** ⊠ 7-11 Kensington High St. London, W8 5NP ☎ 020/8907-2400 ⊕ www.canbedone.co.uk. **DIAL** ☎ 01302/310123. **Holiday Care** ⊠ 7th Floor Sunley House, 4 Bedford Pk., Croydon, Surrey, CR0 2AP ☎ 0845/124-9971 ⊕ www.holidaycare.org.uk. **London Transport's Unit for Disabled Passengers** ⊠ 172 Buckingham Palace Rd., London, SW1 9TN ☎ 020/7918-3312 ☎ 020/7918-3876 ⊕ www.londontransport.co.uk. **RADAR** ⊠ 12 City Forum, 250 City Rd., London, EC1V 8AF ☎ 020/7250-3222 ⊕ www.radar.org.uk. **Trip-scope** ⊠ The Vassall Centre, Gill Ave., Bristol, BS16 2QQ ☎ 0845/758-5641 ⊕ www.tripscope.org.uk. **Wheelchair Travel & Access Mini Buses** ⊠ 1 Johnston Green, Guildford, Surrey, GU2 6XS ☎ 01483/233-640 ⊕ www.wheelchair-travel.co.uk.

LODGING

The definition of accessibility may differ from hotel to hotel, so it's best to ask questions. If you have mobility problems, ask for the lowest floor on which accessible services are offered. If you have a hearing impairment, check whether the hotel has devices to alert you visually to the ring of the telephone, a knock at the door, and a fire/emergency alarm. Some hotels provide these devices without charge. Discuss your needs with hotel personnel if this equipment isn't available, so that a staff member can personally alert you in the event of an emergency. If you're bringing a guide dog, get authorization ahead of time and write down the name of the person with whom you spoke.

If you book directly through Holiday Care, rates at some hotels with special facilities for visitors with disabilities can be discounted.

RESERVATIONS

When discussing accessibility with an operator or reservations agent, **ask hard questions.** Are there any stairs, inside *or* out? Are there grab bars next to the toilet *and* in the shower/tub? How wide is the doorway to the room? To the bathroom? For the most extensive facilities meeting the latest legal specifications, **opt for newer accommodations.** If you reserve through a toll-free number, consider also calling the hotel's local number to confirm the information from the central reservations office. Get confirmation in writing when you can.

SIGHTS & ATTRACTIONS

The London Tourist Board can provide information on city attractions with accessible facilities. It is best to phone ahead to check on the details of different venues around Britain. Alternatively, you could put yourself in the hands of a tour company such as Tour Guides Ltd.; they not only tailor custom tours but also have a dynamic Blue Badge guide who is a wheelchair user.

Local Resources **Tour Guides Ltd.** ☎ 020/7495-5504 ⊕ www.tourguides.co.uk.

TRANSPORTATION

Complaints **Aviation Consumer Protection Division** (➪ Air Travel) for airline-related problems. **Departmental Office of Civil Rights** ⊠ For general inquiries, U.S. Department of Transportation, S-30, 400 7th St. SW, Room 10215, Washington, DC 20590 ☎ 202/366-4648 🖷 202/366-9371 ⊕ www.dot.gov/ost/docr/index.htm. **Disability Rights Section**

⊠ NYAV, U.S. Department of Justice, Civil Rights Division, 950 Pennsylvania Ave. NW, Washington, DC 20530 📠 ADA information line 202/514-0301; 800/514-0301; 202/514-0383 TTY; 800/514-0383 TTY ⊕ www.ada.gov. **U.S. Department of Transportation Hotline** ☎ For disability-related air-travel problems, 800/778-4838 or 800/455-9880 TTY.

TRAVEL AGENCIES

In the United States, the Americans with Disabilities Act requires that travel firms serve the needs of all travelers. Some agencies specialize in working with people with disabilities.

Travelers with Mobility Problems **Access Adventures/B. Roberts Travel** ⊠ 206 Chestnut Ridge Rd., Scottsville, NY 14624 ☎ 585/889-9096 ⊕ www.brobertstravel.com, run by a former physical-rehabilitation counselor. **CareVacations** ⊠ No. 5, 5110-50 Ave., Leduc, Alberta, Canada T9E 6V4 ☎ 780/986-6404 or 877/478-7827 🖷 780/986-8332 ⊕ www.carevacations.com, for group tours and cruise vacations. **Flying Wheels Travel** ⊠ 143 W. Bridge St., Box 382, Owatonna, MN 55060 ☎ 507/451-5005 🖷 507/451-1685 ⊕ www.flyingwheelstravel.com.

DISCOUNTS & DEALS

Be a smart shopper and **compare all your options** before making decisions. A plane ticket bought with a promotional coupon from travel clubs, coupon books, and direct-mail offers or purchased on the Internet may not be cheaper than the least expensive fare from a discount ticket agency. And always keep in mind that what you get is just as important as what you save.

DISCOUNT PASSES

If you plan to visit castles, gardens, and historic houses during your stay in Britain, **look into discount passes or organization memberships** that can provide significant savings. The National Trust, English Heritage, and the Historic Houses Association are involved with hundreds of properties. Some passes, including VisitBritain's Great British Heritage pass and English Heritage's Overseas Visitor pass, are for specific amounts of time from four days to a month; memberships in organizations such as the National Trust (the Royal Oak Foundation is the U.S. affiliate), English Heritage, and the Historic Houses Association are generally annual. Some passes can be purchased on-line. The VisitBritain Web site (⇨ Visitor Information) has information about these and other discounts. Be sure to **match what the pass or membership offers against your itinerary** to see if its worthwhile. For London Pass information, *see* London A to Z *in* Chapter 1. For passes specifically for Wales and Scotland, *see* Wales A to Z *in* Chapter 9 and Scotland A to Z *in* Chapter 15.

F English Heritage ☎ 0870/333-1181 ⊕ www. english-heritage.org.uk. **Historic Houses Association** ☎ 020/7259-5688 ⊕ www.hha.org.uk. **Royal Oak Foundation** ⊠ 26 Broadway, Suite 950, New York, NY 10004 ☎ 212/480-2889 or 800/913-6565 ⊕ www.royal-oak.org.

DISCOUNT RESERVATIONS

To save money, **look into discount reservations services** with Web sites and toll-free numbers, which use their buying power to get a better price on hotels, airline tickets (⇨ Air Travel), even car rentals. When booking a room, always **call the hotel's local toll-free number** (if one is available) rather than the central reservations number—you'll often get a better price. Always ask about special packages or corporate rates.

When shopping for the best deal on hotels and car rentals, **look for guaranteed exchange rates,** which protect you against a falling dollar. With your rate locked in, you won't pay more, even if the price goes up in the local currency.

F Airline Tickets Air 4 Less ☎ 800/AIR4LESS, low-fare specialist.

F Hotel Rooms Accommodations Express ☎ 800/444-7666 or 800/277-1064 ⊕ www. accommodationsexpress.com. **Hotels.com** ☎ 800/ 246-8357 or 214/369-1246 ⊕ www.hotels.com. **Steigenberger Reservation Service** ☎ 800/223-5652 ⊕ www.srs-worldhotels.com. **Travel Interlink** ☎ 800/888-5898 ⊕ www.travelinterlink.com. **Turbotrip.com** ☎ 800/473-7829 ⊕ www.turbotrip. com.

PACKAGE DEALS

Don't confuse packages and guided tours. When you buy a package, you travel on your own, just as though you had planned the trip yourself. Fly/drive packages, which combine airfare and car rental, are often a good deal. In cities, ask the local visitor's bureau about hotel packages that include tickets to major museum exhibits or other special events. If you **buy a rail/drive pass,**

you may save on train tickets and car rentals. All Eurailpass holders get a discount on Eurostar fares through the Channel Tunnel and often receive reduced rates for buses, hotels, ferries, and car rentals. BritRail Pass holders can purchase Eurostar tickets with their rail passes, too.

EATING & DRINKING

The stereotypical notion of British meals as parade of roast beef, overcooked vegetables, and stodgy puddings is gradually being replaced—particularly in London and other major cities—with a more contemporary picture of Britain as hot foodie territory. From trendy gastro-pubs to the see-and-be-seen dining shrines, Britain is shedding its tired image and becoming one of the most global palates on earth.

The restaurants reviewed in this book are the cream of the crop in each price category. Properties indicated by ✕☐ are lodging establishments whose restaurant warrants a special trip. Price-category information is given in each chapter. In general, restaurant prices are high. If you're watching your budget, **seek out pubs and ethnic restaurants,** which offer excellent food at reasonable prices.

CATEGORY	COST
££££££	over £22
££££	£18-£22
£££	£13-£17
££	£7-£12
£	under £7

Prices are for a main course at dinner and are given in pounds.

MEALS & SPECIALTIES

Local cafés serving the traditional English breakfast of eggs, bacon, beans, half a grilled tomato, and strong tea are often the cheapest—and best—places for breakfast. For lighter morning fare (or for real brewed coffee), try the Continental-style sandwich bars offering croissants and other pastries.

At lunch, you can grab a sandwich between sights, pop into the local pub, or sit down in a restaurant. Dinner, too, has no set rules, but a three-course meal is standard in most mid-range or high-end restaurants. Pre- or post-theater menus, offering two or three courses for a set price, are usually a good value. Note that most pubs do not have any waitstaff and that you are expected to go to the bar, order a beverage and your meal, and inform them of your table number.

These days, especially in London, "local" could mean nearly any global flavor, but for pure Britishness, a traditional roast beef dinner still tops the list. Its typical accompaniment is Yorkshire pudding—a savory soufflé-like batter of eggs, milk, and flour oven-baked until crisp, then topped with a rich, dark gravy. Shepherd's pie, a classic pub dish, is made with diced or minced lamb and a mashed potato topping. In the pubs, you'll also find a ploughman's lunch—crusty bread, English cheese (perhaps cheddar, blue Stilton, crumbly Cheshire, or smooth red Leicester), and pickles. And of course, there's also fish-and-chips, usually made from cod or haddock deep-fried in a crispy batter and served with thick "chips"—what Americans know as French fries. Take time for afternoon tea—whether with scones (with cream and jam) or cucumber sandwiches, it's still a civilized respite.

You can eat your way around the country seeking out regional specialties. Every region has its own cheese, beer, cake, and candy—from the crumbly, sharp cheeses of the Yorkshire and Derbyshire dales to the hard cheddars of Somerset, the creamy goats' rounds in Wales, and the nutty Cornish yarg. In Devon and Cornwall, look for tooth-tingling fudge and toffee made with clotted cream.

MEALTIMES

Breakfast is generally served between 7:30 and 9 and lunch between noon and 2. Tea—often a meal in itself—is taken between 4 and 5:30, dinner or supper between 7:30 and 9:30, sometimes earlier, seldom later except in large cities. High tea, at about 6, replaces dinner in some areas like the north, where lunch is always called dinner. Sunday roasts at pubs last from 11 AM or noon to 3 or 5 PM.

Unless otherwise noted, the restaurants listed in this guide are open daily for lunch and dinner.

PAYING

Be sure that you **don't double pay a service charge.** Many restaurants exclude service charges from the printed menu (which the law obliges them to display outside), then add 10%–15% to the check, or else stamp

SERVICE NOT INCLUDED along the bottom, in which case you should add the 10%–15% yourself. Just don't pay twice for service—some restaurateurs have been known to add service, but leave the total on the credit card slip blank. Larger establishments generally accept major credit cards; pubs, small cafés, or ethnic restaurants may be cash-only.

RESERVATIONS & DRESS

Reservations are always a good idea; we mention them only when they're essential or not accepted. Book as far ahead as you can, and reconfirm as soon as you arrive. (Large parties should always call ahead to check the reservations policy.) We mention dress only when men are required to wear a jacket or a jacket and tie.

WINE, BEER & SPIRITS

Traditional British beer is not the golden-colored designer stuff in fancy bottles served in trendy cafés. Although hundreds of varieties are brewed around the country, the traditional brew is known as bitters. Lighter American-style beer is called lager, and the black brew is called stout (with Guinness the major brand). You may also find traditional "hard" cider made from pressed apples, which can pack an alcoholic punch. If you're a wine aficionado, you'll generally find the selection and quality higher in a wine bar or café, rather than in a pub. Pub hours are 11–11, with last orders called about 20 minutes before closing time, though the law may change to allow later closings. The legal drinking age is 18; unless there's a special family room or a beer garden, children are not welcome in some pubs (⇨ Children in Great Britain).

ELECTRICITY

To use electric-powered equipment purchased in the United States or Canada, **bring a converter and adapter.** The electrical current in Great Britain is 230 volts (in line with the rest of Europe), 50 cycles alternating current (AC); wall outlets take three-pin plugs, and shaver sockets take two round, oversize prongs. Blackouts and brownout are rare and are usually fixed in a few hours.

If your appliances are dual-voltage, you'll need only an adapter. Don't use 110-volt outlets marked FOR SHAVERS ONLY for high-wattage appliances such as blow-dryers. Most laptops operate equally well on 110 and 220 volts and so require only an adapter. For converters, adapters, and advice, contact the British Airways Travel Shop.

🔁 **British Airways Travel Shop** ✉ 156 Regent St., W1B 5SN ☎ 020/7434-4725.

EMBASSIES

🔁 Australia **Australia House** ✉ Strand, London, WC2 ☎ 020/7379-4334 ⊕ www.australia.org.uk.

🔁 Canada **MacDonald House** ✉ 38 Grosvenor St., London, W1 ☎ 020/7258-6600 ⊕ www.canada.org. uk.

🔁 New Zealand **New Zealand House** ✉ 80 Haymarket, London, SW1 ☎ 020/7930-8422 ⊕ www. nzembassy.com.

🔁 United States **American Embassy** ✉ 24 Grosvenor Sq., London, W1 ☎ 020/7499-9000 ⊕ www.usembassy.org.uk; for passports, go to the **U.S. Passport Unit** ✉ 55 Upper Brook St., London, W1 ☎ 020/7499-9000.

EMERGENCIES

If you need to report a theft or an attack, go to the nearest police station, listed in the Yellow Pages or the local directory. For severe emergencies, dial 999 for police, fire, or ambulance. Be prepared to give the telephone number you're calling from. National Health Service hospitals give free, 24-hour treatment in Accident and Emergency sections, although delays can be an hour or more. Prescriptions are valid only if made out by doctors registered in the U.K. For additional information, see the A to Z sections in each chapter.

🔁 **Ambulance, fire, police** ☎ 999.

ETIQUETTE & BEHAVIOR

The traditional British reserve is starting to thaw. Particularly with the younger generations, spontaneous displays of delight or displeasure are becoming more commonplace. But in the theater, the opera, and the church, and in other traditional spots, decorum is the word. If you're visiting a family home, a simple bouquet of flowers is a welcome gift. If you're invited for a meal, bringing a bottle of wine is appropriate, if you wish, as is some candy for the children. Kissing on greeting is still too Continental for most Brits (except among the fashion and

media types, who go for two or three air kisses); a warm handshake is just fine. The British can never say please or thank you too often, and to thank a host for hospitality, either a phone call or thank-you card is always appreciated.

BUSINESS ETIQUETTE

Punctuality is of prime importance, so **call ahead if you anticipate a late arrival.** Spouses do not generally attend business dinners, unless invited. If you invite someone to dine, it's usually assumed that you will pick up the tab. However, if you are the visitor, your host may insist on paying.

GAY & LESBIAN TRAVEL

Most major cities (particularly Birmingham, Brighton, Edinburgh, Glasgow, Manchester, and London) have gay communities and social centers. In London, the main gay areas are in the center city—Soho, Old Compton Street, and west to Kensington and Earl's Court. There's a thriving social scene of clubs and cafés; for London event notices, contact Gay's the Word bookshop. The *Pink Paper*, available at libraries, large bookstores, and gay bars, *Gay Times*, and *Time Out* have comprehensive London listings. The round-the-clock London Lesbian & Gay Switchboard is a font of information on London's gay scene. VisitBritain has a brochure and Web site for gay and lesbian travelers.

🔁 Local Resources **Gay Times** ☎ 020/8340-8644 ⊕ www.gaytimes.co.uk. **Gay's the Word** ✉ 66 Marchmont St., London, WC1N 1AB ☎ 020/ 7278-7654 ⊕ www.gaystheword.co.uk. **London Lesbian & Gay Switchboard** ☎ 020/7837-7324 ⊕ www.llgs.org.uk. **VisitBritain** ☎ 800/462-2748 ⊕ www.gaybritain.org.

🔁 Gay- & Lesbian-Friendly Travel Agencies **Different Roads Travel** ✉ 8383 Wilshire Blvd., Suite 520, Beverly Hills, CA 90211 ☎ 323/651-5557 or 800/ 429-8747 (Ext. 14 for both) 🖷 323/651-3678 ✒ lgernert@tzell.com. **Kennedy Travel** ✉ 130 W. 42nd St., Suite 401, New York, NY 10036 ☎ 212/840-8659 or 800/237-7433 🖷 212/730-2269 ⊕ www. kennedytravel.com. **Now, Voyager** ✉ 4406 18th St., San Francisco, CA 94114 ☎ 415/626-1169 or 800/ 255-6951 🖷 415/626-8626 ⊕ www.nowvoyager. com. **Skylink Travel and Tour** ✉ 1455 N. Dutton Ave., Suite A, Santa Rosa, CA 95401 ☎ 707/546-9888 or 800/225-5759 🖷 707/636-0951, serving lesbian travelers.

GUIDEBOOKS

Plan well and you won't be sorry. Guide-books are excellent tools—and you can take them with you. You may want to check out the comprehensive *Fodor's London*; color-photo-illustrated *Fodor's Exploring Britain* and *Exploring London*, thorough on culture and history; *Fodor's Around London with Kids*, great for families; and *Citypack London*, with a super-size city map. All are available at on-line retailers and bookstores everywhere.

HEALTH

Great Britain enjoys high standards of health, from safe drinking water to pasteurized foods. That noted, all travelers should pack medicines to help cope with diet changes and consequent irregularity, although these are also available over the counter in British pharmacies. If you take prescription drugs, keep a supply in your carry-on luggage and make a list of all your prescriptions to keep on file at home while you are abroad. You will not be able to renew a U.S. prescription at a pharmacy in Britain. Prescriptions are accepted only if issued by a U.K.-registered physician.

In recent years, there has been concern in Great Britain and throughout Europe about Bovine Spongiform Encephalopathy (BSE), commonly known as Mad Cow Disease, a fatal disease believed to have spread to cattle through the use of feed enriched with body parts of sheep infected with a related disease. It's possible for humans to contract Creutzfeldt-Jakob Disease, an extremely rare, fatal, brain-wasting illness, by eating meat from infected cattle. Although the chance of catching the disease is extremely small, you may wish to avoid eating beef or choose beef or beef products, such as solid pieces of muscle meat (as opposed to burgers or sausages), that might have a reduced opportunity for contamination with tissues that might harbor the BSE agent. For more information, contact the Centers for Disease Control and Prevention.

🄵 Health Warnings **National Centers for Disease Control and Prevention (CDC)** ✉ National Center for Infectious Diseases, Division of Quarantine, Travelers' Health, 1600 Clifton Rd. NE, Atlanta, GA 30333 ☎ 877/394-8747 international travelers' health line; 404/498-1600 Division of Quarantine; 800/311-3435 other inquiries 🖷 888/232-3299 ⊕ www.cdc.gov/travel.

HOLIDAYS

ENGLAND & WALES

Holidays are New Year's Day; Good Friday and Easter Monday on Easter weekend; May Day (first Monday in May); spring and summer bank holidays (last Monday in May and August, respectively); Christmas Day; and Boxing Day (day after Christmas). If any of these holidays falls on a weekend, then the holiday is observed on the following Monday. During the Christmas holidays, many restaurants, as well as museums and other attractions, may close for at least a week—call ahead to verify hours. Book hotels for Christmas travel well in advance, and check whether the hotel restaurant will be open.

SCOTLAND

Holidays are the same as in England, but Scots take the day after New Year's Day to nurse the frantic celebrations of Hogmanay, an end-of-the-year festival. Easter Monday is not a holiday.

INSURANCE

The most useful travel-insurance plan is a comprehensive policy that includes coverage for trip cancellation and interruption, default, trip delay, and medical expenses (with a waiver for preexisting conditions).

Without insurance you'll lose all or most of your money if you cancel your trip, regardless of the reason. Default insurance covers you if your tour operator, airline, or cruise line goes out of business. Trip-delay covers expenses that arise because of bad weather or mechanical delays. Study the fine print when comparing policies.

If you're traveling internationally, a key component of travel insurance is coverage for medical bills incurred if you get sick on the road. Such expenses aren't generally covered by Medicare or private policies. Australian citizens need extra medical coverage when traveling abroad.

Always **buy travel policies directly from the insurance company**; if you buy them from a cruise line, airline, or tour operator that goes out of business, you probably won't be covered for the agency or operator's default, a major risk. Before making any purchase, **review your existing health and home-owner's policies** to find what they cover away from home.

🔳 Travel Insurers In the U.S.: **Access America** ✉ 6600 W. Broad St., Richmond, VA 23230 ☎ 800/284-8300 🖷 804/673-1491 or 800/346-9265 ⊕ www.accessamerica.com. **Travel Guard International** ✉ 1145 Clark St., Stevens Point, WI 54481 ☎ 715/345-0505 or 800/826-1300 🖷 800/955-8785 ⊕ www.travelguard.com.

🔳 In the U.K.: **Association of British Insurers** ✉ 51 Gresham St., London, EC2V 7HQ ☎ 020/7600-3333 🖷 020/7696-8999 ⊕ www.abi.org.uk. In Canada: **RBC Insurance** ✉ 6880 Financial Dr., Mississauga, Ontario, L5N 7Y5 ☎ 800/565-3129 🖷 905/813-4704 ⊕ www.rbcinsurance.com. In Australia: **Insurance Council of Australia** ✉ Insurance Enquiries and Complaints, Level 3, 56 Pitt St., Sydney, NSW 2000 ☎ 1300/363683 or 02/9251-4456 🖷 02/9251-4453 ⊕ www.iecltd.com.au. In New Zealand: **Insurance Council of New Zealand** ✉ Level 7, 111-115 Customhouse Quay, Box 474, Wellington ☎ 04/472-5230 🖷 04/473-3011 ⊕ www.icnz.org.nz.

LODGING

Hotels, bed-and-breakfasts, or small country houses—there's a style and price to suit most travelers. The lodgings listed are the cream of the crop in each price category. Wherever you stay, make reservations well in advance; Great Britain is popular.

Properties are assigned price categories based on a range that includes the cost of the least expensive standard double room in high season (excluding holidays) and the most expensive. Lodgings are indicated in the text by 🔳. Properties indicated by ✕🔳 are lodging establishments whose restaurant warrants a special trip. Price-category information is given in each chapter. Unless otherwise noted, all lodgings listed have a private bathroom, air-conditioning, a room phone, and a television. For camping, *see* Sports & Outdoors.

We always list the facilities that are available—but we don't specify whether they cost extra: when pricing accommodations, always ask what's included and what costs extra. Throughout Britain, lodging prices often include breakfast of some kind, but this is generally not the case in London. Assume that hotels operate on the **European Plan** (EP, with no meals) unless we

specify that they use the **Continental Plan** (CP, with a Continental breakfast), **Breakfast Plan** (BP, with a full breakfast), or the **Modified American Plan** (MAP, with breakfast and dinner). Meal plan symbols appear at the end of a review.

CATEGORY	LONDON	ELSEWHERE
££££££	over £250	over £160
££££	£180–£250	£115–£160
£££	£110–£180	£80–£115
££	£60–£110	£50–£80
£	under £60	under £50

Prices are for two people in a standard double room in high season, including VAT, and are given in pounds.

APARTMENT & VILLA RENTALS

If you want a home base that's roomy enough for a family and comes with cooking facilities, **consider a furnished rental.** These can save you money, especially if you're traveling with a group. Home-exchange directories sometimes list rentals as well as exchanges. Also *see* Cottages.

🔳 International Agents **At Home Abroad** ✉ 405 E. 56th St., Suite 6H, New York, NY 10022 ☎ 212/421-9165 🖷 212/752-1591 ⊕ www.athomeabroadinc.com. **Hideaways International** ✉ 767 Islington St., Portsmouth, NH 03801 ☎ 603/430-4433 or 800/843-4433 🖷 603/430-4444 ⊕ www.hideaways.com, membership $145. **Home-tours International** ✉ 1108 Scottie La., Knoxville, TN 37919 ☎ 865/690-8484 or 866/367-4668 ⊕ http://thor.he.net/~hometour. **Interhome** ✉ 1990 N.E. 163rd St., Suite 110, North Miami Beach, FL 33162 ☎ 305/940-2299 or 800/882-6864 🖷 305/940-2911 ⊕ www.interhome.us. **Vacation Home Rentals Worldwide** ✉ 235 Kensington Ave., Norwood, NJ 07648 ☎ 201/767-9393 or 800/633-3284 🖷 201/767-5510 ⊕ www.vhrww.com. **Villas and Apartments Abroad** ✉ 370 Lexington Ave., Suite 1401, New York, NY 10017 ☎ 212/897-5045 or 800/433-3020 🖷 212/897-5039 ⊕ www.ideal-villas.com. **Villas International** ✉ 4340 Redwood Hwy., Suite D309, San Rafael, CA 94903 ☎ 415/499-9490 or 800/221-2260 🖷 415/499-9491 ⊕ www.villasintl.com.

🔳 Local Agents **The Apartment Service** ✉ 5 Francis Grove, Wimbledon, SW19 4DT ☎ 020/8944-1444 🖷 020/8944-6744 ⊕ www.apartmentservice.com. **English Country Cottages** ✉ Stoney Bank, Earby, Barnoldswick, BB94 0AA ☎ 0870/444-1101 ⊕ www.english-country-cottages.co.uk, from studio apartments to castles. In **the English Manner** ✉ Lancych, Boncath, Pembrokeshire, SA37 0LJ ☎ 0123/969-8444 🖷 0123/969-8686 ⊕ www.english-manner.co.uk ✉ American agent ✉ 515 S. Figueroa St., Suite 1000, Los

Angeles, CA 90071-3327 ☎ 213/629-1811 or 800/422-0799 ⊟ 213/629-4759, apartments and cottages.

B&BS

A special British tradition, and the backbone of budget travel, bed-and-breakfasts (B&Bs) are usually in a family home; few have private bathrooms, and most offer only breakfast. Guest houses are a slightly larger, somewhat more luxurious version. Upscale B&Bs, more along the line of American B&Bs, are now appearing around the country.

Tourist Information Centres around the country can help you find a B&B. Bed & Breakfast (GB) reservation service offers rooms in a range of prices and has discounts for families and off-peak reductions. It represents tourist board–accredited places in London, across the country, and in France. Wolsey Lodges, a consortium of 200 private homes mostly in Britain, includes many luxurious country homes and some more modest houses. Guests are encouraged to dine with their hosts at least one night of their stay. For reservation services in London, *see* London A to Z *in* Chapter 1.

▶ Reservation Services **Bed & Breakfast (GB)** ☎ 800/454-8704; 01491/578803 in U.K. ⊟ 01491/410806 ⊕ www.bedbreak.com. **Wolsey Lodges** ⊠ 9 Market St., Hadleigh, Ipswich, 1P7 5DL ☎ 01473/822058; 01473/827500 for brochure ⊟ 01473/827444 ⊕ www.wolsey-lodges.co.uk.

CAMPING

Camping and caravanning (traveling in a motor home or with a trailer) are popular, and campgrounds are well maintained. Most campgrounds have everything from a restaurant and bar to activities such as fishing, golf, sailing, swimming, and tennis. If you plan to travel between June and September, make reservations months in advance. The most popular camping areas are in Snowdonia, the Lake District, Devon, Cornwall, and the New Forest. Contact VisitBritain in the United States or the Camping and Caravanning Club for information.

The Youth Hostels Association (YHA; ⇨ Hostels) maintains a series of "camping barns"—barns converted into sleeping areas for 6 to 24 people. Facilities are basic, but barns are characterful and are operated by the farmers who own them. Prices start at £3.50 per night. Contact the

Forestry Commission for campgrounds and log cabins for rent in Britain's seven forests. Prices are about £4 to £7 per night.

▶ **Camping and Caravanning Club** ⊠ Greenfields House, Westwood Way, Coventry, West Midlands, CV4 8JH ☎ 02476/694995 ⊕ www.campingandcaravanningclub.co.uk. **Forestry Commission** ⊠ 231 Corstorphine Rd., Edinburgh, EH12 7AT, Scotland ☎ 0131/334-0303 ⊟ 0131/334-3047 ⊕ www.forestholidays.co.uk.

COTTAGES

Houses and cottages are available for weekly rental in all areas of the country. These vary from quaint older homes to brand-new buildings set in scenic surroundings. For families and large groups, they offer the best value-for-money accommodations, but because they are often in isolated locations, a car is vital. Lists of rental properties are available free of charge from VisitBritain (⇨ Visitor Information). Some National Trust properties have cottages available on the estates of stately homes. Luxury Cottages Direct deals exclusively in four- and five-star properties. You may find discounts of up to 50% on rentals during the off-season (October–March).

▶ **Luxury Cottages Direct** ⌂ The Old Mill House, Brook St., Chipping Sodbury, Bristol, BS37 6AZ ☎ 01454/852516 ⊟ 01454/324840 ⊕ www.findcottages.co.uk. **National Trust** ⌂ Box 536, Melksham, Wiltshire, SN12 8SX ☎ 0870/458-4422 ⊕ www.nationaltrust.org.uk/cottages. **Rural Retreats** ⊠ Retreat House, Station Rd., Blockley, Moreton-in-Marsh, Gloucestershire, GL56 9DZ ☎ 01386/701177 ⊕ www.ruralretreats.co.uk.

FARMHOUSES

Farmhouses have become increasingly popular in recent years; their special appeal is the rustic, rural experience. Consider this option only if you are touring by car. Prices are generally very reasonable. Ask VisitBritain (⇨ Visitor Information) for the booklet "Stay on a Farm" or contact Farm Stay UK.

▶ **Farm Stay UK** ⊠ National Agricultural Centre, Stoneleigh Park, Kenilworth, Warwickshire, CV8 2LZ ☎ 0247/669-6909 ⊟ 0247/669-6630 ⊕ www.farmstayuk.co.uk.

HISTORIC BUILDINGS

Want to spend your vacation in a Gothic banqueting house, an old lighthouse, a seaside castle, or maybe in an apartment at

Hampton Court Palace? Several organizations, such as the Landmark Trust, National Trust (⇨ Cottages), and Vivat Trust have specially adapted historic buildings to rent. Most are self-catering (meaning that they include kitchens).

🏠 **Landmark Trust** ⊠ Shottesbrooke, Maidenhead, Berkshire, SL6 3SW ☎ 01628/825925 ⊕ www. landmarktrust.co.uk. **Portmeirion Cottages** ⊠ Hotel Portmeirion, Gwynedd, Wales, LL48 6ET ☎ 01766/770228 ⊕ www.portmeirion-village.com. **Vivat Trust** ⊠ 61 Pall Mall, London, SW1Y 5HZ ☎ 020/7930-8030 ⊕ www.vivat.org.uk.

HOME EXCHANGES

If you would like to exchange your home for someone else's, **join a home-exchange organization,** which will send you its updated listings of available exchanges for a year and will include your own listing in at least one of them. It's up to you to make specific arrangements.

🏠 Exchange Clubs **HomeLink International** ⊘ Box 47747, Tampa, FL 33647 ☎ 813/975-9825 or 800/638-3841 🖶 813/910-8144 ⊕ www.homelink. org; $110 yearly for a listing, on-line access, and catalog; $70 without catalog. **Intervac U.S.** ⊠ 30 Corte San Fernando, Tiburon, CA 94920 ☎ 800/ 756-4663 🖶 415/435-7440 ⊕ www.intervacus.com; $105 yearly for a listing, on-line access, and a catalog; $50 without catalog.

HOSTELS

No matter what your age, you can **save on lodging costs by staying at hostels.** In some 4,500 locations in more than 70 countries around the world, Hostelling International (HI), the umbrella group for a number of national youth-hostel associations, offers single-sex, dorm-style beds and, at many hostels, rooms for couples and family accommodations. Membership in any HI national hostel association, open to travelers of all ages, allows you to stay in HI-affiliated hostels at member rates; one-year membership is about $28 for adults (C$35 for a two-year minimum membership in Canada, £13.50 in the U.K., A$52 in Australia, and NZ$40 in New Zealand); hostels charge about $10–$30 per night. Members have priority if the hostel is full; they're also eligible for discounts around the world, even on rail and bus travel in some countries.

🏠 Organizations **Hostelling International–USA** ⊠ 8401 Colesville Rd., Suite 600, Silver Spring, MD 20910 ☎ 301/495-1240 🖶 301/495-6697 ⊕ www. hiayh.org. **Hostelling International–Canada**

⊠ 205 Catherine St., Suite 400, Ottawa, Ontario, K2P 1C3 ☎ 613/237-7884 or 800/663-5777 🖶 613/ 237-7868 ⊕ www.hihostels.ca. **YHA England and Wales** ⊠ Trevelyan House, Dimple Rd., Matlock, Derbyshire DE4 3YH, U.K. ☎ 0870/870-8808; 0870/ 770-8868; 0162/959-2700 🖶 0870/770-6127 ⊕ www.yha.org.uk. **YHA Australia** ⊠ 422 Kent St., Sydney, NSW 2001 ☎ 02/9261-1111 🖶 02/9261-1969 ⊕ www.yha.com.au. **YHA New Zealand** ⊠ Level 4, Torrens House 195, Hereford St.,, Box 436, Christchurch ☎ 03/379-9970 or 0800/278-299 🖶 03/365-4476 ⊕ www.yha.org.nz.

HOTELS

Great Britain is a popular vacation destination, so be sure to **reserve hotel rooms weeks (months for London) in advance.** The country has everything from budget chain hotels to luxurious retreats in converted country houses. In many towns and cities you will find old inns that are former coaching inns, which served travelers as they journeyed around the country in horse-drawn carriages and stagecoaches. Most hotels have rooms with "en suite" bathrooms—as private bathrooms are called in Great Britain—although some older ones may have only washbasins; in this case, showers and bathtubs (and toilets) are usually just down the hall. When you book a room in the mid-to-lower price categories, it's best to confirm your request for a room with en suite facilities. Tourist Information Centres will reserve rooms for you, usually for a small fee. A great many hotels offer special weekend and off-season bargain packages.

HOTEL GRADING SYSTEM

Hotels in England are graded from one to five stars, and guest houses, inns, and B&Bs are graded from one to five diamonds by VisitBritain in association with the Automobile Association (AA) and the Royal Automobile Association (RAC). Basically, the more stars or diamonds a property has, the more facilities it has. A property with one star or diamond has the minimum necessary for a night's sleep and won't include any extras such as minibars, a concierge, or on-site dining. At the top of the scale, five-star properties will have luxurious decor, a broad range of facilities such as a swimming pool and health club, and a highly trained staff.

In Scotland and Wales, the star system is based on quality and comfort, and properties are graded more subjectively by inspectors; they do not use a checklist of facilities. It's a fairly good reflection of lodging from campsites to palatial hotels. Five stars are for the most luxurious hotels; one star is for fair and acceptable. Hostels are graded from one to three stars.

UNIVERSITY HOUSING

In larger cities and in some towns, certain universities offer their residence halls to paying vacationers between terms. The facilities available are usually compact single sleeping units that share bath facilities, and they can be rented on a nightly basis.
⁊ Universities **British Universities Accommodation Consortium** 🏛 **University Park, Box 1564, Nottingham, NG7 2RD** ☏ **01159/504571.**

MAIL & SHIPPING

Stamps may be bought from post offices (open weekdays 9–5:30, Saturday 9–noon), from stamp machines outside post offices, and from news dealers' stores and newsstands. Mailboxes are known as post or letter boxes and are painted bright red; large tubular ones are set on the edge of sidewalks, and smaller boxes are set into post-office walls. Allow seven days for a letter to reach the United States and about 10 days to two weeks to Australia or New Zealand by air mail. Surface mail service can take up to four or five weeks. The useful Royal Mail Web site has information on everything from buying stamps to finding a post office.
⁊ Contact **Royal Mail** ⊕ www.royalmail.com.
⁊ London Post Offices ✉ **17 Euston Rd., NW1** ✉ **125–131 Westminster Bridge Rd., SW1** ✉ **54 Great Portland St., W1** ✉ **43 Seymour St., Marble Arch, W1** ✉ **The Science Museum, Exhibition Rd., SW7** ✉ **24 William IV St., Trafalgar Sq., WC2.**

OVERNIGHT SERVICES

Contact the services listed below for information about the nearest office or package drop-off point.
⁊ Major Services **DHL** ✉ **Unit 24 Mastmaker Ct., Mastmaker Rd., London, E14 9UB** ☏ **0870/110–0300** ⊕ **www.dhl.co.uk. Federal Express** ✉ **27 Poland St., London, W1V 3DB** ☏ **0800/123800** ⊕ **www.fedex.com. Parcelforce** ☏ **0800/224466** ⊕ **www.parcelforce.co.uk.**

POSTAL RATES

Airmail letters up to 10 grams to North America cost 45p; postcards, 40p. The same rates apply to Australia and New Zealand. Letters within Britain are 27p for first-class, 19p for second-class. Always check rates before sending mail, because they are subject to change.

RECEIVING MAIL

If you're uncertain where you'll be staying, **arrange to have your mail sent to American Express.** The service is free to cardholders and traveler's check holders; all others pay a small fee. You can also collect letters at any main or sub post office throughout Britain, so mail can reach you while you are traveling. Ask the sender to mark the envelope "Poste Restante" or "To Be Called For." The letter must be marked with the recipient's full name (as it appears on your passport), and you'll need your passport or another official form of identification for collection.

SHIPPING PARCELS

Most department stores and retail outlets can arrange to ship your goods back home. You should check your insurance for coverage of possible damage. If you want to ship goods yourself, use an overnight postal service, such as Federal Express, DHL, or Parcelforce. Shipping to North America, New Zealand, or Australia can take anywhere from overnight to a month, depending on how much you pay.

MEDIA

NEWSPAPERS & MAGAZINES

For the latest information about shops, restaurants, and art events, peruse Britain's glossy monthly magazines—*Tatler, Country Living, Harpers & Queen, Vogue, Wallpaper, World of Interiors, House & Garden, The Face,* and *Time Out.* Many of these are available in major cities around the world, if you wish to read up before your trip. Many better newsstands around the world also carry the Sunday editions of the leading British newspapers, such as the *Times,* the *Evening Standard,* the *Independent,* and the *Guardian;* the "Arts" sections of these papers often have news of future events. In addition, these London newspapers have Web sites of their own, full of tips and reviews of the hottest eateries, most chic restaurants, and newest hotels. The British tabloids, such as the *Sun, Mirror* and

Daily Mail, present a lively version of the news, with an emphasis on the sensational.

Scotland's major newspapers include the *Scotsman*—a conservative sheet that styles itself as the journal of record—and the moderate *Glasgow Herald,* along with the tabloid *Daily Record.* The *Sunday Post,* conservative in bent, is the leading Sunday paper; *Scotland on Sunday* competes directly with London's *Sunday Times.* The *Sunday Herald,* an offshoot of the *Glasgow Herald,* is another major title. *List,* a twice-monthly magazine with listings comparable to London's *Time Out,* covers the Glasgow and Edinburgh scenes.

RADIO & TELEVISION

The main television channels are BBC1 and BBC2 from the British Broadcasting Corporation. BBC2 is considered the more eclectic and artsy, with a higher proportion of alternative humor, drama, and documentaries. The independent channels are ITV (Independent Television), which regionalizes into many companies across the country. Channel 4 is a mixture of mainstream and off-the-wall, whereas Channel 5 has more sports and films. You'll see big-budget highbrow productions on television occasionally (most often on the BBC), but there are more mainstream soaps, both homegrown—*Brookside* and *Coronation Street* (which the Queen is rumored to watch)—and international (the Australian *Neighbors*), and the U.S. daytime talk shows such as *Oprah* and general interest shows. Cable channels (many of which are available in hotel rooms) have increased the diet of entertainment.

Radio has seen a similar explosion for every taste, from 24-hour classical music on Classic FM (100.9 FM), and rock on Capital FM (95.8 FM) and Branson's Virgin (105.8 FM), to nostalgic on Heart (106.2 FM) and talk on Talk Radio (1053 AM)—and that's just a sample of the independents. The BBC's Radio 1 (98.8 FM) is for the young and hip; 2 (89.1 FM) for middle-of-the-roadsters; 3 (91.3 FM) for classics, jazz, and arts; 4 (93.5 FM) for news, current affairs, drama (such as *The Archers* radio soap), and documentary; 5 Live (693 AM) for sports and news with phone-ins; and BBC World Service (648 AM) for the best of the BBC.

MONEY MATTERS

A cup of coffee will run from 60p to £3, depending on where you buy it; a pint of beer is about £1 in the countryside and £2 in a city, and a ham sandwich costs £1.75–£3.50. A short taxi ride averages £6.

Prices throughout this guide are given for adults. Substantially reduced fees are almost always available for children, students, and senior citizens. For information on taxes, *see* Taxes.

ATMS

A debit card, also known as a check card, deducts funds directly from your checking account, which can help you stay within your budget. When you want to rent a car, though, you will need a credit card. Although you can usually *pay* for your car with a debit card, agencies will not allow you to *reserve* a car with a debit card.

Otherwise, the two types of plastic are virtually the same. Both credit and debit cards offer excellent, wholesale exchange rates. And both protect you against unauthorized use if the card is lost or stolen. Your liability is limited to $50, as long as you report the card missing.

Both cards will get you cash advances at ATMs worldwide if your card is properly programmed with your personal identification number (PIN). **Make sure before leaving home that your card has been programmed for ATM use there**—ATMs in Great Britain accept PINs of four or fewer digits only; if your PIN is longer, ask about changing it. If you know your PIN as a word, learn the numerical equivalent, since most Great Britain keypads show numbers only, no letters. Most ATMs are on both the Cirrus and Plus networks. ATMs are available at most main-street banks, at most large supermarkets, such as Sainsbury's and Tesco's, some tube stops in London, most rail stations, and large shops such as John Lewis or Virgin Megastore.

CREDIT CARDS

Throughout this guide, the following abbreviations are used: **AE**, American Express; **DC**, Diners Club; **MC**, MasterCard; and **V**, Visa. The Discover card is not accepted in Britain.

☎ Reporting Lost Cards **American Express** ☎ 01273/696933. **Diners Club** ☎ 0800/460800. **MasterCard** ☎ 0800/964767. **Visa** ☎ 0800/891725.

CURRENCY

The unit of currency in Britain is the pound sterling (£), divided into 100 pence (p). The bills (called notes in Britain) are 50, 20, 10, and 5 pounds. Scotland and the Channel Islands have their own bills, and the Channel Islands their own coins, too. The Scottish bills are accepted in the rest of Britain, but you cannot use Channel Islands currency outside the islands. Coins are £2, £1, 50p, 20p, 10p, 5p, 2p, and 1p.

CURRENCY EXCHANGE

At press time, the exchange rate was about Australian $2.48, Canadian $2.20, New Zealand $2.80, and U.S. $1.63 to the pound (also known as quid). Britain's entry into the European Union's currency—the euro—continues to be debated.

For the most favorable rates, **change money through banks.** Although ATM transaction fees may be higher abroad than at home, ATM rates are excellent because they're based on wholesale rates offered only by major banks. The currency exchange at Marks & Spencer department stores is also good; they usually have favorable rates and do not charge commission. You won't do as well at exchange booths in airports or rail and bus stations, in hotels, in restaurants, or in stores. To avoid lines at airport exchange booths, **get a bit of local currency before you leave home.**

🔳 Exchange Services International Currency Express ✉ 427 N. Camden Dr., Suite F, Beverly Hills, CA 90210 ☎ 888/278-6628 orders 🖷 310/278-6410 🌐 www.foreignmoney.com. Thomas Cook International Money Services ☎ 800/287-7362 orders and retail locations 🌐 www.us.thomascook.com.

TRAVELER'S CHECKS

Do you need traveler's checks? It depends on where you're headed. If you're going to rural areas and small towns, go with cash; traveler's checks are best used in cities. Lost or stolen checks can usually be replaced within 24 hours. To ensure a speedy refund, buy your own traveler's checks—don't let someone else pay for them: irregularities like this can cause delays. The person who bought the checks should make the call to request a refund. If you plan to use traveler's checks in Britain, buy them in pounds.

PACKING

Britain can be cool, damp, and overcast, even in summer. You'll want a heavy coat for winter and a lightweight coat or warm jacket for summer. There's no time of year when a raincoat or umbrella won't come in handy. For the cities, **pack as you would for an American city:** coats and ties for expensive restaurants and nightspots, casual clothes elsewhere. Jeans are popular in Britain and are perfectly acceptable for sightseeing and informal dining. Casual blazers are popular here with men. For women, ordinary street dress is acceptable everywhere.

If you plan to stay in budget hotels, take your own soap. Many do not provide soap, and some give guests only one tiny bar per room. In your carry-on luggage, **pack an extra pair of eyeglasses or contact lenses and enough of any medication** you take to last a few days longer than the entire trip. In luggage to be checked, **never pack prescription drugs, valuables, or undeveloped film.** And don't forget to carry with you the addresses of offices that handle refunds of lost traveler's checks. Check *Fodor's How to Pack* (available at on-line retailers and bookstores everywhere) for more tips.

To avoid customs and security delays, carry medications in their original packaging. Don't pack any sharp objects in your carry-on luggage, including knives of any size or material, scissors, and corkscrews, or anything else that might arouse suspicion.

To avoid having your checked luggage chosen for hand inspection, don't cram bags full. The U.S. Transportation Security Administration suggests packing shoes on top and placing personal items you don't want touched in clear plastic bags.

CHECKING LUGGAGE

You're allowed to carry aboard one bag and one personal article, such as a purse or a laptop computer. Make sure what you carry on fits under your seat or in the overhead bin. Get to the gate early, so you can board as soon as possible, before the overhead bins fill up.

Baggage allowances vary by carrier, destination, and ticket class. On international flights, you're usually allowed to check two bags weighing up to 70 pounds (32 kilograms) each, although a few airlines allow checked bags of up to 88 pounds (40 kilograms) in first class. Some international carriers don't allow more than 66 pounds (30 kilograms) per bag in business class and 44 pounds (20 kilograms) in economy. On domestic flights, the limit may be usually 50 to 70 pounds (20 to 32 kilograms) per bag. In general, carry-on bags shouldn't exceed 40 pounds (18 kilograms). Most airlines won't accept bags that weigh more than 100 pounds (45 kilograms) on domestic or international flights. Check baggage restrictions with your carrier before you pack.

Airline liability for baggage is limited to $2,500 per person on flights within the United States. On international flights it amounts to $9.07 per pound or $20 per kilogram for checked baggage (roughly $640 per 70-pound bag), with a maximum of $634.90 per piece, and $400 per passenger for unchecked baggage. You can buy additional coverage at check-in for about $10 per $1,000 of coverage, but it often excludes a rather extensive list of items, shown on your airline ticket.

Before departure, **itemize your bags' contents** and their worth, and label the bags with your name, address, and phone number. (If you use your home address, cover it so potential thieves can't see it readily.) Include a label inside each bag and **pack a copy of your itinerary**. At check-in, **make sure each bag is correctly tagged** with the destination airport's three-letter code. Because some checked bags will be opened for hand inspection, the U.S. Transportation Security Administration recommends that you leave luggage unlocked or use the plastic locks offered at check-in. TSA screeners place an inspection notice inside searched bags, which are resealed with a special lock.

If your bag has been searched and contents are missing or damaged, file a claim with the TSA Consumer Response Center as soon as possible. If your bags arrive damaged or fail to arrive at all, file a written report with the airline before leaving the airport.

🔲 **Complaints** U.S. Transportation Security Administration Consumer Response Center ☎ 866/289-9673 ⊕ www.tsa.gov.

PASSPORTS & VISAS

When traveling internationally, **carry your passport** even if you don't need one (it's always the best form of I.D.) and **make two photocopies of the data page** (one for someone at home and another for you, carried separately from your passport). If you lose your passport, promptly call the nearest embassy or consulate and the local police.

U.S. passport applications for children under age 14 require consent from both parents or legal guardians; both parents must appear together to sign the application. If only one parent appears, he or she must submit a written statement from the other parent authorizing passport issuance for the child. A parent with sole authority must present evidence of it when applying; acceptable documentation includes the child's certified birth certificate listing only the applying parent, a court order specifically permitting this parent's travel with the child, or a death certificate for the nonapplying parent. Application forms and instructions are available on the Web site of the U.S. State Department's Bureau of Consular Affairs (⊕ www.travel.state.gov).

ENTERING GREAT BRITAIN

U.S. and Canadian citizens need only a valid passport to enter Great Britain for stays of up to six months. Australian citizens need a passport with at least six months' validity and can stay in Britain for up to six months without a visa when on vacation. New Zealand citizens need a valid passport and can stay up to six months on vacation. Travelers should be prepared to show sufficient funds to support and accommodate themselves while in Britain and to show a return or onward ticket. Health certificates are not required.

PASSPORT OFFICES

The best time to apply for a passport or to renew is in fall and winter. Before any trip, check your passport's expiration date, and, if necessary, renew it as soon as possible.

🔲 **Australian Citizens** Passports Australia ☎ 131-232 ⊕ www.passports.gov.au.
🔲 **Canadian Citizens** Passport Office ✉ To mail in applications: 200 Promenade du Portage, Hull, Québec J8X 4B7 ☎ 819/994-3500; 800/567-6868; 866/255-7655, TTY ⊕ www.ppt.gc.ca.

New Zealand Citizens **New Zealand Passports Office** ☎ 0800/22-5050 or 04/474-8100 ⊕ www.passports.govt.nz.

U.S. Citizens **National Passport Information Center** ☎ 900/225-5674 or 900/225-7778 TTY (calls are 55¢ per minute for automated service or $1.50 per minute for operator service), 888/362-8668 or 888/498-3648 TTY (calls are $5.50 each) ⊕ www.travel.state.gov.

REST ROOMS

Public toilets are sparse in Britain. Most big cities maintain public facilities that are clean and modern. If there is an attendant, you are expected to pay admission (usually 30p). Rail stations and department stores have public toilets that occasionally charge a small fee. Most pubs, restaurants, and even fast-food chains reserve toilets for customer use only. Hotels and museums are usually a good place to find clean, free toilets. Some upscale London establishments have attendants who expect a small tip—about £1. On the road, gas station facilities are usually clean and welcoming.

SAFETY

Great Britain has a low incidence of violent crime. However, petty crime is on the rise, and tourists can be the target. **Don't wear a money belt or a waist pack,** both of which peg you as a tourist. If you wear a backpack, don't store anything valuable in it. **Keep your wallet in your front pocket** where you can feel it and protect it. If you carry a purse, choose one with a zipper and a thick strap. Store only enough money in the purse to cover casual spending. Distribute the rest of your cash and any valuables (including credit cards and your passport) among a deep front pocket, an inside jacket or vest pocket, and a hidden money pouch. When paying at a shop or a restaurant, **never put your wallet down or let your bag out of your hand.** When sitting on a chair in a public place, keep your purse on your lap. Always **use the bag hooks in public toilet stalls** instead of putting your bag on the floor where it may be snatched.

Don't wear expensive jewelry or watches, as they are easily lifted. **Store your passport in the hotel safe;** use your driver's license for identification. **Don't leave anything in your car**—take valuables with you and put everything else, even a coat, out of sight in your trunk.

Over the years there have been terrorist incidents in England and Northern Ireland, and although U.S. citizens are not targeted, some have been injured. Since the September 2001 attacks on the World Trade Center in New York and the Pentagon in Washington, D.C., London has become a possible target of terrorist violence. Bomb threats are taken seriously. **Don't leave any bags unattended,** as they may be viewed as a security risk and taken away by the authorities. (For U.S. State Department advisories, *see* Visitor Information.)

LOCAL SCAMS

Although scams do occur in Britain, they are not pervasive. Do, however, **watch out for pickpockets,** particularly in London and other large cities. They often work in pairs, with one distracting you in some way (asking for directions or bumping into you) while the other takes your valuables. Always take a licensed black taxi or call a car service (sometimes called minicabs) recommended by your hotel. Passengers have been robbed or overcharged by unlicensed drivers in fake cabs. Avoid using minicab services offered by drivers on the street. In most cases, they will drive an indirect route and overcharge you. When withdrawing cash from an ATM, be sure to cover the number pad with one hand while inputting your PIN. Always buy theater tickets from a reputable dealer. If you are driving in from a British port, beware of thieves posing as fake customs officials. The thieves stop travelers after they have followed them away from the port. Then they flag them down and "confiscate illegal goods."

WOMEN IN GREAT BRITAIN

Women are unlikely to be harassed, but the usual precautions apply—be vigilant if walking alone at night and avoid dimly lit or deserted areas.

SENIOR-CITIZEN TRAVEL

Many museums and galleries in Britain offer free admission to anyone over age 60, and stately homes and gardens may give discounts of up to 40%. To qualify for age-related discounts, **mention your senior-citizen status up front** when booking hotel reservations (not when checking out) and before you're seated in restaurants (not when paying the bill). Be sure to have identification on hand. When renting a car, ask about promotional car-rental discounts, which can be cheaper than senior-citizen rates.

F Educational Programs Elderhostel ⊠ 11 Ave. de Lafayette, Boston, MA 02111-1746 ☎ 877/426-8056; 978/323-4141 international callers; 877/426-2167 TTY 🖶 877/426-2166 ⊕ www.elderhostel.org. **Interhostel** ⊠ University of New Hampshire, 6 Garrison Ave., Durham, NH 03824 ☎ 603/862-1147 or 800/733-9753 🖶 603/862-1113 ⊕ www.learn.unh.edu.

SHOPPING

Britain is a global market: Europe's best labels and fashion boutiques can be found in London and in many of the country's major cities, and several U.S. chain stores operate here as well. Department stores, including John Lewis, Selfridges, and Debenhams, have a wide range of everyday items and goods that make great gifts for the folks back home. If you followed no other pursuit save shopping, you could really exercise your plastic—but the prices may well exhaust it. Yet in any shopping excursion, seek out original designs, ethnic finds (from the many craft markets and fairs), and historical items, which you'll find in abundance, since nearly every village has at least one antiques shop.

KEY DESTINATIONS

London is the center of the shopper's universe. Whatever department store, boutique, or specialty shop there is in the whole of the kingdom, you need look no farther than London's Oxford and Regent streets, Knightsbridge, and Kensington areas. Antiques hunters head for the capital's markets and auction rooms, particularly in the Portobello, Bermondsey, and Bond Street areas. For bespoke tailoring from top to toe, anything can be made to measure—at a price—on Savile Row and Jermyn Street. For fine china, department stores and specialty shops are fruitful hunting grounds. And for one-stop shopping for art, crafts, and beautiful clothes, head for Covent Garden.

To seek out Britain's most famous products on their home turf, you must travel beyond London. If you're seeking true tartans, Shetland sweaters, shortbread, and whisky, Edinburgh should top your shopping itinerary. For Welsh wool rugs and woolen clothing, visit Cardiff and the Welsh folk museums. In Stoke-on-Trent, you can visit museums of pottery and china and purchase these items from the many stores and outlets. The Isle of Wight in the south produces designs to rival the Venetians' Murano glass. Hay-on-Wye, on the Welsh border, is a bibliophiles' center, full of bookshops.

SMART SOUVENIRS

Shops in museums, galleries, and stately homes around the country are often good choices for interesting merchandise, such as high-quality art reproductions, stationery, and beautifully packaged foods such as jam, toffee, and tea. Bookshops and antiques stores stock a plethora of unique and interesting souvenirs. For British crafts and jewelry, the Victoria & Albert Museum shop in London is a smart choice, and for souvenirs with a historical bent, visit the British Museum shop.

WATCH OUT

For art or antiques more than 100 years old, get a Certificate of Age and Origin for customs from the Association of Art and Antique Dealers (LAPADA) or from the dealer selling the piece. Anything more than 50 years old and valued at £39,600 or more needs a certificate, too. Beware of antique items that contain anything from an endangered species, such as tortoiseshell or ivory. You need a permit from the Department of Environment, Food and Rural Affairs to take such items out of Britain.

F Association of Art and Antiques Dealers ⊠ 535 Kings Rd. London SW10 0SZ ☎ 020/7823-3511 ⊕ www.lapada.co.uk. **Department of Environment, Food and Rural Affairs** ⊠ Global Wildlife Division, 2 The Square, Temple Quay, Bristol BS1 6EH ☎ 0117/372-8433.

SPORTS & OUTDOORS

In addition to the associations listed below, VisitBritain and local Tourist Information Centres can recommend places to enjoy your favorite sport.

BIKING

The national body promoting cycle touring is the Cyclists' Touring Club (CTC: £25 a year, £15 for students and those under 18, £15 for those over 65, and £40 for a family of more than three). Members get free advice and route information, a B&B handbook, and a magazine. The CTC and VisitBritain (⇨ Visitor Information) publish a free guide, "Britain for Cyclists." Both the CTC and BTA provide lists of travel agencies specializing in cycling vacations. Also *see* Bike Travel for further information.

◪ Cyclists' Touring Club ✉ Cotterell House, 69 Meadrow, Godalming, Surrey, GU7 3HS ☎ 01483/417217 or 0870/873-0060 ⊕ www.ctc.org.uk.

BOATING

Boating can be a leisurely way to explore the countryside. For boat-rental operators along Britain's several hundred miles of historic canals and waterways, from the Norfolk Broads to the Lake District, contact the Association of Pleasure Craft Operators or Waterway Holidays UK. British Waterways has maps and other information. U.K. Waterway Holidays arranges boat accommodations of all kinds, from traditional narrow boats (small, slender barges) to motorboats and sailboats.

◪ Association of Pleasure Craft Operators ✉ 35A High St., Newport, Shropshire, TF10 7AT ☎ 01952/813572. **British Waterways** ✉ Customer Services, Willow Grange, Church Rd., Watford, WD17 4QA ☎ 01923/201120 ⊕ www.britishwaterways.co.uk. **U.K. Waterway Holidays** ✉ 1 Port Hill, Hertford, SG14 1PJ ☎ 01992/550616 ⊕ www.ukwh.freeserve.co.uk. **Waterway Holidays UK** ☎ 0870/241956 ⊕ www.waterwayholidaysuk.com.

GOLF

Originally from Scotland, golf is a beloved pastime all over Great Britain. Some courses take advantage of spectacular natural settings, from the ocean to mountain backdrops. Most courses are reserved for club members and adhere to strict rules of protocol and dress. However, many famous courses, such as St. Andrews in Scotland, can be used by visiting golfers if they reserve well in advance. Package tours with companies such as Golf International and Owenoak International Golf Travel allow visitors into usually exclusive clubs. VisitBritain has a "Golf in Britain" map and brochure that covers 147 courses. For further information on courses, fees, and locations, try the Web sites UK Golf Guide and Golfcourses.org.

◪ Golf Courses ⊕ www.golfcourses.org. **Golf International** ✉ 14 E. 38 St., New York, NY 10016 ☎ 212/986-9176 or 800/833-1389 ⊕ www.golfinternational.com. **Owenoak International Golf Travel** ✉ 40 Richards Ave., Norwalk, CT 06854 ☎ 203/854-9000 or 800/426-4498 🖷 203/854-1606 ⊕ www.owenoak.com. **UK Golf Guide** ⊕ www.uk-golfguide.com.

WALKING

Walking and hiking, from the slowest ramble to a mountainside climb requiring technical equipment, are enormously popular in Britain. Chapters in this book contain information about a number of long-distance paths. The Ramblers' Association publishes a magazine and a yearbook full of resources, and a list of B&Bs within 2 mi of selected long-distance footpaths.

◪ Countryside Commission ✉ John Dower House, Crescent Pl., Cheltenham, Gloucestershire, GL50 3RA ☎ 01242/521381 ⊕ www.countryside.gov.uk and www.nationaltrail.co.uk. **Long Distance Walkers Association** ✉ Membership Secretary, 63 Yockley Close, Camberley, Surrey, GU15 1QQ ☎ 01753/866685 ⊕ www.ldwa.org.uk. **The Ramblers' Association** ✉ Camelford House, 87–90 Albert Embankment, London, SE1 7TW ☎ 020/7339-8500 ⊕ www.ramblers.org.uk.

STUDENTS IN GREAT BRITAIN

To save money, **look into deals available through student-oriented travel agencies.** To qualify, you'll need a bona fide student I.D. card. Members of international student groups are also eligible.

◪ I.D.s & Services STA Travel ✉ 10 Downing St., New York, NY 10014 ☎ 212/627-3111, 800/777-0112 24-hr service center 🖷 212/627-3387 ⊕ www.sta.com. **Travel Cuts** ✉ 187 College St., Toronto, Ontario, Canada M5T 1P7 ☎ 800/592-2887 in the U.S., 416/979-2406 or 866/246-9762 in Canada 🖷 416/979-8167 ⊕ www.travelcuts.com.

TAXES

An airport departure tax of £20 (£10 for within U.K. and EU countries) per person is payable, and may be subject to more government increases; it's included in the price of your ticket.

VALUE-ADDED TAX

The British sales tax (VAT, Value Added Tax) is 17½%. The tax is almost always included in quoted prices in shops, hotels, and restaurants. The most common exception is at high-end hotels, where prices often exclude VAT. Be sure to verify whether the room price includes VAT.

Most travelers can **get a VAT refund** by either the Retail Export or the more cumbersome Direct Export method. Refunds apply for VAT only on goods being taken out of Britain, and purchases must exceed a minimum limit (check with the store—generally £50–£100). Many large stores provide VAT-refund services, but only if you request them; they will handle the paperwork. For the Retail Export method, you must ask the store to complete Form VAT 407 (you must have identification—passports are best), to be given to customs at your last port of departure. Have the form stamped like any customs form by customs officials when you leave the country or, if you're visiting several European Union countries, when you leave the EU. Be ready to show customs officials what you've bought (pack purchases in your carry-on luggage); budget extra time at the airport for this. After you're through passport control, take the form to a refund-service counter for an on-the-spot refund (if the retailer has an agreement with the firm running the counter; ask the store when you make your purchase), or mail it back to the store or a refund service from the airport or after you arrive home. The refund will be forwarded to you in about eight weeks, minus a service charge, either in the form of a credit to your charge card or as a British check, which American banks charge you to convert.

With the Direct Export method, the goods are mailed directly to your home; you must have a Form VAT 407 certified by customs, police, or a notary public when you get home and then sent back to the store, which will refund your money. For inquiries, call the local Customs & Excise office listed in the telephone directory. Remember, VAT refunds can't be processed after you arrive back home.

A refund service can save you some hassle, for a fee. Global Refund is a Europe-wide service with 190,000 affiliated stores and more than 700 refund counters—at every major airport and border crossing. Its refund form is called a Tax Free Check. The service issues refunds in the form of cash, check, or credit-card adjustment, minus a processing fee. If you don't have time to wait at the refund counter, you can mail in the form instead.

🏢 **VAT Refunds Global Refund** ✉ 99 Main St., Suite 307, Nyack, NY 10960 ☎ 800/566-9828 📠 845/348-1549 ⊕ www.globalrefund.com.

TELEPHONES

British Telecom runs the telephone service in Great Britain and is generally reliable.

AREA & COUNTRY CODES

The country code for Great Britain is 44. When dialing a British number from abroad, drop the initial 0 from the local area code. For example, let's say you're calling Buckingham Palace—020/7839–1377—from the United States. First, dial 011 (the international access code), then 44 (Great Britain's country code), then 20 (London's center city code—without its initial 0), then the remainder of the telephone number.

Dialing from Great Britain to back home, the country code is 1 for the United States and Canada, 61 for Australia, and 64 for New Zealand.

DIRECTORY & OPERATOR ASSISTANCE

To call the operator, dial 100; directory inquiries (information), 192; international directory assistance, 153.

INTERNATIONAL CALLS

For direct overseas dialing, dial 00, then the country code, area code, and number. For the international operator, credit card, or collect calls, dial 155. Bear in mind that hotels usually levy a hefty (up to 300%) surcharge on calls; it's better to use the pay phones in most hotel foyers or a U.S. calling card.

LOCAL CALLS

You do not need to dial the area code if you are making a call within the same area code.

LONG-DISTANCE CALLS

For long-distance calls within Britain, dial the area code (which usually begins with 01, except in London), followed by the telephone number. The area code prefix is used only when you are dialing from outside the region. In provincial areas, the dialing codes for nearby towns are often posted in the phone booth.

LONG-DISTANCE SERVICES

AT&T, MCI, and Sprint access codes make calling long-distance relatively convenient, but you may find the local access number blocked in many hotel rooms. First ask the hotel operator to connect you. If the hotel operator balks, ask for an international operator, or dial the international operator yourself. One way to improve your odds of getting connected to your long-distance carrier is to travel with more than one company's calling card (a hotel may block Sprint, for example, but not MCI). If all else fails, call from a pay phone.

Access Codes AT&T Direct In the U.K., there are AT&T access numbers to dial the U.S. using three different phone types: ☎ 0500/890011 Cable & Wireless; 0800/890011 British Telecom; 0800/0130011 AT&T. **MCI WorldPhone** ☎ 0800/890222 in the U.K. for the U.S. via MCI. **Sprint International Access** ☎ 0800/890877.

PHONE CARDS

Public card phones operate with British Telecom (BT) chip cards that you can buy from post offices or newsstands. They are ideal for longer calls; are composed of units of 20p; and come in values of £2, £5, £10, and £20. To use a card phone, lift the receiver, insert your card, and dial the number. An indicator panel shows the number of units used. At the end of your call, the card will be returned. Where credit cards are taken, slide the card through, as indicated. Beware of buying cards that require you to dial a free phone number; some of these are not legitimate. It's better to get a BT card.

PUBLIC PHONES

There are three types of phones: those that accept (a) only coins, (b) only British Telecom (BT) phone cards, or (c) BT phone cards and credit cards.

The coin-operated phones are of the push-button variety; their workings vary, but there are usually instructions on each unit. Most take 10p, 20p, 50p, and £1 coins. Insert the coins *before* dialing (minimum charge is 20p). If you hear a repeated single tone after dialing, the line is busy; a continual tone means the number is unobtainable (or that you have dialed the wrong—or no—prefix). The indicator panel shows how much money is left; add more whenever you like. If there is no answer, replace the receiver and your money will be returned.

All calls are charged according to the time of day. Standard rate is weekdays 8 AM–6 PM; cheap rate is weekdays 6 PM–8 AM and all day on weekends, when it's even cheaper. A local call before 6 PM costs 15p for three minutes; this doubles to 30p for the same from a pay phone. A daytime call to the United States will cost 24p a minute on a regular phone (weekends are cheaper), 80p on a pay phone.

TIME

England sets its clocks by Greenwich Mean Time, five hours ahead of the U.S. East Coast. British summer time (GMT plus one hour) requires an additional adjustment from about the end of March to the end of October.

TIPPING

Some restaurants, bars, and most hotels add a service charge of 10%–15% to the bill. In this case, you are not obliged to tip extra. If no service charge is indicated, add 10%–15% to your total bill. Beware when signing credit-card slips that you fill in the correct total; some restaurants leave the gratuity entry empty even when they have levied a service charge. Taxi drivers should also get 10%–15%. If you get help from a hotel concierge, a tip of £1–£2 is appropriate. You are not expected to tip theater or cinema ushers, elevator operators, or bartenders in pubs. Hairdressers and barbers should receive 10%–15%.

TOURS & PACKAGES

Because everything is prearranged on a prepackaged tour or independent vacation, you spend less time planning—and often get it all at a good price.

BOOKING WITH AN AGENT

Travel agents are excellent resources. But it's a good idea to collect brochures from several agencies, as some agents' suggestions may be influenced by relationships with tour and package firms that reward them for volume sales. If you have a special interest, **find an agent with expertise in that area**; the American Society of Travel Agents (ASTA; ➪ Travel Agencies) has a database of specialists worldwide. You can log on to the group's Web site to find an ASTA agent in your neighborhood.

Make sure your travel agent knows the accommodations and other services of the place being recommended. Ask about the hotel's location, room size, beds, and whether it has a pool, room service, or programs for children, if you care about these. Has your agent been there in person or sent others whom you can contact?

Do some homework on your own, too: local tourism boards can provide information about lesser-known and small-niche operators, some of which may sell only direct.

BUYER BEWARE

Each year consumers are stranded or lose their money when tour operators—even large ones with excellent reputations—go out of business. So **check out the operator.** Ask several travel agents about its reputation, and try to **book with a company that has a consumer-protection program.** (Look for information in the company's brochure.) In the United States, members of the National Tour Association and the United States Tour Operators Association are required to set aside funds to cover payments and travel arrangements in the event that the company defaults. It's also a good idea to choose a company that participates in the American Society of Travel Agents' Tour Operator Program; ASTA will act as mediator in any disputes between you and your tour operator.

Remember that the more your package or tour includes, the better you can predict the ultimate cost of your vacation. Make sure you know exactly what is covered, and **beware of hidden costs.** Are taxes, tips, and transfers included? Entertainment and excursions? These can add up.

🛈 Tour-Operator Recommendations **American Society of Travel Agents** (⇨ Travel Agencies). **National Tour Association** (NTA) ✉ 546 E. Main St., Lexington, KY 40508 ☎ 859/226-4444 or 800/682-8886 🖷 859/226-4404 🌐 www.ntaonline.com. **United States Tour Operators Association** (USTOA) ✉ 275 Madison Ave., Suite 2014, New York, NY 10016 ☎ 212/599-6599 or 800/468-7862 🖷 212/599-6744 🌐 www.ustoa.com.

TRAIN TRAVEL

Privatization of rail service in Britain has produced some difficulties, with more service delays and more accidents than in past years. Despite these concerns, the train system, offering service by more than two dozen companies, is extensive and helpful. Changes in the next few years will include the introduction of high-speed trains on popular routes such as London to Manchester. Ask about express or high-speed service if you plan to travel by train.

When traveling by train, **make a reservation whenever possible;** there are often discounts for early booking. Specify if you require nonsmoking or smoking; most trains have one or two carriages designated for smokers. On long-distance runs, some rail lines have buffet cars, whereas in others, you can purchase snacks from a mobile snack cart.

Britain has some fabulously scenic rail routes, often on steam trains, which generally run from April to October. In Wales, the Vale of Rheidol Railway from Aberystwyth climbs up sheer rock faces to Devil's Bridge. In the north of England, the Settle-to-Carlisle Railway travels the Yorkshire Dales; in the west country, the West Somerset Railway's Dunster-to-Minehead route takes in glorious coastline; and in the east, the Romney Marsh-to-Dymchurch runs along the marshland, skirting the Kent coast. A tour on the Orient-Express train *Northern Belle* takes in London, York, Edinburgh, Chester, Wales, and Bath. Steam Dreams runs steam trains on regular lines out of London stations to Bath, Canterbury, Chichester, Ely, Norwich, Portsmouth, Salisbury, and Winchester.

CLASSES

Most rail lines have a couple of first-class carriages on each train, which have superior seating and tables—but the difference in price between a first-class and standard ticket varies considerably between rail companies. Check with National Rail Enquiries for details.

CUTTING COSTS

To save money, **look into rail passes.** But be aware that if you don't plan to cover many miles, you may come out ahead by buying individual tickets.

If you plan to travel by train in Great Britain, **consider purchasing a BritRail Pass,** which gives unlimited travel over the entire British rail network and will save you money. You must **buy your BritRail Pass before you leave home.** They are available from most travel agents or from BritRail, DER, or Rail Europe; check their Web sites for complete details. Note that EurailPasses are not honored in Britain and that the rates listed here are subject to change.

BritRail passes come in two basic varieties. The Classic pass allows travel on consecutive days, and the FlexiPass allows a number of travel days within a set period of time. The cost (in U.S. dollars) of a BritRail Classic pass adult ticket for 8 days is $269 standard and $405 first-class; for 15 days, $405 standard and $609 first-class; for 22 days, $515 and $769; and for a month, $609 and $915. The cost of a BritRail FlexiPass adult ticket for 4 days' travel in two months is $235 standard and $355 first-class; for 8 days' travel in two months, $349 standard and $519 first-class; and for 15 days' travel in two months, $525 standard and $779 first-class. Prices drop by about 25% for off-peak travel passes between October and March. Passes for students, seniors, and ages 16–25 are discounted, too.

If you want the flexibility of a car combined with the speed and comfort of the train, try BritRail/Drive (from $473 for one adult, with a $166 supplement for additional adults and $72.50 for children 5–15); this gives you a three-day BritRail FlexiPass and three vouchers valid for Hertz car rental from more than 100 locations throughout Great Britain. A six-day rail pass with seven days of car rental is also available (from $958 car and driver, with $241 adult supplement, $105 children, with a "free child per adult" deal for children under 5 traveling gratis). Prices listed are for compact, automatic transmission cars, with first-class seats; other options—manual transmission, larger cars, and so on—are available at different prices. If you call your travel agency or Hertz's international desk (⇨ Car Rental), the car of your choice will be waiting for you at the train station.

The Freedom of Scotland Travelpass allows unlimited standard-class travel: $139 for 4 days, $180 for 8 days, and $215 for any 12 or 15 days. There's a Freedom of Wales pass as well, and you can purchase a Eurostar ticket for Paris or Brussels in conjunction with a BritRail Pass.

Many travelers assume that rail passes guarantee them seats or sleeping accommodations on the trains they wish to ride. Not so. You need to **book seats ahead even if you are using a rail pass,** especially on trains that may be crowded, particularly in summer on popular routes.

There are also some discount passes for travel within regions; individual chapters have information, or you can call National Rail Enquiries (⇨ Fares & Schedules).

📑 Discount Passes **BritRail** ☎ 877/677-1066 🌐 www.britrail.net. **DER Travel Services** ✉ 9501 W. Devon Ave., Rosemont, IL 60018 ☎ 800/782-2424 📠 800/282-7474 for information; 800/860-9944 for brochures 🌐 www.der.com. **Rail Europe** ✉ 226 Westchester Ave., White Plains, NY 10604 ☎ 877/456-7245 🌐 www.raileurope.com ✉ 94 Cumberland St., Toronto, Ontario M5R 1A3 ☎ 416/482-1777 or 800/361-7245 ✉ 179 Piccadilly, London, W1V 0BA ☎ 0870/584-8848.

FARES & SCHEDULES

The monthly *OAG Rail Guide* (about £6.95 and available from WH Smith branches and most larger main line rail stations) covers all national rail services and Eurostar, including private, narrow-gauge, and steam lines, as well as special services, buses, ferries, and rail-based tourist facilities. You can find timetables of rail services in Britain and some ferry services in the *Thomas Cook European Timetable,* issued monthly and available at travel agents and some bookstores in the United States.

National Rail Enquiries provides an up-to-date railways schedule. Rail travel can be expensive: for instance, a round-trip ticket to Bath from London can cost around £60 per person at peak times. The fee reduces to around £30 at other times, so it's best to travel before or after the commuter rush (before 4 PM and after 10 AM).

📑 Train Information **National Rail Enquiries** ☎ 0845/748-4950; 01332/387601 outside Britain 🌐 www.nationalrail.co.uk. **Orient-Express** ☎ 800/524-2420 🌐 www.orient-express.com. **Royal Scotsman** ☎ 0131/555-1344 🌐 www.royalscotsman.com **Steam Dreams** ☎ 01483/209888 🌐 www.steamdreams.co.uk. **UK Public Transport Information** ☎ 0870/608-2608 🌐 www.traveline.org.uk.

PAYING

You can pay in cash, and credit cards are accepted for train fares paid both in person and by phone.

RESERVATIONS

Reserving your ticket in advance is always recommended. Even a reservation 24 hours in advance can provide a substantial discount. Look into cheap day returns if you plan to travel a round-trip in one day.

TRANSPORTATION AROUND GREAT BRITAIN

Ask any Briton about public transportation in the country and the answer will be long and woeful. Air travel within a relatively small country is best saved for the longest trips; trains can be faster and cheaper. The train system is extensive but probably in the worst shape, suffering from frequent delays, cancellations, and even accidents and strikes. Buses are convenient but can take up to twice as long as the train; service can be infrequent in the most rural areas.

However, most tourists are not affected by the souring of the British public transportation system. Compared with the United States, it's easy to get around by train or bus. For day trips, the train will do just fine, but for longer trips or wanderings around the countryside, a car will make the trip more flexible—and wonderfully scenic, if you choose the slower roads. Buses and cars face the rising problem of congestion, especially in and around London and on the major highways. If you avoid rush hour, you can escape much of this. If you really want to go slow, perhaps the best way is by foot or canal boat. Britain has a well-developed network of footpaths and waterways, and both offer a relaxing way of getting around with the added benefit of getting to stop and talk to locals.

TRAVEL AGENCIES

A good travel agent puts your needs first. Look for an agency that has been in business at least five years, emphasizes customer service, and has someone on staff who specializes in your destination. In addition, **make sure the agency belongs to a professional trade organization.** The American Society of Travel Agents (ASTA)—the largest and most influential in the field with more than 20,000 members in some 140 countries—maintains and enforces a strict code of ethics and will step in to help mediate any agent-client disputes involving ASTA members if necessary. ASTA (whose motto is "Without a travel agent, you're on your own") also maintains a Web site that includes a directory of agents. (If a travel agency is also acting as your tour operator, *see* Buyer Beware *in* Tours & Packages.)

Local Agent Referrals American Society of Travel Agents (ASTA) ⊠ 1101 King St., Suite 200, Alexandria, VA 22314 ☎ 703/739-2782; 800/965-2782 24-hr hot line 🖷 703/739-3268 ⊕ www.astanet.com. **Association of British Travel Agents** ⊠ 68-71 Newman St., London, W1T 3AH ☎ 020/7637-2444 🖷 020/7637-0713 ⊕ www.abta.com. **Association of Canadian Travel Agencies** ⊠ 130 Albert St., Suite 1705, Ottawa, Ontario, K1P 5G4 ☎ 613/237-3657 🖷 613/237-7052 ⊕ www.acta.ca. **Australian Federation of Travel Agents** ⊠ Level 3, 309 Pitt St., Sydney, NSW 2000 ☎ 02/9264-3299 🖷 02/9264-1085 ⊕ www.afta.com.au. **Travel Agents' Association of New Zealand** ⊠ Level 5, Tourism and Travel House, 79 Boulcott St., Box 1888, Wellington, 6001 ☎ 04/499-0104 🖷 04/499-0786 ⊕ www.taanz.org.nz.

VISITOR INFORMATION

Learn more about foreign destinations by checking government-issued travel advisories and country information. For a broader picture, consider information from more than one country.

The main London Tourist Information Centre is at Victoria Station Forecourt, with branches at Heathrow Airport (Terminals 1, 2, and 3). Britain Visitor Centre, open weekdays 9–6:30, weekends 10–4, provides details about travel, accommodations, and entertainment for the whole of Britain, but you need to visit the center in person to get information. London Line (accessible only in Britain) is the London Tourist Board's 24-hour phone service—it's a premium-rate (60p per minute at all times) recorded information line, with different numbers for theater, events, museums, sports, getting around, and so on.

VisitBritain has a vast amount of information, both printed and on its Web site; you can even check out information on-line about film locations in the Harry Potter movies and obtain a Harry Potter map or information about Potter tours.

In London Britain Visitor Centre ⊠ 1 Regent St., Piccadilly Circus, SW1Y 4NX ☎ No phone ⊕ www.visitbritain.com. **London Line** ☎ 09068/663344. **London Tourist Information Centre** ⊠ Victoria Station Forecourt, Buckingham Palace Rd. ☎ No phone

⊕ www.visitlondon.com. **London Visitor Centre** ⊠ Arrivals Hall, Waterloo International Terminal, Waterloo Rd. ☎ No phone.
🔁 In the U.S. **VisitBritain** ⊠ 551 5th Ave., 7th fl., New York, NY 10176 ☎ 212/986-2200 or 800/462-2748 ⊕ www.travelbritain.org ⊠ 625 N. Michigan Ave., Suite 1510, Chicago, IL 60611 ☎ 800/462-2748.
🔁 In Canada **VisitBritain** ⊠ 5915 Airport Rd., Suite 120, Mississauga, Ontario, L4V 1T1 ☎ 905/405-1840 or 800/847-4885 ⊕ www.visitbritain.com/ca.
🔁 Government Advisories **U.S. Department of State** ⊠ Overseas Citizens Services Office, Room 4811, 2201 C St. NW, Washington, DC 20520 ☎ 202/647-5225 interactive hot line; 888/407-4747 ⊕ www.travel.state.gov; enclose a cover letter with your request and a business-size SASE. **Consular Affairs Bureau of Canada** ☎ 800/267-6788 or 613/944-6788 ⊕ www.voyage.gc.ca. **Australian Department of Foreign Affairs and Trade** ☎ 02/6261-1299 Consular Travel Advice Faxback Service ⊕ www.dfat.gov.au. **New Zealand Ministry of Foreign Affairs and Trade** ☎ 04/439-8000 ⊕ www.mft.govt.nz.

WEB SITES

Do check out the World Wide Web when planning your trip. You'll find everything from weather forecasts to virtual tours of famous cities. Be sure to **visit Fodors.com** (⊕ www.fodors.com), a complete travel-planning site. You can research prices and book plane tickets, hotel rooms, rental cars, vacation packages, and more. In addition, you can post your pressing questions in the Travel Talk section. Other planning tools include a currency converter and weather reports, and there are loads of links to travel resources.

VISITOR INFORMATION

The VisitBritain Web site is at ⊕ www.visitbritain.com. Its U.S. gateway Web site, ⊕ www.travelbritain.org, focuses on information most helpful to Britain-bound U.S. travelers, from practical information to money-saving deals. The official London Web site is ⊕ www.visitlondon.com. The London Tourist Board's site for kids, ⊕ www.kidslovelondon.com, has interactive features and virtual tours. British In-

formation Services, part of the British Embassy in Washington, D.C., maintains ⊕ www.britainusa.com, a site loaded with practical travel information. The British government's Foreign and Commonwealth Office runs ⊕ www.i-uk.com, with information about culture, business, and education in Britain, as well as tourism information.

SPECIAL INTERESTS

Anyone planning to visit Britain's stately homes, castles, and gardens should study the Web sites of the National Trust (⊕ www.nationaltrust.org.uk), the National Trust for Scotland (⊕ www.nts.org.uk), and English Heritage (⊕ www.english-heritage.org.uk). Gardens are the subject of VisitBritain's site at ⊕ www.visitbritain.com/gardens; also check out ⊕ www.ngs.org.uk, the site of Britain's National Gardens Scheme, which organizes the opening of private gardens to the public. You can find information about more than 100 arts festivals from the British Arts Festivals Association (⊕ www.artsfestivals.co.uk), and U.K. Theatre Web (⊕ www.uktw.co.uk) covers theater around Britain. The official Web site of the British monarchy is ⊕ www.royal.gov.uk. If you're looking for smoke-free establishments, check ⊕ www.smokefreeworld.com or ⊕ www.nonsmokerstravel.com. Other Web sites are given throughout Smart Travel Tips.

LONDON ARTS

Many travelers often wonder how to find out about London events and news in advance; sometimes a box-office phone call is needed. You can start by using *Time Out*'s weekly listings— ⊕ www.timeout.co.uk—but these listings often don't extend more than a few weeks. For news and arts and reviews, click on the daily newspaper site (⊕ www.thetimes.co.uk). Theatergoers should log on to ⊕ www.officiallondontheatre.co.uk, which provides a rundown of theater and opera events months down the road.

LONDON

1

FODOR'S CHOICE

busabe eathai, *restaurant*

Changing of the Guard, Buckingham Palace

County Hall Travel Inn Capital

Covent Garden Hotel

The Dorchester, *hotel*

The Eagle, *gastro-pub*

Gordon Ramsay at Claridge's, *restaurant*

Houses of Parliament, *view at sunset*

Kew Gardens, *Kew*

Locanda Locatelli, *restaurant*

Morgan Hotel

myhotel bloomsbury

New England Hotel

Rules, *restaurant*

The Social, *restaurant*

Westminster Abbey

Many other great sights, hotels, and restaurants enliven the city. For other favorites, look for the black stars as you read this chapter.

Updated by
Catherine
Belonogoff,
Jacqueline
Brown, Julius
Honnor, Alex
Wijeratna

LONDON IS AN ANCIENT CITY whose history greets you at every turn. To gain a sense of its continuity, stand on Waterloo Bridge at sunset. To the east, the great globe of St. Paul's Cathedral glows golden in the fading sunlight as it has since the 17th century, still majestic amid the modern towers of glass and steel that hem it in. To the west stand the mock-medieval ramparts of Westminster, home to the "Mother of Parliaments," which has met here or hereabouts since the 1250s. Past them both snakes the swift, dark Thames, following the same course as when it flowed past the Roman settlement of Londinium nearly 2,000 years ago. If the city contained only its famous landmarks—the Tower of London, Big Ben, Westminster Abbey, Buckingham Palace—it would still rank as one of the world's top cities. But London is so much more.

For much of its history, innumerable epigrams and observations have been coined about London by enthusiasts and detractors. The great 18th-century author and wit Samuel Johnson said that a man who is tired of London is tired of life. Oliver Wendell Holmes said, "No person can be said to know London. The most that anyone can claim is that he knows something of it." In short, the capital of Great Britain is simply one of the most interesting cities on earth. There's no other place like it in its agglomeration of architectural sins and sudden intervention of almost rural sights, in its medley of styles, in its mixture of the green loveliness of parks and the modern gleam of neon. Thankfully, the old London of Queen Anne and Georgian architecture can still be discovered under the hasty routine of later additions.

A city that loves to be explored, London beckons with great museums, royal pageantry, and history-steeped houses. Discovering it takes a bit of work, however. Modern-day London still largely reflects its medieval layout, a willfully difficult tangle of streets. This swirl of spaghetti will be totally confusing to anyone brought up on the rigidity of a grid system. Even Londoners, most of whom own a dog-eared copy of the indispensable A–Z street finder (these books come under different names), get lost in their own city. But the bewildering street patterns will be a plus for anyone who likes to get lost in atmosphere. London is a walker's city and will repay every moment you spend exploring on foot. If you want to penetrate beyond the crust of popular knowledge, you are well advised not only to visit St. Paul's Cathedral and the Tower of London, but also to set aside some time for random wandering. Walk in the city's backstreets and mews, around Park Lane and Kensington. Pass up Buckingham Palace for Kensington Palace, beautifully situated in regal gardens. Take in the National Gallery, but don't forget London's "time machine" museums, such as the 19th-century homes of Lord Frederic Leighton and Sir John Soane. Abandon the city's standard-issue chain stores to discover the gentlemen's outfitters of St. James's. In such ways can you best visualize the shape or, rather, the various shapes of Old London, a curious city that engulfed its own past for the sake of modernity but still lives and breathes the air of history.

Today, that sense of modernity is stronger than ever, as swinging-again London holds its own as one of the coolest cities in the world. Millennium fever left its trophies on the capital, with the opening of buildings and bridges and impressively revamped museums, and the city's art, style, fashion, and dining scenes make headlines around the world. London's chefs have become superstars. Its fashion designers have conquered Paris, avant-garde artists have caused waves at the august Royal Academy of Arts, the city's raging after-hours scene is packed with music mavens ready to catch the Next Big Thing, and the theater continues its tradition of radical, shocking productions.

In a city with as many richly stocked museums and marvels as London, you risk seeing half of everything and all of nothing. You could easily spend two weeks exploring the city, but if time is limited you'll need to plan carefully.

If you have 1 day

Touring the largest city in England in a single day sounds like an impossible goal, but it can actually—almost—be done in a single sunrise-to-sunset span. Think London 101, though many of these sights merit an extended visit. Begin at the Houses of Parliament, best viewed from Westminster Bridge. If you're lucky, you'll hear Big Ben chiming. Move on to centuries-old Westminster Abbey—site of many a coronation—then tube it from the Westminster stop to Charing Cross (if you want to catch a glimpse of Her Majesty's two mounted sentries at Horse Guards Parade, bus it up to Whitehall) to arrive at Trafalgar Square for your photo op with Nelson's Column. Take in the treasures of the National Gallery; history buffs might opt instead for a flip-book-fast tour of the adjacent National Portrait Gallery, heavy on the likes of England's heroes and literateurs. Break for lunch in the Brasserie of the National Gallery, then take a short taxi trip to a sight dear to your heart: for connoisseurs, this might be the Wallace Collection, the Tate Britain, or the Tate Modern; for time travelers, Apsley House (the home of the duke of Wellington) or Sir John Soane's Museum; for kids, the London Dungeon or Madame Tussaud's. For a midafternoon session, choose between royal monuments. First choice: heading west from Trafalgar Square, taxi through the Admiralty Arch down the Mall to Buckingham Palace. In summer, the State Rooms are open to the public. Theatreland awaits palace trekkers with a hit West End musical—a refreshing finale to the day. Second choice: eastward lies the Tower of London, with the Beefeaters, the Crown Jewels, and the resident ravens. At dusk, after leaving the Tower, head across the way to the East End for a spine chiller, a Jack the Ripper guided walking tour. Or board the British Airways London Eye at twilight for an aerial view.

If you have 3 days

A breakneck first day in London has been outlined above. On your second day, begin at the legendary British Museum, resting place of such wonders as the Rosetta Stone and the Elgin Marbles. If the idea of traipsing through "mankind's attic" doesn't grab you, head for the fun house, Sir John Soane's Museum, with interiors that will transport you to Regency-era England. Here in Bloomsbury other treats beckon: Pollock's Toy Museum or the Charles Dickens House. For an early lunch, tube it from Russell Square to Tottenham Court Road in Soho, for dim sum in Chinatown, or the menu du jour at a cute French bistro. Next, for a dose of magisterial grandeur, hop back on the tube to arrive at the St. Paul's stop and St. Paul's Cathedral. Walk off lunch by strolling south through Blackfriars—a district full of crooked streets and minuscule cul-de-sacs—to the Thames River. After downing a pint at the Black Friar, cross Blackfriars Bridge (or take the pedestrian-only Millennium Bridge, which ends near the Tate Modern) to Southwark's riverside embankment for a splendid view of St. Paul's dome. A stone's throw away is the rebuilt Shakespeare's Globe Theatre. If you're not catching a performance at the Globe (held only in warm-weather months), tour the museum beneath the theater. Keep heading west along the river, past the London Eye, and cross Waterloo Bridge to Somerset House, which you can walk through the courtyard to the Strand at the foot of Covent Garden. Dine at one of the area's chic restaurants, then watch the street performers, called buskers, or attend a gala evening (book ahead) at the Royal Opera House.

Start your third day with Buckingham Palace's Changing of the Guard, held April–July at 11:30 daily, August–March at the same hour on alternate days. Warm up for this ceremony by viewing the treasures in the Queen's Gallery and the nearby Royal Mews. If the State Rooms of the palace are closed to viewing, head through Green Park to Apsley House, the 18th-century mansion of the Duke of Wellington. Wander up Park Lane into ritzy Mayfair and stroll past Grosvenor Square and Oxford Street to Manchester Square and the Wallace Collection, whose gilded interiors are stuffed with 18th-century art. For retail therapy, return south, then east to scout three great shopping destinations: Bond Street for glitz, Regent Street for savvy sophistication, and Carnaby Street for some rocker-style street gear. For an evening highlight, pick a play of your choice.

If you have
7 days

Each section of London provides distinct clues to the city's past. Kick off day four at the South Kensington museums, a district planned by the Victorians to induce gallery gout and museum feet: the Victoria & Albert, the Natural History Museum, and the Science Museum. Art lovers will want to explore the first, whereas budding Einsteins will run for either of the latter. All three cultural palaces could easily consume an entire day, so pick one. Then head over to Knightsbridge to mercantile-and-fashion giants Harrods or Harvey Nichols. Move on to Kensington Gardens, where almost everyone throws a kiss to the statue of *Peter Pan*, and to Kensington Palace, the home of royals from Queen Anne to today's Windsors, to see the State Rooms.

Day 5 dawns at the City—London's ancient core. Built up around St. Paul's, the area has numerous attractions, including Dr. Johnson's House, the Museum of London, and several Christopher Wren churches. After lunch, serious folk will want to tube westward over to Holborn (Chancery Lane, Temple stops) to visit the Inns of Court and the Temple, the historic foundations of legal London. Farther along lies that storybook icon, Tower Bridge, which you cross to reach the South Bank, where the London Dungeon awaits—this waxworks show is devoted to the more gory aspects of British history.

On Day 6, leave the city behind for pleasures along the Thames, at Greenwich or the storied palace and gardens of Hampton Court—don't even *consider* attempting both. Begin your last day by taking the tube to the Knightsbridge stop and heading south for an early morning stroll through Belgravia; it's London at its most Edwardian. Head over to the emporiums of Sloane Street and Sloane Square and enjoy some high-style shopping. Chelsea, along King's Road, is where much of London comes to shop and stroll. Relax over lunch at a King's Road eatery, then bus over to Millbank to take in the Tate Britain's collection of paintings by J. M. W. Turner, the romantic-period artist who painted the most beautiful sunsets of any century. As dusk settles, head over to the South Bank Centre for a play in the Olivier Theatre or a concert in the Queen Elizabeth Hall. Don't fret if the performances are booked—London itself is the most wonderful free show in the world.

On the other hand, although the outward shapes may alter and the inner spirit may be warmer, the base-rocks of London's character and tradition remain the same. Deep down, Britons have a sense of the continuity of history. Even in the modern metropolis, some things rarely change. The British bobby is alive and well. The tall, red, double-decker buses still lumber from stop to stop, although their aesthetic match at street level, the glossy red telephone booth, is disappearing. And, of course, teatime is still a hallowed part of the day, with, if you search hard enough, toasted crumpets honeycombed with sweet butter. Then, of course, there's that greatest living link with the past—the Royal Family. Don't let the tag of "typical tourist" stop you from enjoying the pageantry of the Windsors; the Changing of the Guard, at Buckingham Palace and at Whitehall, is one of the greatest free shows in the world.

The London you might discover may include some enthusiastic recommendations from this guide, but be prepared to be taken by surprise as well. The best that a great city has to offer often comes in unexpected ways. Armed with energy and curiosity, you can find, to quote Dr. Johnson again, "in London all that life can afford."

EXPLORING LONDON

London grew from a wooden bridge built over the Thames in the year AD 43 to its current 600 square mi and 7 million souls in haphazard fashion, meandering from its two official centers: Westminster, seat of government and royalty, to the west, and the City, site of finance and commerce, to the east. However, London's *un*official centers multiply and mutate year after year, and it would be a shame to stop only at the postcard views. Life is not lived in monuments, as the patrician patrons of the great Georgian architects understood when they commissioned the city's elegant squares and town houses. Westminster Abbey's original vegetable patch (or convent garden), which became the site of London's first square, Covent Garden, is now an unmissable stop.

If the great, green parks such as Hyde Park are, as in Lord Chatham's phrase, "the lungs of London," then the River Thames is its backbone. The South Bank of the river absorbs the reconstruction of Shakespeare's original Globe Theatre, the concert hall from the '50s Festival of Britain, the arts complex from the '70s, and—farther downstream—the gorgeous 17th- and 18th-century symmetry of Greenwich, where the world's time is measured.

Westminster & Royal London

Westminster and Royal London might be called "London for Beginners." If you went no farther than these few acres, you would have seen many of the famous sights, from the Houses of Parliament, Big Ben, Westminster Abbey, and Buckingham Palace, to two of the world's greatest art collections, in the National and Tate Britain galleries. You can truly call this area Royal London, since it is bounded by the triangle of streets that make up the route that the Queen usually takes when journeying from Buckingham Palace to Westminster Abbey or to the Houses of Parliament on state occasions. The three points on this royal triangle are Trafalgar Square, Westminster, and Buckingham Palace. Naturally, in an area that regularly sees the pomp and pageantry of royal occasions, the streets are wide and the vistas long. St. James's Park lies at the heart of the triangle, which has a feeling of timeless dignity—flower beds bursting with color, long avenues of trees framing classically proportioned buildings, glimpses of pinnacles and towers over the treetops, the distant *bong!* of Big Ben counting off the hours. This is concentrated sight-seeing, so pace yourself. For a large part of the year, much of Royal London is floodlighted at night, adding to the theatricality of the experience.

Numbers in the text correspond to numbers in the margin and on the London map.

a good walk

Trafalgar Square ❶ ☞, the obvious place to start, is the geographical core of London, by dint of a plaque on the corner of the Strand and Charing Cross Road from which distances on U.K. signposts are measured. After taking in the instantly identifiable **Nelson's Column** in the center (read about the area on a plaque marking its 150th anniversary), head for the **National Gallery** ❷ on the north side, Britain's greatest trove of masterpieces. Detour around the corner to see the **National Portrait Gallery** ❸—a parade of the famous that can be rewarding to anyone interested in what makes the British tick. East of the National Gallery, still on Trafalgar Square, see the much-loved church of **St. Martin-in-the-Fields** ❹. Then, stepping through grand Admiralty Arch down on the southwest corner, enter the Mall, the royal pink road, the Mall, with **St. James's Park** running along the south side. On your right is the **Institute of Contemporary Arts** ❺, in the great Regency architect John Nash's **Carlton House Terrace**. At the foot of the Mall is one of London's most famous sights, **Buckingham Palace** ❻, home, of course, to the monarch of the land, with the **Queen's Gallery** ❼—showing some of Her Majesty's vast art collection—and the **Royal Mews** ❽ nearby. Turning left and left again, almost doubling back, follow the southern perimeter of St. James's Park around Birdcage Walk, passing the headquarters of the Queen's foot guard, the **Wellington Barracks** ❾, on your right. Cross Horse Guards Road at the eastern edge of the park, walk down Great George Street, and across Parliament Square, and you come to another of the great sights of London, the **Houses of Parliament** ❿. A mock-medieval extravaganza designed by two Victorian-era architects, it was built along the Thames and includes the famous Clock Tower, known as Big Ben after the nickname of the bell that chimes the hour. A clockwise turn around the square brings you to historic **Westminster Abbey** ⓫. Complete the circuit and head north up Whitehall, where you'll see a simple monolith in the middle of the street—the Cenotaph, designed by Edwin Lutyens in 1920 in commemoration of the 1918 Armistice. The gated alley there on your left leads to **Ten Downing Street** ⓬, where England's modest "White House" stands. Soon after that you pass **Horse Guards Parade** ⓭, setting for the Queen's birthday celebration, Trooping the Colour, with the Inigo Jones–designed neoclassical **Banqueting House** ⓮, scene of Charles I's execution, opposite. The hub of the execution of Sir Winston's war is back down toward Westminster on the left, deep in Foreign Office government buildings, in the **Cabinet War Rooms** ⓯. If it's art you're mad about, skip the last three sights and head down Millbank to the **Tate Britain** ⓰—the most famous museum for British painting and sculpture.

TIMING You could finish this walk of roughly 3 mi in just over an hour or spend a week's vacation on this route alone. Allow as much time as you can for the three great museums—the National Gallery and the Tate Britain require *at least* two hours each, the National Portrait Gallery less than one. Westminster Abbey can take a half day—especially in summer, when lines are long. In summer, you can get inside Buckingham Palace, too; a half-day's operation will be increased to a whole day if you see the Royal Mews or the Queen's Gallery. If the Changing of the Guard is a priority, make sure you time this walk correctly.

1

Great Flavors

London ranks among the world's top dining scenes. Newspapers and magazines devote many pages to food and restaurant reviews, and everyone dines out to the point where London has become the most significant foodies' town in Europe. The haute cuisine scene powers on, and creative menus seem to evolve every 10 minutes. The days are long gone when British cuisine was best known for shepherd's pie—ubiquitously available in pubs—and fish-and-chips. As it turns out, there's a real interest in British favorites, with old standbys like bangers and mash getting modish treatments: the bangers may be of venison or wild boar, with potato puree flavored with pesto. This thriving dining scene rests on a solid foundation of ethnic cuisines. Thousands of Indian restaurants have long ensured that Londoners view access to a tasty tandoori as a birthright. Chinese—Cantonese, primarily—restaurants in London's tiny Chinatown and beyond have been around a long time, as have Greek tavernas, and there are even more Italian restaurants than Indian. Now add Thai, Malaysian, Spanish, and Japanese cuisines to those easily found in England's capital. After all this, traditional British food appears as one more exotic cuisine in the pantheon. If, in fact, you're out for traditional fare but with a stylish twist (often less fancy prices, too), head for a gastro-pub. It's a growing craze in London and across the country.

Museums & Marvels

A blizzard of blue plaques all over town proclaims the historic importance of structures such as Dickens House and the Handel House Museum, turning London itself into something of a living museum. High culture and low, it's all here. The National Gallery holds the richest trove of old-master paintings in Britain and the Tate Modern some of art's latest creations, whereas the London Dungeon and Madame Tussaud's take a more populist approach to history. The British Museum is a jumbo time capsule, with treasures from civilizations around the world. Sir John Soane's Museum, in contrast, is a Regency-era phantasmagoria of unusual perspectives and objets d'art. Whether you like stately homes such as Spencer House and Hampton Court Palace, national monuments such as the Tower of London, or exquisite, specialized fare such as the French art in the Wallace Collection, London has plenty to fascinate you.

Pub Scene

London's pubs include some of the most gorgeous and historic interiors in the city. An integral part of the British way of life, public houses dispense beer "on tap" and usually a basic, inexpensive menu of sandwiches, quiche, and salads, and other snacks at lunchtime. But you don't go to a "local" for just pub grub or even the fancier fare at the increasingly popular gastro-pubs. Rather, pubs are the best place to get to meet the locals in their habitat. Sit at a table if you want privacy; better, help prop up the bar, where no introductions are needed, and watch that legendary British reserve fade away.

Theater

From Shakespeare to the glossiest musical, London's West End has the cream of the city's theater offerings. But you can see more in London than the offerings of Theatreland and the national companies: of the 100 or so legitimate theaters operating in the capital, only about half are officially "West

End," and the remainder fall under the blanket title of "Fringe," which encompasses everything from off-the-wall "physical theater" to premieres of new plays and revivals of old ones.

Shakespeare supplies the backbone to the theatrical life of the city. You can see his plays in the reconstructed Globe Theatre—the fabled "Wooden O"—on the banks of the Thames 200 yards from where it stood in the 16th century. Elsewhere in London, the plays have survived being turned into musicals (from Purcell to rock); they have made the reputations of generations of famous actors (and broken not a few); they have seen women playing Hamlet and men playing Rosalind. Though the Bard of Bards remains a headliner around town, the theater scene is amazingly varied. From a West End *My Fair Lady* revival to an East End feminist staging of *Ben-Hur*, London remains a theatergoer's town.

What to See

⑭ Banqueting House. Commissioned by James I, Inigo Jones (1573–1652), one of England's great architects, created this banqueting hall in 1619–22 out of an old remnant of the Tudor Palace of Whitehall. Influenced by Andrea Palladio's work, which he saw during a sojourn in Tuscany, Jones remade the palace with Palladian sophistication and purity. James I's son, Charles I, enhanced the interior by employing the Flemish painter Peter Paul Rubens to glorify his father all over the ceiling. These allegorical paintings, depicting a wise monarch being received into heaven, were the last thing Charles saw before he was beheaded on a scaffold outside in 1649. ⊠ *Whitehall, Westminster SW1* ☎ *020/7930–4179* ⊕ *www.hrp.org.uk* ⊡ *£4, includes audio guide* ☉ *Jan.–late Dec., Mon.–Sat. 10–5; may close on short notice for banquets* Ⓤ *Charing Cross, Embankment, Westminster.*

❻ Buckingham Palace. Supreme among the symbols of London, indeed of Britain generally and of the Royal Family, Buckingham Palace tops many must-see lists—although the building itself is no masterpiece and has housed the monarch only since Victoria (1819–1901) moved here from Kensington Palace on her accession in 1837. Its great gray bulk sums up the imperious splendor of so much of the city: stately, magnificent, and ponderous. In 1824 the palace was substantially rebuilt by John Nash, that tireless architect, for George IV, that tireless spendthrift. Compared with other great London residences, it is a fairly recent affair: the Portland stone facade dates from 1913, and the interior was renovated and redecorated after World War II bombs damaged it. It contains some 600 rooms, including the State Ballroom and, of course, the Throne Room. These State Rooms are where much of the business of royalty is played out—investitures, state banquets, receptions. The royal apartments are in the north wing; when the Queen is in, the royal standard is raised. The State Rooms can be toured from August to early October, when the Royal Family is away. The **Changing of the Guard**—which, with all the pomp and ceremony monarchists and children adore, remains one of London's best free shows—culminates in front of the palace. Marching to live music, the **Queen's guards** proceed up the Mall from St. James's Palace to Buckingham Palace. Shortly afterward, the replacement guard approaches from Wellington Barracks via Birdcage Walk. Once the old and new guards are in the forecourt, the old guard symbolically hands over the keys to the palace. The ceremony takes place daily at 11:30 AM April–July and on alternating days August–March,

FodorsChoice
★

but the guards sometimes cancel because of bad weather; check the signs in the forecourt or phone. Arrive by 10:30 AM for a decent view of all the panoply. Be sure to prebook tour reservations of the palace with a credit card by phone. ⊠ *Buckingham Palace Rd., St. James's SW1* ☎ *020/7839–1377; 020/7799–2331 24-hr information; 020/7321–2233 credit-card reservations (50p booking charge)* ⊕ *www.royal.gov.uk* ✉ *£12, prices change annually* ☾ *Early Aug.–early Oct. (confirm dates, which are subject to Queen's mandate), daily 9:30–4:15* Ⓤ *St. James's Park, Victoria.*

☾ ⑮ **Cabinet War Rooms.** From this small maze of bombproof underground rooms—in the back of the hulking Foreign Office—Britain's World War II fortunes were directed. During air raids, the cabinet met here, and the Cabinet Room is still arranged as if a meeting were about to convene. In the Map Room, the Allied campaign is charted. The Prime Minister's Room holds the desk from which Winston Churchill made his morale-boosting broadcasts, and the Telephone Room has his hot line to FDR. The rest of the rooms have been preserved as they were when the last light was turned off, at the end of the war. ⊠ *Clive Steps, King Charles St., Westminster SW1* ☎ *020/7930–6961* ⊕ *www.iwm. org.uk* ✉ *£7* ☾ *Apr.–Sept., daily 9:30–5:15; Oct.–Mar., daily 10–5:15* Ⓤ *Westminster.*

Carlton House Terrace. A glorious example of Regency architect John Nash's genius, Carlton House Terrace was built between 1812 and 1830, under the patronage of George IV (Prince Regent until George III's death in 1820). Nash was responsible for a series of West End developments, of which the white-stucco facades and massive Corinthian columns on this street may be the most imposing. Today No. 12 houses the **Institute of Contemporary Arts,** one of Britain's leading modern-art centers. ⊠ *The Mall, St. James's W1* Ⓤ *Charing Cross, Piccadilly Circus.*

⑬ **Horse Guards Parade.** Once the tiltyard of Whitehall Palace, where jousting tournaments were held, the Horse Guards Parade is now notable mainly for the annual Trooping the Colour ceremony, in which the Queen takes the Royal Salute, her official birthday gift, on the second Saturday in June. (Like Paddington Bear, the Queen has two birthdays; her real one is on April 21.) There's pageantry galore, and throngs of onlookers. Covering the vast expanse of the square that faces Horse Guards Road, opposite St. James's Park at one end and Whitehall at the other, the ceremony is televised. You can also attend the queenless rehearsals on the preceding two Saturdays. At the Whitehall facade of Horse Guards, the changing of two mounted sentries known as the **mounted guard** provides what may be London's most popular photo opportunity. ⊠ *Whitehall, Westminster SW1* ☾ *Queen's mounted guard ceremony: Mon.–Sat. 11 AM, Sun. 10 AM* Ⓤ *Westminster.*

⑩ **Houses of Parliament.** Seat of Great Britain's government, the Houses of Parliament are, arguably, the city's most famous and photogenic sight. Facing them you see, from left to right, Big Ben—keeping watch on the corner—the Houses of Parliament themselves, Westminster Hall (the oldest part of the complex), and the Victoria Tower. The most romantic view of the complex is from the opposite, south side of the river, a vista especially dramatic at night when the spires, pinnacles, and towers of the great building are floodlighted green and gold. After a catastrophic fire in 1834, these buildings arose, designed in a delightful mock-medieval style by two Victorian-era architects, Sir Charles Barry and Augustus Pugin. The Palace of Westminster, as the complex is still properly called, was established by Edward the Confessor in the 11th century. It has served as the seat of English administrative power, on and off, ever

London

TO HAMPSTEAD

Regent's Park

Inner Circle

Abbey Road Studios

Euston Station

BLOOM

Telecom Tower

SOHO

Manchester Square

Paddington Station

BAYSWATER

NOTTING HILL

Peter Pan Statue

U.S. Embassy

Royal Academy

Kensington Gardens

Hyde Park

MAYFAIR

Serpentine Gallery

The Serpentine

KNIGHTSBRIDGE

KENSINGTON

Harrods

BELGRAVIA

Victoria Station

VICTORIA

SOUTH KENSINGTON

CHELSEA

Thames

Battersea Park

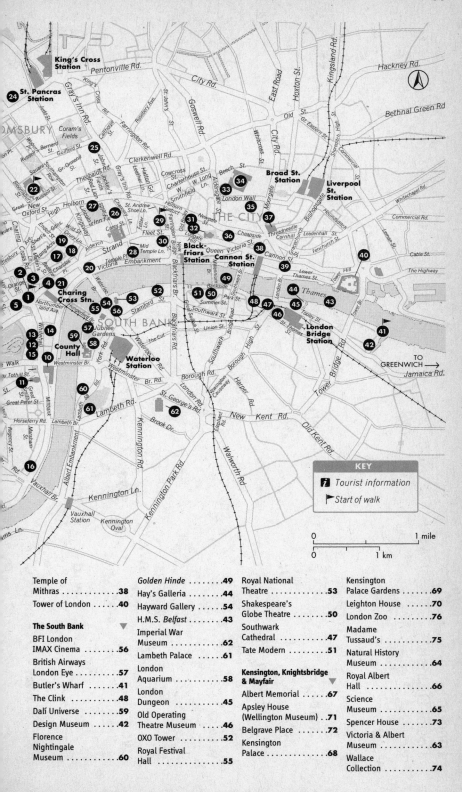

London
Postal Districts

since. Now virtually the symbol of London, the 1858 **Clock Tower** designed by Pugin contains the bell known as **Big Ben** that chimes the hour (and the quarters). Weighing a mighty 13 tons, the bell takes its name from Sir Benjamin Hall, the far-from-slim Westminster building works commissioner. At the other end of Parliament is the 336-foot-high **Victoria Tower.** There are two houses, the Lords and the Commons. The **Visitors' Gallery,** known as the Strangers' Gallery, is open while the House of Commons sits. You'll need to get in line at the main St. Stephen's entrance at least an hour in advance—and even then you might not get a space—for the most popular session, the prime minister's Question Time, on Wednesday. Other days are easier, though you should still arrive an hour before the session starts. Foreign visitors get priority in line if they have applied to their embassy in London for a "card of introduction," but each embassy issues only four of these each day. A complete tour of the public galleries is available year-round (even when Parliament is in recess), but foreign visitors may take advantage of this only during the summer opening (late July–August and mid-September–early October). The **Lord Chancellor's Residence** within the Palace of Westminster is spectacular; be sure to have your name placed in advance on the waiting list for the twice-weekly tours. ⊠ *St. Stephen's Entrance, St. Margaret St., Westminster SW1* ☎ *020/7219–4272 Commons information; 020/7219–3107 Lords information; 020/7219–2184 Lord Chancellor's Residence; 0870/906–3773 for summer and recess tours* ⊕ *www.parliament.uk and www.firstcalltickets.com for summer and recess tours* 🎫 *Free, £7 summer tours* ⊙ *Commons Mon. 2:30–10, Tues. and Wed. 11:30–7:30, Thurs. 11:30–7:30, Fri. 9:30–3; Lords Mon.–Thurs. 2:30–10; Lord Chancellor's Residence Tues. and Thurs. 10:30–12:30* ⊙ *Closed Easter wk, and 3 wks at Christmas* Ⓤ *Westminster.*

need a break? The **Wesley Café** (⊠ Storey's Gate, Westminster SW1 ☎ 020/7222–8010), a popular budget haunt, is almost opposite the abbey itself, in Central Hall. In the crypt of this previous Methodist church, you can grab a hot or cold meal for around a fiver (£5).

❺ Institute of Contemporary Arts. A handsome Regency building houses the ICA, one of Britain's leading modern-art centers. It has provided a stage for the avant-garde in theater, dance, visual art, and music since 1947. There are two cinemas, a library of video artists' works, a bookshop, a café and a popular, hip bar, and a team of adventurous curators. ⊠ *The Mall, 12 Carlton House Terr., St. James's W1* ☎ *020/7930–3647* ⊕ *www.ica.org.uk* 🎫 *£1.50 weekdays, £2.50 weekends, additional charge for specific events* ⊙ *Daily noon–7:30, later for some events* Ⓤ *Charing Cross, Piccadilly Circus.*

★ ❷ National Gallery. Jan Van Eyck's *Arnolfini Marriage,* Leonardo da Vinci's *Virgin and Child,* Diego Velázquez's *Rokeby Venus,* John Constable's *Hay Wain* . . . you get the picture. There are approximately 2,200 other paintings in this museum, many of them among the most treasured works of art anywhere. The museum's low, gray, colonnaded, neoclassical facade fills the north side of Trafalgar Square. The National's collection ranges from painters of the Italian Renaissance and earlier—housed in the modern extension, the Sainsbury Wing, designed by the U.S. architect Robert Venturi—through the Flemish and Dutch masters, the Spanish school, and of course the English tradition, including William Hogarth, Thomas Gainsborough, George Stubbs, and Constable.

The museum is really too overwhelming to absorb in a single viewing. The **Micro Gallery,** a computer information center in the Sainsbury Wing, might be the place to start. You can access in-depth information on any work here, choose your favorites, and print out a free personal tour map that marks the paintings you most want to see. Rounding out the top-10 list (the first four lead off above) are Paolo di Dono Uccello's *Battle of San Romano* (children love its knights on horseback), Giovanni Bellini's *Doge Leonardo Loredan* (notice the snail-shell buttons), Sandro Botticelli's *Venus and Mars*, Michelangelo da Caravaggio's *Supper at Emmaus* (almost cinematically lit), J. M. W. Turner's *Fighting Téméraire* (one of the artist's greatest sunsets), and Georges Seurat's *Bathers at Asnières*. Note that free admission encourages repeat visits: the National Gallery reveals more gems the more one explores. For a great time-out or lunch, head for the Brasserie in the Sainsbury Wing. ⊠ *Trafalgar Sq., Covent Garden WC2* 🕾 *020/7747–2885* ⊕ *www.nationalgallery.org. uk* 🖃 *Free, charge for special exhibitions* ☉ *Thurs.–Tues. 10–6, Wed. 10–9; 1-hr guided tour starts at Sainsbury Wing daily at 11:30 and 2:30, and also 6:30 Wed.* Ⓤ *Charing Cross, Leicester Sq.*

★ ❸ **National Portrait Gallery.** An idiosyncratic collection that presents a potted history of Britain through its people, past and present, this museum is an essential stop for all history and literature buffs. As an art collection it is eccentric, because the subject, not the artist, is the point. Highlights range from Hans Holbein to David Hockney. Many of the faces are obscure, because the portraits outlasted their sitters' fame—not so surprising when the portraitists are such greats as Sir Joshua Reynolds, Gainsborough, Sir Thomas Lawrence, and George Romney. But the annotation is comprehensive, and the chronological layout easy to negotiate. The spacious, bright galleries are accessible via glass escalator, through which you can view the paintings as you ascend to a skylit Tudor Gallery, displaying the oldest works. At the summit, a restaurant with classy British cuisine, open beyond gallery hours, will satiate skyline droolers. A separate research center (with bookshop and café in the basement) assists those who get hooked on particular personages. Don't miss the Victorian and early-20th-century portrait galleries. ⊠ *St. Martin's Pl., Covent Garden WC2* 🕾 *020/7312–2463 recorded information* ⊕ *www. npg.org.uk* 🖃 *Free* ☉ *Mon.–Wed. and weekends 10–6, Thurs. and Fri. 10–9* Ⓤ *Charing Cross, Leicester Sq.*

Nelson's Column. Centerpiece of Trafalgar Square, this famed landmark is topped with E. H. Baily's 1843 statue of Admiral Lord Horatio Nelson (1758–1805), who keeps watch from his 145-foot-high granite perch. The celebrated naval hero died at the battle of Trafalgar (hence the name of the square) during a spectacular victory against the combined French and Spanish fleets. The bas-reliefs depicting scenes of Nelson's life, installed around the base, were cast from cannons he captured. The four majestic lions, designed by the Victorian painter Sir Edwin Landseer, were added in 1867. The calling cards of generations of pigeons have been a corrosive problem for the statue; this may have been finally solved by the addition of a gel coating to it. ⊠ *Trafalgar Sq., Covent Garden WC2* Ⓤ *Charing Cross, Leicester Sq.*

★ ❼ **Queen's Gallery.** Housed in a former chapel at the south side of **Buckingham Palace**, this selection of treasures from the Queen's vast art collection has been wonderfully expanded and updated to give greater space and computer access to pictures on show and in storage. The main room, the Pennethorne Gallery, is dominated by the larger-than-life portrait of Charles I (Van Dyck) in equestrian mode, which almost overshadows works by Holbein, Frans Hals, Jan Vermeer, and Rubens. These contrast starkly with the frank portrait of Queen Elizabeth II by Lucian Freud in the Nash Gallery. Between and beneath the paintings are cabinets and tables, vases and silverwork. The E-gallery reveals hidden de-

WHERE TO SEE THE ROYALS

YOU'VE SEEN BIG BEN, *the Tower, and Westminster Abbey. But somehow you feel something is missing: a close encounter with Britain's most famous attraction—Her actual Majesty. True, you've toured Buckingham Palace, but the Windsors are notorious for never standing at a window (the London Times once suggested that the palace mount a mechanical procession of royal figures to parade in and out of the palace, on the hour, in cuckoo-clock fashion), and the odds are that you won't bump into Elizabeth II on the tube. But at many royal events, you can catch a glimpse of her, along with other Windsor personages. Fairs and fetes, polo matches and horse races galore—her date book is crammed with such events. On one of them—who knows?—you might even meet her on a royal walkabout.*

The Queen and the Royal Family attend some 400 functions a year, and if you want to know what they are doing on any given date, turn to the Court Circular printed in the major London dailies. You might catch Prince Charles launching a ship or the Queen at a hospital's ribbon-cutting ceremony. But most people want to see the Royals in all their dazzling pomp and circumstance. For this, the best bet is the second Saturday in June, when the Trooping the Colour is usually held to celebrate the Queen's official birthday. This spectacular parade begins when she leaves Buckingham Palace in her carriage and rides down the Mall to arrive at Horse Guards Parade at 11 AM exactly. (Well, occasionally the clock has been timed to strike as she arrives and not vice versa.)

If you wish to obtain one of the 7,000 seats (no more than two per request, distributed by ballot), enclose a letter and self-addressed, stamped envelope or International Reply Coupon—January to February 28 only—to Ticket Office, Headquarters Household Division, Horse Guards, London SW1A 2AX, ☎ 020/ 7414–2479. Of course, you can also just line up along the Mall with your binoculars.

Another time you can catch the Queen in all her regalia is when she and the Duke of Edinburgh ride in state to Westminster to open the Houses of Parliament. The famous gilded coach is escorted by the brilliantly uniformed Household Cavalry—on a clear day, it is to be hoped, for this ceremony takes place in late October or early November, depending on the exigencies of Parliament. As the Queen enters the building, the air shakes with the booming of heavy guns, and all London knows that the democratic processes that have so long protected England from oppression have once again been renewed with all their age-old ceremony.

Perhaps the nicest time to see the Queen is during Royal Ascot, held at the racetrack near Windsor Castle—just a short train ride out of London—usually during the third week of June (Tuesday to Friday). After several races, the Queen invariably walks down to the paddock on a special path, greeting race goers as she proceeds. U.S. citizens wishing a seat in the Royal Enclosure—fashion note: the big party hats come out on Ladies Day, normally the Thursday of the meet—should apply to the American Embassy, 24 Grosvenor Square, London W1, before the end of March (note: you must be sponsored by two guests who have attended Ascot at least seven times before!).

If you're lucky enough to meet the Queen, you'll be in for a treat—contrary to her stodgy public persona, she's actually a great wit. Should you miss seeing the Queen, or if you just want to read about the Royals, visit ⊕ www.royal.gov.uk, the official Web site of the British monarchy.

tails of some of the artworks, allowing you to open lockets, remove a sword from its scabbard, or take apart the tulip vases. Admission is by timed ticket, which you can prebook. ⊠ *Buckingham Palace, Buckingham Palace Rd., St. James's SW1* ☎ *020/7321–2233; 020/7766–7301 tickets* ⊕ *www.royal.gov.uk* ⊠ *£6.50* ☉ *Daily 10–5:30; last admission at 4:30* Ⓤ *St. James's Park, Victoria.*

☙ ❽ **Royal Mews.** Unmissable children's entertainment, this museum is the home of Her Majesty's Coronation Coach. Standing nearly next door to the Queen's Gallery, the Royal Mews were designed by Regency-era architect John Nash. Mews were falcons' quarters (the name comes from their "mewing," or feather-shedding), but horses gradually eclipsed birds of prey. Now some of the royal beasts live here alongside the bejeweled coaches. ⊠ *Buckingham Palace Rd., St. James's SW1* ☎ *020/7839–1377* ⊕ *www.royal.gov.uk* ⊠ *£5* ☉ *Oct.–July, Mon.–Thurs. noon–4; Aug. and Sept., Mon.–Thurs. 10:30–4:30; last admission 30 mins before closing. Call to confirm hrs; the Royal Mews often closes for holidays or for royal events* Ⓤ *St. James's Park, Victoria.*

St. James's Park. London's smallest, most ornamental park and the oldest of its royal ones, St. James's Park makes a spectacular frame for the towers of Westminster and Victoria—especially at night, when the illuminated fountains and the skyline beyond the trees look like a floating fairyland. Its current shape more or less reflects what John Nash designed under George IV, turning the canal into a graceful lake (cemented in at a depth of 4 feet in 1855) and generally naturalizing the gardens. More than 17 species of birds—including swans that belong to the Queen—congregate on Duck Island at the east end of the lake. On summer days, the deck chairs (which you must pay to use) are often crammed with office lunchers being serenaded by music from the bandstands. Along the northern side of the park, you'll find the grand thoroughfare known as the **Mall.** ⊠ *Entrances at the Mall, Horse Guards approach, or Birdcage Walk, St. James's SW1* ⊕ *www.royalparks.gov.uk* Ⓤ *St. James's Park, Westminster.*

❹ **St. Martin-in-the-Fields.** One of Britain's best-loved churches, St. Martin's was completed in 1726; James Gibbs's classical temple-with-spire design became a familiar pattern for churches in colonial America. The church is also a haven for music lovers, since the Academy of St. Martin-in-the-Fields, an internationally known orchestra, was founded here, and a popular program of lunchtime and evening concerts (often free) continues today. The church's fusty interior is wonderful for music making—but the wooden benches can make it hard to give your undivided attention to the music. The **London Brass-Rubbing Centre,** where you can make your own souvenir knight from reproduction tomb brasses, with metallic waxes, paper, and instructions provided for about £5, is in the crypt, along with a café and bookshop. ⊠ *Trafalgar Sq., Covent Garden* ☎ *020/7766–1100; 020/7839–8362 evening-concert credit-card bookings* ⊕ *www.stmartin-in-the-fields.org* ☉ *Church daily 8–8; crypt Mon.–Sat. 10–8, Sun. noon–6; box office Mon.–Sat. 10–5, or purchase tickets on-line* Ⓤ *Charing Cross, Leicester Sq.*

★ ⑯ **Tate Britain.** This museum, which first opened in 1897 with funding by sugar magnate Sir Henry Tate, became Tate Britain with the opening in 2000 of its offspring gallery, Tate Modern, on the South Bank. The gallery is a brilliant celebration of great British artists from the 16th century to the present day, with theme rooms that display key works from different eras alongside one another. Noteworthy artists include Hogarth, Gainsborough, Reynolds, and Stubbs from the 18th century, and Constable,

William Blake, and the Pre-Raphaelite painters from the 19th. Also from the 19th century is the J. M. W. Turner Bequest, housed magnificently in the James Stirling–designed **Clore Gallery,** the largest collection of work by this leading British romantic artist. The **Linbury Galleries** on the lower floors present changing exhibitions. Upper floors, reached by a wide, sweeping staircase, bring many works to permanent view that had been consigned to storage. ⊠ *Millbank, Westminster SW1* ☎ *020/7887–8000; 020/7887–8008 recorded information* ⊕ *www.tate.org.uk* 🖂 *Free, special exhibitions £3–£7* ⊙ *Daily 10–5:50* Ⓤ *Pimlico.*

⑫ Ten Downing Street. The British version of the White House occupies three unassuming 18th-century houses. No. 10 has been the official residence of the prime minister since 1732. The cabinet office, hub of the British system of government, is on the ground floor; the prime minister's private apartment is on the top floor. The chancellor of the exchequer traditionally occupies No. 11. Downing Street is cordoned off, but you should be able to catch a glimpse of it from Whitehall. Just south of Downing Street, in the middle of Whitehall, you'll see the **Cenotaph,** a stark white monolith designed in 1920 by Edward Lutyens to commemorate the 1918 Armistice. ⊠ *Whitehall, Westminster SW1* Ⓤ *Westminster.*

▶ **① Trafalgar Square.** Permanently alive with people—Londoners and tourists alike—and pigeons and roaring traffic, Trafalgar Square remains London's "living room." Great events, such as royal weddings, elections, and sporting triumphs, will always see crowds gathering in the city's most famous square. It is a commanding open space—originally built to reflect the width and breadth of an empire that once reached to the farthest corners of the globe—containing a bevy of attractions, including **Nelson's Column** and the **National Gallery.** A redesign has joined the front of the National Gallery to the rest of the square, so that buses, cars, and taxis no longer roar around the north side. The square's pigeons have also been moved on, although quite a few still insist on making the most of the tourists. Celebratory occasions here peak in December, first when the lights on the gigantic Christmas tree (an annual gift from Norway to thank the British for harboring its royal family during World War II) are turned on, and then when thousands see in the New Year. ⊠ *Trafalgar Sq., Covent Garden SW1* Ⓤ *Charing Cross, Leicester Sq.*

⑨ Wellington Barracks. These are the headquarters of the Queen's five regiments of foot guards, who protect the sovereign and patrol her palace dressed in tunics of gold-purled scarlet and tall busbies of black bearskin. If you want to learn more about the guards, you can visit the **Guards Museum;** the entrance is next to the Guards Chapel. ⊠ *Wellington Barracks, Birdcage Walk, Westminster SW1* ☎ *020/7414–3271* 🖂 *£2* ⊙ *Daily 10–4; last admission at 3:30* Ⓤ *St. James's Park.*

⑪ Westminster Abbey. Nearly all of Britain's monarchs have been crowned
Fodor's Choice here since the coronation of William the Conqueror on Christmas Day
★ 1066—and most are buried here, too. The majestic main nave is packed with memories (and, often, crowds), as it has witnessed many splendid coronation ceremonies and royal weddings. Other than the mysterious gloom of the vast interior, the first thing that strikes most people is the proliferation of statues, tombs, and commemorative tablets: in parts, the building seems more like a stonemason's yard than a place of worship. But in its latter capacity, this landmark truly comes into its own. Although attending a service is not something to undertake purely for sightseeing reasons, it provides a glimpse of the abbey in its full majesty, accompanied by music from the Westminster choristers and the organ that Henry Purcell once played.

The current abbey is a largely 13th- and 14th-century rebuilding of the 11th-century church founded by Edward the Confessor, with one notable addition being the 18th-century twin towers over the west entrance, designed by Sir Christopher Wren and completed by Nicholas Hawksmoor. Entering by the north door, what you see first on your left are the extravagant 18th-century monuments of statesmen in the north transept, as well as the north-transept chapels. Look up to your right to see the painted-glass rose window, the largest of its kind. At many points the view of the abbey is crowded by the many statues and screens; to your right is the 19th- (and part 13th-) century choir screen, while to the left is the sacrarium, containing the medieval kings' tombs that screen the **Chapel of St. Edward** (because of its fragility, the shrine is closed off, unless you take a tour with the verger—see the admission desk). Continuing to the foot of the Henry VII Chapel steps, you can still see the hot seat of power, the **Coronation Chair,** which has been graced by nearly every royal posterior. Then proceed into one of the architectural glories of Britain, the **Henry VII Chapel,** passing the huge white marble tomb of Elizabeth I, buried with her half-sister, "Bloody" Mary I. All around are magnificent sculptures of saints, philosophers, and kings, with mermaids and monsters carved on the choir-stall misericords (undersides), and exquisite fan vaulting above (binoculars will help you spot the statues high on the walls)—the last riot of medieval design in England and one of the miracles of Western architecture.

Continue to **Poets' Corner;** in 1400 Geoffrey Chaucer became the first poet to be buried here. There are also memorials to William Shakespeare, William Blake, and Charles Dickens (who is also buried here). Exit the abbey by a door from the south transept. Outside the west front is an archway into the quiet, green **Dean's Yard** and the entrance to the **Cloisters.** If time allows, visit the **Chapter House;** for a small fee you can see the stunning octagonal room, adorned with 14th-century frescoes, where the King's Council met between 1257 and 1547. The **Abbey Museum** is in the **Undercroft,** which survives from Edward the Confessor's original church. The museum includes effigies made from the death masks and actual clothing of Charles II and Admiral Lord Nelson, among other fascinating relics. The **Pyx Chamber** contains the abbey's treasure. As you return to the abbey, look again at the truly awe-inspiring nave. Pause finally for the poignant **Tomb of the Unknown Warrior,** an anonymous World War I martyr who lies buried here in memory of the soldiers fallen in both world wars.

Arrive early if possible, but be prepared to wait in line to tour the abbey. Photography is not permitted. ⊠ *Broad Sanctuary, Westminster SW1* ☎ *020/7222–5152* ⊕ *www.westminster-abbey.org* ⊠ *Abbey and museum £6, Chapter House £2.50* ⊙ *Weekdays 9–4:45, Sat. 9–2:45; last admission 1 hr before closing. Museum daily 10:30–4. Chapter House Apr.–Oct., daily 10–5:30; Nov.–Mar., daily 10–4:30. The abbey is closed weekdays and Sun. to visitors during services.* Ⓤ *Westminster.*

Soho & Covent Garden

A quadrilateral bounded by Regent Street, Coventry and Cranbourn streets, Charing Cross Road, and the eastern half of Oxford Street encloses Soho, the most entertaining part of the West End. This appellation, unlike the New York City neighborhood's similar one, is not an abbreviation of anything, but a blast from the past—derived from the shouts of "So-ho!" that royal huntsmen in Whitehall Palace's parklands were once heard to cry. One of Charles II's illegitimate sons, the duke of Monmouth, was an early resident, his dubious pedigree setting the tone for the future: for many years Soho was London's strip show–peep show–sex shop–brothel center. The mid-1980s brought legislation that granted expensive licenses to a few such establishments and closed down the rest. Today, Soho remains the address for many wonderful ethnic restaurants, including those of London's Chinatown.

Eliza Doolittle's stomping grounds in George Bernard Shaw's *Pygmalion* and Alan Jay Lerner and Frederick Loewe's *My Fair Lady*, the former Covent Garden Market became the Covent Garden Piazza in 1980, and it still functions as the center of a neighborhood—one that has always been alluded to as "colorful." It was originally the "convent garden" belonging to the Abbey of St. Peter at Westminster (later Westminster Abbey). Centuries of magnificence and misery, vice and mayhem, and periods of art-literary bohemia followed, until Covent Garden became the vegetable supplier of London when its market building went up in the 1830s, followed by the Flower Market in 1870. When the produce moved out to the bigger, better Nine Elms Market in Vauxhall in 1974, the (now defunct) Greater London Council stepped in with a rehabilitation scheme, and a neighborhood was born.

a good walk

Soho, being small, is easy to explore, although it's also easy to mistake one narrow, crowded street for another. Enter from the northwest corner, Oxford Circus, and head south for about 200 yards down Regent Street, turn left onto Great Marlborough Street, and head to the top of **Carnaby Street** ▶. Turn right off Broadwick Street onto Berwick (pronounced *ber*-rick) Street, famed as central London's best fruit and vegetable market. Then step through tiny Walker's Court, cross Brewer and Wardour streets, and you'll have arrived at Soho's hip hangout, Old Compton Street. From here, Wardour, Dean, Frith, and Greek streets lead north, all of them bursting with restaurants and clubs. Either of the latter two leads north to Soho Square—its Tudor-style cottage is a perfect backdrop for a picnic—but for lunch, head one block south instead, to Shaftesbury Avenue, heart of Theatreland, across which you'll find Chinatown's main drag, **Gerrard Street.** Below Gerrard Street is **Leicester Square,** and running along its west side is Charing Cross Road, a bibliophile's dream. You'll find some of the best of the specialty bookshops in little Cecil Court, running east just before Trafalgar Square. During your Soho sojourn, visit the neighborhood's wonderful rival patisseries: the old-style French Maison Bertaux at 8 Greek Street or the busy Italian-run but French-accented Pâtisserie Valerie at 44 Old Compton Street. Both serve divine cakes, croissants, and éclairs.

The easiest way to find the **Covent Garden Piazza** ⑰ is to walk down Cranbourn Street, next to Leicester Square tube, then down Long Acre, and turn right at James Street. Near here are St. Paul's—the actors' church—and **London's Transport Museum** ⑱, shops, and cafés. (If your aim is to shop, Neal Street, Floral Street, the streets around Seven Dials, and the Thomas Neal's mall all repay exploration.) At the northwest corner of the Piazza is the **Royal Opera House** ⑲. A detour down Wellington Street to the Strand brings you to **Somerset House** ⑳ and the impressionist-stocked **Courtauld Institute Gallery.** Follow the Strand west to the **Adelphi** ㉑, cross the Victoria Embankment Gardens to the river, and by sticking to the embankment walk and returning east, you'll pass Waterloo Bridge, where (weather permitting) you can catch some of London's finest views, toward the City and Westminster around the Thames bend.

TIMING

The distance covered here is around 5 mi, if you include the lengthy walk down the Strand and riverside stroll back. Skip that, and it's a couple of miles, but you will probably get lost, because the streets in Covent Garden and Soho are winding and chaotic. You can whiz around both neighborhoods in an hour, but if the area appeals at all, you'll want all day—for shopping, lunch, the transportation museum, and Somerset House. You might start at Leicester Square at 2 PM, when tkts, the Society of London Theatre (SOLT) half-price ticket kiosk, opens, pick up tickets for later, and walk, shop, and eat in between.

What to See

㉑ Adelphi. Near Victoria Embankment Gardens, this once-regal riverfront row of houses was the work of all four brothers Adam (John, Robert, James, and William: hence the name, from the Greek *adelphoi,* meaning "brothers"), the noted 18th-century Scottish architects. The best mansions are Nos. 1–4 Robert Street and 7 Adam Street. At the **Royal Society of Arts** (⊠ 8 John Adam St. ☎ 020/7930–5115 ⊕ www.rsa.org. uk ⊠ free ☉ 1st Sun. of month, 10–1), you can see a suite of Adam rooms; no booking is required. ⊠ *The Strand, Covent Garden WC2* Ⓤ *Charing Cross, Temple.*

▶ **Carnaby Street.** The '60s synonym for swinging London fell into a post-party depression, re-emerging sometime during the '80s as the main drag of a public-relations invention called West Soho. Blank stares would greet anyone asking directions to such a place, but it's geographically logical, and the tangle of streets around Carnaby—Foubert's Place, Broadwick Street, Marshall Street—do cohere, at least, in type of merchandise (youth accessories, mostly, with a smattering of designer boutiques). ⊠ *Carnaby St., Soho W1* Ⓤ *Oxford Circus.*

Courtauld Institute Gallery. The collection is housed in a place worthy of its fame: an 18th-century classical mansion, **Somerset House.** Founded in 1931 by textile maven Samuel Courtauld, it is London's finest impressionist and postimpressionist collection (Édouard Manet's *Bar at the Folies-Bergère* is the star), with bonus baroque works thrown in. The collection has been expanded with key works by modernists including Henri Matisse, Maurice Vlaminck, and Raoul Dufy. Other parts of Somerset House can be enjoyed for free. ⊠ *The Strand, Covent Garden WC2* ☎ *020/7848–2526* ⊕ *www.courtauld.ac.uk* ⊠ *£5, free Mon. 10–2 (not bank holiday Mon.); joint ticket with one other collection at Somerset House, £1 discount* ☉ *Mon.–Sat. 10–6, Sun. noon–6; last admission at 5:15* Ⓤ *Covent Garden, Holborn, Temple (closed Sun.).*

⑰ Covent Garden Piazza. The original "convent garden" produced vegetables for the 13th-century Abbey of St. Peter at Westminster. In 1630 the duke of Bedford, having become owner, commissioned Inigo Jones to lay out a square, with **St. Paul's Church** (designed by Jones and known as the actors' church) at one end. Open-air entertainers known as buskers perform under the church's portico, where George Bernard Shaw set the first scene of *Pygmalion* (reshaped as the musical *My Fair Lady*). The fruit, flower, and vegetable market established in the 1700s flourished until 1974, when it moved south of the Thames. Since then, the area has been transformed into the Piazza, a mostly higher-class shopping mall that has a couple of cafés and beauty and gift stores. A superior crafts market, the **Apple Market,** is open daily; the less upscale **Jubilee Market** is across the cobbles in the Jubilee Hall. ⊠ *Bordered by Henrietta St., King St., Russell St., and Bedford St., Covent Garden WC2* Ⓤ *Covent Garden.*

Gerrard Street. Pedestrianized Gerrard Street, south of Shaftesbury Avenue, is the hub of London's compact Chinatown, with restaurants, dim sum houses, Chinese supermarkets, and Chinese New Year's celebrations, plus a brace of scarlet pagoda-style archways and a pair of phone booths with pictogram dialing instructions.

Leicester Square. This is the big magnet for nightlife lovers. Looking at the neon of the major movie houses, the fast-food outlets, and the disco entrances, you'd never guess the square—it's pronounced *les*-ter—was laid out around 1630. The Odeon, on the east side, is the venue for all the Royal Film Performances, and a jaunty little statue of Charlie Chaplin in the opposite corner continues the movie theme. Shakespeare sulks in the middle, chin on hand, clearly wishing he were somewhere else. One landmark worth visiting is **tkts**, the Society of London Theatre (SOLT) ticket kiosk, on the southwest corner, which opens at 2 and sells half-price tickets for many of that evening's performances. ⊠ *Leicester Sq., Covent Garden WC2* Ⓤ *Covent Garden.*

Ⓒ ⑱ **London's Transport Museum.** Occupying the old Flower Market at the southeast corner of the piazza, this museum tells the story of mass transportation in the capital. For children there are lots of touch-screen interactives, old rolling stock, period smells and sounds, and, best of all, a tube-driving simulator. The shop sells the wonderful old London Transport posters, printed with the tube map. ⊠ *Covent Garden Piazza, Covent Garden WC2* ☎ *020/7379–6344; 020/7565–7299 recorded info* ⊕ *www. ltmuseum.co.uk* ⊠ *£5.95* ☉ *Sat.–Thurs. 10–6, Fri. 11–6; last admission at 5:15* Ⓤ *Covent Garden.*

⑲ **Royal Opera House.** After mammoth renovations, the fabled home of the Royal Ballet and Britain's finest opera company has been brought smartly into the 21st century. Here, in days of yore, Joan Sutherland brought down the house as Lucia di Lammermoor, and Rudolf Nureyev and Margot Fonteyn became the greatest ballet duo of all time. London's premier opera venue was designed in 1858 by E. M. Barry, son of Sir Charles, the House of Commons architect. Without doubt, the glass-and-steel Floral Hall is the most wonderful jaw-dropping feature, and you can wander in during the day, when there may be free lunchtime concerts and events. You can also visit the Amphitheatre Bar and Piazza concourse, which give a splendid panorama across the city. ⊠ *Bow St., Covent Garden WC2* ☎ *020/7240–1200 or 020/7304–4000* ⊕ *www. royaloperahouse.org* Ⓤ *Covent Garden.*

★ ⑳ **Somerset House.** This grand 18th-century pile, constructed during the reign of George III, was designed to house government offices, principally those of the navy. The gracious rooms on the south side of the building, by the river, are on view for free, including the Seamen's Waiting Hall and the Nelson Stair. The **Courtauld Institute Gallery** occupies most of the north building, facing the busy Strand. Cafés and a river terrace adjoin the property, and a footbridge leads on to Waterloo Bridge. In the vaults of the house is the **Gilbert Collection**, a museum of intricate works of silver, gold snuffboxes, and Italian mosaics. **The Hermitage Rooms** have changing exhibitions of treasures from the State Hermitage Museum in Russia. ⊠ *The Strand, Covent Garden WC2* ☎ *020/7845–4600; 020/7485–4630 Hermitage information* ⊕ *www.somerset-house.org.uk, www.hermitagerooms.com* ⊠ *Somerset House free, Courtauld Institute Gallery £5, Gilbert Collection £5 (free after 4:30), Hermitage Rooms £6. Visit 2 collections, save £1; visit all 3, save £2* ☉ *Daily 10–6; last admission at 5:15* Ⓤ *Charing Cross.*

Bloomsbury & Legal London

The character of an area of London can change visibly from one street to the next. Nowhere is this so clear as in the contrast between fun-loving Soho and intellectual Bloomsbury, a mere 100 yards to the northeast, or between arty, trendy Covent Garden and—on the other side of Kingsway—sober Holborn. Both Bloomsbury and Holborn (pronounced *hoe*-bun) are almost purely residential and should be seen by day. The first district is best known for its famous flowering of literary-arty bohemia, personified during the first three decades of the 20th century by the clique known as the Bloomsbury Group, and for the British Museum and the University of London, which dominate it now. The second sounds as exciting as, say, a center for accountants or dentists, but don't be put off—filled with ancient buildings, Holborn is more interesting and beautiful than you might suppose.

Many people head here to find the ghosts of all those great Bloomsbury figures such as Virginia Woolf, E. M. Forster, Vanessa Bell, and Lytton Strachey. Ghosts of their literary salons soon lead into the time-warp territory of interlocking alleys, gardens and cobbled courts, and town houses and halls where London's legal profession grew up. The Great Fire of 1666 razed most of the city but spared the buildings of legal London, and all of Holborn oozes history. Leading landmarks here are the Inns of Court, where the country's top solicitors and barristers have had their chambers for centuries.

a good walk

From Russell Square tube station, walk south down Southampton Row and west on Great Russell Street, passing Bloomsbury Square on the left, en route to London's biggest and most important collection of antiquities, the **British Museum** 22 ☞. Leaving this via the back exit leads you to Montague Place; then head left to Malet Street if you want to walk around the University of London. For a delightful detour, head west toward the Goodge Street tube stop on Tottenham Court Road to Scala Street to find the Victorian-era wonders of **Pollock's Toy Museum** 23. Back at the university, head north on Gordon Street to busy Euston Road and east toward St. Pancras and the bold redbrick **British Library** 24. But if time is short, head south through the university, veering left down Guilford Street past Coram's Fields, then right to Doughty Street and the **Dickens House** 25. Two streets west, parallel to Doughty Street, is Lamb's Conduit Street (whose pretty pub, the Lamb, Dickens frequented). At the bottom of Lamb's Conduit Street you reach Theobalds Road, where you enter the first of the Inns of Court, Gray's Inn, emerging from here onto High Holborn—the noisy main route from the City to the West End and Westminster—and Hatton Garden, running north from Holborn Circus and still the center of London's diamond and jewelry trade. Pass another ghost of former trading, Staple Inn, and turn left down tiny Great Turnstile Row to reach **Lincoln's Inn** 26. Cross to the north side of Lincoln's Inn Fields to **Sir John Soane's Museum** 27. Head south and cross the Strand to the **Temple** 28, and pass through the elaborate stone arch to Middle Temple Lane, which you follow to the Thames.

TIMING This is a substantial walk of 3 to 4 mi, and it has two distinct halves. The first half, around Bloomsbury, is not so interesting on the surface, but it includes the British Museum, where you could spend two hours—or two days. The Dickens House is also worth a stop. The second half, legal London, is a real walker's walk: most of the highlights are in the architecture, with the exception of Sir John Soane's Museum. The walk alone can be done comfortably in two hours.

What to See

24 **British Library.** Since 1759, the British Library had been housed in the British Museum—but space ran out in the 1990s, necessitating this grand edifice, a few blocks north of the museum, between Euston and St. Pancras stations. The collection includes 18 million volumes, and the library's treasures are on public view: the John Ritblat Gallery displays the Magna Carta, the Gutenberg Bible, Jane Austen's manuscripts, Shakespeare's First Folio, and musical manuscripts by George Fridric

Handel and Sir Paul McCartney. You'll find headphones to listen to some interesting snippets in a small showcase of the **National Sound Archive** (which is the world's largest collection, but not on view), such as the voice of Florence Nightingale and an extract from the Beatles' last tour interview. ⊠ *96 Euston Rd., Bloomsbury NW1* ☎ *020/7412-7332* ⊕ *www.bl.uk* ☎ *Free* ⊙ *Mon. and Wed.–Fri. 9:30–6, Tues. 9:30–8, Sat. 9:30–5, Sun. 11–5* Ⓤ *Euston or King's Cross.*

★ ☺ ☞ ㉒ **British Museum.** With a facade like a great temple, this celebrated treasure house, filled with plunder of incalculable value and beauty from around the globe, occupies a ponderous Greco-Victorian building that makes a suitably grand impression. Inside you'll find some of the greatest relics of humankind: the Elgin Marbles, the Rosetta Stone, the Sutton Hoo Treasure—almost everything, it seems, but the Ark of the Covenant. The museum has shaken off its dust and opened new galleries, and many sections have been updated, particularly in ethnography, including the impressive **Sainsbury African Galleries.** The focal point is the **Great Court,** a brilliant techno-classical design with a vast glass roof, which highlights and reveals the museum's most well-kept secret—an inner courtyard. The revered **Reading Room** has also been carefully restored. If you want to navigate the highlights of the almost 100 galleries, join at least one of the free "Eyeopener" 50-minute tours by museum guides (details at the information desk).

The collection began in 1753 and grew quickly, thanks to enthusiastic kleptomaniacs during the Napoleonic Wars—most notoriously the seventh earl of Elgin, who acquired the marbles from the Parthenon and Erechtheum during his term as British ambassador in Constantinople. Here follows a highly edited résumé (in order of encounter) of the British Museum's greatest hits: close to the entrance hall, in Room 4, is the **Rosetta Stone,** found by French soldiers in 1799, and carved in 196 BC with a decree of Ptolemy V in Egyptian hieroglyphics, demotic (a cursive script developed in Egypt), and Greek. This inscription provided the French Egyptologist Jean-François Champollion with the key to deciphering hieroglyphics. Maybe the **Elgin Marbles** ought to be back in Greece, but since these graceful sculptures are here, make a beeline for them in Room 18, west of the entrance in the Parthenon Galleries. These galleries also include the spectacular remains of the Parthenon frieze that girdled the cella of Athena's temple on the Acropolis, carved around 440 BC. Also in the West Wing is one of the Seven Wonders of the Ancient World—in fragment form—in Room 21: the **Mausoleum of Halikarnassos.** The **JP Morgan Chase North American Gallery** (Room 26) has one of the largest collections of native culture outside the North American continent, going back to the earliest hunters 10,000 years ago.

Upstairs are some of the most popular galleries, especially beloved by children: Rooms 62–63, where the **Egyptian mummies** live. The Roxie Walker Galleries display even more Egyptian relics. Nearby are the glittering 4th-century **Mildenhall Treasure** and the equally splendid 8th-century Anglo-Saxon **Sutton Hoo Treasure.** A more prosaic exhibit is that of Pete Marsh, sentimentally named by the archaeologists who unearthed the **Lindow Man** from a Cheshire peat marsh; poor Pete was ritually slain, probably as a human sacrifice. The **Korean Gallery** (Room 67) delves into the art and archaeology of the country, including precious porcelain and colorful screens. ⊠ *Great Russell St., Bloomsbury WC1* ☎ *020/ 7636–1555* ⊕ *www.thebritishmuseum.ac.uk* ☎ *Free, suggested donation £2* ⊙ *Museum Sat.–Wed. 10–5:30, Thurs. and Fri. 10–8:30. Great Court Sun.–Wed. 9–6, Thurs.–Sat. 9 AM–11 PM* Ⓤ *Holborn, Russell Sq., Tottenham Court Rd.*

> **need a break?**

The British Museum's **restaurant and café** get very crowded but serve a reasonably tasty menu beneath a plaster cast of a part of the Parthenon frieze. The restaurant is open Monday–Saturday noon–4:30, Sunday noon–5:30; the café, Monday–Saturday 10–3. The self-service café in the Great Court concourse is open Sunday–Wednesday 9–5:30 and Thursday–Saturday 9–9.

㉕ Dickens House. This is the only one of the many London houses Charles Dickens (1812–70) inhabited that's still standing. The great novelist wrote *Oliver Twist* and *Nicholas Nickleby* and finished *The Pickwick Papers* here between 1837 and 1839. The house looks exactly as it would have in Dickens's day, complete with first editions, letters, and tall clerk's desk, plus a treat for Lionel Bart fans—his score of *Oliver!* Special exhibitions give insight into the Dickens family and the author's works, with sessions where, for example, you can try your own hand with a quill pen. During Christmas, the rooms are decorated in traditional style. ⊠ *48 Doughty St., Bloomsbury* ☎ *020/7405–2127* ⊕ *www.dickensmuseum. com* ⊠ *£4* ☉ *Mon.–Sat. 10–5, Sun. 11–5; last admission at 4:30* Ⓤ *Chancery La., Russell Sq.*

⟳ King's Cross Station. Known for its 120-foot-tall clock tower, this yellow brick, Italianate building with large, arched windows was constructed in 1851–52 as the London terminus for the East Coast main line. Harry Potter and fellow aspiring wizards took the Hogwarts Express to school from the imaginary platform 9¾ (platforms 4 and 5 were the actual shooting site) in the movies based on J. K. Rowling's popular novels. The station has put up a sign for platform 9¾ if you want to take a picture there. ⊠ *Euston Rd. and York Way, Euston* ☎ *0845/ 748–4950* Ⓤ *King's Cross.*

㉖ Lincoln's Inn. One of the oldest, best preserved, and most attractive of the Inns of Court, Lincoln's Inn offers plenty to see—from the Chancery Lane Tudor brick gatehouse to the wide-open, tree-lined, atmospheric Lincoln's Inn Fields and the 15th-century chapel remodeled by Inigo Jones in 1620. The wisteria-clad New Square is London's only complete 17th-century square. ⊠ *Chancery La., Bloomsbury WC2* ☎ *020/7405–1393* ⊠ *Free* ☉ *Gardens weekdays 7–7; chapel weekdays noon–2:30; public may also attend Sun. service at 11:30 in chapel during legal terms* Ⓤ *Chancery La.*

⟳ ㉓ Pollock's Toy Museum. For some, this will merit a visit whether they have children or not. A small, magical museum in a warren of rooms in an 18th-century town house, Pollock's displays dolls, dollhouses, teddy bears, folk toys—and those bedazzling mementos of Victorian childhood, Pollock's famed cardboard cutout miniature theaters, all red velvet and gold trim, with movable scenery and figurines. The store sells reproductions of these cut-and-paste theater kits. ⊠ *1 Scala St., Bloomsbury W1* ☎ *020/7636–3452* ⊕ *www.pollocksweb.co.uk* ⊠ *£3* ☉ *Mon.–Sat. 10–5; last admission at 4:30* Ⓤ *Goodge St.*

★ ㉗ Sir John Soane's Museum. Guaranteed to raise a smile from the most blasé traveler, this collection hardly deserves the burden of its dry name. Sir John, architect of the Bank of England, who lived here from 1790 to 1831, created one of London's most idiosyncratic and fascinating houses. Everywhere mirrors and colors play tricks with light and space, and split-level floors worthy of a fairground fun house disorient you. In a basement chamber sits the vast 1300 BC sarcophagus of Seti I, lit by a skylight two stories above. ⊠ *13 Lincoln's Inn Fields, Bloomsbury WC2* ☎ *020/7405–2107* ⊕ *www.soane.org* ⊠ *Free* ☉ *Tues.–Sat. 10–5; also 6–9 on 1st Tues. of every month* Ⓤ *Holborn.*

28 **Temple.** This is the collective name for the **Inner Temple** and **Middle Temple**, and its entrance, the exact point of entry into the City, is marked by a young (1880) bronze griffin, the **Temple Bar Memorial**. In the buildings opposite is an elaborate stone arch through which you pass into Middle Temple Lane, past a row of 17th-century timber-frame houses, and on into Fountain Court. If the Elizabethan **Middle Temple Hall** is open, don't miss its hammer-beam roof—among the finest in the land. ⊠ *2 Plowden Bldgs., Middle Temple La., Bloomsbury* ☏ *020/7427–4800* ⊙ *Weekdays 10–11 and (when not in use) 2–4* Ⓤ *Temple.*

The City

When people in London tell you that they work in the City, they aren't being vague: they're using the British equivalent of Wall Street. The City extends eastward from Temple Bar to the Tower of London, and north from the Thames to Chiswell Street. Despite its small size (it's known as the Square Mile), this area is the financial engine of Britain and one of the world's leading centers of trade. The City also holds two of London's most notable sights, the Tower of London and St. Paul's, one of the world's greatest cathedrals—truly, a case of the money changers encompassing the temple. The pedestrian-only Millennium Bridge connects the area with the South Bank.

Twice, the City has been nearly wiped off the face of the earth. The Great Fire of 1666 necessitated a total reconstruction, in which Sir Christopher Wren had a big hand, contributing not only his masterpiece, St. Paul's Cathedral, but 49 additional parish churches. The second wave of destruction was dealt by the German bombers of World War II. The ruins were rebuilt, but slowly, and with no overall plan, leaving the City a patchwork of the old and the new, the interesting and the flagrantly awful. Since a mere 8,000 or so people call it home, the financial center of Britain is deserted on weekends, with restaurants shuttered.

a good walk

Begin at the gateway to the City, the Temple Bar, a bronze griffin on the Strand opposite the Royal Courts of Justice. Walk east to Fleet Street and turn left on Bolt Court to Gough Square, and **Dr. Johnson's House** **29** ⌐, passing Ye Olde Cheshire Cheese on Wine Office Court en route back to Fleet Street and the journalists' church, **St. Bride's** **30**. At the end of Fleet Street, cross Ludgate Circus to Ludgate Hill to reach the **Old Bailey** **31** and the Central Criminal Courts. Continuing along Ludgate Hill, you reach **St. Paul's Cathedral** **32**, Wren's masterpiece.

Retrace your steps to Newgate Street to reach London's meat market, Smithfield—where, for centuries, livestock was sold. From Smithfield Market, cross Aldersgate Street and take the right fork to London Wall, named for the Roman rampart that stood along it, with a remaining section of 2nd- to 4th-century wall at St. Alphege Garden. There's another bit outside the **Museum of London** **33**, behind which is the **Barbican Centre** **34**, an important arts venue. Back on London Wall, turn south onto Coleman Street, then right onto Masons Avenue to reach Basinghall Street and the **Guildhall** **35**, then follow Milk Street south to Cheapside. Here is another symbolic center of London, the church of **St. Mary-le-Bow** **36**.

Walk to the east end of Cheapside, where seven roads meet, and you will be facing the **Bank of England** **37**. Turn your back on the bank and there's the Lord Mayor's Palladian-style abode, the Mansion House, with Wren's St. Stephen Walbrook church—considered his finest effort by architectural historians—behind it, and the Royal Exchange in between Threadneedle Street and Cornhill. Now head down Queen Victoria Street, where you'll pass the remains of the Roman **Temple of Mithras** **38**, then, after a sharp left turn onto Cannon Street, you'll come upon the **Monument** ㊴, Wren's memorial to the Great Fire of London. Just south of it is London Bridge. Turn left onto Lower Thames Street, for almost a mile's walk—passing Billingsgate, London's principal fish market for 900 years, until 1982, and the Custom House, built early in the last century—to the **Tower of London** ㊵, which may be the single most unmissable of London's sights. Children of all ages will be enchanted by that Thames icon, the **Tower Bridge.**

TIMING   This is a marathon. Unless you want to walk all day, without a chance to do justice to London's most famous sights, the Tower of London (take the tube here) and St. Paul's Cathedral—not to mention the Museum of London, Tower Bridge, and the Barbican Centre—you should consider splitting the walk into segments. However, if you're not planning to go inside, this walk makes for a great day out, with lots of surprising vistas, river views, and history. The City is a wasteland on weekends and after dark, so choose your time accordingly.

What to See

㊲   **Bank of England.** Known for the past couple of centuries as "the Old Lady of Threadneedle Street," the bank has been central to the British economy since 1694. Sir John Soane designed the neoclassical hulk in 1788, wrapping it in windowless walls (which are all that survive of his building) to project a facade of unshakable stability. This and other facets of the bank's history are traced in the Bank of England Museum, around the corner. ⊠ *Bartholomew La., The City EC4* ☎ *020/7601–5545* ⊕ *www.bankofengland.co.uk* ⊠ *Free* ☉ *Weekdays 10–5 and Lord Mayor's Show Day (2nd Sat. in Nov.)* Ⓤ *Bank, Monument.*

㉞   **Barbican Centre.** An enormous concrete maze Londoners love to hate, the Barbican is home to the London Symphony Orchestra and its auditorium, the Guildhall School of Music and Drama, two movie theaters, a convention center, and The **Barbican Art Gallery,** which showcases modern, populist topics from the Shaker movement to *Star Wars.* The center's dance, music, and theater programs, transformed into a yearlong fest called Barbican International Theatre Events (BITE), focus on the contemporary and new but also present established companies and artists. The **Museum of London** is also part of the complex. ⊠ *Silk St., The City EC2* ☎ *020/7638–8891 box office* ⊕ *www.barbican.org.uk* ⊠ *Barbican Centre free, gallery £5* ☉ *Barbican Centre Mon.–Sat. 9 AM–11 PM, Sun. noon–11; gallery Mon.–Sat. 10–7:30, Sun. noon–7:30* Ⓤ *Barbican, Moorgate.*

▶ ㉙   **Dr. Johnson's House.** Samuel Johnson lived here between 1746 and 1759, while in the worst of health, compiling his famous *Dictionary of the English Language* in the attic. Like Dickens, he lived all over town, but, like Dickens House, this is the only one of Johnson's abodes remaining today. The 17th-century house is a shrine to the man possibly more attached to London than anyone else has ever been, and it includes a first edition of his dictionary among the Johnson-and-Boswell mementos. After your visit, repair around the corner in Wine Office Court to the Ye Olde Cheshire Cheese pub, once Johnson's and James Boswell's favorite watering hole. ⊠ *17 Gough Sq., The City EC4* ☎ *020/7353–3745* ⊠ *£4* ☉ *May–Sept., Mon.–Sat. 11–5:30; Oct.–Apr., Mon.–Sat. 11–5* Ⓤ *Blackfriars, Chancery La.*

㉟   **Guildhall.** In the symbolic nerve center of the City, the Corporation of London ceremonially elects and installs its Lord Mayor as it has done for 800 years. The Guildhall was built in 1411, and although it failed to escape either the 1666 or 1940 flames, its core survived. The fabulous hall is a psychedelic patchwork of coats of arms and banners of the City Livery Companies. Also here is the Worshipful Company of Clockmakers Museum in the Guildhall Library, with more than 600 time-pieces; to the right of Guildhall Yard is the **Guildhall Art Gallery,** the corporation's collection of London scenes and portraits of royals and statesmen. During construction of the art gallery, London's only Roman amphitheater was discovered and excavated, and you can walk among the remains. The Museum of London displays additional relics from the dig. Entry to the amphitheatre is included in admission to the art gallery. ⊠ *Gresham St., The City EC2* ☎ *020/7606–3030; 020/7332–1632 gallery; 020/7332–3700 recorded information* ⊕ *www.guildhall-art-gallery.org.uk* ✉ *Free, gallery and amphitheatre £2.50* ⊙ *Mon.–Sat. 9:30–5; Clockmakers Museum weekdays 9:30–4:45; gallery Mon.–Sat. 10–5, Sun. noon–4* Ⓤ *Bank, Mansion House, Moorgate, St. Paul's.*

off the beaten path

JACK THE RIPPER'S LONDON – *Cor blimey, guv'nor, Jack the Ripper woz here!* Several organizations offer tours of "Jack's London"—the (still) mean streets of the East End, the working-class neighborhood directly to the east of the City. Here, in 1888, the Whitechapel murders traumatized Victorian London. At the haunting hour, tour groups head out to Bucks Row and other notorious scenes of the crime. Even with a large group, this can be a spooky and unforgettable experience. Original London Walks (☎ 020/7624–3978 ⊕ www.walks.com) has frequent tours leaving at 7 PM from the Tower Hill tube stop. The Jack the Ripper Mystery Walk (☎ 020/8558–9446) departs at 8 PM from the Aldgate tube stop Wednesday and Sunday; Friday 7 PM. The Blood and Tears Walk: London's Horrible Past (☎ 020/8348–9022) goes beyond Jack the Ripper, although he is the star criminal, and details some of the City's other gruesome murderers. Tours depart from the Barbican tube; phone for times.

Lloyd's of London. Architect Richard Rogers's (of Paris Pompidou Centre fame) fantastical 1980s steel-and-glass medium-rise of six towers around a vast atrium, with his trademark inside-out ventilation shafts, stairwells, and gantries, is one of the most exciting modern structures in London. This fun house of a building, which contains the offices of the world-famous insurance agency, is best seen at night, when cobalt and lime spotlights make it leap out of the gray skyline. ⊠ *1 Lime St., The City EC3* Ⓤ *Aldgate, Bank, Liverpool St., Monument.*

Millennium Bridge. Norman Foster and sculptor Anthony Caro designed this strikingly modern, pedestrian-only bridge of aluminum and steel. The bridge connects the City—St. Paul's Cathedral area—with the Tate Modern art gallery. On the South Bank side, the bridge marks the middle of the **Millennium Mile,** a walkway taking in a clutch of popular sights. The city views from the bridge are breathtaking, with perhaps the best-ever view of St. Paul's. ⊠ *Peters Hill to Bankside, The City, South Bank EC4, SE1* Ⓤ *Mansion House, Blackfriars, or Southwark.*

㊴ Monument. Commemorating the "dreadful visitation" of the Great Fire of 1666, this is the world's tallest isolated stone column—the work of Christopher Wren. The viewing gallery is 311 steps up the 202-foot-high structure. ⊠ *Monument St., The City EC3* ☎ *020/7626–2717* ✉ *£1.50, combination ticket with Tower Bridge gives £1 discount off entry to Tower Bridge* ⊙ *Daily 10–5:40; hrs subject to change, phone before visiting* Ⓤ *Monument.*

off the beaten path

MUSEUM IN DOCKLANDS – This museum, in a converted quayside warehouse, focuses on the days when ships and sailors, rather than towering office blocks, filled this part of London. Displays and interactive zones tell the story: Early Years, Water Zone, Dock Work, and Building. ⊠ *No. 1 Warehouse, Hertsmere Rd., West India Quay, East End E14* ☎ *020/7001–9800* ⊕ *www.museumindocklands.org. uk* ⊠ *£5* ⊙ *Daily 10–6; call to confirm hrs* Ⓤ *West India Quay.*

★ ⚅ ❸❸ **Museum of London.** Anyone with the least interest in how this city evolved will adore this museum, especially its reconstructions and dioramas of the Great Fire (flickering flames! sound effects!), a 1940s air-raid shelter, a Georgian prison cell, and a Victorian street complete with stocked shops. Come right up to date in the London Now gallery. World City charts one of the city's most dynamic periods, from the French Revolution to World War I, and the Medieval Gallery is a time journey to an age when London depended on the Thames. The remains unearthed at the Roman amphitheater at the Guildhall are on display. ⊠ *London Wall, The City EC2* ☎ *020/7600–0807* ⊕ *www.museumoflondon.org.uk* ⊠ *Free* ⊙ *Mon.–Sat. 10–5:50, Sun. noon–5:50* Ⓤ *Barbican.*

❸❶ **Old Bailey.** The present-day Central Criminal Court is where legendary Newgate Prison stood from the 12th century right until the beginning of the 20th century. Dickens visited Newgate several times—Fagin ends up in the Condemned Hold here in *Oliver Twist*. Ask the doorman which current trial is likely to prove juicy, if you're that kind of ghoul—you may catch the conviction of the next Crippen or Christie (England's most notorious wife murderers, both tried here). There are restrictions on entry (cameras, drinks, large bags, and children under 14 are not allowed), and you will be searched before you enter; call the information line first. The court has no storage facilities for items. ⊠ *Newgate St., The City EC4* ☎ *020/7248–3277* ⊙ *Public Gallery weekdays 10:30–1 and 2–4:30; line forms at Newgate St. entrance* Ⓤ *Blackfriars.*

❸❶ **St. Bride's.** One of the first of Christopher Wren's city churches, St. Bride's was also one of those bomb-damaged in World War II, to be reconsecrated in 1960 after a 17-year-long restoration. From afar, study its extraordinary steeple. Its tiered shape gave rise, legend has it, to the traditional wedding cake. ⊠ *Fleet St., The City EC4* ☎ *020/7427–0133* ⊕ *www.stbrides.com* ⊠ *Free* ⊙ *Weekdays 8–4:30, Sat. 10–3:30, Sun. for services only 11–2; crypt closed Sun.* Ⓤ *Chancery La.*

❸❻ **St. Mary-le-Bow.** Christopher Wren's 1673 church has one of the most famous sets of bells around—a Londoner must be born within the sound of Bow Bells to claim to be a true cockney. The origin of that idea was probably the curfew rung on the Bow Bells during the 14th century, even though "cockney" came to mean "Londoner" three centuries later, and then it was an insult. The Bow in the name comes from the bow-shape arches in the Norman crypt. Packed during weekday lunchtimes, it's also open for breakfast. ⊠ *Cheapside, The City EC2.* ☎ *020/7248–5139* ⊕ *www.stmarylebow.co.uk* ⊙ *Mon.–Thurs. 6:30–5:45, Fri. 6:30–4* Ⓤ *Mansion House.*

need a break?

The Place Below (⊠ Cheapside, The City EC2 ☎ 020/7329–0789) occupies St. Mary-le-Bow's crypt. The self-service vegetarian menu includes particularly good soups and quiches. Lunches are served from 10:30 until 2:30, weekdays only, or you can stop by for breakfast (from 7:30) and morning coffee, or for snacks (until 3:30).

★ ㉜ **St. Paul's Cathedral.** The symbolic heart of London, St. Paul's will take your breath away. The dome—the world's third largest—will already be familiar, since you see it peeping through on the skyline from many an angle. The structure is Sir Christopher Wren's masterpiece, completed in 1710 after 35 years of building, and then, much later, miraculously spared (mostly) by World War II bombs. Wren's first plan, known as the New Model, did not make it past the drawing board. The second, known as the Great Model, got as far as the 20-foot oak rendering you can see here today before it also was rejected, whereupon Wren is said to have burst into tears. The third, however, was accepted, with the fortunate coda that the architect be allowed to make changes as he saw fit. Without that, there would be no dome, since the approved design had a steeple. When you enter and see the dome from the inside, you may find that it seems smaller than you expected. You aren't imagining things; it *is* smaller, and 60 feet lower than the lead-covered outer dome. Beneath the lantern is Wren's famous epitaph, which his son composed and had set into the pavement, and which reads succinctly: *Lector, si monumentum requiris, circumspice*—"Reader, if you seek his monument, look around you." The epitaph also appears on Wren's memorial in the Crypt. Up 259 spiral steps is the **Whispering Gallery,** an acoustic phenomenon; you whisper something to the wall on one side, and a second later it transmits clearly to the other side, 107 feet away. Ascend farther to the **Stone Gallery,** which encircles the outside of the dome and has a spectacular panorama of London.

The poet John Donne, who had been dean of St. Paul's for his final 10 years (he died in 1631), lies in the south choir aisle. The vivacious choir-stall carvings nearby are the work of Grinling Gibbons, as are the organ's, which Wren designed and Handel played. Behind the high altar, you'll find the **American Memorial Chapel,** dedicated in 1958 to the 28,000 GIs stationed here who lost their lives in World War II. Among the famous whose remains lie in the **Crypt** are the duke of Wellington and Admiral Lord Nelson. The Crypt also has a gift shop and a café. ⊠ *St. Paul's Churchyard, The City EC4* ☎ *020/7236–4128* ⊕ *www. stpauls.co.uk* ⊠ *£6, audio tour £3.50, guided tour £2.50* ⊙ *Cathedral Mon.–Sat. 8:30–4, closed occasionally for special services; ambulatory, Crypt, and galleries Mon.–Sat. 9–5:15. Shop and Crypt Café also Sun. 10:30–5* Ⓤ *St. Paul's.*

㊳ **Temple of Mithras.** Unearthed on a building site in 1954 and taken, at first, for an early Christian church, this was a minor place of pilgrimage in Roman London. In fact, worshipers here favored Jesus' chief rival, Mithras, the Persian god of light, during the 3rd and 4th centuries. You can see the foundations of the temple on this site. ⊠ *Temple Court, Queen Victoria St., The City EC4* Ⓤ *Bank.*

Ⓒ **Tower Bridge.** Despite its venerable appearance, this Victorian youngster dates from 1894. Constructed of steel, then clothed in Portland stone, the bridge was built in the Gothic style to complement the Tower of London next door and is famous for its enormous bascules, the "arms," which open to allow large ships through—a rare occurrence these days. The **Tower Bridge Experience** exhibition is a fun tour inside the building to discover how one of the world's most famous bridges actually works. Through hands-on displays and film, you will see how the original engine-room workers kept the power stoked up by coal; today electricity powers the lifts that raise the bridge. One highlight is the glorious view from up high on the covered walkway between the turrets. ☎ *020/7403–3761* ⊕ *www. towerbridge.org.uk* ⊠ *£4:50, joint ticket available for the Monument* ⊙ *Daily 9:30–5:30; last entry at 5* Ⓤ *Tower Hill.*

★ **Tower of London.** Nowhere else does London's history come to life so vividly as in this minicity of melodramatic towers stuffed to bursting with heraldry and treasure, the intimate details of lords and dukes and princes and sovereigns etched in the walls (literally, in some places), and quite a few pints of royal blood spilled on the stones. This is one of Britain's most popular sights, and you can save time and avoid lines by buying a ticket in advance on the Web site, by phone, or at any tube station; arriving early (before 11) can also help at busy times. Moving walkways within the prize exhibit, the Crown Jewels, hasten progress there at the busiest times. Allow at least three hours for exploring, and don't forget to stroll along the battlements before you leave; from them, you get a wonderful overview of the whole Tower.

The Tower holds the royal gems because it's still one of the royal palaces, although no monarch since Henry VII has called it home. It has also housed the Royal Mint, the Public Records, the Royal Menagerie (which formed the basis of the London Zoo), and the Royal Observatory, although its most renowned and titillating function has been, of course, as a jail and place of torture and execution.

A person was mighty privileged to be beheaded in the peace and seclusion of **Tower Green** instead of before the mob at Tower Hill. In fact, only seven people were ever important enough—among them Anne Boleyn and Catherine Howard, wives two and five of Henry VIII's six; Elizabeth I's friend Robert Devereux, earl of Essex; and the nine-day queen, Lady Jane Grey, age 17. The executioner's block and ax, along with the equally famous rack, plus assorted thumbscrews, "iron maidens," and so forth, have been moved to the Royal Armouries in Leeds, Yorkshire. Fans of this niche of heavy metal might want to pay a call on the London Dungeon attraction, just across the Thames.

Free tours depart every half hour or so from the Middle Tower. They are conducted by the 39 Yeoman Warders, better known as Beefeaters—ex-servicemen dressed in resplendent navy-and-red (scarlet-and-gold on special occasions) Tudor outfits. Beefeaters have been guarding the Tower since Henry VII appointed them in 1485. One of them, the Yeoman Ravenmaster, is responsible for making life comfortable for the Tower ravens (six birds plus reserves)—an important duty, because if the ravens were to desert the Tower, goes the legend, the kingdom would fall. Today, the Tower takes no chances: the ravens' wings are clipped.

In prime position stands the oldest part of the Tower and the most conspicuous of its buildings, the **White Tower.** This central keep was begun in 1078 by William the Conqueror; Henry III (1207–72) had it whitewashed, which is where the name comes from. The spiral staircase is the only way up, and here you'll find the **Royal Armouries,** with a collection of arms and armor. Most of the interior of the White Tower has been altered over the centuries, but the **Chapel of St. John the Evangelist,** downstairs from the armories, is a pure example of 11th-century Norman style—very rare, very simple, and very beautiful. Across the moat, **Traitors' Gate** lies to the right. Immediately opposite Traitors' Gate is the former Garden Tower, better known since about 1570 as the **Bloody Tower.** Its name comes from one of the most famous unsolved murders in history, the saga of the "little princes in the Tower." In 1483 the uncrowned boy king, Edward V, and his brother Richard were left here by their uncle, Richard of Gloucester, after the death of their father, Edward IV. They were never seen again, Gloucester was crowned Richard III, and in 1674 two little skeletons were found under the stairs to the White Tower. The obvious conclusions have always been drawn—and were, in fact, even before the skeletons were discovered. The **New Armouries** have become a restaurant.

The most famous exhibits here are the **Crown Jewels**, housed in the Jewel House, Waterloo Block. You get so close to the fabled gems you feel you could polish them (if it weren't for the wafers of bulletproof glass), if your eyes weren't so dazzled by the sparkle of the gems, enhanced with special lighting. Before you see them, you view a short film that includes scenes from Elizabeth's 1953 coronation. Security is tight because the jewels—even though they would be impossible for thieves to sell—are so priceless that they're not insured. However, they are polished every January by the crown jewelers. A brief résumé of the top jewels: finest of all is the Royal Sceptre, containing the earth's largest cut diamond, the 530-carat Star of Africa. This is also known as Cullinan I, having been cut from the South African Cullinan, which weighed 20 ounces when dug up from a De Beers mine at the beginning of the century. Another chip off the block, Cullinan II, lives on the Imperial State Crown made for Queen Victoria's coronation in 1838; Elizabeth II also wore this crown at her coronation and wears it annually for the State Opening of Parliament. Another famous gem is the Koh-i-noor, or "Mountain of Light." The legendary diamond, which was supposed to bring luck to women, came from India, and was given to the Queen in 1850. You can see it, in cut-down shape, in the late Queen Mother's Crown.

The little chapel of **St. Peter ad Vincula** is the second church on the site, and it conceals the remains of some 2,000 people executed at the Tower, Anne Boleyn and Catherine Howard among them.

One of the more evocative towers is **Beauchamp Tower,** built west of Tower Green by Edward I (1272–1307). It was soon designated as a jail for the higher class of miscreant, including Lady Jane Grey, who is thought to have added her Latin graffiti to the many inscriptions carved by prisoners that you can see here.

For tickets to the Ceremony of the Keys (locking of main gates, nightly at 9:30–10), write well in advance to the Resident Governor and Keeper of the Jewel House (at the Queen's House, address below). Give your name, the dates you wish to attend (including alternate dates), and number of people (up to seven) in your party, and enclose a self-addressed, stamped envelope. ✉ *H. M. Tower of London, Tower Hill, The City EC3N* ☎ *0870/756–7070 recorded information and advance booking* ⊕ *www. hrp.org.uk* 🎫 *£12* ⊙ *Mar.–Oct., Mon.–Sat. 9–5, Sun. 10–5; Nov.–Feb., Tues.–Sat. 9–4, Sun. and Mon. 10–4; Tower closes 1 hr after last admission time and all internal bldgs. close 30 mins after last admission. Yeoman Warder guided tours leave daily from Middle Tower (subject to weather and availability), at no charge, about every 30 mins until 3:30 Mar.–Oct., 2:30 Nov.–Feb.* Ⓤ *Tower Hill.*

The South Bank

There's an old North London quip about needing a passport to cross the Thames. Visitors rarely frequented the area unless they were departing from Waterloo Station. Times have changed dramatically. The Tate Modern is the star attraction, installed in a 1930s power station, with the eye-catching Millennium Bridge linking its main door across the river to the City. At the South Bank Centre, the world's largest observation wheel, the British Airways London Eye, gives you a flight over the city. Even from a great height, the South Bank—which occupies the riverside stretch between Waterloo Bridge and Hungerford Bridge—isn't beautiful, but this area of theaters and museums has Culture with a capital C. Starting with the 1976 construction of the South Bank Centre, developers and local authorities have expanded the area's potential farther east, turning this once-neglected district into an exciting neighborhood. The '80s brought renovations and innovations such as Hay's Galleria and Butler's Wharf. In the '90s came the OXO Tower, the London Aquarium, and the reconstruction of Shakespeare's Globe. Cultural options have also increased with the arrival of art galleries such as Dalí Universe and the Hayward Gallery at the South Bank Centre.

It's fitting that so much of London's artistic life should once again be centered on the South Bank—in the past, Southwark was the location for the theaters, taverns, and cockfighting arenas. The Globe Theatre, in which Shakespeare acted and held shares, was one of several here. In truth the Globe was as likely to stage bearbaiting as Shakespeare, but today, at the reconstructed "Wooden O," you can see only the latter. Be sure to take a walk along Bankside, the embankment along the Thames from Southwark to Blackfriars Bridge.

a good walk

Start at the south end of Tower Bridge, finding the steps on the east (left) side, which descend to the start of a pedestrians-only street, Shad Thames. From here, you cannot miss the massive glass, mushroomlike building designed by Norman Foster; it is City Hall, which houses the London Assembly. Now turn your back on the bridge and follow this path between cliffs of the good-as-new warehouses that now constitute **Butler's Wharf** ㊶ ▶ but were once the dangerous shadowlands where Dickens kills off Bill Sikes in *Oliver Twist*. See the foodies' center, the Gastrodrome, and the **Design Museum** ㊷; then just before you get back to Tower Bridge, turn away from the river along Horselydown Lane, follow Tooley Street, and take the right turn at Morgan's Lane to **HMS Belfast** ㊸, or continue to **Hay's Galleria** ㊹ with the **London Dungeon** ㊺ beyond. Next, turn left onto Joiner Street underneath the arches of London's first (1836) railway, then right onto St. Thomas Street, where you'll find the **Old Operating Theatre Museum** ㊻, with **Southwark Cathedral** ㊼ across Borough High Street, and then down Cathedral Street. See the west wall, with rose window outline, of Winchester House, palace of the bishops of Winchester until 1626, built into it, and **The Clink** ㊽ next door. Detouring left up Rose Alley, where the remains of the Jacobean **Rose Theatre** were unearthed, you can view an exhibition about the excavation. Also near St. Mary Overie Dock is a replica of Sir Francis Drake's ship the ***Golden Hinde*** ㊾. Nearby on New Globe Walk is **Shakespeare's Globe Theatre** ㊿. Continue west to reach Bankside Power Station, now the **Tate Modern** ㊛. The pedestrian Millennium Bridge crosses the Thames near here.

Ahead lies Blackfriars Bridge, which you pass beneath to join the street called Upper Ground, spending some time in the Coin Street Community Builders' fast-emerging neighborhood, which includes the **OXO Tower** ㊜ and Gabriel's Wharf, a marketplace of shops and cafés. Farther along Upper Ground, you reach the **South Bank Centre**, with the **Royal National Theatre** ㊝, **Hayward Gallery** ㊞, and the **Royal Festival Hall** ㊟. The **BFI London IMAX Cinema** ㊠ sits just down Waterloo Road behind the Hayward Gallery. Walk on around the curve of the river, passing another restored footbridge, this time the Hungerford, running parallel to the Charing Cross rail line, and you come to the Jubilee Gardens with the magnificent **British Airways London Eye** ㊡. Look to the opposite bank for the postcard vista of the Houses of Parliament. Just after the London Eye, you reach the **London Aquarium** ㊢ and the surrealist museum, **Dalí Universe** ㊣. Farther along the river, beyond the **Florence Nightingale Museum** ㊤, **Lambeth Palace** ㊥—for 800 years the London base of the archbishop of Canterbury, top man in the Church of England—stands by Lambeth Bridge. A little farther east along Lambeth Road you will reach the **Imperial War Museum** ⑥.

TIMING   On a fine day, this 2- to 3-mi walk makes for a very scenic wander, since you're following the south bank of the Thames nearly all the way. Views across to the north bank include everything from St. Paul's to the Houses of Parliament, and you pass—under, over, or around—no fewer than nine bridges, from the Tower to Lambeth. Allow a full day to see the sights. The Tate Modern, the Imperial War Museum, Shakespeare's Globe, the Design Museum, and the Aquarium each could take more than an hour, but the London Dungeon doesn't take long, unless you have kids in tow. The other museums are compact enough to squeeze together en route to your main event, evening theater tickets. Remember, though, that the theaters stay dark on Sundays. Dinner or a riverside drink at the OXO Tower Brasserie, Gastrodome, or the People's Palace is another idea for a big finish. Public transportation is thin here, so pick a day when you're feeling energetic; there are few shortcuts.

What to See

⊛ ⑤⑥ **BFI London IMAX Cinema.** With the largest screen in London—it's the height of five double-decker buses and wide enough to fill your eye—you're guaranteed an eyeful of technological and celluloid innovation. Choose from 2-D or 3-D films, generally on educational topics from archaeology to natural science. ⊠ *Waterloo Bridge at Stamford St., South Bank SE1* ☎ *020/7902–1234* ⊕ *www.bfi.org.uk/imax* ⊠ *£7.50* ⊗ *Daily 10:30–7:30* Ⓤ *Waterloo, Exit 5.*

⊛ ⑤⑦ **British Airways London Eye.** If you want a pigeon's-eye view of London, this is the place to get it. The highest observation wheel in the world, at 500 feet, towers over the South Bank from the Jubilee Gardens next to County Hall. For 25 minutes, passengers hover over the city in a slow-motion flight. You can book by phone or on-line, or buy tickets in advance at the Eye itself; it's very popular. ⊠ *Jubilee Gardens, South Bank SE1* ☎ *0870/500–0600* ⊕ *www.ba-londoneye.com* ⊠ *£11* ⊗ *Mon.–Thurs. 9:30–8, Fri.–Sun. 9:30–9, but subject to change, so call ahead* Ⓤ *Embankment, Waterloo.*

▶ ④① **Butler's Wharf.** An '80s development that is maturing gracefully, this wharf is full of loft-style warehouse conversions and swanky buildings housing restaurants and galleries. People flock here thanks partly to London's saint of the stomach, Sir Terence Conran (also responsible for high-profile restaurants Bibendum, Mezzo, and Quaglino's). He gave it his Gastrodome of four restaurants, a vintner's, a deli, and a bakery. ⊠*South Bank SE1* Ⓤ *London Bridge or Tower Hill, then walk over bridge.*

④⑧ **The Clink.** Giving rise to the term "the clink," which still refers to a jail, this institution was originally the prison attached to Winchester House, palace of the bishops of Winchester until 1626. It was one of the first prisons to detain women, most of whom were called "Winchester Geese"—a euphemism meaning prostitutes. The world's oldest profession was endemic in Southwark; a museum traces the history of prostitution here and shows what the Clink was like in its 16th-century prime. ⊠ *1 Clink St., South Bank SE1* ☎ *020/7403–0900* ⊕ *www.clink.co. uk* ⊠ *£4* ⊗ *Daily 10–6; last admission 5:30* Ⓤ *London Bridge.*

⑤⑨ **Dalí Universe.** Here is Europe's most important collection of art by master surrealist Salvador Dalí (1904–89). Neatly arranged into three areas, "Sensuality and Femininity," "Religion and Mythology," and "Dreams and Fantasy," the museum reflects the artist's eclectic work, from sculpture to painting to drawings. ⊠ *County Hall, Riverside Bldg., Westminster Bridge Rd., South Bank SE1,* ☎ *020/7620–2720* ⊕ *www.daliuniverse. com* ⊠ *£8.50* ⊘ *Daily 10–5:30* Ⓤ *Waterloo, Westminster.*

㊷ Design Museum. This was the first museum in the world to elevate everyday design to the status of art, presenting designs in their social and cultural context. Fashion, creative technology, and architecture are explored in thematic displays, and temporary exhibitions provide an indepth focus. Check out the very good Blueprint Café, with its own river terrace. ⊠ *28 Shad Thames, South Bank SE1* ☎ *020/7403–6933; 020/ 7940–8790 recorded information* ⊕ *www.designmuseum.org* ⊠ *£6* ⊘ *Sat.–Thurs. 10–5:45; last admission at 5:15* Ⓤ *London Bridge, Tower Gateway (DLR), Tower Hill.*

㊿ Florence Nightingale Museum. Here you can learn all about that most famous of health care reformers, the "Lady with the Lamp." On view are fascinating reconstructions of the barracks ward at Scutari (Turkey), where Nightingale tended soldiers during the Crimean War (1854–56) and earned her nickname, and a Victorian East End slum cottage, to show what she did to improve living conditions among the poor. The museum is in **St. Thomas's Hospital.** ⊠ *2 Lambeth Palace Rd., South Bank SE1* ☎ *020/ 7620–0374* ⊕ *www.florence-nightingale.co.uk* ⊠ *£4.80* ⊘ *Weekdays 10–5, weekends 11:30–4:30; last admission 1 hr before closing* Ⓤ *Waterloo or Westminster, then walk over the bridge.*

㊾ *Golden Hinde.* In the late 16th century, Sir Francis Drake circumnavigated the globe in this little galleon, or one just like it, anyway. This exact reproduction finished a 23-year, round-the-world voyage—much of it spent along American coasts, both Pacific and Atlantic—and has settled here to continue its educational mission. ⊠ *St. Mary Overie Dock, Cathedral St., South Bank SE1* ☎ *020/7403–0123* ⊕ *www.goldenhinde. co.uk* ⊠ *£2.75* ⊘ *Apr.–Oct., daily 9:30–5:30; Nov.–Mar., daily 9:30–5; last admission 30 mins before closing; may close Christmas wk and for special events* Ⓤ *London Bridge.*

㊹ Hay's Galleria. Once known as "London's larder" because of the edibles sold here, Hay's Galleria was reborn in 1987 as a Covent Garden–esque parade of bars and restaurants, offices, and shops, all weatherproofed by an arched glass atrium roof supported by tall iron columns. Jugglers, string quartets, and crafts stalls abound. ⊠ *2 Battle Bridge La., South Bank SE1* ☎ *020/7940–7770* ⊕ *www.haysgalleria. co.uk* ⊘ *Varies from shop to shop* Ⓤ *London Bridge.*

�554 Hayward Gallery. This is the one gallery you can't miss, thanks to the multicolor neon tube sculpture topping the building, which blinks away through the night. The windowless bunker tucked behind the South Bank Centre concert halls is getting a foyer extension that gives more daylight and exhibit space; the highlight is an elliptical mirrored glass pavilion by New York–based artist Dan Graham. The gallery is due to reopen in fall 2003; it presents changing exhibitions that focus on cross-cultural patterns or on reinterpretations of established masters. ⊠ *South Bank Centre, Belvedere Rd., South Bank SE1* ☎ *020/7928–3144* ⊕ *www.hayward.org.uk* ⊠ *Admission varies according to exhibition* ⊘ *Thurs.–Mon. 10–6, Tues. and Wed. 10–8* Ⓤ *Waterloo.*

☾ ㊸ HMS *Belfast.* At 656 feet, this is one of the largest cruisers the Royal Navy has ever had. It played a role in the D-Day landings off Normandy. An outpost of the **Imperial War Museum** is on board. ⊠ *Morgan's La., Tooley St., South Bank SE1* ☎ *020/7940–6300* ⊕ *www.iwm.org.uk* ⊠ *£6* ⊘ *Mid-Mar.–Oct., daily 10–6; Nov.–mid-Mar., daily 10–5; last admission 45 mins before closing* Ⓤ *London Bridge.*

Hungerford Bridge. Actually two pedestrian bridges, this stunning suspension update on the previous version provides a convenient crossing from Charing Cross to Jubilee Gardens and South Bank sights. The name comes from a grand 17th-century marketplace built in the gardens of Edward Hungerford's old mansion, long before Charing Cross Station. ⊠ *Jubilee Gardens, South Bank SE1.*

62 **Imperial War Museum.** This museum of 20th-century warfare does not glorify bloodshed but attempts to evoke what it was like to live through the two world wars. There's hardware—a Battle of Britain Spitfire, a German V2 rocket—but there's an equal amount of war art (John Singer Sargent to Henry Moore) and interactive material. One very affecting exhibit, "The Blitz Experience," provides a 10-minute taste of an air raid in a street of acrid smoke, sirens, and searchlights. There's also a Holocaust exhibition. The museum is in an elegantly colonnaded 19th-century building that was once the home of the infamous insane asylum called Bedlam. ⊠ *Lambeth Rd., South Bank SE1* ☎ *020/ 7416–5320* ⊕ *www.iwm.org.uk* ⊠ *Free* ☉ *Daily 10–6* Ⓤ *Lambeth N.*

61 **Lambeth Palace.** The London residence of the archbishop of Canterbury, the senior archbishop of the Church of England since the 13th century, is closed to the public, but you can admire the fine Tudor gatehouse. ⊠ *Lambeth Palace Rd., South Bank SE1* ⊕ *www.archbishopofcanterbury. org* Ⓤ *Waterloo.*

☺ 58 **London Aquarium.** County Hall was the original name of this curved, colonnaded neoclassical hulk, which took 46 years (1912–58; two world wars interfered) to build. It housed London's local government, the Greater London Council, until it disbanded in 1986. The three-level aquarium is full of sharks and stingrays, educational exhibits, and exotic piscine sights. ⊠ *Westminster Bridge Rd., South Bank SE1* ☎ *020/7967–8000* ⊕ *www.londonaquarium.co.uk* ⊠ *£8.75* ☉ *Daily 10–6; last admission at 5* Ⓤ *Waterloo, or Westminster and walk over the bridge.*

☺ 45 **London Dungeon.** Did you ever wonder what a disembowelment actually looks like? See it here. Preteens seem to adore this place, which, although grisly, usually has long lines. Inside, realistic waxwork people are subjected to the horrors that you hear about at the Tower of London. Tableaux depict bloody historic moments—like Anne Boleyn's decapitation—alongside the torture and ritual slaughter of more anonymous victims, all to a sound track of agonized moaning. The Great Fire and the Great Plague are brought to life, too, and a whole section is devoted to Jack the Ripper. ⊠ *28–34 Tooley St., South Bank SE1* ☎ *020/7403–7221* ⊕ *www.thedungeons.com* ⊠ *£10.95* ☉ *Apr.–mid-July, daily 10–5:30; mid-July–Aug., daily 10–8; Sept.–Mar., daily 10–5* Ⓤ *London Bridge.*

National Film Theatre. The NFT has the best repertory programming in London; it's also home to the British Film Institute and to numerous international film festivals, such as the London Film Festival during November, the Gay and Lesbian Film Festival in April, and a Crime Thriller Festival. ⊠ *South Bank Centre, South Bank SE1* ☎ *020/7928–3232* ⊠ *£7.20* ☉ *Daily 11:30–8:30* ⊕ *www.bfi.org.uk/nft* Ⓤ *Waterloo.*

46 **Old Operating Theatre Museum.** One of England's oldest hospitals stood here from the 12th century until the railway forced it to move in 1862. Its operating theater has been restored into an exhibition of early-19th-century medical practices: the operating table onto which the gagged and blindfolded patients were roped, the box of sawdust underneath for catching blood, the knives, pliers, and handsaws the surgeons wielded, and—this was a theater-in-the-round—the spectators' seats. ⊠ *9A*

St. Thomas St., South Bank ☎ *020/7955–4791* ⊕ *www.thegarret.org.
uk* 🎫 *£4* ☉ *Early Jan.–mid-Dec., daily 10:30–5:30* Ⓤ *London Bridge.*

52 OXO Tower. Long a London landmark to the cognoscenti, this wonderful art deco tower has graduated from its former incarnations as power-
generating station and warehouse into a vibrant community of artists'
and designers' workshops, a pair of restaurants, and cafés, as well as
five floors of the best low-income housing in the city, thanks to Coin
Street Community Builders. A rooftop viewing gallery adjacent to the
well-regarded OXO Tower Restaurant and Brasserie provides the best
river vista in town, and the first floor has a performance area. ⊠ *Barge
House St., South Bank SE1* ☎ *020/7401–3610* 🎫 *Free* ☉ *Studios and
shops Tues.–Sun. 11–6* Ⓤ *Blackfriars, Waterloo.*

Rose Theatre. If you're thrilled by the reconstruction of Shakespeare's
Globe, you'll be fascinated by an even earlier model of which much of
the original is still in existence. Built in 1587, the Rose preceded its near
neighbor, the Globe, which opened in 1599. The original foundations
uncovered in 1989 were under wraps until 1999, when an exhibition
opened concerning the history of this fascinating little theater. A trial
dig in 2001 revealed timbers from the theater boundaries, but it will take
£5 million before major work can proceed again. ⊠ *56 Park St., South
Bank SE1* ☎ *020/7593–0026* ⊕ *www.rosetheatre.org.uk* 🎫 *£4, joint
ticket available with Shakespeare's Globe Theatre exhibition*
☉ *May–Sept., daily 11–5* Ⓤ *London Bridge.*

55 Royal Festival Hall. The largest auditorium of the South Bank Centre has
superb acoustics and a 3,000-plus capacity. It's the oldest of the riverside blocks raised as the centerpiece of the 1951 Festival of Britain, a
postwar morale-boosting exercise. The London Philharmonic resides here;
symphony orchestras from around the world visit; and choral works,
ballet, serious jazz and pop, and even films with live accompaniment
are staged. There's a good restaurant, the People's Palace, and a fine
bookstore. An adjacent building contains two concert halls, the **Queen
Elizabeth Hall** and the **Purcell Room.** ⊠ *South Bank Centre, Belvedere
Rd., South Bank SE1* ☎ *020/7960–4242* ⊕ *www.rfh.org.uk* Ⓤ *Waterloo.*

53 Royal National Theatre. Londoners generally felt the same way about Sir
Denys Lasdun's stolid building when it opened in 1976 as they would
a decade later about the far nastier Barbican. But the interior of the Royal
National Theatre—still abbreviated colloquially to the pre–royal warrant "NT"—makes up for its exterior. Three auditoriums—the Olivier,
named after Sir Laurence, first artistic director of the National Theatre
Company; the Lyttelton; and the Cottesloe—host ever-changing productions. The NT attracts many of the nation's top actors in addition
to launching stars and star productions. ⊠ *South Bank Centre, South
Bank SE1* ☎ *020/7452–3000 box office; 020/7452–3400 tour availability*
⊕ *www.nationaltheatre.org.uk* 🎫 *Tour £5* ☉ *1-hr backstage tours
Mon.–Sat. at 10:15, 12:30, and 5:30* Ⓤ *Waterloo.*

★ **50 Shakespeare's Globe Theatre.** Stratford-upon-Avon remains the primary
shrine for Shakespeare, but the Globe Theatre is a cathedral for his works.
In 1644, the Puritans closed the fabled "Wooden O," the open-air
polygonal structure on London's South Bank, for which Shakespeare
wrote *Hamlet, King Lear,* and *Julius Caesar,* among other peerless plays.
Now the famous playhouse has been re-created 200 yards from its original site. For several decades, American actor and director Sam Wana-
maker worked ceaselessly to raise funds for a reconstruction of the
theater. The late actor's dream was realized in 1996 when an exact reproduction of Shakespeare's open-roof Globe Playhouse (built in 1599;

incinerated in 1613; rebuilt 1614) was completed, using authentic Elizabethan materials and craft techniques and the first thatched roof in London since the Great Fire. A second, indoor theater is built to a design of the 17th-century architect Inigo Jones. You step past the entrance into a 45-foot-tall arena, made intimate by three half-timber galleries. Ahead of you is the "pit," or orchestra level, filling up with 500 standees—or "groundlings," to use the historic term—massed in front of the high stage. Soaring overhead are a twin-gabled stage canopy—the "heavens"—framed by trompe l'oeil marble columns, and a "lords' " gallery, all fretted with painted planets, and celestial stars.

A repertory season of three or four Shakespeare plays is presented during the summer, usually mid-May to late September, in natural light (and sometimes rain), to 1,000 people on wooden benches in the "bays," plus the standees. The audience becomes as much a part of the proceedings as the actors on stage. Although the main theater is open only for performances during the summer season, it can be viewed year-round (unless a performance is scheduled; check in advance). The **Shakespeare's Globe Exhibition,** touted as the largest ever to focus on Shakespeare, his work, and his contemporaries, is in the Underglobe, beneath the Globe site. ⊠ *New Globe Walk, Bankside, South Bank SE1* ☎ *020/7401–9919 box office; 020/7902–1500 New Shakespeare's Globe Exhibition* ⊕ *www.shakespeares-globe.org* ⊠ *£8 for exhibition and tour; joint ticket available with Rose Theatre* ⊙ *Exhibition daily 10–5, plays May–Sept.; call for schedule* Ⓤ *Mansion House, then walk across Southwark Bridge; Blackfriars, then walk across Blackfriars Bridge; or Southwark, then walk down to the river.*

South Bank Centre. On either side of Waterloo Bridge is London's chief arts center. Along Upper Ground is the **Royal National Theatre,** three auditoriums that present some of the finest theater in Britain. Underneath Waterloo Bridge is the **National Film Theatre.** Also here are the **Royal Festival Hall,** the **Queen Elizabeth Hall,** and the **Purcell Room,** three of London's finest venues for classical music. Finally, tucked away behind the concert halls is the **Hayward Gallery,** a venue for impressive, ever-changing art exhibitions. Along the wide paths of the complex you'll find distractions of every sort—secondhand bookstalls, entertainers, and arrogant pigeons. ⊠ *South Bank Centre, South Bank* ☎ *020/ 7401–2636* Ⓤ *Embankment, Waterloo.*

㊼ Southwark Cathedral. This cathedral (pronounced *suth*-uck) is the second-oldest Gothic church in London, next to Westminster Abbey. Look for the gaudily renovated 1408 tomb of the poet John Gower, friend of Chaucer, and for the Harvard Chapel, named after John Harvard, founder of the United States college, who was baptized here in 1608. Also buried here is Edmund Shakespeare, brother of William. ⊠ *Montague Close, South Bank SE1* ☎ *020/7367–6700* ⊕ *www.dswark.org* ⊠ *Free, suggested donation £4* ⊙ *Daily 8–6* Ⓤ *London Bridge.*

★ **㊿ Tate Modern.** This former power station has glowered on the banks on the Thames since the 1930s, and after a dazzling renovation by Herzog & de Meuron, provides a magnificent space for a massive collection of international modern art. The vast Turbine Hall is a dramatic entrance point. On permanent display in the galleries are classic works from 1900 to the present day, by Matisse, Pablo Picasso, Dalí, Henry Moore, Francis Bacon, Andy Warhol, and the most-talked-about British upstarts. They are not grouped by artist but are arranged in themes that mix the historic with the contemporary—Landscape, Still Life, and The Nude—on different levels, reached by a moving staircase that is a feature in itself. The changing exhibitions (for which there's a charge, and often very long lines to get in) are always the talking point of Londoners who have their fingers on the pulse. ⊠ *25 Summer St., South Bank SE1* ☎ *020/ 7887–8000* ⊕ *www.tate.org.uk* ⊠ *Free* ☾ *Sun.–Thurs. 10–6, Fri. and Sat. 10–10* Ⓤ *Blackfriars, Southwark.*

Kensington, Knightsbridge & Mayfair

Splendid houses with pillared porches line the streets of this elegant area of the Royal Borough of Kensington, but other notable attractions draw your attention as well. These include some fascinating museums, stylish squares, glittering antiques shops, and Kensington Palace (the former home of both Diana, Princess of Wales, and Queen Victoria), which put the district literally on the map back in the 17th century. To Kensington's east is one of the highest concentrations of important artifacts anywhere, the "museum mile" of South Kensington, with the rest of Kensington offering peaceful strolls, a noisy main street, and another palace. Kensington first became the *Royal* Borough of Kensington (and Chelsea) when William III, who suffered terribly from the Thames mists over Whitehall, decided in 1689 to buy Nottingham House in the rural village of Kensington so that he could breathe more easily. Courtiers and functionaries and society folk soon followed where the crowns led, and by the time Queen Anne was on the throne (1702–14), Kensington was overflowing. In a way, it still is, since most of its grand houses have been divided into apartments, or are serving as foreign embassies.

Hyde Park and Kensington Gardens together form by far the biggest of central London's royal parks. It's probably been centuries since any major royal had a casual stroll here, but the parks remain the property of the Crown, and it was the Crown that saved them from being devoured by the city's late-18th-century growth spurt.

Around the borders of Hyde Park are several of London's poshest and most beautiful neighborhoods. To the south of the park and a short carriage ride from Buckingham Palace is the splendidly aristocratic enclave of Belgravia. Its stucco-white buildings and grand squares—particularly Belgrave Square—are Regency-era jewels. On the eastern border of Hyde Park is Mayfair, which gives Belgravia a run for its money as London's wealthiest district. Three mansions here allow you to get a peek into the lifestyles of London's rich and famous—19th- and 20th-century versions: Apsley House, the home of the duke of Wellington; Spencer House, home of Princess Diana's ancestors; and the Wallace Collection, a mansion on Manchester Square stuffed with great art treasures.

a good
walk

When you surface from the Knightsbridge tube station, you are immediately engulfed by the manic drivers, professional shoppers, and ladies-who-lunch who compose the local population. Walk west down Brompton Road, past **Harrods** ►, to the junction of Cromwell Road and the pale, Italianate Brompton Oratory, which marks the beginning of museum territory. The **Victoria & Albert Museum** ⓖ, or V&A, is first, at the start of Cromwell Road, followed by the **Natural History Museum** ⓖ and the **Science Museum** ⓖ behind it. Turn left to continue north up Exhibition Road, a kind of unfinished cultural main drag that was Prince Albert's conception, toward the road after which British moviemakers named their fake blood, Kensington Gore, to reach the giant round Wedgwood china box of the **Royal Albert Hall** ⓖ and the gilded **Albert Memorial** ⓖ opposite, on the edge of **Kensington Gardens**.

Walk northwest through the park to reach **Kensington Palace** ⓖ. From here you can either head west to check out some of London's current sanctuaries of the rich and famous at **Kensington Palace Gardens** ⓖ or take an extra leg of the journey to see **Leighton House** ⓱ or the **Linley Sambourne House.** If opulent 19th-century interiors are not your cup of tea, head east instead to explore **Kensington Gardens.** When you cross the bridge over the Serpentine, you leave Kensington Gardens and enter **Hyde Park.** Walk to the southern perimeter and along the sand track called Rotten Row. It's still used by the Household Cavalry (the brigade that mounts the guard at the palace), who live at the Knightsbridge Barracks to the left. Then head toward the Hyde Park Corner exit of the park and discover glorious **Apsley House (Wellington Museum)** ⓶. If you decided to skip Hyde Park, tube it from Kensington High Street (and Leighton House) over to Hyde Park Corner to take in the Wellington Museum, then head south to see chic **Belgrave Place** ⓷ or north for some more palatial treats: several blocks northeast is **Spencer House** ⓸, and farther north through elegant Mayfair—custom-built for expansive strolling—is the **Wallace Collection** ⓹. For sights to delight children, head northward to discover the sights around **Regent's Park** and the park itself: **Madame Tussaud's** ⓺ and the **London Zoo** ⓻.

TIMING   This walk is at least 4 mi long, with many places to stop along the way; you'll need plenty of time and some money for taxis or the tube. A jaunt from Belgrave Square up to the Apsley and Spencer houses (note that Spencer House is open Sundays only) and on to the Wallace Collection would add another 2 mi. You could cut out a lot of Hyde Park without missing essential sights, and walk the whole thing in a good five hours. The best way (time permitting) to approach these neighborhoods is to treat Knightsbridge shopping and the South Kensington museums as separate days out, although you may find the three vast museums too much to take in at once. The parks are best in the growing seasons and during fall, when the foliage is turning, although the summer roses in Regent's Park are stunning. On Sunday, the Hyde Park and Kensington Gardens railings all along the Bayswater Road are hung with mediocre art, which may slow your progress; this is prime perambulation day for locals.

What to See

ABBEY ROAD STUDIOS – Strawberry Fields Forever. Here, outside the Abbey Road Studios, is the world's most famous zebra crossing. Immortalized on the Beatles's *Abbey Road* album of 1969, this footpath is a spot beloved by Beatlemaniacs and baby boomers. The studios (closed to the public) are where the Beatles recorded their entire output from "Love Me Do" on, including *Sgt. Pepper's Lonely Hearts Club Band* (1967). To see Fab Four sites, Original London Walks (☎ 020/7624–3978 ⊕ www.walks.com) offers two Beatles tours: "The Beatles In-My-Life Walk" and "The Beatles Magical Mystery Tour." Abbey Road is a 10-minute ride on the Jubilee tube line from central London. After you exit, head southwest three blocks down Grove End Road. ✉ *3 Abbey Rd., Hampstead NW8* ⊕ *www. abbeyroad.co.uk* Ⓤ *St. John's Wood.*

off the beaten path

❻ **Albert Memorial.** This gleaming, neo-Gothic shrine to Prince Albert created by George Gilbert Scott epitomizes the Victorian era. The 14-foot bronze statue of Albert looks as if it had been created yesterday, thanks to its fresh coat of gold leaf. Albert's grieving widow, Queen Victoria, had this elaborate confection erected on the spot where his Great Exhibition had stood a decade before his early death, from typhoid, in 1861. ✉ *Kensington Gore, opposite Royal Albert Hall, Hyde Park, Kensington SW7* Ⓤ *Knightsbridge.*

★ ⑦ **Apsley House (Wellington Museum).** Once known, quite simply, as Number 1, London, this was celebrated as the best address in town. Built by Robert Adam in the 1770s, the mansion was the home of the celebrated conqueror of Napoléon, the duke of Wellington, who lived here from the 1820s until his death in 1852. The great Waterloo Gallery—scene of legendary dinners—is a veritable orgy of opulence. Not to be missed, in every sense, is the gigantic Antonio Canova statue of a nude (but fig-leafed) Bonaparte in the entry stairwell. The current duke of Wellington still lives here. During special weekends, entrance to the house is free, and there are special events and costumed guides. These include the weekend closest to June 18 (the day of the battle of Waterloo) and a weekend before Christmas. Imposing statues flank the house: opposite is the 1828 Decimus Burton **Wellington Arch** with the four-horse chariot of peace as its pinnacle; renovated by English Heritage, it's open to the public as an exhibition area and viewing platform. ✉ *149 Piccadilly, Mayfair* ☎ *020/7499–5676* ⊕ *www.apsleyhouse.org.uk* 🎫 *£4.50 includes audio guide* ☉ *Tues.–Sun. 11–5* Ⓤ *Hyde Park Corner.*

⑦ **Belgrave Place.** One of the main arteries of Belgravia—London's swankiest neighborhood—Belgrave Place is lined with grand, imposing Regency-era mansions, now mostly embassies. Walk down this street toward Eaton Place to pass two of Belgravia's most beautiful mews—Eaton Mews North and Eccleston Mews, both fronted by grand Westminster-white rusticated entrances right out of a 19th-century engraving. There are few other places where London is so elegant. ✉ *Belgravia* Ⓤ *Hyde Park Corner.*

Handel House Museum. The former home of the composer, where he lived for more than 30 years until his death in 1759, celebrates his genius in its fine Georgian rooms. You can linger over original manuscripts (others are in the British Library) and gaze at portraits and art illustrating the times. Some of Handel's most famous pieces were created here, including *Messiah* and *Music for the Royal Fireworks*. The museum occupies No. 25 and the adjoining house, which contains exhibits on life in Georgian London. ✉ *25 Brook St., Mayfair W1* ☎ *020/7495–1685* ⊕ *www.handelhouse.org* 🎫 *£4.50* ☉ *Tues., Wed., Fri., and Sat. 10–6, Thurs. 10–8, Sun. noon–6* Ⓤ *Bond St.*

☺ ▶ **Harrods.** Just in case you hadn't noticed it, this well-known shopping destination outlines its domed terra-cotta Edwardian bulk in thousands of white lights at night. Owned by Mohamed Al Fayed, whose son Dodi was killed in the car crash that also claimed Princess Diana's life in 1997, the 15-acre store has world-class, frenetic sale weeks. Don't miss the extravagant **Food Hall,** with its art nouveau tiling. This is the department in which to acquire your green-and-gold-logo souvenir Harrods bag, since food prices are competitive. ✉ *87–135 Brompton Rd., Knightsbridge SW1* ☎ *020/7730–1234* ⊕ *www.harrods.com* ☉ *Mon.–Sat. 10–7, Sun. noon–6* Ⓤ *Knightsbridge.*

☺ **Hyde Park.** Along with the smaller St. James's and Green parks to the east, Hyde Park started as Henry VIII's hunting grounds. Along its south side runs **Rotten Row,** once Henry's royal path to the hunt—hence the name, a corruption of *route du roi.* It's still used by the Household Cavalry, who live at the **Knightsbridge Barracks**—a high-rise and a low, ugly red block to the left. This brigade mounts the guard at the palace, and you can see them leave to perform this duty, in full regalia, at about 10:30, or await the return of the ex-guard about noon. Hyde Park is wonderful for strolling, watching the locals, or just relaxing by the **Serpentine,** the long body of water near its southern border. On Sunday, **Speakers' Corner,** in the park near Marble Arch, is an unmissable spectacle of vehement, sometimes comical, and always entertaining orators.

☎ *020/7298–2100* ⊕ *www.royalparks.gov.uk* ⊙ *Daily 5 AM–midnight* Ⓤ *Hyde Park Corner, Lancaster Gate, Marble Arch.*

🕐 **Kensington Gardens.** More formal than neighboring Hyde Park, Kensington Gardens was first laid out as palace grounds. The paved Italian garden at the top of the Long Water, **The Fountains,** is a reminder of this, although, of course, **Kensington Palace** itself is the main clue to its royal status, with the early-19th-century Sunken Garden north of it. Nearby is George Frampton's beloved 1912 *Peter Pan,* a bronze of the boy who lived on an island in the Serpentine and never grew up, and whose creator, J. M. Barrie, lived at 100 Bayswater Road, not 500 yards from here. The **Round Pond** is a magnet for model-boat enthusiasts and duck feeders. The fabulous **Princess Diana Memorial Playground** has, besides the usual play equipment, specially designed structures and areas on the theme of Barrie's Neverland. ⊕ *www.royalparks.gov.uk* ⊙ *Daily dawn–dusk* Ⓤ *Lancaster Gate, Queensway.*

68 Kensington Palace. The long and regal history of this palace has been somewhat eclipsed by the woman some might call its most famous inhabitant, the late Princess Diana. Kensington was put on the map, socially speaking, when King William III, "much incommoded by the Smoak of the Coal Fires of London," decided in the 17th century to vacate Whitehall and relocate to a new palace outside the center city in the village of Kensington. Royals have lived here since William and Mary—and some have died here, too. In 1760, poor George II burst a blood vessel while on the toilet. The **State Apartments,** where Victoria had her ultrastrict upbringing, depict the life of the Royal Family through the centuries. This palace is an essential stop for royalty vultures, because it's the only one where you may actually catch a glimpse of the real thing. The Duke and Duchess of Gloucester and Prince and Princess Michael of Kent all have apartments here. The palace also holds the **Royal Ceremonial Dress Collection.** Extending back centuries, the collection shows state and occasional dresses, hats, and shoes worn by Britain's Royal Family. Some dazzlers of note are the coronation robes of Queen Mary and George V and a regal mantua (a 6-foot-wide court dress), as well as dresses worn by Princess Diana. ✉ *The Broad Walk, Kensington Gardens, Kensington W8* ☎ *0870/751–5180 advance tickets and information* ⊕ *www.hrp.org.uk* 🎟 *£10.20* ⊙ *Daily 10–5* Ⓤ *High St. Kensington.*

need a break? A separate building from the rest of Kensington Palace, the **Orangery** (✉ The Broad Walk, Kensington Gardens, Kensington W8 ☎ 020/7376–0239) was built for Queen Anne. The setting, beneath the bright white-and-gold arches, is perfect for teatime. Light lunches, coffee, and kids' menus are also offered daily from 10 to 6.

69 Kensington Palace Gardens. Immediately behind Kensington Palace is Kensington Palace Gardens (called Palace Green at the south end), a wide, leafy avenue of mid-19th-century mansions that used to be one of London's most elegant addresses. Today, it's largely Embassy Row, including those of Russia and Israel. Ⓤ *High St. Kensington.*

70 Leighton House. The exotic richness of late-19th-century aesthetic tastes is captured in this fascinating home, once the abode of Lord Frederic Leighton (1830–96)—painter, sculptor, and president of the Royal Academy. Persian tiles and pieced woodwork lavishly line the Arab Hall. The neighborhood was one of the principal artists' colonies of Victorian London. If you are interested in 19th-century domestic architecture, wander through the surrounding streets. ✉ *12 Holland Park Rd.,*

Kensington W14 ☎ *020/7602–3316* ⊕ *www.rbkc.gov.uk* ✉ *Free* ⊙ *Wed.–Mon. 11–5:30* Ⓤ *High St. Kensington.*

Linley Sambourne House. Stuffed with Victorian and Edwardian antiques, fabrics, and paintings, this 19th-century house was built and furnished in the 1870s. It was the home of Edward Linley Sambourne, who for more than 30 years was the political cartoonist for the satirical magazine *Punch.* The Italianate house was the scene for society parties when Anne Messel lived here in the 1940s. Because this is Kensington, there's a royal connection, too: her son, Antony Armstrong-Jones, married the late Princess Margaret, and their son has preserved the connection by taking the name Viscount Linley. ✉ *18 Stafford Terr., Kensington W8* ☎ *020/7602–3316* ⊕ *www.rbkc.gov.uk* ⊙ *Call for hrs and admission.*

☙ ⑦⑥ **London Zoo.** Opened in 1828 and now housing an extensive collection of animals from all over the world, this zoo has long been a local favorite. A modernization program progresses gradually. Many traditional cages remain, but elephants have been moved to the zoo's countryside branch, Whipsnade. One modern highlight is the Web of Life—a conservation and education center. Some of the thrills include a desert swarming with locusts, meerkats perching on termite mounds, and an otter exhibit with underwater viewing. The Reptile House is a draw for Harry Potter fans—it's where Harry, in the book and film versions of *Harry Potter and the Sorcerer's Stone,* discovers that he can converse with snakes and make magic happen. ✉ *Regent's Park NW1* ☎ *020/7722–3333* ⊕ *www.zsl.org* ✉ *£12* ⊙ *Mar.–Oct., daily 10–5:30; Nov.–Feb., daily 10–4; last admission 1 hr before closing* Ⓤ *Camden Town, then Bus 274.*

☙ ⑦⑤ **Madame Tussaud's.** This is nothing more, nothing less, than the world's premier exhibition of lifelike waxwork models of celebrities. Madame T. learned her craft while making death masks of French Revolution victims and in 1835 set up her first show of the famous ones near this spot. You can see everyone from Shakespeare to Benny Hill here, but top billing still goes to the murderers in the Chamber of Horrors, who stare glassy-eyed at you—one from the electric chair, one next to the tin bath where he dissolved several wives in quicklime. Next door is the London Planetarium, which offers a special combo ticket with Tussaud's. Beat the crowds by booking on-line or calling in advance for timed entry tickets. ✉ *Marylebone Rd., Regent's Park NW1* ☎ *020/7935–6861; 0870/400–3000 advance tickets* ⊕ *www.madame-tussauds.com* ✉ *£14, £16.95 combined ticket with planetarium* ⊙ *Sept.–June, weekdays 10–5:30, weekends 9:30–5:30; July and Aug., daily 9:30–5:30* Ⓤ *Baker St.*

★ ☙ ⑥④ **Natural History Museum.** When you want to heed the call of the wild, discover this fun place—enter to find Dinosaurs on the left and the Ecology Gallery on the right. Both these exhibits (the former with life-size moving dinosaurs, the latter complete with moonlit "rain forest") make essential viewing in a large museum that has overhauled itself creatively. Don't miss the ambitious Earth Galleries or the Creepy Crawlies Gallery, which includes a nightmarish super-enlarged scorpion. In the basement, hands-on activities can be experienced in Investigate, which allows you to do just that, with actual objects from old bones to bugs. The Darwin Centre showcases all the museum's creatures great and small in their pickling jars and vats, from a tiny frog to the giant Komodo dragon lizard. Daily Explore tours leave from the museum's main information desk. ✉ *Cromwell Rd., Kensington SW7* ☎ *020/7942–5000* ⊕ *www.nhm. ac.uk* ✉ *Free* ⊙ *Mon.–Sat. 10–5:50, Sun. 11–5:50* Ⓤ *S. Kensington.*

Notting Hill. Currently the best place to wear sunglasses, smoke Gauloises, and contemplate the latest issue of *Wallpaper,* "the Hill" now ranks as one of London's coolest neighborhoods. Centered around the Portobello Road antiques market, this district is bordered on the west by Lansdowne Crescent—address of the Hill's poshest 19th-century terraced row houses—and to the east by Chepstow Road, with Notting Hill Gate and Westbourne Grove Road marking the southern and northern boundaries. In between, Rastafarians rub elbows with wealthy young British types (aka "Trustafarians"), and residents such as fashion designer Rifat Ozbek, CNN's Christiane Amanpour, and historian Lady Antonia Fraser can be spotted at the chic shops on Westbourne Grove and the cafés on Kensington Park Road. No historic sites here, so just wander the streets to shop or savor the flavor. Ⓤ *Notting Hill Gate, Ladbroke Grove.*

Regent's Park. Laid out in 1812 by John Nash for the Prince Regent (hence the name), who was crowned George IV in 1820, the park was designed to re-create the atmosphere of a grand country residence close to the center of town. A walk around the Outer Circle, with the white stucco terraces of grand houses facing the park, including the famous **Cumberland Terrace,** shows that it succeeds magnificently. The Inner Circle has many garden themes, the most impressive being **Queen Mary's Gardens,** a scented riot of roses in summer. From June to August, the **Regent's Park Open-Air Theatre** (☎ 020/7486–2431) mounts Shakespeare productions. ☎ *020/7486–7905* ⊕ *www.openairtheatre.org* Ⓤ *Baker St. or Regent's Park.*

Royal Albert Hall. This famous theater was made possible by the Victorian public, who donated funds for the domed, circular 8,000-seat auditorium. The Albert Hall is best known for its annual July through September Henry Wood Promenade Concerts (the "Proms"), with bargain-price standing (or promenading, or sitting-on-the-floor) tickets sold on the night of the classical concerts. ✉ *Kensington Gore, Kensington SW7* ☎ *020/7589–4185* ⊕ *www.alberthall.co.uk* ✆ *Admission varies according to event* Ⓤ *S. Kensington.*

Science Museum. Up-to-date, hands-on exhibits make this museum enormously popular. Highlights include the Launch Pad gallery, the Computing Then and Now show, *Puffing Billy,* the oldest steam locomotive in the world, and the actual *Apollo 10* capsule. A must-do attraction is the spectacular **Wellcome Wing,** devoted to contemporary science, medicine, and technology, which also includes a 450-seat IMAX cinema. ✉ *Exhibition Rd., Kensington SW7* ☎ *020/7942–4000* ⊕ *www. sciencemuseum.org.uk* ✆ *Free* ☉ *Daily 10–6* Ⓤ *S. Kensington.*

Spencer House. Ancestral abode of the Spencers, the family of Princess Diana, this great mansion is perhaps the finest London example of 18th-century elegance on a domestic scale. Superlatively restored by Lord Rothschild, the house was built in 1766 for the first earl Spencer, heir to the first duchess of Marlborough. James "Athenian" Stuart decorated the gilded State Rooms, including the Painted Room, the first completely neoclassical room in Europe. The most ostentatious part of the house is the florid bow window of the Palm Room: covered with stucco palm trees, it conjures up both ancient Palmyra and modern Miami Beach. Children under 10 are not admitted. ✉ *27 St. James's Pl., St. James's SW1* ☎ *020/7499–8620* ⊕ *www.spencerhouse.co.uk* ✆ *£6* ☉ *Feb.–July and Sept.–Dec., Sun. 10:30–5:30; 1-hr guided tour leaves about every 25 mins (tickets on sale Sun. at 10:30)* Ⓤ *Green Park.*

★ **Victoria & Albert Museum.** Recognizable by the copy of Victoria's Imperial Crown it wears on the lantern above the central cupola, this huge museum showcases the decorative arts of all disciplines, all periods, all nationalities, and all tastes. The collections of the V&A, as it's always called, are *so* all-encompassing that confusion is a hazard. One minute you're gazing on the Jacobean oak 12-foot-square four-poster Great Bed of Ware (one of the V&A's most prized possessions, given that Shakespeare immortalized it in *Twelfth Night*), and the next, you're in the 20th-century end of the equally celebrated Dress Collection, coveting a Jean Muir frock. Prince Albert was responsible for the genesis of this permanent version of the 1851 Great Exhibition, and Victoria laid its foundation stone in her final public London appearance in 1899. The British Galleries present British art and design from 1500 to 1900 (from Henry VIII through Victoria), with displays such as George Gilbert Scott's model of the Albert Memorial and the first English fork ever made (1632). Free one-hour tours whirl you by some of the museum's prized treasures. To rest your overstimulated eyes, head for the brick-walled restaurant for daily brunch and lunch, candlelit dinners on Wednesday, or traditional roasts on Sunday. ✉ *Cromwell Rd., Kensington* ☎ *020/7942–2000* 🌐 *www.vam.ac.uk* 🎫 *Free* 🕙 *Thurs.–Tues. 10–5:45, Wed. 10–10* Ⓤ *S. Kensington.*

★ 74 **Wallace Collection.** Assembled by four generations of marquesses of Hertford, the Wallace Collection is important, exciting, undervisited—and free. Hertford House itself, a fine late-18th-century mansion, is part of the show. The eccentric fourth marquess really built the collection, snapping up paintings by François Boucher, Jean-Honoré Fragonard, Antoine Watteau, and Nocolas Lancret for a song after the French Revolution rendered this art dangerously unfashionable. A highlight is Fragonard's *The Swing*, which conjures up the 18th-century's let-them-eat-cake frivolity. Don't forget to smile back at Frans Hals's *Laughing Cavalier* in the Big Gallery. ✉ *Hertford House, Manchester Sq., Marylebone W1* ☎ *020/7935–0687* 🌐 *www.the-wallace-collection.org.uk* 🎫 *Free* 🕙 *Mon.–Sat. 10–5, Sun. 2–5* Ⓤ *Bond, Baker St.*

Up & Down the Thames

Downstream—meaning seaward, or east—from central London, Greenwich has enough riches, especially if the maritime theme (strong in an island nation) is your thing, that you should allow a very full day to see them. Meanwhile, upstream, the royal palaces and grand houses that dot the area were built not as town houses but as country residences with easy access to London by river; Hampton Court Palace is the best and biggest of all.

Greenwich

8 mi east of central London.

Greenwich makes an ideal day out from central London, thanks to its historic and maritime attractions. Sir Christopher Wren's Royal Naval College and Inigo Jones's Queen's House reach architectural heights; the Old Royal Observatory measures time for the entire planet; and the Greenwich Meridian divides the world in two. You can stand astride it with one foot in either hemisphere. The National Maritime Museum and the clipper ship *Cutty Sark* will appeal to seafaring types, and landlubbers can stroll the parkland that surround the buildings, the pretty 19th-century houses, and the weekend crafts and antiques markets.

Once, Greenwich was considered remote by Londoners, with only the river as a direct route. With direct transportation links in the form of the Docklands Light Railway (DLR) and the tube's Jubilee Line, getting here is both easy and inexpensive. The quickest route to maritime Greenwich is the tube to Canary Wharf and the Docklands Light Rail to the Greenwich stop. However, river connections to Greenwich (you can take the tube and DLR one way and a ferry the other) make the journey memorable in itself. On the way, the boat glides past famous London sights and the ever-changing Docklands. **Ferries** (☎ 020/7987–1185 from Embankment and Tower piers, 020/7930–4097 from Westminster Pier, 020/8305–0300 from Barrier Gardens Pier) from central London to Greenwich take 30–55 minutes and leave from various piers.

☺ *Cutty Sark.* This romantic tea clipper was built in 1869, one of a multitude of similar wooden tall-masted clippers that during the 19th century plied the seven seas, trading in exotic commodities—tea, in this case. The *Cutty Sark,* the last to survive, was also the fastest, sailing the China–London route in 1871 in only 107 days. Now the photogenic vessel lies in dry dock, a museum of one kind of seafaring life—and not a comfortable kind for the 28-strong crew, as you'll see. The collection of figureheads is amusing, too. ✉ *King William Walk, Greenwich SE10* ☎ *020/8858-3445* ⊕ *www.cuttysark.org.uk* 🎫 *£3.95* ⏰ *Daily 10–5; last admission at 4:30* Ⓤ *DLR: Cutty Sark.*

★ ☺ **National Maritime Museum.** One of Greenwich's outstanding attractions contains everything to do with the British at sea, in the form of paintings, models, maps, globes, sextants, and uniforms (including the one Nelson died in at Trafalgar, complete with bloodstained bullet hole). Explorers such as Captain James Cook and Robert F. Scott are celebrated, along with the valuable research gleaned from their grueling voyages. Best of all, there are actual boats, including an ornately gilded royal barge. New exhibitions, such as the excellent interactive All Hands gallery for kids, and an immense glazed roof that creates an indoor courtyard have revitalized this museum. Don't miss the Nelson galleries. ✉ *Romney Rd., Greenwich SE10* ☎ *020/8858-4422* ⊕ *www.nmm.ac.uk* 🎫 *Free* ⏰ *Apr.–Sept., daily 10–6; Oct.–Mar., daily 10–5* Ⓤ *DLR: Greenwich.*

need a break? The old **Trafalgar Tavern** (✉ Park Row, Greenwich SE10 ☎ 020/8858–2437), with views of the Thames, is a grand place to have a pint and some upscale pub grub. In warm weather, the terrace has outdoor seating overlooking the now-closed Millennium Dome.

Old Royal Observatory. Founded in 1675 by Charles II, this observatory (now a museum) was designed the same year by Christopher Wren for John Flamsteed, the first Astronomer Royal. The red ball you see on its roof has been there since 1833. It drops every day at 1 PM, and you can set your watch by it, as the sailors on the Thames always have. Everyone comes here to be photographed astride the **Prime Meridian,** a brass line laid on the cobblestones at zero degrees longitude, one side being the eastern, one the western, hemisphere. An exhibit on the solution to the problem of measuring longitude includes John Harrison's famous clocks, H1–H4. ✉ *Greenwich Park, Greenwich SE10* ☎020/8312–6565 ⊕ *www.rog.nmm.ac.uk* 🎫 *Free* ⏰ *Apr.–Sept., daily 10–6; Oct.–Mar., daily 10–5; last admission 30 mins before closing* Ⓤ *DLR: Greenwich.*

Queen's House. The queen for whom Inigo Jones began designing the house in 1616 was James I's Anne of Denmark, but she died three years later, and it was Charles I's French wife, Henrietta Maria, who inherited the building when it was completed in 1635. Britain's first classical building to use the lessons of Italian Renaissance architecture, it is of enormous importance in the history of English architecture. Paintings of the Muses, the Virtues, and the Liberal Arts decorate the Great Hall, a perfect cube exactly 40 feet in all three directions. ✉ *Romney*

Rd., Greenwich SE10 ☎ *020/8858–4422* ⊕ *www.nmm.ac.uk* ✉ *Free*
⊘ *Weekends 10–5, weekdays guided visits only, departing on the hr 11–4;
phone for extended hrs Apr.–Sept.* Ⓤ *DLR: Greenwich.*

Royal Naval College. Designed by Christopher Wren in 1694 as a home
for ancient mariners, these buildings became a school for young ones
in 1873; today the University of Greenwich uses them for classes. You'll
notice how the two main blocks part to reveal the Queen's House behind the central lawns, one of England's most famous architectural set
pieces. Wren, with the help of his assistant, Nicholas Hawksmoor, was
at pains to preserve the river vista from the house, and there are few
more majestic views in London than the awe-inspiring symmetry he
achieved. The **Painted Hall** and the **College Chapel** are the two outstanding
interiors on view here. ⊠ *King William Walk, Greenwich SE10* ☎ *0800/
389–3341 recorded information* ⊕ *www.greenwichfoundation.org.uk*
✉ *Free, guided tours £5* ⊘ *Painted Hall and Chapel Mon.–Sat. 10–5,
Sun. 12:30–5, last admission at 4:15; grounds 8–6* Ⓤ *DLR: Greenwich.*

Hampton Court Palace
★ *20 mi southwest of central London.*

On a loop of the Thames lies Hampton Court, one of London's oldest
royal palaces and more like a small town in size; it requires a day to do
it justice. The magnificent Tudor brick house was begun in 1514 by Cardinal Wolsey, the ambitious and worldly lord chancellor (roughly, prime
minister) of England and archbishop of York. He wanted it to be the
best palace in the land, and he succeeded so well that Henry VIII grew
deeply envious, whereupon Wolsey felt obliged to give Hampton Court
to the king. Henry moved in during 1525, added a great hall and chapel,
and proceeded to live much of his astonishing life here. Later, during
the reign of William and Mary, Christopher Wren expanded the palace
substantially. The site beside the slow-moving Thames is perfect. The
palace itself, steeped in history, hung with priceless paintings, and full
of echoing cobbled courtyards and cavernous Tudor kitchens complete
with deer pies and cooking pots, is in a fantastic setting of ornamental
gardens, lakes, and ponds. Best of all is the celebrated maze; it was planted
in 1714 and is truly fiendish. Six theme routes, including Henry VIII's
State Apartments and the King's (William III's) Apartments help you
plan your visit; special guides in period costume add to the fun. To get
here, take the tube or a train. Trains run frequently from London Waterloo to Hampton Court Station, with the trip taking about 30 minutes. The palace is a five-minute walk from the station. ⊠ *A308, East
Molesey* ☎ *0870/753–7777* ⊕ *www.hrp.org.uk* ✉ *Apartments and
maze £11.50, maze £2.30, park grounds free* ⊘ *State Apartments
Apr.–Oct., Tues.–Sun. 9:30–6, Mon. 10:15–6; Nov.–Mar., daily 9:30–4:30.
Grounds daily 7 AM–dusk* Ⓤ *Richmond, then Bus R68.*

Kew Gardens
FodorśChoice *6 mi southwest of central London.*
★

Kew Gardens, or more formally the Royal Botanic Gardens at Kew, is
the headquarters of the country's leading botanical institute as well as
a spectacular public garden of 300 acres and more than 30,000 species
of plants. The highlights of a visit are the two great 19th-century greenhouses filled with tropical plants, many of which have been there as long
as their housing. The bold glass roofs of the ultramodern Princess of
Wales Conservatory shelter no fewer than 10 climatic zones. Two 18th-
century royal ladies, Queen Caroline and Princess Augusta, were responsible for the garden's founding. Kew Palace, on the grounds (not
open to the public because of renovation), was the home of George III

for much of his life. ✉ *Kew Rd., Kew* ☎ *020/8332–5655* ⊕ *www.kew. org* 🖫 *£7.50* ⊙ *Gardens Apr.–Aug., weekdays 9:30–6:30, weekends 9:30–7:30; Sept.–Mar., daily 9:30–4:30* Ⓤ *Kew Gardens.*

WHERE TO EAT

No longer would Somerset Maugham be justified in saying, "If you want to eat well in England, have breakfast three times a day." London is in the midst of a restaurant revolution, and its dining scene is one of the hottest around. The city has fallen head over heels in love with its restaurants—all 6,700 of them—from its vast, glamorous eateries to its tiny neighborhood joints, from pubs where young foodies find their feet to swank trendsetters where celebrity chefs launch their ego flights.

This restaurant renaissance is due to talented entrepreneurs and chefs: Sir Terence Conran, Marco Pierre White, Gordon Ramsay, Jamie Oliver, and Oliver Peyton lead the list. Read all about them, and many others, when you get here, which you can easily do by picking up any newspaper. To keep up with the onslaught, each has reviewers aplenty. Luckily, London also does a good job of catering to people more interested in satisfying their appetites without breaking the bank than in following the latest food fashions. The listings here strike a balance between these extremes and include hip-and-happening places, neighborhood spots, ethnic alternatives, and old favorites.

A caveat: many restaurants are closed on Sunday, especially for dinner; the same is true on public holidays. Over the Christmas period, the London restaurant community all but shuts down—only hotels will be prepared to feed you. When in doubt, call ahead.

Prices

London is not an inexpensive dining city, although set-price menus at lunchtime may bring even the finest establishments within reach. Prix-fixe dinners are beginning to proliferate, too. Few places these days mind if you order a second appetizer instead of an entrée. Ethnic restaurants have always been a good bet here, especially the thousands of Indian restaurants. The law obliges all British restaurants to display their prices, including VAT (sales tax) outside, but watch for extras such as bread and vegetables charged separately, and service. Most restaurants add 10%–15% to the check, or else stamp SERVICE NOT INCLUDED along the bottom, in which case you should add the 10%–15% yourself. Beware of paying twice for service—restaurateurs have been known to add service, then leave the total on the credit-card slip blank, hoping for more.

WHAT IT COSTS In pounds				
£££££	**££££**	**£££**	**££**	**£**
AT DINNER over £22	£18–£22	£13–£17	£7–£12	under £7

Prices are for a main course at dinner.

Bloomsbury

FRENCH
£££–££££

✗ **Elena's L'Etoile.** London's most popular maitre d', Elena Salvoni presided for years over L'Escargot in Soho, where she made so many friends she opened her own restaurant. This century-old place is one of London's few remaining unreconstructed French bistros. The traditional dishes of duck braised with cabbage, salmon cakes, and *co-queletrôti* (roast chicken) are joined by newer treats, and most diners are guaranteed a warm smile from Elena even if they're not her politi-

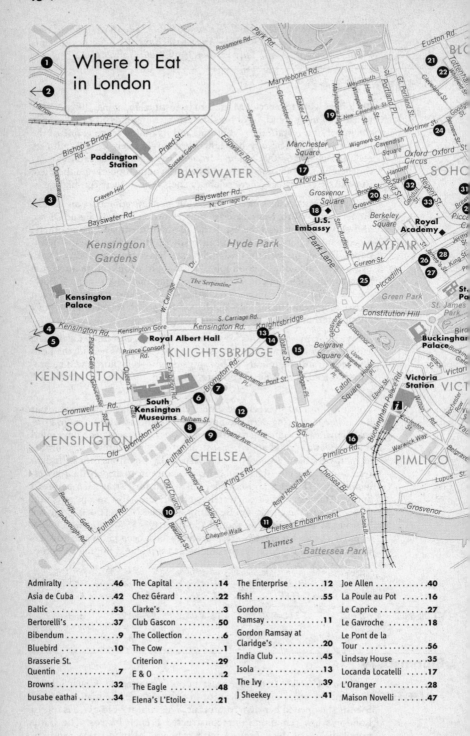

Where to Eat in London

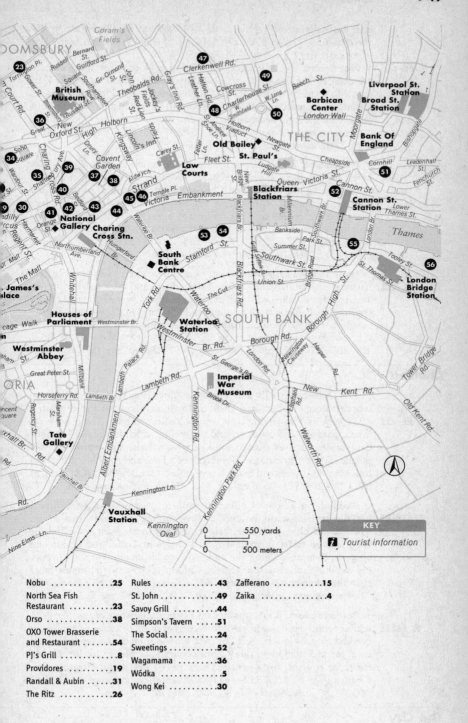

cian-journalist-actor regulars. ⊠ *30 Charlotte St., Bloomsbury W1* ☎ *020/7636–7189* ▭ *AE, DC, MC, V* ☺ *Closed Sun. No lunch Sat.* Ⓤ *Goodge St.*

ff–fff ✕**Chez Gérard.** One of an excellent chain of steak-frites restaurants (there are eight across London), this one has widened the choice on the Gallic menu to include more for those who don't eat red meat and serves Icelandic cod with mussels, leeks, and saffron, for instance. Steak with shoestring fries and béarnaise sauce remains the reason to visit, though. ⊠ *8 Charlotte St., Bloomsbury W1* ☎ *020/7636–4975* ▭ *AE, DC, MC, V* Ⓤ *Tottenham Court Rd.*

JAPANESE ✕**Wagamama.** Londoners drain bowls and bowls of Japanese noodles
f–ff in this big basement. It's high-tech, high-volume, and high-turnover, with a fast-moving line at the door. Choose ramen in or out of soup (topped with sliced meat) or "raw energy" vegetarian dishes and juices. This formula is so successful that the restaurant now has a clothing line. London has 13 branches; see www.wagamama.com. ⊠ *4A Streatham St., Bloomsbury WC1* ☎ *020/7323–9223* ⌲ *Reservations not accepted* ▭ *AE, DC, MC, V* Ⓤ *Tottenham Court Rd.*

SEAFOOD ✕**North Sea Fish Restaurant.** Come here and nowhere else for the British
ff–fff national dish of fish-and-chips—battered cod and deep-fried whitefish and thick fries shaken with salt and vinegar. It's tricky to find: three blocks south of St. Pancras station, down Judd Street. They serve only freshly caught fish, which you can order grilled—though that would defeat the purpose. You can take out or eat in. ⊠ *7–8 Leigh St., Bloomsbury WC1* ☎ *020/7387–5892* ▭ *AE, DC, MC, V* ☺ *Closed Sun.* Ⓤ *Russell Sq.*

Chelsea

AMERICAN/ ✕**PJ's Grill.** Enter PJ's and you've adopted the Polo Joe lifestyle—
CASUAL wooden floors and stained glass, a slowly revolving propeller from a
ff–fff 1911 Vickers Vimy flying boat, and polo memorabilia. The place is relaxed, friendly, and efficient, and the menu, which includes all-American staples such as steaks, smoked ribs, salads, and brownies, will please all but vegetarians. PJ's stays open late, and the bartenders can mix anything. Weekend brunch is popular. ⊠ *52 Fulham Rd., Chelsea SW3* ☎ *020/7581–0025* ▭ *AE, DC, MC, V* Ⓤ *S. Kensington.*

CONTEMPORARY ✕**Bluebird.** Sir Terence Conran presents a "gastrodome"—food mar-
fff–ffff ket, florist, fruit stand, butcher, kitchen shop, a café, and a restaurant. The place is blue and white, bright, and not in the least cozy, and the food can be fairly formulaic: veal kidneys and shallots, rabbit and spinach, then chocolate cake and espresso ice cream. Go for the people-watching and visual excitement: Conran's chefs tend to promise more than they deliver. ⊠ *350 King's Rd., Chelsea SW3* ☎ *020/7559–1000* ⌲ *Reservations essential* ▭ *AE, DC, MC, V* Ⓤ *Sloane Sq.*

FRENCH ✕**Gordon Ramsay.** Ramsay whips up a storm with white beans, foie gras,
★ **fffff** scallops, and truffles. He's Britain's current number one, and tables are booked months in advance. For £80, blow out on the seven-course option, for £65 wallow in three dinner courses, or plump for lunch (£35 for three courses) for a gentler check. ⊠ *68–69 Royal Hospital Rd., Chelsea SW3* ☎ *020/7352–4441* ⌲ *Reservations essential* ▭ *AE, DC, MC, V* ☺ *Closed weekends* Ⓤ *Sloane Sq.*

The City

CONTEMPORARY ✕**Maison Novelli.** Jean-Christophe Novelli is a hero of the Modern Brit
fff–ffff movement, and he's drawn foodies from day one to this hip Clerkenwell restaurant. Favorites on the menu include French onion soup with

Beaufort cheese, smoked haddock Monte Carlo, and the famed pig's trotter stuffed "following the mood of the day." ✉ *29–31 Clerkenwell Green, The City EC1* ☎ *020/7251–6606* ⚕ *Reservations essential* ☰ *AE, DC, MC, V* Ⓤ *Farringdon.*

££–£££ ✕ **St. John.** You either love or hate Fergus Henderson's ultra-British cooking at this converted smokehouse: one appetizer is sliced pig spleen. Main courses (venison liver and boiled egg, haddock and fennel, deviled crab) appear stark on the plate but always have style. Expect an all-French wine list with plenty of affordable bottles, plus malmseys and ports. Try the rice pudding with plums, or the English Eccles cakes. ✉ *26 St. John St., The City EC1* ☎ *020/7251–0848* ⚕ *Reservations essential* ☰ *AE, DC, MC, V* ☸ *Closed Sun. No lunch Sat.* Ⓤ *Farringdon.*

ENGLISH ✕ **Simpson's Tavern.** A bastion of English tradition, this back-alley chop-
£–££ house was founded in 1759 but did not admit women until 1916. It's popular with City traders and stockbrokers, who come for the traditional fare: steak-and-kidney pie, liver and bacon, chops from the grill, Simpson's salmon cakes, or the house specialty, stewed cheese (melted Cheddar cheese with béchamel and Worcestershire sauce spread on toast). The tavern fills up at lunch, so wander in early. ✉ *38½ Cornhill, at Ball Ct., The City EC3* ☎ *020/7626–9985* ⚕ *Reservations not accepted* ☰ *AE, DC, MC, V* ☸ *Closed weekends. No dinner* Ⓤ *Bank.*

FRENCH ✕ **Club Gascon.** You can struggle to find a sexier scene than this in all
★ London. Maybe it's the restrained, leather-walled interior, the spot-on
£££–£££££ service, the cut flowers, or the way the tapas-style new French cuisine is served: on a slab of rock rather than on a plate. Foie gras runs through the menu from start to finish; you can even have it for dessert, with fortified wine, gingerbread, and grapes. Bliss out on roast zander (a kind of pike perch) or foie gras steeped in Montilla-Moriles sherry and shot through with 10-year-old Maury wine. ✉ *57 W. Smithfield, The City EC1* ☎ *020/7796–0600* ⚕ *Reservations essential* ☰ *AE, MC, V* ☸ *Closed Sun. No lunch Sat.* Ⓤ *Barbican.*

MEDITERRANEAN ✕ **The Eagle.** It's the gastro-pub of gastro-pubs, and it belongs here by
£–£££ virtue of the amazingly good-value Portuguese-Spanish food. There are
FodorsChoice about nine dishes on the menu each day—a pasta, two vegetarian
★ choices, and a risotto always among them. Quite a few places in London charge three times the price for similar food; the Eagle all but started the welcome trend toward pubs serving good meals. ✉ *159 Farringdon Rd., The City EC1* ☎ *020/7837–1353* ⚕ *Reservations not accepted* ☰ *AE, DC, MC, V* Ⓤ *Farringdon.*

SEAFOOD ✕ **Sweetings.** Uniquely English, this time warp from the old City of Lon-
££–££££ don was established in 1830. There are many things Sweetings doesn't do: dinner, reservations, weekends, and coffee. It does, however, do seafood. It's not far from St. Paul's, and City gents come for "luncheon." They like tankards of Black Velvet (Guinness and champagne) and are reassured by potted shrimps, poached haddock, West Mersey oysters, and Welsh rarebit. The puddings are schoolboy favorites such as spotted dick (suet pudding with currants). ✉ *39 Queen Victoria St., The City EC4* ☎ *020/7248–3062* ⚕ *Reservations not accepted* ☰ *AE, MC, V* ☸ *Closed weekends. No dinner* Ⓤ *Mansion House.*

Covent Garden

AMERICAN ✕ **Joe Allen.** Long hours (thespians flock here after the curtains fall) and
££–£££ a welcoming interior mean New York Joe's London branch still swings after more than two decades. The fun menu helps: roasted poblano peppers and black-bean soup are typical starters, and entrées include bar-

becued ribs and monkfish with sun-dried-tomato salsa. There are Yankee desserts, too, such as grilled banana bread with ice cream and hot caramel sauce. ⊠ *13 Exeter St., Covent Garden WC2,* ☎ *020/7836–0651* ⌂ *Reservations essential* ⊟ *AE, MC, V* Ⓤ *Covent Garden.*

CONTEMPORARY ⨯ **The Ivy.** This is London's favorite restaurant, and thus hard to get into.
★ **££–££££** In a wood-paneled, latticed, art deco room with stained glass and blinding-white tablecloths, the theater set eat Caesar salad, kedgeree, salmon cakes, and baked Alaska. For star-trekking ("Don't look now, dear, but there's Ralph Fiennes"), this is the primo spot in London. The weekend three-course lunch is a deal at £17.50. Try walking in off the street for a table on short notice—it's been known to work. ⊠ *1 West St., Covent Garden WC2* ☎ *020/7836–4751* ⌂ *Reservations essential* ⊟ *AE, DC, MC, V* Ⓤ *Covent Garden.*

CONTINENTAL ⨯ **Savoy Grill.** The grill in the Savoy hotel continues in the first rank of
££££–£££££ power-dining locations. Politicians, newspaper barons, and tycoons like the comforting food and impeccably discreet service in the low-key, rather dull, yew-paneled salon. On the menu, an omelet Arnold Bennett (cheese and smoked haddock) is perennial, as are such standards as beef Wellington and saddle of lamb. Diners can take to the dance floor at Saturday's "Stompin' at the Savoy" event. ⊠ *The Strand, Covent Garden WC2* ☎ *020/7836–4343* ⌂ *Reservations essential* 🏛 *Jacket and tie* ⊟ *AE, DC, MC, V* ⊙ *Closed Sun. No lunch Sat.* Ⓤ *Covent Garden.*

ENGLISH ⨯ **Rules.** Come, escape from the 21st century at what is probably the
£££–£££££ single most beautiful dining salon in London. More than 200 years old
FodorsChoice (it opened in 1798), this institution has welcomed everyone from Dick-
★ ens to the current Prince of Wales. The decoration is delicious: plush red banquettes and lacquered Regency yellow walls crammed with oil paintings and engravings. The menu includes fine historical dishes—try the steak-and-kidney pudding for a taste of the 18th century. For a main dish, pick something from the list of daily specials, which may include game from Rules's Teesdale estate. ⊠ *35 Maiden La., Covent Garden WC2* ☎ *020/7836–5314* ⊟ *AE, DC, MC, V* Ⓤ *Covent Garden.*

FRENCH ⨯ **Admiralty.** It's a restaurant worthy of the grand courtyard setting of
£££££ Somerset House, just off the Strand. London is turning away from fusion food, and Admiralty does fine French cuisine very simply. The snail ravioli in Chablis with artichokes and garlic is a classic French starter, and the monkfish and asparagus tastes as good as it looks on the plate. Political heavy-hitters flock for the splendid cooking, and (surely?) their hard hearts melt when they break the steaming hot chocolate *moelleux* (pudding). ⊠ *Somerset House, Strand, Covent Garden, WC2* ☎ *020/ 7845–4646* ⊟ *AE, DC, MC, V* ⊙ *No dinner Sun.* Ⓤ *Charing Cross.*

ITALIAN ⨯ **Orso.** Sharing the same snappy staff and glitzy clientele of showbiz
£££ types and hacks, this is the sister restaurant of Joe Allen. The Tuscan menu changes daily but always includes excellent pizza and pasta dishes plus entrées based, perhaps, on grilled rabbit or roast sea bass. Food here is never boring, nor is the place itself. Orsino, at 119 Portland Road, W11, is a stylish offshoot, serving much the same food. ⊠ *27 Wellington St., Covent Garden WC2* ☎ *020/7240–5269* ⌂ *Reservations essential* ⊟ *AE, MC, V* Ⓤ *Covent Garden.*

££–£££ ⨯ **Bertorelli's.** Across from the stage door of the Royal Opera House, Bertorelli's is quietly chic, the food tempting and just innovative enough: sea bass with walnut pesto, monkfish ragout with fennel, wonder beans, Swiss chard, and lime butter. Even more decorous and delicious is the branch at 19–23 Charlotte Street (check out its amazing marble-clad restrooms). ✉ *44A Floral St., Covent Garden WC2* ☎ *020/7836–3969* ⊟ *AE, DC, MC, V* ☉ *Closed Sun.* Ⓤ *Covent Garden.*

INDIAN
£

✕ **India Club.** Defying convention, this idiosyncratic Indian canteen in the Strand Continental Hotel is going strong after 50 years. The Formica, linoleum, and faded photos aren't pretty, but the place is a favorite with London University students, BBC World Service workers, and Indian High Commission staff. You need to be a member of the hotel drinking club (£1) to get a beer from the bar (down two flights), so stick with the *masala dosai* (pancakes stuffed with onion and potato). ✉ *143 The Strand, Covent Garden WC2* ☎ *020/7836–0650* ⚑ *Reservations not accepted* ⊟ *No credit cards* Ⓤ *Charing Cross.*

PAN-ASIAN
£££–£££££

✕ **Asia de Cuba.** A trendy restaurant, in a trendy hotel, in a trendy city: Asia de Cuba is the star turn at Ian Schrager's St. Martin's Lane Hotel. Philippe Starck–designed, it's sexy and loud—check out the dangling lightbulbs, Latin music, stacks of books, portable TVs, and satin-clad pillars. The food is Pan-Asian fusion and you're encouraged to share (as the British do with curry). The Thai beef salad with Asian greens and coconut is delicious, as is the lobster with rum and red curry. ✉ *45 St. Martin's La., Covent Garden WC2* ☎ *020/7300–5588* ⊟ *AE, DC, MC, V* Ⓤ *Leicester Sq.*

SEAFOOD
££–£££££

✕ **J Sheekey.** The stars gather here as an alternative to the Ivy and Le Caprice (it's run by the same owners). Sleek and discreet, in the heart of Theatreland, the popularity of this seafood haven is evidenced by the photos on the walls—Peter O'Toole, Charlie Chaplin, Noel Coward, and Peter Sellers. And sultry J Sheekey really charms: cracked tiles, lava-rock bar tops, American oak paneling. Sample the wonderful jellied eels, Dover sole, Cornish fish stew, and the famous Sheekey fish pie. The weekend fixed-price lunch is £17.50. ✉ *28–32 St. Martin's Ct., Covent Garden WC2* ☎ *020/7240–2565* ⊟ *AE, DC, MC, V* Ⓤ *Leicester Sq.*

Kensington

POLISH
££–£££

✕ **Wódka.** This smart restaurant serves modern Polish food. It's popular with elegant locals and often seems like it's hosting one big dinner party. Alongside the salmon, herring, caviar, and eggplant blinis, you might find venison or roast duck. Order a carafe of the purest vodka in London; encased in ice, it is flavored (with bison grass, cherries, and rowanberries) by the owner, who is a Polish prince. ✉ *12 St. Alban's Grove, Kensington W8* ☎ *020/7937–6513* ⚑ *Reservations essential* ⊟ *AE, DC, MC, V* ☉ *No lunch weekends* Ⓤ *High St. Kensington.*

Knightsbridge

FRENCH
£££££

✕ **The Capital.** Elegant and clublike, the dining room has a grown-up atmosphere and formal service. Chef Eric Chavot carries out classy French cooking, and many of his dishes astonish, including turbot with creamed baby leeks and mushroom ravioli. Desserts follow the same exciting route. Set-price menus at lunch (£26.50) make it somewhat more affordable. ✉ *22–24 Basil St., Knightsbridge SW3* ☎ *020/7589–5171* ⚑ *Reservations essential* ⊟ *AE, DC, MC, V* Ⓤ *Knightsbridge.*

£££–££££

✕ **La Poule au Pot.** One of London's most charming restaurants is superb for proposals or romantic evenings. The Chelsea set—and Americans—love this candlelit corner of France. The country cooking is fairly good, not spectacular. The *poule au pot* (stewed chicken) and *lapin à la moutarde* (rabbit with mustard) are strong and hearty, and there are fine classics, such as beef bourguignonne and French onion soup. Service comes with bonhomie. ✉ *231 Ebury St., Knightsbridge SW1* ☎ *020/7730–7763* ♨ *Reservations essential* ▤ *AE, DC, MC, V* Ⓤ *Sloane Sq.*

££–££££ ✕ **Brasserie St. Quentin.** French expatriates and locals alike frequent this popular slice of Paris. Every inch of culinary France is explored—queen scallops, escargots, pheasant and partridge, fillet of beef brioche, tarte Tatin—in the bourgeois provincial comfort that so many London chains (the Dômes, the Cafés Rouges) try for but fail to achieve. ✉ *243 Brompton Rd., Knightsbridge SW3* ☎ *020/7589–8005* ▤ *AE, DC, MC, V* Ⓤ *S. Kensington.*

ITALIAN ✕ **Zafferano.** Any number of wealthy Belgravians flock here, one of London's best exponents of *cucina nuova.* The fireworks are in the kitchen: buckwheat pasta with leek and sage, lamb cutlets with hazelnut crust and white truffle polenta. The desserts are *delizioso,* especially the nougat parfait with chestnuts and the poached pears and mascarpone ice cream. ✉ *15 Lowndes St., Knightsbridge SW1* ☎ *020/7235–5800* ♨ *Reservations essential* ▤ *AE, DC, MC, V* Ⓤ *Knightsbridge.*

££££–£££££

££–££££ ✕ **Isola.** An island of glam in Knightsbridge, Isola guns to be a cool London restaurant. Upstairs you'll find Iso-bar, a stylish place for cocktails, and downstairs is fine dining. You sit on leather sofas amid the sparkle of chrome and mirrors. Try the rack of lamb and potato gratin, or the carpaccio of Scottish beef. The all-Italian wine list is one of the best in town. ✉ *145 Knightsbridge, Knightsbridge SW1* ☎ *020/7838–1044* ♨ *Reservations essential* ▤ *AE, DC, MC, V* Ⓤ *Knightsbridge.*

Marylebone

ECLECTIC ✕ **Providores.** New Zealander Peter Gordon scores a perfect 10 with his Pacific Rim fusion food at Providores in trendy Marylebone. Have a charming meal upstairs or go down to the relaxed ground-floor Tapa Rooms—try the sweet potato and miso, the cassava fritters, and the roast *chioca* (a tuber similar to Jerusalem artichoke). ✉ *109 Marylebone High St., Marylebone W1* ☎ *020/7935–6175* ▤ *AE, MC, V* Ⓤ *Baker St.*

★ ££–£££

ENGLISH ✕ **The Social.** London's a groovy city, and the Social is the best and by far the friendliest of the new wave of hip DJ-bars springing up around town, offering great sounds with decent grub. The weekly and monthly DJ sessions are a knockout—you'll hear anything from electronica to Latino dub salsa—and the food is English old-school comfort: meat pie (or steak and Guinness), fish sandwiches, or beans on toast. Watch trendy London groove. ✉ *5 Little Portland St., Marylebone W1* ☎ *020/ 7636–4992* ▤ *MC, V* Ⓤ *Oxford Circus.*

£–££

Fodor'sChoice

★

Mayfair

ENGLISH ✕ **Browns.** Unpretentious, crowd-pleasing, child-friendly English food is delivered at the former establishment of the bespoke tailors Messrs. Cooling and Wells, now converted to Edwardian style by the group behind the successful Browns eateries. The classic Browns steak-and-Guinness pie is on the menu, but king prawns, lamb shanks, roasted peppers, salads, and pastas predominate. ✉ *47 Maddox St., Mayfair W1* ☎ *020/ 7491–4565* ▤ *AE, DC, MC, V* Ⓤ *Oxford Circus.*

££–£££

FRENCH ✕ **Gordon Ramsay at Claridge's.** Ramsay is Britain's greatest chef, and Claridge's is booked six months in advance. They do breakfast, bargain three-course lunches (£25), and stunning dinners for £50 and £60. Try the eight-hour roast shoulder of lamb, braised halibut, or brill in red wine. Arrive early for dinner and have a drink at Claridge's art deco bar, the best cocktail lounge in London. ✉ *Claridge's Hotel, Brook St.,*

£££££

Fodor'sChoice

★

Mayfair W1 ☎ *020/7499–0099* ⌨ *Reservations essential* 🏛 *Jacket and tie* 🖃 *AE, MC, V* Ⓤ *Bond St.*

★ **£££££** ✗ **Le Gavroche.** Michel Roux, who inherited the family cooking gene, runs one of London's finest restaurants. He's a master of classical French cooking—formal, flowery, decorated. The fixed-price lunch is relatively affordable at £40 (for canapés and three courses, plus mineral water, a half bottle of wine, coffee, and petits fours). In fact it's the only way to eat here if you don't have an expense account. Book at least a week in advance. 🖃 *43 Upper Brook St., Mayfair W1* ☎ *020/7408–0881* ⌨ *Reservations essential* 🖃 *AE, DC, MC, V* ☉ *Closed Sun. and 10 days at Christmas. No lunch Sat.* Ⓤ *Marble Arch.*

ITALIAN ✗ **Locanda Locatelli.** Everything chef Giorgio Locatelli touches turns to
£££–£££££ gold—hence the six-week waiting list at London's top Italian restaurant,
Fodor'sChoice an elegant David Collins–designed restaurant at the Churchill Inter-Con-
★ tinental, complete with convex mirrors, etched glass, swivel chairs, and banquettes. The food is incredibly accomplished—superb risottos, silky handmade pastas. Be bold: try the ravioli osso bucco or the sweet-breads with Roman *agro-dolce* (sweet and sour sauce). 🖃 *8 Seymour St., Mayfair W1* ☎ *020/7935–9088* ⌨ *Reservations essential* 🖃 *AE, MC, V* ☉ *Closed Sun.* Ⓤ *Marble Arch.*

JAPANESE ✗ **Nobu.** Packed with stars, this is London's hottest destination restau-
£££–£££££ rant. Nobuyuki Matsuhisa wows 'em with new-style sashimi with a Pe-
ruvian touch—he sells 300 pounds of Alaskan black cod a day. Nobu is in the Metropolitan, a hip hotel, with staff, attitude, clientele, and prices to match. Ubon (that's Nobu backward), a sister restaurant, operates in Canary Wharf. 🖃 *Metropolitan Hotel, 19 Old Park La., Mayfair W1* ☎ *020/7447–4747* ⌨ *Reservations essential* 🖃 *AE, DC, MC, V* ☉ *No lunch weekends* Ⓤ *Hyde Park.*

Notting Hill

CONTEMPORARY ✗ **Clarke's.** There's no choice on the evening menu at Sally Clarke's restau-
£££££ rant; her four-course dinners contain fresh ingredients, plainly but per-
fectly cooked and accompanied by home-baked breads. The flower-and-art-speckled room is similarly home-style, if your home hap-pens to be one of the £3 million white town houses with a stucco fa-cade that you see around here. 🖃 *124 Kensington Church St., Notting Hill W8* ☎ *020/7221–9225* ⌨ *Reservations essential* 🖃 *AE, DC, MC, V* ☉ *Closed Sun. and 2 wks in Aug. No lunch Sat.* Ⓤ *Notting Hill Gate.*

£££ ✗ **The Cow.** Not *another* Conran: the Cow belongs to Tom, son of Sir Terence, although it's a million miles from Quaglino's and Mezzo. This chic gastro-pub includes a faux-Dublin back-room bar that serves oys-ters, salmon cakes, and baked brill. Upstairs the chef whips up Anglo-French specialties—cod and mash is one temptation. Notting Hillbillies love the house special—a half-dozen Irish rock oysters with a pint of Guinness. 🖃 *89 Westbourne Park Rd., Notting Hill W2* ☎ *020/7221–0021* ⌨ *Reservations essential* 🖃 *MC, V* Ⓤ *Westbourne Park.*

PAN-ASIAN ✗ **E&O.** This is the scene restaurant of London's scene restaurants, full
★ **££–££££** of luxurious charm. E&O stands for Eastern and Oriental, and the Pan-Asian cuisine is an intelligent mix of Chinese, Japanese, Vietnamese, and Thai. Don't skip the Thai rare-beef salad with red *nam jhim* (bean sprouts) or the albacore sashimi, and remember to look up and then look away when an A-list star settles in at Table 5. 🖃 *14 Blenheim Crescent, Notting Hill W11* ☎ *020/7229–5454* ⌨ *Reservations essential* 🖃 *AE, DC, MC, V* Ⓤ *Ladbroke Grove.*

St. James's

CONTEMPORARY ✕ **Le Caprice.** Secreted behind the Ritz Hotel, Le Caprice commands the
★ **££–££££** deepest loyalty of any restaurant in London because it gets everything
right: the glossy Eva Jiricna interior; the perfect service; the menu,
halfway between Euro-peasant and fashion plate. This food—crispy duck
and watercress salad, San Daniele ham and figs—has no business being
so good. Expect the best people-watching in town (apart from its sister
restaurants, the Ivy and J Sheekey). ✉ *Arlington House, Arlington St.,
St. James's SW1* ☎ *020/7629–2239* ⌕ *Reservations essential* ⊟ *AE,
DC, MC, V* Ⓤ *Green Park.*

CONTINENTAL ✕ **The Ritz.** This palace of marble, gilt, and trompe l'oeil would moisten
£££££ Marie Antoinette's eye. Add the view over Green Park and the Ritz's
sunken garden, and it seems beside the point to eat. The cuisine stands
up to the visual onslaught, with super-rich morsels—foie gras, lobster,
truffles, caviar—all served with a flourish. Englishness is wrested from
Louis XVI by a daily roast from the trolley. A three-course lunch at £35
and a four-course dinner at £51 make the check more bearable than the
£59 you'll pay for the Friday and Saturday dinner dance, a dying tradition. ✉ *150 Piccadilly, St. James's W1* ☎ *020/7493–8181* ⌕ *Reservations essential* 🏛 *Jacket and tie* ⊟ *AE, DC, MC, V* Ⓤ *Green Park.*

FRENCH ✕ **L'Oranger.** The food here reaches perfection: duck with fondant potato
££££–£££££ and foie gras sauce; scallops with cured Iberico ham; John Dory with
crushed cocoa beans; and hazelnut soufflé with praline ice cream. The
conservatory is highly romantic, plus there's a little courtyard where the
last duel in London was fought. The waiters are French, courteous, and
friendly. ✉ *5 St. James's St., St. James's SW1* ☎ *020/7839–3774*
⌕ *Reservations essential* ⊟ *AE, DC, MC, V* ☾ *Closed Sun. No lunch
Sat.* Ⓤ *Green Park.*

£££–£££££ ✕ **Criterion.** You'll appreciate the glamour of this spectacular, neo-Byzan-
tine mirrored marble hall, which first opened in 1874. It's heavy on the
awe factor, with dishes to match, and Marco Pierre White's team scores
highly. Some of his well-known dishes appear on the menu, such as the
ballotine of salmon with herbs and *fromage blanc* (soft, fresh cream
cheese), and grilled calves' liver and Lyonnais sauce. The soaring golden
ceiling, oil paintings, and attentive Gallic service add up to a first-rate
night out. ✉ *Piccadilly Circus, St. James's W1* ☎ *020/7930–0488*
⊟ *AE, DC, MC, V* Ⓤ *Piccadilly Circus.*

NORTH AFRICAN ✕ **Momo.** It's a hot ticket—go if you can. Mourad Mazouz—Momo to
★ **££–££££** friends—storms beau London with his Casbah-like North African restaurant behind Regent Street. The seats are low and close together, and there's
a resident DJ and often live North African music. Downstairs is the mem-
bers-only Kemia Bar, and next door is Mô—a Moroccan tearoom, open
to all. The menu, based on *pastilla* (a pie-like dish with phyllo), *tagine*
(a meat or chicken stew with vegetables and olives), and couscous,
doesn't match the excitement of the scene. ✉ *23–25 Heddon St., St.
James's W1* ☎ *020/7434–4040* ⌕ *Reservations essential* ⊟ *AE, DC,
MC, V* Ⓤ *Piccadilly Circus.*

Soho

CHINESE ✕ **Wong Kei.** One of the cheapest Chinese restaurants in Chinatown has
£–££ famously rude waiters. The interior is jazzed up these days and things
are less brusque than before. You'll find it full of London's Chinese residents enjoying tasty food at rockbottom prices. The all-in-one meals
are good, and the soups—such as the hot-and-sour—are decent, pun-

gent broths. ✉ *41–43 Wardour St. W1* ☎ *020/7437–8408* 🚭 *No credit cards* Ⓤ *Piccadilly Circus.* ·

IRISH ✕ **Lindsay House.** Richard Corrigan brings his Irish country charm to
★ **££££** Soho and fills up the warren of rooms in this Georgian town house with his large personality. Start with celeriac soup or Amaretto-soaked figs, and move on. Corrigan wraps rabbit and black pudding in Bayonne ham and excels with mash and Irish beef, and his white asparagus and langoustine dish can't be bettered. Petits fours with coffee will send you home oh-so-happy. ✉ *21 Romilly St., Soho W1* ☎ *020/7439–0450* 🚭 *AE, DC, MC, V* ⏾ *Closed Sun.* Ⓤ *Leicester Sq.*

SEAFOOD ✕ **Randall & Aubin.** Ex-Armani model Ed Baines's converted French
££–££££ butcher's shop, complete with white tiles, meat hooks, and marble tabletops, is one of London's buzziest champagne-oyster bars—bang in Soho's sexland. Go for the Loch Fyne oysters, dressed crab, or a half lobster with chips. At peak time you'll spend 15 minutes at the bar waiting for a seat. Another outpost has opened at 329–331 Fulham Road in Chelsea. ✉ *16 Brewer St.; Soho W1* ☎ *020/7287–4447* ⌕ *Reservations not accepted* 🚭 *AE, DC, MC, V* Ⓤ *Piccadilly Circus.*

THAI ✕ **busabe eathai.** One of Londoners' favorite cheap spots in Soho, this
£–££ superior Thai canteen is fitted with rattan, benches, hardwood tables,
Fodor'sChoice low lights, and paper lamp shades. It's no less seductive for its commu-
★ nal tables. The menu lists noodles, curries, stir-fries, rice, and side dishes. Try chicken with butternut squash, cuttlefish curry, or seafood vermicelli (prawns, squid, and scallops). The mantra here is *gan gin gan yuu:* "as you eat, so you are." ✉ *106–110 Wardour St., Soho W1* ☎ *020/7255–8686* ⌕ *Reservations not accepted* 🚭 *AE, MC, V* Ⓤ *Leicester Sq.*

South Bank

CONTEMPORARY ✕ **OXO Tower Brasserie and Restaurant.** London has a room with a view—
££££–£££££ and *such* a view. On the eighth floor of the OXO Tower is this elegant space serving Euro-Asian food with trendy ingredients (such as spinach pie with quail and pumpkin salad). The ceiling slats turn from white to blue, but who notices, with the London Eye wheel and St. Paul's Cathedral across the water? The Brasserie is slightly less expensive than the restaurant, but both have great river views. Terrace tables in summer have some of the best panoramas in London. ✉ *Barge House St., South Bank SE1* ☎ *020/7803–3888* 🚭 *AE, DC, MC, V* Ⓤ *Waterloo.*

EASTERN ✕ **Baltic.** To eat well in Southwark while visiting the Young Vic or Tate
EUROPEAN Modern, come to this bustling vodka-party playground—a good spot for
££–£££ drinks at the bar or a decent East European meal in sexy surroundings. Owned by the guy behind Wódka in Kensington, Baltic serves fine blinis—with herring, smoked salmon, or caviar—and great *leniwe* (potato dumplings) and gravlax. The vodkas are fruity and eclectic: rose petal, Siberian, peppercorn, bison grass, rye and honey. ✉ *74 Blackfriars Rd., South Bank SE1* ☎ *020/7928–1111* 🚭 *AE, MC, V* Ⓤ *Southwark.*

FRENCH ✕ **Le Pont de la Tour.** This is a perfect spot in summer, when sitting at
£££–£££££ the outside tables feels heavenly. Inside you'll find a wine merchant, bakery, deli, seafood bar, brasserie, and the diner-style restaurant, smart as the captain's table. Fish and seafood (lobster salad, halibut and hollandaise) and meat and game (Denham-estate venison and Gressingham duck) are prominent. Prune-and-Armagnac tart is a fine finish to a glamorous meal. ✉ *36D Shad Thames, Butler's Wharf, South Bank SE1* ☎ *020/7403–8403* ⌕ *Reservations essential* 🚭 *AE, DC, MC, V* Ⓤ *Tower Hill.*

SEAFOOD ✕ **fish!** A sensation on London's scene, this sleek modern diner sits in
££–£££ the shadow of Southwark Cathedral, near Borough Market. The fish
at fish! is excellent and politically correct. The langoustines are creel-
caught, the salmon organic, and the scallops landed by divers. There
are eight types of fish on the menu, including swordfish, brill, skate, and
turbot. The formula's struck a chord; five more fish! have come on-stream.
Call for locations. ✉ *Cathedral St., South Bank SE1* ☎ *020/7407–3803*
⊟ *AE, DC, MC, V* Ⓤ *London Bridge.*

South Kensington

CONTEMPORARY ✕ **Bibendum.** This converted 1911 Michelin showroom, adorned with
£££–£££££ art deco prints and brilliant stained glass, remains one of London's dining showplaces. Chef Matthew Harris cooks with Euro-Brit flair. Good
choices are deep-fried calf brains, any of the risottos, steak au poivre,
or Pyrenean milk-fed lamb with garlic and mint gravy. The £25 fixed-
price lunch menu is money well spent. ✉ *Michelin House, 81 Fulham
Rd., South Kensington SW3* ☎ *020/7581–5817* ⚄ *Reservations essential* ⊟ *AE, DC, MC, V* Ⓤ *S. Kensington.*

££–£££ ✕ **The Enterprise.** A hot spot near Harrods and Brompton Cross, the Enterprise is filled with decorative types who complement the striped wallpaper, Edwardian side tables covered with baskets, vintage books piled
up in the windows, and white linen and fresh flowers on the tables. The
menu is fairly subtle—braised lamb shank with rosemary and celeriac
puree—and the heartiness of the room contributes to a fun experience.
✉ *35 Walton St., South Kensington SW3* ☎ *020/7584–3148* ⊟ *AE,
MC, V* Ⓤ *S. Kensington.*

INDIAN ✕ **Zaika.** At one of London's finest Indian restaurants, Vineet Bhatia pushes
£££–£££££ the boundaries of Indian cuisine by mixing old flavors with modern sen-
sibilities. You can't top the *samundri Zaika* (tandoor-smoked salmon,
king prawn, swordfish, and cardamom), nor can you better the scallops
in coconut milk, with masala mashed potato. Sign off with chocolate
samosas ("chocomosas") and Indian ice cream. ✉ *1 Kensington High
St., South Kensington W8* ☎ *020/7795–6533* ⚄ *Reservations essential* ⊟ *AE, MC, V* Ⓤ *High St. Kensington.*

MEDITERRANEAN ✕ **The Collection.** Enter this former Katharine Hamnett shop through the
££–££££ spotlighted tunnel over the glass drawbridge, make your way past the
style police, and you'll find yourself engulfed by a fashionable crowd.
The warehouse setting, adorned with industrial wood beams and steel
cables, and a suspended gallery, makes a great theater for people-watching. Well-dressed wannabes peck at Mediterranean food with Japanese
and Thai accents. ✉ *264 Brompton Rd., South Kensington SW3* ☎ *020/
7225–1212* ⊟ *AE, DC, MC, V* Ⓤ *S. Kensington.*

Pubs

The city's pubs, or public houses, dispense beer, good cheer, and casual
grub in settings that range from ancient wood-beam rooms to ornate
Victorian interiors to utilitarian modern rooms. London's culinary fever
has not passed pubs by, however, and gastro-pub fever is still sweeping
the city. At many places, char-grills are being installed in the kitchen out
back, and up front the faded wallpapers are being replaced by abstract
paintings (the best of these luxe pubs are reviewed earlier). Some of the
following also showcase nouveau pub grub, but whether you have Moroccan chicken or the usually dismal ploughman's special, you'll want
to order a pint. Note that American-style beer is called "lager" in
Britain, whereas the real British brew is "bitters" (usually served warm).
You can order up your choice in two sizes—pints or half pints. If this

is your first taste of British beer, order a half. Some London pubs also sell "real ale," which is less gassy than bitters and, many would argue, has a better flavor. When doing a London pub crawl, remember that arcane licensing laws forbid the serving of alcohol after 11 PM (10:30 on Sunday; there are different rules for restaurants)—a circumstance you see in action at 10 minutes to 11, when the "last orders" bell triggers a stampede to the bar. However, a new law under review at press time may allow more places to serve alcohol later.

✕ **Black Friar.** A step from Blackfriars Tube stop, this spectacular pub has an Arts-and-Crafts interior that is entertainingly, satirically ecclesiastical, with inlaid mother-of-pearl, wood carvings, stained glass, and marble pillars all over the place. In spite of the finely lettered temperance tracts on view just below the reliefs of monks, fairies, and friars, there's a nice group of beers on tap from independent brewers. ✉ *174 Queen Victoria St., The City EC4* ☎ *020/7236–5474* Ⓤ *Blackfriars.*

✕ **Dove Inn.** Read the list of famous ex-regulars, from Charles II to Ernest Hemingway, as you wait for a beer at this very popular, very comely 16th-century riverside pub by Hammersmith Bridge. If the Dove is too full, stroll upstream to the Old Ship or the Blue Anchor. ✉ *19 Upper Mall, Hammersmith W6* ☎ *020/8748–5405* Ⓤ *Hammersmith.*

✕ **George Inn.** The current building, with a courtyard where Shakespeare's plays were once staged, dates from the late 17th century and is central London's last remaining galleried inn. Dickens was a regular, and the George is featured in *Little Dorrit.* ✉ *77 Borough High St., South Bank SE1* ☎ *020/7407–2056* Ⓤ *London Bridge.*

✕ **Lamb & Flag.** This 17th-century pub was once known as the Bucket of Blood because the upstairs room was used as a ring for bare-knuckle boxing. Now it's a trendy, friendly, and entirely bloodless pub, serving food (lunchtime only) and real ale. It's on the edge of Covent Garden, off Garrick Street. ✉ *33 Rose St., Covent Garden WC2* ☎ *020/ 7497–9504* Ⓤ *Covent Garden.*

✕ **Mayflower.** An atmospheric 17th-century riverside inn with exposed beams and a terrace, this is practically the very place from which the Pilgrims set sail for Plymouth Rock. The inn is licensed to sell American postage stamps. ✉ *117 Rotherhithe St., South Bank SE16* ☎ *020/ 7237–4088* Ⓤ *Rotherhithe.*

✕ **Museum Tavern.** Across the street from the British Museum, this gloriously Victorian pub makes an ideal resting place after the rigors of the culture trail. With lots of fancy glass, gilded pillars, and carvings, the heavily restored hostelry once helped Karl Marx unwind after a hard day in the library. ✉ *49 Great Russell St., Bloomsbury WC1* ☎ *020/ 7242–8987* Ⓤ *Tottenham Court Rd.*

✕ **Sherlock Holmes.** This pub used to be known as the Northumberland Arms, and Arthur Conan Doyle popped in regularly for a pint. It figures in *The Hound of the Baskervilles,* and you can see the hound's head and plaster casts of its huge paws among other Holmes memorabilia. ✉ *10 Northumberland St., Euston WC2* ☎ *020/7930–2644* Ⓤ *Charing Cross.*

✕ **Ye Olde Cheshire Cheese.** Yes, it's a tourist trap, but this most historic of all London pubs (it dates from 1667) deserves a visit for its sawdust-covered floors, low wood-beam ceilings, and the 14th-century crypt of Whitefriars' monastery under the cellar bar. This was the most regular of Dr. Johnson's and Dickens's *many* locals. ✉ *145 Fleet St., The City EC4* ☎ *020/7353–6170* Ⓤ *Blackfriars.*

Afternoon Tea

In the grandest places, teatime is still a ritual, so be prepared for a dress code: Claridge's, the Ritz, and the Savoy all require jacket and tie.

✕ **Brown's Hotel.** Famous for its teas, the hotel lounge does rest on its laurels somewhat, with a packaged aura and nobody around but fellow tourists. Still, everyone swears by the divine armchairs. For £25 you get sandwiches, a scone with cream and jam, tart, fruitcake, and shortbread. Champagne tea is £36. ⊠ *33 Albermarle St., Mayfair W1* ☎ *020/ 7518–4108* ⊟ *AE, DC, MC, V* ☉ *Tea daily 2–6.* Ⓤ *Green Park.*

✕ **Claridge's.** This is the real McCoy, with liveried footmen proffering sandwiches, scones, and superior patisseries (£22, £26, or £35) in the palatial yet genteel foyer, to the sound of the resident "Hungarian orchestra" (actually a string quartet). ⊠ *Brook St., Mayfair W1* ☎ *020/ 7629–8860* ⊟ *AE, DC, MC, V* ☉ *Tea daily 3–5:30* Ⓤ *Bond St.*

✕ **Fortnum & Mason.** Upstairs at the Queen's grocers, three set teas are ceremoniously served: standard afternoon tea (sandwiches, scone, cakes, £17.50), old-fashioned high tea (the traditional nursery meal, adding something more robust, £20), and champagne tea (£24). ⊠ *St. James's Restaurant, 4th fl., 181 Piccadilly, St. James's W1* ☎ *020/7734–8040* ⊟ *AE, DC, MC, V* ☉ *Tea Mon.–Sat. 3–5:45* Ⓤ *Green Park.*

✕ **Harrods.** The fourth-floor Georgian Restaurant at this ridiculously well-known department store has a high tea—£18.50, or £22.50 with a glass of champagne—that will give you a sugar rush for a week. ⊠ *Brompton Rd., Knightsbridge SW3* ☎ *020/7730–1234* ⊟ *AE, DC, MC, V* ☉ *Tea Mon.–Sun. 3:45–5:30* Ⓤ *Knightsbridge.*

✕ **The Ritz.** The huge, stagey, sometimes cold and overly formal Palm Court has tiered cake stands, silver pots, a harpist, and Louis XVI chaises, plus a great deal of rococo gilt and glitz, all for £27. Reserve at least four weeks ahead, more for weekends. ⊠ *150 Piccadilly, St. James's W1* ☎ *020/7493–8181* ⊟ *AE, DC, MC, V* ☉ *Tea daily 1:30–5:30* Ⓤ *Green Park.*

✕ **The Savoy.** The glamorous Thames-side hotel does one of the most pleasant teas (£24 or £27). Its triple-tiered cake stands are packed with goodies, and its tailcoated waiters are wonderfully polite. ⊠ *The Strand, Covent Garden WC2* ☎ *020/7836–4343* ⊟ *AE, DC, MC, V* ☉ *Tea daily 3–5:30* Ⓤ *Charing Cross.*

WHERE TO STAY

Staying at one of London's grand-dame hotels is the next best thing to—some say better than—being a guest at the palace. Royally resplendent furnishings set the tone, and armies of extra-solicitous staff are stuck in the pampering mode. Even in more affordable choices, classic British style brings you a taste of home, with tea-makers and pastel wallpapers. Still not cozy enough? Borrow some door keys, and be a bed-and-breakfast guest. Happily, there is no dearth of options where friendliness outdistances luxe. The latest trends are new hotels with chic, contemporary furnishings, cookie-cutter but convenient budget chain offerings in the heart of town, and new hotels in areas far outside the West End, Kensington, and Knightsbridge.

Where you stay can affect your experience. The West End is equivalent to downtown, but there's a big difference between, say, posh Park Lane and bustling, touristy Leicester Square. Hotels in Mayfair and St. James's are central and yet distant in both mileage and sensibility from funky, youthful neighborhoods such as Notting Hill and from major tourist sights such as the Tower of London, St. Paul's Cathedral, and the Kensington museums. On the edges of the West End, Soho and Covent Garden are crammed with eateries and entertainment options. South Kensington, Kensington, Chelsea, and Knightsbridge are patrician and peaceful, which will give you a more homey feeling than anything in the West End; Belgravia is super elegant. From Bloomsbury it's a stroll to the shops and restaurants of Covent Garden, to Theatreland, and to the British Museum; Hampstead and Islington are close enough to explore easily, too. Bayswater is an affordable haven north of Hyde Park. The South Bank, with all its cultural attractions, is another option.

Reservations

Wherever you decide to stay, be sure to reserve in advance. London is a popular city, and special events can fill hotel rooms suddenly. If you arrive in the capital without a room, the **London Tourist Board Information Centres** at Heathrow, Victoria Station Forecourt, and Waterloo International Terminal can help. **London Line** (☎ 09068/663344, calls cost 60p per minute) provides general advice 24 hours a day. The **VisitLondon Accommodation Booking Service** (☎ 020/7932–2020) is open weekdays 9–6, Saturday 10–2.

Prices

London is an expensive city, and in the £££££ category, you can often pay considerably more than £250 per room. In any event, you should confirm *exactly* what your room costs before checking in. British hotels are obliged by law to display a price chart at the reception desk; study it carefully. In January and February you'll often find reduced rates, and large hotels with a business clientele have frequent weekend packages. The usual practice these days in all but the cheaper hotels is for quoted prices to cover room alone; breakfast, whether Continental or "full English," costs extra. VAT (Value Added Tax—sales tax) follows the same rule, with the most expensive hotels excluding a hefty 17.5%, whereas middle-of-the-range and budget places include it in the initial quote.

WHAT IT COSTS In pounds				
£££££	**££££**	**£££**	**££**	**£**
For Two People over £250	£180–£250	£110–£180	£60–£110	under £60

Prices are for two people in a standard double room in high season, including VAT, with no meals or, if indicated, CP (with Continental breakfast), BP (Breakfast Plan, with full breakfast), or MAP (Modified American Plan, with breakfast and dinner).

Bayswater & Notting Hill

£££–££££   🏨 **Abbey Court.** Elegant and gracious, this small hotel occupies a white mansion in a quiet street off Notting Hill Gate. Abbey Court is deep in the era of Victoria—dark red wallpaper, Murano glass, gilt-framed mirrors, framed prints, mahogany, and plenty of antiques. The sitting room and the conservatory are lovely places to relax. Bathrooms look the part but are entirely modern: gray Italian marble, with brass fittings and whirlpool baths. ⊠ *20 Pembridge Gardens, Notting Hill W2 4DU* ☎ *020/7221–7518* 🖷 *020/7792–0858* ⊕ *www.abbeycourthotel.co.uk* ⇆ *19 rooms, 3 suites* ⚭ *Restaurant, room service, fans, in-room data ports, in-room safes, in-room hot tubs, cable TV, dry cleaning, laundry service, concierge, car rental, no-smoking rooms; no a/c* ☰ *AE, DC, MC, V* ⏃ *CP* Ⓤ *Notting Hill Gate.*

★ **£££–££££**   □ **Miller's Residence.** From the moment you are ushered up the winding staircase flanked by antiques and curios, you know this is a place where history is paramount. Jacobean, Victorian, Georgian, and Tudor antiques create a rich lesson in bygone days. Run by Martin Miller of the *Miller's Antique Price Guides,* this town house serves as his home, gallery, and B&B. Sip a complimentary evening cocktail in the long, candlelit drawing room with fireplace. The rooms are named for romantic poets. ⊠ *111a Westbourne Grove, Notting Hill W2 4UW* ☎ *020/ 7243–1024* ≜ *020/7243–1064* ⊕ *www.millersuk.com* ↩ *6 rooms, 2 suites* ⚹ *Dining room, fans, in-room data ports, some in-room faxes, lounge, dry cleaning, laundry service, concierge, Internet, meeting room; no a/c* ⊟ *AE, DC, MC, V* |⊙| *CP* Ⓤ *Notting Hill Gate.*

££   □ **Abbey House.** This pretty, white-stucco 1860 Victorian town house— once the home of a bishop and a member of Parliament before World War II—is in an excellent location close to trendy Notting Hill. You can spend the cash you save by staying here in the surrounding antiques shops. Rooms are spacious, with quads suitable for families, and have washbasins, but every room shares a bath with another. Note that there is no elevator. ⊠ *11 Vicarage Gate, Notting Hill W8 4AG* ☎ *020/ 7727–2594* ≜ *020/7727–1873* ⊕ *www.abbeyhousekensington.com* ↩ *16 rooms without bath* ⚹ *Lounge, concierge; no a/c, no room phones* ⊟ *No credit cards* |⊙| *BP* Ⓤ *High St. Kensington.*

££   □ **The Columbia.** The public rooms in these five adjoining Victorians are as big as museum halls. Some of the clean, high-ceiling bedrooms are very large (three to four beds) and have park views and balconies. Teak veneer, khaki-beige-brown color schemes, and avocado bathrooms dominate the design, but who expects Regency Revival at these prices? It's popular with tour groups. ⊠ *95–99 Lancaster Gate, Bayswater W2 3NS* ☎ *020/7402–0021* ≜ *020/7706–4691* ⊕ *www.columbiahotel.co.uk* ↩ *103 rooms* ⚹ *Restaurant, in-room safes, bar, lobby lounge, dry cleaning, laundry service, concierge, meeting room; no a/c* ⊟ *AE, MC, V* |⊙| *BP* Ⓤ *Lancaster Gate.*

££   □ **Vancouver Studios.** This little hotel is run like an apartment building: rooms are actually studios with kitchens, and the front door has a security entry system. Each studio has daily maid service as well as room service. Some rooms have working fireplaces, and there is a garden for guests to enjoy. ⊠ *30 Prince's Sq., Bayswater W2 4NJ* ☎ *020/7243–1270* ≜ *020/7221–8678* ⊕ *www.vancouverstudios.co.uk* ↩ *45 studios* ⚹ *Room service, in-room data ports, kitchens, microwaves, refrigerators, dry cleaning, laundry facilities, parking (fee); no a/c* ⊟ *AE, DC, MC, V* Ⓤ *Bayswater, Queensway.*

££   □ **The Vicarage.** Family-owned and set on a leaf-shaded street just off Kensington Church Street, the Vicarage occupies a large white Victorian house that is full of heavy and dark-stained wood furniture, patterned carpets, and brass pendant lights. All in all, this remains a charmer, but it's beginning to fray around the edges. A few doubles have their own showers. ⊠ *10 Vicarage Gate, Notting Hill W8 4AG* ☎ *020/ 7229–4030* ≜ *020/7792–5989* ⊕ *www.londonvicaragehotel.com* ↩ *14 rooms, 8 with bath* ⚹ *Lounge; no a/c, no room TVs* ⊟ *No credit cards* |⊙| *BP* Ⓤ *High St. Kensington.*

Bloomsbury, Covent Garden & Soho

£££££   □ **Covent Garden Hotel.** A former 1880s hospital in the midst of artsy,
Fodor'sChoice   boisterous Covent Garden, is now the London home-away-from-home
★   for a mélange of off-duty celebrities, actors, and style mavens. The public salons keep even the most picky happy: with painted silks, style *anglais* ottomans, and 19th-century romantic oils, they are perfect places

to decompress over sherry from the honesty bar. Stylish guest rooms show-case matching-but-mixed couture fabrics to stunning effect. ⊠ *10 Monmouth St., Covent Garden WC2H 9HB* ☎ *020/7806–1000* ⌨ *020/7806–1100* ⊕ *www.firmdale.com* ⤴ *55 rooms, 3 suites* ⚐ *Restaurant, room service, in-room data ports, some in-room faxes, in-room safes, minibars, cable TV, in-room VCRs, gym, massage, spa, cinema, library, baby-sitting, dry cleaning, laundry service, concierge, Internet, business services, meeting rooms, car rental* ⊟ *AE, MC, V* Ⓤ *Covent Garden.*

£££££ **Sanderson.** Sister to the St. Martins Lane hotel, this stylish urban oasis sits in the revamped box that was the Sanderson fabrics headquarters. From the Japanese garden to the billowy cloth that separates the bathrooms from the bedrooms, this hotel walks to the beat of its own whimsical drum. The furniture mixes French Louis XV and industrial, and bedrooms have sleigh beds. Some might find Agua (the "holistic bath house"), the in-room spa services, and the fitness classes just what the doctor ordered. Foodies favor the Spoon+ restaurant. ⊠ *50 Berners St., Soho W1T 3NG* ☎ *020/7300–1400* ⌨ *020/7300–1401* ⊕ *www.ianschragerhotels.com* ⤴ *150 rooms* ⚐ *Restaurant, room service, in-room data ports, some in-room faxes, in-room safes, minibars, cable TV, in-room VCRs, gym, massage, sauna, spa, billiards, 2 bars, lobby lounge, shop, baby-sitting, dry cleaning, laundry service, concierge, Internet, business services, meeting room, parking (fee), no-smoking rooms* ⊟ *AE, DC, MC, V* Ⓤ *Oxford Circus or Tottenham Court Rd.*

★ £££££ **The Savoy.** This grand hotel hosted Elizabeth Taylor's first honeymoon in one of its famous river-view rooms, and it poured one of Europe's first dry martinis in its equally famous American Bar, which is haunted by Ernest Hemingway, F. Scott Fitzgerald, and George Gershwin. Does it measure up to this high profile? Absolutely. The art deco rooms are especially fabulous, but all rooms are impeccably maintained, spacious, elegant, and comfortable. A room facing the Thames costs a fortune and requires an early booking, but it's worth it. Bathrooms have original fittings, with sunflower-size showerheads. Top-floor rooms are newer and less charming. ⊠ *The Strand, Covent Garden WC2R 0EU* ☎ *020/7836–4343* ⌨ *020/7240–6040* ⊕ *www.savoy-group.com* ⤴ *263 rooms, 19 suites* ⚐ *3 restaurants, room service, in-room data ports, in-room fax, in-room safes, minibars, cable TV with movies, in-room VCRs, indoor pool, gym, hair salon, sauna, spa, steam room, 2 bars, lobby lounge, theater, shop, baby-sitting, dry cleaning, laundry service, concierge, Internet, business services, meeting rooms, parking (fee), no-smoking rooms* ⊟ *AE, DC, MC, V* Ⓤ *Aldwych.*

££££ **Hazlitt's.** Three connected, early-18th-century houses, one of which was the last home of essayist William Hazlitt (1778–1830), make up this charming hotel. It's a disarmingly friendly place, full of personality but devoid of elevators. Robust antiques are everywhere, assorted prints crowd every wall, and every room has a Victorian claw-foot tub in its bathroom. There are tiny sitting rooms, wooden staircases, and, outside, more restaurants within strolling distance than you could patronize in a year. This is *the* London address of antiques dealers and theater and literary types. ⊠ *6 Frith St., Soho W1V 5TZ* ☎ *020/7434–1771* ⌨ *020/7439–1524* ⊕ *www.hazlittshotel.com* ⤴ *20 rooms, 3 suites* ⚐ *Room service, fans, in-room data ports, minibars, cable TV, in-room VCRs, dry cleaning, laundry service, concierge, Internet, meeting rooms, parking (fee), some pets allowed, no-smoking floors; no a/c in some rooms* ⊟ *AE, DC, MC, V* Ⓤ *Tottenham Court Rd.*

££££ **myhotel bloomsbury.** Before you arrive, you'll be asked to fill out a
preferences sheet so that your room will be just as you like it. If anything should go wrong, just contact your personal assistant for help. Rooms are minimalist, with wooden floors and simple color schemes;

Where to Stay in London

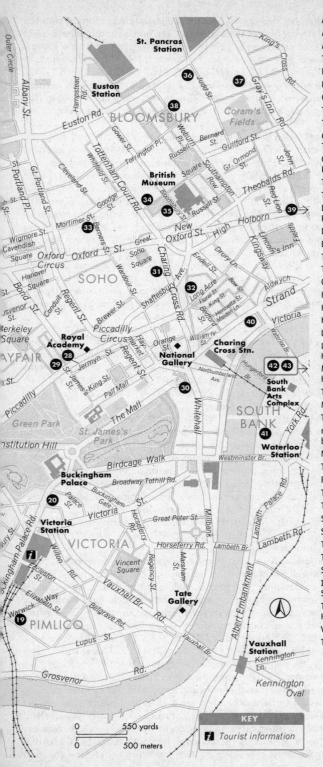

superior doubles are bigger and have separate sitting rooms. From the "jinja" spa to the library stocked with CDs, books, and free beverages, myhotel takes on the traveler who wants a hotel to be a new experience; its novel approach succeeds brilliantly. ⊠ *11–13 Bayley St., Bedford Sq., Bloomsbury WC1B 3HD* ☎ *020/7667–6000* 🖷 *020/7667–6001* ⊕ *www.myhotels.com* ↪ *76 rooms* ♿ *Restaurant, room service, in-room data ports, in-room safes, cable TV with movies, gym, massage, spa, bar, library, baby-sitting, concierge, business services, no-smoking floors* ⊟ *AE, DC, MC, V* Ⓤ *Tottenham Court Rd.*

££££ 🔲 **Trafalgar London Hilton.** Fresh and contemporary, this hotel defies the Hilton's norm. The rooms, in either sky blue or beige color schemes, keep many of the 19th-century office building's original features, and some have floor-to-ceiling windows with expansive views of Trafalgar Square. Twenty-one rooms are split-level, with upstairs space for chilling out with a CD or DVD and sleeping space below. Bathrooms take the cake with deep baths, full-size toiletries, eye masks, and mini-televisions. Go up to the roof garden for spectacular views of the Houses of Parliament, Westminster Abbey, and the British Airways London Eye. ⊠ *2 Spring Gardens, Covent Garden SW1A 2TS* ☎ *020/7870–2900* 🖷 *020/7870–2911* ⊕ *www.hilton.com* ↪ *127 rooms, 2 suites* ♿ *Restaurant, room service, in-room data ports, in-room safes, minibars, cable TV with movies and video games, bar, dry cleaning, laundry service, concierge, Internet, business services, meeting rooms, parking (fee), no-smoking floors* ⊟ *AE, DC, MC, V* Ⓤ *Charing Cross.*

££ 🔲 **Harlingford Hotel.** The Harlingford is by far the sleekest and most contemporary of the Cartwright Gardens hotels, which include the Crescent Hotel. Bold color schemes and beautifully tiled bathrooms make this family-run hotel a bargain for contemporary style. The quad rooms are an excellent choice for traveling families. ⊠ *61–63 Cartwright Gardens, Bloomsbury WC1H 9EL* ☎ *020/7387–1551* 🖷 *020/7383–4616* ⊕ *www.harlingfordhotel.com* ↪ *43 rooms* ♿ *Tennis court, lounge; no a/c* ⊟ *AE, DC, MC, V* ⦿ *BP* Ⓤ *Russell Sq.*

££ 🔲 **Morgan Hotel.** This is a Georgian row-house hotel, family-run with

Fodor'sChoice charm and panache. Rooms are small and functionally furnished, yet

★ friendly and cheerful. The apartments (in the £££ category) are particularly pleasing: three times the size of normal rooms, complete with kitchens and private phone lines. The tiny, paneled breakfast room is straight out of an 18th-century dollhouse. Back rooms overlook the British Museum. ⊠ *24 Bloomsbury St., Bloomsbury WC1B 3QJ* ☎ *020/ 7636–3735* 🖷 *020/7636–3045* ↪ *15 rooms, 5 apartments* ♿ *In-room safes, some refrigerators, cable TV* ⊟ *MC, V* ⦿ *BP* Ⓤ *Tottenham Court Rd. or Russell Sq.*

££ 🔲 **St. Margaret's.** A popular hotel near the British Museum, St. Margaret's has well-lit rooms with high ceilings, telephones, and TVs in a Georgian-era building. The friendly Italian family that runs the hotel is sure to welcome you by name if you stay long enough. Back rooms have garden views, and each room retains Georgian touches such as a fireplace and beautiful cornice moldings. ⊠ *26 Bedford Pl., Bloomsbury WC1B 5JL* ☎ *020/7636–4277* 🖷 *020/7323–3066* ⊕ *www. stmargaretshotel.co.uk* ↪ *64 rooms, 12 with bath* ♿ *Dining room, cable TV, lounge, no-smoking rooms; no a/c* ⊟ *MC, V* ⦿ *BP* Ⓤ *Russell Sq.*

£ 🔲 **The Generator.** Easily the grooviest youth hostel in town, this former police barracks has a friendly, funky, and international vibe. Talking Heads, the Internet café, provides handy maps and leaflets, plus a chance to get on-line. The Generator Bar has cheap drinks and a rowdy, young clientele, and the Fuel Stop cafeteria provides inexpensive meals. Rooms are designed on a prison-cell theme, complete with bunk beds and dim views. There are singles, doubles, and dormitory rooms (the cheapest option), each with a washbasin, locker, and free bed linen. ✉ *MacNaghten House, Compton Pl. off 37 Tavistock Pl., Bloomsbury WC1H 9SE* ☎ *020/7388–7666* 🖷 *020/7388–7644* ⊕ *www.generatorhostels.com* ⬄ *215 beds* ⌂ *Restaurant, fans, lobby lounge, pub, sports bar, recreation room, shop, concierge, Internet, meeting rooms, airport shuttle, travel services, parking (fee), no-smoking floors; no a/c, no room phones, no room TVs* ☱ *MC, V* ⭕ *BP* Ⓤ *Russell Sq.*

The City

£££££ 🏨 **Great Eastern.** Another style coup for designer and food maven Sir Terence Conran, this hotel is a sturdy pillar of the modern establishment, loaded with amenities. Choose among the five restaurants (serving sushi, fish, brasserie fare, pub grub, and haute cuisine), visit the florist, or browse in the Ren bath-products shop. Some rooms overlook Liverpool Street and Bishopsgate; others look inward to the stained-glass dome of the Aurora restaurant or the Gallery. All rooms modern and sleeke. ✉ *Liverpool St. at Bishopsgate, The City E2M 7QN* ☎ *020/7618–5010* 🖷 *020/7618–5011* ⊕ *www.great-eastern-hotel.co.uk* ⬄ *246 rooms, 21 suites* ⌂ *5 restaurants, room service, in-room data ports, some in-room faxes, in-room safes, minibars, cable TV with video games, in-room VCRs, gym, spa, bar, pub, library, baby-sitting, dry cleaning, laundry service, concierge, Internet, business services, meeting rooms, car rental, no-smoking rooms* ☱ *AE, DC, MC, V* Ⓤ *Liverpool St.*

Kensington & South Kensington

★ £££££ 🏨 **Blakes.** Designed by owner Anouska Hempel, Blakes is another world. Each room is a fantasy packed with precious Biedermeier, Murano glass, and modern pieces collected from all over the world. Cinematic mood lighting, with recessed halogen spots, compounds the impression that you, too, are a movie star in a big-budget biopic. The foyer sets the tone with piles of cushions, Phileas Fogg valises and trunks, black walls, rattan, and bamboo. ✉ *33 Roland Gardens, South Kensington SW7 3PF* ☎ *020/7370–6701* 🖷 *020/7373–0442* ⊕ *www.blakeshotels.com* ⬄ *38 rooms, 11 suites* ⌂ *Restaurant, room service, in-room data ports, some in-room faxes, in-room safes, minibars, cable TV, in-room VCRs, bar, baby-sitting, dry cleaning, laundry service, concierge, Internet, business services, meeting rooms, car rental, parking (fee); no a/c in some rooms* ☱ *AE, DC, MC, V* Ⓤ *S. Kensington.*

££££–£££££ 🏨 **The Pelham.** The second of Tim and Kit Kemp's gorgeous hotels is just like the Dorset Square, except that this one looks more like the country house to end all country houses. There's 18th-century pine paneling in the drawing room, flowers galore, quite a bit of glazed chintz and antique-lace bed linen, and the occasional four-poster bed and fireplace. The first-floor (American second-floor) suites are extra spacious, with high ceilings and chandeliers; some top-floor rooms under the eaves have sloping ceilings and casement windows. ✉ *15 Cromwell Pl., South Kensington SW7 2LA* ☎ *020/7589–8288* 🖷 *020/7584–8444* ⊕ *www.firmdale.com* ⬄ *51 rooms* ⌂ *Restaurant, room service, in-room data ports, some in-room safes, minibars, cable TV, in-room VCRs, bar, concierge, business services, meeting rooms, parking (fee)* ☱ *AE, MC, V* Ⓤ *S. Kensington.*

£££ 🏨 **Aster House.** Rooms in this delightful guest house are country casual. The friendly owners go out of their way to make you feel at home and answer questions. Breakfast is served in the airy, light conservatory, and the small garden at the back has a charming pond. Note that this is a five-story building with no elevator. Rooms have tea- and coffeemakers. ✉ *3 Sumner Pl., South Kensington SW7 3EE* ☎ *020/7581–5888*

🖼 020/7584–4925 ⊕ *www.welcome2london.com/asterhouse* ⊅ *14 rooms* ⚑ *Dining room, in-room safes, cable TV, lounge, Internet, no smoking* ⊟ *MC, V* 🍴 *BP* Ⓤ *S. Kensington.*

£££ 🖼 **The Gallery.** Across the street from its sister property, the Gainsborough hotel, the Gallery has a Victorian Arts and Crafts–style living room complete with a piano, lush carpets, cozy fires, and sturdy furniture. The rooms are a good size with solid, comfortable beds; bathrooms have London's ubiquitous polished granite. ⊠ *10 Queensberry Pl., South Kensington SW7 2E8* 🖼 *020/7915–0000; 800/270–9206 in U.S.* 🖼 *020/7915–4400* ⊕ *www.eeh.co.uk* ⊅ *34 rooms, 2 suites* ⚑ *Room service, in-room data ports, some in-room fax, in-room safes, some in-room hot tubs, some minibars, cable TV, bar, dry cleaning, laundry service, concierge, Internet, meeting rooms, airport shuttle; no a/c in some rooms* ⊟ *AE, DC, MC, V* 🍴 *BP* Ⓤ *S. Kensington.*

££ 🖼 **Swiss House Hotel.** Behind its ivy-and-flower-bedecked entrance, this is a sweet little guest house with a friendly proprietor. Dried flower arrangements, pine furniture, and simple dark blue rugs and throws make the rooms welcoming and soothing. Ask for a back room for a garden view. The triple and quad rooms, with more space and beds, are convenient for families. ⊠ *171 Old Brompton Rd., South Kensington SW5 OAN* 🖼 *020/7373–2769* 🖼 *020/7373–4983* ⊕ *www.swiss-hh.demon. co.uk* ⊅ *15 rooms, 1 without bath* ⚑ *Fans, baby-sitting, parking (fee), no-smoking rooms; no a/c* ⊟ *AE, DC, MC, V* 🍴 *CP* Ⓤ *Gloucester Rd.*

Knightsbridge, Chelsea & Belgravia

£££££ 🖼 **The Berkeley.** This luxury hotel mixes the old and the new in its modern building with a splendid penthouse swimming pool. The bedrooms either have swags of William Morris prints or are art deco. All have sitting areas, CD players, and big bathrooms with bidets. There are spectacular penthouse suites with their own conservatory terrace, and others with saunas or balconies. The posh, European-style restaurant, La Tante Claire, is wonderful. ⊠ *Wilton Pl., Belgravia SW1X 7RL* 🖼 *020/7235–6000; 800/637–2869 in U.S.* 🖼 *020/7235–4330* ⊕ *www.theberkeley.com* ⊅ *103 rooms, 55 suites* ⚑ *Restaurant, room service, in-room safes, in-room fax, some kitchens, minibars, cable TV, in-room VCRs, indoor-outdoor pool, gym, hair salon, massage, sauna, spa, Turkish bath, bar, cinema, baby-sitting, dry cleaning, laundry service, concierge, Internet, business services, meeting rooms, airport shuttle, car rental, parking (fee), no-smoking floors* ⊟ *AE, DC, MC, V* Ⓤ *Knightsbridge.*

★ £££££ 🖼 **Mandarin Oriental Hyde Park.** Stay here, and the three greats of Knightsbridge are on your doorstep—Hyde Park, Harrods, and Harvey Nichols. The Mandarin Oriental, built in 1880, is one of the poshest places to stay in London. Bedrooms are traditional Victorian with hidden high-tech gadgets and luxurious touches—potted orchids, chocolates, and fruit. The service here is legendary and includes butlers on every floor. Some rooms facing the park have balconies. Shopping, spa, and theater packages are available. ⊠ *66 Knightsbridge, Knightsbridge SW1X 7LA* 🖼 *020/7235–2000* 🖼 *020/7235–2001* ⊕ *www. mandarinoriental.com* ⊅ *177 rooms, 23 suites* ⚑ *2 restaurants, room service, in-room data ports, some in-room faxes, in-room safes, minibars, cable TV, in-room VCRs, gym, hot tub, massage, sauna, spa, steam room, bar, baby-sitting, dry cleaning, laundry service, concierge, Internet, business services, meeting rooms, airport shuttle, car rental, parking (fee), no-smoking rooms* ⊟ *AE, DC, MC, V* Ⓤ *Knightsbridge.*

££££ 🖼 **Knightsbridge Hotel.** Just off glamorous Knightsbridge in quiet Beaufort Gardens, this is Tim and Kit Kemp's—of Covent Garden Hotel, Charlotte Street, Dorset Square, and Pelham fame—newest property. The hotel succeeds in being cheap (relatively) and chic (enormously). The balconied suites and regular rooms benefit from CD players, writing desks, and large granite-and-oak bathrooms. The fully loaded honesty bar is an excellent place to unwind amid African sculptures and modern art. ⊠ *10 Beaufort Gardens, Knightsbridge SW3 1PT* ☎ *020/7584–6300; 800/ 553–6674 in U.S.* 🖷 *020/7584–6355* ⊕ *www.knightsbridgehotel.co.uk* ⪢ *42 rooms, 2 suites* ⬥ *Room service, in-room data ports, in-room safes, minibars, cable TV, some in-room VCRs, gym, bar, library, baby-sitting, dry cleaning, laundry service, concierge, Internet, meeting rooms, parking (fee)* ⊟ *AE, MC, V* ⦿ *CP* Ⓤ *Knightsbridge.*

£££–££££ ⊞ **The Sloane.** Many hotels use the word "unique" to describe their identical canopy beds or garden views, but the tiny Sloane really *is* unique. You can lie in your canopy bed, pick up the phone, and buy the bed–or any of the covetable Victorian antiques. No tacky price tags besmirch the gorgeous decor; instead, the staff maintains a price list. The roof terrace, which has garden furniture and a panoramic view of Chelsea, is a great spot. ⊠ *29 Draycott Pl., Chelsea SW3 2SH* ☎ *020/7581–5757* 🖷 *020/7584–1348* ⊕ *www.sloanehotel.com* ⪢ *14 rooms, 8 suites* ⬥ *Dining room, in-room data ports, in-room safes, cable TV, in-room VCRs, lobby lounge, dry cleaning, laundry service, concierge, business services, Internet, parking (fee)* ⊟ *AE, DC, MC, V* Ⓤ *Sloane Sq.*

★ £££ ⊞ **L'Hotel.** Rooms at this upscale B&B have an air of provincial France, with white bedcovers, pine furniture, and beige color schemes. Delicious breakfast croissants and baguettes are served in Le Metro cellar wine bar. It's like staying in a house—you're given your own front-door key, there's no elevator, and the staff leaves in the evening. Ask for a fire-place room: they're the biggest. All rooms have tea- and coffeemakers; some rooms have only handheld showerheads. You have access to the restaurant and concierge services of the plush Capital hotel, run by the same family, a few doors down the street. ⊠ *28 Basil St., Knights-bridge SW3 1AT* ☎ *020/7589–6286* 🖷 *020/7823–7826* ⊕ *www.lhotel. co.uk* ⪢ *11 rooms, 1 suite* ⬥ *Restaurant, fans, cable TV, in-room VCRs, bar, baby-sitting, dry cleaning, laundry service, concierge, park-ing (fee)* ⊟ *AE, V* ⦿ *CP* Ⓤ *Knightsbridge.*

£££ ⊞ **The Diplomat.** From its aristocratically elegant exterior, this hotel looks like a Cecil Beaton stage set: a Wedgwood-white "palazzo" ter-race house built by 19th-century architect Thomas Cubitt, a flatiron shape (it stands at the confluence of two streets), and decked with hanging pots of geraniums. It's the picture of Belgravian chic. Inside, the reception area gives way to a circular staircase lit by a Regency-era chandelier and topped with a winter-garden dome. Rooms are pleasantly decorated; some are large enough for families. Room service is available from 1 PM to 8:30 PM. ⊠ *2 Chesham St., Belgravia SW1X 8DT* ☎ *020/7235–1544* 🖷 *020/7259–6153* ⊕ *www.btinternet.com/~diplomat.hotel* ⪢ *26 rooms* ⬥ *Room service, fans, in-room data ports, in-room safes, some refrigerators, cable TV, lobby lounge, dry cleaning, laundry service, business services, airport shuttle, car rental; no a/c* ⊟ *AE, DC, MC, V* ⦿ *BP* Ⓤ *Sloane Sq. or Knightsbridge.*

Mayfair, Marylebone & St. James's

£££££ ⊞ **Brown's.** Founded in 1837 by Lord Byron's "gentleman's gentle-man," James Brown, this hotel made up of 11 Georgian town houses is patronized by many Anglophilic Americans—a habit that was estab-lished by the two Roosevelts. Bedrooms are thickly carpeted and have soft armchairs, brass chandeliers, and brocade wallpapers. The public rooms retain their cozy, oak-paneled, chintz-laden, grandfather-clock-ticking-in-the-parlor sensibility. In the Drawing Room, one of London's best-known afternoon teas is served. ✉ *34 Albemarle St., Mayfair W1X 4BT* ☎ *020/7493–6020* 🖶 *020/7493–9381* 🌐 *www. brownshotel.com* ⇆ *108 rooms, 10 suites* ⚭ *2 restaurants, room service, in-room data ports, in-room safes, minibars, cable TV, gym, bar, lounge, meeting rooms* 🚭 *AE, DC, MC, V* Ⓤ *Green Park.*

★ **£££££** 🏨 **Claridge's.** Stay here, and you're staying at a hotel legend (founded in 1812) with one of the world's classiest guest lists. The friendly, liveried staff is not in the least condescending, and the rooms are never less than luxurious. The bathrooms are spacious, as are the bedrooms (Victorian or art deco), with bells to summon a maid, waiter, or valet. Enjoy a cup of tea in the lounge, or retreat to the stylish bar for cocktails—or, better, to Gordon Ramsay's inimitable restaurant. The grand staircase and magnificent elevator complete with sofa and driver are equally glamorous. ✉ *Brook St., St. James's W1A 2JQ* ☎ *020/ 7629–8860; 800/637–2869 in U.S.* 🖶 *020/7499–2210* 🌐 *www.claridges. co.uk* ⇆ *203 rooms* ⚭ *Restaurant, in-room data ports, in-room fax, in-room safes, some in-room hot tubs, minibars, cable TV with movies, in-room VCRs, gym, hair salon, spa, bar, lobby lounge, shop, baby-sitting, dry cleaning, laundry service, concierge, Internet, business services, airport shuttle, car rental, parking (fee), meeting rooms, no-smoking rooms* 🚭 *AE, DC, MC, V* ⦿| *BP* Ⓤ *Bond St.*

★ **£££££** 🏨 **The Connaught.** Make reservations well in advance for this very exclusive small hotel—the most understated of any of London's grand hostelries, and the London base for those who have inherited the habit of staying here from their great-grandfathers. The bar and lounges have the air of an ambassadorial residence, an impression reinforced by the imposing oak staircase and dignified staff. Each bedroom has a foyer, antique furniture (if you don't like the desk, they'll change it), and fresh flowers. If you value privacy, discretion, and the kind of luxury that eschews flashiness, this is the place for you. ✉ *Carlos Pl., Mayfair W1K 6AL* ☎ *020/ 7499–7070* 🖶 *020/7495–3262* 🌐 *www.savoy-group.co.uk* ⇆ *75 rooms, 27 suites* ⚭ *2 restaurants, room service, in-room data ports, in-room fax, in-room safes, minibars, cable TV, gym, massage, 2 bars, lobby lounge, baby-sitting, dry cleaning, laundry service, concierge, Internet, business services, meeting rooms, airport shuttle, car rental, travel services, parking (fee), no-smoking rooms* 🚭 *AE, DC, MC, V* Ⓤ *Bond St.*

£££££
FodorśChoice
★

🏨 **The Dorchester.** No other hotel this opulent manages to be this charming. The glamour level is off the scale: 1,500 square yards of gold leaf and 1,100 square yards of marble. Bedrooms (some not as spacious as you might expect) have Irish-linen sheets on canopy beds, brocades and velvets, and Italian marble and etched-glass bathrooms with Floris toiletries. Furnishings are opulent English country-house style, with more than a hint of art deco, in keeping with the original 1930s building. You can take afternoon tea, drink, lounge, or pose in the catwalk-shape Promenade lounge. ✉ *Park La., Mayfair W1A 2HJ* ☎ *020/7629–8888* 🖶 *020/7409–0114* 🌐 *www.dorchesterhotel.com* ⇆ *195 rooms, 55 suites* ⚭ *3 restaurants, in-room data ports, in-room safes, minibars, cable TV with movies, in-room VCRs, gym, hair salon, health club, spa, hot tub, massage, sauna, steam room, bar, lobby lounge, nightclub, shop, baby-sitting, dry cleaning, laundry service, concierge, Internet, business services, meeting rooms, car rental, parking (fee), no-smoking rooms* 🚭 *AE, DC, MC, V* Ⓤ *Marble Arch or Hyde Park Corner.*

★ **£££££** 🏨 **The Metropolitan.** This supertrendy hotel is one of the only addresses for fashion, music, and media folk in London. Its Met bar has an exclusive guest list and is a hotel resident–only bar, and the restaurant is the famed Nobu, leased by Japanese wonder chef Nobu Matsuhisa. The lobby is sleek and postmodern, as are the bedrooms, which have identical minimalist taupe-and-white furnishings. The best rooms overlook Hyde Park, but all have a groovy minibar hiding the latest alcoholic and health-boosting beverages, as well as an emergency kit with aspirin. ⊠ *Old Park La., Mayfair W1K 1LB* ☎ *020/7447–1000; 800/337–4685 in U. S.* ☐ *020/7447–1100* ⊕ *www.metropolitan.co.uk* ↪ *137 rooms, 18 suites* ↻ *Restaurant, room service, in-room data ports, in-room fax, in-room safes, minibars, cable TV with movies and video games, some in-room VCRs, gym, massage, bar, shop, baby-sitting, dry cleaning, laundry service, concierge, Internet, business services, meeting room, parking (fee), no-smoking floors* ⊟ *AE, DC, MC, V* Ⓤ *Hyde Park Corner.*

£££££ ⬚ **The Ritz.** The name conjures the kind of Edwardian opulence associated with swagged curtains, handwoven carpets, and the smell of cigars, polish, and fresh lilies. The only thing that has been lost is a certain vein of moneyed naughtiness that someone like F. Scott Fitzgerald, at least, would have banked on. The bedrooms are bastions of pastel Louis XVI style with gilded furniture and crystal chandeliers. With a ratio of two staff to every bedroom, you're guaranteed personal service despite the massive size of the hotel. Formal dress is encouraged, and jeans are not allowed in public areas. ⊠ *150 Piccadilly, St. James's W1J 9BR* ☎ *020/ 7493–8181* ☐ *020/7493–2687* ⊕ *www.theritzhotel.co.uk* ↪ *133 rooms* ↻ *2 restaurants, room service, in-room data ports, some in-room faxes, in-room safes, cable TV, some in-room VCRs, gym, hair salon, bar, baby-sitting, dry cleaning, laundry service, concierge, Internet, business services, meeting rooms, car rental, parking (fee), no-smoking rooms* ⊟ *AE, DC, MC, V* Ⓤ *Piccadilly Circus.*

★
£££–£££££ ⬚ **Dorset Square Hotel.** This special boutique hotel off Baker Street was the first London address for husband and wife Tim and Kit Kemp, hoteliers extraordinaire. They decanted the English country look into a fine pair of Regency town houses. Everywhere you look are antiques, rich colors, and ideas *House & Garden* subscribers will steal. Every room is different, but the first-floor balconied "Coronet" rooms are the largest. The marble-and-mahogany bathrooms have power showers; glossy magazines and a half bottle of claret are complimentary. There's a reason for the ubiquitous cricket memorabilia: Dorset Square was the first Lord's cricket grounds. ⊠ *39–40 Dorset Sq., Marylebone NW1 6QN* ☎ *020/7723–7874* ☐ *020/7724–3328* ⊕ *www.firmdale.com* ↪ *38 rooms* ↻ *Restaurant, room service, minibars, cable TV, in-room VCRs, bar* ⊟ *AE, MC, V* Ⓤ *Baker St.*

£££ ⬚ **Durrants.** A hotel since the late 18th century, Durrants occupies a quiet corner almost next to the Wallace Collection, a stone's throw from Oxford Street and the smaller, posher shops of Marylebone High Street. It's a good value for the area, especially if you like the old English style, with wood paneling, leather armchairs, and dark-red patterned carpets. ⊠ *26–32 George St., Mayfair W1H 5BJ* ☎ *020/7935–8131* ☐ *020/ 7487–3510* ⊕ *www.durrantshotel.co.uk* ↪ *87 rooms, 5 suites* ↻ *Restaurant, dining room, room service, in-room data ports, cable TV, bar, baby-sitting, dry cleaning, laundry service, concierge, meeting rooms; no a/c in some rooms* ⊟ *AE, MC, V* Ⓤ *Bond St.*

£££ ⬚ **10 Manchester Street.** Tucked away on a quiet street between bustling Oxford Street and posh Marylebone High Street, "Number 10" promises no frills, good value, and high quality—and it delivers. The early-20th-century town house has been refurbished to a high standard. Simple, modern rooms have CD players with radios, trouser presses, and tea-and coffeemakers. The small doubles are indeed small, but for the price and location these no-frills rooms are great. ⊠ *10 Manchester St., Mayfair W1U 5DG* ☎ *020/7486–6669* ☐ *020/7224–0348* ⊕ *www.10manchesterstreet.com* ↪ *51 rooms* ↻ *Fans, in-room data ports, refrigerators,* cable TV, dry cleaning, concierge, Internet, no-smoking rooms; no a/c ▤ AE, MC, V ¶⊙¶ CP Ⓤ Baker St.

££ 🏨 **Edward Lear.** This family-run guest house, just a minute's walk from Oxford Street, is in a Georgian town house that was formerly the home of the master of nonsense verse, Edward Lear. Its location is the biggest selling point, as rooms tend to be small and the furnishings worn. The management is proud of the English breakfasts—it uses the same butcher as the Queen. ⊠ 28–30 Seymour St., Mayfair W1H 5WD ☎ 020/7402–5401 🖷 020/7706–3766 ⊕ www.edlear.com 🛏 31 rooms, 15 with shower (no toilet), 4 with full bath ↺ Cable TV, lounge, baby-sitting, Internet; no a/c ▤ MC, V ¶⊙¶ BP Ⓤ Marble Arch.

South Bank

££££ 🏨 **London Bridge Hotel.** Just steps away from the London Bridge rail and tube station, this thoroughly modern, stylish hotel is popular with business travelers. Most of the South Bank's attractions are within walking distance. Each sleek room is decorated in understated, contemporary style. Two-bedroom apartments (£££££) come with kitchen, living room, and dining room. Foodies will want to stop in at the delightful Borough Market, open Fridays and Saturdays, just across the street. ⊠ 8–18 London Bridge St., South Bank SE1 9SG ☎ 020/7855–2200 🖷 020/7855–2233 ⊕ www.london-bridge-hotel.co.uk 🛏 138 rooms, 3 apartments ↺ Restaurant, room service, in-room data ports, in-room safes, some kitchens, minibars, cable TV with movies, gym, sauna, bar, lobby lounge, dry cleaning, laundry service, concierge, meeting rooms, parking (fee); no-smoking floors ▤ AE, DC, MC, V Ⓤ London Bridge.

££ 🏨 **County Hall Travel Inn Capital.** Don't get too excited—this neighbor of the fancy Marriott lacks the river view (it's at the back of the grand former seat of local government). Still you get an incredible value, with the standard facilities of the cookie-cutter rooms of this chain. Best of all for families on a budget are the foldout beds that let you accommodate two kids at no extra charge. That's a bargain. ⊠ Belvedere Rd., South Bank SE1 7PB ☎ 0870/238–3300 🖷 020/7902–1619 ⊕ www.travelinn.co.uk 🛏 313 rooms ↺ Restaurant, coffee shop, fans, in-room data ports, bar, business services, meeting rooms, parking (fee), no-smoking floors ▤ AE, DC, MC, V Ⓤ Westminster.

Fodor'sChoice ★

££ 🏨 **Premier Lodge South Bank.** Practically riverside, this branch of the chain has an excellent location across the cobbled road from Vinopolis, a wine center. Rooms have desks, tea- and coffeemakers, and the chain's signature 6-foot-wide beds (really two zipped together). Family rooms can accommodate four people. The nautical Anchor restaurant and pub is adjacent to the hotel. ⊠ 34 Park St., South Bank SE1 9EF ☎ 0870/700–456 🖷 0870/700–1456 ⊕ www.premierlodge.co.uk 🛏 56 rooms ↺ In-room data ports, cable TV, parking (fee), no-smoking rooms ▤ AE, DC, MC, V Ⓤ London Bridge.

Westminster & Victoria

£££££ 🏨 **The Rubens at the Palace.** This hotel likes to say it treats you like royalty. In fact you're only a stone's throw from the real thing, because Buckingham Palace is just across the road. The elegant Rubens, which looks out over the Royal Mews, provides the sort of deep comfort needed to soothe away a hard day's sightseeing, with cushy armchairs crying out for you to sink into them with a cup of Earl Grey. With decent-size rooms—furnished nicely if not quite like the ones at the palace—and a location that couldn't be more central, this hotel is a favorite for many travelers. ⊠ 39 Buckingham Palace Rd., Westminster SW1W OPS

☎ 020/7834–6600 ⊟ 020/7233–6037 ⊕ *www.rubenshotel.com* ⊷ *160 rooms, 13 suites* ⬧ *2 restaurants, room service, in-room data ports, some in-room fax, in-room safes, some minibars, cable TV with movies, some in-room VCRs, lobby lounge, piano bar, baby-sitting, dry cleaning, laundry service, concierge, Internet, business services, meeting rooms, parking (fee), no-smoking floors* ⊟ *AE, DC, MC, V* Ⓤ *Victoria.*

££   ⊡ **New England Hotel.** Family-run, this guest house in a 19th-century town
FodorsChoice house is a find. The power showers, comfortable beds, and electronic
★ key cards are unexpected in this price category. There is nothing trend-
setting about the interior, but the plaid-and-floral motif is as welcoming as the staff. ⊠ *20 Saint George's Dr., Victoria SW1V 4BN* ☎ *020/
7834–8351* ⊟ *020/7834–9000* ⊕ *www.newenglandhotel.com* ⊷ *25
rooms* ⬧ *Fans, in-room data ports, cable TV, parking (fee), no-smok-
ing floors; no a/c* ⊟ *AE, DC, MC, V* ⦿*| BP* Ⓤ *Victoria.*

NIGHTLIFE & THE ARTS

There isn't a single London nightlife or arts scene but an infinite variety of them. As long as audiences exist for Feydeau revivals, drag queens,
teenage rock bands, hit musicals, body-painted dancers, and improvised
stand-up comedy, someone will find a space or stage for them in London. Admission prices are not always bargain basement, but when you
consider how much a London hotel room costs, the city's arts and
nightlife diversions are a bargain.

Nightlife

London is one of the party capitals of Europe. Despite draconian liquor
laws and the inconvenience of tubes that stop running around midnight,
Londoners still go out every night. The restrictions on late-night drinking have relaxed in the past few years, however, and are set to become
even more liberal. There are already a staggering number of places with
late licenses where you can party after 11 PM when the neighborhood
pubs close their doors.

In one night, whether you're in the West End, trendier-than-thou East
London, or racially diverse Brixton, you can drop into half a dozen bars
and in each one find a completely unique world. Ultraswank hotel bars,
wine-soaked experimental jazz clubs, industrial microbreweries, and Asian-
themed cocktail bars are just a few of the choices. Once 2 AM arrives,
much of the bar scene moves on to the clubs, where you can dance until
9 AM to any kind of music.

Bars

★ **American Bar.** Festooned with club ties, signed celebrity photographs, and
baseball caps, this sensational bar rakes in praise for its martinis and cocktails. ⊠ *Stafford Hotel, 16–18 St. James's Pl., St. James's SW1A* ☎ *020/
7493–0111* ◷ *Weekdays 11:30 AM–midnight, Sat. 11:30 AM–3 PM and
5:30–midnight, Sun. noon–2:30 PM and 6:30–10:30* Ⓤ *Green Park.*

Atlantic Bar. A marble staircase spirals dramatically into this glamorous
art deco bar. The original furnishings are intact, and the impeccable service, the superb cocktails, and Oliver Peyton's excellent restaurant keep
pulling in the crowds. ⊠ *20 Glasshouse St., Soho W1* ☎ *020/7734–4888
◷ Weekdays noon–3 AM, Sat. 5 PM–3 AM* Ⓤ *Piccadilly Circus.*

★ **Che.** Occupying a stylish former bank building with high ceilings, suede
walls, leather banquettes, and Che Guevara portraits, this colorful back-
lit bar claims to have the largest range of spirits in Europe. Cuba's finest
are available in the subdued cigar lounge. ⊠ *23 St. James's St., St. James's
SW1* ☎ *020/777–9380* ◷ *Mon.–Sat. 11–11* Ⓤ *Green Park.*

Hoxton Square Bar & Kitchen. The rectangular concrete bar, reminiscent of an airport hangar, has long, comfortable sofas, a plate-glass window at the back, and tables overlooking leafy Hoxton Square. The vibe is less pretentious than at neighboring bars, and creative types keep it packed. ⊠ *2–4 Hoxton Sq., Islington E1* ☎ *020/7613–0709* ◷ *Mon.–Sat. 11:30 AM–midnight, Sun. 11:30–10:30* Ⓤ *Old St.*

Opium. Fashionable young things sip exotic cocktails amid the trappings of the East. Amber light, delicate wooden carvings, and small alcoves dripping in velvet and gold re-create French colonial Vietnam. The cocktails are impressive and pricey, as is the nouvelle Vietnamese cuisine. ⊠ *1 Dean St., Soho W1* ☎ *020/7287–9608* ◷ *Weekdays 5 PM–3 AM, Sat. 7:30 PM–3 AM* Ⓤ *Tottenham Court Rd.*

Comedy

Comedy Store. At what is known as the birthplace of alternative comedy, Britain's funniest stand-ups have cut their teeth before being launched onto prime-time TV. Weekends have up-and-coming comedians performing on the same stage as established talent. ⊠ *1A Oxendon St., Soho SW1* ☎ *020/7344–0234* 🎫 *£12–£18* ◷ *Shows Tues.–Thurs. and Sun. 8 PM–10:15 PM, Fri. and Sat. 8 PM–10:15 PM and midnight–2:30 AM* Ⓤ *Piccadilly Circus or Leicester Sq.*

Dance Clubs

The End. Top-name DJs, a state-of-the-art sound system, and minimalist steel-and-glass decor—clubbing doesn't get much better than this. Next door, the aka Bar (owned by the same people) is a stylish split-level Manhattan-esque cocktail bar with excellent food and a movie theater. ⊠ *16A West Central St., Holborn WC1* ☎ *020/7419–9199* 🎫 *£4–£15* ◷ *Mon. 10 PM–3 AM, Thurs. 9 PM–4 AM, Fri. 10 PM–4 AM, Sat. 10 PM–7 AM; also some Sun.* Ⓤ *Tottenham Court Rd.*

★ **Fabric.** This sprawling subterranean club has been *the* place to be for the past few years. *Fabric Live* hosts hip-hop crews and live acts on Fridays, and big-name international DJs play slow bass lines and cutting-edge music on Saturdays. Sunday is Polysexual Night. Arrive early to avoid a lengthy line, and don't wear a suit. ⊠ *77A Charterhouse St., East End EC1* ☎ *020/7336–8898* 🎫 *£12–£15* ◷ *Fri. and Sun. 10 PM–5 AM, Sat. 10 PM–7 AM* Ⓤ *Farringdon.*

Hanover Grand. A former Masonic Hall is now an extravagant and opulent West End club, popular with a glamorous, glitzy crowd. There is an elaborate sound-and-light show and a large dance floor. Glam disco and chart-bound house and garage nights attract long lines, so dress up to impress the bouncers. ⊠ *6 Hanover St., Mayfair W1* ☎ *020/7499–7977* 🎫 *£5–£15* ◷ *Wed. 10:30 PM–3:30 AM, Thurs. and Fri. 10:30 PM–4 AM, Sat. 10:30 PM–5 AM* Ⓤ *Oxford Circus.*

Eclectic Music

The Borderline. This important small venue has a solid reputation for booking everything from metal to country and beyond. Oasis, Pearl Jam, Blur, Sheryl Crow, PJ Harvey, Jeff Buckley, and Counting Crows have all played here. ⊠ *Orange Yard off Manette St., Soho W1* ☎ *020/7395–0777* 🎫 *£6–£15* ◷ *Mon.–Sat. 8 PM–11 PM* Ⓤ *Tottenham Court Rd.*

Brixton Academy. This legendary Brixton venue has seen it all—mods and rockers, hippies and punks. Despite a capacity of 4,000 people, this refurbished Victorian hall with original art deco fixtures retains a club-like charm; it has plenty of bars, and upstairs seating. ⊠ *211 Stockwell Rd., Brixton SW9* ☎ *0870/771–2000* 🎫 *£10–£20* Ⓤ *Brixton.*

Union Chapel. Excellent acoustics and sublime architecture distinguish this beautiful old chapel. The world fusion music program has hosted performances by Bjork, Talvin Singh, Goldfrapp, and Tori Amos.

✉ *Compton Ave., Islington N1* ☎ *020/7226–1686 or 0870/120–1349*
🎫 *Free–£15* Ⓤ *Highbury, Islington.*

Jazz

★ **Jazz Café.** A palace of high-tech cool remains an essential hangout for fans of both the mainstream end of the repertoire and hip-hop, funk, rap, and Latin fusion. Book ahead for a prime table overlooking the stage, in the balcony restaurant. ✉ *5 Parkway, Camden Town NW1* ☎ *020/ 7916–6060 or 020/7344–0044* 🎫 *£6–£20* ☼ *Mon.–Thurs. 7 PM–1 AM, Fri. and Sat. 7 PM–2 AM, Sun. 7 PM–midnight* Ⓤ *Camden Town.*

Pizza Express. The capital's best-loved pizza chain is also a principal jazz club. The darkly lit Soho venue hosts top-quality international jazz acts every night except Mondays, and eight other branches also have live music. ✉ *10 Dean St., Soho W1* ☎ *020/7437–9595 or 020/7439–8722* 🎫 *£10–£20* ☼ *From 11:30 AM for food; music nightly 9 PM–midnight* Ⓤ *Tottenham Court Rd.*

Ronnie Scott's. Since the '60s, this legendary jazz club has attracted big names. It's usually crowded and hot, the food isn't great, and service is slow—but the atmosphere can't be beat, even since the sad departure of its eponymous founder and saxophonist. Reservations are recommended. ✉ *47 Frith St., Soho W1* ☎ *020/7439–0747* 🎫 *£15–£25 nonmembers, £5–£10 members, annual membership £60* ☼ *Mon.–Sat. 8:30 PM–3 AM, Sun. 7:30 PM–11 PM* Ⓤ *Leicester Sq.*

Rock

Barfly Club. At one of the finest small clubs in the capital, punk, indie guitar bands, and new metal rock attract a nonmainstream crowd. Weekend club nights at the Club Monarch, upstairs, host DJs who rock the decks. ✉ *49 Chalk Farm Rd., Camden Town NW1* ☎ *020/7691–4246* 🎫 *£6* ☼ *Mon.–Thurs. 7:30 PM–midnight, Fri. and Sat. 8 PM–2 AM, Sun. 7:30 PM–11 PM* Ⓤ *Camden Town, Chalk Farm.*

Forum. The best medium-to-big-name rock performers consistently play at this 2,000-capacity club, a converted 1920 art deco movie theater, with a balcony overlooking the dance floor. Saturday club night, "House of Fun," focuses on '70s and '80s nostalgia. ✉ *9–17 Highgate Rd., Kentish Town NW5* ☎ *020/7284–1001* 🎫 *£10–£15* ☼ *Most nights 7–11, Sat. until 2 AM* Ⓤ *Kentish Town.*

The Arts

Whether you prefer your art classical or modern, or as a contemporary twist on a time-honored classic, you'll find that London's arts scene pushes the boundaries. Celebrity divas sing original-language librettos at the Royal Opera House, whereas the Almeida Opera focuses on radical productions of new opera and musical theater. Shakespeare's plays are brought to life at the reconstructed Globe Theatre, and challenging new writing is produced at the Royal Court.

To find out what's showing during your stay, the weekly magazine *Time Out* (it comes out every Tuesday) is an invaluable resource. The *Evening Standard,* especially the Thursday edition, also carries listings, as do the "quality" Sunday papers and the Saturday *Independent, Guardian,* and *Times.* You'll find leaflets and fliers in most cinema and theater foyers, and you can pick up the free bimonthly *London Theatre Guide* leaflet from most hotels and tourist information centers.

Classical Music

It's possible to hear first-rank musicians in outstanding venues almost every day of the year. The London Symphony Orchestra is in residence at the Barbican Centre, although other top orchestras—including the

Philharmonia and the Royal Philharmonic—also perform here. The Barbican also hosts chamber music concerts with such celebrated orchestras as the City of London Sinfonia. Wigmore Hall, a lovely venue for chamber music, is renowned for its recitals by up-and-coming young instrumentalists. The South Bank Centre has an impressive international music season, held in the Royal Festival Hall (one of the finest concert halls in Europe), the Queen Elizabeth Hall, and the small Purcell Room. Full houses are rare, so even at the biggest concert halls you should be able to get a ticket for £12–£45. If you can't book in advance, arrive at the hall an hour before the performance for a chance at returns.

Lunchtime concerts take place in smaller concert halls, the big arts-center foyers, and churches. They usually cost less than £5 or are free, and will showcase string quartets, singers, jazz ensembles, or gospel choirs. St. John's in Smith Square and St. Martin-in-the-Fields are popular locations. Performances usually begin about 1 PM and last one hour.

A great British tradition, the **Henry Wood Promenade Concerts** (known more commonly as the "Proms") lasts eight weeks, from July to September, at the Royal Albert Hall. It's renowned for its last night, a madly jingoistic display of singing "Land of Hope and Glory," Union Jack waving, and general madness. Demand for tickets is so high you must enter a lottery. For regular Proms, where the best music is heard, tickets run £4–£30, with hundreds of standing tickets for £4 available at the hall on the night of the concert. The last night is broadcast in Hyde Park on a jumbo screen, but even here a seat on the grass requires a paid ticket.

Kenwood House. Concerts are held in the grassy amphitheater in front of Kenwood House on Saturday evening from July to early September. ⊠ *Hampstead Heath, Hampstead* ☎ *020/7973–3427.*
Royal Albert Hall. Built in 1871, this splendid iron-and-glass domed auditorium hosts a varied music program, including Europe's most democratic music festival, the Henry Wood Promenade Concerts—the Proms. ⊠ *Kensington Gore, Kensington SW7* ☎ *020/7589–4185; 020/ 7589–8212 information about Proms concerts* Ⓤ *S. Kensington.*
St. John's in Smith Square. This baroque church behind Westminster Abbey presents chamber music and solo recitals. ⊠ *Smith Sq., Westminster W1* ☎ *020/7222–1061* Ⓤ *Westminster.*
St. Martin-in-the-Fields. Free lunchtime concerts are held in this lovely 1726 church. ⊠ *Trafalgar Sq., Covent Garden WC2* ☎ *020/7839–1930* Ⓤ *Charing Cross.*
South Bank Centre. The Royal Festival Hall hosts large-scale choral and orchestral works, the Queen Elizabeth Hall hosts chamber orchestras and A-list soloists, and the Purcell Room has chamber music and recitals. ⊠ *South Bank, SE1* ☎ *020/7960–4242* Ⓤ *Waterloo.*
★ **Wigmore Hall.** Hear chamber music and recitals in this hall with near perfect acoustics. Don't miss the midmorning Sunday concerts. ⊠ *36 Wigmore St., Marylebone W1* ☎ *020/7935–2141* Ⓤ *Bond St.*

Contemporary Art

For centuries, Britain has accumulated extraordinary collections of art in national institutions such as the National Gallery, National Portrait Gallery, the Tate, and the Victoria & Albert Museum. No less high profile is London's contemporary art scene, displayed in publicly funded exhibition spaces such as the Barbican Gallery, Hayward Gallery, Institute of Contemporary Arts, Serpentine Gallery, and Whitechapel Art Gallery. And with the arrival of the Tate Modern, London has a flagship modern art gallery. Since the early 1990s, the contemporary art scene here has exploded, and Young British Artists (YBA)—Damien Hirst,

Tracey Emin, Gary Hume, Rachel Whiteread, Jake and Dinos Chapman, Sarah Lucas, Gavin Turk, Steve McQueen, and others—have made London one of the most dynamic spots for contemporary art in the world.

In addition to the trendy, Arts Council–funded scene, hundreds of other small galleries exist all over London. Check the weekly listings for details. Expect to pay around £8 for entry into touring exhibitions, but most permanent displays and commercial galleries are free.

Barbican Centre. Innovative exhibitions of 20th-century and current art and design are presented here. ⊠ *Silk St., The City EC2* ☎ *020/7638–8891* 🖭 *£5–£7* 🕙 *Mon. and Tues. and Thurs.–Sat. 10–6, Wed. 10–9, Sun. noon–6* Ⓤ *Barbican.*

Hayward Gallery. This example of 1960s brutalist architecture is one of London's major venues for touring exhibitions. ⊠ *South Bank Centre, Belvedere Rd., South Bank SE1* ☎ *020/7960–5226* 🖭 *Varies by exhibition* 🕙 *Thurs.–Mon. 10–6, Tues. and Wed. 10– 8* Ⓤ *Waterloo.*

Institute of Contemporary Arts. Visual art, contemporary drama, film, new media, literature, and photography are the focus at this center in a Regency terrace. ⊠ *The Mall, 12 Carlton House Terr., St. James's SW1* ☎ *020/7930–3647 or 020/7930–0493* 🖭 *Weekdays £1.50, weekends £2.50* 🕙 *Daily noon–7:30* Ⓤ *Charing Cross.*

Lisson. This respected gallery represents more than 40 blue-chip artists. ⊠ *52–54 Bell St., Marylebone NW1* ☎ *020/7724–2739* 🖭 *Free* 🕙 *Weekdays 10–6, Sat. 10–5* Ⓤ *Edgware Rd.*

Photographer's Gallery. Cutting-edge photography is the draw at this distinguished gallery. ⊠ *5 & 8 Great Newport St., Covent Garden WC2* ☎ *020/7831–1772* 🖭 *Free* 🕙 *Mon.–Sat. 11 –6, Sun. noon–6* Ⓤ *Leicester Sq.*

Saatchi Gallery. This headline-grabbing gallery favors high-profile, provocative modern art. ⊠ *County Hall, South Bank SE1* ☎ *020/ 7823–2363* 🖭 *£5* 🕙 *Daily 10–10* Ⓤ *Waterloo.*

Serpentine Gallery. A tea pavilion in Kensington Gardens houses a gallery that has earned a reputation for exhibitions of modern and contemporary art. ⊠ *Kensington Gardens, South Kensington W2* ☎ *020/ 7402–6075* 🖭 *Donation* 🕙 *Daily 10–6* Ⓤ *S. Kensington.*

Tate Modern. This converted power station is the largest modern art gallery in the world. ⊠ *25 Summer St., South Bank SE1* ☎ *020/7887–8008* 🖭 *Free–£8.50* 🕙 *Sun.–Thurs. 10–6, Fri. and Sat. 10–10* Ⓤ *Southwark.*

★ **Whitechapel Art Gallery.** Established in 1897, this independent East End gallery is one of London's most innovative. ⊠ *80–82 Whitechapel High St., East End E1* 🖭 *Free* 🕙 *Tues., Thurs., and Fri. 11–5, Wed. 11–8, weekends 11–6* Ⓤ *Aldgate E.*

White Cube. Jay Joplin's influential gallery is in a 1920s light industrial building on trendy Hoxton Square. ⊠ *48 Hoxton Sq., East End N1* ☎ *020/ 7930–5357* 🖭 *Free* 🕙 *Tues.–Sat. 10 AM–6 PM* Ⓤ *Old St.*

Dance

The **English National Ballet** and visiting international companies usually perform at the London Coliseum; because of renovations, these companies will use the Hammersmith Apollo and Sadler's Wells until February 2004. The **Royal Ballet,** world renowned for its classical excellence, as well as innovative contemporary dance from several companies and scores of independent choreographers, can be seen at the Royal Opera House. **Royal Festival Hall** in the South Bank Centre has a fine contemporary dance program that hosts top international companies and British choreographers. **The Place** presents the most daring, cutting-edge

★ dance performances. **Sadler's Wells** hosts ballet companies and regional and international modern dance troupes. The biggest annual event,

Dance Umbrella (☎ 020/874–5881 ⊕ www.danceumbrella.co.uk), a six-week season in October and November, showcases international and British-based artists at various venues across the city.

DANCE BOX
OFFICES **London Coliseum** (✉ St. Martin's La., Covent Garden WC2N ☎ 020/7632–8300 Ⓤ Leicester Sq.).

The Place (✉ 17 Duke's Rd., Bloomsbury WC1 ☎ 020/7380–1268 Ⓤ Euston).

South Bank Centre (✉ Belvedere Rd., South Bank SE1 ☎ 020/7960–4242 Ⓤ Embankment, Waterloo).

Royal Opera House (✉ Bow St., Covent Garden WC2 ☎ 020/7304–4000 Ⓤ Covent Garden).

Sadler's Wells (✉ Rosebery Ave., Islington EC1 ☎ 020/7863–8000 Ⓤ Angel).

Film

There are many lovely movie theaters in London and several that are committed to nonmainstream cinema, in particular, the National Film Theatre. West End movie theaters continue to do good business. Most of the major houses (Odeon Leicester Square and UCI Empire) are in the Leicester Square–Piccadilly Circus area, where tickets average £8. Mondays and matinees are often cheaper, at around £5, and crowds are smaller. Check out *Time Out* or *The Guardian*'s "Guide section" (free with the paper on Saturdays) for listings.

National Film Theatre. The NFT's three theaters show more than 2,000 titles each year, including foreign-language films, documentaries, cult Hollywood features, and animation. The Regus London Film Festival, held in November, is based here. ✉ *South Bank Centre, Belvedere Rd., South Bank SE1* ☎ *020/7633–0274 information; 020/7928–3232 box office* Ⓤ *Waterloo.*

Opera

The two key players in London's opera scene are the Royal Opera (which ranks with the Metropolitan Opera in New York) and the more innovative English National Opera (ENO), which presents English-language productions at the London Coliseum (at the Barbican until February 2004, because of renovation at the Coliseum). Only the Theatre Royal, Drury Lane, has a longer theatrical history than the Royal Opera House, and the current theater—the third to be built on the site since 1858—completed a monumental renovation in 1999. The new building has been well received, especially the restored Victorian auditorium and the Floral Hall foyer, which beautifully integrates with the Covent Garden Piazza.

The Royal Opera House struggles to shrug off its reputation for elitism and mismanagement. Ticket prices go up to £150. Since the renovation, it has, however, made good on its promise to be more accessible—the cheapest tickets are just £3 (for a matinee). Conditions of purchase vary; call for information. Prices for ENO are generally lower, ranging from £5 to £55. ENO sells same-day balcony seats for as little as £2.50.

Almeida Opera and BAC Opera (at the Battersea Arts Centre) produce festivals that showcase new opera and cutting-edge music theater. During the summer months, Holland Park Opera presents the usual chestnuts in the open-air theater of leafy Holland Park.

OPERA BOX
OFFICES **Almeida Theatre** (✉ Almeida St., Islington N1 ☎ 020/7359–4404 Ⓤ Angel or Highbury & Islington).

BAC Opera (✉ Lavender Hill, Battersea SW11 ☎ 020/7223–2223 Ⓤ Clapham Junction).

English National Opera (✉ London Coliseum, St. Martin's La., Covent Garden WC2 ☎ 020/7632–8300 Ⓤ Leicester Sq.).
Holland Park Opera (✉ Holland Park, Kensington High St., Kensington W8 ☎ 020/7602–7856 Ⓤ Covent Garden).
★ **Royal Opera House** (✉ Bow St., Covent Garden WC2 ☎ 020/7304–4000 Ⓤ Covent Garden).

Theater

One of the special experiences the city has to offer is great theater. London's theater scene consists, broadly, of the state-subsidized companies, the Royal National Theatre and the Royal Shakespeare Company; the commercial West End, equivalent to Broadway; and the Fringe—small, experimental companies. Another category could be added: known in the weekly listings magazine *Time Out* as Off-West End, these are shows staged at the longer-established fringe theaters. Most of the West End theaters are in the neighborhood nicknamed Theatreland, around the Strand and Shaftesbury Avenue.

The Royal Shakespeare Company and the Royal National Theatre Company often stage contemporary versions of the classics. The Almeida, Battersea Arts Centre (BAC), Donmar Warehouse, Royal Court Theatre, Soho Theatre, and the Young Vic attract famous actors and have excellent reputations for new writing and innovative theater. These are the places that shape the theater of the future, the venues where you'll see an original production before it becomes a (more expensive) hit in the West End. From mid-May through mid-September you can see the Bard served up at the open-air reconstruction of Shakespeare's Globe Theatre on the South Bank.

Theatergoing isn't cheap. Tickets under £10 are a rarity; in the West End you should expect to pay from £15 for a seat in the upper balcony to at least £25 for a good one in the stalls (orchestra) or dress circle (mezzanine). However, much of London theater has struggled because the number of U.S. visitors to London has declined since 2001, and you may find some good deals. Tickets may be booked at the individual theater box offices or over the phone by credit card; most theaters still don't charge a fee for the latter. You can also book through ticket agents or go to the theater box office, as the vast majority of theaters have some tickets (returns and house seats) available on the night of performance. All the larger hotels offer theater bookings, but they tack on a hefty service charge. Fringe tickets are always considerably less expensive than tickets for West End productions.

Warning: Be *very* careful of scalpers and unscrupulous ticket agents outside theaters and in the line at tkts, the discount ticket booth. They will try to sell tickets at five times the price of the ticket at legitimate box offices, and you'll pay a stiff fine if caught buying a scalped ticket.

Edwards & Edwards (✉ 1 Times Sq. Plaza, 12th fl., New York, NY 10036 ☎ 800/223–6108 ⊕ www.globaltickets.com) sells tickets from its U.S. office. **First Call** (☎ 020/7420–0000 ⊕ www.firstcalltickets.com) sells theater tickets. **Keith Prowse** (✉ 234 W. 44th St., Suite 1000, New York, NY 10036 ☎ 212/398–1430 or 800/669–8687) can book London tickets in the U.S. **Ticketmaster** (☎ 020/7344–0055; 800/775–2525 in U.S. ⊕ www.ticketmaster.com) sells tickets to various theaters.

The **Society of London Theatre** (✉ 32 Rose St., Covent Garden, London WC2 E9E5 ☎ 020/7557–6700 ⊕ www.officiallondontheatre.co.uk) operates tkts, the half-price ticket booth (no phone) on the southwest corner of Leicester Square, and sells the best available seats to performances at about 25 theaters. It's open Monday–Saturday 10–7, Sunday noon–3; there's a £2 service charge. All major credit cards are accepted. The society has good information about theatrical events.

SELECTED
THEATERS

Almeida. Hollywood stars often perform at this Off-West End venue that premieres excellent new plays and exciting twists on the classics. ⊠ *Almeida St., Islington N1* ☎ *020/7359–4404* Ⓤ *Angel or Highbury & Islington.*

Barbican Centre. Barbican International Theatre Events (BITE) presents groundbreaking performance, dance, drama, and music theater. ⊠ *Silk St., The City EC2* ☎ *020/7638–8891* Ⓤ *Barbican.*

BAC. Battersea Arts Centre has an excellent reputation for producing innovative new work. Check out Scratch, a night of low-tech cabaret theater by emerging artists, and the BAC October Festival of innovative performance. ⊠ *176 Lavender Hill, Battersea SW11* ☎ *020/7223–2223* Ⓤ *National Rail: Clapham Junction.*

★ **Donmar Warehouse.** Hollywood stars often perform in diverse and daring new works, bold interpretations of the classics, and small-scale musicals. It works both ways, too—director Sam Mendes went straight from here to directing *American Beauty.* ⊠ *41 Earlham St., Covent Garden WC2* ☎ *020/7369–1732* Ⓤ *Covent Garden.*

Open Air Theatre. On a warm summer evening, classical theater in pastoral Regent's Park is hard to beat. Enjoy a supper before the performance and during the interval on the picnic lawn, and drinks in the spacious bar. ⊠ *Inner Circle, Regent's Park NW1* ☎ *020/7486–2431* Ⓤ *Baker St., Regent's Park.*

Players' Theatre. This long-running music hall takes you back to the reign of Queen Victoria, as actors in period costume perform bawdy Victorian songs. Dinner is served before and after performances in the restaurant. ⊠ *The Arches, Villiers St., The Strand, Covent Garden WC2* ☎ *020/7839–1134* Ⓤ *Charing Cross or Embankment.*

Royal Court Theatre. Britain's undisputed epicenter of new writing, the RCT has produced gritty British and international drama since the mid-20th century. Don't miss the best deal in town–£5 tickets on Mondays. ⊠ *Sloane Sq., Chelsea SW1* ☎ *020/7565–5000* Ⓤ *Sloane Sq.*

Royal National Theatre. The NT has three theaters: the 1,160-seat Olivier, the 890-seat Lyttelton, and the 400-seat Cottesloe. Musicals, classics, and new plays are staged. It's closed Sunday. ⊠ *South Bank Centre, Belvedere Rd., South Bank SE1* ☎ *020/7452–3000* Ⓤ *Waterloo.*

Royal Shakespeare Company. The RSC schedules its high-quality productions in different West End theaters; in 2003 performances took place at the Old Vic and the Theatre Royal Haymarket. ☎ *0870/609–1110 for reservations.*

Shakespeare's Globe Theatre. This reconstruction of the open-air playhouse where Shakespeare wrote many of his greatest plays re-creates the 16th-century theatergoing experience. Standing room costs £5. The season runs May through September, with a winter season in the indoor Inigo Jones Theatre. ⊠ *New Globe Walk, Bankside, South Bank SE1* ☎ *020/7401–9919* Ⓤ *Southwark, Mansion House (walk across Southwark Bridge), or Blackfriars (walk across Blackfriars Bridge).*

Soho Theatre + Writers' Centre. This sleek theater is devoted to new writing and work by emerging writers. ⊠ *21 Dean St., Soho W1* ☎ *020/7478–0100* Ⓤ *Tottenham Court Rd.*

Tricycle Theatre. The focus here is the best in Irish, African-Caribbean, and Asian works, as well as political drama and new plays. ⊠ *269 Kilburn High Rd., Kilburn NW6 7JR* ☎ *020/7328–1000* Ⓤ *Kilburn.*

Young Vic. Big names perform in innovative productions of classic plays. No one sits more than five rows from the stage in this theater-in-the-round auditorium. The seats are unreserved; each has a perfect view. ✉ *66 The Cut, South Bank SE1* ☎ *020/7928–6363* Ⓤ *Waterloo.*

SPORTS & THE OUTDOORS

There are the Wimbledon Tennis Championships, and there's cricket, and then there's football (soccer in the United States), and that's about it for the sports fan in London, right? Wrong. London is a great city for the weekend player of almost anything. It comes into its own in summer, when the parks sprout nets and goals and painted white lines, outdoor swimming pools open, and a season of spectator events gets under way. If you feel like joining in, *Time Out* magazine, available at newsstands, is a great resource. Bring your gear, and branch out from that hotel gym.

Cricket

★ **Lord's** (✉ St. John's Wood Rd., St. John's Wood NW8 ☎ 020/7432–1066) has been hallowed turf for worshipers of England's summer game since 1811. Tickets can be hard to procure for the five-day Test Matches (full internationals) and one-day internationals played here. Top-class county matches can usually be seen by lining up on the day of the match.

Football

Three of London's football (soccer in the U.S.) clubs competing in the **Premier League** and the Football Association's FA Cup are particularly popular, though not always correspondingly successful: **Arsenal** (✉ Highbury, Avenell Rd., Islington N5 ☎ 020/7413–3366), **Chelsea** (✉ Stamford Bridge, Fulham Rd., Fulham SW6 ☎ 020/7386–7789), and **Tottenham Hotspur** (✉ White Hart La., 748 High Rd., Tottenham N17 ☎ 08700/112–222). Try to buy tickets in advance, and don't get too carried away by the excitement a vast football crowd can generate.

Gyms

The **Central YMCA** (✉ 112 Great Russell St., Bloomsbury WC1 ☎ 020/7343–1700) has every facility and sport, including a great 25-meter pool and a well-equipped gym. Weekly membership is £41, a "one-day taster" £15. At **Jubilee Hall** (✉ 30 The Piazza, Covent Garden WC2 ☎ 020/7379–0008), the day rate is £7.10, monthly £55. This is a very crowded but happening and super-well-equipped central gym. The trendy yoga school **Life Centre** (✉ 15 Edge St., Kensington W8 ☎ 020/7221–4602) specializes in the energetic Ashtanga Vinyasa yoga technique. Classes cost £8–£10.

Running

Green Park and St. James's Park are convenient to the Piccadilly hotels. It's about 2 mi around the two parks. Hyde Park and Kensington Gardens together supply a 4-mi perimeter route, or you can do a 2½-mi run in Hyde Park if you start at Hyde Park Corner or Marble Arch and encircle the Serpentine. Near the Park Lane hotels, Regent's Park has the Outer Circle loop, measuring about 2½ mi. **London Hash House Harriers** (☎ 020/8995–7879) organizes daily noncompetitive hour-long runs (£1) around interesting parts of town, with loops, shortcuts, and pubs built in.

The **Flora London Marathon** (☎ 020/7620–4117) starts at 9:30 AM on a Sunday in April, with some 30,000 athletes running from Blackheath or Greenwich to the Mall. Entry forms for the following year are available between August and October.

Swimming

Chelsea Sports Centre (⊠ Chelsea Manor St., Chelsea SW3 ☎ 020/ 7352–6985), with a renovated, turn-of-the-century 32-by-12-meter pool, is just off King's Road, so it's usually busy. It's packed with kids on weekends. **Oasis** (⊠ 32 Endell St., Covent Garden WC2 ☎ 020/ 7831–1804) is just that, with a heated outdoor pool, open year-round, right in Covent Garden, and a 30-by-10-yard pool indoors.

Tennis

The **Wimbledon Lawn Tennis Championships,** the most prestigious of the four Grand Slam tournaments, are also one of London's most eagerly awaited annual events. To enter the lottery for show-court tickets, send a self-addressed, stamped envelope between October and December to **All England Lawn Tennis & Croquet Club** (⊡ Box 98, Church Rd., Wimbledon SW19 5AE ☎ 020/8946–2244) for an application form. Alternatively, during the last-week-of-June, first-week-of-July tournament, tickets collected from early departing spectators are resold (profits go to charity). These can provide grandstand seats with plenty to see: play continues until dusk. You can also line up (start as early as possible) for tickets for the outside courts.

SHOPPING

Napoléon must have known what he was talking about when he called Britain a nation of shopkeepers. The finest emporiums are in London, still. You can shop like royalty at Her Majesty's glove maker, discover an uncommon Toby jug in a Kensington antiques shop, or find a leather-bound edition of *Wuthering Heights* on Charing Cross Road. If you have a yen to keep up with the Windsors, head for stores proclaiming they are "By Appointment" to H. M. the Queen—or to Prince Philip or the Prince of Wales. The fashion-forward crowd favors places such as Harvey Nichols or Browns of South Molton Street, whereas the most ardent fashion victims will shoot to Notting Hill, London's prime fashion location. If you have only limited time, zoom in on one or two of the West End's grand department stores, such as Harrods or Marks & Spencer, where you'll find enough booty for your entire gift list. Below is a brief introduction to the major shopping areas.

CHELSEA Chelsea centers on King's Road, once synonymous with ultra-high fashion; it still harbors some designer boutiques, plus antiques and home furnishings stores.

COVENT GARDEN This something-for-everyone neighborhood has chain clothing stores and top designers, stalls selling crafts, and shops selling gifts of every type—bikes, kites, tea, herbs, beads, hats—you name it.

FULHAM Newly popular, Fulham is divided into two postal districts, SW6 (farther away from the center of town) and SW10 (which is the closer, beyond Chelsea) on the high-fashion King's Road. There are many different shops to tease you to spend.

KENSINGTON Kensington's main drag, Kensington High Street, houses some small, classy shops, with some larger stores at the eastern end. Try Kensington Church Street for expensive antiques, plus a little fashion.

KNIGHTSBRIDGE Knightsbridge, east of Kensington, has Harrods, of course, but also Harvey Nichols, the top clothes stop, and many expensive designers' boutiques along Sloane Street, Walton Street, and Beauchamp Place.

MARYLEBONE Behind Oxford Street lies this quiet backwater with Marylebone High Street as its main artery. Restaurants once coexisted peacefully along with delis and practical stores until the arrival of designer furniture stores. Satellite streets have designer women's wear and menswear.

MAYFAIR   In Mayfair are the two Bond streets, Old and New, with desirable dress designers, jewelers, and fine art. South Molton Street has high-price, high-style fashion—especially at Browns—and the tailors of Savile Row have worldwide reputations.

NOTTING HILL   Go westward from the famous Portobello Road market and explore the Ledbury Road–Westbourne Grove axis, Clarendon Cross, and Kensington Park Road for a mix of antiques and up-to-the-minute must-haves for body and lifestyle. Toward the more bohemian foot of Portobello are Ladbroke Grove and Golborne Road, where, in among the tatty stores, Portuguese cafés, and patisseries, you can bag bargains.

REGENT STREET   At right angles to Oxford Street is Regent Street, with possibly London's most pleasant department store, Liberty, plus Hamleys, the capital's favorite toy store. Shops around once-famous Carnaby Street stock designer youth paraphernalia and 57 varieties of the T-shirt.

ST. JAMES'S   Here the English gentleman buys everything but the suit (which is from Savile Row): handmade hats, shirts and shoes, silver shaving kits, and hip flasks. Nothing in this neighborhood is cheap, in any sense.

Department Stores

Debenhams (⊠ 334–348 Oxford St., Mayfair W1 ☎ 020/7580–3000 Ⓤ Oxford Circus) has moved up the fashion stakes with the pretty, affordable, Jasper Conran collection for women. Other creations—for men, too—by in-house designers are desirable. **Harrods** (⊠ 87 Brompton ★   Rd., Knightsbridge SW1 ☎ 020/7730–1234 Ⓤ Knightsbridge), one of the world's most famous department stores, can be forgiven its immodest motto, *Omnia, omnibus, ubique* ("everything, for everyone, everywhere"), because it has more than 230 well-stocked departments. The food halls are stunning—so are the crowds, especially during the sales that usually run during the last three weeks of January. **Harvey Nichols** (⊠ 109 Knightsbridge, Knightsbridge SW1 ☎ 020/7235–5000 Ⓤ Knightsbridge) is famed for five floors of ultimate fashion; every label any chic, well-bred London lady covets is here. There's a home furnishings department. It's also known for the restaurant, Fifth Floor. **John Lewis** (⊠ 278 Oxford St., Mayfair SW1 ☎ 020/7629–7711 Ⓤ Oxford Circus) claims as its motto "Never knowingly undersold." This traditional department store carries a good selection of dress fabrics and curtain and uphol-★   stery materials. **Liberty** (⊠ 200 Regent St., Mayfair SW1 ☎ 020/7734–1234 Ⓤ Oxford Circus), full of nooks and crannies, is famous principally for its fabulous fabrics. It also carries Asian goods, menswear, womenswear, fragrances, soaps, and accessories. **Selfridges** (⊠ 400 Oxford St., Mayfair SW1 ☎ 020/7629–1234 Ⓤ Bond St.), London's mammoth version of Macy's, includes a food hall, a theater ticket counter, and a Thomas Cook travel agency. Miss Selfridge (which has branches nationwide) is its outpost for trendy, affordable young women's clothes.

Specialty Stores

Antiques

Antiquarius (⊠ 131–145 King's Rd., Chelsea SW3 ☎ 020/7351–5353 Ⓤ Sloane Sq.), near Sloane Square, is an indoor antiques market with more than 200 stalls offering collectibles, including smaller items: art deco brooches, meerschaum pipes, silver salt cellars. It's closed Sunday. **Facade** (⊠ 196 Westbourne Grove, Notting Hill W11 ☎ 020/7727–2159

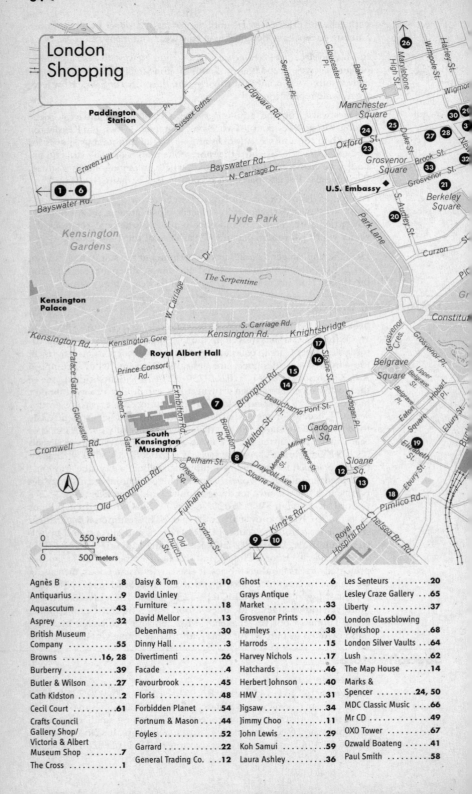

London Shopping

Paddington Station

Sussex Gdns.

Seymour Pl.

Edgware Rd.

Gloucester Pl.

Baker St.

Harley St.

High St.

Marylebone

Wimpole St.

26

Manchester Square

Wigmor

30 **29**

24 **25** Duke St. **27** **28** **3**

Oxford St.

23

Grosvenor Square

Brook St.

33

32

Craven Hill

Bayswater Rd.

N. Carriage Dr.

Grosvenor St.

21

U.S. Embassy ◆

Berkeley Square

1 – 6

Bayswater Rd.

S. Audley St.

Park Lane

20

Curzon

Kensington Gardens

Hyde Park

The Serpentine

Constitut

Kensington Palace

W. Carriage Dr.

S. Carriage Rd.

Kensington Rd.

Knightsbridge

Grosvenor Cres.

Grosvenor Pl.

Gr

Kensington Rd.

Kensington Gore

Royal Albert Hall

Prince Consort Rd.

17

Sloane St.

16

Belgrave Square

Upper Belgrave St.

Hobart Pl.

15

Brompton Rd.

Beauchamp Pl.

14

Pont St.

Cadogan Pl.

Belgrave Pl.

Eaton Square

Palace Gate

Queen's Gate

Exhibition Rd.

7

Walton St.

Cadogan Sq.

Ebury St.

South Kensington Museums

Brompton Rd.

Milner St.

Moore St.

19

Cromwell Rd.

Pelham St.

8

Draycott Ave.

Sloane Sq.

Elizabeth St.

Onslow Sq.

Sloane Ave.

12

13

Old Brompton Rd.

Fulham Rd.

11

Ebury St.

18

Pimlico Rd.

Sydney St.

Old Church St.

9 – 10

King's Rd.

Royal Hospital Rd.

Chelsea Br. Rd.

0 ___ 550 yards

0 ___ 500 meters

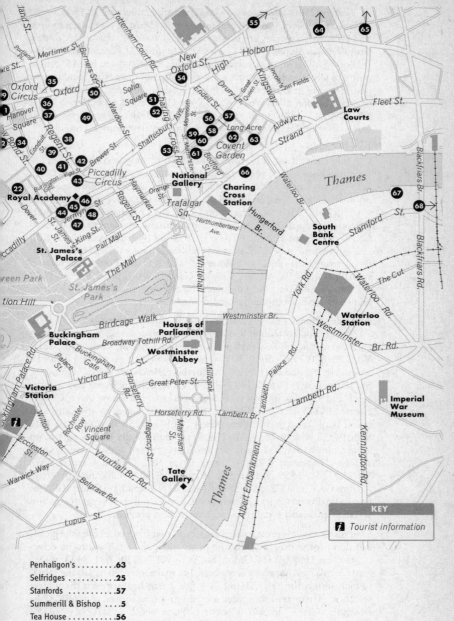

Ⓤ Notting Hill Gate) stocks a large, eclectic collection of French and Italian chandeliers, sconces, and table lamps. Most of them aren't wired and polished, so prices are reasonable. It's closed Sunday and Monday. **Grays Antique Market** (⊠ 58 Davies St., Mayfair W1 ☎ 020/7629–7034 Ⓤ Bond St.) assembles dealers specializing in everything from Sheffield plates to Chippendale furniture. Bargains are not impossible, and proper pedigrees are guaranteed. It's closed Saturday (except December) and Sunday. **London Silver Vaults** (⊠ 53–64 Chancery La., Holborn WC2 ☎ 020/7242–3844 Ⓤ Chancery La.) has 36 dealers specializing in antique silver and jewelry. It's closed Saturday afternoon and Sunday.

Books, CDs & Records

BOOKS Charing Cross Road is London's "booksville," with a couple dozen antiquarian booksellers, and many mainstream bookshops, too. **Cecil Court,** off Charing Cross Road, is a pedestrian-only lane filled with specialty bookstores. **Bell, Book and Radmall** (⊠ 4 Cecil Ct., Covent Garden WC2 ☎ 020/7240–2161 Ⓤ Tottenham Court Rd.) offers quality antiquarian tomes and specializes in modern first editions. **Marchpane** (⊠ 16 Cecil Ct., Covent Garden WC2 ☎ 020/7836–8661 Ⓤ Tottenham Court Rd.) stocks rare and antique illustrated children's books with many first editions, from 18th-century volumes to today's Harry Potter. **Pleasures of Past Times** (⊠ 11 Cecil Ct., Covent Garden WC2 ☎ 020/7836–1142 Ⓤ Tottenham Court Rd.) indulges the collective nostalgia for Victoriana in its stock of modern and old books.

Forbidden Planet (⊠ 71 New Oxford St., Bloomsbury WC1 ☎ 020/7420–3666 Ⓤ Tottenham Court Rd.) is the place for sci-fi, fantasy, horror, and comic books. **Foyles** (⊠ 113–119 Charing Cross Rd., Soho WC2 ☎ 020/7437–5660 Ⓤ Tottenham Court Rd.) is so vast it can be
★ confusing, but you can find almost anything. **Hatchards** (⊠ 187 Piccadilly, St. James's W1 ☎ 020/7439–9921 Ⓤ Piccadilly Circus) has a huge stock and a well-informed staff. **Stanfords** (⊠ 12–14 Long Acre, Covent Garden WC2 ☎ 020/7836–1321 Ⓤ Covent Garden) specializes in travel books and maps. **Waterstone's** (⊠ 121–125 Charing Cross Rd., Soho WC2 ☎ 020/7434–4291 Ⓤ Tottenham Court Rd.) is part of an admirable chain with long hours and a program of author readings and signings. **Zwemmer** (⊠ 72 Charing Cross Rd., Covent Garden WC2 ☎ 020/7240–1559 Ⓤ Tottenham Court Rd. ⊠ 80 Charing Cross Rd., Covent Garden WC2 ☎ 020/7240–4157 Ⓤ Tottenham Court Rd.) has two locations on Charing Cross Road: No. 72 sells books on design and related fields, and No. 80 covers cinema and photography.

CDS & RECORDS London created the great music megastores that have taken over the globe, but don't forget to check out the many independents for a more eclectic selection. **HMV** (⊠ 150 Oxford St., Soho W1 ☎ 020/7631–3423 Ⓤ Oxford Circus) has branches everywhere, but make a special trip to the HMV (which stands for "His Majesty's Voice") flagship store for the widest selection. There are autograph sessions and free shows, too. **MDC Classic Music** (⊠ 437 Strand, Covent Garden WC2 ☎ 020/7240–2157 Ⓤ Charing Cross) has helpful staff who will guide you to the best deals on any diva. There's some jazz, too. **Mr CD** (⊠ 80 Berwick St., Soho W1 ☎ 020/7439–1097 Ⓤ Oxford Circus) stocks a wide selection for all tastes in a tiny shop where you must delve to find the bargains. **Virgin Megastore** (⊠ 14–16 Oxford St., Soho W1 ☎ 020/7631–1234 Ⓤ Tottenham Court Rd.), Richard Branson's pride and joy, carries music of all kinds, books, magazines, and computer games under one roof.

China & Glass

David Mellor (⊠ 4 Sloane Sq., Chelsea SW1 ☎ 020/7730–4259 Ⓤ Sloane Sq.) sells practical Dartington crystal along with more unique porcelain and pottery pieces by British craftspeople. **Divertimenti** (✉ 33–34 Marylebone High St., Regent's Park W1 ☎ 020/7935–0689 Ⓤ Oxford Circus) specializes in beautiful kitchenware and French pottery from Provence. **Summerill & Bishop** (✉ 100 Portland Rd., Notting Hill W11 ☎ 020/7221–4566 Ⓤ Notting Hill Gate), a little piece of French country, supplies French embroidered linen, Portuguese and Tuscan stoneware, and designer culinary ware. **Thomas Goode** (✉ 19 S. Audley St., Mayfair W1 ☎ 020/7499–2823 Ⓤ Bond St.) stocks vast ranges of formal china and lead crystal, including English Wedgwood and Minton, and is one of the world's top shops for these items.

Clothing

Aquascutum (✉ 100 Regent St., Soho W1 ☎ 020/7675–8200 Ⓤ Piccadilly Circus) is known for its classic raincoats but also stocks expensive garments to wear underneath, for both men and women. Styles keep up with the times but are firmly on the safe side. **Burberry** (✉ 21–23 New Bond St., Mayfair W1 ☎ 020/7839–5222 Ⓤ Piccadilly Circus ✉ 165 Regent St., Soho W1 ☎ 020/7734–4060 Ⓤ Piccadilly Circus) tries to evoke English tradition, with mahogany closets and merchandise with the trademark "Burberry Check" tartan—scarves, umbrellas, shortbread tins, and of course, those famous raincoat linings. **Daisy & Tom** (✉ 181–183 King's Rd., Chelsea SW3 ☎ 020/7352–5000 Ⓤ Sloane Sq.) is for cool kids and smart parents. On one floor are high-fashion junior clothes (Kenzo, IKKS, and Polo), shoes aplenty (for newborns to 10-year-olds), a bookshop, and a soda fountain café. **Marks & Spencer** (✉ 458 Oxford St., Mayfair W1 ☎ 020/7935–7954 Ⓤ Marble Arch ✉ 173 Oxford St., Soho ☎ 020/7437–7722 Ⓤ Tottenham Court Rd., Oxford Circus) is a major chain that's an integral part of the British way of life—sturdy practical clothes and good materials. What it *is* renowned for is underwear; the English all buy theirs here. **Topshop** (✉ 214 Oxford St., Soho W1 ☎ 020/7636–7700 Ⓤ Oxford Circus), one of the niftiest retail fashion operations for teens and women, favors top young designers. Topman is the male version of the chain.

MENSWEAR **Favourbrook** (✉ 18 Piccadilly Arcade, St. James's W1 ☎ 020/7491–2337 Ⓤ Piccadilly Circus) tailors exquisite handmade vests, jackets, ties, and cummerbunds. **Herbert Johnson** (✉ 54 St. James's St., St. James's W1 ☎ 020/7408–1174 Ⓤ Piccadilly Circus) is one of a handful of gentleman's hatters who still know how to construct deerstalkers, bowlers, flat caps, and panamas—and Ascot-worthy hats for women, too. **Ozwald Boateng** (✉ 9 Vigo St., Mayfair W1 ☎ 020/7734–6868 Ⓤ Piccadilly Circus) is one of the modern breed of bespoke tailors not on Savile Row but on the fringe. His made-to-measure suits are sought after by rock luminaries for their shock-color linings as well as great classic cuts. **Paul Smith** (✉ 40–44 Floral St., Covent Garden WC2 ☎ 020/7379–7133 Ⓤ Covent Garden) can do the job if you don't want to look outlandish but you're bored with plain pants and sober jackets. **Turnbull & Asser** (✉ 72–73 Jermyn St., St. James's W1 ☎ 020/7808–3000 Ⓤ Piccadilly Circus) is *the* custom shirtmaker. Unfortunately, the first order must be for a minimum of six shirts, from about £100 each. There are less expensive, still exquisite ready-to-wear shirts, too.

WOMENSWEAR **Agnès B** (✉ 111 Fulham Rd., South Kensington SW3 ☎ 020/7225–3477 Ⓤ S. Kensington) has oh-so-pretty, timeless, understated French clothing. Prices are midrange and worthy for the quality. There are branches in Marylebone High Street (W1) and Heath Street, Hampstead (NW3); Floral Street (WC2) has elegant men's suits. **Browns** (✉ 23–27 South Molton St., Mayfair W1 ☎ 020/7491–7833 Ⓤ Bond St. ✉ 6C Sloane St., Knightsbridge SW1 ☎ 020/7514–0040 Ⓤ Knightsbridge), the first notable store to populate the South Molton Street pedestrian mall, seems to sprout offshoots every time you visit. Well-established designers (Donna Karan, Romeo Gigli, Jasper Conran) rub shoulder pads here with younger, funkier names (Dries Van Noten, Jean Paul Gaultier, Hussein Chalayan). The July and January sales are famed. **Cath Kidston** (✉ 8 Clarendon Cross, Notting Hill W11 ☎ 020/7221–4000 Ⓤ Notting Hill Gate) translates fresh ginghams and flower-sprig cotton prints into nightclothes, bed linens, and bath wear. There are also cozy hand-knit sweaters, skirts in flouncy wools, and a children's wear line. **Ghost** (✉ 36 Ledbury Rd., Notting Hill W11 ☎ 020/7229–1057 Ⓤ Notting Hill Gate) presents up-to-the-minute offerings such as willowy dresses and skirts in silks, velvets, and viscose. It's also at 14 Hinde Street (W1). **Jigsaw** (✉ 126–127 New Bond St., Mayfair W1 ☎ 020/7491–4484 Ⓤ Bond St.) wins points for its reasonably priced separates, which don't sacrifice quality for fashion and suit women in their twenties to forties. **Jimmy Choo** (✉ 169 Draycott Ave., Chelsea SW3 ☎ 020/7584–6111 Ⓤ S. Kensington), the name on every supermodel's and fashion editor's feet, creates exquisite, elegant shoes; nothing is less than £100.

Koh Samui (✉ 65 Monmouth St., Covent Garden WC2 ☎ 020/7240–4280 Ⓤ Covent Garden) stocks the clothing of around 40 hot young designers. Discover the next fashion wave before *Vogue* gets there. **Laura Ashley** (✉ 256–258 Regent St., Soho W1 ☎ 020/7437–9760 Ⓤ Oxford Circus) has designs from the firm founded by the late high priestess of English traditional. **Vivienne Westwood** (✉ 6 Davies St., Mayfair W1 ☎ 020/7629–3757 Ⓤ Bond St.), one of the top British designers, produces Pompadour-punk ball gowns, Lady Hamilton vest coats, and foppish getups that still represent the apex of high-style British couture. **Zara** (✉ 118 Regent St., Soho W1 ☎ 020/7534–9500 Ⓤ Piccadilly Circus) has swept Europe. The style is young and snappy, and the prices are low. Don't expect durability—these are fun pieces, for men and kids, too.

Crafts

The Crafts Council Gallery Shop/Victoria & Albert Museum Shop (✉ Cromwell Rd., South Kensington SW7 ☎ 020/7589–5070 Ⓤ S. Kensington) showcases a microcosm of British crafts—jewelry, glass, ceramics, toys. **David Linley Furniture** (✉ 60 Pimlico Rd., Chelsea SW1 ☎ 020/7730–7300 Ⓤ Sloane Sq.) is the outpost for Viscount Linley—the only gentleman in the kingdom who can call the Queen "Auntie" and one of the finest furniture designers of today. The large pieces are expensive, but small desk accessories and objets d'art are available. The **Lesley Craze Gallery** (✉ 33–35 Clerkenwell Green, Clerkenwell EC1 ☎ 020/7608–0393 Ⓤ Farringdon) carries exquisite jewelry by some 100 young British designers. The adjacent Two gallery specializes in nonprecious metals and sumptuous scarves and textiles. **London Glassblowing Workshop** (✉ 7 The Leathermarket, Weston St., South Bank SE1 ☎ 020/7403–2800 Ⓤ London Bridge) showcases glassblowers and designers who make decorative and practical pieces on-site. On weekdays you can see them at work, and buy or commission your own variation. In the Leathermarket are other craftspeople, most notably a silversmith and papermaker. **OXO Tower** (✉ Barge House St., South Bank SE1 ☎ 020/7401–2255 Ⓤ Southwark) holds shops and studios, open Tuesday–Sunday 11–6, that sell excellent handmade goods. At Gabriel's Wharf, a few steps farther west along the river, a collection of craftspeople sell porcelain, jewelry, clothes, and more.

Gifts

The **British Museum Company** (✉ 22 Bloomsbury St., Bloomsbury WC1 ☎ 020/7637–9449 Ⓤ Tottenham Court Rd.) carries cute gift items—

Egyptian scarabs in ceramic, Rosetta stone tins, and the like. You can also buy ancient pottery pieces, and the bookshop is a mine of information. **The Cross** (⊠ 141 Portland Rd., Notting Hill W11 ☎ 020/7727–6760 Ⓤ Notting Hill Gate), is big with the high-style crowd, thanks to its hedonistic, beautiful things: silk scarves, brocade bags, and jew-

★ eled baubles. **Floris** (⊠ 89 Jermyn St., St. James's W1 ☎ 020/7930–2885 Ⓤ Piccadilly Circus) is one of London's most beautiful shops, with 19th-century glass and mahogany showcases filled with swan's-down

★ powder puffs, cut-glass bottles, and faux tortoiseshell combs. **Fortnum & Mason** (⊠ 181 Piccadilly, St. James's W1 ☎ 020/7734–8040 Ⓤ Piccadilly Circus), the Queen's grocer, is, paradoxically, the most egalitarian of gift stores, with plenty of luxury foods, stamped with the gold "By Appointment" crest, for less than £5. Try the teas, preserves, tins of pâté, or turtle soup. **General Trading Company** (⊠ 2 Symons St., Sloane Sq., Chelsea SW3 ☎ 020/7730–0411 Ⓤ Sloane Sq.) "does" just about every upper-class wedding gift list, but caters also to slimmer pockets with its merchandise shipped from far shores but moored securely to English taste. **Hamleys** (⊠ 188–196 Regent St., Soho W1 ☎ 0870/333–2455 Ⓤ Oxford Circus) has six floors of toys and games for children and adults.

Les Senteurs (⊠ 71 Elizabeth St., Belgravia SW1 ☎ 020/7730–2322 Ⓤ Sloane Sq.), an intimate, unglossy gem of a perfumery, sells little-known yet timeless fragrances, such as Creed, worn by Eugenie, wife of Emperor Napoléon III. **Lush** (⊠ 11 The Piazza, Covent Garden WC2 ☎ 020/7240–4570 Ⓤ Covent Garden) is crammed with fresh, very wacky, handmade cosmetics. **Penhaligon's** (⊠ 41 Wellington St., Covent Garden WC2 ☎ 020/7836–2150 Ⓤ Covent Garden), established by William Penhaligon, court barber to Queen Victoria, was parfumier to Lord Rothschild and Winston Churchill. The **Tea House** (⊠ 15A Neal St., Covent Garden WC2 ☎ 020/7240–7539 Ⓤ Covent Garden) purveys everything to do with the British national drink. Dispatch your gift list here with "teaphernalia"—strainers, trivets, infusers, and such.

Jewelry

Asprey (⊠ 165 New Bond St., Mayfair W1 ☎ 020/7493–6767 Ⓤ Bond St.), described as the "classiest and most luxurious shop in the world,"

★ offers exquisite jewelry and gifts, both antique and modern. **Butler & Wilson** (⊠ 20 South Molton St., Mayfair W1 ☎ 020/7409–2955 Ⓤ Bond St.) has irresistible retro costume jewelry and is strong on diamanté, jet, and French gilt. You can also find some nostalgic gowns here. There's another branch at 189 Fulham Road, South Kensington SW3. **Dinny Hall** (⊠ 200 Westbourne Grove, Notting Hill W11 ☎ 020/7792–3913 Ⓤ Notting Hill Gate) sells simple designs in gold and silver, including dainty gold and diamond earrings or chokers with delicate curls. There's another branch at 54 Fulham Road, SW3. **Garrard** (⊠ 24 Albemarle St., Mayfair W1 ☎ 020/7758–8520 Ⓤ Bond St.), after sharing premises with Asprey, has returned to its original site; Jade Jagger is the designer employed by the company to draw in the younger market. Garrard is the royal jeweler, in charge of the upkeep of the Crown Jewels.

Prints

Besides individual print stores, browse around the gallery shops, such as those at the Tate Britain and Tate Modern. In the open air, try hunting around Waterloo Bridge along the Riverside Walk Market, at St. James's Craft Market at St. James's Church in Piccadilly, and at the Apple Market near The Piazza, Covent Garden. **Grosvenor Prints** (⊠ 28 Shelton St., Covent Garden WC2 ☎ 020/7836–1979 Ⓤ Covent Garden) sells antiquarian prints, with an emphasis on views and architecture of London—and dogs. The **Map House** (⊠ 54 Beauchamp Pl., Knightsbridge SW3 ☎ 020/7589–4325 Ⓤ Knightsbridge) has antique maps in all price ranges, and fine reproductions of maps and prints, especially of botanical subjects and cityscapes.

Street Markets

Bermondsey is the market the dealers frequent for small antiques, which gives you an idea of its scope. The real bargains start going at 5 AM, but there'll be a few left if you arrive later. Take Bus 15 or 25 to Aldgate, then Bus 42 over Tower Bridge to Bermondsey Square; or take the tube to London Bridge and walk. ⊠ *Tower Bridge Rd., South Bank SE1* ۞ *Fri. 5 AM–noon* Ⓤ *London Bridge.*

Borough Market, a foodie's delight, carries whole-grain, organic everything, mainly from Britain but with an international flavor. ⊠ *Borough High St., South Bank SE1* ۞ *Fri. noon–6, Sat. 9–4* Ⓤ *London Bridge, Borough.*

Camden Passage is hugged by curio stores and is dripping with jewelry, silverware, and other antiques. Saturday and Wednesday are when the stalls go up; the rest of the week, only the stores are open. Bus 19 or 38 or the tube will get you there. ⊠ *Off Upper St., Islington N1* ۞ *Wed. and Sat. 8:30–3* Ⓤ *Angel.*

Covent Garden has craft stalls, jewelry designers, clothes makers, potters, and other artisans, who congregate in the undercover central area known as the Apple Market. The Jubilee Market, toward Southampton Street, is less classy (printed T-shirts and the like), but on Monday the selection of vintage collectibles is worthwhile. ⊠ *The Piazza, Covent Garden WC2* ۞ *Daily 9–5* Ⓤ *Covent Garden.*

★ **Portobello Market,** London's most famous market, still wins the prize for the all-round best. There are 1,500 antiques dealers here, so bargains are still possible. Nearer Notting Hill Gate, prices and quality are highest; the middle is where locals buy fruit and vegetables and hang out in trendy restaurants. Under the Westway elevated highway you'll find a great flea market, and more bric-a-brac and bargains appear as you walk toward Golborne Road. Take Bus 52 or the tube here. ⊠ *Portobello Rd., Notting Hill W11* ۞ *Fruit and vegetables Mon.–Wed. and Fri. 8–5, Thurs. 8–1; antiques Fri. 8–3; food market and antiques Sat. 6–5* Ⓤ *Ladbroke Grove, Notting Hill Gate.*

Spitalfields, an old 3-acre indoor fruit market near Petticoat Lane, has turned into Trendsville, with crafts and design shops. It also has food and clothes stalls, cafés, and performance areas. On Sunday the place comes alive, with stalls selling antique clothing, handmade rugs, and cookware. The resident stores have lovely things for body and home. For refreshment, you can eat anything from Spanish tapas to Thai. ⊠ *Brushfield St., East End E1* ۞ *Organic market Fri. and Sun. 10–5; general market weekdays 11–3, Sun. 10–5* Ⓤ *Liverpool St., Aldgate, Aldgate East.*

LONDON A TO Z

To research prices, get advice from other travelers, and book travel arrangements, visit www.fodors.com.

ADDRESSES

Central London and its surrounding districts are divided into 32 boroughs—33, counting the City of London. More useful for finding your way around, however, are the subdivisions of London into postal districts. The first one or two letters give the location: N means north, NW means northwest, etc. You won't find W2 next to W3, but the general rule is that the lower numbers, such as W1 or SW1, are closest to the city center. Abbreviated (for general location) or full (for mailing information) postal codes are given for many listings in this chapter. Neighborhood names such as Mayfair or Soho are also provided.

AIR TRAVEL TO & FROM LONDON
For information, *see* Air Travel *in* Smart Travel Tips.

AIRPORTS & TRANSFERS
For information about Heathrow, Gatwick, and Stansted airports, *see* Airports *in* Smart Travel Tips. Airport Travel Line has information on transfers between Heathrow and Gatwick and into London by bus. However, you may be directed to some of the numbers listed below.

From Heathrow, the least-expensive route into London is by train, via the Piccadilly line of the Underground. Trains on the tube run every four to eight minutes from all four terminals; the 50-minute trip costs £3.70 one-way and connects with London's extensive tube system. The first train departs at 5:08 AM (5:57 on Sunday), and the last at 11:49 PM (10:57 on Sunday). The quickest way into London is the Heathrow Express, which takes just 15 minutes to and from Paddington Station (in the city center and a main hub on the Underground). One-way tickets cost £12 for standard-express class (£23 round-trip). Daily service departs every 15 minutes, from 5:02 AM to 11:47 PM.

Bus service to London is available from the Heathrow Central Bus Station. Airbus A2 costs £8 one-way and £12 round-trip; travel time is about one hour and 40 minutes. Buses leave for King's Cross and Euston, with stops at Marble Arch and Russell Square, every 30 minutes 5:30 AM–9:45 PM from Terminal 4, 5:45 AM –10:08 PM from Terminal 3, but can be tedious because there are more than a dozen stops en route. National Express buses (incorporating Jetlink service) leave every 30 minutes to Victoria Coach Station from Heathrow Central Bus Station—connected to arrival terminals by a pedestrian underpass, and next to Heathrow Underground Station for Terminals 1–3: cost is £7 one-way, from 5:40 AM to 9:35 PM.

From Gatwick, the fast, nonstop Gatwick Express train has frequent departures to Victoria Station. From 5:20 AM to 6:50 AM trains leave every 30 minutes, then every 15 minutes until 8:50 PM, and back to every 30 minutes until the last departure at 1:35 AM. The 30-minute trip costs £11 one-way, £21.50 round-trip. A frequent local train also runs all night. National Express Jetlink bus services from North and South terminals do not go to London, but to many other major cities, such as Bristol, Cambridge, and Oxford.

Stansted serves mainly European destinations. The Stansted Express train to Liverpool Street station runs every half hour and costs £13 one-way, £21 round-trip; travel time is about 40 minutes. Monday to Saturday departures are from 6 AM to 11:59 PM. Airbus 6, by National Express, runs cheaper hourly bus services to Victoria Coach Station from 12:03 AM to 11:20 PM; the cost is £8 one-way, £10 round-trip, and travel time is about an hour and 40 minutes.

If you are thinking of taking a taxi from Heathrow and Gatwick, remember that they can get caught in traffic; the trip from Heathrow, for example, can take more than an hour and costs about £35. From Gatwick, the taxi fare is about £75; the ride takes about an hour and

20 minutes. From Stansted, the £75 journey takes a little over an hour. Your hotel may be able to recommend a car service for airport transfers. Charges are usually about £35 to any of the airports. Add a tip of 10% to 15% to the basic fare.

You can get discounts on many tickets if you book on the Internet. The Web site for British Airports Authority has links to all the previously mentioned services, with fare details and timetables.

🚖 Taxis & Shuttles **Airbus A2** ☎ 0870/574-7777. **Airport Travel Line** ☎ 0870/574-7777. **British Airports Authority** ⊕ www.baa.co.uk. **Gatwick Express** ☎ 0870/530-1530 ⊕ www.gatwickexpress.co.uk. **Heathrow Express** ☎ 0845/600-1515 ⊕ www.heathrowexpress.co.uk. **London Transport** ☎ 020/7222-1234 ⊕ www.thetube.com or www.transportforlondon.gov.uk. **National Express** ☎ 0870/580-8080 ⊕ www.nationalexpress.com. **Stansted Express** ☎ 0845/850-0150 ⊕ www.stanstedexpress.co.uk.

BUS TRAVEL TO & FROM LONDON

Buses, or "coaches," as long-distance services are known, operate mainly from London's Victoria Coach Station to more than 1,200 major towns and cities. Buses are about half as expensive as the train, but trips can take twice as long. For information, *see* Bus Travel *in* Smart Travel Tips.

BUS TRAVEL WITHIN LONDON

In central London, London Transport (LT) buses are traditionally bright red double- and single-deckers, although there are now many privately owned buses of different colors. Not all buses run the full length of their route at all times, so check with the driver or conductor. On some buses you pay the conductor after finding a seat; on others you pay the driver upon boarding. On Bendy buses, which have three doors, you purchase tickets from machines at bus stops along the routes before you board. Bus stops are clearly indicated; the main stops have a red LT symbol on a plain white background. When the word REQUEST is written across the sign, you must flag the bus down. Buses are a good way to see the town, but don't take one if you are in a hurry. Single fares start at 65p for short hops in the central zone.

London is divided into six concentric zones for both bus and tube fares: the more zones you cross, the higher the fare. However, for buses only, short single fares in the city center (Zone 1) are 65p, then for travel through any number of outer zones, just add an extra 70p. A One-Day Bus Pass for zones one through four is a good deal at £2 (a seven-day pass is £8.50) but must be bought before boarding the bus, from one of the machines at bus stops, most newsagents, or underground stations. Off-peak Day Travelcards (£4.10–£5.10) allow unrestricted travel on bus *and* tube after 9:30 AM and all day on weekends and national holidays (except on N-prefixed Night Buses). Day Travelcards (peak) are more expensive (£5.10–£10.70). Other options are Weekend Travelcards, for the two days of the weekend and on any two consecutive days during public holidays (£6.10–£7.60); Family Travelcards, which are one-day tickets for one or two adults with one to four children (£2.70–£3.40 per adult, with one child; additional children cost 80p each); or the Carnet, a book of 10 single Underground tickets valid for central Zone 1 (£11.50) to use anytime over a year—a savings of £4.50. Visitor Travelcards are similar to the Day Travelcards but with the bonus of a booklet of money-off vouchers to major attractions (available only in the United States, for three, four, and seven days). Visitor Travelcards are available from BritRail or Rail Europe.

Traveling without a valid ticket makes you liable for an on-the-spot fine (£10 at press time), so always pay your fare before you travel. For more information, there are London Transport Travel Information Centres at the following tube stations: Euston (closed weekends), Hammersmith (closed Sunday), King's Cross, Liverpool Street, North Greenwich, Oxford Circus (closed Sunday), Paddington, Piccadilly Circus, St. James's Park (closed weekends), Victoria, and Heathrow (in Terminals 1, 2, and 4). Most are open in daytime only; call London Transport for hours.

Night Buses can prove helpful when traveling in London from 11 PM to 5 AM—these buses add the prefix "N" to their route numbers and don't run as frequently and don't operate on quite as many routes as day buses. You'll probably have to transfer at one of the Night Bus nexuses: Victoria, Westminster, and either Piccadilly Circus or Trafalgar Square. For safety reasons, avoid sitting alone on the top deck of a Night Bus.

FARES & SCHEDULES   ▪ **BritRail** ☎ 877/677–1066 ⊕ www.britrail.net. **London Transport** ☎ 020/7222–1234 ⊕ www.londontransport.co.uk. **Rail Europe** ☎ 888/274–8724 ⊕ www.raileurope.com.

CAR TRAVEL

The major approach roads to London are motorways (six-lane highways; look for an "M" followed by a number) or "A" roads; the latter may be "dual carriageways" (divided highways), or two-lane highways. Motorways (from Heathrow, M4; from Gatwick, M23 to M25, then M3; Stansted, M11) are usually the faster option for getting in and out of town, although rush-hour traffic is horrendous. Stay tuned to local radio stations for regular traffic updates.

The simple advice about driving in London is: don't. Because the city grew as a series of villages, there was never a central street plan, and the result is a chaotic winding mass, made no easier by the one-way street systems. If you must drive in London, remember to drive on the left and stick to the speed limit (30 mph on most city streets).

A £5 "congestion charge" is levied on all vehicles entering central London (bounded by the Inner Ring Road; street signs note the area) on weekdays from 7 to 6:30, excluding bank holidays. Pay in advance or on that day until 10 PM if you're entering the central zone. You can pay by phone, mail, or Internet, or at retail outlets (look for signs indicating how and where you can pay). There are no tollbooths; cameras monitor the area. The penalty for not paying is stiff: £80 (£40 for prompt payment). For current information, check ⊕ www.cclondon.com.

DISCOUNTS & DEALS

All national collections (such as the Natural History Museum, Science Museum, Victoria & Albert Museum) are free, a real bargain for museum goers. The London Pass, a smart card, offers entry to more than 60 top attractions such as museums and tours on boats and buses. It also includes restaurant discounts and free travel in London on the tube and buses, though you can buy the pass without these features for less. You can purchase the pass in one-, two-, three-, or six-day options for £32, £55, £71, or £110; the cost for children is much less. You may recoup your cost if you visit two major attractions. London Pass is available by phone, on-line, or from the Britain Visitor Centre and Tourist Information Centre branches. For other discounts, *see* Discounts & Deals *in* Smart Travel Tips.

▪ **London Pass** ☎ 0870/242-9988 ⊕ www.londonpass.com.

EMBASSIES

For information, *see* Embassies *in* Smart Travel Tips.

EMERGENCIES

For hospitals in different areas of London that provide free 24-hour accident and emergency facilities, the following are listed: in the west of London is Charing Cross Hospital; in the city center is University College Hospital; to the north of the center is the Royal Free Hospital; and on the south bank of the city center is St. Thomas's Hospital. Bliss Chemist is open daily 9 AM–midnight. NHS Direct offers 24-hour general expert medical advice from the National Health Service.

Emergency Services Ambulance, fire, police ☎ 999. NHS Direct ☎ 0845/4647. **Hospitals** Charing Cross Hospital ⊠ Fulham Palace Rd., Hammersmith W6 ☎ 020/8846-1234. Royal Free Hospital ⊠ Pond St., Hampstead Hampstead, NW3 ☎ 020/7794-0500. St. Thomas's Hospital ⊠ Lambeth Palace Rd., South Bank SE1 ☎ 020/7928-9292. University College Hospital ⊠ Grafton Way, Bloomsbury WC1 ☎ 020/7387-9300.

Late-night Pharmacies Bliss Chemist ⊠ 5 Marble Arch, Bayswater W1 ☎ 020/7723-6116.

LODGING

BED-AND-BREAKFASTS & APARTMENT RENTALS — Bed-and-breakfasts (rooms in private homes) or apartment rentals may be an economical choice for your stay. A number of agencies offer rooms and apartments in different neighborhoods. In some cases you can check out many of the properties on-line before you book. Of the firms listed below, the Bulldog Club and Uptown Reservations offer tonier accommodations; London B&B also represents some fancier homes; Primrose Hill B&B is committed to affordable lodgings. For other suggestions, *see* Lodging *in* Smart Travel Tips.

Reservation Services Bulldog Club ⊠ 14 Dewhurst Rd., West Kensington W14 0ET ☎ 020/7371-3202 ⎙ 020/7371-2015 ⊕ www.bulldogclub.com. London B&B ✍ Box 124859, San Diego, CA 92112 ☎ 800/872-2632 ⊕ www.londonbandb.com. Primrose Hill B&B ⊠ 14 Edis St., Primrose Hill NW1 8LG ☎ 020/7722-6869. Uptown Reservations ⊠ 41 Paradise Walk, Chelsea SW3 4JL ☎ 020/7351-3445 ⎙ 020/7351-9383.

TAXIS

Hotels and main tourist areas have taxi ranks; you can also hail taxis on the street. If the yellow FOR HIRE sign is lighted on top, the taxi is available. But drivers often cruise at night with their signs unlighted, so if you see an unlighted cab, keep your hand up. Fares start at £1.40 and increase by units of 20p per 281 yards or 55.5 seconds until the fare exceeds £8.60. After that, it's 20p for each 188 yards or 37 seconds. Surcharges are added after 8 PM and on weekends and public holidays. Over Christmas and New Year's Eve, the surcharge rises to £2—and there's 40p extra for each additional passenger. Note that fares are usually raised each April. Tips are extra, usually 10%–15% per ride.

TOURS

BOAT TOURS — In summer, narrow boats and barges cruise London's two canals, the Grand Union and Regent's Canal. Most vessels operate on the latter, which runs between Little Venice in the west (the nearest tube is Warwick Avenue on the Bakerloo Line) and Camden Lock (about 200 yards north of Camden Town tube station). Jason's Trip operates one-way and round-trip narrow-boat cruises on this route. The London Waterbus Company operates this route year-round with a stop at London Zoo: trips run daily April–October and weekends only November–March. Canal Cruises offers three or four cruises daily March–October on the *Jenny Wren* and all year on the cruising restaurant *My Fair Lady* from Walker's Quay, Camden.

Boats cruise the Thames throughout the year. Most leave from West-minster Pier, Charing Cross Pier, and Tower Pier. Downstream routes go to the Tower of London, Greenwich, and the Thames Barrier; up-stream destinations include Kew, Richmond, and Hampton Court. De-pending on the destination, river trips may last from 30 minutes to four hours. For trips downriver from Charing Cross to Greenwich Pier and historic Greenwich, call Catamaran Cruisers or Westminster Passenger Services (which runs the same route from Westminster Pier). Thames Cruises goes to Greenwich and onward to the Thames Barrier. West-minster Passenger Service (Upriver) runs through summer to Kew and Hampton Court from Westminster Pier. A Rail and River Rover ticket combines the modern wonders of Canary Wharf and Docklands devel-opment by Docklands Light Railway with the historic riverside by boat. Tickets are available year-round from Westminster, Tower, and Green-wich piers, and Dockland Light Railway stations. London Transport (⇨ Bus Travel) should be able to give information on all companies.
🎬 **Canal Cruises** ☎ 020/7485-4433. **Catamaran Cruisers** ☎ 020/7987-1185 ⊕ www. catamarancruisers.co.uk. **Jason's Trip** ☎ 020/7286-3428. **Rail and River Rover** ☎ 020/ 7363-9700. **Thames Cruises** ☎ 020/7930-3373. **Westminster Passenger Services** ☎ 020/7930-4097. **Westminster Passenger Service (Upriver)** ☎ 020/7930-2062 ⊕ www.wpsa.co.uk.

BUS TOURS   Guided sightseeing tours provide a good introduction to the city from double-decker buses, which are open-topped in summer. Tours run daily and depart from Haymarket, Baker Street, Grosvenor Gardens, Mar-ble Arch, and Victoria. You may board or alight at any of about 21 stops to view the sights, and then get back on the next bus. Tickets (£12) may be bought from the driver; several companies run tours. The Original London Sightseeing Tour also offers frequent daily tours and has in-formative staff on easily recognizable double-decker buses. Tours de-part from 8:30 AM from Baker Street (Madame Tussaud's), Marble Arch (Speakers'Corner), Piccadilly (Haymarket), or Victoria (Victoria Street) around every 12 minutes (less often outside peak summer sea-son). The Big Bus Company runs a similar operation with a Red and Blue tour. The Red is a two-hour tour with 18 stops, and the Blue, one hour with 13. Both start from Marble Arch, Speakers' Corner. Evan Evans offers good bus tours that also visit major sights just outside the city. Another reputable agency for bus tours is Frames Rickards.

Green Line, Evan Evans, and Frames Rickards all offer day excursions by bus to places within easy reach of London, such as Hampton Court, Oxford, Stratford, and Bath.
🎬 **Big Bus Company** ☎ 020/7233-9533 ⊕ www.bigbus.co.uk. **Evan Evans** ☎ 020/ 7950-1777 ⊕ www.evanevans.co.uk. **Frames Rickards** ☎ 020/7837-3111; 800/992-7700 in U.S. ⊕ www.etmtravelgroup.com. **Green Line** ☎ 0870/608-7261 ⊕ www. greenline.co.uk. **Original London Sightseeing Tour** ☎ 020/8877-1722 ⊕ www. theoriginaltour.com.

PRIVATE GUIDES   Black Taxi Tour of London is a personal tour by cab direct from your hotel. The price is per cab, so the fare can be shared among as many as five people. An introductory two-hour tour is £75 by day, £85 by night.
🎬 **Black Taxi Tour of London** ☎ 020/7935-9363 ⊕ www.blacktaxitours.co.uk.

WALKING TOURS   One of the best ways to get to know London is on foot, and there are many guided walking tours from which to choose. Original London Walks has theme tours devoted to the Beatles, Sherlock Holmes, Dickens, Jack the Ripper—you name it. If horror and mystery are your interest, then the City holds plenty of that, as you'll discover on a Blood and Tears tour (not suitable for younger children). For a more historical accent, check the tours from Historical Walks. Peruse the leaflets at a London Tourist Information Centre for special-interest walks. You can tailor your own walking tour of the city with a Blue Badge guide.

🚶 **Blood and Tears Walk** ☎ 020/8348-9022. **Blue Badge** ☎ 020/7495-5504 ⊕ www. blue-badge.org.uk. **Historical Walks** ☎ 020/8668-4019. **Original London Walks** ☎ 020/7624-3978 ⊕ www.walks.com.

TRAIN TRAVEL

London has 15 major train stations, each serving a different area of the country, all accessible by Underground or bus. The once-national British Rail is now various private companies, under National Rail, but there is a central rail information number. For further information on train travel, *see* Train Travel *in* Smart Travel Tips.

🚆 **National Rail Enquiries** ☎ 0845/748-4950 ⊕ www.nationalrail.co.uk.

TRAVEL AGENCIES

🚆 Local Agent Referrals **American Express** ✉ 30-31 Haymarket, St. James's SW1 ☎ 020/7484-9600 ✉ 89 Mount St., Mayfair W1 ☎ 020/7659-0701. **Thomas Cook** ✉ 1 Woburn Pl., Bloomsbury WC1 ☎ 020/7837-0393 ✉ 184 Kensington High St., Kensington W8 ☎ 020/7707-2300.

UNDERGROUND TUBE TRAVEL

London's extensive Underground system has color-coded routes, clear signage, and extensive connections. Trains run out into the suburbs, and all stations are marked with the London Underground circular symbol. (In Britain, the word "subway" means "pedestrian underpass.") Trains are all one class; smoking is *not* allowed on board or in the stations. Some lines have branches (Central, District, Northern, Metropolitan, and Piccadilly), so be sure to note which branch is needed for your particular destination. Electronic platform signs tell you the final stop and route of the next train and how many minutes you'll have to wait for the train to arrive. The zippy Docklands Light Railway runs through the Docklands with an extension to Greenwich.

FARES & SCHEDULES London is divided into six concentric zones (ask at Underground ticket booths for a map and booklet, which give details of the ticket options), so make sure to buy a ticket for the correct zone or you may be liable for an on-the-spot fine (£10 at press time). You can buy a single or return ticket, the equivalent of a one-way and a round-trip, for travel anytime on the day of issue. Singles vary in price from £1.60 to £3.70. For information, including discount passes for bus and tube travel, *see* Bus Travel Within London.

Trains begin running just after 5 AM Monday–Saturday; the last services leave central London between midnight and 12:30 AM. On Sunday, trains start two hours later and finish about an hour earlier. Frequency of trains depends on the route and the time of day, but normally you should not have to wait more than 10 minutes in central areas. Travelers with disabilities should get the free leaflet "Access to the Underground."

🚇 **"Access to the Underground"** ☎ 020/7918-3312. **London Transport** ☎ 020/7222-1234 ⊕ www.londontransport.co.uk.

VISITOR INFORMATION

The main London Tourist Information Centre at Victoria Station Forecourt is open in summer, Monday–Saturday 8–7 and Sunday 8–5; winter, Monday–Saturday 8–6 and Sunday 8:30–4; also at Heathrow Airport (Terminals 1, 2, and 3). Britain Visitor Centre, open weekdays 9–6:30, weekends 10–4, provides details about travel, accommodations, and entertainment for the whole of Britain, but you need to visit the center in person to get information. London Line is the London Tourist Board's 24-hour phone service—it's a premium-rate (60p per minute at all times) recorded information line, with different numbers for theater, events, museums, sports, getting around, and so on. The London Tourist Board also has a helpful Web site with links to other sites.

📗 **Britain Visitor Centre** ✉ 1 Regent St., Piccadilly Circus, St. James's SW1Y 4NX ☎ No phone ⊕ www.visitbritain.com. **London Line** ☎ 09068/663344, calls cost 60p per minute. **London Tourist Board** ⊕ www.visitlondon.com. **London Tourist Information Centre** ✉ Victoria Station Forecourt, Victoria ☎ No phone.

THE SOUTHEAST

CANTERBURY, DOVER, BRIGHTON, TUNBRIDGE WELLS

FODOR'S CHOICE

City Fish Bar, *restaurant in Canterbury*

Ightham Mote, *manor house near Sevenoaks*

Knole, *stately home in Sevenoaks*

Petworth House, *stately home in Petworth*

Sissinghurst Castle Garden, *Cranbrook*

Wisley, *garden near Guildford*

HIGHLY RECOMMENDED

SIGHTS Bodiam Castle, *Bodiam*

Brighton Pier, *Brighton*

Canterbury Cathedral, *Canterbury*

Chilham

Dover Castle, *Dover*

Hever Castle, *Hever*

Leeds Castle, *near Maidstone*

Lewes

Museum of Canterbury, *Canterbury*

Penshurst Place, *stately home in Penshurst*

Royal Pavilion, *Brighton*

Rye

Sculpture at Goodwood, *Goodwood*

Many other great hotels and restaurants enliven this area. For other favorites, look for the black stars as you read this chapter.

Updated by
Julius Honnor

IN AN ERA WHEN EVERYTHING SMALL IS FASHIONABLE, from radios to cameras, the Southeast will inevitably have great appeal. Where ancient hedgerows have been allowed to stand, this is still a landscape of small-scale features and pleasant hills. From the air, the tiny fields, neatly hedged, form a patchwork quilt. On the ground, once away from the motorways and London commuter tract housing, the Southeast, including Surrey, Kent, and Sussex, East and West, reveals some of England's loveliest countryside, where gentle hills and woodlands are punctuated with farms and storybook villages rooted in history and with cathedral cities waiting to be explored. Rivers wind down to a coast that is alternately sweeping chalk cliff and seaside resort. This area farthest from the unpredictable influences of the Atlantic is England at its warmest. Fruit trees and even vineyards flourish in archetypal English landscapes and, often, atypical English sunshine.

Although it is one of the most densely populated areas of Britain because of its proximity to London, the Southeast includes Kent, the "Garden of England." Fields of hops and acre upon acre of orchards burst into a mass of pink and white blossoms in spring and stretch away into the distance, though even here large-scale modern farming has done much to homogenize the landscape. In the Southeast, too, are ancient Canterbury, site of the mother cathedral of England, and Dover, whose chalky white cliffs and brooding castle have become symbols of Britain. Medieval castles and a trove of superb stately homes such as Petworth House and Knole are found throughout the region.

Famous seaside towns and resorts dot the coasts of Sussex and Kent, the most famous being that eccentric combination of carnival and culture, Brighton, site of 19th-century England's own Xanadu, the Royal Pavilion. Also on the coast, the busy ports of Newhaven, Folkestone, Dover, and Ramsgate have served for centuries as gateways to continental Europe. The Channel Tunnel, linking Britain to France by rail, runs from near Folkestone.

Indeed, because the English Channel is at its narrowest here, a great deal of British history has been forged in the Southeast. The Romans landed in this area and stayed to rule Britain for four centuries. So did the Saxons—Sussex means "the land of the South Saxons." William ("the Conqueror") of Normandy defeated the Saxons at a battle near Hastings in 1066. Canterbury has been the seat of the Primate of All England, the Archbishop of Canterbury, since Pope Gregory the Great dispatched St. Augustine to convert the heathen hordes of Britain in 597. And long before any of these invaders, the ancient Britons blazed trails that formed the routes for today's modern highways.

Exploring the Southeast

For sightseeing purposes, the Southeast can be divided into four sections. The eastern part of the region takes in the cathedral town of Canterbury, in the heart of Kent, as well as Dover, England's Continental gateway, to the south. Another area is the coast, from pretty Rye in the east to Lewes in the west, including historic seaside towns along the way. A third area begins in the coastal resort of Brighton and takes in Chichester, in West Sussex, and then swings north into Surrey, taking in Guildford and East Grinstead. The fourth region takes in the spa town of Royal Tunbridge Wells and western Kent, with its rich collection of stately homes, castles, and historic landmarks. Many towns can be reached by public transportation from London for a day trip. Buses, trains, and occasionally even steam trains provide service to most major sights. If you're interested in stately homes or quiet villages, it's wiser to rent a car.

About the Restaurants & Hotels

All around this coast, resort towns stretch along beaches, their hotels standing cheek by jowl. Of the smaller hotels and guest houses only a few remain open year-round, as most do business only from mid-April to September or October. Some hotels have all-inclusive rates for a week's stay, which is cheaper than taking room and meals by the day. Prices rise in July and August, when the seaside resorts can get solidly booked, especially Brighton, which is also a popular conference center. Places in Brighton may not take a booking for a single night in summer.

WHAT IT COSTS In pounds				
	££££££	££££	£££	££	£
RESTAURANTS	over £22	£18–£22	£13–£17	£7–£12	under £7
HOTELS	over £160	£115–£160	£80–£115	£50–£80	under £50

Restaurant prices are for a main course at dinner. Hotel prices are for two people in a standard double room in high season, including VAT, with no meals or, if indicated, CP (with Continental breakfast), BP (Breakfast Plan, with full breakfast), or MAP (Modified American Plan, with breakfast and dinner).

Timing

Because the counties of Kent, Surrey, and Sussex offer some of the most scenic landscape in southern England, lovers of the open air will want to get their fill of the many outdoor attractions here. In addition, most of the privately owned castles and mansions are open only between April and September or October, so it's best to tour the Southeast in the spring, summer, or early fall. Failing that, however, the great parks surrounding the stately houses are often open all year. In Canterbury and in the seaside towns, you would do well to avoid August, Sunday, and national holidays if you don't like crowds.

CANTERBURY TO DOVER

The ancient city of Canterbury, worldwide seat of the Church of England, shrine of Thomas à Becket, and immortalized in Geoffrey Chaucer's *Canterbury Tales,* is a prime historic center. Even in prehistoric times, this part of England was relatively well settled. Saxon settlers, Norman conquerors, and the folk who lived here in more settled late-medieval times all left their mark—most notably in the city's magnificent cathedral, the Mother Church of England. You can make endless excursions through the countryside between Canterbury and the busy port of Dover. Here, the Kentish landscape ravishes the eye in the spring with apple blossoms. It is a county of orchards, market gardens, and round, red-roof oasthouses, used for drying hops.

Canterbury

► *56 mi southeast of London.*

For many people, Geoffrey Chaucer's *Canterbury Tales,* about a pilgrimage to Canterbury Cathedral, brings back memories of high school English classes. Judging from the tales, however, medieval Canterbury was as much a party for people on horses as it was a spiritual center. The height of Canterbury's popularity came in the 12th century, when thousands of pilgrims flocked here to see the shrine of the murdered Archbishop Thomas à Becket, making this southeastern town one of the most visited in England, if not Europe. Buildings that served as pilgrims' inns still dominate the streets of Canterbury's center.

The relatively compact Southeast is densely packed with points of interest. Most of the essential sights are contained in and around the towns, whereas the rustic attractions such as castles, country homes, and gardens invite a more leisurely appreciation. Note that your own transportation is essential for some. You could spend several weeks here and still have more to see, but if you have only three days, confine your travels to one or two specific areas. A visit of seven days or so will allow you to explore a number of highlights as well as some of the Southeast's better-kept secrets.

2

Numbers in the text correspond to numbers in the margin and on the Southeast, Canterbury, and Brighton maps.

If you have 3 days You could opt for the glories of historic 🏛 **Canterbury** ❶–❸ ▶ as a first choice. Stay one night here, making a cathedral visit your priority, and spend any extra time meandering through the old streets, taking in the city's secondary sights. For your next two nights, pencil in 🏛 **Brighton** ㉚–㊲, where the Royal Pavilion is a must on any itinerary. Keeping Brighton as your base, you could spend a third day exploring **Lewes** ㉙, with its castle in a commanding position over the town and Tudor timber-frame buildings scattered along its steep lanes. Or, if you're lucky enough, you might attend a performance at the nearby Glyndebourne Opera House.

If you have 7 days Your first two nights will be spent in the ancient city of 🏛 **Canterbury** ❶–❸ ▶. If you're traveling east from London, you can stop en route and spend half a day at the dockyards at Chatham and the castle and cathedral at neighboring **Rochester** ㊵, both of which should be a great hit with children. In the morning, explore the cathedral and other sights in Canterbury, reserving the afternoon for a foray to the coast, tracing it down from **Broadstairs** ⑱, with its Dickensian associations, to **Dover** ㉒. On your third morning, head back west, veering south near Maidstone for **Leeds Castle** ㊶, whose lovely grounds vie for your attention with the treasures within. Farther south, **Sissinghurst Castle Garden** ㊷ is likely to convert even those who have never lifted a trowel. Overnight in pretty 🏛 **Rye** ㉓; take in nearby **Winchelsea** ㉔ the next day; then continue west to the site of the Battle of Hastings at **Battle** ㉖, where the remains of an abbey founded by William the Conqueror mark one of the most momentous events in English history. **Hastings** ㉕ is a typical south-coast town, but Herstmonceux, 12 mi farther west, has beautiful **Herstmonceux Castle** ㉗. From here, head to 🏛 **Brighton** ㉚–㊲, which deserves a two-night stay. After a morning of ambling around the promenades of this bustling seaside town and shopping in the Lanes and North Laine area, visit nearby **Lewes** ㉙, where some advance planning may get you seats at the Glyndebourne Opera for an evening treat.

Proceeding west along the coast on your sixth morning, take in 🏛 **Arundel** ㊳ and 🏛 **Chichester** ㊴, either of which would make a wonderful place for your sixth night. Arundel is dominated by Arundel Castle, whereas Chichester has a Norman cathedral in town and a Roman villa outside. For your last day, you can opt to travel north and toward London, which will bring you through 🏛 **Guildford** ㊹, a commuter town with some good 18th-century remnants and, east of here, a graceful Italianate palace, **Clandon Park** 45 . An alternative is to drive northeast back into Kent, where you can choose among the magnificent historic houses around 🖼 **Royal Tunbridge Wells** 49 . Some of the most stirring are the medieval manor house **Penshurst Place** 50 ; **Hever Castle** 51 , associated with two famous families, the Boleyns of the Tudor era and the Astors of the present day; medieval **Ightham Mote** 54 ; and **Chartwell** 52 , home of Sir Winston Churchill for more than 40 years.

Dig a little deeper and there is evidence of prosperous society in the Canterbury area as early as the Bronze Age (around 1000 BC). An important Roman city, an Anglo-Saxon center in the Kingdom of Kent, and currently headquarters of the Anglican Church, Canterbury remains a lively place, a fact that has impressed visitors since 1388, when Chaucer wrote his stories. Today, most pilgrims come in search of history and picture-perfect moments rather than spiritual enlightenment, and magnificently medieval Canterbury, with its ancient city walls, leaning Tudor buildings, and remnants of its Roman past, obliges. The absence of cars in the center brings some tranquillity to its streets, but to see Canterbury at its best, walk around early, before the tourist buses arrive, or wait until after they depart.

Canterbury is bisected by a road running northwest, beside which lie all the major tourist sites. This road, which crosses a branch of the River Stour in the city, begins as St. George's Street, becomes High Street, and finally turns into St. Peter's Street. On St. George's Street a lone church tower marks the site of **St. George's Church**—the rest of the building was destroyed in World War II—where playwright Christopher Marlowe was baptized in 1564.

❷ The **Canterbury Roman Museum,** including the colorful mosaic Roman pavement of a town house and a hypocaust (the Roman version of central heating), is below ground, at the level of the Roman town. Displays of excavated objects (some of which you can hold in the Touch the Past area) and computer-generated reconstructions of Roman buildings and the marketplace help re-create the past. ⊠ *Butchery La.* ☎ *01227/ 785575* ⊕ *www.canterbury.co.uk* ✉ *£2.60* ☉ *June–Oct., Mon.–Sat. 10–5, Sun. 1:30–5; Nov.–May, Mon.–Sat. 10–5; last admission at 4. Closed last wk Dec.*

Mercery Lane, with its medieval-style cottages and massive, overhanging timber roofs, runs right off High Street and ends in the tiny **Buttermarket,** an old market square where dairy products were sold. The immense **Christchurch Gate,** built in 1517, leads into the cathedral close. As you pass through, look up at the sculpted heads of two young figures: Prince Arthur, elder brother of Henry VIII, and the young Catherine of Aragon, to whom Arthur was betrothed. After Arthur's death, Catherine married Henry. Her failure to produce a male heir after 25 years of marriage led to Henry's decision to divorce her, creating an irrevocable breach with the Roman Catholic Church and altering the course of English history.

★ ❺ **Canterbury Cathedral,** the focal point of the city, was the first of England's great Norman cathedrals. Nucleus of worldwide Anglicanism, the Cathedral Church of Christ Canterbury (its formal name) is a living textbook of medieval architecture. The building was begun in 1070, demolished, begun anew in 1096, and then systematically expanded over the next three centuries. When the original choir section burned to the ground in 1174, another replaced it, designed in the Gothic style, with tall, pointed arches. The North Choir aisle holds two windows that show Jesus in the Temple, the three kings asleep, and Lot's wife turned to a pillar of salt. The windows are among the earliest parts of the cathedral, but only 33 of the original 208 survive.

The cathedral was only a century old, and still relatively small in size, when Thomas à Becket, the archbishop of Canterbury, was murdered here in 1170. Becket, an uncompromising defender of ecclesiastical interests, had angered his friend Henry II, who was heard to exclaim, "Who will rid me of this troublesome priest?" Thinking they were carrying out the king's wishes, four knights burst in on Becket in one of the side chapels and killed him. Two years later Becket was canonized, and Henry II's subsequent submission to the authority of the Church and his penitence helped establish the cathedral as the undisputed center of English Christianity. Becket's tomb, destroyed by Henry VIII in 1538 as part of his campaign to reduce the power of the Church and confiscate its treasures, was one of the most extravagant shrines in Christendom. In **Trinity Chapel,** which held the shrine, you can still see a series of 13th-century stained-glass windows illustrating Becket's miracles. So hallowed was this spot that in 1376, Edward, the Black Prince, warrior son of Edward III and a national hero, was buried near it. The actual site of Becket's murder is down a flight of steps just to the left of the nave. In the corner, a second flight of steps leads down to the enormous Norman **undercroft,** or vaulted cellarage, built in the early 12th century. A row of squat pillars whose capitals dance with fantastic animals and strange monsters supports the roof.

If time permits, be sure to explore the **cloisters** and other small monastic buildings to the north of the cathedral. The 12th-century octagonal water tower is still part of the cathedral's water supply. The Norman staircase in the northwest corner of the Green Court dates from 1167 and is a unique example of the domestic architecture of the times. The cathedral is very popular, so arrive early or late in the day to avoid the worst crowds. ⊠ *Cathedral Precincts* ☎ 01227/762862 ⊕ *www. canterbury-cathedral.org* ⊠ *£4, free for services and for ½ hr before closing* ⊙ *Easter–Sept., Mon.–Sat. 9–6:30, Sun. 12:30–2:30 and 4:30–5:30; Oct.–Easter, Mon.–Sat. 9–5, Sun. 12:30–2:30 and 4:30–5:30. Restricted access during services.*

need a break? **The Custard Tart** (⊠ 35a St. Margaret's St. ☎ 01227/785178), a short walk from the cathedral, serves a great selection of freshly made sandwiches, pies, tarts, and cakes. You can take your choice upstairs to the seating area. It's not open for dinner.

❻ **The Canterbury Tales** exhibition, in an unused church just off High Street, dramatizes 14th-century English life in an entertaining way. You'll "meet" Chaucer's pilgrims at the Tabard Inn near London and view tableaus illustrating five tales. Then, passing through a reconstruction of the city gate, you enter the marketplace. An actor in period costume often performs a charade as part of the scene. ⊠ *St. Margaret's St.* ☎ 01227/479227 ⊕ *www.canterburytales.org.uk* ⊠ *£6.50* ⊙ *Feb.–June, daily 10–5; July and Aug., daily 9:30–5:30; Sept. and Oct., daily 10–5; Nov. and Dec., daily 10–4:30.*

❼ Huguenot weavers who settled here after fleeing from religious persecution in France occupied the 16th-century **Weavers' Houses,** a lopsided group of half-timber buildings. The houses are just past where St. Peter's **❽** Street crosses a branch of the River Stour. The 12th-century **Eastbridge Hospital of St. Thomas** (which would now be called a hostel) lodged pilgrims who came to pray at the tomb of Thomas à Becket. The refectory, the chapel, and the crypt are open to the public. ✉ *25 High St.* ☎ *01227/462395* 🎫 *£1* ☉ *Mon.–Sat. 10–5; last admission at 4:30.*

★ ❾ The medieval Poor Priests' Hospital is the site of the enlarged **Museum of Canterbury** (previously the Canterbury Heritage Museum), whose exhibits provide an excellent overview of the city's history and architecture from Roman times to World War II. Special displays explore the Blitz, Rupert Bear, and the mysterious death of Christopher Marlowe. Visit early in the day to avoid the crowds. The building is off High Street. ✉ *20 Stour St.* ☎ *01227/452747* ⊕ *www.canterbury.gov.uk* 🎫 *£2.60* ☉ *Jan.–May, Nov., and Dec., Mon.–Sat, 10:30–5; June–Oct., Mon.–Sat, 10:30–5, Sun. 1:30–5; last admission at 4.*

🖑 ❿ One of the city's seven medieval gatehouses survives, complete with twin castellated towers; it now contains the **West Gate Museum**. Inside are medieval bric-a-brac and armaments used by the city guard, as well as more contemporary weaponry. The building became a jail in the 14th century, and you can view the prison cells. Climb to the roof for a panoramic view of the city. ✉ *St. Peter's St.* ☎ *01227/452747* ⊕ *www.canterbury.gov. uk* 🎫 *£1* ☉ *Mon.–Sat. 11–12:30 and 1:30–3:30. Closed Christmas wk.*

⓫ One essential Canterbury experience is to follow the circuit of the 13th- and 14th-century **medieval city walls,** built on the line of the original Roman walls. Those to the east survive intact, towering some 20 feet high and offering a sweeping view of the town. You can access these from a number of places, including Castle Street and Broad Street.

⓬ Augustine, England's first Christian missionary, was buried in 597 at **St. Augustine's Abbey,** one of the oldest monastic sites in the country. When Henry VIII seized the abbey in the 16th century, he destroyed some buildings and converted others into a royal manor for his fourth wife, Anne of Cleves. A free interactive audio tour puts the abbey's history into context. ✉ *Longport* ☎ *01227/767345* ⊕ *www.english-heritage.org.uk* 🎫 *£3* ☉ *Apr.–Sept., daily 10–6; Oct., daily 10–5; Nov.–Mar., daily 10–4.*

⓭ The **Dane John Mound,** just opposite the Canterbury East train station, was originally part of the city defenses.

Where to Stay & Eat

★ ££–££££ ✕ **Lloyds.** The magnificent beamed barn roof of this older building remains, but the interior—stripped wooden floor, white walls enlivened by contemporary paintings—and the cooking are definitely up-to-the-minute. A young crew of chefs creates such dishes as salad of spiced eggplant, caviar, and eggplant crisps with roasted cumin, and chicken and crayfish with braised fennel. The ice creams are homemade. ✉ *89–90 St. Dunstan's St.* ☎ *01227/768222* 🖃 *AE, MC, V.*

££–£££ ✕ **Weavers.** In the Old Weavers House, one of the Weavers' Houses on the River Stour, this popular restaurant in the center of town is an ideal place to feast on Tudor atmosphere as well as generous portions. The menu lists traditional English, seafood, and pasta dishes, and a good choice of wines. ✉ *1 St. Peter's St.* ☎ *01227/464660* 🖃 *AE, MC, V.*

£ ✕ **City Fish Bar.** Long lines and lots of satisfied finger-licking attest to the deserved popularity of this excellent fish-and-chips outlet in the center of town. Everything is freshly fried, the batter crisp and the fish tasty; the fried mushrooms are also surprisingly good. It closes at 7. ✉ *30 St. Margarets St.* ☎ *01227/760873* 🖃 *No credit cards.*

FodorśChoice
★

£ ✕ **Tapas en las Trece.** Interesting tapas in this atmospheric small restaurant include rabbit and bacon, and lamb in orange and chili. There are also some good vegetarian options. The dim lighting hides the fact that

2

Great Flavors
If you're in a seaside town, look for that great British staple, fish-and-chips. Perhaps "look" isn't the word—just follow your nose. In all the coastal areas, seafood, much of it locally caught, is a specialty. You'll discover local dishes such as Sussex smokies (smoked mackerel) and some of the most succulent oysters in Britain. In the larger towns, trendy restaurants tend (as ever) to spring up for a time and then disappear. This is an area in which to experiment.

Stately Homes & Castles
Britain has a rich heritage of stately homes scattered all over the nation, but this region has one of the greatest concentrations. To select the superlatives: Petworth House holds remarkable art; Chartwell was home and is permanent memorial to Sir Winston Churchill; Hever Castle was the abode of Henry VIII's second wife, Anne Boleyn, and was restored in the last century by William Waldorf Astor; Ightham Mote is perhaps the most enchanting medieval house in all Europe; Knole, one of the largest houses in Europe, is built around seven romantic courtyards; Leeds Castle, pretty as a picture, stands in the middle of a lake; Penshurst Place, dating from 1340, was once the home of poet Sir Philip Sidney, whose descendants still live there; and Sissinghurst Castle Garden won renown through the horticultural vision of author Vita Sackville-West.

Walking
Long sweeps of chalky downland—open, rolling terrain used mainly for pasture—characterize the Southeast and make walking a pleasure. Ardent walkers can explore both the North Downs Way (141 mi) and the South Downs Way (106 mi), following ancient paths along the tops of the downs. Both trails give you wide views over the countryside. The North Downs Way follows in part the ancient Pilgrim's Way to Canterbury. The South Downs Way crosses the chalk landscape of Sussex Downs, with parts of the route going through deep woodland. You can easily walk short sections of both trails. Along the way, plenty of towns and villages, mostly just off the main trail, have old inns that offer refreshment and/or accommodations. The 30-mi (north–south) Downs Link joins the two routes. Along the Kent coast, the Saxon Shore Way, 143 mi from Gravesend to Rye, passes many historical sites, including four Roman forts. Guides to all these walks are available from the Southeast England Tourist Board.

---

this is not quite the Mediterranean. ⊠ *13 Palace St.* ☎ *01227/762637* ▤ *MC, V.*

£££ ✕▥ **Falstaff Hotel.** This old coaching inn with a courtyard sits right outside Westgate. Some of the beamed and oak-furnished bedrooms overlook the River Stour; rooms have a mix of old features and new, and some have four-posters. Classic English fare at the restaurant includes pan-fried salmon, roast leg of lamb, and medallions of pork. The central location is a big plus: reserve well in advance. ⊠ *8 St. Dunstan's St., CT2 8AF* ☎ *01227/462138* 🖷 *01227/463525* ⊕ *www.corushotels. com* ⊅ *48 rooms* ⌂ *Restaurant, in-room data ports, cable TV, bar; no a/c* ▤ *AE, DC, MC, V.*

The
Southeast

Thames

Hampstead

LONDON

Windsor

Hounslow
Heathrow
Airport

Richmond

Woolwich

Thames

Egham

Staines

Merton

Sydenham

Dartford

Bromley

Sidcup

Beckenham

Woking

Leatherhead

Great Bookham **46**

Westerham

Knole **53**

A25

Clandon Park **45**

M25

52

Chartwell

A21

54
Ightham
Mote

Guildford **44**

Box Hill **47**

A246

A25

Hever Castle **51**

B2007

A31

Dorking

Reigate

M23

Penshurst Place
Penshurst

50 B2176 Tonbrid

NORTH DOWNS

A248

Hartfield

A26

Farnham

A3

A287

SURREY

Gatwick
Airport
Crawley

A264

Royal
Tunbridge Wells

A264

49 Lam

Milford

A24

East
Grinstead

48

A267

THE

B
W

Haslemere

A286

A283

Horsham

Handcross

A22

Wadhurst

Midhurst

A272

A286

Wisborough Green

A29

Cuckfield

Haywards Heath

Rother

Burwash

43 Petworth
House

WEST
SUSSEX

A283

Uckfield

EAST
SUSSEX

A265

SOUTH

A285

Storrington

Burgess
Hill

Ouse

A26

Singleton **42**

B2139

A281

A23

Lewes **29**

Glyndebourne

27

DOWNS

Amberley

A27

Herstmor
Castle

Sculpture at
Goodwood **41**

38

Arundel

A27

Rodmell

Fishbourne
Roman Palace

A259

Hove

A259

Wilmington **28** A27

40 **39** Chichester

A259

Worthing

Eastbourne

A259

Bognor Regis

Brighton
30 – **37**
see detail
map

English Channel

KEY
▶ Start of itinerary

GREAT
BRITAIN

North
Sea

ESSEX

Chelmsford
Maldon
Blackwater
Crouch
Rayleigh
Basildon
CANVEY
ISLAND
Southend-
on-Sea
Thames
Grays
Sheerness
Queenborough
Herne Bay
Birchington
Margate
Whitstable
Broadstairs **18**
Rochester **55**
Gillingham
Chatham
The Swale
Faversham **17**
Fordwich
Ramsgate
Harbledown **15**
14
Sandwich **19**
Maidstone
Canterbury
1–**13**
see detail
map
Deal **20**
Leeds **56**
Castle
Chilham **16**
Walmer **21**
Castle
Headcorn
KENT
Wye
Great Stour
Ashford
Dover **22**
Finchcocks **61**
Biddenden
Sissinghurst Castle **57**
and Garden
Cranbrook
Folkestone
Channel Tunnel
WEALD
Hawkhurst
Bewl
Water
Romney Marsh
Hythe
Great Dixter **59**
House and Gardens
Northiam
New Romney
Bodiam **58**
Castle
60
Rye **23**
Lydd
Battle
26
Winchelsea **24**
Rye Bay
27
monceux
Bexhill
Hastings **25**
Pevensey
Pevensey
Bay
Strait of Dover

0   5 miles
0   5 km

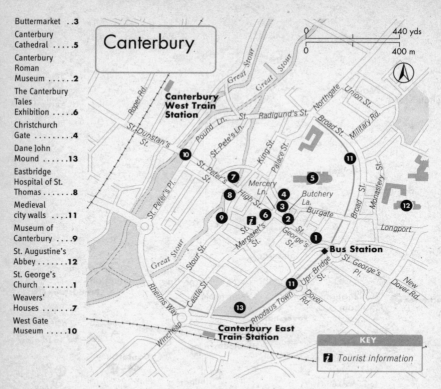

ff–fff ✕⊡ **County Hotel.** First licensed in 1588, the year of the Spanish Armada, this hotel includes up-to-date comforts, but touches such as old wood and antiques keep the past alive. A number of more expensive specialty bedrooms are done in Tudor, Georgian, or Colonial style; others are standard modern. The bar and tea rooms are pleasantly old-fashioned, and the formal Sully's Restaurant is known for traditional English dining. ⊠ *High St., CT1 2RX* ☎ *01227/766266* 🖷 *01227/451512* ⊕ *www.macdonaldhotels.co.uk* 🛏 *73 rooms* ♧ *Restaurant, coffee shop, bar, meeting rooms, some pets allowed; no a/c* ⊟ *AE, DC, MC, V* ❧ *BP.*

fff ⊡ **Magnolia House.** Kept in apple-pie order, this Georgian detached house is charmingly elegant, with a lovely walled garden for relaxation. Bedrooms have floral motifs and traditional furnishings; one has a four-poster. Evening meals are available in winter. ⊠ *36 St. Dunstan's Terr., CT2 8AX* 🖷🖷 *01227/765121* ⊕ *http://freespace.virgin.net/magnolia.canterbury* 🛏 *7 rooms* ♧ *No a/c, no room phones, no kids under 12, no smoking* ⊟ *AE, DC, MC, V* ❧ *BP.*

f–fff ⊡ **Cathedral Gate Hotel.** Older even than the adjoining cathedral gateway, this hotel was originally built as a hostelry for pilgrims in 1438. The large beams, sloping floors, and twisting corridors are evidence of its medieval origins; the plainly furnished rooms, however, have been sympathetically modernized. The bow-window restaurant looks out over the Buttermarket. ⊠ *36 Burgate, CT1 2HA* ☎ *01227/464381* 🖷 *01227/462800* ⊕ *www.cathgate.co.uk* 🛏 *27 rooms* ♧ *Restaurant, bar, some pets allowed; no a/c* ⊟ *AE, DC, MC, V* ❧ *CP.*

ff ⊡ **Pointers.** This homey redbrick Georgian hotel stands within easy walking distance of the cathedral and city center; it looks down to the Westgate and overlooks the 10th-century church of St. Dunstans. Some of the simply furnished rooms are on the small side, but you can stretch out a bit more in the sitting room. Extra window glazing ensures quiet, despite the location on a busy road. ✉ *1 London Rd., CT2 8LR* ☎ *01227/456846* 🖷 *01227/452786* ⊕ *www.pointers.hotel.dial.pipex. com* ↩ *12 rooms* ♿ *Dining room, bar; no a/c* ⊟ *AE, DC, MC, V* ✪ *Closed late Dec.–mid-Feb.* ⊠❘ *BP.*

Nightlife & the Arts
The two-week-long, mixed-arts **Canterbury Festival** (☎ 01227/452853 ⊕ www.canterburyfestival.co.uk) is held every October. The **Gulbenkian Theatre** (✉ Giles La. ☎ 01227/769075), at the University of Kent, mounts all kinds of plays, particularly experimental works. The **Marlowe** (✉ St. Margaret's St. ☎ 01227/787787), named after the Elizabethan playwright, who was born in Canterbury, is a venue for touring drama and opera companies.

Shopping
Hawkin's Bazaar (✉ 34 Burgate ☎ 01227/785809) carries an exceptional selection of traditional and modern toys and games. The **National Trust Shop** (✉ 24 Burgate ☎ 01227/457120) stocks the National Trust line of household items, ideal for gifts.

Fordwich

⑭ *1½ mi east of Canterbury.*

The village of Fordwich was originally the river port for Canterbury; the Caen stone quarried in Normandy and shipped across the Channel to be used in the construction of the cathedral was brought ashore here. Don't miss England's smallest town hall, with stocks and ducking stool outside.

Harbledown

⑮ *1 mi west of Canterbury.*

Along the old Roman road to London (now A2) lies Harbledown; once a separate village, it's now part of Canterbury. The main sight here is the cluster of pretty almshouses, built in the 11th century to house the poor. Harbledown was customarily the spot from which pilgrims caught their first glimpse of Canterbury Cathedral.

Chilham

★ ⑯ *5 mi southwest of Canterbury.*

From this hilltop village, midway between Canterbury and Ashford on the A252 (off the A28), you can walk the last few miles of the traditional Pilgrim's Way back to Canterbury. The village square is filled with textbook examples of English rural architecture with gabled windows beneath undulating roofs. The church dates from the 14th century.

Where to Eat
££ ✕ **White Horse.** This 16th-century inn shadowed by Chilham's church has a pleasant beer garden and provides lunchtime and evening meals superior to the usual pub grub, with many good pasta dishes. There's a log fire in winter. ✉ *The Square* ☎ 01227/730355 ⊟ *MC, V.*

Faversham

⑰ *9 mi west of Canterbury, 11 mi northwest of Chilham.*

In Roman times, Faversham was a thriving seaport. Today the port is hidden from sight, and you could pass through this pretty market town without knowing it was there. Still, Faversham is a must for those in search of Ye Quaint Olde Englande: the town center, with its Tudor houses grouped around the 1574 guildhall and covered market, looks like a perfect stage set.

Where to Stay & Eat

★ **£££££**   ✕ **Read's.** The glorious food in this elegant restaurant is assuredly British, but with an audacious spin on old favorites. The accent falls firmly on local ingredients, many of which come from the vegetable garden (in which you are welcome to stroll). After a main course of duck breast marinated in honey or Kentish lamb with rosemary, try the scrumptious "chocoholics anonymous" dessert. Prices are fixed, with good three-course lunch options at £19.50 and a three-course dinner costing £42. You can also overnight here in one of six spacious rooms in Georgian style. ✉ *Macknade Manor, Canterbury Rd.* ☎ *01795/535344* ▤ *AE, DC, MC, V* ☉ *Closed Sun. and Mon.*

£   ✕ **Sun Inn.** The flagship of the Shepherd Neame Brewery chain, established in Faversham in the 17th century, this clapboard pub is even older, dating to the 1400s. The inn follows the local tradition of hanging up hops in September; they add a distinctive fragrance. At press time plans were in the works to open for dinner and to add some accommodations. ✉ *10 West St.* ☎ *01795/535098* ▤ *MC, V* ☉ *No dinner.*

★ **££**   ✕▥ **White Horse Inn.** Mentioned in Chaucer's *Canterbury Tales,* this 15th-century coaching inn outside Faversham on the old London-to-Dover road (now A2) retains much of its traditional character. The pale blue guest rooms have antique furniture. Besides the friendly bar, there's an excellent restaurant in what used to be a courtroom; you might find shark steak on the list of daily specials. ✉ *The Street, Boughton, ME13 9AX* ☎ *01227/751343* 🖷 *01227/751090* ⊕ *www.shepherd-neame.co.uk* ⬎ *13 rooms* ⚘ *Restaurant, bar; no a/c* ▤ *AE, MC, V* �‖ *BP.*

Broadstairs

⑱   *25 mi east of Faversham, 17 mi east of Canterbury.*

Like other towns such as Margate and Ramsgate on this stretch of coast, Broadstairs was once the playground of vacationing Londoners. Charles Dickens spent many summers here between 1837 and 1851 and wrote glowingly of its bracing freshness. One of Dickens's favorite abodes in the town was **Bleak House,** perched on a cliff overlooking Viking Bay, where he wrote much of *David Copperfield* and drafted *Bleak House,* after which the house was later renamed. His study and other rooms have been preserved. Displays explore local history, including the wrecks at nearby Goodwin Sands, and the cellars have exhibits about the smuggling, a longtime local activity. ✉ *Fort Rd.* ☎ *01843/862224* ⊕ *www. bleakhouse.ndo.co.uk* ☒ *£3* ☉ *Feb.–June and Sept.–mid-Dec., daily 10–6; July and Aug., daily 10–9.*

The **Dickens House Museum** was the setting Dickens imagined as the home of Betsy Trotwood, David Copperfield's aunt. There's a reconstruction of her room, and prints and photographs commemorate Dickens's association with Broadstairs. ✉ *2 Victoria Parade* ☎ *01843/861232* ⊕ *www.dickenshouse.co.uk* ☒ *£1.50* ☉ *Apr.–mid-Oct., daily 2–5.*

Nightlife & the Arts

Each June, Broadstairs holds a **Dickens Festival** (☎ 01843/865265), lasting about a week, with readings, people in Dickensian costume, a Dickensian cricket match, and Victorian vaudeville, among other entertainments. Aficionados of the author are also drawn to another Dickens festival in Rochester.

Sandwich

⑲ *11 mi south of Broadstairs, 12 mi east of Canterbury.*

The coast near Canterbury holds three of the ancient **Cinque Ports** (pronounced sink ports), a confederacy of ports along the southeast seaboard whose heyday lasted from the 12th through the 14th centuries. These towns, originally five in number (hence *cinque,* from the Norman French)—Sandwich, Dover, Hythe, Romney, and Hastings—are rich in history and are generally less crowded than the other resorts of Kent's northeast coast.

In Saxon times Sandwich stood in a sheltered bay; it became the most important of the Cinque Ports in the Middle Ages and later England's chief naval base. From 1500 the port began to silt up, however, and the pretty town is now 2 mi inland, though the River Stour still flows through it. The 16th-century checkerboard barbican (gatehouse) by the toll bridge is one of many medieval and Tudor buildings; Strand Street has many half-timber structures.

Deal

⑳ *7 mi south of Sandwich, 8 mi northeast of Dover.*

The large seaside town of Deal is famous in history books as the place where Caesar's legions landed in 55 BC, and it was from here that William Penn set sail in 1682 on his first journey to the American colony he founded, Pennsylvania.

Deal Castle, erected in 1540 and intricately built to the shape of a Tudor rose, is the largest of the coastal defenses built by Henry VIII. A moat surrounds its gloomy passages and austere walls. The castle museum has exhibits of prehistoric, Roman, and Saxon Britain. ⊠ *Victoria Rd.* ☎*01304/372762* ⊕*www.english-heritage.org.uk* ☜*£3.20* ⊙ *Apr.–Sept., daily 10–6; Oct., daily 10–5; Nov.–Mar., Wed.–Sun. 10–4.*

Walmer Castle

㉑ *7 mi northeast of Dover, 1 mi south of Deal.*

Walmer Castle, one of Henry VIII's fortifications, was converted in 1730 into the official residence of the lord warden of the Cinque Ports, and it now resembles a cozy country house. Among the famous lord wardens were William Pitt the Younger; the duke of Wellington, hero of the Battle of Waterloo, who lived here from 1829 until his death here in 1852 (a small museum contains Wellington memorabilia); and Sir Winston Churchill. The Queen Mother held the post until her death in 2002. The drawing and dining rooms are open to the public, and attractive gardens and a grassy walk fill what was the moat. ⊠ *A258* ☎ *01304/364288* ⊕ *www.english-heritage.org.uk* ☜ *£5* ⊙ *Apr.–Sept., daily 10–6; Oct., daily 10–5; Mar., Nov., and Dec., Wed.–Sun. 10–4; Jan. and Feb., weekends 10–4.*

Dover

㉒ *7 mi south of Walmer Castle, 78 mi east of London.*

One of the busiest passenger ports in the world, Dover has for centuries been Britain's gateway to Europe. Its chalk **White Cliffs** are a famous and inspirational sight. You may find the town disappointing; the savage bombardments of World War II and the shortsightedness of postwar developers have left their scars on the city center. Roman legacies include a lighthouse, adjoining a stout Anglo-Saxon church. The **Roman Painted House,** believed to have been a hotel, includes some well-preserved wall paintings, along with the remnants of an ingenious heating system. ⊠ *New St.* ☎ *01304/203279* 🖼 *£2* ⊙ *Apr.–Sept., Tues.–Sun. 10–5.*

★ ♻ Spectacular **Dover Castle,** towering high above the ramparts of the White Cliffs, was one of the mightiest medieval castles in Western Europe and served as an important strategic center over the centuries. Most of the castle, including the keep, dates back to Norman times. It was begun by Henry II in 1181 but incorporates additions from almost every succeeding century. There's a lot to see here besides the castle rooms: exhibits, many of which will appeal to kids, include the Siege of 1216, the Princess of Wales Regimental Museum, and Castle Fit for a King. You can tour the secret wartime tunnels, a medieval and Napoleonic-era underground tunnel system that was used as a World War II command center during the evacuation of Dunkirk in 1940. ⊠ *Castle Rd.* ☎ *01304/ 211067* ⊕ *www.english-heritage.org.uk* 🖼 *£7.50* ⊙ *Apr.–Sept., daily 10–6; Oct., daily 10–5; Nov.–Mar., daily 10–4.*

The Victorian cells of the **Old Town Gaol,** beneath the town hall, evoke the misery endured by convicted felons. Audiovisual gadgetry enhances the reconstructed courtroom and exercise yard. ⊠ *Biggin St.* ☎ *01304/ 202723* 🖼 *£3.50* ⊙ *June–Sept., Tues.–Sat. 10–4:30, Sun. 2–4:30; Oct.–May, Wed.–Sat. 10–4:30, Sun. 2–4:30.*

Where to Stay

★ **£–££** 🏠 **Number One Guest House.** This popular, family-run guest house with garage parking is a great bargain. Mural wallpapers and porcelain collections decorate the cozy corner terrace home built in the early 19th century, and you can even have breakfast in your own room. The walled garden has a fine view of the castle. ⊠ *1 Castle St., CT16 1QH* ☎ *01304/ 202007* 🖨 *01304/214078* ⊕ *www.number1guesthouse.co.uk* 🛏 *4 rooms* ⚹ *No a/c, no room phones* ▭ *No credit cards* ❍I *BP.*

RYE TO GLYNDEBOURNE

From Dover, the coast road winds west through Folkestone (a genteel resort, small port, and Channel Tunnel terminal), across Romney Marsh (reclaimed from the sea and famous for its sheep and, at one time, its ruthless smugglers), to the delightful town of Rye. The region along the coast is noted for pretty Winchelsea, the history-rich sites of Hastings and Herstmonceux, and the famous Glyndebourne Opera House festival, based outside Lewes, a town celebrated for its architectural heritage. One of the three steam railroads in the Southeast services part of the area: the Romney, Hythe, and Dymchurch Railway, a main-line service that uses locomotives one-third the regular size.

Rye

★ ㉓ *68 mi southeast of London, 34 mi southwest of Dover.*

With cobbled streets and timbered dwellings, pretty Rye on its hill remains an artist's dream, sprinkled with such historic buildings as the Mermaid Inn as well as the secret places that made it a smuggler's strategic retreat. In fact, today the former port of Rye lies nearly 2 mi inland, overlooking the Romney Marshes. The town is famous for its pottery, produced by four working potteries and shipped all over the world. The tourist office has a good audio guided tour of Rye.

Rye Castle Museum, below the castle, displays watercolors and examples of Rye pottery, including 19th-century hopware decorated with hop motifs in relief. Among the exhibits on local history is an 18th-century fire engine. ⊠ *3 East St.* ☎ *01797/226728* ⊕ *www.rye.org.uk* ⊡ *£1.90, £2.90 including Ypres Tower* ⊘ *Apr.–Oct., Mon., Thurs., and Fri. 2–5, Sat. 10:30–1, Sun. 10:30–2; last admission 30 mins before closing.*

On an elevation behind Church Square, **Ypres Tower** was built as part of the town's fortifications in 1249; it later served as a prison. The stone chambers hold a motley collection of local items, such as smuggling bric-a-brac and shipbuilding mementos. A topographical map of Romney Marsh shows the changes in sea level. ⊠ *Gungarden* ☎ *01797/226728* ⊡ *£1.90, £2.90 including Rye Castle* ⊘ *Apr.–Oct., Mon., Thurs., and Fri. 10–1 and 2–5; Sat. 10:30–1, Sun. 10:30–2; Nov.–Mar., weekends 10:30–3:30; last admission 30 mins before closing.*

Several well-known writers have lived in **Lamb House**, an early 18th-century structure. The most famous was the novelist Henry James, who lived here from 1898 to 1916. E. F. Benson, one-time mayor of Rye and author of the witty *Lucia* novels (written in the 1920s and 1930s, with some set in a town based on Rye), was a later resident. The ground-floor rooms contain some of James's furniture and personal belongings. ⊠ *West St.* ☎ *01892/890651* ⊕ *www.nationaltrust.org.uk* ⊡ *£2.60* ⊘ *Apr.–Oct., Wed. and Sat. 2–6; last admission at 5:30.*

A wonderfully nostalgic tour of the exhibits at the **Rye Treasury of Mechanical Music** treats you to tunes from music boxes, barrel organs, and a 1920s dance organ. ⊠ *20 Cinque Ports St.* ☎ *01797/223345* ⊡ *£3* ⊘ *Mar.–Oct., daily 10–5; Nov.–Feb., Wed.–Mon. 11–4.*

Where to Stay & Eat

★ **££–£££** ✕ **Landgate Bistro.** Although definitely a bistro, this restaurant in a small shop unit near one of the ancient gateways is serious about its food. Fish is always a good choice, or you can opt for the wild rabbit or griddle-cooked cutlets of Gloucester Old Spot pork with sage, applesauce, and potatoes. A fixed-price menu (about £17) is available Tuesday–Thursday. ⊠ *5–6 Landgate* ☎ *01797/222829* ⊟ *DC, MC, V* ⊘ *Closed Sun., Mon., last wk Dec., 1st wk Jan. No lunch.*

★ ✕▣ **The Mermaid.** Once the headquarters of a notorious smuggling **££££–£££££** gang, this classic half-timber inn has served Rye for nearly six centuries. Sloping floors, oak beams, low ceilings, and a huge open hearth in the bar testify to its age. Rooms vary in size but are comfortable; some have four-posters. The main restaurant allows you to soak up the period details while choosing from an extensive English menu. An adjacent bar serves pub meals, and in summer the Tudor Tearoom offers a lovely cuppa. Be warned: the Mermaid is *very* popular, and you must book well ahead. ⊠*Mermaid St., TN31 7EY* ☎*01797/223065* 🖷*01797/225069* ⊕ *www.mermaidinn.com* ⇗ *31 rooms* ⚭ *Restaurant, bar, meeting room; no a/c* ⊟ *AE, MC, V* ⦿*BP.*

£££ ▣ **Jeake's House.** Antiques and books fill the cozy bedrooms of this rambling 1689 house, and print fabrics and brass or mahogany beds add charm. The snug painted and paneled parlor has a wood-burning stove for cold days. Breakfast, which might include deviled kidneys or kippers, is served in a galleried room formerly used for Quaker meetings and as a Baptist chapel. Book well in advance. ⊠ *Mermaid St., TN31 7ET* ☎ *01797/222828* 🖷 *01797/222623* ⊕ *www.jeakeshouse.com* ⇗ *11 rooms, 10 with bath* ⚭ *Bar, some pets allowed (fee); no a/c, no kids under 12* ⊟ *MC, V* ⦿ *BP.*

££ ▣ **The Old Vicarage.** Roses frame the door of this pretty, bay-front Georgian house in a peaceful location close to the church (double glazing ensures that the peal of the bells does not intrude). The sunny rooms combine Victorian, Edwardian, and French furniture. You can breakfast on scrumptious homemade bread, scones, and locally produced eggs and bacon in a dining room that overlooks a walled garden. ⊠ *66 Church Sq., TN31 7HF* ☎ *01797/222119* 🖷 *01797/227466* ⊕ *www. oldvicaragerye.co.uk* 🖙 *4 rooms* ⚘ *No a/c, no room phones, no kids under 8, no smoking* 🖃 *No credit cards* ⊘ *Closed last wk Dec.* ⵙⵔ *BP.*

Winchelsea

㉔ *2 mi southwest of Rye, 71 mi southeast of London.*

Like Rye, Winchelsea perches atop its own small hill amid farmland and tiny villages. One of the prettiest places to visit in the region, it has many attractive houses, some with clapboards, and a splendid (though damaged) church built in the 14th century with Caen stone from Normandy. The town was built on a grid system devised in 1283, after the sea destroyed an earlier settlement at the foot of the hill. The sea later receded, leaving the town high and dry. Some of the original town gates still stand.

Where to Stay & Eat

££ ✕▦ **The New Inn.** This 18th-century hostelry in the heart of town is an excellent place to stop for a pub lunch or a bed for the night. The quiet, refurbished rooms have deep-pile carpets and pleasant views. The bar serves up juicy roasts and quaffable cask ales, and there's a warming log fire. ⊠ *German St.* ☎ *01797/226252* 🖙 *6 rooms* ⚘ *Restaurant; no a/c, no room phones* 🖃 *MC, V* ⵙⵔ *BP.*

Hastings

㉕ *9 mi southwest of Winchelsea, 68 mi southeast of London.*

Hastings, famous as the base for the invasion led by William, duke of Normandy, in 1066, is now a large, slightly run-down seaside resort. A visit to the old town provides an interesting overview of 900 years of English maritime history. Below the East Cliff, tall wooden towers called **net shops**, unique to the town, are still used for drying fishermen's nets. The 250-foot **Hastings Embroidery,** in the White Rock Theatre opposite the pier, was made in 1966 to mark the battle's 900th anniversary. Twenty-seven panels depict 81 great events in British history. ⊠ *White Rock* ☎ *01424/781010* 🎫 *£2* ⊘ *Daily 11–4; last admission at 3:30.*

You can take the West Hill Cliff Railway from George Street precinct to the Norman **Hastings Castle,** built by William the Conqueror in 1069. All that remains are fragments of the fortifications, some ancient walls, and a number of gloomy dungeons. Nevertheless, you get an excellent view of the chalky cliffs, the coast, and the town below. "The 1066 Story" retells the Norman invasion using audiovisual technology. ⊠ *West Hill* ☎ *01424/781112* ⊕ *www.hastings.gov.uk* 🎫 *£3.20* ⊘ *Apr.–Sept., daily 10–5:30 (10–6 in Aug.); Oct.–Mar., daily 11–4; last admission 30 mins before closing.*

Ⓒ Waxworks and exhibits recall the history of coastal smuggling at **Smuggler's Adventure,** in a labyrinth of caves and passages a 5- or 10-minute walk above Hastings Castle. ⊠ *St. Clement Caves* ☎ *01424/422964* ⊕ *www.smugglersadventure.co.uk* 🎫 *£5.25* ⊘ *Apr.–Sept., daily 10–6; Oct.–Mar., daily 11–5; last admission 30 mins before closing.*

Where to Stay & Eat

£££–££££ ✕ **Bonaparte's.** A hands-on approach to food distinguishes this slightly haughty seafront restaurant, which has dark walls with booths for dining. Owner Bob Bone shoots his own game and buys fish fresh from the market to create dishes such as game pie in beer and wine sauce and halibut steak with crayfish tails. His inventive vegetarian choices include a Tibetan roast with buckwheat, spinach, mushrooms, and walnuts. ⊠ 64 *Eversfield Pl., St. Leonards* ☎ *01424/712218* ⊟ *AE, DC, MC, V* ⊗ *Closed Mon. No lunch Sun.*

££ 🏠 **Eagle House.** Its own attractive garden surrounds this guest house in a large Victorian building. Guest rooms and public areas have Victorian touches, and the restaurant uses fresh produce from local farms. The lodging is in St. Leonards, the western section of Hastings, within easy reach of the town center. ⊠ *12 Pevensey Rd., St. Leonards, TN38 0JZ* ☎ *01424/430535* 🖷 *01424/437771* ⊕ *www.eaglehousehotel.com* 🖙 *18 rooms* ⚎ *Restaurant; no a/c* ⊟ *AE, DC, MC, V* ⦿❘ *BP.*

Battle

❷ *7 mi northwest of Hastings, 61 mi southeast of London.*

Battle is the actual site of the crucial Battle of Hastings, at which, on October 14, 1066, the more disciplined forces of William of Normandy trounced King Harold's Anglo-Saxon army. Harold II was killed, and the Norman state was established with the coronation of William I—also known as William the Conqueror—in Westminster Abbey in London on Christmas Day.

The ruins of **Battle Abbey,** the great Benedictine abbey William the Conqueror erected after his victory, and the surrounding area still convey the sense of past conflict. A memorial stone marks the high altar, which stood on the spot where Harold II was killed. The abbey was destroyed in 1539 during Henry VIII's dissolution of the monasteries, but you can take the mile-long Battlefield Walk around the edge of the battlefield and see the remains of many of the domestic buildings. The **Abbot's House** (closed to the public) is now a girls' school. ⊠ *High St.* ☎ *01424/ 773792* ⊕ *www.english-heritage.org.uk* 🎟 *£4.50* ⊗ *Apr.–Sept., daily 10–6; Oct., daily 10–5; Nov.–Mar., daily 10–4.*

Where to Stay & Eat

£££–££££ ✕🏠 **Powder Mills Hotel.** The grounds of this Georgian house, close to Battle Abbey and adjoining the 1066 battlefield, include 150 acres of parkland. Among the bedrooms lavishly furnished in country-house style are one used by the duke of Wellington and another supposedly haunted by a "lady in white." The seafood receives high marks at the conservatory-style Orangery Restaurant. There's a fixed-price menu at lunch and dinner. ⊠ *Powdermill La., TN33 0SP* ☎ *01424/775511* 🖷 *01424/ 774540* 🖙 *40 rooms* ⚎ *Restaurant, cable TV, pool, fishing, meeting rooms, some pets allowed; no a/c* ⊟ *AE, DC, MC, V* ⦿❘ *BP.*

£££ ✕🏠 **Little Hemingfold Hotel.** The surrounding 40 acres of fields and woodland, including a trout lake, provide the main enticement of this informal, early Victorian farmhouse hotel. Guest rooms, done in simple country style, are bright and serene, and there's a piano in one of the sitting rooms. The fixed-price dinner in the candelit dining rooms uses homegrown fruit and vegetables. The hotel is 2 mi south of Battle off the A2100. ⊠ *Hastings Rd., Telham, TN33 0TT* ☎ *01424/774338* 🖷 *01424/775351* ⊕ *www.smoothhound.co.uk* 🖙 *12 rooms* ⚎ *Restaurant, tennis court, lake, boating, fishing, croquet, bar, some pets allowed; no a/c, no kids under 7* ⊟ *AE, MC, V* ⦿❘ *BP.*

Herstmonceux Castle

❷ *11 mi southwest of Battle, 61 mi southeast of London.*

Back in the Edwardian era, square-shape Herstmonceux was famous as the quintessential romantic English castle, complete with moat and rose-color brick and limestone crenellations. In 1911 rich connoisseurs so completely renovated the structure that the magic nearly evaporated, but Herstmonceux remains a fabled name for castle lovers. Sir Roger Fiennes, ancestor of actor Ralph Fiennes, originally built it in 1444. Now housing the International Study Centre owned by Queen's University of Canada, the castle is open for guided tours only, and you can explore the gardens and grounds. There are no deluxe salons, but the interior still has some fine Elizabethan-era staircases and ceilings. ⊠ *Hailsham* ☎ *01323/834444* ⊕ *www.herstmonceux-castle.com* ☜ *Castle tours £2.50, grounds £4* ⊘ *Mid-Apr.–Sept., daily 10–6; Oct., daily 10–5; last admission 1 hr before closing.*

Where to Eat

£££–££££ ✕ **The Sundial.** This 17th-century brick farmhouse holds a popular French restaurant run by chef Vincent Rongier and his wife, Mary. The extensive, frequently changing menu lists imaginative choices: foie gras and truffles vie with smoked salmon from the Shetland Isles. The fixed-price options are a good value. ⊠ *Gardner St., Herstmonceux* ☎ *01323/832217* ▭ *AE, DC, MC, V* ⊘ *Closed Mon. No dinner Sun.*

Wilmington

㉘ *9 mi southwest of Herstmonceux Castle, 7 mi west of Pevensey on A27.*

Pretty Wilmington has a famous landmark. High on the downs to the south of the village (signposted off A27), a 226-foot-tall white figure, known as the **Long Man of Wilmington,** is carved into the chalk; he has a club in each hand. His age is a subject of great debate, but some researchers think he might have originated in Roman times.

㋛ Specifically designed for children, **Drusilla's Park** is one of the best small zoos in England, with gardens, a miniature railroad, and an adventure playground. The zoo is 1½ mi west of Wilmington in the pretty Cuckmere Valley. ⊠ *A27, Alfriston* ☎ *01323/874100* ⊕ *www.drusillas.co. uk* ☜ *£9.50* ⊘ *Apr.–Oct., daily 10–6; Nov.–Mar., daily 10–5; last admission 1 hr before closing.*

Lewes

★ **㉙** *10 mi northwest of Wilmington, 8 mi northeast of Brighton, 54 mi south of London.*

The town nearest to the celebrated Glyndebourne Opera House, Lewes is so rich in architectural history that the Council for British Archaeology has named it one of the 50 most important English towns. A walk is the best way to appreciate the town's appealing jumble of building styles and materials—flint, stone, brick, tile—and the secret lanes (called "twittens") behind the castle with their huge beeches. Here and there you'll find smart antiques shops and secondhand-book dealers. Buildings of all ages, styles, and descriptions line High Street, including a timber-frame house once occupied by Thomas Paine (1737–1809), author of *The Rights of Man.*

Lewes is one of the few towns left in England that still celebrate in high style Guy Fawkes Night (November 5), the anniversary of Fawkes's attempt to blow up the Houses of Parliament in 1605. It's rather like an autumnal Mardi Gras, with costumed processions and flaming tar barrels rolled down High Street.

High above the valley of the River Ouse stand the majestic ruins of **Lewes Castle,** begun in 1100. For a panoramic view of the surrounding region, climb the keep. The **Barbican House Museum** inside the castle includes the Town Model, a re-creation of Lewes in the 19th century. ⊠ *169 High*

St. ☎ *01273/405730* ⊕ *www.sussexpast.co.uk* ✉ *£4.20, £5.80 includes Anne of Cleves House* ⊙ *Tues.–Sat. 10–5:30 or dusk, Sun. 11–5:30 or dusk; last admission 30 mins before closing.*

The 16th-century **Anne of Cleves House,** a fragile timber-frame building, holds a notable collection of Sussex ironwork and other items of local interest such as Sussex pottery. A famous painting of the local Guy Fawkes procession is also here. The house was part of Anne of Cleves's divorce settlement from Henry VIII, but she did not live in it. To get to the house, walk down steep, cobbled Keere Street, past lovely Grange Gardens, to Southover High Street. ⊠ *52 Southover High St.* ☎ *01273/474610* ⊕ *www.sussexpast.co.uk* ✉ *£2.80, £5.80 includes Lewes Castle* ⊙ *Mar.–Oct., Tues.–Sat. 10–5, Sun. and Mon. noon–5; Nov.–Mar., Tues.–Sat. 10–5; last admission at 4.*

Of interest to serious Bloomsbury fans, **Monk's House** was the home of novelist Virginia Woolf and her husband, Leonard Woolf, who purchased it in 1919. Leonard lived here until his death in 1969. Rooms in the small cottage include Virginia's study, where she wrote a number of her books, and her bedroom. Artists Vanessa Bell (Virginia's sister) and Duncan Grant helped decorate the house. ⊠ *C7, off A27, 3 mi south of Lewes, Rodmell* ☎ *01892/890651* ⊕ *www.nationaltrust.org.uk* ✉ *£2.60* ⊙ *Apr.–Oct., Wed. and Sat. 2–5:30.*

Art and life mixed at **Charleston,** the farmhouse Vanessa Bell bought in 1916 and decorated with Duncan Grant (who resided here until 1978), painting the walls, doors, and furniture. The house became a refuge for writers and artists of the Bloomsbury Group and holds ceramics and textiles of the Omega Workshop—in which Bell and Grant participated— and paintings by Picasso and Renoir as well as by Bell and Grant. The house is seen on a guided tour, except on Sunday. ⊠ *Off A27, 7 mi east of Lewes, Firle* ☎ *01323/811265* ⊕ *www.charleston.org.uk* ✉ *£6, gardens only £2.50* ⊙ *May, June, Sept., and Oct., Wed.–Sun. 2–6; July and Aug., Wed.–Sat. 11:30–6, Sun. 2–6; last admission at 5.*

Where to Stay & Eat

★ ✕🛏 **Horsted Place.** Perfect for outdoor activities or relaxation, this lux-
££££–£££££ urious hotel sits on 1,100 acres, a few minutes' drive from Glyndebourne. Built as a private home in 1850 with Gothic Revival elements by Augustus-Charles Pugin, it is richly furnished in country-house style and has a magnificent Victorian staircase and a Gothic library with a secret door that leads to a courtyard. The dining room, also Gothic, prepares such elegant fare as roasted quail cutlet. ⊠ *Little Horsted, 2½ mi south of Uckfield, 6 mi north of Lewes, TN22 5TS* ☎ *01825/750581* 🖷 *01825/ 750459* ⊕ *www.horstedplace.co.uk* 🛏 *15 rooms, 5 suites* & *Restaurant, cable TV with movies, golf privileges, tennis court, croquet, library, business services, meeting rooms; no a/c* ⊟ *AE, DC, MC, V* ⍟ *BP.*

££££–£££££ 🛏 **Shelleys.** A 17th-century building, this hotel on the hilly main road is a traditional overnight stop for Glyndebourne operagoers. Public rooms are on the grand scale, furnished throughout with antiques, and the garden is a joy. The hotel maintains a reputation for old-fashioned, friendly service. ⊠ *High St., BN7 1XS* ☎ *01273/472361* 🖷 *01273/ 483152* ⊕ *www.shelleys-hotel-lewes.com* 🛏 *19 rooms* & *Restaurant, bar, meeting rooms, some pets allowed; no a/c* ⊟ *AE, DC, MC, V.*

Nightlife & the Arts

Glyndebourne Opera House (⊠ Glyndebourne, near Lewes ☎ 01273/ 813813 ⊕ www.glyndebourne.com) is one of the world's leading opera venues. Nestled beneath the downs, Glyndebourne combines first-class productions, in a state-of-the-art auditorium, with a beautiful setting.

Seats are *very* expensive (£25–£140) and often difficult to acquire, but they're worth every cent to aficionados, some of whom wear evening dress and bring a hamper for a picnic in the gardens. The main season runs from the end of May to the end of August. The Glyndebourne Touring Company performs here in October, when seats are cheaper and slightly easier to obtain.

BRIGHTON TO EAST GRINSTEAD

The self-proclaimed belle of the coast, Brighton is an upbeat, friendly old-new sprawl. It started as a tiny fishing village called Brighthelmstone, with no claim to fame until a certain Dr. Russell sent his patients there for its dry, bracing, crystal-clear air. In the late 18th century the prince regent, later George IV, discovered sea bathing in Brighton, and for nearly 200 years, the place prospered—deservedly so, for few British resorts have ever catered so well as Brighton to its appreciative patronage from London and the world over. Today the city is a lively mixture of carnival and culture, and it contains one of the must-sees of Britain—the mock-Asian Royal Pavilion. The city's second iconic structure, the West Pier, has been closed to the public since 1975. After the children have had their fill of Brighton's amusement parks, the surrounding area beckons with great residences, including Arundel Castle, Petworth House, and Polesden Lacey. Along the way, you'll discover the largest Roman villa in Britain, the bustling city of Guildford, and Chichester, whose cathedral is a poem in stone.

Brighton

9 mi southwest of Lewes, 54 mi south of London.

Ever since the prince regent first visited in 1783, Brighton has been England's most exciting seaside city, and today it remains as vibrant, eccentric, and cosmopolitan as ever. A rich cultural mix—Regency architecture, pleasure pier, specialty shops, sidewalk cafés, lively arts, a flourishing gay scene, and the exotic Royal Pavilion—makes the city truly unique. In decades gone by, it became known for its faded glamor. Happily, a young, bustling spirit has given a face-lift to this ever-popular resort, which shares its city status with neighboring Hove, as genteel a retreat as Brighton is abuzz.

The city owes its modern fame and fortune to the supposed healing attributes of seawater. In 1750 physician Richard Russell published a book recommending seawater treatment for glandular diseases. The fashionable world flocked to Brighton to take Dr. Russell's "cure," and sea bathing became a popular pastime. The next windfall for the town was the arrival of the prince of Wales (later George IV). "Prinny," as he was called, created the Royal Pavilion, a pleasure palace that attracted London society. The influx of visitors triggered a wave of villa building. Fortunately, this was one of the most creative periods in the history of English architecture, and the elegant terraces of Regency houses are today among the town's greatest attractions. The coming of the railroad set the seal on Brighton's popularity: the luxurious *Brighton Belle* brought Londoners to the coast within an hour. They expected to find the same comforts they had in London, and Brighton obliged, which explains the town's remarkable assortment of restaurants, hotels, and pubs. Horse racing was, and still is, another strong attraction.

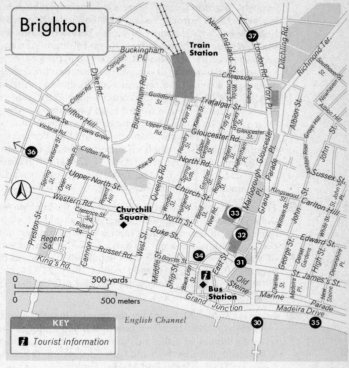

Although fast rail service to London has made Brighton an important base for commuters, the town has unashamedly set out to be a pleasure resort. The very first examples of that peculiarly British institution, the amusement pier, appeared in Sussex in the 1850s, and the restored ★ ⓷⓪ **Brighton Pier** (⊕ www.brightonpier.co.uk), built in 1899, follows the great tradition. Amusement piers traditionally had music halls, with a certain brand of slapstick, ribald humor, and popular theater, and they've always had games and rides. The town museum exhibits some of the original mechanical amusements, including the celebrated flip-card device, "What the Butler Saw," and you can still admire the pier's handsome ironwork. The **West Pier,** built in 1866 and still for many the most recognizable landmark of the city, is closed; in 2003 a renovation program was put under pressure by winter storms, which left parts of the grand old structure scattered around Brighton Beach.

⓷⓵ The heart of Brighton is the **Steine** (pronounced steen), a large open area close to the seafront. This was a river mouth until the Prince of Wales had it drained in 1793. One of the houses here was the home of Mrs. Maria Fitzherbert, later the prince's wife.

The most remarkable building on the Steine, perhaps in all Britain, is unquestionably the Prince of Wales's extravagant fairy-tale palace, the ★ ⓷⓶ domed and pinnacled **Royal Pavilion.** First planned as a simple seaside villa and built in the fashionable classical style of 1787, the Pavilion was rebuilt between 1815 and 1822 by John Nash for the prince regent, who favored an exotic, Indian-inspired design with Chinese interiors. When Queen Victoria came to the throne in 1837, she so disapproved of the palace that she stripped it of its furniture and planned to demolish it. Fortunately, Brighton Council bought it from her, and it is now recognized as unique in all Europe. Today, the Pavilion looks much as it did in its Regency heyday. Quantities of superb period furniture and ornaments, some given or lent by the current Royal Family, fill the interior. The two great set pieces are the **Music Room,** styled in the form of an Asian pavilion, and the **Banqueting Room,** with its enormous flying-dragon "gasolier," or gaslight chandelier, a revolutionary invention in the early 19th century. In the kitchens, palm-tree columns support the ceilings. The upstairs bedrooms contain a selection of cruel caricatures of the prince regent, most produced during his lifetime. The gardens, too, recall Regency splendor, following John Nash's design of 1826. For an elegant time-out, repair to one of the Pavilion's bedrooms, where a tearoom serves snacks and light meals. ⊠ *Old Steine* ☎ *01273/290900* ⊕ *www.royalpavilion. org.uk* ✑*£5.35* ☉ *Oct.–Mar., daily 10–5:15; Apr.–Sept., daily 9:30–5:45; last admission 45 mins before closing.*

㉝ The grounds of the Royal Pavilion contain the **Brighton Museum and Art Gallery,** whose buildings were designed as a stable block for the prince's horses. The museum includes especially interesting art nouveau and art deco collections. Look out for Salvador Dali's famous sofa in the shape of Mae West's lips, and pause at the Balcony Café for its bird's-eye view over the 20th-century Art and Design Gallery. ⊠ *Church St.* ☎ *01273/ 290900* ⊕ *www.brighton.virtualmuseum.info* ✑ *Free* ☉ *Tues. 10–7, Wed.–Sat. 10–5, Sun. 2–5.*

㉞ Just west of the Old Steine lies **the Lanes,** a maze of alleys and passageways filled with restaurants, boutiques, and antiques shops that were once the homes of fishermen and their families. Vehicular traffic is barred from the area. Fish and seafood restaurants line the heart of the Lanes, at Market Street and Market Square.

㉟ **Volk's Electric Railway,** built by inventor Magnus Volk in 1883, was the first public electric railroad in Britain; mid-April through September you can take the 1¼-mi trip along Marine Parade. ⊠ *Marine Parade* ☎*01273/292718* ✑*£1.20 one-way, £2.20 round-trip* ☉ *Mid-Apr.–Sept., weekdays 10:30–5, weekends 10:30–6.*

㊱ The **British Engineerium,** a restored Victorian pumping station, houses hundreds of steam engines, electric motors, motorcycles, and interactive children's exhibits. Note that boilers are lighted and engines set in full steam only on the first Sunday of the month and on major public holidays. ⊠ *Nevill Rd., Hove* ☎ *01273/559583* ⊕ *www.britishengineerium. com* ✑ *£4* ☉ *Daily 10–5; last admission at 4. Closed last wk Dec.*

㊲ Beautifully preserved **Preston Manor,** with its paintings, silver, porcelain, and furniture, evokes the opulence of the Edwardian lifestyle. You can tour formal rooms, bedrooms, and a nursery in the attic, as well as the kitchens and servants' quarters. Take time to wander through the grounds. The house is north of the town center, on the main London road. ⊠ *Preston Park* ☎ *01273/292770* ⊕ *www.prestonmanor.virtualmuseum.info* ✑ *£3.40* ☉ *Mon. 1–5, Tues.–Sat. 10–5, Sun. 2–5.*

Where to Stay & Eat

££££ ✕**One Paston Place.** Bare floorboards and plenty of pictures help give the relaxed mood of a bistro to this roomy, well-established restaurant. The menu changes regularly, but you might expect roasted scallops, grilled cauliflower, and hazelnuts as a starter, and lamb with almonds and juniper berries as a main dish. Prices are a bit high, but set lunches at £16.50 and £19 are a good deal. ⊠ *1 Paston Pl.* ☎ *01273/606933* ☰ *AE, DC, MC, V* ☉ *Closed Sun., Mon., 1st 2 wks Jan., and 1st 2 wks Aug.*

ALL HAIL THE REGENT

The term "Regency" comes from the last 10 years of the reign of George III (1811–20), who was deemed unfit to rule because of advancing insanity. Real power was officially given to the prince of Wales, also known as the prince regent, who became King George IV. Throughout his regency, George spent grand sums indulging his flamboyant tastes in architecture and interior decorating—while failing in affairs of state. The distinctive architecture of the Royal Pavilion is a prime, if extreme,

example of the Regency style, popularized by architect John Nash (1752–1835) in the early part of the 19th century. This style is characterized by a diversity of influences: French, Greek, Italian, Persian, Japanese, Chinese, Roman, Indian—you name it. Nash was King George IV's favorite architect, beloved for his interest in Indian and Asian designs and for Nash's neoclassical designs, as evidenced in his plans for Regent's Park and its terraces in London.

★ ££–££££ ✕ **English's of Brighton.** One of the few old-fashioned seafood havens left in England is buried in the Lanes. It has been a restaurant for more than 150 years and a family business for more than 50. You can eat succulent oysters and other seafood dishes at the counter or take a table in the restaurant section. ⊠ 29–31 East St. ☎ 01273/327980 ☐ AE, DC, MC, V.

£££ ✕ **The Mangerie.** At one of the Brighton and Hove area's best bring-your-own restaurants, you can turn up with a bottle of cheap (or not so cheap) wine and drink it with your meal. This small place is friendly and French, and the food (£15 for a three-course fixed-price menu) ranges from duck breast with mango sauce to deep-fried ice cream. ⊠ Church Rd., Hove ☎ 01273/327329 ☐ MC, V.

£–£££ ✕ **Havana.** The high ceilings, dark wood and leather furnishings, and sophisticated food at Havana might make you think you're in London. Don't let that deter you, however—this place is a pleasure. Expect modern twists on British classics: chicken pie, for example, includes a delectable mound of sautéed baby vegetables topped with a triangle of puff pastry. The bar area is a perfect place to rest your feet at the end of the day. ⊠ 32 Duke St. ☎ 01273/773388 ☐ AE, MC, V.

★ ££ ✕ **Terre à Terre.** This inspiring vegetarian restaurant is popular, so come early for a light lunch or a more sophisticated evening meal. The Jerusalem artichoke soufflé, sumac-scented almond eggplant, and an eclectic choice of salads should satisfy most palates. ⊠ 71 East St. ☎ 01273/729051 ☐ AE, DC, MC, V ⊙ No lunch Mon.

£££££ ✕☐ **Brighton Thistle Hotel.** This well-designed modern, four-story hotel, a little east of the Grand Hotel, is built around a huge, airy atrium and is a popular choice of conference delegates. Bedrooms have bright colors and traditional dark-wood furniture. The restaurant, La Noblesse, serves delicious fare such as a trio of salmon starter and a wild mushroom and red wine risotto main course, with not-too-expensive fixed menus. ⊠ King's Rd., BN1 2GS ☎ 01273/206700; 800/847–4358 in U.S. ☐ 01273/820692 ⊕ www.thistlehotels.com ⇨ 208 rooms ⚬ Restaurant, in-room data ports, cable TV, indoor pool, gym, sauna, business services, meeting rooms, some pets allowed ☐ AE, DC, MC, V ⦿ BP.

££££ ✕☐ **Hotel du Vin.** Brighton has attracted some trendy new hotels such as this stylish newcomer near the seafront and the Lanes, part of a small Anglo-French chain. Guest rooms are crisply modern, with pampering touches such as Egyptian linens and large showers. The bistro restaurant offers classic fare that makes good use of local seafood, and the extensive wine list includes many good values. The wine bar will satisfy connoisseurs (special events take place throughout the year), and you can have a cigar from the cigar gallery before you play billiards. ✉ *Ship St., BN1 1AD* ☎ *01273/718588* 🖷 *01273/718599* ⊕ *www. hotelduvin.com* ↙ *33 rooms, 3 suites* ☖ *Restaurant, billiards, wine bar, meeting rooms* ▭ *AE, DC, MC, V.*

£££££   ▣ **Grand Hotel.** A Brighton classic that lives up to its name, this imposing but elegant hotel built in 1864 overlooks and dominates this part of the seafront. The high-ceiling public rooms tend toward the chandelier-and-marble variety; the spacious bedrooms are traditional in style, with luxurious drapes and large bathrooms. ✉ *King's Rd., BN1 2FW* ☎ *01273/ 321188* 🖷 *01273/202694* ⊕ *www.grandbrighton.co.uk* ↙ *200 rooms* ☖ *Restaurant, in-room data ports, cable TV with movies, indoor pool, gym, sauna, lounge, business services, meeting rooms, some pets allowed (fee); no a/c in some rooms* ▭ *AE, DC, MC, V* ⦿ *BP.*

★ ££££   ▣ **Blanch House.** A theatrical experience as much as a night's rest lies behind this small hotel's typical Georgian facade. You can take your pick from the eclectic mix of superbly executed theme rooms, from '70s-style Boogie Nights to Moroccan and rich Renaissance; the over-the-top suites are double the price. Beds are queen- and king-size, and bathrooms are stylish. The hip cocktail bar (the owner is a former manager of London's Groucho Club) and sleek modern restaurant complete the picture. ✉ *17 Atlingworth St., BN2 1PL* ☎ *01273/603504* 🖷 *01273/689813* ⊕ *www.blanchhouse.co.uk* ↙ *9 rooms, 3 suites* ☖ *Restaurant, in-room data ports, bar, meeting rooms; no a/c* ▭ *MC, V* ⦿ *BP.*

£££–£££££   ▣ **Granville Hotel.** Three former grand residences facing the sea make up this hotel opposite the West Pier on hotel row, to the west of the Grand. Bedrooms, beautifully decorated and themed, include the pink-and-white Brighton Rock and the art deco Noel Coward rooms. Trogs, the restaurant, uses free-range chickens and organic products and caters to vegetarians. ✉ *124 King's Rd., BN1 2FA* ☎ *01273/326302* 🖷 *01273/ 728294* ⊕ *www.granvillehotel.co.uk* ↙ *24 rooms* ☖ *Restaurant, coffee shop, bar, some pets allowed; no a/c* ▭ *AE, DC, MC, V* ⦿ *BP.*

£££–££££   ▣ **Nineteen.** Definitely urban in style, but on a quiet side street close to Brighton Pier, this hotel is a calm oasis of white. Original contemporary works of art and designer accessories set the style in the guest rooms, and beds are supported on platforms of glass bricks that filter an ocean-blue light. A basement kitchen with snacks is for guests' use. ✉ *19 Broad St., BN2 1TJ* ☎ *01273/675529* 🖷 *01273/675531* ⊕ *www.hotelnineteen. co.uk* ↙ *7 rooms* ☖ *In-room VCRs, some pets allowed; no a/c, no kids, no smoking* ▭ *MC, V* ⦿ *BP.*

££–£££   ▣ **The Dove.** Washes of light, modern prints on the walls and an uncluttered feel are the keynotes of this immaculate Regency house. Rooms at the front have sea views; all have crisp cotton bed linens and luxurious pillows. There's no elevator, and the stairs to the attic rooms are steep. Breakfasts are generous. ✉ *18 Regency Sq., BN1 2FG* ☎ *01273/779222* 🖷 *01273/746912* ⊕ *www.brighton.co.uk/hotels/dove* ↙ *9 rooms* ☖ *Dining room; no a/c* ▭ *AE, MC, V* ⦿ *BP.*

£–££   ▣ **Genevieve.** This Regency guest house, near the seafront and Brighton Pier, has large, freshly decorated rooms, some with sea views. Less expensive rooms are done in pastels; some more expensive ones have four-posters. All rooms have private baths, but some bathrooms are outside the bedrooms. Breakfast is served in the basement dining room. ✉ *18 Madeira Pl., BN2 1TN* ☎ *01273/681653* 🖷 *01273/681653* ⊕ *www. genevievehotel.co.uk* ↙ *11 rooms* ☖ *No a/c* ▭ *MC, V* ⦿ *BP.*

Nightlife & the Arts

NIGHTLIFE   Live music is played most nights, and on weekends a lively club scene pulls in crowds from across the Southeast. East of Brighton Pier, try the popular **Escape Club** (✉ 10 Marine Parade ☎ 01273/606906). The **Zap Club** (✉ 188–193 King's Rd. Arches ☎ 01273/202407) is Brighton's most well-established club, but there are several others on the seafront between the two piers.

THE ARTS The three-week-long **Brighton Festival** (☎ 01273/706771 ⊕ www. brighton-festival.org.uk), one of England's biggest and liveliest arts festivals, takes place every May in venues around town. The more than 600 events include drama, music, dance, and visual arts.

The **Brighton Dome** (✉ New Rd. ☎ 01273/709709), just west of the Royal Pavilion, was converted from the prince regent's stables in the 1930s. It includes a theater and a concert hall that stage pantomime (a British theatrical entertainment with songs and dance) and classical and pop concerts. The **Gardner Arts Centre** (✉ Off A27, Falmer ☎ 01273/685861), on the University of Sussex campus a few miles northeast of town, presents plays, concerts, and cabaret. The Regency **Theatre Royal** (✉ New Rd. ☎ 01273/328488), close to the Royal Pavilion, has a gem of an auditorium that is a favorite venue for shows either on their way to or fresh from London's West End.

The **Cinematheque** (✉ 9–12 Middle St. ☎ 01273/384300) screens arthouse fare. The **Duke of York's Picture House** (✉ Preston Circus ☎ 01273/ 626261), a 10-minute walk north of the main train station, is one city option for art-house movies.

Shopping

The main shopping area to head for is **the Lanes,** especially for antiques or jewelry. It also has clothing boutiques, coffee shops, and pubs. Across North Street from the Lanes lies the **North Laine,** a network of narrow streets full of little stores, less glossy than those in the Lanes, but fun, funky, and exotic.

Colin Page (✉ 36 Duke St. ☎ 01273/325954), at the western edge of the Lanes, stocks a wealth of antiquarian and secondhand books at all prices. The **Pavilion Shop** (✉ 4–5 Pavilion Bldgs. ☎ 01273/292798), next door to the Royal Pavilion, carries well-designed souvenirs of Regency Brighton and high-quality fabrics, wallpapers, and ceramics based on material in the Pavilion itself. The old-fashioned **Pecksniff's Bespoke Perfumery** (✉ 45–46 Meeting House La. ☎ 01273/723292) will mix and match ingredients to suit your wishes. **Simultane** (✉ 37 Trafalgar St. ☎ 01273/818031), a boutique in the North Laine, displays women's fashions from its own label—contemporary looks inspired by the styles of the 1940s and 1950s—and clothing from other designers.

Arundel

38 *23 mi west of Brighton, 60 mi south of London.*

The little hilltop town of Arundel is dominated by its great castle, the much-restored home of the dukes of Norfolk for more than 700 years, and an imposing neo-Gothic Roman Catholic cathedral—the duke is Britain's leading Catholic peer. The town itself is full of interesting old buildings, well worth a stroll.

Begun in the 11th century, vast **Arundel Castle** remains rich with the history of the Fitzalan and Howard families and with paintings by Van Dyck, Gainsborough, and Reynolds. It suffered destruction during the Civil War and was later remodeled during the 18th century and the Victorian era. The keep, rising from its conical mound, is as old as the original castle, whereas the barbican and the Barons' Hall date from the 13th century. The castle interior was reconstructed in the fashionable Gothic style of the 19th century. Among the treasures on view are the rosary beads and prayer book used by Mary, Queen of Scots, in preparing for her execution. The ceremonial entrance to Arundel Castle is at the top of High Street, but you enter at the bottom, close to the parking lot. ⊠ *Mill Rd.* ☎ *01903/882173* ⊕ *www.arundelcastle.org* ᵂ *£9.50, grounds only £3.50* ⊙ *Apr.–Oct., Sun.–Fri. noon–5; last admission at 4.*

Where to Stay & Eat

£–££ ✕ **Black Rabbit.** This renovated 18th-century pub is a find, and you must persevere along Mill Road to find it. Its location by the River Arun, with views of the castle and a bird sanctuary, makes it ideal for a summer lunch. There's a good salad bar and an all-day restaurant. ⊠ *Mill Rd.* ☎ *01903/882828* ▭ *DC, MC, V.*

★   ▦ **Amberley Castle.** The lowering of the portcullis every night at mid-
££££–£££££ night is a sure sign that you're in a genuine medieval castle, one that celebrated its 900th birthday in 2003. Across the dry moat, you'll find present-day luxury. Antiques and rich drapery furnish the individually designed bedrooms, and many have lattice windows, beamed ceilings, and curtained four-posters. You can dine in either the Queens restaurant, beneath a 12th-century barrel-vaulted ceiling, or in the presence of suits of armor in the Great Room. The castle is 5 mi north of Arundel. ⊠ *Off B2139, Amberley, BN18 8ND* ☎ *01798/831992* ᵇ *01798/ 831998* ⊕ *www.amberleycastle.co.uk* ⊅ *19 rooms* ⚭ *Restaurant, in-room hot tubs, in-room VCRs, putting green, tennis court, bar, meeting rooms; no a/c, no kids under 12* ▭ *AE, DC, MC, V* ❮❘❯ *CP.*

£££–£££££ ▦ **Hilton Avisford Park.** This converted Georgian house on 89 acres of parkland began as the home of an admiral and became a hotel in the 1970s. Bedrooms are in floral or classic style, with close attention to detail. The least expensive prices do not include breakfast. The hotel is 3 mi west of Arundel off A27, on B2132. ⊠ *Yapton La., Walberton, BN18 0LS* ☎ *01243/551215* ᵇ *01243/552485* ⊕ *www.arundel.hilton. com* ⊅ *139 rooms* ⚭ *Restaurant, 18-hole golf course, 2 tennis courts, indoor-outdoor pool, gym, sauna, croquet, squash, meeting rooms, helipad; no a/c* ▭ *AE, DC, MC, V* ❮❘❯ *BP.*

££££ ▦ **Norfolk Arms Hotel.** Like the cathedral and the castle in Arundel, this 18th-century coaching inn on the main street was built by one of the dukes of Norfolk. The main body of the hotel is traditional in appearance, with narrow passages and cozy little rooms. An annex in the courtyard block holds modern rooms. ⊠ *22 High St., BN18 9AD* ☎ *01903/882101* ᵇ *01903/884275* ⊕ *www.norfolkarmshotel.com* ⊅ *34 rooms* ⚭ *Restaurant, 2 bars, business services, meeting rooms, some pets allowed (fee); no a/c* ▭ *AE, DC, MC, V* ❮❘❯ *BP.*

Nightlife & the Arts

The **Arundel Festival** (☎ 01903/883690 ⊕ www.arundelfestival.co.uk) presents drama productions and classical and pop concerts in and around the castle grounds for a week in August and September.

Chichester

❸❾ *10 mi west of Arundel, 66 mi southwest of London.*

The Romans founded Chichester, the capital city of West Sussex, on the low-lying plains between the wooded South Downs and the sea. Although it has its own large cathedral and all the trappings of a commercial city, Chichester is not much bigger than many of the towns around it. The city walls and major streets follow the original Roman plan; the intersection of the four principal streets is marked by a cross dated 1501.

Norman **Chichester Cathedral,** near the corner of West and South streets, stands on Roman foundations and includes sections from later periods, such as a freestanding bell tower from the 15th century. Inside, a glass panel reveals Roman mosaics uncovered during restoration. Other treasures are the wonderful, moving Saxon limestone reliefs of the raising of Lazarus and Christ arriving in Bethany, both in the choir area, and some outstanding contemporary art, notably a stained-glass window by Marc Chagall, a colorful tapestry by John Piper, and a painting by Graham Sutherland. ⊠ *West St.* ☎ *01243/782595* ⊕ *www.chichester-cathedral.org.uk* ✍ *£2 suggested donation* ⊙ *Easter–Sept., daily 7:30–7; Oct.–Easter, daily 7:30–6. Tours Mon.–Sat. at 11 and 2:15.*

Today Chichester is mainly Georgian, with countless 18th-century houses, and one of the best is **Pallant House,** built in 1712 as a wine merchant's mansion. At that time, its state-of-the-art design showed the latest in complicated brickwork and superb wood carving. Appropriate antiques and porcelains furnish the faithfully restored rooms. The **Pallant House Gallery** showcases a small but important collection of mainly modern British art. Admission includes entry to the **Hans Fiebusch Studio,** nearby in St. Martin's Square, with an exact re-creation of the St. John's Wood (London) studio of this exiled German artist (1898–1998) who was the last member of the so-called degenerate art group. ⊠ *9 N. Pallant* ☎ *01243/774557* ⊕ *www.pallant.co.uk* ✍ *£4* ⊙ *Tues.–Sat. 10–5, Sun. and national holidays 12:30–5.*

Where to Stay & Eat

£££–£££££ ✕ **Comme Ça.** Its location, about a five-minute walk across the park from the Chichester Festival Theatre, makes this attractively converted pub a good spot for a meal before a performance. Bunches of dried hops, suspended from the ceiling, and antique children's toys decorate the dining room. The owner, Michel Navet, is French, and his chef produces authentic French dishes; simpler fare is served in the bar at much lower prices, and the fixed-price lunchtime menu is £15. ⊠ *67 Broyle Rd.* ☎ *01243/788724* ⊟ *AE, DC, MC, V* ⊙ *Closed Mon. No dinner Sun.*

£££–££££ 🛏 **Ship Hotel.** Staying in this hotel close to the Chichester Festival Theatre is something of an architectural experience. Built in 1790, it was originally the home of Admiral Sir George Murray, one of Admiral Nelson's right-hand men. Among the outstanding elements are the flying (partially freestanding) staircase and colonnade. The house has been carefully restored to its 18th-century elegance. Reproduction period furniture fills the pastel guest rooms, which are simpler than the public areas. ⊠ *North St., PO19 1NH* ☎ *01243/778000* ☎ *01243/788000* ⊕ *www.shiphotel.com* ↩ *36 rooms* ⚴ *Restaurant, cable TV, bar, meeting rooms, some pets allowed; no a/c* ⊟ *AE, DC, MC, V* ⊧◎ *BP.*

Nightlife & the Arts

The **Chichester Festival Theatre** (⊠ Oaklands Park ☎ 01243/781312) presents classics and modern plays from May through September and is a venue for touring companies the rest of the year. Built in 1962, it has an international reputation and can be the evening focus for a relaxed day out of London.

Fishbourne Roman Palace

40 ½ *mi west of Chichester, 66 mi southwest of London.*

Intricate mosaics and painted walls lavishly decorate many of the 100 rooms of Fishbourne Roman Palace, the largest and grandest Roman villa in Britain. Sophisticated bathing and heating systems remain, and the Roman garden, the only known example extant in northern Europe, is laid out in the style of the 1st century AD. A museum displays artifacts from the site and provides a history of the building. ⊠ *Salthill Rd., Fishbourne* ☎ *01243/785859* ⊕ *www.sussexpast.co.uk* ⊠ *£5* ⊙ *Mar.–July, Sept., and Oct., daily 10–5; Aug., daily 10–6; Nov.–mid-Dec. and mid-Feb.–end Feb., daily 10–4; mid-Dec.–mid-Feb., weekends 10–4.*

Sculpture at Goodwood

★ ❹❶ *3 mi north of Chichester, 63 mi southwest of London.*

Twenty acres of woodland provide a backdrop for this collection of contemporary British sculpture, specially commissioned by the Hat Hill Sculpture Foundation. A third of the approximately 40 exhibits change annually, and the pieces, sited to maximize their effect, are connected by walks through glades and green fields. A gallery displays models of new sculptures. The park is signposted on the right off A286. ⊠ *Hat Hill Copse, Goodwood* ☎ *01243/538449* ⊕ *www.sculpture.org.uk* ⊠ *£10* ⊙ *Apr.–Oct., Thurs.–Sat. 10:30–4:30.*

Singleton

❹❷ *5 mi north of Chichester, 59 mi south of London.*

Singleton, a secluded village, merits a stop for its excellent open-air museum. The **Weald and Downland Open Air Museum** gives sanctuary to endangered historical buildings. Among the 45 structures on 50 acres of wooded meadows are a cluster of medieval houses, a working water mill, a Tudor market hall, and an ancient blacksmith's shop. ⊠ *A286* ☎ *01243/ 811348* ⊕ *www.wealddown.co.uk* ⊠ *£7* ⊙ *Mar.–Oct., daily 10:30–6; Nov.–Feb., weekends 10:30–4; last admission 1 hr before closing.*

Petworth House

❹❸ *8 mi northeast of Singleton, 12 mi northwest of Arundel, 54 mi south of London.*

FodorsChoice ★

One of the National Trust's greatest treasures and still the home of Lord and Lady Egremont, Petworth House stands in a scenic patch of Sussex. A 13th-century chapel is all that remains of the original manor house, and most of the current building was constructed between 1688 and 1696; the celebrated landscape architect Capability Brown (1716–83) later added a 700-acre deer park. Among the house's outstanding collection of English paintings are works by Gainsborough, Reynolds, Van Dyck, and J. M. W. Turner, the great proponent of romanticism, who immortalized Petworth's sumptuous interiors in evocative watercolors. Other highlights include Greek and Roman sculpture and Grinling Gibbons wood carvings, such as those in the spectacular Carved Room. Six rooms in the servants' quarters, among them the old kitchen, are open to the public, and the Servants Block serves light lunches. Explore the town of Petworth, too, a jewel studded with narrow old streets and timbered houses. You can access the house off A272 and A283 (parking lots are off the latter). ⊠ *Petworth* ☎ *01798/342207* ⊕ *www.nationaltrust.org.uk* ⊠ *£7, gardens only £1.50* ⊙ *House late Mar.–early Nov., Sat.–Wed. 11–5:30; last admission at 5. Gardens late Mar.–early Nov., Sat.–Wed. 11–6. Park daily 8–dusk.*

Guildford

❹❹ *22 mi north of Petworth House, 28 mi southwest of London, 35 mi north of Chichester.*

Guildford, the largest town in Surrey and the county's capital, is an important commuter town, but it retains a faint 18th-century air. No other English town can claim such a brilliant succession of royal visits, from Alfred the Great down to the current queen. Gabled merchants' houses line the steep, pleasantly provincial High Street, now filled with upscale fashion and household shops. You can't miss the massive Tudor facade of the ancient **Hospital of the Blessed Trinity.** George Abbot, Archbishop of Canterbury, founded it in 1619 as almshouses—a function it still performs as a senior-citizens' home. Abbot, one of the translators of the King James Bible, was born in Guildford. ⊠ *High St.* ☎ *01483/ 562670* ⊙ *Chapel and common room by appointment.*

Displays in the **Guildford Museum,** in the old castle building, include interesting exhibits on local history and archaeology, as well as memorabilia of Charles Dodgson, better known as Lewis Carroll, the author of *Alice in Wonderland.* Dodgson spent his last years in a house on nearby Castle Hill. He was buried in the Mount Cemetery, up the hill on High Street. **Castle Arch,** all that remains of the entrance of the old castle, displays a slot for a portcullis. Beyond the arch lie the remains of the castle. ⊠ *Quarry St.* ☎ *01483/444750* ⊕ *www.guildfordborough.co. uk* 🖼 *Free* ⊙ *Mon.–Sat. 11–5.*

Guildford Cathedral, looming on its hilltop across the River Wey, is only the second Anglican cathedral to be built on a new site since the Reformation in the 1500s. It was consecrated in 1961. The redbrick exterior is severely simple, whereas the interior, with its stone and plaster, looks bright and cool. Call several weeks in advance if you want to arrange a guided tour. ⊠ *Stag Hill* ☎ *01483/565287* ⊕ *www.guildfordcathedral.org* 🖼 *Donation accepted, tours £3* ⊙ *Daily 8:30–5.*

Fodor's Choice ★ In a nation of gardeners, **Wisley,** the Royal Horticultural Society's showpiece, is one of Britain's most popular gardens. Both an ornamental and scientific center, it claims to have greater horticultural diversity than any other garden in the world. Founded by businessman and inventor George Ferguson Wilson in 1878, Wisley has expanded to 240 innovative, colorful acres. The alpine meadow in spring, the lilies, the rose gardens, and the year-round conservatories are some highlights, along with a plant center that sells more than 10,000 types of plants. The garden, near Woking, is 10 mi northeast of Guildford. ⊠ *A3, Woking* ☎ *01483/224234* ⊕ *www.rhs.org/gardens/wisley* 🖼 *£6* ⊙ *Mar.–Oct., weekdays 10–6, weekends 9–6, until 9 on Wed. June and July; Nov.–Feb., weekdays 10–4:30, weekends 10–4:30.*

Where to Stay & Eat

££–£££ ✕ **Café de Paris.** An 18th-century building holds this busy, family-owned French restaurant and brasserie. The menu focuses on game and fish: try the venison in juniper berry and sloe gin sauce, bouillabaisse, or one of the couscous dishes, but leave enough room for a sorbet. The brasserie has a good blackboard menu, too. ⊠ *35 Castle St.* ☎ *01483/534896* 🖽 *AE, MC, V* ⊙ *Closed Sun.*

★ ££ ✕ **Rumwong.** The elegant waitresses at this Thai restaurant wear traditional long-skirted costumes, so at busy times the dining room looks like a swirling flower garden. On the incredibly long menu, the Thai name of each dish appears with a clear English description. Good choices are the fisherman's soup, a spicy mass of delicious saltwater fish in a clear broth, or *yam pla muek,* a hot salad with squid. ⊠ *16–18 London Rd.* ☎ *01483/536092* 🖽 *MC, V* ⊙ *Closed Mon.*

★ ✕🖽 **Angel Posting House and Livery.** Guildford was famous for its old
££££–£££££ coaching inns, and this luxurious, 400-year-old hotel is the last of them. The courtyard, where coaches and horses clattered to a stop, still opens

to the sky, and light lunches are offered here in summer. Individually designed guest rooms have attractive fabrics, reproductions of antiques, and marble-lined bathrooms; 10 are in a modern annex. There's a salon with a fireplace and minstrel's gallery, and the 13th-century stone-vaulted crypt serves as the backdrop for fine modern British food. ⊠ *91 High St., GU1 3DP* ☎ *01483/564555* 🖹 *01483/533770* ⊕ *www.slh. com* 📭 *21 rooms* ⚹ *Restaurant, coffee shop, in-room data ports, meeting rooms, some pets allowed; no a/c* ▤ *AE, DC, MC, V.*

Nightlife & the Arts

The **Yvonne Arnaud Theatre** (⊠ Millbrook ☎ 01483/440000), a horseshoe-shape building on an island in the River Wey, frequently previews West End productions; it also has a restaurant.

Clandon Park

㊺ *3 mi east of Guildford, 29 mi southwest of London.*

Venetian architect Giacomo Leoni built the grand Clandon Park for Lord Onslow in the 1730s in the graceful Palladian style. Capability Brown landscaped the park, but the real glory of the mansion is its interior, especially the magnificent two-story Marble Hall.On display are fine collections of 18th-century furniture, needlework, and porcelain, and weapons and medals fill a regimental museum on the grounds. The gardens, too, deserve a look, with a parterre, grotto, and sunken garden. ⊠ *A247, West Clandon* ☎ *01483/222482* ⊕ *www.nationaltrust.org.uk* 🎫 *£6* ☉ *Apr.–early Nov., Tues.–Thurs. and Sun. 11–5; last admission at 4:30. Gardens open daily 11–5.*

Great Bookham

㊻ *8 mi northeast of Guildford, 25 mi southwest of London.*

Great Bookham has some fine old buildings at its core, including a 12th-century church, one of the most complete medieval buildings extant in Surrey. The town is identified with the Highbury of Jane Austen's *Emma.* The most absorbing historic attraction is **Polesden Lacey,** a Regency mansion built in 1824 by Thomas Cubitt on the site of one owned by the famed 18th-century playwright Richard Brinsley Sheridan. Edwardian society hostess Mrs. Ronald Greville lived here from 1906 to 1942 and remodeled the house substantially. Elizabeth, the late Queen Mother, and her husband, the Duke of York (later George VI), stayed here in 1923 for part of their honeymoon. Polesden Lacey contains beautiful collections of furniture, paintings, porcelain, and silver. In summer, open-air theatrical performances are given on the grounds. You can also rent equipment from the house (book in advance) and take advantage of the croquet lawns. ⊠ *Off A246* ☎ *01372/458203* ⊕ *www. nationaltrust.org.uk* 🎫 *£7, grounds only £4* ☉ *House late Mar.–early Nov., Wed.–Sun. 11–5; grounds daily 11–6 or dusk.*

en route   As you make your way southeast to Tunbridge Wells via Dorking (about 28 mi), you'll pass **Box Hill** (⊠ A24 ☎ 01306/885502 ⊕ www.nationaltrust.org.uk), the site of the famous picnic in Jane Austen's *Emma.* It's a favorite spot for walking excursions, with lovely views of the South Downs. At the bottom of Box Hill, the Burford Bridge Hotel was where Keats wrote the last sections of *Endymion;* Admiral Nelson also stayed there when traveling down to Portsmouth, and on to fame and death at Trafalgar.

Dorking

47 *6 mi south of Great Bookham, 29 mi south of London.*

The southeasterly route to Royal Tunbridge Wells leads to the commuter town of Dorking, a pleasant neighborhood that has inspired the pens of many writers. The cemetery holds the remains of the writer George Meredith (1828–1909). On the wide High Street stands the White Horse Inn, or the Marquis o' Granby, as Dickens dubbed it in *Pickwick Papers.*

Where to Eat

££££££ ✗ **Partners and Sons.** Behind the 16th-century, half-timber facade, this comfortable, air-conditioned restaurant specializes in modern English fare with Mediterranean influences. The chef uses fresh area produce. The local lamb and beef dishes are recommended, as well as the homemade organic desserts. There's a fixed-price menu at dinner. ⊠ *2–4 West St.* ☎ *01306/882826* ▤ *AE, DC, MC, V* ⊙ *Closed Sun. and Mon.*

East Grinstead

48 *15 mi southeast of Dorking, 32 mi south of London.*

The small country town of East Grinstead claims the longest continuous run of 14th-century timber-frame buildings in the country. Six miles to the east is the village of Hartfield, where A. A. Milne wrote his Winnie the Pooh stories in the 1920s.

Tours of **Saint Hill Manor,** 2 mi southwest of town, concentrate on the five families who have occupied the house since its construction in 1795. The house was for many years the home of L. Ron Hubbard (1911–86), science fiction writer and founder of the Church of Scientology. He left his 530 published works on display in the library. Pride of place must go to the 100-foot Monkey Mural, in which Winston Churchill's nephew John Spencer Churchill depicted famous personalities (including his uncle) as monkeys. ⊠ *Off A22* ☎ *01342/326711* ⊕ *www.sainthillmanor. org.uk* ▤ *Free* ⊙ *Daily 2–5; tours at 2, 3, 4, and 5.*

A well-preserved family country house dating from the 1890s and set in a beautiful hillside garden, **Standen** typifies the Arts and Crafts movement. Designed by the influential architect Philip Webb (1831–1913), it contains a wealth of William Morris carpets, wallpapers, and fabrics, and even the original electric light fittings. The house is 2 mi south of East Grinstead. ⊠ *Off B2110* ☎ *01342/323029* ⊕ *www.nationaltrust.org. uk* ▤ *£5.50, garden only £3* ⊙ *House late Mar.–early Nov., Wed.–Sun. 11–5. Garden late Mar.–early Nov., Wed.–Sun. 11–6; early Nov.–mid-Dec., Fri.–Sun. 11–3.*

At lush **Nymans Garden,** exotic plants collected by the gardener Ludwig Messel beginning in 1885 mingle with more homely varieties. The garden reflects the tastes of three generations of the family. Spring is the best time to appreciate the prolific rhododendrons and the rare Himalayan magnolias in the romantic walled garden; in summer the roses are lovely. The garden is 10 mi southwest of East Grinstead. ⊠ *B2114, Handcross* ☎ *01444/400321* ⊕ *www.nationaltrust.org.uk* ▤ *£6* ⊙ *Mar.–early Nov., Wed.–Sun. 11–6 or dusk; Nov.–Feb., weekends 11–4.*

Where to Stay & Eat

★ ££££££ ✗▣ **Gravetye Manor.** This Elizabethan stone mansion, built in 1598, stands on a hilltop site in 1,000 acres of grounds landscaped by William Robinson (1838–1935), an advocate of natural rather than formal gardens. Restored with oak paneling and ornamental plaster ceilings, it represents the epitome of the luxurious English country-house hotel; guest rooms are appropriately plush. The superb if expensive restaurant (fixed-price menu; reservations essential) favors seafood and has an excellent wine list. ✉ *Off B2110, 5 mi south of East Grinstead, RH19 4LJ* ☎ *01342/810567* 📠 *01342/810080* 🌐 *www.gravetyemanor.co.uk* 🛏 *18 rooms ⌂ 2 restaurants, cable TV, lake, fishing, croquet, bar, meeting rooms; no a/c, no kids under 7 except babes in arms* ⊟ *MC, V.*

MASTERPIECES & MOATS
TUNBRIDGE WELLS TO FINCHCOCKS

One of England's greatest attractions is its many magnificent stately homes and castles. But for people with limited time, the dismaying fact is that the greatness is thinly spread, with many houses scattered across the country. Within a 15-mi radius of Tunbridge Wells, however, in that area of hills and hidden dells known as the Weald, lies a remarkable group of historic homes, castles, gardens, and monuments: Penshurst Place, Hever Castle, Chartwell, Knole, Ightham Mote, Leeds Castle, Sissinghurst Castle Garden, Bodiam Castle, Great Dixter House and Gardens, Rudyard Kipling's Batemans, and Finchcocks.

Royal Tunbridge Wells

49 *13 mi east of East Grinstead, 39 mi southeast of London.*

Tunbridge Wells has been the butt of humorists who have made it out to be unbelievably straitlaced, but it's a pleasant town favored by many London commuters. Although the city's official name is Royal Tunbridge Wells, locals ignore the prefix "royal," which was added only in 1909, during the reign of Edward VII. The city owes its prosperity to the 17th- and 18th-century passion for spas and mineral baths, initially as medicinal treatments and later as social gathering places. In 1606 a spring of chalybeate (mineral) water was discovered here, drawing legions of royal visitors. It's still possible to drink the waters when a "dipper" (the traditional water dispenser) is in attendance, from Easter through September. Tunbridge Wells reached its zenith in the mid-18th century, when Richard "Beau" Nash presided over its social life. The buildings at the lower end of High Street are mostly 18th century, but as the street climbs the hill north, changing its name to Mount Pleasant Road, the buildings become more modern.

A good place to begin a visit is at the **Pantiles**, a famous promenade with colonnaded shops near the spring on one side of town, which derives its odd name from the Dutch "pan tiles" that originally paved the area. Now bordered on two sides by busy main roads, the Pantiles remains an elegant, tranquil oasis. The **Church of King Charles the Martyr** (✉ Chapel Pl.), across the road from the Pantiles, dates from 1678, when it was dedicated to Charles I, who was executed by Parliament in 1649. Its plain exterior belies its splendid interior; take special note of the beautifully plastered baroque ceiling.

Tunbridge Wells Museum and Art Gallery, at the northern end of Mount Pleasant Road, contains a fascinating jumble of local artifacts, prehistoric relics, and Victorian toys, as well as a permanent exhibition of Tunbridge Ware pieces: small, wooden items inlaid with tiny pieces of colored woods. ✉ *Civic Centre, Mount Pleasant Rd.* ☎ *01892/554171* 🌐 *www.tunbridgewells.gov.uk* 🎟 *Free* ☉ *Mon.–Sat. 9:30–5.*

off the
beaten
path

ALL SAINTS CHURCH – A modest building dating from the 13th and 14th centuries holds one of the glories of 20th-century church art. The church is awash with the luminous yellows and blues of 12 windows by Marc Chagall (1887–1985), commissioned as a tribute by the family of a young girl who was drowned in a sailing accident in 1963. The church is 4 mi north of Tunbridge Wells; turn off A26 before Tonbridge and continue a mile or so east along B2017. ✉ *B2017, Tudeley* ☎ *0870/744–1456* 🎫 *Free* ⊙ *Daily 9–6 or dusk.*

Where to Stay & Eat

£££–££££ ✕ **Gracelands Palace.** Fun elements—not least of which is owner Paul Chan's cabaret of Elvis songs—as well as the food have made this popular Chinese restaurant famous. The fixed-price menu includes Szechuan and Cantonese fare. ✉ *3 Cumberland Walk* ☎ *01892/540754* ⊟ *AE, MC, V* ⊙ *Closed Sun. No lunch Mon.*

£££–££££ ✕ **Thackeray's House.** This mid-17th-century tile-hung house, once the home of Victorian novelist William Makepeace Thackeray, is now an elegant restaurant known for creative, modern French cuisine. Specialties include cauliflower soup with truffle cream, caramelized pork with baby vegetables, and roast salmon with red onion marmalade. ✉ *85 London Rd.* ☎ *01892/511921* ⊟ *AE, MC, V* ⊙ *Closed Mon. and last wk Dec. No dinner Sun.*

★ £–££ ✕ **Himalayan Gurkha Restaurant.** It's not necessarily what you might expect to find in the cozy confines of Tunbridge Wells, but the Nepalese cuisine of this friendly spot seems popular with the locals. Spicy mountain dishes are cooked with great care in traditional clay ovens or barbecued on flaming charcoal. There are good vegetarian options. ✉ *31 Church Rd.* ☎ *01892/527834* ⊟ *MC, V.*

£ ✕ **Hogshead and Compasses.** This spacious well-kept pub claims to be the oldest in town. Besides notable real ales, the pub serves tasty homemade food at lunchtime, from salads and wraps to traditional dishes such as liver and bacon, bubble and squeak (cabbage fried with potatoes and meat), and steak pies. In winter you can snuggle up to the open fires. The pub lies on a tiny, steep lane off High Street. ✉ *Little Mount Sion* ☎ *01892/530744* ⊟ *MC, V* ⊙ *No dinner.*

£££–££££ ✕▣ **Hotel du Vin.** Formerly a private house, this elegant sandstone building dating from 1762 has been transformed into a chic boutique hotel with polished wood floors and luxurious armchairs and sofas. Oriental rugs give public rooms an air of warmth that is both intimate and grand, and guest rooms are modern, with pampering bathrooms. The Burgundy Bar stocks a fine selection of wines from the eponymous region of France. The contemporary menu in the bistro changes daily but is strong on creamy soups and crisp salads. ✉ *Crescent Rd., near Mount Pleasant Rd., TN1 2LY* ☎ *01892/526455* 🖷 *01892/512044* ⊕ *www. hotelduvin.com* ➪ *32 rooms* ⚭ *Restaurant, cable TV, billiards, 2 bars, meeting rooms* ⊟ *AE, DC, MC, V.*

£££–££££ ▣ **Spa Hotel.** The Goring family, which also runs the noted Goring Hotel in London, owns this plush hotel loaded with amenities. Carefully chosen furnishings and details help maintain the country-house flavor of the 1766 Georgian mansion, although guest rooms come with many modern extras. There are superb views from the 14-acre grounds across the town and into the Weald of Kent. The traditional English fare of the Chandelier Restaurant is popular with locals. ✉ *Mount Ephraim, TN4 8XJ* ☎ *01892/520331* 🖷 *01892/510575* ⊕ *www.spahotel.co.uk* ➪ *71 rooms* ⚭ *Restaurant, cable TV, tennis court, indoor pool, 2 gyms, hair salon, sauna, spa, croquet, meeting rooms, some pets allowed; no a/c in some rooms* ⊟ *AE, DC, MC, V.*

££–£££ ⊡ **Old Parsonage.** This friendly guest house, 2 mi south of Tunbridge Wells via A267, stands at the top of a quiet lane beside the village church. Built in 1820, the Georgian manor has lovely antique furniture, a dining room with oak refectory table, and a big conservatory for afternoon tea. Two pubs and a restaurant lie within a short walk of the house. ⊠ *Church La., Frant, TN3 9DX* ☎☎ *01892/750773* ⊕ *www.theoldparsonagehotel.co.uk* ⋑ *3 rooms* ⚘ *No a/c* ⊟ *MC, V* ▯◉▯ *BP.*

Penshurst Place

★ ➄ *7 mi northwest of Royal Tunbridge Wells, 33 mi southeast of London.*

At the center of the hamlet of Penshurst stands one of England's finest medieval manor houses, hidden behind tall trees and walls. Although it has retained its 14th-century hall, Penshurst is mainly Elizabethan, with additions from later periods. It has been in the Sidney family since 1552, giving the house particular historical interest. The most famous Sidney is the Elizabethan poet, Sir Philip, author of *Arcadia*. The **Baron's Hall**, topped in 1341 with a chestnut roof, is the oldest and one of the grandest to survive from the early Middle Ages. Family portraits, furniture, tapestries, and armor help tell the story of the house. The grounds include a 10-acre walled Tudor garden, and there's a toy museum and a restaurant. Although Penshurst is basically an appendage of the "Great House," the village is a delightful destination. It centers around Leicester Square, which has late-15th-century half-timber structures adorned with soaring brick chimneys. ⊠ *Off B2188, from Tunbridge Wells, follow A26 and B2176* ☎ *01892/870307* ⊕ *www.penshurstplace.com* ⬰ *£6.50, grounds only £5* ⊘ *Mar., weekends noon–5:30; Apr.–Oct., daily noon–5. Grounds daily 10:30–6. Last admission 30 mins before closing.*

Where to Stay & Eat

££–££££ ✕ **Spotted Dog.** This pub first opened its doors in 1520; today, it tempts you with an inglenook fireplace, heavy beams, imaginative food, and a splendid view of Penshurst Place. ⊠ *Smarts Hill* ☎ *01892/870253* ⊟ *AE, MC, V.*

£££–££££ ⊡ **Rose and Crown.** Originally a 16th-century inn, this hotel on the main street in Tonbridge (5 mi east of Penshurst, 5 mi north of Tunbridge Wells) has a distinctive portico, added later. Inside, low-beam ceilings and Jacobean woodwork make the bar and the restaurant snug and inviting. Guest rooms in the main building are traditionally furnished, whereas rooms in the newer annex are more modern in style. ⊠ *125 High St., Tonbridge, TN9 1DD* ☎ *01732/357966* ⊟ *01732/357194* ⊕ *www.rose-andcrownhotel.co.uk* ⋑ *50 rooms* ⚘ *Restaurant, cable TV, bar, meeting rooms; no a/c* ⊟ *AE, MC, V* ▯◉▯ *BP.*

Hever Castle

★ ➄ *3 mi west of Penshurst, 10 mi northwest of Royal Tunbridge Wells, 30 mi southeast of London.*

For some, 13th-century Hever fits the stereotype of what a castle should look like, all turrets and battlements, the whole encircled by a water lily–bound moat. For others, it's too squat in structure (and perhaps too renovated). Here the ill-fated Anne Boleyn, second wife of Henry VIII and mother of Elizabeth I, was courted and won by Henry, who had her beheaded in 1536. He later gave Hever to his fourth wife, Anne of Cleves. American millionaire William Waldorf Astor acquired the castle in 1903, and the Astor family owned it until 1983. Astor built a Tudor village to house his staff (it's now a hotel for corporate functions) and

VISITING THE TREASURE HOUSES

CURIOSITY AS TO HOW the other half lives is undoubtedly one of the most deep-seated traits of human nature, and it's extremely pleasing to know you can satisfy your healthy desire to snoop through stately homes, including the many glorious specimens in Kent, for the payment of a small amount of conscience money. The fact that you will see some of the world's greatest treasures at the same time is a bonus.

Even the most highly developed sense of curiosity isn't enough to explain why millions of people have surged on to England's stately home trail. They have been urged to move by a great deal of exposure—the houses all over the country touched by Royal Family upheavals, such as Althorp, the ancestral home of Princess Diana, and the Mountbatten home, Broadlands; the numerous television serials, which have brought further fame to such spectacular houses as Castle Howard and Blenheim Palace; the continuing spate of historical movies shot on location, including the numerous versions of Jane Austen's novels, The Madness of King George (the spectacular interiors of Wilton House dazzled here), Sense and Sensibility (partly shot at Saltram), or the over-the-top style of Charles II on view in Restoration. Here, in Kent, Penshurst Place and Knole are still the homes of the aristocratic families who built them more than half a millennium ago.

The reason owners of stately homes open them to the public is simply that they need the ready money. Spiritually rewarding as it must be to own vast tracts of countryside, paintings by Rembrandt and Gainsborough, a house designed by one of the Adam brothers and furnished by Chippendale, and tapestries by the mile and porcelain by the ton—it is all a dead loss as far as cash flow (and death duties) are concerned.

What you get for your entrance fee differs enormously from one house to another. In some houses you are left completely free to wander at will, soaking up the splendor. In some you are organized into groups that then proceed through the house like bands of prisoners behind enemy lines. Occasionally you may find that your mentor is a member of the family, who will gleefully relate stories of uncles, aunts, and cousins back to the Crusades. Those are often the most memorable experiences.

A number of facts should be kept in mind when you're "doing the statelies" and touring these treasure houses. Depending on your itinerary, you may be able to save money by purchasing a special pass or joining an organization such as the National Trust (⇨ Discounts & Deals in Smart Travel Tips). Also keep in mind that many houses are unreachable except by car; be sure to plan your journey in advance. Hours are always subject to change, so be sure to call the day before and inquire: at times, people arrive at published times to stand on the doorstep and stare at a bolted door.

Although most houses are open only in the warm-weather seasons, from April to October, some of these houses have celebrated parks—Blenheim Palace and Chatsworth come to mind—that are utter delights and are open through much of the year. The most popular houses can be extremely busy in the peak summer months. You may want to plan off-season visits or, if that's not possible, arrive early in the day to avoid crowds.

Everyone has a top-10 list of favorite houses—Knole, Longleat, Woburn, and so on—but don't forget lesser-known neoclassical abodes and those wonderful mock-medieval Victorian piles, such as Castle Drogo in Devon, designed for Sir Julius Drewe, the founder of a chain of grocery stores. There is something keenly appropriate about the fact that the last great castle built in Britain was created for a shopkeeper. Napoléon, who echoed Adam Smith in observing that England was a nation of shopkeepers, would have approved.

had the stunning gardens laid out, with Italian and Tudor plantings, a yew maze, and topiary. ✉ *Off B2026, Hever* ☎ *01732/865224* ⊕ *www.hevercastle.co.uk* ✐ *£8.40, grounds only £6.70* ☉ *Castle Apr.–Oct., daily noon–6; Mar. and Nov., daily noon–4. Grounds Apr.–Oct., daily 11–6; Mar. and Nov., daily 11–4. Last admission 1 hr before closing.*

Chartwell

52 *9 mi north of Hever Castle, 12 mi northwest of Tunbridge Wells, 28 mi southeast of London.*

Chartwell was Sir Winston Churchill's home from 1924 until his death in 1965. The Victorian house was acquired by the National Trust, and today it appears much as it did in Churchill's lifetime, with personal memorabilia and even a half-smoked cigar in an ashtray. In the garden you can see a wall he built himself. ✉ *Off B2026, Westerham* ☎ *01732/866368* ⊕ *www.nationaltrust.org.uk* ✐ *£6.50, garden and studio only £3.25* ☉ *Late Mar.–June and Sept.–early Nov., Wed.–Sun. 11–5; July and Aug., Tues.–Sun. 11–5; last admission at 4:15.*

Knole

53 *8 mi east of Chartwell, 11 mi north of Royal Tunbridge Wells, 27 mi*
Fodor'sChoice *southeast of London.*
★

The town of Sevenoaks lies in London's commuter belt, a world away from the baronial air of its premier attraction, Knole, the grand home of the Sackville family since the 16th century. Begun in the 15th century and enlarged in 1603 by Thomas Sackville, Knole, with its complex of courtyards and buildings, resembles a small town. You'll need most of an afternoon to explore it thoroughly. The house is noted for its tapestries, embroidered furnishings, and the most famous set of 17th-century silver furniture to survive. Most of the salons are in the pre-baroque mode, rather dark and armorial. Paintings on display include family portraits by 18th-century artists Thomas Gainsborough and Sir Joshua Reynolds. The magnificently florid staircase was a novelty in its Elizabethan heyday. The noted writer Vita Sackville-West grew up at Knole and set her novel *The Edwardians,* a witty account of life among the gilded set, here. Encompassed by a 1,000-acre deer park, the house lies in the center of Sevenoaks, opposite St. Nicholas Church. To get there from Chartwell, drive north to Westerham, then pick up A25 and head east for 8 mi. ✉ *Off A225* ☎ *01732/450608* ⊕ *www.nationaltrust.org.uk* ✐ *House £5, gardens £2* ☉ *Late Mar.–Oct., Wed.–Sun. and national holidays 11–4, last admission at 3:30; gardens May–Sept., 1st Wed. of each month 11–4, last admission at 3.*

Ightham Mote

54 *7 mi southeast of Knole, 10 mi north of Royal Tunbridge Wells, 31 mi*
Fodor'sChoice *southeast of London.*
★

Finding Ightham Mote requires careful navigation, but it's worth the effort to see a vision right out of the Middle Ages. To enter this outstanding example of a small manor house, you cross a stone bridge over one of the dreamiest moats in England—the absolute quintessence of medieval romanticism. This moat, however, does not relate to the "mote" in the name, which refers to the role of the house as a meeting place, or "moot." Ightham (pronounced *i*-tem) Mote's magical exterior has changed little since it was built in the 14th century, but within you'll find that it encompasses styles of several periods, Tudor to Victorian. The Great Hall is an antiquarian's delight, both comfy and grand, and the magnificent Tudor chapel, drawing room, and billiards room in the northwest quarter are highlights. Ongoing restoration may mean that parts of the house are sometimes closed. Take time to explore the 14-acre garden and the woodland walks or to eat at the restaurant. To reach the house from Sevenoaks, follow A25 east to A227 (8 mi) and follow the signs. ☒ *Off A227, Ivy Hatch, Sevenoaks* ☎ *01732/810378* ⊕ *www.nationaltrust.org.uk* ☞ *£5.40* ☉ *Apr.–Oct., Mon., Wed.–Fri., and Sun. 10:30–5:30; last admission at 4:30.*

Rochester

🏛 *15 mi north of Ightham Mote, 28 mi southeast of London.*

Kent is Charles Dickens country, and all Dickens aficionados will want to head to Rochester, the place outside of London most closely associated with the great author. He lived for many years at Gad's Hill Place, just outside of town. You can find out all about Dickens and his connections with the town at the **Charles Dickens Centre**, with life-size models of scenes from the author's books that can amuse and horrify at the same time (parents, be warned). Opposite the center, look for the abode of Uncle Pumblechook in *Great Expectations,* one of the many buildings in High Street still "full of gables with old beams and timbers," as Dickens described them. ☒ *Eastgate House, High St.* ☎ *01634/844176* ☞ *£3.60* ☉ *Apr.–Sept., daily 10–6; Oct.–Mar., daily 10–4.*

Rochester Castle is one of the finest surviving examples of Norman military architecture. The keep, built in the 1100s and partly based on the Roman city wall, is 125 feet high, the tallest in England. ☒ *Boley Hill* ☎ *01634/402276* ⊕ *www.english-heritage.org.uk* ☞ *£3.70* ☉ *Apr.–Sept., daily 10–6; Oct., daily 10–5; Nov.–Mar., daily 10–4; last admission 30 mins before closing.*

In AD 604, Augustine of Canterbury ordained the first English bishop in a small cathedral on the site of the **Rochester Cathedral.** The current cathedral, England's second-oldest, is rather a jumble of architectural styles. Work was started in 1077 by the Norman Bishop Gundulph, who also built the castle. The elaborate Norman west front is striking, as is the crypt. ☒ *Boley Hill* ☎ *01634/843366* ☞ *£2 donation requested* ☉ *Mon.–Sat. 7:30–6, Sun. 7:30–5.*

The buildings and 47 retired ships at the **Historic Dockyard** across the River Medway from Rochester constitute the world's most complete Georgian–early Victorian dockyard. The dockyard's origins go back to the time of Henry VIII, and some 400 naval ships were built here over as many years, as shown in the museum and the "Wooden Walls" exhibit. There's a guided tour of the submarine HMS *Ocelot,* the last warship to be built for the Royal Navy at Chatham. ☒ *Chatham* ☎ *01634/823800* ⊕ *www.chdt.org.uk* ☞ *£9.50* ☉ *Apr.–Oct., daily 10–6, last admission at 4; Feb.–Mar., daily 10–dusk, last admission at 3; Nov., weekends 10–dusk, last admission at 3.*

Where to Stay

£ 🏠 **Mrs. Thomas' Bed & Breakfast.** This small B&B in an 1851 building tries to re-create the atmosphere of a Dickens-era town house, complete with period furnishings and an early Victorian four-poster in one bedroom. It's a two-minute walk from the railway station. ☒ *255 High St., ME1 1HQ* ☎ *01634/842737* 🛏 *3 rooms, 1 with bath* ♿ *No a/c* 🍽 *BP.*

Nightlife & the Arts

Rochester sponsors a **Dickens festival** (☎ *01634/306000*) in late May or early June, at which thousands of people in period dress attend enactments of scenes from the author's novels. Another important Dickens festival takes place in Broadstairs (40 mi east).

Leeds Castle

★ ⑤ *12 mi south of Rochester, 19 mi northwest of Royal Tunbridge Wells, 40 mi southeast of London.*

The bubbling River Medway runs through Maidstone, Kent's county seat, with its backdrop of chalky downs. Nearby, the fairy-tale stronghold of Leeds Castle commands two small islands on a peaceful lake. Dating back to the 9th century and rebuilt by the Normans in 1119, Leeds (not to be confused with Leeds in the North of England) became a favorite home of many medieval English queens. Henry VIII liked it so much he had it converted from a fortress into a grand palace. The house (much restored) offers a fine collection of paintings and furniture, plus an unusual dog-collar museum. Other attractions include a maze, a grotto, an aviary of native and exotic birds, and woodland gardens. The castle is 5 mi east of Maidstone. ⊠ *A20* ☎ *01622/765400* ⊕ *www. leedscastle.org.uk* ▣ *Nov.–Feb. £9.50, Mar.–June, Sept., and Oct. £11, July and Aug. £12* ⊙ *Apr.–Oct., daily 10–5; Nov.–Mar., daily 10–3. Castle closed Sat. last weekend June and 1st weekend July.*

Sissinghurst Castle Garden

⑤⑦ *10 mi south of Leeds Castle, 53 mi southeast of London.*

Fodor'sChoice ★

One of the most famous gardens in the world, Sissinghurst rests deep in the Kentish countryside around the remains of a moated Tudor castle. Unpretentiously beautiful, quintessentially English, the gardens were laid out in the 1930s around the remains of a former wing of the castle by the writer Vita Sackville-West (one of the Sackvilles of Knole) and her husband, the diplomat Harold Nicolson. The grounds are at their best in June and July, when the roses are in bloom. The gardens are informal in style; the White Garden, with its white flowers and silver-gray foliage, is a classic, and the herb garden and cottage garden show Sackville-West's knowledge of plants. Children may feel restricted in the gardens, and strollers (push chairs, in Britain) are not allowed. From Leeds Castle, make your way south on B2163 and A274 through Headcorn, then follow signs. ⊠ *A262, Cranbrook* ☎ *01580/710701* ⊕ *www. nationaltrust.org.uk* ▣ *£6.50* ⊙ *Mar.–Nov., Mon., Tues., and Fri. 11–6:30, weekends 10–6:30; last admission at 5:30. Admission often restricted because of limited space; a timed ticket system may be in effect, usually May–July.*

Where to Stay & Eat

£ ✕ **Claris's Tea Shop.** Claris's, near Sissinghurst Castle Garden, serves traditional English teas in a half-timber room and displays attractive English crafts items. There's a pretty garden for summer, and a gift shop stocks pottery, china, and glass. ⊠ *3 High St., Biddenden* ☎ *01580/ 291025* ▤ *No credit cards* ⊙ *Closed Mon. No dinner.*

★ ££ ▥ **Frogshole Oast.** This converted 18th-century oasthouse, in a rural setting 2 mi east of Sissinghurst Castle Garden, has three kilns that were once used for drying hops. The house retains many period features, and the rooms and sitting area have some antiques. There's a garden and a natural duck pond. ⊠ *Sissinghurst Rd., Biddenden, TN27 8HB* ☎☎ *01580/291935* ✎ *hartley@frogsholeoast.freeserve.co.uk* ⇨ *3 rooms* ⚐ *No a/c* ⊙▮ *BP.*

en route As you leave Sissinghurst Castle Garden, continue south along A229 through Hawkhurst, a little village that was once the headquarters of a notorious gang of smugglers. Turn left onto the B2244 and left at the Curlew pub to arrive in the tiny Sussex village of Bodiam.

Bodiam Castle

★ ⑤⑧ *9 mi south of Cranbrook, 15 mi southeast of Royal Tunbridge Wells, 57 mi southeast of London.*

Immortalized in 1,001 travel posters, Bodiam Castle is one of Britain's most picturesque medieval strongholds, despite being virtually a shell. Built in 1385 to withstand a threatened French invasion, it was "slighted" (partly demolished) during the English Civil War of 1642–46 and has been uninhabited ever since. Nevertheless, you can climb some of the towers. Surrounded by a lovely moat and adorned with battlements and turrets, this castle seems designed to be photographed. ☒ *Off B2244, Bodiam* ☎ *01580/830436* ⊕ *www.nationaltrust.org.uk* ☒ *£4* ☉ *Mid-Feb.–Oct., daily 10–6 or dusk; Nov.–mid-Feb., weekends 10–4 or dusk; last admission 1 hr before closing.*

Great Dixter House & Gardens

⑤⑨ *3 mi east of Bodiam, 18 mi southeast of Royal Tunbridge Wells, 60 mi southeast of London.*

Combining one of the largest timber-frame halls in the country with a cottage garden on a grand scale, this place will get your green fingers twitching. The house dates back to 1464 and was restored in 1910 by architect Edwin Lutyens, who also designed the garden. From these beginnings, horticulturist and writer Christopher Lloyd, whose birthplace this is, has developed a series of "garden rooms" and a dazzling herbaceous Long Border. There's a nursery on site. ☒ *Off A28, Northiam* ☎ *01797/252878* ⊕ *www.greatdixter.co.uk* ☒ *£6.50, gardens only £5* ☉ *Apr.–Oct., Tues.–Sun. 2–5:30; last admission at 5.*

Burwash

⑥⓪ *13 mi west of Northiam, 14 mi south of Royal Tunbridge Wells, 58 mi southeast of London.*

Burwash, a pretty Sussex village, is known for its association with writer Rudyard Kipling. Close by, between Burwash Common and the River Dudwell, is the setting for *Puck of Pook's Hill,* one of Kipling's well-known children's books.

Kipling lived from 1902 to 1936 at **Bateman's,** a beautiful 17th-century house a half mile south of the village that was built for a prominent ironmaster when Sussex was the center of England's iron industry. Many of the rooms, including Kipling's study, look as they did when the writer lived here. In the garden, a water mill still grinds flour (most Saturdays in summer at 2 PM); it's thought to be one of the oldest working water turbines. ☒ *Off A265* ☎ *01435/882302* ⊕ *www.nationaltrust.org.uk* ☒ *£5.20, £2.60 in Mar.* ☉ *Mar., weekends 11–4, garden only; Apr.–Oct., Sat.–Wed. 11–5 (house), 11–5:30 (grounds); last admission 1 hr before closing.*

Sports & the Outdoors

Bewl Water, one of England's largest reservoirs, has aquatic sports, waterside walks, bicycle rentals, and boat trips. There are also special events and an adventure playground. You pay a small parking fee. ⊠ *Off B2099, 5 mi north of Burwash* ☎ *01892/890661* ⊕ *www.bewl. co.uk* ⊙ *Open daily 9–sunset.*

Finchcocks

61 *13 mi north of Burwash, 10 mi east of Tunbridge Wells, 48 mi southeast of London.*

Finchcocks, an elegant Georgian mansion between Lamberhurst and Goudhurst, contains a magnificent collection of nearly 100 historic keyboard instruments. They are played whenever the house is open; admission includes demonstration recitals. A festival is held on September weekends. ⊠ *Off A262, Goudhurst* ☎ *01580/211702* ⊕ *www. finchcocks.co.uk* ⊠ *£7.50* ⊙ *Mid-Apr.–July and Sept., Sun. 2–6; Aug., Wed.–Thurs. and Sun. 2–6.*

Where to Stay & Eat

££ ✕⊞ **Star and Eagle.** Pints and hospitality have been served at this traditional, gabled half-timber village inn since 1600. Exposed beams and open fireplaces recall the past. Rooms come in all shapes and sizes; some overlook the village graveyard. Food includes Spanish, Mexican, and Italian dishes, in addition to English favorites such as beef Wellington. Great views make it good for outdoor eating in summer. ⊠ *High St., Goudhurst, TN17 1AL* ☎ *01580/211512* 🖷 *01580/211416* ⇘ *10 rooms* ⚗ *Restaurant, bar; no a/c* ▭ *MC, V* ⦿ *BP.*

SOUTHEAST A TO Z

To research prices, get advice from other travelers, and book travel arrangements, visit www.fodors.com.

AIRPORTS

Gatwick Airport, 27 mi south of London, has direct flights from many U.S. cities and is more convenient for this region than Heathrow. The terminal for the British Rail line is in the airport buildings, and there are connections to major towns in the region. *See* London A to Z *in* Chapter 1 for information about transfers from Gatwick to London.
🚩 **Gatwick Airport** ⊠ M23, Junction 9, Crawley ☎ 0870/000–2468 ⊕ www.baa.co.uk.

BUS TRAVEL

National Express serves the region from London's Victoria Coach Station. Trips to Brighton and Canterbury take less than two hours; to Chichester, about three hours. For regional bus transport inquiries, contact Traveline. Maps and timetables are available at bus depots, train stations, local libraries, and tourist information centers.

FARES &   🚩 **National Express** ☎ 0870/580–8080 ⊕ www.nationalexpress.com.
SCHEDULES   **Traveline** ☎ 0870/608–2608 ⊕ www.traveline.org.uk.

CAR RENTAL

🚩 **Local Agencies Avis** ⊠ 6A Brighton Marina, Brighton ☎ 01273/673738 ⊠ Eastern Docks, Dover ☎ 01304/206265. **Hertz** ⊠ 47 Trafalgar St., Brighton ☎ 01273/738227 ⊠ C/o Elf Garage, Broad Oak Rd., Canterbury ☎ 01227/470864 ⊠ 173–177 Snargate St., Dover ☎ 01304/207303 ⊠ Guildford Railway Station, Station Approach, Guildford ☎ 01483/536677.

CAR TRAVEL

Major routes radiating outward from London to the Southeast are, from west to east, M23/A23 to Brighton (52 mi); A21, passing by Royal Tunbridge Wells to Hastings (65 mi); A20/M20 to Folkestone; and A2/M2 via Canterbury (56 mi) to Dover (71 mi).

A good link route for traveling through the region, from Hampshire across the border into Sussex and Kent, is A272 (which becomes A265). It runs through the Weald, which separates the North Downs from the more inviting South Downs. Although smaller, less busy roads forge deeper into the downs, even the main roads take you through lovely country-side and villages. The main route east from the downs to the Channel ports and resorts of Kent is A27. To get to Romney Marsh (just across the Sussex border in Kent), take A259 from Rye. Be warned that more traffic tickets are issued per traffic warden in Brighton than anywhere else in the country.

EMERGENCIES

Ambulance, fire, police ☎ 999. **Royal Sussex County Hospital** ✉ Eastern Rd., Brighton ☎ 01273/696955. **Canterbury Hospital** ✉ Ethelbert Rd., Canterbury ☎ 01227/766877.

TOURS

BUS TOURS City Sightseeing's hop-on, hop-off bus tour of Brighton leaves Brighton Pier every 20–30 minutes and lasts about an hour. It operates April–October; cost is £6.50.

City Sightseeing ☎ 01789/294466 ⊕ www.city-sightseeing.com.

PRIVATE GUIDES The Southeast England Tourist Board (⇨ Visitor Information) can arrange private tours with qualified Blue Badge guides. The Canterbury Guild of Guides provides guides who have a specialized knowledge of the city and its surrounding area.

Canterbury Guild of Guides ✉ Arnett House, Hawks La. ☎ 01227/459779 ⊕ www.canterburyguidedwalksuk.com.

TRAIN TRAVEL

Connex South Eastern and Connex South Central serve the area from London's Victoria and Charing Cross (for all areas) and Waterloo (for the west). From London, the trip to Brighton takes about one hour by the fast train, and to Dover, about two hours. South West Trains runs service to Guildford. The line running west from Dover passes through Ashford, where you can change trains for Hastings and Eastbourne. There are connections from Eastbourne for Lewes, and from Brighton for Chichester. For local and regional information, call National Rail Enquiries.

CUTTING COSTS A Network Railcard costing £20, valid throughout the southern and south-eastern regions for a year, entitles you and three companions to one-third off many off-peak fares.

FARES & SCHEDULES **National Rail Enquiries** ☎ 0845/748–4950 ⊕ www.nationalrail.co.uk.

TRAVEL AGENCIES

Besides those listed below, Thomas Cook has offices in Dover, Eastbourne, Folkestone, Guildford, Hastings, Hove, Maidstone, Ramsgate, and Sevenoaks.

Local Agent Referrals American Express ✉ 82 North St., Brighton ☎ 01273/712905. **Thomas Cook** ✉ 9 Rose La., Brighton ☎ 01227/596054 ✉ 9 High St., Canterbury ☎ 01227/597800 ✉ 109 Mount Pleasant Rd., Royal Tunbridge Wells ☎ 01892/791500.

VISITOR INFORMATION

The Southeast England Tourist Board will send you useful illustrated booklets, *South East Breaks* and *Walk South East England,* and can give you information on tours and excursions. The office is open Monday to Thursday 9–5:30, Friday 9–5. Local tourist information centers (TICs) are normally open Monday–Saturday 9:30–5:30, but hours vary seasonally; offices are listed below by town.

🛈 **Southeast England Tourist Board** ✉ The Old Brew House, 1 Warwick Park, Royal Tunbridge Wells, TN2 5TU ☎ 01892/540766 ⌨ 01892/511008 ⊕ www.southeastengland. uk.com. **Arundel** ✉ 61 High St., BN18 9AJ ☎ 01903/882268 ⊕ www.sussex-by-the-sea.co.uk. **Brighton** ✉ 10 Bartholomew Sq., BN1 1JS ☎ 0906/711–2255 ⊕ www. visitbrighton.com. **Canterbury** ✉ 12–13 Sun St., CT1 2HX ☎ 01227/378100 ⊕ www. canterbury.co.uk. **Chichester** ✉ 29A South St., PO19 1AH ☎ 01243/775888 ⊕ www. chichester.gov.uk. **Dover** ✉ Townwall St., CT16 1JR ☎ 01304/205108. **Guildford** ✉ 14 Tunsgate, GU1 3QT ☎ 01483/444333 ⊕ www.guildfordborough.co.uk. **Hastings** ✉ Queens Sq., Priory Meadow, TN34 1TL ☎ 01424/781111 ✉ In summer only ✉ 2 The Stade ☎ 01424/781111. **Lewes** ✉ 187 High St., BN7 2DE ☎ 01273/483448 ⊕ www.lewes.gov. uk. **Maidstone** ✉ The Gatehouse, Palace Gardens, Mill St., ME15 6YE ☎ 01622/602169 ⊕ www.digitalmaidstone.co.uk. **Royal Tunbridge Wells** ✉ The Old Fish Market, The Pantiles, TN2 5TN ☎ 01892/515675 ⊕ www.visittunbridgewells.com. **Rye** ✉ The Heritage Centre, Strand Quay, TN31 7AY ☎ 01797/226696 ⊕ www.rye.org.uk.

THE SOUTH
WINCHESTER, SALISBURY & STONEHENGE

FODOR'S CHOICE

Lamperts Cottage, *B&B near Cerne Abbas*

Salisbury Cathedral, *Salisbury*

Stonehenge, *near Amesbury*

Stourhead, *garden, in Stourton*

HIGHLY RECOMMENDED

RESTAURANTS Bishopstrow House, *Warminster, near Longleat House*

Chewton Glen, *New Milton, near Bournemouth*

Howard's House, *near Salisbury*

HOTELS Bishopstrow House, *Warminster, near Longleat House*

Casterbridge Hotel, *Dorchester*

Chewton Glen, *New Milton, near Bournemouth*

Howard's House, *near Salisbury*

Streamside Hotel, *near Weymouth*

Yalbury Cottage, *near Dorchester*

SIGHTS Avebury Stone Circles, *Avebury*

Carisbrooke Castle, *Carisbrooke*

Corfe Castle, *Corfe*

Jane Austen's House, *Chawton*

Longleat House, *Warminster*

Maiden Castle, *near Dorchester*

Portsmouth Historic Dockyard, *Portsmouth*

Wilton House, *Wilton*

Winchester Cathedral, *Winchester*

Updated by
Robert
Andrews

CATHEDRALS, STATELY HOMES, STONE CIRCLES—the South, made up of Hampshire, Dorset, and Wiltshire counties, holds all kinds of attractions, and not a few quiet pleasures. Two important cathedrals, Winchester and Salisbury (pronounced *sawls*-bree), are here, as well as stately homes—Longleat, Stourhead, and Wilton House, among them—pretty market towns, and literally hundreds of haunting prehistoric remains, two of which, Avebury and Stonehenge, should not be missed. These are but the tourist-brochure superlatives. Sooner or later, anyone spending time in these parts should rent a bike and set out to discover the back-road villages—much favored by those who migrate here from every corner of the country in search of upward mobility—*not* found in those brochures. After a drink in the village pub and a look at the cricket game on the village green, take a break at a strawberry farm, where you can lie on straw strewn between the rows and gorge yourself on sun-warmed berries, or collapse in a grassy field that has "nap time" written all over it. *This* is what summer in England is all about.

Hampshire has been called the Cinderella County because for many it is just a county to be crossed in the feverish holiday migration from London to the cliffs and coves of Devon and Cornwall in the west. To many others, Hampshire means the last sight of England from departing steamers, or a first solid acquaintance with her on stepping ashore at Southampton. The county may seem but the gateway to England, through which to pass hurriedly. Nothing could be further from the truth, for the sandwich shire holds much for the perceptive.

One of the area's many historical highlights was when Alfred the Great, teaching religion and letters, made Winchester the capital of 9th-century England and helped lay plans for Britain's first navy, sowing the seeds of its Commonwealth. This well-preserved market town is dominated by its cathedral, an imposing edifice dotted with the Gothic tombs of 15th-century bishops, who lie peacefully behind grillwork, their marble hands crossed for eternity. Winchester is a good center from which to visit quiet villages where so many of England's once great personages, from Florence Nightingale to Lord Mountbatten, lived or died. Jane Austen and her works are enduringly popular, and thanks to a spate of filmed versions of her classic novels, her home at Chawton has become a favored pilgrimage spot. But everywhere the unscheming hand of time has scattered over Hampshire pretty villages, many with cottages grouped around a green.

Moving beyond the gentle, gardenlike landscape of Hampshire, you can explore the somewhat harsher terrain of Salisbury Plain. Two monuments, millennia apart, stand sentinel over the plain. One is the 404-foot stone spire of Salisbury Cathedral, which dominates the entire Salisbury valley and has been immortalized in oil by John Constable. Not far away is the most imposing and dramatic prehistoric structure in Europe: Stonehenge. The many theories about its construction and purpose only add to its attraction, which endures despite the hordes of visitors.

Each of the numerous other districts to explore has its own pleasures, and many have literary or historical associations. Turn your sights to the Dorset heathland, the countryside explored in the novels of Thomas Hardy. This district is spanned by grass-covered chalk hills—the downs—wooded valleys, and meadows through which course meandering rivers. Along the coastline you'll find Lyme Regis, where the tides and currents strike fear into the hearts of sailors, and Cowes on the Isle of Wight—Queen Victoria's favorite getaway—which welcomes high-flyers who enter their yachts in the famous regattas.

3

You could spend weeks exploring the South, but you can do a good sampling of the area in seven days or less. On a three-day visit, you can see the highlights of Winchester and Salisbury, plus Stonehenge and a stately home or two. A weeklong visit allows time to see areas and sights off the beaten path—to see Avebury in addition to Stonehenge, for example—and to explore the New Forest or relax by the shore a bit.

Numbers in the text correspond to numbers in the margin and on the South, Winchester, and Salisbury maps.

If you have
3 days

With limited time, you will want to combine the most sights with the least amount of traveling. If you're coming from London or southeast England, 🖼 **Winchester** ❶ – ❽ ▶ will be your first stop, a quiet, solid town, conducive to walking about, with the great cathedral at its heart. Other historic sites include the Great Hall and Winchester College, one of the country's noted "public" schools. Spend a night here, then move west to another cathedral city, 🖼 **Salisbury** ㉑ – ㉙. Surely few cathedrals have a more beautiful setting than this town—worth a two-night stay to take in the city sights and nearby **Stonehenge** ㊲. Even closer to Salisbury are **Wilton House** ㉚ and its gardens, which you can see on your way to visit the village of **Shaftesbury** ㉛, and two more country estates, **Stourhead** ㉝ and **Longleat House** ㉞. The former holds—many believe—the most beautiful garden in England; the latter marries an African game park with a famous Elizabethan house.

If you have
7 days

Spend your first day and night in 🖼 **Winchester** ❶ – ❽ ▶, then head down to Portsmouth to take a ferry across to **Cowes** ⑮ on the Isle of Wight, a favorite island haven for both Queen Victoria and Charles Dickens. The former vacationed at Osborne House, an Italianate villa, whereas one of her forebears, Charles I, was the unwilling guest of the Parliamentary army during his incarceration in **Carisbrooke Castle** ⑳. Overnight in nearby 🖼 **Ryde** ⑯. Leave the Isle of Wight from Cowes, disembarking at **Southampton** ⑬, which is not particularly noteworthy but has several absorbing museums as well as the Pilgrim Fathers' Memorial. North of town, **Romsey** ⑭ is an attractive village, with the 18th-century mansion of Broadlands lying just outside. From here, you are well placed to spend two nights in 🖼 **Salisbury** ㉑ – ㉙ to take in the city and nearby attractions such as **Stonehenge** ㊲, traveling as far north as the stone circles of **Avebury** ㉟ and **Marlborough** ㊱, said to be the burial place of Merlin. If you have already toured this area, you might swoop down instead to the leafy New Forest; **Lyndhurst** ㊳ is an excellent place to take a breather and some exercise, including riding. Heading westward, stop in at 🖼 **Bournemouth** ㊶, containing the Russell-Cotes Art Gallery and Museum, a Victorian edifice brimming with treasures, and the burial place of Mary Shelley, author of *Frankenstein*. If the seaside frivolity doesn't grab you, carry on as far as **Corfe Castle** ㊹. Farther west is the genteel resort of **Weymouth** ㊽, where you can dine on fish by the harborside. South of Weymouth lies the **Isle of Portland** ㊾, which, together with Chesil Beach, will provide both beach fun and interest to anyone intrigued by geological phenomena. 🖼 **Dorchester** ㊺ and **Maiden Castle** ㊼ lie just north of here, and a few miles west, **Abbotsbury** ㊿ contains a famous 600-year-old swannery. Farther along Lyme Bay is the pretty port of **Lyme Regis** �51.

The South has been quietly central to England's history for well over 4,000 years, occupied successively by prehistoric man, the Celts, the Romans, the Saxons, and the modern British. History continues to be made here, right up to the modern era. On D-Day, forces sailed for Normandy from ports along this coast; nearly 40 years later, they set out to recover the Falklands.

Exploring the South

The South of England ranges from the broad plains of Wiltshire, including the Marlborough Downs, the Vale of Pewsey, and the great Salisbury Plain, to the gaudy bucket-and-spade resorts of the coast, and the sedate retirement homes of the Isle of Wight. The wide-open windblown feel of the inland county of Wiltshire offers a sharp contrast both to the tame, sequestered villages of Hampshire and Dorset, and the self-important bustle of Southampton and Portsmouth. On the whole, you will not want to spend much time in these two ports; instead, spend your nights in the more compelling cities of Salisbury and Winchester.

This good-size area holds a number of distinctive, self-contained destinations for touring. The cathedral city of Winchester makes a useful base for visiting a handful of villages before you move on to the historic ports of Southampton and Portsmouth. You can end your tour on the Isle of Wight. The city of Salisbury, with its own lovely cathedral, is another major starting point. The obvious draw outside town is Stonehenge, but you are also within reach of an equally interesting prehistoric monument, Avebury. From there, you can swing south to the cultivated woodlands of the New Forest. The southern coast of Dorset is another major area, with a couple of popular holiday resorts, Bournemouth and Weymouth, and a string of ancient sites: Corfe Castle, Maiden Castle, and Cerne Abbas. Lyme Regis, on the Devon border at the center of the wide arc of Lyme Bay, is a favorite holiday destination in this area. It provides a gateway to the World Heritage Site called the Jurassic Coast, with fossil-rich cliffs from Swanage in the east to Exmouth in the west.

About the Restaurants

Fertile soil, well-stocked rivers, and a long coastline ensure excellent farm produce and a plentiful stock of fish throughout the South. Try fresh-grilled river trout or sea bass poached in brine, or dine like a king on the New Forest's renowned venison. Hampshire especially is noted for its pig farming, and you should zero in on pork products on local restaurant menus.

About the Hotels

Modern hotel chains are well represented, and in rural areas you can choose among elegant country-house hotels, traditional coaching inns, and modest guest houses. Note that some seaside hotels do not accept one-night bookings in summer. If you plan to visit Cowes on the Isle of Wight during Cowes Week, the annual yachting jamboree in late July or early August, book well in advance.

WHAT IT COSTS In pounds				
	££££request	££££	£££	££	£
RESTAURANTS	over £22	£18–£22	£13–£17	£7–£12	under £7
HOTELS	over £160	£115–£160	£80–£115	£50–£80	under £50

Restaurant prices are for a main course at dinner. Hotel prices are for two people in a standard double room in high season, including VAT, with no meals or, if indicated, CP (with Continental breakfast), BP (Breakfast Plan, with full breakfast), or MAP (Modified American Plan, with breakfast and dinner).

3

Ancient Sites
All around Britain, prehistoric monuments dot the landscape, silent but tantalizing reminders of civilizations long vanished. Ceremonial stone circles, barrows used for burials, and Iron Age hill forts attract endless speculation about the motives and methods of their ancient builders. The South contains not only the 5,000-year-old Stonehenge, one of the great treasures of Britain and, indeed, Europe, but also an abundance of other sites, sometimes overlaid with reminders of other eras. At Old Sarum, near Salisbury, the earthwork ramparts of an Iron Age hill fort survive although Romans and Normans took over the site. The evocative Avebury Stone Circles surround part of a village; nearby is the West Kennett Long Barrow, a chambered tomb. Close to Dorchester, Maiden Castle is a stone and earth hill fort with ramparts that enclose 45 acres. If all this fuels your imagination, the shop at Stonehenge sells plenty of books with plenty of theories, and the Salisbury and South Wiltshire Museum in Salisbury and the Alexander Keillor Museum in Avebury provide helpful background. Start by visiting one site, and you may find yourself rerouting your trip to seek out others.

Literary Landmarks
Like a library, the South is tailor-made for browsing, thanks to its many literary shrines. In Dorset, Thomas Hardy country, you can get far from the madding crowd. The Victorian novelist brought immortality to the peaceful countryside and to towns such as Shaftesbury and Dorchester, which appear in a number of his works, though with different names. In addition to Hardy landmarks, Jane Austen sites and shrines abound in the South of England, including the house in which she lived, in Chawton, and her burial place in Winchester Cathedral. Lyme Regis, an important setting for Austen's *Persuasion*, was where John Fowles set his classic novel of pseudo-Victoriana, *The French Lieutenant's Woman*.

Markets
The tradition of local markets is alive and well in the South, and the numerous open-air markets in towns and villages sell everything from mundane housewares to crafts and foodstuffs. Exploring a local market can provide a unique sense of place; for a complete list, ask the Southern Tourist Board. Among the best are Salisbury's traditional city market (Tuesday and Saturday), Kingsland Market in Southampton for bric-a-brac (Thursday), and a general country market (Wednesday) at Ringwood, near Bournemouth. At the country's biggest farmers' market, held in Winchester's Middle Brook Street on the last Sunday of the month, all produce and goods sold must be grown, reared, baked, or caught in Hampshire or within 10 mi of its borders.

Timing
Make sure you don't see the cathedrals of Salisbury and Winchester on a Sunday, when your visit will be restricted, or during services, when it won't be overly appreciated. Places such as Stonehenge and Longleat House attract plenty of people at all times, so bypass such sights on weekends or public holidays. In summer, day-trippers and longer-stay tourists crowd the coastal resorts of Bournemouth and Weymouth; it may be difficult to find suitable accommodations. The Isle of Wight, too, gets its fair share of summer visitors, especially during the weeklong Cowes

The South

GLOUCESTERSHIRE

Bristol Channel

Avon

Bristol

Avebu

Calne

A4

M5

A37

A46

Bath

Melksham

Devizes

M4

Avon

WILTSHI

Trowbridge

B3098

Westbury

A361

Frome

A3098

Warminster

B390

34 **Longleat House**

SALISBURY PLAIN

A303

Wylye

A.

Wells

Shepton Mallet

33 **Stourhead**

Mere

B3092

A362

B30

Teffont Evias

Tisbury

Nadder

SOMERSET

A37

B3092

Swallowcliffe

A30

B3091

31 **Shaftesbury**

Yeovil

A303

32 **Sherborne**

A352

Farnham

Illminster

A354

DORSET

43 **Blandford Forum**

46 **Cerne Abbas**

42 **Wimborne Minster**

Godmanstone

Tolpuddle

A349

51 **Lyme Regis**

Puddletown

A35

A35

Bridport

Frome

Poole

Bo

Lyme Bay

West Bexington

B3157

45 **Dorchester**

47 **Maiden Castle**

Abbotsbury

Puddle

A351

Brownsea Island

50

Portesham

A352

Wareham

A35

A364

A353

PURBECK HILLS

Chesil Beach

B3107

West Lulworth

B3070

44 **Corfe Castle**

B3351

48 **Weymouth**

Lulworth Cove

Swanage

49 **Isle of Portland**

GREAT BRITAIN

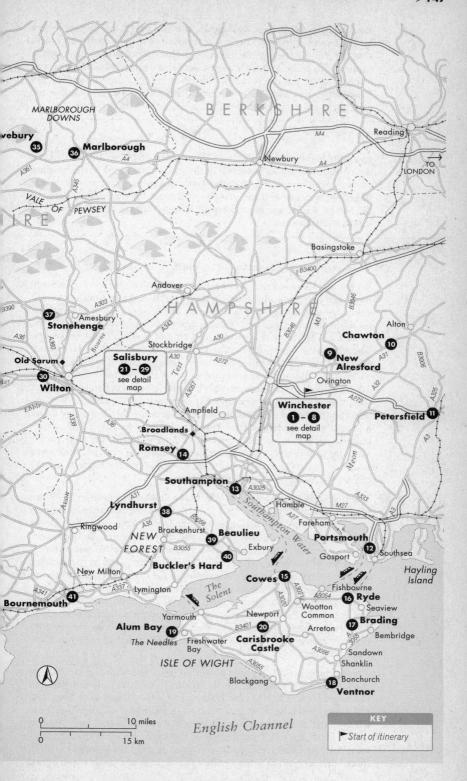

MARLBOROUGH
DOWNS

B E R K S H I R E

Reading

TO
LONDON

Newbury

M4

A4

ebury

35

A361

36 **Marlborough**

A4

VALE OF PEWSEY

IRE

Basingstoke

B3400

Andover

H A M P S H I R E

B3046

M3

Chawton

Alton

37 Amesbury

Stonehenge

A303

9 **New
Alresford**

10

A36

A360

Stockbridge

A30

A30

A272

A31

B3006

Old Sarum

30 **Wilton**

Salisbury
21 – 29
see detail
map

A3057

Ovington

A32

A325

Ebble

A338

A36

Ampfield

Winchester
1 – 8
see detail
map

Petersfield 11

Broadlands

Romsey 14

Meon

Avon

Southampton

13 A3025

Hamble

M27

A333

A3

Lyndhurst 38

Ringwood

A35

B3056

Brockenhurst

NEW
FOREST

B3055

39 **Beaulieu**

Exbury

Fareham

Portsmouth

A27

Southampton Water

Gosport

12

Southsea

Hayling
Island

New Milton

A341

A337

Buckler's Hard

40

Lymington

The Solent

Yarmouth

Cowes 15

A3020

A3021

A3054

Fishbourne

16 **Ryde**

Seaview

Bournemouth

41

Alum Bay 19

The Needles

Freshwater
Bay

Newport

B3401

**Carisbrooke
Castle**

20

Wootton
Common

Arreton

17 **Brading**

Bembridge

A3056

Sandown

Shanklin

ISLE OF WIGHT

A3055

Blackgang

18 **Bonchurch**

Ventnor

English Channel

0   10 miles
0   15 km

KEY

▶ Start of itinerary

Regatta in late July or early August, and you may have to wait longer
for the ferries. The New Forest is at its most alluring in spring and early
summer (for the foaling season) and fall (for the colorful foliage), while
summer can be quite busy with walkers and campers. In fall, take waterproof boots for the puddles. Wherever you go, choose smaller, less
frequented stops when the going gets tough. Otherwise, the South is one
area of the country you will enjoy visiting at any time of year.

FROM WINCHESTER TO SOUTHAMPTON

From the lovely cathedral city of Winchester, 70 mi southwest of London, you can meander southward to the coast, stopping at the bustling
ports of Southampton and Portsmouth to explore their maritime heritage. From either of these you can strike out for the restful shores of
the Isle of Wight, vacation home of Queen Victoria and thousands of
modern-day Britons.

Winchester

▶ *70 mi southwest of London, 14 mi north of Southampton.*

Winchester is among the most historic of English cities, and as you walk
its graceful streets and wander its many gardens, a sense of the past envelops you. Although it is now merely the county seat of Hampshire,
for more than four centuries Winchester served as England's capital. Here,
in AD 827, Egbert was crowned first king of England, and his succes-
sor, Alfred the Great, held court until his death in 899. In late Saxon
times the town became the home of the finest school of calligraphy and
manuscript illumination in Europe. After the Norman Conquest in
1066, William I ("the Conqueror") had himself crowned in London, but
took the precaution of repeating the ceremony in Winchester. William
also commissioned the local monastery to produce the Domesday Book,
a record of the general census begun in England in 1085. The city remained the center of ecclesiastical, commercial, and political power
until the 13th century. Winchester's power has long vanished, and some
fast-food outlets and retail chains have moved onto High Street, but the
city still preserves much of its past glory.

★ ❶ The city's greatest monument, **Winchester Cathedral,** begun in 1079 and
consecrated in 1093, presents a sturdy, chunky appearance in keeping
with its Norman construction, so that the Gothic lightness within is even
more breathtaking. Its tower, transepts, and crypt, and the inside core
of the great Perpendicular nave, reveal some of the world's best surviving
examples of Norman architecture. Other features, such as the arcades,
the presbytery (behind the choir, holding the high altar), and the windows, are Gothic alterations carried out between the 12th and 14th centuries. Little of the original stained glass has survived, however, thanks
to Cromwell's Puritan troops, who ransacked the cathedral in the 17th
century during the English Civil War, but you can still see the sumptuously illuminated 12th-century Winchester Bible in the Library and Triforium Gallery.

Among the many well-known people buried in the cathedral are William
the Conqueror's son, William II ("Rufus"), mysteriously murdered in
the New Forest in 1100; Izaak Walton (1593–1683), author of *The Compleat Angler,* whose memorial window in Silkestede's Chapel was paid
for by "the fishermen of England and America"; and Jane Austen,
whose grave lies in the north aisle of the nave. Firmly in the 20th century, Antony Gormley's evocative statue of a figure, *Sound II* (1986),
looms in the crypt, as often as not standing in water (as it was designed

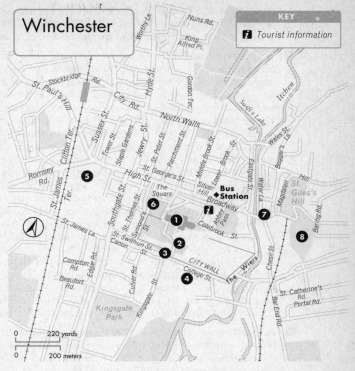

Winchester

KEY

ℹ️ Tourist information

to do), because of seasonal flooding. You can also explore the bell tower—with views as far as the Isle of Wight in fair weather—and other recesses of the building on a special tour. Occasionally, special services or ceremonies may mean the cathedral is closed for visits, so telephone first to avoid disappointment. ✉ *The Close, Cathedral Precincts* ☎ *01962/857225* 🌐 *www.winchester-cathedral.org.uk* 💷 *£3.50 donation requested; Library and Triforium Gallery £1, bell tower tour £2* 🕐 *Daily 8:30–6, longer for services. Free tours on the hr daily 10–2, bell tower tours Wed. 2:15 and Sat. 11:30 and 2:15.*

②
③ The **Close,** behind the cathedral, is an area containing neat lawns and the Deanery, Dome Alley, and Cheyney Court. **King's Gate,** on St. Swithun Street on the south side of the Close, was built in the 13th century and is one of two gates remaining from the original city wall. **St. Swithun's Church** is built over the ancient King's Gate. The saint himself is interred in Winchester Cathedral; it is said that it rained for 40 days when his body was transferred there from the churchyard, giving rise to the legend that rain on St. Swithun's Day (July 15) means another 40 days of wet weather. Nearby, at 8 College Street, is the house where Jane Austen died on July 18, 1817, three days after writing a comic poem about the legend of St. Swithun's Day (copies are usually available in the cathedral).

④ **Winchester College,** one of England's oldest "public" (i.e., private) schools, was founded in 1382 by Bishop William of Wykeham, who has his own chapel in Winchester Cathedral. The school chapel is notable for its delicately vaulted ceiling. Among the original buildings still in use is Chamber Court, center of college life for six centuries. Notice the "scholars"—students holding academic scholarships—clad in their traditional gowns. ⊠*College St.* ☎*01962/621209* ⊕*www.winchestercollege. org* 🖾 *£3.50* ⊙ *1-hr tours Mon., Wed., Fri., and Sat. 10:45, noon, 2:15, and 3:15; Tues. and Thurs. 10:45 and noon; Sun. 2:15 and 3:15.*

❺ The historic **Great Hall,** a few blocks west of the cathedral, is all that remains of the city's Norman castle. The English Parliament met here for the first time in 1246; Sir Walter Raleigh was tried for conspiracy against King James I and condemned to death here in 1603 (although he wasn't beheaded until 1618); and Dame Alice Lisle was sentenced to death by the infamous Judge Jeffreys for sheltering fugitives, after Monmouth's Rebellion in 1685. A huge and gaudy sculpture of Victoria, carved by Sir Alfred Gilbert (responsible for *Eros* in Piccadilly Circus) to mark the queen's Golden Jubilee in 1887, dominates the floor of the Great Hall. But the greatest relic hangs on the hall's west wall, the object fondly known as King Arthur's Round Table, which has places for 24 knights and a portrait of Arthur bearing a remarkable resemblance to King Henry VIII. In fact, the table dates back no further than the 13th century and was repainted by order of Henry on the occasion of a visit by the Holy Roman Emperor Charles V; the real Arthur was probably a Celtic cavalry general who held off the invading Saxons after the fall of the Roman Empire in the 5th or 6th century AD. The Tudor monarchs revived the Arthurian legend for political purposes. Take time for a brief wander in Queen Eleanor's Medieval Garden—a re-creation of a noblewoman's shady retreat. ⊠ *Castle Hill* ☎ *01962/846476* 🖾 *Free* ⊙ *Mar.–Oct., daily 10–5; Nov.–Feb., weekdays 10–5, weekends 10–4.*

❻ Across from the cathedral, the **City Museum** interprets Winchester's past through displays of Celtic pottery, Roman mosaics, Saxon coins, and reconstructed Victorian shop fronts. ⊠ *The Square* ☎ *01962/848269* ⊕ *www.winchester.gov.uk/heritage* 🖾 *Free* ⊙ *Apr.–Oct., Mon.–Sat. 10–5, Sun. noon–5; Nov.–Mar., Tues.–Sat. 10–4, Sun. noon–4.*

❼ The **City Mill** is a working 18th-century water mill, complete with small island garden, at the east end of High Street. Part of the premises is a National Trust gift shop open year-round, and part is used as a youth hostel. Call ahead for milling days. ⊠ *Bridge St.* ☎ *01962/870057* ⊕*www.nationaltrust.org.uk* 🖾*£2* ⊙ *Mar., weekends 11–4:30; Apr.–June, Sept., and Oct., Wed.–Sun. 11–4:30; July and Aug., daily 11–4:30.*

❽ To top off a tour of Winchester, you can climb **St. Giles's Hill** for a panoramic view of the city. A walk down High Street and Broadway will bring you to the hill.

Where to Stay & Eat

£££££ ✕ **Chesil Rectory.** The building may be old—15th-century—but the highly regarded cooking is essentially innovative. The high price of main courses (£30), such as the house specialty, pork and black pudding, is offset by the low price (£5) of starters, such as Roquefort cheese soufflé, and desserts, which include fruity sorbets. Service and the antique charm of the surroundings match the quality of the food. ⊠ *1 Chesil St.* ☎ *01962/851555* ⊟ *DC, MC, V* ⊙ *Closed Sun. and Mon.*

£–££ ✕ **Cathedral Refectory.** The bold, modern style of this self-service eatery next to the cathedral helps make it a refreshing lunch or snack stop. The menu ranges from traditional soups to Welsh rarebit and Hampshire fish pie, but do sample the local "trenchers." This thick bread was used in medieval times as a plate from which to eat meat; once soaked in the meat juices, the bread was passed down to the poor. Today the trenchers, soaked in toppings such as meat or fish, are grilled. ⊠ *Inner Close* ☎ *01962/857258* ⊟ *MC, V* ⊙ *No dinner.*

£–££ ✕ **The Royal Oak.** Try a half pint of draft bitter or dry cider at this lively traditional pub, which claims to have Britain's oldest bar (it has a Saxon wall). The two no-smoking bars—a British rarity—are in the cellar and on the upper level. Bar meals are served until 9 PM ('til 7 on Friday and Saturday). ✉ *Royal Oak Passage, off High St.* ☎ *01962/842701* ▭ *AE, MC, V.*

£££–££££ ✕▭ **Winchester Royal.** Formerly a bishop's house and then a Benedictine convent, this classy hotel dating to the 15th century lies within easy reach of the cathedral on a quiet side street. Bedrooms, decorated with floral fabrics and dark wood, surround a large inner garden; rooms in the main building have more period features. You can have an excellent lunch in the bar or a fuller, fixed-price meal in the conservatory restaurant. ✉ *St. Peter St. near High St., SO23 8BS* ☎ *01962/840840* ⊠ *01962/ 841582* ⊕ *www.marstonhotels.com* ➷ *75 rooms* △ *Restaurant, in-room data ports, cable TV, bar, business services, meeting rooms, some pets allowed; no a/c* ▭ *AE, DC, MC, V* ⦿ *BP.*

£££ ✕▭ **Hotel du Vin.** Rooms in this elegant redbrick Georgian town house are richly furnished in modern style, with Oriental rugs enhancing the polished wooden floors. Egyptian cotton bed linens, huge baths, and power showers make for a luxurious stay. The many eclectic wine selections in the stylish bistro complement traditional fare such as calves' liver with bacon and braised lamb with swede (rutabaga) mash. Call ahead to arrange a private wine-tasting session. In summer food is served in the walled garden. ✉ *14 Southgate St., SO23 9EF* ☎ *01962/ 841414* ⊠ *01962/842458* ⊕ *www.hotelduvin.com* ➷ *23 rooms* △ *Restaurant, in-room data ports, cable TV, bar, meeting rooms; no a/c* ▭ *AE, DC, MC, V.*

£££ ✕▭ **Wykeham Arms.** This old inn is centrally located, close to the cathedral and the college. Bedrooms at the inn itself are cozy and furnished in pine; those across the road in the St. George annex are more elegant, with period touches. The bars, happily cluttered with prints and pewter, make use of old school desks for tables. A good wine list sets off the French and English dishes at the restaurant, which is very popular with locals; call ahead. ✉ *75 Kingsgate St., SO23 9PE* ☎ *01962/853834* ⊠ *01962/854411* ➷ *14 rooms* △ *Restaurant, some cable TV, sauna, 2 bars, some pets allowed, no-smoking rooms; no a/c, no kids under 14* ▭ *AE, DC, MC, V* ⦿ *BP.*

££££–£££££ ▭ **Lainston House.** Dating from 1668, this elegant country-house hotel is set in a 63-acre park, its discreet seclusion an obvious attraction for such eminent guests as Margaret Thatcher, who stayed here to write her memoirs. Inside, cedar and oak paneling and other restored 17th-century details adorn the public rooms. Bedrooms, many of which are beamed, are done in warm colors and rich fabrics. Ground-floor suites have the added attraction of access to the gardens, and a converted stable holds luxury rooms. The hotel is 2½ mi northwest of Winchester. ✉ *Off B3049, Sparsholt, SO21 2LT* ☎ *01962/863588* ⊠ *01962/776672* ⊕ *www.exclusivehotels.co.uk* ➷ *41 rooms* △ *Restaurant, some in-room hot tubs, 2 tennis courts, gym, croquet, meeting rooms, helipad, some pets allowed; no a/c in some rooms* ▭ *AE, DC, MC, V* ⦿ *BP.*

£ ▭ **Church Cottage.** Five minutes from High Street, this ancient and tiny bed-and-breakfast adjacent to the graveyard of St. John's Church could be in a remote village, but for the odd glimpse of the cathedral from the top windows. Cramped but characterful accommodation is in one thick-beamed double bedroom (the preferred option) with a private but separate bathroom, and a room with twin beds and a minuscule single share some facilities. A spiral staircase serves all three rooms. ✉ *20 St. John's St., SO23 0HF* ☎ *01962/865058* ✎ *junerowlands@petuchio.freeserve.*

co.uk ⟿ *3 rooms, 1 with bath* ⟍ *No a/c, no room phones, no smoking* 🖃 *No credit cards* 🍽 *BP.*

Shopping

A complete list of local antiques stores is available from the **Winchester Tourist Information Centre** (⊠ The Guildhall, Broadway ☎ 01962/840500). **Antique and Craft Centre** (⊠ King's Walk, off Friarsgate ☎ 01962/864855) sells crafts and gift items and antiques. **P&G Wells** (⊠ 11 College St. ☎ 01962/852016), the oldest bookshop in town, stocks new titles and also carries a small selection of secondhand books and prints in an annex in nearby Kingsgate Street.

Britain's largest **farmers market** (☎ 01962/845135 ⊕ www.hampshirefarmersmarkets.co.uk), held in Middle Brook Street on the last Sunday of each month, specializes in local produce and goods. Look for Dexter beef, the products of water buffalo and Manx Loughton sheep, and walking sticks made from local wood. In September, the market is the focal point of Hampshire Hog Day, the hog being the symbol of Hampshire. Pig farmers from around the county sell all kinds of pig-related products.

New Alresford

❾ *8 mi northeast of Winchester, by A31 and B3046.*

New Alresford (pronounced *awls*-ford) has a pleasant village green crossed by a stream and some Georgian houses and antiques shops. The village is the starting point of the **Watercress Line,** a 10-mi railroad reserved for steam locomotives that runs to Alton. The line (named for the watercress beds formerly in the area) takes you on a nostalgic tour through reminders of 19th-century England. ⊠ *Railway Station* ☎ *01962/733810* ⊕ *www.watercressline.co.uk* 🎫 *£9* ⊗ *May–early Sept., daily departures; Feb.–Apr. and mid-Sept.–Oct., weekends and national holidays; call for details.*

Chawton

❿ *8 mi east of New Alresford.*

Jane Austen (1775–1817) lived the last eight years of her life in the village of Chawton; she moved to Winchester only during her final illness. The site now draws literary pilgrims. Here, in an unassuming redbrick house, Austen revised *Sense and Sensibility,* created *Pride and Prejudice,* and worked on *Emma, Persuasion,* and *Mansfield Park.* Now a museum,
★ the rooms of **Jane Austen's House** retain the atmosphere of restricted gentility suitable to the unmarried daughter of a clergyman. In the left-hand parlor, Jane would play her piano every morning, then repair to her mahogany writing desk in the family sitting room—leaving her sister Cassandra to do the household chores ("I find composition impossible with my head full of joints of mutton and doses of rhubarb," Jane wrote). In the early 19th century, the house was much closer to a bustling thoroughfare, and one traveler reported that a window view proved that the Misses Austen were "looking very comfortable at breakfast." Jane was famous for working through interruptions, but one protection against the outside world was the famous door that creaked, whose hinges she asked might remain unattended to because they gave her warning that someone was coming. ⊠ *Signed off the A31/A32 roundabout* ☎ *01420/83262* ⊕ *www.janeaustenmuseum.org.uk* 🎫 *£4* ⊗ *Mar.–Nov., daily 11–4:30; Dec.–Feb., weekends 11–4:30; last admission 30 mins before closing.*

IN SEARCH OF JANE AUSTEN

A TOUR OF "JANE AUSTEN COUNTRY" in the lovely South of England invariably leads to or enhances the experience of reading Austen's novels, and today, thanks to the 1990s film adaptations of Sense and Sensibility, Emma, Persuasion, and Pride and Prejudice, the great author has captured another audience eager to peer into the decorous 18th- and early-19th-century world of Austen's circle. By visiting one or two main locales—such as Chawton and Winchester—it is possible to imagine hearing the tinkle of teacups raised by the likes of Elinor Dashwood, Emma Woodhouse, and the bold and dashing Mr. Darcy. Serious Janeites will want to retrace the complete itinerary of her life—starting out in the hamlet of Steventon, southwest of Basingstoke, where she spent the first 25 years of her life, then moving on to Bath, Southampton, Chawton, and Winchester.

It is easy to see the self-contained world that is Jane Austen country—a pleasant landscape filled with intimately scaled villages, gently rolling downland, and tree-canopied paths—as a perfectly civilized stage on which her characters organized visits to stately homes and husband-hunting expeditions. As Austen herself described this terrain in Emma, "It has a sweet view—sweet to the eye and the mind. English verdure, English culture, English comfort, seen under a sun bright, without being oppressive." Entering that world, you'll find its heart is not Bath, nor London, nor Winchester, but the tiny Hampshire village of Chawton. Here at a former bailiff's cottage on her brother's estate that is now a museum, Austen produced three of her greatest novels, writing at the minute, pedestaled table still standing in the dining parlor. Her 6-mi-a-day walks often took her to Chawton Manor—her brother's regal Jacobean mansion, which opened in 2003 as Chawton House Library, a center for the study of 16th–18th-century women's literature (for consultation, call ☎ 01420/541010—or to nearby Lyards Farm, where her favorite niece, Anna Lefroy (thought to be the model for Emma Woodhouse, with "a disposition to think a little too well of herself") came to live in 1815. She would use a little donkey cart, still at the cottage, to shop in nearby Alton. A bit farther away is Great Bookham—closely identified with the "Highbury" of Emma, and nearby lies Box Hill (to the east of A24 between Leatherhead and Dorking), the probable inspiration for the locale of the famous walking expedition that left Miss Woodhouse in tears.

Driving southwest from Chawton, take A31 for about 15 mi to Winchester, where you can visit Austen's austere grave within the cathedral; then take in No. 8 College Street, where her losing battle with Addison's disease ended with her death on July 18, 1817. Heading 110 mi southwest, you can visit Lyme Regis, the lovely 18th-century seaside resort on the Devon border where Austen spent the summers of 1804–05. Here, at the Cobb, the stone jetty that juts into Lyme Bay, Louisa Musgrove suffers her terrible accident when she jumps off the steps known as Granny's Teeth—a turning point in Chapter 12 of Persuasion. Northwest of Winchester by some 60 mi is Bath, the elegant setting that served as the backdrop for some of Austen's razor-sharp observations on the social order of the day. The Jane Austen Centre explores the relationship between Bath and the writer.

"It is the only place for happiness," Austen once said of the county of Kent, some 150 mi to the east of Chawton. "Everybody is rich there." Godmersham Park, another of her brother's estates (off the A28 between Canterbury and Ashford), offered her an escape to the countryside, where baronets lived "in unrepentant idleness." The magnificent redbrick mansion is privately owned, but you can take a nearby public footpath to pass the little Grecian temple where she completed Sense and Sensibility; views of the Palladian house from this spot may have inspired her visions of Pemberley and Mansfield Park. Whether you search for Jane Austen country in Hampshire or Kent, you can revisit it again and again in its home base: English literature.

Petersfield

⑪ *10 mi south of Chawton, along B3006 and A325.*

The Georgian market town of Petersfield is set in a wide valley between wooded hills and open downs. **Queen Elizabeth Country Park,** part of an Area of Outstanding Beauty in the South Downs, 4 mi south of town, has 1,400 acres of chalk hills and shady beeches with scenic hiking trails. You can climb to the top of Butser Hill (888 ft) to take in a splendid view of the coast. ⊠ *A3* ☎ *023/9259–5040* ⊕ *www.hants.gov.uk/countryside/qecp* ⊠ *Free; car park £1, £1.50 Sun.* ⊘ *Park open 24 hrs; visitor center (including café and shop) Apr.–Oct., daily 10–5:30; Nov. and Dec., daily 10–dusk; Jan.–Mar., weekends 10–dusk.*

Portsmouth

⑫ *15 mi south of Petersfield, 77 mi southwest of London.*

This city has been England's naval capital and principal port of departure for centuries. Plenty of ferries still leave here for the Continent and the Isle of Wight. The harbor covers about 7 square mi, incorporating the world's first dry dock (built in 1495) and extensive defenses. Portsmouth is not particularly scenic, but the waterfront area possesses England's richest collection of maritime memorabilia, including the Royal Naval Museum and some well-preserved warships. The newly developed Gunwharf Quays demonstrates the city's ongoing vitality.

Portchester Castle, built as a Roman fort more than 1,600 years ago, contains the most complete set of Roman walls in northern Europe. In the 12th century a castle (now in ruins) was built inside the impressive fortifications. From the keep's central tower you can take in a sweeping view of the harbor and coastline. ⊠ *Off A27, near Fareham* ☎ *023/9237–8291* ⊕ *www.english-heritage.org.uk* ⊠ *£3.50* ⊘ *Apr.–Sept., daily 10–6; Oct., daily 10–5; Nov.–Mar., daily 10–4.*

★ The city's most impressive attraction, the **Portsmouth Historic Dockyard,** includes an unrivaled collection of historic ships and the comprehensive Royal Naval Museum. The youngest ship, **HMS *Warrior 1860,*** was England's first ironclad battleship. Admiral Lord Horatio Nelson's flagship, **HMS *Victory,*** has been painstakingly restored to appear as she did at the battle at Trafalgar (1805). You can inspect the cramped gun decks, visit the cabin where Nelson entertained his officers, and stand on the spot where a French sniper mortally wounded him. Visits aboard the *Victory* are by guided tour only and may entail a long wait. The *Mary Rose,* former flagship of the Tudor navy, which capsized and sank in the harbor in 1545, was raised in 1982. Described at the time as "the flower of all the ships that ever sailed," the *Mary Rose* is now housed in a special enclosure, where water continuously sprays her timbers to prevent them from drying out and breaking up. Exhibits in the intriguing *Mary Rose* Museum hold artifacts from the ship. The **Royal Naval Museum** has a fine collection of painted figureheads, exhibits about Nelson and the battle of Trafalgar, and galleries of paintings and mementos recalling different periods of naval history from King Alfred to the present. **Action Stations,** an interactive attraction, gives you insight into life in the modern Royal Navy through a swashbuckling movie and tests your sea legs with tasks such as piloting boats through gales. ⊠ *Historic Dockyard, Portsmouth Naval Base* ☎ *023/9286–1512* ⊕ *www.historicdockyard.co.uk* ⊠ *£13.75 includes harbor tour; valid for return visits* ⊘ *Apr.–Oct., daily 9:45–5:30; Nov.–Mar., daily 10–5; last admission 1 hr before closing.*

need a break?

After a slog around the Historic Dockyard, you'll find rest and replenishment, including seafood, at the harborside **Still & West Country House** (✉ Bath Sq. ☎ 023/9282–1567), a pub with outdoor seating. It faces the Spice Island Inn, another pub.

In the popular **D-Day Museum,** in nearby Southsea, exhibits reconstruct the planning and logistics involved in the D-Day landings, as well as the actual invasion on June 6, 1944. The museum's centerpiece is the Overlord Embroidery ("Overlord" was the code name for the invasion), a 272-foot tapestry with 34 panels illustrating the history of World War II, from the Battle of Britain in 1940 to D-Day and the first days of the liberation. ✉ *Clarence Esplanade, Southsea* ☎ *023/9282–7261* ⊕ *www.portsmouthmuseums.co.uk* ✆ *£5* ⊙ *Apr.–Oct., daily 10–5:30 Nov.–Mar., daily 10–5; last admission 30 mins before closing.*

The highlight of **Submarine World** is the tour of the World War II submarine HMS *Alliance* by an ex-submariner. You can see the cramped quarters and complex engine room. The museum fills you in on submarine history and lets you view Portsmouth harbor through a periscope. There are plenty of historic subs, weapons, and diving paraphernalia around the extensive site. From Portsmouth Harbour, take the ferry to Gosport and walk along Millennium Promenade past the huge sundial clock. ✉ *Haslar Jetty Rd.* ☎ *023/9252–9217* ⊕ *www.rnsubmus.co.uk* ✆ *£4* ⊙ *Apr.–Oct., daily 10–5:30; Nov.–Mar., daily 10–4:30.*

Where to Stay & Eat

££££–£££££ ✕ **Bistro Montparnasse.** Modern paintings on terra-cotta walls add a contemporary touch to this bustling restaurant. Dishes on the fixed-price menu may include sugar snap pea and sorrel soup, and roasted lamb with an apple and celeriac purée. ✉ *103 Palmerston Rd., Southsea* ☎ *023/9281–6754* ▭ *MC, V* ⊙ *Closed Sun. and Mon.*

££ ✕▦ **Sally Port.** This timber-frame old tavern opposite the cathedral in Old Portsmouth has numerous subtle nautical associations, such as the top spar around which the handsome Georgian staircase is built, a 40-foot mast said to have come from a frigate in 1798. Sloping floors and marine pictures are additional details. The street-level bar and first-floor restaurant provide good light meals or fuller fare, such as sea bass, Dover sole, steaks, and lamb fillets. Rooms are comfortable and fully equipped, with private washbasins and showers; toilets are shared. ✉ *57–58 High St., PO1 2LU* ☎ *023/9282–1860* 🖷 *023/9282–1293* ☞ *10 rooms without bath* ♿ *Restaurant, bar* ▭ *AE, DC, MC, V* ⅼ⊙ⅼ *BP.*

££–£££ ▦ **Westfield Hall.** Portsmouth is well supplied with chain offerings, but this pleasant smaller establishment has personal service and character. It occupies two converted early 20th-century houses close to the water in the resort of Southsea. Rooms (seven of which are on the ground floor) have satellite TV and large bay windows, and are restfully furnished in greens and creams; three sitting rooms provide a place to relax. ✉ *65 Festing Rd., off Eastern Parade, PO4 0NQ* ☎ *023/9282–6971* 🖷 *023/9287–0200* ⊕ *www.whhotel.info* ☞ *26 rooms* ♿ *Dining room, no-smoking rooms; no a/c* ▭ *AE, DC, MC, V* ⅼ⊙ⅼ *BP.*

Southampton

⓭ *21 mi northwest of Portsmouth, 25 mi southwest of Salisbury, 79 mi southwest of London.*

Seafaring Saxons and Romans used Southampton's harbor, Southampton Water, as a commercial trading port for centuries, and the city thrived, becoming one of England's wealthiest. But Plymouth eventually supplanted it, and Southampton has been going downhill ever since.

Still, it remains England's leading passenger port, and as the home port of Henry V's fleet bound for Agincourt, the *Mayflower,* the *Queen Mary,* and the ill-fated *Titanic,* along with countless other great ocean liners of the 20th century, Southampton has one of the richest maritime traditions in England. Much of the city center is shoddy, having been hastily rebuilt after World War II bombing, but bits of the city's history peek out from between modern buildings. The Old Town retains its medieval air, and considerable parts of Southampton's castellated walls remain. Other attractions include a good art gallery, extensive parks, and a couple of superb museums. The Southampton International Boat Show, a 10-day event in mid-September, draws huge crowds.

Incorporated in the town walls are a number of old buildings, including **God's House Tower,** originally a gunpowder factory and now the local archaeology museum. Displays focus on the Roman, Saxon, and medieval periods of Southampton's history, and an interactive computer allows access to the archaeological collections. ⊠ *Winkle St.* ☎ *023/ 8063–5904* ⊕ *www.southampton.gov.uk* ✄ *Free* ☉ *Tues.–Fri. 10–noon and 1–5, Sat. 10–noon and 1–4, Sun. 2–5.*

Mayflower Park and the Pilgrim Fathers' Memorial on Western Esplanade commemorate the sailing of the *Mayflower* from Southampton to the New World on August 15, 1620. (The ship was forced to stop in Plymouth for repairs.) John Alden, the hero of Longfellow's poem *The Courtship of Miles Standish,* was a native of Southampton.

The **Southampton Maritime Museum** brings together models, mementos, and items of furniture from the age of the great clippers and cruise ships, including a wealth of memorabilia relating to the *Titanic*—footage, photos, crew lists, etc. Boat buffs will relish plenty of other vital statistics dealing with the history of commercial shipping. ⊠ *Bugle St.* ☎ *023/ 8022–3941* ⊕ *www.southampton.gov.uk* ✄ *Free* ☉ *Tues.–Fri. 10–1 and 2–5, Sat. 10–1 and 2–4, Sun. 2–5.*

Where to Stay & Eat

££–£££ ✕ **Langley's.** At this busy bistro centrally located near Southampton's docks, dishes such as Mediterranean fish soup and baked chicken breast with tomato and mozzarella share the menu with more native fare. Modern art adorns the walls, and ceiling fans keep things cool in summer. ⊠ *10–11 Bedford Pl.* ☎ *023/8022–4551* ▤ *DC, MC, V* ☉ *Closed Sun.*

££–£££ ✕ **Oxford Brasserie.** This is a busy spot at lunchtime, popular with the business community, although it quiets down in the evening. Fresh fish is always available (the set-price menus are a particularly good value), along with French and international fare, and the decor is straightforward and not gimmicky. ⊠ *33–34 Oxford St.* ☎ *023/8063–5043* ▤ *AE, DC, MC, V* ☉ *Closed Sun. No lunch Sat.*

££ ▨ **Dolphin Hotel.** Originally a Georgian coaching inn—although there's been an inn of some sort on this site for seven centuries—the Dolphin has seen past visitors such as Queen Victoria, Lord Nelson, and Jane Austen. You'll find modern, dark wood furniture and patterned quilts in the bedrooms, and wood paneling in the lounge. The Thackeray Restaurant and Nelson Bar serve good meals and bar snacks, respectively. ⊠ *35 High St., SO14 2HN* ☎ *023/8033–9955* 🖷 *023/8033–3650* ⊕ *www.corushotels.com* ⇄ *73 rooms* ♨ *Restaurant, cable TV with movies, bar, business services, meeting rooms, some pets allowed; no a/c* ▤ *AE, DC, MC, V* ⋈ *BP.*

Nightlife & the Arts

The refurbished **Mayflower Theatre** (✉ Commercial Rd. ☎ 023/ 8071–1811) is among the larger theaters outside London, and all kinds of entertainment, from the Royal Shakespeare Company to Barnum on Ice, has packed the house. The **Nuffield Theatre** (☎ 023/8067–1771), on the Southampton University campus, has its own repertory company and also hosts national touring groups.

Romsey

⑭ *10 mi northwest of Southampton.*

This small town on the River Test has an authentic Norman abbey church and, in the marketplace, an iron bracket said to have been used to hang two of Cromwell's soldiers. The flint and stone house near the marketplace, known as King John's Hunting Box, dates from the 13th century. Florence Nightingale lies under a simple stone in East Wellow churchyard in Romsey, near her former house at Embley Park.

Broadlands, outside Romsey, was the home of the late Lord Mountbatten (1900–79), uncle of Queen Elizabeth II, and is undoubtedly the grandest house in Hampshire. Ornate plaster moldings and paintings of British and Continental royalty decorate the 18th-century Palladian mansion. Noted landscape designer Capability Brown laid out the gardens, and the wide lawns sweep down to the banks of the River Test. Personal mementos trace Lord Mountbatten's distinguished career in the navy and in India. In 1947 the Queen and the Duke of Edinburgh spent their honeymoon here, and Prince Charles and the late Princess Diana spent a few days here after their wedding in 1981. ✉ *A3090 Romsey bypass* ☎ *01794/505010* ⊕ *www.broadlands.net* 🎫 *£6.50* ⊙ *Early June–early Sept., daily noon–5:30; last admission 4.*

Where to Stay

£££ 🏨 **Potters Heron Hotel.** An ideal place to stay if you're visiting Broadlands, this modern hotel sits behind the original thatched building. Some bedrooms have floral themes and are paneled in pine, whereas others are plainer; many have balconies. Dining is in the oak-beam Potters Pub or the Garden Restaurant. ✉ *Ampfield, SO51 9ZF, 3 mi east of Romsey* ☎ *023/8026–6611* 🖷 *023/8025–1359* ⊕ *www.corushotels.com* 🛏 *54 rooms* ↻ *Restaurant, cable TV with movies, sauna, pub, business services, meeting rooms, some pets allowed; no a/c in some rooms* ▭ *AE, DC, MC, V.*

Sports

Hilly parkland cradles the par-68, 5,767-yard golf course of the **Dunwood Manor Country Club** (✉ Danes Rd., Awbridge, near Romsey ☎ 01794/340549).

ISLE OF WIGHT

The Isle of Wight (pronounced white) has a very special atmosphere, quite distinct from that of the mainland: it is essentially Victorian. Although the island was known to the Romans and the ill-fated Stuarts, Queen Victoria put it on the map by choosing it for the site of Osborne House. She lived here as much as she could, and ultimately she died here. Clearly she created a great vogue, because most of the domestic architecture is Victorian. The islanders are fiercely chauvinistic; like Tennyson, once an inhabitant of the island until tourist harassment drove him away, they resent vacationers somewhat. But every season the day-trippers arrive—thanks to the ferries, hovercraft, and hydrofoils that connect the

Isle of Wight with Southampton, Portsmouth, Southsea, and Lymington. People come to this 23-mi-long island for its holiday resorts—Ryde, Bembridge, Ventnor, Freshwater (stay away from tacky Sandown and Shanklin)—its rich vegetation, narrow lanes, thatched cottages, curving bays, sandy beaches, and walking paths. The fabulous ocean air, to quote Tennyson, is "worth six pence a pint." All is not sea and sails, however. There is splendid driving to be done in the interior of the island, in such places as Brading Down, Ashley Down, and Mersely Down, and the occasional country house to visit, none more spectacular than Queen Vicky's own Osborne House.

Cowes

🔟 *11 mi northwest of Ryde.*

If you embark from Southampton, your ferry will cross the Solent channel and dock at Cowes (pronounced cows), a magic name in the sailing world and internationally known for the Cowes Week annual yachting festival, held in July or August. Fifty years ago, the Cowes Regatta was a supreme event, attended by imperial majesties and serene highnesses from all over the world; the world's most famous figures crowded the green lawns of the Royal Yacht Squadron. Although elegance is a thing of the past, the Cowes Regatta remains an important yachting event and is occasionally attended by that royal seaman, the Duke of Edinburgh. At the north end of High Street, on the Parade, a tablet commemorates the 1633 sailing from Cowes of two ships carrying the first English settlers of the state of Maryland.

Queen Victoria's **Osborne House,** designed by Prince Albert after a villa in the stodgiest Italian Renaissance style, holds enormous interest for anyone drawn to the domestic side of history. The queen spent much of her time here in seclusion after Albert's death in 1861, mourning her loss. In this massive pile, one sees the engineer manqué in Prince Albert and his clever innovations—even central heating—as well as evidence of Victoria's desperate attempts to give her children a normal but disciplined upbringing. A carriage ride will take you to the Swiss Cottage, a superior version of a playhouse, especially built for the children. The antiques-filled state rooms have scarcely been altered since Victoria's death here in 1901. The house and grounds were used as a location for the 1998 movie *Mrs. Brown.* ⊠ *Off A3021, 1 mi southeast of Cowes* ☎ *01983/200022* ⊕ *www.english-heritage.org.uk* 🎫 *£8, grounds only £4.50* ☉ *Apr.–Oct., daily 10–5 (last admission to house at 4); phone for prebooked guided tours in winter.*

Where to Stay

£££ 🏨 **New Holmwood Hotel.** This Best Western hotel occupies an unrivaled location above the Esplanade—ideal for watching yachters in the Solent. The three sitting rooms include one with an open fire on winter evenings and one for nonsmokers, and the sun terrace and pool take full advantage of fine weather. Patterned fabrics contrast with plain walls in the guest rooms. ⊠ *Queens Rd., Egypt Point, PO31 8BW* ☎ *01983/292508* 🖷 *01983/295020* ⊕ *www.newholmwoodhotel.co.uk* 📠 *26 rooms* ⚏ *Restaurant, in-room data ports, cable TV, pool, bar, meeting rooms, some pets allowed; no a/c* 🖃 *AE, DC, MC, V* ⭗ *BP.*

Ryde

🔟 *11 mi southeast of Cowes.*

The town of Ryde has long been one of the Isle of Wight's most popular summer resorts, with several family attractions. After the construction of Ryde Pier in 1814, elegant (and occasionally ostentatious) town houses sprang up along the seafront and on the slopes behind, commanding fine views of the harbor. In addition to its long, sandy beach, Ryde has a large boating lake (rowboats and pedal boats can be rented) and children's playgrounds. To get here from Cowes, leave on A3021, then follow the signs on A3054.

Where to Stay & Eat

£££–££££   ✕🏨 **Seaview Hotel.** A strong maritime flavor defines this smart hotel, a converted house dating to around 1800, in the heart of a harbor village just outside Ryde. Guest rooms are furnished with antiques, original watercolors, and bold fabrics. The main attractions, however, are the restaurants, which specialize in seafood and fresh island produce. Try the hot crab ramekin, baked with cream and tarragon with a cheese topping, to start, and don't pass up desserts; floating islands (poached meringues) are a must. For a fee, guests can use the well-equipped Isle of Wight Sports Club nearby. ⊠ *High St., Seaview, PO34 5EX* ☎ *01983/612711* 🖷 *01983/613729* ⊕ *www.seaviewhotel.co.uk* ⇆ *16 rooms, 1 cottage* ♨ *2 restaurants, 2 bars, some pets allowed, no-smoking rooms; no a/c* ⊟ *AE, DC, MC, V* ⦿ *BP.*

££££–£££££   🏨 **Priory Bay Hotel.** This hotel, part of which dates back to medieval times, has been sympathetically developed in country house style. Lawns and woodlands on the 70-acre estate, as well as a beach, help make for a pampered, private sojourn. Antiques furnish the public rooms, and guest rooms are light and airy. On the grounds are nine chalets, four of them with kitchens; pets are allowed in these. ⊠ *Priory Dr., Seaview, PO34 5BU* ☎ *01983/613146* 🖷 *01983/616539* ⊕ *www.priorybay.co.uk* ⇆ *16 rooms, 9 chalets* ♨ *Restaurant, 9-hole golf course, tennis court, pool, beach, bar, business services, meeting rooms; no a/c* ⊟ *AE, DC, MC, V* ⦿ *BP.*

Brading

17 *3 mi south of Ryde on A3055.*

In Brading, St. Mary's Church, dating from Norman times, holds monuments to the local Oglander family. Next to the Old Town Hall stands the 16th-century rectory, said to be the oldest inhabited dwelling on the island; it now holds a wax museum.

The remains of the substantial 3rd-century **Brading Roman Villa,** a mile south of Brading, include splendid mosaic floors and a well-preserved heating system. The villa may be closed in 2004 for rebuilding work; call ahead. ⊠ *Off A3055* ☎ *01983/406223* 💷 *£2.95* 🕙 *Apr.–Oct., daily 9:30–5; last admission 4:30.*

Ventnor

18 *11 mi south of Ryde.*

The south coast resorts are the sunniest and most sheltered on the Isle of Wight. Handsome Ventnor itself rises from such a steep slope that the ground floors of some of its houses are level with the roofs of those across the road. The lovely **Ventnor Botanic Gardens,** laid out over 22 acres, contain more than 3,500 species of trees, plants, and shrubs. A pavilioned visitor center puts the subtropical and display gardens into context. ⊠ *Undercliff Dr.* ☎ *01983/855397* ⊕ *www.botanic.co.uk* 💷 *Free* 🕙 *Jan.–Mar., weekends 10–4; Apr.–Oct., daily 10–6; Nov. and Dec., Tues.–Thurs. 10–3, weekends 10–4.*

Sports

James Braid, who designed the Gleneagles golf course in Scotland, helped create the challenging par-70, 5,804-yard, heathland **Shanklin and Sandown** (⌧ The Fairway, Sandown ☎ 01983/403170) course.

en route   The coast road from Ventnor to the Needles passes the fantasy theme park **Blackgang Chine,** built in a deep chine (cleft in the cliffs) overlooking a former smugglers' landing place. There's a film about the history of the area, as well as Dinosaurland, Smugglersland, Cowboytown, Water Force (a large water slide), and other attractions for ages 3–12. ⌧ A3055, Ventnor ☎ 01983/730330 ⊕ *www. blackgangchine.com* ⌧ *£7.50* ⊙ *Apr.–mid-July and early Sept.–late Oct., daily 10–5:30; mid-July–early Sept., daily 10–10; late Oct.–early Nov., daily 10–5.*

Alum Bay & the Needles

⑲ *19 mi northwest of Ventnor, 18 mi southwest of Cowes.*

At the western tip of the Isle of Wight is the island's most famous natural landmark, the **Needles,** a long line of jagged chalk stacks jutting out of the sea like monstrous teeth, with a lighthouse at the end. It's part of the Needles Pleasure Park, which has various attractions, mostly for kids. Adjacent is **Alum Bay,** accessed from the Needles by chairlift. Here you can catch a good view of the multicolor sand in the cliff strata or take a boat to view the lighthouse.

Dimbola Lodge is the former home of Julia Margaret Cameron (1815–79), the eminent Victorian portrait photographer and friend of Lord Tennyson. The gallery in the building includes more than 60 examples of her work, as well as a bookshop and café. ⌧ *Terrace La., Freshwater Bay* ☎ *01983/756814* ⊕ *www.dimbola.co.uk* ⌧ *Gallery £3.50* ⊙ *Tues.–Sun. and national holidays 10–5.*

Where to Stay

£££   🏨 **Farringford Hotel.** For more than 40 years this splendid 18th-century house was the home of the Victorian poet laureate Alfred, Lord Tennyson. Now a gracious hotel on 33 acres of parkland, it also includes self-catering accommodations. Victorian mahogany and rich damask fabrics reign supreme in the bedrooms in the main house. ⌧ *Bedbury La., Freshwater Bay, near Alum Bay, PO40 9PE* ☎ *01983/752500* 🖷 *01983/ 756515* ⊕ *www.farringford.co.uk* ⇋ *15 rooms, 23 suites, 5 apartments, 4 cottage rooms* ♨ *2 restaurants, 9-hole golf course, tennis court, pool, croquet, lawn bowling, some pets allowed (fee); no a/c* ▭ *AE, DC, MC, V* ⍾⍥⍾ *BP.*

Sports

Overlooking the bay, the par-68/69, 5,725-yard **Freshwater Bay Golf Club** (⌧ Southdown Rd., Freshwater Bay ☎ 01983/752955) is on land owned by the National Trust.

Carisbrooke Castle

★ **⑳** *14 mi east of Alum Bay, 1¼ mi southwest of Newport, 5 mi south of Cowes.*

Standing above the village of Carisbrooke, this castle built by the Normans and enlarged in Elizabethan times had its moment of historical glory when King Charles I was imprisoned here during the English Civil War. Note the small window in the north curtain wall through which he tried unsuccessfully to escape. A museum holds items from his incarceration.

You can stroll along the battlements to watch the donkey wheel, where a team of donkeys draws water from a deep well. The castle is a short distance outside the Isle of Wight's modern-day capital, Newport. ⊠ *Off B3401* ☎ *01983/522107* ⊕ *www.english-heritage.org.uk* ⌑ *£5* ⊙ *Apr.–Sept., daily 10–6; Oct., daily 10–5; Nov.–Mar., daily 10–4.*

SALISBURY TO THE NEW FOREST
STOURHEAD, AVEBURY & STONEHENGE

This roster of famous sights kicks off in the attractive city of Salisbury, renowned for its glorious cathedral, then loops west around Salisbury Plain, up to Avebury, and back to Stonehenge. A trio of stately homes reveals the ambitions and wealth of their builders—Wilton House with its Inigo Jones–designed state rooms, Stourhead and its exquisite gardens, and the Italian Renaissance pile of Longleat. From Stonehenge you can dip south into Hampshire, to the wild, scenic expanse of the New Forest, ancient hunting preserve of William the Conqueror. Your own transportation is essential to see anything beyond Salisbury.

Salisbury

25 mi northwest of Southampton, 55 mi southeast of Bristol, 90 mi southwest of London.

The unique silhouette of Salisbury Cathedral's majestic spire signals your approach to this historic city long before you arrive. Although the cathedral is the principal interest in the town, and the Cathedral Close itself one of the country's most atmospheric spots (best experienced on a foggy night), Salisbury has much more to see, not least its largely unspoiled—and relatively traffic-free—old center. Here you'll find stone shops and houses from many periods that grew up in the shadow of the great church. You're never far from any of the three rivers that meet here, or from the bucolic water meadows that stretch out to the west of the cathedral and provide the best views of it.

Salisbury did not become important until the early 13th century, when the seat of the diocese was transferred here from Old Sarum, the original settlement 2 mi to the north, of which only ruins remain today. In the 19th century, novelist Anthony Trollope based his tales of ecclesiastical life, notably *Barchester Towers,* on life here, although his fictional city of Barchester is really an amalgam of Salisbury and Winchester. The local tourist office organizes walks—of differing lengths for varying stamina—to lead you to the treasures.

㉑
FodorśChoice
★

Salisbury continues to be dominated by the towering **Salisbury Cathedral,** a soaring hymn in stone. It is unique among cathedrals in that it was conceived and built as a whole, in the amazingly short span of only 38 years (1220–58). The spire, added in 1320, is the tallest in England and a miraculous feat of medieval engineering—even though the point, 404 ft above the ground, is 2½ ft off vertical. For a fictional, keenly imaginative reconstruction of the drama underlying such an achievement, read William Golding's novel *The Spire.* The excellent model of the cathedral in the north transept, the "arm" of the church to your left as you look toward the altar, shows the building about 20 years into construction, and makes very clear the ambition of Salisbury's medieval builders. For all their sophistication, the height and immense weight of the great spire have always posed structural problems. In the late 17th

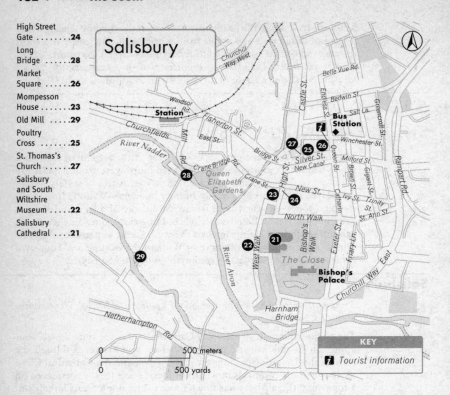

Salisbury

KEY

Tourist information

century Sir Christopher Wren was summoned from London to strengthen
the spire, and in the mid-19th century Sir George Gilbert Scott, a leading Victorian Gothicist, undertook a major program of restoration on
it. At the same time, he began a clearing out of the interior and removed
some less-than-sympathetic 18th-century alterations. For all that, the
interior still seems spartan and a little gloomy, but check out the remarkable lancet windows and sculpted tombs of crusaders and other
medieval heroes. The clock in the north aisle—probably the oldest
working mechanism in Europe, if not the world—was made in 1386.
You can join a free 45-minute tour of the church leaving two or more
times a day, and there are also tours to the roof and spire at least once
a day. The spacious **cloisters** are the largest in England, and the octagonal **Chapter House** contains a marvelous 13th-century frieze showing
scenes from the Old Testament. In the chapter house you can also see
one of the four original copies of the **Magna Carta,** the charter of rights
the English barons forced King John to accept in 1215; it was sent here
for safekeeping in the 13th century. ✉ *Cathedral Close* ☏ *01722/
555120* ⊕ *www.salisburycathedral.org.uk* ✉ *Cathedral £3.80 requested
donation, roof tour £4, Chapter House free* ☉ *Cathedral June–Aug.,
daily 7:15 AM–7:15 PM; Sept.–May, daily 7–6:15. Chapter House
June–Aug., Mon.–Sat. 9:30–6:45, Sun. noon–5:30; Sept.–May, Mon.–Sat.
10–5:30, Sun. noon–5:30.*

Salisbury's **Cathedral Close** forms probably the finest backdrop of any
British cathedral, with its smooth lawns and splendid examples of architecture of all ages (except modern) creating a harmonious background. Some of the historic houses are open to the public.

㉒ Models and exhibits at the Stonehenge Gallery of the **Salisbury and South Wiltshire Museum** arm you with helpful background information for a visit to the famous stones. Also on view are collections of costumes, lace, embroidery, and Wedgwood, all dwarfed by the medieval pageant figure of St. Christopher, a 14-foot red-cloaked giant and his companion hobbyhorse, Hob Nob. ⊠ *The King's House, 65 The Close* ☎ *01722/ 332151* ⊕ *www.salisburymuseum.org.uk* ✍ *£3.50* ☼ *July and Aug., Mon.–Sat. 10–5, Sun. 2–5; Sept.–June, Mon.–Sat. 10–5.*

㉓ Elegant **Mompesson House,** on the north side of Cathedral Close, dates from 1701 and can justifiably be called one of Britain's most appealing Queen Anne houses. There are no treasures per se, but there is some fine original paneling and plasterwork, as well as a fascinating collection of 18th-century drinking glasses. Tea and refreshments are served in an attractive walled garden. ⊠ *The Close* ☎ *01722/335659* ⊕ *www.nationaltrust. org.uk* ✍ *£3.90* ☼ *Apr.–Sept., Sat.–Wed. 11–5; last admission 4:30.*

㉔ On the north side of the Cathedral Close is **High Street Gate,** one of the four castellated stone gateways built to separate the close from the rest of the city. Passing through it, you enter into the heart of the modern **㉕** town. One of Salisbury's best-known landmarks, the hexagonal **Poultry Cross** (⊠ Silver St.) is the last remaining of the four original market crosses, and dealers still set up their stalls beside it. One of southern England's **㉖** most popular markets fills **Market Square** on Tuesday and Saturday. Permission to hold an annual fair here was granted in 1221, and that right is still exercised for four days every October, when the Charter Fair takes place. A narrow side street links Poultry Cross to Market Square.

㉗ **St. Thomas's Church** contains a rare medieval doom painting of Judgment Day, the best-preserved and most complete of the few such works left in Britain. Created around 1470 and covering the chancel arch, the scenes of heaven and hell served to instill the fear of damnation into the congregation. It's best seen on a spring or summer evening when the light through the west window illuminates the details. ⊠ *Silver St.* ☎ *01722/ 322537* ✍ *Free* ☼ *Apr.–Oct., Mon.–Sat. 9:30–6, Sun. noon–6; Nov.–Mar., Mon.–Sat. 9:30–3:30, Sun. noon–6.*

㉘ For a classic view of Salisbury, head to the **Long Bridge** and the town path. From High Street walk west to Mill Road, which leads you across Queen Elizabeth Gardens. Cross the bridge and continue on the town path; along here you can find the very spot where John Constable set down his easel to create that 19th-century icon *Salisbury Cathedral,* now hung in the Constable Room of London's National Gallery. Reached via a 20-minute walk southwest of the town center along the town path, **㉙** the **Old Mill** (⊠ Town Path, West Harnham), dating from the 12th century, makes a pleasant destination. It is now a restaurant and coffee shop under the same management as the Old Mill Hotel next door.

Massive earthwork ramparts in a bare sweep of Wiltshire countryside are all that remain of the impressive Iron Age hill fort of **Old Sarum,** which was successively taken over by Romans, Saxons, and Normans (who built a castle and cathedral within the earthworks). The site was still fortified in Tudor times, though the population had mostly decamped in the 13th century for the more amenable site of New Sarum, or Salisbury. You can clamber over the huge banks and ditches and take in the bracing views over the chalk downland. ⊠ *Off A345, 2 mi north of Salisbury* ☎ *01722/335398* ⊕ *www.english-heritage.org.uk* ✍ *£2.50* ☼ *Apr.–June and Sept., daily 10–6; July and Aug., daily 9–6; Oct., daily 10–5; Nov.–Mar., daily 10–4.*

Where to Stay & Eat

££–£££ ✕Harper's. The cuisine at this popular second-floor restaurant overlooking Market Square mingles English and French dishes. Specialties include fillet of salmon and New Forest venison, and there are good-value early bird lunches and dinners. ⊠ 7 Ox Row ☎ 01722/333118 ☰ AE, DC, MC, V ☉ Closed Sun. Oct.–May; no lunch Sun. June–Sept.

££–£££ ✕ LXIX. A stone's throw from the cathedral, this small no-smoking restaurant has a cool, modern, elegant style that doesn't stop it from being convivial and relaxed. Dishes such as smoked river eel and calves' liver with sage butter are presented with care and with an eye to design. The sister bistro next door, Après LXIX, serves similar fare at more modest prices. ⊠ 69 New St. ☎ 01722/340000 ☰ AE, DC, MC, V ☉ Closed Sun. and last wk in Dec., first wk in Jan. No lunch Sat.

£–£££ ✕Haunch of Venison. This place opposite the Poultry Cross has been going strong for more than six centuries, and the wood-paneled restaurant brims with period details, such as the mummified hand of an 18th-century card player still clutching his cards that was found by workmen in 1903. You can choose between simple bar food or more substantial meals such as venison sausages and steaks, and fortify yourself with any of the 50 malt whiskeys. ⊠ 1 Minster St. ☎ 01722/322024 ☰ AE, MC, V ☉ No dinner Sun. in winter, usually Oct.–Easter.

£–££ ✕ Le Hérisson. It's just a few steps from Cathedral Close and the High Street Gate to this café-bistro that doubles as a delicatessen. There's a good selection of snacks and meals, from brownies and coffees, teas, and fruit drinks to hot dishes such as pasta with pesto and roasted hock (lower leg of pork). Alternatively, choose from the impressive hams, pâtés, and cheeses on sale at the counter. You can sit in the small, busy conservatory or in the garden. ⊠ 90–92 Crane St. ☎ 01722/333471 ☰ MC, V ☉ Closed Sun. No dinner.

★ ££££ ✕▥ Howard's House. If you're after complete tranquillity, head for this early 17th-century house 10 mi west of Salisbury, set on 2 acres of grounds in the Nadder valley. French windows lead from the tidy lawns into the restaurant, which serves sophisticated contemporary fare such as pan-seared scallops with lemongrass couscous. The inviting sitting room mixes pastels and bright fabrics, and the soothing bedrooms use subtle colors. ⊠ Off B3089, Teffont Evias, SP3 5RJ ☎ 01722/716392 ☐ 01722/716820 ⊕ www.howardshousehotel.com ⬩9 rooms 㐂 Restaurant, meeting rooms, some pets allowed (fee); no a/c ☰ AE, DC, MC, V ⑩ BP.

£££ ✕▥ Red Lion Hotel. A former coaching inn—parts of the building date from 1220—this centrally located hotel in the Best Western consortium makes a good base for exploring the city on foot. It's packed with old clocks and other relics from its long past. Rooms are in either modern or antique style, with an abundance of drapery and rich red, gold, and blue colors. Room 22 has a restored fireplace dating from the inn's original construction. The Vine restaurant (reservations essential) serves mainly modern British dishes such as roast pork with a mustard sauce. ⊠ Milford St., SP1 2AN ☎ 01722/323334 ☐ 01722/325756 ⊕ www.the-redlion.co.uk ⬩ 51 rooms 㐂 Restaurant, cable TV, business services, meeting rooms; no a/c ☰ AE, DC, MC, V.

££££ ▥ White Hart. Behind the pillared portico and imposing facade of this 17th-century hotel in the heart of Salisbury lie cozily old-fashioned yet spacious public rooms. The muted cream and brown color scheme complements the unhurried pace, and the freshly refurbished bedrooms are grouped around the inner courtyard. ⊠ 1 St. John St., SP1 2SD ☎ 0870/400–8125 ☐ 01722/241–2761 ⊕ www.whitehart-salisbury.co.uk ⬩ 68 rooms 㐂 Restaurant, cable TV, bar, business services, meeting rooms, some pets allowed; no a/c ☰ AE, DC, MC, V ⑩ BP.

££ ⬚ **Cricket Field House Hotel.** As the name suggests, this modernized gamekeeper's cottage overlooks a cricket ground, allowing you to puzzle over the intricacies of the game at leisure. Some rooms are in the main house and others in the pavilion annex, but all are individually furnished in soft shades. The hotel is on the main A36 road, a mile or so west of Salisbury's center. ✉ *Wilton Rd., SP2 9NS* ☎☎ *01722/322595* ⊕ *www. cricketfieldhousehotel.co.uk* ⥂ *14 rooms* ⌂ *Dining room; no a/c, no kids under 14* ⊟ *AE, MC, V* ❙⦿❙ *BP.*

£ ⬚ **Wyndham Park Lodge.** This solid Victorian house in a quiet part of town (off Castle Street) provides an excellent B&B and a garden. Furnishings are in keeping with the period, with antiques and elegant patterned wallpapers and drapes, and one room has its own patio. ✉ *51 Wyndham Rd., SP1 3AB* ☎ *01722/416517* 🖷 *01722/328851* ⊕ *www. wyndhamparklodge.co.uk* ⥂ *4 rooms* ⌂ *No a/c, no room phones, no smoking* ⊟ *MC, V* ❙⦿❙ *BP.*

Nightlife & the Arts

The **Salisbury Festival** (✉ 75 New St. ☎ 01722/332241 ⊕ www. salisburyfestival.co.uk), held in May and June, has outstanding classical concerts, recitals, plays, and outdoor events. The **Salisbury Playhouse** (✉ Malthouse La. ☎ 01722/320333) presents high-caliber drama all year and is the main venue for the Salisbury Festival.

Sports

Hayball's Cycle Shop (✉ 26–30 Winchester St. ☎ 01722/411378) rents bikes for about £10 per day or £55 per week, £25 cash deposit.

Shopping

Trevan's Old Books (✉ 30 Catherine St. ☎ 01722/325818) stocks all kinds of tax-free secondhand books, including some rare first editions. **Watsons** (✉ 8–9 Queen St. ☎ 01722/320311) specializes in Aynsley and Wedgwood bone china, Waterford and Dartington glass, Royal Doulton, and fine ornaments. The buildings, dating from 1306 and 1425, have their original windows and an oak mantelpiece.

Wilton

③⓪ *4 mi west of Salisbury.*

Five rivers—the Avon, the Bourne, the Nadder, the Wylye, and the Ebble—wind slowly from Salisbury into the rich heart of Wiltshire. Following the valley of the Nadder will lead you to the ancient town of Wilton, from which the county takes its name. A traditional market is held here every Thursday, and the Wilton Carpet Factory Shop draws people (Wilton is renowned for its carpets), but the main attraction is Wilton House.

★ The home of the 17th earl of Pembroke, **Wilton House** would be noteworthy if it contained no more than the magnificent state rooms designed by Inigo Jones, Ben Jonson's stage designer and the architect of London's Banqueting House. John Webb rebuilt the house in neoclassical style after fire damaged the original Tudor mansion in a fire in 1647. In fine weather, the lordly expanse of sweeping lawns that surrounds the house, bisected by the River Avon and dotted with towering oaks and a gracious Palladian bridge, is a quintessential English scene. Wilton House contains one of the most extravagantly beautiful rooms in the history of interior decoration, the aptly named Double Cube Room. The name refers to its simple proportions, evidence of Jones's classically inspired belief that beauty in architecture derives from the harmony and balance. The room's headliner is the spectacular Van Dyck portrait of the Pembroke family. Adorned with gilded William Kent furniture, the

Double Cube was where Eisenhower prepared some of his plans for the Normandy invasion; it has been used in many period films, including *The Madness of King George,* and Emma Thompson's adaptation of *Sense and Sensibility.* Other delights include superb old master paintings, an exhibition of 7,000 toy soldiers, and the Wareham Bears (200 dressed teddy bears). Be sure to explore the extensive gardens; children will appreciate the large playground. ⊠ *Off A30* ☎ *01722/746729* ⊕ *www.wiltonhouse.co.uk* ⊠ *£9.25, grounds only £4* ☉ *Apr.–Oct., daily 10:30–5:30; last admission 4:30.*

Shaftesbury

③ *18 mi west of Wilton, 22 mi west of Salisbury.*

The pretty village of Shaftesbury—the model for the town of Shaston in Thomas Hardy's *Jude the Obscure*—lies just inside the Dorset county border. From the top of **Gold Hill,** a steep, relentlessly picturesque street lined with cottages, you can catch a sweeping view of the surrounding countryside. Although Gold Hill itself is something of a tourist cliché (it has even appeared in TV commercials), it's still well worth visiting.

Sherborne

㉜ *15 mi west of Shaftesbury.*

Once granted cathedral status, until deferring to Old Sarum in 1075, this unspoiled market town is awash with medieval buildings honed from the honey-color local stone. The focal point of the winding streets is the abbey church. Also worth visiting here are the ruins of the 12th-century Old Castle and the grounds and Sherborne Castle.

The glory of **Sherborne Abbey,** a warm, "old gold" stone church, is the delicate and graceful 15th-century fan vaulting that extends the length of the soaring nave and choir. If you're lucky, you might hear "Great Tom," one of the heaviest bells in the world, pealing out from the bell tower. Guided tours are offered in summer on Tuesday morning and Friday afternoon, or by prior arrangement. ⊠ *Abbey Close* ☎ *01935/812452* ⊠ *Free, guided tour £1.50* ☉ *Apr.–Sept., daily 9–6; Oct.–Mar., daily 9–4.*

Sherborne Castle, built by Sir Walter Raleigh in 1594, remained his home for 10 years before it passed to the custodianship of the Digby family. The interior has been remodeled in 19th-century Gothic style, and ceilings have splendid plaster moldings. After admiring the extensive collections of Meissen and Asian porcelain, stroll around the lake and landscaped grounds, the work of Capability Brown. The house is a half mile southeast of town. ⊠ *Off A352* ☎ *01935/813182* ⊕ *www.sherbornecastle.com* ⊠ *£6, gardens only £3.25* ☉ *Apr.–Oct., Tues.–Thurs., Sun., and national holidays 11–4:30, Sat. 2:30–4:30.*

Stourhead

㉝ *15 mi northeast of Sherborne, 30 mi west of Salisbury.*

Fodor'sChoice
★

Close to the village of Stourton lies one of Wiltshire's most breathtaking sights—Stourhead, a country-house-and-garden combination that has few parallels for beauty anywhere in Europe. Most of Stourhead was built between 1721 and 1725 by Henry the Magnificent, the wealthy banker Henry Hoare. Many rooms in the Palladian mansion contain Chinese and French porcelain, and some have furniture by Chippendale. The elegant library and floridly colored picture gallery were both built for the cultural development of this exceedingly civilized family. Still, the house must take second place to the adjacent gardens designed by

Hoare's son, Henry Hoare II, which are the most celebrated example of the English 18th-century taste for "natural" landscaping. Temples, grottoes, and bridges have been skillfully placed among colorful shrubs, trees, and flowers to make the grounds look like a three-dimensional oil painting. A walk around the lake (1½ mi) reveals changing vistas that conjure up the 17th-century landscapes of Claude and Poussin. The best time to visit is early summer, when the massive banks of rhododendrons are in full bloom, but it's beautiful at any time of year. You can get a fine view of the estate from Alfred's Tower, a 1772 folly. In summer there are occasional concerts, sometimes accompanied by fireworks and gondoliers on the lake. A restaurant and plant shop are on the grounds. From London by train, get off at Gillingham and take a five-minute cab ride to Stourton. ⊠ *Off B3092, Stourton, northwest of Mere* ☎ *01747/841152* ⊕ *www.nationaltrust.org.uk* 🎫 *£8.90, house only £5.10, gardens only £5.10 (Mar.–Oct.) or £3.95 (Nov.–Feb.)* ☉ *House Apr.–Oct., Fri.–Tues. 11–5 or dusk; last admission 30 mins before closing, or 4 in Oct.; gardens daily 9–7 or dusk.*

Where to Stay & Eat

£££ ╳▥ **Spread Eagle Inn.** You can't live at Stourhead, but this very popular hostelry, built at the beginning of the 19th century at the entrance to the landscaped park, is the next best thing. Guest rooms are elegant and understated, with period features. The restaurant serves traditional English fare from wood pigeon to prime fillet steak, and there are seafood and vegetarian choices. ⊠ *Stourton, northwest of Mere, BA12 6QE* ☎ *01747/840587* 🖶 *01747/840954* ⊕ *www.latonahotels.co.uk* 🛏 *5 rooms* ⚭ *Restaurant, bar; no a/c* ▭ *AE, MC, V* ⧖ *BP.*

Longleat House

★ ☯ ❸ *6 mi north of Stourhead, 19 mi south of Bath, 27 mi northwest of Salisbury.*

Home of the marquess of Bath, Longleat House is one of southern England's most famous private estates. The blocklike Italian Renaissance building was completed in 1580 (for just over £8,000, an astronomical sum at the time) and contains outstanding tapestries, paintings, porcelain, and furniture, as well as notable period features such as the Victorian kitchens, the Elizabethan minstrels' gallery, and the great hall with its massive wooden beams. Giant antlers of the extinct Irish elk decorate the walls. In 1966 the grounds of Longleat became Britain's first safari park, with giraffes, zebras, rhinos, and lions all on view. Longleat also has dollhouses, a butterfly garden, a private railroad, the world's longest hedge maze, and an adventure castle, all of which make it extremely popular, particularly in summer and during school vacations. You can easily spend a whole day here, in which case it's best to visit the house in the morning, when tours are more relaxed, and the safari park in the afternoon. Call to confirm opening hours in winter. ⊠ *Off A362, Warminster* ☎ *01985/844400* ⊕ *www.longleat.co.uk* 🎫 *£16, house £9, safari park £9* ☉ *House Apr.–Oct., daily 10–5:30; Nov.–Mar., daily 11–3; guided tours only (hourly on the hr). Safari park Apr.–Oct., weekdays 10–4, weekends and school vacations 10–5. Other attractions Apr.–Oct., daily 11–5:30.*

Where to Stay & Eat

★ £££££ ╳▥ **Bishopstrow House.** It's not often that you'll find a Georgian house converted into a luxurious but refreshingly relaxed hotel that combines antiques and fine carpets with modern amenities such as whirlpool baths and CD players. There's an airy conservatory, and the lavish, chintz-filled guest rooms overlook either the grounds (27 acres) or an interior courtyard. The Mulberry restaurant creates imaginatively prepared French meals (fixed-price menus) with a penchant toward the piquant. Bishopstrow House is 1½ mi out of town. ✉ *Boreham Rd., Warminster, BA12 9HH* ☎ *01985/212312* 🖷 *01985/216769* ⊕ *www.slh.com* 🛏 *32 rooms ₺ Restaurant, some in-room hot tubs, golf privileges, 2 tennis courts, 2 pools (1 indoor), gym, hair salon, sauna, fishing, croquet, bar, piano bar, business services, meeting rooms, helipad, some pets allowed; no a/c* ▤ *AE, DC, MC, V* ⦿ *BP.*

---

en route   Four miles west of Avebury, on A4, **Cherhill Down** is a prominent hill carved with a vivid white horse and topped with a towering obelisk. It's one of a number of hillside etchings in Wiltshire, but unlike the others, this one isn't an ancient symbol—it was put there in 1780 to indicate the highest point of the downs between London and Bath. The views from the top are well worth the half-hour climb. (The best view of the horse is from A4, on the approach from Calne.)

Avebury

③⑤ *25 mi northeast of Longleat, 27 mi east of Bath, 34 mi north of Salisbury.*

The village of Avebury was built far later than the stone circles that brought
★ it fame. The **Avebury Stone Circles** are one of England's most evocative prehistoric monuments—not so famous as Stonehenge, but all the more powerful for their lack of commercial exploitation. The stones were erected around 2500 BC, some 500 years after Stonehenge was started but about 500 years before that much smaller site assumed its present form. As with Stonehenge, the specific purpose of this stone circle has never been ascertained, although it most likely was used for similar ritual purposes as the more famous site. Unlike Stonehenge, however, there are no astronomical alignments at Avebury, at least none that have survived. The main site consists of a wide, circular ditch and bank, about 1,400 ft across and well over half a mile around; it actually surrounds part of the village of Avebury. Entrances break the perimeter at roughly the four points of the compass, and inside stand the remains of three stone circles. The largest one originally had 98 stones, although only 27 remain. Many of the stones on the site were destroyed centuries ago, especially in the 17th century when they were the target of religious fanaticism. Some stones were pillaged to build the thatched cottages you see flanking the fields. You can walk around the circles at any time; early morning and early evening are recommended. ✉ *1 mi north of A4* ☎ *No phone* ⊕ *www.english-heritage.org.uk* 🎫 *Free* ⊙ *Daily.*

In the **Alexander Keiller Museum and Barn Gallery,** finds from the Avebury area, and charts, photos, models, and home movies taken by the archaeologist Keiller himself, put the Avebury Stone Circles and the site into context. Recent revelations suggest that Keiller, responsible for the excavation of Avebury in the 1930s, may have adapted the site's layout more in the interests of presentation than authenticity. ✉ *1 mi north of A4* ☎ *01672/539250* ⊕ *www.english-heritage.org.uk* 🎫 *£4* ⊙ *Apr.–Oct., daily 10–6; Nov.–Mar., daily 10–4.*

The Avebury monument lies at the end of the **Kennett Stone Avenue,** a sort of prehistoric processional way leading to Avebury. The avenue's stones were spaced 80 ft apart, but only the half mile nearest the main monument survives intact. The lost ones are marked with concrete.

Where to Eat

££ ✕ **Waggon and Horses.** This spot just beside the traffic circle linking A4 and A361, a two-minute drive from the Avebury site, serves an excellent sandwich lunch beside a blazing fire. The thatch-roof pub, mentioned in Dickens's *Pickwick Papers,* is built of stones taken from the Avebury site. ⊠ *Beckhampton* ☎ *01672/539418* ▭ *AE, MC, V.*

---

en route | Relics of the prehistoric age dot the entire Avebury area; be sure to stop off at the **West Kennett Long Barrow,** a chambered tomb dating from about 3250 BC, 1 mi east of Avebury on A4. As you turn right at the traffic circle onto A4, **Silbury Hill** rises up on your right. This man-made mound, 130 ft high, dates from about 2500 BC. Excavations over 200 years have provided no clue as to its original purpose, but the generally accepted notion is that it was a massive burial chamber.

Marlborough

36 *7 mi east of Avebury, 28 mi north of Salisbury.*

The attractive town of Marlborough developed as an important staging post on the old London–Bath stagecoach route. Today it is better known for its unusually wide main street, its Georgian houses—these replaced the medieval town center, which was destroyed in a great fire in 1653—and its celebrated public school. The grounds of the school, on the west side of town, enclose a small, man-made hill called Castle Mound, or Maerl's Barrow, which gave the town its name. This was said to be the grave of Merlin, King Arthur's court wizard, but it is clearly much older than the period when the historic Arthur may have lived.

Where to Stay

£££ 🏠 **Ivy House.** This redbrick Georgian house on the colonnaded High Street makes an excellent touring base. Public rooms are clubby, and the bedrooms are predominantly beige and cream, some with exposed beams or arches. Those in the Vines annex are less expensive. A courtyard bar serves light meals, and a more formal restaurant has views overlooking the sun terrace. ⊠ *43 High St., SN8 1HJ* ☎ *01672/515333* 🖷 *01672/ 515338* ⊕ *www.ivyhousemarlborough.co.uk* ⌇ *36 rooms* ⌂ *Restaurant, cable TV, bar, meeting room; no a/c* ▭ *AE, MC, V* ¶⊙¶ *BP.*

Sports

The **Marlborough Golf Club** (⊠ The Common ☎ 01672/512147), with a par-72, 6,514-yard course, has fine views down the Og Valley.

Stonehenge

37 *21 mi south of Marlborough, 8 mi north of Salisbury.*

Fodor'sChoice ★

One of England's most visited and most puzzling monuments, Stonehenge is dwarfed by its lonely isolation on the wide sweep of Salisbury Plain. Sadly, the great circle of stones has been enclosed by barriers to control both the relentless throngs of tourists and, during the summer solstice, crowds of New Age druids intent on celebrating, in the monument's imposing shadows, an obscure pagan festival. But if you visit in the early morning, when the crowds have not yet arrived, or in the evening, when the sky is heavy with scudding clouds, you can experience Stonehenge as it once was: a magical, mystical, awe-inspiring place.

Stonehenge was begun about 3000 BC, enlarged between 2100 and 1900 BC, and altered yet again by 150 BC. It has been excavated and rearranged several times over the centuries. The medieval term "Stonehenge" means "hanging stones." Many of the huge stones that ringed the center were brought here from great distances. The original 80 bluestones (dolerite), which made up the two internal circles, were transported from the Preseli mountains, near Fishguard on the Atlantic coast of Wales, presumably by raft over sea and river. Next they were dragged on rollers across country—a total journey of 130 mi as the crow flies, but closer to 240 by the practical route. The labor involved in quarrying, transporting, and carving these stones is astonishing, all the more so when you realize that it was accomplished about the same time that the major pyramids of Egypt were built.

Although some of the mysteries concerning the site have been solved, the reason Stonehenge was originally built remains unknown. It is fairly certain that it was a religious site, and that worship here involved the cycles of the sun; the alignment of the stones to point to sunrise at midsummer and sunset in midwinter makes this clear. For some historians one thing is certain: the druids had nothing to do with the construction. The monument had already been in existence for nearly 2,000 years by the time they appeared. Most historians think Stonehenge may have been a kind of neolithic computer, with a sophisticated astronomical purpose—an observatory of sorts.

A paved path for visitors surrounds Stonehenge, so that you can't get very close to the monoliths except in one section of the site. Bring a pair of binoculars to help make out the details more clearly. It pays to walk all about the site, near and far, to get that magical Kodak shot. If you're a romantic, you'll want to view Stonehenge at dawn or dusk, or by a full moon. You can rent an audio tour, but in general, visitor amenities at Stonehenge are rather squalid, with no indoor seating; there are plans to improve them. Visitors coming from Marlborough should join A345 south for Stonehenge, turning west onto A303 at Amesbury. The monument stands near the junction with A344. ✉ *Junction of A303 and A344/A360, near Amesbury* ☎ *01980/624715* 🌐 *www.english-heritage.org.uk* 🎫 *£5* ⏲ *Mid-Mar.–May and Sept.–mid-Oct., daily 9:30–6; June–Aug., daily 9–7; mid-Oct.–mid-Mar., daily 9:30–4.*

Lyndhurst

38 *26 mi southeast of Stonehenge, 18 mi southeast of Salisbury, 9 mi west of Southampton.*

Lyndhurst is famous as the capital of the New Forest. To explore the depths of this natural wonder, take A35 out of Lyndhurst (the road continues southwest to Bournemouth). To get here from Stonehenge, head south along A360 to Salisbury, then follow A36, B3079, and continue along A337 another 4 mi or so. The New Forest **Visitor Information Centre** (✉ High St. ☎ 023/8028–2269) in the town's main car park is open daily year-round. Lewis Carroll's *Wonderland* fans should note that Alice Hargreaves (*née* Liddell) is buried in the **churchyard at Lyndhurst.**

The **New Forest** (☎ 01590/689000 🌐 www.thenewforest.co.uk) consists of 150 square mi of mainly open, unfenced countryside interspersed with dense woodland, a natural haven for herds of free-roaming deer, cattle, and, most famously, hardy New Forest ponies. The forest was "new" in 1079, when William the Conqueror cleared the area of farms and villages and turned it into his private hunting grounds. Although some favorite spots can get crowded in summer, there are ample parking lots, picnic areas, and campgrounds. Miles of walking trails crisscross the region.

Sports & the Outdoors

GOLF You may see New Forest ponies grazing on the par-69, 5,772-yard **New Forest Golf Course** (⊠ Southampton Rd. ☎ 023/8028–2752), right in the middle of the New Forest.

HORSEBACK RIDING The New Forest was created for riding, and there's no better way to enjoy it than on horseback. You can arrange a ride at the **Forest Park Riding Stables** (⊠ Rhinefield Rd., Brockenhurst ☎ 01590/623429 ☎ £18 for 1 hr). The **New Park Manor Stables** (⊠ New Park, Brockenhurst ☎ 01590/623919 ☎ £17 for 1 hr) gives full instruction.

WALKING The **New Forest** is more domesticated than, for example, the Forest of Dean, and the walks it provides are not much more than easy strolls. For one such walk (about 4 mi), start from Lyndhurst and head directly south for Brockenhurst, a commuter village. You will pass through woods, pastureland, and leafy river valleys—and you may even see some New Forest ponies.

Beaulieu

39 *7 mi southeast of Lyndhurst.*

The unspoiled village of Beaulieu (pronounced *byoo*-lee) has three major attractions in one. **Beaulieu**, with a ruined abbey, a stately home, and an automobile museum, may have something for everyone. In 1204 King John established **Beaulieu Abbey** for the Cistercian monks, who gave their new home its name, which means "beautiful place" in French. It was badly damaged during the reign of Henry VIII, leaving only the cloister, the doorway, the gatehouse, and two buildings. A well-planned exhibition in one building re-creates daily life in the monastery. **Palace House** incorporates the abbey's 14th-century gatehouse and has been the home of the Montagu family since they purchased it in 1538, after the dissolution of the monasteries. In this stately home you can see drawing rooms, dining halls, and a number of very fine family portraits. The present Lord Montagu is noted for his work in establishing the **National Motor Museum,** which traces the development of motor transport from 1895 to the present. More than 250 classic cars, buses, and motorcycles are displayed. Museum attractions include a monorail, audiovisual presentations, and a trip in a 1912 London bus (weekends only in winter, excluding January). **Beaulieu Cycle Hire** (☎ 01590/611029), on the grounds of the motor museum, rents bicycles. ⊠ *Off B3056* ☎ *01590/612123* ⊕ *www.beaulieu.co.uk* ☎ *Abbey, Palace House, and Motor Museum £11.95* ☉ *May–Sept., daily 10–6; Oct.–Apr., daily 10–5; last admission 40 mins before closing.*

Buckler's Hard

40 *2 mi south of Beaulieu.*

Among local places of interest around Beaulieu is the museum village of Buckler's Hard, an almost perfectly restored 18th-century hamlet of 24 brick cottages, leading down to an old shipyard on the River Beaulieu. The fascinating **Maritime Museum** tells the story of Lord Nelson's favorite ship, HMS *Agamemnon,* which was built here of New Forest oak. Exhibits and model ships trace the shipbuilding history of the town. Also part of the museum are four building interiors in the hamlet that re-create 18th-century village life. Easter through October, you can arrange to take a cruise on the Beaulieu River. ☎ *01590/616203* ⊕ *www.bucklershard.co.uk* ☎ *£5* ☉ *Easter–Oct., daily 10:30–5; Nov.–Easter, daily 11–4.*

en route

From Beaulieu, take any of the minor roads leading west through wide-open heathland to Lymington and pick up A337 for the popular seaside resort of Bournemouth, a journey of about 18 mi.

BOURNEMOUTH TO LYME REGIS
FAR FROM THE MADDING CROWD

"I am convinced that it is better for a writer to know a little bit of the world remarkably well than to know a great part of the world remarkably little," wrote Thomas Hardy, the immortal author of *Far from the Madding Crowd* and other classic Victorian-era novels. His "little bit" was the county of Dorset, the setting for most of his books and, today, a green and hilly area that is largely unspoiled. A visit to one of the last remaining corners of old, rural England follows the Dorset coastline, immortalized by Hardy and, more recently, by John Fowles. Places of historic interest such as Maiden Castle and the chalk-cut giant of Cerne Abbas are interspersed with the seaside resorts of Bournemouth and Weymouth, although you may find the quieter towns of Lyme Regis and the smaller villages scattered along the route closer to your ideal of rural England. Chief glory of the county is Dorchester, an ancient agricultural center with a host of historical and literary associations, and worth a prolonged visit.

Bournemouth

41 *30 mi southwest of Southampton, 30 mi south of Salisbury, 30 mi east of Dorchester.*

The beach resort of Bournemouth was founded in 1810 by Lewis Tregonwell, an ex-army officer who had taken a liking to the area when stationed there some years before. He settled near what is now the Square and planted the first pine trees in the steep little valleys—or chines—cutting through the cliffs to the famous Bournemouth sands. The scent of fir trees was said to be healing for consumption (tuberculosis) sufferers, and the town grew steadily. Gardens laid out with trees and lawns link the Square and the beach. This is an excellent spot to relax and listen to music wafting from the Pine Walk bandstand. Regular musical programs take place at the Pavilion and at the Winter Gardens (home of the Bournemouth Symphony Orchestra) nearby.

Taking the zigzag paths through the leafy public gardens, you can descend to the seafront, where Bournemouth Pier juts into the channel from the pristine sandy beach. Bournemouth has 7 mi of beaches, and the waters are said to be some of southern England's cleanest. If you're not tempted to swim, you can always saunter along the wide promenade behind the beach.

Concerts and shows are staged at the **Bournemouth International Centre** (✉ Exeter Rd. ☎ 01202/456400), which includes a selection of restaurants and bars, and a swimming pool. For an old-fashioned tea, try the **Cumberland Hotel** (✉ E. Overcliffe Dr. ☎ 01202/290722), which serves outdoors in summer.

On the corner of Hinton Road stands **St. Peter's** parish church, easily recognizable by its 200-foot-high tower and spire. Lewis Tregonwell is buried in the churchyard. Here, too, is the elaborate tombstone of Mary Shelley, author of *Frankenstein* and wife of the great Romantic poet Percy Bysshe Shelley, whose heart is buried with her.

The **Russell-Cotes Art Gallery and Museum,** a late Victorian mansion perched on top of East Cliff, overflows with Victorian paintings and miniatures, cases of butterflies, and treasures from Asia, including an exquisite suit of Japanese armor. The Russell-Cotes family, wealthy hoteliers who traveled widely, collected the items. Fine landscaped gardens surround the house. ⊠ *East Cliff* ☎ *01202/451800* ⊕ *www.russell-cotes.bournemouth.gov. uk* ☞ *Free* ⊘ *Tues.–Sun. 10–5.*

Where to Stay & Eat

£–££££   ✕ **CH2.** Shiny, metallic, and elegant with wooden flooring, this busy modern restaurant specializes in steaks and mussels, served with inventive sauces such as red Thai curry and garlic and shallot. It's close to the sea and not far from the International Centre. ⊠ *37 Exeter Rd.* ☎ *01202/ 296296* ☰ *AE, MC, V* ⊘ *Closed Sun., Mon.*

★ £££££   ✕⌂ **Chewton Glen.** Once the home of Captain Frederick Marryat, author of *The Children of the New Forest,* this early-19th-century country house on extensive grounds is now a supremely luxurious hotel, among Britain's most expensive. All the rooms are sumptuously decorated in rich fabrics and upholstered furniture, with an eye to the minutest detail. Many diners consider its contemporary restaurant, the Marryat Room, and the cooking of its chef, Pierre Chevillard, worthy of a pilgrimage. The staff is genuine and friendly. Chewton Glen is 12 mi east of Bournemouth. ⊠ *Christchurch Rd., New Milton, BH25 6QS* ☎ *01425/ 275341; 800/344–5087 in U.S.* ☐ *01425/272310; 800/398–4534 in U. S.* ⊕ *www.chewtonglen.com* ↝ *59 rooms* ↺ *Restaurant, in-room data ports, cable TV, 9-hole golf course, 4 tennis courts, 2 pools (1 indoor), gym, spa, croquet, business services, meeting rooms, helipad; no a/c in some rooms, no kids under 6* ☰ *AE, DC, MC, V* ❚◯❚ *BP.*

£££–££££   ✕⌂ **Langtry Manor Hotel.** Edward VII built this house for his mistress Lillie Langtry in 1877, and it still preserves its Edwardian atmosphere, even in the newer annex. Individually named rooms continue the theme. In the restaurant (fixed-price menu), lacy tablecloths, silver cutlery, and other details set off the dishes, which are mainly British with French trimmings and include Lillie's Special—meringue in the shape of a swan. There's an Edwardian banquet every Saturday. Guests have access to a health club across the street. ⊠ *26 Derby Rd., East Cliff, BH1 3QB* ☎ *01202/553887* ☐ *01202/290115* ⊕ *www.langtrymanor.com* ↝ *27 rooms* ↺ *Restaurant, in-room data ports, meeting rooms; no a/c* ☰ *AE, DC, MC, V* ❚◯❚ *BP.*

Nightlife & the Arts

Bournemouth holds a **Music Festival** (☎ 0906/802–0234) June–July, with choirs, brass bands, and orchestras, some from overseas.

Wimborne Minster

㊷ *7 mi northwest of Bournemouth.*

The impressive minster of this quiet market town makes it seem like a miniature cathedral city. To get here from Bournemouth, follow the signs northwest on A341. The crenellated and pinnacled twin towers of **Wimborne Minster** present an attractive patchwork of gray and reddish-brown stone. The church's powerful Norman nave has zigzag molding interspersed with carved heads, and the Gothic chancel has tall lancet windows. Stop in to see the chained library (accessed via a spiral staircase), where valuable books have been kept on chains since 1686, and look out for the 14th-century astronomical clock on the inside wall of the west tower. ⊠ *High St.* ☎ *01202/884753* ⊕ *www.wimborneminster.org.uk* ☞ *£1 donation requested for church, chained library free* ⊘ *Church Mar.–Dec., Mon.–Sat. 9:30–5:30, Sun. 2:30–5:30; Jan. and Feb., Mon.–Sat. 9:30–4, Sun. 2:30–4. Chained library Easter–Oct., Mon.–Thurs. 10–12:30 and 2–4, Fri. 10–2:30.*

The **Priest's House Museum,** on the main square in a Tudor building with a garden, includes rooms furnished in various period styles and a Victorian kitchen. It also has Roman and Iron Age exhibits, including a cryptic, three-faced Celtic stone head. ✉ *23 High St.* ☎ *01202/882533* 🖃 *£2.50* ⊙ *Apr.–Oct., Mon.–Sat. 10–4:30.*

Kingston Lacy, a grand 17th-century house built for the Bankes family (who had lived in Corfe Castle), was altered in the 19th century by Sir Charles Barry, co-architect of the Houses of Parliament in London. The building holds a choice picture collection with works by Titian, Rubens, Van Dyck, and Velásquez, as well as the fabulous Spanish Room, lined with gilded leather and topped with an ornate Venetian ceiling. There's also a fine collection of Egyptian artifacts. Parkland with walking paths surrounds the house. ✉ *B3082, 1½ mi northwest of Wimborne Minster* ☎ *01202/883402* ⊕ *www.nationaltrust.org.uk* 🖃 *£6.80, park and garden only £3.50* ⊙ *House late Mar.–Oct., Wed.–Sun. 11–5 (last admission 4). Garden and park Feb.–mid-Mar., weekends 10:30–4; late Mar.–Oct., daily 10:30–6; Nov. and Dec., Fri.–Sun. 10:30–4.*

Where to Eat

££–£££ ✕ **Primizia.** This popular bistro serves dishes with French and Italian influences; try the pasta and bean soup for starters, followed by carpaccio of beef with wild mushrooms, and crème brûlée for dessert. ✉ *26 Westborough* ☎ *01202/883518* 🖃 *MC, V* ⊙ *Closed Sun.–Mon.*

Blandford Forum

㊸ *11 mi northwest of Wimborne Minster.*

Endowed with perhaps the handsomest Georgian town center in the southwest, this market town of brick and stone on the River Stour was Thomas Hardy's "Shottesford Forum." The Church of St. Peter and St. Paul, with an imposing cupola and dating from 1739, deserves a look.

Where to Stay & Eat

££–££££ ✕🏠 **Museum Inn.** It's worth making the detour 9 mi northeast of Blandford Forum to find this characterful inn. Despite a stylish transformation, the building remains in harmony with its 17th-century beginnings, retaining its flagstone floors and inglenook fireplace. Bedrooms are rustic but smart. Good fresh fare, from grilled venison sausage to fettuccine with king prawns, is available daily in the bar, and on weekends you can dine more formally in the Shed restaurant. ✉ *Farnham, DT11 8DE* ☎ *01725/516261* 🖷 *01725/516988* ⊕ *www.museuminn.co.uk* ⌂ *8 rooms* ♿ *Restaurant, bar, some pets allowed; no a/c, no kids under 8* 🖃 *MC, V* ⦿ *BP.*

Corfe Castle

★ ㊹ *20 mi south of Blandford Forum, 15 mi south of Poole, 6 mi south of Wareham.*

One of the most impressive ruins in Britain, the remains of Dorset's Corfe Castle overlook the pretty, gray limestone village of Corfe. The castle site guards a gap in the surrounding Purbeck Hills and has been fortified from very early times. The present ruins are of the castle built between 1105, when the great central keep was erected, and the 1270s, when the outer walls and towers were built. It owes its ramshackle state to Cromwell's soldiers, who blew up the castle in 1646 during the Civil War after Lady Bankes led its defense during a long siege. ✉ *A351* ☎ *01929/481294* ⊕ *www.nationaltrust.org.uk* 🖃 *£4.40* ⊙ *Mar., daily 10–5; Apr.–Oct., daily 10–6; Nov.–Feb., daily 10–4.*

off the
beaten
path

CLOUDS HILL – A tiny, spartan, brick-and-tile cottage served as the retreat of T. E. Lawrence (Lawrence of Arabia) before he was killed in a motorcycle accident on the road from Bovington in 1935. The house remains very much as he left it, with photos and memorabilia from the Middle East. It's particularly atmospheric on a gloomy day, as there's no electric light. ⊠ *Wareham, 8 mi northwest of Corfe, off B3390* ☎ *01929/405616* ⊕ *www.nationaltrust.org.uk* ☜ *£2.90* ⊘ *Apr.–Oct., Thurs.–Sun. and national holidays noon–5 or dusk.*

Where to Stay & Eat

£–££ ✕ **The Fox.** An age-old pub, the Fox has a fine view of Corfe Castle from its flower garden. There's an ancient well in the lounge bar and more timeworn stonework in an alcove, as well as a pre-1300 fireplace. The bar cheerfully doles out soups and sandwiches, as well as steaks and curries, but things can get uncomfortably congested in summer. ⊠ *West St., Corfe* ☎ *01929/480449* ▭ *MC, V.*

£–££ ▦ **Castle Inn.** This thatched hotel, 10 mi west of Corfe and just five minutes' walk from the sea, has a flagstone bar and other 15th-century features. Bedrooms are individually furnished, some with four-posters, and there's an extensive garden to sit in, including a rose garden. An extensive bar menu is available daily, and on weekend evenings the good restaurant has an à la carte menu. Satisfying walks are nearby. ⊠ *Main Rd., West Lulworth, BH20 5RN* ☎ *01929/400311* 🖶 *01929/400415* ⊕ *www.thecastleinn-lulworthcove.co.uk* ⇨ *15 rooms, 12 with bath* ⚐ *Restaurant, bar, some pets allowed; no a/c, no phones in some rooms* ▭ *AE, DC, MC, V* ⦿ *BP.*

Dorchester

⑮ *21 mi west of Corfe on A351 and A352, 30 mi west of Bournemouth, 43 mi southwest of Salisbury.*

In many ways Dorchester, the Casterbridge of Thomas Hardy's novel *The Mayor of Casterbridge,* is a traditional southern country town. The town owes much of its fame to its connection with Hardy, whose bronze statue looks westward from a bank on Colliton Walk. Born in a cottage in the hamlet of Higher Bockhampton, about 3 mi northeast of Dorchester, Hardy attended school in the town and was apprentice to an architect here.

Roman history and artifacts abound in Dorchester. The Romans laid out the town about AD 70, and if you walk along Bowling Alley Walk, West Walk, and Colliton Walk, you will have followed the approximate line of the original Roman town walls. On the north side of Colliton Park lies an excavated Roman villa with a marvelously preserved mosaic floor.

Dorchester is also associated with Monmouth's Rebellion of 1685, when Charles II's illegitimate son, the duke of Monmouth, led a rising against his unpopular uncle, James II. The rising was ruthlessly put down, and the chief justice, Lord Jeffreys, arrived from London to try the rebels and sympathizers for treason. A bullying drunkard, Jeffreys was the prototypical hanging judge, and memories of his mass executions lingered for centuries throughout the South. The trials became known as the Bloody Assizes. Jeffreys's courtroom in Dorchester was in what is now the Antelope Hotel on South Street.

To appreciate the town's character, visit the local Wednesday market in the **Market Square,** where you can find handcrafted items and Dorset delicacies such as Blue Vinney cheese (which some connoisseurs prefer to Blue Stilton). Things have changed a bit since the days when, to quote Hardy, "Bees and butterflies in the cornfields at the top of the town, who desired to get to the meads at the bottom, took no circuitous route, but flew straight down High Street . . ."

The **Dorset County Museum** contains ancient Celtic and Roman remains but is better known for possessing a large collection of Hardy memorabilia. ⊠ *High West St.* ☎ *01305/262735* ⊕ *www.dorsetcountymuseum. org* ⊠ *£3.75* ⊙ *May–Oct., daily 10–5; Nov.–Apr., Mon.–Sat. 10–5.*

The small thatch and cob **Hardy's Cottage,** where the writer was born in 1840, was built by his grandfather and is little altered since that time. From here Thomas Hardy would make his daily 6-mi walk to school in Dorchester. Among other things, you can see the desk at which the author completed *Far from the Madding Crowd.* ⊠ *½ mi south of Blandford Rd. (A35), Higher Bockhampton* ☎ *01305/262366* ⊕ *www. nationaltrust.org.uk* ⊠ *£2.80* ⊙ *Apr.–Oct., Thurs.–Mon. 11–5 or dusk.*

Thomas Hardy lived in **Max Gate** from 1885 until his death in 1928. An architect by profession, Hardy designed the house, in which the dining room and the light, airy drawing room are now open. He wrote much of his poetry here and many of his novels, including *Tess of the d'Urbervilles* and *The Mayor of Casterbridge.* ⊠ *Allington Ave., 1 mi east of Dorchester on A352* ☎ *01305/262538* ⊕ *www.nationaltrust. org.uk* ⊠ *£2.30* ⊙ *Apr.–Sept., Mon., Wed., and Sun. 2–5.*

The **Maumbury Rings** (⊠ Maumbury Rd.), the remains of a Roman amphitheater on the edge of town, were built on a prehistoric site that later served as a place of execution. (Hardy's *Mayor of Casterbridge* contains a vivid evocation of the Rings.) As late as 1706, a girl was burned at the stake here.

☾ The popular **Dinosaur Museum** has life-size models, interactive displays, and a hands-on Discovery Gallery. ⊠ *Icen Way, off High East St.* ☎ *01305/269880* ⊕ *www.dinosaur-museum.org.uk* ⊠ *£5.50* ⊙ *Apr.–Oct., daily 9:30–5:30; Nov.–Mar., daily 10–4:30.*

It's hardly what you might expect from a small county town, but the ☾ **Tutankhamun Exhibition,** in a former Catholic church, re-creates the young pharaoh's tomb and treasures in all its glory. The smells of ointments and cedarwood oil complement the displays; the same ticket admits you to the small Mummies Exhibition next door, showing the process of mummification with copies of mummies. ⊠ *High West St.* ☎ *01305/269571* ⊕ *www.tutankhamun-exhibition.co.uk* ⊠ *£5.50* ⊙ *Apr.–Oct., daily 9:30–5:30; Nov.–Mar., weekdays 9:30–5, Sat. 10–5, Sun. 10–4:30; last admission 45 mins before closing.*

need a break? Soak up some of the region's darker history at **Judge Jeffreys** (⊠ 6 High West St. ☎ 01305/264369), where you can have coffee, cream teas, and light meals in the original beamed building where Judge Jeffreys held his Bloody Assizes in 1685.

Fine 19th-century gardens complement an outstanding example of 15th-century domestic architecture at **Athelhampton House and Gardens,** 5 mi east of Dorchester and 1 mi east of Puddletown. Thomas Hardy called this place Athelhall in some of his writings, referring to the legendary King Aethelstan, who had a palace on this site. The current house includes the Great Hall, with much of its original timber roof intact, and the King's Room. The 10 acres of landscaped gardens contain water features and

HARDY'S DORSET

Among this region's proudest claims is its connection with Thomas Hardy (1840–1928), one of England's most celebrated novelists. If you read some of Hardy's novels before visiting Dorset—re-created by Hardy as his part-fact, part-fiction county of Wessex—you'll already have a feeling for it, and indeed, you'll recognize some places immediately from his descriptions. The tranquil countryside surrounding Dorchester, in particular, is lovingly described in Far from the Madding Crowd, *and Casterbridge, in* The Mayor of Casterbridge, *stands for Dorchester itself. Any pilgrimage to Hardy's Wessex begins at the author's birthplace in Higher Bockhampton, 3 mi east of Dorchester. Salisbury makes an appearance as "Melchester" in* Jude the Obscure. *Walk in the footsteps of Jude Fawley by climbing Shaftesbury—"Shaston"—and its steeply pretty Gold Hill. Today, many of these sights seem frozen in time, and Hardy's spirit is ever present.*

the Great Court with its 12 giant yew pyramids. The property may close on some Friday afternoons in summer, so call ahead. ✉ *A35* ☎ *01305/848363* 🌐 *www.athelhampton.co.uk* 🎫 *£7, gardens only £4.95* ⏲ *Mar.–Oct., Sun.–Fri. 10:30–5; Nov.–Feb., Sun. 10:30–5.*

Where to Stay & Eat

£££–£££ ✕ **Potters Café-Bistro.** This café on two floors of a 17th-century cottage is just the place for a break during the day, for teas, coffees, and delicious cakes and pastries, as well as sandwiches and light lunches. In the evening, the menu may list scallops and vegetarian caviar for starters, and mille-feuille of Mediterranean vegetables and duck breast with wild rice for main courses. The inglenook fireplace adds coziness in winter, and the garden is pleasant in summer. ✉ *19 Durngate St.* ☎ *01305/260312* 💳 *AE, DC, MC, V* ⏲ *Closed Sun. No dinner Mon.–Wed.*

★ £££ ✕🏨 **Yalbury Cottage.** A thatch roof and inglenook fireplaces enhance the traditional appeal of this 300-year-old cottage, just 2½ mi east of Dorchester and close to Hardy's birthplace. The three-course fixed-price menu of superior modern British fare might include herb-crusted rack of lamb (with tomato and basil jus) or roast halibut with celeriac confit. Pine-furnished bedrooms are available in a discreet extension overlooking gardens or adjacent fields. ✉ *Lower Bockhampton, DT2 8PZ* ☎ *01305/262382* 📠 *01305/266412* 🌐 *www.smoothhound.co.uk* 🛏 *8 rooms* ♨ *Restaurant, some pets allowed (fee); no a/c* 💳 *MC, V* ⏲ *Closed Jan. No lunch* 🍽 *BP.*

★ £££ 🏨 **Casterbridge Hotel.** Small but full of character, this Georgian building (1790) reflects its age, with period furniture and elegance. Guest rooms are each individually and impeccably furnished in traditional style, and the conservatory overlooks a leafy courtyard garden. You'll be looked after by the congenial husband-and-wife team who own and run the hotel. ✉ *49 High East St., DT1 1HU* ☎ *01305/264043* 📠 *01305/260884* 🌐 *www.casterbridgehotel.co.uk* 🛏 *14 rooms* ♨ *In-room data ports, bar; no a/c* 💳 *AE, DC, MC, V* 🍽 *BP.*

Sports & the Outdoors

From April through October the **Thomas Hardy Society** (📮 Box 1438, Dorchester, DT1 1YH ☎📠 01305/251501) organizes walks that follow in the steps of Hardy's novels. Readings and discussions accompany the walks, which take the largest part of a day.

Cerne Abbas

46 *6 mi north of Dorchester.*

The village of Cerne Abbas, worth a short exploration on foot, has some appealing Tudor houses on the road beside the church. Nearby you can also see the original village stocks. Tenth-century **Cerne Abbey** is now a ruin, with little left to see except its old gateway, although the nearby Abbey House is still in use.

Cerne Abbas's main claim to fame is the colossal and unblushingly priapic **figure of a giant,** cut in chalk on a hillside overlooking the village. The 180-foot-long giant carries a huge club and bears a striking resemblance to Hercules, although he may have originated as a tribal fertility symbol long before Roman times; authorities disagree. His outlines are formed by 2-foot-wide trenches. The present giant is thought to have been carved in the chalk about AD 1200. The best place to view the figure is from the A352 itself, where you can park in any of the numerous turnouts.

Where to Stay

£ Fodor'sChoice ★ **Lamperts Cottage.** This idyllic thatch-roof B&B, about 2 mi southwest of Cerne Abbas, has a stream in front and back, so you must cross a little bridge to reach it. In summer roses cover the cottage. The house, dating from the 16th century, is very comfortable although small; the rooms share two baths. The interior has exposed beams and fireplaces. ✉ *10 Dorchester Rd., Sydling St. Nicholas, DT2 9NU* ☎ *01300/341659* 📠 *01300/341699* *nickywillis@tesco.net* *3 rooms without bath* *No a/c, no room phones, no room TVs, no kids under 8* *MC, V* *BP.*

Maiden Castle

★ 47 *2 mi southwest of Dorchester.*

After Stonehenge, Maiden Castle (✉ A354) is the most important pre-Roman archaeological site in England. It's not really a castle at all, but an enormous, complex hill fort of stone and earth with ramparts that enclose about 45 acres. England's mysterious prehistoric inhabitants built the fort, and many centuries later it was a Celtic stronghold. In AD 43, the invading Romans, under the general (later emperor) Vespasian, stormed the fort. Finds from the site are on display in the Dorset County Museum in Dorchester. To experience an uncanny silence and sense of mystery, climb Maiden Castle early in the day (access to it is unrestricted). Leave your car at the lot at the end of Maiden Castle Way, a 1½-mi lane signposted off the A354.

Weymouth

48 *8 mi south of Dorchester.*

Dorset's main coastal resort, Weymouth, is known for its wide, safe, sandy beaches and its royal connections. King George III took up sea bathing here for his health in 1789, setting a trend among the wealthy and fashionable people of the day. Its popularity left Weymouth with many fine buildings, including the Georgian row houses lining the esplanade. Striking historical details clamor for attention: a wall on Maiden Street, for example, holds a cannonball that was embedded in it during the Civil War. Nearby, a column commemorates the launching of the United States forces from Weymouth on D-Day, June 6, 1944.

Where to Stay & Eat

£££ ✕ **Perry's.** A busy, family-run restaurant right by the harbor, Perry's specializes in simple dishes using the best local seafood. Try the lobster, crab, or medallions of monkfish with mussels and leeks. The meat dishes, such as roast rack of lamb, are tasty, too. ⊠ *The Harbourside, 4 Trinity Rd.* ☎ *01305/785799* ▤ *AE, MC, V* ⊘ *No lunch Mon. and Sat.; no dinner Sun. Sept.–June.*

£–££ ✕ **Old Rooms.** A fisherman's pub full of maritime clutter and low beams, this popular choice has great views over the harbor. The long menu includes pastas, curries, and meat pies. There's a separate dining area, or you can mix with the locals at the bar. ⊠ *7 Cove Row* ☎ *01305/771130* ▤ *AE, MC, V.*

★ ££ ⌂ **Streamside Hotel.** This black-and-white timbered hotel on the outskirts of town is a stone's throw from the beach and has spectacular gardens. Bedrooms are furnished in pine with white bed linens, and the restaurant serves English fare, with steaks, smoked salmon, and various fish in season. ⊠ *29 Preston Rd., Overcombe, DT3 6PX* ☎ *01305/833121* ⌂ *01305/832043* ⟐ *11 rooms* ⌂ *Restaurant, meeting rooms, some pets allowed (fee); no a/c* ▤ *MC, V* ⊙| *BP.*

Isle of Portland

㊾ *4 mi south of Weymouth.*

A 5-mi-long peninsula jutting south from Weymouth leads to the Isle of Portland, well known for its limestone. The peninsula is the eastern end of the unique geological curiosity known as **Chesil Beach**—a 200-yard-wide, 30-foot-high bank of pebbles that decrease in size from east to west. The beach extends for 18 mi. A powerful undertow makes swimming dangerous, and tombstones in local churchyards attest to the many shipwrecks the beach has caused.

Abbotsbury

㊿ *10 mi northwest of Weymouth.*

The attractive village of Abbotsbury is at the western end of Chesil Beach. A lagoon outside the village serves as the **Abbotsbury Swannery,** a famous breeding place for swans. Introduced by Benedictine monks as a source of meat in winter, the swans have remained for centuries, building new nests every year in the soft, moist pampas grass. ⊠ *New Barn Rd.* ☎ *01305/871684* ⊕ *www.abbotsbury.co.uk* ⌸ *£5.80* ⊙ *Late Mar.–Oct., daily 10–6; last admission 5.*

On the hills above Abbotsbury stands the **Hardy Monument**—dedicated not to the novelist but to Sir Thomas Masterman Hardy, Lord Nelson's flag captain at Trafalgar, to whom Nelson's dying words, "Kiss me, Hardy," were addressed. The monument is without much charm, but in clear weather you can scan the whole coastline between the Isle of Wight and Start Point in Devon. ⊠ *Black Down, Portesham* ☎ *01297/561900* ⊕*www.nationaltrust.org.uk* ⌸*£1* ⊙ *Apr.–Sept., weekends 11–5. Subject to closure in bad weather.*

Where to Stay & Eat

£££ ✕⌂ **Manor Hotel.** The pedigree of this honey-color hotel and restaurant goes back more than 700 years—note its flagstone floors, oak paneling, and beamed ceilings. Among the English and French dishes in which the Manor specializes are seafood and game; the fixed-price menu changes daily. Some guest rooms, which are individually decorated in pastel colors and furnished with antiques, have sea views, and Chesil Beach is a couple of minutes' walk away. Self-catering facilities are also available.

✉ *Beach Rd., 3 mi west of Abbotsbury, West Bexington, DT2 9DF*
☎ *01308/897785* 🖷 *01308/897035* ⊕ *www.manorhotel.com* ⇪ *13*
rooms ⚲ *Restaurant, playground; no a/c* ▤ *AE, MC, V* ⍾❙ *BP.*

Lyme Regis

🖲 *19 mi west of Abbotsbury.*

"A very strange stranger it must be, who does not see the charms of
the immediate environs of Lyme, to make him wish to know it better,"
wrote Jane Austen in *Persuasion*. Judging from the summer crowds,
most people appear to be not at all strange. The ancient, scenic town
of Lyme Regis and the so-called Jurassic Coast (a World Heritage Site,
including the coast from Exmouth in the west to Swanage in the east,
that encompasses 185 million years of the Earth's geological history)
are highlights of southwest Dorset. The crumbling seaside cliffs in this
area are especially fossil rich. In 1810 a local child named Mary An-
ning dug out a complete ichthyosaur here (it's on display in London's
Natural History Museum). Exhibits in the Philpot Museum and the Lyme
Regis Marine Aquarium provide insight into local history and marine
life, respectively.

Lyme Regis is famous for its curving stone breakwater, **The Cobb,** built
by King Edward I in the 13th century to improve the harbor. The duke
of Monmouth landed here in 1685 during his ill-fated attempt to over-
throw his uncle, James II. The Cobb figured prominently in the movie
The French Lieutenant's Woman, based on John Fowles's novel, as
well as in the film version of Jane Austen's *Persuasion*. Fowles is Lyme's
most famous current resident.

The lively **Philpot Museum,** in a gabled and turreted Victorian building, contains engaging items that illustrate the town's maritime and domestic history, as well as a section on local writers and a good selection of local
fossils. ✉ *Bridge St.* ☎ *01297/443370* ⊕ *www.lymeregismuseum.co.uk*
🎫 *£1.60* ⊘ *Apr.–Oct., Mon.–Sat. 10–5, Sun. 11–5; Nov.–Mar., weekends
10–5, Sun. 11–5.*

🖑 The **Dinosaurland Fossil Museum,** in a former church, displays an excellent collection of local fossils and gives the background on regional geology and how fossils develop. Although the museum is aimed at
children, most people will find it informative. Ask here about guided
fossil-hunting walks. The **Lyme Regis Fossil Shop** on the ground floor
sells books and fascinating real fossils from around the world as well
as copies, some fashioned into jewelry or ornaments. ✉ *Coombe St.*
☎ *01297/443541* ⊕ *www.dinosaurland.co.uk* 🎫 *£4* ✉ *Daily 10–5.*

Where to Stay & Eat

£   ✕ **Bell Cliff Restaurant.** This friendly little place at the bottom of Lyme's
main street makes a great spot for a light lunch or tea, although it can
get noisy and cramped. Apart from teas and coffees, you can order seafood,
including whitebait, plaice, and the chef's salmon fish cakes, or a gam-
mon steak (a thick slice of cured ham) or nut roast. The restaurant occasionally stays open in the evenings in summer. ✉ *5–6 Broad St.*
☎ *01297/442459* ▤ *MC, V* ⊘ *No dinner.*

££–££££ ✕⊡ **Alexandra.** A short walk from the Cobb, the Alexandra is a genteel,
old-fashioned haven with a high, panoramic location. Informal lunches
and teas are served in a sunny conservatory that overlooks an expanse
of lawn. The formal restaurant has an impressive wine list to complement the fixed-price four-course dinners, with straightforward entrées
such as poached salmon and duckling in orange sauce. Depending on the

cost, some guest rooms have a restrained elegance and others are purely functional, although you're almost guaranteed a view over garden and sea. ⊠ *Pound St., DT7 3HZ* ☎ *01297/442010* 🖷 *01297/443229* ⊕ *www.hotelalexandra.co.uk* 📞 *26 rooms* ♻ *Restaurant, bar, some pets allowed (fee); no a/c* ▭ *MC, V* ☺ *Closed Jan.* ⧖⧖ *BP.*

£ 🖵 **Coombe House.** The main building of this B&B tucked away on one of the oldest lanes in Lyme (dating from the 16th century) has spacious and tasteful guest rooms. Across the yard is a larger studio with a kitchen. Breakfast is brought to your room. ⊠ *41 Coombe St., DT7 3PY* ☎🖷 *01297/443849* 📞 *3 rooms, 1 studio* ♻ *No a/c, no room phones, no smoking* ▭ *No credit cards* ⧖⧖ *BP.*

Sports & the Outdoors

The 72-mi **Dorset Coast Path** (⊠ South West Coast Path Association, Windlestraw, Penquit, Ermington ☎ 01752/896237) runs east from Lyme Regis to Poole, bypassing Weymouth and taking in the quiet bays, shingle beaches, and low chalk cliffs of the coast. Some highlights are Golden Cap, the highest point on the South Coast; the Swannery at Abbotsbury; Chesil Beach; and Lulworth Cove (between Weymouth and Corfe Castle). Villages and isolated pubs dot the route, as do many rural B&Bs.

THE SOUTH A TO Z

To research prices, get advice from other travelers, and book travel arrangements, visit www.fodors.com.

AIRPORTS

The small international airport at Southampton is useful for flights to the Channel Islands and some European destinations.

🖪 **Southampton International Airport** ⊠ M27, Junction 5 ☎ 023/8062–0021 ⊕ www.baa.co.uk.

BOAT & FERRY TRAVEL

Wightlink operates a car-ferry service between the mainland and the Isle of Wight. The crossing takes about 30 minutes from Lymington to Yarmouth; 40 minutes from Southsea (Portsmouth) to Fishbourne. It also operates catamaran service between Portsmouth and Ryde (15 minutes). Red Funnel runs a car-ferry (one hour) and hydrofoil service (25 minutes) between Southampton and Cowes. Hovertravel has a hovercraft shuttle between Southsea and Ryde (10 minutes).

FARES & SCHEDULES 🖪 **Hovertravel** ☎ 01983/811000 or 023/9281–1000 ⊕ www.hovertravel.co.uk. **Red Funnel** ☎ 0870/444–8898 ⊕ www.redfunnel.co.uk. **Wightlink** ☎ 0870/582–7744 ⊕ www.wightlink.co.uk.

BUS TRAVEL

National Express buses at London's Victoria Coach Station on Buckingham Palace Road depart hourly for Bournemouth (2½ hours) and every two hours for Southampton (2½ hours), Portsmouth (2½ hours), and Winchester (2 hours). There are three buses daily to Salisbury (2¾ hours). Solent Blue and Stagecoach Hampshire Bus operate a comprehensive service in the Southampton, New Forest, Winchester, and Bournemouth areas. Southern Vectis covers the Isle of Wight. Traveline can provide information about travel throughout the region.

CUTTING COSTS Wilts (Wiltshire) & Dorset Bus Co. offers both one-day Explorer and seven-day Busabout tickets; in summer, it also conducts Explorer Special open-top tours around Bournemouth. Also ask about the Rover tickets offered by Solent Blue and Southern Vectis.

FARES & SCHEDULES
National Express ☎ 0870/580–8080 ⊕ www.nationalexpress.com. Solent Blue ☎ 023/8061–8233 ⊕ www.solentblueline.com. Southern Vectis ☎ 01983/532373 ⊕ www.svoc.co.uk. Stagecoach Hampshire Bus ☎ 0845/121–0180 ⊕ www.stagecoachbus.com. Traveline ☎ 0870/608–2608 ⊕ www.traveline.org.uk. Wilts (Wiltshire) & Dorset Bus Co. ☎ 01722/336855 ⊕ www.wdbus.co.uk.

CAR RENTAL

Local Agencies Avis ⊠ 33–39 Southcote Rd., Bournemouth ☎ 01202/296942. Enterprise Rent-a-Car ⊠ Train Station, Winchester ☎ 01962/844022. Esplanade ⊠ 9–11 George St., Ryde ☎ 01983/562322. Europcar ⊠ c/o Ibis Hotel, 1 West Quay Rd., Southampton ☎ 023/8033–2973. Hertz ⊠ Hinton Rd., Bournemouth ☎ 01202/291231 ⊠ 1 Queensway, Southampton ☎ 023/8063–8437. Thrifty ⊠ Brunel Rd., Churchfields Industrial Estate, Salisbury ☎ 01722/336444.

CAR TRAVEL

The South is linked to London and other major cities by a well-developed road network, which includes M3 to Winchester (59 mi) and Southampton (77 mi); A3 to Portsmouth (70 mi); and M27 along the coast, from the New Forest and Southampton to Portsmouth. For Salisbury, take M3 to A303, then A30. A31 and A35 connect Bournemouth to Dorchester and the rest of Dorset.

ROAD CONDITIONS Driving is very easy in this area. In northeast Hampshire and in many parts of neighboring Wiltshire there are pretty lanes overhung by trees and lined with thatched cottages and Georgian houses. Often these lanes begin near the exits of main highways. Salisbury Plain has long, straight roads surrounded by endless vistas; the problem here is staying within the speed limit.

EMERGENCIES

Ambulance, fire, police ☎ 999. Dorset County Hospital ⊠ Williams Ave., Dorchester ☎ 01305/251150. Queen Alexandra Hospital ⊠ Southwick Hill Rd., Cosham, Portsmouth ☎ 023/9228–6000. St. Mary's Hospital ⊠ Parkhurst Rd., Newport, Isle of Wight ☎ 01983/524081. Salisbury District Hospital ⊠ Odstock Rd., Salisbury ☎ 01722/336262. Southampton General Hospital ⊠ Tremona Rd., Southampton ☎ 023/8077–7222.

TOURS

City Sightseeing/Guide Friday has a daily Stonehenge tour from Salisbury, May through September, costing £15 check for availability. A. S. Tours arranges day tours of Stonehenge and Avebury, year-round, in six-seater minibuses. Salisbury City Guides run a program of daily summer (weekends in winter) walks in Salisbury, starting at 11. The Southern Tourist Board and Wessexplore can reserve qualified Blue Badge guides who will arrange to meet you anywhere in the region for private tours of different lengths and themes.

A. S. Tours ☎ 01980/862931. City Sightseeing/Guide Friday ☎ 01789/294466 ⊕ www.city-sightseeing.com. Salisbury City Guides ☎ 01725/518658 ⊕ www.salisburycityguides.co.uk. Southern Tourist Board ☎ 023/8062–5400 ⊕ www.southerntb.co.uk. Wessexplore ☎ 01722/326304 ⊕ www.dmac.co.uk/wessexplore.

TRAIN TRAVEL

South West Trains serves the South from London's Waterloo Station. Travel times average 1 hour to Winchester, 1¼ hours to Southampton, 2 hours to Bournemouth, and 2½ hours to Weymouth. The trip to Salisbury takes 1⅓ hours, and Portsmouth about 2 hours. There is at least one fast train every hour on all these routes. For local information throughout the region, contact National Rail Enquiries.

CUTTING COSTS   A Network card, valid throughout the South and Southeast for a year, entitles you to one-third off particular fares.

FARES & SCHEDULES   **National Rail Enquiries** ☎ 08457/484950 ⊕ www.nationalrail.co.uk. **South West Trains** ☎ 08457/484950 ⊕ www.swtrains.co.uk.

TRAVEL AGENCIES
Local Agent Referrals American Express ⊠ 99 Above Bar, Southampton ☎ 023/8071-6802. **Thomas Cook** ⊠ 7 Richmond Hill, Bournemouth ☎ 01202/452800 ⊠ 18 Queen St., Salisbury ☎ 01722/313500 ⊠ 9 Palmerston Rd., Southsea ☎ 023/9230-2100 ⊠ 30 High St., Winchester ☎ 01962/743100.

VISITOR INFORMATION
The Southern Tourist Board is open Monday–Thursday 8:30–5, Friday 8:30–4:30. Local tourist information centers are normally open Monday–Saturday 9:30–5:30.

Southern Tourist Board ⊠ 40 Chamberlayne Rd., Eastleigh, S050 5JH ☎ 023/8062-5400 🖷 023/8062-0010 ⊕ www.southerntb.co.uk. **Bournemouth** ⊠ Westover Rd., near the bandstand, BH1 2BU ☎ 0906/802-0234 (calls cost 60p per min) ⊕ www.bournemouth.co.uk. **Dorchester** ⊠ 11 Antelope Walk, DT1 1BE ☎ 01305/267992 ⊕ www.westdorset.com. **Lyme Regis** ⊠ Guildhall Cottage, Church St., DT7 3BS ☎ 01305/442138. **Lyndhurst** ⊠ Main Car Park, High St., S043 7NY ☎ 023/8028-2269 ⊕ www.thenewforest.co.uk. **Marlborough** ⊠ Car Park, George La., SN8 1EE ☎ 01672/513989. **Portsmouth** ⊠ The Hard, PO1 3QJ ☎ 023/9282-6722 ⊕ www.visitportsmouth.co.uk ⊠ Clarence Esplanade, Southsea, PO5 3PB. ☎ 023/9282-6722. **Ryde** ⊠ 81 Union St., PO33 2LW ☎ 01983/813813 ⊕ www.islandbreaks.co.uk. **Salisbury** ⊠ Fish Row, off Market Sq., SP1 1EJ ☎ 01722/334956 ⊕ www.visitsalisbury.com. **Sherborne** ⊠ 3 Tilton Ct., Digby Rd., DT9 3NL ☎ 01935/815341 ⊕ www.westdorset.com. **Southampton** ⊠ 9 Civic Centre Rd., SO14 7FJ ☎ 023/8083-3333 ⊕ www.southampton.gov.uk. **Winchester** ⊠ The Guildhall, Broadway, SO23 9LJ ☎ 01962/840500 ⊕ www.visitwinchester.com.

THE WEST COUNTRY

SOMERSET, DEVON, CORNWALL

4

FODOR'S CHOICE

Clovelly, *coastal village in Devon*

Eden Project, *garden and conservatories near St. Austell*

Herbie's, *restaurant in Exeter*

Lanhydrock, *stately home near Bodmin*

The Old Rectory, *B&B near Boscastle*

The Seafood Restaurant, *Padstow*

T'Gallants, *guest house in Charlestown*

Tintagel Castle, *Tintagel*

HIGHLY RECOMMENDED

SIGHTS   A la Ronde, *house near Topsham*

Cathedral Church of St. Andrew, *Wells*

Cotehele House and Quay, *St. Dominick*

Glastonbury

Land's End, *Cornwall*

Lizard Peninsula, *Cornwall*

Lydford Gorge, *Lydford*

Montacute House, *Yeovil*

Mousehole

National Marine Aquarium, *Plymouth*

Saltram, *stately home in Plympton*

St. Just in Roseland, *hamlet near Trelissick*

St. Michael's Mount, *island near Marazion*

Tate St. Ives, *St. Ives*

Many other great hotels and restaurants enliven this area. For other favorites, look for the black stars as you read this chapter.

Updated by
Robert
Andrews

LEAFY, NARROW COUNTRY ROADS all around the Southwest lead through miles of buttercup meadows and cider apple orchards to countless mellow villages of stone and thatch and heathery heights overlooking the sea. This can be one of Britain's most relaxing regions to visit. The secret of exploring it is to ignore the main highways and just follow the signposts—or, even better, to let yourself get lost. The village names alone are music to the ears: there's Tintinhull, St. Endellion, Huish Episcopi, and Bower Hinton—just to name a few hamlets that *haven't* been covered below.

Somerset, Devon, and Cornwall are the three counties that make up the long southern peninsula known as the West Country. Each has its own distinct flavor, and each also comes with a regionalism that borders on patriotism. Somerset is noted for its rolling green countryside; Devon's wild and dramatic moors—bare, boggy upland heath dominated by heathers and gorse, with a scattering of trees—contrast with the restfulness of its many sandy beaches and coves; and Cornwall has managed to retain a touch of its old insularity, despite the annual invasion of thousands of people lured by the ocean or the English Channel.

Bristol is where you'll come across the first unmistakable burrs of the western brogue. Its historic port retains a strong maritime flavor, and Georgian architecture and a dramatic gorge create a backdrop to what has become one of Britain's most dynamic cities. You might weave south through the lovely Chew Valley on your way to the cathedral city of Wells, in Somerset. The county's mellow green countryside is best seen in a cloak of summer heat when its orchards give ample shade, its bees are humming, and its old stone houses and inns welcome you with a breath of coolness. Abutting the north coast are the Quantock and Mendip hills, and the heather-covered expanse of Exmoor, the setting for R. D. Blackmore's historical romance, *Lorna Doone*.

Devon, farther west, is famed for its wild moorland—especially Dartmoor, home of the mysterious beast in Sir Arthur Conan Doyle's novel "Hound of the Baskervilles," and actual home to ponies and an assortment of strange tors, rocky outcroppings eroded into weird shapes. Devon's large coastal towns are as interesting for their cultural and historical appeal—many were smugglers' havens—as for their scenic beauty. Some propagandists of east Devon speak of the "red cliffs" of Devon in contrast to the more famous "white cliffs of Dover." Parts of south Devon, on the other hand, resemble some balmy Mediterranean shore—hence its soubriquet, the English Riviera.

Cornwall, England's southernmost county, has a mild climate, and here you are never more than 20 mi from the sea. The county has always regarded itself as separate from the rest of Britain, and it was here that the Arthurian legends really took root, not least at Tintagel Castle, the legendary birthplace of Arthur. High, jagged cliffs line Cornwall's Atlantic coast—the dangerous and dramatic settings that Daphne du Maurier often waxed eloquent about—and indeed pose a menace to passing ships. The south coast, Janus-like, is filled with sunny beaches, delightful coves, and popular resorts. England's last outpost, the flower-filled Isles of Scilly, claims the most hours of sunshine in the country.

Exploring the West Country

A circular tour of the West Country covers a large territory, from the bustling city of Bristol, two hours outside London, to the remote and rocky headlands of Devon and Cornwall to the west. Stark contrasts abound in this peninsula, and the farther west you travel, the more the sea becomes an overwhelming presence. On the whole, the northern coast is more rugged, the cliffs dropping dramatically to tiny coves and beaches, whereas the south coast shelters many more resorts and wider expanses of sand. The crowds gravitate to the south, but there are plenty of remote inlets and estuaries along this southern littoral, and you do not need to go far to find a degree of seclusion.

Unless you confine yourself to a few choice towns—for example, Exeter, Penzance, and Plymouth—you will be at a huge disadvantage without your own transport. The region has a few main arteries, but you should take minor roads whenever possible, if only to see the real West Country at a leisurely pace. Rail travelers can make use of a fast service connecting Exeter, Plymouth, and Penzance, and there's also a good network of bus services.

About the Restaurants & Hotels

The more established restaurants are often completely booked on a Friday or Saturday night, so reserve in advance; the same is true for hotels and other lodgings. Room availability can be scarce on the coasts during August.

Accommodations in the West Country range from national hotel chains, represented in all the region's principal centers, to ancient inns and ubiquitous bed-and-breakfast places. Many farmhouses also rent out rooms, offering tranquillity in rural surroundings, yet these lodgings are often difficult to reach without a car. It's worth finding out about weekend and winter deals that many hotels offer.

WHAT IT COSTS In pounds				
	££££££	££££	£££	££	£
RESTAURANTS	over £22	£18–£22	£13–£17	£7–£12	under £7
HOTELS	over £160	£115–£160	£80–£115	£50–£80	under £50

Restaurant prices are for a main course at dinner. Hotel prices are for two people in a standard double room in high season, including VAT, with no meals or, if indicated, CP (with Continental breakfast), BP (Breakfast Plan, with full breakfast), or MAP (Modified American Plan, with breakfast and dinner).

Timing

Come July and August, traffic chokes the roads leading into the West Country. Somehow the region absorbs all the "grockles," or tourists, although the chances of finding a remote oasis of peace and quiet are severely curtailed. The beaches heave with sunseekers, and the resort towns are either bubbling with zest or unbearably tacky, depending on your point of view. If you must visit in summer, your best option would be to find a secluded hotel and make brief excursions from there. Try to avoid traveling on Saturday, when weekly rentals start and finish and the roads are jammed with vehicles; the August bank holiday (the last weekend of August) is notorious for congested roads. Otherwise, time your visit to coincide with the beginning or end of the summer. The West Country enjoys more hours of sunshine than most other parts of Britain, so you can take your chances with the weather. Fall and spring are good times to escape the crowds, although most people find the sea too cold for swimming and there is often a strong ocean breeze. Most properties not open all year open for Easter and close in late September or October. Those that remain open have reduced hours. Winter has its own special appeal, when the Atlantic waves crash dramatically against the coast and the austere Cornish cliffs are at their most spectacular.

The West Country requires some time to explore. Three days will provide only a sadly limited view of what Somerset and Devon have to offer, and you should avoid excessive traveling at the expense of exploring. If Cornwall in particular beckons, a four-day tour would take in many of its highlights. Even a week would not do justice to this dense region, but it would give you a chance to push on into Cornwall and get a more balanced idea of the West Country.

Numbers in the text correspond to numbers in the margin and on the West Country and Plymouth maps.

If you have 3 days

Start off from the gateway to the West, **Bristol** ❶ ▶, where you should make a point of crossing the Avon Gorge, before heading down the motorway to spend the best part of a day and your first night in 🏨 **Exeter** ❺❻. The cathedral here commands the most attention, but the city has plenty more to offer, with its quayside and fine period architecture. The next morning, follow A30 back east, along the coast to the fishing village of **Beer** ❺❽ before heading inland to **Honiton** ❺❾, a handsome Georgian town renowned for its delicate lace, a collector's delight. Spend your second overnight in 🏨 **Glastonbury** ❹, a small town awash in Arthurian and early Christian myth. Explore the abbey here in the morning—run up to the tor if you're feeling energetic—before making the short hop to the tiny city of **Wells** ❸. Its cathedral is different from Exeter's but is equally grand.

If you have 4 days

This itinerary focuses exclusively on Cornwall. Traveling down along the North Devon coast, stop at the harbor village of **Boscastle** ❶❸ ▶ before steeping yourself in Arthurian legends at **Tintagel** ❶❹, ideally taking a coastal walk here. Overnight in 🏨 **Padstow** ❶❻ and dine on excellent seafood (reserve ahead). The next day, head for **St. Ives** ❶❾, popular with art lovers and beach fans, and push on to the country's westernmost tip, **Land's End** ❷⓪. Stay in 🏨 **Penzance** ❷❸ for your second night; from here you can visit the island castle of **St. Michael's Mount** ❷❹. Then either follow the coast around to tour the **Lizard Peninsula** ❷❻, or head straight for Pendennis Castle in **Falmouth** ❷❼. Across the Carrick Roads estuary basin, explore the sequestered creeks of the Roseland Peninsula, spending your third night in 🏨 **St. Mawes** ❷❾, which has a fine castle. Start early the next day to visit the **Eden Project** ❸❷, a must for anyone with horticultural leanings, and then choose between two superb country piles: Victorian Lanhydrock, near **Bodmin** ❸❹, and **Cotehele House** ❹❼, a Tudor manor house.

If you have 7 days

Once out of **Bristol** ❶ ▶, first up is a tour of the northern coast of Somerset and Devon, making stops at **Dunster** ❻, site of a turreted and battlemented castle, and the twin towns of **Lynton** and **Lynmouth** ❽, in a narrow cleft once likened to a fragment of Switzerland, but, thankfully, outliving the hype. Any of these would make a good place to break for lunch before continuing on to your overnight destination, the cliff-top village of 🏨 **Clovelly** ❶❷. The second day, continue into Cornwall to take in **Tintagel** ❶❹, which, with or without the Arthurian associations, presents a dramatic sight perched on its black rock above the waves. Enjoy a refined seafood lunch in **Padstow** ❶❻ and make a stop in **Newquay** ❶❼ if you want to sample the more down-to-earth fish-and-chips atmosphere and generous beaches of this typical seaside resort. Pull into ⊠ **St. Ives** ⑲ for your second night; the town has a great deal to offer in the way of art and a good selection of hotels and restaurants. After taking in St. Ives the third day, set out for the very tip of the peninsula, **Land's End** ⑳, which is worth exploring on foot. Head for your next overnight, ⊠ **Penzance** ㉓. Nearby, the island fortress of **St. Michael's Mount** ㉔ is clearly visible and demands a closer inspection. Now make a brief sortie into the **Lizard Peninsula** ㉖, basing yourself in the resort of ⊠ **Falmouth** ㉗, which has plenty of accommodations as well as a brace of castles—the imposing Pendennis and its sibling across the estuary, **St. Mawes** ㉙. On your fifth day, begin by exploring seaside **Charlestown** ㉛, leaving the main part of the day for the eye-popping plant collection of the **Eden Project** ㉜, outside St. Austell. Spend the night either in ⊠ **Fowey** ㉝, still a thriving commercial and sailing port, or in ⊠ **Plymouth** ㊲–㊹. Explore Plymouth in the morning and then track north to Dartmoor, making a stop at Castle Drogo, near **Chagford** ㊶; spend your sixth night in ⊠ **Exeter** ㊻. Once you've soaked up the sights of this historic city, head up the M5, swinging east to see the majestic ruins of ⊠ **Glastonbury** ④ and the cathedral at nearby **Wells** ③.

The most notable festivals, with plenty of crowds and congestion, are Padstow's Obby Oss, a traditional celebration of the arrival of summer that takes place around May 1; Helston's Flora Day parades on May 8; the Cornish-themed, weeklong Golowan Festival in Penzance in late June; the Exeter Arts Festival in July; and the St. Ives Festival of Music and the Arts for eight days in mid-September. In addition, many West Country maritime towns host regattas over summer weekends. The best times to visit Devon are late summer and early fall, during the end-of-summer festivals, especially popular in the small towns of eastern Dartmoor.

BRISTOL TO NORTH DEVON

Starting out from Bristol, your journey takes you south to the cathedral city of Wells and continues on via Glastonbury, possibly the Avalon of Arthurian legend. Taunton, to the west, is the capital of cider country and was the focus of fierce skirmishes during the English Civil War. Proceed west along the Somerset coast into Devon, skirting the moorlands of Exmoor and tracing the northern shore via Clovelly.

Bristol

▶ ❶ *120 mi west of London, 46 mi south of Birmingham, 13 mi northwest of Bath.*

A treasure of great historic interest, Bristol can be called the "birthplace of America" with some confidence, for John Cabot and his son Sebastian sailed from the old city docks in 1497 to touch down on the North American mainland, which he claimed for the English crown. Bristol was also the home of William Penn, developer of Pennsylvania, and a haven for John Wesley, whose Methodist movement played a significant role in the history of colonial Georgia. The city had been a major center since medieval times, but in the 17th and 18th centuries it became an important port for the North American trade. Now that the city's industries no longer rely on the docks, the historic harbor along the River Avon has been largely given over to pleasure craft. Arts and entertainment complexes, museums, stores, pubs, and restaurants fill the quayside; and carnivals, speedboat races, and regattas take place here in summer.

Queen Elizabeth I called the rib-vaulted, 14th-century **Church of St. Mary Redcliffe** "the fairest in England." It was built by Bristol merchants who wanted a place in which to pray for the safe (and profitable) voyages of their ships. A chapel holds the arms and armor of Sir William Penn, father of the founder of Pennsylvania. The church is a five-minute walk from Temple Meads train station toward the docks. ✉ *Redcliffe Way* ☎ *0117/929–1487* ☼ *Mon.–Sat. 9–5 (until 4 in winter), Sun. 8–8.*

The **British Empire and Commonwealth Museum,** in engineer Isambard Kingdom Brunel's 19th-century railway station by the modern Temple Meads train station, helps put Bristol in the context of the growth of Britain's colonial empire and the trading organization that succeeded it. It's an absorbing whirl through history and geography, with a fascinating collection of photographs, slides, and grainy film of missionaries and pith-helmeted memsahibs. You'll also find horned Ghanaian headwear made from cowrie shells and beaver-skin hats, the huge demand for which fueled the Canadian beaver-pelt trade. The darker side of the story of the empire is not ignored, with space devoted to slavery, the Opium Wars, and the transportation of convicts to Australia. The interactive exhibits will appeal to children. ✉ *Station Approach, Temple Meads* ☎ *0117/ 925–4980* ⊕ *www.empiremuseum.co.uk* ✑ *£4.95* ☼ *Daily 10–5.*

Among the Dissenters from the Church of England who found a home in Bristol were John Wesley and Charles Wesley, and in 1739 they built the **New Room,** a meeting place that became the first Methodist chapel. Its simplicity contrasts both with Anglican churches and with the modern shopping center hemming it in. The rooms upstairs contain mementos of the early Methodists and material relating to their proselytizing work in Georgia. Call ahead to arrange a tour that can include **Charles Wesley's House** (a 10-minute walk away), a well-restored 18th-century town house where the Wesleys lived while in Bristol. ✉ *Broadmead* ☎ *0117/926–4740* ⊕ *www.methodist.org.uk/new.room* ✑ *Free, tour of New Room and house £4.50, New Room only £2.80* ☼ *Mon.–Sat. and national holidays 10–4.*

☾ **@Bristol,** in the rebuilt Harbourside area, has three science- and nature-theme attractions with innovative exhibits. Explore@Bristol provides a "hands-on, minds-on" experience of science, and Wildwalk@Bristol includes interactive natural history exhibits and a walk through a rain forest aflutter with exotic birds and butterflies. The region's only giant-screen IMAX cinema shows mostly science-related films. Open spaces linking the sites act as a venue for live performances and multimedia activities, with shops, cafés, and restaurants nearby. ✉ *Anchor Rd.* ☎ *0117/909– 2000* ⊕ *www.at-bristol.org.uk* ✑ *£6.50 for 1 attraction (£7.50 for Explore@Bristol), £11 or £12 for 2 attractions, £15.50 or £16.50 for 3 attractions* ☼ *Daily 10–6.*

need a break? The excellent café-restaurant upstairs at the **Watershed Media Centre** (✉ 1 Canon's Rd. ☎ 0117/927–6444) overlooks part of the harborside. Sandwiches, salads, and hot snacks are served during the day, as well as coffees and cakes; there's a bar, too.

On view in the harbor stands the **SS *Great Britain,*** the first iron ship to cross the Atlantic. Built by the great English engineer Isambard Brunel in 1843, it remained in service until the end of the century, first on the North American route and then on the Australian. Moored alongside is a replica of the *Matthew,* the tiny craft that carried John Cabot to

North America in 1497. Your entry ticket also admits you to the **Maritime Heritage Centre,** which gives the lowdown on both vessels as well as an overview of Bristol's seafaring history. ⊠ *Great Western Dockyard, Gas Ferry Rd.* ☎ *0117/926–0680* ⊕ *www.ss-great-britain.com* 🖃 *£6.25* ⊙ *Apr.–Oct., daily 10–5:30; Nov.–Mar., daily 10–4:30.*

In the Georgian suburb of Clifton—a sort of Bath in miniature—you can take in a monument to Victorian engineering, the 702-foot-long **Clifton Suspension Bridge** (⊠ Suspension Bridge Rd., Clifton), which spans the Avon Gorge. Work began on Isambard Brunel's design in 1831, but the bridge was not completed until 1864. In spring 2004, the **Clifton Suspension Bridge Visitor Centre** (☎ 0117/974–4664 ⊕ .www.clifton-suspension-bridge.org.uk) will open on a site adjacent to the Bristol end of the bridge. It will have an exhibition on the bridge and its construction, including a model that illustrates how the engineering works.

☝ **Bristol Zoo Gardens,** alongside the leafy expanse of Clifton Downs, is one of the country's most famous zoos. More than 300 animal species live in 12 acres of landscaped gardens; the Seal and Penguin Coasts, with underwater viewing, are rival attractions for Gorilla Island, Bug World, Twilight World, and the walk-through aviary. ⊠ *Clifton Down* ☎ *0117/ 973–8951* ⊕ *www.bristolzoo.org.uk* 🖃 *£8.90* ⊙ *June–Aug., daily 9–5:30; Sept.–May, daily 9–5.*

> **off the beaten path**

TYNTESFIELD – The National Trust rescued this extravagant, 35-bedroom Victorian Gothic Revival mansion in 2002 and will gradually restore it, but you can explore the house and formal gardens if you prebook a two-hour tour. Besides magnificent woodwork, stained glass, and original furniture and fabrics, the house contains the latest modern conveniences of the 1860s, such as a heated billiard table and gaslights in the garden. The ornate chapel, with its mosaics and ironwork, is remarkable. Tyntesfield is 7 mi south of Bristol. ⊠ *Wraxall* ☎ *0870/241–4500 for tours* ⊕ *www. nationaltrust.org.uk, www.ticketmaster.co.uk for tours* 🖃 *£10* ⊙ *Late Mar.–early Nov., Sun., Mon., Wed., and Thurs. 10–2.*

Where to Stay & Eat

For a notable overture to your West Country excursion, you might book a night at Thornbury Castle, 12 mi north of Bristol in Thornbury (⇨ Berkeley Castle *in* Chapter 7).

££–££££ ✕ **Bell's Diner.** A local institution, this bistro in the Montpelier area occupies a converted corner shop and has Bristol prints on its pale gray walls and polished wooden floors. The inventive Mediterranean menu changes regularly and includes organic and wild ingredients, as well as toothsome desserts such as goat cheese ice cream with figs. Bell's is rather hidden—take A38 (Stokes Croft) north, then turn right on Ashley Road and immediately left at Picton Street, which will lead you to York Road. ⊠ *1 York Rd.* ☎ *0117/924–0357* ▤ *AE, MC, V* ⊙ *Closed Sun. and Dec. 24–30. No lunch Sat. and Mon.*

££–£££ ✕ **Old India.** Bristol's former stock exchange has found a new role as a fashionable Indian eatery. All the opulent trimmings have been restored, including the mahogany paneling, rich drapes, and a tiled staircase overlooked by elegant statuary. It's the perfect setting for classic Indian cuisine and such innovative dishes as *niljiri korma* (chicken breast in a mild curry sauce with rose petals) and *macchi mazadaar* (salmon with mustard seeds, coconut, curry leaves, and tamarind water). The two-course lunch menu is a particularly good deal. ⊠ *34 St. Nicholas St.* ☎ *0117/922–1136* ▤ *AE, DC, MC, V.*

4

Great Flavors From cider to cream teas, there are specialties to tempt your palate in the West Country. Lamb, venison, and, in Devon and Cornwall, seafood are favored in the region's restaurants, which have improved markedly, notably through the influence of Rick Stein's culinary empire in Padstow, in Cornwall. Seafood is celebrated at fishy frolics that include the Newlyn Fish Fair (late August) and Falmouth's Oyster Festival (early October). Somerset is the home of Britain's most famous cheese—the ubiquitous cheddar, from the Mendip Hills village. Do try to taste real farmhouse cheddar, made in the traditional barrel shape known as a truckle. Devon's caloric cream teas consist of a pot of tea, homemade scones, and lots of thickened clotted cream and strawberry jam (clotted, or specially thickened cream, is a regional specialty and is sometimes called Devonshire cream). Cornwall's specialty is the pasty, a pastry shell filled with chopped meat, onions, and potatoes. The pasty was devised as a handy way for miners to carry their dinner to work; today's versions are rather pale imitations of the original. Scrumpy, a homemade dry cider, is refreshing but carries a kick. Look out, too, for perry, similar to cider but made from pears. English wine, similar to German wine, is made in Somerset, and in Cornwall you can find a variant of age-old mead made from local honey.

Walking The coasts and moors of the West Country provide wonderfully varied walking. A fine 10-mi walk is a cliff-top hike along the coast from Hartland Quay, near Clovelly, down to Lower Sharpnose Point, just above Bude. Longer hikes in the bleak, unpeopled region of Dartmoor—for example, the tors south of Okehampton—are appropriate only for the most experienced walkers, though the areas around Widgery Cross, Becky Falls, and the Bovey Valley, and the short but dramatic walk along Lydford Gorge, will appeal to everyone. Walking on Exmoor is less rigorous and offers spectacular views over the Bristol Channel. In Cornwall, the coast around Tintagel is also splendidly scenic. If you are interested in longer "theme" walks, note the Saints Way, a 30-mi walk between Padstow and the Camel Estuary on Cornwall's north coast to Fowey on the south coast. Britain's longest national trail, the South West Coast Path, runs for 630 mi from Minehead (Somerset) to South Haven Point, near Poole (Dorset).

Water Sports The beaches lining parts of the peninsula have made the West Country one of Britain's main family vacation destinations. Natives don't mind the water's temperature, but foreigners, many of them pampered by the warm waves of the Mediterranean, are not so eager to brave the elements. The sea—even in Cornwall, where it seems to be warmer than anywhere else in the British Isles—is not to be enjoyed in a sensuous way: it is a bracing experience that sometimes leaves you shivering and breathless. At many major resorts, flags show the limits of safe swimming. There can be strong undertows, especially on the northern coast, which has the region's best surfing beaches. Looe, on the south coast of Cornwall, is known for shark fishing, and you can rent boats for shark or mackerel fishing from harbors along the south coast. This is a good sailing area, with plenty of safe harbors, marinas, and deepwater channels, mainly at Falmouth, Plymouth Sound, and Torbay.

The West Country

GREAT
BRITAIN

ATLANTIC OCEAN

Bideford Bay

Braunto
Burrow
Natur
Reserv

Clovelly **12**

Hartland Quay ○

D E V C

Lower Sharpnose
Point ○

A39

Bude ○

B3254

A388

Bude Bay

Boscastle ▶
13 B3263

A39

Tintagel **14**
B3314

Launceston

Lewdown

A30

Port Isaac
15 B3314

A388

36

Padstow
Wadebridge **16**

Bolventor ○

Lydfo
Gor

B3276

BODMIN
MOOR

Dozmary
35 Pool

Cotehele
House
& Quay

4

Newquay **17**

A30

Bodmin **34** A38

A391

Perranporth **18**

Eden
Project

Fral

32

33 Fowey

Looe ○

Truro **30**

St. Austell ○

St. Ives

B3289

A390

31 Charlestown

Zennor

19

A30

Portloe ○

B3306

Pendeen ○

CORNWALL

28 Trelissick

Penzance

St. Michael's
Mount

A394

Falmouth **27** **29**

Carrick Roads

Newlyn

23 **24**

A394

St. Mawes

Land's
End **20**

22

25

Helston

Gweek

B3291

Porthcurno B3315

21

Mousehole

A3083

*GOONHILLY
DOWNS*

TO ISLES OF SCILLY

*Kynance
Cove*

B3293

26

Lizard
Peninsula

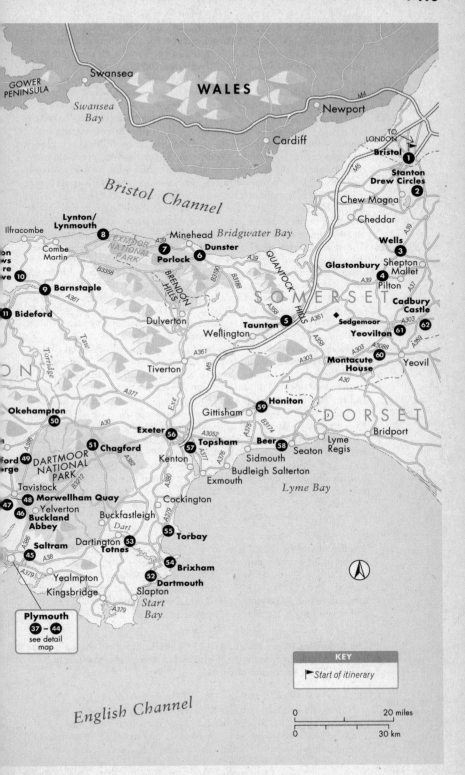

GOWER
PENINSULA

Swansea

WALES

*Swansea
Bay*

Newport

Cardiff

M4

Bristol Channel

TO
LONDON

Bristol ①

M5

**Stanton
Drew Circles** ②

Chew Magna

Cheddar

A39

Wells ③

Shepton
Mallet

Glastonbury

Pilton

A39

A37

Ilfracombe

Combe
Martin

**Lynton/
Lynmouth**

⑧ EXMOOR
NATIONAL
PARK

A39 Minehead *Bridgwater Bay*

⑦ **Porlock**

⑥ **Dunster**

A39

B3190

A39

QUANTOCK

B3188

S O M E R S E T

**Cadbury
Castle**

⑩

B3358

BRENDON
HILLS

Sedgemoor ◆

A303

⑥②

Yeovilton ⑥①

⑨ **Barnstaple**

A361

Dulverton

A358

HILLS

A361

A303

A3088

⑥⓪

A361

⑪ **Bideford**

Taw

Torridge

Wellington

Taunton ⑤

A358

A303

A358

**Montacute
House**

A30

Yeovil

Yeovil

Tiverton

M5

Exe

A377

Honiton ⑤⑨

D O R S E T

Okehampton

⑤⓪

A386

A30

Gittisham

A3052

B3174

Bridport

Exeter ⑤⑥

Topsham ⑤⑦

A376

Beer ⑤⑧

Seaton

Lyme
Regis

⑤① **Chagford**

A382

Kenton

A377

Sidmouth

ford ④⑨
rge

DARTMOOR
NATIONAL
PARK

A386

B3212

Budleigh Salterton

Exmouth

Lyme Bay

Tavistock

④⑧ **Morwellham Quay**

Yelverton

Cockington

A379

④⑦

④⑥ **Buckland
Abbey**

A386

Buckfastleigh

Dart

Torbay

⑤⑤

④⑤ **Saltram**

A38

Dartington

Totnes ⑤③

Dartmouth

⑤④ **Brixham**

Yealmpton

Kingsbridge

⑤②
Slapton

*Start
Bay*

A379

Plymouth

③⑦ – ④④
see detail
map

English Channel

KEY

▶*Start of itinerary*

0   20 miles

0   30 km

£–££ ✕ **Wagamama.** Part of a chain that has expanded from London, this centrally located noodle bar is a convenient spot for nourishing chicken ramen (soup and noodles topped with grilled chicken breast) or salmon *karoke* (salmon and potato cakes in a sweet tamarind sauce). White walls and plain wooden tables and benches make a minimalist statement. Helpings are abundant, and the service is fast and courteous. ⊠ *63 Queens Rd.* ☎ *0117/922–1188* 🖃 *AE, DC, MC, V.*

££££ ✕🖻 **Hotel du Vin.** This hip Anglo-French minichain has established an ambitious outlet in the Sugar House—six former sugar-refining warehouses—close to the docklands and the city center. Rooms are crisply contemporary in style, with CD players and huge showers, but retain many of the original industrial features. The restaurant's wine list is extensive—visit the cellar for a private tasting session—and the menu entices with modern but robust French flavors. ⊠ *Narrow Lewins Mead, BS1 2NU* ☎ *0117/925–5577* 🖷 *0117/925–1199* ⊕ *www.hotelduvin.com* 📡 *35 rooms, 5 suites* ♨ *Restaurant, in-room data ports, cable TV, billiards, bar, meeting rooms; no a/c in some rooms* 🖃 *AE, DC, MC, V.*

££££ 🖻 **Redwood Lodge Hotel.** Primarily a business hotel and health center, this makes a handy stopover for anyone touring by car—it's just off A4, close to the Clifton Suspension Bridge. Modern and attractively furnished, the hotel has a number of amenities, including 16 acres of woodland surroundings. Weekend rates are a good value. ⊠ *Beggar Bush La., Failand, BS8 3TG* ☎ *01275/393901* 🖷 *01275/392104* ⊕ *www.regalhotels. co.uk* 📡 *112 rooms* ♨ *2 restaurants, cable TV, tennis court, indoor-outdoor pool, gym, squash, cinema; no a/c* 🖃 *AE, DC, MC, V.*

££ 🖻 **Naseby House Hotel.** On a tree-lined street in the heart of elegant Clifton, this Victorian hotel is not far from Bristol's major sights. The basement holds the plushest, most expensive bedroom, with a four-poster and a French door opening onto the garden. Period pieces fill the sitting room, and the breakfast room is also impressive. ⊠ *105 Pembroke Rd., BS8 3EF* ☎ *0117/973–7859* ⊕ *www.nasebyhousehotel.co.uk* 📡 *16 rooms, 15 with bath* ♨ *Some pets allowed; no a/c* 🖃 *MC, V* ⏣ *BP.*

£ 🖻 **Sunderland Guest House.** The rooms at this simple Georgian town house are small and plain, but clean and comfortable enough to ensure a tranquil night's sleep. The main advantage here is a location in a quiet Clifton lane, very close to the city center. Breakfast is self-service. ⊠ *4 Sunderland Pl., BS8 1NA* ☎ *0117/973–7249* ✍ *sunderland. gh@blueyonder.co.uk* 📡 *10 rooms, 4 with bath* ♨ *No a/c, no smoking* 🖃 *No credit cards* ⏣ *CP.*

Nightlife & the Arts

The **Bristol Old Vic** (⊠ King St. ☎ 0117/987–7877), the oldest working theater in the country, dates to 1766. Performances, from classics to new works, are staged in three spaces. **St. George's** (⊠ Great George St., off Park St. ☎ 0117/923–0359), a former church built in the 18th century, serves as one of the country's leading acoustic venues for classical, jazz, and world music. Regular lunchtime concerts are scheduled.

Sports

The **Badminton Horse Trials** (☎ 01454/218272) are held annually during four days in May at the duke of Beaufort's magnificent estate in Badminton, 12 mi northeast of Bristol.

en route   The area south of Bristol is notable for its scenery and walks, attractive villages, and ancient stone circles. Take A38 (follow signs for the airport), then B3130 and B3114 to the villages of Chew Magna and Chew Stoke. At Chew Magna note the gargoyles on the ancient church. Continue on to Chew Valley Lake, a reservoir in a drowned valley surrounded by woods that shelter 240 species of birds.

Stanton Drew Circles

2 *6 mi south of Bristol, 10 mi west of Bath.*

Three rings, two avenues of standing stones, and a burial chamber make up the Stanton Drew Circles, one of the grandest and most mysterious monuments in Britain, dating from 3000 to 2000 BC. Excavations beneath the circles in 1997 revealed evidence of an older site, from around 3000 BC, consisting of a wood henge, or timber circle. Its great size suggests that it was once as important as Stonehenge for its ceremonial functions, although little of great visual impact remains. The site lies in a field reached through a farmyard—you'll need suitable shoes to visit it. English Heritage supervises the stones, which stand on private land. Access is given at any reasonable time, and a small admission may be requested. To get here from Chew Magna, turn east on B3130; the circles are just east of the village of Stanton Drew. ⊠ *B3130, Stanton Drew* ☎ *0117/975-0700* ⊕ *www.english-heritage.org.uk.*

Wells

3 *16 mi south of Stanton Drew Circles, 22 mi south of Bristol, 132 mi west of London.*

England's smallest cathedral city, with a population of 10,000, lies at the foot of the Mendip Hills. Although it feels more like a quiet country town than a city, Wells contains one of the masterpieces of Gothic architecture, its great cathedral—the first to be built in the early English style. The city's name refers to the underground streams that bubble up into St. Andrew's Well within the grounds of the Bishop's Palace. Spring water has run through High Street since the 15th century. Seventeenth-century buildings surround the ancient marketplace in the city center. Wells has market days on Wednesday and Saturday.

★ The great west towers of the medieval **Cathedral Church of St. Andrew,** the oldest surviving English Gothic church, can be seen for miles. Dating from the 12th century, the cathedral derives its beauty from the perfect harmony of all of its parts, the glowing colors of its original stained-glass windows, and its peaceful setting among stately trees and majestic lawns. To appreciate the elaborate west front facade, approach the building on foot from the cathedral green, accessible from Market Place through a great medieval gate called "penniless porch" (named after the beggars who once waited here to collect alms from worshipers). The cathedral's west front is twice as wide as it is high, and some 300 statues of kings and saints adorn it. Inside, vast inverted arches were added in 1338 to stop the central tower from sinking to one side. The cathedral also has a rare medieval clock, consisting of the seated figure of a man called Jack Blandiver, who strikes a bell on the quarter hour while mounted knights circle in mock battle. Near the clock is the entrance to the Chapter House—a small wooden door opening onto a great sweep of stairs worn down on one side by the tread of pilgrims over the centuries. Free 45-minute guided tours begin at the information desk. Tours are suspended April–October during Quiet Hour between noon and 1. ⊠ *Cathedral Green* ☎ *01749/674483* ⊕ *www.wellscathedral. org.uk* ⊠ *£4.50 suggested donation* ☉ *Apr.–Sept., Mon.–Sat. 9:30–7, Sun. 12:30–2:30; Oct.–Mar., Mon.–Sat. 9:30–6, Sun. 12:30–2:30. Open longer on Sun. for services.*

The Bishop's Eye gate leading from Market Place takes you to the magnificent moat-ringed **Bishop's Palace,** which still contains most of the original 12th- and 13th-century residence. You can also see the ruins of a late-13th-century great hall. The hall lost its roof in the 16th century because Edward VI needed to use the lead it contained. ⊠ *Market Pl.* ☎ *01749/678691* ⊠ *£3.50* ☉ *Apr.–July, Sept., and Oct., Tues.–Fri. and national holidays 10:30–6, Sun. 1–6; Aug., daily 10:30–6 (may close Sat. or Mon. in Aug.); last admission at 5.*

To the north of the cathedral, the cobbled **Vicar's Close,** one of Europe's oldest streets, has terraces of handsome 14th-century houses with strange, tall chimneys. A tiny medieval chapel here is still in use.

off the beaten path

WOOKEY HOLE CAVES – Signs in Wells's town center direct you 2 mi north to limestone caves in the Mendip Hills that may have been the home of Iron Age people. Here, according to ancient legend, the Witch of Wookey turned to stone. You can tour the caves, including an underground lake, and visit a museum, a working paper mill, and a penny arcade full of Victorian amusement machines worked by predecimal pennies. ☎ *01749/672243* ⊕ *www.wookey.co.uk* ⊠ *£8.80* ☉ *Apr.–Oct., daily 10–5; Nov.–Mar., daily 10:30–4:30.*

Where to Stay & Eat

££££–£££££ ✕ **Ritcher's.** You can choose between eating downstairs in the bistro or in the more formal, plant-filled restaurant upstairs. Both serve good-value two- or three-course fixed-price meals. Among the dishes are rump of lamb with mushroom and truffle risotto and pan-fried pheasant breast with bubble and squeak (a fried mixture of mashed potatoes and greens such as cabbage). ⊠ *5 Sadler St.* ☎ *01749/679085* ⊟ *MC, V.*

£££–££££ ✕▥ **Swan Hotel.** A former coaching inn built in the 15th century, the Swan faces the cathedral. Bedrooms, furnished with antiques, are done in subtle, restful colors; nine rooms have four-posters. The restaurant prepares traditional English roasts and fish dishes and displays costumes owned by the great Victorian actor Sir Henry Irving. ⊠ *11 Sadler St., BA5 2RX* ☎ *01749/836300* 🖷 *01749/836301* ⊕ *www.Bhere.co.uk* ☞ *50 rooms* ♨ *Restaurant, in-room data ports, bar, meeting rooms; no a/c* ⊟ *AE, DC, MC, V* ⎥⊙⎢ *BP.*

££–£££ ✕▥ **The Crown.** This hotel has been a landmark in Wells since the Middle Ages; William Penn was arrested here in 1695 for preaching without a license. A period atmosphere remains, although guest rooms (with the exception of four rooms with four-posters) are furnished in Swedish modern style. The Penn Bar serves salads and such hot dishes as steak-and-kidney pie, or you can eat in the more comfortable French bistro, Anton's. ⊠ *Market Pl., BA5 2RP* ☎ *01749/673457* 🖷 *01749/679792* ⊕ *www.crownatwells.co.uk* ☞ *15 rooms* ♨ *Restaurant, bar, some pets allowed; no a/c, no room phones* ⊟ *AE, MC, V* ⎥⊙⎢ *BP.*

££ ✕▥ **Ancient Gate House.** The guest rooms of this centrally located restaurant run by Franco Rossi and his two sons make a convenient base. The premises, dating back to 1473, incorporate the Great West Gate and are full of character. There's an ancient stone staircase, and many rooms have four-posters. You can dine well on either Italian or English dishes, made largely from local produce, in the Rugantino restaurant. ⊠ *20 Sadler St., BA5 2SE* ☎ *01749/672029* 🖷 *01749/670319* ⊕ *www.ancientgatehouse.co.uk* ☞ *9 rooms* ♨ *Restaurant, bar, some pets allowed; no a/c* ⊟ *AE, DC, MC, V* ⎥⊙⎢ *BP.*

Glastonbury

★ ❹ *5 mi southwest of Wells, 27 mi south of Bristol, 27 mi southwest of Bath.*

A town steeped in history, myth, and legend, Glastonbury lies in the lee of Glastonbury Tor, a grassy hill rising 520 feet above the Somerset Levels (drained marshes). In legend, Glastonbury is identified with Avalon, the paradise into which King Arthur was reborn after his death. It is also said to be the burial place of Arthur and Guinevere, his queen. According to Christian tradition, it was to Glastonbury, the first Christian settlement in England, that Joseph of Arimathea brought the Holy Grail, the chalice used by Christ at the Last Supper. Partly because of these associations, the town has acquired renown as a New Age center, mixing crystal gazers with Druids, yogis, and aging hippies, who are variously in search of Arthur, Merlin, Jesus—and even Elvis.

At the foot of **Glastonbury Tor** is **Chalice Well,** the legendary burial place of the Grail. It's a stiff climb up the tor, but you'll be rewarded by the fabulous view across the Vale of Avalon. At the top stands a ruined tower, all that remains of **St. Michael's Church,** which collapsed after a landslide in 1271.

The ruins of the great **Glastonbury Abbey,** in the center of town, are on the site where, according to legend, Joseph of Arimathea built a church in the 1st century. A monastery had certainly been erected here by the 9th century, and the site drew many pilgrims. The ruins are those of the abbey completed in 1524 and destroyed in 1539, during Henry VIII's dissolution of the monasteries. A sign south of the Lady Chapel marks the sites where Arthur and Guinevere were supposedly buried. ⊠ *Magdalene St.* ☎ *01458/832267* ⊕ *www.glastonburyabbey.com* 🎫 *£3.50* ⊘ *Feb., daily 10–5; Mar., daily 9:30–5:30; Apr.–May and Sept., daily 9:30–6; June–Aug., daily 9–6; Oct., daily 9:30–5; Nov., daily 9:30–4:30; Dec.–Jan., daily 10–4:30; last admission 30 mins before closing.*

The **Somerset Rural Life Museum** occupies an impressive 14th-century tithe barn, named the Abbey Barn. More than 90 feet in length, it once stored the one-tenth portion of the town's produce that was owed to the church. Exhibits (some in a Victorian farmhouse) illustrate 19th-century farming. Events especially designed for children take place most weekends during school holidays. ⊠ *Chilkwell St.* ☎ *01458/831197* ⊕ *www.somerset.gov.uk/museums* 🎫 *Free* ⊘ *Weekdays 10–5, weekends 2–6.*

Where to Stay

££ 🏨 **George and Pilgrims Hotel.** Pilgrims en route to Glastonbury Abbey stayed here in the 15th century. Today the stone-front hotel is equipped with all the modern comforts but retains its flagstone floors, wooden beams, and antique furniture; three rooms have four-posters. ⊠ *1 High St., BA6 9DP* ☎ *01458/831146* 🖷 *01458/832252* ⊕ *www.georgeandpilgrims. activehotels.com* 🛏 *13 rooms* 🍴 *Restaurant, bar, meeting rooms, some pets allowed (fee); no a/c* ☰ *MC, V* ⧉ *BP.*

Nightlife & the Arts

Held annually a few miles away in Pilton, the **Glastonbury Festival** (☎ 01749/890470) is the biggest and perhaps the best rock festival in England. For three days over the last weekend in June, it hosts hundreds of bands—a mix of established and up-and-coming, with a few big names from the past—on five stages. Pick up an issue of *New Musical Express* for the complete lineup. Festival tickets are steep—around £90—but include entertainment, a camping area, and service facilities.

Shopping

Glastonbury's market day is Tuesday. **Morlands Factory Shop** (✉ 25 High St. Street ☎ 01458/448811), 2 mi southwest of Glastonbury in the village of Street, is one of several good outlets for sheepskin products in Somerset sheep country, selling coats, slippers, and rugs.

en route

West of Glastonbury, take A39 and A361 toward Taunton to cross the Somerset Levels, marshes that were drained by open ditches (known as "rhines") for peat digging, an industry that is now heavily restricted. The broad, marshy expanse of **Sedgemoor** is where, in 1685, the troops of James II routed those of his nephew, the duke of Monmouth, in the last battle fought on English soil; a flagstaff and memorial stones indicate the site. R. D. Blackmore's novel *Lorna Doone*, published in 1869, is set during Monmouth's Rebellion.

Taunton

❺ *22 mi southwest of Glastonbury, 50 mi southwest of Bristol, 18 mi northeast of Exeter.*

Somerset's principal town lies in the heart of cider-making country in the fertile Vale of Taunton. Two of the loveliest examples of the county's famous pinnacled and battlemented churches, St. James and St. Mary Magdalene, overlook the county cricket ground in the center of town. Taunton is most celebrated for its cider, which is the traditional beverage in these parts. Beware—it can be far more potent than beer. In the fall, some cider mills open their doors to visitors. The grounds of **Sheppys,** a local farm and cider museum, include orchards and a fishpond and are always open for picnickers. There's a café (summer only) and farm shop. ✉ *Three Bridges, on A38 west of Taunton, Bradford-on-Tone* ☎ *01823/461233* ⊕ *www.sheppyscider.com* 🔒 *Museum £2, guided tour (2½ hrs) £4.75* ⊙ *Mid-Apr.–Dec. 25, Mon.–Sat. 8:30–6, Sun. noon–2; late Dec.–mid-Apr., Mon.–Sat. 8:30–6.*

Where to Stay & Eat

££–£££ ✕ **Brettons.** This small, casual spot serves both light lunches, such as pastas and curries, and more substantial meals, including John Dory, medallions of pork, and vegetarian choices. It's a 10-minute walk from the center of town. ✉ *49 East Reach* ☎ *01823/256688* 🖃 *MC, V* ⊙ *Closed Sun. No lunch Sat., Mon.*

★ **£££££** ✕🖭 **The Castle.** The battlements and turrets of this 300-year-old stone building look particularly fine from April to June, when the 150-year-old wisteria covering the facade is in flower. Rooms are individually decorated with chintz and period furniture. The outstanding restaurant has creative daily-changing, fixed-price menus. Specialties include jellied tomato consommé and pan-fried Brixham scallops, and there's a great cheese board. Softer on the wallet, the informal Brazz dishes up pastas, salads, and deluxe burgers and french fries. ✉ *Castle Green, TA1 1NF* ☎ *01823/272671* 🖷 *01823/336066* ⊕ *www.the-castle-hotel.com* 🖘 *39 rooms, 5 suites* ♨ *2 restaurants, bar, meeting rooms, in-room data ports, some pets allowed (fee); no a/c* 🖃 *AE, DC, MC, V* ⭐ *BP.*

en route

North of Taunton you will see the outlines of the **Quantock and Brendon hills.** Herds of red deer live in the beech-covered eastern Quantocks. Climb to the top of the hills for a spectacular view of the Vale of Taunton Deane and, to the north, the Bristol Channel.

Dunster

6 *21 mi northwest of Taunton, 43 mi north of Exeter.*

Lying between the Somerset coast and the edge of Exmoor National Park, Dunster is a picture-book village with a broad main street. The eight-sided yarn-market building on High Street dates from 1589. **Dunster Castle**, a 13th-century fortress remodeled in 1868–72, dominates the village. Acres of parkland surround the building, which has fine plaster ceilings and a magnificent 17th-century oak staircase. The climb up to the castle from the parking lot is steep. ⊠ *Off A39* ☎ *01643/823004* ⊕ *www. nationaltrust.org.uk* ⊡ *£6.40, gardens only £3.50* ☉ *Castle late Mar.–late Oct., Sat.–Wed. 11–5; last wk Oct., Sat.–Wed. 11–4. Gardens late Mar.–late Oct., daily 10–5; late Oct.–late Mar., daily 11–4.*

Exmoor National Park

20 mi northwest of Taunton.

Less wild and forbidding than Dartmoor to its south, 267-square-mi Exmoor National Park is no less majestic for its bare heath and lofty views. The park extends right up to the coast and straddles the county border between Somerset and Devon. Although more interwoven with cultivated farmland and pasturage than Dartmoor, Exmoor can be just as desolate. Taking one of the many paths and bridleways through the bracken and heather (at its best in the fall), you might glimpse the ponies and red deer for which the region is noted, and you may well encounter a local hunt at full gallop. Be careful: the proximity of the coast means that mists and squalls can descend with alarming suddenness. There are national park visitor centers at Combe Martin, County Gate, Dulverton, Dunster, and Lynmouth. *Exmoor National Park Authority,* ⊠ *Exmoor House, Dulverton, TA22 9HL* ☎ *01398/323665* ⊕ *www. exmoor-nationalpark.gov.uk* ⊡ *Free.*

Porlock

7 *6 mi west of Dunster, 45 mi north of Exeter.*

Buried at the bottom of a valley, with the slopes of Exmoor all about, the small, unspoiled town of Porlock lies near the fabled Doone Country, setting for R. D. Blackmore's swashbuckling saga *Lorna Doone*. Porlock had already achieved a small place in literary history after Coleridge declared it was a "man from Porlock" who interrupted his opium trance while the poet was composing "Kubla Khan."

The small harbor in the town of **Porlock Weir** is the starting point for an undemanding 2-mi walk along the coast through chestnut and walnut trees to **St. Culbone** (☎ 01598/741270), reputedly the smallest and most isolated church in England. Saxon in origin, it has a small Victorian spire and is lighted by candles only. It would be hard to find a more enchanting spot.

Where to Stay & Eat

££–£££ ✕⊡ **Andrew's on the Weir.** Calling itself a restaurant with rooms, this waterfront Georgian hotel is pure relaxed English country house with touches of glamour. Guest rooms have pretty drapes and patchwork quilts. The ambitious contemporary menu takes advantage of seafood, local pork, and duckling, and you can expect interesting desserts, such as grapefruit mousse, and excellent local cheeses. ⊠ *Porlock Weir, TA24 8PB* ☎ *01643/863300* ⊟ *01643/863311* ⊕ *www.andrewsontheweir.co.uk* ⟿ *5 rooms* ⟋ *Restaurant, bar, some pets allowed; no a/c, no kids under 12* ⊟ *AE, DC, MC, V* ☉ *Closed mid-Jan. and mid-Nov.* ⊺⊙⎸ *BP.*

> en route As you're heading west from Porlock to Lynton, the coast road A39 mounts **Porlock Hill,** an incline so steep that signs encourage drivers to "keep going." The views across Exmoor and north to the Bristol Channel and Wales are worth it.

Lynton & Lynmouth

⑧ *13 mi west of Porlock, 60 mi northwest of Exeter.*

A steep hill separates this pretty pair of Devonshire villages, which are linked by a water-powered cliff railway. Lynmouth, a fishing village at the bottom of the hill, crouches below 1,000-foot cliffs at the mouths of the East and West Lynne rivers. To 19th-century visitors, the place evoked an Alpine scene. The grand landscape of Exmoor lies all about, with undemanding walks possible to Watersmeet or the Valley of the Rocks, two local beauty spots.

Where to Stay & Eat

£££–££££ ✗◻ **Rising Sun.** A 14th-century inn and a row of thatched cottages make up this attractive hotel with great views over the Bristol Channel. One cottage is said to have hosted the poet Percy Bysshe Shelley on his honeymoon. In the main building, creaking staircases and corridors lead to cozy rooms decorated in stylish print fabrics and furnished with pine or older pieces. The traditional restaurant specializes in local cuisine, including such dishes as Devonshire beef fillet, and there's a superb game menu December through February. ✉ *Harbourside, Lynmouth, EX35 6EQ* ☎ *01598/753223* 🖷 *01598/753480* ⊕ *www.risingsunlynmouth.co.uk* ➷ *19 rooms, 1 cottage* ⌂ *Restaurant, fishing, bar; no a/c, no kids under 7, no smoking* ☰ *AE, DC, MC, V* ⬤ *BP.*

★ ££–£££ ◻ **Shelley's Hotel.** The second of Lynmouth's two hotels that claim to be Percy Bysshe Shelley's honeymoon haunt does not have such a fine location as the Rising Sun, but it's more spacious and modern inside. Bright rooms have big windows and good views, and the staff is cheerful and helpful. Shelley and his 16-year-old bride, Harriet Westbrook, apparently left without paying their bill—although the poet later mailed £20 of the £30 owed. During his nine-week sojourn in Lynmouth, Shelley found time to write his polemical *Queen Mab.* ✉ *8 Watersmeet Rd., Lynmouth, EX35 6EP* ☎ *01598/753219* 🖷 *01598/753751* ⊕ *www.shelleyshotel.co.uk* ➷ *11 rooms* ⌂ *Restaurant, bar; no a/c, no smoking* ☰ *MC, V* ⬤ *BP.*

Barnstaple

⑨ *21 mi southwest of Lynton, 42 mi northwest of Exeter.*

Northern Devon's largest town sits on the banks of the River Taw, with a bustling center that retains its traditional role as the region's principal market. West of Barnstaple, along the Taw estuary, desolate stretches of sand dunes offer long vistas of marram grass and sea.

Off the crowded High Street, you can catch the colorful scene at the timber-roofed **Pannier Market,** where crafts are traded on Monday and Thursday, antiques on Wednesday, and general goods and local produce on Tuesday, Friday, and Saturday. The 33 arches of **Butchers Row,** opposite the Pannier Market, still hold a handful of mainly identical butcher's shops, as well as other food stores. The 14th-century **St. Anne's Chapel,** between High Street and Boutport Street, became a grammar school in 1549; John Gay (1685–1732), author of *The Beggar's Opera,* was a pupil here.

Where to Stay & Eat

££–£££ ╳⌘ **Royal and Fortescue Hotel.** Edward VII, who stayed here when he was prince of Wales, gave this Victorian hotel the royal part of its name. It's set by the river in the center of town, although the functionally furnished rooms have no view to speak of. You can dine in the excellent bistro, 62 The Bank, or in the self-service Lord Fortescue's. ⌂ *Boutport St., EX31 1HG* ☎ *01271/342289* 🖷 *01271/340102* ⊕ *www. royalfortescue.co.uk* ⇔ *51 rooms* ⌂ *2 restaurants, cable TV, bar; no a/c* ⊟ *AE, DC, MC, V* ⍾⌐ *BP.*

Braunton Burrows Nature Reserve

❿ *5 mi west of Barnstaple, 18 mi southwest of Lynton.*

Miles of trails run through the dunes at this nature reserve on the north side of the Taw estuary. Bird-watching is first class, especially in winter, and the reserve warden can put people in touch with organized walks. Talks are held in the **Countryside Centre** (⌂ Caen Car park, Braunton ⊙ Easter–Oct., Mon.–Sat. 10–4). ⌂ *Off B3231, 2 mi west of Braunton* ☎ *01271/812552 for warden.*

Bideford

⓫ *8 mi southwest of Barnstaple, 49 mi northwest of Exeter.*

The confluence of the rivers Taw and Torridge feeds Broad Bideford Bay. Bideford lies on the Torridge, which you can cross either by the 14th-century 24-arch bridge or by the more modern structure to reach the scenic hillside sheltering the town's elegant houses. The area was a mainstay of 16th-century shipbuilding; the trusty vessels of Sir Francis Drake were built here. From the Norman era until the 18th century, the port was the property of the Grenville family, whose most celebrated scion was Sir Richard Grenville (circa 1541–91), commander of the seven ships that carried the first settlers to Virginia, and later a key player in the defeat of the Spanish Armada.

Clovelly

⓬ *12 mi west of Bideford, 60 mi northwest of Exeter.*

Fodor'sChoice
★

Lovely Clovelly always seems to have the sun shining on its flower-lined cottages and stepped and cobbled streets. Alas, its beauty is well known, and day-trippers can overrun the village. Perched precariously among cliffs, a steep, cobbled road—tumbling down at such an angle that it's closed to cars—leads to the toylike harbor with its 14th-century quay. The climb back has been likened to the struggles of Sisyphus, but, happily, a Land Rover service (in summer) will take you to and from the parking lot at the top. You pay £3.50 to park and use the visitor center; this is the only way to enter the village.

Where to Stay & Eat

£££ ╳⌘ **Red Lion Hotel.** One of only two hotels in this coastal village, the 18th-century Red Lion sits right on the harbor. Guest rooms, some small, are decorated along a nautical theme; all have sea views. The climb up through Clovelly is perilously steep, but hotel guests can bring cars via a back road to and from the Red Lion. The sophisticated restaurant (fixed-price menu at dinner) specializes in seafood dishes and homemade ice creams and sorbets. ⌂ *The Quay, EX39 5TF* ☎ *01237/431237* 🖷 *01237/431044* ⊕ *www.clovelly.co.uk* ⇔ *11 rooms* ⌂ *Restaurant, 2 bars; no a/c* ⊟ *AE, MC, V* ⍾⌐ *BP.*

CORNWALL
COAST & MOOR

Cornwall stretches west into the sea, with plenty of coastline to see. One way to explore it all is to travel southwest from Boscastle and the cliff-top ruins of Tintagel Castle, the legendary birthplace of Arthur, along the north Cornish coast to Land's End. From this westernmost tip of Britain, known for its savage land- and seascapes and panoramic views, turn northeast, stopping in the popular seaside resort of Penzance, the harbor city of Falmouth, and a string of pretty Cornish fishing villages. Leave time to visit the Eden Project, with its large, surrealistic-looking conservatories in an abandoned clay pit, and to explore the boggy, heath-covered expanse of Bodmin Moor.

Boscastle

▶ ⓭   *15 mi north of Bodmin, 30 mi south of Clovelly.*

In tranquil Boscastle, some of the stone and slate cottages at the foot of the steep valley date from the 1300s. The town is centered around a little harbor, set snug within towering cliffs. Nearby, 2 mi up the valley of the Valency, is St. Juliot's, the "Endelstow" referred to in Thomas Hardy's *A Pair of Blue Eyes*—the young author was involved with the restoration of this church while he was working as an architect.

Where to Stay

££   ▦ **The Old Rectory.** Hardy stayed here while restoring St. Juliot's church, and this is where he first met his wife-to-be, Emma, the rector's sister-in-law. The stone house, set on 3 acres of attractive grounds, has been in the same family for five generations, and updates are mainly in Victorian style. Breakfast may include organic produce from the kitchen garden, and Hardy-related workshops are available. ✉ *Off B3263, St. Juliot, Boscastle, PL35 0BT* ☎ *01840/250225* ⊕ *www.stjuliot.com* ⇔ *4 rooms, 2 with bath* ⬙ *Croquet; no a/c, no room phones, no kids under 12, no smoking* ▭ *MC, V* ⊘ *Closed Dec.–Feb.* ⦿❘ *BP.*

Fodor'sChoice
★

Tintagel

⓮   *5 mi southwest of Boscastle.*

The romance of Arthurian legend thrives around Tintagel's ruined castle on the coast. Ever since the somewhat unreliable 12th-century chronicler Geoffrey of Monmouth identified Tintagel as the home of Arthur, son of Uther Pendragon and Ygrayne, devotees of the legend cycle have revered the site. In the 19th century, Alfred, Lord Tennyson, described Tintagel's Arthurian connection in *The Idylls of the King*. The historical Arthur is likely to have been a Christian Celtic chieftain battling against the heathen Saxons in the 6th century. Today the village itself has more than its share of tourist junk—including Excaliburgers.

The **Old Post Office**, a 14th-century stone manor house with smoke-blackened beams, has been restored to its appearance during Victorian times, when one room served as a post office. ✉ *3–4 Tintagel Centre* ☎ *01840/ 770024* ⊕ *www.nationaltrust.org.uk* ⊠ *£2.40* ⊘ *Apr.–Sept., daily 11–5:30; Oct., daily 11–4.*

Fodor'sChoice   Although all that remains of the ruined cliff-top **Tintagel Castle**, legendary
★   birthplace of King Arthur, is the outline of its walls, moats, and towers, it requires only a bit of imagination to conjure up a picture of Sir Lancelot and Sir Galahad riding out in search of the Holy Grail over the narrow causeway above the seething breakers. Archaeological evi-

dence, however, suggests that the castle dates from much later—about 1150, when it was the stronghold of the earls of Cornwall; long before that, Romans may have occupied the site. The earliest identified remains at the castle are of Celtic (5th-century) origin, and these may have some connection with the legendary Arthur. Legends aside, nothing can detract from the castle ruins, dramatically set off by the wild, windswept Cornish coast, on an island connected by a narrow isthmus. (There are also traces of a Celtic monastery here.) Paths lead down to the pebble beach, to a cavern known as **Merlin's Cave.** Exploring Tintagel Castle involves some arduous climbing on steep steps, but even on a summer's day, when people swarm over the battlements and a westerly Atlantic wind sweeps through Tintagel, you can feel the proximity of the distant past. ⊠ *Castle Rd., ½ mi west of village* ☎ *01840/770328* ⊕ *www.english-heritage.org.uk* ☜ *£3.20* ۞ *Apr.–mid-July and Sept., daily 10–6; mid-July–Aug., daily 10–7; Oct., daily 10–5; Nov.–Mar., daily 10–4.*

Displays in the **Arthurian Centre** provide background to the story of King Arthur. Highlights include Arthur's Stone, dated to 540 BC, and a woodland walk to the site of Arthur's "last battle." There's also a gift shop and tea garden. The center is 5 mi southeast of Tintagel Castle, on the edge of Bodmin Moor. ⊠ *Slaughterbridge, Camelford* ☎ *01840/212450* ⊕ *www.arthur-online.com* ☜ *£2.50* ۞ *Apr.–Oct., daily 10–dusk.*

Port Isaac

⑮ *5 mi southwest of Tintagel.*

A mixture of granite, slate, and whitewashed cottages tumble precipitously down the cliff to the tiny harbor at Port Isaac, still dedicated to the crab and lobster trade. Low tide reveals a pebbly beach and rock pools. Relatively unscathed by tourists, it makes for a peaceful and secluded stay. For an extra slice of authentic Cornwall life, the local choir sings shanties at the harborside on Friday nights in summer.

Where to Stay & Eat

£££ ✕⌂ **Slipway Hotel.** This 16th-century inn right on the harborfront has low ceilings, exposed timbers, and steep staircases that lead to cozily furnished rooms. The split-level restaurant, held up by unusual slate pillars, serves the freshest fish, lobster, and crab dishes. ⊠ *Harbourfront, PL29 3RH* ☎ *01208/880264* 🖷 *01208/880408* ⊕ *www.portisaac.com* ⇨ *11 rooms* ⌂ *Restaurant, bar, some pets allowed (fee); no a/c* ⊟ *AE, MC, V* ۞ *Closed Jan.* ⍟❘ *BP.*

Padstow

⑯ *10 mi southwest of Port Isaac.*

At the mouth of the Camel River, this small fishing port has attracted considerable attention as a center of culinary excellence, largely because of the presence here since 1975 of pioneering seafood chef Rick Stein, who has made this an essential stop on any foodie's itinerary. Stein's empire now includes two restaurants, a café, a seafront delicatessen (open April–October) good for food to go, a cooking school (classes fill up months in advance), a gift shop, and some elegant accommodations. However, Padstow is worth visiting even if seafood is not your favorite fare. The cries of seagulls fill its lively harbor, a string of fine beaches lies within a short ride—including some choice strands highly prized by surfers—and two scenic walking routes await: the Saints Way across the peninsula to Fowey, and the Camel Trail, a footpath and cycling path that follows the river as far as Bodmin Moor.

£££–£££££ ✕▣ **St. Petroc's Hotel and Bistro.** Rick Stein's cream-color bistro is a French-inspired take on his Seafood Restaurant—simpler, less expensive, and with more options for carnivores and vegetarians. Both diners and hotel guests have use of the sunny walled garden. Those who stay the night can also take advantage of the stylishly decorated rooms. ⊠ *4 New St., PL28 8EA* ☎ *01841/532700* ☒ *01841/532942* ⊕ *www.rickstein.com* ↪ *10 rooms* ♿ *Restaurant, bar, some pets allowed; no a/c* ☰ *MC, V* ☉ *Closed 1 wk around Christmas* |◯| *BP.*

£££–£££££
Fodor'sChoice
★ ✕▣ **The Seafood Restaurant.** Rick Stein's flagship restaurant, just across from where the lobster boats and trawlers unload their catch, has built its reputation on the freshest fish and high culinary artistry. The fixed-price dinners are the best option and may include stir-fried mussels with black beans and grilled haddock with spring onion mash. If you don't want to move after your meal, book one of the sunny, individually designed guest rooms furnished in a modern or more traditional style. ⊠ *Riverside, PL28 8BY* ☎ *01841/532700* ☒ *01841/532942* ⊕ *www.rickstein.com* ↪ *13 rooms* ♿ *Restaurant, some pets allowed; no a/c* ♿ *Reservations essential* ☰ *MC, V* ☉ *Closed 1 wk around Christmas* |◯| *BP.*

£££££ ▣ **St. Edmond's House.** The most luxurious Rick Stein venture opts for a cool minimalist look. Excellently equipped, the shuttered bedrooms have wooden floors, in-room DVD players, and French doors facing the harbor. Booking here guarantees a table at the Seafood Restaurant, where breakfast is taken, but you should reserve as far ahead as possible. ⊠ *St. Edmond's La., PL28 8BZ* ☎ *01841/532700* ☒ *01841/532942* ⊕ *www.rickstein.com* ↪ *6 rooms* ♿ *Minibars, cable TV* ☰ *MC, V* ☉ *Closed 1 wk around Christmas* |◯| *BP.*

BIKING Bikes of all shapes and sizes can be rented at **Brinham's** (⊠ South Quay ☎ 01841/532594).

SURFING **Harlyn Surf School** (⊠ 16 Boyd Ave. ☎ 01841/533076) can arrange half- to five-day surfing courses.

WALKING The **Saints Way,** a 30-mi path between Padstow and the Camel Estuary on Cornwall's north coast to Fowey on the south coast, follows a Bronze Age trading route, later used by Celtic pilgrims to cross the peninsula. Several relics of such times can be seen along the way. Contact the tourist offices in Padstow or Fowey or the Cornwall Tourist Board for information.

Newquay

⑰ *14 mi southwest of Padstow, 30 mi southwest of Tintagel.*

The principal resort on the north Cornwall coast is a fairly large town established in 1439. It was once the center of the trade in pilchards (a small herringlike fish), and on the headland you can still see a white hut where a lookout known as a "huer" watched for pilchard schools and directed the boats to the fishing grounds. Newquay has become Britain's surfing capital, and in summer young California-dreaming devotees can pack the wide beaches.

Perranporth

⑱ *8 mi south of Newquay, 13 mi northwest of Truro.*

Past the sandy shores of Perran Bay, Perranporth is one of Cornwall's most popular seaside spots and becomes extremely crowded in high season. The swells off this 3-mi stretch of beach attract swarms of surfers, too. The best times to visit are the beginning and end of the summer. Enchanting coastal walks extend along the dunes and cliffs.

St. Ives

⑲ *20 mi southwest of Perranporth on A30, 10 mi north of Penzance.*

James McNeill Whistler came here to paint his landscapes, Daphne du Maurier and Virginia Woolf to write their novels. Today sand, sun, and world-class art continue to attract thousands of stylish vacationers to the fishing village of St. Ives, named after St. Ia, a 5th-century female Irish missionary said to have arrived on a floating leaf. The town has long played host to a well-established artists' colony, and there are plenty of craftspeople, too. Day-trippers often crowd St. Ives, so it's best to park outside the town.

The house of Dame Barbara Hepworth (1903–75), who pioneered abstract sculpture in England, is now the **Barbara Hepworth Museum and Sculpture Garden.** London's prominent Tate gallery runs the museum. The artist lived here for 26 years. ⊠ *Trewyn Studio, Barnoon Hill* ☎ *01736/796226* ⊕ *www.tate.org.uk* ⊠ *£3.95, combined ticket with Tate St. Ives £6.95* ⊗ *Mar.–Oct., daily 10–5:30; Nov.–Feb., Tues.–Sun. and national holidays 10–4:30.*

★ The spectacular **Tate St. Ives** displays the work of artists who lived and worked in St. Ives, mostly from 1925 to 1975, and has selections from the rich collection of the Tate in London. It occupies a modernist building—a fantasia of seaside deco-period architecture with a panoramic view of turquoise rippling ocean. The four-story gallery, set at the base of a cliff fronted by Porthmeor Beach, may be the only art museum with a special storage space for visitors' surfboards. The rooftop café is excellent. ⊠ *Porthmeor Beach* ☎ *01736/796226* ⊕ *www.tate.org.uk* ⊠ *£4.25, combined ticket with Barbara Hepworth Museum and Sculpture Garden £6.95* ⊗ *Mar.–Oct., daily 10–5:30; Nov.–Feb., Tues.–Sun. and national holidays 10–4:30.*

At the **St. Ives Society of Artists Gallery,** local artists display selections of their current work for sale in the Old Mariners' Church. The Crypt is rented out for private exhibitions. ⊠ *Norway Sq.* ☎ *01736/795582* ⊕ *www.stivessocietyofartists.com* ⊠ *25p* ⊗ *Mid-Mar.–Oct., Mon.–Sat. and national holidays 10–4:30.*

Where to Stay & Eat

££ ✕ **The Sloop Inn.** One of Cornwall's oldest pubs, the harborfront Sloop Inn was built in 1312. Pub lunches and evening meals are available in the wood-beam rooms, where you can also see the work of local artists. ⊠ *The Wharf* ☎ *01736/796584* ⊟ *MC, V.*

★ £££–££££ ✕▥ **Garrack Hotel.** A family-run, ivy-clad hotel with panoramic sea views from its hilltop location, the Garrack is relaxed and undemanding. Some rooms are furnished in traditional style; others are more modern. The excellent restaurant specializes in fresh local fish, including grilled or sautéed lobster, as well as Cornish lamb. Breads are made in-house, and the wine list features some Cornish vineyards. ⊠ *Burthallan La., TR26 3AA* ☎ *01736/796199* 🖷 *01736/798955* ⊕ *www.garrack.com* ↪ *18 rooms* ⌂ *Restaurant, indoor pool, gym, sauna, bar, meeting rooms, some pets allowed (fee); no a/c* ⊟ *AE, DC, MC, V* ⦿⦿ *BP.*

£–££ ▥ **The Grey Mullet.** Everything in St. Ives seems squeezed into the tiniest of spaces, and this cottage B&B a few yards from the harbor is no exception. Pictures and decoration cover the walls, and even the outside is thickly hung with flowers. Built in 1776, the former fisherman's abode claims to be the oldest house in town. The bedrooms manage to accommodate four-posters, and an old-fashioned cellar dining room is open for afternoon teas. The galleries are minutes away. ✉ *2 Bunkers Hill, TR26 1LJ* ☎ *01736/796635* ✏ *greymulletguesthouse@lineone. net* ⇆ *9 rooms* ♿ *Tea shop; no smoking* ▤ *MC, V* ⏸ *BP.*

en route The winding B3306 coastal road southwest from St. Ives passes through some of Cornwall's starkest yet most beautiful countryside. Barren hills crisscrossed by low stone walls drop abruptly to granite cliffs and wide bays. Evidence of the ancient tin-mining industry—the remains of smokestacks and pumping houses—is everywhere. Now a fascinating mining heritage center, the early 20th-century **Geevor Tin Mine** was the only mine left in the St. Just district by the 1930s. At its peak Geevor employed 400 men, but in October 1985, the collapse of the world tin market wiped Cornwall from the mining map. Make sure you have suitably sturdy footwear for the surface and underground tours. A museum, shop, and café are on the site. ✉ *B3306, Pendeen* ☎ *01736/788662* ⊕ *www.geevor.com* 🎫 *£6.50* ⊙ *Apr.–Oct., Sun.–Fri. 10–5; Nov.–Mar., Sun.–Fri. 10–4; last admission 1 hr before closing.*

Land's End

★ ⑳ *10 mi southwest of St. Ives, 10 mi west of Penzance.*

The coastal road, B3306, ends at the western tip of Britain at what is, quite literally, Land's End. The sea crashes against its rocks and lashes ships battling their way around it. Approach it from one of the coastal footpaths for the best panoramic view. Over the years, sightseers have caused some erosion of the paths, but new ones are constantly being built, and Cornish "hedges" (granite walls covered with turf) have been planted to prevent future erosion. The scenic grandeur of Land's End remains undiminished, although the point draws crowds of people from all over the world. A low-key theme park, the **Land's End Experience** (☎ 0870/458–0099), runs a poor second to nature.

Nightlife & the Arts

The open-air **Minack Theatre** perches high above a beach 3 mi southeast of Land's End. The slope of the cliff forms a natural amphitheater, with bench seats on the terraces and the sea as a magnificent backdrop. Different companies present plays from classic dramas to modern comedies afternoons and evenings in summer. An exhibition center recounts the theater's creation. ✉ *Off B3315, Porthcurno* ☎ *01736/810181* 🎫 *Exhibition center £2.50, performances £5.50 and £7* ⊙ *Apr.–Sept., daily 9:30–5:30; Oct.–Mar., daily 10–4* ⊙ *Closed during matinees, currently May–Sept., Wed. and Fri. noon–4:30.*

Mousehole

★ ㉑ *7 mi east of Land's End, 3 mi south of Penzance.*

On B3315 between Land's End and Penzance, Mousehole (pronounced *mow-*zel, with the first syllable rhyming with "cow") merits a stop—and plenty of people do stop—to see this archetypal Cornish fishing village of tiny stone cottages. It was the home of Dolly Pentreath, supposedly the last native Cornish speaker, who died in 1777.

Newlyn

㉒ *2 mi north of Mousehole.*

Long the county's most important fishing port, Newlyn became the magnet for a popular artists' colony at the end of the 19th century. Few of the fishermen's cottages that attracted artists to the area remain, however. To see the works of the Newlyn School, drop in at the Penlee House Gallery in Penzance. The Pilchard Works, a museum that is also an active factory, presents the history of Cornish pilchard fishing.

Penzance

㉓ *1½ mi north of Newlyn, 10 mi south of St. Ives.*

Superb views over Mount's Bay are one lure of this popular seaside resort. The town's isolated position has always made it vulnerable to attack from the sea. During the 16th century, Spanish raiders destroyed most of the original town, and the majority of old buildings date from as late as the 18th century. The main street is Market Jew Street, a folk mistranslation of the Cornish expression "Marghas Yow," which means "Thursday Market." Look for Market House, constructed in 1837, an impressive, domed granite building that is now a bank.

The former main street and one of the prettiest thoroughfares in Penzance, **Chapel Street** winds down from Market House to the harbor. Its predominantly Georgian and Regency houses suddenly give way to the extraordinary **Egyptian House,** whose facade recalls ancient Egypt. Built around 1830 as a geological museum, today it houses vacation apartments. Across Chapel Street is the 17th-century **Union Hotel,** where in 1805 the death of Lord Nelson and the victory of Trafalgar were first announced from the minstrels' gallery in the assembly rooms. Near the Union Hotel on Chapel Street is one of the few remnants of old Penzance, the **Turk's Head,** an inn said to date from the 13th century.

The small collection at the **Penlee House Gallery and Museum,** in a gracious Victorian house set in a park, focuses on paintings by members of the so-called Newlyn School from about 1880 to 1930. These works evoke the life of the inhabitants of Newlyn, mostly fisher folk. The museum also covers 5,000 years of history in West Cornwall, with archaeology, decorative arts, costume, and photography exhibits. ⊠ *Penlee Park* ☎ *01736/363625* ⊕ *www.penleehouse.org.uk* ✉ *£2, Sat. free* ⊙ *May–Sept., Mon.–Sat. 10–5; Oct.–Apr., Mon.–Sat. 10:30–4:30; last admission ½ hr before closing.*

off the beaten path

ISLES OF SCILLY – Fondly regarded in folklore as the lost land of Lyonesse, this compact group of more than 100 islands 30 mi southwest of Land's End is equally famed for the warm summer climate and ferocious winter storms. In fair weather, you'll find peace, a profusion of flowers—wild, cultivated, and subtropical— swarms of seabirds, and unspoiled beaches galore. If you have time, take the 2½-hour ferry service from Penzance; otherwise there's plane and helicopter service. All arrive at the largest of the five inhabited islands, St. Mary's, which has the bulk of the lodgings, from palatial retreats to humble but comfortable and friendly B&Bs.

Where to Stay & Eat

£££ ✕ **Harris's.** Tucked away off Market Jew Street, the two small, elegant rooms here are a rare outpost of high-quality cuisine in Penzance. Seafood is the main event: whatever the boats bring in. Crab Florentine, grilled on a bed of spinach with cheese sauce, is usually available. Meat dishes might include medallions of West Country venison with wild mushrooms. ⊠ *46 New St.* ☎ *01736/364408* ⊟ *AE, MC, V* ☉ *Closed Sun., also Mon. Nov.–May, and 4 wks Nov.–Mar.*

★ **££–£££** ✕ **Admiral Benbow Inn.** One of the most famous inns in Penzance, the 15th-century Admiral Benbow was once a smugglers' pub—look for the armed smuggler on the roof. Seafaring memorabilia, a brass cannon, model ships, ropes, and figureheads fill the inn. In the restaurant area, decorated to resemble a ship's galley, you can dine on seafood or a steak-and-Guinness pie. ⊠ *46 Chapel St.* ☎ *01736/363448* ⊟ *MC, V.*

★ **£££–££££** ✕▣ **Abbey Hotel and Restaurant.** Owned by former model/icon Jean Shrimpton and her husband, this small, 17th-century hotel is marvelously homey. Books fill the drawing room, and antiques and chintz furnish many of the rooms; there's also a comfortable small apartment. The sleekly modern restaurant next door (closed Sunday and Monday) has a short but intriguing menu (fixed-price Tuesday–Friday) that lists wild mushroom and celeriac lasagna, bourride of turbot, and iced apple and Calvados parfait, among other succulent creations. ⊠ *Abbey St., TR18 4AR* ☎ *01736/366906 hotel; 01736/330680 restaurant* 🖷 *01736/351163* ⊕ *www.abbey-hotel.co.uk* ➳ *6 rooms, 1 apartment* ♿ *Restaurant, croquet, some pets allowed; no a/c* ⊟ *AE, MC, V* ⍾⃝ *BP.*

£–££ ▣ **Camilla House.** This flower-bedecked Georgian house stands on a road parallel to the promenade, close to the harbor. Guest rooms are cheerfully decorated; ones at the front have sea views, and the top room is coziest. The owners are agents for the ferry line and can help with trips to the Isles of Scilly. ⊠ *12 Regent Terr., TR18 4DW* 🖷🖷 *01736/363771* ⊕ *www.camillahouse-hotel.co.uk* ➳ *9 rooms, 4 with bath* ♿ *In-room data ports; no a/c, no room phones, no smoking* ⊟ *AE, MC, V* ⍾⃝ *BP.*

£ ▣ **Holbein House.** A stout Edwardian house set in its own garden, this family-run B&B west of the center of Penzance is quiet, friendly, and clean, and offers exceptionally good value. Breakfast is taken in the bedrooms, which are spacious and bright, with modern furnishings. Penlee House is a pleasant walk from here across the park. ⊠ *Alexandra Rd., TR18 4LZ* ☎ *01736/332625* ➳ *7 rooms* ♿ *No a/c, no room phones* ⊟ *No credit cards* ⍾⃝ *CP.*

Sports & the Outdoors

Many ships have foundered on Cornwall's rocky coastline, resulting in an estimated 3,600 shipwrecks. The area around Land's End has some of the best diving in Europe, and the convergence of the Atlantic and the Gulf Stream results in impressive visibility and unusual subtropical marine life. **Undersea Adventures** (⊠ 15a Cuxhaven Way, Long Rock Industrial Estate ☎ 01736/333040) offers courses and guided dives for beginners and experts.

St. Michael's Mount

★ ㉔ *3 mi east of Penzance on A394.*

Rising out of Mount's Bay just off the coast, this spectacular granite and slate island is one of Cornwall's greatest natural attractions. A 14th-century castle perched at the highest point—200 feet above the sea—was built on the site of a Benedictine chapel founded by Edward the Confessor. In its time, the island has served as a church (Brittany's island abbey of Mont St. Michel served as a model), a fortress, and a private residence. The castle rooms you can tour include the Chevy Chase Room—a name probably associated with the Cheviot Hills or the French word *chevaux* (horses), after the hunting frieze that decorates the walls of this former monks' refectory. The battlements also offer splendid views.

Around the base of the rock are buildings that range from medieval to Victorian but appear harmonious. Fascinating gardens surround the Mount, and many kinds of plants flourish in its microclimates. To get to the island, follow the cobbled causeway from the village of Marazion or, when the tide is in during the summer, take the ferry. There are pubs and restaurants in the village, but the island also has a café and restaurant. Wear stout shoes for your visit to this site, which is unsuitable for anyone with mobility problems. ⊠ *Marazion* ☎ *01736/710507* ⊕ *www. stmichaelsmount.co.uk* ⊡ *£4.80, £1 for ferry each way* ☉ *Apr.–June, Sept., and Oct., weekdays 10:30–5:30, last admission 4:45; July and Aug., daily 10:30–5:30, last admission 4:45; Nov.–Mar., phone for hrs.*

Helston

㉕ *13 mi east of Marazion, 14 mi east of Penzance, 18 mi southwest of Truro.*

The attractive Georgian town of Helston is most famous for its annual "Furry Dance," which takes place on Floral Day, May 8 (unless the date is a Sunday or Monday, in which case it takes place on the previous Saturday). Flowers deck the whole town, and dancers weave their way in and out of the houses along a 3-mi route.

Ⓒ Besides the usual rides, **Flambards Theme Park** has an aircraft collection, a re-creation of a wartime street during the Blitz, and a reconstructed Victorian village. Family Saver tickets are a good deal. ⊠ *Off A394, 2 mi from Helston* ☎ *01326/573404; 0845/601–8684 24-hr information line* ⊕ *www.flambards.co.uk* ⊡ *£12.25* ☉ *Apr.–Oct., daily 10–5; may close later in summer. Call about possible Mon. and Fri. closings in Oct.*

Where to Stay & Eat

££–££££ ✕⊡ **Nansloe Manor.** Although near Helston's center, this peaceful 17th-century manor house gives the impression of being deep in the country, with its ½-mi driveway and 4 acres of grounds. Public areas and guest rooms are done in country-house style, with upholstered furniture and chintz fabrics. In the restaurant, the fixed-price four-course menu favors traditional English fare. ⊠ *Meneage Rd., TR13 0SB* ☎ *01326/574691* 🖷 *01326/564680* ⊕ *www.nansloe-manor.co.uk* ⇄ *7 rooms* ♿ *Restaurant, croquet, bar; no a/c, no kids under 10* ▤ *AE, MC, V* ⏍ *BP.*

Lizard Peninsula

★ **㉖** *10 mi south of Helston.*

The southernmost point on mainland Britain, this peninsula is an officially designated Area of Outstanding Natural Beauty. The huge, eerily rotating dish antennae of the Goonhilly Satellite Communications Earth Station are visible from the road as it crosses Goonhilly Downs, the backbone of the peninsula. A path, close to the tip of the peninsula, plunges down 200-foot cliffs to the tiny **Kynance Cove**, with its handful of pint-size islands. The sands here are reachable only in the 2½ hours before and after low tide. The peninsula's cliffs are made of greenish serpentine rock, interspersed with granite; local souvenirs are carved out of the stone.

Falmouth

㉗ *7 mi northeast of Gweek, 12 mi south of Truro.*

The bustle of this resort town's fishing harbor, yachting center, and commercial port only adds to its charm. In the 18th century, Falmouth was the main mail-boat port for North America, and in Flushing, a village across the inlet, you can see the slate-covered houses built by prosperous mail-boat captains. A ferry service now links the two towns. On Custom House Quay, off Arwenack Street, is the King's Pipe, an oven in which seized contraband was burned.

🕙 Opened in 2002, the granite and oak-clad **National Maritime Museum, Cornwall,** is an excellent place to come to grips with Cornish maritime heritage, weather lore, and navigational science. You can view the collection of 140 or so boats, study the tools associated with Cornish sail makers and boatbuilders, and wander through a sail loft and pilchard cellar. In the glass-fronted tidal gallery below sea level, you come face to face with the sea itself. ☒ *Discovery Quay* ☎ *01326/313388* ⊕ *www. nmmc.co.uk* 🎟 *£5.90* 🕙 *Daily 10–5.*

At the end of its own peninsula stands the formidable **Pendennis Castle,** built by Henry VIII in the 1540s and later improved by his daughter, Elizabeth I. You can explore the different defenses developed over the centuries. The castle has sweeping views over the English Channel and across the water known as Carrick Roads to St. Mawes Castle, designed as a companion fortress to guard the roads. Open-air plays and concerts are usually staged here in July and August. ☒ *Pendennis Head* ☎ *01326/316594* ⊕ *www.english-heritage.org.uk* 🎟 *£4.20* 🕙 *Apr.–Sept., daily 10–6; Oct., daily 10–5; Nov.–Mar., daily 10–4.*

Where to Stay & Eat

££–£££ ✕ **Pandora Inn.** Four miles north of Falmouth, this thatched pub on a creek is a great retreat, with both a patio and a moored pontoon for summer dining. Maritime memorabilia and fresh flowers provide decoration, and you can eat in the bar (lunch or dinner) or in the candlelit restaurant (dinner only). The menu highlight is fresh seafood—try the creamy crab thermidor or check out the catch of the day. ☒ *Restronguet Creek, Mylor Bridge* ☎ *01326/372678* ▤ *MC, V.*

★ ££–£££ ✕ **Seafood Bar.** The window of this restaurant on the quay is a fish tank, and beyond it is the very best seafood. Try thick crab soup, locally caught lemon sole, or, in summer, turbot cooked with cider, apples, and cream. ☒ *Quay St.* ☎ *01326/315129* ▤ *MC, V* 🕙 *Closed Sun. Oct.–June, Mon. Oct.–Easter. No lunch.*

£££ 🏨 **St. Michael's Hotel.** The gardens sweep down to the sea at this seaside hotel in a long, low, white building overlooking Falmouth Bay. A top-to-bottom refurbishing has made the public areas and guest rooms sleek and contemporary, and the staff welcomes families. ☒ *Stracey Rd., TR11 4NB* ☎ *01326/312707* 🖷 *01326/211772* ⊕ *www.corushotels. com* 🛏 *65 rooms* 🍴 *Restaurant, indoor pool, gym, hot tub, sauna, bar, meeting rooms; no a/c* ▤ *AE, MC, V.*

Trelissick

❷❽ *6 mi north of Falmouth.*

A ferry point, Trelissick also has colorful Trelissick Garden, owned by the National Trust. The **King Harry Ferry** (☎ *01872/862312* ⊕ www. kingharryferry.co.uk), a chain-drawn car ferry, runs to the scenically splendid Roseland Peninsula three times hourly every day. From its decks you can see up and down the Fal, a deep, narrow river with steep, wooded banks. The river's great depth provides mooring for old ships waiting to be sold; these mammoth shapes lend a surreal touch to the riverscape.

★ Taking the King Harry Ferry, you can visit **St. Just in Roseland,** one of the most beautiful spots in the West Country. This tiny hamlet made up of stone cottage terraces and a 13th-century church is set within a subtropical garden, often abloom with magnolias and rhododendrons on a summer's day. St. Just is 9 mi south of Truro.

St. Mawes

㉙ *16 mi east of Falmouth by road, 1½ mi east by sea, 11 mi south of Truro by ferry.*

At the tip of the Roseland Peninsula is the pretty, quiet village of St. Mawes. The well-preserved Tudor-era **St. Mawes Castle,** outside the village, has a cloverleaf shape that makes it seemingly impregnable, yet during the Civil War, its Royalist commander surrendered without firing a shot. (In contrast, Pendennis Castle held out at this time for 23 weeks before submitting to the siege.) ⊠ *A3078* ☎ *01326/270526* ⊕ *www.english-heritage.org.uk* ☞ *£2.90* ⊙ *Apr.–Sept., daily 10–6; Oct., daily 10–5; Nov.–Mar., Wed.–Sun. 10–1 and 2–4.*

Where to Stay & Eat

£££££ ✕🏠 **Lugger Hotel.** It's worth the winding drive through some of Cornwall's narrowest roads to get to this chic hideaway by the water in a tiny fishing village. Several 17th-century cottages have been transformed in an eclectic modern style with bleached Portuguese wood and subdued hues. Seafood is a good choice at the excellent restaurant (fixed-price menu), which overlooks the diminutive harbor. There's a terrace for drinks and sunbathing. On either side of the hotel, the rugged coastline tempts you with exhilarating walks. The Lugger is 8 mi east of St. Mawes and 12 mi southeast or Truro. ⊠ *Portloe, TR2 5RD* ☎ *01872/501322* 🖷 *01872/501691* ⊕ *www.luggerhotel.com* ⇦ *21 rooms* ⚕ *Restaurant, spa* ☐ *MC, V* ⊙ *Closed 2 wks in Jan.* ⊺⊙⊺ *BP.*

£££££ ✕🏠 **Tresanton Hotel.** It's the Cornish Riviera, Italian style: this former yachtsman's club, owned by Olga Polizzi, daughter of grand hotelier Charles Forte, makes for a luxuriously relaxed stay. Decorated in sunny whites, blues, and yellows, with terra-cotta pots on the terrace, the Tresanton seems distinctly Mediterranean, and the yacht and speedboat available in summer to guests reinforces the jet-set spirit. In the restaurant, the Italian-inspired menu includes steamed langoustine with fettuccine and pan-fried Dover sole. ⊠ *Lower Castle Rd., TR2 5DR* ☎ *01326/270055* 🖷 *01326/270053* ⊕ *www.tresanton.com* ⇦ *24 rooms, 2 suites* ⚕ *Restaurant, boating, fishing, bar, cinema, meeting rooms; no a/c* ☐ *AE, MC, V* ⊺⊙⊺ *BP.*

en route The shortest route from St. Mawes to Truro is via the ferry. The longer way swings in a circle on A3078 for 19 mi through attractive countryside, where subtropical shrubs and flowers thrive, past Portloe and the 123-foot church tower in Probus, flaunting its gargoyles and pierced stonework.

Truro

㉚ *12 mi north of Falmouth, 19 mi north of St. Mawes.*

Truro is a compact, elegant Georgian city, nestled in a crook at the head of the River Truro. Although Bodmin is the county seat, Truro is Cornwall's only real city. For an overview of the Georgian house fronts, take a stroll down steep, broad Lemon Street. The 18th-century facades are of pale stone—unusual for Cornwall, where granite predominates. Like Lemon Street, Walsingham Place is a typical Georgian street, a curving, flower-lined pedestrian oasis.

Truro Cathedral, the **Cathedral Church of St. Mary,** dominates the city. Although comparatively modern (built 1880–1910), it evokes the feeling of a medieval church, with an exterior in early English Gothic style. The interior is filled with relics from the 16th-century parish church that originally stood on this site, part of which has been incorporated in a side chapel. An open, cobbled area called High Cross lies in front of the west porch, and the city's main shopping streets fan out from here. ⊠ *14 St. Mary's St.* ☎ *01872/276782* ⊕ *www.trurocathedral.org.uk* 🖃 *£4 suggested donation* ☉ *Mon.–Sat. 7:30–6, Sun. noon–4; free tours Easter–Oct. at 11:30, also at 2 during school vacations.*

The **Royal Cornwall Museum**, in a Georgian building, displays some fine examples of Cornwall-inspired art, a sampling of Cornish archaeology, an absorbing hodgepodge of local history, and an extensive collection of minerals. There's a café and shop. ⊠ *River St.* ☎ *01872/272205* ⊕ *www.royalcornwallmuseum.org.uk* 🖃 *£4* ☉ *Mon.–Sat. 10–5.*

Where to Stay & Eat

££££ ✕🖼 **Alverton Manor.** A former bishop's house and then a convent, this up-to-date hotel is both efficient and atmospheric. The chapel makes an unusual conference room. Guest rooms are large and have French cherrywood furniture. Quiet elegance is the keynote of the public areas, and in the Terrace restaurant (fixed-price menu), standards are kept high with the use of the best local produce in traditional and modern English recipes. ⊠ *Tregolls Rd., TR1 1ZQ* ☎ *01872/276633* 🖃 *01872/222989* ⊕ *www.connexions.co.uk/alvertonmanor* 🛏 *32 rooms* ♿ *Restaurant, cable TV, bar, meeting rooms, some pets allowed (fee); no a/c* ⊟ *AE, MC, V* ☉ *Closed 4 days over New Year* ﹙◯﹚ *BP.*

Charlestown

③ *15 mi east of Truro.*

This port was built by a local merchant in 1791 to export the huge reserves of china clay from St. Austell, 1 mi to the north, and it became one of the ports from which 19th-century emigrants left for North America. Charlestown has managed to avoid overdevelopment since its heyday in the early 1800s, preserving its Georgian harbor, which often appears in period film and television productions.

Where to Stay

£ 🖼 **T'Gallants.** This refurbished Georgian house directly behind the harbor takes its name from top gallant, one of the sails of a square-rigged sailing ship. Ask for a south-facing room to enjoy the tranquil morning view. The garden at the front is ideal for afternoon tea, and bag lunches are provided in summer. ⊠ *6 Charlestown Rd., PL25 3NJ* ☎ *01726/70203* 🛏 *8 rooms* ♿ *No a/c* ⊟ *MC, V* ﹙◯﹚ *CP.*

Fodor'sChoice
★

Eden Project

③ *3 mi northeast of Charlestown.*

Fodor'sChoice
★

Spectacularly set in a former china clay pit, the Eden Project presents the world's major plant systems in microcosm. The crater contains more than 70,000 plants, many belonging to rare or endangered species, from three climate zones. Two of the zones are housed in biomes—hexagonally paneled geodesic domes—the largest conservatories in Britain. In one dome, olive and citrus groves rub shoulders with cacti and other plants indigenous to a warm temperate climate, whereas the tropical dome steams with heat, resounds to the gushing of a waterfall, and blooms with exotic flora. The emphasis is on conservation and ecology, yet without the slightest hint of moralizing. A free shuttle, the Land Train, helps the footsore, and well-informed guides provide information. An entertaining exhibition in the visitor center gives you the lowdown on the project. To avoid the biggest crowds, visit on a Friday or Saturday or early in the morning; you'll need at least half a day to see everything. ⊠ *Bodelva, signposted off the A30, A390, and A391, St. Austell* ☎ *01726/811911* ⊕ *www.edenproject.com* ⊠ *£10* ⊙ *Apr.–Oct., daily 10–6; Nov.–Mar., daily 10–dusk; last admission 1½ hrs before closing.*

Fowey

③ *7 mi northeast of the Eden Project, 10 mi northeast of Charlestown.*

Nestled in the mouth of a beautiful wooded estuary, Fowey (pronounced Foy) is still very much a working china clay port as well as the focal point for the sailing fraternity. Increasingly, it's also the favored home of the rich and famous. Good and varied eating and sleeping options abound; these are most in demand during Regatta Week in mid-August and the annual Daphne du Maurier Festival in mid-May. The Bodinnick Ferry takes cars as well as foot passengers across the river for the coast road on to Looe.

Where to Stay & Eat

£–££ ✕ **Sam's.** You should be prepared to wait at this small and buzzing bistro. Then squeeze onto the green benches and savor dishes made with local seafood, including a bouillabaisse fit for kings. ⊠ *20 Fore St.* ☎ *01726/ 832273* ♤ *Reservations not accepted* ▤ *No credit cards* ⊙ *Closed Jan.–mid-Feb.*

££££ ▥ **Fowey Hall.** A showy Victorian edifice, all turrets, castellations, and elaborate plasterwork, this friendly, relaxed hotel set in 5 acres of gardens is very family centered—despite the abundance of antiques. Guest rooms are spacious, and there are great facilities for children. ⊠ *Hanson Dr., PL23 1ET* ☎ *01726/833866* ☒ *01726/834100* ⊕ *www. foweyhall.com* ⇄ *12 rooms, 12 suites* ♧ *2 restaurants, cable TV with movies, in-room VCRs, indoor pool, Ping-Pong, bar, meeting rooms, helipad, some pets allowed (fee); no a/c* ▤ *AE, MC, V* ¶◎¶ *BP.*

Sports & the Outdoors

Between Easter and September, **Fowey River Canoe Expeditions** (⊠ 17 Passage St. ☎ 01726/833627) runs daily canoe trips up the tranquil River Fowey, the best way to observe the abundant wildlife.

Bodmin

③ *12 mi north of Fowey.*

Bodmin, the county seat, was the only Cornish town recorded in the 11th-century Domesday Book, William the Conqueror's census. During World War I, the Domesday Book and the Crown Jewels were sent to Bodmin Prison for safekeeping. From the Gilbert Memorial on Beacon Hill, you can see both of Cornwall's coasts.

Fodor'sChoice
★
One of Cornwall's greatest country piles, **Lanhydrock,** former home of the powerful, wealthy Robartes family, was originally constructed in the 17th century but was totally rebuilt after a fire in 1881. The granite exterior remains true to its original form, however, and the long picture gallery in the north wing, with its barrel-vaulted plaster ceiling depicting 24 biblical scenes, survived the devastation. A small museum in the north wing shows photographs and letters relating to the family. The house's endless pantries, sculleries, dairies, nurseries, and linen and livery cupboards bear testimony to the immense amount of work involved in maintaining this lifestyle. Nine hundred acres of wooded parkland border the River Fowey, and in spring the gardens present an exquisite ensemble of magnolias, azaleas, and rhododendrons. ⊠ *3 mi southeast of Bodmin, signposted off A30, A38, and B3268* ☎ *01208/73320*

⊕ *www.nationaltrust.org.uk* ⌦ *£7.20, grounds only £3.90* ⊙ *House Apr.–Sept., Tues.–Sun. 11–5:30; Oct., Tues.–Sun. 11–5; garden daily 10–6; last admission 30 mins before closing.*

Dozmary Pool

㉟ *10 mi northeast of Bodmin.*

For a taste of Arthurian legend, follow A30 northeast out of Bodmin across the boggy, heather-clad granite plateau of Bodmin Moor, and turn right at Bolventor to get to Dozmary Pool. A lake of considerable size rather than a pool, it was here that King Arthur's legendary magic sword, Excalibur, was supposedly returned to the Lady of the Lake after Arthur's final battle.

Where to Stay

££ 🛏 **Jamaica Inn.** This inn near the middle of Bodmin Moor was made famous by Daphne du Maurier's 1936 novel of the same name, and it makes a good base for excursions onto the moor. Originally a farmstead, Cornwall's best-known pub incorporates a reproduction of du Maurier's study, an entertaining museum of curiosities, and a smugglers' museum, all worth a look. The bedrooms are functional and traditional in style, and three have four-posters. ⊠ *Off A30, Bolventor, PL15 7TS* ☎ *01566/86250* 📠 *01566/86177* ⊕ *www.jamaicainn.co.uk* ⌦ *6 rooms* ♨ *Restaurant, bar; no a/c* ⊟ *AE, DC, MC, V* ⑪ *BP.*

Launceston

㊱ *25 mi northwest of Plymouth.*

Cornwall's ancient capital, Launceston (pronounced *larn*-ston), on the eastern side of Bodmin Moor, retains parts of its medieval walls, including the South Gate. For a fine view of the surrounding countryside, you can climb up to the ruins of 14th-century **Launceston Castle.** ☎ *01566/ 772365* ⊕ *www.english-heritage.org.uk* ⌦ *£2.20* ⊙ *Apr.–Sept., daily 10–6; Oct., daily 10–5; Nov.–Mar., Fri.–Sun. 10–4.*

Where to Stay & Eat

££££–£££££ ✕🛏 **Lewtrenchard Manor.** Paneled rooms, stone fireplaces, ornate leaded windows, and handsome gardens enhance this spacious 1620 manor house on the northwestern edge of Dartmoor. Victorian hymn writer Sabine Baring Gould is responsible for the eclectic mix of architectural styles. Prints, chintzes, and upholstered furniture create comfort in the individually decorated guest rooms. The restaurant (fixed-price menu), with its big log fire and family portraits, serves good, fresh fish caught an hour away, and is noted for exemplary presentation. ⊠ *Lewdown, between Launceston and Okehampton, EX20 4PN* ☎ *01566/783256* 📠 *01566/783332* ⊕ *www.lewtrenchard.co.uk* ⌦ *9 rooms* ♨ *2 restaurants, in-room data ports, fishing, croquet, bar, meeting rooms, helipad, some pets allowed; no a/c* ⊟ *AE, DC, MC, V* ⑪ *BP.*

SOUTH DEVON TO CADBURY CASTLE
PLYMOUTH, DARTMOOR & EXETER

Just over the border from Cornwall, Plymouth, Devon's largest city, has an unprepossessing air, but its historic old core and splendid harbor recall a rich maritime heritage. North of Plymouth, you can explore the vast, boggy reaches of Dartmoor (setting for the Sherlock Holmes classic "The Hound of the Baskervilles"). Another choice is to continue east of Plymouth along Start Bay to Torbay, known as the English Riviera.

Both options lead north to Exeter, Devon's county seat, a historic city that has kept some of its medieval character despite wartime bombing. From Exeter you can meander south to Exmouth, then turn northeast to Yeovil in Somerset, reentering King Arthur Country at Cadbury Castle, the legendary Camelot.

Plymouth

48 mi southwest of Exeter, 124 mi southwest of Bristol, 240 mi southwest of London.

Devon's largest city has long been linked with England's commercial and maritime history. Much of the city center was destroyed by air raids in World War II and has been rebuilt in an uninspiring style, but there are worthwhile sights. From the **Hoe**, a wide, grassy esplanade with crisscrossing walkways high above the city, you can take in a magnificent view of the inlets, bays, and harbors that make up Plymouth Sound. The lighthouse **Smeaton's Tower**, transferred here at the end of the 19th century from its original site 14 miles out to sea, provides a sweeping vista over Plymouth Sound and the city as far as Dartmoor. ⊠ *Plymouth Hoe* ☎ *01752/603300* ⌨ *£2, £6 includes Plymouth Dome* ⊙ *Apr.–Oct., daily 10–4; Nov.–Mar., Tues.–Sat. 10–3.*

Plymouth Dome, next to Smeaton's Tower, presents an exhibition that takes in exploration, battles, and the Blitz in its overview of local history, with plenty of high-tech reconstructions. One section covers the construction and reconstruction of Smeaton's Tower. The kids will love it, and it makes a great haven on a wet afternoon. ⊠ *Plymouth Hoe* ☎ *01752/603300* ⌨ *£4.50, £6 includes Smeaton's Tower* ⊙ *Apr.–Oct., daily 10–5; Nov.–Mar., Tues.–Sat. 10–4; last admission 1 hr before closing.*

The huge **Royal Citadel** was built by Charles II in 1666 and still operates as a military center. ⊠ *End of the Hoe* ☎ *0870/225–4950* ⊕ *www. english-heritage.org.uk* ⌨ *£3* ⊙ *May–Sept., Tues. 1¼-hr guided tours at 2:30.*

The **Barbican**, east of the Royal Citadel, is the oldest surviving section of Plymouth. Here, Tudor houses and warehouses rise from a maze of narrow streets leading down to the fishing docks and harbor. Many of these buildings have become antiques shops, art shops, and bookstores. By the harbor you can visit the **Mayflower Steps**, where the Pilgrims embarked in 1620; the **Mayflower Stone** marks the exact spot.

Near the Barbican, just off the Royal Parade, the largely 18th-century **Merchant's House** is a museum of local history. ⊠ *33 St. Andrew's St.* ☎ *01752/304774* ⌨ *£1.10* ⊙ *Apr.–Sept., Tues.–Fri. 10–1 and 2–5:30, Sat. 10–1 and 2–5.*

The excellent **National Marine Aquarium**, on a central harborside site, presents aqueous environments from freshwater stream to seawater wave tank and huge "shark theater." Not to be missed are the extensive collection of sea horses, part of an important breeding program, and the chance to walk under sharks in the Mediterranean tank. Try to visit at shark-feeding time, which takes place three times a week. ⊠ *Rope Walk, Coxside* ☎ *01752/600301* ⊕ *www.national-aquarium.co.uk* ⌨ *£8* ⊙ *Apr.–Oct., daily 10–6; Nov.–Mar., daily 10–5; last admission 1 hr before closing.*

Plymouth Boat Cruises Ltd. (⊠ 8 Anderton Rise, Millbrook, Torpoint ☎ 01752/822797) runs several harbor and river sightseeing trips between Easter and October; boats depart every 30 minutes in peak season from Phoenix Wharf. **Tamar Cruising** (⊠ Cremyll Quay, Cremyll,

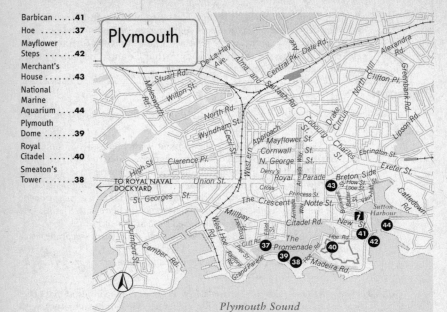

Torpoint ☎ 01752/822105) has harbor cruises and longer scenic trips on the Rivers Tamar and Yealm between Easter and October. Boats leave from the Mayflower Steps and Cremyll Quay.

Where to Stay & Eat

★ **£££££** ✕ **Chez Nous.** This pleasant, relaxed French—*très* French—restaurant is worth searching for among the stores in the shopping precinct. Fresh local fish is the draw. The pricey fixed-price menu, chalked up on the blackboard, usually repays the splurge with interest. ⊠ *13 Frankfort Gate* ☎ *01752/266793* ☐ *AE, DC, MC, V* ☉ *Closed Sun. and Mon. and 1st 3 wks in Feb. and Sept. No lunch.*

£££ ✕ **Piermaster's.** Fresh fish landed at nearby piers, notably squid, mussels, and oysters, appears high on the menu at this Barbican eatery. The decoration is basic seafront, with a tiled floor and wooden tables. ⊠ *33 Southside St.* ☎ *01752/229345* ☐ *AE, MC, V* ☉ *Closed Sun.*

££–££££ ▥ **Copthorne Hotel Plymouth.** This efficient, modern hotel downtown delivers the expected comforts and amenities. Guest rooms are contemporary in style, with a coral, turquoise, and cream color scheme. The Burlington Restaurant has an Edwardian look, and there is also a brasserie. ⊠ *Armada Way, PL1 1AR* ☎ *01752/224161or 0500/303030; 800/843–3311 in U.S.* ☐ *01752/670688* ⊕ *www.millenniumhotels. com* ⇆ *135 rooms* ⚹ *2 restaurants, cable TV with movies, indoor pool, gym, steam room, bar, business services, meeting rooms, free parking; no a/c* ☐ *AE, DC, MC, V* ¶◯¶ *BP.*

££ ▥ **Bowling Green Hotel.** Friendly and unpretentious, this Victorian house overlooks Sir Francis Drake's bowling green on Plymouth Hoe. Pine pieces and floral print fabrics decorate the guest rooms. The house is centrally located for shopping and sightseeing. ⊠ *9–10 Osborne Pl., Lockyer St.,*

PL1 2PU ☎01752/209090 🖶01752/209092 ⊕*www.bowlingreenhotel. com* ⇆ *12 rooms* ♿ *Parking (fee); no a/c* 🖃 *AE, DC, MC, V* ❙◎❙ *BP.*

Nightlife & the Arts

Plymouth's **Theatre Royal** (🖂 Royal Parade ☎ 01752/267222) presents ballet, musicals, and plays by some of Britain's best companies.

Saltram

★ ⓸⓹ *3½ mi east of Plymouth city center.*

A lovely 18th-century home with many of its original furnishings, Saltram was built around the remains of a late Tudor mansion. Its jewel is one of Britain's grandest neoclassical rooms, a vast, double-cube salon designed by Robert Adam and adorned with paintings by Sir Joshua Reynolds, first president of the Royal Academy of Arts, who was born nearby in 1723. The Axminster carpet was specially created for the room. Fine plasterwork adorns many rooms, and three have their original Chinese wallpaper. The house's beautiful garden includes rare trees and shrubs. Saltram appeared as Norland Park in the 1995 film *Sense and Sensibility.* There is a restaurant in the house and a cafeteria in the Coach House. 🖂 *South of A38, Plympton* ☎ *01752/333500* ⊕ *www.nationaltrust.org.uk* 🖾 *£6.30, garden only £3.30* ☉ *House Apr.–Sept., Sat.–Thurs. noon–4:30; Oct., Sat.–Thurs. 11:30–3:30; last admission 30 mins before closing. Garden Apr.–Oct., Sat.–Thurs. 11–5; Nov.–Mar., Sat.–Thurs. 11–4.*

| en route | From Plymouth, you have a choice of routes northeast to Exeter. If rugged, desolate, moorland scenery appeals to you, take A386 and B3212 northeast across Dartmoor. You'll find plenty to stir the imagination, no matter what the weather is. |

Dartmoor National Park

13 mi west of Exeter.

Even on a summer's day the scarred, brooding hills of this sprawling wilderness appear a likely haunt for such monsters as the hound of the Baskervilles, and it seems entirely fitting that Sir Arthur Conan Doyle set his Sherlock Holmes thriller in this landscape. Sometimes the wet, peaty wasteland vanishes in rain and mist, although in very clear weather you can see as far north as Exmoor. Much of northern Dartmoor consists of open heath and moorland, unspoiled by roads—wonderful walking and horseback-riding territory but an easy place to lose your bearings. Dartmoor's earliest inhabitants left behind stone monuments, burial mounds, and hut circles that help you envision prehistoric man roaming these bogs and pastures. Today ponies, sheep, and birds are the main animals to be seen.

Several villages scattered along the borders of this 368-square-mi reserve—one-third of which is owned by Prince Charles—make useful bases for hiking excursions. **Okehampton** is a main gateway, and other scenic spots include **Buckland-in-the-Moor,** a hamlet with thatched-roof cottages, **Widecombe-in-the-Moor,** whose church is known as the Cathedral of the Moor, and **Grimspound,** the Bronze Age site featured in Conan Doyle's tale. Transmoor Link buses connect most of Dartmoor's towns and villages. Park information centers include the main High Moorland Visitor Centre in Princetown and centers in Newbridge, Postbridge, and Haytor. The park also works with tourist information centers in Ivybridge, Okehampton, Tavistock, and Totnes. 🖂 *Dartmoor National Park*

Authority, Parke, Haytor Rd., Bovey Tracey, Newton Abbot, TQ13 9JQ ☎ *01626/832093* ⊕ *www.dartmoor-npa.gov.uk* ✉ *Free.*

Buckland Abbey

46 *8 mi north of Plymouth.*

This 13th-century Cistercian monastery became the home of Sir Francis Drake in 1581. Today it is filled with mementos of Drake and the Spanish Armada and has a restaurant. From Tavistock, take A386 south to Crapstone, then west. ⊠ *Yelverton* ☎ *01822/853607* ⊕ *www. nationaltrust.org.uk* ✉ *£5, grounds only £2.70* ⊙ *Mid-Feb.–Mar., weekends 2–5; Apr.–Oct., Fri.–Wed. 10:30–5:30; Nov.–Dec., weekends 2–5; last admission 45 mins before closing.*

> off the beaten path

GARDEN HOUSE – Terraced around the remains of a 16th-century vicarage, this rich, naturalistic garden, developed since 1945, is vivid with wisterias cascading over ancient brick walls, azaleas, roses, and 6,000 other flowering plants, many of them rare. The 8-acre garden is a mile northwest of Buckland Abbey. ⊠ *Off A386, Buckland Monachorum, near Yelverton* ☎ *01822/854769* ⊕ *www. thegardenhouse.org.uk* ✉ *£4* ⊙ *Mar.–Oct., daily 10:30–5.*

Cotehele House & Quay

★ **47** *4 mi west of Buckland Abbey, 15 mi north of Plymouth.*

This was formerly a busy port on the River Tamar, but it is now usually visited for the well-preserved late-medieval manor, home of the Edgcumbe family for centuries. The house has original furniture, tapestries, embroideries, and armor; there are also impressive gardens, a restored mill, and a quay museum. A limited number of visitors are allowed per day, so arrive early and be prepared to wait. Choose a bright day, because the rooms have no electric light. Shops, an arts and crafts gallery, a restaurant, and a tearoom provide other diversions. ⊠ *St. Dominick, north of Saltash, signposted off A390* ☎ *01579/352739* ⊕ *www. nationaltrust.org.uk* ✉ *£6.60, gardens and mill only £3.80* ⊙ *House late Mar.–Sept., Sat.–Thurs. 11–5; Oct., Sat.–Thurs. 11–4:30. Mill Apr.–June and Sept., Sat.–Thurs. 1–5:30; July and Aug., daily 1–6; Oct. and Nov., Sat.–Thurs. 1–4:30. Gardens daily 10:30–dusk.*

Morwellham Quay

48 *2 mi east of Cotehele House & Quay, 5 mi southwest of Tavistock, 18 mi north of Plymouth.*

In the 19th century, Morwellham (pronounced More-wel–ham) Quay was England's main copper-exporting port, and it has been carefully restored as a working museum, with quay workers and coachmen in costume, and a copper mine open to visitors. The museum is off the Gunnislake-to-Tavistock road. ☎ *01822/832766; 01822/833808 recorded information* ⊕ *www.morwellham-quay.co.uk* ✉ *Easter–Oct. £8.90, Nov.–Easter £5* ⊙ *Easter–Oct., daily 10–5:30; Nov.–Easter, daily 10–4:30; last admission 2 hrs before closing.*

Where to Stay & Eat

★
£££–£££££ ✕🛏 **Horn of Plenty.** A "country house hotel and restaurant" is the way this establishment in a Georgian house describes itself. The restaurant (no lunch Monday) has magnificent views across the wooded, rhododendron-filled Tamar Valley. Peter Gorton's cooking takes inspiration from around the world, and includes pigeon salad and pan-fried medal-

lions of beef. There are three- and five-course fixed-price menus, the best value being Monday's potluck menu. A converted coach house and the main house contain sumptuously furnished guest rooms, many with balconies. Rates tumble in winter. ⊠ *Gulworthy, 3 mi west of Tavistock on A390, PL19 8JD* ☎ *01822/832528* ⊕ *www.thehornofplenty.co. uk* ⇄ *9 rooms, 1 suite* ☖ *Restaurant, in-room VCRs, meeting rooms, some pets allowed; no a/c* ☰ *AE, MC, V* ¶⦶ *BP.*

Lydford Gorge

★ ㊾ *12 mi north of Morwellham Quay, 7 mi north of Tavistock, 9 mi east of Launceston, 24 mi north of Plymouth.*

The River Lyd has carved a spectacular 1½-mi chasm through the rock at Lydford Gorge. Two paths follow the gorge past gurgling whirlpools and waterfalls with names such as the Devil's Cauldron and the White Lady. Sturdy footwear is recommended. Although the walk can be quite challenging, the paths can still get congested during busy periods. From Launceston, continue east along A30, following the signs. ⊠ *Off A386, Lydford* ☎ *01822/820320* ⊕ *www.nationaltrust.org.uk* ⓢ *£3.80, free Nov.–Mar.* ⊘ *Apr.–Sept., daily 10–5:30; Oct., daily 10–4; Nov.–Mar., daily 10:30–3 (walk restricted to main waterfall).*

Where to Stay & Eat

£££–££££ ✕ **Dartmoor Inn.** Locals and visitors alike make a beeline for this pretty 16th-century pub, a good spot for a lunchtime snack such as farmhouse sausages and mash, or something more substantial in the evening. You can try imaginative contemporary fare such as a casserole of sea fish, and a lemon and Strega (an herbal liqueur) tart. The pub is at the Lydford junction. ⊠ *A386, Lydford* ☎ *01822/820221* ☰ *MC, V* ⊘ *Closed Mon. No dinner Sun.*

££–£££ ▦ **Castle Inn.** The heart of Lydford village, this 16th-century inn lies midway between Okehampton and Tavistock next to Lydford Castle. Rose trellises frame its rosy brick facade. The public rooms are snug, lamp lit, and full of period clutter. Strong colors fill the stylish guest rooms, and one room has its own roof garden. ⊠ *Lydford, 1 mi off A386, EX20 4BH* ☎ *01822/820241* ⓕ *01822/820454* ✉ *info@dartmoorinn.co. uk* ⇄ *8 rooms* ☖ *Restaurant, bar, some pets allowed (fee); no a/c* ☰ *MC, V* ¶⦶ *BP.*

Sports & the Outdoors

Lydford has one of the most popular Dartmoor riding facilities, the **Lydford House Riding Stables** (⊠ Lydford House Hotel, off A386 ☎ 01822/ 820321), open Easter–September.

Okehampton

㊿ *8 mi northeast of Lydford Gorge, 28 mi north of Plymouth, 23 mi west of Exeter.*

This town at the confluence of the Rivers East and West Okement is a good base for exploring North Dartmoor. It has numerous pubs and cottage tearooms, as well as a helpful tourist office. On the riverbank a mile southwest of the town center, the jagged ruins of the Norman **Okehampton Castle** occupy a verdant site with a picnic area and woodland walks. ☎ *01837/52844* ⊕ *www.english-heritage.org.uk* ⓢ *£2.60* ⊘ *Apr.–Sept., daily 10–6; Oct., daily 10–5.*

The informative **Museum of Dartmoor Life** contains interactive models, a working waterwheel, and photos of traditional farming methods, spread over three floors. The museum will be closed until mid-2004 for renovation, so call to confirm opening times. ⊠ *3 West St.* ☎ *01837/52295* ⊕ *www.museumofdartmoorlife.eclipse.co.uk* ☎ *£2.50* ⊙ *Easter–May and Oct., Mon.–Sat. 10–4:30; June–Sept., daily 10–5; Nov.–Easter, weekdays 10–4.*

Sports & the Outdoors
Skaigh Stables Farm (⊠ Skaigh La., Higher Sticklepath, near Okehampton ☎ 01837/840917) arranges day horseback rides and longer trips from Easter through September.

Chagford

🗐 *9 mi southeast of Okehampton, 30 mi northeast of Plymouth.*

Chagford was once a tin-weighing station and an area of fierce fighting between the Roundheads and the Cavaliers in the Civil War. A Roundhead was hanged in front of a pub on the village square. The town makes a convenient base from which to explore North Dartmoor.

The intriguing **Castle Drogo,** east of Chagford across A382, looks like a medieval castle, complete with battlements, but construction actually took place between 1910 and 1930. Designed by Sir Edwin Lutyens for Julius Drewe, a wealthy grocer, the castle is only half finished (funds ran out). The existing pile resembles a magisterial vision out of the Dark Ages. Take the A30 Exeter–Okehampton road to reach the castle, which is 4 mi northeast of Chagford and 6 mi south of A30. ⊠ *Drewsteignton* ☎ *01647/433306* ⊕ *www.nationaltrust.org.uk* ☎ *£5.90, grounds only £3* ⊙ *Castle Apr.–Oct., Wed.–Mon. 11–5:30. Grounds daily 10:30–5:30 or dusk.*

Where to Stay & Eat

★ **£££££** ✕🖾 **Gidleigh Park.** One of England's foremost hotels and restaurants, lauded in poetry by Ted Hughes, is set in its own enclave of landscaped gardens and streams within Dartmoor. Antiques and luxurious country-house furnishings fill the long, black-and-white Tudor-style residence, and the extremely pricey contemporary French restaurant (reservations essential), directed by chef Michael Caines, has been showered with culinary awards. You'll see why when you tuck into the tartlet of quail's eggs or the apple mousse with cider coulis. The locally pumped spring water is like no other. ⊠ *Gidleigh Park, TQ13 8HH* ☎ *01647/432367* 🖶 *01647/432574* ⊕ *www.gidleigh.com* 🗇 *14 rooms, 1 estate cottage* ⚲ *Restaurant, putting green, tennis court, croquet, meeting rooms, helipad, some pets allowed; no a/c* ▤ *DC, MC, V* ○ *BP.*

££ 🖾 **Easton Court.** Discerning travelers such as C. P. Snow, Margaret Mead, John Steinbeck, and Evelyn Waugh—who completed *Brideshead Revisited* here—made this their Dartmoor home-away-from-home. The pretty, Tudor thatched-roof manse has a garden and simple but elegant cottage-style rooms in an Edwardian wing, all with views over the Teign Valley. ⊠ *Easton Cross, TQ13 8JL* ☎ *01647/433469* 🖶 *01647/433654* ⊕ *www.easton.co.uk* 🗇 *5 rooms* ⚲ *No a/c* ▤ *MC, V* ○ *BP.*

Dartmouth

🗐 *35 mi east of Plymouth, 35 mi south of Exeter.*

An important port in the Middle Ages, Dartmouth is today a favorite haunt of yacht owners. Traces of its past include the old houses in Bayard's Cove near Lower Ferry, the 16th-century covered Butterwalk, and the two castles guarding the entrance to the River Dart. The Royal Naval College, built in 1905, dominates the town.

Where to Stay & Eat

★ **£££££** ✕ **Carved Angel.** Picture windows provide harbor views at this quayside restaurant with a long-standing reputation as one of Britain's finest eateries. Its offerings embrace international cuisine and fresh local products, such as Dartmouth crab with cucumber jelly and smoked pepper relish, and black-currant soufflé. There are two fixed-price evening menus. ✉ *2 S. Embankment* ☎ *01803/832465* 🖃 *MC, V* ☻ *No dinner Sun., no lunch Mon.*

££ ✕ **Carved Angel Café.** Bright and light, this offshoot of the Carved Angel is more modestly priced. Meals run the gamut from breakfasts and light lunches to high teas (sandwiches, cakes, and scones) and bistro-type dinners that show Mediterranean and Thai influences. Leave room for dessert, too. Kids are made to feel especially welcome. ✉ *7 Foss St.* ☎ *01803/834842* 🖃 *MC, V* ☻ *Closed Sun. No dinner Mon.–Thurs.*

££££–£££££ 🏠 **Royal Castle Hotel.** This hotel has truly earned the name "Royal"— several monarchs have slept here. Part of Dartmouth's historic waterfront (and consequently a hub of activity), it was built in the 17th century, reputedly of timber from wrecks of the Spanish Armada. Fireplaces and beamed ceilings are traditional features. Rooms come in different shapes and sizes, but all are thoughtfully and richly furnished, with a liberal sprinkling of antiques. Number 6 has its own priest hole, a secret room used to hide Roman Catholic priests. ✉ *11 The Quay, TQ6 9PS* ☎ *01803/833033* 🖷 *01803/835445* ⊕ *www.royalcastle.co. uk* ⇆ *25 rooms* ♿ *Restaurant, in-room data ports, cable TV, 2 bars, meeting rooms, some pets allowed; no a/c* 🖃 *AE, MC, V* ⏐⭕⏐ *BP.*

en route Two ferries cross the River Dart at Dartmouth; in summer, lines can be long, and you may want to try the inland route, heading west via A3122 to Halwell and then taking A381 north to Totnes.

Totnes

🟢 *9 mi northwest of Dartmouth, 28 mi southwest of Exeter.*

This busy market town preserves some of its past, particularly on summer Tuesdays and Saturdays, when most of the shopkeepers dress in Elizabethan costume. Its historic buildings include a guildhall and St. Mary's Church. You can climb up the hill in town to the ruins of **Totnes Castle**— a fine Norman motte and bailey design—for a wonderful view of Totnes and the River Dart. ☎ *01803/864406* ⊕ *www.english-heritage.org.uk* 🎟 *£1.80* ☻ *Apr.–Sept., daily 10–6; Oct., daily 10–5; Nov.–Mar., Wed.–Sun. 10–4.*

☙ Steam trains of the **South Devon Railway** run through 7 wooded mi of the Dart Valley between Totnes and Buckfastleigh, on the edge of Dartmoor. ✉ *Littlehempston, near Totnes* ☎ *01364/642338* ⊕ *www. southdevonrailway.org* 🎟 *£7.50 round-trip* ☻ *Easter–Oct., daily; call for winter times, including specials at Christmas and New Year's.*

Where to Stay & Eat

££ ✕🏠 **Cott Inn.** The exterior of this inn—a long, low, thatched building— has remained almost unchanged since 1320. Flagstone floors, thick ceiling beams, and open fireplaces are other signs of age. The snug bedrooms, tucked beneath the eaves, are furnished in modern style. Good rustic English meals are available from the restaurant, and there's a carvery with roasted meats. ✉ *Dartington, 2 mi west of Totnes on A385, TQ9 6HE* ☎ *01803/863777* 🖷 *01803/866629* ⊕ *www.thecottinn.co.uk* ⇆ *4 rooms* ♿ *Restaurant, bar; no a/c* 🖃 *AE, MC, V* ⏐⭕⏐ *BP.*

Shopping

Near Dartington Hall (2 mi northwest of Totnes), a collection of stores and two restaurants inside an old cider press make up the **Dartington Cider Press Centre** (⊠ Shinner Bridge, Dartington ☎ 01803/847500), which markets handmade Dartington crystal glassware, kitchenware, crafts, and toys from Devon and elsewhere. The farm shop sells fudge, ice cream, and cider, as well as local produce, and Cranks is an excellent vegetarian restaurant.

Brixham

54 *10 mi southeast of Totnes by A385 and A3022.*

Brixham, at the southern point of Tor Bay, has kept much of its original charm, partly because it is still an active fishing village. Much of the catch goes straight to restaurants as far away as London. Sample a portion of the local fish-and-chips on the quayside, where there is a (surprisingly petite) full-scale reproduction of the vessel on which Sir Francis Drake circumnavigated the world.

Torbay

55 *5 mi north of Brixham via A3022, 23 mi south of Exeter.*

The most important resort area in South Devon, Torbay envisions itself as the center of the "English Riviera." Since 1968, the towns of Paignton and Torquay (pronounced tor-*kee*) have been amalgamated under the common moniker of Torbay. Torquay is the supposed site of the hotel in the popular British television comedy *Fawlty Towers,* and was the home of mystery writer Agatha Christie. Fans should check out the exhibition devoted to Christie at the town museum and her reconstructed study at Torre Abbey Mansion.

The town has shed its old-fashion image in recent years, with modern hotels, luxury villas, and apartments that climb the hillsides above the harbor. Palm trees and other semitropical plants flourish in the seafront gardens. The sea is a clear and intense blue, and in summer the whole place has that unmistakable air of what was once called Continental. To sun and swim, head for Anstey's Cove, a favorite spot for scuba divers, with more beaches farther along at neighboring Babbacombe.

Just outside Torbay lies the most Devonish hamlet in England, **Cockington,** which has thatched cottages, a 14th-century forge, and the square-towered Church of St. George and St. Mary. Repair to the Old Mill for a café lunch or head to the Drum Inn, designed by Sir Edwin Lutyens to be an archetypal pub. On the village outskirts lies Cockington Court—a grand estate with shops and an eatery. Although the whole has more than a touch of the faux (cottages that don't sell anything put up signs to this effect), who can resist this dreamy dollop of Devon?

Where to Stay & Eat

£££ ✕ **Remy's.** Torquay's oldest-established French restaurant is known for delightful, straightforward traditional French cooking. Scallops with wild mushrooms and shallots, and guinea fowl with Roquefort cheese and spinach typify the choices on the fixed-price menu. The wine list concentrates on French vintages. ⊠ *3 Croft Rd., Torquay* ☎ *01803/292359* 🖃 *MC, V* ☺ *Closed Sun. and Mon. No lunch.*

★ ££–££££ ✕ **Capers.** A spot for anyone who likes enthusiasm along with the food, this small, select restaurant goes in for serious cooking. Local fish ranks high on the menu, accompanied by vegetables and herbs grown by the chef. Try sea bass with mint and spring onions, or curried crayfish risotto. ✉ *7 Lisburne Sq., Torquay* ☎ *01803/291177* 🚪 *AE, MC, V* 🕐 *Closed Sun. and 1 wk mid-Aug. No lunch.*

★
££££–£££££ 🏨 **The Imperial.** This is arguably Devon's most luxurious hotel, perched above the sea, overlooking Torbay. Magnificent gardens surround the property, and the interior of the 1866 hotel is, well, imperial, with chandeliers, marble floors, and the general air of a bygone world. Most of the traditionally furnished bedrooms are large and comfortable, and many have private balconies. ✉ *Park Hill Rd., Torquay, TQ1 2DG* ☎ *01803/294301* 🖨 *01803/298293* ⊕ *www.paramount-hotels.co.uk* 🛏 *153 rooms, 17 suites* ♿ *2 restaurants, cable TV with movies, tennis court, 2 pools (1 indoor), health club, sauna, squash, business services, meeting rooms; no a/c* 🚪 *AE, DC, MC, V* ❄ *BP.*

££ 🏨 **Fairmount House Hotel.** Near the village of Cockington, on the edge of Torquay, this relaxed, family-run Victorian hotel has a pretty south-facing garden. Guest rooms are solidly furnished; two have private access to the garden, as does the Victorian Conservatory Bar. The restaurant favors homegrown and local produce. ✉ *Herbert Rd., Chelston, Torquay, TQ2 6RW* ☎🖨 *01803/605446* ⊕ *www.smoothhound.co.uk* 🛏 *8 rooms* ♿ *Restaurant, bar, some pets allowed (fee); no a/c, no room phones* 🚪 *MC, V* ❄ *BP.*

Exeter

🅖 *23 mi north of Torbay, 48 mi northeast of Plymouth, 85 mi southwest of Bristol, 205 mi southwest of London.*

Devon's county seat, Exeter, has been the capital of the region since the Romans established a fortress here 2,000 years ago. Little evidence of the Roman occupation exists, apart from the great city walls. Although it was heavily bombed in 1942, Exeter retains much of its medieval character, as well as examples of the gracious architecture of the 18th and 19th centuries.

At the heart of Exeter, the great Gothic **Cathedral of St. Peter** was begun in 1275 and completed almost a century later. Its twin towers are even older survivors of an earlier Norman cathedral. Rising from a forest of ribbed columns, the nave's 300-foot stretch of unbroken Gothic vaulting is the longest in the world. Myriad statues, tombs, and memorial plaques adorn the interior. In the minstrels' gallery, high up on the left of the nave, stands a group of carved figures singing and playing musical instruments, including bagpipes. The **Close,** a pleasant green space for relaxing on a sunny day, surrounds the cathedral. Don't miss the 400-year-old door to No. 10, the bishop of Crediton's house, ornately carved with angels' and lions' heads. ✉ *Cathedral Close* ☎ *01392/214219* ⊕ *www.exeter-cathedral.org.uk* 🖂 *£3.50 suggested donation* 🕐 *Weekdays 8–6:30, Sat. 8–5, Sun. 8–7:30; free guided tours Apr.–Oct., daily at 11 and 2:30.*

With its half-timber facade bearing the coat of arms of Elizabeth I, **Mol's Coffee House** (now a store), on the corner of Cathedral Close, is redolent of bygone times. It is said that Sir Francis Drake met his admirals here to plan strategy against the Spanish Armada in 1588. Opposite the cathedral, the 1769 **Royal Clarence Hotel** was England's first inn to be described as a "hotel"—a designation applied by an enterprising French manager. It is named after the duchess of Clarence, who stayed here in 1827 on her way to visit her husband, the future William IV.

The **Guildhall,** just behind the Close, is said to be the oldest municipal building in the country still in use. The current hall, with its Renaissance portico, dates from 1330, although a guildhall has occupied this site since at least 1160. Its timber-braced roof, one of the earliest in England, dates from about 1460. ⊠ *High St.* ☎ *01392/265500* 🎫 *Free* ⊙ *Weekdays 10:30–1 and 2–4, Sat. 10–noon (alternate Sat. only in winter), unless in use for a civic function.*

Devon's fine **Royal Albert Memorial Museum** houses natural-history displays, a superb collection of Exeter silverware, and the work of some West Country artists. There is also an excellent international gallery and a fine archaeological section. ⊠ *Queen St.* ☎ *01392/265858* ⊕ *www.exeter.gov.uk* 🎫 *Free* ⊙ *Mon.–Sat. 10–5.*

The **Rougemont Gardens** (⊠ Off Queen St.), behind the Royal Albert Memorial Museum, were first laid out at the end of the 18th century. The land was once part of the defensive ditch of Rougemont Castle, built in 1068 by decree of William the Conqueror. Here you will find the original Norman gatehouse and the remains of the Roman city wall, the latter forming part of the ancient castle's outer wall; nothing else remains.

Just off the High Street, the **Underground Passages,** which once served as conduits for fresh water to the city, are the only medieval vaulted passages open to the public in England. They date back to the mid-14th century, although many now have a Victorian veneer. An exhibition and video precede the 40-minute guided tour. Many of the passages are narrow and low; be prepared to stoop. ⊠ *Romangate Passage* ☎ *01392/ 665887* ⊕ *www.exeter.gov.uk* 🎫 *June–Sept. £3.75, Oct.–May £3* ⊙ *June–Sept. and school vacations, Mon.–Sat. 10–5; Oct.–May, Tues.–Fri. noon–5, Sat. 10–5.*

need a break? At **The Prospect Inn** (⊠ The Quay ☎ 01392/273152), you can contemplate the quayside comings and goings over a pint of beer or ale and a hot or cold meal. The nautical theme comes through in pictures and the ship's wheel hanging from the ceiling.

Exeter's historic waterfront on the River Exe was once the center of the city's medieval wool industry, and the **Custom House,** built in 1682 on The Quay, attests to its prosperity. Victorian warehouses flank the city's earliest surviving brick building. The **Quay House,** a late-17th-century stone warehouse, houses the Heritage Centre, with documents on the maritime history of the city and an audiovisual display. ⊠ *The Quay* ☎ *01392/265213* 🎫 *Free* ⊙ *Apr.–Oct., daily 10–5; Nov.–Mar., weekends 11–4.*

off the beaten path **POWDERHAM CASTLE** – Seat of the earls of Devon, this notable stately home 8 mi south of Exeter is famed for its staircase hall, a soaring fantasia of white stuccowork on a turquoise background, constructed in 1739–69. Other sumptuous rooms, adorned with family portraits by Sir Godfrey Kneller and Reynolds, were used in the Merchant-Ivory film *Remains of the Day.* A tower built in 1400 by Sir Philip Courtenay, ancestor of the current owners, stands in the deer park. The restaurant serves traditional English fare, and there's a farm shop and plant center. ⊠ A379, Kenton ☎ 01626/ 890243 ⊕ www.powderham.co.uk 🎫 £6.90 ⊙ Apr.–Oct., Sun.–Fri. 10–5:30.

Where to Stay & Eat

★ **✕ St. Olaves.** One of the finest dining spots in the West Country, this
££££–£££££ restaurant in a Georgian house with a walled garden is part of St. Olaves Court Hotel. The bar overlooks the lovely garden. From the fixed-price menus, you might try the pan-roasted venison with shallots or steamed fillet of lemon sole with lobster and crab mousse, followed by

hot chocolate fondant with rosemary ice cream. ✉ *Mary Arches St.* ☎ *01392/217736* ▭ *DC, MC, V.*

£–££ ✕**Hansons.** Near the cathedral, this spot is ideal for lunch, coffee, or snacks when you're seeing the sights. You can also sample one of Devon's famous cream teas, served with jam, scones, and clotted cream. ✉ *1 Cathedral Close* ☎ *01392/276913* ▭ *AE, DC, MC, V* ⊙ *Closed Sun. No dinner.*

£–££ ✕**Ship Inn.** Here you can lift a tankard of stout in the very rooms where Sir Francis Drake and Sir Walter Raleigh enjoyed their ale. Drake, in fact, once wrote, "Next to mine own shippe, I do most love that old 'Shippe' in Exon." The pub dishes out casual bar fare, and the upstairs restaurant serves the usual grilled lemon sole and other English dishes. ✉ *St. Martin's La.* ☎ *01392/272040* ▭ *MC, V* ⊙ *No dinner upstairs restaurant on weekends.*

£ ✕**Herbie's.** A mellow stop for lunch or dinner, this friendly, no-frills veg-
Fodor's Choice etarian restaurant is ideal for unwinding over leisurely conversation. You
★ can snack on pita bread with hummus and cottage cheese fillings, or tackle the carrot and cashew nut loaf or spinach and mushroom lasagna. All wines and the superb ice cream are organic. ✉ *15 North St.* ☎ *01392/ 258473* ▭ *MC, V* ⊙ *Closed Sun. No dinner Mon.*

££££ ✕▥**Royal Clarence Hotel.** This hotel is wonderfully situated within the Cathedral Close. It has a branch of the ultrachic Michael Caines (of Gidleigh Park fame) restaurants, with fine French-accented contemporary fare. The restaurant's modern look includes smart pinstripe upholstery, but the rest of the hotel is traditional in style; many rooms have oak paneling. ✉ *Cathedral Yard, EX1 1HB* ☎ *01392/319955* ☎ *01392/ 439423* ⊕ *www.corushotels.co.uk* ⇌ *56 rooms* ♦ *Restaurant, 2 bars, meeting rooms, some pets allowed (fee); no a/c* ▭ *AE, DC, MC, V.*

£££ ✕▥**Hotel Barcelona.** Sister to the Kandinsky in Cheltenham, this hip, classy hotel occupies the old redbrick eye hospital, as the long corridors and big elevators testify. Bright furnishings and ornaments from the 1930s to the 1960s give rooms an individual appeal, and the aquamarine bathrooms are luxurious. You'll find Spanish and other Mediterranean flavors in the semicircular bistro-style restaurant. ✉ *Magdalen St., EX2 4HY* ☎ *01392/281000* ☎ *01392/281001* ⊕ *www.hotelbarcelona-uk. com* ⇌ *46 rooms* ♦ *Restaurant, in-room data ports, cable TV with movies, in-room VCRs, croquet, bar, nightclub, meeting rooms, some pets allowed (fee); no a/c* ▭ *AE, DC, MC, V.*

££ ✕▥**White Hart.** It is said that Oliver Cromwell stabled his horses here, and guests have been welcomed since the 15th century. Beyond the lovely cobbled entrance, the main building retains all the trappings of a period inn—beams, stone walls, a central courtyard—but there are also fully modern bedrooms in one wing. The hotel has an English restaurant, a wine bar, and a more casual ale-and-port house. Try the local salmon or the chicken and chestnut pie. ✉ *66 South St., EX1 1EE* ☎ *01392/279897* ☎ *01392/250159* ⊕ *www.roomattheinn.info* ⇌ *55 rooms* ♦ *Restaurant, bar, wine bar; no a/c* ▭ *AE, DC, MC, V* ⊙❙ *BP.*

£ ▥**Hotel Maurice.** There's nothing fancy in this quiet hotel close by Exeter Central train station, just clean, neat, and cheerful rooms, small in size but more than adequate for a night or two. The main benefit is the location in a calm Georgian square, just a stroll away from all the sights. ✉ *5 Bystock Terr., EX4 4HY* ☎ *01392/213079* ⊕ *www. hotelmaurice.eclipse.co.uk* ⇌ *8 rooms* ♦ *No a/c, no smoking* ▭ *MC, V* ⊙❙ *BP.*

Nightlife & the Arts

Among the best known of the West Country's festivals, the **Exeter Festival** (☎ 01392/265205) mixes musical and theater events each July. Some of London's best companies often stage plays at the **Northcott Theatre** (⊠ Stocker Rd. ☎ 01392/493493).

Shopping

Until 1882 Exeter was the silver-assay office for the West Country, and it's possible to find Exeter silver, particularly spoons, in some antiques and silverware stores. The earliest example of Exeter silver (now a museum piece) dates from 1218, and Victorian pieces are still sold. The Exeter assay mark is three castles. **William Bruford** (⊠ 17 The Guildhall Centre, Queen St. ☎ 01392/254901) stocks antique jewelry and silver.

Topsham

🔟 *4 mi southeast of Exeter on B3182.*

The town of Topsham is full of narrow streets and hidden courtyards. This once-bustling port remains rich in 18th-century houses and inns. Occupying a 17th-century Dutch-style merchant's house beside the river, the **Topsham Museum** includes period-furnished rooms and an eclectic collection, displaying everything from local history and wildlife to memorabilia belonging to the late actress Vivien Leigh. ⊠ *25 The Strand* ☎ *01392/873244* 🔳 *Free* ☉ *Easter–Oct., Mon., Wed., and weekends 2–5.*

★ The 16-sided, nearly circular **A la Ronde,** surely one of the most unusual houses in England, was built in 1798 and inspired by the Church of San Vitale in Ravenna, Italy. Among the 18th- and 19th-century curiosities here is an elaborate display of feathers and shells. The house is 5 mi south of Topsham. ⊠ *Summer La., on A376 near Exmouth* ☎ *01395/265514* ⊕ *www.nationaltrust.org.uk* 🔳 *£3.50* ☉ *Apr.–Oct., Sun.–Thurs. 11–5:30; last admission at 5.*

en route The Devon coast from Exmouth to the Dorset border 26 mi to the east has been designated an Area of Outstanding Natural Beauty. The reddish, grass-topped cliffs of the region are punctuated by quiet seaside resorts such as Budleigh Salterton, Sidmouth, and Seaton.

Beer

🔟 *22 mi east of Topsham, 26 mi east of Exeter, 33 mi south of Taunton.*

Beer, just outside Seaton, was once a favorite smugglers' haunt, and this fishing village has remained fairly unchanged. It was also the source of the white stone used for numerous Devon churches, Exeter Cathedral, and, farther afield, Winchester Cathedral, Westminster Abbey, and the Tower of London. A tour of the **Beer Quarry Caves**, worked from Roman times until 1900, guides you around the impressive underground network. A small exhibition includes tools and examples of carved stone. ⊠ *Quarry La.* ☎ *01297/680282* ⊕ *www.beerquarrycaves.fsnet.co.uk* 🔳 *£4.75* ☉ *Easter–Sept., daily 10–5; Oct., daily 11–4; last admission 30 mins before closing.*

Honiton

🔟 *10 mi northwest of Beer on A3052/A375, 19 mi south of Taunton.*

Handsome Georgian houses line Honiton's long High Street. Modern storefronts have intruded, but the original facades remain at second-floor level. For 300 years the town was known for lace making, and the industry was revived when Queen Victoria selected the fabric for her wedding veil in 1840. Lace has not been made here commercially since the early 20th century, but individuals still keep up the craft.

After viewing the splendid collection of lace at **Allhallows Museum**, it's worth delving into the antiques shops where prized early examples are sold. ⊠ *High St.* ☎ *01404/44966* ⊕ *www.honitonmuseum.co.uk* ⊠ *£2* ⊙ *Mid-Apr.–Oct., weekdays 9:30–4:30, Sat. 9:30–12:30.*

Where to Stay & Eat

£–££ ✕ **Dominoes.** For a satisfying lunch or dinner, try this wine bar, extravagantly decorated with murals, cherubs, and other Parisian frippery. You can get everything from nachos to rack of lamb. ⊠ *178 High St.* ☎ *01404/47707* ☐ *MC, V.*

££££ ▦ **Combe House Hotel.** Rolling parkland surrounds this Elizabethan manor house. From the imposing entrance hall, with its huge, open fireplace, to the spacious, individually decorated bedrooms, the emphasis is on country-house style that mixes antiques and modern comfort. You can fish on a 1½-mi stretch of the River Otter and explore the pretty village of Gittisham, just west of Honiton. ⊠ *Gittisham, EX14 3AD* ☎ *01404/540400* 🖷 *01404/46004* ⊕ *www.thishotel.com* ⇝ *14 rooms, 1 suite* ⚒ *Restaurant, in-room data ports, fishing, meeting rooms, some pets allowed (fee); no a/c* ☐ *AE, DC, MC, V* ⦿ *BP.*

Shopping

Honiton has several dozen fine antiques stores. The **Lace Shop** (⊠ *44 High St.* ☎ *01404/42416*) has everything needed for lace making and examples of old and new work for sale.

Montacute House

★ ⑥ *30 mi northeast of Honiton on A30 and A303, 30 mi southeast of Taunton, 44 mi south of Bristol.*

Rich with fine Elizabethan details, this house was built in the late 16th century of the golden limestone found in this part of Somerset and used in many local villages and mansions. The 189-foot-long gallery brims with Elizabethan and Jacobean portraits, most on loan from the National Portrait Gallery, and the house also contains a good collection of textiles. Pick a bright day to visit: some rooms do not have electric light. ⊠ *A3088, Yeovil, turn south off A303 at Stoke sub Hamdon* ☎ *01935/ 823289* ⊕ *www.nationaltrust.org.uk* ⊠ *£6.50, garden and park only £3.50 Apr.–Oct., £2 Nov.–Mar.* ⊙ *House Apr.–Oct., Wed.–Mon. 11–5; last admission at 4:30. Garden and park Apr.–Oct., Wed.–Mon. 11–6 or dusk; Nov.–Mar., Wed.–Sun. 11–4.*

Where to Stay & Eat

£££ ✕▦ **King's Arms.** This nicely decorated 16th-century inn was constructed with the same warm golden stone as nearby Montacute House. Much of the interior incorporates the local stone, harmoniously integrated with details such as an engraved archway rescued from Coventry Cathedral (bombed in World War II). The pastel guest rooms are quite modern, however. The menu in the Abbey Room lists a huge selection of dishes, but the fare is mostly British, from rib-eye steak to baked duck breast. ⊠ *Bishopston, Montacute, TA15 6UU* ☎ *01935/822513* 🖷 *01935/ 826549* ⇝ *15 rooms* ⚒ *2 restaurants, bar; no a/c* ☐ *AE, MC, V* ⦿ *BP.*

Yeovilton

⑥ *7 mi north of Yeovil.*

☉ The village of Yeovilton has a Royal Naval Air Station. The **Fleet Air Arm Museum** displays more than 50 historic aircraft, among them the Concorde 002. The spectacular "Carrier" exhibit includes a simulated helicopter ride over the ocean to an aircraft carrier and a unique re-creation of the flight deck of a working carrier, complete with 12 actual planes from the 1960s and 1970s. ⊠ *Royal Naval Air Station Yeovilton, signposted on B3151 at Ilchester from A303 or A37* ☎ *01935/840565* ⊕ *www.fleetairarm.com* ✉ *£8.50* ⊙ *Apr.–Oct., daily 10–5:30; Nov.–Mar., daily 10–4:30.*

Cadbury Castle

62 *7 mi northeast of Yeovilton, 17 mi south of Wells.*

Cadbury Castle (⊠ Off A303, South Cadbury) is said to be the site of Camelot—it's one among several contenders for the honor. Glastonbury Tor, rising dramatically in the distance across the plain, adds to the atmosphere of Arthurian romance. A legend says that every seven years the hillside opens and Arthur and his followers ride forth to water their horses at nearby Sutton Montis. Cadbury Castle is, in fact, an Iron Age fort (circa 650 BC), with grass-covered, earthen ramparts forming a green wall 300 feet above the surrounding fields. You can park off A303 and then walk about a mile, mostly uphill, to the site; the path is signposted.

THE WEST COUNTRY A TO Z

To research prices, get advice from other travelers, and book travel arrangements, visit www.fodors.com.

AIRPORTS

Bristol International Airport, a few miles southwest of the city on the A38, has flights to and from destinations in Britain and Europe. Plymouth has a small airport 3 mi from town. Exeter International Airport is 5 mi east of Exeter, 2 mi from the M5 motorway. All three airports have flights to the Isles of Scilly during the summer; Land's End Airport also connects daily, and British International operates helicopter flights to the islands from Penzance.

🛈 **Bristol International Airport** ⊠ Bridgwater Rd., Lulsgate, Bristol ☎ 0870/121-2747 ⊕ www.bristolairport.co.uk. **British International** ⊠ Penzance Airport, A30, Penzance ☎ 01736/363871 ⊕ www.scillyhelicopter.co.uk. **Exeter International Airport** ⊠ M5, Junction 29, Exeter ☎ 01392/367433 ⊕ www.exeter-airport.co.uk. **Plymouth City Airport** ⊠ Plymbridge Rd., Plymouth ☎ 01752/204090 or 0845/773-3377. **Skybus** ⊠ Land's End Airport, St. Just ☎ 0845/710-5555; 01736/334220 outside U.K. ⊕ www.ios-travel.co.uk.

BOAT & FERRY TRAVEL

The Isles of Scilly Steamship Company operates ferries from Penzance to St. Mary's at least four times weekly from late March through October. Travel time is 2½ hours, and the trip can be rough. The company also has air service to St. Mary's from Land's End, Newquay, and, from March through October, Bristol and Exeter.

🛈 **Isles of Scilly Steamship Company** ☎ 0845/710-5555; 01736/334220 outside U.K. ⊕ www.ios-travel.co.uk.

BUS TRAVEL

National Express buses leave London's Victoria Coach Station for Bristol (2½ hours), Exeter (3¾ hours), Plymouth (4¾ hours), and Penzance (about 8 hours).

The bus company Stagecoach Devon covers mainly South Devon. First runs most of the services in North Devon, in Plymouth, and throughout Cornwall. Truronian operates in West Cornwall. Ask any of these companies about money-saving one-, three-, and seven-day Explorer passes good for unlimited travel. Buses serve the main towns, but it's best to have a car if you want to explore off the beaten path. For public transportation information, contact Traveline.

FARES &
SCHEDULES 🚌 **First** ☎ 01271/345444 for North Devon; 01752/402060 for Plymouth and Cornwall ⊕ www.firstgroup.com. **National Express** ☎ 0874/580–8080 ⊕ www.nationalexpress.com. **Stagecoach Devon** ☎ 01392/427711 ⊕ www.stagecoachbus.com. **Traveline** ☎ 0870/608–2608 ⊕ www.traveline.org.uk. **Truronian** ☎ 01872/273453 ⊕ www.truronian.co.uk.

CAR RENTAL

🚌 Local Agencies **Avis** ✉ 29 Marsh Green Rd., Marsh Barton Trading Estate, Exeter ☎ 01392/259713 ✉ 20 Commercial Rd., Coxside, Plymouth ☎ 01752/221550 ✉ Tregolls Rd., Truro ☎ 01872/262226. **Enterprise Rent-a-Car** ✉ 8 The Octagon, off Union St. Plymouth ☎ 01752/601000. **Hertz** ✉ Sutton Rd., Coxside, Plymouth ☎ 01752/207207.

CAR TRAVEL

The fastest way from London to the West Country is via the M4 and M5 motorways, bypassing Bristol (115 mi) and heading south to Exeter, in Devon (172 mi). The main roads heading west are A30—which burrows through the center of Devon and Cornwall all the way to Land's End at the tip of Cornwall—A39 (near the northern shore of the peninsula), and A38 (near the southern shore of the peninsula, south of Dartmoor and taking in Plymouth). West of Plymouth, there are few main roads, which results in heavy traffic in summer.

ROAD
CONDITIONS Driving can be tricky, especially as you travel farther west. Most small roads are twisting country lanes flanked by high stone walls and thick hedges that severely restrict visibility.

EMERGENCIES

🚑 **Ambulance, fire, police** ☎ 999. **Derriford Hospital** ✉ Derriford, Plymouth ☎ 01752/792511. **Royal Cornwall Hospital (Treliske)** ✉ A390, Higher Town, Truro ☎ 01872/250000. **Royal Devon and Exeter Hospital** ✉ Barrack Rd., Exeter ☎ 01392/411611.

NATIONAL PARKS

🏞 **Dartmoor National Park Authority** ✉ Parke, Haytor Rd., Bovey Tracey, Newton Abbot, TQ13 9JQ ☎ 01626/832093 ⊕ www.dartmoor-npa.gov.uk. **Exmoor National Park Authority** ✉ Exmoor House, Dulverton, TA22 9HL ☎ 01398/323665 ⊕ www.exmoor-nationalpark.gov.uk.

OUTDOORS & SPORTS

WALKING For information about walking in Dartmoor or Exmoor, contact the National Parks Authority (⊳ National Parks). The South West Coast Path Association has information about the 630-mi-long coastal path.
🥾 **South West Coast Path Association** ✉ Windlestraw, Penquit, Ermington, PL21 0LU ☎ 01752/896237 ⊕ www.swcp.org.uk.

TOURS

South West Tourism (⊳ Visitor Information) and local tourist information centers have lists of qualified guides. West Country Tour Guides (Blue Badge) offers walking tours around Plymouth's old town and can arrange tours throughout Devon and Cornwall.
🚶 **West Country Tourist Guides (Blue Badge)** ☎ 01726/813463 ⊕ www.luxsoft.demon.co.uk/awctg.

TRAIN TRAVEL

First Great Western and South West Trains serve the region from London's Paddington and Waterloo stations; contact National Rail Enquiries for details. Average travel time to Exeter is 2½ hours; to Plymouth, 3½ hours; and to Penzance, about 5½ hours.

Regional Rail Rover tickets provide seven days' unlimited travel throughout the West Country, and localized Rovers cover Devon or Cornwall.

🚹 **National Rail Enquiries** ☎ 0845/748–4950 ⊕ www.nationalrail.co.uk.

TRAVEL AGENCIES
🚹 Local Agent Referrals **American Express** ✉ 139 Armada Way, Plymouth ☎ 01752/502706. **Thomas Cook** ✉ c/o HSBC Bank, 38 High St., Exeter ☎ 01392/425712 ✉ 9 Old Town St., Plymouth ☎ 01752/612600.

VISITOR INFORMATION
Local tourist information centers are usually open Monday–Saturday 9:30–5:30; they are listed after the regional offices below by town.
🚹 **South West Tourism** ✉ Woodwater Park, Pynes Hill, Exeter, EX2 5WT ☎ 01392/360050 🖷 01392/445112 ⊕ www.westcountrynow.com. **Cornwall Tourist Board** ✉ Pydar House, Pydar St., Truro, TR1 1EA ☎ 01872/274057 🖷 01872/322895 ⊕ www.cornwalltouristboard.co.uk. **Devon Tourist Information Service** 🕭 Box 55, Barnstaple, EX32 8YR ☎ 0870/608–5531 ⊕ www.devon.gov.uk. **Somerset Visitor Centre** ✉ Sedgemoor Service Station, M5 Southbound ☎ 01934/750833 🖷 01934/750646 ⊕ www.somerset.gov.uk/tourism.

Bristol ✉ The Annexe, Wildscreen Walk, Harbourside ☎ 0870/586–2313, at cost of 60p per min ⊕ www.visitbristol.co.uk ✉ written inquiries, Bristol Tourism and Conference Bureau, St. Nicholas St., BS1 1UE. **Exeter** ✉ Civic Centre, Paris St., EX1 1JJ ☎ 01392/265700 ⊕ www.exeter.gov.uk. **Falmouth** ✉ 28 Killigrew St., TR11 3PN ☎ 01326/312300 ⊕ www.go-cornwall.com. **Glastonbury** ✉ The Tribunal, High St., BA6 9DP ☎ 01458/832954. **Isles of Scilly** ✉ Hugh St., Hugh Town, St. Mary's ☎ 01720/422536 ⊕ www.simplyscilly.co.uk. **Okehampton** ✉ Okehampton Museum Yard, West St., EX20 1HQ ☎ 01837/53020 **Penzance** ✉ Station Approach, TR18 2NF ☎ 01736/362207 ⊕ www.go-cornwall.com. **Plymouth** ✉ Island House, 9 The Barbican, PL1 2LS ☎ 0870/225–4950 ⊕ www.visitplymouth.co.uk. **St. Ives** ✉ The Guildhall, Street-an-Pol, TR26 2DS ☎ 01736/796297 ⊕ www.go-cornwall.com. **Taunton** ✉ Paul St., TA1 3XZ ☎ 01823/336344 ⊕ www.heartofsomerset.com. **Truro** ✉ City Hall, Boscawen St., TR1 2NE ☎ 01872/274555 ⊕ www.truro.gov.uk. **Wells** ✉ Town Hall, Market Pl., BA5 2RB ☎ 01749/672552 ⊕ www.wells-uk.com.

THE THAMES VALLEY

WINDSOR, HENLEY-ON-THAMES, OXFORD, BLENHEIM PALACE

5

FODOR'S CHOICE

Blenheim Palace, *Woodstock*

Cliveden hotel, *Taplow*

Grand Café, *Oxford*

Le Manoir aux Quat' Saisons, *restaurant in Great Milton*

Punting on the river, *Oxford*

Stowe Landscape Garden, *near Aylesbury*

HIGHLY RECOMMENDED

RESTAURANTS Le Petit Blanc, *Oxford*

Rosamund the Fair, *Oxford*

HOTELS Old Parsonage, *Oxford*

The Bear, *Woodstock*

The Feathers, *Woodstock*

SIGHTS Eton College, *Eton*

Magdalen College, *Oxford*

Mapledurham House, *Mapledurham*

Radcliffe Camera and Bodleian Library, *Oxford*

Runnymede, *Egham*

Windsor Castle, *Windsor*

Woburn Abbey, *Woburn*

Woodstock

Updated by
Catherine
Belonogoff

THE RIVER GLIDETH AT HIS OWN SWEET WILL was how Wordsworth described the Thames in "Upon Westminster Bridge." Like other great rivers, such as the Seine and the Danube, it creates the illusion of flowing not only through the prosperous countryside of Berkshire and Oxfordshire, but through long centuries of history, too. The past seems to rise from its swiftly moving waters like an intangible mist. In London, where it's a broad oily stream, the Thames speeds almost silently past great buildings, menacingly impressive. Higher upstream it's a busy part of the living landscape, flooding meadows in spring and fall and rippling past places holding significance not just for England but also the world. Runnymede is one of these. Here, on a riverside greensward, the Magna Carta was signed, a crucial step in the Western world's progress toward democracy.

Nearby rises the medieval bulk of Windsor Castle, home of monarchs from eight successive royal houses. Anyone who wants to understand the mystique of the British monarchy should visit Windsor, where a fraction of the current Queen's vast wealth is on display in surroundings of heraldic splendor. Farther upstream lie the quadrangles and turrets of Oxford, where generations of the ruling elite have been educated. Close by Oxford are the storybook village of Woodstock and Blenheim Palace, one of the grandest houses in all the land.

Along the River Thames, scattered throughout the unfolding landscape of trees, meadows, and hills, are numerous small villages and larger towns, some spoiled by ill-considered modern building, many still sleepily preserving their ancient charm. The railroads and superhighways carrying heavy traffic between London, the West Country, and the Midlands have turned much of this area into commuter territory, but you can easily depart from these beaten tracks to discover timeless villages whose landscapes are kept green by the river and its tributaries. The stretches of the Thames near Marlow, Henley, and Sonning-on-Thames are havens for relaxation, with rowing clubs, piers, and well-built cottages and villas. Anyone who comes to London in summer and has some time to spare would be well advised to spend it touring the Thames Valley.

Exploring the Thames Valley

An exploration of the Thames Valley can begin in the lively town of Windsor, favorite home-away-from-home of Britain's Royal Family. From there you can follow the river to Henley, site of the famous regatta, and then make a counterclockwise sweep west to Wallingford—the countryside immortalized by *The Wind in the Willows*. You can head north to Oxford next, and end with a visit to some stately homes and palaces. The area also abounds with tiny villages hidden from the major highways.

About the Restaurants & Hotels

The Thames Valley is a popular escape for Londoners as well as a commuter area, so it's highly advisable to make restaurant reservations, especially on weekends.

From converted country houses to refurbished Elizabethan inns, the region's accommodations are rich in history and distinctive in appeal. Many hotels cultivate traditional gardens and retain a sense of the past with impressive collections of antiques, whereas others have embraced the future with fully modern amenities. Book ahead, particularly in summer; you're competing for rooms with many Londoners in search of a getaway.

5

With your own transportation, you can see all the places outlined below on day trips from London, but to get the most out of the region, it's worth staying at that perfect riverside inn or High Street hotel and settling in for a night—or more. Evenings in Windsor or Oxford will allow you to take in some world-class theater, and to make the most out of the mornings for touring the surrounding countryside. The area offers the greatest pleasure to those willing to leave the main roads to explore the smaller centers; to best appreciate the Thames itself, set off on foot along the towpath that runs alongside much of the river. You could spent a month exploring the Thames Valley, but three days will give you a taste of Windsor, a few towns, Blenheim Palace, and Oxford. Five days allows you to spend more time in Oxford and to explore additional villages and the area's many stately homes.

Numbers in the text correspond to numbers in the margin and on the Thames Valley and Oxford maps.

If you have 3 days

Begin at ▦ **Windsor** ❶ ▶, where royalty is the predominant note, and spend a morning visiting the castle, leaving part of the day for Eton College and Windsor Great Park. The next day, follow the river upstream, taking in the grandeur of the great Astor estate at **Cliveden** ❺ and the pretty village of **Marlow** ❻, where the pubs offer decent snacks for lunch. Head toward **Henley** ❼, where the Thames forms a harmonious dialogue with the medieval buildings alongside, and easy and tranquil walks beckon upstream or down. Reserve the last morning for ▦ **Oxford** ⑫–㉕, whose scholastic air does not dampen the aesthetic and gastronomic pleasures on tap, with an afternoon visit to nearby **Woodstock** ㉖—a lovely English village—and **Blenheim Palace** ㉗, birthplace of Winston Churchill and one of the most spectacular houses in England.

If you have 5 days

Make your base at ▦ **Windsor** ❶ ▶ for your first night. From there you can take excursions to **Ascot** ❹, for some of England's finest horse racing, and, to the north, **Cliveden** ❺. For your second night, consider staying in ▦ **Henley** ❼, from which it's an easy trip to the aristocratic **Mapledurham House** ❾ and a cluster of attractive Thames-side villages, such as **Sonning-on-Thames** ❽ and **Dorchester-on-Thames** ㉜. Reserve the third day and night for the medieval wonders of ▦ **Oxford** ⑫–㉕; then head on your fourth day to the nearby 18th-century village of ▦ **Woodstock** ㉖, site of magisterial **Blenheim Palace** ㉗. For the final day, swing eastward to the town of **Great Milton** ㉝ for perhaps the grandest luncheon of your English trip, at Le Manoir aux Quat' Saisons. Next, pay a call on one or two of a trio of stately homes: Waddesdon Manor near **Aylesbury** ㉞, **Woburn Abbey** ㊱, or **Althorp** ㊲.

WHAT IT COSTS In pounds				
	£££££	££££	£££	££	£
RESTAURANTS	over £22	£18–£22	£13–£17	£7–£12	under £7
HOTELS	over £160	£115–£160	£80–£115	£50–£80	under £50

Restaurant prices are for a main course at dinner. Hotel prices are for two people in a standard double room in high season, including VAT, with no meals or, if indicated, CP (with Continental breakfast), BP (Breakfast Plan, with full breakfast), or MAP (Modified American Plan, with breakfast and dinner).

Timing

Although the verdant countryside around the Thames can be alluring year-round, the depths of winter may not be the time most conducive to appreciating its special beauty. High summer is lovely, but droves of visitors descend on popular sights in the area; avoid August and September if you can. June and July are the times for Henley's Royal Regatta and Ascot's Royal Meeting. Spring and autumn reveal the countryside at its best. Remember, however, that visiting at Eton and the Oxford colleges is much more restricted during term time. Most stately homes are open March through September or October only, and a number have very limited opening hours. Check in advance if you're planning an itinerary. Avoid any driving in the London area during the rush hour, which starts an hour or two earlier than usual on Friday.

WINDSOR & ENVIRONS

Windsor Castle is one of the jewels of the area known as Royal Windsor, but a journey around this section of the Thames has other classic pleasures. The town of Eton holds the eponymous public school, Ascot has its famous racecourse, and Cliveden is a stately home turned into a very grand hotel. At Runnymede you can honor an early step toward democracy.

Windsor

▶ ❶ *21 mi west of London.*

Only a small part of old Windsor—the settlement that grew up around the town's famous castle in the Middle Ages—has survived. Windsor Town is not what it used to be in the time of Sir John Falstaff and the *Merry Wives of Windsor*, when it was famous for its inns, of which, in 1650, it boasted about 70. Today only a handful remain, and the beer is not so strong and the wit not so rapier-sharp. The presence of sightseers can be overwhelming at times, but seekers of romantic history will appreciate narrow, cobbled Church Lane and Queen Charlotte Street, opposite the castle entrance. The venerable buildings of Windsor Town now house antiques shops and restaurants.

★ **Windsor Castle,** the longtime home of England's monarchs, was built to be visible for miles around, a monumental symbol of authority. From William the Conqueror to Queen Victoria, the kings and rulers of England added towers and wings to the brooding structure, and it is today the largest inhabited castle in the world. Yet despite the multiplicity of hands that have gone into its design, the palace has managed to emerge with a unity of style and character. Easily accessible from London, the castle and its surrounding town make for a rewarding day trip.

The most impressive view of Windsor Castle is from the A332 road, on the southern approach to the town. William the Conqueror began work

5

Great Flavors

Londoners weekend here, and where they go, Cordon Bleu restaurants follow. Ascot, Henley, and Woodstock claim some of Britain's best tables—beginning with Le Manoir aux Quat' Saisons in Great Milton (whose eight-course *menu gourmand* is the perfect topper to an afternoon spent exploring *le style Rothschild* at nearby Waddesdon Manor) and continuing on with the Oak Leaf in Oakley Court near Windsor and the jewel-like Feathers in Woodstock. Simple pub food, as well as classic French cuisine, can be enjoyed in waterside settings at many restaurants beside the Thames. Even in towns away from the river, well-heeled commuters and Oxford professors support top-flight establishments.

Henley Royal Regatta

During the cusp of June and July Henley hosts rowing's most elegant race, the Henley Royal Regatta. Its riverbanks become one gigantic, opulent lawn party as 500,000 visitors, including members of the Royal Family, descend en masse during the week. Each day, the racing pauses twice, at noon for luncheon and at 4 PM for tea (more likely a bottle of Pimm's "champers"—champagne—and some Kent strawberries with fresh Henley cream). If you're lucky enough to get a spot near the finish line, you'll swear you're back in Edwardian England.

Hiking & Walking

The Thames Valley is a good area for gentle walking; it's not too hilly, and handy eateries, especially pubs, and plenty of easily accessible, comfortable lodgings dot the riverside and small towns. For long-distance walkers, the Oxfordshire Way runs 65 mi from Henley-on-Thames to Bourton-on-the-Water, on the eastern edge of the Cotswolds. A 13-mi ramble starts in Henley, runs north through the Hambleden Valley, and returns to Henley via the Assendons, Lower and Middle. The Thames is almost completely free of car traffic along the Thames Path, a 180-mi route following the river from the London flood barrier to its source near Kemble, in the Cotswolds. The path follows towpaths from the outskirts of London, through Windsor, to Oxford and Lechlade. Good public transportation in the region makes it possible to start and stop easily anywhere along this route. In summer the walking is fine and no special gear is necessary, but in winter the path often floods—check before you head out.

---

on the castle in the 11th century, and Edward III modified and extended it in the mid-1300s. One of Edward's largest contributions was the enormous and distinctive **Round Tower.** Finally, between 1824 and 1837, George IV transformed the still essentially medieval castle into the fortified royal palace you see today. Most kings and queens of England have demonstrated their undying attachment to the castle, the only royal residence that has been in continuous use by the Royal Family since the Middle Ages.

Just outside the castle, on St. Albans Street, is the **Royal Mews,** where the royal horses are kept, with carriages, coaches, and splendid crimson and gold harnesses. The **Jubilee Garden,** created in 2002, has a central stone bandstand used for concerts on summer Sunday afternoons. The garden begins at the main gates and extends to St. George's Gate on Castle Hill.

The Thames Valley

Warwick

Middle Tysoe
Lower Tysoe
Upper Tysoe
Banbury

OXFORDSHIRE

Chipping
Norton

Bourton-
on-the-Water

Weston-on-
the-Green

Woodstock 26
Blenheim Palace 27
28 **Bladon**

Burford

Witney

Wolvercote

Oxford
12 – 25
see detail
map

Garsington

**Stanton
Harcourt
Manor** 29

Cumnor

Thames

**Kelmscott
Manor**
30

Abingdon

Faringdon

**Dorchester-
on-Thames** 32

VALE OF WHITE HORSE

Wallingford 11

Uffington 31

Wantage

Thames

Swindon

LAMBOURN
DOWNS

Pangbourn

M4

Marlborough   Hungerford

Hungerford
Newtown

BERKSHIR

Newbury

WILTSHIRE

KEY

▶ *Start of itinerary*

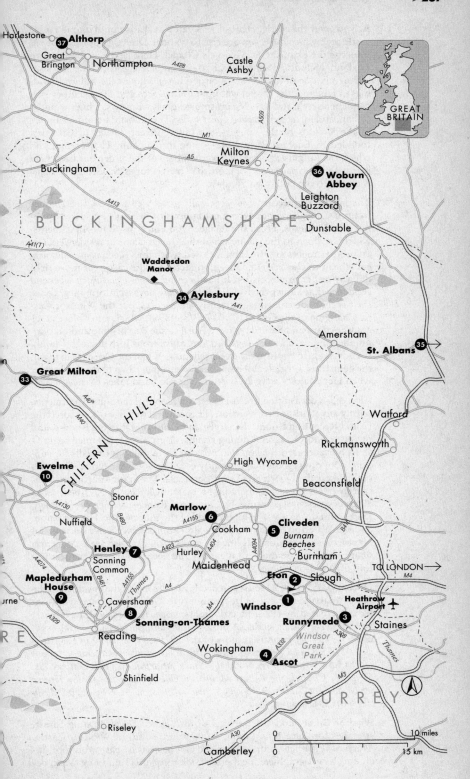

As you enter the castle, **Henry VIII's gateway** leads uphill into the wide castle precincts, where you are free to wander. Directly opposite the entrance is the exquisite **St. George's Chapel.** Here lie 10 of the kings of England, including Henry VI, Charles I, and Henry VIII (Jane Seymour is the only one of his six wives buried here). One of the noblest buildings in England, the chapel was built in the 15th- and 16th-century Perpendicular style and has elegant stained-glass windows, a high, vaulted ceiling, and intricately carved choir stalls. The colorful heraldic banners of the Knights of the Garter—the oldest British Order of Chivalry, founded by Edward III in 1348—hang in the choir. The ceremony in which the knights are installed as members of the order has been held here with much pageantry for more than five centuries. St. George's Chapel is closed to the public on Sunday.

The **North Terrace** provides especially good views across the Thames to Eton College, perhaps the most famous of Britain's exclusive "public" boys' schools. From the terrace, you enter the **State Apartments,** which are open to the public when the Queen is not in residence. (The State Apartments are sometimes closed when the Queen is in residence; call ahead to check.) The Queen, in fact, uses the castle far more than did any of her predecessors. It has become a sort of country weekend residence that allows the Royal Family a few days of informality. To see the royal abode come magnificently alive, check out the Windsor Castle **Changing of the Guard** (☎ 01753/869898), which takes place at 11 AM weekdays and Saturdays from April to the end of June and on odd-numbered days on weekdays and Saturdays from July through March. It's advisable to confirm the exact schedule. When the Queen is in town, the guard and a regimental band parade through town to the castle gate; when Her Majesty is away, a drum-and-fife band takes over.

Although a devastating fire in 1992 gutted some of the State Apartments, hardly any works of art were lost. Phenomenal repair work restored the **Grand Reception Room,** the **Green and Crimson Drawing Rooms,** and the **State and Octagonal dining rooms.** A green oak hammer-beam (a short horizontal roof beam that projects from the tops of walls for support) roof now looms magnificently over the 600-year-old **St. George's Hall,** where the Queen gives state banquets. The State Apartments contain priceless furniture, including a magnificent Louis XVI bed; Gobelin tapestries; and paintings by Canaletto, Rubens, Van Dyck, Holbein, Dürer, and del Sarto. The high points of the tour are the **Throne Room** and the **Waterloo Chamber,** where Sir Thomas Lawrence's portraits of Napoléon's victorious foes line the walls. You can also see a collection of arms and armor, much of it exotic, and an exhibition on the restoration of Windsor Castle.

Queen Mary's Doll's House, on display to the left of the entrance to the State Apartments, is a perfect miniature Georgian palace-within-a-palace, created in 1923. Electric lights work, the doors all have keys, and there is running water. A library holds Lilliputian-size books especially written by famous authors of the 1920s. ☎ 020/7321–2233 tickets; 01753/83118 recorded information ⊕ www.royalresidences.com ☒ £11.50 for the Precincts, the State Apartments, the Gallery, St. George's Chapel, the Albert Memorial Chapel, and the Doll's House ⊙ Mar.–Oct., daily 9:45–5:15, last admission 4; Nov.–Feb., daily 9:45–4:15, last admission 3.

Windsor Great Park, the remains of an ancient royal hunting forest, stretches for some 8 mi (about 5,000 acres) south of Windsor Castle. Much of it is open to the public and can be seen by car or on foot, including its geographical focal points, the romantic 3-mi **Long Walk,** designed by Charles II to join castle and park, and **Virginia Water,** a 2-mi-long lake. The park contains Frogmore, one of Queen Victoria's most treasured residences and still a retreat for the Royal Family. On rare occasions, however, the public is invited to **Frogmore House** (☎ 01753/869898 ⊕ www.royalresidences.com ✉ House, gardens, and mausoleum £5.20 ⊙ May, selected days only [check by phone, 10–6]; Aug., selected days only [check by phone, 11–4]). Nearby, at the Royal Mausoleum at Frogmore, two famous royal couples are buried: inside, Victoria and Albert; outside, the Duke and Duchess of Windsor. This is open only a few days a year, with prebooked guided tours also possible on selected weekdays August–October. The main horticultural delight of Windsor Great Park, the exquisite **Savill Garden** (✉ Wick La., Englefield Green, Egham ☎ 01753/847518 ⊕ www.savillgarden.co.uk ✉ £3–£5 ⊙ Mar.–Oct., daily 10–6; Nov.–Feb., daily 10–4), contains a tremendous diversity of trees and shrubs.

☺ An extensive theme park, **Legoland,** 2 mi outside Windsor, celebrates the versatile Lego building brick. Ingenious models small and large, rides and interactive activities, a lakeside picnic area, 150 acres of parkland, and restaurants allow you to make a day of it. ✉ *Winkfield Rd.* ☎ *08705/040404* ⊕ *www.legoland.co.uk* ✉ *£22.95* ⊙ *Apr.–June and Sept.–Jan., daily 10–6; July and Aug., daily 10–8.*

Where to Stay & Eat

£ ✕ **Two Brewers.** Two small low-ceilinged rooms make up this 17th-century pub where locals congregate. Children are not welcome, but adults will find a suitable collection of wine, espresso, and local beer, plus an excellent little menu with dishes from salmon fish cakes to chili and pasta. Reservations are essential on Sunday, when the pub serves a traditional roast. ✉ *34 Park St.* ☎ *01753/855426* ⊟ *AE, DC, MC, V.*

£££££ ✕⊞ **Oakley Court.** A romantic getaway with plenty of pampering amenities, this Victorian-era mock castle stands on landscaped grounds beside the Thames, 3 mi west of Windsor. Its bristling towers and spires have been used in several films (including the *Rocky Horror Picture Show*); note, however, that half the rooms are in a modern annex. At the excellent Oak Leaf Restaurant, serving French and English fare, Prince Charles has been known to enjoy the fillet of beef with Stilton mousse. ✉ *Windsor Rd., Water Oakley, SL4 5UF* ☎ *01753/609988* 🖷 *01628/ 637011* ⊕*www.moathousehotels.com* ⮡ *106 rooms, 12 suites* ₺ *Restaurant, room service, in-room data ports, in-room safes, minibars, room TV with movies, 9-hole golf course, putting green, 2 tennis courts, indoor pool, gym, hot tub, sauna, spa, steam room, billiards, croquet, bar, lobby lounge, dry cleaning, laundry service, concierge, business services, meeting rooms, no-smoking rooms; no a/c in some rooms* ⊟ *AE, DC, MC, V.*

£££££ ✕⊞ **Stoke Park Club.** On a 350-acre estate 4 mi southwest of Windsor, Stoke Park can make Windsor Castle, off in the distance, seem almost humble in comparison. Architect James Wyatt perfected this version of neoclassical grandeur when he built the house for the Penn family in 1791. Antiques, paintings, and original prints decorate the elegant bedrooms. The Brasserie serves traditional English cuisine. Both *Goldfinger* and *Bridget Jones's Diary* were partly filmed here. ✉ *Park Rd., Stoke Poges, SL2 4PG* ☎ *01753/717171* 🖷 *01753/717181* ⊕ *www. stokeparkclub.com* ⮡ *21 rooms* ₺ *2 restaurants, in-room data ports, cable TV, 27-hole golf course, 12 tennis courts, indoor pool, fitness classes, gym, hot tub, hair salon, massage, spa, steam room, fishing, croquet, squash, 2 bars, meeting rooms* ⊟ *AE, MC, V* ⊚*l BP.*

££££–£££££ ✕⊞ **Sir Christopher Wren's House Hotel.** A private mansion built by the famous architect in 1676, this impressively sober house has a brick facade lightened by white columns and perfectly proportioned windows. Wren's Bedroom, the star of the hotel, has dark wood walls and antique furniture. All rooms are different but tastefully appointed. The riverside Strok's Restaurant has a good fixed-price Continental dinner menu and a Thames-side wooden terrace. ⊠ *Thames St. at Eton Bridge, SL4 1PX* ☎ *01753/861354* 🖷 *01753/442490* ⊕ *www.wrensgroup.com* ⇔ *79 rooms, 5 suites* ♨ *Restaurant, café, in-room data ports, some in-room hot tubs, cable TV, health club, bar, meeting rooms* ⊟ *AE, DC, MC, V* ⦿l *BP.*

£££–£££££ 🏨 **The Castle Hotel.** Past and present lie behind the Georgian facade of this hotel, which includes a main building, built in 1528 as a coaching inn, and a modern wing. Rooms in the older section have gently tilting floors and flowery bedspreads; some rooms have four-poster beds. Piano recitals take place in cozy lounges with beamed ceilings and plush, antique furnishings—perfect for afternoon cream tea. To take advantage of lower prices, book a weekend leisure break with breakfast or half board. ⊠ *High St., SL4 ILJ* ☎ *0870/400–8300* 🖷 *01753/856930* ⊕ *www.macdonaldhotels.co.uk* ⇔ *111 rooms* ♨ *Restaurant, room service, cable TV, bar, lounge, laundry service, meeting rooms, no-smoking rooms; no a/c* ⊟ *AE, DC, MC, V.*

££££ 🏨 **Ye Harte & Garter Hotel.** The location couldn't be better—right across the street from Windsor Castle, with a good view of it from many rooms. Some rooms have balconies and others have whirlpool tubs. Expect a muted rose tone and floral prints in the rooms, which vary in size. ⊠ *31 High St., SL4 1PH* ☎ *01753/863426* 🖷 *01753/830527* ⇔ *31 rooms, 7 suites* ♨ *Restaurant, some in-room hot tubs, some minibars, cable TV, bar, dry cleaning, laundry service, meeting rooms; no a/c* ⊟ *AE, DC, MC, V.*

££ 🏨 **Alma Lodge.** This friendly little bed-and-breakfast in an early Victorian town house is just one of many that can be booked through the Windsor tourist office. Ornate ceilings and ornamental fireplaces are some of the house's original features, and each well-maintained room is decorated in an uncluttered Victorian style. ⊠ *58 Alma Rd., SL4 3HA* ☎ *01753/862983* 🖷 *01753/862983* ✉ *almalodge@aol.com* ⇔ *4 rooms* ♨ *Some pets allowed; no a/c, no room phones, no smoking* ⊟ *MC, V* ⦿l *BP.*

Nightlife & the Arts

Windsor's **Theatre Royal** (⊠ Thames St. ☎ 01753/853888), where productions have been staged since 1910, is one of Britain's leading provincial theaters. It puts on plays and musicals year-round, including a pantomime for the six weeks after Christmas.

Concerts, poetry readings, and children's events highlight the two-week **Windsor Festival** (☎ 020/8883–8740 ⊕ www.windsorfestival.com), usually held in early September or October, with events occasionally taking place in the castle.

Sports & the Outdoors

Windsor Cycle Hire (⊠ Alexandra Gardens, Alma Rd. ☎ 01753/830220) rents bikes and in-line skates.

Shopping

Most Windsor stores are open on Sunday, particularly the antiques stores along Peascod Street, High Street, and King Edward Court. The **Windsor Royal Station shopping center** (⊠ Central Train Station ☎ 0800/923–0017) includes Jaeger, Pied-à-Terre, and an outpost of the quintessential London department store, Liberty. **Past Times** (⊠ 126 Peascod St. ☎ 01753/867762) sells reproductions of items from England's past and displays them according to era.

Eton

❷ *23 mi west of London, linked by a footbridge across the Thames to Windsor.*

Some observers may find it symbolic that almost opposite Windsor Castle—which embodies the continuity of the royal tradition—stands Eton, a school that for centuries has educated many future leaders of the country. With its single main street leading from the river to the famous school, the old-fashioned town itself is a much quieter place than Windsor.

★ The splendid redbrick Tudor-style buildings of **Eton College**, founded in 1440 by King Henry VI, border the north end of High Street; signs warn drivers of "Boys Crossing." During the college semesters, the schoolboys dress in their distinctive pinstripe trousers, swallow-tailed coats, and stiff collars (top hats have not been worn by the boys since the '40s), but don't let the dapper duds fool you. Some of the more mischievous Etonians have been known to fill visitors' heads with fantastic stories about the supposedly mythic origins of their alma mater.

The Gothic **Chapel** rivals St. George's at Windsor in size and magnificence, and is both impressively austere and intimate at the same time. Beyond the cloisters are the school's playing fields where, according to the duke of Wellington, the Battle of Waterloo was really won, since so many of his officers had learned discipline in their school days there. The **Museum of Eton Life** has displays on the school's history. You can also take a guided tour of the school and chapel. ⊠ *Main entrance Brewhouse Yard* ☎ *01753/671177* ⊕ *www.etoncollege.com* 🎫 *£3.70, £4.70 with tour* ⊙ *Mid-Mar.–mid-Apr., July, and Aug., daily 10:30–4:30; mid-Apr.–June and Sept., daily 2–4:30; guided tours mid-Mar.–Sept., daily at 2:15 and 3:15.*

Where to Stay & Eat

££–£££ ✕ **Gilbey's Bar & Restaurant.** Just over the bridge from Windsor, this restaurant sits at the center of Eton's Antiques Row and serves a fine, changing menu of English fare from apricot-coated loin of pork to pan-fried duck breast. Well-priced French wines are a specialty here. The conservatory is a particularly nice place to sit in fine weather. ⊠ *82–83 High St.* ☎ *01753/854921* ▤ *AE, DC, MC, V.*

£££ ✕▥ **Christopher Hotel.** Sister to Sir Christopher Wren's Hotel in Windsor, this former coaching inn on the main shopping street has spacious rooms in the main building as well as the courtyard mews. All are done in traditional style, but the courtyard rooms have more privacy. The fine Renata's restaurant, serving dinner every day except Sunday, has a modern European menu. ⊠ *110 High St., SL4 6AN* ☎ *01753/852359* 🖷 *01753/830914* ⊕ *www.christopher-hotel.co.uk* ➟ *33 rooms* ⚬ *Restaurant, room service, cable TV, bar, some pets allowed, no-smoking rooms* ▤ *AE, DC, MC, V.*

Runnymede

★ ❸ *5 mi southeast of Windsor.*

A giant step in the history of democracy was taken at Runnymede on the Thames outside Egham. Here King John, under his barons' compulsion, signed the Magna Carta in 1215, affirming the individual's right to justice and liberty. On the wooded hillside, in a meadow given to the United States by Queen Elizabeth in 1965, stands a **memorial to President John F. Kennedy.** Nearby is another memorial, a classical temple in style, erected by the American Bar Association for the 750th anniversary of the signing. There is no visitor center at Runnymede, just informational plaques and a parking lot (small charge). The site is on the south side of A308; on the opposite bank of the Thames are the ruins of the 11th-century St. Mary's Priory and the 2,000-year-old Ankerwycke Yew. ⊠ *A308, Egham* ☎ *01784/432891* ⊕ *www.nationaltrust.org.uk.*

Ascot

❹ *10 mi southwest of Runnymede, 8 mi southwest of Windsor, 28 mi southwest from London.*

The town of Ascot (pronounced *as*-cut) has for centuries been famous for horse racing and for style. Queen Anne chose to have a racecourse here, and the first race meeting took place in 1711. Every third week of June (Tuesday–Friday), the titled and the gentry watch the world's finest thoroughbreds pound the turf during the **Royal Meeting,** or Royal Ascot, at **Ascot Racecourse.** The impressive show of millinery for which the Royal Meeting is also known was immortalized in Cecil Beaton's Ascot sequence in *My Fair Lady,* in which osprey feathers and black and white silk roses held high transformed Eliza Doolittle into a grand lady. Today more than a quarter of a million race goers continue to bet, sip champagne, and be seen. The racecourse is divided into several enclosures, the Royal Enclosure being the most famous. Morning dress—meaning tailcoat, top hat, and striped pants—must be worn by gentlemen, whereas hats are de rigueur for the ladies in the Royal Enclosure. The two main public enclosures, the Grandstand and the Silver Ring, have great views and all the fun for less cash and less snobbery. Budget travelers can even try for the Ascot Heath, which costs £3. With around 100 bars and four large catering facilities, no one wants for food or drink.

The Royal Meeting may be the most chichi and the best known, but racing goes on year-round (except March) at England's largest racecourse. Diamond Day, the fourth Saturday in July, or the Ascot Festival, the last Saturday and Sunday in September, are a little more low-key. During most of the year the Royal Enclosure becomes the Members' Enclosure and seats are readily bookable, although it is always advised to phone ahead; for the Royal Meeting, book many months ahead. ⊠ *A329* ☎ *01344/622211 racecourse; 01344/876876 credit card hot line* ⊕ *www.ascot-authority.co.uk* ✍ *Royal Ascot: grandstand and paddock £52, Silver Ring £16, Ascot Heath £3. Diamond Day and Ascot Festival: Members' Enclosure £33, grandstand and paddock £22, Silver Ring £10. All other race days: general admission £6, with special enclosures £13–£18.*

Where to Stay

£££££   🏨 **Berystede Country House Hotel.** With its turrets and half-timbering, this Victorian-era hotel is a magnificent neo-Gothic fantasy on 9 acres of traditional British countryside. Inside, every square inch pays homage to the horsey culture of Ascot, and horse and jockey prints line the walls. Most of the rooms are pleasantly standard (in the annex); a few (in the main house) are nothing short of extraordinary. The Hyperion restaurant serves modern British cuisine. ⊠ *Bagshot Rd., SL5 9JH* ☎ *01344/ 623311* 🖷 *01344/872301* ⊕ *www.heritagehotels.co.uk* ✍ *90 rooms, 4 suites* ⌂ *Restaurant, room service, in-room data ports, cable TV, pool, croquet, bar, lounge, library, baby-sitting, dry cleaning, laundry service, Internet, meeting rooms, some pets allowed, no-smoking rooms; no a/c* ▭ *AE, DC, MC, V.*

Cliveden

⑤ *8 mi northwest of Windsor, 16 mi north of Ascot, 26 mi west of London.*

Deemed by Queen Victoria a "bijou of taste," this magnificent country mansion has for more than 300 years lived up to its Georgian heritage as a bastion of aesthetic delights. The house, set in 376 acres of gardens and parkland high above the River Thames, was rebuilt for the Duke of Sutherland by Sir Charles Barry in 1861; the Astors, who purchased it in 1893, made it famous. In the 1920s and '30s the Cliveden Set met here at the strongly conservative (not to say fascist) salon presided over by Nancy Astor, who—though she was an American—was the first woman to sit in Parliament, in 1919. Cliveden now belongs to the National Trust, which has leased it for use as a *very* exclusive hotel. The public can visit the spectacular grounds and formal gardens that run down to bluffs overlooking the Thames and, by timed ticket, three rooms in the west wing of the house. ☒ *Off A404, Taplow, near Maidenhead* ☎ *01628/605069; 01494/755562 recorded information* ⊕ *www.nationaltrust.org.uk* ☜ *Grounds £6; house additional £1* ☉ *Grounds mid-Mar.–Oct., daily 11–6; Nov. and Dec., daily 11–4. House Apr.–Oct., Thurs. and Sun. 3–5:30. Restaurant in the Orangery mid-Mar.–Oct., Wed.–Sun. 11–5; Nov.–mid-Dec., weekends 11:30–2:30.*

Where to Stay & Eat

£££££ ✕🏨 **Cliveden.** If you've ever wondered what it would feel like to be an
Fodor's Choice Edwardian grandee, splurge for a stay at this stately home, one of
★ Britain's grandest hotels. Cliveden's opulent interior includes historic portraits such as Sargent's portrait of Nancy Astor in the Great Hall, suits of armor, and a richly paneled staircase. The plush traditional bedrooms continue the historic note—each bears the name of someone famous who has stayed here. Since people lease many of the rooms, you may feel you're in a home rather than a hotel. Waldo's, one of three restaurants, is known for contemporary British and French cuisine. ☒ *Off A404 near Maidenhead, Taplow, SL6 0JF* ☎ *01628/668561* 🖷 *01628/661837* ⊕ *www.clivedenhouse.co.uk* ☜ *38 rooms, 1 cottage* ☍ *2 restaurants, room service, in-room data ports, in-room safes, cable TV with movies, in-room VCRs, 2 tennis courts, indoor-outdoor pool, gym, hair salon, outdoor hot tub, massage, sauna, spa, steam room, boating, horseback riding, squash, lounge, library, baby-sitting, dry cleaning, laundry service, meeting rooms, some pets allowed, no-smoking rooms; no a/c in some rooms* 🗎 *AE, DC, MC, V* ⦿*BP.*

TO HENLEY & BEYOND
"WIND IN THE WILLOWS" COUNTRY

"Believe me, my young friend, there is nothing—absolutely nothing—half so much worth doing as simply messing about in boats. Simply messing." You'll probably agree with Water Rat's opinion, voiced in Kenneth Grahame's classic 1908 children's book *The Wind in the Willows,* if you do some of your own "messing about" in this stretch of the Thames Valley, from Marlow to Wallingford. Boat-borne or by foot, you'll discover some of the region's most delightful scenery. On each bank are fine wooded hills, with spacious houses, greenhouses, flower beds, and neat lawns that stretch to the water's edge. It was to Pangbourne, along this stretch of the river, that Grahame retired to write his beloved book. His illustrator, E. H. Shepard, used the great house at Mapledurham as the model for Toad Hall. A Victorian boathouse, not far from Pangbourne, was immortalized in pen and ink as Rat's House. The Henley Royal Regatta is one of the region's most famous attractions.

Marlow

6 *7 mi west of Cliveden, 15 mi northwest of Windsor.*

Just inside the Buckinghamshire border, Marlow overflows with Thames-side prettiness, and tourism can often overwhelm it on summer weekends. Take particular note of its unusual suspension bridge, which William Tierney Clark built in the 1830s. Marlow has a number of striking old buildings, particularly the stylish, privately owned Georgian houses along Peter and West streets. In 1817 the Romantic poet Percy Bysshe Shelley stayed with friends at 67 West Street and then bought **Albion House** on the same street. His second wife, Mary, completed her Gothic novel *Frankenstein* here. **Marlow Place**, on Station Road, dates from 1721 and has been lived in by several princes of Wales. Marlow hosts its own miniregatta in mid-June for one day. The town is a good base from which to join the Thames Path to Henley-on-Thames.

Swan-Upping (☎ 01628/523030), a traditional event that dates back 800 years, takes places in the third week of July. The Queen owns most of the swans on the Thames. Swan-markers in Thames skiffs start from Sunbury-on-Thames, catching the new cygnets and marking their beaks to establish ownership. The Queen's swan keeper, dressed in scarlet livery, presides over this colorful ceremony.

Where to Stay

££££ ⊡ **Compleat Angler.** Fishing aficionados might consider this luxurious, 17th-century Thames-side inn the ideal place to stay. The name comes from Izaak's Walton 1653 masterpiece of angling advice and philosophy, which he wrote in this area. Plenty of fishy touches enhance the chintz and floral bedrooms; most rooms and the Riverside Restaurant have views over the Thames. A cozy conservatory serves afternoon tea. ⊠ *Marlow Bridge, Bisham Rd., SL7 1RG* ☎ *01628/484444* 🖷 *01628/486388* ⊕ *www.heritagehotels.co.uk* ⤴ *61 rooms, 3 suites* ⅋ *2 restaurants, room service, minibars, cable TV with video games, fishing, 2 bars, meeting rooms, some pets allowed (fee), no-smoking rooms; no a/c* ⊟ *AE, DC, MC, V.*

Henley

7 *7 mi southwest of Marlow on A4155, 8 mi north of Reading, 36 mi west of central London.*

Henley's identity manifests itself in one word: rowing. The Henley Royal Regatta, held in early July (in 2004, June 30–July 4) on a long straight stretch of the River Thames, has made the little riverside town famous throughout the world. Townspeople launched the Henley Regatta in 1839, initiating the Grand Challenge Cup, the most famous of its many trophies. After 1851, when Prince Albert, Queen Victoria's consort, became its patron, it was known as the Royal Regatta. The best amateur oarsmen from around the globe compete in crews of eight, four, or two, or as single scullers. For many of the spectators, however, the social side of the event is far more important and on par with Royal Ascot and Wimbledon. Elderly oarsmen wear brightly colored blazers and straw boater hats; businesspeople entertain wealthy clients, and everyone admires the ladies' fashions.

The town is set in a broad valley between gentle hillsides. Henley's historic buildings, including half-timber Georgian cottages and inns (as well as one of Britain's oldest theaters, the Kenton), are all within a few minutes' walk. The river near Henley is alive with boats of every shape and size, from luxury cabin cruisers to tiny rowboats. The 16th-century "checkerboard" tower of **St. Mary's Church** overlooks Henley's bridge on Hart Street. If the church's rector is about, ask permission to climb to the top to take in the superb views up and down the river. The adjacent **Chantry House**, built in 1420, is one of England's few remaining merchant houses from the period. Converted into a school for impoverished boys in 1604, it is an unspoiled example of the rare timber-frame design, with upper floors jutting out. ⊠ *Hart St.* ☎ *01491/577062* ☒ *Free* ☉ *Church services or by appointment.*

The handsome **River & Rowing Museum** focuses not just on the history and sport of rowing but on the Thames and the town itself. One gallery interprets the Thames and its surroundings as the river flows from its source to the ocean; another explores Henley's history and the regatta. Galleries devoted to rowing display models and actual boats, from Greek triremes to lifeboats to sleek modern rowing boats. David Chipperfield's striking building, combining traditional oak and modern steel, takes full advantage of its riverside location. ⊠ *Mill Meadows* ☎ *01491/415600* ⊕ *www.rrm.co.uk* ☒ *£4.95* ☉ *Sept.–Apr., daily 10–5; May–Aug., daily 10–5:30.*

Where to Stay & Eat

££££ ✕⊡ **Red Lion.** Ivy-draped and dignified, this redbrick 16th-century hotel overlooks the river and the town bridge. Guests have included King Charles I; Samuel Johnson, the 18th-century critic, poet, and lexicographer; and the duke of Marlborough, who used the hotel as a base during the building of Blenheim Palace. Rooms are furnished with antiques, and some bedrooms have river views. The restaurant serves contemporary fare such as lasagna of woodland mushrooms or beef fillet with leek and Stilton mousse; the bar has a lighter menu. ⊠ *Hart St., RG9 2AR* ☎ *01491/572161* 🖷 *01491/410039* ⊕ *www.redlionhenley.co.uk* 🛏 *26 rooms* ♿ *Restaurant, room service, in-room data ports, cable TV, bar, lobby lounge, baby-sitting, dry cleaning, laundry service, Internet, meeting rooms, car rental; no a/c* ▭ *AE, MC, V.*

££££ ✕⊡ **Stonor Arms.** A popular formal dining salon, one of the region's showpiece restaurants, draws many to this 18th-century country hotel. The sophisticated menu at the Stonor Arms ranges from venison in white bean sauce to roast cod with Thai noodles. A sister restaurant, Blades, has two glass conservatories and a slightly less expensive menu. Bedrooms are comfortable and antiques-bedecked, if somewhat cramped; some desirable ones open out onto the walled garden. The hotel is 4 mi north of Henley. ⊠ *B480, off A4130, Stonor, RG9 6HE* ☎ *01491/638866* 🖷 *01491/638863* ⊕ *www.stonor-arms.co.uk* 🛏 *11 rooms* ♿ *2 restaurants, room service, in-room data ports, massage, bar, dry cleaning, meeting rooms, airport shuttle; no a/c* ▭ *AE, MC, V* ℺ *CP.*

££–£££ ⊡ **Little White Hart.** There aren't many better views of the boat races than those from the balcony rooms of this Victorian version of a riverside retreat. Topped by three imposing gables, the hotel recalls a chalet, and traditional furnishings dominate the guest rooms and public spaces. A brasserie and an adjacent pub serve affordable food and locally brewed ales. ⊠ *Riverside, RG9 2LJ* ☎ *01491/574145* 🖷 *01491/411772* ✉ *barberwhite@aol.com* 🛏 *23 rooms* ♿ *Restaurant, bar, meeting rooms* ▭ *AE, MC, V* ℺ *BP.*

Nightlife & the Arts

The popular **Henley Festival** (☎ 01491/843400 ⊕ www.henley-festival.co.uk) takes place each July, during the week after the regatta. All kinds of open-air concerts and events are staged.

GOLF At **Badgemore Park** (✉ A4130 ☎ 01491/573667), a parkland 18-hole course, visitors are welcome on weekdays, and on weekends by arrangement.

ROWING **Henley Royal Regatta** (☎ 01491/572153 ⊕ www.hrr.co.uk), a series of rowing competitions that draw participants from many countries, takes place over five days at the beginning of July each year. Large tents go up, especially along both sides of the unique straight stretch of river here known as Henley Reach (1 mi, 550 yds), and every surrounding field becomes a parking lot. The most prestigious place for spectators is the Stewards' Enclosure, but admission here is by invitation only. Fortunately, there is plenty of space on the public towpath from which to watch the early stages of the races. If you want to attend, make your plans and book a room months in advance.

Sonning-on-Thames

⑧ *5 mi south of Henley, 4 mi northeast of Reading.*

It is plausible that Sonning's reputation as the prettiest village on the Thames goes back as far as its Saxon bishops. The 18th-century bridge spanning the Thames, the Georgian houses, the ancient mill mentioned in the 11th-century Domesday Book, and the black, white, and yellow cottages make it an all-too-perfect Thames-side village.

Where to Stay & Eat

££££ ✕▢ **French Horn.** Elegance is the keynote of this Thames-side hotel with a lawn graced with a willow tree and calming river views. Guest rooms, some in the main building and others in cottages, are spacious. Most have sitting rooms, and the light green walls and rose-festooned fabrics are typically English. The restaurant serves inspired French cooking. ✉ *Thames St., RG4 6TN* ☎ *0118/969–2204* ☎ *0118/944–2210* ⊕ *www.thefrenchhorn.co.uk* ↗ *11 rooms, 10 suites* ⚘ *Restaurant, in-room data ports, some minibars, bar, lobby lounge, laundry service, meeting rooms; no a/c in some rooms* ▭ *AE, DC, MC, V* ¶◎¶ *BP.*

Mapledurham House

★ **⑨** *5 mi west of Sonning-on-Thames, 10 mi southwest of Henley.*

The section of the Thames from Caversham to Mapledurham inspired Kenneth Grahame's 1908 children's book *The Wind in the Willows,* which began as a bedtime story for Grahame's son Alastair while the Grahames were living at Pangbourne. Some of E. F. Shepard's illustrations are of specific sites along the river—none more fabled than this redbrick Elizabethan mansion, bristling with tall chimneys, mullioned windows, and battlements, which became the inspiration for Shepard's vision of Toad Hall. The Eyston family, descendants of longtime owners of the estate, still lives at Mapledurham, and the house seems warm and friendly even with all the family portraits, magnificent oak staircases, and Tudor plasterwork ceilings. Here you can see a 15th-century water mill—the last working grain mill on the Thames. On summer weekends you can reach the house in true *Wind-in-the-Willows* fashion by a **Thames River Cruises** (☎ 0118/948–1088) boat from Caversham Promenade in Reading. The boat leaves at 2 PM, and travel time is about 45 minutes. You can linger in the area at one of the 11 rental cottages around the estate (£265–£620 a week). ✉ *Mapledurham, near Reading* ☎ *0118/972–3350* ⊕ *www.mapledurham.co.uk* ▢ *House and mill £5, house only £4, grounds and mill £3* ◷ *Easter–Sept., weekends only 2–5:30.*

Ewelme

⑩ *12 mi north of Mapledurham House, 10 mi northwest of Henley off A4130.*

One of England's most unspoiled villages lies near the town of Benson, in Oxfordshire. Its picture-book almshouses, church, and school—one of the oldest in Britain—huddle close together, as they did more than 500 years ago. The church shelters the carved alabaster tomb of Alice, duchess of Suffolk, the granddaughter of medieval poet Geoffrey Chaucer. Jerome K. Jerome, author of the humorous book *Three Men in a Boat,* describing a 19th-century Thames-side vacation, is also buried here.

Wallingford

⑪ *2 mi west of Ewelme, 13 mi southeast of Oxford on A4074.*

The busy marketplace of this typical riverside market town is bordered by a town hall, built in 1670, and an Italianate corn exchange, now a theater and cinema. Nice walks and fishing opportunities are plentiful along this section of the Thames, and excellent antiques shops fill the town. Market day is Friday.

The Outdoors

Rent a boat from **Maidline Cruisers** (✉ Chalmore Meadow ☎ 01491/ 836088) to spend a leisurely day cruising the Thames.

OXFORD

With arguably the most famous university in the world, Oxford has been a center of learning since the 12th century, with only the Sorbonne preceding it. To get the city placed in your mind's eye, say the phrase "dreaming spires" (the words are Matthew Arnold's) over and over, as all tour guides do, and think *Brideshead Revisited,* Sebastian Flyte, and Evelyn Waugh—not to mention Percy Bysshe Shelley, Oscar Wilde, and W. H. Auden. Except for the modern storefronts, the city stands as it has for hundreds of years, in part because Adolf Hitler had designs on making it his European capital and so spared it from bombings. When arriving, try to stop on one of the low hills that surround the city and look at the skyline. Stretched out in front of you is this ancient home of erudition and scholarship, where students are still required to take their exams in "sub fusc" attire (cap, gown, and white bow tie). Oxford is 55 mi northwest of London, at the junction of the Thames and Cherwell rivers. The city is bigger and more cosmopolitan than Cambridge, with two major industrial complexes on its outskirts: the Rover car factory and the Pressed Steel works. Plenty of traffic and even suburban sprawl lie beyond the hushed quadrangles, chapels, and gardens.

Exploring Oxford

Oxford University is not one unified campus but a collection of many colleges and buildings, new as well as old, scattered across the city. Undergraduates live and study at 40 different colleges. Most of the college grounds and magnificent dining halls and chapels are open to visitors, though the opening times (displayed at the entrance lodges) vary greatly. Some colleges are open only in the afternoons during university semesters, when the undergraduates are in residence; access is often restricted to the chapels and dining rooms (called halls) and sometimes the libraries, too, and you are requested to refrain from picnicking in the quadrangles. All are closed certain days during exams, usually from mid-April to late June, when the

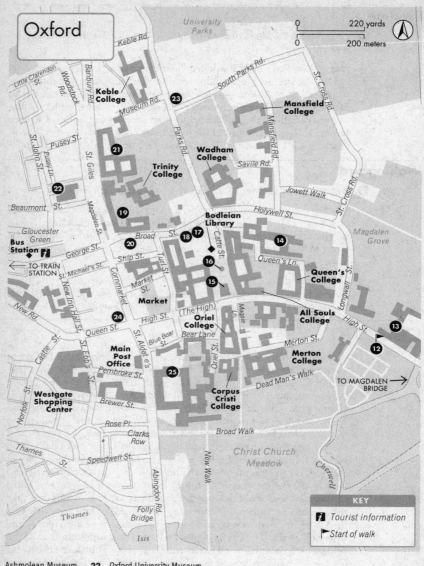

Oxford

0 ——— 220 yards
0 ——— 200 meters

Little Clarendon St.

Keble Rd.

University Parks

South Parks Rd.

St. Cross Rd.

Woodstock Rd.

Banbury Rd.

Keble College

Museum Rd.

23

Mansfield College

Mansfield Rd.

St. John St.

Pusey St.

St. Giles

21

Parks Rd.

Wadham College

Savile Rd.

Jowett Walk

22

Beaumont St.

Magdalen St.

Trinity College

19

Bodleian Library

Holywell St.

Magdalen Grove

Gloucester Green

Broad St.

18 17

Catte St.

14

St. Cross Rd.

Bus Station 🛈

George St.

20

16

Queen's Ln.

Queen's College

Longwall St.

TO TRAIN STATION

St. Michael's St.

Ship St.

Turl St.

15

Oriel College

All Souls College

New Inn Hall St.

Cornmarket

Market St.

Market

(The High)

Bear Lane

High St.

13

High St.

New Rd.

Queen St.

St. Aldate's

Blue Boar St.

Oriel St.

Magpie Ln.

Merton St.

Merton College

12

Castle St.

24

St. Ebbe's

Main Post Office

Pembroke St.

25

Dead Man's Walk

TO MAGDALEN BRIDGE

Norfolk St.

Westgate Shopping Center

Brewer St.

Rose Pl.

Corpus Cristi College

Thames St.

Clarks Row

Speedwell St.

Broad Walk

Christ Church Meadow

New Walk

Cherwell

Abingdon Rd.

Folly Bridge

Thames

Isis

KEY

🛈 Tourist information

▶ Start of walk

May Balls are held. The best way to gain access is to join a walking tour led by a Blue Badge guide. These two-hour tours leave up to five times daily from the Tourist Information Centre. As you walk through this scholastic wonderland, try to spot as many Gothic gargoyles as you can; after all, this *was* the home turf of Alice and Lewis Carroll.

The St. Clement's car park before the roundabout that leads to Magdalen Bridge is one of the only places with public parking, so pay the price if you're making a day trip.

a good walk

The most picturesque approach to a college tour is from the east, over Magdalen (pronounced *maud*-lin) Bridge. After crossing the bridge, turn left off gently curving High Street for a sojourn through the **University of Oxford Botanic Garden** ⑫ ▶ and Christ Church Meadow, or turn right into **Magdalen College** ⑬. Its quadrangle is a quiet area enclosed by ancient vaulted cloisters covered with wisteria. Almost halfway up High Street, turn right onto Queen's Lane and take in the extensive gardens and the row of gargoyles at **New College** ⑭. A little farther up High Street turn right at the 14th-century tower of the **University Church of St. Mary the Virgin** ⑮ and behold the gilded gates of All Souls College and the magnificent 17th-century dome of the **Radcliffe Camera** ⑯. The Bridge of Sighs and Bodleian Library lie straight ahead, and left at Broad Street brings you to Christopher Wren's **Sheldonian Theatre** ⑰. Step past its iron gates and those fabulous megabusts of the Roman emperors to check out the schedule for evening concerts here. Next door to the Sheldonian is the **Museum of the History of Science** ⑱, the original site of the Ashmolean, the oldest public museum in Britain. Book lovers will want to cross the street to Blackwell's before heading down St. Giles to see **Balliol College** ⑲.

If you have time, go back to Broad Street and stop in at the **Oxford Story Exhibition** ⑳, an imaginative presentation of 800 years of Oxford life. You may want to continue north along St. Giles to a possible lunch stop, the Eagle and Child pub, where J. R. R. Tolkien often met his friends, the "Inklings." Next, check out either the lovely gardens of **St. John's College** ㉑ or the **Ashmolean Museum** ㉒, Oxford's finest art and archaeology museum, on Beaumont Street. After viewing Oliver Cromwell's death mask you may be up for a spot of tea, so dip into the Randolph across the way for a reviving cuppa in its Victorian Gothic interior. If you're a natural history buff, you may want to head over to the **Oxford University Museum of Natural History** ㉓ on Parks Road. Late afternoon should lure you south, down Cornmarket, passing **Carfax Tower** ㉔, Oxford's preeminent lookout point, to St. Aldate's and **Christ Church** ㉕, Oxford's snobbiest college, with its vast Tom Quad, 800-year-old chapel, medieval dining hall, and scholarly Picture Gallery.

TIMING You can walk this route in 1½ hours, but it's easy to spend a full day here if you visit each of the key museums for an hour and take more time to absorb the scene by exploring the colleges. Be sure to note college opening hours and check in advance for special closures. If you're arriving at the train station for a day in Oxford, you might wish to start at the Ashmolean Museum above and work your way backward.

What to See

㉒ **Ashmolean Museum.** Britain's oldest public museum contains among its priceless collections (all university owned) many Egyptian, Greek, and Roman artifacts uncovered during archaeological expeditions conducted by the university. Michelangelo drawings, the Alfred jewels, and a Chinese gallery are some highlights. ⊠ *Beaumont St.* ☎ *01865/278000* ⊕ *www.ashmol.ox.ac.uk* ⊠ *Free* ☉ *Tues.–Sat. 10–5, Sun. 2–5.*

⑲ Balliol College. The wooden doors between the inner and outer quadrangles of Balliol (founded 1263) still bear scorch marks from 1555 and 1556, when during the reign of Mary ("Bloody Mary"), Bishops Latimer and Ridley and Archbishop Cranmer were burned alive on huge pyres in Broad Street for their Protestant beliefs. A cross on the roadway marks the spot. The **Martyrs' Memorial** at St. Giles and Beaumont Street also commemorates the three men. ⊠ *Broad St. and St. Giles* ☎ *01865/277777* ⊕ *www.balliol.ox.ac.uk* ⊡ *£1* ⊗ *Daily 2–5.*

㉔ Carfax Tower. Passing through Carfax, where four roads meet, you will see this tower, all that remains of **St. Martin's Church,** where Shakespeare once stood as godfather for William Davenant, who himself became a playwright. Every 15 minutes, little mechanical "quarter boys" mark the passage of time on the tower front. You can climb up the dark stairwell for a good view of the town center. ⊠ *Corner of Carfax and Cornmarket* ☎ *01865/792653* ⊡ *£1.20* ⊗ *Apr.–Oct., daily 10–5:15; Nov.–Mar., daily 10–3:30.*

㉕ Christ Church. Built in 1546, the college of Christ Church is referred to by its members as "The House." This is the site of Oxford's largest quadrangle, Tom Quad, named after the huge bell (6¼ tons) that hangs in the gate tower and still rings 101 times at five past nine every evening in honor of the original number of Christ Church scholars. The vaulted, 800-year-old chapel in one corner has been Oxford's cathedral since the time of Henry VIII. The college's medieval dining hall contains portraits of many famous alumni, including John Wesley, William Penn, and 13 of Britain's prime ministers. (A reproduction of this room appears in the banquet scenes at Hogwarts School in the film versions of *Harry Potter and the Sorcerer's Stone* and *Harry Potter and the Chamber of Secrets.*) Lewis Carroll was a teacher of mathematics here for many years; a shop opposite the meadows on St. Aldate's sells Alice paraphernalia. ⊠ *St. Aldate's* ☎ *01865/286573* ⊕ *www.chch.ox.ac.uk* ⊡ *£4* ⊗ *Mon.–Sat. 9:30–5:30, Sun. 2–5:30.*

Christ Church Picture Gallery. This connoisseur's delight in Canterbury Quadrangle exhibits works by the Italian masters as well as Hals, Rubens, and Van Dyck. Drawings in the 2,000-strong collection are shown on a changing basis. ⊠ *Oriel Sq.* ☎ *01865/276172* ⊕ *www.chch.ox. ac.uk* ⊡ *£2* ⊗ *Mon.–Sat. 10:30–1 and 2–4:30, Sun. 2–4:30.*

★ **⑬ Magdalen College.** Founded in 1458, with a handsome main quadrangle and a supremely monastic air, Magdalen is one of the richest and most impressive of Oxford's colleges. A stroll around the Deer Park and along Addison's Walk is a good way to appreciate the place. Alumni have included such diverse people as Cardinal Wolsey, Edward Gibbon, Oscar Wilde, and Dudley Moore. ⊠ *High St.* ☎ *01865/276000* ⊕ *www. magd.ox.ac.uk* ⊡ *£2* ⊗ *June–Sept., daily noon–6.*

⑱ Museum of the History of Science. The Ashmolean, Britain's oldest public museum, was originally housed in this 1638 building, which now holds centuries of scientific and mathematical instruments from astrolabes to quadrants to medical equipment. You can also visit the restored 18th-century chemical laboratory in the basement. ⊠ *Broad St.* ☎ *01865/ 277280* ⊕ *www.mhs.ox.ac.uk* ⊡ *Free* ⊗ *Tues.–Sat. noon–4; call for additional hrs.*

⑭ New College. Founded in 1379, New College has extensive gardens, partly enclosed by the medieval city wall, and an outstanding row of gargoyles. Famous alumni include actor Hugh Grant and Richard Mason, who published his international best-seller, *The Drowning People,* only months after first "coming up" to Oxford. ⊠ *Holywell St.* ☎ *01865/279555*

⊕ *www.new.ox.ac.uk* ✉ *£2* ⊙ *Easter–Sept., daily 10–5, Oct.–Easter, daily 2–4.*

☞ ⑳ **Oxford Story Exhibition.** This imaginative presentation in a converted warehouse revisits 800 years of Oxford life with models, sounds, and smells. You ride through the exhibition in small cars shaped like medieval students' desks. ✉ *6 Broad St.* ☎ *01865/728822* ⊕ *www.oxfordstory. org.uk* ✉ *£6.50* ⊙ *July and Aug., daily 9:30–5; Sept.–June, Mon.–Sat. 10–4:30, Sun. 11–4:30.*

㉓ **Oxford University Museum of Natural History.** Eclectic collections relating to entomology, geology, mineralogy, and zoology are stored in this massive Victorian Gothic structure. Among the myriad exhibits are local dinosaur remains and the head and left foot of an extinct dodo bird. The museum is across the street from the Rhodes House, in which hangs a portrait of former president Bill Clinton, who attended University College on High Street. ✉ *Parks Rd.* ☎ *01865/272950; 01865/270949 recorded information* ⊕ *www.oum.ox.ac.uk* ✉ *Free* ⊙ *Daily noon–5.*

★ ⑯ **Radcliffe Camera and Bodleian Library.** One of the largest domes in Britain tops Oxford's most spectacular building, built in 1737–49 by James Gibbs in Italian Baroque style. The Camera contains part of the **Bodleian Library**'s collection, which was begun in 1602 and has grown to more than 6 million volumes, including a copy of every book ever printed in Great Britain. Although visitors are not allowed in the Camera, the general public may stop into another part of the Bodleian, the Divinity School, a superbly vaulted room dating back to 1462. In the film *Harry Potter and the Sorcerer's Stone*, some interior scenes at Hogwarts School take place in parts of the Bodleian, including the Divinity School. (For another scholarly library, medieval in vintage, check out the library at Merton College on Merton Street.) ✉ *Broad St.* ☎ *01865/277224 for information on tour* ⊕ *www.bodley.ox.ac.uk* ✉ *£3.50, extended tour £7* ⊙ *Tours of part of Bodleian Mar.–Oct., weekdays 10:30, 11:30, 2, 3 and Sat. 10:30, 11:30; Nov.–Feb., weekdays 2, 3 and Sat. 10:30, 11:30. Children under 14 not admitted. Divinity School weekdays 9–4:45, Sat. 9–12:30.*

⑰ **Sheldonian Theatre.** This fabulously ornate theater is where Oxford's impressive graduation ceremonies are held, conducted almost entirely in Latin. Dating to 1663, it was the first building designed by Sir Christopher Wren when he served as professor of astronomy. The D-shape theater has pillars, balconies, and an elaborately painted ceiling. Outside, stone pillars are topped by 18 massive stone heads, sculpted in the 1970s to replace originals destroyed by air pollution. ✉ *Broad St.* ☎ *01865/277299* ⊕ *www.sheldon.ox.ac.uk* ✉ *£1.50* ⊙ *Mon.–Sat. 10–12:30 and 2–4:30; mid-Nov.–Feb., closes at 3:30. Closed for 10 days at Christmas and Easter and for degree ceremonies and events.*

㉑ **St. John's College.** For a quiet pause, step inside St. John's (1555) to see its huge gardens, among the city's loveliest. ✉ *St. Giles* ☎ *01865/ 277300* ⊕ *www.sjc.ox.ac.uk* ⊙ *Daily 1 PM–dusk.*

> **need a break?** The **Eagle and Child** pub (✉ 49 St. Giles ☎ 01865/310154) is a tourist favorite not only for its good beer and snacks but for its literary history. C. S. Lewis was a visitor, and this was the meeting place of J. R. R. Tolkien and his friends, the "Inklings." The pub's narrow interior leads to a conservatory and small terrace.

⑮ **University Church of St. Mary the Virgin.** From the top of the church's 14th-century tower, you get a panoramic view of the city's skyline with nearly every architectural style since the 11th century. Seven hundred years' worth of funeral monuments crowd the interior, including one belonging to Amy Robsart, the wife of Robert Dudley, Elizabeth I's favorite. One pillar marks the site of Thomas Cranmer's trial under Bloody Mary for his marital machinations on behalf of Henry VIII. The Convocation House, a part of the church accessible from Radcliffe Square, serves generous portions—cafeteria style—under the room in which OxFam was founded. ⊠ *High St.* ☎ *01865/279111* ⊕ *www.university-church.ox.ac.uk* ☜ *Church free, tower £1.60* ☉ *Church and tower Sept.–June, daily 9–5 ('til 4:30 in winter); July and Aug. daily 9–7.*

▶ ⑫ **University of Oxford Botanic Garden.** Founded in 1621 as a physic (healing) garden, this is the oldest of its kind in the British Isles. The compact but diverse garden displays 7,000 species from lilies to palms in greenhouses, a small walled garden, and special gardens (such as rock and bog gardens) outside the walled area. ⊠ *Rose La.* ☎ *01865/286690* ⊕ *www.botanic-garden.ox.ac.uk* ☜ *Free* ☉ *Apr.–Sept., garden daily 9–4:30, greenhouses daily 10–4:30; Oct.–Mar., garden daily 9–4, greenhouses daily 10–4.*

Where to Eat

Restaurants in the Old Bank and Old Parsonage hotels also have worthwhile restaurants.

★ **£££££** ✕ **Rosamund the Fair.** You can watch swans and eat delicious classic cuisine with a modern twist while you glide smoothly down the Isis past Folly Bridge and the university boathouse. For £57 per person, you get dinner from a set menu and a three-hour cruise on the lovely *Rosamund the Fair*, which seats about 20 people. Vegetarians can be accommodated if they contact the chef in advance. Dinner cruises leave at 7:45, weekend lunch cruises at 12:15. ⊠ *Castle Mill Boatyard, Cardigan St.* ☎ *01865/553370* ⚓ *Reservations essential* ▭ *AE, MC, V* ☉ *Closed Mon. and Jan.*

★ **£££** ✕ **Le Petit Blanc.** Raymond Blanc's sophisticated brasserie, a more hip cousin of Le Manoir aux Quat' Saisons in Great Milton, is the finest place to eat in Oxford. The changing menu always lists innovative, visually stunning adaptations of bourgeois French fare, sometimes with Mediterranean or Asian influences. Try the herb pancakes with mushrooms, Gruyère, and ham. The set menus here are a good value. ⊠ *71–72 Walton St.* ☎ *01865/510999* ▭ *AE, DC, MC, V.*

££–£££ ✕ **Gee's.** With its glass and steel framework, this former florist's shop just north of the town center resembles a quintessential English conservatory. The constantly changing menu highlights French and English dishes with seasonal variations, and the place is popular with both town and gown. ⊠ *61 Banbury Rd.* ☎ *01865/553540* ▭ *AE, MC, V* ⌿ *No smoking.*

££ ✕ **Café Joe's.** For some of the best eggs Benedict in the valley, cross the Magdalen Bridge out of town, take the center fork, and continue past the café's takeout sibling, Espresso Joe, on the left. Students "living out" sip lattés and eat goat cheese salad and grilled chicken with couscous in comfortable style. ⊠ *21 Cowley Rd.* ☎ *01865/201120* ▭ *MC, V.*

£–££ ✕ **Grand Café.** Golden-hue tiles, columns, and antique marble tables make
FodorsChoice this café both architecturally impressive and an excellent spot for a light
★ meal or leisurely drink. The tasty menu lists sandwiches, salads, and tarts as well as perfect coffee drinks and desserts. ⊠ *84 High St.* ☎ *01865/204463* ▭ *AE, MC, V.*

£–££ ✕ **Trout Inn.** More than a century ago, Lewis Carroll took three children on a Thames picnic. "We rowed up to Godstow, and had tea beside a haystack," he told a friend at Christ Church; "I told them the fairy tale of Alice's adventures in Wonderland." The haystacks are gone, but you can still stop at the creeper-covered Thames-side pub 2 mi north of the city center for mixed grills and baked trout. There's a corner devoted to Carroll, and a Morse bar with Morse memorabilia, as the fictional inspector often drank here; his novelist creator, Colin Dexter, still does. ⊠ *195 Godstow Rd., Wolvercote* ☎ *01865/302071* 🚞 *AE, DC, MC, V.*

Where to Stay

Oxford is pricey; for the cheapest lodging, contact the tourist information office for bed-and-breakfasts in locals' homes.

£££££ 🏨 **The Randolph.** A 19th-century neo-Gothic landmark in its own right, the hotel faces both the Ashmolean and the Martyrs' Memorial. If their parents are feeling generous, undergraduates are treated to tea in the Morse Bar or dinner in the Spires Restaurant. Scenes from PBS's Inspector Morse *Mystery* series and the film *Shadowlands* were shot here. The floorboards can be *too* historic; in some rooms, squeaky ceilings can lead to sleepless nights. ⊠ *Beaumont St., OX1 2LN* ☎ *0870/400–8200* 🖳 *01865/791678* ⊕ *www.macdonald-hotels.co.uk* ⋺ *99 rooms, 10 suites* ♿ *Restaurant, room service, fans, in-room data ports, minibars, cable TV, bar, lobby lounge, dry cleaning, laundry service, concierge, Internet, business services, meeting rooms, airport shuttle, car rental, parking (fee), some pets allowed (fee), no-smoking floors; no a/c* 🚞 *AE, DC, MC, V* ❯❮ *BP.*

★ 🏨 **Old Parsonage.** This hotel, a 17th-century, gabled stone house in a
££££–£££££ small garden next to St. Giles Church, provides a dignified escape from the surrounding city center. Dark wood paneling in the lobby and the guest rooms' tasteful chintzes and marble baths are far from trendy, but memorable meals by an open fire (or in the walled garden terrace in summer) keep people coming back. The inspired international menu includes monkfish with prawn Thai curry and wild mushroom tart. Afternoon cream teas are excellent. ⊠ *1 Banbury Rd., OX2 6NN* ☎ *01865/ 310210* 🖳 *01865/311262* ⊕ *www.oxford-hotels-restaurants.co.uk* ⋺ *26 rooms, 4 suites* ♿ *Restaurant, room service, in-room data ports, in-room safes, cable TV, bar, lobby lounge, baby-sitting, dry cleaning, laundry service, business services, car rental, free parking* 🚞 *AE, DC, MC, V* ❯❮ *BP.*

££££ 🏨 **Old Bank Hotel.** From its sleek lobby to the 20th-century British paintings on display and the subdued modern furnishings in the guest rooms, the former Barclay's Bank has brought some style to a city that favors the traditional. Oxford's most centrally located hotel also holds the contemporary Quod Bar and Grill, serving creative pastas and dishes such as duck confit. ⊠ *92–94 High St., OX1 4BN* ☎ *01865/799599* 🖳 *01865/799598* ⊕ *www.oxford-hotels-restaurants.co.uk* ⋺ *43 rooms* ♿ *Restaurant, room service, in-room data ports, in-room safes, cable TV, bar, lounge, baby-sitting, dry cleaning, laundry service, meeting room, free parking, no-smoking rooms* 🚞 *AE, DC, MC, V.*

££££ 🏨 **Royal Oxford Hotel.** One of Oxford's newest hotels, opened in 2002, is just a few steps away from the train station, but don't let that deter you. Rooms are bright, light, and modern, with contemporary furniture—think Ikea. Tea and coffeemakers and hospitality trays of chocolates, fruit, and biscuits are welcome touches. ⊠ *17 Park End St., OX1 1HR* ☎ *01865/248431* 🖳 *01865/250049* ⊕ *www.royaloxfordhotel.co. uk* ⋺ *26 rooms* ♿ *Restaurant, room service, in-room data ports, cable TV, dry cleaning, laundry service, business services, meeting rooms, parking (fee), no-smoking rooms; no a/c* 🚞 *AE, MC, V* ❯❮ *BP.*

££££ 🖼 **Bath Place Hotel.** Down a cobbled alleyway off Holywell Street stand these 17th-century weavers' cottages converted into a small hotel. A number of rooms have four-poster beds; nearly all have slanting floors and exposed beams. Some rooms have their own entrances, and others are in the main building. There's only a breakfast room, but the adjacent Turf Tavern serves ale and bar food. ⊠ *4–5 Bath Pl., OX1 3SI* ☎ *01865/791812* 🖷 *01865/791834* ⊕ *www.bathplace.co.uk* ⟋ *14 rooms* ⟋ *Fans, minibars, bar, laundry service, free parking, some pets allowed; no a/c, no smoking* ⊟ *AE, DC, MC, V* ⧖ *CP.*

££££ 🖼 **Victoria House Hotel.** Basic, modern rooms at a low (for Oxford) price are the draw at this no-nonsense hotel aimed at the business set. Don't expect breakfast here, but on your doorstep are a fine selection of cafés. The downstairs Mood bar attracts the trendy with its resident DJ; on weekends, clubbers use the hotel as a base. ⊠ *29 George St., OX1 2AY* ☎ *01865/727400* 🖷 *01865/727402* ⊕ *www.victoriahouse-hotel.co.uk* ⟋ *14 rooms* ⟋ *Bar; no a/c, no smoking* ⊟ *AE, DC, MC, V.*

Nightlife & the Arts

Nightlife

Nightlife in Oxford centers around student life, which in turns centers around the local pubs, though you'll find a few surprises, too. **Branca** (⊠ 111 Walton St. ☎ 01865/556111) is the trendy bar of an Italian brasserie. **Frevd** (⊠ 119 Walton St. ☎ 01865/311171), in a renovated neoclassical church, serves up light meals and cocktails as well as nightly live jazz or funk. The **Kings Arms** (⊠ 40 Holywell St. ☎ 01865/242369), popular with students and fairly quiet during the day, carries excellent local brews as well as inexpensive pub grub. The **Turf Tavern** (⊠ Bath Pl. ☎ 01865/243235), off Holywell Street, includes a higgledy-piggledy collection of little rooms and outdoor space good for a quiet drink and inexpensive pub food.

The Arts

FESTIVALS & CONCERTS **Choral music** at the city's churches is a calming way to spend the early evening. Drop by weekdays except Wednesday during term time at 6 PM at Christ Church, Magdalen, or New College to hear evensong.

The **Jacqueline Du Pre Music Building** (⊠ St. Hilda's College ☎ 01865/276821), endowed with the city's best acoustics, showcases rising talent at recitals. **Music at Oxford** (☎ 01865/798600), an acclaimed series of weekend classical concerts, takes place mid-September–June in such surroundings as Christ Church Cathedral and Sir Christopher Wren's Sheldonian Theatre. At the **Oxford Coffee Concerts** (⊠ Holywell Music Room, Hollywell Rd. ☎ 01865/305305), a program of Sunday chamber concerts, string quartets, piano trios, and soloists present baroque and classical pieces in a venerable 1748 hall. Reasonably priced tickets are available from the Oxford Playhouse on Beaumont Street.

Blenheim Palace (☎ 01993/811091) in Woodstock is occasionally the venue for classical concerts in summer, sometimes combined with fireworks displays.

OPERA The **Garsington Opera** (⊠ Garsington ☎ 01865/361636), a well-regarded event staged in a covered outdoor auditorium, uses Garsington Manor's magical gardens as a backdrop for classic and little-known operas for a month each summer. The manor is 5 mi southeast of Oxford; you can dine in the Great Barn.

THEATERS During term time, undergraduate productions are often given in the colleges or local halls. In summer outdoor performances may take place in quadrangles or college gardens. Look for announcement posters.

The Apollo (✉ George St. ☎ 0870/606–3500), Oxford's main theater, stages plays, opera, ballet, pantomime, and concerts. It's the recognized second home of the Welsh National Opera and the Glyndebourne Touring Opera. **Old Fire Station** (✉ 40 George St. ☎ 01865/794490), an alternative theater, showcases student productions, small-scale opera, and new musicals. The **Oxford Playhouse** (✉ Beaumont St. ☎ 01865/798600) is a serious theater presenting classical and modern dramas.

Sports & the Outdoors

Biking

Bikes can be rented at **Bike Zone** (✉ Market St. ☎ 01865/728877).

Punting

FodorsChoice
★

You may choose, like many an Oxford student, to spend a summer afternoon **punting,** while dangling your champagne bottle in the water to keep it cool. Punts—shallow-bottomed boats that are poled slowly up the river—can be rented in several places.

From mid-March through mid-October, **Cherwell Boathouse** (✉ Bardwell Rd. ☎ 01865/515978), a punt station and restaurant a mile north of the heart of Oxford, will rent you a boat and, if you wish, someone to punt it. Rentals are £8–£10 per hour. At the foot of **Magdalen Bridge** (✉ High St. ☎ 01865/515978) you can rent a punt for £10 an hour, plus a £25 refundable deposit.

Spectator Sports

At the end of May, during **Oxford's Eights Week,** men and women rowers from the university's colleges compete to be "Head of the River." Because the river is too narrow and twisting for teams of eight to race side by side, the boats set off, 13 at a time, one behind another. Each boat tries to catch and bump the one in front. Spectators can watch all the way.

Oxford University Cricket Club competes against leading county teams and, each summer, the major foreign team visiting Britain. In the middle of the sprawling University Parks—itself worthy of a walk—the club's playing field is one of the loveliest in England.

Shopping

Small shops line High Street, Cornmarket, and Queen Street, and the Clarendon and Westgate centers, which lead off them, have branches of several nationally known stores. **Alice's Shop** (✉ 83 St. Aldate's ☎ 01865/723793) sells all manner of *Alice in Wonderland* paraphernalia. **Blackwell's** (✉ 48–50 Broad St. ☎ 01865/792792), family owned and run since 1879, stocks one of the world's widest selections of books. The **Covered Market** (✉ Off High St.) is a good place for a cheap sandwich and a leisurely browse; the smell of pastries follows you from cobbler to jeweler to cheese monger. **Shepherd & Woodward** (✉ 109 High St. ☎ 01865/249491), a traditional tailor, specializes in university gowns, ties, and scarves. The **University of Oxford Shop** (✉ 106 High St. ☎ 01865/247414), run by the university, sells authorized clothing, ceramics, and tea towels, all emblazoned with university crests.

BLENHEIM PALACE TO ALTHORP

The River Thames takes on a new graciousness as it flows along the borders of Oxfordshire for 71 mi; each league it increases in size and importance. Three tributaries swell the river as it passes through the landscape: the Windrush, the Evenlode, and the Cherwell. Tucked among the hills and dales are one of England's most impressive stately homes, one of its most Edenic villages, and a former Rothschild estate. Closer to London in Hertfordshire is St. Albans, with its cathedral and Roman remains.

Woodstock

★ ❷   *8 mi northwest of Oxford on A44.*

Handsome 17th- and 18th-century houses line the trim streets of Woodstock, which sits at the edge of the Cotswolds and is best known for nearby Blenheim Palace. In summer tour buses clog the village's ancient streets, and the lofty halls of Blenheim echo with the clamor of voices from around the world. On a quiet fall or spring afternoon, however, Woodstock is a sublime experience: a mellowed 18th-century church and town hall mark the central square, and along its back streets you'll find flower-bedecked houses and quiet lanes right out of a 19th-century etching. A public bus route runs (usually every half hour) from Oxford to Woodstock.

Where to Stay & Eat

★ **££££**   ✕🖼 **The Feathers.** Flowery, antiques-bedecked guest rooms fill a stylish hotel in the heart of town that was created from five 17th-century houses. The courtyard is a favored spot for a summertime meal, and in winter log fires make the public rooms cozy. The seasonal menu and upscale dining room are worth the restaurant's hefty prices. You might opt for a rich risotto topped with foie gras or duck confit or seafood such as roasted sea bass. ⊠ *Market St., 0X20 1SX* ☎ *01993/812291* 🖷*01993/813158* ⊕*www.feathers.co.uk* ⬎*22 rooms, 5 suites* ⚿ *Restaurant, room service, cable TV, lounge, dry cleaning, laundry service, meeting rooms; no a/c* ⊟ *AE, DC, MC, V* ⦸ *BP.*

★   🖼 **The Bear.** This is an archetypal English coaching inn, with Tudoresque
££££–£££££   wood paneling, beamed ceilings, wattle-and-daub walls, and dancing fireplaces in winter. The guest rooms, overlooking either a quiet churchyard or the town square, have plenty of carved oak; the duplex suites would make a Stuart king feel at home, thanks to their timbered loft-balconies and gargantuan four-posters. Legend has it that the Bear is where Richard Burton finally popped the question to Elizabeth Taylor. ⊠ *Park St., OX20 1SZ* ☎ *0870/400–8202* 🖷 *01993/813380* ⊕ *www. heritagehotels.co.uk* ⬎ *47 rooms, 6 suites* ⚿ *Restaurant, room service, minibars, cable TV, bar, laundry service, meeting rooms, no-smoking rooms* ⊟ *AE, DC, MC, V* ⦸ *BP.*

££   🖼 **Blenheim Guest House & Tea Rooms.** The Cinderella of all British hotels, this small three-story guest house stands in the quiet village cul-de-sac that leads to the back gates of Blenheim Palace. Its facade still bears a Victorian-era banner that says "Views and Postcards of Blenheim," and there's a storefront tearoom. The unassuming guest rooms have modern furnishings, but the Marlborough room is unique—its bathroom offers a view of Blenheim. ⊠ *17 Park St., OX20 1SJ* ☎ *01993/813814* 🖷 *01993/813810* ⊕ *www.theblenheim.com* ⬎ *6 rooms* ⚿ *Tea shop, laundry service; no a/c, no smoking* ⊟ *MC, V* ⦸ *BP.*

Blenheim Palace

❷   *8 mi northwest of Oxford via A44 to A4095.*

So grandiose is Blenheim's masonry and so breathtaking are its articulations of splendor, that some have pondered why it hasn't been named a wonder of the world. Built by Sir John Vanbrugh in the early 1700s, Blenheim was given by Queen Anne and the nation to General John

Churchill, first duke of Marlborough. The exterior is mind-boggling, with its huge columns, enormous pediments, and obelisks, all exemplars of English baroque. Inside, lavishness continues in monumental extremes. In most of the opulent rooms, great family portraits look down at sumptuous furniture, tapestries illustrating important battles, and immense pieces of silver. For some, however, the most memorable room is the small, low-ceiling chamber where Winston Churchill (his father was the younger brother of the then-duke) was born in 1874, he is buried in nearby Bladon.

Sir Winston once wrote that the unique beauty of Blenheim lay in its perfect adaptation of English parkland to an Italian palace. Indeed the 2,000 acres of grounds, the work of Capability Brown, 18th-century England's most gifted landscape gardener, are arguably the best example of the "cunningly natural" park in the country. Brown declared that his object at Blenheim was to "make the Thames look like a small stream compared with the winding Danube." At points he almost succeeds—the scale of these grounds must be seen to be believed. At dusk, flocks of sheep are let loose to become living mowers for the magnificent lawns. Tucked away here is the Temple of Diana, where Winston Churchill proposed to his future wife, Clementine. Blenheim's formal gardens include notable water terraces and an Italian garden with a mermaid fountain, all built in the 1920s.

The Pleasure Gardens, reached by a train that stops just outside the main entrance to the palace, contain some child pleasers: a butterfly house, giant hedge maze, playground, and giant chess set. The fragrant herb and lavender garden is also delightful. The train runs every 30 minutes from 11 AM until 5 PM. ⊠ *Woodstock* ☎ *01993/811325* ⊕ *www. blenheimpalace.com* 🗐 *£10* ⊙ *Palace mid-Mar.–Oct., daily 10:30–4:45; park daily 9–4:45; special events, fairs, and concerts throughout year.*

Bladon

㉘ *2 mi southeast of Woodstock on A4095; 6 mi north of Oxford.*

A small tree-lined churchyard holds the burial place of Sir Winston Churchill, his grave the more impressive for its simplicity.

Stanton Harcourt Manor

㉙ *9 mi south of Bladon, 9 mi southwest of Oxford.*

Reached through twisting lanes, this outstanding example of an early medieval unfortified manor house lies among streams, small lakes, and woods. It was here, in 1718, that Alexander Pope translated Homer's *Iliad*. The manor—stuffed with silver, pictures, and antique furniture— is worth a visit apart from this association; it has a complete medieval kitchen and 12 acres of gardens. ⊠ *Stanton Harcourt* ☎ *01865/881928* 🗐 *£5, garden only £3* ⊙ *Easter–Sept., every other Thurs. and Sun., and bank holiday Mon.; check locally for opening times.*

Kelmscott Manor

㉚ *11 mi west of Stanton Harcourt, 20 mi southwest of Oxford.*

Behind its dignified 16th- and 17th-century exterior, limestone Kelmscott Manor was, in its Victorian heyday, a site of social and domestic unrest. Here, artist, writer, and socialist William Morris (1834–96) launched his anti-industrial Arts and Crafts movement. At the manor his wife, Jane, openly cohabited with her lover, the painter Dante Gabriel Rossetti (1828–82), Morris's business partner. Today the house displays textiles, furniture, and ceramics by Morris and his associates. The surrounding landscape was an obvious source of Morris's inspiration. Oxford University now owns the house, a unique monument to the "Brotherhood." Morris died at Kelmscott and is buried in the local churchyard. ⊠ *Off A417, Kelmscott, Lechlade* ☎ *01367/252486* ⊕ *www.kelmscottmanor. co.uk* ⊠ *£7, garden £2* ⊙ *Apr.–Sept., Wed. 11–1 and 2–5; Apr.–June and Sept., 3rd Sat. 2–5; July and Aug., 1st and 3rd Sat. 2–5.*

Uffington & the Vale of the White Horse

㉛ *7 mi southeast of Kelmscott Manor, 18 mi southwest of Oxford, 9 mi northeast of Swindon.*

Stretching up into the foothills of the Berkshire Downs between Swindon and Oxford is a wide fertile plain known as the Vale of the White Horse. Here, off B4507, cut into the turf of the hillside to expose the underlying chalk, is the 374-foot-long, 110-foot-high **figure of a white horse,** one of the most important of Britain's prehistoric sites. Some historians believed that the figure might have been carved to commemorate King Alfred's victory over the Danes in 871, whereas others dated it back to the Iron Age, around 750 BC. More current research suggests that it is at least 1,000 years older, created at the beginning of the second millennium BC. Nearby **Dragon Hill** is equally mysterious; an unlikely legend suggests that St. George slew his dragon on Dragon Hill. **Uffington Castle,** above the horse, is a prehistoric fort. English Heritage maintains these sites. To reach the Vale of the White Horse from Oxford, follow A420, then B4508 to the village of Uffington. The 85-mi **Ridgeway National Trail** (⊕ www.nationaltrail.gov.uk), which runs from south of Aylesbury to near Avebury, passes through the area.

Where to Stay

££ ▣ **The Craven B&B.** Rose-filled gardens and antiques-filled rooms are among the traditional elements at this pretty thatch-roof, 17th-century cottage on the outskirts of Uffington. Bedrooms have beamed ceilings and country cottage prints. Family photographs and the shared breakfast at the kitchen table keep the B&B convivial. Creative seasonal menus are available for dinner. ⊠ *Fernham Rd., Uffington, SN7 7RD* ☎ *01367/820449* ⊕ *www.thecraven.co.uk* ⇱ *6 rooms, 4 with bath* ♨ *Dining room, lounge, laundry service; no a/c, no room phones, no room TVs, no smoking* ⊟ *MC, V* ⦿ *BP.*

Dorchester-on-Thames

㉜ *15 mi east of Uffington, 7 mi southeast of Abingdon, 9 mi southeast of Oxford.*

An important center in Saxon times, when it was the seat of a bishopric, Dorchester deserves a visit chiefly for its ancient abbey. The main street, once a leg of the Roman road to Silchester, has timber houses, thatch cottages, and ancient inns. Crossing the Thames at Day's Lock and turning left at Little Wittenham takes you on a pleasant walk past the remains of the village's Iron Age settlements.

In addition to secluded cloisters and gardens, **Dorchester Abbey** has a spacious church (1170) with traceried medieval windows and a lead baptismal font. The east window was restored in 1966 by the American Friends of the Abbey in memory of Sir Winston Churchill. The abbey is a popular concert venue. ⊠ *Off A4074* ☎ *01865/340007* ⊕ *www. dorchester-abbey.org.uk* ⊠ *Free* ⊙ *May–Sept., daily 8:30–7; Oct.–Apr., daily 8:30–dusk, except during services.*

Where to Stay

£££ 🖼 **George Hotel.** Overlooking Dorchester Abbey, this 500-year-old hotel was built as a coaching inn—there's still an old coach parked outside—and it retains whitewashed walls, exposed beams, and log fires. Each room has an individual style and two have four-poster beds. The modern rooms in the annex have less character, however. ⊠ *25 High St., OX10 7JX* ☏ *01865/340404* ⊟ *01865/341620* ☞ *17 rooms* ⚭ *Restaurant, room service, in-room data ports, pub, dry cleaning, laundry facilities, meeting rooms, free parking, some pets allowed, no-smoking rooms; no a/c* ⊟ *AE, MC, V* ❀ *CP.*

Great Milton

❸❸ *8 mi northeast of Dorchester-on-Thames, 7 mi southeast of Oxford.*

With attractive thatch cottages built of local stone and a single street about a mile long with wide grass verges, this is another stop on the literary pilgrim's route. The poet John Milton, author of *Paradise Lost* (1667), was married in the local church, which holds an unusual collection of old musical instruments. The town is also a haunt of culinary pilgrims.

Where to Stay & Eat

£££££ ✕🖼 **Le Manoir aux Quat' Saisons.** Standards run high at this 15th-cen-
Fodor'sChoice   tury stone manor house, which has one of England's finest kitchens (com-
★   plete with cooking school) and luxurious rooms in styles from rococo fantasy to chic chinoiserie. Chef Raymond Blanc's epicurean touch shows at every turn. Spare yourself the trouble of deciding among the innovative French creations and treat yourself to the *menu gourmand*—eight courses of haute cuisine for £95. ⊠ *Church Rd., OX44 7PD* ☏ *01844/278881* ⊟ *01844/278847* ⊕ *www.manoir.com* ☞ *32 rooms* ⚭ *Restaurant, some in-room data ports, baby-sitting, kennel; no a/c in some rooms* ⊟ *AE, DC, MC, V* ❀ *BP.*

Aylesbury

❸❹ *17 mi northeast of Great Milton, 22 mi east of Oxford, 46 mi north-west of London.*

Aylesbury makes a good base for exploring the surrounding country-side. The area around the 13th-century St. Mary's Church is the only hint of the 17th-century town with its small Tudor lanes and cottages.

Many regal residences created by the Rothschild family throughout Europe are gone now, but **Waddesdon Manor** remains, a vision of the 19th century at its most sumptuous. G. H. Destailleur built the house in 1880–89 for Baron Ferdinand de Rothschild in the style of a French chateau. Furnished with Savonnerie carpets, Sèvres porcelain, furniture made by Riesener for Marie Antoinette, and numerous paintings by Rubens, Watteau, Gainsborough, and Reynolds, the mansion underwent a top-to-bottom renovation, thanks to Lord Rothschild, current head of the English branch of the family. The National Trust now owns Waddesdon Manor. The splendid Victorian gardens and the aviary deserve a look, and you can dine on English or French fare at restaurants on the grounds. ⊠ *Waddesdon, on the A41 near Aylesbury* ☏ *01296/653226* ⊕ *www.waddesdon.org.uk* ☏ *£10, grounds £3* ☉ *House Apr.–Oct., Wed.–Sun. and bank holiday Mon. 11–4; gardens Mar.–late Dec., Wed.–Sun. and bank holiday Mon. 10–5.*

Fodor'sChoice   A superb example of a Georgian garden, **Stowe Landscape Garden** was
★   created for the Temple family by the most famous gardeners of the 18th century. Capability Brown, Charles Bridgeman, and William Kent all

worked on the land to create 980 acres of pleasing greenery in the valleys and meadows. More than 30 striking monuments, follies, and temples dot the landscape of lakes, rivers, and pleasant vistas. Stowe House, at its center, is now a fancy school; it's closed to the public. The gardens are about 3 mi northwest of Buckingham, which is a half mile from Aylesbury. ⊠ *Stowe Ave., off 422 Buckingham–Banbury Rd., Buckingham* ☎ *01280/822850* ⊕ *www.nationaltrust.org.uk* ⊠ *£4.80* ☉ *Mar.–Oct., Wed.–Sun 10–5:30; Nov. and Dec., Wed.–Sun. 10–4.*

Where to Stay & Eat

£££ ✕⊞ **Five Arrows.** Patterned brick chimneys and purple gables decorate this Tudor-style Victorian building next to the main entrance of Waddesdon Manor. Originally constructed to house the manor's workers, it now holds a hotel with traditional-style bedrooms that are sweet if small. The delightful suites in the Courtyard Stables are big enough for families. A fine restaurant and pub serves inspired modern fare with a Mediterranean twist; the wine list is excellent. ⊠ *High St., Waddesdon, HP18 0JE* ☎ *01296/651727* 🖷 *01296/658596* ⊕ *www.waddesdon.org.uk* ⇄ *9 rooms, 2 suites* ♧ *Restaurant, bar; no a/c, no smoking* ⊟ *MC, V* ⧖⧘ *BP.*

£££££ ⊞ **Hartwell House.** Part Jacobean, part Georgian, this magnificent stately home provides formal luxury and modern pampering in the countryside. Chandeliers, valuable oil paintings, and carved ceilings adorn the marvelously ornate public areas. Bedrooms are suitably grand, and some have direct access to the gardens, including 90 acres of landscaped parkland for strolls. This is the kind of place where you must dress for dinner. ⊠ *Oxford Rd. (A418), HP17 8NL* ☎ *01296/747444* 🖷 *01296/747450* ⊕ *www.hartwell-house.com* ⇄ *46 rooms* ♧ *Restaurant, café, room service, in-room data ports, 2 tennis courts, indoor pool, gym, hair salon, hot tub, sauna, spa, steam room, fishing, croquet, bar, lounge, library, dry cleaning, laundry service, meeting rooms, concierge, car rental, some pets allowed, no-smoking floors; no kids under 8* ⊟ *AE, MC, V.*

St. Albans

㉟ *25 mi east of Aylesbury, 27 mi northwest of London.*

St. Albans, a pleasant town on the outskirts of London, has a Norman cathedral and a number of reminders of its long history, which extends back to the Romans. From AD 50 to 440, Verulamium was one of the largest towns in Roman Britain, and splendid Roman ruins and the Verulamium museum recall that past. The surrounding countryside gave birth to Beatrix Potter's *Peter Rabbit* and inspired George Bernard Shaw. Every Wednesday and Saturday, the Market Place comes alive with traders from all over England. St. Albans is just 20 minutes by fast train from Kings Cross station in central London, and London and industry continue to encompass the town.

Medieval pilgrims came from far and wide to hilltop **St. Albans Cathedral** to worship St. Alban, the Roman soldier turned Christian martyr. Construction of the impressive, mainly Norman cathedral began in the early 11th century, but the nearly 300-foot-long nave dates from 1235. The tower contains bricks that were part of Roman buildings. ⊠ *Holywell Hill at High St.* ☎ *01727/860780* ⊕ *www.stalbanscathedral.org. uk* ⊠ *Free* ☉ *Daily 8:30–5:45.*

With exhibits on everything from Roman food to burial practices, the **Verulamium Museum,** on the site of the ancient Roman city, explores life 2,000 years ago. The re-created Roman rooms contain colorful mosaics that are some of the finest in Britain. Every second weekend of the month,

"Roman soldiers" invade the museum and demonstrate the skills of the Imperial Army. ⊠ *St. Michael's St.* ☎ *01727/751810* ⊕ *www.verulamium. co.uk* ☞ *£3.20* ☼ *Mon.–Sat. 10–5:30, Sun. 2–5:30.*

☾ **Verulamium Park,** adjacent to the Verulamium Museum, contains the usual (playground, summer wading pool, duck-filled lake) and the unusual— **Roman ruins** that include part of the Roman town hall and a hypocaust, a central heating system. The hypocaust dates to AD 200 and included one of the first heated floors in Britain. Brick columns supported the floor, and hot air from a nearby fire was drawn underneath the floor to keep bathers in the ancient baths warm. ⊠ *St. Michael's St.* ☎ *01727/ 751810* ⊕ *www.verulamium.co.uk* ☞ *Free* ☼ *Hypocaust Mon.–Sat. 10–5:30, Sun. 2–5:30.*

Imagination can take you back to AD 130 and to a Roman stage drama as you walk around the ruins of the **Roman Theater,** one of the few in Britain. Next to the theater are the ruins of a Roman town house, shops, and a shrine. ⊠ *Bluehouse Hill* ☎ *01727/854051* ☞ *£1.50* ☼ *Easter–Nov., daily 10–5; Dec.–Easter, daily 10–4.*

Hatfield House, an outstanding brick mansion surrounded by formal gardens, stands as a testament to the magnificence of Jacobean architecture. Robert Cecil, earl of Salisbury, built Hatfield in 1611, and his descendants still live here today. The interior, with its dark wood paneling, lush tapestries, and Tudor and Jacobean portraits, reveals much about the era. Perhaps the finest feature is the ornate Grand Staircase, with carved wooden figures on the banisters. Friday is Connoisseurs' Day; entrance is £10 and includes an extended tour and additional gardens. ⊠ *Hatfield,, 6 mi east of St. Albans, off A1* ☎ *01707/287010* ⊕ *www.hatfield-house.co.uk* ☞ *House, gardens, and park £7.50 (£10 on Fri.), gardens £4.50, park £2* ☼ *Easter–Sept., daily noon–4; west gardens Easter–Sept., daily 11–5:30; east gardens Easter–Sept., Fri. 11–6. Guided tours weekdays only.*

From 1906 to his death in 1950, the famed playwright George Bernard Shaw lived in the small village of Ayot St. Lawrence. Today his small Edwardian home, **Shaw's Corner,** remains much as he left it. The most delightful curiosity is his little writing hut in the garden, which can be turned to face the sun. ⊠ *Off Hill Farm La., Ayot St. Lawrence, 9 mi northeast of St. Albans* ☎ *01438/820307; 01494/755567 recorded information* ⊕ *www.nationaltrust.org.uk* ☞ *£3.60* ☼ *Apr.–Nov., Wed.–Sun. 1–5.*

Where to Stay & Eat

£ ╳ **Waffle House.** Indoors or outside, you can have a great budget meal at the 16th-century Kingsbury Watermill, near the Verulamium Museum. The organic flour for the high-quality, sweet and savory Belgian waffles comes from Redbournbury Watermill just north of the city; daily specials add variety. In the main dining room, you can see the wheel churn the water of the River Ver. ⊠ *Kingsbury Watermill, St. Michael's St.* ☎ *01727/730458* ⊟ *AE, DC, MC, V.*

£ ╳ **Ye Olde Fighting Cocks.** Some claim this is England's oldest pub, and the octagonal building certainly looks suitably aged. The small rooms with low ceilings make a cozy stop in cold weather for a pint and simple pub grub. Be prepared for crowds; this place is popular. ⊠ *Abbey Mill La.* ☎ *01727/865830* ⊟ *MC, V.*

££££ ╳▥ **St. Michael's Manor.** The Newling Ward family has owned this luxurious 16th-century manor house in the heart of St. Albans for three generations. The 5 acres of grounds, complete with a lake, add a sense of seclusion, and plush furniture helps make the antique- and painting-filled public areas inviting. Bedrooms, some of which have a view of the lake, are decorated in Victorian style and have books and games. The Terrace Room presents a daily set menu of fine modern British cooking, from red onion tart with goat cheese to pan-fried sea bass with Chinese ginger. ⊠ *Fishpool St., AL3 4RY* ☎ *01727/864444* 🖷 *01727/848909* ⊕ *www.stmichaelsmanor.com* ⇆ *23 rooms* ♿ *Restaurant, room service, cable TV, fishing, croquet, bar, lounge, dry cleaning, laundry service, meeting room, no-smoking rooms; no a/c* 🖃 *AE, DC, MC, V* ⦿ *BP.*

Woburn Abbey

★ ❸❻ *30 mi west of St. Albans, 10 mi northeast of Aylesbury.*

Still the ancestral residence of the duke of Bedford, Woburn Abbey houses countless Grand Tour treasures and old master paintings, including 20 Canalettos that practically wallpaper the crimson dining salon—one of the most sumptuous rooms in England. Works by Gainsborough and Reynolds are also notable. The Palladian mansion contains a number of etchings by Queen Victoria, who left them behind when she stayed here. Nine species of deer roam the grounds, where an antiques center and small restaurant add to the list of attractions. (**Woburn Safari Park,** a very popular drive-through experience that takes you past a number of endangered African species, is entered separately.) To get to Woburn from London, head north on M1; to get there from Oxford, head for Milton Keynes, the nearest large town to the house, on A5. ⊠ *Woburn* ☎ *01525/290666* ⊕ *www.woburnabbey.co.uk* 🖾 *House and deer park £7.50, safari £12.50* 🕑 *Jan.–Mar., weekends and national holiday Mon. 10:30–4; Apr.–Oct., Mon.–Sat. 11–4, Sun. 11–5.*

Althorp

❸❼ *27 mi northwest of Woburn Abbey.*

Deep in the heart of Northamptonshire sits Althorp, the ancestral home of the Spencers, the family of Diana, Princess of Wales. Here, set on a tiny island within the estate park, is Diana's final resting place. Back in 1765 Horace Walpole described the setting as "one of those enchanted scenes which a thousand circumstances of history and art endear to a pensive spectator." As it turns out, Princess Diana and her siblings found the house ugly and melancholy, calling it "Deadlock Hall." What the house does have are room after room of Van Dycks, Reynoldses, and Rubens—all portraits of the Spencers going back 500 years—and an entry hall that architectural historian Nikolaus Pevsner called "the noblest Georgian room in the country." To these attractions, Earl Spencer has added a visitor center devoted to Diana. Tickets to Althorp, which is 5 mi west of Northampton, must be booked in advance. On the west side of the estate park is Great Brington, the neighboring village where the church of **St. Mary the Virgin** (🕑 *daily noon–4*) holds the Spencer family crypt; it's best reached by the designated path from Althorp. ⊠ *Rugby Rd., off the A428* ☎ *01604/770107 house; 0870/167–9000 advance tickets* ⊕ *www. althorp.com* 🖾 *£10.50* 🕑 *July–Sept., daily 10–5* 🕑 *Closed Aug. 31.*

THAMES VALLEY A TO Z

To research prices, get advice from other travelers, and book travel arrangements, visit www.fodors.com.

AIR TRAVEL

The Thames Valley is convenient to major airports in London (⇨ Air Travel *in* Smart Travel Tips).

BUS TRAVEL

Traveling by bus continues to be the preferred method of transportation to the Thames Valley. Oxford's bus companies have service every 12 minutes (24 hours a day); pick-up points in London are Victoria train and bus stations, and Baker Street and Marble Arch by the Underground stops. They also offer shuttle service to Gatwick and Heathrow every half hour, and—at £9.50 for round-trip service—are considerably cheaper than the train.

The Oxford Bus Company and other local bus services, such as Stagecoach, link the towns between Oxford and Henley with services to Heathrow Airport and London. Reading Buses also accesses Oxford and Reading to the airports, and First of Bracknell serves the smaller towns of Berkshire. For information about buses and other forms of public transportation, contact Traveline.

CUTTING COSTS   The Oxford Bus Company offers a one-day ticket and a seven-day Freedom ticket, for unlimited bus travel within Oxford.

FARES &   🚌 **First** ☎ 0870/608–2608 ⊕ www.firstgroup.com. **Oxford Bus Company**
SCHEDULES   ☎01865/785400 ⊕www.oxfordbus.co.uk. **National Express** ☎0870/580–8080 ⊕ www.nationalexpress.com. **Reading Buses** ☎ 0118/959–4000. **Stagecoach Oxford Tube** ☎ 01865/772250 ⊕ www.stagecoach-oxford.co.uk. **Traveline** ☎ 0870/608–2608 ⊕ www.traveline.org.uk.

CAR RENTAL

🚗Local Agencies **A. A. Clark Self-Drive** ✉72–74 Arthur Rd., Windsor ☎01753/800600. **Europcar Interrent** ✉ BP Petrol Station, Hartford Motors, Seacourt Tower, Botley, 4 mi north of Oxford ☎ 01865/246373. **Hertz** ✉ City Motors Ltd., Wolvercote Roundabout, Woodstock Rd., Oxford ☎ 01865/319972.

CAR TRAVEL

The M4 and M40 radiate west from London, bringing Oxford (55 mi) and Reading (42 mi) within an hour's drive, except in rush hour. Although the roads are good, this wealthy section of the commuter belt has surprisingly heavy traffic, even on the smaller roads. Parking in towns can be a problem, too, so allow plenty of time.

EMERGENCIES

The John Radcliffe Hospital is accessible by Bus 13 from Carfax Tower in Oxford or from the A40.

🚑**Ambulance, fire, police** ☎ 999. **John Radcliffe Hospital** ✉ Marston Ferry Rd., Oxford ☎ 01865/741166. **Princess Christian's Hospital** ✉ 12 Clarence Rd., Windsor ☎ 01753/853121.

SPORTS & THE OUTDOORS

The Countryside Agency has been charting and preserving Thames paths for years and offers publications about them. For maps and advice, contact the National Trails Office or the Ramblers' Association.

🚶Walking **Countryside Agency** ✉ John Dower House, Crescent Pl., Cheltenham, GL50 3RA ☎ 01242/521381 ⊕ www.countryside.gov.uk ✉ Dacre House, 19 Dacre St., London, SW1H 0DH ☎ 020/7340–2900. **National Trails Office** ✉ Cultural Services, Holton, Oxford, OX33 1QQ ☎ 01865/810224 ⊕ www.nationaltrails.gov.uk. **Ramblers' Association** ✉ Camelford House, 87–90 Albert Embankment, 2nd fl., London, SE1 7TW ☎ 0207/339–8500 ⊕ www.ramblers.org.uk.

TOURS

BOAT TOURS   The ideal way to see the Thames region is from the water; summertime trips range from 30 minutes to all day. Hobbs and Sons covers the Henley Reach and also rents boats. Salter Brothers runs daily steamer cruises, mid-May to mid-September from Windsor, Oxford, Abingdon, Henley,

Marlow, and Reading. Thames River Cruises conducts outings from Caversham Bridge, Reading, Easter–September. French Brothers operates river trips from the Promenade, Windsor, and from Runnymede, as far as Hampton Court.

◪ **French Brothers** ✉ The Promenade, Windsor ☎ 01753/851900 ⊕ www.boat-trips. co.uk. **Hobbs and Sons** ✉ Station Rd., Henley-on-Thames ☎ 01491/572035. **Salter Brothers** ✉ Folly Bridge, Oxford ☎ 01865/243421 ⊕ www.salterbros.co.uk. **Thames River Cruises** ✉ Caversham Bridge, Reading ☎ 0118/948-1088.

BUS TOURS   City Sightseeing runs guided, open-top bus tours, mid-March–November, of Windsor (£6) and Oxford (£9).

◪ **City Sightseeing** ☎ 01865/790522 ⊕ www.city-sightseeing.com.

WALKING TOURS   Theme walking tours (£4.50), including one on Inspector Morse, leave several times daily from outside Oxford's tourist office (⇨ Visitor Information) and from Carfax Tower on Saturday and Sunday.

TRAIN TRAVEL

Trains to Oxford (1¼ hours) and the region depart from London's Paddington station. Ascot (½ hours) is easily accessible from London: trains leave Waterloo on the half hour. Trains to St. Albans (20 minutes) leave from Kings Cross station. Confirm that your train is on time before going to the station—train service in this area is the busiest in all Britain. For timetables, call or log on to National Rail Enquiries. Contact Thames Trains directly for timetables and special offers, including a £50 Trio Ticket for unlimited travel on any three days within a seven-day period during summer in the Thames Valley.

◪ **National Rail Enquiries** ☎ 0845/748-4950 ⊕ www.nationalrail.co.uk. **Thames Trains** ☎ 0800/358-3567 ⊕ www.thamestrains.co.uk.

TRAVEL AGENCIES

◪ Local Agent Referrals **Thomas Cook** ✉ 5 Queen St., Oxford ☎ 01865/447000 ✉ King Edward Ct., Windsor ☎ 01753/851966.

VISITOR INFORMATION

◪ **Aylesbury** ✉ 8 Bourbon St., HP20 2RR ☎ 01296/330559. **Henley** ✉ Town Hall, Market Pl., RG9 2AQ ☎ 01491/578034. **Marlow** ✉ 31 High St., SL7 1AU ☎ 01628/483597. **Oxford** ✉ 15/16 Broad St., OX1 3AS ☎ 01865/726871 ⊕ www.oxford.gov.uk. **Oxford University** ⊕ www.ox.ac.uk. **St. Albans** ✉ Town Hall, Market Pl., AL3 5DJ ☎ 01727/864511 ⊕ www.stalbans.gov.uk. **Windsor** ✉ 24 High St., SL4 1LH ☎ 01753/743900 ⊕ www.windsor.gov.uk. **Woodstock** ✉ Park St., Oxfordshire Museum, OX20 1SN ☎ 01993/813276.

SHAKESPEARE COUNTRY

STRATFORD-UPON-AVON & ENVIRONS

6

FODOR'S CHOICE

Royal Shakespeare Theatre, *Stratford-upon-Avon*

HIGHLY RECOMMENDED

RESTAURANTS   Desport's, *Stratford-upon-Avon*

Lambs, *Stratford-upon-Avon*

HOTELS   Caterham House, *Stratford-upon-Avon*

SIGHTS   Anne Hathaway's Cottage, *Shottery*

Baddesley Clinton, *near Chadwick End*

Lord Leycester Hospital, *Warwick*

Warwick Castle, *Warwick*

Updated by
Catherine
Belonogoff

MUCH ADO ABOUT NOTHING? Far from it. Even if you know little about William Shakespeare, one flourish through his home territory will leave you referring to him familiarly as the Bard. Synonymous with Shakespeare, Stratford-upon-Avon has overshadowed other villages in the region with its popularity. But it was an important market town and malt-making center for more than 300 years before the Bard came along, and the surrounding area does not seem to mind the association with the Shakespeare juggernaut. Stratford has carefully preserved its ancient buildings, creating what is in many ways a perfect specimen of a four-centuries-old provincial town. It's also a home base of the Royal Shakespeare Company, where thespians pay their finest tribute to the master.

Warwickshire—the ancient county of which Stratford is the southern nexus—is a land of sleepy villages, thatch-roof cottages, and solitary farmhouses. It was the birthplace of the image of Britain that has been spread around the world by the works of Shakespeare. This is, quintessentially, the realm of the yeoman, the wooded land of Arden, the home of the prosperous tradesman and the wealthy merchant, the region where landowners still pasture deer as they have for the last 900 years, and the county of peace and prosperity that is the fire in the heart of what Shakespeare called "this precious stone set in the silver sea."

A rich selection of historic sites stud the verdant landscape. Three of England's most memorable abodes are here: the home of Anne Hathaway, Shakespeare's wife; Charlecote, a grand Elizabethan manor house; and Baddesley Clinton, a superb example of late medieval domestic architecture. Other treasure houses include Ragley Hall, Coughton Court, and Broughton Castle, brimming with art treasures. Also near Stratford is "medieval England in stone"—Warwick Castle, which provides a glimpse into England's turbulent history. Little wonder Henry James once wrote that Warwickshire "is the core and center of the English world."

The core and center of Warwickshire is, of course, Stratford. In addition to charting Shakespeare's achievements, the town's historic monuments give a thrilling insight into English life in late-medieval, Tudor, and Elizabethan times. Pride of place goes to the five properties administered by the Shakespeare Birthplace Trust, including Shakespeare's Birthplace. These not only give you a picture of Shakespeare as writer and man of wealth and property but also help trace the social pattern of his family, following its rise from humble beginnings to a position of eminence through the generations.

The price you pay for absorbing these scenes and treading the streets once frequented by Shakespeare is the press of the thousands of others who also come to pay their respects, and the sometimes ruthless commercialization. If the hustle and bustle become too much, just take a hint from the young Shakespeare. He often turned his back on the town and followed the Avon as it wended its way through meadows and small villages. Today, you, too, can wander through a landscape seemingly untouched by the brasher aspects of modern life.

Exploring Shakespeare Country

Stratford-upon-Avon is neighbor to a number of villages that have legends connected with the Bard, as well as architecture dating from his time. Complementing these humble hamlets, and often in the midst of them, is an impressive gathering of country houses open to the public, each of which requires a good half day to explore and is easily reachable from Stratford. To the north lie two magnificent castles, Warwick and Kenilworth. Warwick has much to offer besides its castle, and it is worth a protracted jaunt.

Stratford-upon-Avon, the lead destination for most travelers, is ideal for day visits or as a convenient base from which to brush up on your Shakespeare. If you can manage only a day here, arrive early and confine your visit to two or three of the Shakespeare Birthplace Trust properties, a few other town sights, a pub lunch, and a walk along the river, capped off by a stroll to the cottage of Anne Hathaway. You can use the train to visit Stratford from London or other major cities; to see most of the sights outside the town, a car is best. A couple of nights in Shakespeare's home city allow you to gather the gist of the place without testing too severely your tolerance for crowds. With four days you can explore the rural delights of the countryside.

Numbers in the text correspond to numbers in the margin and on the Shakespeare Country and Stratford-upon-Avon maps.

If you have 2 days

Stratford-upon-Avon ❶–❾ deserves at least a full day and a drama-packed night—that is, if you wish to catch a performance of the Bard's works at the Royal Shakespeare Theatre. Five historic properties are must-sees: three are in town—**Shakespeare's Birthplace** ❶ and the Shakespeare Centre, on Henley Street, the **Nash's House and New Place** ❸ property, and **Hall's Croft** ❻—whereas the others, **Anne Hathaway's Cottage** ❼ and **Mary Arden's House** ❿, are just a few minutes out of town. (If you spend both days in Stratford and wish to enjoy these and other sights in a leisurely manner, follow the self-guiding Town Heritage Trail or the black-and-gold signposts that direct you to the landmarks.) After your Stratford sojourn, spend the next day touring selected sights, including the mansions of **Baddesley Clinton** ⓭ and **Charlecote Park** ⓱. In between, take in some of the villages nearby, ideal for lunch. Spend your second night back in Stratford or in one of the inns along the rural way.

If you have 4 days

After two days spent touring the august abodes of **Stratford-upon-Avon** ❶–❾ and the Shakespeare-linked attractions of the immediate vicinity—including **Henley-in-Arden** ⓫, the setting for *As You Like It*—you will be ready for a change of scene. Dedicate a couple of mornings to visiting two or three of the stately houses within easy driving distance. Plan your route along minor roads to take in some off-the-beaten-track hamlets. Nearest of these is fetching **Welford-on-Avon** ⓴, hugging the river as it loops west from Stratford. A short distance north, on either side of the village of **Alcester** ㉑, an appealing one-horse town, lie two of the area's most notable country houses, the Palladian **Ragley Hall** ㉒ and the Elizabethan **Coughton Court** ㉓, both surrounded by inviting parkland. After spending your first night in Stratford, plan for your second in **Warwick** ⓮, devoting the next morning to exploring the town's medieval castle. Other lower-key attractions are worth an hour or two. If castles are your thing, you should also see **Kenilworth Castle** ⓯, a short drive north, whose red sandstone ruins are redolent of royal pageantry. South of Stratford, **Alderminster** ⓳, the largest of another cluster of villages well worth driving through, makes a suitable night stop and is en route to **Broughton Castle** ⓲.

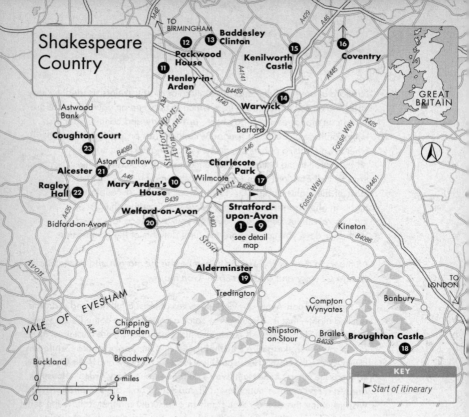

Shakespeare Country

About the Restaurants

Although Stratford has little in the way of high-class dining establishments, many reasonably priced bistros and unpretentious restaurants offer a broad international cuisine. For fancier fare, find one of the better hotels, whose kitchens have drawn some of the foremost chefs from London and beyond. Warwick and Kenilworth have their share of excellent eateries, ideal for a midday lunch or a more substantial evening meal, and the countryside has many old pubs.

About the Hotels

Stratford holds the highest concentration of lodgings in the area, from bed-and-breakfasts to hotels. Here you can find accommodations to fit every pocket, and for the most part they are well maintained. The best establishments are the older, centrally located ones, often with fine period architecture; national chains own most of these. Because the town is *so* popular with theatergoers, book ahead whenever possible. Most hotels offer discounted two- and three-day packages. Outside town, some top-notch country hotels guarantee discreet but attentive service—at very fancy prices. At the other end of the scale, almost every village has a gnarled old inn with rooms at very reasonable rates.

WHAT IT COSTS In pounds					
	£££££	££££	£££	££	£
RESTAURANTS	over £22	£18–£22	£13–£17	£7–£12	under £7
HOTELS	over £160	£115–£160	£80–£115	£50–£80	under £50

Restaurant prices are for a main course at dinner. Hotel prices are for two people in a standard double room in high season, including VAT, with no meals or, if indicated, CP (with Continental breakfast), BP (Breakfast Plan, with full breakfast), or MAP (Modified American Plan, with breakfast and dinner).

Shakespearean Theater

Stratford's Royal Shakespeare Theatre is the home of the Royal Shakespeare Company (RSC), arguably the finest repertory troupe in the world and long the backbone of the theatrical life of the country. The company also mounts its productions in London and around the country, but seeing a play in Stratford is a favored experience. The current theater, built in 1932, was quickly dubbed a "factory for Shakespeare" because of its modern utilitarian aspect. No matter: "The play's the thing." Here, the Bard's plays have made the reputations of generations of actors (and broken not a few), have been staged as archaeological reconstructions and science fiction, and have seen women playing Hamlet and men playing Rosalind. However Shakespeare's plays are reshaped by directors and actors, they continue to reveal new facets of some eternal truth about humanity.

6

Walking

This part of England has glorious, gentle countryside, and many of the local historic houses are surrounded by parkland with scenic walks. Even Stratford can be the base for easy walks along the River Avon or the canal. The towpath bordering the Stratford-upon-Avon Canal provides a chance to escape the throng. Pick up a leaflet on the Avon Valley walk from the town's tourist office.

Timing

In Stratford, avoid visits on weekends and school holidays, and take in the main Shakespeare shrines in the early morning to see them at their least frenetic. One of the high points of Stratford's calendar is the Shakespeare Birthday Celebrations, usually on the weekend nearest to April 23. If you visit during this time, make hotel reservations as early as possible. Warwick Castle, too, usually brims with visitors, and you should arrive early in the day to beat the rush. Some country properties fill up quickly on weekends. Note that a number of these close for the winter, as do most of the stately homes.

STRATFORD-UPON-AVON

▶ "Famous people do seem to have a habit of being born in pretty places—Mozart in Salzburg, Wordsworth in the Lake District, Hardy in Dorset, the Brontës in Yorkshire," begins Susan Hill's 1987 travel book *Shakespeare Country* (now out of print). "And Stratford's charms are very evident." Under the busloads of visitors, Strat-forde—to use the old Saxon name, which means "a ford over a river"—has hung on to its original character as an English market town on the banks of the slow-flowing River Avon. It is close to Birmingham, which lies 37 mi to the northwest, and London, 102 mi to the southeast.

Still, it is Shakespeare who counts. Born in a half-timber, early-16th-century building in the center of Stratford on April 23, 1564, Shakespeare died on April 23, 1616, his 52nd birthday, in a more imposing house at New Place. Although he spent much of his life in London as a leading figure of the theater, the world still associates him with "Shakespeare's Avon." Here, in the years between his birth and 1587, he played as a young lad, attended the local grammar school, and married

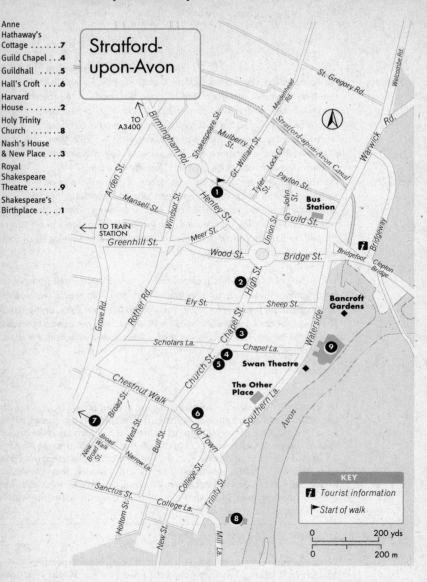

Stratford-
upon-Avon

KEY

i   *Tourist information*

▶ *Start of walk*

0   200 yds

0   200 m

Anne Hathaway; here he returned to the town a man of prosperity. Today you can see his birthplace on Henley Street; his burial place in Holy Trinity Church; Anne Hathaway's Cottage; his mother's home at Wilmcote; New Place and the neighboring Nash's House, home of Shakespeare's granddaughter; and Hall's Croft, home of the Stratford physician who married the Bard's daughter. Whether or not their connections to Shakespeare are historically valid, these sites reveal Elizabethan England at its loveliest. Then, of course, there is the Royal Shakespeare Theatre, with its unrivaled productions.

Stratford-upon-Avon is a fascinating town, so take Antonio's advice (*Twelfth Night*, Act 3, scene 3) and "beguile the time, and feed your knowledge with viewing the town." By the 16th century it was already a prosperous market town with thriving guilds and industries. Its characteristic half-timber houses from this era have been preserved, and they are set off by the charm of later architecture, such as the elegant Georgian storefronts on Bridge Street, with their 18th-century porticoes and arched doorways. By 1769 the town's literary preeminence was confirmed by a three-day festival commemorating Shakespeare, supported by the great actor David Garrick. Since then Stratford's flame has shone ever more brightly, yet the town is far from being a museum piece or a tourist trap. Although full of souvenir shops—every back lane seems to have been converted into a shopping mall—Stratford isn't overly strident in its search for a quick buck.

Exploring Stratford-upon-Avon

The town is easily manageable on a walking tour. Most sights cluster around Henley Street (off the roundabout as you come in on the A3400 Birmingham road), High Street, and Waterside, which skirts the public gardens through which the River Avon flows. Bridge Street and Sheep Street (parallel to Bridge) are Stratford's main thoroughfares and site of most of the banks, shops, and eating places. The town's tourist office lies at Bridgefoot, between the canal and the river, next to Clopton Bridge—"a sumptuous new bridge and large of stone" built in the 15th century by Sir Hugh Clopton, once lord mayor of London and one of Stratford's richest and most philanthropic residents.

The **Shakespeare Birthplace Trust** runs the main places of Shakespearean interest: Anne Hathaway's Cottage, Hall's Croft, Mary Arden's House, Nash's House and New Place, and Shakespeare's Birthplace. They all have similar opening times, and you can buy a combination ticket to three or five properties or pay separate entry fees if you want to visit only one or two. The trust also hosts events by the Tudor Group, costumed interpreters who bring the past alive through demonstrations and talks on subjects such as how Tudor England celebrated Christmas. ☎ *01789/204016* ⊕ *www.shakespeare.org.uk* ✉ *Joint ticket to 5 properties £13; joint ticket to Shakespeare's Birthplace, Hall's Croft, and Nash's House–New Place £9.*

a good walk

To begin at the beginning, pay your respects at **Shakespeare's Birthplace** ① ► on Henley Street. Elizabethan antiques and theater memorabilia are on view. Next door is the Shakespeare Centre, with its impressive library. Then head east down Henley Street to the old city center. Take High Street to the right, passing several half-timber buildings, including the magnificent, twin-gabled **Harvard House** ②, which contains the Museum of British Pewter; at the nearby corner of Sheep Street is a stone bust of the Bard mounted on the north front of the Town Hall. Where High Street becomes Chapel Street, one block down on the left, stands the timber-and-daub **Nash's House and New Place** ③, home of Shakespeare's granddaughter. You can count the varieties of roses in the Elizabethan knot gardens of New Place next door. On Chapel Street is the Shakespeare Hotel—its five gables make one of the longest Elizabethan facades extant. Continue south, and where Chapel Street becomes Church Street are several buildings, seen on the left, that were old when Shakespeare was young: the **Guild Chapel** ④ and the timbered **almshouses** (notice the high chimneys that carried sparks safely above what were once thatch roofs), and the **Guildhall** ⑤, with Shakespeare's school. A left turn at the end of Church Street leads to Old Town and to **Hall's Croft** ⑥, an impressive Tudor residence associated with the poet's daughter. Detour now, taking the footpath from Evesham Place 1 mi northwest to the country hamlet of Shottery and **Anne Hathaway's Cottage** ⑦. After viewing this romantic house, stroll back to **Holy Trinity Church** ⑧, by the banks of the Avon. Here is Shakespeare's tomb *and* the north aisle font where he was christened. Twilight—and your performance at the **Royal Shakespeare Theatre** ⑨—may be approaching now, so head over to Southern Lane. Opt for dinner at the theater restaurant or toast the Bard at the nearby Black Swan—with an evening aperitif in its garden.

TIMING
If you don't tour the sites themselves, this walk takes about three hours, including the walk to Anne Hathaway's Cottage. A more thorough exploration, with an hour for lunch, could last seven hours.

What to See

Almshouses. Immediately beyond the Guildhall on Church Street lies a delightful row of timber-and-daub almshouses. These were built to accommodate the poor by the Guild of the Holy Cross in the early 15th century and still serve as housing for pensioners. ⊠ *Church St.*

★ ❼ **Anne Hathaway's Cottage.** The most perfectly picturesque of the Shakespeare Trust properties, set on the western outskirts of Stratford, was the family home of the woman Shakespeare married in 1582. The "cottage," actually a substantial farmhouse, has latticed windows and a grand thatch roof; inside there is period furniture such as the rare carved-wood canopied Elizabethan bed. Set in a garden (now planted with Victorian herbs and flowers), the cottage is one of the loveliest spots in Shakespeare Country. In a nearby field the **Shakespeare Tree Garden** has 40 trees mentioned in works by the Bard, a yew maze, and sculptures with Shakespearean themes. The best way to get here is to walk, especially in late spring when the apple trees are in blossom. There are two main footpaths, one via Greenhill Street by the railroad bridge, the other leaving from Holy Trinity Church up Old Town and Chestnut Walk. ⊠ *Cottage La., Shottery* ☎ *01789/204016* ⊕ *www. shakespeare.org.uk* ⊠ *£5, Shakespeare Trust joint ticket £13* ⊘ *Apr., May, Sept., and Oct., Mon.–Sat. 9:30–5, Sun. 10–5; June–Aug., Mon.–Sat. 9–5, Sun. 9:30–5; Nov.–Mar., Mon.–Sat. 10–4, Sun. 10:30–4; last entry 30 mins before closing.*

Bancroft Gardens. Between the Royal Shakespeare Theatre and Clopton Bridge lie these well-tended expanses of lawns and flower beds. The swans gliding gracefully along the river are permanent residents, coexisting with the pleasure craft on the river and the nearby canal. The centerpiece of the gardens (incidentally, Bancroft means "croft on the banks") is the **Gower Memorial statue,** designed in 1888 by Lord Gower, and adorned with bronze figures of Hamlet, Lady Macbeth, Falstaff, and Prince Hal—symbols of philosophy, tragedy, comedy, and history, respectively. ⊠ *Off Waterside.*

need a
break?
At Cox's Yard Tea Shop (⊠ *Bridgefoot* ☎ *01789/404600.*), next to Bancroft Gardens in the town center, you can sample a sweet cake and some tea or coffee for a rapid sugar and caffeine infusion before more sightseeing or a riverside walk.

☺ **Butterfly Farm.** The farm houses Europe's largest display of butterflies, a mock rain forest, and displays of spiders, caterpillars, and insects from all over the world. It's a two-minute walk past the Bridgefoot footbridge. ⊠ *Swan's Nest La.* ☎ *01789/299288* ⊕ *www.butterflyfarm.co.uk* ⊠ *£4.25* ⊘ *June–Aug., daily 10–6; Sept.–May, daily 10–dusk.*

❹ **Guild Chapel.** This chapel is the noble centerpiece of Stratford's Guild buildings, including the Guildhall, the Grammar School, and the almshouses—all structures well known to Shakespeare. The ancient structure was rebuilt in the late Perpendicular style in the first half of the 15th century, thanks to the largesse of Stratford resident Hugh Clopton. The otherwise plain interior includes fragments of a remarkable medieval fresco of the Last Judgment. The chapel is currently used for occasional functions, and the bell, also given by Sir Hugh, still rings as it did to tell Shakespeare the time of day. ⊠ *Chapel La. at Church St.* ☎ *01789/293351* ✉ *Free* ⊘ *Daily 9–5.*

5 **Guildhall.** Dating to 1416–18, the Guildhall is occupied by **King Edward's Grammar School,** which Shakespeare probably attended as a boy and, which is still used as a school. On the first floor is the Guildhall proper, where traveling acting companies came to perform. Many historians believe that it was after seeing the troupe known as the Earl of Leicester's Men in 1587 that Shakespeare got the acting bug and set off for London. Upstairs is the classroom in which the Bard is reputed to have learned "little Latin and less Greek." A brass plate at its far end records the traditional position of Master Will's seat. Students still use the classroom today, so visits may be made by prior arrangement only, during after-school hours or vacation time. Contact the tourist information office to schedule a visit. ⊠ *Church St.*

6 **Hall's Croft.** One of the finest surviving Jacobean (early 17th-century) town houses, this impressive residence has a delightful walled garden. Tradition has it that Hall's Croft was the home of Shakespeare's elder daughter Susanna and her husband, Dr. John Hall, whose dispensary is on view along with the other rooms, all containing Jacobean furniture of heavy oak. ⊠ *Old Town* ☎ *01789/204016* ⊕ *www.shakespeare.org. uk* ✉ *£3.50, Shakespeare Trust joint ticket £13* ⊘ *Nov.–Mar., daily 11–4; Apr., May, Sept., and Oct., daily 11–5; June–Aug., Mon.–Sat. 9:30–5, Sun. 10–5; last entry 30 mins before closing.*

7 **Harvard House.** This is the grand half-timber 16th-century home of Katherine Rogers, mother of the John Harvard who founded Harvard University in 1636. The twin-gabled facade, dating from about 1600, is one of Stratford's glories. Note the exterior beams carved with fleurs-de-lis in relief, the sculpted human faces on the corbels, and the bear and staff (symbols of the Warwick earls) on the bracket heads. Inside, the **Museum of British Pewter** displays pewter toys, tankards, and teapots, dating from Roman times to the present. ⊠ *High St.* ☎ *01789/ 204507* ⊕ *www.shakespeare.org.uk* ✉ *£1.50* ⊘ *May, June, and Sept.–Nov., Fri.–Sun. 11:30–4:30; July–Sept., Thurs.–Sun. 11:30–4:30.*

8 **Holy Trinity Church.** The fabled burial place of William Shakespeare, this 13th-century church sits on the banks of the Avon, with an avenue of lime trees framing its entrance. Shakespeare's final resting place is in the chancel, rebuilt in 1465–91 in the late-Perpendicular style. He was buried here, incidentally, not because he was a famed poet but because he was a lay rector of Stratford, owning a portion of the township tithes. Here, on the north wall of the sanctuary over the altar steps, you'll find the famous marble bust created by Gerard Jansen in 1623; along with the Droeshout engraving in the First Folio, this is one of the only two contemporary portraits of the Bard. Rigidly stylized in the Elizabethan mode, the bust offers a more human, even humorous, perspective when viewed from the side. Also in the chancel are the graves of Shakespeare's wife, Anne; his daughter Susanna; his son-in-law, John Hall; and his granddaughter's husband, Thomas Nash. Nearby, the Parish Register is displayed, containing both Shakespeare's baptismal entry (1564) and his burial notice (1616). ⊠ *Trinity St.* ✉ *Small fee for chancel* ⊘ *Mar., Mon.–Sat. 9–5, Sun. 12:30–5; Apr.–Oct., Mon.–Sat. 8:30–6, Sun. 12:30–5; Nov.–Feb., Mon.–Sat. 9–4, Sun. 12:30–5; last admission 20 mins before closing.*

❸ Nash's House and New Place. This is the home of the Thomas Nash who married Shakespeare's last direct descendant, his granddaughter Elizabeth Hall. The heavily restored house has been furnished in 17th-century style, and it also contains a local museum. In the gardens (where there's an intricately laid-out Elizabethan knot garden) are the foundations of **New Place,** the house in which Shakespeare died in 1616. Built in 1483 "of brike and tymber" for a lord mayor of London, it was Stratford's grandest piece of real estate when Shakespeare bought it in 1597 for £60; tragically it was torn down in 1759. The man responsible for this, the Reverend Francis Gastrell, had already shown his ire at the hordes of sightseers by cutting down a mulberry tree said to have been planted by Shakespeare himself. The townspeople were in such an uproar at Gastrell's vandalism that they stoned his house. Today you can see what is claimed to be a descendant of the mulberry tree in the middle of the lawn. The **Great Garden** of New Place, beyond the knot garden, has a sculpture trail with bronze works inspired by Shakespeare's plays. ⊠ *Chapel St.* ☎ *01789/204016* ⊕ *www.shakespeare.org.uk* ✉ *£3.50, Shakespeare Trust joint ticket £13* ☉ *Nov.–Mar., daily 11–4; Apr., May, Sept., and Oct., daily 11–5; June–Aug., Mon.–Sat. 9:30–5, Sun. 10–5; last entry 30 mins before closing.*

❾ Royal Shakespeare Theatre. The beloved Stratford home of the Royal Shakespeare Company (RSC) is set amid lovely gardens along the River Avon. Throughout the year some of the finest productions in the world of the Bard's plays are presented here. The theater company has existed since 1879, established by brewer Charles Edward Flower, although the original building burned down in 1926. Six years later the current building was erected, according to a design by Elizabeth Scott, cousin of the more-famous Sir Giles Gilbert Scott, architect of Liverpool's Anglican Cathedral. Many people criticize the modern appearance of the building, calling it "a factory for Shakespeare." As of this writing, plans for a new theater are being debated. At the rear is the **Swan Theatre,** created in the only part of the Victorian theater to survive a fire in the 1930s. This theater follows the lines of Shakespeare's original Globe and is one of the most exciting performing spaces in Britain. Beside the Swan is an art gallery, where you can see theater-related exhibitions and portraits and depictions of scenes from the plays. You might also consider taking a tour of the theater complex, but book well in advance. Farther down Southern Lane toward Holy Trinity Church is **The Other Place,** a modern auditorium for experimental productions. ⊠ *Waterside* ☎ *01789/403403 box office; 01789/296655 information; 01789/403405 tours* ⊕ *www.rsc.org.uk* ✉ *Tour £4, gallery £1.50* ☉ *Tour weekdays (except matinee days) 1:30 and 5:30; matinee days 5:30 and after show; Sun. noon, 1, 2, and 3. No tours when shows are being prepared. Gallery Mon.–Sat. 9:30–6:30, Sun. noon–4:30.*

▶ **❶ Shakespeare's Birthplace.** A half-timber house typical of its time, the Bard's birthplace has been much altered and restored since Shakespeare lived here but remains a much-visited shrine. Entrance is through the **Shakespeare Centre,** the headquarters of the Shakespeare Birthplace Trust. Scholars head for the library here; lay visitors enjoy an informative exhibition about the life and times of the Bard. Furnishings in the house reflect comfortable middle-class Elizabethan domestic life. Shakespeare's father, John, a glove maker and wool dealer, purchased the house; a reconstructed workshop shows the tools of the glover's trade. An auction notice describes the property as it was when it was offered for sale in 1847. Until then, two widowed ladies had maintained the house in a somewhat ramshackle state, but with the approach of the tercentennial of the Bard's birth, and in response to a rumor that the building was to be purchased by P. T. Barnum and shipped across the Atlantic, the city shelled out £3,000 for the relic, whereupon it was tidied up and made the main attraction for the stream of Shakespeare devotees that was steadily growing into a torrent. You can see the signatures of earlier pilgrims cut into the windowpanes, including those of Mark Twain and Charles Dickens. ☒ *Henley St.* ☎ *01789/204016* ⊕ *www.shakespeare.org.uk* 🎟 *£6.50, Shakespeare Trust joint ticket £13* ⊙ *Nov.–Mar., Mon.–Sat. 10–4, Sun. 10:30–4; Apr. and May, Mon.–Sat. 10–5, Sun. 10:30–5; June–Aug., Mon.–Sat. 9–5, Sun. 9:30–5; Sept. and Oct., Mon.–Sat. 10–5, Sun. 10:30–5; last entry 30 mins before closing.*

🐾 **Teddy Bear Museum.** A diversion from Shakespeareana, this museum contains hundreds of the furry creatures in all shapes and sizes from around the world, including Paddington Bear and bears previously owned by Margaret Thatcher and Tony Blair. ☒ *19 Greenhill St.* ☎ *01789/293160* ⊕ *www.theteddybearmuseum.com* 🎟 *£2.50* ⊙ *Daily 9:30–5:30.*

Where to Eat

££££ ✕ **Quarto's.** Views of the River Avon and its resident swans enhance this attractive spot in the Royal Shakespeare Theatre, where you can dine decently before or after a play. The lounge offers pretheater canapés and champagne. The fixed-price menu is contemporary British, so look for dishes such as lamb with rosemary and goat-cheese salad. ☒ *Royal Shakespeare Theatre, Waterside* ☎ *01789/403415* ⟁ *Reservations essential* 🖃 *AE, MC, V* ⊙ *Closed when theater is closed.*

★ £££ ✕ **Desport's.** A small unassuming restaurant serves what is probably the most sophisticated food in town. The wood floors and wattle-and-daub ceiling of the 16th-century building lend an antique air, but the food is thoroughly modern. Chef Paul Desport's menu blends Mediterranean and Asian influences; try the crab cakes with Thai spices or fresh pasta with olives, roast peppers, and tomatoes topped with pine nuts, basil, and Parmesan. ☒ *14 Meer St.* ☎ *01789/269304* ⟁ *Reservations essential* 🖃 *AE, DC, MC, V* ⊙ *Closed Sun. and Mon.*

★ ££–£££ ✕ **Lambs.** Sit downstairs in the no-smoking section to appreciate the hardwood floors and oak beams of this local epicurean favorite. The modern updates of tried-and-true dishes include roast chicken with lime butter and char-grilled sausages with leek mash. Daily specials keep the menu seasonal. The two- and three-course set menus are particularly good deals. ☒ *12 Sheep St.* ☎ *01789/292554* ⟁ *Reservations essential* 🖃 *AE, MC, V.*

££–£££ ✕ **Opposition.** Pre- and post-theater meals are offered at this informal, family-style restaurant in a 16th-century building on the main dining street near the theater. The American and Continental dishes on the menu win marks with the locals. Try the smoked haddock or, among the vegetarian options, the mushrooms and asparagus in cream sauce. ☒ *13 Sheep St.* ☎ *01789/269980* 🖃 *MC, V.*

££–£££ ✕ **Russons.** A 16th-century building holds a quaint dining room that's a favorite with theatergoers. The fare, though inexpensive, doesn't skimp on quality. The daily-changing menu is chalked on a blackboard and includes English specialties such as roast lamb and guinea fowl. ☒ *8 Church St.* ☎ *01789/268822* ⟁ *Reservations essential* 🖃 *AE, MC, V* ⊙ *Closed Mon.*

££–£££ ✕ **The Vintner.** The imaginative bistro-inspired menu changes daily at this café and wine bar. Shoulder of lamb ranks among the favorite main courses; tapas are also popular, and a children's menu is available. To dine before curtain time, arrive early or make a reservation. The building, largely unaltered since the late 1400s, has lovely flagstone floors and oak beams. ☒ *5 Sheep St.* ☎ *01789/297259* 🖃 *AE, MC, V.*

£–££ ✕ **Black Swan.** Known locally as the Dirty Duck, one of Stratford's most celebrated pubs has attracted actors since Garrick's days. Its little veranda overlooks the theaters and the river. You can sample English grill specialties, as well as bar meals such as mussels and fries, Cajun chicken, or fish and chips, all while sipping a pint of lager. ⊠ *Southern La.* ☎ *01789/297312* ═ *AE, MC, V* ⊘ *No dinner Sun.*

£ ✕ **1564.** The meals and snacks at this informal cafeteria below Quarto's in the theater are crowd pleasers. The river views make the simple food and hot tea seem all the more pleasant. ⊠ *Royal Shakespeare Theatre, Waterside* ☎ *01789/403415* ⌂ *Reservations not accepted* ═ *No credit cards* ⊘ *Closed when theater is closed.*

Where to Stay

The Ettington Park Hotel, in nearby Alderminster, is an alternative to hotels in town.

£££££ ▥ **Welcombe Hotel & Golf Course.** With its mullioned bay windows, gables, and tall chimneys, this hotel in an impressive 1886 neo-Jacobean-style building evokes the luxury of bygone days. You can relax in the clubby bar or the Italianate garden terrace. Public rooms such as the Great Hall, with its wood paneling, chandeliers, and marble fireplace, complement the spacious main-house guest rooms, all with period-style furnishings and some with garden views. Garden rooms in the adjacent building are comfortable but not as big. The fancy Trevelyan Restaurant (jacket and tie required) relies on a French foundation to present English cuisine. The Welcombe is a 10-minute drive from Stratford. ⊠ *Warwick Rd., CV37 0NR* ☎ *01789/295252* ⌂ *01789/414666* ⊕ *www.welcombe.co.uk* ⇆ *64 rooms* ⌂ *2 restaurants, room service, in-room data ports, cable TV, 18-hole golf course, tennis court, pool, gym, fishing, bar, lounge, baby-sitting, dry cleaning, laundry service, meeting rooms, car rental, free parking, no-smoking rooms* ═ *AE, D, MC, V* ⎟◉⎟ *BP.*

££££ ▥ **Alveston Manor.** This redbrick Elizabethan manor house surrounded by lawns and a terrace has traditional Tudor-style rooms with four-poster beds in the main house. To the rear of the hotel are modern rooms done up in sea green and beige. Legend says the grounds were the setting for the first production of *A Midsummer Night's Dream.* The Alveston is across the river from the Royal Shakespeare Theatre. ⊠ *Clopton Bridge, CV37 7HP* ☎ *08704/008181* ⌂ *01789/414095* ⊕ *www.heritage-hotels.com* ⇆ *110 rooms, 4 suites* ⌂ *Restaurant, room service, in-room data ports, cable TV, bar, 2 lounges, dry cleaning, laundry service, meeting rooms, free parking, some pets allowed (fee), no-smoking rooms; no a/c in some rooms* ═ *AE, DC, MC, V* ⎟◉⎟ *BP.*

££££ ▥ **Shakespeare Hotel.** Built in the 1400s, this Elizabethan town house in the heart of town is a vision right out of *The Merry Wives of Windsor,* with five gables and one of the longest black-and-white half-timber fronts in England. The comfortably modernized interiors have a touch of luxury, and Shakespeareana and old playbills adorn the public areas. Upstairs, rooms are named after the Bard's characters and leading thespians. Hewn timbers carved with rose-and-thistle patterns decorate some rooms; all have CD players. ⊠ *Chapel St., CV37 6ER* ☎ *08704/008182* ⌂ *01789/415411* ⊕ *www.heritage-hotels.com* ⇆ *64 rooms, 6 suites* ⌂ *Restaurant, room service, cable TV, bar, lounge, laundry service, meeting rooms, parking (fee), some pets allowed (fee), no-smoking rooms; no a/c* ═ *AE, DC, MC, V.*

££££ ▥ **Stratford Victoria.** Although the modern Victoria may lack the period charm of older hotels, its up-to-date facilities, spacious rooms, and ample grounds are making it a Stratford standard. Rooms, all in dark wood with burgundy and green color schemes, come in several shapes: some have four-poster beds, others accommodate four people, some are geared to business travel. ⊠ *Arden St., CV37 6QQ* ☎ *01789/271000* 🖷 *01789/271001* ⊕ *www.marstonhotels.com* ➲ *102 rooms* ⟁ *Restaurant, room service, in-room data ports, cable TV, gym, hot tub, massage, bar, lounge, baby-sitting, laundry service, meeting rooms, free parking, no-smoking floors; no a/c* ☰ *AE, DC, MC, V* ⑩ *BP.*

££££ 🏠 **Thistle Stratford-Upon-Avon.** Three converted 18th-century town houses opposite the Swan Theatre make up this fairly standard chain offering, which also has a modern wing. The excellent central location is its greatest appeal, and there are some good packages. Beam ceilings, period furniture, and river views enhance the best rooms. ⊠ *44 Waterside, CV37 6BA* ☎ *01789/294949; 800/847–4358 in U.S.* 🖷 *01789/415874* ⊕ *www.thistlehotels.com* ➲ *63 rooms* ⟁ *Restaurant, room service, cable TV with movies, bar, lounge, meeting rooms, parking (fee), some pets allowed (fee), no-smoking rooms; no a/c* ☰ *AE, DC, MC, V* ⑩ *BP.*

£££–££££ 🏠 **Falcon Hotel.** Licensed as an alehouse since 1640, this black-and-white timber-frame hotel in the center of town retains the feeling of a friendly inn. The heavily beamed rooms in the older part are small and quaint; those in the modern extension are standard. In the Oak Bar, wood panels salvaged from New Place, the Bard's last home, accent the impressive room. ⊠ *Chapel St., CV37 6HA* ☎ *01789/279953 or 0845/602–6787* 🖷 *01789/414260* ⊕ *www.regalhotels.co.uk* ➲ *84 rooms* ⟁ *Restaurant, room service, in-room data ports, 2 bars, lounge, baby-sitting, dry cleaning, laundry service, meeting rooms, free parking, some pets allowed (fee); no a/c* ☰ *AE, DC, MC, V* ⑩ *BP.*

★ £££ 🏠 **Caterham House.** Full of information and recommendations, Dominique and Olive Maury welcome you to their comfortable B&B as if you were friends. Rooms in this building dating from 1830 are individually decorated in early-19th-century style with brass beds, antique furnishings, and knickknacks; one has a bathtub, and the rest have showers. The public areas, too, show discriminating taste. You may spot an actor or two among the guests. ⊠ *58–59 Rother St., CV37 6LT* ☎ *01789/267309* 🖷 *01789/414836* ➲ *10 rooms* ⟁ *Room service, bar, lounge, free parking, some pets allowed, no-smoking rooms; no a/c, no room phones* ☰ *MC, V* ⑩ *BP.*

££–£££ 🏠 **Sequoia House Hotel.** The two Victorian houses that make up the Sequoia House are a good budget option in the middle of Stratford. The extensive gardens surrounding the property are delightful in good weather, and the antique-filled lounge is a quiet place to relax. ⊠ *51-53 Shipston Rd., CV37 7LN* ☎ *01789/268852* 🖷 *01789/414559* ⊕ *www.stratford-upon-avon.co.uk/sequoia.htm* ➲ *24 rooms* ⟁ *Bar, lounge, free parking; no a/c, no smoking* ☰ *AE, DC, MC, V* ⑩ *BP.*

££ 🏠 **Mary Arden Inn.** The biggest attraction of this 18th-century pub-hotel in a pleasant village 3½ mi northwest of Stratford is its location away from the tourist madness that is Stratford in summer. Other pluses are the good food and nicely furnished bedrooms with small bathrooms and showers. The four-poster suite (£100) has a whirlpool tub. A copy of the complete works of Shakespeare is left in the rooms for reading. ⊠ *Off A3400, The Green Wilmcote, CV37 9XJ* ☎ *01789/204875* 🖷 *01789/204875* ⊕ *www.oldenglish.co.uk* ➲ *11 rooms, 1 suite* ⟁ *Restaurant, bar, meeting rooms, free parking, no-smoking rooms; no a/c* ☰ *AE, MC, V* ⑩ *BP.*

££ 🏠 **Penryn House.** Traditional English prints and furnishings as well as some simple modern pieces fill this budget choice at the low end of the category. It's an easy walk from the city center, Anne Hathaway's Cottage, and the rail station. ⊠ *126 Alcester Rd., CV37 9DP* ☎ *01789/*

293718 ☎ 01789/266077 ⊕ *www.penrynguesthouse.co.uk* ⇥ *7 rooms, 6 with bath ♿ Laundry service, Internet, free parking; no a/c, no smoking* ⊟ *MC, V* ⦿ *BP.*

££ ▦ **Stratheden Hotel.** One advantage of this family-run budget choice is its location in the center of town. Wall-to-wall carpeting and flowery bedspreads decorate the simple rooms; one has a canopy bed previously owned by Victorian novelist Marie Corelli. The spacious rooms have either a shower or tub, and all have coffeemakers. Garret rooms are smaller but charming. ✉ *5 Chapel St., CV37 6EP* ☎ 01789/297119 ⇥ *9 rooms ♿ Baby-sitting, parking (fee), no-smoking rooms; no a/c* ⊟ *MC, V* ⦿ *BP.*

££ ▦ **Victoria Spa Lodge.** This grand B&B lies 1½ mi outside town, within view of the Stratford Canal. The clematis-draped building dates from 1837; you can see Queen Victoria's coat of arms in two of its gables. Victoria herself stayed here before ascending the throne. Dark-wood and plain white furnishings tastefully decorate the lounge–breakfast room and spacious guest rooms. ✉ *Bishopton La., Bishopton, CV37 9QY* ☎ 01789/267985 ☎ 01789/204728 ⊕ *www.stratford-upon-avon.co. uk/victoriaspa.htm* ⇥ *7 rooms ♿ Free parking; no a/c, no room phones, no smoking* ⊟ *MC, V* ⦿ *BP.*

Nightlife & the Arts

Festivals

The **Stratford-upon-Avon Shakespeare Birthday Celebrations** (✉ Shakespeare Centre, Henley St., Stratford-upon-Avon, CV37 6QW ☎ 01789/ 204016 ⊕ www.shakespeare.org.uk) take place on and around the weekend closest to April 23 (unless Easter occurs around that date). The events, spread over four days, include a formal reception, lectures, free concerts, processions, and a special performance of one of the plays. For tickets for the three-course birthday luncheon in the marquee on the Avon Paddock, write the Shakespeare Birthday Celebrations secretary at the address above, call 01789/415536, or check the Web site.

The **Mop Fair,** dating from medieval times, takes place on or around October 12, traditionally the time when laborers and apprentices from the surrounding area came to seek work. The fair still attracts entertainers and fairground amusements and includes a ceremony attended by local dignitaries, the whole in essence little changed from the past.

Theater

Fodor'sChoice ★ The **Royal Shakespeare Theatre** (✉ Waterside, Stratford-upon-Avon, CV37 6BB ☎ 01789/403403 box office; 01789/296655 general information ☎ 01789/403413 ⊕ www.rsc.org.uk) usually puts on five of Shakespeare's plays in a season lasting from November into October. In September and October, visiting companies often perform opera, ballet, and musicals. The Swan Theatre, at the rear, stages plays by Shakespeare contemporaries such as Christopher Marlowe and Ben Jonson. In the Other Place, the RSC performs some of its most adventurous work. Prices usually range from £7 to £45. Book ahead, as seats go fast, but "day of performance" (two per person to personal callers only) and returned tickets are often available. You can also book tickets from London with **Ticketmaster** (☎ 0870/534-4444 ⊕ www.ticketmaster.co. uk), operating 24 hours a day. You can book tickets in the United States (a 20% surcharge applies) with **Global Tickets** (☎ 212/332-2435 or 800/ 223-6108 ⊕ www.globaltickets.com), **Keith Prowse** (☎ 212/398-1430 or 800/669-8681 ⊕ www.keithprowse.com), or **Edwards and Edwards** (☎ 800/223-6108).

Sports & the Outdoors

Avon Cruises (⊠ The Boatyard, Swan's Nest La. ☎ 01789/267073) rents boats and provides half-hour river excursions and some longer trips by arrangement. **Bancroft Cruises** (⊠ The Boatyard, Clopton Bridge ☎ 01789/269669) runs half-hourly excursions on the river. Hour-long trips farther afield can also be scheduled. You can rent a boat by the hour or by the day.

Shopping

Stratford-upon-Avon's bustling shopping district sells plenty of tourist junk. That said, established shops specializing in silver, jewelry, and china sell some high-quality items. There's an open market (good for bargains) every Friday in the Market Place at Greenhill and Meer streets. The **Antique Market** (⊠ Ely St.) contains 50 stalls of jewelry, silver, linens, porcelain, and memorabilia. **B&W Thornton** (⊠ 23 Henley St. ☎ 01789/269405), above Shakespeare's Birthplace, stocks exclusive Moorcroft pottery and glass. **Once a Tree** (⊠ 8 Bard's Walk ☎ 01789/297790) is thoroughly "green," selling items crafted from sustainable wood sources—animals, bowls, and dozens of imaginative articles. **Robert Vaughan** (⊠ 20 Chapel St. ☎ 01789/205312) is the best of Stratford's many secondhand bookshops. The **Shakespeare Bookshop** (⊠ 39 Henley St. ☎ 01789/292176), run by the Shakespeare Birthplace, sells Elizabethan plays, Tudor history books, children's books, and other Bard paraphernalia.

AROUND SHAKESPEARE COUNTRY

Although the section of Warwickshire known as Shakespeare Country is, in reality, no more than a continuation of that familiar Midlands scene of green fields, slow-moving, mirrorlike rivers, quiet villages, and time-burnished halls, castles, and churches, it becomes an area apart through its role as the homeland of England's greatest dramatist. Warwick and Kenilworth castles are highlights here.

Mary Arden's House

⑩ *3 mi northwest of Stratford.*

This bucolic site in tiny Wilmcote attracted attention in 2000 because a Tudor farmhouse here, considered to have been the home of Shakespeare's mother (and so named), was proved to have been the home of Adam Palmer instead. That farmhouse has been renamed Palmer's Farm. However, research showed that Mary Arden lived in a house on the adjoining Glebe Farm; this farm has now assumed the name Mary Arden's House. The Tudor farmhouse and farm form the **Shakespeare Countryside Museum,** with crafts exhibits, a café, and a garden of trees mentioned in the plays. Rare breeds of poultry, longhorn cows, and Cotswold sheep live on the grounds, and there are demonstrations of farming techniques from the last 400 years. ⊠ *Off A3400, Wilmcote* ☎ *01789/204016; 01789/293455 information on special events* ⊕ *www. shakespeare.org.uk* ⊠ *£5.50; Shakespeare Trust joint ticket £13* ⊙ *Nov.–Mar., Mon.–Sat. 10–4, Sun. 10:30–4; Sept., Oct., Apr., and May, Mon.–Sat. 10–5, Sun. 10:30–5; June–Aug., Mon.–Sat. 9:30–5, Sun. 10–5; last entry 30 mins before closing.*

en route From Wilmcote, continue west for 1½ mi on minor roads to reach **Aston Cantlow.** Shakespeare's parents, Mary Arden and John Shakespeare, were wed at the church here.

Henley-in-Arden

⓫ *8 mi northwest of Stratford.*

A brief drive out of Stratford on the A3400 will take you under the Stratford-upon-Avon Canal aqueduct to pretty Henley-in-Arden, whose wide main street is an architectural pageant of various periods. You are now in the area of what was once the Forest of Arden, where Shakespeare set one of his greatest comedies, *As You Like It*. Among the buildings to look out for are the former Guildhall, dating from the 15th century, and the White Swan pub, built in the early 1600s.

Packwood House

⓬ *12 mi north of Stratford-upon-Avon, 5 mi north of Henley-in-Arden.*

Packwood House draws garden enthusiasts to its re-created 17th-century gardens, highlighted by a remarkable topiary Tudor garden in which yew trees depict Christ's Sermon on the Mount. The house combines red-brick and half-timbering, and its tall chimneys are another Tudor characteristic. The interiors are a 20th-century version of Tudor architecture, but there are good collections of period furniture and textiles. ✉ *Off B4439 near Hockley Heath* ☎ *01564/783294* ⊕ *www.nationaltrust.org.uk* 🎫 *£5.20, garden only £2.60, combined ticket with Baddesley Clinton £8.50* ☉ *House Mar.–Oct., Wed.–Sun. noon–4:30. Garden Mar., Apr., and Oct., Wed.–Sun. 11–4:30; May–Sept., Wed.–Sun. 11–5:30.*

Baddesley Clinton

★ ⓭ *2 mi east of Packwood House, 15 mi north of Stratford-upon-Avon.*

"As you approach Baddesley Clinton, it stands before you as the perfect late medieval manor house. The entrance side of grey stone, the small, creeper-clad Queen Anne brick bridge across the moat, the gateway with a porch higher than the roof and embattled—it could not be better." So wrote the eminent architectural historian Sir Nikolaus Pevsner, and the house lives up to his fervent praise. Set off a winding back road, the moated manor retains its great fireplaces, 17th-century paneling, and priest holes (secret chambers for Roman Catholic priests, who were persecuted at various times throughout the 16th and 17th centuries). The café is an idyllic spot for tea and cakes. Admission to the house is by timed ticket. ✉ *Rising La., off A4141 near Chadwick End* ☎ *01564/783294* ⊕ *www.nationaltrust.org.uk* 🎫 *£5.80, garden only £2.90, combined ticket with Packwood House £8.50* ☉ *House Mar., Apr., and Oct., Wed.–Sun. 1:30–5; May–Sept., Wed.–Sun. 1:30–5:30. Garden Mar., Apr., and Oct., Wed.–Sun. noon–5; May–Sept., Wed.–Sun. noon–5:30; Nov.–mid-Dec., Wed.–Sun. noon–4:30.*

Warwick

⓮ *7½ mi southeast of Baddesley Clinton, 4 mi south of Kenilworth, 9 mi northeast of Stratford-upon-Avon.*

Most famous for Warwick Castle—that vision out of the feudal ages—Warwick (pronounced *wa*-rick) is an interesting architectural mix of Georgian redbrick and Elizabethan half-timbering. Much of the town center has been spoiled by unattractive postwar development, but look for the

★ 15th-century half-timber **Lord Leycester Hospital,** which has been a home—offering "hospitality"—for old soldiers since the earl of Leicester dedicated it to that purpose in 1571. Within the complex are a chapel and a fine courtyard, complete with a wattle-and-daub balcony and 500-year-old gardens. ⊠ *High St.* ☎ *01926/491422* ⊠ *£3.20* ⊙ *Apr.–Sept., Tues.–Sun. 10–5; Oct.–Mar., Tues.–Sun. 10–4.*

Crowded with gilded, carved, and painted tombs, the **Beauchamp Chapel** of the **Collegiate Church of St. Mary** is the essence of late-medieval and Tudor chivalry—although it was built (1443–64) to honor the somewhat-less-than-chivalrous Richard Beauchamp, who consigned Joan of Arc to the flames. Brightly colored bosses, fan tracery, and flying ribs distinguish the chapel, which holds many monuments to the Beauchamps (several of whom became earl of Warwick), including Richard Beauchamp's impressive effigy in bronze and the alabaster table tomb of Thomas Beauchamp and his wife. Robert Dudley, earl of Leicester, adviser and favorite of Elizabeth I, is also buried here. There's a brass-rubbing center, and you can climb the tower in summer. ⊠ *Church St., Old Sq.* ☎ *01926/403940* ⊕ *www.saintmaryschurch.co.uk* ⊠ *Free* ⊙ *Apr.–Oct., daily 10–6; Nov.–Mar., daily 10–4:30.*

★ The vast bulk of medieval **Warwick Castle** rests on a cliff overlooking the Avon—"the fairest monument of ancient and chivalrous splendor which yet remains uninjured by time," to use the words of Sir Walter Scott. Two soaring towers mark the castle, the 147-foot-high Caesar's Tower, built in 1356, and the 128-foot-high Guy's Tower, built in 1380. The towers bristle with battlements, and their irregular form allowed defenders to shoot from numerous points. The castle's most powerful commander was Richard Neville, earl of Warwick, known during the Wars of the Roses as the Kingmaker. He was killed in battle near London in 1471 by Edward IV, whom he had just deposed in favor of Henry VI. Warwick Castle's monumental walls now enclose one of the best collections of medieval armor and weapons in Europe, as well as historic furnishings and paintings by Peter Paul Rubens, Anthony Van Dyck, and other old masters. Twelve rooms are devoted to an imaginative Madame Tussaud's wax exhibition, "A Royal Weekend Party—1898" (the Tussaud's Group owns the castle). Another exhibit displays the sights and sounds of a great medieval household as it prepares for an important battle. The year chosen is 1471, when the earl of Warwick was killed. At the Mill and Engine House, you can see the turning water-mill and the engines used to generate electricity early in the 20th century. Below the castle, along the Avon, strutting peacocks patrol 60 acres of grounds elegantly landscaped by Capability Brown in the 18th century. Banquets (extra charge) and special events, including festivals and tournaments, take place throughout the year. A restaurant in the cellars serves lunch. Head to the bridge across the river to get the best view of the castle. ⊠ *Castle La.* ☎ *01926/495421; 0870/442–2000 recorded information* ⊕ *www.warwick-castle.co.uk* ⊠ *Sept.–June £10.75, July–Aug. £12.50* ⊙ *Apr.–Sept., daily 10–6; Oct.–Mar., daily 10–5.*

need a break? After a vigorous walk around the ramparts at Warwick Castle, you can drop by the brightly painted, vaulted, 14th-century **Undercroft** (☎ 01926/495421) for a refreshing spot of tea or a hot meal from the cafeteria.

The half-timber Oken's House, near the castle entrance, houses the **Warwickshire Doll Museum** and its large collection of antique dolls, toys, and games. ⊠ *Castle St.* ☎ *01926/495546* ⊠ *£1* ⊙ *Easter–Oct., Mon.–Sat. 10–5, Sun. 11–5; Nov.–Easter, Sat. 10–dusk.*

🖐 Kids as well as adults appreciate **St. John's House,** a Jacobean building on the site of a medieval hospital and now surrounded by beautiful gardens. The interior displays period costumes and scenes of domestic life, as well as a Victorian schoolroom. ☒ *Smith St.* ☎ *01926/412132* 🖅 *Free* 🕓 *May–Sept., Tues.–Sat. 10–5, Sun. 2:30–5; Oct.–Apr., Tues.–Sat. 10–5.*

Where to Stay & Eat

££–£££ ✕ **Fanshawe's.** Cheerful prints and vases of flowers decorate this friendly, centrally located restaurant on the market square. The menu is eclectic—you can have simple open-face sandwiches for a light lunch, or try the Wellington lamb with spinach-and-mushroom stuffing or the cod with chervil butter. Game is offered in season. ☒ *22 Market Pl.* ☎ *01926/410590* 🖃 *AE, MC, V* 🕓 *Closed 1 wk in mid-Apr. and 2nd wk in Oct. No dinner Sun., no lunch Mon.*

££–£££ ✕ **Findon's.** The imaginative menu at this posh-Georgian town-house restaurant takes its inspiration from Asia and Europe as well as England. Among the delicious choices are king scallops with baby chard and timbale of butternut squash, and sautéed langoustines with penne topped with mascarpone and basil sauce. The terrace is a lovely spot to dine in summer. For the best deal, try the fixed-price menus. ☒ *7 Old Sq.* ☎ *01926/411755* 🖃 *AE, DC, MC, V* 🕓 *Closed Sun.*

££££ 🏨 **The Glebe.** Built in the 1820s, the redbrick Glebe served as the rectory of the adjacent St. Peter's Church. Today the house has been converted into a small hotel with modern amenities. Bedrooms tend toward prints and pastels, and beds are four-posters or have canopies. The hotel is a 10-minute drive from Warwick. ☒ *Church St., Barford, CV35 8BS* ☎ *01926/624218* 🖶 *01926/624171* 🌐 *www.glebehotel.co.uk* 🛏 *39 rooms* 🍴 *Restaurant, cable TV, indoor pool, exercise equipment, hot tub, sauna, steam room, croquet, bar, meeting rooms, some pets allowed; no a/c* 🖃 *AE, DC, MC, V* ¶◎¶ *BP.*

££–£££ 🏨 **Lord Leycester Hotel.** Built in 1726, this manor house with an appealing central location became a hotel in 1925. Signs of age and history abound, adding character. However, the small yet comfortably furnished rooms and even smaller bathrooms with showers are not to everyone's taste. ☒ *17 Jury St., CV34 4EJ* ☎ *01926/491481* 🖶 *01926/491561* 🌐 *www.lord-leycester.co.uk* 🛏 *51 rooms* 🍴 *2 restaurants, room service, room TVs with movies, bar, lounge, baby-sitting, laundry service, meeting rooms, free parking, some pets allowed (fee), no-smoking rooms; no a/c* 🖃 *AE, DC, MC, V* ¶◎¶ *BP.*

££ 🏨 **Tudor House Inn.** A simple hotel of genuine character, this half-timber inn dates from 1472, having survived the great Warwick fire of 1694 because it was on the road to Stratford, outside the devastated medieval town center. Guest rooms are beamed and basic, and the floors creak satisfactorily. The pub dishes up hearty portions of inexpensive food. ☒ *90–92 West St., CV34 6AW* ☎ *01926/495447* 🖶 *01926/492948* 🛏 *11 rooms, 8 with bath* 🍴 *Restaurant, cable TV, bar; no a/c* 🖃 *AE, DC, MC, V* ¶◎¶ *BP.*

Kenilworth Castle

⑮ *5 mi north of Warwick.*

The great red ruins of Kenilworth Castle loom over the somewhat nondescript village of Kenilworth. Begun in 1120, this castle remained one of the most formidable fortresses in England until it was finally dismantled by Oliver Cromwell after the Civil War in the mid-17th century. Still intact are its keep (central tower) with 20-foot-thick walls; its great hall; and its curtain walls (low outer walls forming the castle's first line of defense). Here the earl of Leicester, one of Queen Elizabeth I's favorites, entertained her four times, most notably in 1575 with 19 days of sumptuous feasting and revelry. Sir Walter Scott's novel *Kenilworth* (1821) presented tales about the earl and Elizabeth, adding to the fascination with the castle. ✉ *Off A452, Kenilworth* ☎ *01926/852078* ⊕ *www. english-heritage.org.uk* 🎟 *£4.40* ⊘ *Apr.–Sept., daily 10–6; Oct., daily 10–5; Nov.–Mar., daily 10–4.*

Where to Eat

££££–£££££ ✕ **Restaurant Bosquet.** This Victorian town-house restaurant serves set menus cooked by the French *patron,* with regularly changing à la carte selections. Try the veal or venison with wild mushrooms, and don't pass up the delicious desserts. Bosquet is mainly a dinner spot, although lunch is available by prior reservation. ✉ *97A Warwick Rd.* ☎ *01926/852463* ▭ *AE, MC, V* ⊘ *Closed Sun., 3 wks in Aug., last wk in Dec. No dinner Mon.*

££££–£££££ ✕ **Simpson's.** The French fixed-price lunch and dinner menus here are a great way to splurge on Kenilworth's finest dining. Crisp white tablecloths and unobtrusive staff make for an elegant experience. Terrine of ham with foie gras and roast sea bass with caramelized endive are among the excellent dishes. ✉ *101 Warwick Rd.* ☎ *01926/864567* ▭ *AE, DC, MC, V* ⊘ *Closed Sun., last 2 wks in Aug. No lunch Sat.*

£–££ ✕ **Clarendon Arms.** A location close to Kenilworth Castle helps make this pub a good spot for lunch. You can order fine home-cooked food at the small bar downstairs, and a larger, slightly pricier restaurant upstairs serves complete meals, from English roasts to more international fare. ✉ *44 Castle Hill* ☎ *01926/852017* ▭ *AE, DC, MC, V.*

Coventry

16 *7 mi northeast of Warwick, 16 mi northeast of Stratford-upon-Avon.*

Coventry thrived in medieval times as a center for the cloth and dyeing industries; in the 19th century it became an industrial powerhouse, but its fortunes have fallen since then. The Germans bombed the city with devastating thoroughness in 1940, and many people decry the postwar industrial architecture, with the notable exception of the rebuilt cathedral. Coventry is where a naked Lady Godiva allegedly rode through the streets to protest high taxes and where the first British automobiles were manufactured.

The modern bulk of **Coventry Cathedral,** designed by Sir Basil Spence and dedicated in 1962, stands beside the ruins of the blitzed St. Michael's, a powerful symbol of rebirth and reconciliation. Outside the sandstone building is Sir Jacob Epstein's *St. Michael Defeating the Devil;* the modern artworks inside include Graham Sutherland's stunning 70-foot-high tapestry, *Christ in Glory.* The undercroft holds a visitor center that shows a film about the cathedral and has a charred cross wired together from timbers from the bombed building. ✉ *Priory Row* ☎ *024/ 7622–7597* ⊕ *www.coventrycathedral.org* 🎟 *Suggested cathedral donation £3, visitor center £2* ⊘ *Daily 9–4:30, services permitting.*

Charlecote Park

17 *13 mi south of Coventry, 6 mi south of Warwick.*

This celebrated house in the village of Hampton Lucy was built in 1572 by Sir Thomas Lucy to entertain Queen Elizabeth (the house is shaped like the letter "E"). According to tradition, Shakespeare was caught poaching deer here soon after his marriage and was forced to flee to London. Years later he supposedly retaliated by portraying Sir Thomas Lucy in

Henry IV Part 2 and the *Merry Wives of Windsor* as the foolish Justice Shallow. Some historians doubt the reference, but the Bard does mention the "dozen white luces"—which figure in the Lucy coat of arms—and Shallow does tax Falstaff with killing his deer. The brick house was renovated in the neo-Elizabethan style by the Lucy family during the mid-19th century. The Tudor gatehouse is unchanged since Shakespeare's day. Capability Brown landscaped the deer park, with its emerald lawns. ⊠ *B4086, off A429, Hampton Lucy* ☎ *01789/470277* ⊕ *www.nationaltrust.org.uk* ✉ *£5.80, grounds only £3* ⊙ *House Mar.–Nov., Fri.–Sun. noon–5. Gardens Mar.–Oct., Fri.–Tues. 11–6; Nov.–mid-Dec., weekends 11–4.*

Where to Stay

££££ 🖼 **Charlecote Pheasant.** Converted farm buildings house this pleasant country-house hotel across from Charlecote Park (follow B4086 east out of Stratford for about 4 mi). The modern wing matches the fine 17th-century redbrick of the original, and all rooms have tasteful chintz and sober wooden furniture. Murder-mystery weekends are popular. ⊠ *Off B4086, Charlecote, CV35 9EW* ☎ *01789/279954* 🖨 *01789/470222* ⊕ *www.corushotels.com* 🛏 *70 rooms* ♿ *Restaurant, tennis court, pool, billiards, bar, lounge, meeting rooms, some pets allowed; no a/c* ⊟ *AE, DC, MC, V* 🍴 *BP.*

Broughton Castle

⑱ *14 mi southeast of Charlecote Park, 18 mi southeast of Stratford-upon-Avon.*

Once owned by the great chancellor and patron William of Wykeham, this impressive moated mansion passed to Lord and Lady Saye and Sele in 1451 and has been occupied by their family ever since. Parts of the building date to around 1300, and it was remodeled in Tudor times. The inside is rich with fireplaces, plasterwork, and exquisite furniture. High points include the Great Chamber, the chapel, and a fine collection of Chinese wallpapers. The house appeared in a few scenes in the movie *Shakespeare in Love* as the home of Viola de Lesseps. Joseph Fiennes, who played Shakespeare, is the baron's third cousin. ⊠ *B4035, Broughton* ☎ *01295/276070* ⊕ *www.broughtoncastle.demon.co.uk* ✉ *£5.50* ⊙ *Mid-May–June and early–mid-Sept., Wed. and Sun. 2–5; July and Aug., Wed., Thurs., and Sun. 2–5; national holiday Mon. 2–5.*

> off the beaten path

COMPTON WYNYATES – This perfect example of Tudor domestic architecture, notable for its timber roof and radiant rose hue, was constructed between 1480 and 1520 from bricks dismantled from a castle given to the family by Henry VIII. Compton Wynyates is 11 mi southeast of Stratford, near Upper Tysoe, but is best reached by turning north from Brailes off the Shipston–Banbury B4035. Today it is the private residence of the marquess of Northampton and should be viewed from the hillside roads that surround its tiny valley.

Alderminster

⑲ *5 mi south of Stratford-upon-Avon on A3400.*

Alderminster is one of the most interesting of the so-called "Stour villages"—those places so characteristic of Shakespeare Country, strung along the winding route of the River Stour south of Stratford. The main street holds an unusual row of old stone cottages, and the church has a Norman nave and a tower dating from the 13th century. Although the interior of the church has been much restored, it's worth a peek for the carved faces between the arches and the old altar stone.

Other Stour villages include Honington, Shipston-on-Stour, and Tredington. A village green anchors Honington, where a lovely five-arched bridge crosses the river. Shipston, the largest of the group, is an old sheep-market town, its handsome batch of Georgian houses formerly owned by wealthy wool merchants. Tredington, an exquisite nutshell of a village, has an old stone church.

Where to Stay & Eat

£££££ ✕🖭 **Ettington Park Hotel.** This luxurious Victorian Gothic house with a modern wing is an ideal spot to stay if you want to see the plays at Stratford but don't want to cope with the crowds. Its 40 acres of grounds contain a ruined church, and the hotel looks across river meadows haunted by herons. Some of the individually decorated rooms have four-poster beds, and there is a Shakespeare suite. The restaurant (fixed-price menu) has extremely good contemporary food. ☒ *Off A3400, CV37 8BU* ☎ *01789/450123* 🖷 *01789/450472* ⊕ *www.ettingtonpark.co. uk* ➥ *48 rooms* ♻ *Restaurant, room service, 2 tennis courts, indoor pool, gym, hot tub, sauna, spa, fishing, bar, lounge, dry cleaning, laundry service, meeting rooms* ⊟ *AE, DC, MC, V* ⦿| *BP.*

£ 🖭 **Horseshoe Inn.** One of a concentration of ancient inns in the village, the 17th-century Horseshoe is timbered outside and has a friendly open fire within. Ales and good coffee are available at the pub, and there are plain guest rooms. ☒ *6 Church St., Shipston-on-Stour, CV36 4AP* ☎ *01608/661225* 🖷 *01608/664743* ➥ *4 rooms* ♻ *Restaurant, bar; no a/c, no room phones* ⊟ *MC, V* ⦿| *BP.*

Welford-on-Avon

⓴ *4 mi southwest of Stratford-upon-Avon.*

Welford is most famous for its May Day revelry, when Morris dancers wearing costumes and bells perform around the maypole on the green. Park in the village, which lies on a loop of the River Avon off B439, and walk over the old bridge. Nearby Boat Lane is lined with timber and whitewashed thatched cottages. Welford also has what is said to be the oldest lych-gate in the county, leading to the church. Close by the church, which is partly Norman, stands Cleavers, an attractive brick-built Georgian house worth the stroll.

Alcester

㉑ *8 mi west of Stratford-upon-Avon.*

The small market town of Alcester (pronounced *al*-ster) holds a cluster of ancient roofs and timber-frame Tudor houses. Search out the narrow **Butter Street,** off High Street, site of the 17th-century Churchill House, and on Malt Mill Lane (off Church Street) the **Old Malt House,** dating from 1500.

Where to Stay & Eat

£££ ✕🖭 **Arrow Mill.** Heavy beams and flagstones recall the history of this inn, which occupies a former mill. Guest rooms, done in warm autumn colors, are individually decorated with pine furnishings. A mill wheel adorns the moderately priced restaurant, known for its hearty country menu. ☒ *Arrow St., B49 5NL* ☎ *01789/762419* 🖷 *01789/765170* ➥ *18 rooms* ♻ *Restaurant, bar, Internet, meeting rooms, some pets* *allowed (fee), no-smoking rooms; no a/c* ⊟ *AE, DC, MC, V* ⊙ *Restaurant closed last wk in Dec., 1st wk in Jan.* ⍩ *BP.*

Ragley Hall

㉒ *2 mi southwest of Alcester.*

A Palladian-style mansion with more than 100 rooms, Ragley Hall was begun in 1680 and worked on by some of the country's most outstanding architects. Inside are architectural and decorative treasures as well as magnificent views of the parkland originally laid out by Capability Brown in the 1750s. The Great Hall has fine baroque plasterwork by James Gibb, and there are portraits by Joshua Reynolds and various Dutch masters, among others, as well as some striking 20th-century murals by Graham Rust. This is the ancestral home of the marquesses of Hertford, the third of whom figured in Thackeray's *Vanity Fair* and the fourth of whom collected many of the treasures in London's Wallace Collection. ⊠ *Off A435 and A46* ☎ *01789/762090* ⊕ *www.ragleyhall. com* ⊠ *£6, state rooms £1* ⊙ *House Apr.–Sept., Thurs.–Sun. 11–6; park Apr.–Sept., daily 11–6; last admission 4:30.*

Coughton Court

㉓ *2 mi north of Alcester.*

Coughton Court, a grand Elizabethan manor house, is the home of the Catholic Throckmorton family, as it has been since 1409. The impressive gatehouse, the centerpiece of a half-timber courtyard, contains a fine fan-vaulted ceiling and various memorabilia, including the dress worn by Mary, Queen of Scots, at her execution. There are children's clothes and Gunpowder Plot exhibitions, and you can wander in the formal gardens and alongside a river and lake. ⊠ *A435* ☎ *01789/400777* ⊕ *www. coughtoncourt.co.uk* ⊠ *£9.45, gardens only £6.95* ⊙ *House mid-Mar.–June and Sept., Wed.–Sun. 11:30–5; July and Aug., Tues.–Sun. 11:30–5; Oct., weekends 11:30–5.*

SHAKESPEARE COUNTRY A TO Z

To research prices, get advice from other travelers, and book travel arrangements, visit www.fodors.com.

AIR TRAVEL

Warwickshire is convenient to major airports in London (⇨ Airports *in* Smart Travel Tips) and Birmingham (⇨ Airports *in* Smart Travel Tips).

BOAT & FERRY TRAVEL

For information about the Stratford towpath and canal, contact British Waterways.

🛈 **British Waterways** ☎ 01564/784634 ⊕ www.britishwaterways.co.uk.

BUS TRAVEL

National Express serves the region from London's Victoria Coach Station with eight buses daily to the Stratford region. Flightlink buses run from London's Heathrow and Gatwick airports to Warwick, and Stagecoach serves local routes throughout the Stratford, Birmingham, and Coventry areas.

FARES & SCHEDULES 🛈 **Flightlink** ☎ 0870/580–8080 ⊕ www.nationalexpress.com. **National Express** ☎ 0870/580–8080 ⊕ www.nationalexpress.com. **Stagecoach** ☎ 01788/535555 or 0870/608–2608 ⊕ www.stagecoachbus.com.

CAR RENTAL

Open Road Classic Car Hire rents sports cars.

Local Agencies **Hertz** ⊠ Rail Station, Stratford-upon-Avon ☎ 01789/298827 ⊕ www. hertz.co.uk. **Listers** ⊠ Western Rd., Stratford-upon-Avon ☎ 01789/294477 ⊕ www. listersgroup.co.uk. **The Open Road Classic Car Hire** ⊠ Stratford-upon-Avon ☎ 01926/ 624891 ⊕ www.theopenroad.co.uk.

CAR TRAVEL

Stratford lies about 100 mi northwest of London; take M40 to Junction 15. The town is 37 mi southeast of Birmingham by the A435 and A46 or by the M40 to Junction 15. Main roads provide easy access between towns, but one pleasure of this rural area is exploring the smaller "B" roads, which lead deep into the countryside.

EMERGENCIES

Ambulance, fire, police ☎ 999. **Saint Michael's Hospital** ⊠ St. Michael's Rd., Warwick ☎ 01926/496241 or 01926/406789. **Stratford-upon-Avon Hospital** ⊠ Arden St., Stratford-upon-Avon ☎ 01926/495321.

TOURS

The Heart of England Tourist Board (⇨ Visitor Information) arranges tours throughout the region. City Sightseeing runs guided tours of Stratford (£8.50) and Warwick (£17.50). Because City Sightseeing charges don't include admission to the Stratford sights—most are within walking distance—some people find the tour unnecessary.

City Sightseeing ☎ 01789/294466 ⊕ www.city-sightseeing.com.

TRAIN TRAVEL

Try to catch one of the four direct trains (two in the morning and two in the afternoon) from London's Paddington Station, which take two hours to reach Stratford; these avoid a change at Leamington Spa. Two direct trains return from Stratford each evening. On winter Sundays there are no direct trains. The fastest route is by train *and* bus using the Shakespeare Connection Road & Rail Link from Euston Station to Coventry, then a City Sightseeing bus.

The Shakespeare Connection trip takes two hours, and there are four departures on weekdays—the three that would allow you to catch an evening performance in Stratford are at 9:15 AM, 10:45 AM, and 4:55 PM; Saturday departures are at 9:05 AM, 10:35 AM, and 5:05 PM; the Sunday departure is at 9:45 AM. Returns to London usually depart around 11:15 PM. Schedules can change, so call to confirm times. National Rail Enquiries has further information.

DISCOUNTS & DEALS
A seven-day Heart of England Rover ticket is valid for unlimited travel within the region; contact National Rail Enquiries for purchasing information. The Shakespeare Country Explorer Pass from Thames Trains offers one-day (£25) or three-day (£30) tickets for rail travel to and from London once and unlimited travel within Shakespeare Country, plus discounts at area sights.

FARES & SCHEDULES
City Sightseeing ☎ 01789/294466 ⊕ www.city-sightseeing.com. **National Rail Enquiries** ☎ 0845/748–4950 ⊕ www.nationalrail.co.uk. **Thames Trains** ☎ 01789/293127 ⊕ www.thamestrains.com. **Virgin Trains** ☎ 0845/ 722–2333 ⊕ www.virgin.co.uk/trains.

TRAVEL AGENCIES

Local Agent Referrals **American Express** ⊠ c/o Tourist Information Centre, Bridgefoot, Stratford-upon-Avon ☎ 01789/415856. **Thomas Cook** ⊠ c/o Midland Bank, 13 Chapel St., Stratford-upon-Avon ☎ 01789/294688.

VISITOR INFORMATION

Local tourist-information centers are normally open Monday–Saturday 9:30–5:30, but times vary according to season.

🚩 **Heart of England Tourist Board** ⊠ Woodside, Larkhill, Worcester, WR5 2EF ☎ 01905/763436 🖶 01905/763450 ⊕ www.visitheartofengland.com. **Shakespeare Country** ⊕ www.shakespeare-country.co.uk. **Coventry** ⊠ Bayley La., CV1 5RN ☎ 024/7622-7264 ⊕ www.coventry.org. **Kenilworth** ⊠ Kenilworth Library, 11 Smalley Pl., CV8 1QG ☎ 01926/852595. **Stratford-upon-Avon** ⊠ Bridgefoot, CV37 6GW ☎ 01789/293127 ⊕ www.stratford-upon-avon.co.uk. **Warwick** ⊠ Court House, Jury St., CV34 4EW ☎ 01926/492212 ⊕ www.warwick-uk.co.uk.

THE HEART OF ENGLAND

BATH, THE COTSWOLDS, GLOUCESTER, THE FOREST OF DEAN

7

FODOR'S CHOICE

Castle Combe, *Wiltshire village*

Cardynham House, *hotel in Painswick*

Hidcote Manor Gardens, *Hidcote Bartrim*

Lacock, *village owned by National Trust*

Lower Slaughter, *Cotswold village*

Queensberry Hotel, *Bath*

HIGHLY RECOMMENDED

SIGHTS Bath

Berkeley Castle, *Berkeley*

Chastleton House, *near Stow-on-the-Wold*

Chedworth Roman Villa, *Yanworth*

Circus, *Bath*

Forest of Dean

Gloucester Cathedral, *Gloucester*

Humblebee Wood, *Winchcombe*

Museum in the Park, *Stroud*

Museum of Costume and Assembly Rooms, *Bath*

Number 1 Royal Crescent, *Bath*

Owlpen, *village*

Roman Baths Museum, *Bath*

Stanway House, *Stanway*

Sudeley Castle, *Winchcombe*

Westonbirt Arboretum, *near Tetbury*

Many other great hotels and restaurants enliven this area. For other favorites, look for the black stars as you read this chapter.

Updated by
Robert
Andrews

THE HEART OF ENGLAND is a term coined by the tourist powers-that-be to designate the heart of *tourist* England, so immensely popular are its attractions. Here it means the county of Gloucestershire, in west-central England, with slices of neighboring Oxfordshire, Worcestershire, and Somerset. Together they make up a sweep of land stretching from Shakespeare Country in the north down through Bath to the Bristol Channel in the south. Bath, among the most alluring small cities in Europe, offers up "18th-century England in all its urban glory," to use a phrase of writer Nigel Nicolson. Northward, beyond Regency-era Cheltenham—like Bath, a spa town adorned with remarkably elegant architecture—the Cotswolds region conjures up "olde Englande" at its most blissfully rural. Urban Gloucester and the ancient Forest of Dean are the western edge of the area.

Bath rightly boasts of being the best-planned town in England. Although the city was founded by the Romans when they discovered here the only true hot springs in England, its popularity during the 17th and 18th centuries ensured its aesthetic immortality. Bath's fashionable period luckily coincided with one of Britain's most creative architectural eras, producing a quite remarkable urban phenomenon—money available to create virtually an entire town of stylish buildings. The city powers have been wise enough to make sure that Bath is kept spruce and welcoming. In the past, Gainsborough, Lord Nelson, and Queen Victoria traveled here to sip the waters, which Dickens described as tasting like "warm flatirons." Today some people come to walk in the footsteps of Jane Austen and take tea and scones with clotted cream. It's also possible to bathe in the hot spring water in an up-to-the-minute spa complex that incorporates the restored 18th-century baths.

North of Bath are the Cotswolds—a region that more than one writer has called the very soul of England. Is it the sun, or the soil? The pretty-as-a-picture villages with the perfectly clipped hedges? The mellow, centuries-old, stone-built cottages festooned with honeysuckle? Whatever the reason, this idyllic region, which from medieval times grew prosperous on the wool trade, remains a vision of rural England. Here are time-defying churches, sleepy hamlets, and ancient farmsteads so sequestered that they seem to offer everyone the thrill of personal discovery. Hidden in sheltered valleys, you'll find fabled abodes—Sudeley Castle, Stanway House, and Snowshill Manor (closed until 2005, though the grounds are open) among them. The Cotswolds can hardly claim to be undiscovered, but, happily, the area's poetic appeal has a way of surviving the crowds who pierce its timeless tranquillity. More than ever, people come here to taste the glories of the old English village—its tile or thatched roofs, low-ceiling rooms, and gardens meticulously built on a gentle slope; its atmosphere is as thick as honey, and equally as sweet.

Exploring the Heart of England

The region's major points of interest—Bath, the Cotswold Hills, and the Gloucester-Cheltenham axis—are one way to organize your explorations. Bath, in the southwestern corner of this area, is a good place to start; it can also be visited on a day out from London. The Cotswold Hills cover some of southern England's most beautiful terrain, with which the characteristic stone cottages found throughout the area are in perfect harmony. Coach parties and antiques shops have overrun some villages, but they have for the most part retained their historic appearance, and can still be fun. To the west of the Cotswolds lie the cities of Gloucester and Cheltenham, a former spa town; beyond them, between

You can get a taste of Bath and the Cotswolds in three days, and a week-long visit will give you plenty of time to wander this relatively small region. Bath is a useful place to start or finish, not far off the M4 motorway on the A46. The cities of Gloucester and Cheltenham also hold many attractions. Once outside the towns, you'll discover that the Cotswold Hills should be relished on a slow schedule, to allow you time to smell the roses and appreciate the moon-daisies.

Numbers in the text correspond to numbers in the margin and on the Bath Environs, Bath, the Cotswolds, and the Forest of Dean maps.

If you have 3 days

A day in **Bath** 1–12 will enable you to tour the Roman Baths, followed by a whirl around Bath Abbey. In the afternoon, stroll along the river or canal, view the ceramics and silverware in the Holburne Museum, then cross town to the Royal Crescent for a promenade. Spend the night here, heading out early for **Cheltenham** 16, whose Regency architecture and fashionable shops will occupy a morning. After lunch, drive northeast on B4632 through **Winchcombe** 17, near which lie the majestic grounds of historic **Sudeley Castle** 18 and **Snowshill Manor** 20. A stop in **Broadway** 21 will allow you to sample its prettiness, or you can press on to that Cotswold showpiece, **Chipping Campden** 22. Now head south on the A429 through the classic Cotswold villages of **Moreton-in-Marsh** 24 and **Stow-on-the-Wold** 25, where cottage pubs are sandwiched between antiques shops. Nearby, don't miss the smaller places such as **Lower and Upper Slaughter** 27. For your final afternoon, head westward on A436 to **Gloucester** 37, with its restored docks and the National Waterways Museum.

If you have 7 days

Two days in **Bath** 1–12 will give you time to explore this Georgian treasure, even browsing its antiques shops and sampling the services of the Thermae Bath Spa. Outside Bath, make sure you see **Castle Combe** 13, "the prettiest village in England," or **Lacock** 14. On your third day, head north to swank **Cheltenham** 16 and walk its Regency-era terraces and promenades. Overnight there, then start out on a circuit of the best of the Cotswold villages and countryside; Cheltenham's tourist office has useful information. Driving north out of Cheltenham, take a look at **Winchcombe** 17 and explore the impressive grounds of **Sudeley Castle** 18 and **Stanway House** 19 (the latter has limited hours). Nearby **Snowshill Manor** 20, in an unspoiled village, has attractive grounds; the house is closed until spring 2005. The popular Cotswold center of **Broadway** 21 lies a couple of miles to the north, on A44.

Spend your fourth night in that Cotswold gem, **Chipping Campden** 22, from which it is an easy drive to the rare shrubs and "garden rooms" of **Hidcote Manor Gardens** 23. From here, head southward, through a pair of Cotswold towns, **Moreton-in-Marsh** 24 and **Stow-on-the-Wold** 25, both deserving a leisurely wander. Four miles east of these towns, Jacobean Chastleton House is something of a time warp, or you might ramble around the ancient Rollright Stones, a few miles farther east. South of Stow, kids may enjoy the museum attractions of **Bourton-on-the-Water** 26 and **Northleach** 28. **Chedworth Roman Villa** 31 recalls the area's importance in Roman times—nearby **Cirencester** 32 was Corinium, an important provincial capital. The chances are that you will already have seen the ideal rural retreat for your fifth night, perhaps in the country around ⌘ **Lower and Upper Slaughter** ㉗. In the morning, an outing eastward might take in idyllic **Bibury** ㉚ and the wool town of **Burford** ㉙. Driving west from Cirencester on A417, make your farewells to the Cotswolds in the model village of **Owlpen** ㉟, immaculate **Painswick** ㉝, and the market town of **Tetbury** ㊱. ⌘ **Gloucester** ㊲ presents an urban contrast to the rustic tone of your last few days. Spend your final day either south of here, exploring the medieval **Berkeley Castle** ㊸ and the celebrated **Slimbridge Wildfowl & Wetland Trust** ㊷, or else west, toward the Wye Valley and Wales, to take a gentle hike through the ancient Forest of Dean with an overnight in ⌘ **Coleford** ㊶. Visit the Dean Heritage Center at Soudley and then put on your walking shoes. If you have children along, the nearby Clearwell Caves can be special fun.

the River Severn and the border of Wales, is the Forest of Dean. The road from Gloucester to Bath takes you by the castle at Berkeley.

About the Restaurants

Good restaurants dot the region, thanks to a steady flow of fine chefs seeking to cater to wealthy locals and waves of demanding visitors. Here, in the heart of England, chefs have never had a problem with a fresh food supply: excellent regional produce, salmon from the Rivers Severn and Wye, local lamb and pork, venison from the Forest of Dean, and pheasant, partridge, quail, and grouse in season. Also look out for Gloucestershire Old Spot pork, bacon, and sausage on area menus.

About the Hotels

While staying at a Cotswold inn during the spring of 1776, the immortal Dr. Johnson uttered his noted panegyric on English hostelries: "There is no private house in which people can enjoy themselves so well as at a capital tavern." The hotels of this region still aim to please, and they are among Britain's most highly rated—from bed-and-breakfasts in village homes and farmhouses to luxurious country-house hotels. Because the region is so popular, book ahead whenever possible, especially if you want to visit Bath during the two weeks in May and June when Bath International Music Festival hits town, or Cheltenham in mid-March when the National Hunt Festival takes place. You should also brace yourself for some high prices. B&Bs are a cheaper alternative to the fancier hotels, and most hotels offer two- and three-day packages. Keep in mind when making reservations that hotels can front on heavily trafficked roads; ask for quiet rooms.

WHAT IT COSTS In pounds				
	££££	££££	£££	££	£
RESTAURANTS	over £22	£18–£22	£13–£17	£7–£12	under £7
HOTELS	over £160	£115–£160	£80–£115	£50–£80	under £50

Restaurant prices are for a main course at dinner. Hotel prices are for two people in a standard double room in high season, including VAT, with no meals or, if indicated, CP (with Continental breakfast), BP (Breakfast Plan, with full breakfast), or MAP (Modified American Plan, with breakfast and dinner).

Timing

This area contains some of Britain's most popular destinations, and you would do well to avoid weekends in the busier areas of the Cotswolds. During the week, even in summer, you will hardly see a soul in the more remote spots. Bath is particularly congested in summer, when students flock to its language schools. On the other hand, Gloucester and Cheltenham are workday places that can absorb the visiting coach tours comfortably; Cheltenham does, however, get very full at festival time and during race meetings. Note that the private properties of Hidcote Manor, Snowshill Manor, and Sudeley Castle close in winter. Hidcote Manor Gardens is at its best in spring and fall, Bowood Gardens in May.

BATH & ENVIRONS

Anyone who listens to the local speech of Bath will note the inflections that herald the beginning of England's West Country. Yet the city retains an inescapable element of the Heart of England: Bath itself is at the bottom edge of the Cotswold Hills, and the Georgian architecture and mellow stone so prominent here are reminders of the stone mansions and cottages of the Cotswolds. In the hinterland of the county of Somerset, the gentle, green countryside harbors country pubs.

Bath

★ ⌐ *13 mi southeast of Bristol, 115 mi west of London.*

"I really believe I shall always be talking of Bath . . . I do like it so very much. Oh! who can ever be tired of Bath," wrote Jane Austen in *Northanger Abbey* and, today, thousands of people heartily agree with the great 19th-century author. One of the delights of staying in Bath is being surrounded by the magnificent 18th-century architecture, a lasting reminder of the vanished world described by Austen. In the 19th century the town lost its fashionable luster and slid into a refined gentility that is still palpable today. Although the 20th century saw some slight harm from World War II bombing and slightly more from urban renewal, the damage was halted before it could ruin the city's Georgian elegance. This doesn't mean that Bath is a museum. It is lively and interesting, with good dining and shopping, excellent art galleries and museums, and theater, music, and other performances throughout the year.

The Romans put Bath on the map in the 1st century, when they built a temple here, in honor of the goddess Minerva, and a sophisticated network of baths to make full use of the mineral springs that gush from the earth at a constant temperature of 116°F (46.5°C). Much later, 18th-century "people of quality" took the city to heart, and Bath became the most fashionable spa in Britain. The architect John Wood created a harmonious city, building graceful terraces, crescents, and villas of the same golden local limestone used by the Romans. His son, called John Wood the Younger, also designed notable buildings in the city. Assembly rooms, theaters, and pleasure gardens were all built to entertain the rich and titled, when they weren't busy attending the parties of Beau Nash (the city's master of ceremonies and chief social organizer) and having their portraits painted by Thomas Gainsborough.

Today, it's once again possible to relive the experience of the Romans and Georgians. You can bathe in the hot springs and sample the therapeutic and aesthetic treatments at the Thermae Bath Spa. Opened in summer 2003, it includes historic baths and a spectacular new building.

a good walk

Start in the traffic-free Abbey Churchyard, at the heart of Bath, and the **Roman Baths Museum** ❶ ⌐ to see the impressive remains of the bath complex. The lively piazza is dominated by **Bath Abbey** ❷, whose facade—itself packed with detail—invites further investigations within. Off Abbey Churchyard, where buskers (strolling musicians) perform,

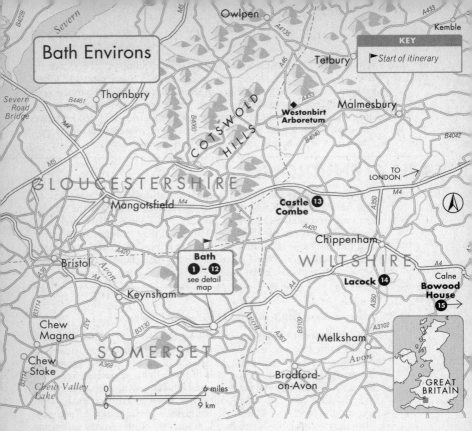

Bath **1** – **12** see detail map

tiny alleys lead to little squares of stores, galleries, and eating places. Walk up Stall and Union streets toward Milsom Street, and you'll find alleyways with fascinating shops. Work your way east to Bridge Street and the graceful, Italianate **Pulteney Bridge 3**, a shop-lined masterpiece over the River Avon. South of here, the Grand Parade looks out over flower-filled gardens. Stroll over the bridge to Great Pulteney Street, a broad thoroughfare that leads to the **Holburne Museum 4**, Bath's finest collection of crafted objects. Cross back over the bridge, and head up Broad Street and its extension, Lansdown Road. Turn left onto Julian Road for insight into the industrial side of Bath at the **Museum of Bath at Work 5**. From here, cross the road to Russell Street; turn right on Bennett Street and visit the **Museum of East Asian Art 6**, with exquisite objets d'art from 5000 BC to the present day. On the opposite side of the road lies the neoclassical **Museum of Costume and Assembly Rooms 7**. The Assembly Rooms were the 18th-century hub of elegant society, and the Museum of Costume provides an overview of some weird and wonderful apparel from the past. From here, it's a short hop to Gay Street and the **Jane Austen Centre 8**, on a street where the author lived in the early 1800s. Returning north on Gay Street, you can study the **Circus 9**, an architectural tour de force compared by some to an inverted Colosseum. The graceful arc of Bath's most dazzling terrace, the Royal Crescent, embraces a swath of green lawns at one end of Brock Street. Stop in at **Number 1 Royal Crescent 10**, a perfectly preserved example of Georgian domestic architecture. Return to the Circus and walk south down Gay Street, which will bring you past **Queen Square**, with its obelisk, to **Theatre Royal 11**, one of the country's most impressive dramatic venues. Wander east from here back to the Roman Baths, opposite which you can relieve tired limbs in a hot spring bath at the **Thermae**

7

Gardens

Perhaps it's the beauty of this area that has inspired the creation of so many superb gardens in a medley of styles. Here, as elsewhere in Britain, the gardens often complement a stately home and deserve as close a look as the house. When you visit Sudeley Castle, the home of Catherine Parr (Henry VIII's last wife), for example, take time to explore the 19th-century Queen's Garden, beloved for its roses. Admirers of the naturalistic landscaping of Capability Brown can see a notable example of his large-scale work in the 2,000-acre park at Bowood House & Gardens; the spectacular Rhododendron Walks here are a later, 19th-century creation. In contrast, the 18th-century Painswick Rococo Garden, with its Gothic screen and other intriguing structures, has a pleasant intimacy. The Arts and Crafts movement in Britain transformed not only interior design but also the world of gardening; at Hidcote Manor Gardens, a much-visited masterpiece of the style, hedges and walls set off vistas and surround distinct themed garden rooms. Britain wouldn't be Britain without a touch of eccentricity, and in this region the garden at the Indian-style manor of Sezincote, with its temple to a Hindu god, supplies a satisfying blend of the stately and the exotic.

Shopping

The antiques shops here are, it is sometimes whispered, "temporary" storerooms for the great families of the region, filled with tole-ware, treen, faience firedogs, toby jugs, and silhouettes, plus lovely country furniture, Edwardiana, and ravishing 17th- to 19th-century furniture. The center of antiquing, with more than 30 dealers, is Stow-on-the-Wold. Other towns that have a number of antiques shops are Burford, Cirencester, Tetbury, and Moreton-in-Marsh. Unfortunately, the Cotswolds now have very few of those "anything in this tray for £5" shops. For information about dealers and special events, contact the Cotswold Antique Dealers' Association. As across England, many towns in the region have market days, when you can purchase local produce, crafts, and assorted items such as clothes, books, and toys. Head for Moreton-in-Marsh on Tuesday, Tetbury on Wednesday, and Cirencester on Monday and Friday.

Walking

Short walks thread the glorious, gentle countryside around the historic towns of the region. The local tourist information centers often route maps for theme walks. If you want to branch out on your own, but not get lost, track the rivers on which many towns are built. Easy-to-follow, scenic towpaths usually run alongside the rivers. However, rivers wind a lot, and you may find yourself walking for much longer than you intended. The Cotswold Way, stretching about 100 mi between Bath and Chipping Campden, traces the ridge marking the edge of the Cotswolds and the Severn Valley and has incomparable views. The densely wooded Forest of Dean is quite special for walking, with interesting villages and monastic ruins. Many of its public footpaths are signposted, as are most of the Forestry Commission trails. You'll find easy walks out of Newland, around New Fancy (great view) and Mallards Pike Lake, and a slightly longer one (three hours), which takes in Wench Ford, Danby Lodge, and Blackpool Bridge. The area has picnic grounds, car parking, and, hidden away, old pubs where you can wet your whistle.

Bath Spa ⑫. Alternatively, head for the abbey and tea shops, including Sally Lunn's, for liquid refreshment of another kind.

TIMING　Allow a full day to see everything, with frequent tea stops; you should save two hours for the Roman Baths Museum. Note that on Sunday many shops close. Bath Abbey is more difficult to visit on Sunday, too. The walk itself takes only about 1½ hours, but in summer the sheer volume of sightseers will hamper your progress.

What to See

American Museum and Gardens. A Greek Revival (19th-century) mansion in a majestic setting on a hill southeast of the city holds the first museum of American decorative arts to be established outside the United States. Some galleries are furnished rooms, and others contain objects—in silver, pewter, and glass, for example—dating from the 17th to 19th centuries. Several rooms are devoted to folk art, Native American culture, and quilts. The parkland includes a reproduction of George Washington's garden at Mount Vernon. ✉ *Warminster Rd. (A36), Claverton Down, 2½ mi southeast of Bath* ☎ *01225/460503* ⊕ *www.americanmuseum.org* ☞ *Museum, grounds, and galleries £6, grounds and galleries £3.50* ⊙ *Late Mar.–July and Sept.–early Nov., Tues.–Sun. 2–5; Aug., daily 2–5; also national holiday Mon. and preceding Sun. 11–5.*

❷ **Bath Abbey.** Dominating Bath's center, this 15th-century edifice of golden, glowing stone has a splendid west front, with carved figures of angels ascending ladders on either side. Notice, too, the miter, olive tree, and crown motif, a play on the name of the current building's founder, Bishop Oliver King. More than 50 stained-glass windows fill about 80% of the building's wall space, giving an impression of lightness. The abbey was built in the Perpendicular (English late-Gothic) style on the site of a Saxon abbey, and the nave and side aisles contain superb fan-vaulted ceilings. Visit the **Heritage Vaults,** accessible from outside the building (the entrance is in the abbey's south wall, off Abbey Church Yard), to see an audiovisual presentation of the history of the abbey and a reconstruction of the Norman cathedral that preceded it. ✉ *Abbey Churchyard* ☎ *01225/422462* ⊕ *www.bathabbey. org* ☞ *Abbey £2.50 donation, Heritage Vaults £2.50* ⊙ *Abbey Easter–Oct., Mon.–Sat. 9–6; Nov.–Mar., Mon.–Sat. 9–4:30; call for Sun. hrs. Heritage Vaults Mon.–Sat. 10–4.*

need a break? The quiet courtyard of two adjacent cafés, the **Café René and Café Parisien** (✉ 2 Shires Yard, off Broad St. ☎ 01225/447147) is handy for coffee and a croissant or a lunchtime baguette.

★ ❾ **Circus.** John Wood designed the masterful Circus, a circle of curving, perfectly proportioned Georgian houses interrupted just three times for intersecting streets. Wood died shortly after work on the Circus began; his son, the younger John Wood, completed the project. Notice the acorns atop the houses; Wood nurtured the myth that Prince Bladud founded Bath, ostensibly with the help of an errant pig rooting for acorns (this is one of a number of variations of Bladud's story), and the architect adopted the acorn motif in a number of places. A garden fills the center of the Circus.

❹ **Holburne Museum.** This elegant 18th-century building houses a small but superb collection of 17th- and 18th-century decorative arts, ceramics, and silverware. Highlights include paintings by Gainsborough (*The Byam Family,* on indefinite loan) and Stubbs (his exquisite portrait, *Reverend Carter Thelwall and Family*), and Rachmaninov's Steinway piano.

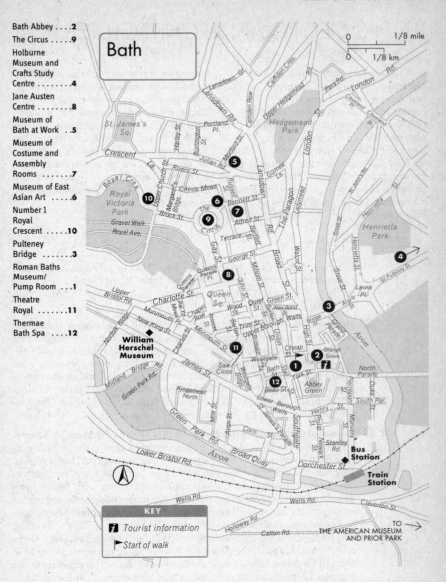

It also displays temporary exhibitions on historical themes. As the Sydney Hotel, the house was once one of the pivots of Bath's high society, who came to perambulate in the pleasure gardens (Sydney Gardens) that still lie behind. One visitor was Jane Austen, whose main Bath residence was No. 4 Sydney Place, a brief stroll across the road from the museum. ✉ *Great Pulteney St.* ☎ *01225/466669* 🌐 *www.bath.ac.uk/holburne* 💷 *£4* 🕐 *Mid-Feb.–mid-Dec., Tues.–Sat. 10–5, Sun. 2:30–5:30.*

⑧ Jane Austen Centre. This cozy Georgian-house-turned-museum, a few doors up from where Jane Austen lived in 1805 (one of several addresses she had in Bath at different times), examines the influence of the city on her writings. If you haven't had time to read *Northanger Abbey* and *Persuasion,* both set in the city, the displays here will give you a pictorial introduction, and the digitally enlarged panorama of Bath in 1800 by Robert Havell helps put it all in context. Jane Austen walking tours leave

BATH'S GEORGIAN ARCHITECTURE

Bath wouldn't be Bath without its distinctive 18th-century Georgian architecture, much of which was conceived by John Wood the Elder (1704–54), an antiquarian and architect obsessed. Wood saw Bath as a city destined for almost mythic greatness along the lines of Winchester and Glastonbury. He sought an architectural style that would do justice to his concept, and found it in the Palladian style, made popular in Britain by Inigo Jones. Influenced by

nearby ancient stone circles as well as round Roman temples, Wood broke loose from convention in his design for Bath's Circus, a full circle of houses broken only three times for intersecting streets. After the death of Wood the Elder, John Wood the Younger carried out his father's plans for the Royal Crescent, an obtuse crescent of 30 interconnected houses. Today you can stop in at No. 1 Royal Crescent for a look at one of these homes.

from the Abbey Churchyard at 1:30 PM daily in July and August and on weekends from September through June. ✉ *40 Gay St.* ☎ *01225/ 443000* ⊕ *www.janeausten.co.uk* 🖃 *£4.45, tours £3.50* ☉ *Mon.–Sat. 10–5:30, Sun. 10:30–5:30.*

❺ **Museum of Bath at Work.** The core of this industrial-history collection, which gives a novel perspective on the city, is a complete engineering works and fizzy drinks factory, relocated to this building. It once belonged to Bath entrepreneur Jonathan Bowler, who started his many businesses in 1872. The tour includes all the original clanking machinery and also offers glimpses into Bath's stone industry and cabinet making. ✉ *Julian Rd.* ☎ *01225/318348* ⊕ *www.bath-at-work.org.uk* 🖃 *£3.50* ☉ *Apr.–Oct., daily 10:30–4:30; Nov.–Mar., weekends 10:30–4:30.*

★ ❼ **Museum of Costume and Assembly Rooms.** In its role as the **Assembly Rooms**, this classical building was the leading center for social life in 18th-century Bath, with a schedule of dress balls, concerts, and choral nights. Jane Austen came here often, and it was here, in the Ballroom, that Catherine Morland had her first, disappointing encounter with Bath's beau monde in *Northanger Abbey;* the Octagon Room became the setting for an important encounter between Anne Elliot and Captain Wentworth in *Persuasion.* Built by John Wood the Younger in 1771, the building was badly damaged by bombing in 1942, but was subsequently faithfully restored. Today, the Assembly Rooms house the entertaining **Museum of Costume,** displaying costumes from Elizabethan times up to the present. Throughout the year, concerts of Vivaldi, Bach, and other classical composers are given in the Ballroom, just as they were in bygone days. ✉ *Bennett St.* ☎ *01225/477789* ⊕ *www.museumofcostume.co. uk* 🖃 *£5.50, including audio guide; combined ticket with Roman Baths £11* ☉ *Daily 10–5; last admission 4:30.*

❻ **Museum of East Asian Art.** Intimate galleries on three floors finely display both ancient and modern pieces from China, Japan, Korea, and Southeast Asia. Highlights are graphic 19th-century watercolors depicting the Chinese idea of hell, Chinese ivory figures, and Japanese lacquerware. ✉ *12 Bennett St.* ☎ *01225/464640* 🖃 *£3.50* ☉ *Tues.–Sat. 10–5, Sun. noon–5.*

★ ❿ **Number 1 Royal Crescent.** The majestic arc of the Royal Crescent, much used as a film location, is the crowning glory of Palladian architecture in Bath. The work of John Wood the Younger, these 30 houses fronted by 114 columns were laid out between 1767 and 1774. A house in the center is now the Royal Crescent Hotel. On the corner of Brock Street and the Royal Crescent, Number 1 Royal Crescent has been turned into a museum and furnished as it might have been at the turn of the 19th century. The museum crystallizes a view of the English class system— upstairs all is elegance, and downstairs is a kitchen display. ☎ 01225/ 428126 ⊕ www.bath-preservation-trust.org.uk ⊠ £4 ۞ Mid-Feb.–Oct., Tues.–Sun. and national holidays 10:30–5; Nov., Tues.–Sun. and national holidays 10:30–4; last admission 30 mins before closing.

Prior Park. A vision to warm Jane Austen's heart, Bath's grandest house lies a mile or so southeast of the center, with splendid views over the Georgian townscape. Built around 1738 by the older John Wood of honey-color limestone, the Palladian mansion was the home of local businessman (he owned a stone quarry) and philanthropist Ralph Allen (1693–1764), whose guests included such luminaries as Pope, Fielding, and Richardson. Today, it is a Roman Catholic school and the interior is not open to the public, but you may wander through the beautiful grounds, designed by Capability Brown and embellished with a Palladian bridge and lake. There is no parking lot here or in the vicinity: unless you relish the uphill trudge, take a taxi, or use the frequent bus service (Nos. 2 or 4 from the center). ⊠ Ralph Allen Dr. ☎ 01225/833422 ⊕ www.nationaltrust.org. uk ⊠ £4.10, £1 discount if arriving by public transportation ۞ Feb.–Nov., Wed.–Mon. 11–dusk; Dec. and Jan., Fri.–Sun. 11–dusk.

❸ **Pulteney Bridge.** Florence's Ponte Vecchio inspired this 18th-century span, one of the most famous landmarks in the city and the only work of Robert Adam in Bath. It's unique in all Britain because shops line both sides of the bridge.

Queen Square. Houses and the Francis Hotel surround the garden in the center of this peaceful, intimate square. An obelisk designed by the older John Wood and financed by Beau Nash celebrates the 1738 visit of Frederick, Prince of Wales.

★ ▶ ❶ **Roman Baths Museum.** The hot springs have drawn people here since prehistoric times, so it's most appropriate to begin an exploration of Bath at this excellent museum on the site of the ancient city's temple complex and primary "watering hole." Here, the patrician elite would gather to immerse themselves, drink the mineral waters, and socialize. With the departure of the Romans, the baths fell into disuse, but when the practice again became fashionable, the site was reopened, and the magnificent Georgian building now standing was erected at the end of the 18th century. During the following century, almost the entire Roman bath complex was rediscovered and excavated, and the museum displays numerous relics of the temple once dedicated to Sulis Minerva. Exhibits include a mustachioed, Celtic-influenced Gorgon's head, fragments of colorful curses invoked by the old Romans against some of their neighbors, and information about Roman bathing practices. The **Great Bath** is now roofless, and the statuary and pillars belong to the 19th century, but much remains from the original complex, and the steaming, somewhat murky waters are undeniably evocative. On August evenings, you can take part in torch-lighted tours of the baths.

Adjacent to the Roman bath complex is the famed **Pump Room,** built in 1792–96, a rendezvous place for 18th-century Bath society, where lords and ladies liked to check on the new arrivals to the city. Here Catherine Morland and Mrs. Allen "paraded up and down for an hour, looking at everybody and speaking to no one," to quote from Jane Austen's Northanger Abbey. Today, you can eat on the premises—or you can simply, for a small fee, taste the fairly vile mineral water. ✉ *Abbey Churchyard* ☎ *01225/ 477785* ⊕ *www.romanbaths.co.uk* ✇ *Pump Room free, Roman Baths £8.50 with audio guide, combined ticket with Museum of Costume and Assembly Rooms £11* ⊙ *Mar.–June, Sept., and Oct., daily 9–6; July and Aug., daily 9 AM–10 PM; Nov.–Feb., daily 9:30–5:30; last admission 1 hr before closing.*

⑪ Theatre Royal. George Dance the younger designed this magnificent auditorium, which opened in 1805 and was restored in 1982 as a vision in damson plush, raspberry-striped silk, and gold grisaille. For £3 you can tour the theater on the first Saturday (11 AM) of the month and the following Wednesday (noon), but call ahead to confirm. ✉ *Saw Close* ☎ *01225/448844* ⊕ *www.theatreroyal.org.uk.*

⑫ Thermae Bath Spa. The only place in Britain where you can bathe in natural hot spring water, and in an open-air rooftop location as well, this state-of-the-art complex designed by Nicholas Grimshaw consists of a Bath stone building surrounded by a glass curtain wall. Opened in summer 2003 in the heart of the city, the spa has four luxurious floors offering all the latest spa treatments and therapies. Close by, the Cross Bath and the Hot Bath, two 18th-century thermal baths, have been brought back into use for bathing and treatments; there's also a café and shop. You can book in advance or call on the day. ✉ *Hot Bath St.* ☎ *01225/ 477051* ⊕ *www.thermaebathspa.com* ✇ *£17 for 2 hrs, £23 for 4 hrs, £35 all day; extra charges for treatments* ⊙ *Daily 9 AM–10 PM.*

William Herschel Museum. In this modest Bath town house, using a handmade telescope of his own devising, William Herschel (1738–1822) identified the planet Uranus. This small museum devoted to his studies and discoveries contains examples of his telescopes, the workshop where he cast his speculum metal mirrors, musical instruments of his time (Herschel came to Bath from his native Hannover as a musician, and was organist at Bath's Octagon Chapel), and the tiny garden where the discovery of Uranus was made. ✉ *19 New King St.* ☎ *01225/311342* ⊕ *www.bath-preservation-trust.org.uk* ✇ *£3.50* ⊙ *Feb.–Nov., Thurs.–Tues. 11–5; Dec. and Jan., weekends 2–5; last admission 4:30.*

Where to Stay & Eat

££££ ✕ Moody Goose. At this modern English restaurant, you descend the stairs to comfy sofas before you enter the creamy, vaulted dining area, highlighted by a green slate floor and French watercolors on the walls. Expect carefully crafted dishes such as turbot with roasted cod and samphire grass; cheeses are served with sultana bread and poached figs. Pretheater meals are a good value. ✉ *7a Kingsmead Sq.* ☎ *01225/466688* ▬ *AE, DC, MC, V* ⊙ *Closed Sun. and 2 wks Jan.*

★ £££–££££ ✕ Popjoy's Restaurant. The former home of Richard "Beau" Nash—the dictator of fashion for mid-18th-century society in Bath—and his mistress Juliana Popjoy provides an elegant choice for a fine, English-style, after-theater dinner. You can dine on the ground floor or in the lovely Georgian drawing room upstairs. The dishes, such as seared loin of lamb with roast garlic and Madeira sauce, show eclectic international touches. ✉ *Beau Nash House, Saw Close* ☎ *01225/460494* ▬ *AE, DC, MC, V* ⊙ *Closed Sun.*

£££ ✕ Number 5 Bistro. An ideal spot for a light lunch, this airy bistro, with its plants, framed posters, and cane-back chairs, is just over the Pulteney Bridge from the center of town. The menu changes daily but includes soups and such dishes as foie gras served with toasted brioche, and roast lamb with aubergine (eggplant) caviar. You can bring your own wine on Monday and Tuesday, and Wednesday is devoted to fish. ✉ *5 Argyle St.* ☎ *01225/444499* ▬ *AE, MC, V* ⊙ *Closed Sun.*

££–£££ ✕ **Eastern Eye.** A magnificent domed Georgian ceiling graces the dining room of one of the country's finest Indian restaurants. Besides many Balti, tandoori, and *tikka* dishes, the menu lists specialties such as king prawn masala. If the choice confounds you, opt for a fixed-price meal or one of the chef's recommendations: chicken *jalfrazi* is hot, whereas *moglai* chicken in a cashew, coconut, and sultana sauce is milder. ⊠ *8a Quiet St.* ☎ *01225/422323* ▭ *AE, MC, V.*

££–£££ ✕ **Retro.** Pull up an old church chair at this bustling, bohemian spot and tuck into contemporary fare such as twice-baked crab soufflé and perhaps a baked cherry and chocolate cheesecake. It's also a great place for a light snack at lunchtime, when club sandwiches and good vegetarian choices are on offer, and there's a Retro-To-Go next door. ⊠ *18 York St.* ☎ *01225/339347* ▭ *AE, MC, V* ☉ *Closed Mon.*

££ ✕ **Pump Room.** The 18th-century Pump Room, next to the Roman Baths Museum, serves morning coffee, lunches of steak sandwiches or chicken and lamb dishes, and afternoon tea, often to music by a string trio. Do sample the English cheese board and homemade Bath biscuits. The Terrace Restaurant has views over the Baths and is also open occasionally for dinner (there's a £22 fixed-price menu for dinner, and reservations are essential). Be prepared to wait in line for a table during the day. ⊠ *Abbey Churchyard* ☎ *01225/444477* ▭ *AE, MC, V* ☉ *No dinner except during Aug., Dec., and Bath Festival.*

£–££ ✕ **Sally Lunn's.** This popular spot near Bath Abbey occupies the oldest house in Bath, dating to 1482. It's famous for the Sally Lunn bun (served here since 1680), actually a light, semisweet bread. You can choose from more than 40 sweet and savory toppings to accompany your bun, or turn it into a meal with such dishes as trencher pork in apple and cider. Daytime diners can view the small kitchen museum in the cellar (free, 30p for visitors). ⊠ *4 North Parade Passage* ☎ *01225/461634* ▭ *MC, V* ☉ *No dinner Dec. and Jan.*

£–££ ✕ **Tilleys Bistro.** The meat and vegetarian menus of this intimate, bow-windowed eatery present an alluring selection of hot and cold dishes in starter-size portions. Typical choices include Somerset mushrooms with smoked ham and cheddar cheese, and spinach, walnut, and Roquefort tart. ⊠ *3 North Parade Passage* ☎ *01225/484200* ▭ *MC, V* ☉ *Closed Sun.*

£ ✕ **The Old Green Tree.** Friendly and unspoiled, this oak-paneled pub is an option for a pint and spot of lunch. You can pick soup, salad, and rolls, or a hearty beef and ale pie, and specials are chalked up on the blackboard. ⊠ *12 Green St.* ☎ *01225/448259* ▭ *No credit cards.*

★ **£££££** ✕▣ **Royal Crescent Hotel.** At the heart of the monumental Royal Crescent, this lavishly converted house is an architectural treasure, with prices to match. The furnishings are consistent with the building's period elegance, and a Palladian villa in the garden provides extra lodging. If some bedrooms are on the small side, there are ample luxuries to compensate. The hotel's superb Pimpernel's restaurant has won consistent praise for modern British fare. ⊠ *16 Royal Crescent, BA1 2LS* ☎ *01225/823333; 888/295–4710 in U.S.* ☒ *01225/339401; 888/295–4711 in U.S.* ⊕ *www.royalcrescent.co.uk* ⤳ *29 rooms, 16 suites* ⚭ *Restaurant, in-room data ports, cable TV, indoor pool, gym, sauna, croquet, bar, meeting rooms, free parking, some pets allowed* ▭ *AE, DC, MC, V.*

££££–£££££
Fodor'sChoice
★
✕▣ **Queensberry Hotel.** Intimate and elegant, this hotel in a residential street near the Circus occupies three 1772 town houses built by John Wood the Younger for the marquis of Queensberry. Renovations have preserved the Regency stucco ceilings and cornices and original marble tiling on the fireplaces, and each room is decorated in pastels, stripes, or flower prints. Downstairs, the Olive Tree restaurant serves top-notch English and Mediterranean dishes. ⊠ *Russell St., BA1 2QF* ☎ *01225/*

447928 🖨 *01225/446065* 🌐 *www.bathqueensberry.com* ⇗ *29 rooms* ♨ *Restaurant, some in-room data ports, bar, meeting rooms, free parking; no a/c* ▭ *MC, V* ⊘ *Closed Dec. 24–30* ⼁OⵏⵏCP.

££££ ✕🖼 **Duke's Hotel.** Refurbishment of this Palladian-style mansion has revealed the true Georgian grandeur of its rooms. Elegant bedrooms (no smoking allowed) are individually decorated in English-, French-, or Italian-inspired style, and some have elaborate plasterwork or large windows facing the street. The informal Fitzroy's restaurant serves the best of British contemporary fare, such as char-grilled minute steak with watercress and butter. The centrally located hotel overlooks Bath's rugby and cricket ground. ✉ *Great Pulteney St., BA2 4DN* ☎ *01225/787960* 🖨 *01225/787961* 🌐 *www.dukesbath.co.uk* ⇗ *24 rooms* ♨ *Restaurant, cable TV, bar, meeting rooms, parking (fee), some pets allowed* ▭ *AE, DC, MC, V* ⼁OⵏCP.

£££££ 🖼 **Bath Spa Hotel.** Its 7 acres of well-kept grounds (complete with grotto) give this splendid golden stone hotel, a converted Georgian mansion, a feeling of seclusion, although you're just a 10-minute walk from the heart of bustling Bath. Public areas have elegant but comfortable sofas and armchairs; many rooms are in wings matching the style of the original building. Guest rooms are modern and neutral in hue, with pampering touches in the large marble bathrooms. ✉ *Sydney Rd., BA2 6JF* ☎ *0870/ 400–8222 or 01225/444424* 🖨 *01225/444006* 🌐 *www.bathspahotel. com* ⇗ *97 rooms, 5 suites* ♨ *2 restaurants, in-room data ports, cable TV, tennis court, indoor pool, gym, sauna, spa, croquet, bar, baby-sitting, meeting rooms, free parking, some pets allowed (fee); no a/c* ▭ *AE, DC, MC, V* ⼁OⵏBP.

£££–££££ 🖼 **Paradise House.** Don't be put off by the 10-minute uphill walk from the center of Bath—you'll be rewarded by a wonderful prospect of the city from the upper stories of this Georgian guest house. Cool pastels and traditional furnishings decorate the rooms attractively, and there are open fires in winter and a lush garden for spring and summer. Rooms 3 and 5 have the best views. If the full English breakfast is too daunting, indulge in coffee and croissants in bed. ✉ *88 Holloway, BA2 4PX* ☎ *01225/317723* 🖨 *01225/482005* 🌐 *www.paradise-house.co. uk* ⇗ *11 rooms* ♨ *Some in-room data ports, croquet, free parking; no a/c, no smoking* ▭ *AE, DC, MC, V* ⊘ *Closed last wk in Dec.* ⼁OⵏBP.

££–£££ 🖼 **Cranleigh.** Standing in a quiet location on the hill high above the city, this Victorian guest house has wonderful views over Bath from the back of the house. Rooms are richly decorated, and extensive breakfasts—pancakes with maple syrup, kippers, eggs with smoked salmon, and vegetarian options—are served in the dining room, which looks out onto the garden. ✉ *159 Newbridge Hill, BA1 3PX* ☎ *01225/310197* 🖨 *01225/423143* 🌐 *www.cranleighguesthouse.com* ⇗ *8 rooms* ♨ *Free parking; no a/c, no kids under 5, no smoking* ▭ *AE, MC, V* ⼁OⵏBP.

££–£££ 🖼 **Holly Lodge.** This large Victorian house overlooking Bath will suit those who like plush B&B accommodations with plenty of frills and flounces, elaborate drapes, and ornaments. Room 4 has the best view. Guests are offered a princely breakfast in the conservatory dining room, and the terraced garden has a gazebo that is floodlit at night. ✉ *8 Upper Oldfield Pk., BA2 3JZ* ☎ *01225/424042* 🖨 *01225/481138* 🌐 *www. hollylodge.co.uk* ⇗ *7 rooms* ♨ *Cable TV with movies, free parking; no a/c, no smoking* ▭ *AE, DC, MC, V* ⼁OⵏBP.

£–££ 🖼 **Albany Guest House.** Homey and friendly, this Edwardian house, close to Victoria Park and the center of town, has simply furnished rooms with a floral motif. The pale blue and yellow attic room is the largest and best. Homemade vegetarian sausages are an option at breakfast. ✉ *24 Crescent Gardens, BA1 2 NB* ☎ *01225/31339* 🌐 *www.bath.org/hotel/*

albany 🍳 *4 rooms, 2 with bath* ♿ *Free parking; no a/c, no room phones, no kids under 5, no smoking* 🚭 *No credit cards* 🍴 *BP.*

Nightlife & the Arts

FESTIVALS The **Bath International Music Festival** (✉ Bath Festival Box Office, 2 Church St. ☎ 01225/463362 ⊕ www.bathfestivals.org.uk), held for two weeks in May and June, presents concerts (classical, jazz, and world music), dance performances, and exhibitions in and around Bath, many in the Assembly Rooms and Bath Abbey.

The **Jane Austen Festival** (☎ 01225/463362) celebrates the great writer with films, plays, walks, and talks during the last week of September.

THEATER The **Theatre Royal** (✉ Box Office, Saw Close ☎ 01225/448844), a lovely Regency playhouse, has a year-round program that often includes pre- or post-London tours. You have to reserve for the best seats well in advance, but you can line up for same-day standby seats or standing room. Check the location—sight lines can be poor.

Sports & the Outdoors

To explore the River Avon by rented punt or canoe, head for the **Bath Boating Station** (✉ Forester Rd. ☎ 01225/466407), behind the Holburne Museum. It's open April–September.

The par-71, 18-hole golf course at **Sham Castle** (✉ North Rd, ☎ 01225/463834), 1 mi southeast of town, is one of the West's finest courses, on high ground with splendid views.

Shopping

Bath has excellent small, family-run, and specialty shops; ⊕ www.bathrealshops.com has information. The shopping district centers on Stall and Union streets (modern stores), Milsom Street (traditional stores), and Walcott Street (arts and crafts). Leading off these main streets are fascinating alleyways and passages lined with galleries and antiques shops. **Bartlett Street Antique Centre** (✉ Bartlett St. ☎ 01225/466689) has more than 100 showcases and stands selling every kind of antique imaginable, including vintage clothing, linens, and furniture. The **Bath Antiques Market** (✉ Paragon Antiques, 3 Bladud Bldgs., The Paragon ☎ 01225/463715), open Wednesday 6:30 AM–3 PM, is a wonderful place to browse; 50 dealers have stalls here, and there's a restaurant. **Beaux Arts Ceramics** (✉ 12–13 York St. ☎ 01225/464850) carries the work of prominent potters and holds eight solo exhibitions a year. **Margaret's Buildings** (✉ Halfway between the Circus and Royal Crescent) is a lane with gift shops and several secondhand and antiquarian bookshops.

Castle Combe

13 *12 mi northeast of Bath, 5 mi northwest of Chippenham.*

Fodor'sChoice
★

This Wiltshire village lived a sleepy existence until 1962, when it was voted the Prettiest Village in England—without any of its inhabitants knowing that it had even been a contender. The village's magic is that it's so toylike, so delightfully all-of-a-piece: you can see almost the whole town at one glance from any one position. It consists of little more than a brook, a pack bridge, a street—which is called the Street—of simple stone cottages, a market cross from the 13th century, and the Perpendicular-style church of St. Andrew. The grandest house in the village (actually, on its outskirts) is the Upper Manor House, built in the 15th century by Sir John Fastolf, chosen to be Dr. Dolittle's house in the 1967 Rex Harrison film, and now the Manor House Hotel.

Where to Stay & Eat

★ ╳▦ **Manor House Hotel.** The partly 14th-century manor house, outside
££££–£££££ the village in a 23-acre park, is a baronial swirl of solid chimney stacks,
carvings, and columns. Inside, a stone frieze depicts characters from Shakespeare's Falstaff plays, to commemorate the fact that Sir John Fastolf,
thought to be the playwright's model for the character, was once lord
of this manor. Antiques abound and bedrooms have lavish bathrooms;
some rooms are in mews cottages. The Bybrook restaurant serves imaginative fixed-price meals—try the loin of lamb with artichoke relish.
✉ *Castle Combe, SN14 7HR* ☎ *01249/782206* 🖷 *01249/782159*
⊕ *www.exclusivehotels.co.uk* 📞 *47 rooms* ⚭ *Restaurant, in-room
data ports, 18-hole golf course, tennis court, pool, bar, meeting rooms,
helipad; no a/c* ▤ *AE, MC, V.*

Lacock

⑭ *3 mi south of Chippenham, 8 mi southeast of Castle Combe.*

Fodor'sChoice
★
This lovely Wiltshire village is the victim of its own charm, its unspoiled
gabled and stone-tiled cottages drawing coach parties aplenty. Left to
its own devices, however, Lacock slips back into its profound slumber,
the mellow stone and brick buildings little changed in 500 years. There
are a few antiques shops, the handsome church of St. Cyriac (built with
money earned in the wool trade), a 14th-century tithe barn, and a scattering of pubs that serve bar meals in atmospheric surroundings.

Well-preserved **Lacock Abbey** reflects the fate of a good number of religious establishments in England—a spiritual center became a home. The
abbey, at the town's center, was founded in the 13th century and closed
down during the dissolution of the monasteries in 1539, when its new
owner, Sir William Sharington, demolished the church and converted
the cloisters, sacristy, chapter house, and monastic quarters into a private dwelling. His last descendant, Mathilda Talbot, donated the property as well as Lacock itself to the National Trust in the 1940s. The abbey's
grounds are also worth a wander, with a Victorian woodland garden
and an 18th-century summer house. Harry Potter fans, take note: Lacock Abbey was used for various scenes at Hogwarts School in the film
version of *Harry Potter and the Sorcerer's Stone.* The **Fox Talbot Museum** (☎ *01249/730459* ⊙ Mid-Mar.–Oct., Wed.–Mon. 1–5:30;
Nov.–mid-Mar., weekends 1–5:30), in a 16th-century barn at the gates
of Lacock Abbey, illustrates the early history of photography with
works by pioneers in the field and also exhibits contemporary artists.
The museum commemorates the work of William Henry Fox Talbot
(1800–77), who developed the first photographic negative at Lacock
Abbey, showing an oriel window in his family home. Look for a copy
of this (the original is in Bradford's National Museum of Photography,
Film, and Television) and other results of his experiments in the 1830s.
✉ *Just east of A350* ☎ *01249/730227* ⊕ *www.nationaltrust.org.uk*
🖾 *Abbey, museum, gardens, and cloisters £6.50; abbey, garden, and
cloisters £5.30; museum, gardens, and cloisters £4.20* ⊙ *Abbey Apr.–Oct.,
Wed.–Mon. 1–5:30; gardens and cloisters Mar.–Oct., daily 11–5:30; last
admission 30 mins before closing.*

Where to Stay & Eat

£££–££££ ╳▦ **At the Sign of the Angel.** An inn since the 15th century, the building measures up to expectations of comfortable antiquity—polished floors,
gleaming silver, antiques, and cottage-style bedrooms (one room contains a bed belonging to famous Victorian engineer Isambard Kingdom
Brunel). The restaurant is known for its Stilton and walnut paté, roasts,
casseroles, and puddings such as meringues with clotted cream and

fresh strawberries. ⊠ 6 *Church St., SN15 2LB* ☎ *01249/730230* 🖷 *01249/730527* ⊕ *www.lacock.co.uk* ⌁ *10 rooms* ♿ *Restaurant, some in-room data ports, meeting rooms, some pets allowed; no a/c* ⊟ *AE, DC, MC, V* ⊘ *Closed last wk Dec.* ⦿ *BP.*

Bowood House & Gardens

👐 ⑮ *3 mi southeast of Chippenham, 3 mi east of Lacock.*

Dating to the mid-18th century, the beautifully proportioned Bowood House sits in magnificent grounds designed by Capability Brown. The family home of the marquess of Lansdowne owes its present appearance to Charles Cockerell, architect of the Ashmolean Museum at Oxford, and to Robert Adam, who was responsible for the south front, the orangery, and the splendid library and sculpture gallery. One room served as the laboratory where Joseph Priestley discovered oxygen gas in 1774. Among the treasures are Lord Byron's Albanian dress, much booty from India, and a dazzling collection of jewelry. The landscaped gardens, complete with Doric temple on the lake and waterfall in the woods, are at their finest in spring, when acres of rhododendrons are in flower. There's also a good adventure playground for children. ⊠ *South of A4, Calne* ☎ *01249/812102* ⊕ *www.bowood.org* 🎟 *£6.25, rhododendron walks £3.50* ⊘ *Apr.–Oct., daily 11–6; rhododendron walks late Apr.–early June.*

THE COTSWOLDS

The Thames rises among the limestone Cotswold Hills, and a more delightful cradle could not be imagined for that historic river. The Cotswolds are among the best-preserved rural districts of England, and the quiet but lovely grays and ambers of the stone buildings here are truly unsurpassed. Much has been written about the area's pretty towns, which age has mellowed rather than withered, but perhaps, on closer inspection, the architecture of the individual villages differs little from that of villages elsewhere in England. Their distinction lies instead in the character of their surroundings: the valleys are deep and rolling, and cozy hamlets appear to drip in foliage from church tower to garden gate. Beyond the village limits, you'll often find the "high wild hills and rough uneven ways" that Shakespeare wrote about.

Over the centuries, quarries of honey-color stone have yielded building blocks for many Cotswold houses and churches and have transformed little towns into realms of gold. Nowhere else in Britain does that superb combination of church tower and gabled manor house shine so brightly, nowhere else are the hedges so perfectly clipped, nor the churchyards so peaceful. There's an elusive spirit about the Cotswolds, so make Chipping Campden, Moreton-in-Marsh, or Stow-on-the-Wold your headquarters for a few days, and wander for a while, going through this valley and along that byroad. Then ask yourself what the area is all about. Its secret seems shared by two things—sheep and stone. The combination is not as strange as it may sound. These were once the great sheep-rearing areas of England, and during the peak of prosperity in the Middle Ages, Cotswold wool was in demand the world over. This made the Cotswold merchants rich, but many gave back to the Cotswolds by restoring old churches (the famous "wool churches" of the region) or building rows of almshouses, of limestone now seasoned to a glorious golden-gray.

Begin with Cheltenham—a gateway to the Cotswolds, but slightly outside the boundaries—then move on to the beauty spots in and around

Winchcombe. Next are Stanway House and Sudeley Castle, among the most impressive houses of the region; the oversold village of Broadway, which has many rivals for beauty hereabouts; Chipping Campden—the Cotswold cognoscenti's favorite; and Hidcote Manor, one of the most spectacular gardens in England. Then circle back south, down through Moreton-in-Marsh, Stow-on-the-Wold, Upper Slaughter, Lower Slaughter, Bourton-on-the-Water, and end with Bibury, Tetbury, and Owlpen. This is definitely a region where it pays to go off the beaten track to take a look at that village among the trees. Many nooks and villages snuggled deep into dells can be rendered invisible by coverings of ivy. Like four-leaf clovers, their discovery must come serendipitously.

Cheltenham

⑯ *50 mi north of Bath, 13 mi east of Gloucester, 99 mi west of London.*

Although Cheltenham has acquired a reputation as the snootiest place in England—and it's undeniable that the population is generally well-heeled and of a conservative persuasion—a vibrant cosmopolitan air fills the place. The town has excellent restaurants and bars, fashionable stores, and a thriving cultural life. Its primary claim to renown, however, is its architecture, rivaling Bath's in its Georgian elegance, with wide, tree-lined streets, crescents, and terraces with row houses, balconies, and iron railings. Like Bath, Cheltenham owes part of its fame to mineral springs. By 1740 the first spa was built, and after a visit from George III and Queen Charlotte in 1788, the town dedicated itself to idleness and enjoyment. "A polka, parson-worshipping place"—in the words of resident Lord Tennyson—Cheltenham gained its reputation for snobbishness when stiff-collared Raj majordomos returned from India to find that the springs—the only purely natural alkaline waters in England—were the most effective cure for their "tropical ailments."

Great Regency architectural set pieces—Lansdown Crescent, Pittville Spa, and the Lower Assembly Rooms, among them—were built solely to adorn the town. The Rotunda building (1826) at the top of Montpellier Walk—now a bank—contains the spa's original "pump room," in which the mineral waters were on draft. More than 30 statues adorn the storefronts of Montpellier Walk. Wander past Imperial Square, with its ironwork balconies, past the ornate Neptune's Fountain, and along the Promenade. In spring and summer, lush flower gardens enhance the town's buildings. Parts of the town may look like something out of a Gilbert and Sullivan stage set, but today Cheltenham is the site of two of England's most progressive arts festivals—the Cheltenham Festival of Literature and the town's music festival—as well as a jazz fest.

From the 1880s onward, Cheltenham was at the forefront of the Arts and Crafts movement, and the **Cheltenham Art Gallery and Museum** contains fine displays of William Morris textiles, furniture by Charles Voysey, and simple wood and metal pieces by Ernest Gimson. Decorative arts, such as Chinese ceramics, are well represented, and British artists, including Stanley Spencer and Vanessa Bell, make their mark in the art gallery. Other exhibits focus on local archaeology and history; one is devoted to Edward Wilson, who traveled with Robert Scott to the Antarctic on Scott's ill-fated 1912 expedition. ⊠ *Clarence St.* ☎ *01242/ 237431* ⊕ *www.cheltenhammuseum.org.uk* ⊠ *Free* ☉ *Mon.–Sat. 10–5:20, Sun. 2–4:20.*

The grandest of the spa buildings remaining in town, the **Pittville Pump Room** is set amid parkland, a 20-minute walk from the town center. The classic Regency structure, built in the late 1820s, now serves mainly as

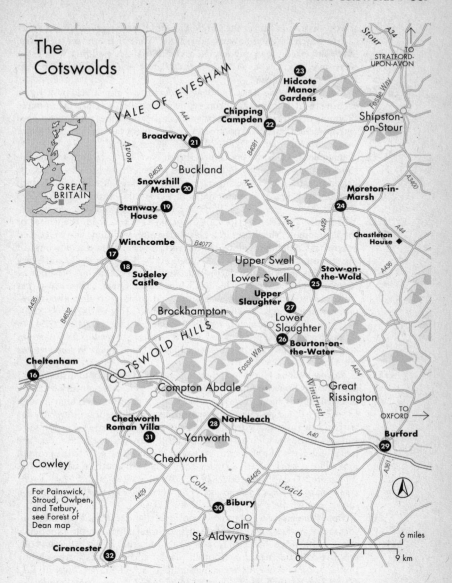

The Cotswolds

GREAT BRITAIN

VALE OF EVESHAM

TO STRATFORD-UPON-AVON

23 Hidcote Manor Gardens

Chipping Campden 22

Shipston-on-Stour

Broadway 21

Buckland

Snowshill Manor 20

Stanway House 19

Moreton-in-Marsh 24

Chastleton House ◆

Winchcombe

17

18 Sudeley Castle

Upper Swell

Lower Swell

Stow-on-the-Wold 25

Brockhampton

Upper Slaughter 27

Lower Slaughter

26 Bourton-on-the-Water

COTSWOLD HILLS

Cheltenham

16

Compton Abdale

Great Rissington

TO OXFORD →

Chedworth Roman Villa

31

28 Northleach

Yanworth

Burford

29

Chedworth

Cowley

For Painswick, Stroud, Owlpen, and Tetbury, see Forest of Dean map

Coln

Bibury

30

Coln St. Aldwyns

0   6 miles

0   9 km

Cirencester

32

a concert hall but still offers its musty mineral waters to the strong of stomach. ⊠ *East Approach Dr., Pittville* ☎ *01242/523852* ⊡ *Free* ⊙ *Wed.–Mon. 10–4.*

Where to Stay & Eat

£££–££££ ✕ **Le Champignon Sauvage.** The relatively short menu at this well-established restaurant is perfectly balanced, and the contemporary French cooking is superb. Indulge your palate with dishes such as lamb fillet roasted with lavender, followed by prune parfait. You can choose among many cheeses as well. Fixed-price menus at lunch and dinner help keep the cost down. ⊠ *24 Suffolk Rd.* ☎ *01242/573449* ⊟ *AE, DC, MC, V* ⊙ *Closed Sun., Mon., 2 wks in summer and 10 days in Dec.*

££–£££ ✕ **The Daffodil.** Brasserie cuisine is the focus of this former cinema that preserves the heyday of 1930s elegance. Admire the art deco trappings as you sip an aperitif in the Circle Bar and then sweep down the staircase to watch the chefs at work "on stage." You can try the seared calves' liver with bacon and puy lentils, and the summer pudding with raspberry purée is a delight. ✉ *18–20 Suffolk Parade* ☎ *01242/700055* ▭ *AE, MC, V* ☾ *Closed Sun.*

££–£££ ✕ **Montpellier Wine Bar.** An ideal place for a light snack or a fuller evening meal, this busy, informal wine bar in Cheltenham's fashionable shopping district serves tapas, pastas, salads, and dishes such as sausages with horseradish mashed potatoes. Get in early for fast service. ✉ *Bayshill Lodge, Montpellier St.* ☎ *01242/527774* ▭ *AE, MC, V.*

£–££ ✕ **Boogaloos.** Choose between the brightly colored, vibrant rooms upstairs or the sofa seating in the relaxed basement for lunches of salads, baked potatoes, or more substantial fare such as shredded lamb with Thai noodles. Leave room for the homemade cakes and puddings. ✉ *16 Regent St.* ☎ *01242/702259* ▭ *MC, V* ☾ *Closed Sun. No dinner.*

££££ ✕▥ **Queen's Hotel.** Overlooking Imperial Gardens from the center of the Promenade, this hotel in a classic Regency building has welcomed people to Cheltenham since 1838. Public areas and rooms leading off the stunning inner stairway are traditionally British in style, and every bedroom is individually decorated. At Le Petit Blanc, an offshoot of renowned chef Raymond Blanc's Manoir aux Quat' Saisons in Great Milton, you can sample French provincial cooking in elegant contemporary surroundings. ✉ *The Promenade, GL50 1NN* ☎ *0870/400–8107; 01242/266800 restaurant; 888/892–0038 in U.S.* 🖷 *01242/224145* ⊕ *www.macdonaldhotels.co.uk* ⇆ *73 rooms* ♧ *2 restaurants, in-room data ports, cable TV, bar, some pets allowed (fee); no a/c in some rooms* ▭ *AE, DC, MC, V* ▯◎ *BP.*

£££££ ▥ **Cowley Manor.** Good-bye, floral prints: this Georgian mansion on 55 acres brings luxury country-house hotels into the 21st century by using modern fabrics and furniture but keeping the comfort level high enough to soothe a chic clientele. Witty sculptures complement lime green sofas with purple pillows, bedrooms are brightly colored, and bathrooms are suitably trendy, with glass walls and large showers. Half the rooms are in the house; the rest fill a transformed stable. The spa, set into the ground, looks like a work of art. Cowley Manor is 5 mi south of Cheltenham. ✉ *Cowley, GL53 9NL* ☎ *01242/870900* 🖷 *01242/870901* ⊕ *www. cowleymanor.com* ⇆ *30 rooms* ♧ *Dining room, 2 pools (1 indoor), gym, sauna, spa, steam room* ▭ *MC, V* ▯◎ *CP.*

£££ ▥ **Hotel Kandinsky.** A fashionably cool style that doesn't stint on the comfort factor makes a stay in this Georgian hotel a memorable experience at a sensible price. Modern teak designer furniture in the bedrooms offsets the colorful rugs, huge potted plants, and antiques in the clubby public rooms. A 1950s-style nightclub is attached. ✉ *Bayshill Rd., GL50 3AS* ☎ *01242/527788* 🖷 *01242/226412* ⊕ *www.hotelkandinsky. com* ⇆ *48 rooms* ♧ *Restaurant, in-room data ports, cable TV, in-room VCRs, bar, nightclub, meeting rooms; no a/c* ▭ *AE, DC, MC, V.*

★ **££–£££** ▥ **Lypiatt House.** This splendid Victorian house—only a short walk from central Cheltenham—is an excellent B&B with attentive service from the friendly husband-and-wife owners. The bedrooms are spacious and have chic bathrooms. The restful drawing room is done in peach and green, and the conservatory makes a good place for a drink. ✉ *Lypiatt Rd., GL50 2QW* ☎ *01242/224994* 🖷 *01242/224996* ⊕ *www. lypiatt.co.uk* ⇆ *10 rooms* ♧ *In-room data ports, bar; no a/c* ▭ *AE, MC, V* ▯◎ *BP.*

££ ▥ **Abbey Hotel.** Relaxed and family-run, this hotel in a quiet terrace near the center of town offers great value. Bedrooms are simple but stylish, decorated in subtle tones, and the breakfast area overlooks the well-stocked garden. ⊠ *14–16 Bath Parade, GL53 7HN* ☎ *01242/516053* 🖷 *01242/ 513034* 📞 *9 rooms* ⚠ *No a/c* ⊟ *AE, MC, V* 🍴 *BP.*

Nightlife & the Arts

The late-19th-century **Everyman Theatre** (⊠ Regent St. ☎ 01242/572573) is an intimate venue for opera, dance, and concerts, as well as plays.

For information on festivals, contact the **Festival Office** (⊠ Town Hall, Imperial Sq., Cheltenham, GL50 1QA ☎ 01242/227979 ⊕ www. cheltenhamfestivals.co.uk). Cheltenham's famous **International Festival of Music,** during the first two weeks of July, highlights new compositions, often conducted by the composers, together with classical pieces. The **International Jazz Festival,** held at the beginning of May, attracts noted jazz musicians. The town's **Festival of Literature** in October brings together world-renowned authors, actors, and critics.

Sports

Important steeplechase races take place at **Cheltenham Racecourse** (⊠ Prestbury Park ☎ 01242/513014), north of the town center; the Gold Cup awards crown the last day of the National Hunt Festival in mid-March.

The hilltop golf course at **Cleeve Hill** (⊠ B4632 ☎ 01242/672592), 3 mi north of Cheltenham, has great views. Book at least a week ahead to play on weekends.

Shopping

A stroll along Montpellier Walk and then along the flower-bedecked Promenade will bring you to high-quality stores. A bubble-blowing Wishing Fish Clock, designed by Kit Williams, dominates the Regent Arcade, a modern shopping area behind the Promenade. General markets are held every Sunday at the racecourse and every Thursday morning off Lower High Street, and an indoor antiques market is open Monday–Saturday at 54 Suffolk Road.

Cavendish House (⊠ 32–48 The Promenade ☎ 01242/521300) is a high-quality department store with designer fashions. **Hoopers** (⊠ 33 The Promenade ☎ 01242/527505) sells select clothes, handbags, and leather goods. **Martin** (⊠ 19 The Promenade ☎ 01242/522821) carries a good stock of modern jewelry. **Scott Cooper** (⊠ 52 The Promenade ☎ 01242/ 522580) sells fine antique jewelry, silver, and china.

Winchcombe

⑰ *7 mi northeast of Cheltenham.*

The sleepy, unspoiled village of Winchcombe, once the capital of the Anglo-Saxon kingdom of Mercia, has some attractive half-timber and stone houses, and a clutch of nice old inns serving food. Almost 40 outlandish gargoyles adorn the mid-15th-century Perpendicular-style **St. Peter's Church,** a typical Cotswold wool church.

★ A bracing 2-mi walk south of Winchcombe on the Cotswold Way leads to the hilltop site of **Belas Knap,** a neolithic long barrow, or submerged burial chamber, above **Humblebee Wood.** There's not much to see of the site itself, but you'll be hiking next to and through one of the most enchanting natural domains in England, with views stretching over to Sudeley Castle. If you have a car, take the scenic Humblebee Wood road down to the villages of Sevenhampton and Brockhampton.

A mile outside Winchcombe, at Greet, you can board a steam-hauled train of the **Gloucestershire and Warwickshire Railway,** which chugs its way along a 13-mi stretch at the foot of the Cotswolds between Toddington Station and Cheltenham Racecourse. ☎ *01242/621405* ⊕ *www. gwsr.plc.uk* 🖾 *£9 round-trip* ⊙ *Mid-Feb.–Oct., weekends 11–5, daily during school holidays and some dates in Dec.*

Where to Stay & Eat

££ ✕☒ **Wesley House.** Beams and stone walls distinguish this 15th-century half-timber building, a restaurant with a few bedrooms. The red-carpeted restaurant makes a fine backdrop for superior Mediterranean-style food; fixed-price menus include nettle and pea soup, breast of Delande duck with cherry and kirsch sauce, and chocolate blinis with brown bread ice cream. Upstairs, the smallish rooms have twisted beams and sloping ceilings. ☒ *High St., GL54 5LJ* ☎ *01242/602366* 🖷 *01242/609046* ⊕ *www.wesleyhouse.co.uk* 🛏 *6 rooms* ♨ *Restaurant; no a/c, no smoking* 🖃 *AE, MC, V* 🍴 *BP.*

Sudeley Castle

★ ⑱   *1 mi southeast of Winchcombe, 9 mi northeast of Cheltenham.*

One of the grand showpieces of the Cotswolds, Sudeley Castle was the home and burial place of Catherine Parr (1512–48), Henry VIII's sixth and last wife, who outlived him by one year. Here, Catherine undertook, in her later years, the education of the ill-fated Lady Jane Grey and the future queen, Princess Elizabeth—Sudeley, for good reason, has been called a woman's castle. The term "castle," however, is misleading, for it appears more like a Tudor-era palace. Today its peaceful air belies its turbulent history. During the 17th century, Charles I took refuge here, causing Oliver Cromwell's army to besiege the castle, leaving it in ruins until the Dent-Brocklehurst family stepped in with a 19th-century renovation. Inside are Tudor and Civil War artifacts, as well as paintings by Van Dyck, Rubens, Turner, and Reynolds. The romantic grounds include the Queen's Garden, with its spectacular roses; a Tudor knot garden; and settings for outdoor Shakespeare performances, concerts, and other events in summer. Accommodations in 14 cottages on the grounds are booked by the week in summer, but these are available for two-night stays or longer in winter. ☒ *Off B4632, Winchcombe* ☎ *01242/604357* ⊕ *www.sudeleycastle.co.uk* 🖾 *£6.70, gardens and exhibitions only £5* ⊙ *Castle Apr.–late Oct., daily 11–5; gardens, grounds, plant center, and shop early Mar.–late Oct., daily 10:30–5:30.*

Stanway House

★ ⑲   *5 mi northeast of Sudeley Castle, 11 mi northeast of Cheltenham.*

Set in the small village of Stanway, this perfect Cotswold manor of glowing limestone dates from the Jacobean era. Its triple-gabled gatehouse is a Cotswold landmark, and towering windows dominate the house's Great Hall. Divided by mullions and transoms into 60 panes, these windows are "so mellowed by time"—to quote Lady Cynthia Asquith (a former chatelaine)—"that whenever the sun shines through their amber and green glass, the effect is of a vast honeycomb." They illuminate a 22-foot shuffleboard table from 1620 and an 18th-century bouncing exercise machine. The other well-worn rooms are adorned with family portraits, tattered tapestries, vintage armchairs, and Lord Neidpath himself, the current owner. On the grounds is a cricket pavilion built by J. M. Barrie, author of *Peter Pan*, who leased the house. To get to Stanway, take B4632 north of Winchcombe, turning right at B4077. ☒ *Stanway* ☎ *01386/584469* 🖾 *£4* ⊙ *July and Aug., Tues. and Thurs. 2–5; other times by appointment only for groups of at least 20.*

Snowshill Manor

20 *4 mi northeast of Sudeley Castle, 3 mi south of Broadway, 13 mi north-east of Cheltenham.*

Snowshill is one of the most unspoiled of all Cotswold villages. Snuggled beneath Oat Hill, with little room for expansion, the hamlet is centered around an old burial ground, the 19th-century St. Barnabas Church, and Snowshill Manor, a splendid 17th-century house that brims with the collections of Charles Paget Wade, gathered between 1919 and 1956. Outside, an imaginative terraced garden provides an exquisite frame for the house. Note that the house is closed until spring 2005, but the grounds remain open. ⊠ *Off A44 Snowshill* ☎ *01386/852410* ⊕ *www.nationaltrust.org.uk* ✉ *£3.60* ✆ *Apr.–Oct., Wed.–Sun. 11–5:30.*

Broadway

21 *3 mi north of Snowshill Manor, 17 mi northeast of Cheltenham.*

The Cotswold town to end all Cotswold towns, Broadway has become a favorite of day-trippers. William Morris first discovered the delights of this village, and J. M. Barrie, Vaughan Williams, and Edward Elgar soon followed. Today some people avoid Broadway in summer, when it's clogged with cars and buses. Named for its handsome, wide main street, the village includes the renowned Lygon Arms and numerous antiques shops, tea parlors, and boutiques. Step off onto Broadway's back roads and alleys and you'll find any number of honey-color houses and pretty gardens.

Among the attractions of **Broadway Tower Country Park**, on the outskirts of town, is its tower, an 18th-century "folly" built by the sixth earl of Coventry and later used by William Morris as a retreat. Exhibits describe the tower's intriguing past, and the view from the top takes in more than 13 counties. Peaceful countryside surrounds you on the nature trails, picnic grounds, and adventure playground; rare animals and birds are on display, too. ⊠ *Off A44* ☎ *01386/852390* ✉ *Park £3, tower £2.50* ✆ *Apr.–Oct., daily 10:30–5; Nov.–Mar. (tower only), weekends 11–4:30.*

☝ If you're a nostalgia buff or love cuddly toys, you may find the **Broadway Dolls and Bears** irresistible. Here are collected "every bear that ever there was," animated snow, circus, and fairground scenes, and dolls and toys. Check out the shop and hospital. ⊠ *76 High St.* ☎ *01386/858323* ✉ *£2.50* ✆ *Feb.–May, Tues.–Sun. 1–4; June–Dec., Tues.–Sun. 10–5.*

Where to Stay & Eat

★ **£££££** ✕⌕ **Buckland Manor.** As an alternative to the razzmatazz of Broadway, you can splurge at this exceptional hotel 2 mi away in the idyllic hamlet of Buckland. The land was valued at £9 in the 11th-century Domesday Book, and the handsome stone building dates back to Jacobean times. Public areas and guest rooms are plushly comfortable, with pleasant old pictures, fine rugs, and antiques everywhere. The garden is lovely and peaceful. In the baronial and expensive restaurant (jacket and tie required), you choose from a menu of contemporary fare from local sources. ⊠ *Off B4632, Buckland, WR12 7LY* ☎ *01386/852626* 🖷 *01386/853557* ⊕ *www.bucklandmanor.com* ➴ *13 rooms* ⌕ *Restaurant, cable TV, tennis court, pool, croquet, bar; no a/c, no kids under 12* ▤ *AE, DC, MC, V* ⍩ *BP.*

£££££ ✕⌕ **Lygon Arms.** Here you'll find modern luxury in perfect symbiosis with old-fashioned charm. In business since 1532, the inn has a multi-gabled facade and mullioned windows dating back to 1620; inside, look for antiques-bedecked parlors, fireplaces, 18th-century paneling, and rooms that once sheltered Charles I and Oliver Cromwell. Behind the house are more modern (and less expensive) bedrooms and 3 acres of formal gardens. One restaurant, the Great Hall, complete with a minstrel's gallery, focuses on creative adaptations of traditional dishes. ⊠ *High St., WR12 7DU* ☎ *01386/852255 or 0800/7671–7671; 800/637–2869 in U.S.* 🖷 *01386/858611* ⊕ *www.savoy-group.co.uk* 🖪 *65 rooms* ⌂ *2 restaurants, in-room data ports, cable TV, in-room VCRs, tennis court, indoor pool, sauna, spa, steam room, croquet, bar, business services, meeting rooms, helipad, some pets allowed (fee); no a/c in some rooms* 🖃 *AE, DC, MC, V* �🍽⊙ *BP.*

★
££££–£££££

✕🖸 **Dormy House Hotel.** Guest rooms in this converted 17th-century farmhouse overlook the Vale of Evesham from high on the Cotswolds ridge, one of the region's most celebrated vistas. Luxury rules at this establishment, where you can relax by a fireplace or in one of the bars. Traditional pieces and a mixture of brass and carved bedsteads furnish the beamed bedrooms. Noted in the region, the restaurant has a superlative wine list and specializes in contemporary fare such as lemon sole with salmon and chive mousse. The hotel is 2 mi north of Broadway. ⊠ *Willersey Hill, WR12 7LF* ☎ *01386/852711* 🖷 *01386/858636* ⊕ *www.dormyhouse.co.uk* 🖪 *48 rooms* ⌂ *Restaurant, café, putting green, gym, sauna, steam room, croquet, 3 bars, meeting rooms, some pets allowed (fee); no a/c* 🖃 *AE, DC, MC, V* ⊙🍽 *BP.*

££££

🖸 **Mill Hay House.** If the rose garden, trout-filled pond, and pet sheep at this 18th-century Queen Anne house aren't appealing enough, then the stone-flagged floors, leather sofas, and grandfather clocks should satisfy. There are only three beautiful, pastel bedrooms at this B&B, so booking ahead is essential. You'll find it a mile from Broadway on the Snowshill road. ⊠ *Snowshill Rd., WR12 7JS* ☎ *01386/852498* 🖷 *01386/858038* ⊕ *www.broadway-cotswolds.co.uk* 🖪 *2 rooms, 1 suite* ⌂ *In-room safes, kitchenettes, some pets allowed, no-smoking rooms; no a/c, no kids under 12* 🖃 *MC, V* ⊙🍽 *BP.*

Chipping Campden

㉒ *4 mi east of Broadway, 18 mi northeast of Cheltenham.*

Undoubtedly one of the most beautiful towns in the heart of England, Chipping Campden is the Cotswolds in a microcosm—it has St. James, the region's most impressive church, frozen-in-time streets, a silk mill that was once the center of the Guild of Handicrafts, and pleasant (and not touristy) shops. One of the area's most seductive settings unfolds before you as you travel on B4081 through sublimely lovely English countryside to happen upon the town, tucked in a slight valley.

The soaring pinnacled tower of **St. James** (⊠ Church St.), a prime example of a Cotswold wool church (rebuilt in the 15th century), announces the town from a distance; it's worth stepping inside to see the lofty nave. It recalls the old saying, because of the vast numbers of houses of worship in the Cotswolds, "As sure as God's in Gloucestershire." Nearby, on Church Street, is an important row of almshouses dating from King James I's reign. The broad High Street, lined with attractive stone houses and shops, follows a picturesque curve; in the center, on Market Street, is the **Market Hall**, a gabled Jacobean structure built by Sir Baptiste Hycks in 1627 "for the sale of local produce."

In 1902 the Guild of Handicrafts took over the **Silk Mill**, and Arts-and-Crafts evangelist C. R. Ashbee (1863–1942) brought 150 acolytes here from London, including 50 guildsmen, to revive and practice such skills as cabinetmaking and bookbinding. The operation folded in 1920, but the refurbished building houses an exhibition and crafts workshops, including a silversmith, sculptor, and printmaker. ⊠ *Sheep St.* ☎ *Free* ⊘ *Weekdays 9–5, Sat. 9–1.*

Where to Stay & Eat

££££–£££££ ✕🗔 **Charingworth Manor.** Views of the Cotswold countryside are limitless from this 14th-century manor-house hotel a short distance outside town. Mullioned windows and oak beams add appeal to the relaxing sitting room, and bedrooms are individually decorated in English floral fabrics, with antique and period furniture. As a guest, T. S. Eliot used to enjoy walking its 50 acres of grounds. The restaurant (fixed-price menu), with its low-beamed ceilings, is attractive but somewhat expensive, with traditional fare such as pea and ham soup and roast beef and Yorkshire pudding. The hotel is 3 mi east of Chipping Campden. ⊠ *Charingworth, GL55 6NS* ☎ *01386/593555* 🖷 *01386/593353* ⊕ *www.englishrosehotels.com* ⇌ *23 rooms, 3 suites* ⚙ *Restaurant, in-room safes, cable TV, tennis court, indoor pool, sauna, steam room, billiards, croquet, meeting rooms; no a/c* ⊟ *AE, DC, MC, V* ⦿⊙ *BP.*

££ ✕🗔 **Churchill Arms.** This small country pub, a mile southeast of Chipping Campden, makes for an intimate stay. Plain wooden tables and benches, sepia prints, a flagstone floor, and a roaring fire provide the backdrop for excellent food. Daily specials—chicken, ham, and leek pie, and cod with star anise sauce, for example—appear on the blackboard. Upstairs bedrooms aren't large, but are nicely furnished with antiques. ⊠ *Paxford, GL55 6XH* ☎ *01386/594000* 🖷 *01386/594005* ⊕ *www.thechurchillarms.com* ⇌ *4 rooms* ⚙ *Restaurant, in-room data ports, in-room VCRs, no-smoking rooms; no a/c* ⊟ *MC, V* ⦿⊙ *BP.*

££££ 🗔 **Noel Arms Hotel.** Dating to the 14th century, the town's oldest inn was built for foreign wool traders. The Noel Arms, in the heart of Chipping Campden, retains its exposed beams and stonework, even though it has been enlarged. The bedrooms—some dating back to the 14th century—are full of reds and golds and dark oak furniture. ⊠ *High St., GL55 6AT* ☎ *01386/840317* 🖷 *01386/841136* ⊕ *www.cotswold-inns-hotels.co.uk* ⇌ *26 rooms* ⚙ *Restaurant, bar, meeting rooms, some pets allowed; no a/c* ⊟ *AE, DC, MC, V* ⦿⊙ *BP.*

Shopping

For all embroidery needs, head for the **Campden Needlecraft Centre** (⊠ High St. ☎ 01386/840583), one of the leading specialty needlecraft shops in the country. At **D. T. Hart** (⊠ The Silk Mill, Sheep St. ☎ 01386/841100), descendants of one of the original members of the Guild of Handicrafts specialize in making silver items. **Martin Gotrel** (⊠ Camperdene House, High St. ☎ 01386/841360) crafts fine traditional and contemporary jewelry.

Hidcote Manor Gardens

㉓ *4 mi northeast of Chipping Campden, 9 mi south of Stratford-upon-*
Fodor's Choice *Avon.*
★

Laid out around a Cotswold manor house, Hidcote Manor Gardens is arguably the most interesting and attractive large garden in Britain, with correspondingly large crowds at the height of the season. A horticulturist from the United States, Major Lawrence Johnstone, created the garden in 1907 in Arts and Crafts style. Johnstone was an imaginative gardener and widely traveled plantsman who brought back specimens from all over the world. The formal part of the garden is arranged in "rooms" without roofs, separated by hedges, often with fine topiary work and walls. The White Garden was probably the forerunner of the popular white gardens at Sissinghurst and Glyndebourne. ⊠ *Hidcote Bar-*

trim ☎ 01386/438333 ⊕ *www.nationaltrust.org.uk* 🎫 £5.90
🕐 *Apr.–Sept., Mon.–Wed. and weekends; 10:30–6; Oct., Mon.–Wed.
and weekends; 10:30–5; last admission 1 hr before closing.*

Hidcote Manor Gardens borders on the hamlet of **Hidcote Bartrim,** set
in another storybook Cotswold dell. A handful of thatched stone
houses, a duck pond, and a well make up the center of this cul-de-sac;
less than a mile away is the equally idyllic hamlet of Hidcote Boyce,
which has a 17th-century manor, Hidcote House.

Moreton-in-Marsh

㉔ *13 mi south of Hidcote Manor Gardens, 18 mi northeast of Cheltenham, 5 mi north of Stow-on-the-Wold.*

In Moreton-in-Marsh, the houses have been built not around a central
square but along a street wide enough to accommodate a market (every
Tuesday). The village has fine views across the hills. A town landmark
is St. David's Church, which has a lovely tower of honey-gold ashlar.
The town also possesses one of the last remaining curfew towers, dated
1633; curfew dates back to the time of the Norman Conquest, when a
bell was rung to "cover-fire" for the night against any invaders. From
Chipping Campden, take B4081 south, then A44 south and east to reach
Moreton-in-Marsh.

It comes as somewhat of an architectural surprise to see the blue onion
domes and miniature minarets of **Sezincote,** a mellow stone house tucked
into a valley near Moreton-in-Marsh. Created in the early 19th century,
the house and estate were the vision of Sir Charles Cockerell, who made
a fortune in the East India Company. He employed his architect brother
Samuel Pepys Cockerell to "Indianize" the residence, which Samuel did
with a mixture of Hindu and Muslim motifs. Note the peacock-tail arches
surrounding the windows of the first floor. The exotic garden, Hindu
temple folly, and Indian-style bridge have appealed to visitors ever since
the prince regent came to the estate in 1807 (and was inspired to create that Xanadu of Brighton, the Royal Pavilion). If you come in spring,
a glorious display of aconites and snowdrops greets you. Note that children are allowed indoors only at the owners' discretion. ✉ *Off A44*
☎ *01386/700444* 🎫 *House and grounds £5, grounds £3.50* 🕐 *House
May–July and Sept., Thurs. and Fri. 2:30–6; grounds Jan.–Nov., Thurs.
and Fri. and national holidays 2–6 or dusk.*

> off the
> beaten
> path

ROLLRIGHT STONES – A reminder of the ancient civilizations of
Britain can be seen about 8 mi east of Moreton, where this stone circle
occupies a high position on the Wolds. It has none of the grandeur of
Stonehenge and Avebury but is almost as important. Legend gives the
stone groups, dating from before 1500 BC, the names of the King's
Men and the Whispering Knights. ✉ *Off A3400.*

Where to Stay & Eat

★ **££–£££** ✕🛏 **Falkland Arms.** It's worth detouring a few miles for this supremely
appealing pub on the village green at Great Tew (12 mi east of Moreton), where you can still buy snuff and smoke a clay pipe. An impressive collection of mugs and jugs hangs from the beams in the bar, and
a spiral stone staircase leads to the intimate bedrooms, which have
brass bedsteads and snowy white bedcovers. The small restaurant (no
dinner Sunday) chalks up a traditional but creative menu each day. Reservations are essential for both staying and eating here. From Moreton,
take A44 to Chipping Norton, then A361 to B4022. ✉ *Great Tew, OX7
4DB* ☎ *01608/683653* ⊕ *www.falklandarms.org.uk* ⇘ *6 rooms*

� *Restaurant, bar, no-smoking rooms; no a/c, no room phones, no kids under 14* ⊟ *AE, MC, V* ⥄⊟ *BP.*

££££ 🏨 **Manor House Hotel.** Secret passages and a priest's hole testify to the age of this 16th-century building, set back from the main thoroughfare. Wing chairs and chintz-covered sofas and drapes adorn the public rooms, and bedrooms, revealing the original stonework, mix stylish modern furnishings and fabrics with antiques. The restaurant serves traditional English dishes. ⊠ *High St., GL56 0LJ* ☎ *01608/650501* 🖷 *01608/651481* ⊕ *www.cotswold-inns-hotels.co.uk* ⥄ *38 rooms* 🛇 *Restaurant, indoor pool; no a/c* ⊟ *AE, DC, MC, V* ⥄⊟ *BP.*

££–£££ 🏨 **Bell Inn.** The coach house of this 18th-century hostelry now holds spacious guest rooms, still with the original beams, and furnished with period pieces, deep carpets, and comfy sofas. The pub has a walled, flower-filled garden, and in summer you can join in the obscure Cotswold game of Aunt Sally, which involves hitting a moving target with something akin to a rolling pin. ⊠ *High St., GL56 0AE* ☎ *01608/651688* 🖷 *01608/652195* ⊕ *www.bellinncotswold.com* ⥄ *5 rooms* 🛇 *Restaurant, bar, some pets allowed; no a/c, no room phones* ⊟ *MC, V* ⥄⊟ *BP.*

Stow-on-the-Wold

㉕ *5 mi south of Moreton-in-Marsh, 15 mi east of Cheltenham.*

At 800 feet, Stow is the highest, as well as the largest, town in the Cotswolds—"Stow-on-the-Wold, where the wind blows cold" is the age-old saying. Built around a wide square, Stow's imposing golden stone houses have been discreetly converted into a good number of high-quality antiques stores. The Square, as it is known, has a fascinating history. In the 18th century, Daniel Defoe wrote that more than 20,000 sheep could be sold here on a busy day; such was the press of livestock that sheep runs, known as "tures," were used to control the sheep, and these narrow streets still run off the main square. Also look for St. Edward's Church and the Kings Arms Old Posting House, its wide entrance still seeming to wait for the stagecoaches that once stopped here on their way to Cheltenham. As well as being a lure for the antiques hunter, Stow is a convenient base: eight main Cotswolds roads intersect here, but all—happily—bypass the town center.

★ **Chastleton House,** one of the most complete Jacobean properties in the country, opts for a beguilingly lived-in appearance, taking advantage of almost 400 years of furniture and trappings accumulated by the many generations of the single family that owned it until the National Trust took over in 1991. The house was built between 1605 and 1612 for William Jones, a wealthy wool merchant. The house has an appealing authenticity: cobwebs and bric-a-brac are strewn around, wood and pewter are unpolished, upholstery uncleaned. The top floor is a glorious, barrel-vaulted long gallery, and throughout the house you can see elaborate plasterwork and paneling, exquisite glassware, and tapestries. The ornamental gardens include England's first-ever croquet lawn (the rules of croquet were codified here in 1865) and rotund topiaries. Chastleton is 6 mi northeast of Stow, signposted off A436 between Stow and A44. ⊠ *Off A436, Moreton-in-Marsh* ☎ *01494/755585 booking line Tues.–Fri. 10–4; 01494/755560 recorded information* ⊕ *www.nationaltrust.org.uk* 🎫 *£5.60* ⊙ *Apr.–Sept., Wed.–Sat. 1–4; Oct., Wed.–Sat. 1–3; admission is by timed ticket, for which prebooking is advised.*

Where to Stay & Eat

£–££ ✕ **Queen's Head.** An excellent stopping-off spot for lunch, this pub has a courtyard out back, perfect for a summer afternoon. The bench in front, under a climbing rose, makes a relaxing spot for imbibing outdoor refreshment. No food is served Sunday, although you can get a drink. ✉ *The Square* ☎ *01451/830563* ▭ *MC, V* ✆ *No lunch or dinner Sun.*

££–££££ ✕▣ **Royalist Hotel.** Certified as the oldest inn in the country (AD 947), this hostelry is jammed with interesting features—witches' marks on the beams, a tunnel to the church across the road—and the owners have stylishly integrated designer bedrooms and a restaurant. If the fixed-price brasserie-style menu doesn't appeal, opt for pub grub in the adjacent Eagle and Child. ✉ *Digbeth St., GL54 1BN* ☎ *01451/830670* ☎ *01451/ 870048* ⊕ *www.theroyalisthotel.co.uk* ⤴ *12 rooms, 1 suite* ♧ *2 restaurants, in-room data ports, 2 bars, meeting rooms, no-smoking rooms; no a/c* ▭ *AE, MC, V* ✆ *No dinner Sun. and Mon.* ◉⧵ *CP.*

Shopping

Stow-on-the-Wold is the leading center for antiques stores in the Cotswolds, with more than 30 dealers centered around the Square, Sheep Street, and Church Street. **Duncan Baggott Antiques** (✉ Woolcomber House, Sheep St. ☎ 01451/830662) displays fine old English furniture, portrait and landscape paintings, and garden statuary and ornaments. A visit to **Huntington Antiques** (✉ Church St. ☎ 01451/830842) is like a step back into the 16th and 17th centuries, with a stock replete with refectory tables, carved wooded reliefs, and Renaissance furniture. **Roger Lamb Antiques** (✉ The Square ☎ 01451/831371) specializes in objects d'art and small pieces of furniture from the Georgian and Regency periods, with Regency "faux bamboo," tea caddies, and antique needlework the particular fortes.

Bourton-on-the-Water

㉖ *4 mi southwest of Stow-on-the-Wold, 12 mi northeast of Cheltenham.*

Bourton-on-the-Water, off A429 on the eastern edge of the Cotswold Hills, is deservedly famous as a classic Cotswold village. The little River Windrush runs through Bourton, crossed by low stone bridges. This village makes a good touring base, but in summer it can be overcrowded. A stroll through Bourton takes you past stone cottages, many converted to little stores and coffee shops.

☾ An old mill, now the **Cotswold Motor Museum and Toy Collection,** contains more than 30 vintage motor vehicles and a collection of old advertising signs (supposedly the largest in Europe), as well as two caravans (trailers) from the 1920s, ancient bicycles, and children's toys. ✉ *Sherborne St.* ☎ *01451/821255* ▭ *£2.75* ✆ *Mid-Feb.–Oct., daily 10–6.*

☾ The **Model Railway Exhibition** displays more than 40 British and Continental trains running on 500 square feet of scenic layout. There are plenty of trains, models, and toys to buy in the shop. ✉ *Box Bush, High St.* ☎ *01451/820686* ⊕ *www.bourtonmodelrailway.co.uk* ▭ *£1.90* ✆ *Apr.–Sept., daily 11–5:30; Oct.–Mar., weekends 11–5.*

An outdoor working reproduction of Bourton, the **Model Village** was built in 1937 to a scale of one-ninth. ✉ *Old New Inn,* ☎ *01451/820467* ▭ *£2.75* ✆ *Apr.–Oct., daily 9–5:45; Nov.–Mar., daily 10–3:45.*

Where to Stay

£££ ▣ **The Old Manse.** Built in 1748 for the local Baptist pastor, this stone hotel is only steps away from the River Windrush. Bedrooms are on the small side and quite simply furnished, and the restaurant serves traditional English fare. There's a garden at the rear and a heated terrace for chilly evenings. ✉ *Victoria St., GL54 2BX* ☎ *01451/820082* ☎ *01451/*

810381 ⊕ www.oldenglish.co.uk ⇨ 15 rooms ⚘ Restaurant, bar, meeting rooms, some pets allowed (fee); no a/c ⊟ MC, V ⚞⚟ BP.

£   🖼 **Rooftrees.** If you go in for frills, flounces, and leprechauns, then this old Cotswold stone house, a 10-minute walk from the center of the village, is the place for you. Ornaments abound within, and hanging baskets and garden gnomes decorate the outside. The amiable Irish hosts dish up substantial breakfasts. ⊠ Rissington Rd., GL54 2DX ☎ 01451/821943 🖨 01451/810614 ⇨ 3 rooms ⚘ No a/c, no room phones, no smoking ⊟ MC, V ⚞⚟ BP.

Shopping

The **Cotswold Perfumery** carries many perfumes that are manufactured here. While deciding what to buy, visit the Exhibition of Perfumery and the Perfumed Garden. Perfume bottles and jewelry are also on sale. ⊠ Victoria St. ☎ 01451/820698 🎟 Exhibition £2 ⊙ Mon.–Sat. 9:30–5, Sun. 10:30–5.

Lower & Upper Slaughter

27   2 mi north of Bourton-on-the-Water, 15 mi east of Cheltenham.

Fodor'sChoice
★

To see the quieter, more typical Cotswold villages, seek out the evocatively named Lower Slaughter and Upper Slaughter (the names have nothing to do with mass murder, but come from the Saxon word *sloh*, which means "a marshy place"). Lower Slaughter is one of the "water villages," with Slaughter Brook running down the center road of the town. Little stone footbridges cross the brook, and the town's resident gaggle of geese can often be seen paddling through the sparkling water. Connecting the two Slaughters is Warden's Way, a mile-long pathway that begins in Upper Slaughter at the town center parking lot. Along the way, you'll pass stone houses, green meadows, ancient trees, and a 19th-century corn mill with a waterwheel and brick chimney. Warden's Way continues south to Bourton-on-the-Water. Lower and Upper Swell are two other quiet towns to explore in the area.

Where to Stay & Eat

£££££   ✕🖼 **Washbourne Court.** This fine 17th-century stone building, standing amid 4 acres of pretty grounds beside the River Wye, has flagstone floors, beams, and open fires. The bedrooms in the main building have a deliberate country feel to them, whereas rooms in the converted barn and cottages are more modern. Choices in the restaurant (fixed-price menu) might include Cotswold lamb in an herb crust or Hereford duck breast with braised red cabbage. ⊠ Lower Slaughter, GL54 2HS ☎ 01451/822143 🖨 01451/821045 ⊕ www.washbournecourt.co.uk ⇨ 27 rooms, 4 suites ⚘ Restaurant, tennis court; no a/c ⊟ AE, DC, MC, V ⚞⚟ BP.

££££–£££££   ✕🖼 **Lords of the Manor Hotel.** A fishing stream threads the rolling fields that surround this rambling 17th-century manor house with Victorian additions. It offers comfort and a warm welcome in a quintessential Cotswold village, with a choice of bedrooms in the main house or more modern ones in the converted granary and barn. Country-house chintz and antiques set the style throughout, including in the acclaimed restaurant, which has a creative British-French menu that might list ravioli of quail or a slow-roasted fillet of Angus beef with horseradish mash. ⊠ Upper Slaughter, GL54 2JD ☎ 01451/820243; 800/872–4564 in U.S. 🖨 01451/820696 ⊕ www.lordsofthemanor.com ⇨ 27 rooms ⚘ Restaurant, fishing, croquet, bar, business services, meeting rooms; no a/c ⊟ AE, DC, MC, V ⚞⚟ BP.

Northleach

28 *7 mi southwest of Lower and Upper Slaughter, 14 mi southeast of Cheltenham.*

Just off the Fosse Way (and fortunately bypassed by the busy A40), Northleach has remained one of the least spoiled of Cotswold towns. Pretty cottages, many with traditional stone-tile roofs, line the streets that converge on the spacious central square. By the 13th century, Northleach had acquired substantial wealth thanks to the wool trade—the local breed of sheep, Cotswold Lion, became the largest in the country, and their fleeces were exported to Flemish weaving towns. The 15th-century church of **St. Peter and St. Paul,** with its soaring slender pillars and clerestory windows, contains notable memorial brasses, monuments to the merchants who endowed the church; each merchant has a wool sack and sheep at his feet. ✉ *Mill End* ☎ *01451/860314* 🎫 *Free, donations accepted* ⏲ *Apr.–Oct., daily 8–6; Nov.–Mar., daily 8–dusk.*

At **Keith Harding's World of Mechanical Music,** the diverting tour explores pianolas, music boxes, and other mechanical instruments from times past, which you can hear played. You'll even listen to the maestros Grieg, Paderewski, Rachmaninoff, and Gershwin themselves on piano rolls. The shop stocks antique and modern music boxes and more. ✉ *The Oak House, High St.* ☎ *01451/860181* 🌐 *www.mechanicalmusic.co.uk* 🎫 *£5* ⏲ *Daily 10–6; last tour at 5.*

Where to Stay & Eat

££ ✕🏨 **Wheatsheaf Inn.** This elegantly remodeled traditional pub has light and stylish rooms in mainly neutral tones, as well as a highly regarded restaurant. On the dinner menu you might find red snapper fillets or chicken and veal roulade, and the wide choice of breakfasts includes smoked kippers and local yogurts. The staff is youthful and friendly. ✉ *West End, GL54 3EZ* ☎ *01451/860244* 📠 *01451/861037* 🛏 *8 rooms* 👍 *Restaurant, some pets allowed; no a/c* 💳 *MC, V* 🍽 *BP.*

Burford

29 *9 mi east of Northleach, 18 mi north of Swindon, 18 mi west of Oxford.*

Burford's broad main street leads steeply down to a narrow bridge across the River Windrush. The village served as a stagecoach stop for centuries and has many historic inns; it's now a popular coach party stop. Hidden away at the end of a lane at the bottom of High Street is the splendid parish church of **St. John,** its interior a warren of arches, chapels, and shrines. The church was remodeled in the 15th century from Norman beginnings. Among the many monuments is one dedicated to Henry VIII's barber, Edmund Harman, that shows four Amazonian Indians, said to be the first depiction of native people from the Americas in Britain. Look out also for the elaborate Tanfield monument and its poignant widow's epitaph. ✉ *Church Green* ☎ *01993/822275* 🎫 *Free, donations accepted* ⏲ *Apr.–Oct., daily 9–5; Nov.–Mar., daily 9–4.*

Where to Stay & Eat

££££–£££££ ✕🏨 **Bay Tree.** This atmospheric inn, set away from Burford's bustle, occupies a 16th-century stone house visited in its prime by both Elizabeth I and James I. Flagstones, beams, and antiques enhance the public areas, and cheerful print and floral fabrics decorate the bedrooms; try for a room in the main house. The restaurant overlooks the rose and herb garden and serves such dishes as liver with haggis mashed potatoes. Among the waist-enhancing desserts is lemon cheesecake with white chocolate sauce. ⊠ *Sheep St., OX18 4LW* ☎ *01993/822791* 📠 *01993/823008* ⊕*www.cotswold-inns-hotels.co.uk* ⇌*21 rooms* ⚘ *Restaurant, bar, meeting rooms; no a/c* ⊟ *AE, DC, MC, V* �⎮ *BP.*

£££ ✕🔲 **The Angel.** Dishes you might see at the farmhouse-style tables of this informal brasserie (closed Sunday and Monday) in a 16th-century former coaching inn include bream with warm potato salad and saffron sauce and venison with caramel peaches. Upstairs, the delightful guest rooms are furnished in a choice of Indian style in deep reds and oranges, French with wooden sleigh bed, or a cool blue contemporary Italian look. ⊠ *14 Witney St., OX18 4SN* ☎ *01993/822714* 📠 *01993/822069* ⊕*www.theangel-uk.com* ⇌*3 rooms* ⚘ *Restaurant; no a/c, no kids under 9* ⊟ *MC, V* ☉ *Closed last 2 wks of Jan. and 1st wk of Feb.* aO⎮ *BP.*

Bibury

③⓪ *10 mi southwest of Burford, 6 mi northeast of Cirencester, 15 mi north of Swindon.*

The tiny town of Bibury, on the B4425, sits idyllically beside the little River Coln; it was famed Arts and Crafts artist William Morris's choice for Britain's most beautiful village. Fine old cottages, a river meadow, and the church of St. Mary's are some of the delights here. **Arlington Row** is a famously pretty stone group of 17th-century weavers' cottages. On a site recorded in the 11th-century Domesday Book stands **Arlington Mill**, a huge 17th-century working corn mill that contains examples of agricultural implements and machinery from the Victorian era, as well as country exhibits. ☎ *01285/740368* 🎫 *£2* ☉ *Daily 10–6.*

Where to Stay & Eat

£££££ ✕🔲 **Swan Hotel.** Chandeliers and displays of plates and glassware adorn this mid-17th-century coaching inn on the banks of the River Coln. The guest rooms, all different though most are traditional in style, come with splendid modern bathrooms—Room 3's is spectacular in black and white. The Signet restaurant, with heavily swagged drapes and an intricate plaster ceiling, offers such dishes as poached free-range chicken breast, as well as a selection of unusual cheeses to round off your meal. ⊠*Bibury, GL7 5NW* ☎*01285/740695; 800/323–5463 in U.S.* 📠*01285/ 740473* ⊕ *www.swanhotel.co.uk* ⇌ *20 rooms* ⚘ *2 restaurants, some in-room data ports, some in-room hot tubs, fishing, meeting rooms, no-smoking rooms; no a/c* ⊟ *AE, DC, MC, V* aO⎮ *BP.*

££££–£££££ ✕🔲 **New Inn.** A hop-bedecked bar leads you to the restaurant in this ancient coaching inn, 2 mi southeast of Bibury in an attractive village. The fixed-price menu changes three times weekly and might include wild mushroom tart or fillet of plaice with brown shrimp and buttered spinach. The pretty bedrooms are of the floral wallpaper and chintz variety. On weekends dinner is included in the price of the stay. ⊠ *Coln St. Aldwyns, GL7 5AN* ☎ *01285/750651* 📠 *01285/750657* ⊕ *www. new-inn.co.uk* ⇌ *11 rooms* ⚘ *2 restaurants, bar, meeting rooms, some pets allowed (fee); no a/c, no kids under 10* ⊟ *AE, MC, V* aO⎮ *BP.*

Chedworth Roman Villa

★ ③① *6 mi northwest of Bibury, 9 mi north of Cirencester, 10 mi southeast of Cheltenham.*

One of the largest and best-preserved Roman villas in England sits in a wooded valley on the eastern fringe of the Cotswolds. Thirty-two rooms, including two complete bath suites, have been identified. The visitor center and museum give a fine picture of Roman life in Britain. From Bibury, go across A429 to Yanworth and Chedworth, where you will pick up the signs; the villa is also signposted from A40. ⊠ *Yanworth* ☎ *01242/890256* ⊕ *www.nationaltrust.org.uk* ⊠ *£3.90* ☉ *Apr.–late Oct., Tues.–Sun. and national holidays 10–5; Mar. and late Oct.–mid-Nov., Tues.–Sun. 11–4.*

Cirencester

32 *9 mi south of Chedworth, 14 mi southeast of Cheltenham.*

Cirencester (pronounced sirensester) has been a hub of the Cotswolds since Roman times, when it was called Corinium and was second only to London in importance. It lay at the intersection of two major Roman roads, the Fosse Way and Ermin Street (today A429 and A417). In the Middle Ages, the town grew rich on wool, which funded its 15th-century parish church. Today this lovely old market town preserves many mellow stone buildings dating mainly from the 17th and 18th centuries, and bow-fronted shops that still have one foot in the past.

At the top of Market Place is the magnificent Gothic parish church of **St. John the Baptist,** known as the cathedral of the "woolgothic" style. Its elaborate three-tiered, three-bayed south porch, the largest in England, once served as the town hall. The chantry chapels and many coats of arms bear witness to the importance of the wool merchants, benefactors of the church. A rare example of a 15th-century wineglass pulpit sits in the nave. ⊠ *Market Pl.* ☎ *01285/659317* ⊠ *Free, donations accepted* ☉ *Mon.–Sat. 9:30–4:45, Sun. 2:15–5:45.*

Not much of the Roman town remains visible, but the **Corinium Museum** displays an outstanding collection of Roman artifacts, including mosaic pavements, as well as full-scale reconstructions of local Roman interiors. Also worth lingering over are the Anglo-Saxon and 18th-century galleries. The museum is closed until spring 2004; call ahead for opening times. ⊠ *Park St.* ☎ *01285/655611* ⊕ *www.cotswold.gov.uk.*

Where to Stay & Eat

£££ ✕🛏 **Wild Duck Inn.** This family-run Elizabethan inn 3 mi south of Cirencester has richly decorated guest rooms in antique style. The mellow, deep red dining room has an abundance of beams and oil portraits, and the menu is strong on fresh fish and such meat dishes as baked chicken in a creamy oregano sauce. Make room reservations in advance, as the inn is very popular. ⊠ *Ewen, GL7 6BY* ☎ *01285/770310* 🖷 *01285/ 770924* ⊕ *www.thewildduckinn.co.uk* 🛏 *11 rooms* ↻ *Restaurant; no a/c* ⊟ *AE, MC, V* ⫿◯⫿ *CP.*

£ 🛏 **Ivy House.** Ivy clings to this stone Victorian house, close to the center of town, that offers excellent value and friendly accommodation. The simple bedrooms have pastel colors and pine furniture. Cyclists and walkers are welcomed. ⊠ *2 Victoria Rd., GL7 1EN* ☎ *01285/656626* ⊕ *www.ivyhousecotswolds.com* 🛏 *4 rooms* ↻ *No a/c, no room phones, no smoking* ⊟ *MC, V* ⫿◯⫿ *BP.*

Nightlife & the Arts

The **Brewery Arts Centre** (⊠ Brewery Ct. ☎ 01285/657181; 01285/ 655522 box office) has studios for more than a dozen artists and craftspeople and a shop that sells their work. The center also includes a theater, exhibition space, and a café.

Sports & the Outdoors

You can indulge in water sports from waterskiing to windsurfing at the **Cotswold Water Park,** 3 mi south of Cirencester. This group of 130 lakes covers 30 square mi and has multiple entrances. There's swimming June–September; the park also draws wildlife enthusiasts, walkers, cyclists, and horseback riders. You pay individual charges for the activities April–October. ⊠ *Keynes Country Park, off B4696, Shorncote* ☎ *01285/861459* ⊕ *www.waterpark.org* ⊡ *£6 parking Apr.–Oct., £1 parking Nov.–Mar.* ⊘ *Daily 9 AM–9 PM.*

Shopping

The **Corn Hall** (⊠ Market Pl.) is the venue for a Friday antiques market and a crafts market on Saturday (unless it's the fifth Saturday in the month). Every Monday and Friday, Cirencester's central **Market Place** is packed with stalls selling a motley assortment of goods, mainly household items but some local produce and craft work, too. **Rankine Taylor Antiques** (⊠ 34 Dollar St. ☎ 01285/652529) concentrates on 17th- and 18th-century furniture, silver, pottery, and glass.

Painswick

33 *16 mi northwest of Cirencester, 8 mi southwest of Cheltenham, 5 mi south of Gloucester.*

This old Cotswold wool town has become a chocolate-box picture of quaintness, attracting plenty of day-trippers and coach parties. But come during the week and you can discover the place in relative tranquility. The huddled gray stone houses and inns date from as early as the 14th century and include a notable group from the Georgian era. The churchyard is renowned for its 99 yew trees (legend has it that the devil prevents the 100th from growing) planted in 1792. Painswick's annual Clypping Ceremony, on the first Sunday after September 19, has nothing to do with topiary—the name derives from the Anglo-Saxon word "clyppan," meaning "encircle." Children with garlands make a ring around the church as traditional hymns are sung. Another good time to visit is the town's Victorian Market Day in early July.

The **Painswick Rococo Garden,** ½ mi north of town, has survived from the short but exuberant rococo period of English garden design (1720–60). After 50 years in its original form, the 6-acre garden became overgrown with woodland, and its central section became a vegetable plot. Beginning in 1984, after the rediscovery of a 1748 painting of the garden by Thomas Robins, the garden was restored. Now you can view the garden's original architectural structures and asymmetrical vistas. There's also a restaurant and a gift shop. ⊠ *B4073* ☎ *01452/813204* ⊕ *www. rococogarden.co.uk* ⊡ *£3.60* ⊘ *Mid-Jan.–Oct., daily 11–5.*

Where to Stay & Eat

££££–£££££ ✕⊡ **Painswick Hotel.** Unstuffy and friendly, this family-run hotel occupies a Georgian house behind Painswick's church. Beautiful fabrics and deep, vibrant colors enhance the individually designed rooms, some of which have antique four-posters and balconies. The menu blends the traditional with the more exotic—Cotswold lamb served with pease pudding or in a samosa with honey and rosemary, for example. ⊠ *Kemps La., GL6 6YB* ☎ *01452/812160* ⊟ *01452/814059* ⊕ *www. painswickhotel.com* ⇨ *19 rooms* ⚫ *Restaurant, meeting rooms; no a/ c* ⊟ *AE, MC, V* ⦿ *BP.*

££–£££ ✕⊡ **Cardynham House.** The Cotswolds are really about the art of liv-
Fodor's Choice ing, as this 16th-century former wool merchant's house demonstrates.
★ The stylish retreat, which retains its beamed ceilings, Jacobean staircase, and Elizabethan fireplace, has four-poster beds in many rooms and creative theme rooms such as the Medieval Garden, Dovecote, or Arabian Nights. One far more expensive room has a private pool. Downstairs, the March Hare dining room (closed Sunday and Monday) serves delicious Thai food (fixed-price menu), such as red snapper curry with co-

conut and lime leaves. ⊠ *The Cross, GL6 6XX* ☏ *01452/814006;
01452/813452 restaurant* 🖶 *01452/812321* ⊕ *www.cardynham.co.uk*
🛏 *9 rooms* ⚠ *Restaurant; no a/c* ⊟ *AE, MC, V* ⦿ *BP.*

Stroud

34 *3 mi south of Painswick, 12 mi west of Cirencester.*

Very much a contrast to the well-heeled, antiques-infused settlements of the Cotswolds, Stroud is a hardworking town with little time for pretensions. For centuries the wool trade dominated the economy. At one time 150 mills operated along the River Frome (pronounced froom), and the town was particularly associated with the famous Stroudwater Scarlet, used for military uniforms. Now the one mill that remains produces the green baize cloth used on snooker tables and felt for tennis balls. Stroud has become noted for its support of ecological issues.

★ ☾ Stroud's main attraction is the excellent **Museum in the Park,** which explores the history of the town and the surrounding countryside. Among the theme exhibits are "Clean, Fit, and Tidy" and "Fire and Theft"; objects displayed include medieval watering cans, 18th-century paintings showing the hanging out of Stroudwater Scarlet cloth on the hillside, eelskin gaiters from the 19th century, and the world's first lawn mower (1830). A fascinating video describes farming in the 1940s. The museum is ½ mi from the town center. ⊠ *Stratford Park, junction of A4171 and A46* ☏ *01453/763394* ⊕ *www.stroud.gov.uk* 🎫 *Free* ⦿ *Apr.–Sept., Tues.–Fri. 10–5, weekends 11–5; Oct.–Mar., Tues.–Fri. 10–4, weekends 11–4:30.*

Where to Eat

£ ✕ **Mills Café.** This busy café, tucked away in a courtyard off the High Street in the center of town, is the best spot for baguettes, homemade soups, and scrumptious cakes, as well as more substantial lunches. ⊠ *Withey's Yard* ☏ *01453/752222* ⊟ *MC, V* ⦿ *Closed Sun. No dinner.*

Owlpen

★ **35** *6 mi southwest of Stroud, 13 mi west of Cirencester.*

Prince Charles described the beauty spot of Owlpen, an off-the-beaten-path hamlet, as "the epitome of the English village." First settled in Saxon days as Olla's Pen (meaning "valley"), the village centers on a church, a Tudor manor house, and pearl-gray stone cottages, all set against a picturesque hillside. A graceful grouping of tithe barns, garden buildings, and grist mills softens the seignorial bearing of the manor house.

The triple-gabled stone **Owlpen Manor** was built between 1450 and 1616, but was restored in the 1920s by local Arts and Crafts artisans, who also created some of the furnishings. Today Nicholas and Karin Mander live here with their family. Inside are oak chests fashioned by William Morris, family portraits, Georgian doorcases, painted cloths from the Tudor and Stuart eras, and Queen Margaret's Room, said to be haunted by the spirit of Queen Margaret of Anjou, wife of Henry VI, who visited here during the Wars of the Roses. You can also explore the terraced garden with its yew topiary, the envy of gardening masters such as Gertrude Jekyll. The Cyder Press restaurant opens at noon. Several cottages have been converted into guest accommodations, available for weekends or longer rentals. ⊠ *Off B4066, near Uley* ☏ *01453/860261* ⊕ *www.owlpen.com* 🎫 *£4.80, gardens only £2.80* ⦿ *Apr.–Sept., Tues.–Sun. and national holidays 2–5.*

Tetbury

36 *6 mi southeast of Owlpen, 8 mi southwest of Cirencester, 12 mi south of Painswick.*

With Prince Charles and Princess Anne both nearby neighbors, Tetbury claims right royal connections. Indeed, the soaring spire of the church that presides over this lovely Elizabethan market town is within sight of Highgrove House, the Prince of Wales's abode. At the center of the village, look for the eye-catching, white-painted stone **Market House** on Market Square, dating from 1655 and built up on rows of Tuscan pillars. The antiques market is held here on Wednesday. The **Church of St. Mary** (⊠ Church St. ☎ 01666/502333), in 18th-century Gothic style, has a spacious galleried interior with pews.

need a break? **Tetbury Gallery and Tea Room** (⊠ 18 Market Pl. ☎ 01666/503412) is an intimate place for coffee, light lunches, and cream teas. Be sure to try the delicious sweet or savory scones. The small walled garden is open in summer.

Tall gate piers and spreading trees frame the family-owned **Chavenage,** a gray Cotswold-stone Elizabethan manor house. The tour includes a room, full of fine tapestries, where Cromwell lodged during the Civil War, and a main hall with minstrels' gallery. ✚ *2 mi northwest of Tetbury between B4104 and A4135* ☎ *01666/502329* ⊕ *www.chavenage. com* 🖼 *£5* ☉ *May–Sept., Thurs., Sun., and national holidays 2–5.*

One of the last English country houses to be constructed using traditional methods and materials, **Rodmarton Manor** (built 1909–29) is furnished with specially commissioned pieces in the Arts and Crafts style. The lovely gardens—wild, winter, sunken, and white—are divided into "rooms" bounded by hedges of holly, beech, and yew. The manor is 5 mi northeast of Tetbury. ⊠ *Off A433, Rodmarton* ☎ *01285/841253* ⊕ *www. rodmarton-manor.co.uk* 🖼 *£6, garden only £3* ☉ *May–Aug., Wed., Sat., and national holidays 2–5; garden June and July, Mon. 11–5.*

★ The 600-acre **Westonbirt Arboretum,** 3 mi southwest of Tetbury, contains one of the most extensive collections of trees and shrubs in Europe. The best times to come for color are in late spring when the rhododendrons, azaleas, and magnolias are blooming and in fall when the maples come into their own. ⊠ *Off A433* ☎ *01666/880220* ⊕ *www.forestry.gov.uk* 🖼 *£5* ☉ *Daily 10–8 or dusk.*

Where to Stay & Eat

ff–fff ✕ **Trouble House.** Simple yet tasty dishes are created at this white-washed pub. Your order from the bar might be five-hour leg of lamb with bean and tomato stew, or sea bass with creamed spinach. The pub is 2 mi northeast of Tetbury on the Cirencester road. ⊠ *A433* ☎ *01666/502206* ▤ *AE, MC, V* ☉ *Closed Mon.*

fffff ✕▦ **Calcot Manor.** Comfortable country-house furnishings with lots of greens and burgundies fill the main house and converted sandstone barns and stables of this family-friendly establishment. Guest rooms are airy and spacious; family suites have bunk beds in a separate room and refrigerators. The more formal conservatory restaurant prepares dishes such as roast rack of Cotswold lamb with a garlic and parsley crust, and the Gumstool provides farmhouse-style fare; dinner is included in the price on weekends. The hotel is 3 mi west of town. ⊠ *A4135, GL8 8YJ* ☎ *01666/890391* 🖷 *01666/890394* ⊕ *www.calcotmanor.co.uk* ⇆ *24 rooms, 4 suites* ⚐ *2 restaurants, tennis court, pool, gym, hair salon, spa, croquet, 2 bars, meeting rooms; no a/c* ▤ *AE, DC, MC, V* ⭐ *BP.*

Shopping

Many of Tetbury's more than 20 antiques shops line Long Street. You're bound to find something from the 40-odd dealers at the **Antiques Emporium** (⊠ Old Chapel, Long St. ☎ 01666/505281), a cornucopia of treasures from kitchenware to miniatures, jewelry, and glass. **Dolphin Antiques** (⊠ 48 Long St. ☎ 01666/504242) specializes in porcelain, including Minton and Royal Worcester. **Fowler and Bateson** (⊠ 51a Long St. ☎ 01666/505083) displays decorative wares and some furniture.

GLOUCESTER TO THE FOREST OF DEAN

West of the Cotswolds a rather urbanized axis connects Gloucester with Cheltenham. Despite their proximity on either side of the M5 motorway, the towns are very different; the down-to-earth Gloucester, built around docks connected to the River Severn, contrasts with the gentrified spa town of Cheltenham. North of Gloucester lies the riverside town of Tewkesbury with its imposing abbey; to the south, easily accessible from M5, stands battlemented Berkeley Castle. Southwest of Gloucester, the low-lying Forest of Dean (officially the Royal Forest of Dean), once a private hunting ground of kings, is now a recreation area for the public, with some of the most beautiful woodlands in the country.

Gloucester

③⑦ *13 mi southwest of Cheltenham, 56 mi south of Birmingham, 105 mi west of London.*

Although much of the ancient heritage of this county seat has been lost to nondescript modern stores and offices, Gloucester has a number of worthwhile sights, most notably its cathedral. The historic **Gloucester Docks**, a short walk from the cathedral along the canal, still function but now cater mainly to pleasure craft. The vast Victorian warehouses have been restored, and shops and cafés added, reviving the area. One warehouse is now the Antiques Centre, and others hold good museums.

★ The magnificent **Gloucester Cathedral**, with its soaring, elegant exterior, was originally a Norman abbey church, consecrated in 1100. Reflecting various periods, the cathedral mirrors perfectly the slow growth of ecclesiastical taste and the development of the Perpendicular style. The interior has largely been spared the sterilizing attentions of modern architects and is almost completely Norman, with the massive pillars of the nave left untouched since their completion. The fan-vaulted roof of the 14th-century cloisters is the finest in Europe, and the cloisters enclose a peaceful garden (used in the filming of *Harry Potter and the Sorcerer's Stone* for some Hogwarts School scenes). The Whispering Gallery has a permanent exhibition about the history of the cathedral, and tours of the tower (269 steps up and down) are available. ⊠ *Westgate St.* ☎ *01452/528095* ⊕ *www.gloucestercathedral.uk.com* ⊠ *Requested donation £2.50, Whispering Gallery £1.50, tours £2.50* ⊙ *Daily 8–6, except during services and special events; tower tours Apr.–Oct., Wed.–Sat. and national holidays at 2:30.*

The **Gloucester Folk Museum,** opposite the cathedral, fills a row of fine Tudor and Jacobean half-timber houses. Illustrating the history of Gloucester and the surrounding areas, the museum includes exhibits on local crafts and domestic life. ⊠ *99–103 Westgate St.* ☎ *01452/526467* ⊕ *www.gloucester.gov.uk* ⊠ *£2* ⊙ *Tues.–Sat. 10–5.*

The **National Waterways Museum,** in a converted Victorian warehouse, displays examples of canal houseboats, including gaily painted "canal

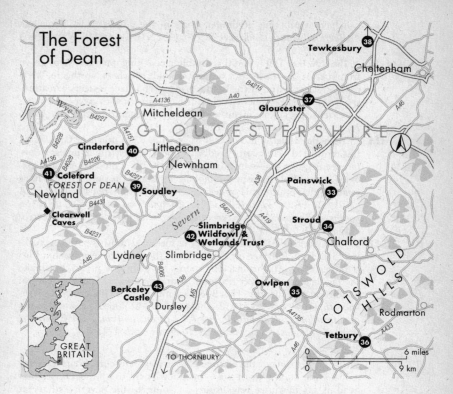

The Forest
of Dean

Tewkesbury **38**

Cheltenham

A4136 Mitcheldean B4215 A40 Gloucester **37** A46

GLOUCESTERSHIRE

Cinderford **40** Littledean

41 Coleford
FOREST OF DEAN **39** Soudley
Newland

◆ Clearwell
Caves

Lydney

Slimbridge

Berkeley
Castle **43**

Dursley

TO THORNBURY

Painswick **33**

Stroud **34**

Chalford

Owlpen **35**

Rodmarton

Tetbury **36**

COTSWOLD HILLS

Slimbridge
Wildfowl &
Wetlands Trust **42**

GREAT
BRITAIN

6 miles
9 km

ware"—ornaments and utensils found on barges. Exhibits interpret the
role of canals in the 18th and 19th centuries, and you can try your foot
at "walking the wall"—the boatmen's way of propelling barges through
tunnels with their feet. Walking tours around the Gloucester Docks start
at the museum every Sunday in August at 2:30. ✉ *Llanthony Warehouse,
Llanthony Rd., Gloucester Docks* ☎ *01452/318054* ⊕ *www.nwm.org.
uk* ✍ *£5* ✆ *Daily 10–5.*

The **Soldiers of Gloucestershire Museum** examines the lives and service of
Gloucestershire soldiers, and the effect of military service on their wives
and families. All the accoutrements of military life since 1694 are here—
medals, uniforms, and souvenirs—as well as a taped sound track of firing from World War I trenches. ✉ *Gloucester Docks, Commercial Rd.*
☎ *01452/522682* ⊕ *www.glosters.org.uk* ✍ *£4.25* ✆ *June–Sept., daily
10–5; Oct.–May, Tues.–Sun. and national holidays 10–5.*

A Georgian mansion holds **Nature in Art**, a museum dedicated to works
of art inspired by nature. Exhibits are mainly contemporary, including
selections by Picasso, Henry Moore, and the wildlife artist David Shepherd, but you'll also come across a Byzantine mosaic and 19th-century
Asian ivory. From February through November you can watch artists
at work. The museum is 2 mi north of Gloucester. ✉ *Wallsworth Hall,
A38, Twigworth* ☎ *01452/731422* ⊕ *www.nature-in-art.org.uk* ✍ *£3.60*
✆ *Tues.–Sun. and national holidays 10–5.*

Where to Stay & Eat

£££–££££ ✕ **Bearland Restaurant.** An informal, brick-vaulted room in the basement
of an 18th-century building in the center of town is the setting for imaginative Mediterranean-influenced dishes such as grilled polenta with wild
mushrooms, or chicken breast with sesame seeds and spring onions. You

can have a relaxing predinner drink in the conservatory wine bar. ⊠ *Bearland House Longsmith St.* ☎ *01452/419966* ▭ *MC, V* ☉ *Closed Sun. and Mon.*

£–££ ✕ **The New Inn.** You'll find this rambling coaching inn a few steps down from the Cross—the historic heart of the old city where Northgate, Westgate, Southgate, and Eastgate streets meet. The place is steeped in atmosphere, not least its galleried courtyard, overgrown with creepers. There's an extensive carvery menu and plenty of vegetarian choices. ⊠ *16 Northgate St.* ☎ *01452/522177* ▭ *MC, V.*

£££ 🏨 **Hatherley Hotel.** On 37 acres of grounds 2 mi north of Gloucester, this renovated 17th-century redbrick house is fairly quiet, unless a conference is going on—which happens frequently. Guest rooms are spacious and restful, furnished in modern style, but the public rooms have retained their beams and low ceilings. ⊠ *Down Hatherley La., GL2 9QA* ☎ *01452/730217* 🖷 *01452/731032* ⊕ *www.hotel-selection.co.uk* ⤶ *56 rooms* ⌂ *Restaurant, gym, croquet, bar, meeting rooms, helipad; no a/c* ▭ *AE, DC, MC, V* ⦿❙ *BP.*

£–££ 🏨 **Ashleworth Court.** Built of stone, this medieval house is part of a working farm tranquilly set on the banks of the River Severn, with a bird blind close by. All the spacious rooms have antique pieces, but make the Jacobean four-poster bedroom your first choice. There are several good food pubs nearby. This B&B is 5 mi north of Gloucester. ⊠ *Ashleworth, GL19 4JA* ☎ *01452/700241* 🖷 *01452/700411* ⊕ *http://members.farmline.com/chamberlayne* ⤶ *3 rooms without bath* ⌂ *No a/c, no room phones, no smoking* ▭ *No credit cards* ⦿❙ *BP.*

The Outdoors

From the pier outside the National Waterways Museum, boats leave for a 45-minute boat tour of the Gloucester Docks or all-day cruises that head as far north as Tewkesbury or south to the Severn Estuary at Sharpness. Tours take place between Easter and October: contact the **National Waterways Museum** (☎ 01452/318054) for dates and prices.

Shopping

The locals say it's best to look in Cheltenham and buy in Gloucester, where prices are lower. The more than 100 dealers in the **Antiques Centre** (⊠ 1 Severn Rd. ☎ 01452/529716) offer some good buys on items—clocks, silver, china, military collectibles, and more—in a five-floor Victorian warehouse by the Gloucester Docks. The **Beatrix Potter Gift Shop** (⊠ 9 College Ct. ☎ 01452/422856), next to the Cathedral Gate, is the house of the tailor in Potter's story *The Tailor of Gloucester*. It also has a small museum.

Tewkesbury

38 *12 mi northeast of Gloucester.*

Tewkesbury is an ancient town of black-and-white half-timber buildings, as well as some fine Georgian ones, on the River Avon. The stonework in the Norman **Tewkesbury Abbey** has much in common with that of Gloucester Cathedral, but this church was built in the Romanesque (12th-century) and Decorated Gothic (14th-century) styles. Its exterior makes an impressive sight, with the largest Norman tower in the world—148 feet high and 46 feet square—and the 65-foot-high arch of the west front. Fourteen stout Norman pillars and myriad gilded bosses on the roof of the nave and choir (best viewed through a mirror on wheels) grace the beautifully kept interior. ⊠ *Church St.* ☎ *01684/ 850959* ⊕ *www.tewkesburyabbey.org.uk* 🖾 *Requested donation £2, tours £2.50* ☉ *Daily 7:30–5:30; tours Apr.–Oct., daily at 11 and 2:15.*

Where to Stay

£££–££££ 🖼 **Royal Hop Pole.** One of the most famous old English inns, the half-timber Hop Pole is mentioned in Charles Dickens's *Pickwick Papers*. The rooms at the rear have wood beams and views of the pretty gardens running down to the river, where there is private mooring for boats. ⊠ *Church St., GL20 5RT* ☎ *0845/602–6787 or 01684/293236* 🖨 *01684/296680* ⊕ *www.regalhotels.co.uk* ↩ *29 rooms* ᠔ *Restaurant, bar, meeting rooms, some pets allowed; no a/c* ⊟ *AE, DC, MC, V.*

££ 🖼 **Abbey Antiques B&B.** If you have yearned to wake up in an antiques shop, this may be the nearest you'll get. This three-story Georgian town house, just across from the abbey, has two gorgeously furnished, antiques-filled rooms above the Aladdin's cave of a shop and one apartment on the top floor. Wooden floorboards, patchwork quilts, and fresh flowers in the house (and free-range hens in the garden) make for a fun, informal stay. ⊠ *61 Church St., GL20 5RZ* ☎☎ *01684/298145* ⊕ *www.simplybedandbreakfast.com* ↩ *2 rooms, 1 apartment* ᠔ *No a/c, no room phones* ⊟ *No credit cards* ⏵ *BP.*

Soudley

➌➒ *27 mi southwest of Tewkesbury, 15 mi west of Gloucester.*

★ Soudley has a museum that provides a useful introduction to the surrounding forest. The ancient **Forest of Dean** (⊕ www.forestofdean.gov.uk) covers much of the valley between the Rivers Severn and Wye. Although the primordial forest has long since been cut down and replanted, the landscape here remains one of strange beauty, hiding in its folds and under its hills deposits of iron, silver, and coal that have been mined for thousands of years. Of the original forest established in 1016 by King Canute, 27,000 acres are preserved by the Forestry Commission. It's still a source of timber, but parking lots and picnic grounds have been created and eight nature trails marked. For a driving tour of the forest, head to Littledean, where SCENIC DRIVE signs direct you through the best of the forest. To get to Littledean from Soudley, backtrack north on B4227, and turn east on A4151.

The **Dean Heritage Centre,** in a restored mill building in a wooded valley on the forest's eastern edge, tells the history of the forest, with reconstructions of a mine and a miner's cottage, a waterwheel, and a "beam engine" (a primitive steam engine used to pump water from flooded coal mines). Within the grounds is a tiny farm, with a resident pig as well as natural-history exhibitions. Craftspeople work in the outbuildings. ⊠ *B4227, near Cinderford* ☎ *01594/822170* ⊕ *www.fweb.org.uk/deanmuseum* 🎫 *£4* ⏰ *Apr.–Sept., daily 10–5; Oct.–Mar., daily 10–4.*

Cinderford

➍➋ *1 mi west of Littledean, 14 mi southwest of Gloucester.*

In Cinderford, a hiking trail links sculptures around Speech House, the medieval verderer's court in the forest's center, and now a restaurant and inn. The verderer was responsible for the enforcement of the forest laws. It was usually a capital offense to kill game or cut wood without authorization.

Where to Stay & Eat

££–££££ ✕🖼 **Speech House.** Dating from 1676, this former royal hunting lodge retains its satisfyingly creaky floors and low-beamed ceilings. Rooms are traditionally furnished with striped and print fabrics; some have four-posters. The wood-paneled Verderer's Court still functions four times a year, but at any other time the courtroom is a restaurant (fixed-price menu) that serves country platters that might include the local Gloucestershire Old Spot pork, and treacle tart. Although the postal address for Speech House is the town of Coleford, it is outside the village of Cinderford. ⊠ *Coleford, GL16 7EL* ☎ *01594/822607* 🖷 *01594/823658* ⊕*www.thespeechhouse.co.uk* ⤴*33 rooms* ⚷ *Restaurant, café, golf privileges, gym, spa, meeting rooms, some pets allowed (fee); no a/c* ⊟ *AE, DC, MC, V* ⦿ *BP.*

Coleford

41 *4 mi west of Cinderford, 10 mi south of Ross-on-Wye.*

The area around Coleford is a maze of weathered and moss-covered rocks, huge ferns, and ancient yew trees—a shady haven on a summer's day. The **tourist information center** (☎ 01594/812388 ⊕ www.forestofdean. gov.uk) at Coleford (drive west from Cinderford on A4151, and then west again on B4226 and B4028) has details of picnic grounds, nature and sculpture trails, and tours of the forest.

A visit to the workings in the spectacular **Clearwell Caves,** 1½ mi south of Coleford, provides insight into the region's mining for iron and coal, which went on continuously from Roman times to 1945. Ocher (for paint pigments) is still mined here today. ⊠ *Off B4228* ☎ *01594/832535* ⊕*www.clearwellcaves.com* ✉*£4, £4.50 Christmas Fantasy* ⊘ *Feb.–Oct., daily 10–5; Nov. and Jan., weekends and school holidays 10–4; Dec., Christmas Fantasy weekends 10–5.*

Where to Stay & Eat

★ £££ ✕ **Wyndham Arms.** This may be a modest, old-fashioned village inn, but its restaurant produces sophisticated cuisine. Try the local wild salmon, guinea fowl, or one of the excellent steaks, followed by sherry trifle or chocolate and walnut fudge cake. ⊠ *The Cross, Clearwell,, near Coleford* ☎ *01594/833666* ⊟ *MC, V.*

££–£££ ✕⬚ **Tudor Farmhouse.** Despite its name, parts of this former farmhouse date to the 13th century. Polished oak staircases, mullioned windows, and a huge stone fireplace in the sitting room imbue the place with antique calm. Most of the bedrooms are in a converted barn, though they retain the traditional style, and four have four-poster beds. The restaurant serves good-quality fare (fixed-price menu) using seasonal ingredients for such dishes as fresh spinach and apple soup and smoked duck salad. ⊠ *High St., Clearwell, near Coleford, GL16 8JS* ☎ *01594/ 833046* 🖷 *01594/837093* ⊕ *www.tudorfarmhousehotel.co.uk* ⤴*23 rooms* ⚷ *Restaurant, some pets allowed; no a/c* ⊟*AE, DC, MC, V* ⦿*BP.*

Slimbridge Wildfowl & Wetlands Trust

42 *38 mi east of Coleford (via Severn Bridge to the south), 12 mi south of Gloucester, 20 mi northeast of Bristol.*

This 73-acre site on the banks of the River Severn encompasses rich marshland that harbors Britain's largest collection of wildfowl. Thousands of swans, ducks, and geese come to winter here; in spring and early summer, you can see the resulting cygnets, ducklings, and goslings. Trails with blinds (called "hides" in Britain) thread the preserve. The flashy visitor center has an observation tower, cinema, gift shop, and restaurant; a gallery of wildlife art presents changing exhibitions. The preserve is outside the village of Slimbridge (head west and across the little swing bridge over the Sharpness Canal). ☎ *01453/890333* ⊕ *www.wwt.org. uk* ✉ *£6.40* ⊘ *Apr.–Oct., daily 9:30–5; Nov.–Mar., daily 9:30–4.*

Berkeley Castle

★ 43 *4 mi southwest of Slimbridge, 17 mi southwest of Gloucester, 21 mi north of Bristol.*

Berkeley Castle, in the sleepy little village of Berkeley (pronounced barkley), is perfectly preserved down to its medieval turrets. It witnessed the gruesome murder of King Edward II in 1327—the cell where it occurred can still be seen. He was deposed by his French consort, Queen Isabella, and her paramour, the earl of Mortimer. They then connived at his imprisonment and subsequent death. Roger De Berkeley, a Norman knight, began work on the castle in 1153, and it has remained in the family ever since. Magnificent furniture, tapestries, and pictures fill the state apartments, but even the ancient buttery and kitchen are interesting. The surrounding meadows, now the setting for pleasant Elizabethan gardens, were once flooded to make a formidable moat. ✉ *Off A38, Berkeley* ☎ *01453/810332* 🌐 *www.berkeley-castle.com* *£6.25* ⏲ *Apr.–Sept. and national holidays, Wed.–Sat. 11–4, Sun. 2–5.*

Where to Stay & Eat

★ **££££–£££££** **Thornbury Castle.** An impressive castle-hotel, Thornbury has everything a genuine 16th-century Tudor castle needs: huge fireplaces, antiques, paintings, and mullioned windows, to say nothing of an extensive garden. There's also plenty of history: Henry VIII, Anne Boleyn, and Mary Tudor spent time here. The standards of comfort and luxury are famous, and the pampering touches in the plushly decorated bedrooms include fine bathrooms. People come from all over to dine on sophisticated fare such as warm smoked salmon with caviar and potato salad and duckling with chestnut potatoes. The hotel is 12 mi north of Bristol. ✉ *Castle St., off A38, Thornbury, BS35 1HH* ☎ *01454/281182; 800/987–7433 in U.S.* *01454/416188* 🌐 *www.prideofbritainhotels.com* *25 rooms* *Restaurant, archery, croquet, bar, business services, meeting rooms, some pets allowed (fee); no a/c* *AE, DC, MC, V* *BP.*

££ **Drakestone House.** This lovely, reasonably priced Cotswold Arts and Crafts house 3 mi east of Berkeley has wooden floors and beamed and plasterwork ceilings. Fine antiques and period furniture complement the architecture. ✉ *Off B4060, Stinchcombe, Dursley, GL11 6AS* ☎ *01453/542140* 🌐 *www.a1tourism.com/uk/cotswol1.html* *3 rooms* *No a/c, no room phones, no smoking* *No credit cards* ⏲ *Closed Dec. and Jan.* *BP.*

THE HEART OF ENGLAND A TO Z

To research prices, get advice from other travelers, and book travel arrangements, visit www.fodors.com.

AIRPORTS

This area is not far from London; Bristol and Birmingham have the closest regional airports. Bristol's airport is 8 mi south of the city.

Birmingham International Airport ✉ A45, off Junction 6 of M42 ☎ 0121/767–5511 🌐 www.bhx.co.uk. **Bristol International Airport** ✉ Bridgwater Rd., Lulsgate ☎ 0870/121–2747 🌐 www.bristolairport.co.uk.

BUS TRAVEL

National Express serves the region from London's Victoria Coach Station. First covers the area around Bath. Stagecoach, Castleways, and Pulhams operate in the Gloucestershire and Cotswolds region. For all bus inquiries, call Traveline. Although you can get around the Cotswolds by bus, service between some towns can be extremely limited, perhaps only twice a week.

Various bus routes to major Cotswold destinations are as follows (when not stated otherwise, routes are serviced by National Express buses and depart from London's Victoria Coach Station). Bourton-on-the-Water: take Pulhams buses from Cheltenham or Stow-on-the-Wold. Broadway: four Castleways coaches serve the town daily (Monday–Saturday from Cheltenham). Burford (A40 turnout): Swanbrook buses leave four times every weekday from Cheltenham; from London, change at Oxford. Cheltenham and Cirencester: buses leave London 11 times daily. Moreton-in-Marsh: buses depart 5 times daily from London, changing at Cirencester. Painswick: 12 Stagecoach buses run from Cheltenham (Monday–Saturday). Stow-on-the-Wold: Pulhams buses run 6 times daily (not Sunday in winter) from Moreton-in-Marsh. Winchcombe: 8 Castleways buses leave Cheltenham (Monday–Saturday).

FARES & SCHEDULES 🏢 **Castleways** ☎ 01242/602949 ⊕ www.castleways.co.uk. **First** ☎ 01225/464446 ⊕ www.firstbadgerline.co.uk. **National Express** ☎ 0870/580–8080 ⊕ www.nationalexpress.com. **Pulhams** ☎ 01451/820369. **Stagecoach** ☎ 01453/763421. **Swanbrook** ☎ 01452/712386 ⊕ www.swanbrook.co.uk. **Traveline** ☎ 0870/608–2608 ⊕ www.traveline.org.uk.

CAR RENTAL
🏢 **Local Agencies Avis** ⊠ Unit 4B, Bath Riverside Business Park, Riverside Rd., Bath ☎ 01225/446680 ⊠ Unit 7, Chancel Close Trading Estate, Eastern Ave., Gloucester ☎ 01452/380356. **Budget** ⊠ 88 Prestbury Rd., Cheltenham ☎ 01242/235222. **Ford Rental** ⊠ Hayden Rd., off Tewkesbury Rd., Cheltenham ☎ 01242/229937.

CAR TRAVEL
M4 is the principal route west from London to Bath and southern Gloucestershire. From Exit 18, take A46 south to Bath. From Exit 20, take M5 north to Gloucester (25 mi), Cheltenham, and Tewkesbury; from Exit 15, take A419 to A429 north to the Cotswolds. From London, you can also take M40 and A40 to the Cotswolds. Driving down the scenic roads of the rural Cotswold Hills can be one of the real joys of a British vacation.

Parking in Bath is restricted within the city, and any car illegally parked is likely to be ticketed. If your car is towed, you may pay hundreds of pounds in fees to retrieve it. Public parking lots in the historic area fill up early, but the Park and Ride lots on the outskirts of town provide shuttle service into the city center. A car can be an encumbrance in Cheltenham and Gloucester; garage your car or leave it at your hotel and forgo the stress of finding parking spaces and negotiating one-way streets.

DISCOUNTS & DEALS
The Bath Pass, an excellent deal if you're planning extensive visits in the Bath and Bristol area, gives you free admission to 30 attractions as well as discounts on boat trips, bicycle rentals, and restaurant meals. A one-day pass costs £22, two-day £29, and three- and five-day passes are £39 and £59 respectively. Tourist offices sell the pass.
🏢 **Bath Pass** ☎ 01664/500107 ⊕ www.bathpass.com.

EMERGENCIES
🏢 **Ambulance, fire, police** ☎ 999. **Cheltenham General Hospital** ⊠ Sandford Rd. ☎ 01242/222222. **Gloucester Royal Hospital** ⊠ Great Western Rd. ☎ 01452/528555. **Royal United Hospital** ⊠ Combe Park, Bath ☎ 01225/428331.

SHOPPING

For information about dealers and special events, contact the Cotswold Antique Dealers' Association.

Cotswold Antique Dealers' Association ✉ Broadwell House, Sheep St., Stow-on-the-Wold, GL54 1JS ☎ 01451/830053 ⊕ www.cotswolds-antiques-art.com.

SPORTS & THE OUTDOORS

For information on hiking the Cotswold Way, contact the National Trail Office or various town tourist centers. For information on hiking in the Forest of Dean, contact the Forestry Commission.

Hiking **Forestry Commission** ✉ Bank House, Bank St., Coleford, GL16 8BA ☎ 01594/833057 ⊕ www.forestry.gov.uk. **National Trail Office** ✉ The Malt House, Standish, Stonehouse, GL10 3DL ☎ 01453/827004 ⊕ www.cotswold-way.co.uk.

TOURS

Based in Oxford, Cotswold Roaming is a stylish outfit offering tours of the Cotswolds (Tuesday and Saturday) and excursions to Bath and Castle Combe (Wednesday and Saturday) in small vehicles. The full-day tour of the Cotswolds takes in Bourton-on-the-Water, Upper Slaughter and Lower Slaughter, Chipping Campden, Sudeley Castle, and Stow-on-the-Wold. Half-day tours are also offered. The pickup point is next to the Playhouse Theatre in Beaumont Street, Oxford.

Gloucester Civic Trust organizes tours of the city and docks by appointment. Contact Gloucester's tourist office (⇨ Visitor Information) for details. City Sightseeing/Guide Friday runs guided tours of Bath year-round and tours from Stratford-upon-Avon into the Cotswolds from Easter through October, in open-top single- and double-decker buses.

Cotswold Roaming ☎ 01865/308300 ⊕ www.oxfordcity.co.uk/cotswold-roaming. **City Sightseeing/Guide Friday** ☎ 01789/294466 in Stratford, 01225/444102 in Bath ⊕ www.city-sightseeing.com.

TRAIN TRAVEL

First Great Western, Wales and West, Virgin, Central, and Thames Trains all serve the region from London's Paddington Station, or, less frequently, from Euston. Travel time from Paddington to Bath is about 90 minutes. Most trains to Cheltenham (2 hours) and Gloucester ($1\frac{3}{4}$ hours) involve a change at Swindon. A three-day or seven-day Heart of England Rover ticket is valid for unlimited travel within the region.

Some pointers for reaching central Cotswold destinations by train follow. Broadway: train to Moreton-in-Marsh or Evesham, then bus or taxi locally to reach the town. Burford: train to Oxford, then buses from the Taylor Institute there. Cirencester: train from London to Kemble (4 mi from town). Bourton-on-the-Water, Chipping Campden, and Stow-on-the-Wold: train to Moreton-in-Marsh, then local bus lines (some lines have minimal schedules). Moreton-in-Marsh is serviced by train from London daily. Contact local tourist offices for details.

FARES & SCHEDULES National Rail Enquiries ☎ 0845/748–4950 ⊕ www.nationalrail.co.uk.

TRAVEL AGENCIES

Local Agent Referrals **American Express** ✉ 5 Bridge St., Bath ☎ 01225/444747. **Thomas Cook** ✉ 20 New Bond St., Bath ☎ 01225/492000 ✉ 159 High St., Cheltenham ☎ 01242/847900 ✉ 24 Eastgate St., Gloucester ☎ 01452/368000.

VISITOR INFORMATION

The Heart of England Tourist Board is open Monday–Thursday 9–5:30, Friday 9–5. South West Tourism has information on Bath. Local tourist information centers are normally open Monday–Saturday 9:30–5:30, but times vary according to season. Note that Cirencester's and Stroud's Web sites serve the whole of the Cotswolds.

🖪 **Heart of England Tourist Board** ✉ Larkhill Rd., Worcester, WR5 2EZ ☎ 01905/761100 🖷 01905/763450 ⊕ www.visitheartofengland.com. **South West Tourism** ✉ Woodwater Park, Pynes Hill, Exeter, EX2 5WT ☎ 01392/360050 🖷 01392/445112 ⊕ www.westcountrynow.com. **Bath** ✉ Abbey Chambers, Abbey Church Yard, BA1 1LY ☎ 01225/477101 ⊕ www.visitbath.co.uk. **Broadway** ✉ 1 Cotswold Court, WR12 7AA ☎ 01386/852937. **Burford** ✉ The Brewery, Sheep St., OX18 4LP ☎ 01993/823558 ⊕ www.oxfordshirecotswolds.co.uk. **Cheltenham** ✉ 77 Promenade, GL50 1PP ☎ 01242/522878 ⊕ www.visitcheltenham.com. **Chipping Campden** ✉ The Old Police Station, High St., GL55 6HB ☎ 01386/841206. **Cirencester** ✉ Corn Hall, Market Pl., GL7 2NW ☎ 01285/654180 ⊕ www.cotswold.gov.uk. **Gloucester Tourist Office** ✉ 28 Southgate St., GL1 2DP ☎ 01452/396572 ⊕ www.visit-glos.org.uk. **Moreton-in-Marsh Tourist Office** ✉ High St., GL56 0AZ ☎ 01608/650881 ⊕ www.moreton-in-marsh.co.uk. **Painswick** ✉ The Library, Stroud Rd., GL6 6UT ☎ 01452/813552. **Stow-on-the-Wold** ✉ Hollis House, The Square, GL54 1AF ☎ 01451/831082. **Stroud** ✉ Subscription Rooms, George St., GL5 1AE ☎ 01453/760960 ⊕ www.visitthecotswolds.org.uk. **Tetbury** ✉ 33 Church St., GL8 8JG ☎ 01666/503552 ⊕ www.tetbury.org.uk. **Tewkesbury** ✉ 64 Barton St., GL20 5PX ☎ 01684/295027 ⊕ www.visitcotswoldsandsevernvale.gov.uk.

THE WELSH BORDERS

BIRMINGHAM, WORCESTER, HEREFORD, SHREWSBURY, CHESTER

FODOR'S CHOICE
Ludlow, *town*
The Merchant House, *restaurant in Ludlow*

HIGHLY RECOMMENDED

RESTAURANTS Brown's, *Worcester*
Café @ All Saints, *Hereford*
Le Petit Blanc, *Birmingham*
Mr. Underhill's, *Ludlow*

HOTELS Chester Crabwall Manor, *Mollington, near Chester*
Library House, *Telford, Ironbridge Gorge*
New Hall, *Birmingham*

SIGHTS Barber Institute of Fine Art, *Birmingham*
Birmingham Museum and Art Gallery, *Birmingham*
Black Country Living Museum, *Dudley*
Eastnor Castle, *Ledbury*
Ironbridge Gorge
Mappa Mundi and Chained Library Exhibition, *Hereford*
Rows, *Chester*
Worcester Cathedral, *Worcester*

Updated by
Robert
Andrews

SOME OF ENGLAND'S PRETTIEST COUNTRYSIDE lies along the 108-mi border with the principality of Wales, which stretches from the town of Chepstow on the Severn estuary in the south to the city of Chester in the north. Much of the land along this border, in the counties of Herefordshire, Shropshire, and southern Cheshire, is remote and tranquil. But today's rural peace belies a turbulent past. Relations between the English and the Welsh have seldom been easy, and from the earliest times the English have felt it necessary to keep the "troublesome" Welsh firmly on the other side of the border. A string of medieval castles bears witness to this history. Many are romantic ruins; some are brooding fortresses. Built to control the countryside and repel invaders, they still radiate a sense of mystery and menace.

For the last 500 years or so, the people of this border country have enjoyed a peaceful existence, with little to disturb the traditional patterns of country life. In the 18th century, however, one small corner of Shropshire heralded the tumultuous birth of the Industrial Revolution. Here, in a wooded stretch of the Severn Gorge, the first coke blast furnace was invented and the first iron bridge was erected (1779).

The ramifications of that technological leap led to the growth of Britain's second-largest city, Birmingham, the capital of the Midlands. Birmingham has transcended its reputation as one of the country's least attractive cities, and its active artistic life draws people who appreciate what remains of its historic civic architecture, some of the most fascinating to be found anywhere.

Herefordshire, in the south, is a county of rich, rolling countryside and river valleys, gradually opening out in the high hills and plateaus of Shropshire. North of the Shropshire hills, the gentler Cheshire plain stretches toward the great industrial cities of Liverpool and Manchester. This is dairy country, dotted with small villages and market towns, many rich in the 13th- and 14th-century black-and-white, half-timber buildings typical of northwestern England. These are the legacy of a forested countryside, where wood was easier to come by than stone. In the market towns of Chester and Shrewsbury, the more elaborately decorated half-timber buildings are monuments to wealth, dating mostly from the early Jacobean period at the beginning of the 17th century. More half-timbered structures are found in the archetypal Borders town of Ludlow, nestled in the lee of its majestic ruined castle.

Exploring the Welsh Borders

The main gateway to the region is bustling Birmingham, now one of the best places in England for the performing arts, having redeemed itself from its reputation as a post–World War II urban disaster zone. The city of Worcester is renowned for its proud cathedral and fine bone china. To the south and west, along the lovely Malvern Hills, lie the peaceful spa town of Great Malvern and the prosperous agricultural city of Hereford. Northward is Bewdley, terminus of the Severn Valley Railway, and beyond, the West Midlands—birthplace of modern British industry.

The handsome medieval city of Shrewsbury is near the wooded banks of the River Severn and a cluster of Ironbridge museums interpreting the region's industrial heritage. To its south lies Ludlow, an architectural and culinary jewel; at the northwestern edge of the region is the ancient city of Chester.

About the Restaurants

Birmingham has splendid international restaurants but is probably most famous for its Asian eateries, the best of which are off the main roads.

Although the region's main towns—Worcester, Hereford, Shrewsbury, and Chester—distill the essence of the surrounding countryside, there's much in between that should not be neglected. It would be easy to base yourself in one of these towns, but you might do better to lodge in some of the smaller centers, or in one of the remoter country inns, to absorb the full flavor of the borderlands. In three days you can take in the highlights of a couple of major centers and visit some smaller towns. A week gives you a chance to explore Birmingham and some major towns, along with more scenic stops.

8

Numbers in the text correspond to numbers in the margin and on the Welsh Borders, Birmingham, and Shrewsbury maps.

If you have 3 days

The city of ⊞ **Worcester** ⑭ ▶ makes a convenient entry to the Welsh Borders. Spend your first night here, making sure you see the majestic cathedral and the Commandery, devoted to the 17th-century tussle between Cavaliers and Roundheads. Take a whirl around the Royal Worcester Porcelain Factory and the adjacent museum. On your second day, take A443 northwest, making a stop at the evocative ruins of **Witley Court** ㉕, a good place for a picnic; or opt for a pub meal in the nearby village. Keep on the same road as far as **Ludlow** ㊶, stopping to view its magnificent castle and its remarkable crowd of Tudor, Jacobean, and Georgian buildings. Plan ahead if you want to have lunch at one of its noted restaurants. Next, head south for ⊞ **Hereford** ㉔, with its stout Norman cathedral and numerous reminders of the city's importance as a market town. See the most interesting sights in the morning, and spend the afternoon exploring **Ross-on-Wye** ⑳, nearby **Goodrich** ㉑, dramatically poised over the River Wye, and the beauty spot of **Symond's Yat** ㉒.

If you have 7 days

Devote at least a day to ⊞ **Birmingham** ①–⑬ ▶, and don't miss the Barber Institute of Fine Arts and the Birmingham Museum and Art Gallery. After an overnight stay, head south to Worcester and the Malvern Hills, dropping in along the way at Hellen's, a 13th-century manor house (opening hours are limited, so check) just outside **Much Marcle** ⑲. You could take a lunch break at the generously timbered village of **Ledbury** ⑱ before continuing on toward the Wye Valley, where the nearby ruins of the castle at **Goodrich** ㉑ and **Symond's Yat** ㉒ provide good excuses to stop traveling and stretch your legs. A night in ⊞ **Hereford** ㉔ will allow you to absorb the flavor of this old market town before heading up to **Ludlow** ㊶ for lunch and a couple of hours' ramble around the castle and its surrounding streets. Spend the next two nights in ⊞ **Worcester** ⑭, taking in the Malverns and, to the north, the quiet riverside town of **Bewdley** ㉖, with its Georgian architecture. From here you can take a trip on the Severn Valley Railway, an old-style steam train. One of the main stops is **Bridgnorth** ㊵, occupying a sandstone ridge high above the Severn, and within a short distance of **Ironbridge Gorge** ㊴, the crucible of the Industrial Revolution. You can stay near Ironbridge or visit it on a day's excursion from ⊞ **Shrewsbury** ㉙–㊱. Outside this historic town lies **Attingham Park** ㊲, an 18th-century mansion with a deer park designed by Humphrey Repton. Your last overnight—entailing a sizable journey northward—can be spent in ⊞ **Chester** ㊷, famous for its black-and-white buildings and worthy of a day's sightseeing.

If you plan to dine in one of Ludlow's noted restaurants, you must book up to three months ahead for dinner (lunch is a better bet).

About the Hotels

The Welsh Borders are full of ancient inns and venerable Regency-style houses converted into hotels. Although some of these can be pricey, bargains can be found. You may have to put up with asthmatic plumbing and creaking beams that masquerade as period charm, but it's usually worth the savings. Birmingham's hotels, geared to the convention crowd, are mostly bland and impersonal, but smart; weekend rates may be up to 50% less than they would be during the week.

WHAT IT COSTS In pounds				
	££££££	££££	£££	££	£
RESTAURANTS	over £22	£18–£22	£13–£17	£7–£12	under £7
HOTELS	over £160	£115–£160	£80–£115	£50–£80	under £50

Restaurant prices are for a main course at dinner. Hotel prices are for two people in a standard double room in high season, including VAT, with no meals or, if indicated, CP (with Continental breakfast), BP (Breakfast Plan, with full breakfast), or MAP (Modified American Plan, with breakfast and dinner).

Timing

Most attractions are open and the countryside is most appealing in the warmer weather between April and September. The official and fringe festivals take place at Malvern at the end of May, the open-air performances at Ludlow Castle at the end of June, and the Shrewsbury International Music Festival in June and July. The Three Choirs Festival, rotating among Hereford, Gloucester, and Worcester, takes place in mid-August (early booking is essential for the best seats). Most rural sights have limited opening hours in winter. Even in the towns, the majority of the attractions close at 5, which leaves several hours of dark and often chilly winter evenings to fill. Be on the road early to catch the best light. In the winter's favor are the creeping mists shrouding the valleys, and the warm hearths at inns and hotels.

BIRMINGHAM

▶ Birmingham's dynamic cultural life—the result of the museums, art galleries, theater, ballet, and symphony that thrive here—comes as a refreshing surprise. The city's appeal, thanks to heavy industry and German bombing during World War II, may be less than instantly evident, but there is satisfaction to be gained from discovering its treasures and the historic civic architecture that remains.

The center of Britain's "second city" has undergone so many injudicious structural alterations in the postwar period that, as an official guidebook put it, "There is more of the future to be seen coming into being than there is of the past left to contemplate." Indeed, Birmingham has become something of a monument to late-20th-century civic architecture—for better or worse. Mercifully, city officials have adopted a policy of humanizing the areas and buildings that their immediate predecessors did so much to ruin, and creative redevelopment and public art have made some areas more attractive.

Birmingham, with a metropolitan area population of 2.6 million, lies 25 mi north of Stratford and 120 mi northwest of London. The city first flourished in the boom years of the 19th century's Industrial Revolution. Its inventive, hardworking citizens accumulated enormous wealth,

8

Great Flavors Outside Birmingham, this is all rich farming country where, for centuries, the orchards have produced succulent fruit, especially apples. Hereford cider, for example, is popular because it tastes much sweeter than the cider brewed farther south in Devon. The meat and milk products, which come from the local black-and-white breed of cattle, are second to none. Ludlow produces a formidable range of local meat products and is particularly noted for its sausages. Despite this natural bounty, formal restaurants are few and far between in this rural area, with the notable exception of Ludlow, which has a remarkable group of superb restaurants.

Walking The Malvern Hills in the southern part of this region have climbs and walks of varying length and difficulty. The best places to start are Great Malvern and Ledbury. The trail designated the Elgar Route extends for 45 mi and touches on Malvern and Worcester as it threads through the Malverns. The hilltop views across the countryside are spectacular—isolated hills rise up from the fairly flat plain, providing vistas for many miles around. The area around Ross-on-Wye has ideal walks with scenic river views. In Shropshire, Wenlock Edge and the uplands of Long Mynd south of Much Wenlock are popular places to walk.

---

and at one time the city had some of the finest Victorian buildings in the country (it still has some of the most ravishingly beautiful Pre-Raphaelite paintings, on view in the Birmingham Museum and Art Gallery). The remaining architectural treasures can be best reached on foot or by public transportation; it's advisable to avoid negotiating the city's convoluted road network. Much of Birmingham is now pedestrian-friendly, the downtown shopping area transformed into pedestrian arcades and buses-only streets. If you *are* driving, note that Birmingham's inner ring road twists right through the city center.

Exploring Birmingham

Most of Birmingham's sights form a tight-knit group and can be easily explored on a pleasant walk in the mostly pedestrianized center. You can also reach the Jewellery Quarter by public transport, which is the best means for arriving at the Barber Institute and Cadbury World, the only two city sites away from the center.

a good walk

Start from the **International Convention Centre** ❶ ▶, where a tourist desk can equip you with information for your explorations. Cross the canal by the footbridge over to Brindleyplace, full of shops and offices in architecturally interesting new buildings. From the aptly named Water's Edge, cut across Central Square, with its fountains, to the ornate red-brick **Ikon Gallery** ❷—a good coffee stop—to find out what's new in British contemporary art. Retracing your steps over the canal bridge and through the convention center will bring you to **Symphony Hall** ❸. You can see its plush wooden and chrome interior if there's no rehearsal in progress. Entering **Centenary Square** ❹, you face the **Birmingham Repertory Theatre** ❺ and, farther down, the imposing **Hall of Memory** ❻. Centenary Way leads through the shopping arcade past the library into Chamberlain Square, where the magnificent **Birmingham Museum and Art**

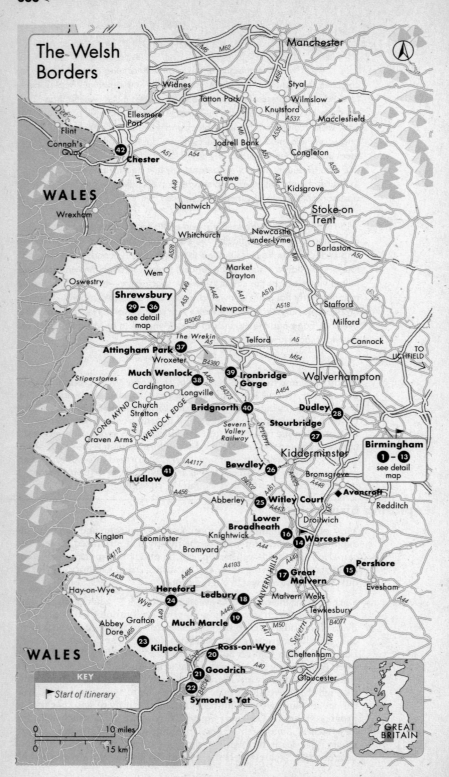

The Welsh Borders

Manchester

Widnes
Ellesmere Port
Flint
Connah's Quay
Chester **42**

WALES

Wrexham

Jodrell Bank
Knutsford
Styal
Wilmslow
Macclesfield
Congleton
Kidsgrove

Crewe

Nantwich
Whitchurch
Newcastle-under-Lyme
Stoke-on-Trent
Barlaston

Oswestry
Wem
Market Drayton
Newport
Stafford
Milford

Shrewsbury **29 – 36**
see detail map

The Wrekin
Telford
Cannock
TO LICHFIELD

Attingham Park **37**
Wroxeter

Stiperstones
Much Wenlock **38** **39** Ironbridge Gorge
Wolverhampton

Cardington
Longville
Church Stretton
WENLOCK EDGE
Bridgnorth **40**
Dudley **28**
Stourbridge **27**

LONG MYND

Craven Arms
Severn Valley Railway
Kidderminster
Birmingham **1 – 13**
see detail map
Bromsgrove

Ludlow **41**
Bewdley **26**
Avoncroft
Redditch

Kington
Abberley
Witley Court **25**
Droitwich

Leominster
Knightwick
Lower Broadheath **16**
Worcester **14**

Bromyard

Hay-on-Wye
Great Malvern **17**
Pershore **15**

Hereford **24**
Ledbury **18**
Malvern Wells
Evesham

Abbey Dore
Grafton
Much Marcle **19**
Tewkesbury

WALES
Kilpeck **23**
Ross-on-Wye **20**
Goodrich
Cheltenham

21
22
Symond's Yat
Gloucester

KEY
▶ Start of itinerary

0   10 miles
0   15 km

GREAT BRITAIN

Gallery ❼ invites a couple of hours' lingering. South of the museum is the classical **Town Hall** ❽, behind which Victoria Square spreads out, with its modern fountains and statues. From here, your route leaves the pedestrianized area and continues northeast through the bustle of Colmore Row to the Georgian **Birmingham Cathedral** ❾, distinguished by its concave tower. Continue north past Snow Hill Station to St. Chad's Circus, where the lofty twin towers of **St. Chad's Roman Catholic Cathedral** ❿ rear incongruously above the busy intersection. Taking the metro from Snow Hill Station the couple of stops to the **Jewellery Quarter** ⓫ would save you the 10-minute walk, but you'd miss some striking examples of redbrick and terra-cotta industrial architecture from the 19th century. The fascinating **Museum of the Jewellery Quarter** ⓬ explores the history of the neighborhood. After perusing this and the surrounding area, a short train ride or walk will take you back to the center. For the tour's grand finale, the **Barber Institute of Fine Arts** ⓭—one of the country's most absorbing collections of European art—you must drive or take a taxi or train (from New Street Station).

TIMING Allow a full day to visit all the sights, which gives you time to linger in the Jewellery Quarter and browse the art museums; allow a half day if you keep your walk to the very central part of the city. Some sights have limited opening hours on Sunday, and the Jewellery Quarter shops are closed on that day.

What to See

off the beaten path

AVONCROFT MUSEUM OF HISTORIC BUILDINGS – You can see the architecture typical of the Midlands in microcosm at this 15-acre open-air museum that has rescued more than 25 structures from destruction. Alongside the half-timber buildings are Victorian chimneys, a collection of phone boxes, and a working windmill. There's also a year-round program of activities and events such as battle reenactments and medieval fairs. Avoncroft is 17 mi southwest of Birmingham. ⊠ *Stokeheath, Bromsgrove* ☎ *01527/831–363* ⊕ *www.avoncroft.org.uk* ☞ *£5.50* ☉ *Mar. and Nov., Tues.–Thurs. and weekends 10:30–4; Apr.–June, Sept., and Oct., Tues.–Sun., 10:30–4:30; July and Aug., daily 10:30–5.*

★ ⓭ **Barber Institute of Fine Art.** Part of the University of Birmingham, the museum has a small but astounding collection of European paintings, prints, drawings, and sculpture, including works by Bellini, Canaletto, Guardi, Poussin, Murillo, Gainsborough, Turner, Whistler, Renoir, Monet, and van Gogh. To get here, take Cross City Line train from New Street Station south to University Station, or Bus 61, 62, or 63 from the city center. ⊠ *Off Edgbaston Park Rd. near East Gate, Edgbaston* ☎ *0121/414–7333* ⊕ *www.barber.org.uk* ☞ *Free* ☉ *Mon.–Sat. 10–5, Sun. noon–5.*

❾ **Birmingham Cathedral.** The early 18th-century cathedral of St. Philip, a few blocks from the renovated Victoria Square, contains some lovely plasterwork in its elegant, gilded Georgian interior. The stained-glass windows behind the altar, designed by the Pre-Raphaelite Edward Burne-Jones (1833–98) and executed by William Morris (1834–96), seem to glow with a garnet hue. ⊠ *Colmore Row, City Centre* ☎ *0121/262–1840* ☉ *Weekdays 7 AM–7 PM, weekends 9–5* ☞ *Free.*

★ ❼ **Birmingham Museum and Art Gallery.** Vast and impressive, this museum holds a magnificent collection of Victorian art and is known internationally for its works by the Pre-Raphaelites. All the big names are here, including William Holman Hunt, John Everett Millais, and Dante

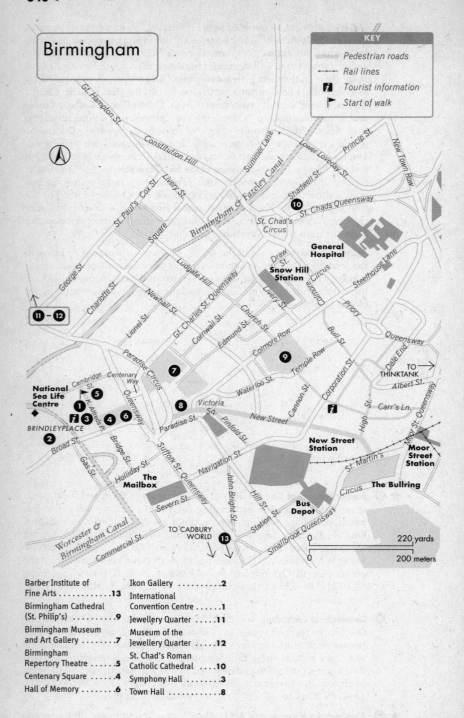

Birmingham

KEY

Pedestrian roads

Rail lines

i Tourist information

Start of walk

Gabriel Rossetti—reflecting the enormous wealth of 19th-century Birmingham and the aesthetic taste of its industrialists. Galleries of metalwork, silver, and ceramics also reveal some of the city's history, and selections of contemporary art are displayed. ⊠ *Chamberlain Sq., City Centre* ☎ *0121/303–2834* ⊕ *www.bmag.org.uk* ✉ *Free* ⊗ *Mon.–Thurs. and Sat. 10–5, Fri. 10:30–5, Sun. 12:30–5.*

❺ **Birmingham Repertory Theatre.** Set to one side of Centenary Square, the building houses one of England's oldest and most esteemed theater companies. The Birmingham Rep—as it's always called—has an excellent cafeteria–restaurant in its foyer, behind sweeping windows that allow for a great view over the square. ⊠ *Centenary Sq., Broad St., City Centre* ☎ *0121/236–4455* ⊕ *www.birmingham-rep.co.uk.*

Cadbury World. The village of Bournville (4 mi south of the city center) contains this museum devoted to—what else?—chocolate. In 1879 the Quaker Cadbury brothers moved the family business to this "factory in a garden" from the less than healthy conditions of the city; they also constructed a model village for the factory workers. In the museum you can trace the history of the cocoa bean and the Cadbury dynasty, walking through a rain forest along the way. Chocoholics can watch (and smell) specialties being made in the factory, enjoy the free samples, and then stock up from the cut-price shop. The restaurant has specialty chocolate cakes as well as lunches. ⊠ *Off A38 (take train from New St. to Bournville Train Station), Bournville* ☎ *0121/451–4159* ⊕ *www.cadburyworld.co.uk* ✉ *£8.50* ⊗ *Mar.–Oct., weekdays 10–3, weekends 10–4; reservations advised, and essential at busy times; times for rest of year vary.*

❹ **Centenary Square.** Just outside the International Convention Centre and near the Birmingham Repertory Theatre and Symphony Hall, the square is at the heart of the city's cultural life. Pavement bricks of different shades form a pattern like a Persian carpet. The creamy sculpture in the center of the square, *Forward,* shows a group of people (and a factory) and represents the city's progressive outlook.

❻ **Hall of Memory.** The octagonal war memorial, neoclassical in style, was built in the 1920s in remembrance of those who fell during World War I and, later, during World War II. Inside, there's a book containing their names and the poppies laid on Armistice Day. ⊠ *Centenary Sq., City Centre* ✉ *Free* ⊗ *Mon.–Sat. 10–4.*

❷ **Ikon Gallery.** This gallery, converted from a Victorian Gothic–style school, serves as the city's main venue for exhibitions of contemporary art from Britain and abroad. The bright, white interior is divided into comparatively small display areas, making the shows easily digestible. ⊠ *1 Oozells Sq., Brindleyplace, City Centre* ☎ *0121/248–0708* ⊕ *www.ikon-gallery.co.uk* ✉ *Free* ⊗ *Tues.–Sun. and national holidays 11–6.*

▶ ❶ **International Convention Centre.** A network of blue struts and gleaming air ducts dominates the main atrium of the high-tech convention center, although indoor trees soften the effect. The **information center** here is useful, but the office at Colmore Row, near the cathedral, is more fully stocked. ⊠ *Broad St., City Centre* ☎ *0121/200–2000* ⊕ *www.necgroup.co.uk* ⊗ *Daily 7 AM–11:30 PM.*

need a break? The balcony of the **Malt House** (⊠ 75 King Edward's Rd. ☎ 0121/633–4171) is just the place to linger over a drink as you watch canal life go by. Former president Bill Clinton had a beer here in 1998.

THE VENICE OF THE NORTH

It may come as a surprise that Birmingham has more canals in its center than Venice: its eight canals include 34 mi of waterways. The city is at the heart of a system of restored waterways built during the Industrial Revolution to connect inland factories to rivers and seaports—by 1840 the canals extended more than 4,000 mi throughout the British Isles. These canals, which carried 9 million tons of cargo a year in the late 19th century and helped make the city an industrial powerhouse,

have undergone extensive renovations and are now a tourist attraction in their own right.

A walk along a canal near the Gas Street Basin will bring you to developments such as Brindleyplace and to pubs and cafés, and you'll see the city from an attractive new perspective. Contact any city tourist office for maps of walks along the towpaths and for details on canal barge cruises.

⑪ **Jewellery Quarter.** For more than two centuries, jewelers have worked in the district of Hockley, northwest of the city center; today more than 200 manufacturing jewelers and 50 silversmiths continue the tradition, producing a third of the jewelry made in Britain. The city has its own Assay Office, which hallmarks 10 million items each year with the anchor symbol denoting Birmingham origin. The ornate green and gilded Chamberlain Clock marks the center of the district. ⊠ *Hockley* ⊕ *www.the-quarter.com.*

off the beaten path

LICHFIELD CATHEDRAL – It's worth a detour (14 mi northeast of Birmingham on A38) to explore the only English cathedral with three spires. The current sandstone building, beautifully sited by a tree-fringed pool, dates mainly from the 12th and 13th centuries, and the Lady Chapel glows with some fine 16th-century stained glass from the Cistercian abbey of Herkenrode, near Liège, in Belgium. Half-timber houses surround the peaceful grounds, and the town itself has attractive Georgian buildings as well as the birthplace museum of lexicographer Dr. Samuel Johnson. ⊠ *Cathedral Close, Lichfield* ☎ *01543/306100* ⊕ *www.lichfield-cathedral.org* ✉ *Suggested donation £3* ☉ *Daily 7:30–6:15; closes Sun. at 5 in winter.*

⑫ **Museum of the Jewellery Quarter.** The museum is built around the workshops of Smith and Pepper, who operated here for more than 80 years until 1981; very little has changed since the early 1900s. The guided factory tour and exhibits explain the history of the neighborhood and the craft of the jeweler, and you can watch jewelry being made. ⊠ *75–79 Vyse St., Hockley* ☎ *0121/554–3598* ⊕ *www.bmag.org.uk* ✉ *£3* ☉ *Weekdays 10–4, Sat. 11–5; last admission 1 hr before closing.*

↻ **National Sea Life Centre.** Even as far from the sea as you can get in Britain, this imaginatively landscaped aquarium allows a glimpse into Davey Jones's locker. An underwater tunnel lets you view sharks and stingrays up close, and there are displays of oceanic and freshwater marine life. Children will gravitate to the touch pools and other interactive activities. ⊠ *The Water's Edge, Brindleyplace, City Centre* ☎ *0121/643–6777* ⊕ *www.sealife.co.uk* ✉ *£8.50* ☉ *Daily 10–5.*

⑩ **St. Chad's Roman Catholic Cathedral.** Dating from 1841, this redbrick pile was the first Roman Catholic cathedral to be built in England since the Reformation. A. W. N. Pugin, leading architect of the Gothic revival, designed St. Chad's, which basically consists of one lofty room—the nave—divided by soaring slender pillars and decorated in red, blue, and gold. Many furnishings are 15th century. ✉ *Queensway, City Centre* ☎ *0121/230–6208* 🖭 *Free* 🕑 *Daily 8–6:30.*

3 Symphony Hall. Attending a concert here is sufficient reason to visit Birmingham. The internationally recognized City of Birmingham Symphony Orchestra has won awards for its recordings under its former conductor, Sir Simon Rattle (who occasionally guest conducts). Symphony Hall occupies the same building as the International Convention Centre. ✉ *Broad St., City Centre* ☎ *0121/780–3333* ⊕ *www.necgroup.co.uk.*

Thinktank. This interactive museum in the state-of-the-art Millennium Point center allows you to explore science and the history of Birmingham over four floors of galleries. You can walk into the giant boiler of a steam engine, explore deep space, program a robot to play the drums, and even perform a hip operation. An IMAX Theatre shows films daily. ✉ *Curzon St., Digbeth* ☎ *0121/202–2222* ⊕ *www.thinktank.ac* 🖭 *Thinktank £6.75, IMAX £6, joint ticket £10.50* 🕑 *Sat.–Thurs. and school vacations 10–5; last admission 4.*

8 Town Hall. Classical columns surround this mid-19th-century performance hall, a copy of the Temple of Castor and Pollux in Rome. The former home of the symphony orchestra heard the premieres of Mendelssohn's *Elijah* and Elgar's *Dream of Gerontius,* and today Town Hall hosts concerts and exhibitions. Locals have affectionately dubbed the statue of a woman in the prominent fountain outside the building "the floozie in the Jacuzzi." ✉ *Victoria Sq., City Centre.*

Where to Eat

££–£££ ✕ **Café Lazeez.** This New Wave Indian restaurant, in a trendy shopping, restaurant, and housing development overlooking a canal, blends the traditional with the contemporary taste for lighter, less oily dishes. Try the Peshawari naan bread as an accompaniment to fillets of salmon in a tomato and yogurt sauce, or herbed breast of chicken. ✉ *116 Wharfside St., The Mailbox, City Centre* ☎ *0121/643–7979* 🖃 *AE, MC, V.*

★ **££–£££** ✕ **Le Petit Blanc.** An outpost of noted chef Raymond Blanc(of Le Manoir aux Quat' Saisons, near Oxford), this brasserie provides a very contemporary showcase of gleaming metal, light wood, and plate glass for the excellent regional French menu. The cherry tomato risotto with Parmesan crisp is one of the fine starters; you might follow up with pan-fried sea bream with ratatouille. ✉ *9 Brindleyplace, City Centre* ☎ *0121/633–7333* 🖃 *AE, DC, MC, V.*

££–£££ ✕ **Shimla Pinks.** Birmingham has some of Britain's finest Indian restaurants, and this is one upbeat choice—the name refers to the "bright young things" of India's upper classes. Both the decoration and the cooking are a mix of modern and traditional, and waiters are elegantly turbaned. Try the Assamese *jalfrezi,* pieces of meat with coriander leaves and red peppers, or *rogan josh* made from fresh tomatoes, paprika, and chili. The Sunday evening buffet is abundant. ✉ *214 Broad St., City Centre* ☎ *0121/633–0366* 🖃 *AE, MC, V.*

££ ✕ **Henry's.** This very popular traditional Cantonese restaurant in the Jewellery Quarter is a haven for lunch during a shopping spree. The menu lists more than 180 dishes; there's also a good-value fixed-price menu and a Sunday buffet. ✉ *27 St. Paul's Sq., City Centre* ☎ *0121/200–1136* 🖃 *AE, DC, MC, V.*

££ ✕ **Thai Edge.** The elegant, contemporary Asian design will draw you into this restaurant. Dishes such as *gang keow waan* (green curry cooked in coconut milk with eggplant, lime leaves, and basil) are excellent. You can eat all you want for £13 at the Sunday lunch buffet. ✉ *7 Oozells Sq., City Centre* ☎ *0121/643–3993* 🖃 *AE, DC, MC, V.*

£–££ ✕ **Brass House.** The city's first foundry is now a useful central location for full meals or bar snacks. Look for such traditional favorites as steak, roast ham and parsley sauce, and even the humble "chip buttie" (a sandwich filled with french fries). The pastel, marbled glass lights on the bar are an attraction in their own right. ✉ *44 Broad St., City Centre* ☎ *0121/633–3383* 🖃 *AE, MC, V.*

Where to Stay

££££–£££££ 🛏 **Birmingham Marriott Hotel.** Once a group of offices, this elegant building from the early 20th century now contains a luxurious hotel. The interior is rich with dark wood and chandeliers; the spacious bedrooms offer all the latest comforts. Note the Egyptian theme in the health club. The fixed-price menu in the formal Sir Edward Elgar restaurant (reservations essential) changes daily, whereas the more casual Langtry's Brasserie serves traditional British dishes. On weekends, a full breakfast is included. ✉ *12 Hagley Rd., Five Ways, B16 8SJ* ☎ *0121/452–1144; 888/236–2427 in U.S.* 🖷 *0121/456–3442* ⊕ *www.marriott.com* 🛏 *98 rooms* ♨ *2 restaurants, in-room data ports, cable TV with movies, pool, health club, spa, meeting rooms, parking (fee), some pets allowed* 🖃 *AE, DC, MC, V* ⦿ *BP.*

★

££££–£££££ 🛏 **New Hall.** A tree-lined drive leads through 26 acres of gardens and open land to this moated 12th-century manor-house-turned-country-hotel. The public rooms include 16th-century oak paneling and Flemish glass, 18th-century chandeliers, and a stone fireplace from the 17th century; guest rooms (most in a more modern section) are done in English country style with print fabrics and marble-tile baths. At the elegant formal restaurant, you can indulge in sophisticated English and French cuisine. A full breakfast is included in the price on weekends. The hotel is 7 mi northeast of the city center. ✉ *Walmley Rd., Sutton Coldfield, Birmingham, B76 1QX* ☎ *0121/378–2442; 800/847–4358 in U.S.* 🖷 *0121/378–4637* ⊕ *www.thistlehotels.com* 🛏 *60 rooms* ♨ *Restaurant, some in-room data ports, cable TV with movies, 9-hole golf course, tennis court, pool, gym, hot tub, sauna, spa, croquet, bar, meeting rooms, free parking, some pets allowed; no a/c in some rooms* 🖃 *AE, DC, MC, V* ⦿ *BP.*

£££–££££ 🛏 **Burlington Hotel.** Wood paneling, marble, and classical columns abound at this traditional hotel, and rooms are individually decorated in a conservative style with dark woods and print fabrics. At the sumptuous Berlioz restaurant, English dishes such as liver with onion mash share menu space with classic French-influenced dishes. On weekends, a full breakfast is included. ✉ *Burlington Arcade, 126 New St., City Centre, B2 4JQ* ☎ *0121/643–9191* 🖷 *0121/628–5005* ⊕ *www.burlingtonhotel.com* 🛏 *112 rooms* ♨ *Restaurant, in-room data ports, cable TV with movies, gym, sauna, business services, meeting rooms, parking (fee), some pets allowed; no a/c* 🖃 *AE, DC, MC, V* ⦿ *BP.*

£££–££££ 🛏 **Hotel du Vin & Bistro.** A Victorian eye hospital, right in the city center, received a makeover from this hip mini-chain but retains details such as the double ironwork stairway and marble columns. Beyond the imposing redbrick exterior, you'll find an inner courtyard with a fountain and garden. Bedrooms are sleek and contemporary, with huge fluffy towels and white linens. The bistro dining room is redolent of fin-de-siècle Paris, and in the Bubble Lounge you can drown in more than 50 varieties of champagne. ✉ *25 Church St., City Centre, B3 2NR* ☎ *0121/200–0600* 🖷 *0121/236–0889* ⊕ *www.hotelduvin.com* 🛏 *66 rooms* ♨ *Restaurant, in-room data ports, cable TV, gym, sauna, spa, steam room, bar, meeting rooms, parking (fee); no a/c* 🖃 *AE, DC, MC, V.*

££–£££   ▣ **City Inn.** This bustling, absolutely up-to-the-minute hotel in the canal-side piazza, near the waterside nightlife scene, represents an excellent value. The crisp modern bedrooms and bathrooms, though on the small side, are beautifully equipped; white and gray, with a splash of red, set off the light wood furniture. ⊠ *1 Brunswick Sq., Brindleyplace, City Centre, B1 2HW* ☎ *0121/643–1003* ☐ *0121/643–1005* ⊕ *www.cityinn. com* ⋗ *238 rooms* ⌂ *Restaurant, in-room data ports, cable TV with movies, gym, meeting rooms, parking (fee)* ⊟ *AE, DC, MC, V.*

££   ▣ **Copperfield House Hotel.** In a quiet location a few minutes' drive from Cadbury World, this Victorian, family-run hotel with secluded lawns and simple rooms is nevertheless convenient to the bustle of the center 2 mi away. The restaurant serves good English cooking, including delicious desserts. ⊠ *60 Upland Rd., Selly Park, Birmingham, B29 7JS* ☎ *0121/472–8344* ☐ *0121/415–5655* ⊕ *www.copperfieldhousehotel. co.uk* ⋗ *17 rooms* ⌂ *Restaurant, bar, free parking, some pets allowed (fee); no a/c* ⊟ *AE, MC, V.*

££   ▣ **Fountain Court.** A five-minute drive from the center, this cheerful family-run hotel is in a leafy, well-heeled neighborhood. Bedrooms are modern and bright, and the more traditional public rooms have patterned carpets and dark wood furniture. ⊠ *339–343 Hagley Rd., Edgbaston, B17 8NH* ☎ *0121/429–1754* ☐ *0121/429–1209* ⊕ *www.fountain-court.net* ⋗ *23 rooms* ⌂ *Restaurant, bar; no a/c* ⊟ *AE, DC, MC, V* ⋔❘ *BP.*

Nightlife & the Arts

Nightlife

Converted from a church, **The Bar** (⊠ The Church, 55 Broad St., City Centre ☎ 0121/632–5501) has turned from God to Mammon. It's a bar in the early evening and later plays commercial dance music for the over-21s. At **52° North** (⊠ Arcadian, Hurst St., City Centre ☎ 0121/622–5250), the bar specializes in classic and contemporary cocktails and mixes up 14 types of martinis.

The Arts

BALLET   The second company of the Royal Ballet, the **Birmingham Royal Ballet** (⊠ Hurst St., City Centre ☎ 0870/730–1234) is based at the Hippodrome Theatre, which also hosts visiting companies such as the Welsh National Opera.

CONCERTS   The distinguished **City of Birmingham Symphony Orchestra** (⊠ International Convention Centre, Broad St., City Centre ☎ 0121/780–3333) performs regularly in Symphony Hall, also the venue for visiting artists.

THEATER   The **Alexandra Theatre** (⊠ Station St., City Centre ☎ 121/643–5536 0870/607–7533) welcomes touring companies on their way to or from London's West End. The **Birmingham Repertory Theatre** (⊠ Centenary Sq., Broad St., City Centre ☎ 0121/236–4455), founded in 1913, is equally at home with modern or classical work.

Sports & the Outdoors

Boating

Birmingham's canals provide a novel perspective on the city. You can take an hour ride on a canal barge from **Sherborne Wharf** (⊠ Sherborne St., City Centre ☎ 0121/455–6163). Trips leave daily mid-April through October at 11:30, 1, 2:30, and 4, and on weekends throughout the rest of the year, departing from the International Convention Centre Quayside.

Cricket

To watch first-class cricket at one of the country's most hallowed venues, head for **Warwickshire County Cricket Club** (⊠ County Ground, Edgbaston ☎0121/446–5506). Tickets for test matches sell out six months ahead, but those at county level are not so sought after.

Shopping

In the **Jewellery Quarter** (⊠ Hockley, ☎ 0121/554–3598) more than 100 shops sell and repair gold and silver handcrafted jewelry, clocks, and watches. The Museum of the Jewellery Quarter sells a selection of contemporary work and has information on individual artisans and retail outlets. **The Mailbox** (⊠ 150 Wharfside St., City Centre ☎ 0121/632–1000), once a Royal Mail sorting office, entices with shops and designer outlets such as Harvey Nichols and Armani, restaurants, and hotels.

FROM WORCESTER TO DUDLEY

In the arc of towns to the west of Birmingham and the cluster of places around the banks of the River Wye, history and tradition rub up against deepest rural England. The cathedral towns of Worcester and Hereford make great bases to soak up the bucolic flavor of the Malverns and Elgar country, or to view the spectacular swing of the Wye at Symond's Yat. En route, there's a taste of Georgian architecture at Pershore and Bewdley, and reminders of the old industrial Midlands at Stourbridge and Dudley.

Worcester

▶ ⑭ *27 mi southwest of Birmingham, 118 mi northwest of London.*

Worcester (pronounced as in Bertie *Wooster*) sits on the River Severn in the center of Worcestershire. It's an ancient place proud of its history, and in particular, its nickname, "the Faithful City," bestowed on the town for steadfast allegiance to the crown during the English Civil War. In that conflict between king and Parliament, two major battles were waged here. The second one, the decisive Battle of Worcester of 1651, resulted in the exile of the future Charles II. Since the mid-18th century the town's name has become synonymous with the fine bone china produced here. Despite unfortunate "modernization" in the 1960s, some of medieval Worcester remains. This ancient section forms a convenient and pleasant walking route around the great cathedral. Worcester's mainly pedestrianized High Street runs through the center of town, from the cathedral to Foregate Street train station.

★ There are few more quintessentially English sights than that of **Worcester Cathedral**, its towers overlooking the green expanse of the county cricket ground, and its majestic image reflected in the swift-flowing—and frequently flooding—waters of the River Severn. A cathedral has stood on this site since the year 680, and much of what remains dates from the 13th and 14th centuries. Notable exceptions are the Norman crypt (built in the 1080s), the largest in England, and the ambulatory, a cloister built around the east end. The most important tomb in the cathedral is that of King John (1167–1216), one of the country's least-admired monarchs, who alienated his barons and subjects through bad administration and heavy taxation and in 1215 was forced to sign the Magna Carta, the great charter of liberty. The cathedral's most beautiful decoration is in the vaulted **chantry chapel of Prince Arthur**, Henry VII's elder son, whose body was brought to Worcester after his death at Ludlow in 1502. The wealthy endowed chantry chapels to enable priests to celebrate masses there for the souls of the deceased. ⊠ *College Yard at High St.* ☎ *01905/28854* ⊕ *www.cofe-worcester.org.uk* ✉ *Suggested donation £3* ⊗ *Daily 8–6:15.*

At the **Royal Worcester Porcelain Factory,** you can browse in the showrooms or rummage in the "seconds" and "clearance" shops; the January and July sales have especially good bargains. Tours of the factory take you through the process of making bone china figurines. The **Museum of Worcester Porcelain** displays the world's largest collection of Worcester porcelain, representing work from the start of manufacturing in 1751 to the present. The factory lies south of Worcester Cathedral (follow Severn Street). ⊠ *Severn St.* ☎ *01905/23221* ⊕ *www. royal-worcester.co.uk* ✉ *Visitor center £2.25, museum £3, 1-hr tour of factory £5; tour, museum, and visitor center £8; prebooked 2-hr Connoisseur Tours £14* ⊗ *Mon.–Sat. 9–5:30, Sun. 11–5; tours weekdays 10:30–2:30, Connoisseur Tours weekdays 10:15 and 1:15. Children under 11 not admitted on tours.*

Now an enthralling museum focusing on the Civil War, the **Commandery** occupies a cluster of 15th-century half-timber buildings that were originally built as a poorhouse and later became the headquarters of the Royalist troops during the Battle of Worcester. The museum presents a colorful audiovisual presentation about the war in the magnificent, oak-beam Great Hall. The Commandery is across the road from the porcelain factory, minutes from the cathedral. ⊠ *Sidbury* ☎ *01905/361821* ✉ *£4* ⊗ *Mon.–Sat. 10–5, Sun. 1:30–5.*

The timber-frame **Museum of Local Life,** on a medieval street, focuses on Worcester's domestic and social history. You can see reconstructions of Victorian and Edwardian shops and homes, as well as changing exhibitions. ⊠ *Friar St.* ☎ *01905/722349* ✉ *Free* ⊗ *Mon.–Wed., Fri. and Sat. 10:30–5.*

Also the location of the tourist information office, the **Guildhall,** set back behind ornate iron railings, has an 18th-century facade with gilded statues of Queen Anne, Charles I, and Charles II. Note the carving of Cromwell's head pinned up by the ears. Inside, impressive patrician portraits hang under a painted ceiling in the Assembly Room; you can admire them over tea and buns. ⊠ *High St.* ☎ *01905/723471* ✉ *Free* ⊗ *Mon.–Sat. 8:30–4:30.*

Where to Stay & Eat

★

££££–£££££ ✕ **Brown's.** A former grain mill contains this light, airy riverside restaurant. The fixed-price menu and daily specialties revolve around simple, well-timed dishes. You might try the roast breast of duck with lentil and tomato vinaigrette, and finish up with rhubarb fool or coconut tart with chocolate sauce. ⊠ *24 Quay St.* ☎ *01905/26263* 🟰 *AE, MC, V* ⊗ *Closed Mon. No lunch Sat., no dinner Sun.*

££££ ✕ **King's Restaurant.** The deluxe Fownes Hotel, a converted Victorian glove factory, houses this classic English restaurant, furnished in white, red, and gold. A good selection of modern and exotic dishes, such as king prawn masala, counter the old-fashioned tone. There's a fixed-price menu at dinner. ⊠ *Fownes Hotel, City Walls Rd.* ☎ *01905/613151* 🟰 *AE, DC, MC, V.*

££–£££ ✕ **King Charles II Restaurant.** A half-timber house in which Charles II hid after the Battle of Worcester is now an oak-paneled, silver-service restaurant that exudes friendliness. Cuisine is mainly French and Italian, but traditional English selections such as beef Wellington and fish dishes including Dover sole meunière also appear on the menu. ⊠ *29 New St.* ☎ *01905/22449* 🟰 *AE, DC, MC, V* ⊗ *Closed Sun.*

£££ ▨ **Diglis House Hotel.** English artist John Constable was a frequent visitor to this idyllically sited 18th-century house overlooking terraced gardens and the river. Service is discreet but friendly, and furnishings are uncluttered but elegant. Choose between views over the garden or river when you dine. ⊠ *Severn St., WR1 2NF* ☎ *01905/353518* 🖷 *01905/ 767772* ⊕ *www.diglishousehotel.co.uk* ⥽ *29 rooms* ⚭ *2 restaurants, bar, meeting rooms; no a/c* ⊟ *AE, MC, V* ⑩ *BP.*

££ ▨ **Ye Olde Talbot Hotel.** The Olde Talbot was originally a courtroom belonging to the cathedral, which stands close by. Modern extensions supplement the 16th-century core of the building. The spacious bedrooms have double-glazed windows and are done in a cheerful, reproduction Victorian style. ⊠ *Friar St., WR1 2NA* ☎ *01905/23573* 🖷 *01905/ 612760* ⊕ *www.yeoldetalbot.co.uk* ⥽ *27 rooms* ⚭ *Restaurant, cable TV, some pets allowed; no a/c* ⊟ *AE, DC, MC, V* ⑩ *BP.*

Nightlife & the Arts

Huntingdon Hall (⊠ Crowngate ☎ 01905/611427), a refurbished Methodist chapel founded in 1773, puts on a varied program of music and poetry recitals year-round. The original pews are—thankfully—provided with cushions.

Sports & the Outdoors

BIKING **Peddlers** (⊠ 46 Barbourne Rd. ☎ 01905/24238) rents bikes.

BOATING In Worcester you can easily rent boats or take short cruises on the Severn. **Bickerline River Trips** (⊠ South Quay near the cathedral ☎ 01905/ 831639 or 0775/375–7424) runs 45-minute excursions on a small passenger boat daily on the hour, March through October.

HORSE RACING You can have a day at the races at **Worcester Racecourse** (⊠ Pitchcroft ☎ 01905/25364), attractively set on the banks of the River Severn. Admission prices start at £5.

Shopping

Many shoppers will first head for the emporium at the **Royal Worcester Porcelain Factory** (⊠ Severn St. ☎ 01905/23221), where, among other merchandise, you can buy "seconds." **Bygones** (⊠ Dean's Way ☎ 01905/ 25388 ⊠ 55 Sidbury ☎ 01905/23132) sells antiques, items of fine craftsmanship, and small gifts in silver, glass, and porcelain. **G. R. Pratley** (⊠ The Shambles ☎ 01905/22678) has tables piled high with fine china, such as Royal Worcester, Wedgwood, and Spode.

Pershore

⓯ *8 mi southeast of Worcester.*

In the fruitful Vale of Evesham sits the peaceful, unspoiled market town of Pershore. This is plum and asparagus country; trees are loaded down with blossoms in spring, and May sees the asparagus harvest. Georgian buildings with elegant facades flank the town's wide streets.

The nave of **Pershore Abbey** did not survive the dissolution of the monasteries, but the beautiful chancel and crossing has been preserved. The choir has a rare plowshare vault (so called because the curved panels resemble the blade of a plowshare) with soaring ribs that culminate in 41 carved bosses; no two are the same. Architect George Gilbert Scott opened up the fine lantern tower in the 1860s to reveal the internal tracery. He replaced the old bell-ringing chamber with a suspended platform that seems to float in space. ⊠ *Church Row* ☎ *01386/552071* ⊕ *www. pershoreabbey.fsnet.co.uk* ⊡ *Free* ⊙ *Daily 9–5.*

Where to Eat

£££££ ✕ **Epicurean.** If you're here on a Friday, direct your steps toward this small, modern, and elegantly simple restaurant where star chef Patrick McDonald—when not cooking for royalty or troubleshooting other restaurants—has made his mark. You can choose between a contemporary British five- or six-course meal meticulously cooked and presented. It's usually necessary to book at least three weeks in advance. ⊠ *76 High St.* ☎ *01386/555576* ⌣ *Reservations essential* ▭ *No credit cards* ☉ *Closed Sat.–Thurs. and 2 wks Dec.–Jan. and 2 wks in Aug.*

Lower Broadheath

16 *10 mi northwest of Pershore, 2 mi west of Worcester.*

Southwest of Worcester lie the Malvern Hills, their long, low, purple profiles rising starkly from the surrounding plain. These hills inspired much of the music of Sir Edward Elgar (1857–1934), as well as his remark that "there is music in the air, music all around us." The village of Lower Broadheath is on the B4204.

The **Elgar Birthplace Museum,** in a peaceful little garden, is the tiny brick cottage in which the composer was born. It now exhibits photographs, musical scores, letters, and such. ⊠ *Crown East La.* ☎ *01905/333224* ⊕ *www.elgar.org* ✑ *£4* ☉ *Feb.–Dec., daily 11–4:15.*

Great Malvern

17 *9 mi south of Lower Broadheath, 7 mi south of Worcester.*

Great Malvern, off the A449, is a Victorian spa town whose architecture has changed little since the mid-1800s. Exceptionally pure spring water is still bottled here and exported worldwide—the Queen never travels without a supply. Great Malvern is known today both as an educational center and as a place for old folks' homes. The town also has a Winter Gardens complex with a theater, cinema, and gardens. The **Priory,** an early Norman Benedictine abbey in Perpendicular style, dominates the steep streets downtown. Vertical lines of airy tracery and fine 15th-century glass decorate the building. ⊠ *Entrance opposite church* ☎ *01684/561020* ⊕ *www.greatmalvernpriory.org.uk* ✑ *Free* ☉ *Apr.–Oct., daily 9–6:30; Nov.–Mar., daily 9–4:30.*

Where to Stay & Eat

£££–££££ ✕▥ **Cottage in the Wood.** This family-run hotel sits on shady grounds high up the side of the Malvern Hills, with splendid views of the countryside. Country-house furnishings in the three buildings include floral prints and white bedspreads; rooms with a view are equipped with binoculars. The mirrored restaurant has the best of the panorama. The food is English, with the accent on country fare, and you can choose from more than 600 wines, among them many local English wines. ⊠ *Holywell Rd., WR14 4LG* ☎ *01684/575859* 🖷 *01684/560662* ⊕ *www.cottageinthewood.co.uk* ✒ *20 rooms* ⌂ *Restaurant, bar, Internet, meeting rooms, some pets allowed; no a/c* ▭ *AE, MC, V* ⦿ *BP.*

£–££ ▥ **Sidney House.** In addition to having stunning views, this dignified Georgian hotel, run by a friendly husband-and-wife team, is near the town center. On a clear afternoon you can gaze out over the Vale of Evesham to the Cotswolds. ⊠ *40 Worcester Rd., WR14 4AA* ☎ *01684/574994* ✒ *8 rooms* ⌂ *Dining room, Internet, some pets allowed; no a/c, no room phones* ▭ *AE, DC, MC, V* ⦿ *BP.*

Nightlife & the Arts

Malvern has historical connections with Sir Edward Elgar as well as with George Bernard Shaw, who premiered many of his plays here. The October **Malvern Festival** (☎ 01684/892277 or 01684/892289), originally devoted to the works of Elgar and Shaw, also presents new music and drama. The spring **Malvern Fringe Festival** (☎ 01684/561017 or 01684/892289) has an exceptional program of alternative events.

Ledbury

🔞 *10 mi southwest of Great Malvern on A449.*

Among the black-and-white half-timber buildings that make up the market town of Ledbury, take special note of two late-16th-century ones: the Feathers Hotel and the Talbot Inn. Almost hidden behind the 17th-century market house, cobbled Church Lane, crowded with medieval, half-timber buildings, leads to St. Michael's Church. The **Old Grammar School,** a heritage center in an old school, traces the history of local industries, with some displays on two literary celebrities linked to the area, John Masefield and Elizabeth Barrett Browning. ⊠ *Church La.* ☎ *01531/636147* 🖾 *Free* ☉ *Apr.–Oct., daily 10:30–4:30.*

★ Completed in 1820, **Eastnor Castle,** a turreted, stone Norman Revival extravaganza on the eastern outskirts of Ledbury, includes some magnificent, ornate, neo-Gothic salons designed by 19th-century architect Augustus Pugin. The Hervey-Bathurst family has restored other grand rooms, all full of lush tapestries, gilded paintings, Regency chandeliers, and Auntie's old armchairs, to the height of *le style anglais,* making Eastnor a must-see for lovers of English interior decoration. ⊠ *A438* ☎ *01531/633160* ⊕ *www.eastnorcastle.com* 🖾 *House and grounds £6, grounds only £4* ☉ *July and Aug., Sun.–Fri. 11–5; late Apr.–June and Sept., Sun. and national holidays 11–5; last admission 30 mins before closing.*

Where to Stay & Eat

£££–££££ ✕🖾 **Feathers Hotel.** You can't miss the striking black-and-white facade of this central hostelry, which dates from the 16th century. The interior has a satisfyingly antique flavor, with creaking staircases and ancient floorboards, and some rooms have four-posters. The hop-bedecked Fuggles Brasserie (so named after a variety of hop) serves plenty of fresh fish, as well as lighter meals. If you're indulging, try the Herefordshire duck or beef. ⊠ *High St., HR8 1DS* ☎ *01531/635266* ☎ *01531/638955* ⊕ *www.feathers-ledbury.co.uk* 🛏 *19 rooms* ♨ *Restaurant, cable TV, indoor pool, health club, bar, Internet, meeting rooms, some pets allowed; no a/c* ☱ *AE, DC, MC, V* 🍽 *BP.*

Much Marcle

🔞 *4 mi southwest of Ledbury.*

Much Marcle is one of the English villages still holding the ancient annual ceremony of "wassailing"—beating the apple trees to make them fruitful in the coming year. The ritual takes place on Twelfth Night, January 6. Effigies and tombs richly endow the beautiful 13th-century church here, notably one of Blanche, Lady Grandison. If you have a detailed map and plenty of time to spare, wander around and discover tiny villages down sleepy lanes overhung by high hedges.

Just outside Much Marcle lies the beautiful 17th-century manor of **Hellen's,** still in singularly authentic and pristine condition. Part of the house dates from the 13th century. The gloom and dust are part of the experience; candles illuminate the house, and central heating has been scorned. ✉ ½ *mi east of Much Marcle* ☎ *01531/660504* 🎫 *£4* ⊙ *Apr.–Sept., Wed. and weekends 2–5; tours on the hr, last tour at 4.*

Ross-on-Wye

⑳ *6 mi southwest of Much Marcle.*

Perched high above the River Wye, Ross-on-Wye seems oblivious to modern-day intrusions and remains at heart a small market town. Its steep streets come alive on Thursday and Saturday—market days—but they're always a happy hunting ground for antiques.

Where to Stay

£££–££££ 🏨 **Chase Hotel.** The public areas in this well-renovated Georgian-style country-house hotel set on 11 acres retain some original elements. Bedrooms in the main house are simply and comfortably furnished in pastels and print fabrics, and those in the newer wing are more modern. ✉ *Gloucester Rd., HR9 5LH* ☎ *01989/763161* 🖨 *01989/768330* ⊕ *www.chasehotel.co.uk* 🛏 *38 rooms* ⌂ *Restaurant, cable TV, Internet, meeting rooms; no a/c* ⊟ *AE, DC, MC, V* ⧮ *BP.*

Goodrich

㉑ *3 mi south of Ross-on-Wye on B4234, 3 mi north of Symond's Yat on B4229.*

The ruins of a castle that is the English equivalent of a Rhineland *Schloss* dominate the village of Goodrich. Looming dramatically over the River Wye crossing at Kerne Bridge, **Goodrich Castle** from the south looks picturesque amid the green fields, but you quickly see its grimmer face from its battlements on the north side. Dating from the late 12th century, the red sandstone castle is surrounded by a deep moat carved out of solid rock, from which its walls appear to soar upward. Built to repel Welsh raiders, Goodrich was destroyed in the 17th century during the Civil War. ✉ *Off A40* ☎ *01600/890538* ⊕ *www.english-heritage.org. uk* 🎫 *£3.70* ⊙ *Apr.–Sept., daily 10–6; Oct., daily 10–5; Nov.–Mar., Wed.–Sun. 10–4.*

Symond's Yat

㉒ *3 mi south of Goodrich, 6 mi south of Ross-on-Wye.*

Outside the village of Symond's Yat ("gate"), the 473-foot-high Yat Rock commands superb views of the River Wye as it winds through a narrow gorge and swings around in a great 5-mi loop.

Kilpeck

㉓ *15 mi northwest of Goodrich, 7 mi southwest of Hereford.*

Tucked away on a minor road off the A465, the tiny hamlet of Kilpeck is blessed with one of the best-preserved Norman churches in Britain. Much of the village, along with the remains of a castle and the church, is protected as a Scheduled Ancient Monument. The red sandstone **Kilpeck church**, completed in the mid-12th century, is lavishly decorated inside and out with sculpted carving exceptional for a country church. The carvings depict all manner of subjects, including animals. Some showed scenes so scandalously frank that high-minded Victorians removed them. (One or two ribald ones remain, however, so look carefully.) Don't miss the gargoyle rainwater spouts, either. ☎ *01981/ 570315* 🎫 *Donations accepted* ⊙ *Daily 9–dusk.*

Hereford

㉔ *7 mi northeast of Kilpeck, 56 mi southwest of Birmingham, 31 mi northwest of Gloucester, 54 mi northeast of Cardiff.*

A busy country town, Hereford is the center of a wealthy agricultural area known for its cider, fruit, and cattle—the white-faced Hereford breed has spread across the world. It's also an important cathedral city, and the massive Norman building towers proudly over the River Wye. Before 1066, Hereford was the capital of the Anglo-Saxon kingdom of Mercia and, earlier still, the site of Roman, Celtic, and Iron Age settlements. Today people come primarily to see the cathedral but quickly discover the charms of a town that has changed slowly but fairly unobtrusively with the passing centuries.

Built of local red sandstone with a large central tower, **Hereford Cathedral** retains some fine 11th-century Norman carvings but suffered considerable "restoration" in the 19th century. Inside, its greatest glories include the 14th-century bishop's throne and some fine misericords (the elaborately carved undersides of choristers' seats). ⊠ *Cathedral Close* ☎ *01432/374200* ⊕ *www.herefordcathedral.co.uk* ✉ *Suggested donation £2, tours £2.50* ☉ *Mon.–Sat. 7:30–6:30, Sun. 8–4:30; tours Apr.–Oct., daily 11 and 2.*

★ The **Mappa Mundi and Chained Library Exhibition,** an extraordinary double attraction, includes the more than 20-square-foot parchment Mappa Mundi. Hereford's own picture of the medieval world shows the Earth as flat, with Jerusalem at its center. It's now thought that it was originally the central section of an altarpiece dating from 1290. The chained library contains some 1,500 books, among them an 8th-century copy of the Four Gospels. Chained libraries, in which the books were attached to cupboards to discourage theft, are extremely rare: they date from medieval times, when books were as precious as gold. ⊠ *Cathedral Close* ☎ *01432/374200* ⊕ *www.herefordcathedral.co.uk* ✉ *£4* ☉ *Apr.–Oct., Mon.–Sat. 10–5, Sun. 11–4; Nov.–Mar., Mon.–Sat. 11–4; last admission 45 mins before closing.*

The half-timber **Old House** is a fine example of domestic Jacobean architecture, furnished in 17th-century style on three floors. You can see a kitchen and hall, among other rooms. ⊠ *High Town* ☎ *01432/260694* ✉ *Free* ☉ *Apr.–Sept., Tues.–Sat. 10–5, Sun. 10–4; Oct.–Mar., Tues.–Sat. 10–5.*

The 13th-century **All Saints Church,** on the west side of High Town, contains superb canopied choir stalls and misericords, as well as an unusual Queen Anne reredos in the south chapel. There's also an excellent coffee bar and restaurant.

A farm cider house and a cooper's workshop have been re-created at the **Cider Museum,** where you can tour ancient cider cellars with huge oak vats. Cider brandy (applejack) is made here, and the museum sells its own brand, along with other cider items. ⊠ *Pomona Pl. at Whitecross Rd.* ☎ *01432/354207* ⊕ *www.cidermuseum.co.uk* ✉ *£2.70* ☉ *Apr.–Oct., daily 10–5:30; Nov.–Mar., daily 11–4; call ahead to confirm.*

Where to Stay & Eat

★ £ ✕ **Café @ All Saints.** The west end and gallery of this community-minded church are given over to a coffee bar and restaurant, giving you a rare opportunity to indulge body and spirit at one sitting. The imaginative vegetarian menu is worth every penny, but for something lighter, try the tasty sandwiches, salads, cakes, and local ice creams. ⊠ *High St.* ☎ *01432/370415* ▭ *MC, V* ☻ *Closed Sun. No dinner.*

££££–£££££ ✕▦ **Castle House.** These conjoined Georgian villas next to the moat (all that remains of Hereford Castle) offer luxury and a warm welcome. Underfoot is parquet flooring, and delicate plasterwork graces the walls. Rooms vary in style, with yellow and gold the preferred colors; each bedroom contains a decanter of cider brandy. The restaurant specializes in French fare with an Asian accent. ⊠ *Castle St., HR1 2NW* ☎ *01432/356321* 🖷 *01432/365909* ⊕ *www.castlehse.co.uk* ➴ *15 rooms* ☖ *Restaurant, in-room data ports, refrigerators, cable TV, in-room VCRs, bar, Internet, business services, meeting rooms, some pets allowed; no a/c in some rooms* ▭ *AE, DC, MC, V* ❙❍❙ *CP.*

£ ▦ **Grafton Villa Farm.** Warm period rooms with antiques and rich furnishings fill this peaceful, early 18th-century farmhouse 2 mi south of the city. For your breakfast, choose between scrambled eggs provided by the resident hens or poached haddock. The farm lies off the A49 road to Ross. ⊠ *Grafton, HR2 8ED* 🖷🖷 *01432/268689* ➴ *3 rooms* ☖ *No a/c, no room phones* ▭ *No credit cards.*

Shopping

Hereford has a different market each day—food, clothing, livestock—on New Market Street.

The stores in **Capuchin Yard** (⊠ Off 29 Church St.) display crafts, including handmade shoes and knitwear; other outlets sell books, posters, and watercolors.For high-quality foods, head for the **Left Bank Village** (⊠ Bridge St. ☎ 01432/340200) development and browse the delicatessen, patisserie, ice cream parlor, and wine shop.

Witley Court

㉕ *27 mi northeast of Hereford, 10 mi northwest of Worcester.*

The romantic shell of Witley Court conjures up the Victorian heyday of the imposing stately home—a huge Italianate pile—that stood here before being ravaged by fire in 1937. In contrast to this ruin, the tiny baroque parish church on the grounds is perfectly preserved. Note its parapet with balustrades, the small golden dome over its cupola, and, inside, a ceiling painted by Bellucci, 10 colored windows, and the ornate case of an organ once used by Handel. Witley Court's glorious gardens are being restored, and the Poseidon and Flora fountains, set to be repaired in 2003, should send their jets skyward "with the noise of an express train." The sculpture park contains works by Elizabeth Frink and Antony Gormley, among others. The house is little less than a mile outside Great Witley. ⊠ *A443* ☎ *01299/896636* ⊕ *www.english-heritage.org.uk* ▭ *£4.60* ☻ *Apr.–Sept., daily 10–6; Oct., daily 10–5; Nov.–Mar., Wed.–Sun. 10–4.*

Where to Stay & Eat

££££–£££££ ✕▦ **Elms Hotel.** Formal gardens and 10 acres of grounds surround this ivy-clad Queen Anne mansion, now a luxurious, traditional country-house hotel 16 mi northeast of Worcester and near Great Witley. Gilbert White, a pupil of Sir Christopher Wren, designed the house, and public areas retain their ornate plasterwork. All rooms are individually decorated in warm colors and include antiques. The restaurant (with a fixed-price menu) creates imaginative contemporary fare using organic produce and vegetables from the garden. ⊠ *Stockton Rd., Abberley, WR6 6AT* ☎ *01299/896666* 🖷 *01299/896804* ⊕ *www.slh.com* ➴ *21 rooms* ☖ *Restaurant, in-room data ports, tennis court, croquet, Internet, meeting rooms, helipad; no a/c* ▭ *AE, DC, MC, V* ❙❍❙ *BP.*

Bewdley

❷❻ *8 mi north of Great Witley, 14 mi north of Worcester, 3 mi west of Kidderminster.*

Bewdley is an exceptionally attractive Severn Valley town, with many tall, narrow-front Georgian buildings clustered around the river bridge. The 18th-century butchers' market, the **Shambles,** now holds a museum of local history, trades, and crafts, with exhibits and demonstrations of rope making and clay-pipe making. Craftspeople working in wood, glass, and felt occupy the nearby workshops. ⊠ *Load St.* ☎ *01299/ 403573* ⚏ *£2.10* ⊘ *Apr.–Sept., daily 11–5; Oct., daily 11–4.*

☾ Bewdley is the southern terminus of the **Severn Valley Railway,** a steam railroad running 16 mi north along the river to Bridgnorth. It stops at a handful of sleepy stations where time has apparently stood still since the age of steam. You can get off at any of these stations, picnic by the river, and walk to the next station to get a train back. ⊠ *Railway Station* ☎ *01299/403816* ⊕ *www.svr.co.uk* ⚏ *£10.50 round-trip* ⊘ *Mid-May–Sept., trains run daily; Oct.–mid-May, weekends only.*

Stourbridge

❷❼ *8 mi northeast of Bewdley via A451, 11 mi west of Birmingham.*

Stourbridge is the home of Britain's crystal glass industry, and although the industry is in decline, the exquisite glassware is still being produced. A number of shops sell "factory seconds" bargains.

Between March and December, you can join the **Stourport Steamer Co.** (⊠ Riverside Walk ☎ 01299/871177 or 0786/046–8792 ⊕ www. riverboathire.co.uk) for short river trips on weekends and national holidays, and for longer journeys as far as Worcester on Wednesday from the first week in July through August.

Shopping

The **Crystal Glass Centre** (⊠ Churton House, Audnam ☎ 01384/354400), a mile from Stourbridge on the A491 Wolverhampton road, stocks international glassware as well as local products; it is open daily. The **Stuart Crystal Visitor Centre and Factory Shop** (⊠ Bridge St., Wordsley ☎ 01384/261777), open daily, carries a good selection of gift items.

Dudley

❷❽ *6 mi northeast of Stourbridge, 8 mi west of central Birmingham.*

★ ☾ It was in Dudley that coal was first used for smelting iron in the 17th century. The town subsequently became known as the capital of the Black Country, a term that arose from the air pollution caused by ironworks foundries and coal mining. The **Black Country Living Museum,** established to interpret the area's industrial heritage, consists of an entire village reconstructed of disused buildings from around the region. Among the exhibits on 26 acres are a chain maker's house and workshop, with demonstrations of chain making; a small trap works that made animal traps; a druggist and general store, where costumed women describe life in a poor industrial community in the 19th century; a Methodist chapel; the Bottle & Glass pub; Stables restaurant, serving such traditional delicacies as faggots and peas (a fried pork-liver dish); and a coal mine and wharf. The reconstructed brick and terra-cotta Rolfe Street Baths building (brought here from Smethwick) gives an overview of the Black Country, and a ride on a barge (extra charge) through a tunnel takes you back to canal travel of yesteryear. ⊠ *Tipton Rd.* ☎ *0121/557–9643*

⊕ *www.bclm.co.uk* ✉ *£8.25, barge trip £3.50* ⊙ *Mar.–Oct., daily 10–5; Nov.–Feb., Wed.–Sun. 10–4.*

At the **New Royal Brierley Experience,** next to the Black Country Living Museum, you can witness the making of glass (all by hand) on a factory tour, view documents and pieces from the Brierley company's 300 years of history, and browse through samples in the shop. ✉ *Tipton Rd.,* ☎ *0121/530–5608* ✉ *£2* ⊙ *Mon.–Sat. 9–5:30, Sun. 10–4; self-guided factory tours finish at 3.*

FROM SHREWSBURY TO CHESTER ⑧

SKIRTING THE "BLACK COUNTRY"

The "peak" of this region—in terms of height—is the Wrekin, a hill geologists claim to be the oldest in the land, and a hill A. E. Housman and others have invested with some of their poetic charm. From its isolated summit you can gaze on a peaceful rural scene, quite different from most people's preconceptions of the industrial Midlands. Ironbridge, several miles from the Wrekin, has two identities, as a place as well as a thing. The thing itself is the first bridge to be made of iron, erected between 1777 and 1779. Now taken over by the Ironbridge Gorge Museum Trust, the bridge is the centerpiece of a vast Industrial Revolution museum complex. The place is the 6-mi stretch of the Ironbridge Gorge, once an awesome scene of mining and charcoal burning, reeking with smoke and the stench of sulfur. The ironworks forges and the coal mining created the pollution that gave this region west of Birmingham its name—the Black Country—during the mid-19th century. The stretch has been transformed into a scene of idyllic beauty, scars grassed over, woodland filling the gaps left by tree felling. Within easy reach of Ironbridge, rural Shropshire spreads invitingly, with towns long famed as beauty spots, such as Bridgnorth and Ludlow. Around this area are two important cities of the Welsh Border region: Shrewsbury and Chester, both famous for their medieval heritage and their wealth of half-timber buildings.

Shrewsbury

47 mi northwest of Dudley, 55 mi north of Hereford, 46 mi south of Chester, 48 mi northwest of Birmingham.

Shrewsbury (usually pronounced *shrose*-bury), the county seat of Shropshire, lies within a great horseshoe loop of the Severn. One of England's most important medieval towns, it has numerous 16th-century half-timber buildings—many built by well-to-do wool merchants—plus elegant ones from later periods. Today the town retains a romantic air (indeed, there are numerous bridal shops, along with churches), and it can be a lovely experience to stroll the Shrewsbury "shuts." These narrow alleys overhung with timbered gables lead off the central market square, which was originally designed to be closed off at night to protect local residents. The town is especially proud of its flower displays; in summer, filled window boxes and hanging baskets make a vivid contrast to the black-and-white buildings.

Walking is an ideal way to see Shrewsbury, and traffic has been banned on some of the most historic streets. A good starting point for a walking tour is the small square between Fish Street and Butcher Row. These streets are little changed since medieval times, when some of them took their names from the principal trades carried on there, but Peacock Alley, Gullet Passage, and Grope Lane clearly got their names from somewhere ❷❾ else. The stone spire of **St. Mary's church** (✉ off Castle St.), built around

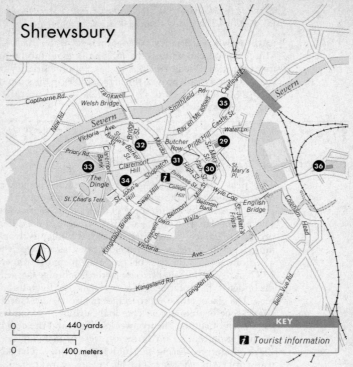

Shrewsbury

0   440 yards
0   400 meters

1200, is one of the three tallest in England. The church merits a visit for its stained glass and superb Victorian encaustic tiles.

30 **St. Alkmund's** (✉ St. Alkmund's Pl., off Fish St.), prominent on the Shrewsbury skyline, is worth seeing for its stained glass. It was built in 1795 on the site of a much earlier church. Bear Steps is a cluster of restored half-timber buildings that link Fish Street with Market Square;

31 the most notable building is the massive **Ireland's Mansion,** built in 1575 with elaborate Jacobean timbering and richly decorated with quatrefoils.

need a
break?

The timbered lace-curtained room and—if the weather is right—the courtyard at **Poppy's Tea Rooms** (✉ Milk St., off Wyle Cop ☎ 01743/232307) make a pleasant stop for coffee, teas, and some satisfying snacks. It's closed Sunday.

32 A magnificent 16th-century timber-frame warehouse and a brick-and-stone mansion built in 1618 house the **Shrewsbury Museum and Art Gallery,** with collections of antique clothing, Shropshire pottery and ceramics, as well as a unique Roman silver mirror from Wroxeter and other items of local history. A reconstructed 17th-century bedroom has oak, holly, and walnut paneling and a four-poster bed. Changing exhibits display contemporary art. ✉ Barker St. ☎ 01743/361196 ⊕ www.shrewsburymuseums.com ✉ Free ☉ Apr. and May, Tues.–Sat. 10–5; June–Sept., Tues.–Sat. 10–5, Sun. and Mon. 10–4; Oct.–Mar., Tues.–Sat. 10–4.

33 Below Swan Hill, the manicured lawn of **Quarry Park** slopes down to the river. In a sheltered corner is the **Dingle,** a colorful garden with floral displays. To reach the park from the center of town, head for Welsh Bridge and stroll along the riverbank, or walk up Claremont Hill.

34 On a hilltop west of the center, the church of **St. Chad,** designed by George Steuart, the architect of Attingham Park, is one of England's most original ecclesiastical buildings. Completed in 1792, the round Georgian church is surmounted by a tower that is in turn square, octagonal, and circular—and finally topped by a dome. When being built, it provoked riots among the townsfolk averse to its radical style. The interior has a fine Venetian east window and a brass Arts and Crafts pulpit. ⊠ *St. Chad's Terrace* ☎ *01743/365478* ⌧ *Free* ☉ *Apr.–Oct., daily 8–5; Nov.–Mar., daily 8–1.*

35 Guarding the northern approaches to the town, **Shrewsbury Castle** rises up over the river at the bottom of Pride Hill. Originally Norman, it was dismantled during the Civil War and later rebuilt by Thomas Telford, the distinguished Scottish engineer who designed a host of notable buildings and bridges at the beginning of the 19th century. The castle holds the **Shropshire Regimental Museum.** ⊠ *Shrewsbury Castle, Castle Gates* ☎ *01743/358516* ⊕ *www.shrewsburymuseums.com* ⌧ *£2* ☉ *Mid-Feb.–Mar. and Oct.–Dec., Wed.–Sat. 10–4; Apr. and May, Tues.–Sat. 10–5; June–Sept., Tues.–Sat. 10–5, Sun. and Mon. 10–4. Castle grounds daily 10–5, 4 in winter.*

36 **Shrewsbury Abbey,** now unbecomingly surrounded by busy roads, was founded in 1083 and later became a powerful Benedictine monastery. The abbey church has survived various vicissitudes, including the dissolution of the monasteries, and retains a good 14th-century west window above a Norman doorway. The abbey figures in the medieval whodunits by Ellis Peters that feature Brother Cadfael; the novels provide an excellent idea of local life in the Middle Ages. To reach the abbey from the center of town, cross the river by the English Bridge. ⊠ *Abbey Church, Abbey Foregate* ☎ *01743/232723* ⊕ *www.virtual-shropshire. co.uk/shrewsbury-abbey* ⌧ *Suggested donation £2* ☉ *Apr.–Oct., daily 9:30–5:30; Nov.–Mar., daily 10:30–3.*

Where to Stay & Eat

£££££ ✕ **Country Friends.** An attractive black-and-white building, 5 mi south of Shrewsbury by the A49, houses this light and airy restaurant overlooking a garden and pond. Typical dishes on the set-price menu include potato cake with smoked salmon, pancetta, and horseradish, and guinea fowl with wild mushroom risotto. The restaurant also has a simple double bedroom available (dinner, bed, and breakfast package for two comes to £130). ⊠ *Dorrington* ☎ *01743/718707* ⊟ *MC, V* ☉ *Closed Sun.–Tues., 2 wks mid-July, mid-wk in Oct.*

£–£££ ✕ **Draper's.** The dark wood paneling, antique furniture, and warm intimate lighting of this 16th-century hall make it a distinctive dining spot. A salad of beetroot leaves, wild mushrooms, and Parmesan flakes is a good starter, and you can fill up on fillet of beef with red onions, or ale-battered vegetables with salsa and aïoli. There are also plenty of cheeses and salad choices. ⊠ *10 St. Mary's Pl.* ☎ *01743/344679* ⊟ *AE, MC, V* ☉ *Closed Mon.*

£–££ ✕ **The Armoury.** This smartly converted warehouse, whose arched windows overlook the river, is well stocked with books, prints, and curiosities, as well as good food, wines, and real ales. Starters include a Shropshire blue cheese, red apple, and walnut salad. Fish stew is one of the main courses, and you can try marmalade bread-and-butter pudding for dessert. ⊠ *Victoria Quay* ☎ *01743/340525* ⊟ *AE, MC, V.*

£££–££££ ▥ **Albright Hussey Hotel.** Lovely gardens surround this Tudor manor house, originally the home of the Hussey family, which dates back to 1524 and combines black-and-white half-timbering with a later (1560) redbrick-and-stone extension. Beams, oak paneling, four-poster beds, and antiques enhance rooms in the original building; those in the extension are plainer. The hotel is 2½ mi north of Shrewsbury on A5228. ⊠ *Ellesmere Rd., SY4 3AF* ☎01939/290571 ☎01939/291143 ⊕*www.albrighthussey. co.uk* ⬩ *14 rooms* ⬩ *Restaurant, 2 bars, meeting rooms, some pets allowed (fee); no a/c, no kids under 3* ⊟ *AE, DC, MC, V* ⦿ *BP.*

£££ ⬩ **The Lion Hotel.** Parts of this once-renowned coaching inn in the heart of town date back to the 14th century; today the hotel envelops you in the 17th century–style luxury for which it became famous. Rooms are small and well-appointed, but the glorious lounge with its high ceiling, oil paintings, and enormous carved-stone fireplace truly sets the Lion apart. Add to this the magnificent Adam Ballroom, and you can see the appeal for former guests such as Charles Dickens, Benjamin Disraeli, and King William IV. ⊠ *Wyle Cop, SY1 1UY* ☎01743/353107 ☎01743/ 352744 ⊕ *www.regalhotels.co.uk/thelion* ⬩ *59 rooms* ⬩ *Restaurant, some in-room data ports, cable TV, bar, lounge, business services, meeting rooms; no a/c* ⊟ *AE, DC, MC, V.*

££ ⬩ **Sandford House.** The hospitable Richards family runs this late-Georgian bed-and-breakfast close to the river and the town center. The original decorative plasterwork is still much in evidence; modern pine furnishes the bedrooms. Room 5 is seven-sided, with a beautiful molded ceiling. You can have dinner here, and packed lunches are also provided. ⊠ *St. Julian Friars, SY1 1XL* ☎01743/343829 ⊕ *www.sandfordhouse. co.uk* ⬩ *10 rooms* ⬩ *Dining room, piano, some pets allowed; no a/c, no room phones* ⊟ *AE, MC, V* ⦿ *BP.*

£ ⬩ **164.** The outside of this centrally located B&B is 16th century, but the bedrooms—all on the ground floor—are contemporary in design, with cheerful orange or lemon walls. An abundant Continental breakfast is brought to your room. ⊠ *164 Abbey Foregate, SY2 6AL* ☎☎ *01743/367750* ⊕ *www.164bedandbreakfast.co.uk* ⬩ *3 rooms* ⬩ *No a/c, no room phones, no smoking* ⊟ *MC, V* ⦿ *CP.*

Nightlife & the Arts
During the **Shrewsbury International Music Festival** (☎ 01606/872633) in June and July, the town vibrates to traditional and not-so-traditional music by groups from Europe and North America.

Shopping
The Parade (☎ 01743/343178), just behind St. Mary's church, is a shopping mall created from the former Royal Infirmary, built in 1830. One of the most appealing malls in England, it has attractive boutiques, apartments upstairs, a restaurant, and a terrace overlooking the river.

Attingham Park

③ *4 mi southeast of Shrewsbury.*

Built in 1785 by George Steuart (architect of the church of St. Chad in Shrewsbury) for the first Lord Berwick, this elegant stone mansion has a three-story portico, with a pediment carried on four tall columns. The building overlooks a sweep of parkland, including a deer park landscaped by Humphrey Repton (1752–1818). A five-year redevelopment of the grounds began in 2001, but there are lovely walks by the river and in the deer park. Inside the house are painted ceilings and delicate plasterwork, a fine picture gallery designed by John Nash (1752–1835), and a collection of 19th-century Neapolitan furniture. ⊠ *B4380, off A5, Atcham* ☎ *01743/708162* ⊕ *www.nationaltrust.org.uk* ⬩ *£5, park and grounds only £2.30* ⦿ *House late Mar.–Oct., Fri.–Tues. 1–4:30,* *national holidays 11–5; last admission 30 mins before closing. Park and grounds Mar.–Oct., daily 9–8; Nov.–Feb., daily 9–5.*

en route   Continuing southeast on B4380, you will see, rising on the left, the **Wrekin**, a strange, conical extinct volcano that is 1,335 feet high. A few miles farther on you enter the wooded gorge of the River Severn.

Much Wenlock

38 *8 mi southeast of Attingham Park, 12 mi southeast of Shrewsbury.*

Much Wenlock, a town on A458, is full of half-timber buildings, including a 16th-century guildhall. The romantic ruins of Norman **Wenlock Priory** are set in an attractive garden full of topiary. ✉ *High St.* ☎ *01952/ 727466* ⊕ *www.english-heritage.org.uk* 🎫 *£3* ⏲ *Apr.–Oct., daily 10–6; Nov.–Mar., Wed.–Sun. 10–1 and 2–4.*

Sports & the Outdoors
The high escarpment of **Wenlock Edge** runs southwest from Much Wenlock and provides a splendid view. This is hiking country, and if a healthful walk sounds inviting, turn off B4371 through Church Stretton into Cardingmill Valley, or to the wide heather uplands on top of Long Mynd. You can park and set off on foot.

Ironbridge Gorge

★ 39 *15 mi east of Shrewsbury, 28 mi northwest of Birmingham.*

Ironbridge Gorge is the name given to a group of villages south of Telford that were crucial in ushering in the Industrial Revolution. The Shropshire coalfields were of enormous importance to the development of the coke smelting process, which helped make producing anything in iron much easier. The nine component sections of the **Ironbridge Gorge Museum**, spread over 6 square mi, preserve and recount the area's fascinating industrial history. There's no public transport between them, so you'll need your own vehicle. Allow at least a full day to appreciate all the major sights and to perhaps take a stroll around the famous iron bridge or hunt for Coalport china in the stores clustered near it. The best starting point is the **Museum of the Gorge**, which has a good selection of literature and an audiovisual show on the gorge's history. In nearby Coalbrookdale, the **Museum of Iron** explains the production of iron and steel. You can see the original blast furnace built by Abraham Darby, who developed the original coke process in 1709. Adjacent to this, the interactive **Enginuity** exhibition is a hands-on, feet-on exploration of engineering, offering the opportunity to pull a locomotive, control a boiler, and even "fly" a magnetic carpet. From here, drive the few miles along the river until the arches of the **Iron Bridge** come into view; it was designed by T. F. Pritchard, smelted by Darby, and erected between 1777 and 1779. This infinitely graceful arch spanning the River Severn can best be seen—and photographed or painted—from the towpath, a riverside walk edged with wildflowers and dense shrubs. The tollhouse on the far side houses an exhibition on the bridge's history and restoration.

A mile farther along the river is the old factory and the **Coalport China Museum** (the china is now made in Stoke-on-Trent). Exhibits show some of the factory's most beautiful wares, and craftspeople give demonstrations. Above Coalport is **Blists Hill Victorian Town,** where you can see old mines, furnaces, and a wrought-iron works. But the main draw is the re-creation of the "town" itself, with its doctor's office, sweet-smelling bakery, grocer's, candle maker's, sawmill, printing shop, and candy store. At the entrance you can change some money for specially minted pennies, which you can use to make purchases from the shops. Shopkeepers, the bank manager, and the doctor's wife are on hand in period dress to give you advice or information. Regular craft demonstrations are scheduled in summer. ⊠ *Ironbridge Gorge Museum Trust, B4380, Ironbridge, Telford* ☎ *01952/433522* ⊕ *www.ironbridge.org. uk* ☑ *Ticket to all sights £12.95* ◷ *Apr.–Oct, daily 10–5; Nov.–Mar., Sat.–Wed. 10–4.*

Where to Stay & Eat

£ ✕ **New Inn.** This Victorian building was moved from Walsall, 22 mi away, so that it could be part of the Blists Hill Victorian Town. It's a fully functioning pub, with gas lamps, sawdust on the floor, and traditional ales served from the cask. For an inexpensive meal, you can try a ploughman's lunch, a pasty from the antique-style bakery, or a pork pie from the butcher's store next door. ⊠ *Blists Hill Victorian Town* ☎ *01952/583003* ▤ *AE.*

£££ ✕▥ **Clarion Hotel at Madeley Court, Telford.** Guest rooms in this restored 16th-century stone manor house, once the home of Abraham Darby, are rich in antiques and period furnishings. Modern rooms are available as well. The Priory Restaurant occupies the original Great Hall and serves contemporary British food (set-price menu). In the garden you'll find a rare example of an Elizabethan stone cube sundial. ⊠ *Castlefields Way, Madeley, Telford, TF7 5DW* ☎ *01952/680068* 🖷 *01952/684275* ⊕ *www.choicehotelseurope.com* ✍ *47 rooms* ⚘ *Restaurant, some in-room data ports, cable TV, bar, Internet, meeting rooms, some pets allowed* ▤ *AE, DC, MC, V* ▯❙ *BP.*

★ ££ ▥ **Library House.** At one point the village's library, this small guest house on the hillside near the Ironbridge museums (and only a few steps away from the bridge itself) has kept its attractive Victorian style while allowing for modern-day luxuries—a video library, for instance. Service is warm without being obtrusive; a glass of wine awaits you on arrival. ⊠ *11 Severn Bank, Ironbridge, Telford, TF8 7AN* ☎ *01952/432299* 🖷 *01952/433967* ⊕ *www.libraryhouse.com* ✍ *4 rooms* ⚘ *Cable TV, in-room VCRs, some pets allowed; no a/c, no room phones, no kids under 10, no smoking* ▤ *No credit cards* ◷ *Closed 1st 3 wks in Jan* ▯❙ *BP.*

Bridgnorth

40 *9 mi south of Ironbridge, 22 mi southeast of Shrewsbury, 25 mi west of Birmingham.*

Perching perilously on a high sandstone ridge on the banks of the Severn, the pretty market town of Bridgnorth has two distinct parts, High Town and Low Town, connected by a winding road, flights of steep steps, and—best of all—a cliff railroad. Even the tower of the Norman castle seems to suffer from vertigo, having a 17-degree list (three times the angle of the Leaning Tower of Pisa). The Severn Valley Railway, which originates in Bewdley, terminates here.

Ludlow

41 *29 mi south of Shrewsbury, 24 mi north of Hereford.*

Fodor'sChoice
★

Pretty Ludlow has medieval, Georgian, and Victorian buildings and a finer display of black-and-white buildings than even Shrewsbury. The great Church of St. Lawrence on College Street dominates the center, its extravagant size a testimony to the town's prosperous wool trade. Cross the River Teme and climb Whitcliff for the most spectacular view.

The town is also a perfect example of how small rural places (the population is around 10,000) can become culinary hot spots, in this case from the buzz generated by its cluster of outstanding restaurants. The **Ludlow and the Marches Food Festival** (☎ 01584/861586 ⊕ www. foodfestival.co.uk) takes place over a weekend in mid-September and consists of demonstrations, competitions, and tastings (including local sausages, ale, and cider).

Dating from 1085, the massive, ruined, red sandstone **Ludlow Castle** dwarfs the town; it served as a vital stronghold for centuries and was the seat of the Marcher Lords who ruled "the Marches," the local name for the border region. The two sons of Edward IV—the little princes of the Tower of London—spent time here before being dispatched to London and their death in 1483. The earl of Powys owns the castle. Follow the terraced walk around the castle for a lovely view. ⊠ *Castle Sq.* ☎ *01584/873355* ⊕ *www.ludlowcastle.com* ☒ *£3.50* ⊙ *Jan., weekends 10–4; Feb., Mar., and Oct.–Dec., daily 10–4; Apr.–July and Sept., daily 10–5; Aug., daily 10–7; last admission 30 mins before closing.*

off the beaten path

STOKESAY CASTLE – Not a castle but an immaculately preserved ensemble of leaning half-timber buildings, this 13th-century fortified manor house originally built by a wealthy merchant is arguably the finest of its kind in England. Inside, the original central fireplace takes pride of place, and outside, the cottage-style gardens create a bewitching backdrop for the magnificent Jacobean timber-frame gatehouse. ⊠ *Craven Arms, off the A49 Shrewsbury road, 7 mi northwest of Ludlow* ☎ *01588/672544* ⊕ *www.english-heritage. org.uk* ☒ *£4.40* ⊙ *Apr.–Sept., daily 10–6; Oct., daily 10–5; Nov.–Mar., Wed.–Sun. 10–4.*

Where to Stay & Eat

£££££
FodorsChoice
★

✕ **The Merchant House.** Tucked away in the northern end of town, this black-and-white Jacobean building could be mistaken for a private terraced house. Service at the small restaurant is not fussy, and the superb daily changing set menu reflects the eclectic preferences of the chef, relying on organic products where possible. Typical dishes include saffron and artichoke risotto, and iced prune and Armagnac parfait. ⊠ *Lower Corve St.* ☎ *01584/875438* ⚛ *Reservations essential* ☐ *MC, V* ⊙ *Closed Sun., Mon., 1 wk in late Dec., and 1 wk in spring. No lunch Tues.–Thurs.*

££££

✕▦ **Dinham Hall.** A converted merchant's town house dating from 1792, this hotel near Ludlow Castle formerly served as a boys' dormitory for the local grammar school. The owners have successfully integrated modern comforts—including comfortable furniture and pretty print fabrics—with the original historic elements. The deep pink dining room serves creative fixed-price meals, with choices such as lobster ravioli with basil sauce for a first course and hot chocolate pudding with pistachio ice cream for dessert. ⊠ *Off Market Sq., SY8 1EJ* ☎ *01584/ 876464* ☐ *01584/876019* ⊕ *www.dinhamhall.co.uk* ⇄ *14 rooms* ♨ *Restaurant, meeting rooms, some pets allowed (fee); no a/c* ☐ *AE, DC, MC, V* ⊙ *BP.*

★ **££–££££**

✕▦ **Mr. Underhill's.** Occupying a converted mill building beneath the castle, this secluded restaurant with rooms looks onto the wooded River Teme. Both restaurant (closed Tuesday; reservations essential) and rooms are informal, with plenty of pictures, and the bright bedrooms are furnished in natural fabrics. The superb modern British fixed-price menu, customized when you book, uses only fresh seasonal ingredients. Dinner could be *pavé* (a cold mousse) of brill with cardamom and wild lime sauce or lamb with sorrel and mint, followed by a luscious chocolate tart. Book well ahead. ✉ *Dinham Weir, SY8 1EH* ☎ *01584/874431* ⊕ *www.mr-underhills.co.uk* ⤶ *7 rooms* ♨ *Restaurant; no a/c, no smoking* ▤ *MC, V* ⊘ *Restaurant closed Tues.* ⫦⊙⫦ *BP.*

££–£££   ▦ **The Feathers.** Even if you're not staying here, you can't help but admire the extravagant half-timber façade of this building, described by the architectural historian Nicholas Pevsner as "that prodigy of timber-framed houses." The interior is equally impressive—dripping with ornate plaster ceilings, carved oak, paneling, beams, and creaking floors. Some guest rooms are done in modern style, but others preserve the antique look. ✉ *The Bull Ring, SY8 1AA* ☎ *01584/875261* 🖷 *01584/ 876030* ⊕ *www.feathersatludlow.co.uk* ⤶ *40 rooms* ♨ *Restaurant, cable TV with movies, Internet, meeting rooms, some pets allowed (fee); no a/c* ▤ *AE, DC, MC, V* ⫦⊙⫦ *BP.*

££   ▦ **Hen and Chickens.** Creaking floors and sloping ceilings abound in this 18th-century former pub. Bedrooms are simply furnished, bathrooms are sizable, and you'll find home-produced eggs and preserves on the breakfast table, as well as the famous local sausages. ✉ *103 Old St., SY8 1NU* ☎ *01584/874318* ⊕ *www.hen-and-chickens.co.uk* ⤶ *4 rooms* ♨ *No a/c, no room phones, no kids under 10, no smoking* ▤ *MC, V* ⫦⊙⫦ *BP.*

Nightlife & the Arts

The two-week **Ludlow Festival** (☎ 01584/872150 ⊕ www.ludlowfestival. co.uk), starting in late June, includes opera, ballet, concerts, and Shakespeare performed by the ruined castle.

Chester

㊷ *75 mi north of Ludlow, 46 mi north of Shrewsbury.*

Cheshire is mainly a land of well-kept farms, supporting their herds of cattle, but numerous places here are steeped in history. Villages contain many fine examples of the black-and-white "magpie" type of architecture more often associated with areas to the east. The thriving center of the region is Chester, a city similar in some ways to Shrewsbury, though it has many more black-and-white half-timber buildings (some of which were built in Georgian and Victorian times), and its medieval walls still stand. Chester has been a prominent city since the late 1st century AD, when the Roman Empire expanded northward to the banks of the River Dee. The original Roman town plan is still evident: the principal streets, Eastgate, Northgate, Watergate, and Bridge Street, lead out from the Cross—the site of the central area of the Roman fortress—to the four city gates, and the partly excavated remains of what is thought to be the country's largest Roman amphitheater lie to the south of Chester's medieval castle. Since Roman times, seagoing vessels have sailed up the estuary of the Dee and anchored under the walls of Chester. The port enjoyed its most prosperous period during the 12th and 13th centuries.

History seems more tangible in Chester than in many other ancient cities. So much medieval architecture remains that the town center is quite compact, and modern buildings have not been allowed to intrude. A negative result of this perfection is that Chester has become a favorite bus-tour destination, with gift shops, noise, and crowds.

★ Chester's unique **Rows,** which originated in the 12th and 13th centuries, are essentially double rows of stores, one at street level and the other on the second floor with galleries overlooking the street. The Rows line the junction of the four streets in the old town. They have medieval crypts below them, and some reveal Roman foundations.

The city **walls,** accessible from various points, provide splendid views of the city and its surroundings. The whole circuit is 2 mi, but if your time is short, climb the steps at Newgate and walk along toward Eastgate to see the great ornamental **Eastgate Clock,** erected to commemorate Queen Victoria's Diamond Jubilee in 1897. Lots of small shops by this part of the walls sell old books, old postcards, antiques, and jewelry. Where the **Bridge of Sighs** (named after the enclosed bridge in Venice that it closely resembles) crosses the canal, descend to street level and walk up Northgate Street into Market Square.

Tradition has it that a church of some sort stood on the site of what is now **Chester Cathedral** in Roman times, but records indicate construction around AD 900. The earliest work traceable today, mainly in the north transept, is that of the 11th-century Benedictine abbey. After Henry VIII dissolved the monasteries in the 16th century, the abbey church became the cathedral church of the new diocese of Chester. The choir stalls reveal figures of people and dragons, and above is a gilded and colorful vaulted ceiling. In the small inner garden a striking modern bronze statue depicts the woman of Samaria offering water to Jesus. ⊠ *St. Werburgh St., off Market Sq.* ☎ *01244/324756* ⊕ *www.chestercathedral. org.uk* ⊠ *Suggested donation £3* ☉ *Daily 8–6.*

Chester Castle, overlooking the River Dee, lost its moats and battlements at the end of the 18th century to make way for the classical-style civil and criminal courts, jail, and barracks. The castle houses the **Cheshire Military Museum,** exhibiting uniforms, memorabilia, and some fine silver. ⊠ *Castle St.* ☎ *01244/327617* ⊠ *£2* ☉ *Daily 10–4:30.*

Ⓒ Beautiful grounds and natural enclosures make the 80-acre **Chester Zoo** one of Britain's most popular zoos, as well as the largest. Highlights include Chimpanzee Island, the jaguar enclosure, and the Islands in Danger tropical habitat. Baby animals are often on display, thanks to the zoo's emphasis on breeding and conservation, and there's a regular feeding program. There are 11 mi of paths, and you can use the waterbus boats or the overhead train to tour the grounds. ⊠ *A41, 2 mi north of Chester* ☎ *01244/380280* ⊕ *www.chesterzoo.org* ⊠ *£10.50, bus £1.30, train £1.70* ☉ *Daily 10–dusk.*

Where to Stay & Eat

££ ✗ **Brasserie 10/16.** Flooded with natural light from a wall of windows, this brasserie has clean, elegant lines. The Mediterranean fare is well presented, too, ranging from roasted cod with mash, red pepper jam, and pesto to numerous salad options. To complete your meal, indulge yourself with the raspberry ripple cheesecake. ⊠ *Brookdale Pl.* ☎ *01244/ 322288* ⊟ *AE, MC, V.*

££ ✗ **Francs.** Beyond the black-and-white half-timber exterior of this French eatery is an intimate dining area, with rustic basketwork on the walls and bentwood chairs. The menu lists choices such as chicken cassoulet and prawn tails with tomatoes, spring onions, and fennel; vegetarians might consider the spiced couscous and roasted vegetables. Fixed-price meals are a great value. ⊠ *14 Cuppin St.* ☎ *01244/317952* ⊟ *MC, V.*

£££££ ✗🏨 **Chester Grosvenor Hotel.** At this deluxe traditional hotel in a Tudor-style building downtown, handmade Italian furniture and French silk furnishings complement the typically English architecture. Floris toiletries, three telephones, and CD players are among the many pampering amenities. The splendid Arkle Restaurant (named after a celebrated racehorse) has marble and stone walls, solid mahogany tables, and gleaming silver; there's an excellent set-price dinner as well as a daily changing gastronomic menu. The wine cellar has more than 600 bins. Good, hearty food is served in the brasserie. ⊠ *Eastgate St., CH1 1LT* ☎ *01244/324024;*

800/525–4800 from U.S. ☎ *01244/313246* ⊕ *www.chestergrosvenor. co.uk* ⇌ *85 rooms* ♨ *2 restaurants, in-room data ports, cable TV, health club, spa, Internet, business services, meeting rooms* ▤ *AE, DC, MC, V* ❘○❘ *BP.*

★   ✕▥ **Chester Crabwall Manor.** Eleven acres of farm and parkland surround
££££–£££££   this dramatic castellated part-Tudor, part-neo-Gothic mansion, a good place to pamper yourself. The hotel has elegant, subtle furnishings in floral chintzes, a wonderful stone staircase, and sumptuously large bedrooms, all with a breakfast table and a sofa or pair of armchairs. At dinner, try such fine English fare as loin of venison with oven-roasted figs. ✉ *A540, Parkgate Rd., Mollington, CH1 6NE* ☎ *01244/851666* ☎ *01244/851400* ⊕ *www.marstonhotels.com* ⇌ *48 rooms* ♨ *Restaurant, cable TV, indoor pool, health club, spa, meeting rooms, no-smoking rooms; no a/c* ▤ *AE, DC, MC, V* ❘○❘ *BP.*

££   ▥ **Redland Hotel.** If you revel in flamboyant Victorian architecture and decoration, then this villa's original wood paneling, ornamental ceilings, colorful period furnishings, and fascinating collection of *objets* should appeal. Some bedrooms have classy four-poster beds, and all have individual character. Breakfasts match the house for quality. The hotel is a mile west of center on A5104. ✉ *64 Hough Green, CH4 8JY* ☎ *01244/ 671024* ☎ *01244/681309* ⊕ *www.redlandhotel.co.uk* ⇌ *13 rooms* ♨ *Sauna, bar; no a/c* ▤ *AE, DC, MC, V* ❘○❘ *BP.*

£–££   ▥ **Ye Olde King's Head.** Creaky stairs and passageways lead through this centrally located black-and-white17th-century inn to well-equipped guest rooms. Lattice windows and oak beams evoke the past, and the rich fabrics and thick green carpeting provide present-day comfort. ✉ *48–50 Lower Bridge St., CH1 1RS* ☎ *01244/324855* ☎ *01244/ 315693* ⇌ *8 rooms* ♨ *Restaurant, cable TV, bar; no a/c* ▤ *MC, V* ❘○❘ *BP.*

£   ▥ **Grove Villa.** The pretty location of this family-run B&B, a 19th-century house on the banks of the River Dee, enhances its appeal. Add to this antique furniture and a sense of calm, and you are guaranteed a soothing stay. ✉ *18 The Groves, CH1 1SD* ☎ *01244/349713* ✎ *Grove. Villa@tesco.net* ⇌ *3 rooms* ♨ *No room phones, no a/c, no smoking* ▤ *No credit cards* ❘○❘ *BP.*

Shopping

Chester has an **indoor market** in the Forum, near the Town Hall, every day except Sunday. **Adam's Antiques** (✉ 65 Watergate Row ☎ 01244/ 319421) specializes in items from the 18th and 19th centuries. **Bookland** (✉ 12 Bridge St. ☎ 01244/347323), in an ancient building with a converted 14th-century crypt, stocks travel and general-interest books.

WELSH BORDERS A TO Z

To research prices, get advice from other travelers, and book travel arrangements, visit www.fodors.com.

AIRPORTS

Birmingham International Airport, 6 mi east of the city center, is the country's second-busiest airport, with connections to all Britain's major cities. Bus 900 runs to the center every 20 minutes; a taxi will cost you around £15.

🛈 **Birmingham International Airport** ✉ A45, off Junction 6 of M42 ☎ 0121/767–5511 ⊕ www.bhx.co.uk.

BUS TRAVEL

National Express serves the region from London's Victoria Coach Station. Average travel time to Chester is five hours; to Hereford, and Shrewsbury, four hours; and to Worcester, 3½ hours. Flightlink operates services from London's Heathrow and Gatwick airports to Birmingham.

Traveline fields all public transport inquiries. You can also contact local companies individually. For information about bus services and Rover tickets for the Birmingham area, contact the Centro Hotline. For Worcester, Hereford, Chester, and surrounding areas, contact First.

FARES & SCHEDULES ▶ **Centro Hotline** ☎ 0121/200–2700 ⊕ www.centro.org.uk. **First (for Chester)** ☎ 01244/381515 ⊕ www.firstgroup.com. **First (for Worcester and Hereford)** ☎ 01905/763888 ⊕ www.firstgroup.com. **Flightlink** ☎ 0870/580–8080 ⊕ www.gobycoach.com. **National Express** ☎ 0870/580–8080 ⊕ www.nationalexpress.com. **Traveline** ☎ 0870/608–2608 ⊕ www.traveline.org.uk.

CAR RENTAL
▶ Local Agencies **Alamo National Car Rental** ✉ 18–20 Bristol St., Birmingham ☎ 0121/200–3010 ✉ Cathedral Service Station, Bromwich Rd., Worcester ☎ 01905/420699. **Avis** ✉ 17 Horsefair, Birmingham ☎ 0121/632–4361 ✉ 128 Brook St., Chester ☎ 01244/311463. **Hertz** ✉ Auto Travel Ltd., Abley House, Trafford St., Chester ☎ 01244/374705. **Practical Car and Van Rental** ✉ 6a Heathfield Rd., Stourport-on-Severn, between Birmingham and Worcester ☎ 01299/879191 ⊕ www.practical.co.uk.

CAR TRAVEL
To reach Birmingham (120 mi), Shrewsbury (150 mi), and Chester (180 mi) from London, take M40 and keep on it until it becomes M42, or else take M1/M6. M4 and then M5 from London take you to Worcester and Hereford in just under three hours. A prettier but slower route to Worcester and vicinity is M40 to Oxford and then A44, which skirts the Cotswolds.

ROAD CONDITIONS Driving can be difficult in the western reaches of this region—especially in the hills and valleys west of Hereford, where steep, twisting roads often narrow down into mere trackways. Winter travel here can be particularly grueling.

EMERGENCIES
▶ **Ambulance, fire, police** ☎ 999. **Birmingham Heartlands Hospital** ✉ Bordesley Green E, Birmingham ☎ 0121/424–2000. **Countess of Chester Hospital** ✉ Liverpool Rd., Chester ☎ 01244/365000.

SPORTS & OUTDOORS
HIKING & WALKING For information on hiking the Malvern Hills, contact the Malvern Tourist Office or the Ross-on-Wye Tourist Office (⇨ Visitor Information).

TOURS
Local tourist offices can recommend day or half-day tours of the region and will have the names of registered Blue Badge guides. Quality Time Travel in Malvern runs chauffeur-driven tours, shopping trips, and evening travel to theaters and concerts. From June to September, City Sightseeing operates tours of Birmingham and Chester in open-top buses.
▶ **City Sightseeing** ✉ Avenue Farm Rd., Stratford-upon-Avon ☎ 01789/299123 ⊕ www.city-sightseeing.com. **Quality Time Travel** ✉ Moel Bryn, 105 Fruitlands, Malvern, WR14 4XB ☎ 01684/566799 ⊕ www.qualitytimetravel.co.uk.

TRAIN TRAVEL
From London, Great Western and Thames Trains serve the region from Paddington station, and Virgin, Central, and Silverlink Trains leave from Euston (call National Rail Enquiries for all schedules and information). Average travel times are Paddington to Hereford, three hours;

to Worcester, 2¼ hours; Euston to Birmingham, 1¾ hour; Euston to Shrewsbury and Chester, with a change at Wolverhampton or Birmingham, 3 hours and 2½ hours, respectively. A direct local service links Hereford and Shrewsbury, with a change at Oswestry or Wrexham for Chester.

CUTTING COSTS   West Midlands Day Ranger tickets and three- and seven-day Heart of England Rover tickets allow unlimited travel.

FARES & SCHEDULES   🚹 **National Rail Enquiries** ☎ 08457/484950 ⊕ www.nationalrail.co.uk.

TRAVEL AGENCIES

🚹 Local Agent Referrals **American Express** ✉ Bank House, 8 Cherry St., Birmingham ☎ 0121/644–5555. **Thomas Cook** ✉ 99 New St., Birmingham ☎ 0121/255–2600 ✉ 10 Bridge St., Chester ☎ 01244/583500 ✉ 4 St. Peter's St., Hereford ☎ 01432/422500 ✉ 36–37 Pride Hill, Shrewsbury ☎ 01743/842000 ✉ 26 High St., Worcester ☎ 01905/871200.

VISITOR INFORMATION

The Heart of England Tourist Board is open Monday–Thursday 9–5:30, Friday 9–5. Local tourist information centers are usually open Monday–Saturday 9:30–5:30.

🚹 **Heart of England Tourist Board** ✉ Larkhill Rd., Worcester, WR5 2EZ ☎ 01905/763436 🖨 01905/763450 ⊕ www.visitheartofengland.com. **Birmingham** ✉ International Convention Centre, Broad St., B1 2EA ☎ 0121/665–6560 ✉ 2 City Arcade, B2 4TX ☎ 0121/202–5099; 0121/202–5005 accommodations ⊕ www.birmingham.org.uk. **Chester** ✉ Town Hall, Northgate St., CH1 2HJ ☎ 01244/402111 ⊕ www.chestertourism.com. **Great Malvern Tourist Office** ✉ 21 Church St., WR14 2AA ☎ 01684/892289 ⊕ www.malvernhills.gov.uk. **Hereford** ✉ 1 King St., HR4 9BW ☎ 01432/268430 ⊕ www.visitorlinks.com. **Ludlow** ✉ Castle St., SY8 1AS ☎ 01584/875053 ⊕ www.ludlow.org.uk. **Much Wenlock** ✉ The Museum, The Square, TF13 6HR ☎ 01952/727679. **Ross-on-Wye** ✉ Swan House, Edde Cross St., HR9 7BZ ☎ 01989/562768 ⊕ www.visitorlinks.com. **Shrewsbury** ✉ The Music Hall, The Square, SY1 1LH ☎ 01743/281200 ⊕ www.shropshiretourism.info. **Worcester** ✉ The Guildhall, High St., WR1 2EY ☎ 01905/726311 ⊕ www.visitworcester.com.

WALES

9

FODOR'S CHOICE
Bodnant Garden, *Tal-y-Cafn, near Conwy*
Conwy Castle, *Conwy*
Portmeirion, *village near Porthmadog*

HIGHLY RECOMMENDED

RESTAURANTS   Fairyhill, *Reynoldston, near Swansea*
Le Gallois, *Cardiff*
Ynyshir Hall, *near Machynlleth*

HOTELS   Bodysgallen Hall, *Llandudno*
Eyarth Station, *Llanfair Dyffryn Clwyd, near Ruthin*
Hotel Maes-y-Neuadd, *Talsarnau, near Porthmadog*
Hotel Portmeirion, *Portmeirion*
Lake Country House, *near Builth Wells*
Lake Vyrnwy Hotel, *Llanwddyn, near Bala*
Llwydiarth Fawr, *Llanerchymedd, near Beaumaris*
St. David's Hotel and Spa, *Cardiff*

SIGHTS   Big Pit Mining Museum, *near Abergavenny*
Bwlch y Groes, *Bala*
Caernarfon Castle, *Caernarfon*
Cardiff Castle, *Cardiff*
Castell Coch, *Tongwynlais, near Cardiff*
Conwy, *Conwy*
Gower Peninsula, *near Swansea*
Hay-on-Wye
Museum of Welsh Life, *St. Fagans, near Cardiff*
National Botanic Garden of Wales, *Llanarthne*
Powis Castle, *Welshpool*
Snowdon Mountain Railway, *Llanberis*

368 < **Wales**

Updated by
Roger Thomas

WALES, KNOWN AS THE LAND OF SONG, is also a land of mountain and flood, where wild peaks challenge the sky and waterfalls thunder down steep, rocky chasms. It is a land of gray-stone castles, ruined abbeys, male-voice choirs, and a handful of cities. Pockets of the southeast and northeast were heavily industrialized in the 19th century, largely with mining and steelmaking, but long stretches of the coast and the mountainous interior remain areas of unmarred beauty. Small self-contained Wales has three national parks (Snowdonia, including Snowdon, highest mountain in England and Wales; the Brecon Beacons; and the Pembrokeshire Coast) and five official Areas of Outstanding Natural Beauty (the Wye Valley, Gower Peninsula, Llŷn Peninsula, Isle of Anglesey, and Clwydian Range), as well as large tracts of unspoiled moor and mountain in mid-Wales, the least-traveled part of the country. Riches of other sorts dot the entire country: medieval castles, seaside resorts, traditional market towns, the glorious Bodnant Garden and the National Botanic Garden, the stately houses of Powis and Plas Newydd, steampowered trains running through Snowdonia and central Wales, and the cosmopolitan capital of Cardiff.

The 1941 film *How Green Was My Valley* depicted Wales as an industrial cauldron filled with coal mines, an image that has lingered in many people's minds. Although mining took place in Wales, the picture was not accurate then and is certainly not accurate now, when the country has only one fully operational mine. In fact, one of the great glories of Wales is the drive through beautiful countryside from south to north without passing through any large towns. The same applies to the country's 750-mi coast, which consists mainly of sandy beaches, grassy headlands, cliffs, and estuaries.

The Welsh are a Celtic race. When, toward the middle of the first millennium AD, the Anglo-Saxons spread through Britain, they pushed the indigenous Celts farther back into their Welsh mountain strongholds. (In fact, "Wales" comes from the Saxon word "Weallas," which means "strangers," the name impertinently given by the new arrivals to the natives.) The Welsh, however, have always called themselves "Y Cymry," the companions. Not until the English king Edward I (1272–1307) waged a brutal campaign to conquer Wales was English supremacy established. Welsh hopes were finally crushed with the death in battle of Llywelyn ap Gruffudd, last native prince of Wales, in 1282.

Today Wales has achieved a measure of independence from its English neighbor. In a 1999 referendum, a narrow majority of the Welsh people voted for partial devolution for the country. Elections were held and the Welsh Assembly was born. Unlike the Scottish Parliament that came into being on the same day, the Welsh Assembly has no law-making powers, but it does have significant administrative responsibilities and considerable control over Welsh affairs. The Assembly will eventually be housed in a new building on Cardiff Bay.

The Welsh language continues to flourish. Although spoken by only a fifth of the population, it has a high profile within the country. Welsh-language schools are popular, there is a Welsh TV channel, and road signs are bilingual. Ironically, although in the 15th and 16th centuries the Tudor kings Henry VII and Henry VIII continued England's domination of the Welsh, principally by attempting to abolish the language, another Tudor monarch, Elizabeth I, ensured its survival by authorizing a Welsh translation of the Bible in 1588. Today many older people say they owe their knowledge of Welsh to the Bible. You'll see Welsh throughout your travels, but there's no need to worry; everyone in Wales speaks English, too.

Although less than 200 mi from south to north, Wales is packed with scenic variety and a daunting number of places to visit. Many people make the mistake of thinking that they can see Wales in a day or so, but that's time only to scratch the surface. Three days gives you time to sample the country's variety, including Cardiff, two national parks, and some towns. A nine-day trip lets you explore cities, coast, and mountains more thoroughly.

Numbers in the text correspond to numbers in the margin and on the Wales and Cardiff maps.

If you have 3 days

Start in **Cardiff** ㉒–㉙ ⌐, Wales's capital city, and spend at least a half day here before driving through the Brecon Beacons National Park to ☒ **Llandrindod Wells** ⑯, a Victorian spa town. On day two, drive via Rhayader and the Elan Valley, Wales's "Lake District," to **Aberystwyth** ⑰, then along the north coast of Cardigan Bay to ☒ **Porthmadog** ⑤ (handy accommodations are in nearby Harlech and Portmeirion). For your final day, drive via **Blaenau Ffestiniog** ④ through the Snowdonia National Park to **Betws-y-Coed** ⑥ and, if possible, drop by medieval **Conwy** ⑩ before leaving Wales via the A55 route to England.

If you have 9 days

Travel to ☒ **Cardiff** ㉒–㉙ ⌐ for a full day's visit and overnight stop, making sure to stop at the Museum of Welsh Life, at St. Fagans. On day two, drive via **Swansea** ㉝ to ☒ **Tenby** ㉟, a resort at the southern gateway to the Pembrokeshire Coast National Park. Day three is taken up by a tour of this wild and beautiful seashore. Drive to ☒ **St. David's** ㊲ in the far west to visit the cathedral built on a religious site founded by Wales's patron saint in the 6th century. You can walk a stretch of the coast path or explore **Fishguard** ㊳. Day four is taken up by more coastline on the way to **Cardigan** ㊴, then a tour along the Vale of Teifi through Cilgerran to Drefach Felindre to explore the Museum of the Welsh Woolen Industry. Continue on to ☒ **Aberystwyth** ⑰ and overnight there. From Aberystwyth, drive along the Cardigan Bay coast via **Machynlleth** ⑱ to **Dolgellau** ⑲, then head inland through the southern section of the Snowdonia National Park to lakeside ☒ **Bala** ③.

You'll see more mountains on day six on the way from Bala to **Blaenau Ffestiniog** ④, where you can visit the caverns that gave this town its past reputation as the "slate capital of North Wales." From here, follow the Vale of Ffestiniog west to **Porthmadog** ⑤. Then continue north to ☒ **Caernarfon** ⑧ and one of Wales's most famous medieval castles. Day seven takes you to the Isle of Anglesey and **Beaumaris** ⑨ for a brief visit, then back along the coast of mainland North Wales via medieval **Conwy** ⑩ to the Victorian seaside resort of ☒ **Llandudno** ⑪. (On this leg, you may replace the trip to Anglesey with a short detour inland from Caernarfon to **Llanberis** ⑦ and Llanberis Pass in the heart of Snowdonia). Borderland Wales is the theme of the next day, the route passing through **Denbigh** ⑫, **Ruthin** ⑬, **Llangollen** ②, **Chirk** ①, and **Welshpool** ㉑ on the way to ☒ **Llandrindod Wells** ⑯. On your last day, visit **Hay-on-Wye** ⑭, the "town of books," then drive on through the mountains to **Brecon** ㉜ in the Brecon Beacons National Park. From here, follow the Vale of Usk through **Crickhowell** ㉛ and **Abergavenny** ㉚ before leaving Wales along the M4 motorway.

Exploring Wales

Wales has three main regions: south, mid, and north. The south is the most varied, for its boundaries include everything from Wales's capital city to unspoiled coastline, grassy mountains to wooded valleys. Mid-Wales is pure countryside, fringed on its western shores by the great arc of Cardigan Bay. North Wales is a mixture of high, rocky mountains, popular sandy beaches, and coastal hideaways.

About the Restaurants

Today even many rural pubs are more interested in offering meals than serving pints of beer, so do consider these as a dining option. Don't over-look hotel restaurants in Wales; many, particularly those in country inns or hotels, are excellent.

About the Hotels

A 19th-century dictum, "I sleeps where I dines," still holds true in Wales, where good hotels and good restaurants often go together. A number of castles, country mansions, and even small railway stations are being transformed into interesting hotels and restaurants. Traditional inns with low-beam ceilings, wood paneling, and cozy fireplaces remain Wales's pride, but they tend to be off the beaten track, making a car a necessity. The same goes for farmhouse accommodations. Cardiff and Swansea have a number of large international hotels, and, for luxury, Wales has a good choice of country-house hotels. An added attraction is that prices are generally lower than they are for equivalent properties in the Cotswolds, Scotland, or southeast England. A service charge may be added to the room cost; ask if it's included.

WHAT IT COSTS In pounds sterling				
	££££££	££££	£££	££	£
RESTAURANTS	over £22	£18–£22	£13–£17	£7–£12	under £7
HOTELS	over £160	£115–£160	£80–£115	£50–£80	under £50

Restaurant prices are for a main course at dinner. Hotel prices are for two people in a standard double room in high season, including VAT, with no meals or, if indicated, CP (with Continental breakfast), BP (Breakfast Plan, with full breakfast), or MAP (Modified American Plan, with breakfast and dinner).

Timing

The weather in Wales, as in the rest of Britain, is a lottery. It can be warm in the spring and cool in the summer, dry in May, and wet in August. Come prepared for rain or shine. Generally speaking, southwest Wales enjoys a milder climate than elsewhere, thanks to the moderating effects of the sea. Spring and autumn are attractive times in Wales; note that spring can arrive very early in Pembrokeshire, while winter may still grip other parts of the country. These seasons can be surprisingly dry and sunny, and you will have the added advantage of quiet surroundings. That noted, crowds are rarely a problem, apart from the main tourist centers, even in the height of summer. Book ahead for major festivals such as the literary Hay Festival, Brecon Jazz, and Llangollen's International Musical Eisteddfod.

NORTH WALES
IN THE REALM OF SNOWDONIA

The north is the region where Wales masses all its savage splendor and fierce beauty. Dominating its southwestern corner is Snowdon, at 3,560

Castles

In Wales, a "Land of Castles," more than 400 fortresses provide an inexhaustible supply of inspiration for any lover of history. These ancient strongholds, some of which were built by Edward I in the 13th century to control the Welsh, dot the landscape from south (Caerphilly) to north (Harlech, Beaumaris, Conwy) and range from romantic ruins to well-preserved fortresses still rising to their original imperious height. The great North Wales castles, such as Caernarfon, are nearly intact and particularly famous. But for many people, the lasting memory of Wales is the sight of weatherbeaten ruins crowning hilltops or guarding mountain passes deep in the lush countryside.

Great Flavors

Talented chefs throughout the country make the best use of Wales's bountiful natural resources. Succulent Welsh lamb is regarded as the best in the world, seafood is plentiful, and cheese making is undergoing a revival. Welsh lamb served with vegetables is an old favorite. Another traditional feast is cawl, a nourishing broth with vegetables and meat. Laverbread, made from seaweed and cooked to resemble a black pureed substance, has a taste all its own and is usually eaten with bacon and eggs.

Steam Railways

Wales is the best place in Britain for narrow-gauge steam railways, many of which wind through extraordinary landscapes. The Great Little Trains of Wales operate during spring, summer, and autumn through the mountains of Snowdonia and central Wales (there are also a few lines in South Wales). The Ffestiniog Railway, which links two British Rail lines at the old slate town of Blaenau Ffestiniog and Porthmadog, climbs the mountainside around an ascending loop. Tiny, copper-knobbed engines haul narrow carriages through deep cuttings and along rocky shelves above oak woods in Snowdonia National Park. Snowdonia also has Britain's only alpine-style steam rack railway, the Snowdon Mountain Railway, where little sloping boiler engines on rack-and-pinion track push their trains 3,000 feet up from Llanberis to the summit of Snowdon.

Walking

An army of bipeds descends on Wales every year for wonderful walking and hiking. Long-distance paths include the Pembrokeshire Coast Path (which runs all along the spectacular shores of southwest Wales), the south–north Offa's Dyke Path, based on the border between England and Wales established by King Offa in the 8th century, and the Glyndŵr Way, a 128-mi-long highland route that traverses mid-Wales from the border town of Knighton via Machynlleth to Welshpool. Signposted footpaths in Wales's forested areas are short and easy to follow. Enthusiasts might prefer the challenging wide-open spaces of the Brecon Beacons National Park or the mountains of Snowdonia.

---

feet the highest mountain in England and Wales. It is impossible to describe the magnificence of the view on a clear day: to the northwest the Menai Strait, Anglesey, and beyond to the Irish Sea; to the south the mountains of Merionethshire, Harlech Castle, and the Cader Idris mountain range; and all around towering masses of wild and barren rock.

Wales

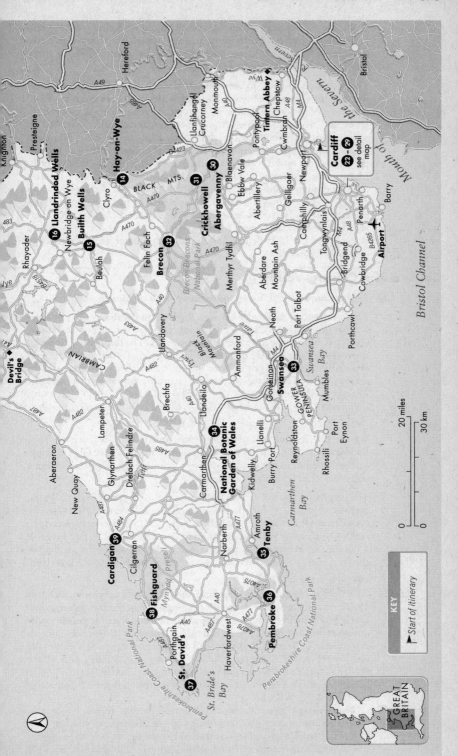

Hereford

Bristol

A49

A465

 Llanfihangel
Crucorney

Monmouth

Wye
Tintern Abbey
Chepstow

Presteigne

Knighton

A438

14 Hay-on-Wye

BLACK MTS.

30

Abergavenny
Crickhowell **31**

Blaenavon

Ebbw Vale

Pontypool
Cwmbran

Newport

A48

M4

Mouth of the Severn

483

16 Llandrindod Wells

Newbridge on Wye

Clyro

A479

A470

15 Builth Wells

Beulah

Felin Fach

Brecon **32**

Brecon Beacons
National Park

A470

Merthyr Tydfil

Aberdare

Mountain Ash

Aberillery

Gelligaer

Caerphilly

Pontywnlais

Cardiff
22 – 29
see detail
map

Penarth

Barry

Barry

Airport

B4265

Cowbridge

Bridgend

Porthcawl

Bristol Channel

Rhayader

Wye

A.

A.

A483

CAMBRIAN

Devil's
Bridge

A487

A482

A482

A44

Llandovery

Llandeilo

A40

Brechfa

A40

A482

Lampeter

A485

Brechfa

Black
Mountain

Ammanford

Tawe

Neath

Port Talbot

M4

Gower
PENINSULA

Swansea **33**

Gorseinon

Swansea
Bay

Mumbles

Port
Eynon

Rhossili

Aberaeron

New Quay

Glynarthen

Dre-fach Felindre

Teifi

A485

34
National Botanic
Garden of Wales

Carmarthen

Llandeilo

Llanelli

Kidwelly

Burry Port

Carmarthen
Bay

A484

A487

A484

Cardigan **39**

Cilgerran

Mynydd Preseli

A478

Narberth

A477

Amroth

35 Tenby

Pembrokeshire Coast National Park

Fishguard **38**

A40

A487

A40

Haverfordwest

A477

A4075

Pembroke **36**

A4075

Porthgain

St. David's

37

St. Bride's
Bay

Pembrokeshire Coast National Park

20 miles

30 km

0

0

GREAT
BRITAIN

If you ascend the peak by the Snowdon Mountain Railway from Llan-beris, telephone from the terminus to ascertain whether Snowdon is free from mist, for you will lose much if you arrive when clouds, as often happens, encircle the monster's brow.

The peak gives its name to **Snowdonia National Park,** which extends south-ward all the way to Machynlleth in mid-Wales. The park consists of 840 square mi of rocky mountains, valleys clothed in oak woods, moorlands, lakes, and rivers, all with one thing in common: natural beauty, and, to a lesser extent, solitude. Increasingly, however, the park has become a popular climbing center, and some fear that Snowdon itself is becom-ing worn away by the boots of too many walkers. Along the sandy, north-facing coast, a string of seaside resorts has also attracted people for well over a century. Llandudno, the dignified "Queen of the North Wales coast," was built in Victorian times as a seaside watering hole. If you prefer away-from-it-all seashore, there are two official Areas of Out-standing Beauty: the Isle of Anglesey (connected by bridge to mainland Wales), and the Llŷn Peninsula, dotted with quieter small resorts and coastal villages.

Chirk & the Ceiriog Valley

❶ *22 mi southwest of Chester, 60 mi southwest of Manchester.*

Chirk, poised on the border between England and Wales, is a handy gate-way to the Ceiriog Valley, a narrowing vale that penetrates the silent, green foothills of the lofty Berwyn Mountains. The impressive medieval fortress of **Chirk Castle,** completed in its original form in 1310, has evolved into a grand home, with interiors furnished in 16th- to 19th-century styles. The castle stands amid beautiful formal gardens and fine 18th-century parkland. ⊠ *Off B4500* ☎ *01691/777701* ⊕ *www.nationaltrust.org.uk* 🖾 *£5.80, garden only £3.60* ☾ *Castle Apr.–Oct., Wed.–Sun. noon–5; garden Apr.–Oct., Wed.–Sun. 11–6.*

West of Chirk is the **Vale of Ceiriog,** nicknamed Little Switzerland. Take B4500 west 6 mi through the lovely valley to the village of Glyn Ceiriog, at the foothills of the remote Berwyn Mountains. The area attracts pony trekkers, walkers, and anglers.

The peat-brown water of **Pistyll Rhaeadr,** the highest waterfall in Wales, thunders down a 290-foot double cascade. To get here, take B4500 south-west from Glyn Ceiriog, and then its unnumbered continuation, to reach Llanrhaeadr ym Mochnant, in the peaceful Tanat Valley. Here, in 1588, the Bible was translated into Welsh, thus ensuring the survival of the language. Turn northwest and go 4 mi up the road to the waterfall.

Where to Stay & Eat

££–£££ ✕▦ **Golden Pheasant.** Antiques and Victorian-style fabrics furnish this 18th-century hotel, and the result is chinoiserie in the bar, horse prints and aspidistras in the lounge, draped curtains and parlor palms in the dining room, and no two bedrooms alike. There's a three-course, fixed-price menu in the restaurant, as well as a bar menu. Specialties include Ceiriog trout and game pie. ⊠ *Glyn Ceiriog, LL20 7BB, near Chirk* ☎ *01691/718281* ⊕ *www.goldenpheasanthotel.co.uk* 🖷 *01691/718479* ⇱ *19 rooms* ☖ *Restaurant, bar, lounge, some pets allowed (fee); no a/c* ▭ *DC, MC, V* ⃝ *BP.*

££ ▦ **Bron Heulog.** Lovingly restored in period style as a guest house, this former Victorian doctor's office has 2 acres of garden with resident don-keys. Fireplaces, high ceilings, and an oak staircase are original elements of the large stone house. Rooms have showers. ⊠ *Waterfall Rd., off*

B4396, Llanrhaeadr ym Mochnant, SY10 0JX ☎01691/780521 ⊕www.
kraines.enta.net ⤵3 rooms ⚄ No-smoking rooms; no a/c, no room
phones ⊟ MC, V ⫣⊙⫤ BP.

Llangollen

❷ *5 mi northwest of Chirk, 23 mi southwest of Chester.*

Llangollen's setting in a deep valley carved by the River Dee gives it typically Welsh appeal. The bridge over the Dee, a 14th-century stone
structure, is named in a traditional Welsh folk song as one of the "Seven
Wonders of Wales." In July the International Musical Eisteddfod takes
place here. For a particularly scenic drive in this area, head for the Horseshoe Pass.

Plas Newydd (not to be confused with the grand estate on the Isle of Anglesey with the same name) was the home from 1778 to 1828 of Lady
Eleanor Butler and Sarah Ponsonby, the eccentric Ladies of Llangollen,
who set up a then-scandalous single-sex household, collected curios and
magnificent wood carvings, and made it into a tourist attraction even
during their lifetimes. Among their celebrated guests were William
Wordsworth, Sir Walter Scott, and the duke of Wellington. The gardens
are quite attractive. ⊠ Hill St. ☎ 01978/861314 ⎙ 01824/708258
⊡ £2.50 ⊙ Apr.–Oct., daily 10–5.

From the **canal wharf** (☎ 01978/860702) you can take a horse-drawn
boat or a narrow boat (a slender barge) along the Llangollen Canal to
☾ the largest navigable aqueduct in the world at Pontcysyllte. The **Llangollen
Railway,** a restored standard-gauge steam line, runs for a few miles along
the scenic Dee Valley. The terminus is near the town's bridge. ☎ 01978/
860979; 01978/860951 24-hr recorded information ⊕ www.llangollen-
railway.co.uk ⊡ £8.50 round-trip ⊙ Apr.–Oct., daily 10–5; Nov.–Mar.,
weekends, limited service.

Where to Stay

££ ⊡ **Oakmere.** This sandstone Victorian residence set in its own grounds
is only a few minutes' walk from Llangollen center. Special features include tile or polished pine floors, period furniture in walnut and mahogany, a conservatory, and spacious, high-ceilinged bedrooms. There
are fine views of the valley and mountains. ⊠ Regent St., LL20 8HS
☎ 01978/861126 ⊕ www.oakmere.llangollen.co.uk ⤵6 rooms ⚄ Tennis court, lounge; no a/c, no room phones, no smoking ⊟ No credit cards
⫣⊙⫤ BP.

Nightlife & the Arts

The six-day **International Musical Eisteddfod** (☎ 01978/862000 ⊕ www.
international-eisteddfod.co.uk), held in early July, brings together amateur choirs and dancers, more than 12,000 participants in all, from all
corners of the globe for a large colorful arts festival. The tradition of
the *eisteddfod,* held throughout Wales, goes back to the 12th century.
Originally gatherings of bards, the *eisteddfodau* of today are more like
competitions or festivals.

Sports & the Outdoors

There are easy walks along the banks of the River Dee or along part of
the lovely **Offa's Dyke Path** (⊕ www.offasdyke.demon.co.uk). The 177-
mi-long National Trail follows the line of an ancient earthen wall, still
surviving in parts, which was built along the border with England in
the 8th century by King Offa of Mercia to keep out Welsh raiders.

Bala

❸ *18 mi southwest of Llangollen.*

The staunchly Welsh town of Bala makes a good base for exploring the eastern and southern sections of Snowdonia National Park as well as the gentler landscapes of borderland Wales. It stands at the head of Llŷn Tegid (Bala Lake), at 4 mi long the largest natural lake in Wales. This is a good place for kayaking and windsurfing. The scenic narrow-gauge **Bala Lake Railway** (☎ 01678/540666 ⊕ www.bala-lake-railway.co.uk), one of the Great Little Trains of Wales, runs along the southern shore of Bala Lake.

★ To experience Wales at its wildest, you can drive over **Bwlch y Groes** (Pass of the Cross), the highest road in Wales, whose sweeping panoramas are breathtaking. To get here, take the narrow road south from Bala through Cwm Hirnant and over the mountain to Lake Vyrnwy. Turn right at the lake and drive for a mile on B4393 before heading west on the mountain road.

Where to Stay & Eat

★ ✕▦ **Lake Vyrnwy Hotel.** Awesome views of mountain-ringed Lake Vyrnwy
££££–£££££ add to the appeal of this country mansion within a 24,000-acre estate. For the ultimate sporting holiday, you can fish, bird-watch, play tennis, or take long walks. Sailboats are also available. Leather chairs, log fires, and a wealth of antiques add luxury, and rooms are quiet and comfortable. The sophisticated contemporary cuisine (four-course prix-fixe menu only) includes trout, pheasant, and duck from the reserve; marinated partridge with saffron vegetables and a casserole of monkfish and scallops are typical dishes. ✉ *Llanwddyn, SY10 0LY* ☎ *01691/870692* ᖴ *01691/870259* ⊕ *www.lakevyrnwy.com* ⤴ *35 rooms* ⚘ *Restaurant, tennis court, boating, fishing, bicycles, meeting rooms; no a/c* ▭ *AE, DC, MC, V* ⎠⎠ *BP.*

£££ ▦ **Cyfie Farm.** This refurbished ivy-clad 17th-century farmhouse in a tranquil area close to Lake Vyrnwy has oak beams and log fireplaces. The luxurious rooms possess all the sophistication of those in a top hotel. ✉ *Llanfihangel-yng-Ngwynfa, near Llanfyllin, SY22 5JE* ☎ *01691/648451* ᖴ *01691/648363* ⊕ *www.wales.little-places.co.uk* ⤴ *3 rooms* ⚘ *Lounge, no-smoking rooms; no a/c, no room phones* ▭ *No credit cards* ⎠⎠ *BP.*

Blaenau Ffestiniog

❹ *22 mi northwest of Bala, 10 mi southwest of Betws-y-Coed.*

Most of the world's roofing tiles once came from this former "slate capital of North Wales," and commercial quarrying continues here. The enterprises that attract attention nowadays, however, remain the old slate mines, which opened to the public in the 1970s.

At the **Llechwedd Slate Caverns,** you can take two trips: a tram ride through floodlighted tunnels where Victorian working conditions have been re-created, and a ride on Britain's deepest underground railway to a mine where you can walk by an eerie underground lake. On the surface of this popular site are a re-created Victorian village, old workshops, and slate-splitting demonstrations. ✉ *Off A470* ☎ *01766/830306* ⊕ *www.llechwedd.co.uk* ▦ *Tour £7.75, surface free* ◷ *Mar.–Sept., daily 10:15–5:15; Oct.–Feb., daily 10:15–4:15.*

Porthmadog

5 *12 mi southwest of Blaenau Ffestiniog, 16 mi south of Caernarfon.*

The little seaside town of Porthmadog, built as a harbor to export slate from Blaenau Ffestiniog, stands at the gateway to Llŷn, an unspoiled peninsula of beaches, wildflowers, and country lanes. Its location between Snowdonia and Llŷn, as well as the good beaches nearby and the many attractions around town, makes it a lively place in summer. A mile-long embankment known as the Cob (the small toll charge goes to charity) serves as the eastern approach to Porthmadog.

The oldest of the Welsh narrow-gauge lines (founded in the early 19th century), the **Ffestiniog Railway** runs from a quayside terminus along the Cob and continues through a lovely wooded vale into the mountains all the way to Blaenau Ffestiniog. ☎ *01766/516073* ⊕ *www.festrail.co.uk* ✉ *£14 round-trip* ⊙ *Apr.–Nov., daily, plus limited winter service.*

Fodor'sChoice One not-to-be-missed site in North Wales is **Portmeirion**, a tiny fantasy-Italianate village said to be loosely modeled after Portofino. Built in 1926 by architect Clough Williams-Ellis (1883–1978), the village has a hotel, restaurant, town hall, shops (selling books, gifts, and Portmeirion pottery), and rental cottages. Williams-Ellis called it his "light-opera approach to architecture," and the result is magical as well as genuinely inspirational, though distinctly un-Welsh. Royalty, political figures, artists, and other celebrities have stayed here, and the cult '60s TV series *The Prisoner* was filmed here. Portmeirion is a short trip east of Porthmadog over the Cob. ✉ *Off A496* ☎ *01766/770228* ⊕ *www.portmeirion-village.com* ✉ *£5.50* ⊙ *Daily 9:30–5:30.*

North of Porthmadog is **Tremadog**, a handsome village that was the birthplace of T. E. Lawrence (1888–1935), better known as Lawrence of Arabia. In the Victorian seaside resort of **Criccieth**, a few miles west of Porthmadog on A497, a medieval castle crowns the headland.

off the beaten path

HARLECH CASTLE – A wealth of legend, poetry, and song is conjured up by this famous 13th-century castle, which dominates the little coastal town of Harlech 12 mi south of Porthmadog. Its mighty ruins, visible for miles and commanding wide views, are as dramatic as its history. The inspiring music of Ceiriog's song *Men of Harlech* typifies the heroic defense of this castle in 1468 by Dafydd ap Eynion, who, summoned to surrender, replied: "I held a castle in France until every old woman in Wales heard of it, and I will hold a castle in Wales until every old woman in France hears of it!" Later in the 15th century the Lancastrians survived an eight-year siege during the Wars of the Roses here, and it was the last Welsh stronghold to fall in the 17th-century Civil War. ✉ *Off B4573* ☎ *01766/780552* ⊕ *www.cadw.wales.gov.uk* ✉ *£3* ⊙ *Late Mar.–late Oct., daily 9:30–6:30; late Oct.–late Mar., Mon.–Sat. 9:30–4, Sun. 11–4.*

Where to Stay & Eat

★ **£££££** ✕▥ **Hotel Maes-y-Neuadd.** Eight acres of gardens and parkland create a glorious setting for this hotel in a manor house dating from the 14th century. Walls of local granite, oak-beam ceilings, and an inglenook fireplace add character; the updated bedrooms have different shapes and details but use prints and pastel fabrics. The restaurant serves a three-course, fixed-price menu of Welsh, English, and French specialties that makes good use of local ingredients, including vegetables grown on the property, fish, and cheeses. The hotel is 3½ mi northeast of Harlech via B4573. ✉ *Talsarnau, LL47 6YA* ☎ *01766/780200 or 800/635–3602*

🕾 *01766/780211* ⊕ *www.neuadd.com* ⇆ *16 rooms* ᐃ *Restaurant, meeting room, some pets allowed (fee), no-smoking rooms; no a/c* 🖃 *AE, DC, MC, V* |◎| *BP.*

★ ✕🖬 **Hotel Portmeirion.** This is one of the most elegant and unusual
££££–£££££ places to stay in Wales. Clough Williams-Ellis built his Italianate fantasy village around this splendid Victorian mansion with a library, mirror room, and curved, colonnaded dining room. Accommodation is also available in cottage suites around the little village and in luxury suites in Castell Deudraeth, a castellated 19th-century house. The restaurant, which serves breakfast and has a three-course, fixed-price dinner menu, highlights local foods with a contemporary touch. ⊠ *Off A496, Portmeirion, LL48 6ET* 🕾 *01766/77000* 🕾 *01766/771331* ⊕ *www. portmeirion-village.com* ⇆ *14 rooms in main hotel, 26 rooms in cottages, 11 suites in Castell Deudraeth* ᐃ *Restaurant, cable TV, in-room VCRs, tennis court, pool, meeting rooms, some pets allowed (fee), no-smoking rooms; no a/c* 🖃 *AE, DC, MC, V* |◎| *BP.*

££ ✕🖬 **Castle Cottage.** Close to Harlech's mighty castle, this friendly hotel is a "restaurant with rooms." The emphasis is on the exceptional cuisine of chef-proprietor Glyn Roberts, who uses fresh ingredients from salmon to lamb to create imaginative, beautifully presented contemporary dishes. There's a fixed-price dinner menu (no lunch). Five small but cozy rooms are in the main building, and the adjoining annex, a former 16th-century pub, contains four spacious rooms. This lodging is a wonderful little find. ⊠ *Near B4573, Harlech, LL46 2YL* 🕾 *01766/780479* 🕾 *01766/781251* ⊕ *www.castlecottageharlech.co.uk* ⇆ *9 rooms, 4 with bath* ᐃ *Restaurant, no-smoking rooms; no a/c* 🖃 *MC, V* |◎| *BP.*

££ ✕🖬 **Yr Hen Fecws.** The name of this welcoming stone "restaurant with rooms" near the quayside means "the old bakehouse." Bold modern colors blend with traditional furnishings at the bistro-style restaurant (dinner only), which serves dishes such as fresh wild bass with ratatouille and pesto. Bedrooms have exposed slate walls, dark wood furniture, and cheerful bed coverings. ⊠ *16 Lombard St., LL49 9AP* 🕾 *01766/514625* ⊕ *www.henfecws.com* ⇆ *7 rooms* ᐃ *Restaurant; no a/c, no smoking* 🖃 *MC, V* |◎| *BP.*

Sports

Below Harlech Castle, on an expanse of land from which the sea has receded over the centuries, are the links of **Royal St. David's** (⊠ Harlech 🕾 01766/780361), one of Wales's best golf courses. Booking in advance is essential.

Betws-y-Coed

❻ *25 mi northeast of Porthmadog, 19 mi south of Llandudno.*

The rivers Llugwy and Conwy meet at Betws-y-Coed, a popular resort village set among wooded hills with excellent views of Snowdonia. Busy in summer, the village has a good selection of hotels and crafts shops. The chief landmark here is the ornate iron Waterloo Bridge (1815) over the Conwy, designed by Thomas Telford (1757–1834), and the magnificent Bodnant Garden south of the town of Conwy makes a delightful excursion. On the western (A5) approach to Betws-y-Coed are the **Swallow Falls** (small admission charge), a famous North Wales beauty spot where the River Llugwy tumbles down through a wooded chasm.

Where to Stay & Eat

££–£££ ✕ **Ty Gwyn.** After a browse through the antiques shop next door, stop for a bite at the restaurant, which is under the same management. Prints and chintz, old beams, and copper pans decorate the 17th-century building, and there's a view of the Waterloo Bridge. King scallops and monk-

THE LANGUAGE OF CYMRU

Welsh, the native language of Wales (Cymru, in Welsh), is revered in the country, but it was not legally recognized in Britain until the 1960s. Today, however, it is surviving more successfully than its closest Celtic cousin, Breton, which is spoken in northwestern France. Welsh may look difficult to pronounce, but it is a totally phonetic language; pronunciation is quite easy once the alphabet is learned. Remember that "dd" is sounded like "th" in they, "f" sounds like "v" in save, and "ff" is the equivalent of the English "f" in forest. The "ll" sound has no English equivalent; the closest match is the "cl" sound in "close." Terms that crop up frequently are bach or fach (small), craig or graig (rock), cwm (valley), dyffryn (valley), eglwys (church), glyn (glen), llyn (lake), mawr or fawr (great, big), mynydd or fynydd (mountain, moorland), pentre (village, homestead), plas (hall, mansion), and pont or bont (bridge).

---

fish or the homemade pâté are good choices on the contemporary menu. ⊠ A5 ☎ 01690/710383 ▭ MC, V.

££ 🏠 **Pengwern Country House.** In Victorian times, this stone-and-slate country house on two acres of woodland was an artists' colony. Today it reflects its original charm, with polished slate floors and beamed bedrooms. You'll find a warm welcome and good food (guests can arrange dinner here). The house is about a mile south of Betws-y-Coed. ⊠ A5, Allt Dinas, LL24 OHF ⊕ www.snowdoniaaccommodation.com ☎☎ 01690/710480 🛏 3 rooms ⚄ Lounge, no-smoking rooms; no a/c ▭ MC, V ⦿ BP.

Llanberis

❼ 17 mi west of Betws-y-Coed, 7 mi southeast of Caernarfon.

Llanberis, like Betws-y-Coed, is a focal point for people visiting the Snowdonia National Park. The town stands beside twin lakes at the foot of the rocky **Llanberis Pass,** which cuts through the highest mountains in the park and is lined with slabs popular with rock climbers. There are hiking trails from the top of the pass, but the going can be rough for the inexperienced. Ask local advice before starting any ramble. At the Pen-y-Gwryd Hotel just beyond the summit of the pass, Lord Hunt and his team planned their successful ascent of Everest in 1953.

★ 🐾 Llanberis's most famous attraction is the rack-and-pinion **Snowdon Mountain Railway,** with some of its track at a gradient of 1 in 5; the train terminates within 70 feet of the 3,560-foot summit. Snowdon, Yr Wyddfa in Welsh, is the highest peak south of Scotland and is set within more than 800 square mi of national park. From May through September, weather permitting, trains go all the way to the summit; on a clear day, you can see as far as the Wicklow Mountains in Ireland, about 90 mi away. In 1998 the National Trust bought the mountain, ensuring its long-term protection. ☎ 0870/458–0033 ⊕ www.snowdonrailway.co. uk 🎟 £18 maximum round-trip fare ☉ Mar.–Oct., daily; schedule depends on customer demand.

On Lake Padarn in the Padarn Country Park, the old Dinorwig slate quarry now serves as the **Welsh Slate Museum.** This living-history museum has quarry workshops and slate-splitting demonstrations, as well as restored worker housing. The narrow-gauge Llanberis Lake Railway runs from here. ⊠ A4086 ☎ 01286/870630 ⊕ www.nmgw.ac.uk 🎟 Free ☉ Easter–Oct., daily 10–5; Nov.–Easter, Sun.–Fri. 10–4.

Caernarfon

8 *7 mi northwest of Llanberis, 26 mi southwest of Llandudno.*

The town of Caernarfon, which has a historic pedigree as a walled medieval settlement, has nothing to rival the considerable splendor of its castle and, in fact, is now overrun with tourist buses. Still, don't miss the garrison church of St. Mary, built into the city walls.

★ Standing like a warning finger, the grim majestic mass of **Caernarfon Castle**, "that most magnificent badge of our subjection," wrote Thomas Pennant (1726–98), looms over the waters of the River Seiont. Numerous bloody encounters were witnessed by these sullen walls, erected by Edward I in the 13th century as a symbol of his determination to subdue the Welsh. Begun in 1283, its towers, unlike those of Edward I's other castles, are polygonal and patterned with bands of different-colored stone. In 1284 the monarch thought of a scheme to steal the Welsh throne. Knowing that the Welsh chieftains would accept no foreign prince, he promised to designate a ruler who could speak no word of English. He sent his queen, Eleanor of Castile, who was expecting a child, to Caernarfon, and in this cold stone fortress the queen gave birth to a son. Edward presented the infant to the assembled chieftains as their prince "who spoke no English, had been born on Welsh soil, and whose first words would be spoken in Welsh." The ruse worked, and on that day was created the first prince of Wales of English lineage. This tradition still holds: in July 1969, Elizabeth II presented Prince Charles to the people of Wales as their prince from this castle. In the Queen's Tower, a museum charts the history of the local regiment, the Royal Welsh Fusiliers. ⊠ *Castle Hill* ☎ *01286/677617* ⊕ *www.caernarfon.com* ☒ *£4.50* ☉ *Late Mar.–late Oct., daily 9:30–6:30; late Oct.–late Mar., Mon.–Sat. 9:30–4, Sun. 11–4.*

Outside Caernarfon, the **Segontium Roman Museum** tells the story of the Roman presence in Wales; it includes material from one of Britain's most famous Roman forts. The extensive excavation site of the fort is here, too. ⊠ *Beddgelert Rd. (A4085)* ☎ *01286/675625* ⊕ *www.nmgw.ac.uk* ☒ *Free* ☉ *Apr.–Oct., Mon.–Sat. 10–5, Sun. 2–5; Nov.–Mar., Mon.–Sat. 10–4, Sun. 2–4.*

☙ You can take a workshop tour and short trip on a coal-fired steam locomotive at the **Welsh Highland Railway–Rheilffordd Eryri**, a narrow-gauge line that operates on the route of an abandoned railway. The terminus is on the quay near Caernarfon Castle. ⊠ *St. Helens Rd.* ☎ *01766/516073* ⊕ *www.festrail.co.uk* ☒ *£12 round-trip* ☉ *Apr.–Oct., daily 10–4; Nov.–Mar., limited weekend service.*

Where to Stay & Eat

££ ✕▥ **Ty'n Rhos.** This immaculate farmhouse between Snowdonia and the sea provides comfortable yet elegant accommodation in rooms furnished with print fabrics and upholstered furniture. A beautifully furnished lounge and dining room has views across the fields to the Isle of Anglesey. The innovative cooking takes advantage of the best local ingredients. Try the fish of the day, the homemade cheeses and yogurt, or the Welsh breakfast, which includes local oysters. ⊠ *Llanddeiniolen, LL55 3AE* ☎ *01248/670489* 🖷 *01248/670079* ⊕ *www.tynrhos.co. uk* 🖙*11 rooms* ☖ *Restaurant, in-room data ports, croquet, lounge, meeting rooms, no-smoking rooms; no a/c* ⊟ *AE, MC, V* ◉❘ *BP.*

££ ▥ **Hafoty.** An 18th-century farmhouse set on the slopes above Caernarfon has wonderful views of the coast and the castle as well as immaculate accommodation. Barns converted to cottages with kitchens are another option here. It's a 10-minute drive from town and a good base for exploring Snowdonia. ✉ *Rhostryfan, LL54 7PH* ☎ *01286/830144* 🖷 *01286/830441* ⊕ *www.hafotyfarmguesthouse.co.uk* ↵ *4 rooms, 4 cottages* ♻ *No-smoking rooms; no a/c* ▭ *MC, V* ⧨ *BP.*

The Outdoors

Caernarfon Airparc operates Pleasure Flights in light aircraft over Snowdon, Anglesey, and Caernarfon; flights are 10–25 minutes. "Hands-on" flying lessons are offered daily (1-hour lesson £110), and there's an aviation museum (£4.50). ✉ *Dinas Dinlle Beach Rd.* ☎ *01286/830800* ⊕ *www.caeairparc.com* 🖾 *£25–£75 per seat* ⊙ *Lessons daily 9–5; flights Apr.–Oct., daily 9–5.*

Beaumaris

❾ *13 mi northeast of Caernarfon.*

Handsome Beaumaris is on the Isle of Anglesey, the largest island directly off the shore of Wales and England. It's linked to the mainland by the Britannia road and rail bridge and by Thomas Telford's remarkable chain suspension bridge, built in 1826 over the dividing Menai Strait. Though its name means "beautiful marsh," Beaumaris has become an elegant town of simple cottages, Georgian terraces, and bright shops. The nearest main-line train station is in Bangor, about 6 mi away on the mainland; a regular bus service operates between it and Beaumaris. Ferries and catamarans to Ireland leave from Holyhead, on the western side of the island.

The town dates from 1295, when Edward I commenced work on impressive **Beaumaris Castle,** the last and largest link in an "iron ring" of fortifications around North Wales built to contain the Welsh. Guarding the western approach to the Menai Strait, the castle (a World Heritage Site) is solid and symmetrical, with concentric lines of fortification, arrow slits, and a moat: a superb example of medieval defensive planning. ✉ *Castle St.* ☎ *01248/810361* ⊕ *www.cadw.wales.gov.uk* 🖾 *£3* ⊙ *Late Mar.–late Oct., daily 9:30–6:30; late Oct.–late Mar., Mon.–Sat. 9:30–4, Sun. 11–4.*

Opposite Beaumaris Castle is the **courthouse** (☎ 01248/810921), built in 1614. A plaque depicts one view of the legal profession: two farmers pull a cow, one by the horns, one by the tail, while a lawyer sits in the middle milking. The **Museum of Childhood Memories** is an Aladdin's cave of music boxes, magic lanterns, trains, cars, toy soldiers, rocking horses, and mechanical savings banks. ✉ *1 Castle St.* ☎ *01248/712498* 🖾 *£3.25* ⊙ *Mar.–Oct. and Dec., Mon.–Sat. 10:30–5, Sun. noon–5; Nov., Tues.–Sat. 10:30–5, Sun. noon–5.*

On Castle Street, look for the **Tudor Rose,** a house dating from 1400 that's an excellent example of Tudor timberwork. To discover the grim life of a Victorian prisoner, head to the old **gaol,** built in 1829 by Joseph Hansom (1803–1882), who was also the designer of the Hansom cab. ✉ *Steeple La.* ☎ *01248/810921* 🖾 *£2.85* ⊙ *May–Sept., daily 11–5:30.*

The 14th-century **Church of St. Mary and St. Nicholas,** opposite the gaol in Steeple Lane, houses the stone coffin of Princess Joan, daughter of King John (1167–1216) and wife of Welsh leader Llewelyn the Great.

off the beaten path

PLAS NEWYDD – Some historians rate the mansion of Plas Newydd on the Isle of Anglesey the finest house in Wales. Built in the 18th century by James Wyatt (1747–1813) for the marquesses of Anglesey, it stands on the Menai Strait about 7 mi southwest of Beaumaris (don't confuse *it with the Plas Newydd at Llangollen). In 1936–40 the society artist Rex Whistler (1905–44) painted the mural in the dining room. A military museum commemorates the Battle of Waterloo, where the first marquess, Wellington's cavalry commander, lost his leg. The interior has some fine 18th-century Gothic Revival decorations, and the gardens have been restored to their original design. The views of Snowdonia across the strait are magnificent. ⊠ Off A4080, southwest of the Britannia Bridge, Llanfairpwll ☎ 01248/714795 ⊕ www. nationaltrust.org.uk ☝ £4.70 ☽ Apr.–Oct., Sat.–Wed. noon–5; last admission ½ hr before closing.*

Nightlife & the Arts

The **Beaumaris Festival** (☎ 01248/811203) takes place annually late May–early June. The whole town is used as a site for special concerts, dance performances, and plays.

Where to Stay & Eat

£££ ✕⊡ **Ye Olde Bull's Head.** Originally a coaching inn built in 1472, this place is small and filled with history, and rooms are comfortably modern if not overly large. Samuel Johnson and Charles Dickens both stayed here. Eat in the stylish brasserie or the excellent oak-beam dining room (reservations essential), dating from 1617. Try the contemporary specialties such as warm salad of pigeon breast with hazelnut oil or the local widgeon (wild duck); seafood dishes win praise, too. ⊠ Castle St., LL58 8AP ☎ 01248/810329 ⌨ 01248/811294 ➴ 13 rooms ♻ Restaurant, bar; no a/c ⊟ AE, MC, V ◐ BP.

★ **££** ⊡ **Llwydiarth Fawr.** It's worth seeking out this exceptional place in the north central part of the Isle of Anglesey, a convenient touring base for the island. The spacious, elegant Georgian house sits on an 850-acre cattle and sheep farm. Guest bedrooms are luxurious, and common areas have antiques and fireplaces. Owner Margaret Hughes serves good country cooking and offers country living with style. ⊠ Llanerchymedd, LL71 8DF ☎ 01248/470321 ⊕ www.wales.little-places.co.uk ➴ 3 rooms ♻ Dining room, fishing, lounge; no a/c, no room phones, no smoking ⊟ MC, V ◐ BP.

Conwy

⑩ *23 mi east of Beaumaris, 48 mi northwest of Chester.*

The still-authentic medieval town of Conwy grew up around its castle on the west bank of the River Conwy. A ring of ancient but well-preserved walls enclose the old town and add to the strong sense of the past. You can walk along sections of the wall and take in impressive views across the huddled rooftops of the town to the castle on the estuary.

FodorsChoice Of all Edward I's fortresses, **Conwy Castle,** a mighty many-turreted
★ stronghold built between 1283 and 1287, preserves most convincingly the spirit of medieval times. The eight large round towers and tall curtain wall provide excellent views of the area and the old city walls. The castle can be approached on foot by a dramatic suspension bridge completed in 1825. Engineer Thomas Telford designed the bridge to blend in with the fortress's presence. ⊠ Castle Sq. ☎ 01492/592358 ⊕ www. cadw.wales.gov.uk ☝ £3.60 ☽ Mid-Mar.–mid-Oct., daily 9:30–6:30; mid-Oct.–mid-Mar., Mon.–Sat. 9:30–4, Sun. 11–4.

What is said to be the **smallest house in Britain** (⊠ Lower Gate St. ☎ 01492/593484) is furnished in mid-Victorian Welsh style. The house, which is 6 feet wide and 10 feet high, was reputedly last occupied in 1900 by a fisherman who was more than 6 feet tall.

Plas Mawr, a jewel in the heart of Conwy, is the best-preserved Elizabethan town house in Britain. Built in 1576 by Robert Wynn (who later became both a member of Parliament and sheriff of Caernarfonshire), this richly decorated house with its ornamental plasterwork gives a unique insight into the lives of the Tudor gentry and their servants. ⊠ *High St.* ☎ *01492/580167* ⊠ *£4.50* ⊙ *Apr.–Oct., Tues.–Sun. 10–6.*

Built in the 14th century, **Aberconwy House** is the only surviving medieval merchant's house in Conwy. Each room in the restored building reflects different eras of its long history. ⊠ *Castle St.* ☎ *01492/592246* ⊠ *£2.20* ⊙ *Apr.–Oct., Wed.–Mon. 11–5.*

Fodor'sChoice ★ With a reputation as the finest garden in Wales, **Bodnant Garden** remains a pilgrimage spot for horticulturists from around the world. Laid out in 1875, the 87 acres are particularly famed for rhododendrons, camellias, magnolias, and a laburnam arch that in May forms a huge tunnel of golden blooms. The mountains of Snowdonia form a magnificent backdrop to the Italianate terraces, rock and rose gardens, and pinetum. The gardens are about 5 mi south of Conwy, in the pretty Vale of Conwy. ⊠ *Off A470, Tal-y-Cafn* ☎ *01492/650460* ⊕ *www.nationaltrust.org. uk* ⊠ *£5.20* ⊙ *Mid-Mar.–Oct., daily 10–5.*

Llandudno

⑪ *3 mi north of Conwy, 50 mi northwest of Chester.*

This appealingly old-fashioned North Wales seaside resort has a wealth of well-preserved Victorian architecture and an ornate pier. A huge selection of attractively painted hotels lines the wide promenade (Llandudno has the largest choice of lodging in Wales). The shopping streets behind also look the part, thanks to their original canopied walkways. Llandudno has little in the way of garish amusement arcades, preferring to stick to its faithful cable car that climbs, San Francisco–style, to the summit of the Great Orme headland above the resort. There's also an aerial cable car to the top, as well as a large, dry ski slope (with an artificial surface you can ski on year-round) and toboggan run.

Llandudno was the summer home of the family of Dr. Liddell, the Oxford don and father of the immortal Alice, inspiration for Lewis Carroll's *Alice's Adventures in Wonderland*. The book's Walrus and the Carpenter may be based on two rocks on Llandudno's West Shore near the Liddell home, which Alice possibly described to Carroll. The Alice in Wonderland connection is explored in the **Alice in Wonderland Centre,** where Alice's adventures come to life in displays of the best-known scenes from the book. Alice merchandise is for sale, too. ⊠ *3–4 Trinity Sq.* ☎ *01492/860082* ⊕ *www.wonderland.co.uk* ⊠ *£3.25* ⊙ *Easter–Oct., daily 10–5; Nov.–Easter, Mon.–Sat. 10–5.*

The prehistoric **Great Orme Mines** are at the summit of the Great Orme (*orme,* a Norse word, means "sea monster"), with its views of the coast and mountains of Snowdonia. Copper was first mined here in the Bronze Age, and you can tour the ancient underground workings. ⊠ *Great Orme* ☎ *01492/870447* ⊕ *www.greatorme.freeserve.co.uk* ⊠ *£4.50* ⊙ *Feb.–Oct., daily 10–5.*

Where to Stay & Eat

★ **£££££** ✕⊡ **Bodysgallen Hall.** Antiques, comfortable chairs by cheery fires, pictures, and polished wood distinguish the part 17th-, part 18th-century Hall, which is set inside walled gardens 2 mi out of town. Bedrooms in the house combine elegance and practicality; those who seek more privacy may prefer the cottage suites scattered around the estate and parkland. The fine restaurant (three-course, fixed-price menu at dinner) uses local ingredients in creative ways, such as beef with a wild mushroom pancake or partridge with pan-fried foie gras. ⊠ *Off A470, LL30 1RS* ☎ *01492/584466* 🖷 *01492/582519* ⊕ *www.bodysgallen.com* ➷ *19 rooms, 16 cottage suites ⟁ Restaurant, tennis court, indoor pool, gym, sauna, spa, croquet, meeting rooms, some pets allowed, no-smoking rooms; no a/c in some rooms, no kids under 8* ⊟ *MC, V* ⟦⟧ *BP.*

££££–£££££ ✕▦ **The Old Rectory.** Michael and Wendy Vaughan take pride in their elegant Georgian home, which resembles a small country house furnished with Victorian antiques rather than a hotel. Another plus is the cooking—Wendy is recognized as one of Wales's top chefs. The fixed-price, three-course dinner menu is strong on creative fish dishes; nonguests must reserve in advance. The Old Rectory overlooks the Conwy Estuary south of Llandudno, with magnificent views across the house's lovely gardens to Conwy Castle and Snowdonia. ⊠ *Off A470, Llansanffraidd Glan, Conwy, LL28 5LF* ☎ *01492/580611* 🖷 *01492/584555* ⊕ *www. oldrectorycountryhouse.co.uk* ➷ *6 rooms ⟁ Restaurant, lounge, some pets allowed; no a/c, no kids under 5, no smoking* ⊟ *MC, V* ⟦⟧ *BP.*

£££–£££££ ✕▦ **St. Tudno Hotel.** One of Britain's top small seaside hotels sits on the seafront in Llandudno. From the outside, it blends unobtrusively with its neighbors, but the interior holds richly decorated and opulently furnished guest rooms and public areas with plenty of print fabrics and chintz. The fine contemporary cuisine includes dishes such as soup of local seafood and saddle of hare with spicy cabbage. ⊠ *Promenade, LL30 2LP* ☎ *01492/874411* 🖷 *01492/860407* ⊕ *www.st-tudno.co.uk* ➷ *19 rooms ⟁ Restaurant, in-room data ports, in-room VCRs, indoor pool, bar, some pets allowed (fee), no-smoking rooms; no a/c in some rooms* ⊟ *AE, DC, MC, V* ⟦⟧ *BP.*

££–£££ ▦ **Bryn Derwen Hotel.** Many hoteliers at British seaside resorts have not upgraded their accommodations and food, but this immaculate Victorian hotel exemplifies how it should be done. There is great attention to detail, and fresh flowers and plush period furnishings set the tone. The hotel offers truly excellent value. ⊠ *34 Abbey Rd., LL30 2EE* ⊕ *www.bryn-derwen-hotel.co.uk* ☎🖷 *01492/876804* ➷ *10 rooms ⟁ Dining room, spa, lounge; no a/c* ⊟ *MC, V* ⟦⟧ *BP.*

en route Inland from Rhyl, **Bodelwyddan Castle,** between Abergele and St. Asaph, is the Welsh home of London's National Portrait Gallery. Gardens, with a maze, aviary, and woodland walks, surround the Victorian castle. Galleries display Regency and Victorian portraits by the likes of Sargent, Lawrence, G. F. Watts, Rossetti, and Landseer. There are also hands-on galleries of Victorian amusements and inventions. ⊠ *Off A55* ☎ *01745/584060* ⊕ *www.bodelwyddan-castle.co.uk* ⊡ *£4.50, grounds only £1.50* ⊙ *Apr.–Oct., Sat.–Thurs. 10:30–5; Nov.–Mar., Tues.–Thurs. and weekends 10:30–4.*

Denbigh

⑫ *25 mi southeast of Llandudno.*

This market town (market day is Wednesday) was much admired by Dr. Samuel Johnson (1709–84). A walk along the riverbank at nearby Lawnt, a spot he loved, brings you to a monumental urn placed in his honor. Not that it pleased him: "It looks like an intention to bury me alive," thundered the great lexicographer.

Denbigh Castle, begun in 1282 as one of Edward I's ring of castles built to subdue the Welsh, is known as "the hollow crown" because it is not much more than a shell—though an impressive one—set on high ground, dominating the town. H. M. Stanley (1841–1904), the intrepid 19th-century journalist and explorer who found Dr. Livingstone in Africa, was born in a cottage below the castle. ☎ 029/2050–0200 ⊕ *www.cadw. wales.gov.uk* ✉ £2 ⊙ *Early Apr.–late Oct., weekdays 10–5:30, weekends 9:30–5:30.*

Ruthin

⑬ *8 mi southeast of Denbigh, 23 mi west of Chester.*

Once a stronghold of Welsh hero Owain Glyndŵr (circa 1354–1416), Ruthin is a delightful market town with elegant shops, good inns, and a fascinating architectural mix of medieval, Tudor, and Georgian buildings. The town also hosts medieval-style banquets and has a crafts complex with displays of the artisans' creations. The 17th-century **Myddleton Arms** in the town square has seven Dutch-style dormer windows, known as the "eyes of Ruthin," set into its red-tiled roof. You can tour **Ruthin Gaol**, where from 1654 to 1916 thousands of prisoners were incarcerated, and learn about conditions over the centuries. ✉ *Clwyd St.* ☎ *01824/708250* ⊕ *www.ruthingaol.co.uk* ✉ *£3* ⊙ *May–Oct., daily 10–5; Nov.–Apr., Tues.–Sun. 10–5.*

Where to Stay

★ **£–££** ▣ **Eyarth Old Railway Station.** This Victorian railway station near Ruthin has been converted into an outstanding bed-and-breakfast. Bedrooms are spacious, with large windows looking out over the Vale of Clwyd. ✉ *Off A525, Llanfair Dyffryn Clwyd, LL15 2EE* ☎ *01824/703643* 🖶 *01824/707464* ⊕ *www.eyarthstation.co.uk* 🛏 *6 rooms* ☌ *Pool; no a/c* ▭ *MC, V* ⊙❘ *BP.*

MID-WALES

THE HISTORIC HEARTLAND

Traditional market towns and country villages, small seaside resorts, quiet roads, and rolling landscapes filled with sheep farms, forests, and lakes make up mid-Wales, the country's green and rural heart. Because this is Wales's quietest vacation region, lodgings are scattered thinly. Outside of one or two large centers, Aberystwyth and Llandrindod Wells, accommodations tend mainly toward country inns, small hotels, and farmhouses. This area also has some splendid country-house hotels. Although green is the predominant color here, the landscape differs around the region. The borderlands are gentle and undulating, rising to the west into high wild mountains. Farther north, around Dolgellau, mountainous scenery becomes even more pronounced in the southern section of the Snowdonia National Park. Mountains meet the sea along Cardigan Bay, a long coastline of headlands, peaceful sandy beaches, and beautiful estuaries that has long been a shelter from the crowd. In the 19th century, Tennyson, Darwin, Shelley, and Ruskin all came to this area to work and relax; today, thousands more come to delight in the numerous antiquarian bookstores of Hay-on-Wye.

Hay-on-Wye

★ ⑭ *57 mi north of Cardiff, 25 mi north of Abergavenny.*

Bookshops and a mostly ruined castle dominate this town on the border of Wales and England. Hay is a lively place, especially on Sunday, when the rest of central Wales seems to be closed down. In 1961 Richard Booth established a small secondhand and antiquarian bookshop here.

Other booksellers soon got in on the act, and bookshops now fill several houses, a movie theater, shops, and a pub. At last count, there were about 25, all in a town of only 1,500 inhabitants. The town is now the largest secondhand bookselling center in the world, and priceless 14th-century manuscripts rub spines with "job lots" selling for a few pounds. Hay also has antiques and crafts centers. The town buzzes in early summer when it hosts the Hay Festival, a celebration of literature that attracts famous writers from all over the world.

need a break? After some hard browsing, take your literary purchases and stop off at **The Granary** (⊠ Broad St. ☎ 01497/820790) by the clock tower. Don't miss the superb homemade soups and flavorful cheese and garlic toast.

Where to Stay & Eat

£££ ✕⊠ **Old Black Lion.** A 17th-century coaching inn close to Hay's center is ideal for a lunch break while you're ransacking the bookshops, or for an overnight stay in one of its country-style rooms. The oak-beamed bar serves its own food, and the breakfasts are especially good. The restaurant's sophisticated cooking with an international twist emphasizes local meats and produce. ⊠ *Lion St., HR3 5AD* ☎ *01497/820841* 🖷 *01497/822960* ⊕ *www.oldblacklion.co.uk* 🖙 *10 rooms* ⚴ *Restaurant, bar, lounge; no a/c, no kids under 5* ▭ *MC, V* ⏺⏺ *BP.*

££ ✕⊠ **Three Cocks Hotel.** Michael and Marie-Jeanne Winstone have beautifully restored this hostelry from its cobbled forecourt to the public rooms filled with antiques and oil paintings. Bedrooms are more modestly decorated. The contemporary cooking is superb, with a strong Continental influence in dishes such as spring lamb with ratatouille. The hotel stands on the western approach to Hay, about 6 mi from town. ⊠ *A438, Three Cocks, LD3 0SL* ☎ *01497/847215* 🖷 *01497/847339* ⊕ *www. threecockshotel.com* 🖙 *7 rooms* ⚴ *Restaurant; no a/c, no room phones, no room TVs* ▭ *MC, V* ⏺⏺ *BP.*

Shopping

Boz Books (⊠ 13a Castle St. ☎ 01497/821277) specializes in 19th-century novels, including first editions of Dickens. A former cinema houses the town's largest book outpost, the **Hay Cinema Bookshop** (⊠ Castle St. ☎ 01497/820071), which stocks 200,000 volumes on subjects from art to zoology at prices from 50 pence to £5,000.

Builth Wells

⑮ *20 mi northwest of Hay-on-Wye, 60 mi north of Cardiff.*

Builth Wells, a farming town and former spa on the banks of the River Wye, hosts Wales's biggest rural gathering. The countryside around Builth and its neighbor, Llandrindod Wells, varies considerably. Some of the land is soft and rich, with rolling green hills and lush valleys, but close by are the wildernesses of Mynydd Eppynt and the foothills of the Cambrian Mountains, the lofty "backbone of Wales."

The annual **Royal Welsh Agricultural Show** (☎ 01982/553683 ⊕ www. rwas.co.uk), held in late July, is not only Wales's prime gathering of farming folk but also a colorful countryside jamboree that attracts huge crowds.

Where to Stay & Eat

★ £££ £–£££££ ✕⊠ **Lake Country House.** This is the place to go for total Victorian country elegance and tranquillity. Its 50 acres of sloping lawns and lush rhododendrons contain a trout-filled lake. Comfortable and quiet, the hotel has first-class service and excellent contemporary cuisine (fixed-price dinner menu) such as salmon with char-grilled eggplant and spicy couscous. Period furniture and fine fabrics furnish the large bedrooms; some have four-posters. The hotel is in a peaceful former spa town about 8 mi west of Builth. ⊠ *Llangammarch Wells, LD4 4BS* ☎ *01591/620202* 🖷 *01591/620457* ⊕ *www.lakecountryhouse.co. uk* ➥ *19 rooms* ♻ *Restaurant, 9-hole golf course, putting green, tennis court, fishing, billiards, croquet, bar, no-smoking rooms; no a/c* 🖃 *AE, DC, MC, V* ⏐◯⏐ *BP.*

Llandrindod Wells

⑯ *7 mi north of Builth Wells, 67 mi north of Cardiff.*

Also known as Llandod, the old spa town of Llandrindod Wells preserves its original Victorian layout and look, with fussy turrets, cupolas, loggias, and balustrades, and greenery everywhere. On a branchline rail route and with good bus service, Llandrindod makes a useful base for exploring the region, and the town itself is easily explored on foot. Cross over to South Crescent, passing the Glen Usk Hotel with its wrought-iron balustrade and the Victorian bandstand in the gardens opposite, and you soon reach Middleton Street, another Victorian thoroughfare. From there, head to Rock Park and the path that leads to the Pump Room. On the other side of town, the lake, with its boathouse, café, and gift shop, has wooded hills on one side and a broad common on the other.

The **Radnorshire Museum,** in Memorial Gardens, presents the spa's development from Roman times and explains some Victorian "cures" in gruesome detail. ☎ *01597/824513* 🖷 *£1* ⏱ *Apr.–Oct., Tues.–Sat. 10–1 and 2–5, Sun. 1–5; Nov.–Mar., Tues.–Fri. 10–1 and 2–5, Sat. 10–1.*

The **Pump Room** (⊠ Rock Park Spa ☎ 01597/822997), where visitors would "take the waters," today serves tea and refreshments and only one type of the many waters that used to be on tap.

During the town's **Victorian Festival** (☎ 01597/823441 ⊕ www. victorianfestival.co.uk), held in late August, shop assistants, hotel staff, and anyone else who cares to join in wear period costume and enjoy "old-style" entertainment.

Where to Stay

££ 🏨 **Guidfa House.** Friendly hosts Tony and Anne Millan run this stylish Georgian guest house with a welcoming log fire and bright, individually furnished bedrooms. Cordon Bleu–trained Anne prepares homemade dinners (for guests only) from fresh local produce; the guinea fowl with apple brandy and mushroom sauce is delicious. All in all, this is an ideal base from which to explore the countryside. ⊠ *Crossgates, near Llandrindod Wells, LD1 6RF* ☎ *01597/851241* 🖷 *01597/851875* ⊕ *www. guidfa-house.co.uk* ➥ *6 rooms* ♻ *Dining room; no a/c, no room phones, no kids under 10* 🖃 *MC, V* ⏐◯⏐ *BP.*

£ 🏨 **Brynhir Farm.** You get a warm welcome at this immaculate, cream-washed farmhouse tucked into the hills on a 200-acre sheep and cattle farm. Country-style furnishings enhance the rooms. ⊠ *Chapel Rd., Howey, LD1 5PB* ☎☎ *01597/822425* ⊕ *www.brynhir.farm.btinternet. co.uk* ➥ *5 rooms* ♻ *No smoking; no a/c* 🖃 *MC, V* ⏐◯⏐ *BP.*

> **en route** From Llandrindod, take A4081/A470 to Rhayader, a good pony-trekking center and gateway town for the **Elan Valley,** Wales's Lake District. This 7-mi chain of lakes, winding between gray-green hills, was created in the 1890s by a system of dams to supply water to

Birmingham, 73 mi to the east. From the Elan Valley, you can follow the narrow Cwmystwyth mountain road west to **Devil's Bridge,** a famous (and popular) beauty spot with a number of bridges over a raging river, before continuing on to Aberystwyth.

Aberystwyth

⑰ *41 mi northwest of Llandrindod Wells via A44, 118 mi northwest of Cardiff.*

Aberystwyth makes the best of several worlds as both a seaside resort and a long-established university town that houses the magnificent National Library of Wales. It also has a little harbor and quite clearly a life of its own. The town, midway along Cardigan Bay, came to prominence as a Victorian watering hole thanks to its curving beach set beneath a prominent headland. The resort is a good gateway for exploring mid-Wales: few towns in Wales present such varied scenery within their immediate neighborhood, from the extraordinary Devil's Bridge to the beautiful Rheidol Valley.

The modern **University of Wales, Aberystwyth,** on the hill above town, includes the **National Library of Wales,** which houses Welsh and other Celtic literary works; the changing exhibitions are worth a look. An arts center, a theater, and a concert hall are also open to visitors. The original university, founded in the 19th century, stands on the seafront. ⊠ *Off Penglais Rd.* ☎ *01970/632800* ⊕ *www.llgc.org.uk* ☜ *Free* ⊘ *Weekdays 9:30–6, Sat. 9:30–5.*

The **castle,** at the southern end of the bay near the New Promenade, was built in 1277 and rebuilt in 1282 by Edward I. It was one of several strongholds to fall, in 1404, to the Welsh leader Owain Glyndŵr. Today it is a romantic ruin on a headland separating the north shore from the harbor shore. At the end of the promenade, a zigzag cliff path–nature trail at **Constitution Hill** leads to a view from the top.

An enjoyable way to reach the summit of Constitution Hill is by the **Aberystwyth Cliff Railway,** the longest electric cliff railway in Britain. Opened in 1896, it has been refurbished without diminishing its Victorian look. ☎ *01970/617642* ☜ *£2.50 round-trip* ⊘ *Mid-Mar.–June and Oct., daily 10–5; July–Sept., daily 10–6.*

At the 430-foot summit of Constitution Hill is the **Great Aberystwyth Camera Obscura** (☎ 01970/617642), a free modern version of a Victorian amusement: a massive 14-inch lens gives a bird's-eye view of more than 1,000 square mi of sea and scenery, including the whole of Cardigan Bay and 26 Welsh mountain peaks.

The fine **Ceredigion Museum,** in a flamboyant 1905 Edwardian theater, displays a fine collection of folk history. Highlights include a reconstructed mud-walled cottage from 1850, exhibits from the building's music hall past, and items illustrating the region's seafaring, lead mining, and farming history. ⊠ *Terrace Rd.* ☎ *01970/633088* ⊕ *www.ceredigion. gov.uk/coliseum/* ☜ *Free* ⊘ *Mon.–Sat. 10–5.*

At Aberystwyth Station you can hop on the narrow-gauge steam-operated **Vale of Rheidol Railway** for an hour ride to the **Devil's Bridge,** where the rivers Rheidol and Mynach meet in a series of spectacular falls. Clamped between two rocky cliffs where a torrent of water pours unceasingly, this bridge well deserves its name—*Pont y Gwr Drwg,* or Bridge of the Evil One. There are actually three bridges (the oldest is 800 years old), and the walk down to the lowest bridge, "the devil's," is magnificent but strictly for the surefooted. ✉ *Alexandra St.* ☎ *01970/625819* ⊕ *www.rheidolrailway.co.uk* ✉ *£11 round-trip* ☉ *Easter–Oct.; call for schedule.*

off the
beaten
path

LLANERCHAERON – This uniquely preserved late-18th-century Welsh gentry estate in the Aeron Valley, 17 mi south of Aberaeron, is a superb example of the early work of John Nash. The walled gardens are spectacular. ✉ *Off A482, Ciliau Aeron,* ☎ *01545/570200* ⊕ *www.nationaltrust.org.uk* ✉ *£4* ☉ *Apr.–Oct., Wed.–Sun. 11:30–4:30; parkland open year-round in daylight.*

Where to Stay & Eat

££ ✕ **Gannets.** A simple, good-value bistro, Gannets specializes in hearty roasts and pies produced from locally supplied meat, fish, and game. Organically grown vegetables and a good French house wine are further draws for a university crowd. ✉ *7 St. James's Sq.* ☎ *01970/617164* ▭ *MC, V* ☉ *Closed Sun., Tues.*

££££ ✕▦ **Conrah Country Hotel.** Part of the appeal of this Edwardian country-house hotel on 20 acres of grounds is its air of seclusion, even though it's just 3 mi south Aberystwyth. Traditional country furnishings and antiques decorate the house, and fresh flowers fill each room. The restaurant is known for its imaginative British cuisine making use of local game, fish, and meat. There's a three-course prix-fixe menu at dinner. ✉ *A487, Chancery, SY23 4DF* ☎ *01970/617941* ▤ *01970/624546* ⊕ *www.conrah.co.uk* ⇆ *17 rooms* ♿ *Restaurant, indoor pool, sauna, croquet; no a/c, no kids under 5* ▭ *AE, DC, MC, V* ⦿❘ *BP.*

££ ✕▦ **Four Seasons.** This family-run hotel in the town center (no relation to the famous chain) is relaxed and friendly. The spacious rooms are simply decorated, with plenty of prints. The restaurant serves à la carte and three-course prix-fixe menus at dinner; roast saddle of Welsh lamb is a specialty. ✉ *50–54 Portland St., SY23 2DX* ☎ *01970/612120* ▤ *01970/627458* ⊕ *www.fourseasonshotel.uk.com* ⇆ *16 rooms* ♿ *Restaurant; no a/c* ▭ *AE, MC, V* ⦿❘ *BP.*

Machynlleth

⑱ *18 mi northeast of Aberystwyth.*

Machynlleth, at the head of the beautiful Dovey Estuary, does not look like a typical Welsh country town. Its long and wide main street (Heol Maengwyn), lined with a mixed style of buildings from sober gray stone to well-proportioned Georgian, creates an atypical sense of openness and space. Machynlleth's busiest day is Wednesday, when the stalls of market traders fill the main street.

At the **Owain Glyndŵr Centre,** a small exhibition celebrates Wales's last native leader, who established a Welsh parliament at Machynlleth in the early 15th century. ✉ *End of Heol Maengwyn* ☎ *01654/702827* ✉ *Free* ☉ *Easter–Sept., Mon.–Sat. 10–5.*

Housed in a cultural and performing arts center in a former chapel is the free **Y Tabernacl Museum of Modern Art** (✉ Heol Penrallt ☎ 01654/703355 ⊕ www.tabernac.dircon.co.uk), a superb art gallery with permanent displays, including works by noted contemporary Welsh artist Kyffin Williams. Changing exhibitions highlight other contemporary artists.

Welsh history of an earlier time is the main theme at **Celtica,** an imaginative exhibition center in the large parkland behind the shops and pubs. Interpretive displays re-create Wales's Celtic past. ☎ *01654/702702*

⊕ *www.celtica.wales.com* ✉ *£4.95* ⊙ *Daily 10–6; last entry to main exhibition 4:40.*

The 128-mi **Glyndŵr's Way** (✉ Tourist Office, Heol Maengwyn ☎ 01654/703376)walking route passes through Machynlleth before it turns east to climb above the Dovey with wonderful views north to Cadair Idris.

⟳ At the unique **Centre for Alternative Technology** in the forested hills just north of Machynlleth, a water-balanced cliff railway transports you to a futuristic village equipped with all things green: alternative energy sources, organic gardens, and a vegetarian café. Interactive displays present ideas about renewable resources. ✉ *Off A487* ☎ *01654/702400* ⊕ *www.cat.org.uk* ✉ *£7* ⊙ *Daily 9–6.*

Where to Stay & Eat

★   ✕▣ **Ynyshir Hall.** Idyllic gardens and grounds surround this supremely
££££–£££££   comfortable country-house hotel in a beautiful Georgian mansion near a wildlife reserve. Owner Rob Reen, an artist, displays his work throughout the house. Antiques and Welsh pottery fill the public areas; the colorful guest rooms, named after artists, have antique beds. The outstanding contemporary cuisine in the candlelit restaurant uses local favorites from wild salmon and venison to farmhouse cheeses. A fixed-price menu is offered at dinner. ✉ *Off A487, Eglwysfach, southwest of Machynlleth, SY20 8TA* ☎ *01654/781209 or 800/777–6536* 🖷 *01654/781366* ⊕ *www.ynyshir-hall.co.uk* ↩ *10 rooms* ⚫ *Restaurant; no a/c, no kids under 9, no smoking* ▭ *AE, DC, MC, V* ¶◎¶ *BP.*

££–£££   ✕▣ **Penhelig Arms.** The delightful little sailing center of Aberdovey is perched at the mouth of the Dovey Estuary, west of Machynlleth. This immaculate harborside inn has a terrace overlooking the harbor and bay, and most rooms have wonderful sea views. Meet the locals in the wood-paneled Fisherman's Bar and dine in style in the fine restaurant (three-course, fixed-price dinner menu), where local seafood is a specialty. ✉ *A493, Aberdovey, LL35 0LT* ☎ *01654/767215* 🖷 *016354/767690* ⊕ *www.penheligarms.com* ↩ *14 rooms* ⚫ *Restaurant, bar; no a/c* ▭ *MC, V* ¶◎¶ *BP.*

Dolgellau

❶❾ *16 mi north of Machynlleth, 34 mi north of Aberystwyth.*

A solidly Welsh town with attractive dark buildings and handsome old coaching inns, Dolgellau (pronounced dol-*geth*-lee) became the center of the Welsh gold trade in the 19th century, when high-quality gold was discovered locally. A nugget of Dolgellau gold is used to make royal wedding rings. You can still try your luck and pan for gold in the Mawddach. The town makes a good base for walks in the area.

The **Museum of the Quakers,** in the town square, commemorates the area's strong links with the Quaker movement and the Quakers' emigration to the American colonies. ☎ *01341/422888* ✉ *Free* ⊙ *Easter–Oct., daily 10–6; Nov.–Easter, Thurs.–Mon. 10–5.*

To the south of Dolgellau rises the menacing bulk of **Cadair Idris** (2,927 feet); the name means "the Chair of Idris," though no one is completely sure who Idris was—probably a warrior bard. It is said that anyone sleeping for a night in a certain part of the mountain will awaken either a poet or a madman, or not at all.

Barmouth

20 *10 mi west of Dolgellau.*

Barmouth, on the northern mouth of the picturesqueMawddach Estuary, is one of the few places along the Welsh coast that can be described as a full-fledged seaside resort, although it's now a bit tired. It has a 2-mi-long promenade, wide expanses of golden beach, and facilities for sea, river, and mountain lake fishing. The splendid location is best appreciated from the footpath beside the railway bridge across the mouth of the estuary. Even in the 19th century Barmouth was a popular holiday resort. Alfred, Lord Tennyson was inspired to write *Crossing the Bar* by the spectacle of the Mawddach rushing to meet the sea. Charles Darwin worked on *The Origin of Species* and *The Descent of Man* in a house by the shore. Essayist and art critic John Ruskin was a frequent visitor and was trustee of the St. George's cottages built there by the Guild of St. George in 1871.

Where to Stay

££ ⊞ **Llwyndu Farmhouse.** This restored 17th-century farmhouse, with its inglenook fireplace, mullioned windows, exposed stone walls, and ancient beams, stands on a hillside with fine views over Cardigan Bay. The country-style rooms in the house or in the adjoining converted barn have modern conveniences as well as some of the charming quirks of age. Guests can dine on traditional and contemporary dishes from Welsh rabbit to stir-fried duck with plum and ginger sauce. ⊠ *A496, Llanaber, LL42 1RR, 1 mi north of Barmouth* ☎ *01341/280144* 🖷 *01341/281236* ⊕ *www.llwyndu-farmhouse.co.uk* ⌖ *7 rooms* ⌂ *Dining room, lounge; no a/c, no smoking* ⊟ *MC, V* ❍❙ *BP.*

Welshpool

21 *48 mi east of Barmouth, 19 mi west of Shrewsbury.*

The border town of Welshpool, "Trallwng" in Welsh, is famous as the home of Powis Castle, one of mid-Wales's greatest treasures, but it also has an appealing town center.

★ In continuous occupation since the 13th century, **Powis Castle** is one of the most opulent residential castles in Britain. Its battlements rear high on a hilltop, and splendid grounds and Italian- and French-influenced terraced gardens surround the castle. Below gigantic yew hedges, the grounds fall steeply down to wide lawns and neat Elizabethan gardens. The interior contains many treasures: Greek vases; paintings by Gainsborough, Reynolds, and Romney, among others; superb furniture, including a 16th-century Italian table inlaid with marble; and the **Clive of India Museum,** with a fine collection of Indian art. The tearoom is excellent. ⊠ *Off A483* ☎ *01938/551920* ⊕ *www.nationaltrust.org. uk* 🖾 *£8, gardens only £5.50* ❍ *Apr.–June, Sept., and Oct., Wed.–Sun.; July and Aug., Tues.–Sun. Hrs: castle and museum 1–5, gardens 11–6; last admission ½ hr before closing.*

The excellent **Powysland Museum,** in a converted warehouse on the banks of the Montgomery canal, focuses on local history from the Stone Age to Victorian times. ⊠ *Canal Wharf* ☎☎ *01938/554656* 🖾 *£1* ❍ *May–Sept., Mon., Tues., Thurs., and Fri. 11–1 and 2–5, weekends 10–1 and 2–5; Oct.–Apr., Mon., Tues., Thurs., and Fri. 11–1 and 2–5, Sat. 2–5.*

SOUTH WALES
FROM CARDIFF TO CARDIGAN

The most diverse of Wales's three regions, the south covers not only the immediate region around Cardiff and the border of Wales and England, but also the southwest as far as the rugged coastline of Pembrokeshire. The very different nature of its two national parks reveals South Wales's scenic variety. The Brecon Beacons park, a short drive north of Cardiff, is an area of high, grassy mountains, lakes, and craggy limestone gorges. In contrast, the Pembrokeshire Coast National Park holds one of Europe's finest stretches of coastal natural beauty, with mile after mile of spectacular sea cliffs, beaches, headlands, and coves. Other pieces of the complicated South Wales jigsaw include traditional farmlands, cosmopolitan urban areas, rolling border country, wooded vales, and the former industrial valleys where coal was mined in huge quantities during the 19th and early 20th centuries.

Cardiff

▶ *20 mi west of the Second Severn Bridge, which carries the M4 motorway across the Severn Estuary into Wales.*

Financially, industrially, and commercially Cardiff is the most important city in Wales, but those attributes, some might point out, are not exactly exciting for visitors. Still, Cardiff is on the upswing, in part because of the presence of the Welsh Assembly. Once you get to know Wales's capital, there is much to delight the eye, including a handsome Civic Centre, magnificent parklands, and a castle with abundant Victorian verve. A regeneration project has totally transformed the city's docklands, once a coal-exporting industrial hub. As part of this, a dam across the Taff and Ely rivers created a huge freshwater lake edged by 8 mi of prime waterfront. Known as Cardiff Bay, this area of promenades, shops, restaurants, and attractions has become very popular.

True to the Welsh tradition of vocal excellence, Cardiff is home base for Britain's most adventurous opera company, the acclaimed Welsh National Opera. Cardiff is also the sporting center of Wales and the Welsh capital of rugby football. To hear crowds singing their support for the Welsh team is a stirring experience.

★ ㉒ **Cardiff Castle** in Bute Park, one section of the city's hundreds of acres of parkland, is an unusual historic site, with Roman, Norman, and especially Victorian associations. Parts of the walls are Roman, the solid keep is Norman, and the whole complex was restored and transformed into a Victorian ego flight by the third marquess of Bute. He employed William Burges (1827–81), an architect obsessed by the Gothic period, and Burges transformed the castle into an extravaganza of medieval color and detailed craftsmanship. It is the perfect expression of the anything-goes Victorian spirit, not to mention of the fortune made by the marquess in Cardiff's booming docklands. ⊠ *Bute Park* ☎ *029/2087–8100* ⊕ *www.cardiff-info.com/castle* ☜ *Grounds and guided tour of castle £5.50, grounds only £2.75* ☉ *Mar.–Oct., daily 9:30–6; Nov.–Feb., daily 9:30–4; call for tour times.*

> **need a break?**
> **Celtic Cauldron** (⊠ 47–49 Castle Arcade ☎ 029/2038–7185), in the Victorian arcade opposite Cardiff Castle, serves snacks and filling dishes with a Welsh flavor. Try the cawl, a lamb and root vegetable stew, and the Glamorgan sausages. It's closed for dinner.

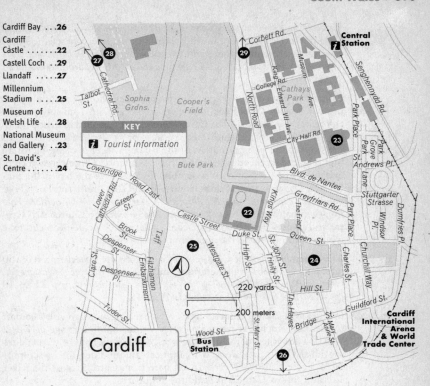

KEY

Tourist information

Cardiff

The **Civic Centre,** two blocks north and east of Cardiff Castle, is a well-designed complex of tree-lined avenues and Edwardian civic buildings with white Portland stone facades. A proud Welsh dragon sits atop the domed City Hall, and inside the building the Marble Hall contains statues of Welsh heroes, including St. David, Henry Tudor, and Owain Glyndŵr (although he razed Cardiff to the ground in 1404). Neoclassical law courts and elegant university campus buildings are also here.

23 The splendid **National Museum and Gallery,** next to City Hall in the Civic Centre, tells the story of Wales through its plants, rocks, archaeology, art, and industry. Its fine collection of modern European art includes a large selection of impressionist and postimpressionist works. Allow at least half a day here, and don't miss *La Parisienne* by Renoir. ✉ *Cathays Park* ☎ *029/2039–7951* ⊕ *www.nmgw.ac.uk* 🎫 *Free* 🕑 *Tues.–Sun. 10–5.*

24 Around **St. David's Centre,** south of the Civic Centre, are the shopping and business areas of Cardiff. A large, modern shopping mall holds **St. David's Hall,** one of Europe's best concert halls, with outstanding acoustics. People come here for classical music, jazz, rock, ballet, and even snooker championships. Nearby is the **Cardiff International Arena,** a multipurpose center for exhibitions, concerts, and conferences.

25 The modern, 72,000-seat **Millennium Stadium** stands beside the River Taff on the site of the famous Cardiff Arms Park, the spiritual home of Welsh rugby. The stadium's retractable roof enables it to be used for concerts and special events throughout the year, as well as for rugby. On a one-hour tour you can walk the player's tunnel and see the Royal Box, dressing rooms, pitch, and broadcasting suite. ⊠ *Entrance Gate 3, Westgate St.* ☎ *029/2082–2228* ⊕ *www.cardiff-stadium.co.uk* ⊠ *£5* ⊙ *Call for times.*

26 Panoramic bay views and appealing promenades, shops, restaurants, and museums make **Cardiff Bay,** the revitalized dockland 1 mi south of the city center, worth a visit. The **Cardiff Bay Visitor Center,** a futuristic building known locally as "the Tube" (because of its distinctive shape), tells the story of the transformation of the bay area. An imposing Victorian building, the **Pierhead,** contains a lively exhibition about the workings and values of the National Assembly. Overlooking the bay is the timber Norwegian seamen's church where Roald Dahl (noted author whose children's books include *Matilda* and *Charlie and the Chocolate Factory*) was baptized. It's now known as **The Norwegian Church Arts Centre** and houses performance space, a gallery, and a café. You can take a bus or taxi to get to the area from the city center.

☾ **Techniquest,** a large science discovery center on the waterfront, has 160 interactive exhibits, a planetarium, and a science theater. ⊠ *Stuart St., Cardiff Bay* ☎ *029/2047–5475* ⊕ *www.techniquest.org* ⊠ *£6.30* ⊙ *Weekdays 9:30–4:30, weekends 10:30–5.*

27 In **Llandaff,** a suburb that retains its village feeling, you can visit **Llandaff Cathedral,** which was renovated after serious bomb damage in World War II. The cathedral includes the work of a number of Pre-Raphaelites as well as *Christ in Majesty,* a 15-foot-tall aluminum figure by sculptor Jacob Epstein (1880–1959). To get here from Cardiff, cross the River Taff and follow Cathedral Road for about 2 mi.

★ ☾ **28** The 100 acres of parklands and gardens at the excellent open-air **Museum of Welsh Life** hold farmhouses, cottages, shops, a school, chapels, St. Fagans castle, and terraced houses that celebrate Wales's rich rural culture and show the evolution of building styles. Special events highlight ancient rural festivals such as May Day, Harvest, and Christmas. The museum is accessible from Junction 33 on the M4. ⊠ *St. Fagans* ☎ *029/2057–3500* ⊕ *www.nmgw.ac.uk* ⊠ *Free* ⊙ *Daily 10–5.*

★ **29** Perched on a hillside, **Castell Coch,** the Red Castle, is a romantically turreted Victorian vision. It was built (on the site of a medieval stronghold) in the 1870s about the time that Ludwig II of Bavaria was creating his fairy-tale castles, and it might almost be one of them. Instead, the castle was another collaboration of the third marquess of Bute and William Burges, builders of Cardiff Castle. Here Burges re-created everything—architecture, furnishings, carvings, murals—in a remarkable exercise in Victorian-Gothic whimsy. ⊠ *A470, Tongwynlais, 4 mi north of Cardiff* ☎ *029/2081–0101* ⊠ *£3* ⊙ *Late Mar.–early May and Oct., daily 9:30–5; late May–Sept., daily 9:30–6; Nov.–Dec. and early Mar., Mon.–Sat. 9:30–4, Sun. 11–4.*

The largest (with more than 30 acres of grounds) and one of the most impressive fortresses in Wales, **Caerphilly Castle** was remarkable at the time of its 13th-century construction. The concentric fortification contained inner and outer defenses. A moat surrounds the castle, but Caerphilly is no longer on guard; some walls have toppled and others lean haphazardly. Exhibits in the gatehouse trace its turbulent history. The castle is 7 mi north of Cardiff. ⊠ *Access off A470–A468, Caerphilly* ☎ *029/2088–3143* ⊠ *£2.50* ⊙ *Apr., May, and Oct., daily 9:30–5; June–Sept., daily 9:30–6; Nov.–Mar., Mon.–Sat. 9:30–4, Sun. 11–4.*

off the beaten path

TINTERN ABBEY – When Wordsworth penned "Lines Written a Few Miles Above Tintern Abbey," he had no idea of all the people who would flock to Tintern to gaze at the substantial ruins of the abbey. Remote and hauntingly beautiful as the site is, Tintern's appeal is diminished in summer because of crowds, so do try to visit early or late in the day to appreciate the complex stonework and tracery of the Gothic church. The abbey, 30 mi northeast of Cardiff, is set on the lovely River Wye. ✉ *A466, Tintern* ☎ *01291/689251* ⊕ *www. cadw.wales.gov.uk* ✒ *£2.50* ⊙ *Late Mar.–late Oct., daily 9:30–6; late Oct.–late Mar., Mon.–Sat. 9:30–4, Sun. 11–4.*

Where to Stay & Eat

★ ££££ ✕ **Le Gallois.** Its fresh modern look and varied menu help make this restaurant, close to Sophia Gardens, one of the city's most popular. The cooking is European in style and makes use of the best of fresh local ingredients. Try the loin of venison with poached pear, celeriac and truffle purée, claret sauce, and chocolate oil. A good-value fixed-price menu is available at lunch. ✉ *8 Romilly Crescent* ☎ *029/2034–1264* 🖃 *AE, MC, V* ⊙ *Closed Sun. and Mon.*

££–£££ ✕ **Armless Dragon.** It's worth the 5-minute drive from the city center to eat at this comfortable restaurant with its cuisine based on Welsh products. Contemporary dishes such as Monmouthshire woodland pork with smoked bacon and creamed leeks are created from locally sourced ingredients. ✉ *97 Wyverne Rd.* ☎ *029/2038–2357* 🖃 *MC, V* ⊙ *Closed Sun. and Mon.*

££ ✕ **Giovanni's.** This popular family-run Italian restaurant in the city center is known for its friendliness rather than for the originality of its fare. Pastas and pizzas are among the choices. ✉ *38 The Hayes* ☎ *029/ 2022–0077* 🖃 *MC, V.*

£–££ ✕ **Harry Ramsden's.** You can dine on the (reputedly) world's most famous fish and chips in a chandeliered, 200-seat dining room with wonderful views across Cardiff Bay. If you like live music with your meal, call ahead to ask for dates of opera and sing-along evenings. ✉ *Landsea House, Stuart St.* ☎ *029/2046–3334* 🖃 *AE, DC, MC, V.*

★ £££££ 🏨 **St. David's Hotel and Spa.** Natural light from a glass atrium floods this striking, modern luxury hotel along the waterfront. Every room, done in soothing neutral tones with modern furniture, has a private balcony and views over Cardiff Bay. You can indulge in a relaxing hydrotherapy spa treatment. The Tides restaurant, under the guidance of noted London chef Marco Pierre White, specializes in modern French fare. ✉ *Havannah St., CF10 6SD* ☎ *029/2045–4045* 🖷 *029/2048–7056* ⊕ *www.roccofortehotels.com* ⇌ *132 rooms* ⚭ *Restaurant, in-room data ports, cable TV, indoor pool, gym, spa, business services, meeting rooms, no-smoking rooms* 🖃 *AE, DC, MC, V* ⊙ *BP.*

££–£££ 🏨 **The Big Sleep Hotel.** Actor John Malkovich is a shareholder in this converted 1960s office tower that cleverly combines chic minimalism with good-value prices. Bright blue-and-white fabrics and Formica furniture add cheer. The city center location is convenient, but avoid the noisier rooms that overlook the nearby railroad tracks. ✉ *Bute Terrace, CF10 2FE* ☎ *029/2063–6363* 🖷 *029/2063–6364* ⊕ *www.thebigsleephotel. com* ⇌ *81 rooms* ⚭ *In-room data ports, cable TV, bar, no-smoking rooms; no a/c* 🖃 *AE, DC, MC, V* ⊙ *CP.*

££ 🏨 **Llanerch Vineyard.** The attractive pine-furnished country-style rooms in the farmhouse and converted outbuildings of this lovely Vale of Glamorgan vineyard are only 15 minutes from Cardiff center. You can walk in the surrounding vineyard and woodlands and arrange your own personal Welsh wine tasting. Take Junction 34 off M4 and follow the brown signs. ✉ *Hensol, Pendoylan, CF72 8GG* ☎ *01443/225877*

🏠 *01443/225546* 🌐 *www.llanerch-vineyard.co.uk* 📠 *11 rooms* ♿ *No a/c, no smoking* 🟰 *MC, V* 🍴 *BP.*

££ 🖼 **Town House.** Cosmopolitan in style, this immaculate guest house near the city center (shops and castle are a short walk away) is well known as Cardiff's best B&B. The tastefully refurbished Victorian building has an elegant hallway and neat, well-equipped bedrooms, and you can savor traditional British or American breakfasts in the beautiful dining room. ✉ *70 Cathedral Rd., CF1 9LL* ☎ *029/2023–9399* 🏠 *029/2022–3214* 🌐 *www.thetownhousecardiff.co.uk* 📠 *8 rooms* ♿ *Lounge; no a/c, no smoking* 🟰 *MC, V* 🍴 *BP.*

Nightlife & the Arts

NIGHTLIFE Cardiff's clubs and pubs support a lively nighttime scene. **Café Jazz** (✉ 21 St. Mary St. ☎ 029/2038–7026) presents live jazz four nights a week and has TV screens in the bar and restaurant so you can view the action on stage. **Clwb Ifor Bach** (✉ Womanby St. ☎ 029/2023–2199), a distinctively Welsh club, has three floors of eclectic music from funk to folk to rock.

THE ARTS The big theaters present a full program of entertainment, from drama to comedy, pop to the classics. The huge **Cardiff International Arena** (✉ Mary Ann St. ☎ 029/2022–4488) showcases artists who can draw huge crowds, from Welshman Tom Jones to Luciano Pavarotti. **St. David's Hall** (✉ The Hayes ☎ 029/2087–8444), a popular venue, presents the Welsh Proms in July, attracting major international orchestras and soloists, and every two years hosts the prestigious Cardiff Singer of the World competition. It also stages rock, pop, jazz, and folk events.

New Theatre (✉ Park Pl. ☎ 029/2087–8889), a refurbished Edwardian playhouse, still attracts big names, including the Royal Shakespeare Company, the National Theatre, and the Northern Ballet.

Wales has one of Britain's four major opera companies, the outstanding **Welsh National Opera** (✉ John St. ☎ 029/2046–4644 for performances). Its home base is the city center New Theatre, but the company spends most of its time touring Wales and England. The WNO may move to the Millennium Arts Centre, which is expected to open in 2004.

Sports

Celtic Manor (✉ Coldra Woods, Newport ☎ 01633/410295), 12 mi northeast of Cardiff via A48, is Wales's most prestigious golf course. It will host the Ryder Cup in 2010.

Shopping

Interesting canopied Victorian and Edwardian shopping arcades, lined with specialty stores, weave in and out of the city's modern shopping complexes. The **Cardiff Antiques Centre** (✉ Royal Arcade ☎ 029/2039–8891), in an 1856 arcade, is a good place to buy antique jewelry. The **Welsh Lovespoon Gallery** (✉ 10 Castle Arcade ☎ 029/2023–1500) specializes in fine Welsh crafts. Cardiff's traditional **covered market** (✉ The Hayes) sells tempting fresh foods beneath its Victorian glass canopy.

Abergavenny

30 *28 mi north of Cardiff.*

The market town of Abergavenny, near Brecon Beacons National Park, is a popular base for walkers and hikers. The **Abergavenny Food Fest** (☎ 01873/857588), held over a weekend in September, has everything from oyster-opening championships and cooking demonstrations to a huge food market. Ruined **Abergavenny Castle,** founded early in the 11th century, has a good local museum. The castle witnessed a tragic event at Christmas in 1176: the Norman knight William de Braose invited the neighboring Welsh chieftains to a feast and, in a crude attempt to gain control of the area, had them all slaughtered as they sat at dinner. Afterward, the Welsh attacked and virtually demolished the castle. Most of what now remains dates from the 13th and 14th centuries. The castle's 19th-century hunting lodge houses the **museum,** with exhibits about area history from the Iron Age to the present. The re-creation of a Victorian Welsh farmhouse kitchen comes complete with old utensils and butter molds. ⊠ *Castle Museum, Castle St.* ☎ *01873/854282* £1 ⊙ *Mar.–Oct., Mon.–Sat. 11–1 and 2–5, Sun. 2–5; Nov.–Feb., Mon.–Sat. 11–1 and 2–4.*

West of Abergavenny lie the valleys—the Rhondda is the most famous— so well described by Richard Llewellyn in his 1939 novel, *How Green Was My Valley* (the basis for the 1941 film). The slag heaps of the coal

★ mines are green now, thanks to land reclamation schemes. The **Big Pit Mining Museum,** southwest of Abergavenny, provides a glimpse of what the area was like when mining was big business. Here, ex-miners take you underground on a tour of an authentic coal mine for a look at the hard life of the South Wales miner. You will also see the pithead baths and workshops. ⊠ *Blaenavon* ☎ *01495/790311* ⊕ *www.nmgw.ac.uk* Free ⊙ *Feb.–Nov., daily 9:30–5; underground tours 10–3:30.*

Where to Stay & Eat

££–£££ ✕ **Clytha Arms.** A converted house on the banks of the River Usk near Abergavenny serves imaginative modern food in a relaxed setting. You can eat very cheaply in the bar (try the real ales) or pay a little more in the restaurant. ⊠ *Off B4598, Clytha* ☎ *01873/840206* ▤ *AE, MC, V* ⊙ *Closed Mon.*

£££ ✕▣ **Llanwenarth House.** Tranquil grounds surround this beautifully restored 16th-century Welsh manor house with spacious bedrooms. Antiques, art, and period furniture enhance the house's original elements. You can dine by candlelight on contemporary cuisine that makes excellent use of local ingredients; a fixed-price menu is offered. King Charles I is said to have kept horses and arms here during the Civil War (1642–51). ⊠ *Govilon, Abergavenny, NP7 9SF* ☎ *01873/830289* 🖷 *01873/832199* ⊕ *www.welsh-hotel.co.uk* ◁ *5 rooms* ⌂ *Restaurant, no-smoking rooms; no a/c, no room phones, no kids under 10* ▤ No *credit cards* |⊙| *BP.*

Crickhowell

㉛ *5 mi northwest of Abergavenny.*

If you take A40 northwest out of Abergavenny, you'll pass Sugar Loaf mountain and come to Crickhowell, a pretty town on the banks of the River Usk with attractive little shops, an ancient bridge, and a ruined castle. **Tretower Court,** 2 mi from Crickhowell, is a splendid example of a fortified medieval manor house. Nearby, and part of the same site, are the ruins of a cylindrical Norman castle. ⊠ *A479* ☎ *01874/730279* ⊕ *www.cadw.wales.gov.uk* £2.50 ⊙ *Mar.–late Oct., daily 10–6.*

Where to Stay & Eat

££–££££ ✕▣ **Bear Hotel.** This old coaching inn in the middle of town is full of character. The bar, decorated with memorabilia from the days stagecoaches stopped here, has a blazing log fire in winter. Rooms in the hotel itself or in a modern addition in the stable yard vary widely; the most luxurious have four-poster beds and antiques. The Bear serves fine contemporary cuisine—both the excellent-value bar food and restaurant offerings such as scallops with Parma ham and venison on creamed spinach. ✉ *A40, NP8 1BW* ☎ *01873/810408* 🖷 *01873/811696* ⊕ *www. bearhotel.co.uk* ⇗ *34 rooms* ⌂ *Restaurant, bar; no a/c* 🖃 *AE, MC, V* 🍴 *BP.*

££ ✕🖾 **Ty Croeso Hotel.** A hillside location with views over the Usk Valley adds to the appeal of this hotel (its name means "House of Welcome") in a stone-walled early-19th-century building. You'll find comfortable rooms with print fabrics, a lounge with a log fire, and imaginative food with a Welsh emphasis, such as Welsh beef flamed in whiskey. ✉ *The Dardy, NP8 1PU* ☎🖷 *01873/810573* ⊕ *www.wiz.to/tycroeso* ⇗ *8 rooms* ⌂ *Restaurant, bar, lounge; no a/c* 🖃 *AE, MC, V* 🍴 *BP.*

Brecon

③② *19 mi northwest of Abergavenny, 41 mi north of Cardiff.*

Brecon, a historic market town of narrow passageways, Georgian buildings, and pleasant riverside walks, is also the gateway to the Brecon Beacons National Park. It's particularly appealing on market days (Tuesday and Friday). You may want to purchase a hand-carved wooden love spoon similar to those on display in the Brecknock Museum.

Cavernous **Brecon Cathedral** (☎ 01874/623857 ⊕ www.breconcathedral. org.uk), with a heritage center that traces its history, stands on the hill above the middle of town. In the colonnaded Shire Hall built in 1842 is the **Brecknock Museum** (☎ 01874/624121), with its superb collection of carved love spoons and its perfectly preserved 19th-century assize court. The rural Welsh custom of giving a hand-carved wooden spoon to one's beloved dates from the mid-17th century. The military exhibits in the **South Wales Borderers' Museum** (✉ The Watton, off the Bulwark ☎ 01874/613310) span centuries of conflict. The Zulu Room recalls the regiment's defense of Rorke's Drift in the Anglo-Zulu war of 1879, an action dramatized in the 1964 film *Zulu,* starring Michael Caine.

South of Brecon, the skyline fills with mountains, and wild, windswept uplands stretch to the horizon in the Brecon Beacons National Park. The **Brecon Beacons National Park Visitor Centre** on Mynydd Illtyd, a high, grassy stretch of upland west of A470, is an excellent source of information for attractions and activities within this 519-square-mi park of hills and open moorlands. It also gives wonderful panoramic views across to Pen-y-fan, at 2,907 feet the highest peak in South Wales. If you plan to explore Wales's high country on foot, come well equipped. Mist and rain can quickly descend, and the Beacons' summits are exposed to high winds. ✉ *Off A470, 5½ mi southwest of Brecon, Brecon, LD3 8ER* ☎ *01874/623366* ⊕ *www.breconbeacons.org* 🖾 *Free, parking fee* ⊙ *Daily 9:30–5; until 4:30 Nov.–Mar.*

Where to Stay & Eat

£££ ✕🖾 **Felin Fach Griffin.** Old and new blend perfectly in this fresh country inn with old wood floors and terra-cotta stone walls hung with bright prints and photos. Some bedrooms have four-posters. The excellent changing menu makes use of fresh local produce. Try the roast partridge with celeriac mash or the salmon fillet with fennel confit. ✉ *A470, east of Brecon, Felin Fach, LD3 0UB* ☎ *01874/620111* 🖷 *01874/620120* ⊕ *www.felinfach.com* ⇗ *7 rooms* ⌂ *Restaurant, no-smoking rooms; no a/c* 🖃 *MC, V* 🍴 *BP.*

££ 🖾 **Cantre Selyf.** Spacious and exquisitely restored, this elegant 17th-century town house with a large garden is close to the center of Brecon. It offers both welcoming hosts and innovative food (for guests only). The rooms have beamed ceilings, Georgian fireplaces, and cast-iron beds.

✉ *5 Lion St., LD3 7AU* ☎ *01874/622904* 🖷 *01874/622315* ⊕ *www.
cantreselyf.co.uk* ⇨ *3 rooms* ☖ *Dining room; no a/c, no room phones*
▭ *No credit cards* ❢❢ *BP.*

Nightlife & the Arts

Theatr Brycheiniog (✉ Canal Wharf ☎ 01874/611622), on the canal, is
the town's impressive venue for the arts. It also has a gallery and waterfront bistro.

Each summer, the town hosts **Brecon Jazz** (☎ 01874/625557 ⊕ www.
breconjazz.co.uk), an international jazz festival that attracts top performers.

Shopping

Crickhowell Adventure Gear (✉ Ship St. ☎ 01874/611586), which also
has smaller shops in Crickhowell itself and Abergavenny, sells outdoor
gear such as clothes and climbing equipment.

Swansea

㉝ *36 mi southwest of Brecon, 40 mi west of Cardiff.*

Swansea, Wales's second-largest city and the birthplace of poet Dylan
Thomas (1914–53), marks the end of the industrial region of South Wales.
Despite typically postwar, rather utilitarian and undistinguished architecture, it has a number of appealing sights. The city was extensively
bombed during World War II, and its old dockland has been transformed
into the splendid **Maritime Quarter,** a modern marina with attractive housing and shops and a seafront that commands wonderful views across
the sweep of Swansea Bay. The maritime museum here will reopen in
2005. Founded in 1841, the **Swansea Museum** contains a quirky and eclectic collection that includes an Egyptian mummy, china, local archaeological exhibits, and the intriguing Cabinet of Curiosity, which holds
artifacts from Swansea's past. The museum is close to the Maritime Quarter. ✉ *Victoria Rd.* ☎ 01792/653763 ➦ *Free* ☉ *Tues.–Sun. 10–4:45.*

The **Dylan Thomas Centre,** on the banks of the Tawe close to the Maritime Quarter, is the National Literature Centre for Wales. The center
houses a permanent Dylan Thomas exhibition and hosts literary events
such as the annual Dylan Thomas Festival (usually the last week in July
and first two weeks of August). The Wales Tourist Board has a leaflet
for a Dylan Thomas Trail around South Wales for those interested in
following in the poet's footsteps. ✉ *Somerset Pl.* ☎ *01792/463980*
⊕ *www.dylanthomas.org* ➦ *Free* ☉ *Tues.–Sun. 10:30–5.*

Swansea's modern shopping center is nothing special, but the **covered
market,** part of Quadrant Shopping Centre, is the best fresh-foods market in Wales. You can buy cockles from the Penclawdd beds on the nearby
Gower Peninsula, and laverbread, that unique Welsh delicacy made
from seaweed, which is usually served with bacon and eggs.

The **Egypt Centre** displays a substantial collection of ancient Egyptian
artifacts, such as bead necklaces from the time of Tutankhamun and the
beautiful painted coffin of a Theban musician. ✉ *Taliesin Centre, University of Wales Swansea, Singleton Park* ☎ 01792/295960 ⊕ *www.
swansea.ac.uk/egypt* ➦ *Free* ☉ *Tues.–Sat. 10–4.*

★ The 14-mi-long **Gower Peninsula,** only minutes away from Swansea's center, was the first part of Britain to be declared an area of Outstanding
Natural Beauty. Its shores are a succession of sheltered sandy bays and
awesome headlands. For the most breathtaking views of all, head to Rhossili on its western tip.

Where to Stay & Eat

££–£££ ✕ **La Braseria.** This lively, welcoming spot resembles a Spanish bodega, with its flamenco music, oak barrels, and whitewashed walls. Among the house specialties are sea bass in rock salt, roast suckling pig, and pheasant (in season). There's a good choice of 140 Spanish and French wines. ⊠ *28 Wind St.* ☎ *01792/469683* ☰ *AE, MC, V* ☾ *Closed Sun.*

★ ✕⬚ **Fairyhill.** Luxuriously furnished public rooms, spacious bedrooms,
££££–£££££ and 24 acres of wooded grounds make this 18th-century country house in the western part of the lovely Gower Peninsula a restful retreat. The hotel is renowned for sophisticated cuisine and a well-chosen wine list; try the Welsh Black beef with beer batter onions or the leek and mushroom strudel. There's a fixed three-course dinner menu. ⊠ *Off B4295, 11 mi southwest of Swansea, Reynoldston, SA3 1BS* ☎ *01792/390139* 🖶 *01792/391358* ⊕ *www.fairyhill.net* ↬ *8 rooms* ⚲ *Restaurant, croquet, helipad; no a/c, no kids* ☰ *AE, MC, V* ❄️ *BP.*

National Botanic Garden of Wales

★ ㉞ *20 mi northwest of Swansea, 60 mi northwest of Cardiff.*

The first modern botanic garden in Britain, opened in 2000, celebrates conservation and education. It's based at Middleton Park, a 568-acre 18th-century estate with seven lakes, cascades, water features, and a Japanese garden. The garden's centerpiece is the spectacular Norman Foster–designed Great Glass House, the largest single-span greenhouse in the world, which blends into the curving landforms of the Tywi valley. The interior landscape includes a 40-foot-deep ravine, 10,000 plants from all the Mediterranean climates of the world, and an interactive educational area called the Bioverse. The garden is signposted off the main road between Swansea and Carmarthen. ⊠ *Off A48 or B4310, Llanarthne* ☎ *01558/668768* ⊕ *www.gardenofwales.org.uk* 🎫 *£6.95* ☾ *Apr.–Oct., daily 9–5:30; Nov.–Mar., daily 10–3.*

Tenby

㉟ *53 mi west of Swansea.*

Pastel-color Georgian houses cluster around a harbor in this attractive seaside resort, where two golden sandy beaches stretch below the hotel-lined cliff top. Medieval Tenby's ancient town walls still stand, enclosing narrow streets and passageways full of shops, inns, and places to eat. From the harbor you can take a boat trip to Caldey Island and visit the monastery, where monks make perfume.

The ruins of a castle stand on a headland overlooking the sea, close to the informative **Tenby Museum** (⊠ Castle Hill ☎ 01834/842809), which recalls the town's maritime history and its growth as a fashionable resort. The late-15th-century **Tudor Merchant's House** (⊠ Quay Hill ☎ 01834/842279 ⊕ www.nationaltrust.org.uk), in town, shows how a prosperous trader would have lived in the Tenby of old.

Where to Stay

££££ ⬚ **Penally Abbey Hotel.** Overlooking the sea close to town, this is a fine base for exploring Pembrokeshire. The dignified 18th-century house built on the site of a former abbey is full of period details, and most bedrooms have four-posters. The atmosphere is relaxed, but service is first-class. ⊠ *Off A4139, Penally, near Tenby, SA70 7PY* ☎ *01834/843033* 🖶 *01834/844714* ⊕ *www.penally-abbey.com* ↬ *16 rooms* ⚲ *Restaurant, indoor pool, billiards; no a/c* ☰ *AE, MC, V* ❄️ *BP.*

Pembroke

36 *13 mi west of Tenby, 13 mi south of Haverfordwest.*

In Pembroke you are entering the heart of Pembrokeshire, one of the most curious regions of Wales. You may begin to doubt whether you are still in Wales, for all around are English names such as Deeplake, New Hedges, and Rudbaxton. Locals more often than not don't seem to understand Welsh, and South Pembrokeshire is even known as "Little England beyond Wales." History is responsible. In the 11th century, the English conquered this region with the aid of the Normans, who intermarried and set about building castles.

One of the most magnificent Norman fortresses is massive **Pembroke Castle,** dating from 1190. Its walls remain stout, its gatehouse mighty, and the enormous cylindrical keep proved so impregnable to cannon fire in the Civil War that Cromwell's men had to starve out its Royalist defenders. You can climb the towers and walk the walls for fine views. This was the birthplace, in 1457, of Henry Tudor, who seized the throne of Britain as Henry VII in 1485, and whose son Henry VIII united Wales and England. ☎ 01646/681510 ⊕ www.pembrokecastle.co.uk ⊠ £3 ☉ Apr.–Sept., daily 9:30–6; Oct. and Mar., daily 10–5; Nov.–Feb., daily 10–4.

St. David's

37 *25 mi northwest of Pembroke, 16 mi west of Fishguard.*

This tiny village holds what has been described as the holiest ground in Great Britain, the Cathedral of St. David and the shrine of the patron saint of Wales, who founded a monastic community here in the 6th century. The entire area around St. David's, steeped in sanctity and history, was a place of pilgrimage for many centuries, two journeys to St. David's equaling one to Rome. Here, on the savagely beautiful coastline, edged by the Pembrokeshire Coast Path—Pembrokeshire at its unspoiled best—you can almost recapture the feeling of those days nearly 1,500 years ago when this shrine was very nearly the solitary outpost of Christianity in the British Isles.

Unlike any other cathedral, the venerable 12th-century **Cathedral of St. David** (⊕ www.stdavidscathedral.org.uk) does not seek to dominate the surrounding countryside with its enormous mass, for it is set in a vast hollow. You must climb down 39 steps (called locally the Thirty-Nine Articles) to enter the cathedral. Its location helped protect the church from Viking raiders by hiding it from the sea. From the outside, St. David's has a simple austerity that harmonizes well with the desolate countryside, but the rich interior more than compensates for this external severity. Treasures include the fan vaulting in Bishop Vaughan's Chapel, the intricate carving on the choir stalls, and the oaken roof over the nave. Across the brook are the ruins of the medieval **Bishop's Palace,** which can be visited.

Where to Stay & Eat

£££££ ✕ **Harbour Lights.** The quality of its local ingredients are the pride of this family-run shore restaurant on an attractive stretch of coast about 7 mi northeast of St. David's, at the tiny harbor of Porthgain. Seafood dishes are a specialty on the fixed-price, three-course menu. The laverbread is handpicked, and the crabs are landed on the quayside. Pictures by local artists hang on the walls, and an adjoining gallery showcases additional work. ⊠ Porthgain ☎ 01348/831549 ▭ MC, V ☉ Call ahead in winter for hrs.

££££–£££££ ✕🖭 **Warpool Court Hotel.** Overlooking a stunning stretch of coastline, this hotel sits on a bluff above St. Non's Bay, near a ruined chapel. Many rooms have wonderful sea views; decorative tiles adorn public areas and some bedrooms. The building dates from the 1860s, when it housed St. David's Cathedral Choir School. Now the well-equipped hotel offers contemporary cuisine (four-course, fixed-price menu at dinner) with fish, including home-smoked salmon, as a specialty. ✉ *St. David's, SA62 6BN* 🕾 *01437/720300* 🖷 *01437/720676* ⊕ *www.stdavids.co.uk/warpoolcourt* ➱ *25 rooms* ♿ *Restaurant, in-room data ports, tennis court, pool, gym, sauna, lounge; no a/c* ▭ *AE, MC, V* ⫶❂⫶ *BP.*

Fishguard

❸❽ *16 mi northeast of St. David's, 26 mi north of Pembroke.*

Fishguard is a town of three parts. The ferry terminal at Goodwick across the sheltered waters of Fishguard Bay sees activity throughout the year as boats sail to Rosslare across the Irish Sea. Fishguard's main town stands on high ground just south of Goodwick, separating the modern port from its old harbor in the Lower Town, where pretty gabled cottages are grouped around the quayside. The Lower Town was the setting for the 1973 film of Dylan Thomas's play *Under Milkwood,* which starred Elizabeth Taylor and Welsh actor Richard Burton.

Cardigan & the Teifi Valley

❸❾ *18 mi northeast of Fishguard.*

The pretty little market town of Cardigan, with its ancient bridge, was the scene of a never-allowed-to-be-forgotten victory by the Welsh over the Norman army in 1136. The town is near the mouth of the Teifi, a river that runs through a wooded valley dotted with traditional market towns and villages, as well as reminders of the area's once-flourishing woolen industry. Wales's first eisteddfod, or folk festival, took place in Cardigan in the 12th century. The eisteddfod tradition, based on the Welsh language and culture, remains strong in Wales, and events large and small are held here (mainly in summer months).

Cilgerran, a village a few miles south of Cardigan, holds the dramatic ruins of 13th-century **Cilgerran Castle,** which stands above a deep wooded gorge where the River Teifi flows. ✉ *Off A478* 🕾 *01239/615136* ⊕ *www.cadw.wales.gov.uk* 🎟 *£2* ◷ *Late Mar.–late Oct., daily 9:30–6:30; late Oct.–late Mar., Mon.–Sat. 9:30–4, Sun. 2–4.*

off the beaten path

MUSEUM OF THE WELSH WOOLEN INDUSTRY – Working exhibits and displays at this museum in what was once the most important wool-producing area in Wales trace the evolution of the industry. There are also crafts workshops and a woolen mill that produces reproduction fabrics. The museum is east of Cenarth, a few miles past Newcastle Emlyn. Call ahead, as the museum has closed but plans to reopen during 2004. ✉ *Off A484, Drefach Felindre* 🕾 *01559/370929* ⊕ *www.nmgw.ac.uk* 🎟 *Free* ◷ *Apr.–Sept., Mon.–Sat. 10–5; Oct.–Mar., weekdays 10–5.*

Where to Stay

£££ 🖭 **Penbontbren Farm Hotel.** This hotel in the peaceful countryside began life as a farm. The one-time barns now serve as cozy, country-style bedrooms and as a high-ceilinged restaurant with exposed stone walls. There's also a fascinating little farm museum. ✉ *Off A487, 9 mi northeast of Cardigan, Glynarthen, SA44 6PE* 🕾 *01239/810248* 🖷 *01239/*

811129 ⊕ *www.penbontbren.com* ⇨ *10 rooms* ᧕ *Restaurant, bil-*
liards, some pets allowed; no a/c ⊟ *AE, MC, V* ❍| *BP.*

WALES A TO Z

To research prices, get advice from other travelers, and book travel arrangements, visit www.fodors.com.

AIR TRAVEL

London's Heathrow and Gatwick airports, with their excellent door-
to-door motorway links with Wales, are convenient gateways (⇨ Airports *in* Smart Travel Tips). Manchester Airport, which offers many
international flights, is an excellent gateway for North Wales, with a
journey time to the Welsh border, via M56, of less than an hour. Wales
International Airport, a 19-mi drive from the center of Cardiff, has a
number of direct international flights to European destinations, connecting
services worldwide via Amsterdam, and flights within the British Isles
to London Stansted, Manchester, Newcastle, Glasgow, Edinburgh, Aberdeen, Cork, and Dublin. A bus service runs from the airport to
Cardiff's central train and bus stations.

AIRPORTS

🏛 **Manchester Airport** ⊠ Near Junctions 5 and 6 of M56 ☎ 0161/489-3000 ⊕ www.
manairport.co.uk. **Wales International Airport** ⊠ A4226, Rhoose ☎ 01446/711111
⊕ www.cardiffairportonline.com.

BUS TRAVEL

Although the overall pattern is a little fragmented, most parts of Wales
are accessible by bus. National Express serves Wales from London's Victoria Coach Station and also direct from London's Heathrow and
Gatwick airports. It also has routes into Wales from almost all other
major towns and cities in England and Scotland. Average travel times
from London to Wales are 3½ hours to Cardiff, 4 hours to Swansea,
5½ hours to Aberystwyth, and 4½ hours to Llandudno.

The three main operators within Wales are Arriva Cymru (for north and
mid-Wales), Stagecoach Red & White (mainly in southeast Wales), and
First Cymru (mainly in southwest Wales). You can also travel cross-country on the Traws Cambria service that runs between Cardiff and Bangor via Aberystwyth. For details of all bus services in Wales, contact
Traveline Cymru. Wales's three national parks also run summer bus services. The Snowdon Sherpa runs into and around Snowdonia and links
with main rail and bus services. The Pembrokeshire Coastal Bus Service operates in the Pembrokeshire Coast National Park, and the Beacons Bus serves the Brecon Beacons National Park.

FARES &
SCHEDULES
🏛 **Beacons Bus** ☎ 01873/853254 ⊕ www.breconbeacons.org. **National Ex-**
press ☎ 0870/580-8080 ⊕ www.nationalexpress.com. **Pembrokeshire**
Coastal Bus Service ☎ 01437/775227 ⊕ www.pembrokeshirecoast.org.
uk. **Snowdon Sherpa** ☎ 01766/770274 ⊕ www.snowdonia.org.uk. **Trav-**
eline Cymru ☎ 0870/608-2608 ⊕ www.traveline.org.uk.

CAR RENTAL

🏛 Local Agencies **Avis** ⊠ 14-22 Tudor St., Cardiff ☎ 029/2034-2111. **Budget Rent-a-**
Car ⊠ 281 Penarth Rd., Cardiff ☎ 029/2066-4499. **Europcar** ⊠ Cardiff Airport, Ar-
rivals Hall, Rhoose, Cardiff ☎ 01446/711924 ⊕ www.europcar.com. **Hertz** ⊠ 9 Central
Sq., Cardiff ☎ 029/2022-4548. **National Car Rental** ⊠ 10 Dominions Way Industrial
Estate, Newport Rd., Cardiff ☎ 029/2049-6256.

CAR TRAVEL

Take the M4 from London for Cardiff (151 mi), Swansea (190 mi), and South Wales. Aberystwyth (211 mi from London) and Llandrindod Wells (204 mi) in mid-Wales are well served by major roads. The A40 is also an important route through central and South Wales. From London, M1/M6 is the most direct route to North Wales. A55, the coast road from Chester in England goes through Bangor. Mid-Wales is reached by the M54, which links with the M6/M5/M1.

ROAD CONDITIONS Distances in miles may not be great in Wales, but getting around takes time because there are few major highways. The mountains mean that there is no single fast route from north to south, although A470 is good and scenic, and A487 does run along or near most of the coastline. Many smaller mountain roads are winding and difficult to maneuver, but they do have magnificent views.

CONSULATES
🔲 Canada ⊠ Wales Airport Hotel, Port Rd., Rhoose, near Cardiff ☎ 01446/719172.

DISCOUNTS & DEALS
The Cadw/Welsh Historic Monuments Explorer Pass is good for unlimited admission to most of Wales's historic sites. The seven-day pass costs £15.50 (single adult), £26 (two adults), or £32 (family ticket); the three-day pass costs £9.50, £16.50, and £23, respectively. Passes are available at any site covered by the Cadw program. All national museums and galleries in Wales are free.
🔲 **Cadw/Welsh Historic Monuments** ⊠ Crown Building, Cathays Park, Cardiff, CF1 3NQ ☎ 029/2050–0200 ⊕ www.cadw.wales.gov.uk. **National Museums and Galleries of Wales** ⊕ www.nmgw.ac.uk.

EMERGENCIES
🔲 **Ambulance, fire, police** ☎ 999. **Bronglais Hospital** ⊠ Cardog Rd., Aberystwyth ☎ 01970/623131. **Morriston Hospital** ⊠ Heol Maes Eglwys, Cwm Rhydyceirw, Swansea ☎ 01792/702222. **University Hospital of Wales** ⊠ Heath Park, Cardiff ☎ 029/2074–7747.

NATIONAL PARKS
🔲 **Brecon Beacons National Park** ⊠ Plas-y-Ffynnon, Cambrian Way, Brecon, LD3 7HP ☎ 01874/624437 ⊕ www.breconbeacons.org. **Pembrokeshire Coast National Park** ⊠ Wynch La., Haverfordwest, SA61 1PY ☎ 01437/764636 ⊕ www.pembrokeshirecoast. org.uk. **Snowdonia National Park** ⊠ Penrhyndeudraeth, LL48 6LF ☎ 01766/770274 ⊕ www.snowdonia.org.uk.

SIGHTSEEING GUIDES
If you are interested in a personal guide, contact the Wales Official Tourist Guide Association. WOTGA uses only guides recognized by the Wales Tourist Board and will create tailor-made tours. You can book a driver-guide or someone to accompany you as you drive.
🔲 **Wales Official Tourist Guide Association** ☎ 01633/774796.

SPORTS & OUTDOORS
Hiking and walking are the most popular outdoor activities in Wales, and a number of organizations can provide you with information.
🔲 **Offa's Dyke Centre** ⊠ West St., Knighton, LD7 1EN ☎ 01547/528753 ⊕ www. offasdyke.demon.co.uk. **Ramblers' Association in Wales** ⊠ Ty'r Cerddwyr, High St., Gresford, Wrexham, LL12 8PT ☎ 01978/855148 ⊕ www.ramblers.org.uk.

TOURS
BUS TOURS A good way to see Wales is by local tour bus; in summer there's a large choice of day and half-day excursions to most parts of the country. In

major resorts and cities you should ask for details at a tourist information center or bus station.

TRAIN TRAVEL

From London's Paddington station it's about two hours to Cardiff and three hours to Swansea on the fast InterCity rail service. Fast InterCity trains also run between London's Euston station and North Wales. Average travel times are from Euston, 3¾ hours to Llandudno in North Wales (some direct trains, otherwise change at Crewe), and about 5 hours to Aberystwyth in mid-Wales (changing at Birmingham).

A regional railway service covers South Wales, western Wales, central Wales, the Conwy Valley, and the North Wales coast on many scenic routes such as the Cambrian Coast Railway, running 70 mi between Aberystwyth and Pwllheli, and the Heart of Wales line, linking Swansea and Craven Arms, near Shrewsbury, 95 mi away.

A ride on one of Wales's many scenic steam railways, including the Great Little Trains of Wales and the Snowdon Mountain Railway, will give you lovely views of the countryside.

CUTTING COSTS For travel within Wales, ask about money-saving unlimited-travel tickets (such as Freedom of Wales Flexi Pass, North and Mid Wales Rover, and the South Wales Flexi Rover), which include the use of bus services. Wanderer tickets are available from participating railways for unlimited travel on the Great Little Trains of Wales: a four-day ticket is £38.

FARES & SCHEDULES ⁊ **Great Little Trains of Wales** ⊠ Tallyllyn Railway, Wharf Station, Tywyn, LL36 9EY ☎ 01654/710472 ⊕ www.greatlittletrainsofwales.co.uk. **Regional & Intercity Railways** ☎ 0845/748–4950 ⊕ www.thetrainline.com. **Snowdon Mountain Railway** ⊠ Llanberis, Caernarfon, LL55 4TY ☎ 01286/870223 ⊕ www.snowdonrailway.co.uk.

RESERVATIONS ⁊ **Flexipass information** ☎ 0870/900–0773 ⊕ www.walesflexipass.com. **National Rail Enquiries** ☎ 0845/748–4950 ⊕ www.thetrainline.com.

TRAVEL AGENCIES

⁊ **Local Agent Referrals American Express** ⊠ 3 Queen St., Cardiff ☎ 029/2064–9304. **Thomas Cook** ⊠ 16 Queen St., Cardiff ☎ 029/2042–2500 ⊠ 3 Union St., Swansea ☎ 01792/332000.

VISITOR INFORMATION

The Wales Tourist Board's Visit Wales Centre provides information and handles reservations; accommodations can also be booked on-line. Tourist information centers are normally open Monday through Saturday 10–5:30 and limited hours on Sunday, but vary by season.

⁊ **Visit Wales Centre** ⌖ Box 113, Bangor, LL54 4WW ☎ 08701/211251 ⊕ www.visitwales.com. **Aberystwyth** ⊠ Terrace Rd. ☎ 01970/612125. **Betws-y-Coed** ⊠ Royal Oak Stables ☎ 01690/710426. **Caernarfon** ⊠ Oriel Pendeitsh, opposite castle entrance ☎ 01286/672232. **Cardiff** national and city information ⊠ 16 Wood St., Central Station ☎ 029/2022-7281 ⊕ www.visitcardiff.info. **Llandrindod Wells** ⊠ Old Town Hall ☎ 01597/822600. **Llandudno** ⊠ 1-2 Chapel St. ☎ 01492/876413. **Llanfair Pwllgwyngyll** ⊠ Station Site, Isle of Anglesey ☎ 01248/713177. **Llangollen** ⊠ Town Hall, Castle St. ☎ 01978/860828. **Machynlleth** ⊠ Owain Glyndŵr Centre ☎ 01654/702401. **Ruthin** ⊠ Craft Centre, Park Rd. ☎ 01824/703992. **Swansea** ⊠ Plymouth St. ☎ 01792/468321 ⊕ www.swansea.gov.uk. **Tenby** ⊠ The Croft ☎ 01834/842402. **Welshpool** ⊠ Vicarage Garden, Church St. ☎ 01938/552043.

LANCASHIRE & THE PEAKS

MANCHESTER, LIVERPOOL & THE PEAK DISTRICT

10

FODOR'S CHOICE
Express by Holiday Inn, *Liverpool*
Haddon Hall, *stately home near Bakewell*
The Lowry Hotel, *Manchester*

HIGHLY RECOMMENDED

RESTAURANTS Fisher's, *Baslow*
Riber Hall, *Matlock*
Simply Heathcote's, *Manchester*
Yang Sing, *Manchester*

HOTELS Buxton's Victorian Guesthouse, *Buxton*
Fischer's, *Baslow*
Riber Hall, *Matlock*

SIGHTS Albert Dock, *Liverpool*
Chatsworth House, *Bakewell*
Hardwick Hall, *Chesterfield*
Manchester Art Gallery, *Manchester*
Museum of Science and Industry, *Manchester*
Walker Art Gallery, *Liverpool*

Updated by
Kate Hughes

FOR THOSE LOOKING FOR THE POSTCARD ENGLAND of little villages and churches, the northwest region of England might not appear at the top of their sightseeing list. After all, the Industrial Revolution thrived nowhere more strongly than the major cities here, including Manchester and Liverpool. Manchester today bustles with redevelopment and youthful culture, but 200 years of smokestack industry, which abated only in the 1980s, have taken a toll on the east Lancashire landscape. Inland, however, in Derbyshire (pronounced "Darbyshire"), lies the spectacular Peak District, a huge, unspoiled national park at the southern end of the Pennines range. In and around this area you'll find Victorian-era spas such as Buxton, pretty towns such as Bakewell, and magnificent stately houses such as Chatsworth, Hardwick Hall, and Haddon Hall.

The areas around Manchester and Liverpool are Britain's equivalent of the Rust Belt, a once-proud bastion of heavy industry and blue-collar values. These cities were the economic engines that propelled Britain in the 18th and 19th centuries. By the mid-18th century, the Lancashire cotton industry had become firmly established in Manchester and enjoyed a special relationship with the port of Liverpool, to the west. Here, at the massive docks, cotton was imported from the United States and sent to the Lancashire mills; the finished cotton goods later returned to Liverpool for export to the rest of the world. Both cities suffered a marked decline during the second half of the 20th century, and today are reestablishing themselves as centers of musical and sporting excellence. Since 1962, the Manchester United, Everton, and Liverpool football (soccer in the United States) clubs have won everything worth winning in Britain and Europe, and in 2002 Manchester hosted the Commonwealth Games. The Beatles launched the Merseysound of the '60s; contemporary Manchester groups often ride both British and U.S. airwaves. On the classical side of music, Manchester is also the home of Britain's oldest leading orchestra, the Hallé (founded in 1857)—just one legacy of 19th-century industrialists' investments in culture.

The Peak District is a wilder part of England, a region of crags that rear violently out of the plain. The Pennines, a line of hills that begins in the Peak District and runs as far north as Scotland, are sometimes called the "backbone of England." In this landscape of rocky outcrops and vaulting meadowland, you'll see nothing for miles but sheep, drystone walls (without mortar), and farms, interrupted—spectacularly—by 19th-century villages and treasure houses. The delight of the Peak District is being able to ramble for days in rugged countryside but still enjoy civilization at its finest.

Exploring Lancashire & the Peak District

Manchester lies at the heart of a tangle of motorways in the northwest of England, about half an hour across the Pennines from Yorkshire. The city spreads west toward the coast and the mouth of the River Mersey, where Liverpool is still centered on its port. For the Northwest's most dramatic scenery—indeed, its only real geological feature of interest—you must travel to the Peak District, a craggy national park less than an hour's drive southeast of Manchester. England at its most grand and ducal can be seen in the Derbyshire valley of the River Wye: majestic 18th-century Chatsworth; Haddon Hall, an enchanting Tudor and Jacobean structure; and Hardwick Hall, the glory of the late Elizabethan age.

About the Restaurants

Dining options in Manchester and Liverpool range from smart café-bars offering modern British and Continental fare to ethnic restaurants. In particular, Manchester has one of Britain's biggest Chinatowns, and locals also set great store in the 40-odd Asian restaurants along Wilmslow Road in Rusholme, a mile south of the city center, where you can savor Bangladeshi, Pakistani, and Indian food.

About the Hotels

If your trip centers on the cities of the Northwest, you can base yourself in Manchester and make Liverpool a day trip. Manchester has a much better choice of accommodations, and because the larger city-center hotels rely on businesspeople during the week, they often markedly reduce their rates on weekends. Smaller hotels and guest houses abound in the nearby suburbs, many just a short bus ride from downtown. The Manchester Visitor Centre operates a room-booking service; you can stop by in person to use it or reserve over the phone with a credit card for a fee. The Peak District has inns, bed-and-breakfasts, and hotels, as well as a network of youth hostels. Local tourist offices have details; reserve well in advance at Easter and in summer.

WHAT IT COSTS In pounds					
	££££££	**££££**	**£££**	**££**	**£**
RESTAURANTS	over £22	£18–£22	£13–£17	£7–£12	under £7
HOTELS	over £160	£115–£160	£80–£115	£50–£80	under £50

Restaurant prices are for a main course at dinner. Hotel prices are for two people in a standard double room in high season, including VAT, with no meals or, if indicated, CP (with Continental breakfast), BP (Breakfast Plan, with full breakfast), or MAP (Modified American Plan, with breakfast and dinner).

Timing

Manchester has a reputation as one of the wettest cities in Britain, and visiting in summer isn't any guarantee of fine weather. Nevertheless, the nature of many sights and cultural activities here and in Liverpool means that wet or cold weather shouldn't spoil a visit. Summer is the optimum time to see the Peak District, especially because early summer sees traditional festivities in many villages. The *only* time to see the great houses of the Derbyshire Wye valley and vicinity—Chatsworth, Haddon Hall, and Hardwick Hall—is from spring through fall.

MANCHESTER

▶ Today Manchester's center hums with the energy of cutting-edge popular music and the swank café-bar culture. Since the late 1980s, events as different as the damage to the city center caused by an IRA bomb in 1996 and the 2002 Commonwealth Games have fueled massive redevelopment of parts of a formerly grim industrial landscape. Canals have been tidied up, cotton mills serve as loft apartments, and contemporary architecture has transformed the skyline. Bridgewater Hall and the Lowry, as well as the Imperial War Museum North, are world-class cultural facilities. Sure, it still rains here, but the rain-soaked streets are part of the city's charm, in a bleak northern kind of way.

For most of its history Manchester, which now has a population of 2.6 million and is Britain's third-largest city, has been a thriving and prosperous place. The Romans built a fort here in AD 79 and named it Mamucium. But the city that stands today—with the elegant Town Hall, Royal Exchange, Midland Hotel, the waterways, and railway—is a product of the Industrial Revolution. Manchester's spectacular rise from a small town to the world's cotton capital (with the nickname Cottonopolis) in only 100 years began with the first steam-powered cotton mill, built in 1783.

10

Greater Manchester and Merseyside form one of the most built-up areas in Britain, but motorway access between the two is fast. One of the main towns of the Peak District, Buxton, could be visited on a day trip from Manchester if you wanted to base yourself in that city. But the Peaks deserve more than just a short drive around the principal sights, and a week's hiking tour here could be constructed easily. If you have only a few days, you might stay in Manchester overnight and take in several of the area's stately homes the rest of the time. If you have a week, you can spend more time in the Peak District as well as explore Manchester and a bit of Liverpool.

Numbers in the text correspond to numbers in the margin and on the Lancashire and the Peaks, Manchester, and Liverpool maps.

If you have
3 days

Base yourself in ⊞ **Manchester** ❶ – ⑫ ⌐ for your first night, which will give you a chance to see the central sights on your first day and attend a concert or a club that night. On the next day, journey to the green Derbyshire Wye valley to visit two of England's most magnificent stately homes, **Haddon Hall** ㉘ and **Chatsworth House** ㉛. Spend your second night in the nearby town of ⊞ **Bakewell** ㉗. If you're traveling when these houses are closed for the season, call in at ⊞ **Liverpool** ⑬ – ㉔ instead for an overnight stay. Enjoy a lunch on the Albert Dock and spend the afternoon in the museums and attractions of this dockside center.

If you have
7 days

It's wisest to split your time between city and national park. Start in **Buxton** ㉖ ⌐ for an afternoon's stroll and spend the night in the pretty town of ⊞ **Bakewell** ㉗. Visit **Haddon Hall** ㉘ and **Chatsworth House** ㉛, both among the top stately homes in Britain, returning to Bakewell for the night. On the morning of the third day, move on to **Matlock** ㉙ and its river, and take a cable-car ride to the Heights of Abraham, or visit **Hardwick Hall** ㉚, which sums up the late Elizabethan era, before aiming for **Castleton** ㉜ and its splendid caverns. If you want to do any walking around the isolated village of **Edale** ㉝, spend the third night back in ⊞ **Buxton** ㉖, making an early start on the day. After walking on the moors, you can take a short drive to ⊞ **Manchester** ❶ – ⑫, where a two-night stay will let you see the best of that city. Move on to enjoy your last night in ⊞ **Liverpool** ⑬ – ㉔.

Dredging made the rivers Irwell and Mersey navigable to ship coal to the factories. The world's first passenger railway opened in 1830, and construction of the Manchester Ship Canal in 1894 provided the infrastructure for Manchester to dominate the industrial world.

A few people acquired wealth, but factory hands worked under appalling conditions. Working-class discontent came to a head in 1819 in the Peterloo Massacre, when soldiers killed 11 workers at a protest meeting. The conditions under which factory hands worked were later recorded by Friedrich Engels (coauthor with Karl Marx of the *Communist Manifesto*), who managed a cotton mill in the city. More formal political opposition to the government emerged in the shape of the Chartist movement (which campaigned for universal suffrage) and the Anti-Corn Law League (which opposed trade tariffs), forerunners of the trade unions

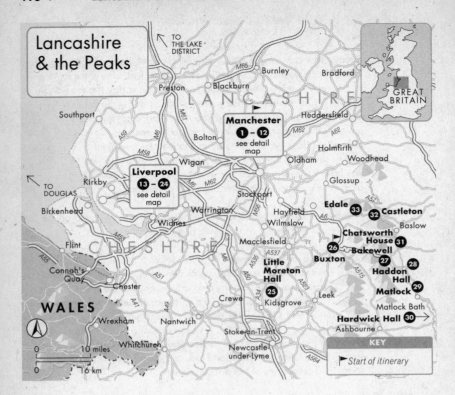

Lancashire & the Peaks

KEY

► Start of itinerary

0   10 miles
0   16 km

in Britain. From Victorian times until the 1960s, daily life for the average Mancunian was so oppressive that it bred the desire to escape, a yearning that is still traceable in the popular culture of the city.

It's impossible to talk about Manchester without mentioning music and football. Out of poverty and unemployment came the brash sounds of punk and the indie record labels. The band New Order produced a unique Mancunian sound that mixed live instruments with digital sound. The now-defunct Haçienda Club marketed New Order to the world, and Manchester became the clubbing capital of England. Joy Division, Morrissey, Stone Roses, Happy Mondays, and Oasis rose to the top of the charts. The triumphant reign of the Manchester United football club, which now faces new challenges because of the departure of team captain David Beckham, has kept many eyes on Manchester.

Exploring Manchester

Manchester is compact enough that you can easily walk across the city center in 40 minutes. The walk below starts at the Town Hall, winds through historic Castlefield, and continues back through the heart of the shopping district to Manchester Cathedral.

a good walk

Begin in Albert Square at the Albert Memorial, built in 1862 with a Gothic-style canopy and spire covering a statue of the Prince Consort. Exit by Lloyd Street, which separates the two parts of the **Town Hall** ❶ ►, a neo-Gothic structure that reflects the economic power of 19th-century Manchester. Turning right at the end of the street will bring you to the Manchester Visitor Centre, a good point to equip yourself with information. Retrace your steps a few yards onto Princess Street, and turn left at Mosley Street, which brings you in front of the neoclassical **Man-**

10

Beatlemania For baby boomers in particular, Liverpool exerts a powerful lure as the birthplace of the Beatles. John, Paul, George, and Pete Best (Ringo arrived a bit later) set up shop at the Cavern in 1961, and the Liverpool Sound soon conquered the world. Today fans can follow in the footsteps of the Fab Four at the Beatles Story, an exhibition at Liverpool's Albert Dock. Many city sites linked with John and Paul have been bulldozed, including Strawberry Field orphanage (a modern structure replaced it), but others, such as childhood homes of John and Paul (now maintained by the National Trust), have survived. The faithful celebrate the Beatles' enduring appeal at the annual International Beatle Week, usually held the last week in August when what seems to be the entire city takes time out to dance, attend John and Yoko fancy-dress parties, and listen to Beatle bands from around the world.

Great Flavors One local dish that has survived in an area that is short on native gustatory delights is the Bakewell pudding (*never* called "tart" in these regions, as its imitations are in other parts of England). The recipe for this tasty treat was allegedly discovered in the 19th century when a cook spilled a rich cake mixture over some jam tarts. Served with custard or cream, the pudding is the joy of Bakewell. Another local creation is the hearty Lancashire hotpot, a casserole of lamb (including the kidneys), potatoes, onions, and carrots that would traditionally have been cooked all day while the family was out at work.

---

chester Art Gallery ❷, where you could spend a couple of hours. Go back to the visitor center and continue to St. Peter's Square and the **Central Library** ❸. Take a peek inside at the glass-domed reading room, inspired by the Pantheon, on the first floor. The Edwardian building on the south side of St. Peter's Square is the Crowne Plaza Manchester— The Midland, a hotel built in 1903.

Continue south on Lower Mosley Street to the G-Mex, a Victorian train shed reconfigured into an exhibition center. Cross Lower Mosley Street to arrive at the striking Bridgewater Hall, where the Hallé Orchestra performs. From Bridgewater Hall, continue down Lower Mosley Street to Whitworth Street West. Turn right and you'll pass Deansgate Locks, a group of trendy bars converted from railway arches, which are the gateway to Castlefield. Turn right on Deansgate and left onto Liverpool Road, and walk several blocks to **Castlefield Urban Heritage Park** ❹, the heart of Manchester's industrial boom.

Liverpool Station, a passenger railway station, is now part of the sprawling **Museum of Science and Industry** ❺, off Liverpool Road, which explores the city's industrial heritage. From the museum, walk north on Lower Byrom Street, turn right onto Quay Street, and go past the Opera House to Deansgate, where you turn left. Continue five blocks until you reach **John Rylands Library** ❻, a red neo-Gothic building on your left. Turn left in front of the library onto Wood Street and follow it to Bridge Street to visit the **PumpHouse: People's History Museum** ❼, which presents Manchester's history from a worker's perspective. Turn right, outside the Pump-House, and follow Bridge Street to Deansgate. Turn left on Deansgate,

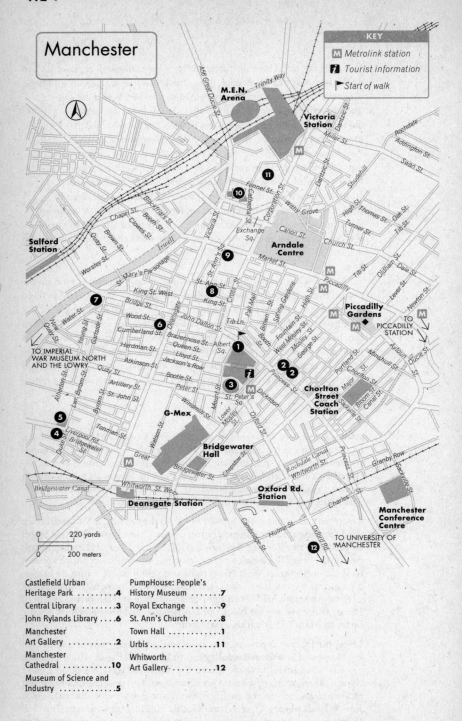

Manchester

KEY

M Metrolink station
i Tourist information
► Start of walk

M.E.N. Arena

Victoria Station

Salford Station

Arndale Centre

Piccadilly Gardens

TO PICCADILLY STATION

Exchange Sq.

TO IMPERIAL WAR MUSEUM NORTH AND THE LOWRY

Chorlton Street Coach Station

G-Mex

Bridgewater Hall

Oxford Rd. Station

Deansgate Station

Manchester Conference Centre

Bridgewater Canal

TO UNIVERSITY OF MANCHESTER

0   220 yards
0   200 meters

Castlefield Urban
Heritage Park 4

Central Library 3

John Rylands Library 6

Manchester
Art Gallery 2

Manchester
Cathedral 10

Museum of Science and
Industry 5

PumpHouse: People's
History Museum 7

Royal Exchange 9

St. Ann's Church 8

Town Hall 1

Urbis 11

Whitworth
Art Gallery 12

right on King Street, left on Cross Street, and left again on St. Ann Street to proceed to **St. Ann's Church** ❽, Manchester's oldest surviving classical building. Exit the church and walk north in a direct line through St. Ann's Square to the **Royal Exchange** ❾, the old cotton market.

From St. Ann's Square walk north past Marks & Spencer, and up Cathedral Street to Exchange Square in the heart of the city's Millennium Quarter. The Triangle, a shopping mall set in the historic facade of the Corn Exchange, is on your left, and the Printworks on your right. **Manchester Cathedral** ❿ sits majestically in the postmodern core of Manchester. To the north of the cathedral, on Fennel Street, is **Urbis** ⓫, a high-tech exploration of city life. If you want to visit the **Whitworth Art Gallery** ⓬ at the University of Manchester, catch any bus with a number in the 40s (except 47) on Oxford Road.

TIMING Although you can complete the walk without stopping in about an hour, you'll need to budget your time carefully at the various sites if you want to see everything in a day. Be sure to save three hours for Castlefield (two of these for the Museum of Science and Industry) and an hour each for the PumpHouse and Manchester Art Gallery. Although many museums are open Sunday, the city will be emptier and some other sights are closed.

What to See

❹ **Castlefield Urban Heritage Park.** Site of an early Roman fort, the district of Castlefield was later the center of the city's industrial boom, which resulted in the building of Britain's first modern canal in 1764 and the world's first railway station in 1830. What had become an urban wasteland has been beautifully restored into an urban park with canal-side walks, landscaped open spaces, and refurbished warehouses. The 7-acre site contains the reconstructed gate to the Roman fort of Mamucium, the buildings of the **Museum of Science and Industry,** and several of the city's hippest bars and restaurants. ⌧ *Off Liverpool Rd., Castlefield.*

❸ **Central Library.** The circular exterior of the city's main library, topped by a line of Doric columns and a massive Corinthian portico facing St. Peter's Square, is a major focus for Manchester's most prestigious civic quarter. Erected in 1930 it was at one time the biggest municipal library in the world; the vast glass-topped social sciences reading room on the first floor is worth seeing. The **Library Theatre** is part of the complex. ⌧ *St. Peter's Sq., City Centre* ☎ *0161/234–1900* ⊕ *www.manchester. gov.uk* ⊗ *Mon.–Thurs. 10–8, Fri.–Sat. 10–5.*

Imperial War Museum North. The thought-provoking exhibits in this imposing, aluminum-clad building, which architect Daniel Libeskind describes as representing three shards of an exploded globe, present the reasons for war and show its effects on society. Three different Big Picture audiovisual shows envelop you in the sights and sounds of conflicts from 1914 to the present, and a rotating storage system allows you to select trays of objects to view. A 100-foot viewing platform gives a bird's-eye view of the city. The museum is on the banks of the Manchester Ship Canal in Salford Quays, across the footbridge from the Lowry. ⌧ *Trafford Wharf Rd., Salford Quays* ☎ *0161/836–4000* ⊕ *www.iwm.org. uk* ⌫ *Free* ⊗ *Daily 10–6.*

❻ **John Rylands Library.** Now owned by the University of Manchester, this Gothic Revival masterpiece designed by Alfred Waterhouse was built by Enriqueta Augustina Rylands as a memorial to her husband, a cotton magnate. Constructed of red sandstone in the 1890s, the library resembles a cathedral. A staircase leads to the reading room, with ornate plaster carvings, a soaring nave, and paneled reading alcoves. The library houses priceless documents and charters, manuscripts, and fine bindings. ⊠ *150 Deansgate, City Centre* ☎ *0161/834–5343* ⊕ *www. rylibweb.man.ac.uk* ☎ *Free, guided tours £1* ⊘ *Weekdays 10–5:15, Sat. 10–12:45; guided tours Wed. at noon.*

The Lowry. This impressive arts center in the heart of Manchester's waterways occupies a dramatic modern building with a steel-gray exterior that reflects the light. L. S. Lowry (1887–1976) was a local artist, and one of the few who painted the industrial landscape. Galleries showcase Lowry's and other contemporary artists' work. The theater, Britain's largest outside London, presents an impressive lineup of touring companies. The nearest Metrolink tram stop is Harbour City. ⊠ *Pier 8, Salford Quays* ☎ *0161/876–2000* ⊕ *www.thelowry.com* ☎ *Free; prices vary for theater tickets and exhibitions; tours £2.50* ⊘ *Building 10* AM–*last performance; galleries, daily 11–5 or 7:30, depending on performances.*

★ ❷ **Manchester Art Gallery.** Beyond its impressive classical portico, this splendid museum does full justice to its fine collections. Outstanding are the Pre-Raphaelite paintings (exemplified by Ford Madox Brown's masterpiece *Work*), Turner watercolors, Dutch masters, and 20th-century British works. The Manchester Gallery illustrates the city's contribution to art, and the Craft and Design Gallery shows off decorative art from ceramics and glass to metalwork and furniture. ⊠ *Mosely St., City Centre* ☎ *0161/235–8888* ⊕ *www.manchestergalleries.org* ☎ *Free* ⊘ *Tues.–Sun. and national holidays 10–5.*

❿ **Manchester Cathedral.** The city's cathedral, set beside the River Irwell and originally a medieval parish church dating in part from the 15th century, is unusually broad for its length and has the widest medieval nave in Britain. Inside, a series of angels with gilded instruments looks down from the roof of the nave, and misericords in the early 16th-century choir stalls reveal intriguing carvings. Note the fine sculpted tomb brass of Warden Huntingdon, who died in 1458, and the octagonal chapter house dating from 1485. ⊠ *Victoria St., Millennium Quarter* ☎ *0161/ 833–2220* ⊕ *www.dws.ndirect.co.uk/mc1.htm* ☎ *Free* ⊘ *Daily 7:30–5.*

★ �™ ❺ **Museum of Science and Industry.** The museum's five buildings, one of which is the world's oldest passenger rail station (1830), hold marvelous collections relating to the city's industrial past and present. You can walk through a reconstructed Victorian sewer, be blasted by the heat and noise of working steam engines, and see cotton looms whirring in action. The Air and Space Gallery fills a graceful cast-iron and glass building, constructed as a market hall in 1877. Allow at least half a day to visit all the sites. ⊠ *Liverpool Rd., main entrance on Lower Byrom Rd., Castlefield* ☎ *0161/832–1830* ⊕ *www.msim.org.uk* ☎ *Free, charges vary for special exhibitions* ⊘ *Daily 10–5.*

☙ ❼ **PumpHouse: People's History Museum.** Not everyone in 19th-century Manchester owned a cotton mill or made a fortune on the trading floor. One of the city's more thought-provoking museums recounts powerfully the struggles of working people in the city since the Industrial Revolution. The museum tells the story of the 1819 Peterloo Massacre and has an unrivaled collection of trade-union banners, tools, toys, utensils, and photographs, all illustrating the working lives and pastimes of the city's people. ⊠ *Bridge St., City Centre* ☎ *0161/839–6061* ⊕ *www. nmlhweb.org* ☎ *£1, free Fri.* ⊘ *Tues.–Sun. 11–4:30.*

| need a break? | The brick-vaulted, waterside **Mark Addy** pub (⊠ Stanley St., off Bridge St., City Centre ☎ 0161/832–4080) is a good spot to have a relaxing drink and sample the excellent spread of pâté and cheeses. |

⑨ Royal Exchange. Throughout its commercial heyday, this was the city's most important building—the cotton market. Built with Victorian panache in 1874, the existing structure accommodated 7,000 traders. The building was refurbished and the giant glass-dome roof restored after damage by the 1996 IRA bombing. Visit to see the lunar module–inspired Royal Exchange Theatre, to have a drink in the café, or to browse in the craft and clothes outlets in the arcade. ⊠ *St. Ann's Sq., City Centre* ☎ *0161/834–3731* ⊕ *www.royalexchange.co.uk.*

⑧ St. Ann's Church. Built in 1712 and sometimes wrongly attributed to Christopher Wren, St. Ann's is Manchester's oldest surviving classical building. The church contains *The Descent from the Cross,* a painting by Annibale Carraci (1561–1609). The verger is usually on hand to show you around. ⊠ *St. Ann's Sq., City Centre* ☎ *0161/834–0239* ⊠ *Free* ⊘ *Daily 10:45–4:30.*

▶ **❶ Town Hall.** Manchester's exuberant Town Hall, with its imposing 280-foot-tall clock tower, speaks volumes about the city's 19th-century sense of self-importance. Alfred Waterhouse designed the Victorian Gothic building (1867–76); extensions were added just before World War II. Over the main entrance is a statue of Roman general Agricola, who founded Mamucium in AD 79. Above him are Henry III, Elizabeth I, and St. George, the patron saint of England. Murals of the city's history, painted between 1852 and 1865 by the Pre-Raphaelite Ford Madox Brown, decorate the Great Hall, with its hammer-beam roof. Guided tours (twice a month) can introduce you to the murals, but ask at the front desk: if the rooms aren't being used, you'll be allowed to wander in. ⊠ *Albert Sq., public entrance on Lloyd St., City Centre* ☎ *0161/234–5000* ⊠ *Free, guided tours £4* ⊘ *Mon.–Sat. 9–4:30; not always open to public access; see the tourist office in Town Hall Extension for tour information.*

⑪ Urbis. A high-tech museum in this striking glass-skinned triangle of a building dissects the modern urban condition with a vengeance, though with mixed success. A glass elevator takes you to the fourth floor, from which you can explore the interactive galleries. Be prepared to be bombarded with light, sound, and images of life in cities as diverse as Tokyo and Paris, as well as Manchester itself. ⊠ *Cathedral Gardens, Millennium Quarter* ☎ *0161/907–9099* ⊕ *www.urbis.org.uk* ⊠ *£5* ⊘ *Sun.–Fri. 10–6, Sat. 10–8; last admission 1½ hrs before closing.*

⑫ Whitworth Art Gallery. This University of Manchester–run art museum has a strong collection of British watercolors, old-master drawings, and postimpressionist works. Captivating rooms full of textiles—Coptic and Peruvian fabrics, Spanish and Italian vestments, tribal rugs, and contemporary weaving—are just what you might expect in a city built on textile manufacture. There's a bistro and a good gift shop. ⊠ *Oxford Rd., University Quarter* ☎ *0161/275–7450* ⊕ *www.whitworth.man.ac.uk* ⊠ *Free* ⊘ *Mon.–Sat. 10–5, Sun. 2–5.*

Where to Eat

Marco Pierre White's River Room at the Lowry Hotel is another excellent dining choice.

££–£££ ✕ **Le Petit Blanc.** Famed chef Raymond Blanc's upscale Manchester brasserie is faithful to its Parisian role models. Conversation buzzes in the relaxed yet elegant surroundings of the mostly white room. The menu combines the best traditions of French bourgeois cuisine with Asian and Mediterranean accents. Try the herb pancakes or fillet of sea bream with saffron potato, followed by the strawberry soup. ⊠ *55 King St., City Centre* ☎ *0161/832–1000* ⊟ *AE, DC, MC, V.*

££–£££ ✕ **The Lincoln.** The innovative cuisine of chef Jem O'Sullivan attracts Manchester's trendiest crowd to this refined restaurant decorated in crisp blue and white. Try the herb-roasted chicken with creamed butter beans or the calves' liver with bacon and onion gravy, but leave room for the chocolate hazelnut cheesecake. ⊠ *1 Lincoln Sq., City Centre* ☎ *0161/834–9000* ⊟ *AE, MC, V.*

££–£££ ✕ **Livebait.** An offshoot of the London-based restaurant serves fresh fish from around the world in an old building across from Albert Square. Tall windows, sage-green walls, a black-and-white tile floor, and green banquettes add fresh style. Among the many good choices are Whitby crab, char-grilled tuna, or traditional cockles and whelks, fish and chips with a twist—in beer batter. Dine early for the fixed-price pretheater menu. ⊠ *22 Lloyd St., City Centre* ☎ *0161/817–4110* ⊟ *AE, DC, MC, V.*

££–£££ ✕ **Mr. Thomas's Chophouse.** The city's oldest restaurant (1872) dishes out good old British favorites such as Lancashire hot pot (lamb stew), with pickled red cabbage and dumplings, and steamed jam sponge puddings. This hearty food is served in a clubby, Victorian-style room with a black-and-white-checked floor, brown ceilings, and wrought-iron screens. The wine list is exceptional. ⊠ *52 Cross St., City Centre* ☎ *0161/832–2245* ⊟ *AE, DC, MC, V.*

££–£££ ✕ **Pacific.** Designed around feng shui principles, this well-regarded split-level concept restaurant fuses old and new Asian culture. The lower floor is China, the upper Thailand; each has a separate kitchen and chef. In China you can sample dim sum and à la carte dishes, with classic favorites as well as unusual Asian delicacies such as abalone in oyster sauce. Thailand has authentic regional cooking and ingredients. ⊠ *58–60 George St., City Centre* ☎ *0161/228–6668* ⊟ *AE, DC, MC, V.*

★ ££–£££ ✕ **Simply Heathcote's.** Lancastrian chef Paul Heathcote earned his reputation as the "cook of the North" for his original, modern food. A diverse clientele that includes pretheater and football crowds packs the massive, minimalist dining room. Some signature dishes are terrine of ham hock with red wine and lentils, honey-glazed duckling, and, for dessert, bread and butter pudding with clotted cream. ⊠ *Jackson's Row, City Centre* ☎ *0161/835–3536* ⊟ *AE, DC, MC, V.*

★ ££ ✕ **Yang Sing.** One of Manchester's best Chinese restaurants, this place is popular with Chinese families, which is always a good sign. The menu of Cantonese dishes is huge, the dim sum are legendary, and there's plenty for those of adventurous spirit—ox tripe with black bean sauce, for example. Vegetarians won't be disappointed, either. ⊠ *34 Princess St., City Centre* ☎ *0161/236–2200* ⊟ *AE, MC, V.*

£–££ ✕ **Tandoori Kitchen.** The menu of this colorful Rusholme legend includes interesting Persian dishes, milder fare that concentrates more on herbs and seasoning, alongside the usual curry offerings. The take-out next door caters to Manchester's nocturnal characters. ⊠ *131–133 Wilmslow Rd., Rusholme* ☎ *0161/224–2329* ⊟ *AE, MC, V.*

Where to Stay

££££–£££££ ⊡ **Crowne Plaza Manchester—The Midland.** The Edwardian splendor of the hotel's public rooms—including a grand lobby—evokes the days when the Midland was Manchester's railroad station hotel. A traditional high tea is served in the lobby. Guest rooms are comfortable but unremarkable, with modern amenities but none of the period flair of the public areas. ⊠ *Peter St., City Centre, M60 2DS* ☎ *0161/236–3333* 🖷 *0161/932–4100* ⊕ *www.manchester-themidland.crowneplaza.com* ⇆ *303 rooms, 7 suites* ⚴ *3 restaurants, in-room data ports, cable TV with movies, in-room VCRs, indoor pool, hair salon, health club, sauna, 2 bars,* *lounge, business services, meeting rooms, free parking, some pets allowed; no a/c* ⊟ *AE, DC, MC, V* ⦿I *BP.*

££££–£££££ 🏨 **The Lowry Hotel.** The modern, ergonomic Italian design of this glass

edifice exudes luxury and spaciousness. Public and guest rooms are washed in soothing neutral tones, enlivened by bright red splashes of furniture; marble bathrooms and walk-in closets enhance the bedrooms. Marco Pierre White oversees the French-inspired menu of the very elegant River Room restaurant. The hotel fronts the River Irwell across from the landmark Trinity Bridge designed by Santiago Calatrava. ⊠ *50 Dearman's Place, City Centre, M3 5LH* ☎ *0161/827–4000; 800/223–6800 in U.S.* 🖷 *0161/827–4001* ⊕ *www.roccofortehotels.com* ⇨ *157 rooms, 7 suites* ⚒ *Restaurant, in-room data ports, cable TV with movies, in-room VCRs, indoor pool, hair salon, health club, sauna, spa, steam room, bar, business services, meeting rooms, parking (fee), no-smoking floors* ⊟ *AE, DC, MC, V.*

££££ 🏨 **Malmaison Hotel.** Stylish and chic, this is the kind of place that's popular with British pop stars. The striking contemporary design, inside an Edwardian facade, includes good-size, individually designed rooms decorated in red, black, and cream. Traditional French cuisine is the focus in the Malmaison Brasserie. The Malmaison is a few minutes' walk to Piccadilly Station, Chinatown, and Canal Street. ⊠ *Piccadilly, City Centre, M1 3AQ* ☎ *0161/278–1000* 🖷 *0161/278–1002* ⊕ *www.malmaison.com* ⇨ *167 rooms* ⚒ *Restaurant, in-room data ports, health club, sauna, spa, steam room, bar, business services, meeting rooms, no-smoking floors; no a/c* ⊟ *AE, DC, MC, V.*

£££–££££ 🏨 **Etrop Grange.** A gracious Georgian mansion with a modern addition, this true gem takes you back in time, even though you're just minutes from the airport rather than out in the country. Fireplaces, chandeliers, tapestry curtains, comfortable sofas, and antiques give a sense of luxurious warmth. Bedrooms are individually furnished, some with antique-style bathtubs. The Coach House Restaurant is known for good British cuisine. ⊠ *Thorley Lā., Manchester Airport, M90 4EG* ☎ *0161/499–0500* 🖷 *0161/499–0790* ⊕ *www.corushotels.com/etropgrange* ⇨ *64 rooms* ⚒ *Restaurant, in-room data ports, cable TV, bar, business services, meeting rooms, airport shuttle, parking (fee), some pets allowed, no-smoking floor; no a/c* ⊟ *AE, DC, MC, V.*

£££–££££ 🏨 **Rossetti.** The girders, parquet flooring, and tiles of this former Victorian textile warehouse (which used to supply floral print dresses to Queen Elizabeth II) are still here, but the feather-soft beds, Molteni furniture, and funky lights are right up to date. There's a help-yourself breakfast bar on each floor, a café-restaurant that dishes up Neapolitan pizzas, and a glitzy nightclub in the basement. ⊠ *107 Piccadilly, City Centre, M1 2DB* ☎ *0161/247–7744* 🖷 *0161/247–7747* ⊕ *www.aliasrossetti.com* ⇨ *56 rooms, 5 suites* ⚒ *Restaurant, in-room data ports, in-room VCRs, bar, nightclub, meeting rooms, parking (fee); no a/c* ⊟ *AE, DC, MC, V* ⦿I *CP.*

££–£££ 🏨 **Castlefield Hotel.** This popular modern redbrick hotel sits near the water's edge in the Castlefield Basin. Public rooms are cheery and traditional, with patterned carpets and plain furnishings; subdued tones help make the bedrooms restful. The leisure facilities and free breakfast make this a good value. ⊠ *Liverpool Rd., Castlefield, M3 4JR* ☎ *0161/832–7073* 🖷 *0161/837–3534* ⊕ *www.castlefield-hotel.co.uk* ⇨ *48 rooms* ⚒ *Restaurant, in-room data ports, cable TV, indoor pool, health club, sauna, bar, meeting rooms, parking (fee)* ⊟ *AE, DC, MC, V* ⦿I *BP.*

££ 🏨 **Jurys Inn.** A good-value outpost of the Irish-based chain, Jurys has a sleek wooden lobby and contemporary design that is light and attractive. Guest rooms are spacious, and you can use a nearby health club. The location is excellent, next to Bridgewater Hall and close to shopping on King Street and the café-bar scenes on Whitworth Street and in Castlefield. ⊠ 56 Great Bridgewater St., Peter's Fields, M1 5LE ☎ 0161/953–8888 🖷 0161/953–9090 ⊕ www.jurysdoyle.com ⇆ 265 rooms ௴ Restaurant, in-room data ports, cable TV, bar, business services, meeting rooms, parking (fee), no-smoking floors ▭ AE, DC, MC, V.

£ ▯ **The Ox.** Friendly and relaxed, this gastro-pub with rooms is a real find. Guest rooms are furnished in light wood, with patterned fabrics and subdued colors, and the buzz-filled restaurant, decorated with local artwork, serves up seafood and vegetarian dishes. Guest ales are on tap, complemented by a good selection of wines. ⊠ 71 Liverpool Rd., Castlefield, M3 4NO ☎ 0161/839–7740 🖷 0161/839–7760 ⊕ www. theox.co.uk ⇆ 9 rooms ௴ Restaurant, bar; no a/c ▭ MC, V ⑩ BP.

Nightlife & the Arts

Manchester vies with London as Britain's capital of youth culture but has vibrant nightlife and entertainment options for all ages. For event listings, buy the twice-monthly City Life magazine.

Nightlife

CAFÉ-BARS & PUBS

Barça (⊠ 8–9 Catalan Sq., Castlefield ☎ 0161/839–7099) is a hip canalside bar-restaurant that has won architectural awards. **Dry Bar** (⊠ 28–30 Oldham St., Northern Quarter ☎ 0161/236–9840), the original café-bar in town, is still full of young people drinking and dancing. The cavernous **Dukes 92** (⊠ 18 Castle St., Castlefield ☎ 0161/839–8646) is a café-bar named after the number of the lock on the Rochdale Canal by which it's situated. **Revolution** (⊠ Whitworth St. W, Peter's Fields ☎ 0161/839–7569), in trendy Deansgate Locks, is a vodka bar. If you're over 25, **Tiger Tiger** (⊠ 5–6 The Printworks, City Centre ☎ 0161/385–8080) is the place to go for a relaxed meal and to drink or dance.

The so-called **Gay Village** has a dozen stylish bars and cafés along the Rochdale Canal. The area is not only the heart of the gay scene but also the nightlife center for the young and trendy. The café-bar **Manto** (⊠ 46 Canal St., Gay Village ☎ 0161/236–2667) draws a chic, mostly gay crowd to its split-level, postindustrial interior.

The Britons Protection (⊠ 50 Great Bridgewater St., Peter's Fields ☎ 0161/236–5895) is a relaxed pub with stained glass and cozy back rooms, a Peterloo Massacre mural, high-quality cask ales, and more than 160 whiskeys and bourbons. **Peveril of the Peak** (⊠ 127 Great Bridgewater St., Peter's Fields ☎ 0161/236–6364), a Victorian pub with a green-tile exterior, draws a crush of locals to its several tiny rooms. **Sinclair's Oyster Bar** (⊠ 2 Cathedral Gates, Millennium Quarter ☎ 0161/834–0430), a half-timber pub built in the 17th century, sells fresh oyster dishes.

DANCE CLUBS

Ascension (⊠ 46–50 Oldham St., City Centre ☎ 0161/228–3300) hosts live music and big name DJs, dishing out everything from house, funk, and hip hop to classic sounds. **Industry** (⊠ 112–116 Princess St., City Centre ☎ 0161/273–5422), a large club on three floors, concentrates on drum and bass, funk, and R&B music.

LIVE MUSIC

Band on the Wall (⊠ 25 Swan St., Northern Quarter ☎ 0161/832–6625) is a cozy room with a formidable reputation for live music—from world fusion to folk, jazz, and rock—and club nights. **Manchester Apollo** (⊠ Stockport Rd., Ardwick Green ☎ 0161/242–2560) showcases diverse acts for all musical tastes. Major rock and pop stars appear at the **Manchester Evening News Arena** (⊠ 21 Hunt's Bank, Hunt's Bank ☎ 0161/930–8000). **The Roadhouse** (⊠ 8 Newton St., City Centre ☎ 0161/237–9789), an intimate live band venue, also hosts funk, hip hop, and drum-and-bass nights.

The Arts

FESTIVALS For information about annual events such as the Manchester Festival (July–August), call the **Visitor Information Centre** (☎ 0161/234–3157 or 0161/234–3158).

FILM The city's major center for contemporary cinema and the visual arts, the **Cornerhouse** (✉ 70 Oxford St., City Centre ☎ 0161/200–1500) has three movie screens plus galleries, a bookshop, a trendy bar, and a café. **The Filmworks** (✉ The Printworks, Exchange Sq., Millennium Quarter ☎ 0870/010–2030) is a state-of-the-art 20-screen complex with an IMAX 3-D screen.

PERFORMING ARTS VENUES **Bridgewater Hall** (✉ Lower Mosley St., Peter's Fields ☎ 0161/907–9000) has concerts by Manchester's Hallé Orchestra and hosts both classical music and a varied light-entertainment program. **The Lowry** (✉ Pier 8, Salford Quays ☎ 0161/876–2000) contains two theaters and presents everything from musicals to dance and performance poetry. The **Opera House** (✉ Quay St., City Centre ☎ 0161/242–2524) is a venue for West End musicals, opera, and classical ballet. The **Palace Theatre** (✉ Oxford St., City Centre ☎ 0161/242–2503) presents large touring shows—major plays, ballet, and opera. **Royal Northern College of Music** (✉ 124 Oxford Rd., University Quarter ☎ 0161/907–5278) hosts classical and contemporary music concerts, jazz, and opera.

THEATRE **Green Room** (✉ 54–56 Whitworth St. W, City Centre ☎ 0161/950–5900) is an alternative space for theater, poetry, dance, and performance art. **Library Theatre** (✉ St. Peter's Sq., City Centre ☎ 0161/236–7110) in the Central Library stages classical drama, Shakespeare, chamber musicals, and new work from local playwrights. **Royal Exchange Theatre** (✉ St. Ann's Sq., City Centre ☎ 0161/833–9833) serves as the city's main venue for innovative contemporary theater.

Sports & the Outdoors

The **Manchester Aquatics Centre** (✉ Oxford Rd., University Quarter ☎ 0161/275–9450) has two 50-meter pools, as well as separate diving and leisure pools. The public can swim here as well as watch competitions. The **Manchester Velodrome** (✉ 1 Stuart St., Beswick ☎ 0161/223–2244) hosts regular cycling, gymnastics, badminton, and basketball events.

Football

Football (soccer in the United States) is *the* major passion in Manchester. Locals support the perennially unsuccessful local club, Manchester City, and glory seekers come from afar to root for Manchester United, based in neighboring Trafford. Matches for both clubs are usually sold out months in advance, but touts (scalpers, legal here) do business outside the grounds. **Manchester City** (✉ Rowsley St., Sportcity ☎ 016/500–5000) plays at the City of Manchester Stadium. **Manchester United** (✉ Sir Matt Busby Way, Trafford Wharf ☎ 0161/868–8000) has home matches at Old Trafford.

You can take a trip to the Theatre of Dreams at the **Manchester United Museum and Tour** (✉ Sir Matt Busby Way, Trafford Wharf ☎ 0870/442–1994), which tells the history of the football club. The tour (not available on match days) takes you behind the scenes, into the changing rooms and players' lounge, and down the tunnel to pitch side. It's open daily 9:30–5; admission for the museum and tour is £8.50, museum only £5.50.

Shopping

Afflecks Palace (⊠ 52 Church St., Northern Quarter ☎ 0161/834–2039) attracts Mancunian youth with four floors of bohemian glam, ethnic crafts and jewelry, and innovative gift ideas. **Barton Arcade** (⊠ 51–63 Deansgate, City Centre ☎ 0161/839–3172) has specialty shopping inside a lovely Victorian arcade. **Chinatown**—surrounded by Portland Street, Mosley Street, Princess Street, and Charlotte Street—is at its liveliest on Sunday when traders from all over the country stock up from the supermarkets and stalls.

The **Lowry Designer Outlet** (⊠ Salford Quays ☎ 0161/848–1832), with 80 stores, has good discounts on top brand names at stores such as Nike and Karen Millen. The **Manchester Craft and Design Centre** (⊠ 17 Oak St., Northern Quarter ☎ 0161/832–4274) houses 16 workshop–cum–retail outlets where you can see craftspeople at work. The world's largest **Marks & Spencer** (⊠ 7 Market St., City Centre ☎ 0161/831–7341) department store offers its own brand of fashion and has an excellent food department. **Oldham Street,** in the Northern Quarter, is littered with urban hip-hop boutiques and music shops. The **Royal Exchange Shopping Centre and Arcade** (⊠ St. Ann's Sq., City Centre ☎ 0161/834–3731) has three floors of restaurants and specialty shops with antiques, Belgian chocolates, teddy bears, and more, inside the former cotton market. **The Triangle** (⊠ Millennium Quarter ☎ 0161/834–8961), a stylish mall in the Victorian Corn Exchange, has more than 30 stores, including independent designer shops.

LIVERPOOL

Lined with one of the most famous waterfronts in England, celebrated around the world as the birthplace of the Beatles, and still the place to catch that "Ferry 'Cross the Mersey," Liverpool has suffered acute decline over the past few decades. New developments, however, such as the Tate Liverpool and the refurbishment of the adjacent Albert Dock, have spurred a reverse in the city's fortunes, and the naming of Liverpool as the European Union's Capital of Culture for 2008 will attract plans and funds for further improvements.

Liverpool, on the east bank of the Mersey River estuary, at the point where it merges with the Irish Sea, developed from the 17th century through the slave trade. It became Britain's leading port for ferrying Africans to North America and for handling cargoes of sugar, tobacco, rum, and cotton, which began to dominate the local economy after the abolition of the slave trade in 1807. Because of its proximity to Ireland, the city was also the first port of call for those fleeing famine, poverty, and persecution in that country. Liverpool was often the last British port of call for thousands of mostly Jewish refugees fleeing the pogroms in Eastern Europe.

Many of the best-known liner companies were based in Liverpool, including Cunard and White Star, whose best-known vessel, the *Titanic,* was registered in Liverpool. The city was dealt an economic blow in 1894 with the opening of the Manchester Ship Canal, which allowed traders to bypass Liverpool and head to Lancashire's other major city, 35 mi east. Liverpool's economy never recovered, and decline gradually set in. Wartime bombing in the 1940s devastated the city's infrastructure, and rebuilding was unsympathetic. The postwar growth of air travel curtailed the services of the oceangoing liners, and a few years later Britain's entry into the European Common Market saw more trade move from the west coast to the east.

As economic decline set in, Liverpool produced its most famous export—the Beatles. The group was one of hundreds that began copying the rock 'n' roll they heard from visiting American GIs and merchant seamen in the late 1950s, and one of many that played local venues such as the Cavern (demolished but since rebuilt nearby). All four Beatles were born in Liverpool, but the group's success dates from the time they left for London. Nevertheless, the city has milked the group's Liverpool connections for all they are worth, and there are a multitude of local attractions connected with the group.

Despite the roughness and shabbiness of parts of the city, a surprising number of people visit Liverpool to tour the Beatles sites, view the paintings in the renowned art galleries, and learn about the city's industrial and maritime heritage at the impressive Albert Dock area.

Exploring Liverpool

Liverpool has a fairly compact center, and you can see many city highlights on foot. This walk includes some civic landmarks and museums, some key Beatles sights, and the renovated Albert Dock and its maritime heritage sights.

A Good Walk

Begin, as many people do, at Lime Street and **Lime Street Station** ⑬ ▶, which is not just the famous railway station but also the city's grandest Classical Revival building, **St. George's Hall** ⑭. To the north lies William Brown Street, a showcase boulevard of municipal buildings, including the outstanding **Walker Art Gallery** ⑮. A left turn at the end of William Brown Street leads into Whitechapel, a street of dowdy-looking stores. However, Nos. 12–14 were once the NEMS (North End Music Stores) record shop owned by Brian Epstein. In 1961 when a teenager asked for a record by Tony Sheridan and the Beat Brothers, Epstein couldn't find it in his catalog. He discovered that the backing band was the Beatles, a local group. The Beatles were playing daily at a nearby club, the Cavern, so he made the short journey—as you can do now—down Whitechapel, turning right at Stanley Street and left onto **Mathew Street** to get to the Cavern at No. 10. The rest is, as they say, history.

The western end of Mathew Street leads into North John Street, and a right turn brings you out at Dale Street, overlooked by the looming mass of the **Royal Liver Building** ⑯, part of Liverpool's famous waterfront skyline. Equally renowned is the palazzolike Cunard Building to the south, once the head office for the famous Cunard Steamship Company. The wide Mersey estuary separating the city from the Wirral Peninsula is usually reached by the ferry, which leaves from the adjacent **Pier Head** ⑰. A riverside walk connects with the museum area that includes the **Merseyside Maritime Museum** ⑱ and **Albert Dock** ⑲, 19th-century brick warehouses that have been redeveloped into boutiques, restaurants, offices, a hotel, and **Tate Liverpool** ⑳. The complex also includes the **Beatles Story** ㉑, detailing the story of the city's best-known sons, and the **Museum of Liverpool Life** ㉒.

From Albert Dock it's a reasonably short walk back into the city center. For a longer walk that takes in the city's two cathedrals, head southeast along Duke Street and Upper Duke Street toward the Gothic-inspired **Anglican Cathedral** ㉓. Hope Street, which runs along the eastern side of the cathedral, links the latter with its Roman Catholic counterpart to the north, the modernistic **Metropolitan Cathedral of Christ the King** ㉔, and includes some romantic Georgian properties such as Gambier Terrace (John Lennon once lived at No. 3) and the College of Art where

Lennon studied. From the Catholic cathedral, it's a five-minute walk north-west back to Lime Street Station.

TIMING   You can do this walk in an hour without stopping, but you'll need a full day to visit all the museums and churches. Remember that 20 Forthlin Road and Mendips, the childhood homes of Paul McCartney and John Lennon, are in Liverpool but lie outside the center city.

What to See

★ **19 Albert Dock.** To understand the city's prosperous maritime past, head straight for waterfront Albert Dock, 7 acres of restored warehouses built in 1846. Albert Dock, named after Queen Victoria's consort, Prince Albert, provided storage for silk, tea, and tobacco from the Far East but ultimately closed in 1972. Rescued by the Merseyside Development Corporation, the fine colonnaded brick warehouse buildings are now England's largest heritage attraction, containing the **Merseyside Maritime Museum, Museum of Liverpool Life, Tate Liverpool,** and the **Beatles Story.** When the weather allows, sit at an outdoor café overlooking the dock or take a boat trip through the docks and out onto the river. Albert Dock is part of the larger area known as **Liverpool's Historic Waterfront.** ✉ *Tourist Information Centre, Atlantic Pavilion, Waterfront* ☎ *0151/708–8854* ⊕ *www.albertdock.com* ⊙ *Information center, daily 10–5:30.*

23 Anglican Cathedral. The largest church in northern Britain overlooks the city and the River Mersey. Built of local sandstone, the Gothic-style cathedral was begun in 1903 by architect Giles Gilbert Scott; it was finally finished in 1978. Take a look at the grand interior, view the exhibit of Victorian embroidery, climb the 331-foot tower, and stop at the visitor center. A refectory serves light meals and coffee. ✉ *St.*

James's Mount, City Centre ☎ *0151/709–6271* ⊕ *www. liverpoolcathedral.org.uk* ✉ *Donation suggested, tower and embroidery exhibition £2.50* ⊙ *Daily 8–6. Tower Mar.–Sept., Mon.–Sat. 11–4:30; Oct.–Feb., Mon.–Sat. 11–3:30.*

need a break? The **Life Café Bar** (✉ 1a Bold St., City Centre ☎ 0151/707–2333) used to be a library and a gentleman's club. Now you can sink into a huge sofa for coffee or cocktails beneath the grand domed ceiling.

㉑ **Beatles Story.** You can follow in the footsteps of the Fab Four at one of the more popular attractions in the Albert Dock complex. It has an entertaining series of scenes re-created from their career, as well as the glasses John Lennon wore when he composed "Imagine." ✉ *Britannia Vaults, Albert Dock, Waterfront* ☎ *0151/709–1963* ⊕ *www.beatlesstory.com* ✉ *£7.95* ⊙ *Mar.–Oct., daily 10–6; Nov.–Feb., daily 10–5; last admission 1 hr before closing.*

⌐ ⑬ **Lime Street Station.** Perhaps the most imposing expression of the city's former industrial might is this railway station, whose cast-iron train shed was the world's largest in the mid-19th century. The opening scene in the film *A Hard Day's Night,* which shows the Beatles on a railway station platform, supposedly Lime Street, was filmed in Marylebone Station, London. ✉ *Lime St., City Centre.*

Liverpool's Historic Waterfront. Liverpool's famous waterside sights include the Royal Liver and Cunard buildings, Pier Head (ferries leave for river trips), and the Albert Dock complex. Also here are the Merseyside Maritime Museum, Museum of Liverpool Life, Tate Liverpool, and the Beatles Story. A shuttle bus (every 20 minutes) runs to the waterfront from the Queen Square bus station, a couple of minutes' walk from Lime Street Station.

Mathew Street. It was at the Cavern on this street that Brian Epstein, who became the Beatles' manager, first heard the group in 1961. The Cavern had opened at No. 10 as a jazz venue in 1957, but beat groups, of whom the Beatles were clearly the most talented, had taken it over. Epstein became their manager a few months after first visiting the club, and within two years the group was the most talked-about phenomenon in music. The Cavern club fell on hard times in the early '70s and was demolished in 1973; it was later rebuilt a few yards from the original site. At No. 31, check out the Beatles Shop.

Mendips. The august National Trust (overseers of such landmarks as Blenheim Palace) also maintains the 1930s semidetached house that was the home of John Lennon from 1946 to 1963. He joined his aunt Mimi here after his parents' separation; she gave him his first guitar but banished him to play in the porch, saying, "The guitar's all very well, John, but you'll never make a living out of it." The house can be seen only on a special tour, for which you must prebook a seat on the minibus that connects the site with Albert Dock or Speke Hall. ✉ *251 Menlove Ave., Woolton* ☎ *0870/900–0256* ⊕ *www.spekehall.org.uk/mendips.htm* ✉ *£10 includes 20 Forthlin Rd. and Speke Hall* ⊙ *Apr.–Oct., Wed.–Sun.; 4 or more departures a day (call for times).*

☝ ⑱ **Merseyside Maritime Museum.** Part of the Albert Dock complex, the museum tells the story of the port of Liverpool by way of models, paintings, and original boats and equipment spread across five floors. In summer full-size vessels are on display. The same admission ticket also grants access to the Transatlantic Slavery and Customs and Excise exhibitions, the former being especially compelling on the human misery engendered by the slave trade, and the latter a testament to man's ingenuity. ✉ *Albert Dock, Waterfront* ☎ *0151/478–4499* ⊕ *www.nmgm.org.uk* ✉ *Free* ⊘ *Daily 10–5; last admission 4.*

㉔ Metropolitan Cathedral of Christ the King. This Roman Catholic cathedral consecrated in 1967 is a modernistic funnel-like structure of concrete, stone, and mosaic, topped with a glass lantern. Long narrow blue-glass windows separate chapels, each with modern works of art. An earlier design by classically inspired architect Edwin Lutyens was abandoned when World War II began (the current design is by Frederick Gibberd), but the crypt shows some of Lutyens's work. ✉ *Mount Pleasant, City Centre* ☎ *0151/709–9222* ⊕ *www.liverpool-rc-cathedral.org.uk* ✉ *Donations welcome* ⊘ *Mon.–Sat. 8–6, Sun. 8–5.*

㉒ Museum of Liverpool Life. This museum in a former Boat Hall takes a somewhat offbeat look at the city's history and culture. Special displays on Merseyside culture focus on matters as diverse as the city's changing trades after the decline of shipping, local sporting prowess, and arts and literature in Liverpool. This is the place to discover what makes "Scousers" (as locals are known) tick. ✉ *Albert Dock, Waterfront* ☎ *0151/478–4080* ⊕ *www.nmgm.org.uk* ✉ *Free* ⊘ *Daily 10–5; last admission 4.*

⑰ Pier Head. Here you can take a ferry across the River Mersey from Pierhead to Birkenhead and back. Ferries leave regularly and offer fine views of the city—a journey celebrated in "Ferry 'Cross the Mersey," Gerry and the Pacemakers' 1964 hit song. It was from Pier Head that 9 million British, Irish, and European emigrants set sail between 1830 and 1930 for new lives in the United States, Canada, Australia, and Africa. ✉ *Pier Head Ferry Terminal, Mersey Ferries, Waterfront* ☎ *0151/330–1444* ⊕ *www.merseyferries.co.uk* ✉ *£1.95 round-trip, cruises £4.30* ⊘ *Ferries every 30 mins 7:45–9:15 AM and 4:15–7:15 PM; cruises hourly 10–3 weekdays and 10–6 weekends.*

⑯ Royal Liver Building. Best seen from the ferry, the 322-foot-tall Royal Liver (pronounced "lie-ver") Building with its twin towers is topped by two 18-foot copper birds. They represent the mythical Liver Birds, the town symbol; local legend has it that if they fly away, Liverpool will cease to exist. For decades Liverpudlians looked to the Royal Liver Society for assistance—it was originally a burial club to which families paid contributions to ensure a decent send-off. ✉ *Water St., Waterfront.*

⑭ St. George's Hall. Built between 1839 and 1847, St. George's Hall is among the world's best Greek Revival buildings. When Queen Victoria visited Liverpool in 1851, she declared it "worthy of ancient Athens." Today the hall serves as a home for music festivals, concerts, and fairs. Refurbishment will be under way throughout 2004, but you can still visit the barrel-vaulted Great Hall. ✉ *Lime St., City Centre* ☎ *0151/707–2391* ⊕ *www.stgeorgeshall.com* ✉ *Free, different charges for events* ⊘ *Weekdays 9–5.*

Speke Hall and Gardens. This black-and-white mansion only 6 mi from downtown Liverpool is one of the best examples of half-timbering in Britain. Built around a cobbled courtyard, the earliest part, the great hall, dates to 1490; an elaborate western bay with a vast chimneypiece was added in 1560. The house, owned by the National Trust, was heavily restored in the 19th century, though a Tudor priest hole and Jacobean plasterwork remain intact. Speke Hall is on the east side of the airport; the Airportxpress 500 bus can drop you at the nearest point, a pleasant 10-minute walk away. ✉ *The Walk, Speke* ☎ *0151/427–7231* ⊕ *www.spekehall.org.uk* ✉ *£5.50, gardens only £2.50* ⊘ *House late*

Mar.–Oct., Wed.–Sun. and national holidays 1–5:30; Nov.–mid-Dec., weekends 1–4:30. Gardens daily 11–5:30 or dusk.

㉑ Tate Liverpool. An offshoot of the London-based art galleries of the same name, the Liverpool museum, a handsome conversion of existing Albert Dock warehouses, was designed in the 1990s by the late James Stirling, one of Britain's leading 20th-century architects. Galleries display changing exhibits of challenging modern art. The excellent shop sells art books, prints, and posters, and there's a children's art-play area and a fashionable dockside café-restaurant. ✉ *The Colonnades, Albert Dock, Waterfront* ☎ *0151/702–7400* ⊕ *www.tate.org.uk* 🎫 *Free, charge for special exhibitions* ⊙ *Tues.–Sun. and national holidays 10–5:50.*

20 Forthlin Road. Paul McCartney lived with his family in this 1950s council house, with its period-authentic windows, doors, and hedges, from 1955 to 1963. A number of the Beatles' songs, including "Love Me Do" and "When I'm Sixty-Four," were written here. The house is viewable only on a special tour, for which you must prebook a seat on the minibus that connects the site with Albert Dock or Speke Hall. ✉ *20 Forthlin Rd., Allerton* ☎ *0870/900–0256* ⊕ *www.spekehall.org.uk* 🎫 *£10 includes Mendips and Speke Hall* ⊙ *Apr.–Oct., Wed.–Sun.; 4 or more departures a day (call for times).*

★ ⑮ Walker Art Gallery. With an excellent display of British art and some superb Italian and Flemish works, the Walker maintains its position as one of the best art collections outside London. Particularly notable are the unrivaled collection of paintings by 18th-century Liverpudlian equestrian artist George Stubbs, and works by J. M. W. Turner, John Constable, Sir Edwin Henry Landseer, and the Pre-Raphaelites. Modern British artists are included, too—on display is one of David Hockney's typically Californian pool scenes. Other exhibits showcase china, silver, and furniture that once adorned the mansions of Liverpool's industrial barons. The Tea Room holds center stage in the airy museum lobby. ✉ *William Brown St., City Centre* ☎ *0151/478–4199* ⊕ *www.nmgm. org.uk* 🎫 *Free* ⊙ *Mon.–Sat. 10–5, Sun. noon–5.*

Where to Eat

£–££££ ✗ **60 Hope Street.** The combination of a ground-floor restaurant and a cheaper basement café-bar make this a popular choice. A light, polished wood floor and blue and cream walls help create the uncluttered backdrop for dishes that reflect a Mediterranean clime, but found only on British shores is the deep-fried jam sandwich with condensed milk ice cream, one of the imaginative desserts. ✉ *60 Hope St., City Centre* ☎ *0151/707–6060* ▭ *MC, V* ⊙ *Closed Sun. No lunch Sat. in restaurant.*

££–£££ ✗ **Blue Bar and Grill.** Expect to rub shoulders with local celebrities in this sophisticated modern restaurant and bar on the waterfront. The focal point is the beautiful Venetian crystal chandelier, a counterpoint to the original open brickwork, chunky furnishings, and plasma screens. Downstairs you can sample tapas, dim sum, and bruschetta; the fare in the upstairs gallery includes a large selection of meat and fish steaks, accompanied by different sauces. ✉ *Edward Pavilion, Albert Dock, Waterfront* ☎ *0151/709–7097* ▭ *AE, MC, V.*

££–£££ ✗ **Chung Ku.** Liverpool has a strong Chinese presence, and here you can sample Asian cuisine with a superb Merseyside view. Panoramic windows wrap around both levels of this stunning, ultramodern restaurant. Choose between 70 different kinds of dim sum, or try one of the "sizzling platters" or something from the extensive seafood selection.

✉ *2 Columbus Quay, Riverside Dr., Waterfront* ☎ *0151/726–8191* ⚇ *AE, MC, V.*

££–£££ ✕ **Simply Heathcote's.** This chic contemporary restaurant, an outpost of chef Paul Heathcote's expanding empire, has a curved glass front, cherrywood furnishings, and a granite floor. You'll find a local accent on the menu—black pudding hash browns, Goosnargh duckling, cherry Bakewell tart—along with dishes from warmer climes. Vegetarians are well served, too. The restaurant is opposite the Royal Liver and Cunard buildings. ✉ *25 The Strand, Waterfront* ☎ *0151/236–3536* ⚇ *AE, DC, MC, V.*

£–££ ✕ **Tate Café.** The Tate Liverpool's café-bar is a winner for daytime sustenance. There are dockside seats for those summer days, and you can pick among sandwiches and salads, as well as more substantial fare such as ham hocks and char-grilled salmon. ✉ *The Colonnades, Albert Dock, Waterfront* ☎ *0151/702–7580* ⚇ *MC, V* ☀ *Closed Mon. No dinner.*

£ ✕ **Coopers.** A popular and cheerful lunch spot, this self-service restaurant dishes up traditional soups and omelets as well as baguettes, toasties (toasted sandwiches), and baked potatoes. Don't look for any frills. ✉ *65–67 Bold St., City Centre* ☎ *0151/707–8251* ⚇ *MC, V* ☀ *Closed Sun. No dinner.*

Where to Stay

£££–££££ 🏨 **Liverpool Marriott Hotel.** This modern city-center hotel is indicative of Liverpool's rise from the economic ashes. Guest rooms have cherry furniture and are decorated in rich gold and burgundy hues. The unbeatable location is a minute from Lime Street Station and the Walker Art Gallery. Breakfast is included in the cost on weekends. ✉ *1 Queen Sq., City Centre, L1 1RH* ☎ *0151/709–7200* 🖪 *0151/708–0743* 🌐 *www. marriott.com* ➙ *143 rooms, 3 suites* ♣ *Restaurant, in-room data ports, cable TV with movies, indoor pool, gym, sauna, bar, business services, meeting rooms, parking (fee)* ⚇ *AE, DC, MC, V.*

£££–££££ 🏨 **Liverpool Moat House.** Some may find this uncompromisingly modern hotel unattractive from the outside, but it lies in landscaped grounds right across from the River Mersey and Albert Dock, which means that many of the main city sights are at your doorstep. Bedrooms, done in cool, soothing colors, are handsome and spacious; most have two large beds. ✉ *Paradise St., City Centre, L1 8JD* ☎ *0151/471–9988* 🖪 *0151/ 709–2706* 🌐 *www.moathousehotels.com* ➙ *263 rooms, 2 suites* ♣ *2 restaurants, in-room data ports, cable TV with movies, indoor pool, gym, sauna, bar, business services, meeting rooms, parking (fee), some pets allowed, no-smoking rooms* ⚇ *AE, DC, MC, V* ➭ *BP.*

£££ 🏨 **Feathers Hotel.** One of a terrace of Georgian brick houses, this smart and efficient hotel close to both the city's cathedrals doesn't stint on decoration. Swags and drapes adorn the public rooms, and bedrooms have modern pine pieces and patterned fabrics in red, blue, and yellow. You can eat your fill at the buffet breakfast and sip a drink at night in the Beatles-themed bar. ✉ *119–125 Mount Pleasant, City Centre, L3 6DX* ☎ *0151/709–9655* 🖪 *0151/709–3838* 🌐 *www.feathers.uk.com* ➙ *75 rooms* ♣ *Restaurant, cable TV, bar, meeting rooms, parking (fee); no a/c* ⚇ *AE, MC, V* ➭ *BP.*

£££ 🏨 **Royal Hotel.** The Royal occupies an 1815 building that overlooks the Marine Gardens and the Mersey estuary, with views of the Wirral Peninsula and North Wales in the distance. The hotel retains much of its original character, with its grand proportions, fireplaces, plasterwork, and maritime features. Bedrooms are modern, done predominantly in prints and cream and red; some have four-posters and whirlpool baths. The hotel is a 10-minute drive from the city center. ⊠ *Marine Terr., Waterloo, L22 5PR* ☎ *0151/928–2332* 🖷 *0151/949–0320* ⊕ *www.liverpool-royalhotel.co.uk* ⇨ *25 rooms* ⌂ *Restaurant, in-room data ports, cable TV, bar, meeting rooms, free parking; no a/c* ⊟ *AE, DC, MC, V* ⊺⊙⊺ *BP.*

£ £ 🖭 **Express by Holiday Inn.** The best central accommodation in terms of
Fodor'sChoice   value, location, and style is this offering in the upper part of the Bri-
    ★   tannia Pavilion, in the heart of the waterfront district. Management is
friendly and helpful, and the rich red and blue decor and thick carpeting reflect the style of the chain. Guest rooms are cool in tone; try for one with views of the dock. ⊠ *Britannia Pavilion, Albert Dock, Waterfront, L3 4AD* ☎ *0151/709–1133 or 0800/434–040* 🖷 *0151/709–1144* ⊕ *www.hiexpress.co.uk* ⇨ *135 rooms* ⌂ *Restaurant, cable TV with movies, bar, meeting room, free parking; no a/c* ⊟ *AE, MC, V* ⊺⊙⊺ *BP.*

£ 🖭 **Liverpool Youth Hostel.** This hostel just a few minutes' walk from Albert Dock really should change its name, because it offers modest hotel standards for bargain prices. The smart rooms (for two, four, or six people) are fully carpeted, with private bathrooms and heated towel rails. You need to be a member of the hostel organization; you can join on the spot (£13), but it's advisable to book well in advance. ⊠ *Chalenor St., Waterfront, L1 8EE* ☎ *0151/709–8888* 🖷 *0151/709–0417* ⊕ *www.yha.org.uk* ⇨ *106 beds* ⌂ *Cafeteria, recreation room, laundry facilities; no a/c* ⊟ *MC, V* ⊺⊙⊺ *BP.*

Nightlife & the Arts

Nightlife

Blue Bar (⊠ Edward Pavilion, Albert Dock, Waterfront ☎ 0151/709–7097), typical of the bars at the Albert Dock, attracts a funky young professional crowd with its late hours, grill, and dockside seating. The **Cavern Club** (⊠ 8–10 Mathew St., City Centre ☎ 0871/222–1957) draws many on the Beatles trail, who don't realize it's not the original spot—that was demolished years ago. The **Cavern Pub** (⊠ 5 Mathew St., City Centre ☎ 0151/236–1957) merits a stop for nostalgia's sake; here are recorded the names of the groups and artists who played in the Cavern Club between 1957 and 1973. **Cream** (⊠ Wolstenholme Sq., City Centre ☎ 0151/709–1693) is one of the hippest nightclubs in Britain. The **Philharmonic** (⊠ 36 Hope St., City Centre ☎ 0151/707–2837), nicest of the city-center pubs and opposite the Philharmonic Hall, is a Victorian-era extravaganza decorated in colorful marble, with comfortable bar rooms and good food.

The Arts

The renowned Royal Liverpool Philharmonic Orchestra plays its concert season at **Philharmonic Hall** (⊠ Hope St., City Centre ☎ 0151/709–3789).

The **Everyman Theatre** (⊠ 5–9 Hope St., City Centre ☎ 0151/709–4776) stages experimental and British theatrical productions. The **Liverpool Empire** (⊠ Lime St., City Center ☎ 0870/606–3536) presents major national and international ballet, opera, drama, and musical performances. **Royal Court Theatre** (⊠ 1 Roe St., City Centre ☎ 0151/709–4321), an art deco building, is one of the city's most appealing sites for pop and rock concerts and stand-up comedy.

Sports & the Outdoors

Football

Football (soccer in the United States) matches are played on weekends and, increasingly, weekdays. Ticket prices vary, but the cheapest seats start at about £20. The tourist offices can give you match schedules and directions to the grounds. **Liverpool** (☎ 0870/220–2345), one of England's top clubs, plays at Anfield, 2 mi north of the city center. **Everton** (☎ 0151/330–2300; 0870/7383–7866 booking line), once a major force but now in a seemingly perpetual rebuilding phase, plays at Goodison Park, about ½ mi north of Anfield.

Horse Racing

Britain's most famous horse race, the Grand National steeplechase, has been run at Liverpool's **Aintree Racecourse** (✉ Ormskirk Rd., Aintree ☎ 0151/523–2600) almost every year since 1839. The race is held every March or April. Admission on race days is £15 (for Grand National, £10–£70). The Grand National Experience (£7, advance booking required), on Tuesday late May–October, includes a tour of the racecourse, admission to the visitor center, and a ride on the race simulator.

Shopping

The **Beatles Shop** (✉ 31 Mathew St., City Centre ☎ 0151/236–8066) may stock the Beatles knickknack of your dreams. **Circa 1900** (✉ India Buildings, Water St., City Centre ☎ 0151/236–1282) specializes in authentic art nouveau and art deco pieces, from ceramics and glass to furniture. The **Stanley Dock Sunday Market** (✉ Great Howard St. and Regent Rd., City Centre) has 400 stalls operating each Sunday, selling bric-a-brac, clothes, and toys from 9 to 4. The **Walker Art Gallery** (✉ William Brown St., City Centre ☎ 0151/478–4199) has a small lobby shop with high-quality glassware, ceramics, and jewelry by local designers.

THE PEAK DISTRICT

BUXTON, BAKEWELL, HADDON HALL, CHATSWORTH

Heading southeast, away from the urban congestion of Manchester and Liverpool, it's not far to the southernmost contortions of the Pennine Hills. Here, sheltered in a great natural bowl, is the spa town of Buxton, about an hour from Manchester: at more than 1,000 feet, it's the second-highest town in England. Buxton makes a convenient base for exploring the 540 square mi of the Peak District, Britain's oldest—and, some say, most beautiful—national park. "Peak" is perhaps misleading; despite being a hilly area, it contains only long, flat-top rises that don't reach much higher than 2,000 feet. Yet touring around destinations such as Bakewell, Matlock, Castleton, and Edale and the grand estates of Chatsworth House, Haddon Hall, and Hardwick Hall, you'll often have to negotiate fairly perilous country roads, each of which repays the effort with enchanting views. Outdoor activities are popular in the Peaks, particularly caving (or "potholing"), walking, and hiking. Bring all-weather clothing and waterproof shoes.

Little Moreton Hall

㉕ *20 mi southwest of Buxton, 45 mi southeast of Liverpool.*

The epitome of "magpie" black-and-white half-timber buildings, this house, in the words of Olive Cook's *The English Country House,* "exaggerates and exalts the typical and humble medieval timber-framed dwelling, making of it a bizarre, unforgettable phenomenon." Covered with zigzags, crosses, and lozenge shapes crafted of timber and daub, the house was built by the Moreton family between 1450 and 1580. The long gallery and Tudor-era wall paintings are spectacular. Little Moreton Hall lies to the west of the Peak District; to get here from Liverpool, take the M6 to the A534 east to Congleton. ⊠ *A34, Congleton* ☎ *01260/ 272018* ⊕ *www.nationaltrust.org.uk* ⊠ *£4.50* ⊙ *Late Mar.–Oct., Wed.–Sun. 11:30–5; Nov.–late Dec., weekends 11:30–4.*

---

off the beaten path

STOKE-ON-TRENT: THE POTTERIES – The area known as the Potteries, about 55 mi southeast of Liverpool, is the center of Britain's ceramic industry. The novels of Arnold Bennett (1867–1931), including *Anna of the Five Towns,* realistically describe life in the area. There are, in fact, six towns, now administered as "the city of Stoke-on-Trent." Four museums here evocatively portray the industrial and social history of this area, and the many factory shops sell all kinds of china.

Ceramica, opened in 2003, occupies an ornate former town hall and uses displays, videos, and interactive technology to explore the area's history, the process of creating china, and some noted companies. In Bizarreland (the name comes from Clarice Cliff's art deco designs) kids can dig for relics from the past and take a virtual "ride" over the Potteries. A shop sells wares from local manufacturers. ⊠ *Market Pl., Burslem* ☎ *01782/832001* ⊕ *www.ceramicauk.com* ⊠ *£3.50* ⊙ *Mon. and Wed.–Sat. 9:30–5, Sun. 10:30–4:30.*

The **Gladstone Pottery Museum,** the city's only remaining Victorian pottery factory, contains examples of the old ovens, surrounded by original workshops where you can watch the traditional skills of throwing, casting, and decorating. The Flushed with Pride galleries tell the story of the toilet from the 1840s onward with many splendidly decorative examples. ⊠ *Uttoxeter Rd., Longton* ☎ *01782/319232* ⊕ *www.stoke.gov.uk/museums* ⊠ *£4.95* ⊙ *Daily 10–5; last admission 4.*

The modern **Potteries Museum and Art Gallery** has a more than 5,000-piece ceramic collection of international repute and is recognized worldwide for its unique Staffordshire pottery. Other excellent galleries are devoted to the fine arts and Arnold Bennett memorabilia. ⊠ *Bethesda St., Hanley* ☎ *01782/232323* ⊕ *www. stoke.gov.uk/museums* ⊠ *Free* ⊙ *Mar.–Oct., Mon.–Sat. 10–5, Sun. 2–5; Nov.–Feb., Mon.–Sat. 10–4, Sun. 1–4.*

At the **Wedgwood Story Visitor Centre** you can learn about the history of Wedgwood from 1759 to the present, watch all the stages of pottery production, and even try your hand at throwing a pot. After visiting the audio-guided exhibition area, shop in the "firsts" and "seconds" stores. ⊠ *Off A5035, Barlaston* ☎ *01782/204218* ⊕ *www. thewedgwoodstory.com* ⊠ *£7.25* ⊙ *Weekdays 9–5, weekends 10–5.*

Buxton

▶ **26** *20 mi northeast of Little Moreton Hall, 25 mi southeast of Manchester.*

The Romans arrived in AD 79 and named Buxton *Aquae Arnemetiae,* loosely translated as "Waters of the Goddess of the Grove," suggesting they considered this Derbyshire hill town special. The mineral springs, which emerge from 3,500 to 5,000 feet below ground at a constant 82°F, were believed to cure assorted ailments and in the 18th century established the town as a popular spa, a minor rival to Bath. You can still drink water from the ancient St. Anne's Well, and it's also bottled and sold throughout Britain.

Buxton's spa days have left a notable legacy of 18th- and 19th-century buildings, parks, and open spaces that give the town an air of faded grandeur. A good place to start exploring is the **Crescent** on the north-west side of the Slopes park (the town hall is on the opposite side); almost all out-of-town roads lead toward this central green. The three former hotels that make up the Georgian-era Crescent, with its arches, Doric colonnades, and 378 windows, were built in 1780 by John Carr for the fifth duke of Devonshire (of nearby Chatsworth House). The thermal baths at the end of the Crescent house a shopping center. The Crescent buildings themselves are closed to the public, except the tourist information center.

The **Devonshire Royal Hospital,** behind the Crescent, also by John Carr, was originally a stable with room for 110 horses. In 1859 the circular area for exercising horses was covered with a massive 156-foot-wide slate-color dome and incorporated into the hospital. Today the University of Derby has taken over the building.

The **Buxton Museum** contains a collection of Blue John stone, a semiprecious mineral found only in the Peak District. It also displays local archaeological finds, including a few pieces from Roman times, and there's a small art gallery. The museum is on the eastern side of the Slopes. ✉ *Terrace Rd.* ☎ *01298/24658* 💷 *Free* ☉ *Tues.–Fri. 9:30–5:30, Sat. 9:30–5, Sun. and national holidays (Apr.–Sept. only) 10:30–5.*

The **Pavilion** (✉ Pavilion Gardens ☎ 01298/23114), with its ornate iron-and-glass roof, was originally a concert hall and ballroom. Erected in the 1870s, it remains a lively place, with a conservatory, several bars, a cafeteria, and a restaurant, set in 25 acres of well-kept gardens. The Pavilion is adjacent to the Crescent and the Slopes on the west.

Buxton Opera House (✉ Water St. ☎ 01298/72190), built in 1903, is one of the most architecturally exuberant structures in town. Its marble bulk, bedecked with carved cupids, is even more impressive inside—so impressive it may be worth buying a ticket to a concert. Otherwise, tours (£2) of the interior are conducted most Saturdays at 11 AM.

The Peak District's extraordinary geology is on show close to Buxton at **Poole's Cavern,** a large limestone cave far beneath the 100 wooded acres of Buxton Country Park. Named after a legendary 15th-century robber, the cave was inhabited in prehistoric times and contains, in addition to the standard stalactites and stalagmites, the source of the River Wye, which flows through Buxton. ✉ *Green La.* ☎ *01298/26978* ⊕ *www.poolescavern.co.uk* 💷 *£5.40 including tour; park and visitor center free* ☉ *Mar.–Oct., daily 10–5.*

Where to Stay & Eat

££££   ✕☐ **Old Hall.** Friendly and central, this hotel in a refurbished 16th-century building overlooks the Opera House. The individually decorated rooms are furnished in a mixture of period and modern styles. One room Mary's Bower, in the oldest section, retains its original ceiling moldings. The Cockerel Bar is popular with theatergoers who stoke up on hearty dishes or salads and *panini* (Italian rolls); there's a more formal restaurant as well. ✉ *The Square, SK17 6BD* ☎ *01298/22841* 🖷 *01298/72437* ⊕ *www.oldhallhotelbuxton.co.uk* ⇨ *38 rooms* ⟡ *Restaurant, bar, meeting rooms, some pets allowed; no a/c* ▤ *AE, DC, MC, V* ⊠⊙⊠ *BP.*

££££   ☐ **The Palace.** A Victorian hotel on a grand scale, the Palace dates from the halcyon days of the spa and sits on 5 acres overlooking the town center and surrounding hills. The interior reveals a sweeping staircase, marble columns, and chandeliers, but the rooms are disappointingly modern in style, with furnishings in orange and brown. ✉ *Palace Rd., SK17 6AG* ☎ *01298/22001* 🖷 *01298/72131* ⊕ *www.paramount-hotels.co.uk* ⇨ *118 rooms, 4 suites* ⟡ *Restaurant, cable TV with movies, indoor* pool, gym, hair salon, sauna, bar, business services, meeting rooms, some pets allowed (fee); no a/c ⊟ AE, DC, MC, V ⧒⦶ BP.

★ **££** ⊞ **Buxton's Victorian Guesthouse.** One of a terrace built by the duke of Devonshire in 1860, this beautifully and imaginatively decorated house stands a stone's throw away from the Opera House. The Oriental dining room has a dragon mural, and the bedrooms have intriguing themes such as the Victorian Craftsman. Victorian and Edwardian antiques and prints furnish all the rooms. ⊠ 3a Broad Walk, SK17 6JE ☏ 01298/78759 ⊟ 01298/74732 ⊕ www.buxtonvictorian.co.uk ⟿ 7 rooms, 1 suite ⟁ Dining room, some in-room data ports; no a/c, no kids under 4 ⊟ No credit cards ⧒⦶ BP.

££ ⊞ **Lakenham Guest House.** This large Victorian structure retains pleasant reminders of its period. Potted plants proliferate and the Victorian-style bedrooms all have excellent views; the house overlooks Pavilion Gardens. ⊠ 11 Burlington Rd., SK17 9AL ☏ 01298/79209 ⊘ lakenhamguesthouse@burlingtonroad11.freeserve.co.uk ⟿ 6 rooms ⟁ Refrigerators, cable TV; no a/c, no kids under 10 ⊟ No credit cards ⧒⦶ BP.

£ ⊞ **Stoneridge.** Built of stone, this Edwardian B&B close to the Opera House has been carefully and richly restored in sympathetic style. Bedrooms are furnished with modern pieces, and there's a complimentary glass of sherry in the evening, and kippers and croissants for breakfast. ⊠ 9 Park Rd., SK17 6SG ☏ 01298/26120 ⊕ www.stoneridge.co.uk ⟿ 4 rooms ⟁ Some pets allowed; no a/c, no room phones, no kids under 10, no smoking ⊟ No credit cards ⊘ Closed Jan. ⧒⦶ BP.

Nightlife & the Arts

Buxton Opera House (⊠ Water St. ☏ 01298/72190; box office 0845/1272–190) presents excellent theater, ballet, and jazz performances year-round; it also hosts an amateur drama festival in summer.

Buxton's renowned **Festival of Music and the Arts** (⊠ Festival Office, The Square ☏ 01298/70395 ⊕ www.buxtonfestival.co.uk), held during the second half of July and early August each year, includes opera, drama, classical concerts, jazz, recitals, and lectures, many of them at the Buxton Opera House.

Shopping

You'll find many kinds of stores in Buxton, especially around Spring Gardens, the main shopping street. Stores in the beautifully tiled **Cavendish Arcade** (⊠ The Crescent), on the site of the old thermal baths, sell antiques, jewelry, fashions, and leather goods in stylish surroundings. A local **market** is held in Buxton every Tuesday and Saturday.

en route Heading southeast from Buxton on the A6, you'll pass through the spectacular valleys of Ashwood Dale, Wyedale, and Monsal Dale before reaching Bakewell.

Bakewell

㉗ 12 mi southeast of Buxton.

Narrow streets and houses built out of the local gray-brown stone and a location on the winding River Wye make Bakewell extremely appealing. A medieval bridge crosses the river in five graceful arches, and the 9th-century Saxon cross that stands outside the parish church reveals the town's great age. Unfortunately, ceaseless traffic through the streets takes the shine off—though there's respite down on the quiet riverside paths. The crowds are really substantial on market day (Monday), attended by local farmers; a similarly popular traditional agricultural show takes place the first week of August. For a self-guided hour-long stroll, pick up a map from the tourist office, where the town trail begins. A museum in the office explains the terrain of the Peak District, with samples of the limestone and grit stone that compose the landscape.

Bakewell is the source of Bakewell pudding, said to have been created inadvertently when, sometime in the 19th century, a cook at the town's Rutland Arms Hotel dropped some rich cake mixture over jam tarts. Every local bakery and tearoom claims an original recipe—it's easy to spend a gustatory afternoon tasting rival puddings.

As in other parts of the Peak District, the inhabitants of Bakewell still practice the early summer custom of "well dressing," when certain wells or springs are elaborately decorated or "dressed" with flowers. Although the floral designs usually incorporate biblical themes, they are just a Christian veneer over an ancient pagan celebration of the water's life-giving powers. In Bakewell the lively ceremony is the focus of several days of festivities in June.

Where to Stay & Eat

£ ✕ **The Old Original Bakewell Pudding Shop.** Given the plethora of local rivals, it takes a bold establishment to claim its Bakewell puddings as "original," but there's certainly nothing wrong with those served here, eaten hot with custard or cream. The oak-beam dining room also turns out commendable main courses of Yorkshireman (batter pudding with meat and vegetables) and steak and stout pie. ⊠ *The Square* ☎ *01629/ 812193* ⊟ *MC, V* ☉ *Closes 6 PM winter, 9 PM summer.*

★ ✕🍴 **Fischer's.** This stately Edwardian manor house run by the Fischer
££££–£££££ family sits just on the edge of the Chatsworth estate. Guest rooms are pretty, with antique pine furniture and muted colors. Rooms in the garden annex show a more contemporary style. You can choose between two set menus: the main dining room (no lunch Sunday and Monday) serves a more expensive full menu, whereas Café Max concentrates on lighter bistro fare. Fish, a specialty, often comes with fresh pastas and delicate sauces; duck, lamb, and game receive similar care. Sunday dinner is for guests only. ⊠ *Baslow Hall, Calver Rd., Baslow, DE45 1RR* ☎ *01246/583259* 🖷 *01246/583818* ⊕ *www.fischers-baslowhall.co.uk* 🛏 *11 rooms* ♧ *Restaurant, some in-room data ports, bar, meeting rooms; no a/c, no kids under 10* ⊟ *AE, DC, MC, V* 🍴 *CP.*

Haddon Hall

28 *2 mi southeast of Bakewell.*

Fodor'sChoice
★
Stately house scholar Hugo Montgomery-Massingberd has called Haddon Hall, a romantic, storybook medieval manor set along the River Wye, "the *beau idéal* of the English country house." Unlike other trophy homes that are marble Palladian monuments to the grand tour, Haddon Hall remains quintessentially English in appearance, bristling with crenellations and stepped roofs and landscaped with rose gardens. It's famous as the setting (perhaps apocryphal) for the shocking 16th-century elopement of Dorothy Vernon and Sir John Manners during a banquet; the tale became a popular Victorian-era love story. Constructed by generations of the Vernon family in the Middle Ages, Haddon Hall passed into the ownership of the dukes of Rutland. After they moved their county seat to nearby Belvoir Castle, time and history literally passed the house by for centuries. In the early 20th century, however, the ninth duke undertook a superlative restoration. The wider world saw the hall to impressive effect in Franco Zeffirelli's 1996 film *Jane Eyre*; part of the 1999 *Elizabeth*, starring Cate Blanchett, was filmed here. The virtually unfurnished house has fine plasterwork and wooden paneling, and

still holds some treasures, including an impressive selection of tapestries, and a famous 1932 painting of Haddon Hall by Rex Whistler. This painting shows the ninth duke and his son gazing at the house from a nearby hillside vantage point. Dorothy and Sir John are buried side by side in Bakewell's parish church. ⊠ *A6* ☎ *01629/812855* ⊕ *www.haddonhall. co.uk* ✉ *£7.25, parking £1* ⊙ *Apr.–Sept., daily 10:30–5; Oct., Thurs.–Sun. 10:30–4:30.*

Matlock

㉙ *5 mi south of Haddon Hall, 8 mi southeast of Bakewell.*

In the heart of the Derbyshire Dales, Matlock and its near neighbor Matlock Bath are former spa towns compressed into a narrow gorge on the River Derwent. Some surviving Regency buildings in Matlock still testify to its former importance, although it's less impressive an ensemble than that presented by Buxton. The surroundings, however, are particularly beautiful. The **Matlock River Illuminations,** a flotilla of lighted boats shimmering after dark along the still waters of the river, takes place on weekends late August–late October.

At Matlock Bath, 2 mi south of Matlock, river and valley views unfold from the curving line of buildings that makes up the village. Aside from riverside strolls, the major attraction is the cable-car ride across the River Derwent that takes you to the bosky ☺ **Heights of Abraham Country Park and Caverns** on the crags above, with a visitor center and café. The all-inclusive ticket allows access to the woodland walks and nature trails of the 60-acre park, as well as entry to a cavern and a guided descent into an old lead mine, where 16th-century workers once toiled by candlelight. ⊠ *A6, Matlock Bath* ☎ *01629/582365* ⊕ *www.heights-of-abraham.co.uk* ✉ *£7.50* ⊙ *Cable car and visitor center Feb. and Mar., weekends 10–4:30; Apr.–Oct., daily 10–5.*

Where to Stay & Eat

★ **£££–££££** ✕▨ **Riber Hall.** Awash with romantic resonance, this partly Elizabethan, partly Jacobean manor-house hotel perches above the town. Antiques and four-poster beds decorate the half-timber bedrooms; some bathrooms have whirlpool tubs. The garden is especially lovely. The restaurant (fixed-price menu) serves imaginative dishes inspired by modern French cuisine; one choice might be roasted monkfish with haricot beans and Parma ham. There's a daily vegetarian menu. ⊠ *Off A615, DE4 5JU* ☎ *01629/582795* 🖷 *01629/580475* ⊕ *www.riber-hall.co.uk* 🛏 *14 rooms* ⚊ *Restaurant, tennis court, bar, business services, meeting rooms, some pets allowed; no a/c* ⊟ *AE, DC, MC, V* ⦾| *BP.*

Sports & the Outdoors

One of the major trails in the Peak District, **High Peak Trail,** runs for 17 mi from Cromford (south of Matlock Bath) to Dowlow, following the route of an old railway. For information, guidebooks, guide services, and maps, contact any Peak District National Park Office.

Hardwick Hall

★ ㉚ *10 mi east of Matlock.*

Few houses in England evoke the late Elizabethan era as vividly as this beautiful stone mansion and all its treasures. The facade glitters with myriad windows, making it easy to see why the house came to be known as "Hardwick Hall, more glass than wall." Choose a sunny day to see the rooms at their best; electric lighting is limited. The vast state apartments of the Long Gallery and High Great Chamber well befit their original

chatelaine, Bess of Hardwick. By marrying a succession of four rich hus-
bands, she had become second only to Elizabeth I in her wealth when
work on this house began. She took possession in 1597, and four years
later made an inventory of the important rooms and their contents—furniture, tapestries, and embroideries. The wonder is that these items still
remain here, very much as she left them. Unique patchwork hangings,
most probably made from clerical copes and altar frontals taken from
monasteries and abbeys, grace the entrance hall, and superb 16th- and
17th-century tapestries cover the walls of the main staircase and first-
floor High Great Chamber. The collection of Elizabethan embroideries—
table carpets, cushions, bed hangings, and pillowcases—is second to
none. There are also fine examples of plasterwork, painted friezes, and
ornamental chimneypieces. Outside, you can visit the attractive walled
gardens. Access is signposted from Junction 29 of the M1 motorway.
✉ *Doe Lea, Chesterfield* ☎ *01246/850430* ⊕ *www.nationaltrust.org.*
uk ✉*£6.60, gardens only £3.50* ⊙ *House Apr.–Oct., Wed., Thurs., week-*
ends, and public holidays 12:30–4:30; gardens Apr.–Oct., Wed.–Mon.
and public holidays 11–5:30.

Chatsworth House

★ ☕ ㉛   *13 mi northwest of Hardwick Hall, 4 mi northeast of Bakewell.*

Glorious parkland leads to Chatsworth House, ancestral home of the
dukes of Devonshire and one of England's greatest country houses. The
vast expanse of greenery, grazed by deer and sheep, sets off the Palladian-style elegance of "the Palace of the Peak." Originally an Elizabethan
house, Chatsworth was conceived on a grand, even monumental, scale.
Unfortunately, it was altered by various dukes over several generations
starting in 1686, and the house's architecture now has a decidedly
hodgepodge look. Death duties have taken a toll on the interior grandeur,
with duke after duke forced to sell off treasures to keep the place going;
still, there is plenty to look at. The house is surrounded by woods, elaborate, colorful gardens, greenhouses, rock gardens, and the most famous
water cascade in the kingdom—all designed by two great landscape artists,
Capability Brown and, in the 19th century, Joseph Paxton, an engineer
as well as a brilliant gardener. Perennially popular with children, the farmyard area has milking demonstrations at 3 PM, and an adventure playground. Plan on at least a half day to explore the grounds; avoid going
on Sunday, when the place is very crowded. A brass band plays on Sunday afternoons in July and August.

Inside are intricate carvings, Van Dyck portraits, superb furniture, and
a few fabulous rooms, including the Sculpture Gallery, the library, and
the Blue Drawing Room, where you can see two of the most famous
portraits in Britain, Sir Joshua Reynolds's *Georgiana, Duchess of De-*
vonshire, and Her Baby, and John Singer Sargent's enormous *Acheson*
Sisters. The magnificent condition of much of the furnishings and decorations is owing to the current duchess's supervision of an ongoing program of repair and restoration. ✉ *Off B6012, Bakewell* ☎ *01246/*
582204 ⊕ *www.chatsworth-house.co.uk* ✉ *House, gardens, and Scots*
rooms £10; house and gardens £8.50; gardens only £5; farmyard and
adventure playground £3.90; parking £1 ⊙ *House Apr.–late Dec., daily*
11–5:30. Garden Apr.–May and Sept.–Dec., daily 11–6; June–Aug.,
daily 10:30–6. Farmyard and adventure playground late-Mar.–Dec.,
daily 10:30–5:30; last admission 1 hr before closing.

Where to Eat

£–££ ✕ **Devonshire Arms.** Once inside this stone 18th-century coaching inn, which
counts Charles Dickens as one of its many visitors, you'll find antique

settles, flagstone floors, and great homemade fare. Sample dishes include cheeses and piccalilli, duck and fig terrine, and beef and horseradish suet pudding. Friday is fresh fish day, and on Sunday you can sample a Victorian breakfast (book ahead), which comes with Buck's Fizz—champagne and orange juice—and newspapers. The inn is 2 mi south of Chatsworth. ⊠ *B6012, Beeley* ☎ *01629/733259* ▤ *AE, MC, V.*

Castleton

32 *10 mi northwest of Chatsworth, 9 mi northeast of Buxton.*

The area around Castleton, in Hope Valley, contains the most famous manifestations of the peculiar geology of the Peak District. The limestone caverns attract people from far and wide, which means that Castleton shows a certain commercialization and tends to be crowded in the peak season. The town has a long pedigree and was probably first established by Henry II in the mid-12th century. It was Henry II who in 1176 added the square tower to the Norman **Peveril Castle**, whose ruins occupy a dramatic crag above the town. The castle has superb views—from here you can clearly see a curving section of the medieval defensive earthworks still visible in the town center below. Peveril Castle is protected on its west side by a 230-foot-deep gorge formed by a collapsed cave. ⊠ *Market Pl., A1687* ☎ *01433/620613* ⊕ *www.english-heritage.org.uk* ⊑ *£2.50* ☉ *Apr.–Sept., daily 10–6; Oct., daily 10–5; Nov.–Mar., Wed.–Sun. 10–4.*

Caves riddle the entire town and the surrounding area, and in the massive **Peak Cavern**—reputedly Derbyshire's largest natural cave—rope making has been done on a great ropewalk for more than 400 years. You can also see the remains of a prehistoric village that has been excavated here. ☎ *01433/620285* ⊕ *www.devilsarse.com* ⊑ *£5.50* ☉ *Apr.–Oct., daily 10–5; Nov.–Mar., weekends 10–5; last tour at 4.*

The Castleton area has a number of caves and mines open to the public, including some former lead mines and Blue John mines (amethystine spar; the unusual name is a local corruption of the French *bleu-jaune*). The most exciting by far is **Speedwell Cavern**, where 105 slippery steps lead down to old lead-mine tunnels, blasted out by 19th-century miners. Here you transfer to a small boat for the claustrophobic ¼-mi chug through an illuminated access tunnel to the cavern itself. At this point you're 600 feet underground, in the deepest public-access cave in Britain, with views farther down to the so-called Bottomless Pit, a water-filled cavern into which the miners dumped their blasted limestone debris. A shop on-site sells items made of Blue John. Speedwell Cavern is at the bottom of Winnats Pass, 1 mi west of Castleton. ⊠ *Winnats Pass* ☎ *01433/620512* ⊕ *www.speedwellcavern.co.uk* ⊑ *£6* ☉ *Apr.–Oct., daily 9:30–5:30; Nov.–Mar., daily 10–5; last tour 45 mins before closing.*

Where to Stay

££ ⊡ **Underleigh House.** Peaceful is the word for the location of this creeper-clad cottage and barn at the end of a lane in lovely walking country. The big lounge has an inglenook fireplace, and the flagstone entrance hall has one big table for breakfasts (expect local specialties such as oatcakes and black pudding). There are plenty of games for rainy days, and lots of books, sweets, and flowers in the tidy modern bedrooms. Hope is 1 mi east of Castleton on A617. ⊠ *Off Edale Rd., Hope, S33 6RF* ☎ *01433/621372* 🖷 *01433/621324* ⊕ *www.underleighhouse.co.uk* 🛏 *6 rooms* ♨ *Some pets allowed; no a/c, no kids under 12, no smoking* ▤ *MC, V* ⊙❘ *BP.*

£ ⊞ **Bargate Cottage.** This cottage dating to 1650, at the top of Market Place opposite the church, is one of Castleton's B&B treasures. The kindly owners scatter rag dolls and teddy bears with abandon, and the cutesy oak-beam rooms incorporate the necessary facilities. Breakfast is served at one table, with plenty of bonhomie and hiking advice on tap. ✉ *Market Pl., S33 8WQ* ☎ *01433/620201* 🖷 *01433/621739* ⊕ *www.peakland. com/bargate* 🛏 *4 rooms* 🖒 *No a/c, no kids under 12, no smoking* ⊟ *No credit cards* 🍽 *BP.*

en route Heading northwest to Edale, the most spectacular route is over **Winnats Pass,** an eye-opening drive through a narrow, boulder-strewn valley. Beyond are the tops of Mam Tor (where there's a lookout point) and the hamlet of Barber Booth, after which you'll run into Edale.

Edale

㉝ *5 mi north of Castleton.*

At Edale, you're truly in the Peak District wilds. This sleepy, straggling village, in the shadow of Mam Tor and Lose Hill and the moorlands of Kinder Scout (2,088 feet), lies among some of the most breathtaking scenery in Derbyshire. Britain can show little wilder scenery than Kinder Scout, with its ragged edges of grit stone and its seemingly interminable leagues of heather and peat. Late summer brings a covering of reddish purple as the heather flowers, but the time to really appreciate the somber beauties of Kinder and its neighbors is in late autumn or early winter, when the clouds hang low and every gully seems to accentuate the brooding spirit of the moor.

The **Old Nag's Head** (☎01433/670291) at the top of the village has marked the official start of the Pennine Way since 1965. Call in at the Hiker's Bar, sit by the fire, and tuck into hearty bar meals and warming hot toddies. On Mondays and Tuesdays in winter, when this pub is closed, the Ramblers' Inn, at the other end of the village, is open.

In the village, the Edale **National Park Information Centre** has maps, guides, and information on all the walks in the area. There's limited accommodation in the village (all B&B-style), but the information center can provide a list of possibilities or point you toward the local youth hostel. ☎ *01433/670207* ⊕ *www.peakdistrict.org* ⊗ *Apr.–Oct., daily 9–1 and 2–5:30; Nov.–Feb., weekdays 9–1 and 2–4:30, weekends 9–1 and 2–5; Mar., daily 9–1 and 2–5.*

Sports & the Outdoors
An extremely popular walking center, Edale is the starting point of the 250-mi **Pennine Way** (⊕ www.nationaltrail.co.uk), which crosses Kinder Scout. If you plan to attempt this, seek local advice first, because bad weather can make the walk treacherous. However, several much shorter routes into the Edale valley, like the 8-mi route west to Hayfield, will give you a taste of the dramatic local scenery.

LANCASHIRE & THE PEAKS A TO Z

To research prices, get advice from other travelers, and book travel arrangements, visit www.fodors.com.

AIRPORTS
Manchester Airport, about 10 mi south of the city, is the third-largest airport in the country. About 100 airlines serve 175 international and

United Kingdom destinations. M56 north leads directly into Manchester via the A5103. Frequent trains run from Manchester Airport to Piccadilly Railway Station (25 minutes); buses go to Piccadilly Gardens Bus Station (55 minutes). A taxi from the airport to Manchester city center costs between £12 and £15. For more details, call the Greater Manchester Passenger Transport Executive (GMPTE) information line.

Liverpool John Lennon Airport, about 8 mi southeast of the city at Speke, covers inland and European destinations. There's bus service to the city center every 30 minutes; contact Airportxpress 500.

🚏 **Airportxpress 500** ☎ 0151/236-7676 ⊕ www.merseytravel.gov.uk/airport_500.html. **GMPTE information line** ☎ 0161/228-7811 ⊕ www.gmpte.com. **Liverpool John Lennon Airport** ✉ Off A561, Speke ☎ 0151/288-4000 ⊕ www.liverpooljohnlennonairport. com. **Manchester Airport** ✉ near Junctions 5 and 6 of M56 ☎ 0161/489-3000 ⊕ www. manairport.co.uk.

BIKING

Special Peak District National Park Hire Centres rent bikes of all descriptions for around £12 per day. The service is restricted to April–October except for Parsley Hay, which opens on weekends only in winter. The most accessible centers are listed below, or contact any Peak District National Park Information Centre.

🚲 Bike Rentals **Peak District National Park Hire Centres** ✉ Hayfield ☎ 01663/746222 ✉ Parsley Hay ☎ 01298/84493 ✉ Middleton Top ☎ 01629/823204 ⊕ www. peakdistrict.org.

BUS TRAVEL

National Express serves the region from London's Victoria Coach Station. Average travel time to Manchester or Liverpool is four hours. To reach Matlock, Bakewell, and Buxton you can take a bus from London to Derby and change to the TransPeak bus service, though you might find it more convenient to travel first to Manchester.

Chorlton Street Coach Station, a few hundred yards west of Piccadilly Railway Station in Manchester's city center, is the main bus station for regional and long-distance buses. Most local buses leave from Piccadilly Gardens Bus Station, the hub of the urban bus network. Centreline Bus Service 1 transports passengers, free of charge, around the city center. It runs daily every five minutes from 7 AM to 7 PM.

In Liverpool, regional and long-distance National Express coaches use the Norton Street Coach Station, and cross-river buses depart from Sir Thomas Street Bus Station. Local buses leave from Queen Square and Paradise Street.

The TransPeak service between Manchester and Derby stops at Buxton and major Peak District destinations, with departures every two hours from Manchester's Chorlton Street Bus Station: Wayfarer tickets are available for 24-hour weekdays (£7) or 48-hour weekends (£10).

FARES & SCHEDULES For Manchester bus information, call the GMPTE information line (⇨ Airports). For timetables and local bus (and train and ferry) service in Liverpool, call the Mersey Travel Line. For local bus information in the Buxton and Peak District area, call Traveline. The *Peak District Timetable* (60p) covers all local public transportation services and is available from tourist offices in the area.

🚌 **Mersey Travel Line** ☎ 0151/236-7676. **National Express** ☎ 0870/580-8080 ⊕ www. nationalexpress.com. **Traveline** ☎ 0870/608-2608 ⊕ www.traveline.org.uk.

CAR RENTAL

Local Agencies Avis ✉ 1 Ducie St., Manchester ☎ 0161/236-6716; 0161/934-2320 airport ✉ 113 Mulberry St., Liverpool ☎ 0151/709-4737. **Europcar** ✉ 79-85 Liverpool St., Manchester ☎ 0161/236-0311; 0161/436-2200 airport ✉ 8 Brownlow Hill, Liverpool ☎ 0151/709-3337; 0151/448-1652 airport. **Hertz** ✉ 31 Aytoun St., Manchester ☎ 0161/236-2747; 0161/437-8208 airport ✉ 141 Vauxhall Rd., Liverpool ☎ 0151/227-2222; 0151/486-7444 airport.

CAR TRAVEL

To reach Manchester from London, take M1 north to M6, leaving M6 at Exit 21a and joining M62 east, which becomes M602 as it enters Greater Manchester. M60 is the ring road around Manchester. Liverpool is reached by leaving M6 at the same junction, Exit 21a, and following M62 west into the city. Travel time to Manchester or Liverpool from London is about 3–3½ hours. Expect heavy traffic out of London on weekends to all destinations in the Northwest; construction work also often slows progress on M6.

Driving from London to the Peak District, stay on the M1 until you reach Exit 29, then head west via the A617/A619/A6 to Buxton. From Manchester, take the A6 southeast via Stockport to Buxton, about an hour's drive.

ROAD CONDITIONS Roads within the region are generally very good, although traffic can get bogged down on M6. In Manchester and Liverpool, try to sightsee on foot—leave your car at your hotel to avoid parking problems in the city centers. In the Peak District, park in signposted parking lots whenever possible and expect heavy summer traffic. In winter, know the weather forecast; moorland roads can quickly become impassable.

CONSULATES

Australian Consulate ✉ Century House, 11 St. Peter's Square, 1st Floor, Manchester ☎ 0161/237-9440.

EMERGENCIES

Ambulance, fire, police ☎ 999. **Royal Liverpool University Hospital** ✉ Prescot St., Liverpool ☎ 0151/706-2000. **Manchester Royal Infirmary & Royal Eye Hospital** ✉ Oxford Rd., Manchester ☎ 0161/276-1234.

NATIONAL PARK

The Peak District National Park head office is in Bakewell. There are also regional offices.

Peak District National Park head office ✉ Baslow Rd., Bakewell, DE45 1AE ☎ 01629/816200 ⊕ www.peakdistrict.org. **Bakewell** ☎ 01629/813227. **Buxton** ☎ 01298/25106. **Castleton** ☎ 01433/620679. **Edale** ☎ 01433/670207. **Matlock** ☎ 01629/583388. **Matlock Bath** ☎ 01629/55082.

TOURS

BOAT TOURS City Centre Cruises in Manchester offers hourly tours on Sunday afternoons, April–September, on a barge traveling from Castlefield to the renovated Salford Quays, and a three-hour Sunday lunch round-trip (all year) to the Manchester Ship Canal.

City Centre Cruises ☎ 0161/902-0222 ⊕ www.citycentrecruises.co.uk.

BUS TOURS Cavern City Tours has a Beatles Magical Mystery Tour of Liverpool, departing from the Beatles Story, Albert Dock, daily at 3 (April–October) or 2:30 (November–March), with additional tours on weekends and during school vacations. The two-hour bus tour (£10.95) runs past Penny Lane, Strawberry Field, and other mop-top landmarks.

A novel way to travel Liverpool is by Liverpool Ducks, amphibious vehicles left over from World War II. Tours run from February to Christmas (£9.95) and leave from Albert Dock.

Tourist offices in Manchester and Liverpool can book you on short city coach tours that cover all the main sights.

🏠 **Cavern City Tours** ✉ Mathew St., Liverpool ☎ 0151/709-3285 ⊕ www.cavern-liverpool.co.uk. **Liverpool Ducks** ☎ 0151/708-7799 ⊕ www.liverpoolducks.co.uk.

WALKING TOURS   In Manchester and Liverpool, Blue Badge Guides can arrange dozens of different tours. The Liverpool Heritage Walk is a self-guided 7½-mi walk through Liverpool city center, following 75 metal markers that point out sights of historic and cultural interest. An accompanying guidebook is available from Liverpool tourist information centers.

🏠 **Blue Badge Guides, Liverpool** ☎ 0151/237-3925 ⊕ www.blue-badge.org.uk. **Blue Badge Guides, Manchester** ☎ 0161/440-0277 ⊕ www.blue-badge.org.uk.

TRAIN TRAVEL
Virgin Trains serves the region from London's Euston Station. Direct service to Manchester and Liverpool takes approximately three hours. To reach Buxton from London take the Manchester train and switch at Stockport.

There are trains between Manchester's Piccadilly Station and Liverpool's Lime Street every half hour during the day; the trip takes approximately 50 minutes. Local service—one train an hour—from Manchester to Buxton takes one hour. In all instances, call National Rail Enquiries for timetable information.

🏠 **National Rail Enquiries** ☎ 0845/748-4950 ⊕ www.nationalrail.co.uk. **Virgin Trains** ☎ 0845/722-2333 ⊕ www.virgintrains.co.uk.

TRAM TRAVEL
In Manchester, Metrolink electric tram service runs through the city center and out to the suburbs. The Eccles extension has stops for the Lowry (Broadway) and for the Manchester United Stadium (Old Trafford).

🏠 **Metrolink** ☎ 0161/228-7811 ⊕ www.gmpte.com.

TRAVEL AGENCIES
🏠 Local Agent Referrals **American Express** ✉ 54 Lord St., Liverpool ☎ 0151/702-4505 ✉ 10-12 St. Mary's Gate, Manchester ☎ 0161/833-7301. **Thomas Cook** ✉ 55 Lord St., Liverpool ☎ 0151/552-1400 ✉ 23 Market St., Manchester ☎ 0161/910-8787.

VISITOR INFORMATION
General information about the region is available from the North West Tourist Board, the Heart of England Tourist Board (for Derbyshire and the Peak District), or from the Manchester Visitor Centre. Local tourist information offices are listed below by town.

🏠 Tourist Information **Heart of England Tourist Board** ✉ Larkhill Rd., Worcester, WR5 2EZ ☎ 01905/761100 ⊕ www.visitheartofengland.com. **North West Tourist Board** ✉ Swan House, Swan Meadow Rd., Wigan Pier, Wigan, WN3 5BB ☎ 0845/600-6040 ⊕ www.visitnorthwest.com. **Bakewell** ✉ Old Market Hall, Bridge St., DE45 1DS ☎ 01629/813227. **Buxton** ✉ The Crescent, SK17 6BQ ☎ 01298/25106. **Liverpool** ✉ Queen Sq., L1 1RG ☎ 0151/709-8111; 0845/601-1125 accommodations ✉ Atlantic Pavilion, Albert Dock, L3 4AE ☎ 0151/708-8854 ⊕ www.visitliverpool.com. **Manchester Visitor Centre** ✉ Town Hall Extension, Lloyd St., M60 2LA ☎ 0161/234-3157 ⊕ www.manchester.gov.uk/visitorcentre ✉ International Arrivals Hall, Manchester Airport Terminal 1 ☎ 0161/436-3344 ✉ International Arrivals Hall, Manchester Airport Terminal 2 ☎ 0161/489-6412. **Matlock Bath** ✉ The Pavilion, DE4 3NR ☎ 01629/55082. **Stoke-on-Trent** ✉ Quadrant Rd., ST1 1RZ ☎ 01782/236000 ⊕ www.visitstoke.co.uk.

THE LAKE DISTRICT

WINDERMERE, GRASMERE, KENDAL, KESWICK

11

FODOR'S CHOICE

Miller Howe, *hotel-restaurant in Bowness-on-Windermere*

Windermere, *England's largest lake*

HIGHLY RECOMMENDED

RESTAURANTS
A Bit on the Side, *Penrith*
Glass House, *Ambleside*
Porthole Eating House, *Bowness-on-Windermere*
Queen's Head Inn, *Penrith*
Quince & Medlar, *Cockermouth*

HOTELS
Britannia Inn, *Elterwater*
Howe Keld, *Keswick*
Old Dungeon Ghyll Hotel, *Great Langdale, near Elterwater*
The Pheasant, *Bassenthwaite*
Sharrow Bay, *Pooley Bridge*
Sun Hotel, *Coniston*
White Moss House, *near Grasmere*

SIGHTS
Aquarium of the Lakes, *near Windermere*
Brantwood, *Coniston*
Bridge House, *Ambleside*
Derwentwater
Dove Cottage, *Grasmere*
Helvellyn, *mountain west of Ullswater*
Levens Hall, *near Kendal*
Towns of Windermere & Bowness-on-Windermere

Updated by
Julius Honnor

LET NATURE BE YOUR TEACHER . . ." Wordsworth's ideal comes true in this region of jagged mountains, waterfalls, wooded valleys, and stone-built villages. The poets Wordsworth and Coleridge, and other English men and women of letters, found the Lake District an inspiring setting for their work, and visitors have followed ever since. In 1951 the Lake District National Park was created here from parts of Cumberland, West-morland, and Lancashire. No mountains in Britain are finer in outline or give a greater impression of majesty; deeper and bluer lakes can be found, but none that fit so readily into the surrounding scene.

Perhaps it is only natural that an area so blessed with natural beauty should have become linked with so many prominent figures in English literature. It may have all started on April 15, 1802, when William Wordsworth and his sister, Dorothy, were walking in the woods of Gowbarrow Park just above Aira Force, and Dorothy noted in her journal that she had never seen "daffodils so beautiful." Two years later Wordsworth was inspired by his sister's words to write one of the best-known lyric poems in English, "I Wandered Lonely as a Cloud." In turn, other English romantic poets came to the region and were inspired by its beauty. Besides Wordsworth, literary figures who made their homes in the Lake District include Samuel Taylor Coleridge, Thomas De Quincey, Robert Southey, John Ruskin, Matthew Arnold, and later, Hugh Walpole, and the children's writers Arthur Ransome and Beatrix Potter.

The Lake District is a contour map come to life, a stunning natural park beloved by outdoor enthusiasts. It covers an area of approximately 885 square mi and holds 16 major lakes and countless smaller stretches of water; it can be crossed by car in about an hour. The mountains are not high by international standards—Scafell Pike, England's highest peak, is only 3,210 feet above sea level—but they can be tricky to climb, especially in inclement weather. In spring, many of the higher summits remain snowcapped long after the weather below has turned mild.

This area can be one of Britain's most appealing reservoirs of calm. Unfortunately, its calm is shattered in summer; a little lakeside town, however appealing it may otherwise be, loses its charm when cars and tour buses clog its narrow streets. Similarly, the walks and hiking trails that crisscross the region seem less inviting when you share them with a crowd that churns the grass into a quagmire. Despite the challenges of popularity, however, the Lake District has managed tourism in a manner that retains both the character of the villages and the natural environment.

Some basic terminology will help you here: if someone gives you directions to walk along the "beck" to the "force" and then climb the "fell" to the "tarn," you've just been told to hike along the stream or river (beck) to the waterfall (force) before climbing the hill or mountain (fell) to reach a small mountain lake (tarn). Moreover, town or place names in the Lake District can also refer to the lake on which the town or place stands. Windermere village is on the lake of that name, for example. And to confuse matters, locals would never say Lake Windermere but just Windermere, since "mere" means "lake" in Old English.

Off-season visits can be a real treat. All those little inns and bed-and-breakfasts that turn away crowds in summer are eager for business the rest of the year (and their rates drop accordingly). It's not an easy task to avail yourself of a succession of sunny days in the Lake District—some malicious statisticians allot to it about 250 rainy days a year—

but when the sun breaks through and brightens the surfaces of the lakes, it is an away-from-it-all place to remember.

Exploring the Lake District

The Lake District is in the northwest of England, north of the industrial belt along the River Mersey that stretches from Liverpool to Manchester, and south of Scotland. The major gateway from the south is Kendal, and from the north, Penrith. Both are on the M6 motorway. Main-line trains stop at Oxenholme, near Kendal, with a branch linking Oxenholme to Kendal and Windermere. The Lake District National Park breaks into two reasonably distinct sections. The southern lakes and valleys contain the park's most popular destinations, incorporating the largest body of water, Windermere, as well as most of what are considered the quintessential Lakeland towns and villages: Kendal, Bowness, Ambleside, Grasmere, Elterwater, Coniston, and Hawkshead. To the north, the landscape opens out across the bleaker fells to reveal challenging (and spectacular) walking country. Here, in the northern lakes, south of Keswick and Cockermouth, you have the best chance to get away from the crowds.

About the Restaurants & Hotels

Some of the area's better restaurants are at hotels. If you are not a guest but want to dine at the hotel, be sure to make reservations in advance. Also inquire if you want to eat in a particular room at the restaurant; guests may have priority.

If the front hall has a row of muddy boots, you've probably made the right choice for a hostelry in the Lake District. At the best of these hotels, people eat heartily and loll about in front of fires in the evenings, sharing an almost religious dedication to the mountains. You'll find everything from small country inns to grand lakeside hotels; at many hotels you'll have the option of paying a higher price that includes dinner as well as breakfast. The regional mainstay is the bed-and-breakfast, from the house on Main Street renting out one room to farmhouses with an entire wing to spare. Most country hotels and B&Bs gladly cater to hikers and climbers and can provide on-the-spot information. The Lake District's more than 25 youth hostels, including small mountain huts and large lakeside mansions, are open to anyone who purchases a membership or has a membership card from their home country's hostel association. Wherever you stay, book well in advance in summer, especially late July and August. In winter many places close for a month or two.

WHAT IT COSTS In pounds				
	££££££	**££££**	**£££**	**££**	**£**
RESTAURANTS	over £22	£18–£22	£13–£17	£7–£12	under £7
HOTELS	over £160	£115–£160	£80–£115	£50–£80	under £50

Restaurant prices are for a main course at dinner. Hotel prices are for two people in a standard double room in high season, including VAT, with no meals or, if indicated, CP (with Continental breakfast), BP (Breakfast Plan, with full breakfast), or MAP (Modified American Plan, with breakfast and dinner).

Timing

The Lake District is one of the rainiest areas in Britain, but June, July, and August hold the best guarantees of fine weather and are the time for all the major festivals. You will, however, be sharing the roads, ho-

You could spend months tramping the hills, valleys, and fells of the Lake District, or, in three days, you could drive through the major towns and villages. The key is not to do too much in too short a time. In three days, you might pick one area—the southern lakes, for example—and spend some time walking, taking a boat out on the water, and relaxing at the inns. With five days, you would have the opportunity to stay the night in towns in both southern and northern Lakeland. If you are traveling by public transportation (scarce at the best of times, much reduced in winter), many places will be off-limits.

11

Numbers in the text correspond to numbers in the margin and on the Lake District map.

If you have 3 days

If you must tour both south and north lakes together in a short time, start in **Kendal** ❶ ➤. After you've looked around the market town, move on to **Windermere and Bowness-on-Windermere** ❷, where you spend the first night. You'll have time to take a boat trip on the lake that afternoon up to pretty **Ambleside** ❹. Next day, cross Windermere by ferry, and drive through **Hawkshead** ❾ and **Coniston** ❽ to rural **Elterwater** ❼, where you can have lunch in one of the fine walkers' inns thereabouts. Spend the afternoon in **Grasmere** ❻ and nearby **Rydal** ❺ touring the sites associated with William Wordsworth, such as Rydal Mount and Dove Cottage. Your second night is in **Keswick** ⑬, and on the third day, you can loop around Derwentwater through **Borrowdale** ⑭ and isolated Seatoller to **Cockermouth** ⑮, Wordsworth's birthplace. From there it's an easy drive east to the market town of **Penrith** ❿ and the M6 motorway, or north to Carlisle.

If you have 5 days

Kendal ❶ ➤, in the southern part of the Lake District, marks the starting point, followed by a drive to **Windermere and Bowness-on-Windermere** ❷ and a cruise on the lake that afternoon up to **Ambleside** ❹. The next morning you can mosey around the shops and museums in Bowness before venturing on to the **Lake District National Park Visitor Centre at Brockhole** ❸. In the afternoon, cross Windermere by ferry, stopping in **Hawkshead** ❾ and **Coniston** ❽, before ending up at **Elterwater** ❼. This is a splendid place to spend the night in peaceful rural surroundings, and you can take in one of the local walks the next morning. Lunch and your overnight can be in **Grasmere** ❻, just a short distance away, giving you plenty of opportunity to explore that lovely village. From Grasmere, **Keswick** ⑬ is the next overnight stop, allowing you to make a day trip into the gorgeous Borrowdale Valley and perhaps take a boat trip on Derwentwater. On the final day, you can see **Cockermouth** ⑮ and **Penrith** ❿.

tels, trails, and lakes with thousands of other people. If you must travel at this time, turn up early at popular museums and attractions, and expect to work to find parking space. April and May, as well as September and October, are appealing alternatives. Later and earlier in the year, there will be even more space and freedom, but you will find many attractions closed and snow on high ground, precluding serious walking without serious equipment.

THE SOUTHERN LAKES
KENDAL, WINDERMERE, GRASMERE & CONISTON

The diverse attractions of the southern lakes range from the small resort towns clustered around Windermere, England's largest lake, to hideaway valleys, rugged walking centers, and monuments rich in literary associations. This is the easiest part of the Lake District to reach, with Kendal, the largest town, just a short distance from the M6 motorway. An obvious route from Kendal takes in Windermere, the natural touring center for this whole area, before moving north through Ambleside and Rydal Water to Grasmere. Some of the loveliest Lakeland scenery is to be found by then turning south, through Elterwater, Hawkshead, and Coniston. From Coniston, it's a simple drive south to the coast or east back to Windermere.

Kendal

▶ ❶ *70 mi north of Manchester.*

The southern gateway to the Lake District is the "Auld Gray Town" of Kendal. The town's motto, Wool Is My Bread, refers to its importance as a textile center in northern England before the Industrial Revolution. It was known for manufacturing woolen cloth, especially Kendal Green, which archers favored. Away from the busy main road are pretty courtyards and quiet, winding medieval streets known locally as "ginnels." Wool merchants used these for easy access to the River Kent. Nearby hills frame Kendal's gray stone houses and provide some delightful walks. Be sure to pack a slab of Kendal mint cake, the local peppermint candy that all British walkers and climbers swear by to provide them with energy. It's on sale in every gift shop in town.

One of the region's finest art galleries, **Abbot Hall**, occupies a Georgian mansion built in 1759. It includes works by Victorian artist and critic John Ruskin, who lived near Coniston, and by 18th-century portrait painter George Romney, who worked (and died) in Kendal. The gallery also displays 18th-century furniture, watercolors of the region, and 20th-century art. There's an excellent café. Abbot Hall is on the River Kent, next to the parish church; the Museum of Lakeland Life is on the same site. ⊠ *Off Highgate* ☎ *01539/722464* ⊕ *www.abbothall.org.uk* ☜ *£3.75, £4.50 combined ticket with Museum of Lakeland Life* ⊙ *Apr.–Oct., Mon.–Sat. 10:30–5; mid-Feb.–Mar., Nov., and Dec., Mon.–Sat. 10:30–4.*

The **Museum of Lakeland Life**, in the former stable block of Abbot Hall, documents Cumbrian life over the past 300 years through excellent exhibits on blacksmithing, wheel-wrighting, farming, weaving, printing, local architecture and interiors, and regional customs. A room is devoted to the curious life of Arthur Ransome (1884–1967), author of the *Swallows and Amazons* series of children's books, set in Coniston. ⊠ *Off Highgate* ☎ *01539/722464* ⊕ *www.lakelandmuseum.org.uk* ☜ *£2.75, £4.50 combined ticket with Abbot Hall* ⊙ *Apr.–Oct., Mon.–Sat. 10:30–5; mid-Feb.–Mar., Nov., and Dec., Mon.–Sat. 10:30–4.*

The **Kendal Museum** focuses on natural history and archaeology and details splendidly the flora and fauna of the Lake District, including displays on the region's great fell walker, Alfred Wainwright. His multivolume, handwritten Lake District walking guides are famous; you can find them in local book and gift shops. The interactive Kendal Castle display charts the town's history from prehistoric times through the

Festivals & Folk Sports

The Lake District hosts some of Britain's most unusual country festivals, featuring traditional music, sports, and entertainment. Major festivals include the Cockermouth and Keswick carnivals (June), Ambleside rushbearing (August) and sports (July), Grasmere rushbearing (August) and sports (August), and Kendal Folk Festival (August), but some sort of event or festival happens somewhere during most weeks throughout the year. Rushbearing dates back to medieval times, when rushes covered church floors; today processions of flower-bedecked children and adults bring rushes to churches in a number of villages. Folk sports, often the highlights at local festivals, include Cumberland and Westmorland wrestling, a kind of traditional English wrestling in which the opponents must maintain a grip around each other's body. Fell running, a sort of cross-country run where the route goes roughly straight up and down a mountain, is also popular. A calendar of events is available at tourist information centers or on the Cumbria Tourist Board Web site.

11

Great Flavors

The region of Cumbria, which encompasses the Lake District, has earned a reputation for good country food. Dishes center on the local Herdwick lamb, beef, game, and fish, including salmon and trout hooked from the district's freshwater streams and lakes. Windermere char and Borrowdale and Ullswater trout are served in many restaurants. Sold in one long strip, the thick, meaty pork and herb Cumberland sausage is another regional specialty. Locally baked bread, cakes, pastries, and scones are scrumptious. Brown sugar, molasses, nutmeg, cinnamon, ginger, and rum—favorite ingredients in traditional cakes—were imported from the West Indies in exchange for wool and are integral to the cakes' unique flavor. Lyth Valley damsons (a kind of plum) have a nutty taste used in everything from beverages and desserts to cheese. Grasmere gingerbread has been baked from a secret recipe for more than 140 years, and Kendal mint cake (a candy marketed as survival food) has a home in many hikers' backpacks.

Walking

The Lake District is rugged and spectacular, and to see it at its best you must get out of the car and walk. You can choose gentle rambles near the most popular towns and villages or challenging hikes and climbs up some of England's most impressive peaks. Information boards at parking lots throughout the region point out the possibilities. British mountaineering began in the Lake District, and there are plenty of notable hikes: the famous Old Man of Coniston, the Langdale Pikes, Scafell Pike, Skiddaw, and Helvellyn are all accessible, though for these you'll need experience, a great deal of energy, and proper hiking boots and clothing. The Cumbria Way (70 mi) crosses the Lake District, starting at the market town of Ulverston and finishing at Carlisle. The Coast-to-Coast Walk (190 mi) runs from St. Bees on the Irish Sea through the Lake District and across the Yorkshire Dales and the North York Moors; it ends at Robin Hood's Bay at the edge of the North Sea in Yorkshire. Guidebooks to these and other Lakeland walks are available in bookstores throughout the region. For short local walks it's best to consult the tourist information centers: those at Ambleside, Cockermouth, Grasmere, Kendal, Keswick, and Windermere provide maps and advice. The other main sources of information are the Lake District National Park information centers. Several climbing organizations offer guided hikes as well as technical rock climbing.

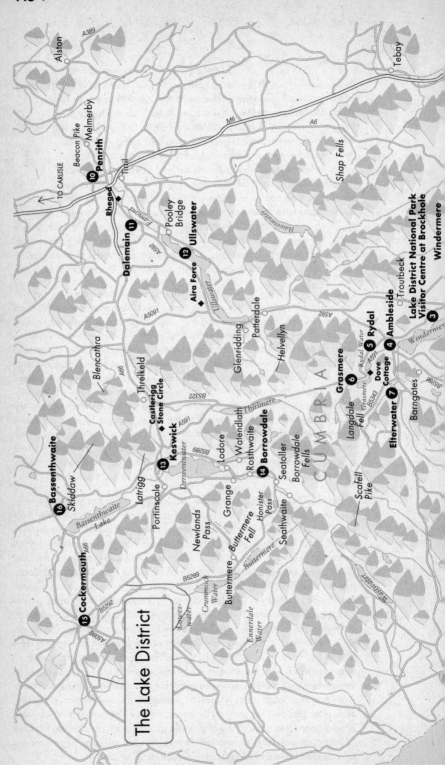

The Lake District

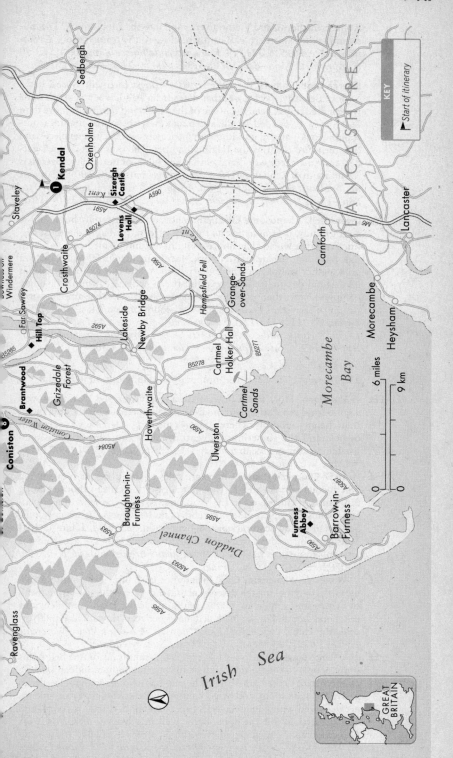

KEY
▶ *Start of itinerary*

Sedbergh

Oxenholme

1 Kendal

Staveley

Sizergh Castle

Kent

A590

Levens Hall

A591

A5074

Southern end of Windermere

Crosthwaite

A590

Kent

Hampsfield Fell

Grange-over-Sands

Carnforth

L A N C A S H I R E

M6

Lancaster

Far Sawrey

Hill Top

Lakeside

Newby Bridge

A592

Cartmel Holker Hall

B5278

B5277

Morecambe

Heysham

B5285

Brantwood

Grizedale Forest

Coniston Water

Haverthwaite

A5084

Cartmel Sands

Morecambe Bay

6 miles

9 km

Coniston

A590

Ulverston

Broughton-in-Furness

A593

A595

Duddon Channel

A5093

A595

Furness Abbey

A590

A5087

Barrow-in-Furness

Ravenglass

A595

Irish Sea

GREAT BRITAIN

Roman, medieval, and Victorian eras and into the 21st century. The museum is at the northern end of town, close to the train station. ⊠ *Station Rd.* ☎ *01539/721374* ⊕ *www.kendalmuseum.org.uk* ⊠ *£3.50* ⊙ *Apr.–Oct., Mon.–Sat. 10:30–5; Nov.–Mar., Mon.–Sat. 10:30–4.*

Sizergh Castle, one of the Lake District's finest fortified houses, has a 58-foot defensive peel tower that dates from 1340, when Scottish raids were feared. It has been the home of the Strickland family for more than 760 years. Expanded in Elizabethan times, the castle includes outstanding oak-paneled interiors with intricately carved chimneypieces and oak furniture, such as the Inlaid Chamber. The estate has a rock garden and an ancient woodland with many kinds of butterflies. Sizergh is 3½ mi south of Kendal. ⊠ *Off A591, Sizergh* ☎ *015395/60070* ⊕ *www.nationaltrust.org.uk* ⊠ *£5, gardens only £2.50* ⊙ *House Apr.–Oct., Sun.–Thurs. 1:30–5:30; gardens Apr.–Oct., Sun.–Thurs. 12:30–5:30.*

★ **Levens Hall,** a handsome Elizabethan house and the family home of the Bagot family, is famous for its topiary garden, probably the most distinctive in the world. The house contains a stunning medieval hall with oak paneling, ornate plasterwork, Jacobean furniture, and Cordova goat leather wallpaper. The topiary garden, laid out in 1694, still has its original design, and the yew and beech hedges, cut into amazingly complex shapes that resemble enormous chess pieces, rise among a profusion of flowers. Levens Hall is 4 mi south of Kendal. ⊠ *Off A590, Levens* ☎ *015395/60321* ⊕ *www.levenshall.co.uk* ⊠ *£7, gardens only £5.50* ⊙ *House mid-Apr.–mid-Oct., Sun.–Thurs. noon–5; gardens mid-Apr.–mid-Oct., Sun.–Thurs. 10–5; last admission 4:30.*

Where to Stay & Eat

The Brewery Arts Centre is another good dining option in Kendal.

££–£££ ✕ **The Moon.** More like a bistro than a restaurant, the Moon has won a good local reputation with high-quality homemade dishes on a menu that changes monthly. There's always a strong selection of vegetarian dishes, and the sometimes adventurous cooking shows occasional Mediterranean and Asian flourishes. ⊠ *129 Highgate* ☎ *01539/729254* ▭ *MC, V* ⊙ *Closed Mon. No lunch.*

£ ✕ **1657 Chocolate House.** Chocolate rules at this pleasant spot serving 38 chocolate drinks and 25 chocolate desserts. You can choose among 300 kinds of chocolates in the shop, too. Aztec Experience hot chocolate blends five spices; the milk chocolate truffle cake is scrumptious. Servers in period costumes also deliver traditional English fare such as Welsh rarebit and ploughman's lunch. Credit cards are accepted for amounts more than £10. ⊠ *54 Branthwaite Brow, Finkle St.* ☎ *01539/740702* ▭ *MC, V* ⊙ *No dinner.*

£ ✕ **Waterside Wholefoods Café.** In summer, grab one of the outdoor picnic tables overlooking the River Kent and order from the vegetarian menu of savory soups, quiches, pizzas, pâtés, nut loafs, salads, and delicious cakes and scones. For the full Lakeland experience, stay at Lakeland Natural, the café's inexpensive guest house. ⊠ *2 Kent View, Waterside* ☎ *01539/729743* ▭ *MC, V* ⊙ *Closed Sun. No dinner.*

££ ✕▦ **Punch Bowl Inn.** Inspired food and a few simply decorated bedrooms draw people to this former 17th-century coaching inn, hidden along a country road in the Lyth Valley. The pub has log fires, minstrel galleries above the main room, and black-painted timbers. Modern British menus are delivered with panache: fresh fish, local lamb, warming soups, and rich desserts all hit the spot. Book well in advance. ⊠ *Off A5074, Crosthwaite, 5 mi west of Kendal, LA8 8HR* ☎ *015395/68237* 🖷 *015395/68875* ⊕ *www.punchbowl.fsnet.co.uk* ⏎ *3 rooms* ⌂ *Pub; no a/c, no room phones* ▭ *MC, V* ⦿ *BP.*

££ 🏨 **Beech House Hotel.** Old-fashioned qualities (this is a town house in a quiet conservation area) combine with modern luxuries (heated floors in bathrooms) in this comfortable option. The rooms are individually designed but share a common homeyness. A full English breakfast includes local smoked bacon, honey-glazed sausages, and pancakes. ✉ 40 *Greenside, LA9 4LD* ☎ *01539/720385* 🖷 *01539/724082* ⊕ *www. beechhouse-kendal.co.uk* ⊷ *5 rooms* ♦ *No a/c* ☰ *MC, V* ⏐◎⏐ *BP.*

Nightlife & the Arts

The **Brewery Arts Centre,** a sophisticated contemporary arts complex in a converted brewery, includes an art gallery, theater, cinemas, and workshop spaces. The Green Room, overlooking lovely gardens, serves lunch and dinner, and Vats Bar offers pizza and ales, lagers, and wines. In November, the Mountain Film Festival presents productions aimed at climbers and walkers. ✉ *Highgate* ☎ *01539/725133* 🖾 *Free, except for special exhibitions* ☉ *Mon.–Sat. 9 AM–11 PM.*

Shopping

Kendal has a pleasant mix of chain names, factory outlet stores, specialty shops, and traditional markets. The most interesting stores are tucked away in the quiet lanes and courtyards around Market Place, Finkle Street, and Stramongate. There's been a **market** in Kendal since 1189, and outdoor market stalls still line the center of town along Stramongate and Market Place every Wednesday and Saturday.

Henry Roberts Bookshop (✉ 7 Stramongate ☎ 01539/720425), in Kendal's oldest house (a 16th-century cottage), stocks a superb selection of regional books. **K Village Outlet Centre** (✉ Lound Rd., Junction 36 of M6 ☎ 01539/732363) sells brand names at discounted prices; the best deals are at the popular K Shoes Factory. The **Kentdale Rambler** (✉ 34 Market Pl. ☎ 01539/729188) is the best local store for walking boots and equipment, maps, and guides, including Wainwright's illustrated guides. **Peter Hall & Son** (✉ Danes Rd., Staveley ☎ 01539/821633), a woodcraft workshop 4 mi north of Kendal along A591, sells ornamental bowls and attractive wood gifts.

Windermere & Bowness-on-Windermere

★ ❷   *10 mi northwest of Kendal.*

For a natural touring base for the southern half of the Lake District, you don't need to look much farther than Windermere. The resort became popular in the Victorian era when the arrival of the railway made the remote and rugged area accessible. Wordsworth and Ruskin opposed the railway, fearing an influx of tourists would ruin the tranquil place. Sure enough, the railway terminus in 1847 brought with it Victorian day-trippers, and the original hamlet of Birthwaite was subsumed by the new town of Windermere, named after the lake. The town has continued to flourish, despite being a mile or so from the water, and the development now spreads to envelop the slate gray lakeside village of Bowness-on-Windermere. Bowness is the more attractive, but they are so close it matters little where you stay. Bus 599, leaving every 20 minutes in summer (hourly the rest of the year) from outside Windermere train station, links the two.

The **Windermere Steamboat Centre** houses the world's finest collection of Victorian and Edwardian steam- and motor-powered yachts and launches. Displays about Windermere's nautical history include the famous names of motorboat racing on the lake. The *Dolly,* built around 1850, is one of the two oldest mechanically powered boats in the world. Among the many other vessels on view are Beatrix Potter's rowing boat and Arthur Ransome's sailing dinghy. For an additional £5, you can take a boat ride on Windermere in an antique vessel—if the weather is good. ⊠ *Rayrigg Rd., Bowness-on-Windermere* ☎ *015394/45565* ⊕ *www. steamboat.co.uk* ⊠ *£3.50* ⊘ *Mid-Mar.–late Oct., daily 10–5.*

The World of Beatrix Potter interprets the tales of Beatrix Potter with three-dimensional scenes of Peter Rabbit raiding Mr. McGregor's garden, Mrs. Tiggy-Winkle in her kitchen, and more. There are also Beatrix Potter souvenirs and a tearoom. You'll find less commercialism in Potter's former home at Hill Top and in the Beatrix Potter Gallery in Hawkshead. ⊠ *The Old Laundry, Crag Brow, Bowness-on-Windermere* ☎ *015394/ 88444* ⊕ *www.hop-skip-jump.com* ⊠ *£3.75* ⊘ *Easter–Sept., daily 10–5:30; Oct.–Easter, daily 10–4:30.*

In 1900, architect H. M. Baillie Scott (1865–45) designed **Blackwell,** a notable Arts and Crafts house full of carved paneling and delicate plasterwork. Lakeland birds, flowers, and trees are artfully integrated into the stained glass, stonework, friezes, and wrought iron. Now exquisitely restored, the house showcases exhibits of works from different periods that embody Arts and Crafts ideals. Peruse the bookshop or relax in the Tea Room overlooking Windermere. ⊠ *B5360, Windermere* ☎ *015394/ 46139* ⊕ *www.blackwell.org.uk* ⊠ *£4.50* ⊘ *Apr.–Oct., daily 10–5; Nov.–late-Dec. and mid-Feb.–Mar., daily 10–4.*

No sights in Windermere or Bowness compete with that of **Windermere** itself. At 11 mi long, 1½ mi wide, and 200 feet deep, the lake is England's largest and stretches from Newby Bridge almost to Ambleside, filling a rocky gorge between steep, thickly wooded hills. The cold waters are superb for fishing, especially for Windermere char, a rare lake trout. In summer, steamers and pleasure craft travel the lake, and a trip across the island-studded waters, particularly the round-trip from Bowness to Ambleside or down to Lakeside, is wonderful. Although the lake's marinas and piers have some charm, you can bypass the busier stretches of shoreline (in summer they can be packed solid) by walking beyond the boathouses. Here, from among the pine trees, is a fine view across the lake. The **car ferry,** which also carries pedestrians, crosses from Ferry Nab on the Bowness side to reach Far Sawrey and the road to Hawkshead. ☎ *0860/813427* ⊠ *Car ferry £2 cars, 40p foot passengers* ⊘ *Ferries every 30 mins Mon.–Sat. 6:50 AM–9:50 PM, Sun. 9:10 AM–9:50 PM; winter 'til 8:50 PM.*

If you take a boat to Lakeside, at the southern end of Windermere, you can spend an hour or so at the excellent **Aquarium of the Lakes,** right on the quayside. Informative wildlife and waterside exhibits culminate in an underwater tunnel walk along a re-created lake bed. ⊠ *C5062, Lakeside* ☎ *015394/30153* ⊕ *www.aquariumofthelakes.co.uk* ⊠ *£5.50* ⊘ *Apr.–Oct., daily 9–6; Nov.–Mar., daily 9–5.*

The **Lakeside & Haverthwaite Railway Company** runs vintage steam trains on the 4-mi branch line between Lakeside and Haverthwaite along the lake's southern tip. Departures coincide with ferry arrivals from Windermere. ☎ *015395/315945* ⊕ *http://ukhrail.uel.ac.uk/lhr.html* ⊘ *Late Mar. and May–late Oct., daily 10:30–6; Apr., weekends 10:30–6.*

off the beaten path

ORREST HEAD – To escape the traffic and have a memorable view of Windermere, set out on foot and follow the signs near the Windermere Hotel (across from the train station) to Orrest Head. The shady, uphill path winds through Elleray Wood, and after a 20-minute hike you arrive at a rocky little summit (784 feet) with a panoramic view that encompasses the Yorkshire fells, Morecambe Bay, and Troutbeck Valley.

Where to Stay & Eat

★ **££–££££** ✕ **Porthole Eating House.** Superb French, Italian, and traditional English dishes have been served in this intimate 18th-century house for more than 30 years. Delicacies include char-grilled partridge with pine nut and rosemary butter sauce, and risotto of wild Lakeland mushrooms and horseradish. The wine cellar stocks more than 350 different vintages. Some nice touches are opera recordings for background music and petits fours presented with coffee. The patio is ideal for alfresco dining. ⊠ *3 Ash St., Bowness-on-Windermere* ☎ *015394/42793* 🖃 *AE, DC, MC, V* ⊗ *Closed Tues. No lunch Mon. and Wed.*

£££ ✕ **Jericho's.** You can watch your meal being prepared in this stylish restaurant with an open kitchen. Some savory choices from the modern British menu are char-grilled Scotch beef and pan-fried black sea bream with salted home fries and Dijon butter. The curried lamb on roasted eggplant and plum tomatoes is especially good. ⊠ *Birch St., Windermere* ☎ *015394/42522* 🖃 *MC, V* ⊗ *Closed Mon. No lunch.*

££–£££ ✕ **Oregano.** Rustic but contemporary, this is an excellent spot for informal Anglo-French dining by candlelight. The inventive menu has all the usual suspects, as well as specialties such as haggis in phyllo pastry with whiskey cream sauce, and ginger pudding with ginger and brandy sauce for dessert. The wine list covers the Americas in addition to France. ⊠ *4 High St., Windermere* ☎ *015394/44954* 🖃 *MC, V* ⊗ *Closed Mon. and 1 wk in Jan. No lunch.*

£££££ ✕🖃 **Miller Howe.** The sumptuous guest rooms in this luxurious Edwardian country-house hotel come with canopy-draped beds and binoculars that allow you to study the dazzling view across Windermere. You can relax in sitting rooms filled with fine antiques and paintings, and have afternoon tea in the conservatory. The modern British fixed-price menu lists sophisticated fare such as warm rabbit salad with apple chutney. Guests have access to a health club, and the hotel arranges activities from archery to pony trekking. ⊠ *Rayrigg Rd., Bowness-on-Windermere, LA23 1EY* ☎ *015394/42536* 🖷 *015394/ 45664* ⊕ *www.millerhowe.com* ⇆ *12 rooms, 3 suites in cottages* ⚘ *Restaurant, croquet, piano, Internet, airport shuttle, helipad, some pets allowed; no a/c, no kids under 8* 🖃 *AE, MC, V* ⦿| *MAP.*

Fodor's Choice
★

££££–£££££ ✕🖃 **Gilpin Lodge.** Hidden in 20 acres of tranquil grounds, this rambling country-house hotel dates back to 1901. The plush but understated public rooms are furnished with sofas and rugs, warmed by log fires, and scattered with books and magazines. Guest rooms embody contemporary rustic chic with wooden furniture and antiques. All have sitting areas; some have four-posters. The food (reservations essential) is superb; local products such as smoked trout, homemade sausages, lamb, and wild mushrooms abound. You can use a nearby health club, and the hotel helps arrange sports activities. ⊠ *Crook Rd., off B5284, Bowness-on-Windermere, LA23 3NE* ☎ *015394/88818* 🖷 *015394/88058* ⊕ *www. gilpin-lodge.co.uk* ⇆ *14 rooms* ⚘ *Restaurant, room service, in-room safes, minibars, pond, croquet, 2 lounges, no-smoking rooms; no kids under 7* 🖃 *AE, DC, MC, V* ⦿| *BP.*

££–£££ ✕🖃 **The Queen's Head Hotel.** Popular with locals, this 17th-century inn north of Windermere is renowned for its innovative twist on pub food such as pan-fried pork with Cajun spices and for real ales served from an Elizabethan four-poster. The intimate dining rooms have oak beams, flagged floors, and roaring log fires. Guest rooms are basic (seven have four-posters) but offer splendid views and good value. ⊠ *A592, Troutbeck, LA23 1PW* ☎ *015394/32174* 🖷 *015394/31938* ⊕ *www.*

queensheadhotel.com ⇆ *15 rooms* ♁ *Restaurant, no-smoking rooms; no a/c, no room phones* ▭ *MC, V* ǀ◎ǀ *BP.*

£££–£££££ **Langdale Chase.** Built in the 19th century and tastefully refurbished, this estate recalls the grandeur of the past with its baronial entrance hall, old-master paintings, oak-paneled lounge, and mosaic floors. But there's genuine comfort here, too, in the pleasing conservatory and terrace. Many guest rooms, done in traditional style with pastels, have views of Windermere; six are in an annex by the lake. The five acres of landscaped gardens are ideal for a stroll. ✉ *Ambleside Rd. near the A591, Windermere, LA23 1LW* ☏ *015394/32201* ⎙ *015394/32604* 🌐 *www.langdalechase.co.uk* ⇆ *27 rooms* ♁ *Restaurant, miniature golf, lake, boating, croquet, bar, Internet, business services, some pets allowed; no a/c* ▭ *AE, DC, MC, V* ǀ◎ǀ *BP.*

££ **Boston House.** Built for railway executives in 1849, this Victorian house is one of Windermere's oldest buildings. It's a five-minute walk from the railway station, where the friendly owners will collect you on request. One of the casual country-style bedrooms has a four-poster. ✉ *The Terrace, Windermere, LA23 1AJ* ☏ *015394/43654* 🌐 *www.bostonhouse.co.uk* ⇆ *5 rooms* ♁ *No a/c, no children under 12, no smoking* ▭ *MC, V* ǀ◎ǀ *BP.*

£ **Brendan Chase.** On a quiet side road in the heart of Windermere, this comfortable Edwardian guest house is close to restaurants and the bus and train stations. The common rooms are pleasantly decorated and the owner is welcoming. Guest rooms, airy and spacious, have some antiques; for the most comfort you'll want to book ahead for a room with private shower. At the cheaper end of the scale, there is a dorm room. ✉ *1–3 College Rd., Windermere, LA23 1BU* ☏⎙ *015394/45638* ⇆ *8 rooms, 3 with bath* ♁ *Some pets allowed, no-smoking rooms; no a/c, no room phones* ▭ *No credit cards* ǀ◎ǀ *BP.*

Sports & the Outdoors

Windermere Lake Holidays Afloat (✉ Gilly's Landing, Glebe Rd., Bowness-on-Windermere ☏ 015394/43415) rents boats from small sailboats to large cabin cruisers.

Shopping

The best selection of shops is at the Bowness end of Windermere, on Lake Road and around Queen's Square: clothing stores, crafts shops, and souvenir stores of all kinds. At **Lakeland Jewellers** (✉ Crag Brow ☏ 015394/42992), the local experts set semiprecious stones in necklaces and brooches. The **Lakeland Sheepskin and Leather Centre** (✉ Lake Rd. ☏ 015394/44466), which also has branches in Ambleside and Keswick, stocks moderately priced leather and sheepskin goods.

Lake District National Park Visitor Centre at Brockhole

❸ *3 mi northwest of Windermere.*

Brockhole, a lakeside 19th-century mansion with terraced gardens sloping down to the water, serves as the park's official visitor center. Exhibits about the Lake District include displays about the local ecology, flora, and fauna. The gardens are at their best in spring, when floods of daffodils cover the lawns and the azaleas burst into bloom. Among the park activities are lectures, guided walks, and demonstrations of traditional Lakeland crafts such as dry-stone-wall building. Some programs are geared toward children, who will also appreciate the adventure playground here. The bookstore carries hiking guides and maps, and you can picnic here or eat at the café-restaurant. Bus *555/556* goes to the center from the Windermere train station. **Windermere Lake Cruises** (☏ 015394/43360) runs a ferry service to the center from Ambleside.

✉ *A591, Ambleside Rd., Windermere* ☎ *015394/46601* ⊕ *www.lake-district.gov.uk* ✉ *Free, parking £3* ☉ *Easter–Oct., daily 10–5.*

Ambleside

④ *4 mi north of Lake District National Park Visitor Centre at Brockhole.*

Unlike Kendal and Windermere, Ambleside seems almost part of the hills and fells. Its buildings, mainly of local stone and many built in the traditional style that forgoes the use of mortar in the outer walls, blend perfectly into their setting. The small town sits at the northern end of Windermere, making it a popular center for Lake District excursions. It has a better choice of restaurants than Windermere or Bowness, and the numerous outdoor shops are handy for fell walkers. The town does, however, suffer from overcrowding in high season. Wednesday, when the local market takes place, is particularly busy.

★ **Bridge House,** a tiny 17th-century stone cottage, perches on an arched stone bridge that spans Stone Beck. This much-photographed building holds a National Trust shop and information center. ✉ *Rydal Rd.* ☎ *015394/35599* ✉ *Free* ☉ *Easter–Oct., daily 10–5.*

need a break? The **Apple Pie Eating House and Bakery** (✉ *Rydal Rd.* ☎ *015394/33679*) is an excellent place to gather the strength for a walk up a mountain or to relax afterward—or both. The hearty, homemade cakes and pies are delicious.

The **Armitt Museum,** a fine local history gallery and library, explores Ambleside's past and its surroundings through the eyes of local people such as William Wordsworth, Thomas De Quincey, Robert Southey, John Ruskin, and Beatrix Potter. You can study Beatrix Potter's natural history watercolors or watch a Victorian lantern slide show. ✉ *Rydal Rd.* ☎ *015394/31212* ⊕ *www.armitt.com* ✉ *£3* ☉ *Daily 10–5.*

Where to Stay & Eat

★ **££–££££** ✕ **Glass House.** What is easily the best restaurant in town occupies a converted medieval mill with waterwheel, adjacent to Adrian Sankey's Ambleside Glass Works. The stylish architecture, with its open plan and use of plate glass, matches the invention in the kitchen. Modern British cuisine comes with a Mediterranean twist in dishes such as spinach, potato, and mozzarella pie or pan-fried scallops with lemon, parsley, and butter. You can have an elegant dinner or just sip a cappuccino in the courtyard. ✉ *Rydal Rd.* ☎ *015394/32137* ⚐ *Reservations essential* ▤ *MC, V* ☉ *Closed Tues. and Jan.*

££–££££ ✕ **Lucy's on a Plate.** This friendly bistro is the perfect spot to relax, whether with a tofu and ginger burger for lunch, a gluten-free chocolate almond torte for afternoon tea, or grilled char for dinner by candlelight. The exquisite food shows influences from around the globe in dishes such as salmon with salsa or Tunisian meatballs. A shop sells Cumbrian foods: sticky toffee pudding, farm cheeses, Cumberland sausage, jams, chutneys, and biscuits. ✉ *Church St.* ☎ *015394/31191* ▤ *MC, V.*

£–££ ✕ **Lucy 4.** You can order wine by the glass and dance to salsa music in this wine bar and bistro that caters to an upbeat crowd. Nibbling is the way to eat, with mostly Mediterranean-influenced tapas such as goat cheese bruschetta, Moroccan couscous salad, and skewered shrimp. The same owner runs Lucy's on a Plate. ✉ *2 St. Mary's La.* ☎ *015394/34666* ▤ *MC, V* ☉ *Closed Tues. and Wed. No lunch.*

£ ▥ **3 Cambridge Villas.** Ambleside has many inexpensive B&Bs, but it's hard to find a more welcoming spot than this lofty Victorian house right in the center, with hosts who know a thing or two about local walks.

Although space is at a premium, the rooms are pleasantly decorated with prints and wood furniture. The sitting room has plenty of books. ✉ *Church St., LA22 9DL* ☎ *015394/32307* ⏎ *7 rooms, 4 with bath* ⚭ *No a/c, no room phones, no smoking* ▤ *No credit cards* ⎮◯⎮ *BP.*

Sports & the Outdoors

The many fine walks in the vicinity include local routes north to Rydal Mount or southeast over Wansfell to Troutbeck. Each walk will take up to a half day, there and back. Ferries from Bowness-on-Windermere dock at Ambleside's harbor, called Waterhead, where you can rent rowboats for an hour or two.

Biketreks (✉ 9 Compston Rd. ☎ 015394/31505) is a good source for bike rentals.

Rydal

❺ *1 mi northwest of Ambleside.*

The village of Rydal, on the small glacial lake called Rydal Water, is rich with Wordsworthian associations. One famous beauty spot linked with the poet is **Dora's Field,** below Rydal Mount next to the church of St. Mary's (where you can still see the poet's pew). In spring the field is awash in yellow daffodils, planted by William Wordsworth and his wife in memory of their beloved daughter Dora, who died in 1847.

If there's one poet associated with the Lake District, it is Wordsworth, who made his home at **Rydal Mount** from 1813 until his death. Wordsworth and his family moved to these grand surroundings when he was nearing the height of his career, and his descendants still live here, surrounded by his furniture, books, and portraits. You'll see the study in which he worked, the family dining room, and the 4½-acre garden, laid out by the poet himself, that gave him so much pleasure. Surrounding Rydal Mount and the areas around Dove Cottage and Grasmere are many footpaths where Wordsworth wandered. His favorite can be found on the hill past White Moss Common and the River Rothay. Spend an hour or two walking them and you'll understand why the great poet composed most of his verse in the open air. ✉ *A591* ☎ *015394/33002* 🔲 *£4* ◷ *Mar.–Oct., daily 9:30–5; Nov.–Feb., Wed.–Mon. 10–4. Closed 3 wks in Jan.*

Grasmere

❻ *3 mi north of Rydal, 4 mi northwest of Ambleside.*

The lovely village of Grasmere, on a tiny, wood-fringed lake, is made up of crooked lanes in which Westmorland slate–built cottages hold shops, cafés, and galleries. The village is a focal point for literary and landscape associations because this area was the adopted heartland of the romantic poets, notably Wordsworth and Coleridge. The Vale of Grasmere has changed over the years, but many features Wordsworth wrote about are still visible. Wordsworth lived on the town's outskirts for almost 50 years and described the area as "the loveliest spot that man hath ever known." The poet walked the hills with his guests, who included the authors Ralph Waldo Emerson and Nathaniel Hawthorne. Wordsworth, his wife, Mary, his sister, Dorothy, and his daughter Dora are buried in the churchyard of **St. Oswald's.** As you leave the churchyard, stop at **The Gingerbread Shop,** in a tiny cottage by the gate—once the schoolhouse—where you can buy fresh gingerbread.

★ William Wordsworth lived in **Dove Cottage** from 1799 to 1808, a prolific and happy time for the poet. During this time he wrote some of his most famous works, including "Ode: Intimations of Immortality" and

POETRY, PROSE & THE LAKES

THE LAKE DISTRICT'S BEAUTY *has whetted the creativity of many a famous poet and artist. Here's a quick rundown of some of the writers inspired by the area's vistas.*

William Wordsworth (1770–1850), one of the first English romantics, redefined poetry by replacing the mannered style of his forerunners with a more conversational style. Many of his greatest works, such as The Prelude, *draw directly from his experiences in the Lake District, where he spent the first 20 and last 50 years of his life. Wordsworth and his work had an enormous effect on Coleridge, Keats, Shelley, Byron, and countless other writers.*

John Ruskin (1819–1900), writer, art critic, and early conservationist, was an impassioned champion of new ways of seeing. He defended contemporary artists such as William Turner and the Pre-

Raphaelites. His five-volume masterwork, Modern Painters, *changed the role of the art critic from that of approver or naysayer to that of interpreter.*

Thomas De Quincey (1785–1859) wrote essays whose impressionistic style influenced 19th-century writers, including Poe and Baudelaire. His most famous work, Confessions of an English Opium Eater *(1822), is a memoir of his young life, which indeed included opium addiction. He settled in Grasmere in 1809.*

Beatrix Potter (1866–1943) spent her childhood studying nature. Her love of the outdoors, and Lakeland scenery in particular, influenced her charmingly illustrated children's books, including The Tale of Jemima Puddle-Duck *and* Squirrel Nutkin.

The Prelude; he was also married here. Originally built in the early 17th century as an inn, this tiny house is beautifully preserved, with an oak-paneled hall and floors of Westmorland slate. It first opened to the public in 1891 and remains as it was when Wordsworth lived there with his sister, Dorothy, and wife, Mary. Bedrooms and living areas contain much of Wordsworth's furniture and many personal belongings. Coleridge was a frequent visitor, as was Thomas De Quincey, best known for his 1822 autobiographical masterpiece *Confessions of an Opium Eater,* who moved in after the Wordsworths left. Your ticket includes admission to the **Wordsworth Museum,** which documents the poet's life and the literary contributions of Wordsworth and the Lake Poets. Besides seeing the poet's original manuscripts, you can hear the poems read aloud on headphones. Books, manuscripts, and artwork capture the spirit of the romantic movement. Work has begun on a center that will house 50,000 letters and manuscripts, but it may not be completed in 2004. Afternoon tea is served at **Dove Cottage Tea Room and Restaurant.** ✉ *A591, 1 mi south of Grasmere* ☎ 015394/35544 ⊕ *www.wordsworth.org.uk* 📷 £5.80 ⊙ *Mid-Feb.–mid-Jan., daily 9:30–5:30.*

need a break? The small, stone-built **Jumble Room Café** (✉ Langdale Rd. ☎ 015394/35188), Grasmere's first shop in the 18th century, is a colorful place for a smoked salmon and dill tartlet and other snacks, or soup such as broccoli and Stilton. The traditional soft Grasmere Rushbearing Gingerbread is still sold here today.

Where to Stay & Eat

£–££ ✕ **Baldry's.** A cheerful café decked out in the yellows and blues often seen in Provence serves the best coffee in the Lake District. The friendly owners offer delicious scones, cakes, pies, and tarts. For a Cumbrian treat, try the sticky gingerbread with rum butter and ginger ice cream. The menu lists quiches, pastas, chestnut and mushroom pâté, and baguettes. ⊠ *Red Lion Sq.* ☎ *015394/35301* ▤ *MC, V* ☺ *No dinner.*

★
££££–£££££   ✕▦ **White Moss House.** Wordsworth purchased this charming house, built in 1730 to overlook Rydal Water, for his son, Willie, whose family lived here until the 1930s. Public areas and bedrooms are prettily decorated with prints and traditional pieces. The current hosts, the Dixons, lavish attention on guests, who hike (or visit a health club to which guests have access) to prepare for dinner in the renowned restaurant. The menu changes daily, but the five courses of contemporary English cuisine always include a soup, local meat and fish, and fine British cheeses. ⊠ *A591, Rydal Water, LA22 9SE* ☎ *015394/35295* 🖷 *015394/35516* ⊕ *www.whitemoss.com* ⇜ *7 rooms, 1 suite* ♿ *Restaurant, fishing, lounge* ▤ *MC, V* ☺ *Closed Dec. and Jan.* ⦿ *MAP.*

££   ▦ **Banerigg House.** You don't have to spend a fortune to find appealing lakeside lodgings in Grasmere. This early 20th-century family house, three-quarters of a mile south of the village, has well-appointed rooms, most with lake views. It's walker-friendly, too, which means local advice from the owners, drying facilities for wet days, and a roaring fire when needed. ⊠ *Lake Rd., LA22 9PW* ☎ *015394/35204* ⇜ *6 rooms, 5 with bath* ♿ *No a/c, no room phones, no room TVs, no smoking* ▤ *No credit cards* ⦿ *BP.*

Sports & the Outdoors

The most panoramic views of lake and village are from the south, from the bare slopes of Loughrigg Terrace, reached along a signposted track on the western side of the lake. It's less than an hour's walk there, though your stroll can be extended by continuing around Rydal Water, passing Rydal Mount and Dove Cottage before returning to Grasmere, a 4-mi (three-hour) walk in total.

Elterwater

❼ *2½ mi south of Grasmere, 4 mi west of Ambleside.*

The delightful little village of Elterwater, at the eastern end of the Great Langdale Valley on B5343, is a good stop in the Lake District for hikers. It's barely more than a cluster of houses around a village green, but from here a selection of excellent circular walks are possible.

Where to Stay & Eat

★ **££–£££**   ✕▦ **Britannia Inn.** You'll sleep peacefully at this family-owned lodging in the heart of superb walking country. Antiques, comfortable chairs, and prints and oil paintings furnish the cozy, beamed public rooms, and guest rooms are modern in style. You can relax with a bar meal and Cumbrian ale on the terrace while taking in the lovely scenery. The hearty food is popular with locals. Two cottages with kitchens can be rented by the week. ⊠ *B5343, LA22 9HP* ☎ *015394/37210* 🖷 *015394/37311* ⊕ *www.britinn.co.uk* ⇜ *13 rooms, 9 with bath, 2 cottages* ♿ *Restaurant, bar, lounge, some pets allowed; no a/c* ▤ *MC, V* ⦿ *BP.*

★ **££–££££**   ▦ **Old Dungeon Ghyll Hotel.** There's no more comforting stop after a day outdoors than the Hiker's Bar of this hotel at the head of the Great Langdale Valley. The stone floor and wooden beams echo to the clatter of hikers' boots, and the roaring stove rapidly dries out wet walking gear. The old inn has provided hospitality for more than 300 years; guest rooms are done in traditional Lakeland style with patterned carpets, wallpaper, and flowered bed linens. You can choose to include dinner in the rate. ⊠ *Off B5343, Great Langdale, LA22 9JY* ☎🖷 *015394/37272*

⊕ *www.odg.co.uk* ⇆ *13 rooms, 5 with bath* ⌂ *Restaurant, bar, lounge; no a/c, no room phones, no room TVs* ⊟ *AE, MC, V* |◯| *BP.*

Sports & the Outdoors

There are access points to Langdale Fell from various places along the main road; look for information boards at local parking places. You can also stroll up the river valley or embark on more energetic hikes to Stickle Tarn or to one of the summits of the Langdale Pikes.

Coniston

⑧ *5 mi south of Elterwater.*

This small lake resort and boating center attracts climbers with the **Old Man of Coniston** (2,635 feet); it also has sites related to John Ruskin. **Coniston Water,** the lake on which Coniston stands, came to prominence in the 1930s when Arthur Ransome made it the setting for *Swallows and Amazons,* one of a series of novels about a group of children and their adventures in the Lake District between the world wars. The lake is about 5 mi long, a tempting stretch that drew boat and car racer Donald Campbell here in 1959 to set a water speed record of 260 mph. He was killed when trying to beat it in 1967. His body and the wreckage of *Bluebird K7* were finally retrieved from the bottom of the lake in 2001. Campbell is buried in St. Andrew's church in Coniston and a stone seat in the village commemorates him.

The **Ruskin Museum** holds manuscripts, personal items, and watercolors by John Ruskin that illuminate his thinking and influence. There's also a gallery about the life of Donald Campbell. ⊠ *Yewdale Rd.* ☎ *015394/41164* ⊕ *www.ruskinmuseum.com* ⧓ *£3.50* ⊙ *Mid-Mar.–mid-Nov., daily 10–5:30; mid-Nov.–mid-Mar., Wed.–Sun. 10:30–3:30.*

★ **Brantwood,** on the eastern shore of Coniston Water, was the cherished home of John Ruskin (1819–1900), the noted Victorian artist, writer, critic, and social reformer, after 1872. The rambling, white 18th-century house (with Victorian alterations) is on a 250-acre estate that stretches high above the lake. Here, alongside mementos such as his mahogany desk and the bath chair he used in later life, is a collection of Ruskin's own paintings, drawings, and books. Also on display is much of the art—he was a great connoisseur—that Ruskin collected, not least superb drawings by the landscape painter J. M. W. Turner (1775–1851). A video on Ruskin's life shows the lasting influence of his thoughts. Ruskin himself laid out the extensive grounds and their woodland walks. It's an easy drive to Brantwood from Coniston, but it's pleasant to travel here by ferry across the lake, via either the Coniston Launch or the *Gondola,* a 19th-century steam yacht. Both depart from Coniston Pier. ⊠ *Off B5285* ☎ *015394/41396* ⊕ *www.brantwood.org.uk* ⧓ *£4.75, gardens only £3, combined ticket with ferry £7* ⊙ *Mid-Mar.–mid-Nov., daily 11–5:30; mid-Nov.–mid-Mar., Wed.–Sun. 11–4:30.*

Where to Stay & Eat

£–££ ✕ **Brantwood's Jumping Jenny's.** This Pre-Raphaelite–style tearoom, named after Ruskin's beloved boat, has an open log fire and mountain views. It serves morning coffee, lunch (soup, pastas, sandwiches, and salads), and afternoon tea with tasty homemade cakes. ⊠ *Off B5285* ☎ *015394/41715* ⊟ *MC, V* ⊙ *Closed Mon. and Tues. mid-Nov.–mid-Mar. No dinner.*

★ **££** ✕🛏 **Sun Hotel.** Standing at the foot of the Old Man of Coniston, this country-house hotel was built at the turn of the century alongside a 16th-century coaching inn that now serves as a pub. The simply furnished guest rooms and conservatory restaurant have exceptional mountain views. The 400-year-old pub, with flagstone walls and floors and exposed beams, fills up most nights with hikers and climbers. Savory pies are the specialty; there are 5 real ales and 35 wines. ⊠ *LA21 8HQ* ☎ *015394/41248* 🖷 *015394/41219* ⊕ *www.thesunconiston.com* 📞 *10 rooms, 9 with bath* ♿ *Restaurant, pub, some pets allowed, no-smoking rooms; no a/c* ▤ *MC, V* ⑩ *BP.*

£ 🖷 **Beech Tree Guest House.** This appealing Victorian stone country house stands on grounds within walking distance of the town center. The individually furnished rooms are done in a country theme, and breakfast is hearty and vegetarian. There's a TV in the sitting room and an interesting garden. ⊠ *Yewdale Rd., LA21 8DX* ☎ *015394/413717* 📞 *8 rooms, 4 with bath* ♿ *Some pets allowed; no a/c, no smoking* ▤ *MC, V* ⑩ *BP.*

Sports & the Outdoors

Steep tracks lead up from the village to the Old Man of Coniston. The trail starts near the Sun Hotel and goes past an old copper mine to the peak, which you can reach in about two hours. Experienced hikers include the peak in a seven-hour circular walk from the village, also taking in the dramatic heights and ridges of Swirl How and Wetherlam.

Coniston Boating Centre (⊠ Lake Rd. ☎ 015394/41366) at the lake rents out launches, canoes, or traditional wooden rowboats. A picnic area and café are near the center.

Hawkshead

🟎 *3 mi east of Coniston.*

Set in the Vale of Esthwaite, this small market town, with its pleasing hodgepodge of tiny squares, cobbled lanes, and whitewashed houses, is perhaps the Lake District's most picturesque village. There's a good deal more history here than in most local villages, however. The Hawkshead Courthouse, just outside town, was originally built by the monks of Furness Abbey in the 15th century. Hawkshead lay within the monastic domain and later derived much wealth from the wool trade, which flourished here in the 17th and 18th centuries. As a thriving market center, it could afford to maintain the **Hawkshead Grammar School,** at which William Wordsworth was a pupil from 1779 to 1787; he carved his name on a desk inside, now on display. A house in the village (Ann Tyson's House) claims the honor of providing the young William with lodgings. The twin draws of Wordsworth and Beatrix Potter—apart from her home, Hill Top, there's also a local Potter gallery—conspire to make Hawkshead overcrowded throughout the year.

The **Beatrix Potter Gallery,** in the solicitor's offices formerly used by Potter's husband, displays an annually changing selection of the artist-writer's original watercolors and drawings from her books, as well as information on her interests as a naturalist. Potter was a conservationist and an early supporter of the National Trust. Admission is by timed ticket. ⊠ *Main St.* ☎ *015394/36355* ⊕ *www.nationaltrust.org.uk* 🖷 *£3* ⊙ *Late Mar.–Oct., Sat.–Wed. 10:30–4:30.*

🄲 **Hill Top** was the home of children's author and illustrator Beatrix Potter (1866–1943), most famous for her *Peter Rabbit* stories. The house looks much the same as when Potter bequeathed it to the National Trust, and fans will recognize details such as the porch and garden gate, old kitchen range, Victorian dollhouse, and 17th-century four-poster, which were used in the book illustrations. Understandably, this is an often crowded spot; admission is by timed ticket, and you can book in advance. Try to avoid visiting on summer weekends and during school vacations. Hill Top lies 2 mi south of Hawkshead by car, though you can also approach via the car ferry from Bowness-on-Windermere. ✉ *Off B5285, Near Sawrey* ☎ *015394/36269* ⊕ *www.nationaltrust.org.uk* 📖 *£4.50* ⊙ *House Easter–Oct., Sat.–Wed. 10:30–4.30; gardens and shop Easter–Oct., daily 11–4.*

Two miles northwest of the village (follow signs on B5285) is one of the Lake District's most celebrated beauty spots, **Tarn Hows**, a tree-lined lake that is considered one of the prettiest in the region. Scenic overlooks let you drink it all in, or you can take about an hour to putter along the paths. A free National Trust bus runs to the beauty spot from Hawkshead and Coniston (Easter–October, Sunday only).

Where to Stay & Eat

£££–£££££ ✕🏠 **Drunken Duck Inn.** After four centuries of serving travelers, this old coaching inn knows about food and lodging. You can nestle into the cozy bar with oak settles and fireplaces and order a real ale brewed at the Duck. The restaurant has a half-dozen intimate rooms with dark wood furniture and deep orange walls adorned with cartoons and hunting prints; superb modern British fare is the specialty. Guest rooms, pleasingly bright and contemporary in style, have wonderful views of the Langdale Pikes. The inn is 2½ mi from Ambleside and Hawkshead. ✉ *Off B5286, Barngates, LA22 ONG* ☎ *015394/36347* 📠 *015394/36781* ⊕ *www.drunkenduckinn.co.uk* 📨 *16 rooms* ⏚ *Restaurant, pub, no-smoking rooms; no a/c* ☰ *AE, MC, V* ⦿❙ *BP.*

Sports & the Outdoors

Grizedale Mountain Bikes (✉ Old Hall Car Park, Grizedale Forest Park Centre ☎ 01229/860369) rents bicycles.

PENRITH & THE NORTHERN LAKES

The scenery of the northern Lakes is considerably more dramatic—some would say bleaker—than much of the landscape to the south. You'll notice the change on your way north from Kendal to Penrith. The easiest approach is a 30-mi drive on the A6 that takes you through the wild and desolate Shap Fells. One of the most notorious moorland crossings in the country, the fells rise to a height of 1,304 feet. Even in summer it's a lonely place to be, and in winter snows the road can be dangerous. From Penrith, the road leads to Ullswater, possibly the grandest of all the lakes, and then there's a steady route west past Keswick, south through the marvelous Borrowdale Valley, and on to Cockermouth and Bassenthwaite.

Penrith

❿ *30 mi north of Kendal.*

The red-sandstone town of Penrith was the capital of Cumbria, part of the Scottish kingdom of Strathclyde in the 9th and 10th centuries. It became rather neglected after the Normans arrived, and the Scots sacked it on several occasions. Even at this time Penrith was a thriving market town; the market still takes place on Tuesday, and it continues to have good shopping.

The tourist information center, in the Penrith Museum, has information about the historic town trail, which takes you through narrow byways to the plague stone on King Street, where food was left for the plague-stricken, to St. Andrew's churchyard with 1,000-year-old "hog back" tombstones (stones carved as stylized "houses of the dead"), and finally to the ruins of Penrith Castle.

The evocative remains of the 14th-century redbrick **Penrith Castle** stand high above a steep, now-dry moat. Home of the maligned Richard, duke of Gloucester (later Richard III), who was responsible for keeping peace along the border, it was one of England's first lines of defense against the Scots. By the Civil War the castle was in ruins, and the townsfolk used some of the fallen stones to build their own houses. The ruins stand across from the town's train station. ⊠ *Off Castlegate* ☎ *No phone* ⊕ *www.english-heritage.org.uk* ⊠ *Free* ☉ *June–Sept., daily 7:30 AM–9 PM; Oct.–May, daily 7:30–4:30.*

The **Penrith Museum,** in a 16th-century building that served as a school from 1670 to the 1970s, contains displays on the history of the Eden Valley, including Roman pottery and a medieval cauldron. The Penrith Tourist Information Centre is here. ⊠ *Robinson's School, Middlegate* ☎ *01768/212228* ⊠ *Free* ☉ *Apr.–Oct., Mon.–Sat. 10–5, Sun. 1–4; Nov.–Mar., Mon.–Sat. 10–5.*

Rheged, the name of the Celtic kingdom of Cumbria that stretched from Strathclyde in Scotland to Lancashire, is also the theme of this grass-covered visitor center that looks like a Cumbrian hill from the outside. Its centerpiece, a large-format cinema, shows the somewhat historically dubious *Lost Kingdom,* which explores the region's past, introducing Celtic warriors, raiders from Scotland, and Arthurian legends; the aerial scenes of lakes and mountains are awesome. The National Mountaineering Exhibition celebrates Everest and mountaineering heroes. Shops showcase Cumbrian produce and crafts, and the Reivers restaurant has mountain views. Rheged is 2 mi southwest of Penrith and 1 mi west of Junction 40 on the M6. ⊠ *A66* ☎ *01768/868000* ⊕ *www.rheged. com* ⊠ *Free, movie £5.50* ☉ *Daily 10–5:30.*

Where to Stay & Eat

★ **££££** ✕ **A Bit on the Side.** Well-regarded chef-owner Archie Bell runs this intimate candlelit restaurant that focuses on local game and fish in season. Pan-fried fillet of Scottish beef comes topped with blue cheese rarebit, and the roast rack of lamb is served in a Parmesan and pesto crust. Another typical choice on the two- or three-course fixed-price menu is a wild mushroom tart with potato dumplings in a tarragon sauce. ⊠ *Brunswick Sq.* ☎ *01768/892526* ═ *MC, V* ☉ *Closed Sun.–Thurs. No lunch.*

★ **££** ✕▦ **Queen's Head Inn.** Once owned by the Wordsworths, this 1719 inn is a true gem. Now the home of the Tirril Brewery, the traditional pub and restaurant is often packed with locals sampling Tirril beers as well as guest ales on tap, malt whiskeys, and wines from family-run vineyards. The sophisticated meals use local produce such as farmhouse cheeses and Ullswater trout but may include more exotic dishes such as ostrich on a cherry brandy flambé. Rambling hallways lead to small, pleasant rooms with plaid bedspreads and simple wood furniture. The inn is 2½ mi south of Penrith. ⊠ *B5320, Tirril, CA10 2JF* ☎ *01768/863219* 🖷 *01768/863243* ⊕ *www.queensheadinn.co.uk* ⇝ *7 rooms* ♨ *Restaurant, pub; no a/c, no room phones* ═ *AE, MC, V* ⅠⓄⅠ *BP.*

££ ▦ **The George.** This large, rambling coaching inn in the center of Penrith has been hosting people for more than 300 years. The lounges are full of wood paneling, antiques, copper and brass fixtures, old paintings, and comfortable chairs. You can stay overnight in one of the modernized rooms, decorated in traditional style. You can also use the local gym and pool. ⊠ *Devonshire St., CA11 7SH* ☎ *01768/862696* 🖷 *01768/ 868223* ⊕ *www.georgehotelpenrith.co.uk* ⇝ *34 rooms, 1 suite* ♨ *Restaurant, bar, lobby lounge, Internet, business services, meeting rooms, some pets allowed (fee); no a/c, no room phones* ═ *AE, MC, V* ⅠⓄⅠ *BP.*

Shopping

Penrith is a delightful place to shop, with its narrow streets, alleyways, and arcades chockablock with family-run specialty shops. Major shopping areas include Devonish Arcade, with its brand-name stores; the pedestrian-only Angel Lane and Little Dockray; and Angel Square. The stalls of the outdoor **market** line Dockray, Corn Market, and Market Square every Tuesday and sell excellent local produce and original crafts.

James & John Graham of Penrith Ltd. (⊠ Market Sq. ☎ 01768/862281), trading from this site since 1793, has a great bakery and a delicatessen that specializes in cheese and local products. **N. Arnison & Sons Ltd.** (⊠ 18 Devonshire St. ☎ 01768/862078), a step back in time, sells high-quality women's and men's fashions and bed linens. **The Saddlers** (⊠ 15 Little Dockray ☎ 01768/862363) carries fine riding gear, leather items, walking sticks, gifts, and travel goods. **The Toffee Shop** (⊠ 7 Brunswick Rd. ☎ 01768/862008) is where the Queen buys her toffee; it may also have the best fudge in England. **Wetheriggs Country Pottery** (⊠ Clifton Dykes ☎ 01768/892733), 2 mi south of Penrith on the A6, sells handmade earthenware and stoneware from Britain's only remaining steampowered pottery.

Dalemain

⑪ *3 mi southwest of Penrith.*

Home of the Hasell family since 1679, Dalemain began with a 12th-century peel tower, built to protect the occupants from raiding Scots, and is now a delightful hodgepodge of architectural styles. An imposing Georgian facade of local pink sandstone encompasses a medieval hall and extensions from the 16th through the 18th centuries. Inside are a magnificent oak staircase, furniture dating from the mid-17th century, a Chinese drawing room, a 16th-century fretwork room with intricate plasterwork, and many fine paintings, including masterpieces by Van Dyck. The gardens are also worth a look. Dalemain is 3 mi west of Junction 40 of the M6. ⊠ A592, Penrith ☎ 01768/486450 ⊕ *www.dalemain. com* ☎ *£5.50, gardens only £3.50* ⊙ *House late Mar.–mid-Oct., Sun.–Thurs. 11–4; gardens Apr.–Oct., Sun.–Thurs. 10:30–5.*

Ullswater

⑫ *3 mi southwest of Dalemain, 6 mi southwest of Penrith.*

Hemmed in by towering hills, Ullswater, the region's second-largest lake, draws outdoor types. Some of the finest views are from the A592 as it sticks to the lake's western shore, through the adjacent hamlets of **Glenridding** and **Patterdale** at the southern end. Lakeside strolls, teashops, and rowboat rental all help provide the usual Lakeland experience. Steamers leave Glenridding's pier for **Pooley Bridge,** offering a pleasant tour along the lake.

At **Aira Force** (⊠ Off A592, 5 mi north of Patterdale), a spectacular series of waterfalls pounds through a wooded ravine to feed into Ullswater. From the parking lot (fee charged for parking), it's a 20-minute walk to the falls. Bring sturdy shoes in wet weather. Just above Aira Force in the woods of Gowbarrow Park is the spot where, in 1802, William Wordsworth's sister, Dorothy, observed daffodils that, as she wrote, " . . . tossed and reeled and danced and seemed as if they verily laughed with the wind that blew upon them." Two years later Wordsworth transformed his sister's words into the famous poem "I Wandered Lonely as a Cloud." And two centuries later, national park wardens patrol Gowbarrow Park in season to prevent tourists from picking the few remaining daffodils.

★ West of Ullswater's southern end, the brooding presence of **Helvellyn** (3,118 feet), one of the Lake District's most formidable mountains, recalls the region's fundamental character. It's an arduous climb to the top, especially via the challenging ridge known as Striding Edge, and the ascent shouldn't be attempted in poor weather or by inexperienced hikers. Signposted paths to the peak run from the road between Glenridding and Patterdale and pass by **Red Tarn**, at 2,356 feet the highest Lake District tarn.

Where to Stay & Eat

★ £££££ ╳▣ **Sharrow Bay.** Sublime views and exceptional service and cuisine add distinction to this country-house hotel on the shores of Ullswater. Salons with oil paintings and fringed lamp shades represent classic Lakeland style. The bedrooms are plushly opulent, although those in the Edwardian Gatehouse and in the Bank House, an Elizabethan farmhouse about 1½ mi away, are somewhat simpler. Your sophisticated dinner (reservations essential, fixed-price menu; request the lake-view dining room) might be roast salmon on scallop risotto or venison with sweet potato confit. Stop by for afternoon tea (£16). ⊠ *Howtown Rd., Pooley Bridge, CA10 2LZ* ☎ *017684/86301* 🖷 *017684/86349* ⊕ *www.sharrow-bay. com* 🛏 *19 rooms, 7 suites* ♨ *2 restaurants, 2 lounges, Internet, business services, some pets allowed, no-smoking rooms; no a/c in some rooms, no kids under 13* ▣ *MC, V* ⊗ *Closed Dec.–mid-Feb.* � *MAP.*

£££–££££ ▣ **Inn on the Lake.** The freshly decorated interior of this inn is as appealing as its spectacular location looking out over Ullswater. The lawns extend to the water's edge, and at the Ramblers Bar on the grounds you can share a pint and some mountain stories with the locals. Bedrooms, some with lake or mountain views, are furnished in traditional style, and there's a pleasant conservatory. ⊠ *Glenridding, CA11 0PE* ☎ *017684/82444* 🖷 *017684/82303* ⊕ *www.innonthelakeullswater. co.uk* 🛏 *46 rooms* ♨ *Restaurant, cable TV, 2 bars, some pets allowed (fee); no a/c, no smoking* ▣ *MC, V* 101 *BP.*

Keswick

🔞 *14 mi west of Ullswater.*

The great mountains of Skiddaw and Blencathra brood over the gray slate houses of Keswick (pronounced kezzick), on the scenic shores of Derwentwater. The town is a natural base for exploring the rounded, heather-clad Skiddaw range to the north, and the hidden valleys of Borrowdale and Buttermere (the latter reached by stunning Honister Pass) take you into the rugged heart of the Lake District. Nearby, five beautiful lakes are set among the three highest mountain ranges in England.

Although tourists pack its cobbled, narrow streets, Keswick doesn't have quite the Victorian charm of Windermere or Ambleside, or the specialty shops of Penrith. It is, however, the best spot in the Lake District to purchase mountaineering gear and outdoor clothing. There are also many hotels, guest houses, restaurants, and pubs, but the best places are a few miles away in the surrounding countryside.

Because traffic congestion can be horrendous in summer, and parking is difficult in the higher valleys, you may want to leave your car behind. The open-top Borrowdale bus service between Keswick and Seatoller runs frequently, and the Honister Rambler minibus is perfect for walkers aiming for the high fells of the central lakes; it makes many stops from Keswick to Buttermere. The Keswick Launch service on Derwentwater links to many walks as well as the Borrowdale bus service.

The handsome 19th-century **Moot Hall** (⊠ Market Pl. ☎ 017687/72645) has served as both the town hall and the local prison. Now it houses the main **tourist information center** for the region.

Exhibits at the **Keswick Museum and Art Gallery** in Fitz Park include original letters by Wordsworth, Southey, and Walpole, a local geological and natural history collection, and an assortment of watercolor paintings. ⊠ *Station Rd.* ☎ *017687/73263* ⌧ *£1* ☉ *Easter–Oct., daily 10–4.*

★ To understand why **Derwentwater** is considered one of England's finest lakes, take a short walk from Keswick's town center to the lakeshore, and follow the **Friar's Crag** path, about a 15-minute level walk from the center. This pine-tree-fringed peninsula is a favorite vantage point, with its view over the lake, the surrounding ring of mountains, and many tiny islands. Ahead you will see the crags that line the **Jaws of Borrowdale** and overhang a dramatic mountain ravine—a scene that looks as if it emerged straight from a romantic painting or poem. For the best lake views, take a wooden-launch cruise with **Keswick-on-Derwentwater Launch Co.** (☎ 017687/72263 ⊕ www.keswick-launch.co.uk) around Derwentwater. Between late March and November, cruises set off every hour in each direction from a dock at the lakeshore. You can also rent a rowboat here. Buy a "hop-on, hop-off" explorer ticket and take advantage of the seven landing stages around the lake that provide access to some hiking trails, such as the two-hour climb up and down Cat Bells, a celebrated lookout point on the western shore of Derwentwater.

A Neolithic monument about 100 feet in diameter, the **Castlerigg Stone Circle** (⊠ Off A66) lies in a brooding natural hollow called St. John's Vale, ringed by peaks and ranged by sheep. The 38 stones are not large, but the site makes them particularly impressive. Wordsworth described them as "a dismal cirque of Druid stones upon a forlorn moor." The circle is 4 mi east of Keswick, and a clearly marked route leads to a 200-foot-long path through a pasture. You can visit the circle during daylight hours, no charge.

Where to Stay & Eat

££–£££ ✕ **Luca's.** The River Greta runs beside this stylish Italian bistro-restaurant, which is somewhat isolated at the north end of town. Choose from a great selection of pastas, risottos, and wood-fired pizzas, as well as traditional Italian dishes with veal, steak, poultry, or fish. The sauces and daily specials are imaginative. ⊠ *Greta Bridge, High Hill* ☎ *017687/74621* ▭ *MC, V* ☉ *Closed Mon. and Jan. and Feb. Sun.–Wed.*

£–££ ✕ **Abraham's Tea Room.** George Fisher's outdoor store has its own welcoming tearoom, with good, honest Cumbrian home cooking—food as fuel for hikers. The tearoom is open shop hours only, usually Monday through Saturday 10–5:30 and Sunday 10:30–4:30. ⊠ *2 Borrowdale Rd.* ☎ *017687/72178* ▭ *No credit cards* ☉ *No dinner.*

£ ✕ **Lakeland Pedlar.** This hip café and bike shop serves inspired vegetarian and vegan cuisine: hearty breakfast burritos, Tex-Mex and Mediterranean food, and fun pizzas such as the Switchback, with sun-dried tomatoes, peppers, and crumbled blue cheese. You can also check out the fresh juices, real espresso, and the best baked goods in town. Admire the fells from the outdoor tables or order takeout and hit the trail. ⊠ *Henderson's Yard, Bell Close* ☎ *017687/74492* ▭ *MC, V* ☉ *Closed Wed. No dinner Sept.–June.*

£££–££££ ✕▭ **Highfield Hotel.** Slightly austere looking, this family-run Victorian hotel overlooks the lawns of Hope Park and has rooms with great character, including turret rooms and a former chapel that now holds a four-poster. The balconies of the common areas have superb valley views. The restaurant's inventive, daily-changing menu takes advantage of local ingredients in dishes such as roast lamb with minted red currant jelly or pan-fried salmon with grilled eggplant and tomatoes. ⊠ *The Heads, CA12 5ER* ☎ *017687/72508* 🖷 *017687/72508* ⊕ *www.highfieldkeswick.co.uk* ⇌ *19 rooms* ⚭ *Restaurant, bar, no-smoking rooms; no a/c, no room phones, no kids under 8* ▤ *AE, MC, V* ☉ *Closed mid-Nov.–Jan.* ⦿ *MAP.*

££ ✕🖾 **Morrel's.** One of the town's better eating places is in this pleasant, good-value hotel. The relaxed kitchen prepares innovative cuisine: jugged hare is served with poached pear and red currant jelly, and a trout and roast pepper tart accompanies the roast cod. The simple but delightful bedrooms are done in cheerful prints and pastels; rooms on the top floor have great views of the fells. ⊠ *34 Lake Rd., CA12 5DQ* ☎ *017687/72666* 🖷 *017687/74879* ⊕ *www.morrels.co.uk* ⇌ *15 rooms* ⚭ *Restaurant, bar, some pets allowed; no a/c, no room phones* ▤ *MC, V* ⦿ *BP.*

★ ££ 🖾 **Howe Keld.** Those in the know bypass the rows of cookie-cutter B&Bs and head here for a bit of budget TLC. The Fisher family puts you at ease in their comfortable, pretty town house–hotel. High-quality breakfasts are the big event; vegetarians do very well here with freshly baked bread and pancakes, or there are traditional meaty Cumbrian fry-ups. Evening meals (on request) are a good value. ⊠ *5–7 The Heads, CA12 5ES* ☎ *017687/72417* ⊕ *www.howekeld.co.uk* ⇌ *15 rooms, 14 with bath* ⚭ *Dining room, some pets allowed, no-smoking rooms; no a/c, no room phones* ▤ *No credit cards* ☉ *Closed Jan.* ⦿ *BP.*

Nightlife & the Arts

The **Keswick Film Club** (☎017687/72398) has an excellent festival in February and a program of international and classical films screened at the Alhambra Cinema on St. John's Street and at the Theatre by the Lake. The popular **Keswick Jazz Festival** (☎ 017687/74411), held each May, consists of four days of music and events. Reservations are taken before Christmas.

The resident company at the **Theatre by the Lake** (⊠ Lake Rd. ☎017687/74411) presents theatrical productions, both classical and contemporary, throughout the year. Touring music, opera, and dance companies also perform here. The Keswick Music Society presents a season September–January, and the Words on the Water literary festival takes place in late October.

Sports & the Outdoors

BIKING **Keswick Mountain Bike Centre** (⊠ Southey Hill ☎ 017687/75202) rents bikes and provides information on trails; it also stocks accessories and clothing. Guided tours can be arranged with advance notice.

FISHING Local permits, for fishing in Derwentwater or Bassenthwaite, are available at **Field & Stream** (⊠ 79 Main St. ☎ 017687/74396).

WATER SPORTS **Derwentwater Marina** (⊠ Portinscale ☎ 017687/72912) offers boat rentals and instruction in canoeing, sailing, windsurfing, and rowing.

Shopping

Keswick has a good choice of bookstores, crafts shops, and wool-clothing stores tucked away in its cobbled streets, as well as excellent outdoor shops. Keswick's **market** is held Saturday.

Bryson's of Keswick (⊠ 42 Main St. ☎017687/71222), a family-run bakery and confectionery, makes more than 250 varieties of baked goods daily and is renowned for hot savory pies and ice cream. You can also sample these goodies in the tearoom. **George Fisher** (⊠ 2 Borrowdale Rd. ☎ 017687/72178), the area's largest specialty outdoor equipment store, sells plenty of sportswear, as well as travel books and maps. Daily weather information is posted in the window. **Needle Sports** (⊠ 56 Main St. ☎ 017687/72227) supplies equipment for mountaineering and for rock and ice climbing. The **Viridian Gallery** (⊠ 13 St. John St. ☎ 017687/71328), a local artists' co-op, presents the paintings, prints, and ceramics of a half-dozen Cumbrian artists.

en route   The finest route from Keswick, B5289 south, runs along the eastern edge of Derwentwater, past turnoffs to several natural attractions such as Ashness Bridge, the idyllic tarn of Watendlath, the Lodore Falls (best in wet weather), and the precariously balanced Bowder Stone. Farther south is the tiny village of **Grange,** a popular walking center at the head of Borrowdale, where there's a riverside café.

Borrowdale

⓮ *7 mi south of Keswick.*

South of Keswick and its lake lies the valley of Borrowdale, whose varied landscape of green valley floor and surrounding crags has long been considered one of the region's most magnificent treasures. **Rosthwaite,** a tranquil farming village, and **Seatoller,** the southernmost settlement, are the two main centers (both are accessible by bus from Keswick), though they are little more than a cluster of aged buildings surrounded by glorious countryside. The **Lake District National Park Information Centre** has displays on the area, books accommodations, and sells maps and guides. ⊠ *Dalehead Base, Seatoller Barn, Seatoller* ☎ *017687/77294* ⊕ *www. lake-district.gov.uk* ☉ *Late Mar.–early Nov., daily 10–5.*

The steep **Borrowdale Fells** rise up dramatically behind Seatoller. Get out and walk whenever inspiration strikes; in spring, keep an eye open and your camera ready for lambs roaming the hillsides. England's highest mountain, the 3,210-foot **Scafell Pike** (pronounced scar-fell) is visible from Seatoller. One route up the mountain, for experienced walkers, is from the hamlet of Seathwaite, a mile south of Seatoller.

Where to Stay & Eat

£–££ ✕ **Yew Tree Restaurant.** Two 17th-century miners' cottages make up this intimate restaurant at the foot of Honister Pass. A low-beam ceiling, open fireplace, and excellent bar add appeal. The menu focuses on local ingredients: Ullswater trout, Derwentwater pike, Herdwick lamb, and wonderful Cumbrian cheeses. ⊠ *B5289, Seatoller* ☎ *017687/77634* ▤ *MC, V* ☉ *Closed Mon. and 3 wks in Jan.*

££££ 🏠 **Hazel Bank Country House.** Hikers and others appreciate the comforts of this stately, lovingly restored Victorian home, which retains original elements such as the stained-glass windows. The spacious, modernized bedrooms are done in a pretty, faux-Victorian theme, and some have four-posters and window seats. All rooms, including the sitting area, have splendid views of the Borrowdale Valley and the central Lakeland peaks. Dinner (guests only) focuses on local ingredients prepared with modern British flair. ⊠ *Off B5289, Rosthwaite, CA12 5XB* ☎ *017687/77248* 🖷 *017687/77373* ⊕ *www.hazelbankhotel.co.uk* ⇌ *8 rooms* ♨ *Dining room, lounge, Internet, business services; no a/c, no kids under 10, no smoking* ▤ *MC, V* ⦿ *MAP.*

en route   Beyond Seatoller, B5289 turns westward through **Honister Pass**
(1,176 feet) and Buttermere Fell. It's a superb drive along one of the
most dramatic of the region's roads, which is lined with huge
boulders and at times channels through soaring rock canyons. The
road sweeps down from the pass to the village of Buttermere,
sandwiched between Buttermere (the lake) and Crummock Water at
the foot of high, craggy fells.

Cockermouth

🖪 *14 mi northwest of Seatoller.*

This attractive little town at the confluence of the Rivers Derwent and
Cocker has the briskness of a busy market town and a maze of narrow
streets that are a delight to wander. There's no public access to the ruined 14th-century castle, but the outdoor market, held each Monday,
still retains its traditions.

Cockermouth was the birthplace of William Wordsworth (and his sister, Dorothy), whose childhood home, **Wordsworth House,** is a handsome
18th-century Georgian town house. Some of the poet's furniture and
personal items are on display, and you can explore the terraced garden
that inspired his childhood poetry, such as "To a Butterfly." The **Old
Kitchen Tea Room** makes traditional Cumbrian cakes and is the perfect spot for afternoon tea. Incidentally, Wordsworth's father is buried
in the All Saints' churchyard, and the church has a stained-glass window in memory of the poet. ⊠ *Main St.* ☎ *01900/824805* ⊕ *www.
nationaltrust.org.uk* 🖾 *£3.50* ♥ *Apr.–May and Sept.–early Oct., weekdays 10:30–4:30; June–Aug., Mon.–Sat. 10:30–4:30.*

Castlegate House Gallery displays an outstanding collection of works for
sale by Cumbrian artists in the Lake District. Eight exhibitions a year
focus on paintings, sculpture, glass, ceramics, and jewelry. ⊠ *Castlegate* ☎*01900/822149* ⊕*www.castlegatehouse.co.uk* 🖾*£3* ♥*Mar.–Dec.,
Mon., Tues., Fri., Sat. 10:30–5, Wed. 10:30–7, Sun. 2–5.*

⊙ The **Cumberland Toy and Model Museum** exhibits mainly British toys
from 1900 to the present. Two buildings contain good model train collections, the re-creation of a 1930s toy shop, and dolls and dollhouses.
There's a play area for younger children. ⊠ *Banks Ct. and Market Pl.*
☎ *01900/827606* ⊕ *www.toymuseum.co.uk* 🖾 *£3* ♥ *Feb. and Nov.,
daily 10–4; Mar.–Oct., daily 10–5; Dec. and Jan., call for times.*

Where to Stay & Eat

★ ££ ✕ **Quince & Medlar.** Sophisticated vegetarian cuisine served by candlelight is the specialty at this wood-paneled Georgian town house. Choose
from at least six main courses such as couscous-crusted eggplant and
poached pear filled with cheese pâté; all come with seasonal vegetables.
Desserts are delicious, especially the pineapple tartlet and chocolate truffle terrine. ⊠ *13 Castlegate* ☎ *01900/823579* ⊟ *MC, V* ♥ *Closed
Sun. and Mon. No lunch.*

££ 🏨 **Allerdale Court Hotel.** At this 17th-century coaching inn, which may
have once been home to famous mutineer Fletcher Christian, original
oak beams provide a touch of old-fashioned charm, although the furnishings are mostly modern. The four-poster rooms verge on the regal.
Pickwick's restaurant serves English fare from Lakeland pheasant to char-
grilled halibut, and Oscar's specializes in grills, pizzas, and Italian dishes.
⊠ *20 Market Pl., CA13 9NQ* ☎ *01900/823654* 🖨 *01900/823033*
⊕ *www.allerdalecourthotel.co.uk* ↪ *28 rooms* ♨ *2 restaurants, in-
room data ports, bar, some pets allowed; no a/c* ⊟ *MC, V* ⦿*I BP.*

Bassenthwaite

16 *6 mi east of Cockermouth, 4 mi north of Keswick.*

The small village of Bassenthwaite, at the northern end of Bassenthwaite Lake, is one of the most beautiful in the Lake District. The lake itself is the only body of water called a lake in the Lake District; the others are known as "meres" or "waters." Bird-watchers know this less-frequented lake well because of the many species of migratory birds here. The shoreline habitat is the best preserved in the national park, in part because most of it is privately owned and also because motorboats are not allowed. A number of posh accommodations and good restaurants dot the area, and the popular walks include Skiddaw (3,054 feet), which, on a clear day, has panoramic views of the Lake District, Pennines, Scotland, and the Isle of Man from its summit.

Where to Stay & Eat

★ £££–££££ ✕🏠 **The Pheasant.** You won't find better service than at this traditional 17th-century coaching inn, which exudes English coziness without the usual Lakeland fussiness. Settle into a sofa by an open fire in the elegant sitting room, painted in subdued tones of butter yellow and sage green. The tasteful modern bedrooms overlook 60 acres of forest, and a beamed restaurant serves superb English fare such as venison with mushrooms and shallots. Varnished walls, oak settles, and hunting prints set the mood in the popular bar. The Pheasant is halfway between Cockermouth and Keswick. ⊠ *Off A66, Bassenthwaite Lake, CA13 9YE* ☎ *017687/76234* ⊕ *www.the-pheasant.co.uk* 🛏 *16 rooms, 2 suites* ♿ *Restaurant, bar, 3 lounges, Internet, business services, some pets allowed; no a/c, no room TVs* ▤ *MC, V* �'⌷I *BP.*

LAKE DISTRICT A TO Z

To research prices, get advice from other travelers, and book travel arrangements, visit www.fodors.com.

AIRPORTS

Manchester Airport has its own rail station with direct service to Carlisle, Windermere, and Barrow-in-Furness. Manchester is 70 mi from the southern part of the Lake District.
🛈 **Manchester Airport** ⊠ Near Junctions 5 and 6 of M56 ☎ 0161/489–3000 ⊕ www.manairport.co.uk.

BIKE TRAVEL

Cycling along the numerous bicycle paths and quiet forest roads in Cumbria is pleasurable and safe. The Cumbria Cycle Way circles the county of Cumbria, and for local excursions guided bike tours are often available, starting at about £25 per day. Contact local tourist offices or bike rental places for details on cycle routes.

BOAT & FERRY TRAVEL

Keswick-on-Derwentwater Launch Company conducts cruises on vintage motor launches around Derwentwater, leaving from Keswick. Coniston Launch connects Coniston with Ruskin's home at Brantwood, offering hourly service for most of the year (service is reduced in winter) on its wooden *Ruskin* and *Ransome* launches. Steam Yacht *Gondola* runs the National Trust's luxurious Victorian steam yacht between Coniston, Brantwood, and Park-a-Moor at the south end of Coniston Water, daily from Easter through October. Ullswater Steamers sends its oil-burning 19th-century steamers the length of Ullswater between Glenridding and Pooley Bridge; service operates April through October.

Windermere Lake Cruises employs its fleet of modern launches and vintage cruisers year-round between Ambleside, Bowness, Brockhole, and Lakeside. Ticket prices vary, though a Freedom of the Lake ticket (£10.50) gives unlimited travel on any of the ferries for 24 hours.

FARES &
SCHEDULES

🛈 **Coniston Launch** ☎ 015394/36216 ⊕ www.conistonlaunch.co.uk. **Keswick-on-Derwentwater Launch Co.** ☎ 017687/72263 ⊕ www.keswick-launch.co.uk. **Steam Yacht** *Gondola* ☎ 015394/41288. **Ullswater Steamers** ☎ 017684/82229 ⊕ www.ullswater-steamers.co.uk. **Windermere Lake Cruises** ☎ 015395/31188 ⊕ www.windermere-lakecruises.co.uk.

BUS TRAVEL

Traveline handles public transportation inquiries. National Express serves the region from London's Victoria Coach Station and from Manchester's Chorlton Street Station. Average travel time to Kendal is just over 7 hours from London; to Windermere, 7½ hours; and to Keswick, 8¼ hours. From Manchester there's one bus a day to Windermere (3½ hours) that stops in Ambleside, Grasmere, and Keswick. There's direct bus service to the Lake District from Carlisle, Lancaster, and York.

Stagecoach in Cumbria provides local service between Lakeland towns and through the valleys and high passes. Contact Traveline for an up-to-date timetable. A one-day Explorer Ticket (£6) is available on the bus and valid on all routes. Service between main tourist centers is fairly frequent on weekdays, but much reduced on weekends and bank holidays. Don't count on reaching the more remote parts of the area by bus. For off-the-beaten-track touring, you'll need a car, or strong legs.

CUTTING COSTS

The YHA Shuttle Bus operates a door-to-door service for guests at eight of the most popular hostels in the Lakes (Easter through October only). Get on and off where you like for £2 a journey, or send your luggage ahead to the next hostel if you want to walk unencumbered. The trip from Windermere station to the Windermere or Ambleside hostel is free. 🛈 **YHA Shuttle Bus** ✉ Ambleside Youth Hostel, Waterhead ☎ 015394/32304.

FARES &
SCHEDULES

🛈 **National Express** ☎ 0870/580–8080 ⊕ www.nationalexpress.com. **Traveline** ☎ 0870/608–2608 ⊕ www.traveline.org.uk.

CAR RENTAL

🛈 **Local Agencies Avis** ✉ Station Rd., Kendal ☎ 01539/733582. **Interental Ltd.** ✉ Brant Cell Garage, Kendal Rd., Bowness-on-Windermere ☎ 015394/44408. **Keswick Motor Company** ✉ Lake Rd., Keswick ☎ 017687/72064.

CAR TRAVEL

To reach the Lake District from London, take M1 north to M6, getting off either at Junction 36 and joining A590/A591 west (around the Kendal bypass to Windermere) or at Junction 40, joining A66 direct to Keswick and the northern lakes region. Travel time to Kendal is about four hours, to Keswick five to six hours. Expect heavy traffic out of London on weekends to all destinations in the Northwest; construction work also often slows progress on M6.

ROAD
CONDITIONS

Roads within the region are generally very good, although many minor routes and mountain passes can be both steep and narrow. Warning signs are normally posted if snow has made a road impassable; always listen to local weather forecasts in winter before heading out. In July and August and during the long public holiday weekends, expect heavy traffic. The Lake District has plenty of parking lots, which should be used to avoid blocking narrow lanes.

EMERGENCIES
Ambulance, fire, police ☎999. **Keswick Cottage Hospital** ✉Croswaithe Rd., Keswick ☎ 017687/72012. **Penrith New Hospital** ✉ Bridge La., Penrith ☎ 017687/245300. **Westmorland General Hospital** ✉ Burton Rd., Kendal ☎ 01539/732288.

NATIONAL PARKS
The Lake District National Park head office (and main visitor center) is at Brockhole, north of Windermere. There are also helpful regional national park information centers.

Lake District National Park ✉ Brockhole, A591, Ambleside Rd., Windermere ☎ 015394/46601 ⊕ www.lake-district.gov.uk. **Bowness Bay** ✉ Glebe Rd., Bowness-on-Windermere ☎015394/42895. **Coniston** ✉Ruskin Ave. ☎015394/41533. **Glenridding** ✉ Beckside Car Park ☎ 017684/82414. **Grasmere** ✉ Red Bank Rd. ☎ 015394/35245. **Hawkshead** ✉ Main Car Park ☎ 015394/36525. **Keswick** ✉ Moot Hall, Main St. ☎ 017687/72645. **Pooley Bridge** ✉ Finkle St. ☎ 017684/86530. **Seatoller** ✉ B5289 ☎ 017687/77294. **Waterhead** ✉ Waterhead, Ambleside ☎ 015394/32729.

TOURS
BUS TOURS Mountain Goat Holidays and Lakes Supertours provide special minibus sightseeing tours with skilled local guides. Half- and full-day tours, which really get off the beaten track, depart from Bowness, Windermere, Ambleside, and Grasmere.

Lakes Supertours ✉1 High St., Windermere ☎ 015394/42751 ⊕ www.lakes-supertours.co.uk. **Mountain Goat Holidays** ✉Victoria St., Windermere ☎015394/45161 ⊕ www.lakes-pages.co.uk/goatmain.html.

WALKING TOURS You can find walks from a gentle stroll with someone who specializes in the area's literary traditions to a challenging ridge hike. The Lake District National Park (⇨ National Parks) or the Cumbria Tourist Board in Windermere (⇨ Visitor Information) can put you in touch with qualified guides. Blue Badge Guides can provide experts on the area. English Lakeland Ramblers organizes single-base and inn-to-inn guided tours of the Lake District from May through October. Go Higher will take you on the more challenging routes and provides technical gear and courses on mountaineering skills.

Blue Badge Guides ☎ 020/7403-1115 ⊕ www.blue-badge.org.uk. **English Lakeland Ramblers** ✉ 18 Stuyvesant Oval, #1A, New York, NY 10009 ☎ 01229/587382 or 212/505-1020; 800/724-8801 in U.S. ⊕ www.ramblers.com. **Go Higher** ✉ High Dyon Side, Distington ☎ 01946/830476.

TRAIN TRAVEL
For schedule information, call National Rail Enquiries. Two train companies serve the region from London's Euston Station: take a Virgin or First North Western train bound for Carlisle, Edinburgh, or Glasgow and change at Oxenholme for the branch line service to Kendal and Windermere. Average travel time to Windermere (including the change) is 4½ hours. If you're heading for Keswick, you can either take the train to Windermere and continue from there by Stagecoach bus (Bus 555/556; 70 minutes), or stay on the main London–Carlisle train to Penrith Station (four hours), from which Stagecoach buses (Bus X5) also run to Keswick (45 minutes). Direct trains from Manchester depart for Windermere five times daily (travel time two hours). First North Western runs a local service from Windermere and Barrow-in-Furness to Manchester Airport.

Train connections are good around the edges of the Lake District, especially on the Oxenholme–Kendal–Windermere line and the Furness and West Cumbria branch line from Lancaster to Grange-over-Sands, Ulverston, Barrow, and Ravenglass. However, these services aren't useful for getting around the central Lakeland region (you must take the bus or drive), and they are reduced, or nonexistent, on Sunday.

FARES &
SCHEDULES

First North Western ☎ 08547/000125 ⊕ www.firstgroup.com. **National Rail Enquiries** ☎ 0845/748–4950 ⊕ www.nationalrail.co.uk. **Virgin Trains** ☎ 0845/722–2333 ⊕ www.virgintrains.co.uk.

TRAVEL AGENCIES

Local Agent Referrals Gates Travel ⊠ 9 Library Rd., Kendal ☎ 01539/720148 ⊠ Ruskin House, Market Pl., Ambleside ☎ 01539/433200.

VISITOR INFORMATION

Cumbria Tourist Board is open Monday–Thursday 9:30–5:30 and Friday 9:30–5.

Cumbria Tourist Board ⊠ Ashleigh, Holly Rd., Windermere, LA23 2AQ ☎ 015394/ 44444 ⊕www.golakes.co.uk. **Youth Hostel Association England and Wales** ⊠ Trevelyan House, Matlock, Derbyshire, DE4 3YH ☎ 0870/870–8808 ⊕ www.yha.org.uk. **Ambleside** ⊠ Central Bldgs., Market Cross, Rydal Rd. ☎ 015394/32582. **Cockermouth** ⊠ The Town Hall, Market St. ☎ 01900/822634. **Coniston** ⊠ Ruskin Ave. ☎ 015394/41533. **Grasmere** ⊠ Red Bank Rd. ☎ 015394/35245. **Hawkshead** ⊠ Main Car Park ☎ 015394/36525. **Kendal** ⊠ Town Hall, Highgate ☎ 01539/725758. **Keswick** ⊠ Moot Hall, Market Sq. ☎ 017687/72645. **Penrith** ⊠ Penrith Museum, Middlegate ☎ 01768/867466. **Ullswater** ⊠ Main Car Park, Glenridding ☎ 017684/82414. **Windermere** ⊠ The Gateway Centre, Victoria St. ☎ 015394/46499.

EAST ANGLIA

CAMBRIDGE, BURY ST. EDMUNDS, NORWICH, LINCOLN

12

FODOR'S CHOICE

Dedham, *village in Essex*

Holkham Hall, *stately home in Wells-next-the-Sea*

Lavenham, *village in Suffolk*

The Lighthouse, *restaurant in Aldeburgh*

Ocean House, *B&B in Aldeburgh*

Victoria at Holkham, *hotel in Wells-next-the-Sea*

HIGHLY RECOMMENDED

RESTAURANTS Adlard's Restaurant, *Norwich*

Jew's House, *Lincoln*

Le Talbooth, *Dedham*

Midsummer House, *Cambridge*

HOTELS Angel Hotel, *Bury St. Edmunds*

Crown and Castle, *Orford*

Ickworth Hotel, *near Bury St. Edmunds*

Lavenham Priory, *Lavenham*

Seckford Hall, *Woodbridge*

White Hart, *Lincoln*

SIGHTS Audley End House and Gardens, *Saffron Walden*

Blickling Hall, *Blickling*

Burghley House, *Stamford*

Bury St. Edmunds

Ely Cathedral, *Ely*

Fitzwilliam Museum, *Cambridge*

King's College Chapel, *Cambridge*

Lincoln

Norwich Cathedral, *Norwich*

Updated by
Catherine
Belonogoff

ONE OF THOSE BEAUTIFUL ENGLISH INCONSISTENCIES, East Anglia has no spectacular mountains or rivers to disturb the storied, quiet land, full of rural delights such as tulip fields, flint churches, and thatched-roof cottages. Occupying an area of southeastern England that juts, knoblike, into the North Sea, its counties of Essex, Norfolk, Suffolk, Lincolnshire, and Cambridgeshire are a bit cut off from the central routes and pulse of Britain. People from London once called the region "silly Suffolk" and referred to the citizens of Norfolk county as "Norfolk Dumplings." In modern times, when life for many is busy and stressful, these terms strike an almost complimentary note.

This area has also been home to some of Britain's greatest thinkers, artists, and poets. John Milton; Francis Bacon; Sir Isaac Newton; Lord Byron; Alfred, Lord Tennyson; and William Thackeray received their education at Cambridge University, one of the world's most important centers of learning and arguably the world's most attractive university town. Here, Oliver Cromwell groomed his Roundhead troops, and Tom Paine, the man who wrote "These are the times that try men's souls," developed his revolutionary ideas. Here, John Constable painted *The Hay Wain,* along with luscious landscapes of the Stour Valley, and Thomas Gainsborough achieved eminence as England's most elegant portraitist. If East Anglia has remained rural to a large extent, its harvest of legendary minds has been just as impressive as its agricultural crops.

Despite its easy access from London, East Anglia remains relatively unfamiliar to visitors, with the notable exception of Cambridge and, to a lesser degree, North Norfolk, where the unspoiled villages have become fashionable. It was a region of major importance in ancient times, as evidenced by the Roman settlements at Colchester and Lincoln; and during the medieval era, trade in wool with the Netherlands made East Anglian towns strong and independent. But with the lack of main thoroughfares and canals, the Industrial Revolution mercifully passed East Anglia by.

As a result of being a historical backwater, the region is enormously rich in quiet villages, presided over by ancient churches, tiny settlements in the midst of otherwise deserted fenland (lowlands), and manor houses surrounded by moats. Few parts of Britain can claim so many stately churches and half-timber houses. The towns are more like large villages; even the largest city, Norwich, has a population of only about 130,000.

If you find the region's mostly quiet, flat spaces dull, you need travel only a few miles to reach the bright lights: four splendid stately houses— Holkham Hall, Blickling Hall, Houghton Hall, and Her Majesty's own Sandringham. There are incomparable cathedrals, at Ely and Lincoln particularly, and the "finest flower of Gothic in Europe," King's College Chapel in Cambridge. These are the superlatives of East Anglia. But half the attraction of the region lies in its subtle landscapes, where the beauties of rural England appear at their enduring best: to rush in search of one or two highlights is to miss these qualities, which only leisurely journeys along the byways can reveal.

Exploring East Anglia

For purposes of sightseeing, East Anglia can be divided into distinct areas: the central area surrounding the ancient university city of Cambridge and including the pretty towns of inland Suffolk; the southeast, taking in the ancient Roman town of Colchester and sweeping upward along the Suffolk Heritage Coast; the northeast, with the region's capital, Norwich, the waterways of Broadland, and the beaches and salt marshes of the North Norfolk coast; and, to the north of Cambridge, the fenland

East Anglia has a reputation for being flat and featureless that is mostly undeserved. But although the lowland marsh country in the west, the fens, may yield more vegetables than it does tourist attractions, you'll need more than a few days to soak up the medieval atmosphere of Norfolk, Suffolk, and the unspoiled coastal villages—including time to linger in a pub over a pint of locally brewed beer. On a three-day trip, it's best to concentrate on one area, probably Cambridge and its surroundings, rather than try to cover the large distances separating major sights and towns. A stay of eight days would enable you to explore more highlights of East Anglia and to match your step to its slow pace and follow some of the tiny country lanes.

12

Numbers in the text correspond to numbers in the margin and on the East Anglia, Cambridge, Norwich, and Lincolnshire maps.

If you have 3 days

🏛 **Cambridge** ❶–⓰ ▶ is easy to visit even as a day trip from London—too easy, some say, to judge by the huge number of visitors year-round. It's also the best base from which to explore a bit of East Anglia. Explore some of the ancient university buildings, stroll along the Backs, or punt down the River Cam to Grantchester. The next day, head for **Ely** ⓱ and spend a few hours exploring the medieval town and its majestic cathedral, before you move on to **Bury St. Edmunds** ㉒, an town with graceful Georgian streets. Spend the third day exploring the medieval Suffolk wool towns of **Sudbury** ⓲, **Long Melford** ⓴, and **Lavenham** ㉑, before returning to Cambridge.

If you have 8 days

Start from 🏛 **Cambridge** ❶–⓰ ▶ and take in the medieval sights on your first day. Spend the night and then head out to **Saffron Walden** ⓲ and northeast, overnighting in 🏛 **Bury St. Edmunds** ㉒. Explore the town the next day, making time to visit the Abbey Ruins and Botanical Gardens, and then head south through **Long Melford** ⓴, **Lavenham** ㉑, and **Sudbury** ⓲ (with a quick stopover to see Gainsborough's House) to 🏛 **Colchester** ㉓, the traditional base for exploring Constable Country. The next day, head for Constable's **Dedham** ㉔, then take the B1084 to 🏛 **Orford** ㉖, a tiny village with a Norman church and castle and traditional smokehouses for preparing fish. Spend the next day exploring Sutton Hoo near 🏛 **Woodbridge** ㉕ or 🏛 **Aldeburgh** ㉗; you may also want to visit **Southwold** ㉘, a seaside town where time seems to have stood still. Travel to 🏛 **Norwich** ㉙–㊳ and visit its cathedral and medieval alleys. The extensive journey northwest to 🏛 **Lincoln** ㊼, where you can spend your sixth night, takes you through flat fenland. En route, you can visit **King's Lynn** ㊹ or detour northward toward the coast to visit one or two spectacular stately homes, such as **Blickling Hall** ㊴, Holkham Hall in **Wells-next-the-Sea** ㊶, **Sandringham House** ㊷, or **Houghton Hall** ㊸. Lincoln is worthy of a day's exploration: on the way back to Cambridge the next day, opt to stop either at **Ely** ⓱, to see its great cathedral, or at **Stamford** ㊻ to visit Burghley House, an Elizabethan extravaganza.

city of Ely with its magnificent cathedral rising out of the flatlands, with Peterborough, a much expanded commercial center, and Lincoln, landmarked by its tall, fluted cathedral towers, lesser luminaries of the region. Farther north, the historic ports of King's Lynn and Boston, from where the Pilgrims made their first, unsuccessful bid to sail to the New World, flank the shallow bay known as the Wash.

About the Restaurants & Hotels

In summer the coast gets so packed with people that reservations are essential at restaurants. Getting something to eat at other than regular mealtime hours is not always possible in small towns; look for cafés if you want a mid-morning or after-lunch snack.

The intimate nature of even East Anglia's larger towns has meant that few hotels have more than 100 rooms. As a result, even the biggest hostelries offer friendly, personal service. In addition, few English regions have quite so many centuries-old, half-timber inns with rooms full of roaring fires and cozy bars. Cambridge has relatively few hotels downtown, and these tend to be rather overpriced: there simply isn't room for hotels among the numerous historic buildings. Bed-and-breakfasts are a cheaper alternative. It's always busy in Cambridge and along the coast in summer, so reserve well in advance.

WHAT IT COSTS In pounds					
	££££	££££	£££	££	£
RESTAURANTS	over £22	£18–£22	£13–£17	£7–£12	under £7
HOTELS	over £160	£115–£160	£80–£115	£50–£80	under £50

Restaurant prices are for a main course at dinner. Hotel prices are for two people in a standard double room in high season, including VAT, with no meals or, if indicated, CP (with Continental breakfast), BP (Breakfast Plan, with full breakfast), or MAP (Modified American Plan, with breakfast and dinner).

Timing

Summer and late spring are the best times to visit. Avoid late fall and winter, as the weather can be cold, windy, and rainy. If you want to escape crowds, stay away from the popular Norfolk Broads in late July and August. The May Bumps, intercollegiate boat races, are, confusingly, held the first week of June in Cambridge. During the summer "long vac," Cambridge is empty of its students, its life and soul. To see the city in full swing, visit October through June, although in summer there are enjoyable festivals, notably the Strawberry Fair (mid-June), and the Folk Festival and Arts Festival (both July). The world-famous Aldeburgh Festival of music and the arts, started in 1948 by Benjamin Britten, takes place in June. King's Lynn and Norwich both have renowned music and arts festivals, in July and October, respectively.

CAMBRIDGE

▶ If you want to think about Cambridge, think Rupert Brooke, the short-lived World War I–era poet ("There is some corner of a foreign field/ That is forever England"), a Cambridgeshire lad, who called his county "The shire for Men who Understand." Think William Wordsworth and Thackeray, Byron and Tennyson, E. M. Forster and C. S. Lewis; and see *Chariots of Fire,* the 1981 film version of the true story of Harold Abrahams, a Cambridge graduate who shone in the 1924 Olympic Games. The exquisite King's College choir defines the season for an entire nation, when the *Festival of Nine Lessons and Carols* is broadcast live on Christmas Eve.

12

Biking

There's a good reason why Cambridge instantly conjures up the image of the undergraduate hurtling along the streets on a bicycle with academic gown flowing behind. It's an ideal city to traverse by bike, and everyone seems to do so. The same can be said for the entire region. "Very flat, Norfolk," Noël Coward's remark, is something of an over-statement; nonetheless, many of the flat coastal areas of East Anglia, although sometimes windswept, are perfect for cycling. A network of cycle routes and bike rental centers provides a good means of getting around the towpaths and backwaters of the Norfolk Broads.

Great Flavors

Look for area specialties, such as duckling, Norfolk black turkey, hare, and partridge, on menus around East Anglia. Among the culinary treats from the sea is samphire, a delicious kind of seaweed that grows in the salt marshes along the North Norfolk and Suffolk coasts. The long coastline also provides tasty Cromer crabs and Yarmouth bloaters (a kind of smoked herring), whereas the Essex coast near Colchester has been producing oysters since Roman times. There's an equally venerable tradition in wine-making. The Romans first introduced vines to Britain, and they took especially well here. Today East Anglia has more than 40 vineyards. If you want to try a bottle (dry whites are best), check wine lists in local restaurants.

The Landscape

For many people, the joy of East Anglia is its very separate-ness, its desolate landscapes and isolated beaches. Of these, the fens (marshy lowlands) of northern Cambridgeshire and the Broads (expanded rivers) of Norfolk are the most dramatic—or depressing, depending on your mood. The water in the marshes and dikes reflects the arching sky, whose cloudscapes are ever-changing, stretching toward seemingly infinite horizons. The sunsets are to be treasured. The fens resemble areas of Holland across the North Sea, and, indeed, work on much of the drainage system here was carried out by Dutch engineers beginning in the 17th century. In both Norfolk and Suffolk, the reed-bordered Broads make a gentle landscape of canals and lakes that are ideal for boating and are alive with birds and animals.

Walking

East Anglia is a walker's dream. The long-distance footpath known as the Peddar's Way follows the line of a pre-Roman road, running from near Thetford through heathland, pine forests, and arable fields, and on through rolling chalk lands to the Norfolk coast near Hunstanton. The Norfolk Coastal Path then continues eastward along the coast, joining at Cromer with the delightfully varied Weaver's Way, which passes through medieval weaving villages and deeply rural parts of the Norfolk Broads on its 56-mi route from Cromer to Great Yarmouth.

With the spires of its university buildings framed by towering trees and expansive meadows, its medieval streets and passages enhanced by gardens and riverbanks, the city of Cambridge is among the loveliest in England. Situated on a bend of the River Cam, 54 mi north of London, and 63 mi southwest of Norwich, this is also one of the most ancient cities in Britain, its foundation lost in the mists of time. This is no mere

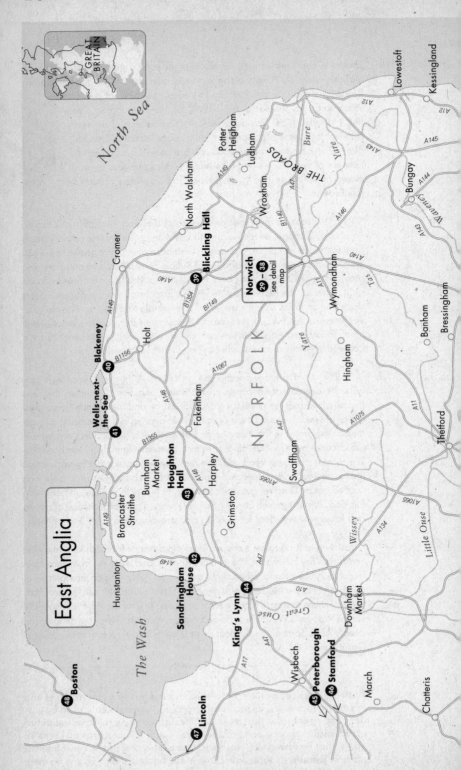

East Anglia

GREAT BRITAIN

North Sea

The Wash

NORFOLK

THE BROADS

Norwich
29 – 38
see detail
map

Lowestoft
Kessingland
A12
A12
A145
Bungay
A144
A143
A146
Waveney
A143
Potter
Heigham
Ludham
Wroxham
A149
A47
B1140
Bure
Yare
Yare
A140
Wymondham
A11
Tas
Banham
Bressingham
Hingham
A11
A1075
Thetford
A47
Yare
A1067
A1065
A1065
Swaffham
Little Ouse
Wissey
A134
Downham
Market
Great Ouse
A10
King's Lynn
44
A47
A134
A17
A17
Wisbech
45 **Peterborough**
46 **Stamford**
March
Chatteris
48 **Boston**
47 **Lincoln**
A149
Hunstanton
Brancaster
Straithe
Burnham
Market
A148
B1355
Sandringham
House
42
A149
Harpley
Grimston
Houghton
Hall
43
A148
Fakenham
Wells-next-
the-Sea
41
Blakeney
40
B1156
Holt
A149
A148
Cromer
A140
B1354
B1149
Blickling Hall
39
North Walsham
A149

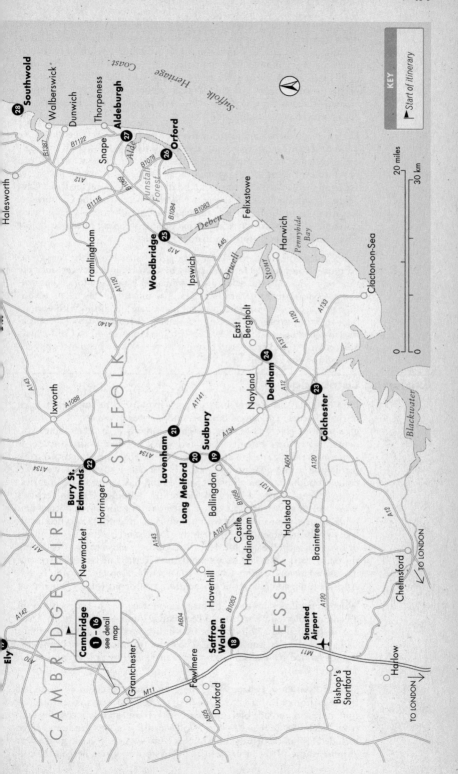

TO LONDON

TO LONDON

KEY

► *Start of itinerary*

20 miles

30 km

Suffolk Heritage Coast

28 **Southwold**
Walberswick
Dunwich
Thorpeness
27 **Aldeburgh**
Snape
26 **Orford**
25 **Woodbridge**
Felixstowe
Harwich
Pennyhide Bay
Clacton-on-Sea

Halesworth
Framlingham
Ipswich
East Bergholt
24 **Dedham**
23 **Colchester**

Ixworth
22 **Bury St. Edmunds**
Horringer
Newmarket
21 **Lavenham**
20 **Long Melford**
19 **Sudbury**
Nayland
Ballingdon
Castle Hedingham
Halstead
Braintree
Chelmsford

SUFFOLK

Tunstall Forest

Deben
Orwell
Stour
Blackwater

CAMBRIDGESHIRE

Ely
Grantchester
Fowlmere
Duxford
Haverhill
18 **Saffron Walden**
Stansted Airport
Bishop's Stortford
Harlow

ESSEX

Cambridge
1 – 16
see detail map

cliché, for the mists that rise from the surrounding water meadows be-devil Cambridge. Certainly the city predates the Roman occupation of Britain. There's similar confusion about when the university itself was founded. Its origins may lie with masters from Oxford who brought their pupils to Cambridge in 1209 to escape the violence of Oxford's town versus gown troubles. Another story attributes its founding to impoverished students from Oxford, who came in search of eels, no less—a cheap source of nourishment.

Keep in mind there is no recognizable campus: the scattered colleges *are* the university. The town reveals itself only slowly, filled with tiny gardens, ancient courtyards, imposing classic buildings, alleyways that lead past medieval churches, and wisteria-hung facades. Perhaps the best views are from the Backs, the green parkland that extends along the River Cam behind several colleges. Here you will feel the essence of Cambridge. Resulting from the larger size of the colleges and from the lack of industrialization in the city center, this broad sweeping openness is just what distinguishes Cambridge from Oxford.

For centuries the University of Cambridge has been among the very greatest universities, rivaled in Britain only by Oxford; indeed, ever since the time of its most famous scientific alumnus, Sir Isaac Newton, it has outshone Oxford in the natural sciences. The university has taken advantage of its scientific prestige, pooling its research facilities with various high-tech industries. As a result, the city is surrounded by IT companies and has been dubbed "Silicon Fen" in comparison to California's Silicon Valley. The prosperity brought by technology businesses has enlivened the city center.

Exploring Cambridge

Exploring the city means, in large part, exploring the university. Each of the 25 oldest colleges is built around a series of courts, or quadrangles, whose velvety lawns are the envy of many a gardener. Since students and fellows (faculty) live and work in these courts, access is sometimes restricted, and at *all* times you are requested to refrain from picnicking in the quadrangles. Visitors are not normally allowed into college buildings other than chapels, dining halls, and some libraries; some colleges charge admission for certain buildings. The university's Web site, ⊕ www.cam.ac.uk, has information about the colleges and other institutions associated with it. Public visiting hours vary from college to college, depending on the time of year, and it's best to call ahead or to check with the city tourist office. Colleges close to visitors during the main exam time, late May to mid-June. Term time (when classes are in session) means roughly October to December, January to March, and April to June; summer term, or vacation, runs from July to September.

When the colleges are open, by far the best way to gain access is to join a walking tour led by an official Blue Badge guide—in fact, many areas are off-limits unless you do. The two-hour tours leave up to five times daily from the city tourist office. The other traditional view of the colleges is gained from a punt—the boats propelled by pole up and down the River Cam.

a good walk

Start at **Peterhouse College** ❶ ┏, the granddaddy of them all, founded by the bishop of Ely in 1281. One of the colleges closest to the train station, it lies on one side of Trumpington Street and stands across the way from **Pembroke College** ❷—the "College of Poets," as graduates have included Edmund Spenser and Thomas Gray—where you can gain a first glimpse of the 17th-century work of Christopher Wren, here in the col-

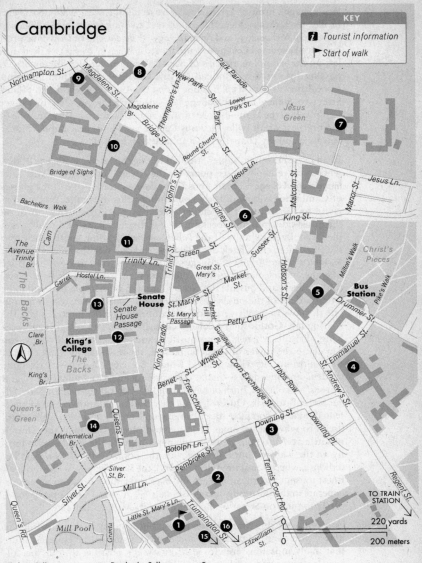

Cambridge

Northampton St.
Magdalene St.
New Park
Park Parade
Magdalene Br.
Thompson's Ln.
Park St.
Lower Park St.
Jesus Green
Bridge St.
Round Church St.
St. John's St.
Jesus Ln.
Jesus Ln.
Bridge of Sighs
Sidney St.
Malcolm St.
Manor St.
Bachelors Walk
Green St.
King St.
Christ's Pieces
The Avenue
Trinity Br.
Cam
Trinity Ln.
Trinity St.
Great St. Mary's
Sussex St.
Hobson's St.
Milton's Walk
Bus Station
Pike's Walk
The Backs
Garret Hostel Ln.
Market St.
Senate House
Drummer St.
Clare Br.
Senate House Passage
St. Mary's
Market Hill
St. Mary's Passage
Petty Cury
Guildhall
St. Emmanuel St.
St. Andrew's St.
King's College
King's Br.
The Backs
King's Parade
Benet St.
Wheeler St.
Corn Exchange St.
St. Tibbs Row
Queen's Green
Mathematical Br.
Queens' Ln.
Free School Ln.
Downing St.
Downing Pl.
Regent St.
Silver St. Br.
Botolph Ln.
Pembroke St.
Tennis Court Rd.
TO TRAIN STATION
Queen's Rd.
Silver St.
Mill Ln.
Little St. Mary's Ln.
Trumpington St.
Fitzwilliam St.
Mill Pool
Granta

220 yards
200 meters

lege's chapel. From the Arts, head over to the Sciences. Walk up to Pembroke Street, turn right, and continue on Downing Street for the engaging **Museum of Archaeology and Anthropology** ❸. At the end of Downing Street you face **Emmanuel College** ❹, and more of Wren's work. You then turn left up the shopping arteries of St. Andrew's Street and Sidney Street, passing the often overlooked **Christ's College** ❺, with fine buildings from different periods. Continue along St. Andrew's Street and Sidney Street to **Sidney Sussex College** ❻—look for the portrait of Oliver Cromwell in the Hall—before turning right down Jesus Lane for one of the prettiest of all colleges, **Jesus College** ❼. Note the Chapter House entrance and the chapel's Pre-Raphaelite stained glass.

Head farther north up Sidney Street and Bridge Street to Magdalene Bridge, where you're likely to see punts on the River Cam. By the river, quiet **Magdalene College** ❽ flanks busy Magdalene Street—one of the glories of Cambridge is how quickly you can move from frantic, modern England to the seclusion of scholarly academe. A little farther north on the other side, museums beckon: the art displays in **Kettle's Yard** ❾ and the city-related exhibits of the **Folk Museum**. Heading south, back into the city center, cross back over the river and down St. John's Street, past **St. John's** ❿ and **Trinity** ⓫ colleges. In St. John's you can view the Bridge of Sighs, modeled after its Venetian namesake. Trinity is Sir Isaac Newton's college, and outside the Great Gate stands an apple tree said to be a descendant of the one whose falling apple caused Newton to formulate the laws of gravity. Ahead lies Cambridge's most famous sight, the soaring late-Gothic **King's College Chapel** ⓬. King's College itself faces King's Parade, where students bustle in and out of the coffee shops; you can climb the tower of **Great St. Mary's**, the university's main church, for a glorious city view. Behind King's, the city's Backs—its riverside gardens and meadows—make their presence felt at **Trinity Hall** ⓭ and **Queens'** ⓮ colleges, both of which will lure you off the beaten path. Silver Street Bridge, by Queens', is another traditional spot to hire a chauffeured punt. To complete the circuit, regain King's Parade and walk south, down to where it becomes Trumpington Street. Call in at the Church of Little St. Mary and pause at the monument to the Washington family on the wall to your left just inside the door. You will then pass Peterhouse, where you started. Just beyond, the **Fitzwilliam** ⓯ is Cambridge's finest museum, with superb art and classical collections, or you can recuperate in the **University Botanic Gardens** ⓰, at least 10 minutes beyond, off Trumpington Street on Bateman Street. Ah, academia!

TIMING You can walk this route in two hours, but it's easy to spend a full day here if you visit the museums and explore some of the colleges. Note that many museums are closed Monday. It's possible to tour the colleges and grounds much of the year except during exams in May and June, but call the Cambridge Tourist Information Centre or the specific college to check in advance; opening hours can be complicated.

What to See

❺ **Christ's College.** To see the way a college has grown over the centuries you could not do better than visit here. The main gateway bears the enormous coat of arms of its patroness, Lady Margaret Beaufort, mother of Henry VII, who established the institution in 1505. It leads into a fine courtyard, with the chapel framed by an ancient magnolia. In the dining hall hang portraits of John Milton and Charles Darwin, two of the college's more famous students. Admitted in 1625 at the age of 16, Milton resided here in a first-floor room on the first stair on the north side of the first court. The unfolding architecture leads you past a fellows' building credited to Inigo Jones, to the spacious garden (once the haunt of Milton), and finally to a modern zigguratlike confection. ⊠ *St. Andrew's St.* ☎ *01223/334900* ⊕ *www.christs.cam.ac.uk* ☉ *Term time, except exam period, daily 9:30–4:30; July–Sept., daily 9:30–noon.*

4 Emmanuel College. The master hand of architect Christopher Wren (1632–1723) is evident throughout much of Cambridge, particularly at Emmanuel, built on the site of a Dominican friary, where he designed the chapel and colonnade. A stained-glass window in the chapel has a likeness of John Harvard, founder of Harvard University, who studied here. The college, founded in 1584, was an early center of Puritan learning; a number of the Pilgrims were Emmanuel alumni, and they remembered their alma mater in naming Cambridge, Massachusetts. ⊠ *St. Andrew's St.* ☎ *01223/334200* ⊕ *www.emma.cam.ac.uk* ☉ *Daily 9–6, except exam period.*

★ **15 Fitzwilliam Museum.** In a classical revival building renowned for its grand Corinthian portico, the Fitzwilliam, founded by the seventh Viscount Fitzwilliam of Merrion in 1816, has one of Britain's most outstanding collections of art (including paintings by John Constable, Gainsborough, the Pre-Raphaelites, and the French impressionists) and antiquities. The opulent interior displays its treasures to marvelous effect, with the Egyptian section in the lower gallery particularly noteworthy. Exhibits range from rare sculptures dating back to the Chinese Han dynasty of the 3rd century BC, inch-high figurines, and burial goods to mummies, painted coffins, and stone inscriptions. Besides its archaeological collections, the Fitzwilliam contains a large display of English Staffordshire and other pottery, as well as a fascinating room full of armor and muskets. ⊠ *Trumpington St.* ☎ *01223/332900* ⊕ *www.fitzmuseum.cam.ac.uk* ☑ *Free* ☉ *Tues.–Sat. 10–5, Sun. 2:15–5; guided tours Sun. at 2:45.*

Folk Museum. In a city where "gown" often dominates "town," this museum adjacent to Kettle's Yard redresses the balance a little. In the former 16th-century White Horse Inn, Cambridgeshire's folk history is brought to life in eight rooms that display crafts, toys, trade utensils, paintings, and domestic paraphernalia in glorious profusion. ⊠ *2–3 Castle St.* ☎ *01223/355159* ⊕ *www.folkmuseum.org.uk* ☑ *£2.50* ☉ *Apr.–Sept., Mon.–Sat. 10:30–5, Sun. 2–5; Oct.–Mar., Tues.–Sat. 10:30–5, Sun. 2–5.*

off the beaten path

GRANTCHESTER – This pretty little village 2 mi up the river from the center of Cambridge is a delightful walk or bicycle ride along a signposted riverside path through college-playing fields and the Grantchester Meadows. It was put on the map by its famous son, Rupert Brooke, whose line "Stands the church clock at ten to three? And is there honey still for tea?" is from his poem *The Old Vicarage, Grantchester.* You also can reach the village enjoyably, if challengingly, by punt upstream along the Cam.

Great St. Mary's. Known as the "university church," Great St. Mary's has its origins in the 11th century, although the current building dates from 1478. The main reason to visit is to climb the 113-foot tower, which has a superb view over the colleges and the colorful marketplace. ⊠ *Market Hill, King's Parade* ☎ *01223/350914* ☑ *Free, tower £2* ☉ *Mon.–Sat. 9:30–5:30, Sun. noon–5:30.*

off the beaten path

IMPERIAL WAR MUSEUM DUXFORD – The buildings and grounds of this former airfield, now Europe's leading aviation museum, house a remarkable collection of 180 aircraft from Europe and the United States. You can trace technological developments as well as military history through the various exhibits. The Land Warfare Hall holds tanks and other military vehicles. The American Air Museum, in a striking Norman Foster–designed building, contains American combat aircraft. It honors the 30,000 Americans who were killed in action flying from Britain during World War II; Duxford itself was the headquarters of the 78th Fighter Group. Check in advance for air shows (extra charge). The museum is 10 mi south of Cambridge, and a shuttle bus runs throughout the day from Cambridge's Crowne Plaza hotel to the Cambridge train station and Duxford. ⊠ *A505, Duxford* ☎ *01223/835000* ⊕ *www.iwm.org.uk* ▣ *£8* ⊙ *Mid-Mar.–Oct., daily 10–6; Nov.–mid-Mar., daily 10–4.*

❼ Jesus College. Unique in Cambridge, the spacious grounds of Jesus College incorporate cloisters, a remnant of the nunnery of St. Radegund, which existed on the site before the college was founded in 1496. Cloister Court exudes a quiet medieval charm, an attribute evident in the adjacent chapel, another part of the nunnery. Victorian restoration of the building includes some Pre-Raphaelite stained-glass windows and ceiling designs by William Morris. ⊠ *Jesus La.* ☎ *01223/339339* ⊕ *www.jesus.cam.ac.uk* ⊙ *Daily 8–7, except exam period.*

❾ Kettle's Yard. Originally a private house owned by a former curator of London's Tate galleries, Kettle's Yard contains a fine collection of 20th-century art, sculpture, furniture, and decorative arts, including works by Henry Moore, Barbara Hepworth, and Henri Gaudier-Brzeska. One gallery shows changing exhibitions of modern art and crafts, and weekly concerts (term time only) and lectures attract an eclectic mix of enthusiasts. ⊠ *Castle St.* ☎ *01223/352124* ⊕ *www.kettlesyard.co.uk* ▣ *Free* ⊙ *House Mar.–Aug., Tues.–Sun. 1:30–4:30; Sept.–Feb., Tues.–Sun. 2–4; Gallery Tues.–Sun. 11:30–5.*

★ ⓬ King's College Chapel. It seems almost impossible to single out one building in Cambridge from the many that are masterpieces, but King's College Chapel is perhaps the supreme architectural work in the city. Based on Sainte Chapelle, the 13th-century private royal chapel in Paris, it was constructed toward the end of the 15th century. Henry VI, the king after whom the college is named, oversaw the work. This was the last period before the classical architecture of the ancient Greeks and Romans, then being rediscovered by the Italians, began to make its influence felt in northern Europe. King's College Chapel is thus the final and perhaps most glorious flowering of Perpendicular Gothic in Britain. From the outside, the most prominent features are the expanses of glass, the massive flying buttresses, and the fingerlike spires that line the length of the building. Inside, the most obvious impression is of great space—the chapel has been described as "the noblest barn in Europe"—and of light flooding in from its huge windows. The brilliantly colored bosses (carved panels at the intersections of the roof ribs) are particularly intense, although hard to see without binoculars. An exhibition in the chantries, or side chapels, explains more about the chapel's construction. Behind the altar is *The Adoration of the Magi,* an enormous and typically lively painting by Peter Paul Rubens, originally painted for a convent in Louvain. Every Christmas Eve, a festival of carols sung by the chapel's famous choir is broadcast worldwide from here. Past students of King's College include the novelist E. M. Forster, the economist John Maynard Keynes, and the World War I poet Rupert Brooke. ⊠ *King's Parade* ☎ *01223/331100 college; 01223/331155 chapel* ⊕ *www.kings.cam.ac.uk* ▣ *Chapel £3.50* ⊙ *Oct.–June, weekdays 9:30–3:30, Sat. 9:30–3:15, Sun. 1:15–2:15; July–Sept., Mon.–Sat. 9:30–4:30, Sun. 1:15–2:15 and 5–5:30. Times may vary; phone in advance.*

8 Magdalene College. Across Magdalene (pronounced *maud*-lin) Bridge, a cast-iron 1820 structure, lies the only one of the older colleges to be sited across the river. Magdalene Street itself is narrow and traffic-heavy, but there's relative calm inside the pretty redbrick courts. It was a hostel for Benedictine monks for more than 100 years before the college was founded in 1542. In the second court, the college's **Pepys Library** (☉ Mid-Apr.–Aug., Mon.–Sat. 11:30–12:30 and 2:30–3:30; Oct.–mid-Mar., Mon.–Sat. 2:30–3:30)—labeled *Bibliotecha Pepysiana*—contains the books and desk of the famed 17th-century diarist Samuel Pepys. ⊠ *Magdalene St.* ☎ *01223/332100* ⊕ *www.magd.cam.ac.uk* ☒ *Free* ☉ *Daily 9–6, except exam period.*

need a break? The 600-year-old **Pickerel Inn** (⊠ 30 Magdalene St. ☎ 01223/355068), one of the city's oldest pubs, makes for a nice stop for a soothing afternoon pint of real ale or lager and a wee snack of greasy chips. Watch for the low beams.

3 Museum of Archaeology and Anthropology. The university maintains some fine museums in its research halls on Downing Street—the wonder is that they are not better known to visitors. Geological collections at the Sedgwick Museum and the exhibits at the Zoological Museum are typically extensive, but be sure to see the Museum of Archaeology and Anthropology, which houses a superb collection of ethnographic objects brought back by early explorers, including members of Captain Cook's pioneering voyages to the Pacific. ⊠ *Downing St.* ☎ *01223/333516* ⊕ *museum-server.archanth.cam.ac.uk* ☒ *Free* ☉ *Sept.–May, Tues.–Sat. 2–4:30; June–Aug., Tues.–Fri. 10–4:30, Sat. 2–4:30.*

2 Pembroke College. Established in 1347, Pembroke has some buildings dating from the 14th century in its first court. On the south side, Christopher Wren's chapel—his first major commission, completed in 1665—looks like a distinctly modern intrusion. You can walk through the college, around a delightful garden, and past the fellows' bowling green. Outside the library you can't miss the resplendent, toga-clad statue of the precocious William Pitt the Younger; he came up to Pembroke at age 15 and was appointed prime minister of Great Britain in 1783, when he was just 24. ⊠ *Trumpington St.* ☎ *01223/338100* ⊕ *www.pem.cam.ac.uk* ☉ *Daily 9–dusk, except exam period.*

1 Peterhouse College. The bishop of Ely founded Cambridge's oldest college in 1281. Parts of the dining hall date from 1290, although the hall is most notable for powerful stained glass by William Morris and his contemporaries. The adjacent church of Little St. Mary's served as the college chapel until 1632, when the current late-Gothic chapel was built. ⊠ *Trumpington St.* ☎ *01223/338200* ⊕ *www.pet.cam.ac.uk* ☉ *Daily 9–5, except exam period.*

14 Queens' College. One of the most eye-catching colleges is Queens', named after the respective consorts of Henry VI and Edward IV. Founded in 1448, the college is tucked away on Queens' Lane, next to the wide lawns that lead down from King's College to the Backs. The secluded "cloister court" looks untouched since its completion in the 1540s. Queens' distinctive masterpiece is the **Mathematical Bridge** (best seen from the Silver Street road bridge), an arched wooden structure that was originally held together without fastenings. The current bridge, dating from 1902, is securely bolted. ⊠ *Queens' La.* ☎ *01223/335511* ⊕ *www.quns.cam.ac.uk* ☒ *£1* ☉ *Apr.–Oct., daily 10–4:30; Nov.–Mar., daily 10–4, except exam period.*

⑩ St. John's College. Two mythical beasts called "yales," with the bodies of antelopes and heads of goats, hold up the coat of arms and guard the gateway of Cambridge's second-largest college. St. John's was founded in 1511 by Henry VII's mother, Lady Margaret Beaufort. Its structures lie on two sites: from the main entrance, walk to the left through the ancient courts—with their turrets, sculpted windows, and clock towers—to where a famous copy of the Bridge of Sighs in Venice reaches across the Cam to the mock-Gothic New Court (1825), whose white crenellations have earned it the nickname "the wedding cake." If you walk through until you reach the riverbank, you'll be able to stroll along the Backs and frame photographs of the elegant bridge (and less-than-elegant New Court buildings). ⊠ *St. John's St.* ☎ *01223/338600* ⊕ *www.joh.cam.ac.uk* ✍ *£1.75* ☉ *Apr.–Oct., weekdays 10–5, Sat. 9:30–5, except exam period.*

❻ Sidney Sussex College. Passing largely unnoticed on busy Sidney Street, Sidney Sussex is smaller than many colleges, yet it has interesting 17th- and 18th-century buildings, most of which were sadly given mock-Gothic "improvements" in 1832. Oliver Cromwell was a student here in 1616; the Hall contains his portrait, and his head has been buried in a secret location in the chapel since 1960. Cromwell charged his painter to include "all these roughnesses, pimples, and warts." ⊠ *Sidney St.* ☎ *01223/ 338800* ⊕ *www.sid.cam.ac.uk* ☉ *Daily 9–5, except exam period.*

⑪ Trinity College. Founded in 1546 by Henry VIII, Trinity replaced a 14th-century educational foundation and is the largest college in either Cambridge or Oxford, with nearly 700 undergraduates. Many of the buildings match its size, not least its 17th-century "great court." Here the massive gatehouse holds a giant clock that strikes each hour with high and low notes. The college's greatest masterpiece is Christopher Wren's library, colonnaded and seemingly constructed with as much light as stone, with wood carving by the 17th-century master Grinling Gibbons. Past alumni include Sir Isaac Newton, William Thackeray, and Lords George Byron, Alfred Tennyson, and Thomas Macaulay. Prince Charles was an undergraduate here in the late 1960s. ⊠ *St. John's St.* ☎ *01223/ 338400* ⊕ *www.trin.cam.ac.uk* ✍ *£1.75, Mar.–Oct.* ☉ *College Mar.–Oct., daily 10–5, except exam period; library weekdays noon–2, Sat. in term time 10:30–12:30; hall and chapel open but hrs vary.*

⑬ Trinity Hall College. The green parkland of the Backs is best appreciated from Trinity College's 14th-century neighbor, Trinity Hall, where you can sit on a wall by the river and watch students in punts maneuver under the ancient ornamental bridges of Clare and King's. Access to the river is down Trinity Lane, off Trinity Street. The **Senate House** (⊠ King's Parade), which stands between Clare College and Trinity Hall, is one of the few strictly university buildings not part of a particular college. A classical building of the 1720s, it's still used for graduation ceremonies and other university events. The building is closed to the public, but if the gate is open you can wander into the court and grounds. ⊠ *Trinity La.* ☎ *01223/332500* ⊕ *www.trinhall.cam.ac.uk* ☉ *Daily 9:15–noon and 2–5:30, except exam period and summer term.*

⑯ University Botanic Gardens. Laid out in 1846, these gardens contain, in addition to many rare specimens, a rock garden. The gardens are a five-minute walk from the Fitzwilliam Museum. ⊠ *Cory Lodge, Bateman St.* ☎ *01223/336265* ⊕ *www.botanic.cam.ac.uk* ✍ *£2.50* ☉ *Garden Nov.–Jan., daily 10–4; Feb. and Oct., daily 10–5; Mar.–Sept., daily 10–6; Glasshouses Feb.–Oct., daily 10–4:30; Nov.–Jan., daily 10–3:45.*

Where to Eat

★ **£££–££££** ✕ **Midsummer House.** An elegant restaurant beside the River Cam, the gray-brick Midsummer House has a comfortable conservatory. Set menus for lunch and dinner list robust yet sophisticated French and Mediterranean dishes. Choices might include tender roast spring lamb or seared sea scallops, adorned with inventively presented vegetables. ⊠ *Midsummer Common* ☎ *01223/369299* ⌂ *Reservations essential* ⊟ *AE, MC, V* ☉ *Closed Mon. No lunch Sat., no dinner Sun.*

££–£££ ✕ **Loch Fyne Oyster Restaurant.** Part of a Scottish chain that both harvests oysters and runs seafood restaurants, this airy, casual place across the street from the Fitzwilliam Museum is open for breakfast, lunch, and dinner. The deservedly popular oysters and other seafood and fish—mussels, salmon, tuna, and more—are fresh and well prepared, including the dauntingly large seafood platters. ⊠ *37 Trumpington St.* ☎ *01223/362433* ⊟ *AE, MC, V.*

££–£££ ✕ **Three Horseshoes.** This early-19th-century pub-restaurant in a thatched cottage has additional dining space in the conservatory. The tempting, beautifully presented dishes focus on modern British cuisine; those fashionable accoutrements sun-dried tomatoes, polenta, and olives accompany char-grilled meats or roast fish. It's 3 mi west of Cambridge, about a 10-minute taxi ride. ⊠ *High St., Madingley* ☎ *01954/210221* ⊟ *AE, DC, MC, V.*

£–££ ✕ **Copper Kettle.** Over the years, students have come to love this coffee shop, where they discuss work, life, and love over frothy coffees, sticky buns, and sandwiches. It's never going to win any gastronomic awards, but for a slice of real university life (and a fine view of King's College) it can't be beat. Closing time is 5:30 PM. ⊠ *King's Parade* ☎ *01223/ 365068* ⊟ *No credit cards* ☉ *No dinner.*

£ ✕ **Dojo Noodle Bar.** Many highlights of Asian cuisine are represented at this trendy spot near the river. If the different kinds of wheat, rice, or mung bean noodles aren't your thing, try a rice dish or pot stickers, tempura prawns, or chicken yakitori. ⊠ *2 Millers Yard, Mill La., off Trumpington St.* ☎ *01223/363471* ⊟ *AE, MC, V.*

Where to Stay

There aren't many hotels downtown. For more (and cheaper) options, consider one of the many guest houses on the arterial roads and in the suburbs. These start at £18–£25 per person per night and can be booked through the tourist information center.

£££££ ▦ **De Vere University Arms Hotel.** Elegant and sympathetically modernized, the 19th-century De Vere is a top choice in the city center. Space is at a premium in central Cambridge, and it shows here: the traditionally furnished guest rooms are comfortable but not overly large. Many rooms have views of Parker's Piece, the green backing the hotel, although you'll pay slightly more for these; Parker's Bar also overlooks the green. The central lounge provides a comfortable place for afternoon tea by the fireplace. Guests can use a health club 2 mi away. ⊠ *Regent St., CB2 1AD* ☎ *01223/351241* 🖷 *01223/315256* ⊕ *www.devere.com* ➳ *116 rooms, 1 suite* ⌂ *Restaurant, room service, in-room data ports, cable TV with movies, 2 bars, lounge, business services, meeting rooms, parking (fee), some pets allowed (fee)* ⊟ *AE, DC, MC, V.*

£££££ ▦ **Garden Moat House Hotel.** Set among the colleges in 3 acres of private grounds, this modern hotel makes the most of its peaceful riverside location. The gardens, bar, and conservatories all have river views, as do most rooms. Request one when you reserve, because some rooms at the rear of the L-shape hotel have less desirable views. As with many chain hotels, the service and standards are high, but the architecture and furnishings are not particularly special. Ask about lower leisure rates, which include breakfast. ⊠ *Granta Pl. and Mill La., CB2 1RT* ☎ 01223/ 259988 🖷 01223/316605 ⊕ *www.moathousehotels.com* ⊷ *117 rooms* ♘ *Restaurant, room service, minibars, cable TV, indoor pool, sauna, steam room, bar, lounge, Internet, business services, meeting rooms, parking (fee), no-smoking rooms; no a/c in some rooms* ⊟ *AE, DC, MC, V.*

££££–£££££   🏨 **Crowne Plaza.** In the middle of historic Cambridge, this late-20th-century building doesn't mesh well with its neighbors but does provide the high standard of accommodation you expect from this chain. Modern amenities such as a writing desk and trouser press enhance the colorful, contemporary rooms. ⊠ *Downing St., CB2 3DT* ☎ 01223/464466 🖷 01223/464440 ⊕ *www.cambridge.crowneplaza.com* ⊷ *198 rooms* ♘ *Restaurant, room service, in-room data ports, in-room safes, minibars, cable TV with movies, gym, sauna, bar, lobby lounge, pub, babysitting, dry cleaning, laundry service, concierge, business services, meeting rooms, parking (fee), no-smoking rooms; no a/c in some rooms* ⊟ *AE, DC, MC, V* ❏ *BP.*

££££   🏨 **Meadowcroft Hotel.** This Victorian house, with its pretty rooms and the stylish Brackenhurst Restaurant, is a pleasant 1-mi walk from the center of Cambridge. English antiques and print fabrics furnish the bedrooms, which overlook a garden. The hotel offers (extra charge) a horse-drawn carriage ride around Cambridge or the nearby village of Grantchester that includes afternoon tea and a game of croquet. ⊠ *16 Trumpington Rd., CB2 2EX* ☎ 01223/346120 🖷 01223/346138 ⊕ *www.meadowcrofthotel.co.uk* ⊷ *12 rooms* ♘ *Restaurant, room service, in-room data ports, cable TV, bicycles, croquet, bar, lounge, meeting room, free parking, some pets allowed; no a/c, no smoking* ⊟ *AE, MC, V* ❏ *BP.*

£££   🏨 **Arundel House Hotel.** Elegantly proportioned, this Victorian row hotel has a fine location overlooking the River Cam, with Jesus Green in the background. The comfortable bedrooms, modern in style, have locally made mahogany furniture. Meals and afternoon teas are available in the Victorian-style conservatory, where rattan chairs, trailing plants, and a patio garden add a certain cachet. The special weekend rates are an excellent value. ⊠ *53 Chesterton Rd., CB4 3AN* ☎ 01223/367701 🖷 01223/367721 ⊕ *www.arundelhousehotels.co.uk* ⊷ *102 rooms* ♘ *2 restaurants, bar, lounge, meeting rooms, free parking, no-smoking rooms; no a/c* ⊟ *AE, DC, MC, V* ❏ *CP.*

££   🏨 **Ashley Hotel.** Sister to the Arundel House Hotel, this pleasant smaller establishment near the center of Cambridge was converted from a private home. Rooms are decent, and you can take advantage of the nearby facilities of Arundel House. ⊠ *74 Chesterton Rd., CB4 1ER* ☎ 01223/ 350059 🖷 01223/350900 ⊕ *www.arundelhousehotels.co.uk* ⊷ *16 rooms* ♘ *Free parking; no a/c, no smoking* ⊟ *AE, DC, MC, V* ❏ *BP.*

£–££   🏨 **Sleeperz.** A low-key budget option, this hostelry right outside the train station has small bedrooms with natural wood floors, white walls, and futon beds. Most double rooms have bunk beds. The sparsely furnished accommodations are recommended only for those who want a cheap, clean place to sleep. ⊠ *Station Rd., CB1 2TZ* ☎ 01223/304050 🖷 01223/357286 ⊕ *www.sleeperz.com* ⊷ *25 rooms* ♘ *Free parking; no a/c, no room phones, no smoking* ⊟ *MC, V* ❏ *CP.*

Nightlife & the Arts

Nightlife

The city's pubs provide the mainstay of Cambridge's nightlife, particularly when students are in town. The **Eagle** (⊠ Bene't St. ☎ 01223/

505020), first among equals, is a 16th-century coaching inn with several bars and a cobbled courtyard that's lost none of its old-time character. It's extremely busy on weekends. **Fort St. George** (✉ Midsummer Common ☎ 01223/354327), which overlooks the university boathouses, gets the honors for riverside views. The **Free Press** (✉ Prospect Row ☎ 01223/368337) is that rare beast, a nonsmoking pub, and all the better for it, attracting a fresh-faced student rowing clientele.

The Arts

Cambridge supports its own symphony orchestra, and regular musical events are held in many colleges, especially those with large chapels. **King's College Chapel** (☎ 01223/331447) has evensong services Tuesday–Saturday at 5:30, Sunday at 3:30. The **Corn Exchange** (✉ Wheeler St. ☎ 01223/357851), beautifully restored, presents concerts (classical and rock), stand-up comedy, musicals, opera, and ballet.

The **ADC Theatre** (✉ Park St. ☎ 01223/503333) hosts mainly student and fringe theater productions, including the famous Cambridge Footlights revue, training ground for much comic talent since the 1970s. The **Arts Theatre** (✉ 6 St. Edward's Passage ☎ 01223/5033333), the city's main repertory theater, was built by economist John Maynard Keynes in 1936 and supports a full program of theater, concerts, and events. It also has a good ground-floor bar and two restaurants, including the conservatory-style Roof Garden.

The **Cambridge Folk Festival** (☎ 01223/357851 ⊕ www.cam-folkfest.co.uk), spread over a late July weekend at Cherry Hinton Hall, attracts major international folk singers and groups. Camping is available on the park grounds—reservations are essential.

Sports & the Outdoors

Biking

It's fun to explore Cambridge by bike. **Geoff's Bike Hire** (✉ 65 Devonshire Rd. ☎ 01223/365629), a short walk from the railroad station, charges from £8 per day and £15 per week, or £5 for up to three hours. Advance reservations are essential in July and August. Geoff's also runs guided cycle tours of Cambridge.

Punting

You can rent punts at several places, notably at Silver Street Bridge–Mill Lane, at Magdalene Bridge, and from outside the Rat and Parrot pub on Thompson's Lane on Jesus Green. Hourly rental costs about £12 (and requires a deposit of £60). Chauffeured punting on the River Cam is also possible at most rental places. Around £5 per head is the usual rate, and your chauffeur will likely be a Cambridge student. **Scudamore's Punting Co.** (✉ Mill La. and Quayside ☎ 01223/359750) rents chauffeured and self-drive punts.

Shopping

Cambridge is a main shopping area for a wide region, and it has all the usual chain stores, many in the Grafton Centre and Lion's Yard shopping precincts. More interesting are the specialty stores found among the colleges in the center of Cambridge, especially in and around Rose Crescent and King's Parade. Bookshops, including antiquarian stores, are Cambridge's pride and joy.

All Saints Garden Art & Craft Market (✉ Trinity St.) displays the wares of local artists outdoors. **Ryder & Amies** (✉ 22 King's Parade ☎ 01223/350371) carries official university wear and even straw boaters.

CloseUp

PUNTING ON THE CAM

To punt is to maneuver a flat-bottomed, wooden, gondolalike boat—in this case, through the shallow River Cam along the verdant Backs behind the colleges of the University of Cambridge. One benefit of this popular activity is that you get a better view of the ivy-covered walls from the water than from the front. Mastery of the sport lies in your ability to control a 15-foot pole, used to propel the punt. Get a bottle of wine, some food, and a small group of people, and you'll find yourself

saying things such as, "It doesn't get any better than this." One piece of advice: if your pole gets stuck, let go. You can use the smaller paddle to go back and retrieve it. The lazier at heart may prefer chauffeured punting. You may even get a fairly informative spiel on the colleges. Some rental places also arrange chauffeured punts, complete with food and drink, and illuminated punts for evening outings.

The **Cambridge University Press bookshop** (⊠ 1 Trinity St. ☎ 01223/333333) stands on the oldest bookstore site in Britain, with books sold here since the 16th century. **Heffer's** (⊠ 20 Trinity St. ☎ 01223/568568 ⊠ Children's branch 30 Trinity St. ☎01223/568551) is one of the world's biggest bookstores, many rare or imported books.

The **Bookshop** (⊠ 24 Magdalene St. ☎ 01223/362457) is the best local secondhand bookshop. **G. David** (⊠ 3 and 16 St. Edward's Passage ☎ 01223/354619), near the Arts Theatre, sells antiquarian books. The **Haunted Bookshop** (⊠ 9 St. Edward's Passage ☎ 01223/312913) carries a great selection of old, illustrated books and British classics.

FROM ELY TO BURY ST. EDMUNDS

This central area of towns and villages within easy reach of Cambridge is testament to the amazing changeability of the English landscape. The town of Ely is set in an eerie landscape of flat, empty, and apparently endless fenland, or marsh. Only a few miles south and east into Suffolk, however, all this changes to pastoral landscapes of—if not rolling, then gently undulating—hills, clusters of villages, and towns whose prettiness is easier to appreciate.

Ely

🔟 *16 mi north of Cambridge.*

Ely is the "capital" of the fens, the center of what used to be a separate county called the Isle of Ely (literally "island of eels"). Until the land was drained in the 17th century, Ely was surrounded by treacherous marshland, which inhabitants crossed wearing stilts. Today Wicken Fen, a nature reserve 9 mi southeast of town (off A1123), preserves the last remaining example of fenland in an undrained state. Enveloped by fields of wheat, sugar beets, and carrots, Ely is a small, dense town dominated by its cathedral. The shopping area and market square lie to the north and lead down to the riverside, and the medieval buildings of the cathedral grounds and the King's School (which trains cathedral choristers) spread out to the south and west. Ely's most famous resident was Oliver Cromwell, whose house is now a museum.

★ Known affectionately as the Ship of the Fens, **Ely Cathedral** can be seen for miles, towering above the flat landscape on one of the few ridges in the whole of the fens. In 1083 the Normans began work on the cathedral, which stands on the site of a Benedictine monastery founded by the Anglo-Saxon princess Etheldreda in 673. In the center of the cathedral you see a marvel of medieval construction—the unique octagonal **Lantern Tower,** a sort of stained-glass skylight of colossal proportions, built to replace the central tower after it collapsed in 1322. The cathedral is also notable for its 248-long **nave,** with its simple Norman arches and Victorian painted ceiling. Much of the decorative carving of the 14th-century **Lady Chapel** was defaced during the Reformation (mostly by knocking off the heads of the statuary), but enough of the delicate tracery remains to show its original beauty. The fan-vaulted, carved ceiling remains intact, as it was too high for the iconoclasts to reach. The cathedral's south triforium gallery houses a wonderful **Stained Glass Museum** (☎ 01353/660347 ⊕ www.sgm.abelgratis.com ☜ £3.50 ☼ May–Oct., weekdays 10:30–5, Sat. 10:30–5:30, Sun. noon–6; Nov.–Apr., weekdays and Sat. 10:30–5, Sun. noon–4:30), with exhibits up a flight of 41 steps. The museum traces the history of stained glass from medieval to Victorian to modern times, with examples from all periods. ⊠ The Gallery ☎ 01353/667735 ⊕ www.cathedral.ely.anglican. org ☜ £4.80, free on Sun., donation requested ☼ May–Sept., daily 7–7; Oct.–Apr., Mon.–Sat. 7:30–6, Sun. 7:30–5.

Oliver Cromwell's House, the half-timber medieval building that was the home of Cromwell and his family, stands in the shadows of Ely Cathedral. During the 10 years he lived here, from 1636, Cromwell was leading the rebellious Roundheads in their eventually victorious struggle against King Charles I. The house contains an exhibit on its former occupant and audiovisual presentations about Cromwell and about the draining of the local fens. It's also the site of Ely's tourist information center. ⊠ 29 St. Mary's St. ☎ 01353/662062 ☜ £2.50 ☼ Apr.–Sept., daily 10–6; Oct.–Mar., Mon.–Sat. 10–5.

Where to Stay & Eat

£££ ✕ **Old Fire Engine House.** Scrubbed pine tables fill the main dining room of this restaurant in a converted fire station near the cathedral. Another dining room, used only for overflow, has an open fireplace and a polished wood floor, and also serves as an art gallery. Among the English dishes are traditional fenland recipes such as pike baked in white wine, as well as eel pie and game in season. ⊠ 25 St. Mary's St. ☎ 01353/ 662582 ▤ MC, V ☼ Closed 2 wks at Christmas. No dinner Sun.

££–£££ ✕ **Dominique's.** A delightful little delicatessen with stripped pine floors, Dominique's serves lunch in a nonsmoking environment. Choose from quiches, salads, cakes, and a lovely selection of cheeses. You can take it all away or eat in the dining room. ⊠ 8 St. Mary's St. ☎ 01353/665011 ▤ MC, V ☼ No dinner.

££ ▥ **Cathedral House.** Run by Jenny and Robin Farndale, this Georgian house makes a pleasant overnight stop in Ely. The cozy bedrooms have antique furniture and coffeemakers, and an oriel window and handsome staircase are original features. ⊠ 17 St. Mary's St., CB7 4ER ☎ 01353/ 662124 ⊕ www.cathedralhouse.co.uk ⇋ 3 rooms, 1 cottage ⸝ No a/ c, no smoking ▤ No credit cards ¶◎¶ BP.

Saffron Walden

⑱ 30 mi south of Ely, 14 mi south of Cambridge.

Best known for its many typically East Anglian timber-frame buildings, this town owes its name to the saffron crocus fields that used to be cultivated in medieval times and processed for their dye. The common at the east end of town has a 17th-century circular earth maze, created from

space left among the crocus beds. Some buildings have elaborate par-
geting (decorative plasterwork), especially the walls of the former Sun
Inn on Church Street, which was used by Cromwell during his campaigns.

★ Palatial **Audley End House and Gardens,** a mile or so west of Saffron Walden,
is a famous example of Jacobean (early-17th-century) architecture. It
was once owned by Charles II, who bought it as a convenient place to
break his journey on the way to the Newmarket races. Remodeled in
the 18th and 19th centuries, it shows the architectural skill of Sir John
Vanbrugh, Robert Adam, and Rebecca Biagio as well as original Jacobean
work in the magnificent Great Hall. You can also walk around the park,
landscaped by Capability Brown in the 18th century, and the fine Victorian gardens. ✉ B1383 ☎ 01799/522842 ⊕ *www.english-heritage.
org.uk* ✍ *£6.95, park only £4.50* ⊙ *Apr.–Sept., Wed.–Sun., park 11–6,
house noon–5; Oct., park and house Wed.–Sun. 10–3.*

Where to Stay

££ 🏠 **Archway Guesthouse.** What must be one of the quirkiest bed-and-breakfasts in Britain embraces the early era of rock 'n' roll by packing its public rooms with rock memorabilia and toys from the 1950s and '60s.
Bedrooms are tasteful, homey, and uncluttered, and hosts Flora and Haydn
Miles are personable. ✉ *Church St., CB10 1JW* ☎ *01799/501500*
🖨 *01799/506003* ✉ *archwayguesthouse@yahoo.co.uk* ➥ *7 rooms*
⚘ *No a/c, no smoking* ▭ *No credit cards* ❙◯❙ *BP.*

en route Hedingham Castle, between Saffron Walden and Sudbury, has a
wonderful 12th-century Norman keep (main tower), built on a hill by
Aubrey de Vere and designed by the archbishop of Canterbury. The
highlight of the 110-foot-tall keep is the Banqueting Hall, which can
be viewed from the minstrels' gallery. In summer the age of
knighthood is re-created through jousting tournaments and medieval
festivals. ✉ B1058, Castle Hedingham ☎ 01787/460261 ⊕ www.
hedinghamcastle.co.uk ✍ £4, special events £5–£8 additional
⊙ Easter–Oct., daily 10–5.

Sudbury

⑲ *23 mi east of Saffron Walden, 16 mi south of Bury St. Edmunds, 14 mi
northwest of Colchester.*

An early silk-weaving industry (which still exists, on a smaller scale) as
well as the wool trade brought prosperity to Sudbury, which has three
fine Perpendicular Gothic churches and a number of half-timber houses.
Today this town of 20,000 is the largest in this part of the Stour Valley.
Its river, the Stour, was once, surprisingly, navigable to the sea, and quays
filled the town. Sudbury was Charles Dickens's model for the fictional
Eatanswill, where Mr. Pickwick stands for Parliament. Thomas Gainsborough, one of the greatest English portrait and landscape painters,
was born here in 1727; a **statue of Gainsborough** holding his palette stands
on Market Hill.

The birthplace and family home of Thomas Gainsborough (1727–88),
Gainsborough's House, is now a museum containing paintings and drawings by the artist (and reproductions of other works of his) and his contemporaries, as well as an arts center with exhibitions. Although it
presents a Georgian facade, with touches of the 18th-century neo-
Gothic style, the building is essentially Tudor. The walled garden behind
the house has a mulberry tree planted in 1620. ✉ *46 Gainsborough St.*
☎ *01787/372958* ⊕ *www.gainsborough.org* ✍ *£3* ⊙ *Apr.–Oct.,
Tues.–Sat. 10–5, Sun. 2–5; Nov.–Mar., Tues.–Sat. 10–4, Sun. 2–4.*

Where to Eat

££–£££ ✕ **Red Onion.** A former motor factory turned trendy bistro serves fixed-price lunch and dinner menus of inspired English comfort food. Try the fresh fish and soups. ✉ *57 Ballingdon St.* ☎ *01787/376777* 🖃 *MC, V.*

Long Melford

❷0 *2 mi north of Sudbury, 14 mi south of Bury St. Edmunds.*

It's easy to see how this village got its name, especially if you walk the full length of its 2-mi-long main street, which gradually broadens to include green squares and trees and finally opens into the large triangular green on the hill. Long Melford grew rich on its wool trade in the 15th century, and the town's buildings are an appealing mixture, mostly Tudor half-timber or Georgian. Many of them house antiques shops. Utility poles are banned to preserve the town's ancient look, although the massed ranks of parked cars down both sides of the street make this a fruitless exercise. Away from the main road, Long Melford returns to its resolutely late-medieval roots.

The mostly 15th-century **Holy Trinity Church,** founded by the rich clothiers of Long Melford, stands on a hill at the north end of the village. Close up, the delicate flint flush-work (shaped flints set into a pattern) and huge Perpendicular Gothic windows that take up most of the church's walls have great impact, especially because the nave is 150 feet long. Much of the superb original stained glass remains, notably the Lily Crucifix window. The Lady Chapel has an unusual interior cloister. ✉ *Main St.* ☎ *01787/310845* ⊕ *www.stedmundsbury.anglican.org/longmelford* ☉ *Daily 10–4.*

Melford Hall, distinguished from the outside by its turrets and topiaries, is an Elizabethan house with a fair number of 18th-century additions and pleasant gardens. Much of the porcelain and many other fine pieces in the house come from the *Santissima Trinidad,* a ship loaded with gifts from the emperor of China and bound for Spain that was captured by one of the house's owners in the 1700s. Children's writer Beatrix Potter, who was related to the owners, visited the house often; there's a small collection of Potter memorabilia. ✉ *Off A134* ☎ *01787/880286* ⊕ *www.nationaltrust.co.uk* 🖃 *£4.50* ☉ *Apr. and Oct., weekends 2–5:30; May–Sept., Wed.–Sun. 2–5:30.*

☙ A wide moat surrounds **Kentwell Hall,** a fine redbrick Tudor manor house with tall chimneys and domed turrets. Built between 1520 and 1550, it was heavily restored inside after a fire in the early 19th century. On some weekends from mid-April through September, costumed "servants" and "farmworkers" perform reenactments of Tudor life or life in the 1940s with great panache and detail. There's also an organic farm with rare-breed farm animals. The house is a half mile north of Long Melford Green. ✉ *Off A134* ☎ *01787/310207* ⊕ *www.kentwell.co.uk* 🖃 *£6.50, £7–£12 during special events* ☉ *Apr.–June, Sun., Wed., Thurs. noon–5; July–Sept., daily noon—5; Oct., Sun. noon–5.*

Where to Stay & Eat

£££ ✕🛏 **The Bull.** The public rooms of the Bull—stone-flagged floors, bowed oak beams, and heavy antique furniture—show its long history. Throughout, the half-timber Elizabethan building is a joy, and whether you eat in the restaurant or the bar with its huge fireplace, you'll be served with efficiency and care. Traditional roasts and a game casserole mix on the menu with modern flavors, such as mullet in a Thai curry sauce. Creature comforts and pleasant bathrooms offset the smallish size of the bedrooms, which retain their original character. ✉ *Hall St., CO10 9JG*

☎ *01787/378494* 🖷 *01787/880307* ⊕ *www.oldenglish.co.uk* ⇋ *23 rooms, 2 suites ♿ Restaurant, bar, lounge, meeting rooms, some pets allowed, no-smoking rooms; no a/c* ⊟ *AE, DC, MC, V* ⍾ *BP.*

Lavenham

㉑ 4 mi northeast of Long Melford, 10 mi south of Bury St. Edmunds.

Fodor'sChoice
★

Virtually unchanged since the height of its wealth in the 15th and 16th centuries, Lavenham is one of the most perfectly preserved examples of a Tudor village in England today. The weavers' and wool merchants' houses occupy not just one show street but most of the town. These are timber-frame in black oak, the main posts looking as if they could last another 400 years. The town has many examples of typical Suffolk pink buildings, in hues from pale pink to apricot. The timber-frame **Guildhall of Corpus Christi** (1529), the most spectacular building in Lavenham, dominates Market Place, a remarkably preserved square with barely a foot in the present. The guildhall is open as a museum of the medieval wool trade. ⊠ *Market Pl.* ☎ *01787/247646* ⊕ *www.nationaltrust.org.uk* 🎟 *£3.50* ⊘ *Mar. and Nov., weekends 11–4; Apr. and Oct., Wed.–Sun. 11–5; May–Sept., daily 11–5.*

The timber-frame **Little Hall,** a former wool merchant's house, shows the building's progress from its creation in the 14th century to its subsequent "modernization" through the 17th century. ⊠ *Market Pl.* ☎ *01787/ 247179* 🎟 *£1.50* ⊘ *Easter–Oct., Wed., Thurs., and weekends 2–5:30.*

A splendid Elizabethan building, the **Swan Hotel** (⊠ High St.) had a long history as a coaching inn and in World War II served as the special pub for the U.S. Air Force's 48th Bomber Group, whose memorabilia cover the walls of the bar. The hotel incorporates the former **Wool Hall,** torn down in 1913 but reassembled at the request of Princess Louise, sister of George V. In 1962, it was joined to the neighboring Swan.

The grand 15th-century Perpendicular **Church of St. Peter and St. Paul** (⊠ Church St.), set apart from the village on a hill, was built with wool money by cloth merchant Thomas Spring between 1480 and 1520. The height of its tower (141 feet) was meant to surpass those of the neighboring churches—and perhaps to impress rival towns. The rest of the church is perfectly proportioned, with intricate woodcarving.

Where to Stay & Eat

££ ✕ **The Angel.** This popular spot overlooks Lavenham's picture-book main square. Modern British cuisine is the draw here, and the specialty of the house—home-smoked fish—earns rave reviews. You can also just sit a spell at the scrubbed pine tables to enjoy one of the local beers on tap. Eight guest rooms are available for about £75 for a double. ⊠ *Market Sq.* ☎ *01787/247388* ⊟ *AE, MC, V* ♿ *Reservations essential.*

£ ✕ **48.** You can shop in the front gallery for locally made jewelry and arts and crafts before you retire to the back room for morning coffee, a vegetarian lunch (noon–2:30), or afternoon cake. The staff is cheerful and the mood relaxed and artsy. ⊠ *High St.* ☎ *01787/248542* ⊟ *MC, V* ⊘ *No dinner.*

££–£££ ✕▣ **Great House.** This 15th-century building on the medieval market square is the town's finest restaurant with rooms. Run by Régis and Martine Crépy, the dining room (reservations essential; closed January) has a changing fixed-price menu of European fare with a French touch. From the fireplace and wooden floors of the restaurant to the walled courtyard garden, dining is a pleasure. The spacious bedrooms have sloping floors, beamed ceilings, and antique furnishings. ⊠ *Market Pl., CO10 9QZ* ☎ *01787/247431* 🖷 *01787/248007* ⊕ *www.greathouse.co.uk*

↝ *5 rooms* ♿ *Restaurant, bar, lounge, baby-sitting, Internet, some pets allowed, no-smoking rooms; no a/c* 🖃 *AE, MC, V* ⦿❘ *BP.*

££££-£ 🏨 **Swan Hotel.** This half-timber 14th-century lodging has aging timbers, rambling public rooms, and open fires. Along corridors so low that cushions are strategically placed on beams, most of the individually styled bedrooms have rich oak cabinets, original wood paneling, and CD players. Bathrooms have been fashioned around ancient timbers and hidden rooms. The restaurant, which has its own minstrels' gallery, serves traditional English cuisine. Full-board and weekend packages can be good deals. ⊠ *High St., CO10 9QA* ☎ *01787/247477* 🖷 *01787/248286* ⊕ *www.heritage-hotels.com* ↝ *49 rooms, 2 suites* ♿ *Restaurant, in-room data ports, minibars, 2 bars, meeting room, some pets allowed (fee); no a/c* 🖃 *AE, DC, MC, V.*

★ £££-££££ 🏨 **Lavenham Priory.** You can immerse yourself in Lavenham's Tudor history at this impressive B&B in a sprawling house that dates in part to the 13th century. The beamed great hall, sitting room (with TV and VCR), and 3 acres of gardens are great places to relax, and a walled herb garden is the scene for evening drinks in warm weather. Prints and wood furnishings fill the beamed bedrooms; each has oak floors and ancient timbered ceilings, and some have four-posters. Reserve well in advance. ⊠ *Water St., CO10 9RW* ☎ *01787/247404* 🖷 *01787/248472* ⊕ *www. lavenhampriory.co.uk* ↝ *5 rooms, 1 suite* ♿ *Lounge; no a/c, no room phones, no kids under 10, no smoking* 🖃 *MC, V* ⦿❘ *BP.*

Bury St. Edmunds

★ ㉒ *10 mi north of Lavenham, 28 mi east of Cambridge.*

Bury St. Edmunds owes its name, and indeed its existence, to Edmund, the last king of East Anglia and medieval patron saint of England, who was hacked to death by marauding Danes in 869. He was subsequently canonized, and his shrine attracted pilgrims, settlement, and commerce. In the 11th century the erection of a great Norman abbey (now only ruins) confirmed the town's importance as a religious center. Robert Adam designed the town hall in 1774. The Georgian streetscape helps make the town one of the area's prettiest, and the nearby Greene King Westgate Brewery adds the smell of sweet hops to the air.

A walk along **Angel Hill** is a journey through the history of Bury St. Edmunds. Along one side, the Abbey Gate, cathedral, Norman Gate Tower, and St. Mary's church make up a continuous display of medieval architecture. Elegant Georgian houses line Angel Hill on the side opposite St. Mary's Church; these include the **Athenaeum**, an 18th-century social and cultural meeting place, which has a fine Adam-style ballroom. The splendid **Angel Hotel** (⊠ 3 Angel Hill) is the scene of Sam Weller's meeting with Job Trotter in Dickens's *Pickwick Papers*. Dickens stayed here while he was giving readings at the Athenaeum.

Originally three churches stood within the walls of the Abbey of St. Edmunds, but only two have survived, including **St. Mary's,** built in the 15th century. It has a blue-and-gold embossed "wagon" (barrel-shape) roof over the choir. Mary Tudor, Henry VIII's sister and queen of France, is buried here. ⊠ *Angel Hill at Honey Hill* ☎ *01284/706668* ⊙ *Daily 10–3; call to confirm.*

St. Edmundsbury Cathedral dates from the 15th century, but the brilliant paint on its ceiling and the stained-glass windows gleaming like jewels are the result of 19th-century restoration by the architect Sir Gilbert Scott. Don't miss the memorial (near the altar) to an event in 1214, when the barons of England gathered here to take an oath to force King John to grant the Magna Carta. The cathedral's original Abbey Gate was destroyed in a riot, and it was rebuilt in the 14th century on defensive lines—you can see the arrow slits. ⊠ *Angel Hill* ☎ *01284/754933* ⊕ *www.stedscathedral.co.uk* ✉ *Free, suggested donation £2* ☉ *June–Aug., daily 8–7; Sept.–May, daily 8–6.*

The **Abbey Ruins and Botanical Gardens** are all that remain of the Abbey of Bury St. Edmunds, which fell during Henry VIII's dissolution of the monasteries. The Benedictine abbey's enormous scale is evident in the surviving Norman Gate Tower on Angel Hill; besides this, only the fortified Abbot's Bridge over the River Lark and a few ruins remain. The **Bury St. Edmunds Tourist Information Centre** (⊠ 6 Angel Hill ☎ 01284/764667 ✉ Audio tour £3 ☉ Easter–Oct., Mon.–Sat. 9:30–5:30, Sun. 10–3; Nov.–Easter, weekdays 10–4, Sat. 10-1) rents a helpful audio tour of the ruins, narrated by the fictitious Brother Jocelin de Brakelond. There are also explanatory plaques amid the ruins, which are now the site of the **Abbey Botanical Gardens,** with roses, elegant hedges, and rare trees, including a Chinese tree of heaven planted in the 1830s. ⊠ *Angel Hill* ✉ *Free* ☉ *Weekdays 7:30 AM–½ hr before dusk, weekends 9 AM–dusk.*

The **Manor House Museum,** a Georgian mansion, contains excellent art collections: paintings, furniture, costumes, and ceramics from the 17th through the 20th centuries. The clocks and watches in the horological collection are extraordinary. ⊠ *Honey Hill* ☎ *01284/757072* ⊕ *www.stedmundsbury.gov.uk/manorhse.htm* ✉ *£3* ☉ *Wed.–Sun. 11–4.*

The 12th-century **Moyse's Hall,** probably the oldest building in East Anglia, is a rare surviving example of a Norman house. The rooms hold local history and archaeological collections. One macabre display relates to the Red Barn murder, a case that gained notoriety in a 19th-century theatrical melodrama, *Maria Marten, or the Murder in the Red Barn;* Maria Marten's murderer was executed in Bury St. Edmunds in 1828. ⊠ *Cornhill* ☎ *01284/706183* ⊕ *www.stedmundsbury.gov.uk/moyses.htm* ✉ *£2.50* ☉ *Weekdays 10:30–4:30, weekends 11–5.*

Pop in for a pint of the local Greene King ale at **The Nutshell** (⊠ Skinner St. ☎ 01905/764867), Britain's smallest pub, measuring just 16 feet by 7 ½ feet.

off the beaten path

ICKWORTH HOUSE – The creation of the eccentric Frederick Hervey, 4th earl of Bristol and bishop of Derry, this unusual 18th-century home was owned by the Hervey family until the 1960s. Inspired by his travels, Hervey wanted an Italianate palace and gardens to match. Today the two wings around a striking central rotunda contain a hotel (east wing) and paintings by William Hogarth, Titian, Diego Velázquez, and Gainsborough (west wing). Behind the house, the rose gardens and vineyards spread out to reach 1,800 acres of woods. A stroll over the hills to see grazing sheep and woodland deer gives the best vistas of the house, which is 7 mi southwest of Bury St. Edmunds. ⊠ *Off A143, Horringer* ☎ *01284/735270* ⊕ *www.nationaltrust.org.uk* ✉ *£6.10, gardens and park £2.80* ☉ *House Apr.–Oct., Tues., Wed., and Fri.–Sun. 1–5. Garden Apr.–Oct., daily 10–5; Nov.–Dec., weekdays 10–4; Jan.–Mar., daily 10–4. Park daily 7–7.*

Where to Stay & Eat

££–£££ ✕ **Maison Bleue.** This French restaurant specializes in locally caught seafood and serves some meat dishes, too. The seafood depends on the day's catch, but mussels and grilled fillets of local trout and salmon are always available, as are cheeses imported from Paris. ⊠ *30 Churchgate*

St. ☎ 01284/760623 ⚠ *Reservations essential* ▤ *AE, DC, V* ☯ *Closed Sun. and late Dec.–late Jan.*

£ ✕ Harriet's Café Tearooms. Harriet's brings back the tearooms of yesteryear. You can munch on a savory sandwich or have a full cream tea while listening to hits from the 1940s in this elegant dining room. ⊠ *57 Cornhill* ☎ *01284/756256* ▤ *MC, V* ☯ *No dinner.*

★ ✕▥ Ickworth Hotel. You can live like nobility in the east wing of the Italianate Ickworth House, 7 mi southwest of Bury St. Edmunds. Unlike many
££££–£££££ other stately home hotels, this one has no dress code, and children are catered to with a day-care room (for kids under 6) and a game room. The splendid public rooms have stylish 1950s and '60s furniture and striking modern art. This look extends to most bedrooms, though some still have period furnishings; all are luxe. Adults can dine in the more formal Frederick's restaurant, and the casual Café Inferno serves pizza. ⊠ *Off A143, Horringer, IP29 5QE* ☎ *01284/735350* 🖷 *01284/736300* ⊕ *www. luxuryfamilyhotels.com* ⟿ *27 rooms, 11 apartments* ☾ *2 restaurants, room service, in-room data ports, some kitchens, cable TV, tennis court, indoor pool, massage, spa, bicycles, croquet, horseback riding, lounge, baby-sitting, dry cleaning, laundry service, meeting rooms, some pets allowed, no-smoking rooms; no a/c* ▤ *AE, DC, MC, V* ❤ *BP.*

★ **£££–££££** ✕▥ Angel Hotel. This spruced-up former coaching inn in the heart of town has spacious, well-furnished rooms. Several have four-posters, and the Charles Dickens Room, where the author stayed, is done in perfect 19th-century English style (the bed is a bit small, however). Morning coffee and afternoon tea are served in the cozy lobby with fireplace. You can dine on English fare in the Abbeygate Restaurant overlooking the abbey's main gate, or try brasserie-style dishes in more informal Vaults, in the cellar. ⊠ *3 Angel Hill, IP33 1LT* ☎ *01284/753926* 🖷 *01284/ 750092* ⊕ *www.theangel.co.uk* ⟿ *66 rooms* ☾ *2 restaurants, in-room data ports, cable TV with movies, bar, business services, meeting rooms, no-smoking rooms; no a/c in some rooms* ▤ *AE, DC, MC, V* ❤ *BP.*

£££ ▥ Ounce House. Small and friendly, this Victorian B&B a three-minute walk from the abbey ruins has a great deal of charm. The stylish guest rooms are furnished with print fabrics and wooden furniture. You can unwind in the antiques-filled drawing room and library, where you can have a drink from the honesty bar. The house is close to Bury's restaurants. ⊠ *Northgate St., IP33 1HP* ☎ *01284/761779* 🖷 *01284/768315* ⊕ *www.ouncehouse.co.uk* ⟿ *4 rooms* ☾ *Bar, lounge; no a/c, no smoking* ▤ *MC, V* ❤ *BP.*

Nightlife & the Arts

The **Theatre Royal,** which presents touring shows, was built in 1819 and is a perfect example of Regency theater design. Guided tours (£2.50) can be booked at the box office. ⊠ *Westgate St.* ☎ *01284/769505* ☯ *Apr.–Oct., guided tours Tues. and Thurs. 11:30 and 2:30, Sat. 11:30, except during rehearsals.*

COLCHESTER & THE ALDEBURGH COAST

Colchester is the oldest town on record in England, dating back to the Iron Age, and the reminders of its long history are well worth visiting. The town also serves as the traditional base for exploring Constable Country, that quintessentially English rural landscape on the borders of Suffolk and Essex made famous by the early-19th-century painter John Constable. This area runs north and west of Colchester along the valley of the River Stour. The 40-mi Suffolk Heritage Coast, which wanders northward from Felixstowe up to Kessingland, is one of the most unspoiled shorelines in the country.

Colchester

㉓ *59 mi northeast of London, 51 mi southeast of Cambridge, 68 mi south of Norwich.*

Evidence of Colchester's four centuries of Roman history is visible everywhere in this ancient town. The Roman walls still stand, together with a Norman castle, a Victorian town hall, and Dutch-style houses built by refugee weavers from the Low Countries in the late 16th century. Archaeological research indicates a settlement at the head of the Colne estuary at least as early as 1100 BC. Two thousand years ago it was the center of the domain of Cunobelin (Shakespeare's Cymbeline), who was king of the Catuvellauni. On Cunobelin's death, the Romans invaded in AD 43. The emperor Claudius built a stronghold here and made it the first Roman colony in Britain, renaming the town *Colonia Victricensis,* the Colony of Victory. (Colchester had to wait another millennium, however, before it received its royal charter in 1189 from King Richard I.) The settlement was burned during the failed revolt in AD 60 by Boudicca, queen of the Iceni, noted for having knives affixed to her chariot wheels. The Romans relocated their administrative center to London after the revolt but maintained a military presence. The English Civil War saw further military conflict in Colchester, as the city endured a three-month siege in 1648 before the Royalist forces surrendered. Colchester has always had a strategic importance and still has a military base; a tattoo (military spectacle) is held in even-numbered years.

Colchester was important enough for the Romans to build massive fortifications around it, and the **Roman Walls,** dating largely from the reign of Emperor Vespasian (AD 69–79, can still be seen, especially along Balkerne Hill (to the west of the town center), with its splendid Balkerne Gate (most of the foundations lie beneath the neighboring Hole-in-the-Wall pub). On Maidenburgh Street, near the castle, the remains of a Roman amphitheater have been discovered. The curve of the foundations is outlined in the paving stones of the roadway, and part of the walls and floor have been exposed and preserved in a building, where they can be viewed through a window.

The castle built by William the Conqueror in about 1076 is today the superb **Colchester Castle Museum.** All that remains is the keep, the largest the Normans built. The castle was constructed over the foundations of the huge Roman Temple of Claudius, and in the vaults you can descend through 1,000 years of history. The museum contains an ever-growing collection of prehistoric and Roman remains. ✉ *Castle Park* ☎ *01206/282931; 01206/282932 information on all Colchester museums* ⊕ *www.colchestermuseums.org.uk* ✆ *£3.90, guided tours £1* ☼ *Mon.–Sat. 10–5, Sun. 11–5.*

The interactive **Hollytrees Museum,** in a Georgian mansion near the castle, tells the story of the daily lives of local people through objects. There are chances to create a silhouette portrait or play with Victorian toys. ✉ *Castle Park* ☎ *01206/282939* ⊕ *www.colchestermuseums.org.uk* ✆ *Free* ☼ *Mon.–Sat. 10–5, Sun. 11–5.*

Halfway down the broad High Street, which follows the line of the main Roman road, the splendid Edwardian **Town Hall** stands on the site of the original Moot (assembly) Hall. On its tower you can see four figures representing Colchester's main industries: fisheries, agriculture, the military, and engineering. The narrow medieval streets behind the Town Hall are called the **Dutch Quarter** because weavers—refugees from the

Low Countries—settled here in the 16th century, when Colchester was the center of a thriving cloth trade.

Tymperleys Clock Museum, off Sir Isaac's Walk, displays a unique collection of Colchester-made clocks in the surviving wing of an Elizabethan house. ⊠ *Trinity St.* ☎ *01206/282932* ⊕ *www.colchestermuseums. org.uk* ✍ *Free* ☉ *May–Sept., Mon.–Sat. 10–5, Sun. 11–5.*

Where to Stay & Eat

££–£££ ✕ **Warehouse Brasserie.** Colchester's most popular eating place has a pastel green and rich red split-level dining room, wooden tables, and large wall mirrors. This cheerful interior contrasts with a fairly anonymous exterior and location: it's tucked away in a converted warehouse, down a cul-de-sac off St. John's Street. The fixed-price lunch and dinner menu mixes brasserie favorites with classic English dishes. ⊠ *12 Chapel St. N* ☎ *01206/765656* ☰ *MC, V* ☉ *No dinner Sun. and Mon.*

£££–££££ ✕⌸ **George Hotel.** This 500-year-old inn in the heart of downtown includes a modern extension but has lost none of its age-old charm. Many rooms incorporate original oak beams and are comfortably furnished in traditional style. The George Bar also retains its ancient beams, and in the cellar a section of Roman pavement and a 16th-century wall painting are on display. The Brasserie restaurant has a good à la carte menu and is popular for afternoon tea or an evening pint. ⊠ *116 High St., CO1 1TD* ☎ *01206/578494* 🖷 *01206/761732* ⊕ *www.bestwestern. com* 📧 *48 rooms* ᝰ *Restaurant, cable TV, bar, no-smoking rooms; no a/c in some rooms* ☰ *AE, DC, MC, V* ⍾ *BP.*

Dedham

㉔ *8 mi northeast of Colchester, off A12 on B1029.*

Fodor'sChoice
★

Dedham is the heart of Constable Country. Here, gentle hills and the cornfields of Dedham Vale, set under the district's delicate, pale skies, inspired John Constable (1776–1837) to paint some of his most celebrated canvases. He went to school in Dedham, a tiny, picture-book kind of place that consists of a single street, a church, and a few timber-frame and brick houses.

From Dedham, on the banks of the River Stour, you can rent a rowboat, which (if you're fit enough) is an idyllic way to travel the 2 mi downriver to **Flatford Mill,** one of the two water mills owned by Constable's father, and the subject of his most famous painting, *The Hay Wain* (1821). Near Flatford Mill is the 16th-century **Willy Lott's House** (not open to the public), which is instantly recognizable from *The Hay Wain.* The National Trust owns Flatford Mill along with the houses around it, including the thatched 16th-century **Bridge Cottage,** on the north bank of the Stour, which has a display about Constable's life. ⊠ *Off B1070, East Bergholt* ☎ *01206/298260* ⊕ *www.nationaltrust.org.uk* ✍ *Free, guided tours or audio tour £2* ☉ *Jan. and Feb., weekends 11–3:30; Mar. and Apr., Wed.–Sun. 11–5:30; May–Sept., daily 10–5:30; Oct., daily 11–5:30; Nov. and Dec., Wed.–Sun. 11–3:30. Guided tours Apr.–Oct. on days open, at 11, 1, and 2:30.*

Two miles northeast of Dedham, off A12, the Constable trail continues in **East Bergholt,** where Constable was born in 1776. Only the stables remain of the house that was his birthplace. As well as many other views of East Bergholt, Constable painted its village church, **St. Mary's,** where his parents lie buried. It has one unusual feature—a freestanding wooden bell house in place of a tower.

Where to Stay & Eat

★ ✕**Le Talbooth.** A longtime favorite, this sophisticated restaurant in a Tudor
fff–fffff house idyllically set beside the River Stour has a floodlighted terrace where
drinks are served in summer. Inside, original beams, leaded-glass windows, and a brick fireplace add to the sense of age. The superb English
fare at lunch and dinner may include venison with wild mushroom
ravioli or cod on roasted artichokes with curry oil. ✉ *Gun Hill* ☎ *01206/
323150* ⌨ *Reservations essential* ♟ *Jacket and tie* ⊟ *AE, MC, V*
☻ *No dinner Sun. Nov.–Mar.*

ff ✕**Marlborough Hotel.** Fine lunches from fisherman's pie to duck are served
at this early-18th-century pub opposite Constable's school. It gets busy
during the summer, so arrive early to ensure a table. ✉ *Mill La.* ☎ *01206/
323250* ⊟ *AE, MC, V.*

fff ✕⊡**Milsoms.** Owned by the Milsoms of Maison Talbooth fame, this sweet
little hotel in a Victorian house maintains their high standards while providing a more modern style. Room decoration is understated but still
maintains the warmth of the countryside. The soothing, split-level
restaurant specializes in updated versions of classic British fare such as
baked mussels or chicken livers, and the relaxed bar is perfect for a cuppa.
In warm weather, sit by the pond in the garden. ✉ *Stratford Rd., CO7
6HW* ☎ *01206/322795* 🖷 *01206/323689* ⊕ *www.talbooth.com* ↩ *14
rooms* ⌂ *Restaurant, room service, minibars, cable TV, bar, lounge, dry
cleaning, laundry service, meeting rooms, no-smoking rooms; no a/c*
⊟ *AE, DC, MC, V.*

ffff–fffff ⊡ **Maison Talbooth.** Constable painted the rich meadowlands in which
this luxurious Victorian country-house hotel is set. Period antiques,
print fabrics, and upholstered furniture decorate each of the elegant, spacious rooms. Continental breakfast is served in your bedroom. Guests
are encouraged to eat in Le Talbooth restaurant, a short walk or free
ride down the lane and owned by the same management. ✉ *Stratford
Rd., CO7 6HP* ☎ *01206/322367* 🖷 *01206/322752* ⊕ *www.talbooth.
com* ↩ *10 rooms* ⌂ *Room service, some in-room hot tubs, minibars,
cable TV, croquet, lounge; no a/c* ⊟ *AE, MC, V* ⏱⊙ *CP.*

Woodbridge

㉕ *18 mi northeast of Dedham.*

One of the first good ports of call on the Suffolk Heritage Coast, Woodbridge, off A12, is a pleasant town whose upper reaches center on a fine
old market square, with two great pubs, the Bull and the King's Head.
Antiques shops fill the surrounding streets, but Woodbridge is at its best
around its old quayside, where boatbuilding has been carried out since
the 16th century—although these days pleasure-craft are built, rather
than working vessels. The most prominent building is a white clapboard
mill, which dates from the 18th century and is powered by the tides.

The visitor center at **Sutton Hoo** helps interpret one of Britain's most significant Anglo-Saxon archaeological sites. In 1938, a local archaeologist excavated three 7th-century burial mounds associated with King
Raedwald of East Anglia. Traces of a buried ship were the most unique
find; many artifacts uncovered are now in the British Museum in London. Later excavations revealed that this was the site of other burials,
some royal. A replica of the 40-oar, 90-foot-long ship stands in the visitor center, which has displays about Anglo-Saxon society and artifacts
on loan from the British Museum. Trails around the 245-acre site explore the area along the River Deben. Sutton Hoo is 2 mi east of Woodbridge. ✉ *B1083* ☎ *01394/389700* ⊕ *www.nationaltrust.org.uk* ⊠ *£4*

🕐 *Mid-Mar.–May and Oct., Wed.–Sun. 10–5; June–Sept., daily 10–5; Nov.–Feb., weekends 10–4.*

---

off the beaten path

FRAMLINGHAM CASTLE – From the outside, this moated castle looks much as it would have in the 12th century. Upon entering, however, you'll see that the keep is missing. (Nearby Orford Castle has an intact keep but no battlements.) An audio tour (included in the admission) leads you on a walk around the curtain wall with its 13 towers. Most of the chimneys along the wall are fake; they were later additions meant to give the impression to passersby that it was a great Tudor mansion. The open-air concerts and reenactments held in the summer are worth seeking out. ✉ B1119 ☎ 01728/724189 🌐 www.english-heritage.org.uk 💷 £3.90 🕐 Apr.–Sept., daily 10–6; Oct., daily 10–5; Nov.–Mar., daily 10–4.

Where to Stay

★ **££££** 🏨 **Seckford Hall.** This magnificent Tudor manor house recalls the days of yore with its wood-paneled walls, oak beams, fireplaces, and impressive antiques, including a 16th-century half-tester bed. The surrounding landscaped grounds are perfect for a stroll to admire the roses or the duck-filled lake. The main restaurant specializes in local lobster. ✉ Off A12, IP13 6NU ☎ 01394/385678 📠 01394/380610 🌐 www.seckford.co.uk 🛏 32 rooms ⚬ 2 restaurants, room service, golf privileges, indoor pool, gym, hot tub, bar, lounge, meeting rooms, laundry service, some pets allowed (fee) 🖃 AE, DC, MC, V ⦿ BP.

Orford

26 *10 mi east of Woodbridge, 35 mi northeast of Colchester.*

Part of the Suffolk Heritage Coast, a 40-mi stretch that runs from Felixstowe northward to Kessingland, the ancient town of Orford is a beautiful example of the coast's many Areas of Special Scientific Interest. There are numerous beaches, marshes, and broads, with an abundance of wildflowers and birds. You can reach other areas on minor roads running east off A12 north of Ipswich.

Small and squat, **Orford Castle** surveys the flatlands from atop a green mound favored by picnickers in summer. Its splendid triple-tower keep was built in 1160 as a coastal defense. Climb it for a view over what was once a thriving medieval port; the 6-mi shingle (coarse gravel) bank of Orford Ness eventually cut off direct access to the sea. ✉ B1084 ☎ 01394/450472 🌐 www.english-heritage.org.uk 💷 £3.20 🕐 Apr.–Oct., daily 10–6; Nov.–Mar., Wed.–Sun. 10–4.

Just a boat ride beyond Orford Quay lies mysterious **Orford Ness**, the biggest vegetated shingle spit in Europe. A 5-mi-long path takes you through beaches and salt marshes to see migrating and native birds and to discover the secret past of the spit—from 1913 until the mid-1980s, it served as a military site. If you'd rather sit than walk, book a seat on the tractor-drawn trailer tour that runs on the first Saturday of the month from July through September. ✉ Orford Quay ☎ 01394/450057 🌐 www.nationaltrust.org.uk 💷 £5.60 including ferry crossing 🕐 Mid-Apr.–June and Oct., Sat. 10–2; July–Sept., Tues.–Sat. 10–2; last ferry at 5.

Where to Stay & Eat

££ ✕ **Butley-Orford Oysterage.** What started as a little café that sold oysters and cups of tea has become a large, bustling, no-nonsense restaurant. It still specializes in oysters and smoked salmon, as well as smoked seafood platters and seasonal fish dishes. The actual smoking takes place in the adjacent smokehouse, and products are for sale in a shop around the corner. ⊠ *Market Hill* ☎ *01394/450277* ▤ *MC, V* ⊘ *No dinner Sun.–Thurs. Nov.–Mar.*

★ **£££–££££** ✕▣ **Crown and Castle.** Artsy, laid-back, and genuinely friendly, this contemporary hotel in an 18th-century building near Orford Castle is a little gem. Many rooms have sunflower-size showerheads; it's best to ask for one of these. The garden rooms are spacious. The Trinity Bistro, run by food writer Ruth Watson, dishes up modern British fare, including plenty of fresh fish and local Butley oysters. In warm weather, the outdoor terrace is a great place for grandstand views of Orford Castle. ⊠ *Market Hill, IP12 2LJ* ☎ *01394/450205* ▤ *01394/450176* ⊕ *www.crownandcastlehotel.co.uk* ↻ *18 rooms* ⌂ *Restaurant, in-room VCRs, bar, lobby lounge, some pets allowed, no-smoking rooms; no a/c* ▤ *AE, DC, MC, V* ⏀ *BP.*

Aldeburgh

➋➐ *20 mi north of Orford, 41 mi northeast of Colchester.*

Aldeburgh (pronounced owl-barrow) is a quiet seaside resort, except in June, when the town fills up with people attending the noted Aldeburgh Festival. Its beach is backed by a promenade lined with candy-color dwellings. Twentieth-century composer Benjamin Britten lived here for some time—although he was actually born in the busy seaside resort of Lowestoft, 30 mi to the north. Britten grew interested in the story of Aldeburgh's native son, the poet George Crabbe (1754–1832), and turned the life story of the poet into the celebrated modern opera *Peter Grimes,* a piece that perfectly captures the atmosphere of the Suffolk coast.

The **Elizabethan Moot Hall,** built of flint and timber, stood in the center of a thriving 16th-century town when first erected. Now it's just a few steps from the beach, a mute witness to the erosive powers of the North Sea. ⊠ *Market Cross, Sea Front* ▨ *70p* ⊘ *Easter–May and Oct., weekends 2:30–5; June and Sept., daily 2:30–5; July and Aug., daily 10:30–12:30 and 2:30–5.*

off the beaten path

THORPENESS – Two miles north of Aldeburgh lies this almost bizarrely perfect—but perfectly fake—Tudor village, as well as the whimsical House in the Clouds, created to disguise a water pump in the local golf course. The whole village was built as a resort in the early 20th century. The white globe that you see farther up the coast is the Sizewell B nuclear power station.

Where to Stay & Eat

££–£££ ✕ **152.** The Mediterranean influences the cooking at this restaurant and brasserie where seafood is the prime attraction. Bright colors, wood floors, and candlelight create a relaxed backdrop for dishes such as baked cod in herb butter, seafood risottos, and grilled duck breast. For picnic fixings or culinary souvenirs, stop by the adjacent delicatessen, which sells quiches, terrines, cold cuts, and cheeses. ⊠ *152 High St.* ☎ *01728/454152* ▤ *MC, V* ⊘ *Closed Mon. and Tues.*

££ ✕ **The Lighthouse.** This low-key brasserie relies exclusively on locally grown
FodorsChoice produce and also focuses on seafood, including oysters and Cromer crabs.
★ All the dishes are simply but imaginatively cooked, usually with an interesting sauce that might just as easily be Asian as English. Desserts, such as the creamy bread-and-butter pudding, are particularly good. ⊠ *77 High St.* ☎ *01728/453377* ▤ *MC, V* ⊘ *Closed 2 wks in Jan. No dinner Sun. Nov.–Mar.*

££££ 🏨 **Wentworth Hotel.** The Wentworth has been owned and managed by the Pritt family since 1920, and the caring attention shows. The huge chairs that fill the public rooms on the ground floor are a great place to sip coffee and watch people stroll by. Sea-view rooms, which are worth the extra cost, come equipped with binoculars for birders. All rooms have a copy of the whimsical children's favorite *Orlando the Marmalade Cat,* by Kathleen Hale, which is set in "Owlbarrow." ⊠ *Wentworth Rd., IP15 5BD* ☎ *01728/452312* 🖷 *01728/454343* ⊕ *www.wentworth-aldeburgh.com* ⟿ *37 rooms, 35 with bath* ⊘ *Restaurant, room service, cable TV, in-room data ports, bar, lobby lounge, meeting rooms, some pets allowed; no a/c, no smoking* ▭ *MC, V* ⦿⦿ *BP.*

££££ 🏨 **White Lion.** Guests have been welcomed at this seafront hotel since 1563, and this heritage shines through in the paneled, oak-beam restaurant, the log fires in the lounges, and the age-old nooks and crannies. All rooms have been updated, but it's worth paying a little extra for the view from the sea-facing ones. The White Lion's more expensive sister hotel, the Brudenell, underwent major refurbishment and reopened in mid-2003. ⊠ *Market Cross Pl., IP15 5BJ,* ☎ *01728/452720* 🖷 *01728/452986* ⊕ *www.whitelion.co.uk* ⟿ *38 rooms* ⊘ *Restaurant, room service, in-room data ports, cable TV, 2 bars, lounge, some pets allowed (fee); no a/c* ▭ *AE, MC, V* ⦿⦿ *CP.*

££ 🏨 **Ocean House.** Juliet and Phil Brereton are your hosts at this 1860s
Fodor'sChoice house near the beach. Antiques and bric-a-brac decorate the public
★ areas and bedrooms, and the two rooms with bath have views of the sea. Breakfast is hearty and home-cooked. ⊠ *25 Crag Path, IP15 5BS* ☎ *01728/452094* ⟿ *6 rooms, 2 with bath* ⊘ *Ping-Pong, lounge, piano; no a/c, no smoking* ▭ *No credit cards* ⦿⦿ *BP.*

Nightlife & the Arts

East Anglia's most important arts festival, and one of the best known in Great Britain, is the **Aldeburgh Festival,** held for two weeks in June in the small village of Snape, 5 mi west of Aldeburgh, at the Snape Maltings Concert Hall. Founded by Benjamin Britten, the festival concentrates on music but includes related exhibitions, poetry readings, and even walks. ⊠ *High St., Aldeburgh, IP15 5AX* ☎ *01728/687100; 01728/453543 box office* ⊕ *www.aldeburgh.co.uk.*

It's well worth a stop to enjoy the peaceful River Alde location of **Snape Maltings** cultural center and pause for a drink at the tea shop or a meal at the Plough & Sail gastro-pub (a pub specializing in trendier fare) between browsing the crafts shops here. Snape Maltings has special events year-round, such as the two-day Aldeburgh Folk Festival, held each July to celebrate traditional English folk music, and the Britten Festival in October. One-hour **river cruises** leave from Snape Bridge during high tide. Tickets cost £5 per person. ⊠ *Snape, near Saxmundham* ☎ *01728/688305* ⊕ *www.snapemaltings.co.uk* ⊙ *Daily 10–5.*

Southwold

28 *15 mi north of Aldeburgh, 32 mi southeast of Norwich.*

This seaside town is an idyllic place to spend a day. Old-fashioned beach huts painted in bright colors huddle together against the wind on the shingle beach, which is lined with small pebbles, and up in the town center a pleasing ensemble of old houses faces the main street and surrounds the central green. The handsome Church of St. Edmund dates to the 15th century. There aren't many "sights," but the whole town gives you the sensation of being transported back in time. George Orwell's parents lived at 3 Queen Street during the 1930s. The **Southwold Museum** displays works of local archaeology, natural history, and pictures of the 17th-century Battle of Sole Bay. It's in a Dutch-gabled cottage, a style typical of Southwold's domestic architecture. ⊠ *Victoria St.* ☎ *01502/722375* ⊠ *Free* ⊙ *Easter–July and Sept. and Oct., daily 2–4; Aug., daily 10:30–noon.*

<table>
<tr><td>off the
beaten
path</td><td>**WALBERSWICK** – For many years this appealing little village, on B1387, was the haunt of arty types (including, during 1914–15, the Scottish art nouveau architect Charles Rennie Mackintosh). The village is separated from Southwold by the mouth of the River Blyth, over which there's a footbridge (about 1 mi inland), but no main road bridge. On summer weekends, a boatman ferries foot passengers over the water in a rowboat every few minutes. ☒ *Ferry £1* ⊙ *Ferry May–Sept., weekends 9–12:30 and 2–5.*</td></tr>
</table>

Where to Stay & Eat

£££–££££ ✕▦ **Swan Hotel.** This 17th-century inn has spacious public rooms and decent-size bedrooms decorated in traditional English-country style. Seventeen secluded and quiet garden rooms are set around the old bowling green. The restaurant's dishes are mainly traditional English fare, accompanied by an excellent wine list. Children under 5 are not allowed in the dining room after 7 PM. ⊠ *Market Pl., IP18 6EG* ☎ *01502/722186* ⊠ *01502/724800* ⊕ *www.adnams.co.uk* ⤳ *43 rooms, 41 with bath* ⊘ *Restaurant, croquet, bar, meeting rooms, some pets allowed; no a/c* ⊟ *AE, DC, MC, V* ⦶⦶ *BP.*

£££ ✕▦ **Crown Hotel.** Like the Swan, the Crown is owned by the old family firm of Adnams brewery, the major employer in Southwold. Bedrooms are suitably small for a 17th-century building, but the antique furniture and friendly staff compensate. The maritime-theme Back Bar or the eclectic brasserie and wine bar provide a cozy place to dine. Seafood dishes are excellent, from pan-fried John Dory to smoked haddock. Children under 5 are not allowed in the restaurant after 7 PM. ⊠ *90 High St., IP18 6DP* ☎ *01502/722275* ⊠ *01502/727263* ⊕ *www.adnams.co.uk* ⤳ *14 rooms, 11 with bath* ⊘ *Restaurant, bar, meeting rooms; no a/c* ⊟ *AE, DC, MC, V* ⦶⦶ *BP.*

NORWICH TO NORTH NORFOLK

Norwich, unofficial capital of East Anglia and the heart of the eastern and northern part of East Anglia's "bump," is dominated by the 15th-century spire of its impressive cathedral. Norfolk's continuing isolation from the rest of the country, and its unspoiled landscape and architecture—bypassed by the Industrial Revolution—have proved to be a draw. Many of the flint-knapped (decorated with broken flint) houses in North Norfolk's pretty villages are, nowadays, weekend or holiday homes. Windmills, churches, and waterways are the area's chief defining characteristics. A few miles inland from the Norfolk coast, the Broads begin, a name that caused much comment among GIs during World War II. In fact, these Broads form a national park, a network of shallow, reed-bordered lakes, many linked by wide rivers. Boating and fishing are great lures; rent a boat for a day or a week and the waterside pubs, churches, villages, and nature reserves all fall within easy reach.

Norwich

63 mi northeast of Cambridge.

It used to be said that Norwich had a pub for each day of the week and a church for each week of the year. Although this is no longer true, both institutions are still much in evidence in this pleasant city of about

130,000. Established by the Saxons because of its prime trading position on the rivers Yare and Wensum, the town has its heart in the triangle between the two waterways, dominated by the castle and cathedral (two of the city's main attractions). The inner beltway follows the line of the old city wall, much of which is still visible. It's worth driving around after dark to see the older buildings, which, thanks to floodlighting, stand out from their newer neighbors. By the time of the Norman Conquest, Norwich was one of the largest towns in England, although much was destroyed by the Normans to create a new town with grand buildings.

Today you can see the flint buildings as you walk down the medieval streets, alleyways, and narrow passageways. Despite its concessions to modernity—some industrial sites and many shopping centers—the town remains accessible, historic, and engaging. The University of East Anglia brings a cosmopolitan touch, including a lively arts scene, to an otherwise remote urban area. Norwich makes a good base from which to explore the Norfolk Broads and the coast.

★ ㉙ **Norwich Cathedral,** the grandest example of Norman architecture in Norwich, has the second-largest monastic cloisters in Britain (Salisbury's are bigger). Although its spire, at 315 feet (also second only to Salisbury's), is visible from everywhere, you cannot see the building itself until you pass through St. Ethelbert's Gate. The cathedral was begun in 1096 by Herbert de Losinga, who had come from Normandy in 1091 to be its first bishop; his splendid tomb is by the high altar. Distinctly Norman elements are the plain west front and dramatic crossing tower, with its austere, geometrical decoration. The remarkable length of the nave is immediately impressive; unfortunately, the similarly striking height of the vaulted ceiling makes it a strain to study the delightful colored bosses, which illustrate Bible stories with great vigor and detail. Binoculars can help. The grave of Norfolk-born nurse Edith Cavell, the British World War I heroine shot by the Germans in 1915, is at the east end of the cathedral. ✉ *62 The Close* ☎ *01603/764385* ⊕ *www.cathedral.org.uk* 📧 *Free* ⊘ *Mid-May–mid-Sept., daily 7:30–7; mid-Sept.–mid-May, daily 7:30–6; free guided tours June–Oct., weekdays at 11 and 2:15, Sat. at 11.*

The Cathedral **Close** (grounds) is one of the most idyllic places in Norwich; past the mixture of medieval and Georgian houses, a path leads ㉚ down to the ancient water gate, **Pulls Ferry.**

㉛ The decorated stone facing of **Norwich Castle,** now a museum high on the hill in the center of the city, makes it look like a children's book illustration for a castle. In fact, the castle is Norman (1130), but a stone keep later replaced the original wooden bailey (wall) on the castle mound. The thick walls and other defenses attest to its military function. For most of its history the castle was a prison, and executions took place here well into the 19th century. Today it houses three museum zones—Natural History, Castle and Archaeology, and Art and Exhibitions. Dioramas in the Natural History section show Norfolk plants and wildlife. The excellent interactive displays in Castle and Archaeology explore topics from ancient Egypt to life in Norman times. You can even try out Queen Boudicca's chariot to relive her attack on Roman Colchester. Art and Exhibitions includes a gallery devoted to the Norwich School of painters who, like the Suffolk artist John Constable, focused their work on the everyday Norfolk landscape and seascape. This museum also holds glass and ceramics and the largest teapot collection in the world. Daily guided tours explore the castle's battlements or dungeons. ✉ *Castle Meadow* ☎ *01603/493625* ⊕ *www.norfolk.gov.uk/tourism/museums* 📧 *Entire museum £4.70, Castle and Archaeology £2.90, Art and Ex-*

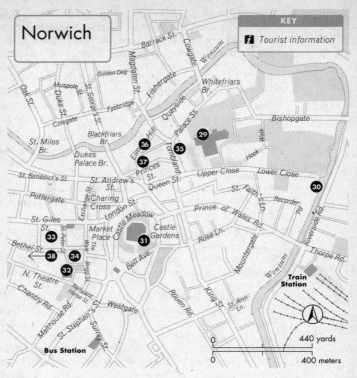

Norwich

KEY

i Tourist information

hibitions £2.90, *guided tours of the battlements or dungeons £1.20* ☉ *Mon.–Sat. 10:30–5, Sun. 2–5.*

🐌 ㉜ On three floors of the modern **Forum, Origins** provides an introduction to Norwich and the surrounding area via a 90-minute interactive tour. The museum delves back 2,000 years to show how the area's inhabitants and landscape have changed over time—from the Vikings and the Romans to the U.S. servicemen and servicewomen who were here during World War II. You can drain a three-dimensional map of the fens, try the Norfolk dialect, and watch a panoramic film about the region on a wraparound screen. The shop stocks lots of made-in-Norfolk souvenirs, and the Forum also houses the Norwich Library, a tourist information center, a few places to eat, and an atrium space for entertainment. ⊠ *Between N. Theatre and Bethel Sts.* ☎ *01603/727920* ⊕ *www.theforumnorfolk.com* 🎟 *£4.95* ☉ *Apr.–Sept., Mon.–Sat. 10–6, Sun. 10:30–4:30; Oct.–Mar., Mon.–Sat. 10–5:30, Sun. 10–4:30.*

With its blanket of brightly striped awnings, the **Market Place,** west of Norwich Castle, has been the heart of the city for 900 years. The large open-air market is closed Sunday. Bronze Norwich lions guard the steps
㉝ of the imposing—if severe—early-20th-century **City Hall** (⊠ St. Peter St.), which overlooks the Market Place. The elaborate church tower of 15th-
㉞ century **St. Peter Mancroft** (⊠ Bethel St.) rises next to the Market Place. Narrow lanes and alleys that used to be the main streets of medieval
㉟ Norwich lead away from the market and end at **Tombland** by the cathedral. Neither a graveyard nor a plague pit, Tombland was the site of the
㊱ Anglo-Saxon trading place, now a busy thoroughfare. **Elm Hill,** off Tombland, is a cobbled and pleasing mixture of Tudor and Georgian houses that hold gift shops and tearooms.

③⑦ St. Peter Hungate, at the top end of Elm Hill, is a 15th-century former church that displays church art and furnishings. You can try your hand at brass rubbing here. ✉ *Princes St.* ☎ *01603/667231* 🎫 *Free, brass rubbing £1.50–£10* ⊘ *Apr.–Oct., Mon.–Sat. 10–5.*

> **need a break?** Next door to Cinema City, the low-key **Take 5** (✉ St. Andrew's St. ☎ 01603/763099) café-bar attracts the local art crowd with its excellent snacks and drinks, including local beers. The little courtyard out back is a great place to unwind in summer.

③⑧ The **Sainsbury Centre for the Visual Arts,** a modern, hangarlike building designed by Norman Foster on the University of East Anglia campus, holds the private art collection of the Sainsbury family, owners of a supermarket chain. It includes a remarkable quantity of tribal art and 20th-century works, especially art nouveau, and has pieces by Pablo Picasso and Alberto Giacometti. The university was designed in the 1960s by architect Denys Lasdun, who used its site on the slopes of the River Yare to give a dramatic, stepped-pyramid effect. Buses 4, 5, 26, and 27 run from Norwich Castle Meadow to the university. ✉ *Earlham Rd.* ☎ *01603/593199* ⊕ *www.uea.ac.uk* 🎫 *£2* ⊘ *Tues.–Sun. 11–5.*

Where to Stay & Eat

★ **£££–££££** ✕ **Adlard's Restaurant.** Wine enthusiast and chef David Adlard runs this relaxed contemporary restaurant with pine floors and white walls. Beautifully presented dishes such as roast turbot with crushed potatoes, roast shallots, and velouté sauce show his ability to bring classical French cooking up to date. Desserts, including prune soufflé with Earl Grey ice cream, compete against excellent cheeses. Choose from a small à la carte menu or one of the set menus for lunch or dinner. ✉ *79 Upper St. Giles St.* ☎ *01603/633522* ▭ *AE, DC, MC, V* ⊘ *Closed Sun. and 1 wk after Christmas. No lunch Mon.*

££–£££ ✕ **St. Benedict's.** This brasserie presents excellent, robust English dishes in tandem with more daring creations. Crispy duck might be paired with creamy mashed potatoes and caramelized apple or a tartlet of smoked chicken and artichoke. ✉ *9 St. Benedict's St.* ☎ *01603/765377* ▭ *AE, DC, MC, V* ⊘ *Closed Sun., Mon., and 1 wk at Christmas.*

£–££ ✕ **Adam and Eve.** Said to be Norwich's oldest pub, this place dates back to 1249. From noon until 7, the kitchen serves such pub staples as beef and ale pie or Irish stew from the short but solid bar menu. Greene King and Adnams beer are available. ✉ *Bishopsgate* ☎ *01603/667423* ▭ *AE, MC, V.*

£ ✕ **Tree House.** Inventive global cuisine such as tofu in coconut-lime sauce, hearty salads, and tasty sweets are the specialties at this co-op vegetarian restaurant. The menu indicates sugar- and gluten-free dishes. ✉ *14 Dove St.* ☎ *01603/763258* ▭ *No credit cards.*

££££ 🛏 **Dunston Hall Hotel & Country Club.** Gables and tall chimneys give this redbrick mansion built in 1859 an Elizabethan look, and extensive additions have transformed a country house into a luxurious retreat. The peaceful landscaped gardens and woodland are ideal for relaxing after a day's sightseeing. If you seek a sense of the past, ask for a four-poster bedroom or one of the small attic bedrooms with original low beamed ceilings. The hotel is 4 mi southwest of the city center. ✉ *Ipswich Rd., NR14 8PQ* ☎ *01508/470444* 🖷 *01508/471499* ⊕ *www.devere-hotels. com* ➥ *127 rooms, 3 suites* ♧ *3 restaurants, room service, in-room data ports, cable TV, driving range, 18-hole golf course, putting green, 2 tennis courts, indoor pool, gym, hot tub, sauna, steam room, billiards, babysitting, dry cleaning, laundry service, concierge, meeting rooms, no-smoking rooms; no a/c* ▭ *AE, DC, MC, V* ⦿ *BP.*

£££ 🏠 **Beeches Hotel.** Three handsome early Victorian houses, set in the Victorian Gardens, make up this family-run hotel. The Governor's House has some rooms with terraces, and the Beeches House has a modern extension. All rooms are simply but pleasantly furnished, and several look out over the gardens with their ornate Gothic fountain and Italianate terrace. The hotel is about a mile west of the city center. ✉ *2–6 Earlham Rd., NR2 3DB* ☎ *01603/621167* 🖷 *01603/620151* ⊕ *www.beeches.co.uk* ➪ *36 rooms* ⌕ *Restaurant, room service, cable TV, bar, dry cleaning, laundry service; no a/c, no smoking, no kids under 12* ▭ *AE, DC, MC, V* ❑ *BP.*

Nightlife & the Arts

Cinema City (✉ St. Andrew's St. ☎ 01603/622047), Norwich's venue for art films, is in a 16th-century building with a café-bar. The **King of Hearts** (✉ Fye Bridge St. ☎ 01603/766129), a restored medieval merchant's house, serves as a small arts center that presents chamber concerts, recitals, and poetry readings. **Norwich Arts Centre** (✉ St. Benedict's St. ☎ 01603/660352) has an eclectic program of live music, dance, and stand-up comedy as well as a good café with free Internet access.

The **Maddermarket Theatre** (✉ St. John's Alley ☎ 01603/620917), patterned after Elizabethan theaters, has been the base of the Norwich Players, an amateur repertory company, since 1911. The theater is closed in August. **Norwich Playhouse** (✉ Gun Wharf, St. George's St. ☎ 01603/598598) is a professional repertory group performing everything from Shakespeare to world premieres of new plays and jazz concerts; it also has a bookshop. Norwich's biggest and best-known theater, the **Theatre Royal** (✉ Theatre St. ☎ 01603/630000), hosts touring companies staging musicals, ballet, opera, and plays.

Sports & the Outdoors

Traffic on the River Yare is now mostly for pleasure rather than commerce, and a summer boat trip with **Southern River Steamers** gives a fresh perspective on Norwich. Longer trips are available down the Rivers Wensum and Yare to the nearer Broads. ✉ *Roaches Ct., Elm Hill; and Thorpe Station Quay by train station* ☎ *01603/624051* 💷 *£2.50–£7.50* 🕘 *May–Sept., 2–3 departures daily.*

Touring by car isn't really an option if you want to see something of the **Norfolk Broads** (⊕ www.broads-authority.gov.uk), because much of this area of shallow lakes linked by wide rivers is inaccessible by road. On a boating holiday, you can cruise with your own launch through 150 mi of waterways. **Broads Tours** (☎ 01603/782207 Wroxham; 01692/670711 Potter Heigham), based at the quaysides in Wroxham, 7 mi northeast of Norwich, and Potter Heigham, 15 mi northeast of Norwich, offers day cruises in the Broads as well as half-day and full-day launch rental (lessons included). Major operators such as **Hoseasons** (☎ 01502/502588 or 0870/543–4434) rent boats by the week. The *Norada, Olive,* and *Hathor* are historic wherry yachts (sailing barges), and all may be chartered from the **Wherry Yacht Centre** (☎ 01603/782470) for luxurious cruises for up to 12 people.

Shopping

The medieval lanes of Norwich, around Elm Hill and Tombland, contain the best antiques, book, and crafts stores. **Peter Crowe** (✉ 75 Upper St. Giles St. ☎ 01603/624800) specializes in antiquarian books. The **Mustard Shop** (✉ 15 Royal Arcade ☎ 01603/627889), perfect for Colman's Mustard enthusiasts, sells collectibles and more than 15 varieties of mustard. The **Norwich Antiques Centre** (✉ 14 Tombland ☎ 01603/619129), opposite the cathedral, is an old house crammed full of shops.

Blickling Hall

★ ❸❾ *15 mi north of Norwich.*

Behind the wrought-iron entrance gate to Blickling Hall, two mighty yew hedges form an imposing allée, creating a magnificent frame for this perfectly symmetrical Jacobean masterpiece. The redbrick mansion has towers and chimneys, baroque Dutch gables, and, in the center, a three-story timber clock tower. The grounds include a formal flower garden and parkland with woods that conceal a temple, an orangery, and a pyramid. The house, belonged to a succession of historic figures, including Sir John Fastolf, the model for Shakespeare's Falstaff; Anne Boleyn's family, who owned it until Anne was executed by her husband, Henry VIII; and finally, Lord Lothian, an ambassador to the United States. The Long Gallery (127 feet) has an intricate plasterwork ceiling decorated with Jacobean emblems, and the superb 17th-century staircase is worth examining. Most of the interior is handsome but somewhat austere, although a sumptuous tapestry of Peter the Great at the Battle of Poltawa hangs in its own room. Next to the main entrance is the Buckinghamshire Arms, a pub. ⊠ *B1354, Blickling* ☎ *01263/738030* ⊕ *www.nationaltrust.org.uk* ⊡ *£6.50, gardens only £3.70* ⊙ *House Mar.–Sept., Wed.–Sun. 1–5; Oct.–Nov., Wed.–Sun. 1–4. Gardens Jan.–Mar., weekends 11–4; Apr.–July, Sept., and Oct., Wed.–Sun. 10:15–5:30; Aug., Tues.–Sun. 10:15–5:30; Nov.–late Dec., Thurs.–Sun. 11–4.*

Blakeney

❹❶ *15 mi northeast of Blickling Hall, 27 mi northeast of Norwich.*

The Norfolk coast begins to feel wild and remote near Blakeney, 15 mi west of Cromer. If you drive along the coast road from Cromer, you'll pass marshes, sandbanks, and coves, as well as a string of villages. Blakeney is one of the most appealing, with harbors used for small fishing boats and yachts. Once a bustling port town exporting corn and salt, it enjoys a quiet existence today with a reputation for excellent wildlife viewing at Blakeney Point.

Blakeney Point, a thousand acres of grassy dunes, is home to nesting terns and about 500 common and gray seals. You can walk 3½ mi from Cley Beach to get here, but a boat trip from Blakeney or Morston quay is fun and educational. **Bishop's Boats** (⊠ Old Lifeboat House ☎ 01263/740753, ⊕ www.norfolksealtrips.co.uk) runs one- or two-hour trips daily from Morston quay and Blakeney harbor for £5.50 per person. ⊠ *A149* ☎ *01263/740480* ⊕ *www.nationaltrust.org.uk* ⊡ *Free.*

Where to Stay & Eat

££ ✕▨ **White Horse at Blakeney.** Fine food is the draw at this former coaching inn. Mussels, crabs, and fish appear on the menu, along with some pub classics such as steak and ale pie and Whitby scampi and chips. The restaurant (reservations essential) opens at 7 PM every day except Monday. A few of the pleasant, simply furnished rooms have sea views that are worth paying extra for. ⊠ *4 High St., NR25 7TE* ☎ *01263/740574* 🖷 *01263/741303* ⊕ *www.blakeneywhitehorse.co.uk* ➷ *9 rooms, 1 suite* ⌂ *Restaurant, pub, lounge, Internet; no a/c* ⊟ *MC, V* ⊙ *Closed 2 wks in Jan.* ⍟ *BP.*

Wells-next-the-Sea

❹❶ *10 mi west of Blakeney, 37 mi northwest of Norwich.*

A quiet base from which to explore, the harbor town of Wells-next-the-Sea and the nearby coastline remain untouched, with many excellent places for bird-watching and walking on the sandy beaches of Holkham Bay, near Holkham Hall. Today the town is a mile from the sea, but in Tudor times, when it was closer to the ocean, it served as one of the main ports of East Anglia. The remains of a medieval priory and two holy wells point to the town's past as a major pilgrimage destination in the Middle Ages. Along the nearby beach, a narrow-gauge steam train makes the short journey to Walsingham in summer.

FodorsChoice
★

The Palladian **Holkham Hall**, one of the most splendid mansions in Britain, is the seat of the Coke family, the earls of Leicester. In the late 18th century, Thomas Coke went on the fashionable grand tour of the Continent, returning with art treasures and determined to build a house according to the new Italian ideas. Centered by a grand staircase and modeled after the Baths of Diocletian, the entryway, the 60-foot-tall Marble Hall (mostly alabaster, in fact), may be the most spectacular room in Britain. Beyond this hall lie salons brilliant with gold and alabaster, each filled with Coke's collection of masterpieces, including paintings by Gainsborough, Sir Anthony Van Dyck, Peter Paul Rubens, Raphael, and other old masters. This transplant from neoclassical Italy is set in extensive parkland landscaped by Capability Brown in 1762. The **Bygones Museum**, in the stable block, has more than 5,000 items, from gramophones to fire engines. ⊠ *Off A149* ☏ *01328/710227* ⊕ *www.holkham.co.uk* ✍ *Hall £6.50, museum £5, combined ticket £10* ⊘ *Late May–Sept., Thurs.–Mon. 1–5, national holiday Mon. 11:30–5.*

Where to Stay & Eat

£££–£££££ ✕🖃 **Hoste Arms.** Paul Whittome and his wife have turned a 17th-century former coaching inn into a small hotel and destination gastro-pub. The menu lists such delights as Cromer crab, Burnham Creek oysters, and North Sea mussels, and the light sauces are more Asian than European. Though the food is trendy, the hotel's style is generally traditional, with prints in the bedrooms, walled gardens, beamed ceilings, and log fires; the six modern rooms in the Zulu Wing are the exception. For less expensive accommodation, try the nearby sister property, the Railway Inn, which has six small rooms with fewer amenities. Burnham Market itself is a lovely town 6 mi west of Wells. ⊠ *The Green, B1155, Burnham Market, PE31 8HD* ☏ *03128/738777* ✍ *01328/730103* ⊕ *www.hostearms.co.uk* ↪ *36 rooms* ⌂ *3 restaurants, bar, meeting rooms, Internet, some pets allowed (fee); no a/c* ⊟ *AE, DC, MC, V* ⫶◯⫶ *BP.*

££££–£££££ ✕🖃 **Victoria at Holkham.** A colorful, whimsical hideaway, the Victoria
FodorsChoice
★
is adjacent to Holkham Hall and owned by the current earl of Leicester. Guest rooms and public areas mix Victorian, colonial, and local themes, all with a touch of Asia. The ornately carved dark-wood furniture was handmade for the hotel in India. In the restaurant you can try game dishes and local seafood such as Cromer crabs, Brancaster mussels, and fresh eels. The dune-backed Holkham Beach (where the ending beach scene from *Shakespeare in Love* was filmed) is only a few minutes' walk away. ⊠ *A149, NR23 1AB* ☏ *01328/711008* ✍ *01328/711009* ⊕ *www.holkham.co.uk/victoria* ↪ *11 rooms* ⌂ *Restaurant, room service, in-room data ports, cable TV, bar, Internet; no a/c in some rooms* ⊟ *AE, DC, MC, V* ⫶◯⫶ *CP.*

Sandringham House

42 *15 mi southwest of Holkham Hall, 8 mi northeast of King's Lynn, 43 mi northwest of Norwich.*

Sandringham House, not far from the old-fashioned but still popular seaside resort of Hunstanton, is one of the Queen's residences—it's where the Royal Family spends Christmas, as well as other vacations.

This huge, redbrick Victorian mansion was clearly designed for enormous country-house parties, with a ballroom, billiard room, and bowling alley, as well as a shooting lodge on the grounds—no wonder George V used to write fondly of "dear old Sandringham." The house and gardens are closed when the Queen is in residence, but the woodlands, nature walks, and museum of royal memorabilia (the latter housed in the old stables) remain open, as does the church, medieval but in heavy Victorian disguise. ⊠ *Sandringham* ☎ *01553/772675* ⊕ *www.sandringhamestate.co.uk* ▧ *House, gardens, and museum £6.50, gardens and museum £5.50* ⊙ *Apr.–mid-July, Aug., and Sept., daily 11–5; Oct., daily 11–3.*

Houghton Hall

㊸ *8 mi east of Sandringham, 35 mi northwest of Norwich.*

This grand Palladian pile, built by British prime minister Sir Robert Walpole in the 1720s, has been carefully restored by its current owner, the seventh marquess of Cholmondeley. The double-height Stone Hall and the sumptuous state rooms, perfect for gatherings of the powerful, reveal designer William Kent's preference for gilt, plush fabrics, stucco, and elaborate carvings. The Common Parlour, one of the original family rooms, is elegant but far simpler. New landscaping, including a 5-acre walled garden, is also part of the picture. ⊠ *Off A148, near Harpley* ☎ *01485/528569* ⊕ *www.houghtonhall.com* ▧ *£6.50, park and grounds only £4* ⊙ *May–Sept., Wed., Thurs., Sun., and bank holiday Mon. 2–5:30; grounds open at 1; last admission at 5.*

King's Lynn

㊹ *12 mi southwest of Houghton Hall, 40 mi northwest of Norwich.*

As Bishop's Lynn, the town thrived as a port on the River Ouse, growing prosperous in the 15th century through the wool and other trade with the continent; a Flemish influence is apparent in the church brasses and the style of the town squares. When Bishop's Lynn became royal property, the name was changed to King's Lynn. Although part of the old center was torn down and rebuilt in the mid-20th century, enough remains of its Georgian town houses, guildhalls, and ancient quayside warehouses (including the 15th-century Hanseatic Warehouse on St. Margaret's Lane) that this is still one of the most English of English towns.

The 15th-century **Trinity Guildhall**, with its striking checkered stone front, contains some civic treasures in the **Regalia Rooms**, in the Guildhall Undercroft. A recorded audio tour calls attention to items such as the unique silver and enamel 14th-century chalice known as King John's Cup. You enter the rooms though the adjacent **Old Gaol House**, site of the town police station until 1954, whose cells form part of an engaging law and order museum. The Guildhall itself is now the Civic Hall of the Borough Council and is not generally open to the public, although you can visit it during the King's Lynn Festival in July and on occasional guided tours in summer. ⊠ *Saturday Market Pl.* ☎ *01533/774297* ▧ *£2.40* ⊙ *Apr.–Oct., daily 10–5; Nov.–Mar., Fri.–Tues. 10–5.*

St. George's Guildhall, the largest surviving medieval guildhall in England, forms part of the **King's Lynn Arts Centre**, an arts and theater complex administered by the National Trust, and the focal point for the annual King's Lynn Festival. There's also a gallery and a crafts fair every December. The **Crofters Coffee House** (☎ 01553/773134), in the guildhall undercroft, is a budget choice for breakfast, lunch, or afternoon tea.

✉ *27–29 King St.* ☎ *01553/765565; 01553/764864 box office* ⊕ *www. kingslynnarts.org.uk* ✍ *Free* ⊙ *Jan.–late Dec., weekdays 10–2.*

> **off the beaten path**

CASTLE RISING – Giant defensive earthworks surround this impressive 12th-century stone castle, which is 4 mi northeast of King's Lynn. The 120-foot-high walls, sadly lacking a roof after all these centuries, contain some well-preserved sections, especially the chapel and the kitchen. Owned by the Howard family since 1544, the castle has been used in the past as a hunting lodge and royal residence and is a fine example of a domestic keep. ✉ *A149* ☎ *01553/631330* ⊕ *www.castlerising.com* ✍ *£3.25* ⊙ *Apr.–Nov., daily 10–6 or dusk; Nov.–Mar., Wed.–Sun. 10–4.*

Where to Stay & Eat

£££–££££ ✕ **Riverside Restaurant.** Part of the King's Lynn Arts Centre, this restaurant reflects the style of the original 15th-century warehouse, with its gnarled oak beams and redbrick walls. Lunches might include local mussels or fresh salmon; dinner is more elaborate, perhaps stuffed Portobello mushrooms followed by halibut steak or venison. When the weather allows, there are tables outside, overlooking the river. ✉ *27 King St.* ☎ *01553/773134* ▭ *MC, V* ⊙ *Closed Sun.*

£££–££££ ✕▭ **Congham Hall.** Parkland surrounds this lovely Georgian manor house, 6 mi southeast of King's Lynn. Neutral colors and traditional print fabrics keep the bedrooms light and airy. Food is taken seriously here—the hotel grows the herbs and vegetables used in the kitchen, smokes its own fish, and collects honey. Cromer crab, Norfolk pheasant, and King's Lynn shrimp all appear on the menu. ✉ *A148, Grimston, PE32 1AH* ☎ *01485/600250* 🖶 *01485/601191* ⊕ *www.conghamhallhotel. co.uk* ◨ *12 rooms, 2 suites* ⚐ *Restaurant, lounge, baby-sitting, meeting rooms, helipad, some pets allowed, kennel, no-smoking rooms; no a/c* ▭ *AE, DC, MC, V* ⦿ *BP.*

£££ ▭ **Duke's Head.** The location couldn't be better: wake up on Tuesday morning and the front rooms at the pink-washed Duke's Head have prime views of the market in full swing below. In the oldest, 17th-century part of the hotel, where age bows the main staircase, no two guest rooms are alike. The floorboards may be creaky, but each room has comfortable beds and relaxing armchairs. You can indulge in a cream tea in the lounge. ✉ *Tuesday Market Pl., PE30 1JS* ☎ *01533/774996* 🖶 *01553/763556* ⊕ *www.regalhotels.co.uk* ◨ *71 rooms* ⚐ *2 restaurants, some in-room data ports, room TVs with movies, 2 bars, lounge, some pets allowed, no-smoking rooms; no a/c* ▭ *AE, DC, MC, V* ⦿ *BP.*

££ ▭ **Tudor Rose.** Dating back to the 16th and 17th centuries, this small hotel, right off Tuesday Market Place, makes an appealing budget choice. Exposed oak beams and sloping floors in the restaurant and the simply furnished rooms recall the building's age. The restaurant serves pub food with world flavors, such as Mediterranean lamb or Mexican chili. ✉ *St. Nicholas Pl., PE30 1LR* ☎ *01553/762824* 🖶 *01553/764894* ⊕ *www.tudorrose-hotel.co.uk* ◨ *13 rooms, 11 with bath* ⚐ *Restaurant, room service, in-room data ports, bar, lounge, no-smoking rooms; no a/c* ▭ *AE, DC, MC, V* ⦿ *BP.*

Nightlife & the Arts

St. George's Guildhall is the venue for much of the **King's Lynn Festival** (☎ 01553/764864 ⊕ www.kingslynn.org), which takes place in July and encompasses concerts, exhibitions, theater, dance, films, literary events, and children's programs. The **Corn Exchange** (✉ Tuesday Market Pl. ☎ 01553/764864), a splendidly revamped 19th-century building, hosts concerts, theater, comedy, and crafts events.

LINCOLN, BOSTON & STAMFORD

The fens of northern Cambridgeshire pass imperceptibly into the three divisions of Lincolnshire: Holland, Kesteven, and Lindsey are all parts of the great county, divided administratively. Holland borders the Isle of Ely and the delightfully named Soke of Peterborough. This marshland spreads far and wide south of the Wash, the names of the district almost reflecting the squelch of mud the inhabitants of pre-drainage times must have encountered. The chief attractions are two towns: Lincoln, with its magnificent cathedral, and Stamford, to the southwest. En route to Lincoln is Peterborough, with its medieval cathedral.

The countryside around Lincoln, especially the Lincolnshire Wolds (chalk hills) to the northeast, consists of hills and copses, with drystone (unmortared) walls dividing well-tended fields. The unspoiled rural area of the Wolds, strikingly evoked in Tennyson's poetry, is particularly worth a visit, whereas the long coastline with its miles of sandy beaches and its North Sea air has all the usual, if occasionally tacky, seaside facilities for the family. Tulips are the pride and joy of south Lincolnshire, drawing thousands from all parts of Britain to view the Holland and Kesteven bulb fields in springtime.

Peterborough

45 *22 mi southwest of King's Lynn, 38 mi north of Cambridge.*

Peterborough's main attraction, the cathedral, is best seen on a day trip from Cambridge. Much of the pedestrianized city center is marred by the commercial shopping center, the Queensgate.

The third building to rise on the site, **Peterborough Cathedral** was begun in 1118, and its history reflects some key events in English history. The first church was founded in 655 by Peada, a nobleman from the early English kingdom of Mercia in central Britain. It was destroyed by the Danes in 870 and reconstructed in 972, only to be burned down again, this time by mistake, in 1116. The next incarnation, consecrated in 1238 after 120 years of building, still towers over Peterborough today. It has seen its fair share of strife, including occupation by Cromwell's forces, who fired muskets into the ceiling and broke most of the statues, stained-glass windows, choir stalls, and high altar. Although the cathedral has been left with few monuments, the result is a startlingly spacious interior into which light streams through the clear glass.

Three soaring arches, each 85 feet high, mark the outstanding West Front. In the peaks of their gables are the three figures of St. Peter, St. Paul, and St. Andrew (the cathedral is consecrated to these three saints), and high up inside the north arch is a modern figure of Queen Elizabeth II. The nave ceiling from 1220 is one of the most significant examples of Romanesque painting in Europe—note the monsters as well as figures of saints, bishops, and kings. Henry VIII buried Catherine of Aragon, his first wife, here after her death (by natural causes) in 1536. In 1541, he conferred cathedral status on the abbey, and over the tomb of his first, most pious wife now hangs the standard of Henry VIII, given by Elizabeth II. The last addition to the cathedral is the New Building, actually built between 1496 and 1508. The exquisite vaulting here is probably by the architect John Wastell, who built the famous fan vaulting in King's College Chapel, Cambridge. An exhibit in the north transept depicts the life of the cathedral throughout its long history. ⊠ *Little Prior's Gate, 12a Minster Precinct* ☎ *01733/453342* ⊕ *www.*

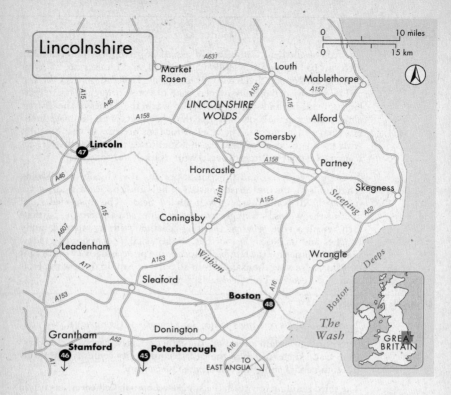

TO
EAST ANGLIA ↓

peterborough-cathedral.org.uk ✉ *Donation requested* ⊘ *Daily 8:30–5:15.*

The **Peterborough Museum and Art Gallery** explores the history of Peterborough from the Jurassic period to the modern day, including both natural and social history. The art gallery displays contemporary art and crafts. The 1816 building, a short walk from the cathedral, was originally built as a town house. ✉ *Priestgate* ☎ *01733/752451* ⊕ *www.peterboroughheritage.org.uk* ✉ *Free* ⊘ *Tues.–Fri. noon–5; Sat. 10–5, Sun. noon–4.*

Stamford

46 *14 mi northwest of Peterborough, 47 mi northwest of Cambridge.*

Serene Stamford, set on a hillside overlooking the River Welland, has a well-preserved center, in part because it was designated England's first conservation area in 1967. This unspoiled town, which grew rich in the medieval wool and cloth trade, is a delightful place to stroll and study the harmonious mixture of Georgian and medieval architecture.

★ **Burghley House,** an architectural masterpiece acknowledged as "the largest and grandest house of the first Elizabethan age," is celebrated for its roof-scape bristling with pepper-pot chimneys and slate-roof towers. It was built between 1565 and 1587 to the design of William Cecil, first Baron Burghley, when he was Elizabeth I's high treasurer; his descendants still occupy the house. The interior was remodeled in the late 17th century with treasures from Europe. The house contains 18 of the most sumptuous state rooms in England, with carvings by Grinling Gibbons and ceiling paintings by Antonio Verrio (including the dramatic Heaven Room and the Hell Staircase), as well as innumerable paint-ings and priceless porcelain. In the 18th century Capability Brown land-scaped the grounds, creating the lake, the Lion Bridge, and the Gothic Revival Orangery, where you can have tea or lunch. A recent chatelain, the sixth marquess of Exeter, was one of the Olympic runners whose life story inspired the 1981 film *Chariots of Fire*. The house is a mile southeast of Stamford. ⌗ *Off A1* ☎ *01780/752451* ⊕ *www.burghley. co.uk* 🖃 *£7.50* ⊘ *Apr.–Oct., daily 11–4:30.*

Lincoln

★ ❹⁷ *93 mi northwest of Cambridge, 97 mi northwest of Norwich.*

Celts, Romans, and Danes all had important settlements here, but it was the Normans who gave Lincoln its medieval stature after William the Conqueror founded Lincoln Castle as a stronghold in 1068. Four years later William appointed Bishop Remigius to run the huge diocese stretch-ing from the Humber to the Thames, resulting in the construction of Lincoln Cathedral, the third largest in England after York Minster and St. Paul's. Since medieval times Lincoln's status has declined. However, its somewhat remote location (there are no major motorways or rail-ways nearby) has helped preserve its traditional character.

In the city center you can walk under the 15th-century Stonebow arch on the site of an old Roman gate. Above it is the Guildhall, which houses the city's civic regalia. The River Witham flows unobtrusively under the incongruously named High Bridge, a low, vaulted Norman bridge topped by timber-frame houses from the 16th century. West of High Bridge, the river opens out into Brayford Pool, busy with river traffic and, unfor-tunately, road traffic. Here you can rent various kinds of boats. In ad-dition, from April through September cruisers tour the River Witham, showing you the city from the water (contact the Lincoln tourist office).

The cathedral is set on the aptly named Steep Hill; to its south, narrow medieval streets cling to the hillside and invite exploration. Jew's House on the Strait, dating from the early 12th century, is one of several well-preserved domestic buildings in this area.

Lincoln's crowning glory, the great **Cathedral of St. Mary,** was for hun-dreds of years the tallest building in Europe, but this magnificent me-dieval building is now among the least known of European cathedrals. The Norman bishop Remigius began work in 1072. The Romanesque church he built was irremediably damaged, first by fire, then by earth-quake (in 1185), but you can still see parts of the ancient structure at the west front. The next great phase of building, initiated by Bishop Hugh of Avalon, is mainly 13th century in character. The unique west front, topped by the two west towers, gives tremendous breadth to the entrance. It is best seen from the 14th-century Exchequer Gate arch in front of the cathedral, or from the castle battlements beyond.

Inside, a breathtaking impression of space and unity belies the many centuries of building and rebuilding. The stained-glass window at the north end of the transept, known as the Dean's Eye, is one of the ear-liest (13th-century) traceried windows, whereas its opposite number at the south end shows a 14th-century sophistication in its interlaced designs. St. Hugh's Choir, in front of the altar, and the Angel Choir at the east end behind it have ceilings with "crazy vaulting," so called be-cause of the irregular pattern. Look for the Lincoln Imp upon the pil-lar nearest St. Hugh's shrine; an angel turned this creature to stone, according to legend. Look even farther up (use binoculars or a telephoto lens) to see the 30 angels who are playing musical instruments and who give this part of the cathedral its name. Through a door on the north side is the chapter house, a 10-sided building that sometimes housed the medieval Parliament of England during the reigns of Edward I and Edward II. The chapter house is connected to the 13th-century cloister, notable for its amusing ceiling bosses. The cathedral library, a restrained building by Christopher Wren, was built onto the north side of the cloisters after the original library collapsed. The roof tours are fascinating. ✉ *Minster Yard* ☎ *01522/544544* ⊕ *www.lincolncathedral. com* ☞ *£3.50* ☾ *June–Aug., Mon.–Sat. 7:15 AM–8 PM, Sun. 7:15–6; Sept.–May, Mon.–Sat. 7:15–6, Sun. 7:15–5. Guided tours Oct.–Apr., daily 11 and 1; May–Sept., daily 11, 1, and 3; roof tours weekdays 2:30, Sat. 11 and 2:30.*

The **Minster Yard,** which surrounds the cathedral on three sides, contains buildings of various periods, including graceful examples of Georgian architecture. A statue of Alfred, Lord Tennyson, who was born in Lincolnshire, stands on the green near the chapter house. The **Medieval Bishop's Palace,** on the south side of Minster Yard, has a garden and exhibits about the former administrative center of the diocese. ✉ *Minster Yard* ☎ *01522/ 527468* ⊕ *www.english-heritage.org.uk* ☞ *£3* ☾ *Apr.–Sept., daily 10–6; Oct., daily 10–5; Nov.–Mar., weekends 10–4.*

☺ **Lincoln Castle,** facing the cathedral across Exchequer Gate, was originally built on two great mounds by William the Conqueror in 1068, incorporating part of the remains of the Roman garrison walls. The castle was a military base until the 17th century, after which it operated as a prison. In the extraordinary prison chapel you can see the cagelike stalls in which Victorian convicts listened to sermons. One of the four surviving copies of the Magna Carta, signed by King John at Runnymede in 1215, is on display in the same building. ✉ *Castle Hill* ☎ *01522/ 511068* ☞ *£2.50* ☾ *Apr.–Oct., Mon.–Sat. 9:30–5:30, Sun. 11–5:30; Nov.–Mar., Mon.–Sat. 9:30–4, Sun. 11–4.*

The **Usher Gallery** has an interesting collection of watches and clocks donated by its benefactor, James Ward Usher, a jeweler who invented the legend of the Lincoln Imp. The gallery also contains memorabilia connected with the poet Tennyson. ✉ *Lindum Rd.* ☎ *01522/527980* ☞ *£2, free on Fri.* ☾ *Tues.–Sat. 10–5:30, Sun. 2:30–5.*

Where to Stay & Eat

★ **£££££** ✕ **Jew's House.** Antique tables and oil paintings enhance this intimate restaurant in one of Lincoln's oldest buildings, a rare survivor of 12th-century Norman domestic architecture that was originally the home of a Jewish merchant. The cosmopolitan fixed-price menu of Continental specialties changes daily, and the restaurant is renowned for its fresh fish and rich desserts, all homemade. ✉ *15 The Strait* ☎ *01522/524851* ⊟ *AE, DC, MC, V* ☾ *Closed Sun. and Mon.*

£–££ ✕ **Wig and Mitre.** This interesting downtown pub-café-restaurant stays open from 8 AM until 11 PM, with everything from breakfast to full evening meals. Produce comes from the local markets, and dishes may include spiced lamb, herbed fish cakes, and a full English breakfast. ✉ *30 Steep Hill* ☎ *01522/535190* ⊟ *AE, DC, MC, V.*

★ **££££** 🛏 **White Hart.** Lincoln's most elegant hotel is luxuriously furnished with a wealth of antiques, including some fine clocks and china. The establishment has been a hotel for 600 years, reflecting a volume of experience. Each bedroom is individually decorated in traditional style; many are outfitted with antiques, and hardwoods such as walnut and mahogany abound. Dinner, bed, and breakfast rates are a particularly good deal here. ✉ *Bailgate, LN1 3AR* ☎ *01522/526222* 🖶 *01522/*

531798 ⊕ *www.heritage-hotels.com* ☞ *36 rooms, 12 suites* ☆ *Restaurant, room service, some in-room data ports, bar, lounge, baby-sitting, dry cleaning, laundry service, meeting rooms, some pets allowed (fee), no-smoking rooms; no a/c* ⊟ *AE, DC, MC, V* ⦿⦿ *BP.*

££–£££ 🏠 **D'Isney Place Hotel.** This pleasant small hotel occupies a converted town house near the cathedral. If you like privacy, it's ideal: there's no lounge or other communal space. A cooked breakfast served on Minton china is delivered to your room. For a little more style, choose one of the deluxe rooms with whirlpool baths. The pretty garden includes a piece of the old city wall. ⊠ *Eastgate, LN2 4AA* ☎ *01522/538881* 🖷 *01522/511321* ⊕ *www.disneyplacehotel.co.uk* ☞ *17 rooms* ☆ *Room service, some in-room hot tubs, baby-sitting, dry cleaning, laundry service, some pets allowed (fee), no-smoking rooms; no a/c* ⊟ *AE, DC, MC, V* ⦿⦿ *BP.*

Nightlife & the Arts

The **Theatre Royal** (⊠ Clasketgate ☎ 01522/525555), a fine Victorian theater, previews shows before their London runs and hosts touring productions. Concerts are occasionally given on Sunday.

Shopping

Chain stores fill the Bailgate Mall and the High Street. The best stores, however, are on Bailgate, Steep Hill, and the medieval streets leading directly down from the cathedral and castle. The **Cobb Hall Craft Centre** (⊠ St. Paul's La., off Bailgate) is a small mall of crafts shops and workshops that sells clocks, candles, and ornaments. **David Hansord** (⊠ Castle Hill ☎ 01522/530044) specializes in antiques, especially scientific instruments. Steep Hill has good bookstores, antiques shops, and crafts and art galleries, including the **Harding House Galleries** (⊠ Steep Hill ☎ 01522/523537).

Boston

48 *31 mi southeast of Lincoln.*

This town on the River Witham prospered during the Middle Ages because of the wool trade with Flanders and revived in the late 18th century after the fens were drained. It was from Boston that, in 1620, Puritans Isaac Johnson and John Winthrop showed their disapproval of the then-prevailing religious conditions by crossing the Atlantic and helping to found the Massachusetts city of the same name. The Puritans had first tried to set sail for Holland in 1607, but they were arrested, tried, and imprisoned. The town's leading landmark is the Boston Stump, the lantern tower of the 14th-century **Church of St. Botolph** (⊠ 1 Wormgate ☎ 01205/362992). With a height of 288 feet, the tower can be seen for 20 mi from both land and sea; it once housed a light that not only guided ships coming to the old port but also directed wayfarers crossing the treacherous marsh. Today it's a directional beacon for aircraft as well.

The 15th-century guildhall, now the **Guildhall Museum,** contains the courtroom where the Pilgrims were tried and the cells where they were held. ⊠ *St. Mary's Guildhall, South St.* ☎ *01205/365954* ⊕ *www. boston.gov.uk* ⊠ *£1.50, includes 45-min audio tour; free on Thurs., when audio tour is not available* ⊙ *Apr.–Sept., Tues.–Sat. 10–5, Sun. 1:30–5; Oct.–Mar., Tues.–Sat. 10–5.*

Among the reminders of Boston's transatlantic links is the early 18th-century **Fydell House,** next to the guildhall, now an adult education center. A room is graciously set aside to welcome visitors from the United States. ⊠ *South St.* ☎ *01205/351520* ⊠ *Free* ⊙ *Weekdays 9:30–12:30 and 1:30–4:30.*

EAST ANGLIA A TO Z

To research prices, get advice from other travelers, and book travel arrangements, visit www.fodors.com.

AIRPORTS

Norwich International Airport serves domestic and European destinations. For information about Stansted Airport in Essex, north of London, *see* Airports *in* Smart Travel Tips.

🚹 **Norwich International Airport** ✉ A140 ☎ 01603/411923 ⊕ www.norwichinternational. com.

BIKE & MOPED TRAVEL

The Broads Authority (⇨ Visitor Information) maintains a network of cycle paths and bike rental centers throughout the Broads. Rentals are £10 per day, and each rental center can provide local maps and route advice. All centers are within 30–40 minutes' drive of Norwich.

BUS TRAVEL

National Express serves the region from London's Victoria Coach Station. Average travel times: 2½ hours to Bury St. Edmunds, 2 hours to Cambridge, 2 hours to Colchester, 4 hours to Lincoln, and 3 hours to Norwich. Information about local bus service for Norfolk and parts of the surrounding counties is available from the Norfolk Bus Information Centre. First buses serve parts of the region. Cambridgeshire's largest bus company is Stagecoach Cambus. Traveline can answer public transportation questions.

CUTTING COSTS   A Ranger ticket (available on board the bus) from First gives a day's unlimited travel on the whole network for £5.50; a family pass for two parents and two children costs £11. Stagecoach Cambus sells Megarider tickets (£5) for seven days' travel within Cambridge.

🚹 **First** ☎ 01268/525251 ⊕ www.firstgroup.com. **National Express** ☎ 0870/580-8080 ⊕ www.nationalexpress.com. **Norfolk Bus Information Centre** ☎ 0500/626116. **Stagecoach Cambus** ☎ 01223/423554 ⊕ www.stagecoachbus.com/cambridge. **Traveline** ☎ 0870/608-2608 ⊕ www.traveline.org.uk.

CAR RENTAL

🚹 **Local Agencies Avis** ✉ 245 Mill Rd., Cambridge ☎ 0990/900500 ✉ 213 Shrub End Rd., Colchester ☎ 0990/900500 ✉ Ermine petrol station, Riseholm Rd., Lincoln ☎ 01522/511200 ✉ Norwich Airport, Cromer Rd., Norwich ☎ 0990/900500. **Budget** ✉ 303–305 Newmarket Rd., Cambridge ☎ 0541/565656 ✉ Hall Rd., Norwich ☎ 0541/565656. **Eurodollar** ✉ Newland Rd., Lincoln ☎ 01522/512233. **Grand Touring Club** ✉ The Model Farm, Rattlesden, Bury St. Edmunds ☎ 01449/737774. **Hertz** ✉ Willhire Ltd., Barnwell Rd., Cambridge ☎ 01223/414600 ✉ Willhire Ltd., Crown Interchange, Old Ipswich Rd., Colchester ☎ 01206/231801 ✉ Norwich Airport, Cromer Rd., Norwich ☎ 01603/404010.

CAR TRAVEL

From London, Cambridge (54 mi) is off M11. At Exit 9, M11 connects with A11 to Norwich (114 mi); A14 off A11 goes to Bury St. Edmunds. A12 from London goes through east Suffolk via Colchester and Ipswich. For Lincoln (131 mi), take A1 via Huntingdon, Peterborough, and Grantham to A46 at Newark-on-Trent. A more scenic alternative is to leave A1 at Grantham and take A607 to Lincoln.

East Anglia has few fast main roads. The principal routes are those mentioned above. Once off the A roads, traveling within the region often means taking country lanes with many twists and turns.

EMERGENCIES

🔁 **Ambulance, fire, police** ☎ 999. **Addenbrooke's Hospital** ✉ Hill's Rd., Cambridge ☎ 01223/245151. **Norfolk and Norwich Hospital** ✉ Brunswick Rd., Norwich ☎ 01603/286286.

TOURS

BUS TOURS   City Sightseeing operates open-top bus tours of Cambridge—the Backs, the colleges, the Imperial War Museum in Duxford, and the Grafton shopping center. The tours start from Cambridge train station but can be picked up at any of the marked bus stops throughout the city. Tickets can be bought from the driver, the City Sightseeing office at Cambridge train station, or the Cambridge Tourist Information Centre for £8. Tours run mid-April through September, every 15 minutes, and October through mid-April, every 30 minutes.

🔁 **City Sightseeing** ✉ Cambridge train station ☎ 01708/866000 ⊕ www.city-sightseeing.com.

WALKING TOURS   Qualified guides for walking tours of the major towns, including Bury St. Edmunds, Cambridge, Ely, Colchester, Norwich, and Lincoln, can be booked through the respective tourist offices (⇨ Visitor Information). Those in Cambridge are particularly popular; book well in advance for tours (£6.50) that depart at 1:30 year-round and more frequently in summer. Ninety-minute audio tours of Lavenham are available for rental from the Lavenham Pharmacy on High Street for £3. For a guided tour (£3) in July and August, meet at the tourist information center on Lady St. on Saturdays at 2:30 and Sundays at 11.

TRAIN TRAVEL

The entire region is served by trains from London's Liverpool Street station; in addition, there are trains to Cambridge, Ely, Lincoln, and Peterborough from King's Cross station. Full information on trains to East Anglia is available from National Rail Enquiries. Average travel times are one hour to Colchester, 50–90 minutes to Cambridge, almost two hours and 50 minutes to Norwich, and two hours to Lincoln.

CUTTING COSTS   A one-day Rover ticket available from any station in either Norfolk or Suffolk for £7.50 lets you disembark to explore any of the little towns en route. Seven-day Regional Rover tickets for unlimited travel in the Anglia Railways region are also available.

🔁 **National Rail Enquiries** ☎ 0845/748-4950 ⊕ www.nationalrail.co.uk.

TRAVEL AGENCIES

🔁 **Local Agent Referrals** **American Express** ✉ 25 Sidney St., Cambridge ☎ 01223/461460. **Thomas Cook** ✉ 18 Market St., Cambridge ☎ 01223/543100 ✉ Grafton Centre, Cambridge ☎ 01223/543000 ✉ 4 Cornhill Pavement, Lincoln ☎ 01522/346400 ✉ 15 St. Stephens St., Norwich ☎ 01603/241200 ✉ 14 London St., Norwich ☎ 01603/241100.

VISITOR INFORMATION

🔁 **East of England Tourist Board** ✉ Toppesfield Hall, Hadleigh, IP7 7DN ☎ 01473/822922 🖷 01473/823063 ⊕ www.eastofenglandtouristboard.com. **Broads Authority** ✉ 18 Colegate, Norwich, Norfolk, NR3 1BQ ☎ 01603/610734 ⊕ www.broads-authority.gov.uk. **Aldeburgh** ✉ 152 High St., IP15 5AQ ☎ 01728/453637 ⊕ www.suffolkcoastal.gov.uk. **Boston** ✉ Market Pl. ☎ 01205/356656 ⊕ www.boston.gov.uk. **Bury St. Edmunds** ✉ 6 Angel Hill ☎ 01284/757084 ⊕ www.stedmundsbury.gov.uk. **Cambridge** ✉ Wheeler St., CB2 3QB ☎ 01223/322640 ⊕ www.tourismcambridge.com. **Cambridge University** ⊕ www.cam.ac.uk. **Colchester** ✉ 1 Queen St. ☎ 01206/282920 ⊕ www.colchester.gov.uk. **Ely** ✉ Oliver Cromwell's House, 29 St. Mary's St., CB7 4HF ☎ 01353/662062 ⊕ www.ely.org.uk. **King's Lynn** ✉ The Custom House, Purfleet Quay, PE30 1HP ☎ 01553/763044 ⊕ www.west-norfolk.gov.uk. **Lavenham** ✉ Lady St. ☎ 01787/248207 ⊕ www.babergh-south-suffolk.gov.uk. **Lincoln** ✉ 9 Castle Hill ☎ 01522/529828 ⊕ www.lincoln.gov.uk. **Norwich** ✉ Forum, between N. Theatre and Bethel Sts. ☎ 01603/666071 ⊕ www. norwich.gov.uk. **Peterborough** ✉ 3 Minster Precints, PE1 6PH ☎ 01733/452336 ⊕ www. peterborough.gov.uk. **Saffron Walden** ✉ 1 Market Pl., Market Sq. ☎ 01799/510444 ⊕ www.uttlesford.gov.uk. **Southwold** ✉ 69 High St. ☎ 01502/724729. **Stamford** ✉ Broad St. ☎ 01780/755611. **Sudbury** ✉ Town Hall, Market Hill ☎ 01787/881320 ⊕ www. babergh-south-suffolk.gov.uk. **Woodbridge** ✉ Station Buildings ☎ 01394/382240 ⊕ www.suffolkcoastal.gov.uk. **Wells-next-the-Sea** ✉ Staithe St., NR23 1AN ☎ 01328/710885.

YORKSHIRE

LEEDS, BRADFORD, HAWORTH, YORK, WHITBY, CASTLE HOWARD

FODOR'S CHOICE

Castle Howard, *Coneysthorpe*

Dairy Guest House, *York*

Magpie Café, *Whitby*

Middlethorpe Hall, *stately home hotel near York*

Whitby, *coastal town*

HIGHLY RECOMMENDED

RESTAURANTS   Betty's, *York*

Endeavour, *Staithes*

19 Grape Lane, *York*

HOTELS   Devonshire Arms, *Bolton Abbey*

Malmaison, *Leeds*

White Horse and Griffin, *Whitby*

SIGHTS   Bolton Priory, *monastic ruins in town of Bolton Abbey*

Brontë Parsonage Museum, *Haworth*

Fairfax House, *York*

Grassington

Harewood House, *Harewood*

Hutton-le-Hole

Malham

National Museum of Photography & Television, *Bradford*

Rievaulx Abbey, *Helmsley*

Robin Hood's Bay

Royal Armouries, *Leeds*

Saltaire, *preserved model factory community near Bradford*

Studley Royal and Fountains Abbey, *near Ripon*

York Minster, *York*

Updated by
Kate Hughes

YORKSHIRE IS ANOTHER COUNTRY, say the locals, and a few days spent exploring this largest of English regions could well convince you they're right. The famous sights, such as the Minster at York, the moorland haunts of the Brontës near Haworth, the ruined monasteries and stately homes, are justifiably popular but provide only half the picture. Nowhere else in England have industry and the natural world collided with such significant effect, offsetting brisk manufacturing towns with untamed scenery. Author J. B. Priestley, in his *English Journey* of 1933, noted that "Industrial Man and Nature sing a rum sort of duet" in Yorkshire, a duet still played out in the hills above Priestley's native Bradford, or in Leeds, or atop the blustery moors.

Yorkshire remains an intensely rural region. The most rugged of its landscapes are the Yorkshire Moors, a vast area of lonely moorland, inspiration of Emily Brontë's 1847 *Wuthering Heights* (and if ever a work of fiction grew out of the landscape in which its author lived, it was surely this). Brilliant at times with spring flowers and heather, the moors can change dangerously, often within a few minutes, to stormy weather, when you'll be lucky to see as far as the next cloud-swept ridge. Between the bleak areas of moorland and the rocky Pennine hills lie lush, green valleys known as the Yorkshire Dales, where the high rainfall produces luxuriant vegetation, swift rivers, sparkling streams, and waterfalls. The villages here, immortalized through the books of the late veterinarian Alf Wight (1916–95), who wrote under the name James Herriot, are among the most utterly peaceful in England, although many burst into life as summer walking bases.

But there's also a gritty, urban aspect to Yorkshire, whose towns have changed the course of British history. Leeds and Bradford, two of Britain's major industrial centers, are now being gradually rejuvenated after the decline of their industrial base. More aesthetically pleasing is the northern, walled city of York, dominated by the towers of its minster—for some, the most noble cathedral in Britain. Settled originally by Romans and Vikings, York was once England's most important northern city, and it is arguably the best-preserved medieval town in the country. Beyond York, more marvels await: Castle Howard and the ruined monastic remains of Rievaulx Abbey, Whitby Abbey, and Fountains Abbey are some of the most impressive sights in Britain.

Yorkshire has historically been split into three divisions or "ridings" (from an old Norse word meaning "third"), and although the county ceased to be run as one administrative entity in 1974, natives still treat Yorkshire as one homogenous unit and tend to ignore the divisions into North, South, and West Yorkshire. York, Haworth—the center of Brontë Country—or the seaside resorts of Scarborough and Whitby make the best touring bases. Those with limited time could see York as a day trip from London; the fastest trains take just two hours to York. Proper exploration of the region, especially of the moors and dales, requires time and effort, well rewarded whether you're out to see untamed natural beauty or great medieval art.

Exploring Yorkshire

Yorkshire is the largest English region to explore (its fiercely proud inhabitants would say the only English region *worth* exploring). You need to plan carefully before launching on a tour around the separate geographic regions. The industrial heartland is West Yorkshire, where the cities of Leeds and Bradford were at the forefront of both the late medieval wool trade and the 19th-century Industrial Revolution. What

You could drive across Yorkshire in less than a day (as many do, on the way to Scotland), but you would have little time to spend anywhere. Three days would give the opportunity for a night in York, followed by a night in rural Yorkshire. However, only with five to seven days does a satisfying itinerary begin to take shape: you could stop longer in York and visit the coast, as well as get off the beaten track to seek out the abbeys, castles, and old moorland villages. You'll still have to move quickly, though, if you want to see every region of Yorkshire in a week.

Numbers in the text correspond to numbers in the margin and on the Yorkshire and York maps.

If you have 3 days

Start in **York** 13 –25 ▶, quintessential city of Yorkshire, where, if you arrive early enough in the day, you'll be able to fit in several of the main medieval city sites, such as York Minster and the Shambles. Then take a bus tour leaving shortly before noon out to spectacular **Castle Howard** 41. Return to York about 4:30 in the afternoon and repair to Betty's tearooms; in the evening you might go on a walking tour. Next morning, continue to see York sights and then travel to Leeds to pick up a bus to **Haworth** 4 for a Brontë pilgrimage. (If you have a car, you can detour to make a quick visit to stunning **Studley Royal and Fountains Abbey** 28.) Spend your final day in Haworth. Don't forget to hike over the moors from Top Withins ("Wuthering Heights") to the Hardcastle Crags valley. Return to Leeds.

If you have 7 days

Starting in **Leeds** 1 ▶, head for **Bradford** 3 and its museums, and make time for a curry lunch on Morley Street before spending the afternoon at the nearby model 19th-century factory community of Saltaire. It's just a short drive to **Haworth** 4 for an overnight stop in Brontë Country, although you'll have to wait until the next morning to see the sights. After this, you can meander up through the Yorkshire Dales, via **Skipton** 6 and **Malham** 8 before stopping for the night in **Grassington** 7. The next day, soak up more remote scenery as you tour the northern dales, Wensleydale and Swaledale, before hitting the main roads and heading south, via **Studley Royal and Fountains Abbey** 28, to the spa town of **Harrogate** 26. After all this driving, you have only a short journey to York the following day. Stay in **York** 13 –25 for two nights, and then early on the morning of departure, aim for **Helmsley** 39 with a sightseeing stop at either **Rievaulx Abbey** 40 or **Castle Howard** 41 before driving across the moors to **Danby** 37 and on to **Whitby** 35 for your overnight stop. The next day, return to York along the coast via **Robin Hood's Bay** 34 and **Scarborough** 33.

---

the tourist office likes to call Brontë Country—basically Haworth, home of the Brontë family—is just to the northwest, and northward spread the hills, valleys, and villages of the Yorkshire Dales, stomping ground of the late James Herriot, the much-loved veterinarian. In the center of the region, York deserves special attention, and there's real interest in its environs, too, from the spa town of Harrogate to the magnificent Fountains Abbey.

Moving east to the coast, Yorkshire reveals itself to be a seaside holiday destination, although never one that will win prizes for summerlike weather. But fine beaches and a fascinating history await you in the resort of Scarborough, the former whaling port of Whitby, Robin Hood's Bay—a cliff-top, one-time smuggler's haunt—and the traditional fishing village of Staithes. Finally, you can strike inland to the North York Moors National Park. Isolated stone villages, moorland walks, Rievaulx Abbey, and elegant Castle Howard are all within easy reach.

About the Restaurants & Hotels

Yorkshire has some fine restaurants, but pubs are often the best (and in small villages, the only) places to find good, hearty meals for a gentle price.

For a high price, you can stay at the stately home of Lady Mary Wortley Montagu and at other luxury hotels, or, to get a real flavor of northern hospitality and cuisine, you can look for farmhouse bed-and-breakfasts. If you're traveling by public transportation, many proprietors of places on the outskirts of town will pick you up at the train station or bus depot. Rooms fill quickly at seaside resorts in July and August, and some places in the dales and moors close in winter. Always call ahead. Hikers and budgeteers love the region's youth hostels, from those in the dales and moorland villages to budget bases in York and Scarborough. Even more basic accommodation is available in camping barns (rural bunkhouses) in the Yorkshire Dales. Tourist offices have reservation numbers and details on these popular budget options.

WHAT IT COSTS In pounds				
	£££££	££££	£££	££	£
RESTAURANTS	over £22	£18–£22	£13–£17	£7–£12	under £7
HOTELS	over £160	£115–£160	£80–£115	£50–£80	under £50

Restaurant prices are for a main course at dinner. Hotel prices are for two people in a standard double room in high season, including VAT, with no meals or, if indicated, CP (with Continental breakfast), BP (Breakfast Plan, with full breakfast), or MAP (Modified American Plan, with breakfast and dinner).

Timing

Summer is undoubtedly the best time to visit Yorkshire, especially the coastal areas and moors, when there are regattas and festivals. However, you can expect resorts and walking centers to be overcrowded, and you must book accommodations well in advance. York's city center will also be packed shoulder to shoulder with visitors. York Minster makes a splendid focal point for the prestigious York Early Music Festival, which takes place in early July. Spring and fall bring their own rewards: less crowded attractions and crisp, clear days, although with an increased risk of rain and fog. Winter is hard to call: with glistening snow and bright days, the coast, moors, and dales are beautiful, but storms and blizzards set in quickly, moorland roads become impassable, and villages can be cut off. During winter, stick to York and the main towns if you must keep to a timetable.

WEST YORKSHIRE & BRONTË COUNTRY

Even before the Industrial Revolution, the towns in the hills and river valleys of West Yorkshire were important commercial centers, whose trade in wool made prodigious fortunes for both local merchants and religious foundations. It's still a region synonymous with wool production, and a large number of "mill shops" sell high-quality knitting wool,

Great Flavors

Exploring Yorkshire, with its fresh air and hilltop walks, positively encourages hearty appetites. Happily, locally produced meat (especially lamb) and vegetables are excellent; roast beef dinners come with Yorkshire pudding, the famous popoverlike batter traditionally cooked under the meat and served with gravy. In the days when meat was a real luxury, it was offered as a first course in hopes of filling you up. Coastal fish are a treat with freshly fried chips (thick french fries); cod or haddock is the main local catch, although sole, crab, and lobster have their seasons. Look for freshly baked bread and homemade cakes, at their best in Yorkshire tearooms. Be sure to try Wensleydale cheese, which has a delicate flavor and honeyed aftertaste.

13

Hiking & Walking

Some of Britain's finest long-distance footpaths cut through the region. Short trails and longer paths crisscross the Yorkshire Dales National Park. The North York Moors National Park has long, empty swaths of land for tramping, and craggy cliff walks follow the dramatic coastline. Leading trails include the Cleveland Way (108 mi), from Helmsley to Filey; the hard-going Lyke-Wake Walk (40 mi), from Osmotherley to Ravenscar; and the eastern section of the Coast-to-Coast Walk (190 mi), which starts or finishes in Robin Hood's Bay. In addition, the Dales Way (80 mi) connects Leeds and Bradford with the Lake District. Perhaps the greatest of all English walks, the Pennine Way, which runs from the Peak District to Scotland, passes through the Yorkshire Dales.

The Monastic Past

The wealth of richly decorated and appointed monastic buildings here is a testament to the monks of medieval Yorkshire, who became some of the richest in Europe by virtue of the international wool trade that they conducted from their vast religious estates in the north. The buildings lie mostly in romantic ruins, a result of the dissolution of the monasteries during the 16th century, part of Henry VIII's struggle with the Catholic church. At places such as Fountains, Rievaulx, and Whitby abbeys, you can learn about the religious and business worlds of the great monasteries. The ruins of Bolton Abbey, praised by 19th-century art critic John Ruskin, are also memorable. Thanks to the countless poems written about these ruins by Victorian poets, and the paintings of them by celebrated 19th-century artists such as J. M. W. Turner, these sites became world famous for their powerful evocation of life in the Middle Ages.

---

sweaters, and woven wool for skirts or suits at factory prices. After industrialization, the towns took to new trades such as textiles, chemicals, and engineering, which transformed the urban scene, leaving many places today rather unattractive at first sight. However, restoration of once-glorious Victorian architecture and the regeneration of inner-city areas is having a beneficial effect, and relief is always close at hand in the region's rural and moorland surroundings.

In the gaunt hills north of the Calder Valley and south of the River Aire is the district immortalized by the writings of the Brontë sisters. Haworth, an otherwise gray West Yorkshire village, might have passed unob-

Yorkshire

GREAT BRITAIN

Swale

Richmond ⑫

Catterick

A6108

B6270

Northallerton

⑩ **Askrigg**

⑪ **Hawes**

Leeming

A684

Aysgarth

Ure

Swale

B6160

YORKSHIRE DALES NATIONAL PARK

A6108

Masham

Thirsk ㉛

A61

Grewelthorpe

North Stainley

A6108

⑨ **Kettlewell**

Ripon

㉙

B6265

⑳ **Newby Hall**

Gouthwaite Res.

Studley Royal & Fountains Abbey ㉘

⑦ **Grassington**

B6265

Pateley Bridge

B6165

Ure

B6265

⑧ **Malham**

Cracoe

Nidd

B6165

B6055

A1(M)

Bolton Priory

Blubberhouses

A59

⑤

⑥ **Skipton**

A65

Ilkley

Askwith

㉗ **Knaresborough**

㉖ **Harrogate**

A661

MARSTON MOOR

A629(T)

AIREDALE

Wharfe

A660

A658

A61

Wetherby

B1224

A659

Keighley

A650

Aire

Pool

② **Harewood House**

A64

A1

④ **Haworth**

A629

B6144

Saltaire

A659

A61

Oxenhope

③ **Bradford**

① **Leeds**

◆ **Temple Newsam**

A63

M1

Aire

A162

KEY

🏁 *Start of itinerary*

M62

TO MANCHESTER ↙

TO SHEFFIELD AND MAGNA ↓

TO LONDON ↘

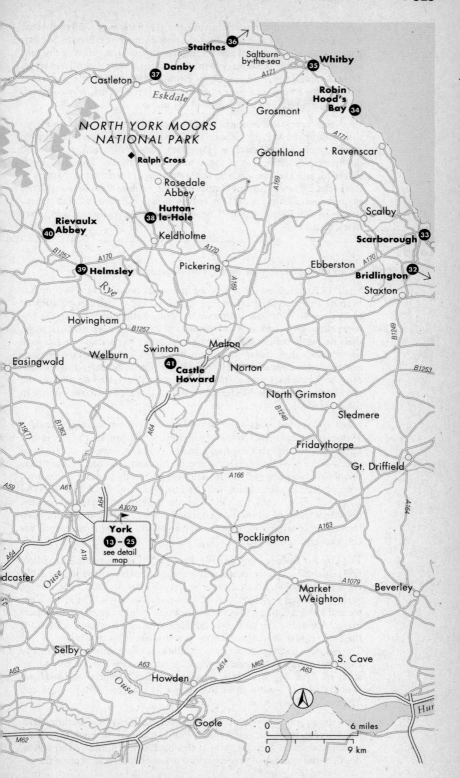

served throughout the years but for the magnetism of the family that lived in the old parsonage, now the museum of the Brontë Society. Every summer, thousands toil up the steep main street to visit the hill-top church and the museum, where all too often Brontë enthusiasm stops. To understand the real spirit of the Brontës it is necessary to go farther afield to the moors and the ruined farm of Top Withins, which legend, but not fact, refers to as Wuthering Heights.

Leeds, easily reached from the west by the trans-Pennine M62 and from the south by the M1, provides an obvious starting point and has its own appeal, including its Victorian shopping architecture and redeveloped downtown. Traditional wool towns to the south, such as Wakefield, Huddersfield, and Halifax, each have a modicum of interest, and Magna at Rotherham draws long lines for its thrilling exploration of steel. But the main thrust of any visit to West Yorkshire is to the west of Leeds, where Bradford and Brontë Country, around Haworth, really begin to repay investigation.

Leeds

▶ **❶** *43 mi northeast of Manchester, 25 mi southwest of York.*

Since 1990, what was formerly an industrial city in severe decline has become an example of urban regeneration. Leeds, with a population of more than 400,000, has a reputation as one of the greenest cities in Europe, although its unkempt industrial outskirts and congested traffic make this difficult to believe at first approach. Besides its parks, Leeds has long green routes that radiate from the city center. Urban heritage projects and redevelopment such as Millennium Square, and trend-setting restaurants and café-bars with outdoor seating have sprouted up all over the city. It's not quite the Mediterranean, but there's a tangible vitality in the air these days.

Leeds had a head start on most comparable cities because its wealthy 19th-century days had left it a fine architectural bequest. The city is well known for its superb Victorian arcades, but the Georgian squares and streets of the West End are just as notable. Tucked away among the streets you'll find old pubs and yards that were originally laid out in the 14th century. The classical **Town Hall** (⊠ The Headrow ☎ 0113/247–8384 ⊕ www.leeds.gov.uk), built in 1853, sits prominently in the city center, one of the finest of all Victorian public buildings in Britain and the masterpiece of local architect Cuthbert Broderick. Today it is a venue for concerts and special events.

The **City Art Gallery,** opposite the Town Hall, showcases a fine collection of painting and sculpture, with particularly strong showings of 20th-century British art, including works by Walter Sickert, L. S. Lowry, Stanley Spencer, and Leeds artist Atkinson Grimshaw. The **Craft Centre and Design Gallery,** also in the museum, exhibits fine contemporary crafts. Adjoining the gallery is the **Henry Moore Institute,** named for the famous British sculptor who was a student at Leeds College of Art. The institute displays temporary exhibitions of modern sculpture. The City Art Gallery has several examples of Moore's own work, or you can study his *Reclining Woman* on the steps outside the gallery. ⊠ *The Headrow* ☎ *0113/247–8248* ⊕ *www.leeds.gov.uk* ⊡ *Free* ☉ *Mon.–Tues. and Thurs.–Sat. 10–5, Wed. 10–8, Sun. 1–5.*

☼ Even the squeamish won't balk at the fun exhibits in the **Thackray Medical Museum,** in which you'll find as much social as medical history. Interactive displays help you take a trip back to the slums of the 1840s, discover the realities of surgery without anesthetics, and explore the experience of having a baby in Victorian times or today. In another exhibit, Sherlock Bones guides you around the human body. The museum is a mile east of the center and accessible by Buses 4, 4C, 42, 49, and 50. ⊠ *Beckett St.* ☎ *0113/244–4343* ⊕ *www.thackraymuseum.org* ⊡ *£4.40, parking £1* ☉ *Tues.–Sun. and national holidays 10–5; last admission 3.*

The **River Aire**, an important trading route in Leeds's early days, has been revitalized after being affected by industrial pollution. **Granary Wharf,** in the Canal Basin, reached via the Dark Arches where the River Aire flows under the City Station, has design and crafts shops, music events, boat trips, and a regular festival market. Farther east at **The Calls,** converted redbrick warehouses hold smart bars, cafés, and restaurants that enliven the cobbled streets and quayside.

★ ☾ Much of the vast, legendary arms and armor collection from the Tower of London fills the **Royal Armouries,** which occupies a redeveloped 13-acre dockland site, a 15-minute walk from the city center. Five theme galleries—War, Tournament, Self-Defense, Hunting, and Arms and Armor of the Orient—trace the history of weaponry. The state-of-the-art building is stunningly designed: expect a full-size elephant in armor, warriors on horseback, and floor-to-ceiling tents, as well as spirited interactive displays and live demonstrations. Shoot a crossbow, direct operations on a battlefield, experience a Wild West gunfight or an Elizabethan joust—it's your choice. ⊠ *Armouries Dr., off M1 or M621* ☎ *0113/220–1999* ⊕ *www.armouries.org.uk* ⊡ *Free* ☉ *Daily 10–5.*

The Leeds City Council uses **Temple Newsam,** a huge Elizabethan and Jacobean building that was altered in the 18th century, to display its rich collections of furniture, paintings, and ceramics. The house was the birthplace in 1545 of Lord Darnley, the doomed husband of Mary, Queen of Scots. Surrounding the house is a large public park with walled rose gardens, greenhouses, and miles of woodland walks, all originally laid out by Capability Brown in 1762. Renovation work has closed the house until fall 2003, but the park remains open. Temple Newsam is 4 mi east of Leeds on A63, and buses leave from Leeds Central Bus Station every 30 minutes. ⊠ *Off Selby Rd.* ☎ *0113/264–7321* ⊕ *www.leeds.gov.uk* ⊡ *Call for house price, park free* ☉ *Call for house hrs; park daily 10–dusk.*

off the beaten path

MAGNA – A 45-minute drive south from Leeds to Rotherham brings you squarely in view of Yorkshire's industrial past. The scale of the former steelworks that houses Magna, a high-tech science museum, is impressive, but the power of the Big Melt show really hits the spot. Smoke, flames, and sparking electricity bring one of the original six arc furnaces roaring to life in a sound-and-light show. In summer former steel workers act as guides; a permanent exhibit explores the world of people who worked in the industry. Four pavilions engagingly illustrate the elements of fire, earth, air, and water, used in the production of steel. ⊠ *Junction 33 or 34 off M1, Sheffield Rd., Rotherham* ☎ *01709/720002* ⊕ *www.magnatrust.org.uk* ⊡ *£4* ☉ *Mar.–Oct., daily 10–5; Nov.–Feb., Tues.–Sun. 10–5.*

Where to Stay & Eat

£££££ ✕**Pool Court at 42.** Elegant and tranquil, this restaurant in the revitalized warehouse district by the river is typical of the fashionable spots becoming popular with northern food fanciers. Good choices on the cosmopolitan contemporary menu include fish, such as griddle-cooked scallops and fresh salmon, and expertly cooked game. There are several set-price options. The adjacent, associated **Brasserie 44** is less formal and less expensive (££). ✉ *42–44 The Calls* ☎ *0113/244–4242; 0113/234–3232 Brasserie 44* ▭ *AE, DC, MC, V* ⊘ *Closed Sun. No lunch Sat.*

££–£££ ✗ **Fourth Floor Restaurant.** If the Harvey Nichols department store has been a roaring success, it's partly because of the lure of its swank Fourth Floor eatery, a standout for both food and dramatic, high-tech design. The well-crafted modern British menu changes several times a week but is sure to have stylish takes on dishes such as oxtail with celeriac purée, char-grilled rib-eye steak, and the freshest lemon sole. On summer days, the terrace comes into its own. ✉ *Harvey Nichols, 107–111 Briggate* ☎ *0113/204–8000* ▭ *AE, DC, MC, V* ⊘ *No dinner Mon.–Wed.*

£–££ ✗ **Whitelocks.** The city's oldest pub (1715), tucked away in an alley right in the city center, recommends itself for traditional Yorkshire pudding and gravy, homemade pies, and real ale. The long, narrow bar has all the trappings of the Victorian era—stained glass, etched mirrors, copper-topped tables, and red plush banquettes. Service is brisk and friendly. ✉ *Turks Head Yard, off Briggate* ☎ *0113/245–3950* ▭ *AE, MC, V.*

★ ££££ ✗▣ **Malmaison.** Passengers who used this building in its days as a tram and bus garage could hardly have envisaged its rebirth as an immaculately chic hotel exuding contemporary class and comfort. Floors have color themes of subtle tones—plum, charcoal, yellow ocher—and guest rooms are beautifully furnished with clean-lined modern pieces. The dark-paneled brasserie concentrates on French food with a Mediterranean twist. ✉ *Sovereign Quay, LS1 1DQ* ☎ *0113/398–1000* 🖷 *0113/398–1002* ⊕*www.malmaison.com* ⇆*100 rooms* ⌂ *Restaurant, in-room data ports, cable TV, gym, spa, bar, meeting rooms* ▭ *AE, DC, MC, V.*

££££–£££££ ▣ **42 The Calls.** Taking an old grain mill in a once-dilapidated waterfront area and converting it into a high-tech, high-comfort hotel took some nerve, but the venture has paid off. Each room shows individual flair but retains such original elements as warehouse skylights, exposed beams, and brickwork. Facilities are up-to-the-minute, including in-room CD players: some rooms even come with fishing rods (bring your own bait). ✉ *42 The Calls, LS2 7EW* ☎ *0113/244–0099* 🖷 *0113/234–4100* ⊕ *www.42thecalls.co.uk* ⇆*41 rooms* ⌂ *2 restaurants, in-room data ports, cable TV with movies, bar, meeting rooms, some pets allowed; no a/c* ▭ *AE, DC, MC, V.*

££££ ▣ **Quebecs.** The grand Leeds and County Liberal Club may have changed its identity when it became a boutique hotel, but the building has lost none of its Victorian verve. The sweeping oak staircase, lit by tall stained-glass windows, leads up to classy bedrooms, all in diverse shapes and sizes, sympathetically decorated in muted colors. The paneled Oak Room, an unusual circular design, is a must for a drink. ✉ *9 Quebec St., LS1 2HA* ☎ *0113/244–8989* 🖷 *0113/244–9090* ⊕ *www.etontownhouse. com* ⇆*45 rooms, 6 suites* ⌂ *In-room data ports, in-room safes, minibars, cable TV, bar, lounge, meeting rooms* ▭ *AE, DC, MC, V.*

Nightlife & the Arts

NIGHTLIFE   At fashionable café-bars all over Leeds, you can grab a bite or sip cappuccino or designer beer until late into the night. There's no shortage of clubs, either; Leeds has one of the best club scenes outside London. **The Atrium** (✉ 6–9 The Grand Arcade ☎ 0113/242–6116) is the place for deep soul and funk. **Bar Norman** (✉ Call La. ☎ 0113/234–3988) has won the local in-crowd with its weird and wonderful design, including curved walls; there's music, too. **Cuban Heels** (✉ The Arches, 28 Assembly St. ☎ 0113/234–6115) kicks out salsa sounds most nights. **Tiger Tiger** (✉ The Light, 117 Albion St. ☎ 0113/236–6999) has dancing to classic disco Thursday–Saturday, or you can sip cocktails in the classy Kaz Bar or the Lodge Bar; it attracts the over-25 set.

THE ARTS   Opera North, a leading provincial opera company, has its home in Leeds at the **Grand Theatre** (✉ 46 New Briggate ☎ 0113/222–6222); the opulent gold-and-plush auditorium is modeled on that of La Scala. Opera North also plays for free each summer on the grounds at Temple Newsam.

The Victorian **Town Hall** (✉ The Headrow ☎ 0113/224–3801) hosts an international concert season (October–May) that attracts top performers and conductors. In September it is the site of the prestigious Leeds International Piano Competition.

The ultramodern **West Yorkshire Playhouse** (✉ Playhouse Sq., Quarry Hill ☎ 0113/213–7700) was built on the slope of an old quarry. Its adaptable staging makes it eminently suitable for new and classic productions as well as touring shows.

Shopping

For ethnic clothes, gifts, jewelry, and accessories, visit the shops inside the old **Corn Exchange** (✉ Call La. ☎ 0113/234–0363). **Harvey Nichols** (✉ 107–111 Briggate ☎ 0113/204–8888), regarded as the crucible of chic, contains an abundance of fashion and a great café-restaurant. The city has some excellent markets, notably **Kirkgate Market** (✉ 34 George St. ☎ 0113/214–5162), an Edwardian beauty that's the largest in the north of England. Specialty shops and designer boutiques fill the Victorian shopping arcades; the glistening **Victoria Quarter** (✉ Briggate ☎ 0113/245–5333) epitomizes fin-de-siècle style.

Harewood House

★ ❷ *7 mi north of Leeds.*

The home of the earl of Harewood, a cousin of the Queen, Harewood House (pronounced *har*-wood) is a spectacular neoclassical mansion, built in 1759 by John Carr of York. Highlights include Robert Adam interiors, important paintings and ceramics, and a large, ravishingly beautiful collection of Chippendale furniture (Chippendale was born in nearby Otley). Capability Brown designed the handsome grounds, and Charles Barry created a notable Italian garden with fountains in the 1840s. Also here are a bird garden with 120 rare and endangered species, an adventure playground, and a butterfly house. ✉ *A61, Harewood* ☎ *0113/288–6331* ⊕ *www.harewood.org* 🎟 *£9.50, bird garden and grounds only £6.75, prices are £1 higher on Sun.* ⊙ *Mid-Mar.–Oct., daily 10–5; bird garden and grounds 10–6; Nov.–mid-Dec., weekends 10–4.*

Bradford

❸ *17 mi southwest of Harewood House, 10 mi west of Leeds, 32 mi northeast of Manchester.*

Bradford was once one of the greatest wool towns in Europe, a trade at which it had excelled since the 16th century. Even as late as the 1960s, wool accounted for a substantial part of its economy, but as with all the other West Yorkshire textile towns, recession and competition from new markets hit hard. Bradford tries hard to be likeable today, and although much of its grandeur has gone, the center still holds the odd Victorian building from its period of greatest prosperity: St. George's Hall on Bridge Street (1851) and the Wool Exchange on Market Street (1864) are two fine examples.

★ ☙   Most people come to Bradford for the museums, particularly the renowned **National Museum of Photography, Film, and Television**, which traces the history of the photographic media. It's a huge, and hugely entertaining, museum, with interactive models, machines, and related ephemera spread out over five galleries and encompassing the world's first negative, up-to-the-minute digital imaging, and all stages between. The Insight: Collections and Research Centre allows you to view material from the museum's holdings. The museum's popularity with children means you should come early or late in the day if you want to see the displays in peace. Allow time, too, for a screening at the museum's 50- by 60-foot IMAX screen. The associated Pictureville cinema has a full repertory program. ⊠ *Pictureville, Prince's Way* ☎ *01274/202030* ⊕ *www.nmpft.org.uk* ✉ *Museum free, IMAX movie £5.80, Pictureville screenings £4.50* ⊙ *Tues.–Sun. and bank holidays 10–6.*

The **Industrial Museum and Horses at Work,** in a former spinning mill 3 mi northeast of the town center, outlines Bradford's history as a wool-producing town. Exhibits include workers' dwellings dating from the 1870s and a mill owner's house from the 19th century. Children love riding in the Shire horse-drawn tram. Moorside Road is off A658 Harrogate Road; or take Bus 608, 609, or 612 from the city center. ⊠ *Moorside Mills, Moorside Rd.* ☎ *01274/435900* ⊕ *www.visitbradford.com* ✉ *Free* ⊙ *Tues.–Sat. 10–5, Sun. noon–5.*

★ A UNESCO World Heritage Site, the former model factory community of **Saltaire** was built by textile magnate Sir Titus Salt in the mid-19th century. It exemplifies the enduring trait of philanthropy among certain Victorian industrialists, who erected modern terraced housing for their workers and furnished them with libraries, parks, hospitals, and schools. Saltaire, fashioned in Italianate style, has been remarkably preserved, its former mills and houses turned into shops, restaurants, and galleries. Salt's Mill, built in 1853, resembles a palazzo and was the largest factory in the world when it was built. Today it holds an art gallery and crafts and furniture shops. One-hour guided tours (£2.50) depart every Saturday at 2 PM and Sunday at 11 AM and 2 PM from the **tourist information center** (⊠ 2 Victoria Rd., Saltaire ☎ 01274/ 774993 ⊕ www.saltaire.yorks.com/touristinfo, www.visitsaltaire.com). The **1853 Gallery** (⊠ Salt's Mill, Victoria Rd. ☎ 01274/531163 ✉ Free ⊙ Daily 10–6) holds a remarkable permanent retrospective exhibition of 400 works by Bradford-born artist David Hockney. A popular restaurant is on site. Saltaire is 4 mi north of Bradford, and there are regular local bus and train services. Drivers should take A650 to Shipley and follow the signs.

Where to Stay & Eat

£ ✕ **Kashmir.** Some of Bradford's finest curry houses line Morley Street, two minutes from the National Museum of Photography, Film, and Television. The Kashmir is one of the best, a simple, no-frills place dishing out authentically spiced food at extremely low prices. ⊠ *27 Morley St.* ☎ *01274/726513* ▭ *AE, DC, MC, V.*

£–££ ✕▦ **Beeties.** In the center of a well-preserved former model factory village, this onetime storage house and fish shop provides intimate accommodation away from downtown Bradford. On the top floor are bedrooms, pleasantly furnished with pine pieces and beautiful bedspreads. Below are a vibrant tapas bar and a more formal restaurant that focuses on fine Mediterranean-style food such as roast cod steak or spicy ratatouille. ⊠ *7 Victoria Rd., Saltaire, BD18 3LA* ☎ *01274/ 595988* ☒ *01274/582118* ⊕ *www.beeties.co.uk* ⇆ *5 rooms* ♿ *Restaurant, tapas bar, meeting rooms; no a/c, no kids under 10, no smoking (in bedrooms)* ▭ *MC, V* ⏀ *BP.*

Haworth: Heart of Brontë Country

4 *10 mi northwest of Bradford, 5 mi southwest of Keighley.*

At first glance there's not much that makes the village of Haworth (pronounced *how*-weth) in West Yorkshire special. It's an old, stone-built spot on the edge of the Yorkshire Moors, superficially much like many other craggy Yorkshire settlements. But Haworth's particular claim to fame makes it probably the most celebrated literary spot in Britain after Stratford-upon-Avon. It was here, in the middle of the 19th century, that the three Brontë sisters—Emily (author of *Wuthering Heights,* 1847), Charlotte (*Jane Eyre,* 1847), and Anne (*The Tenant of Wildfell Hall,* 1848)—lived. This unlikely trio, daughters of the local vicar, were responsible for some of the most romantic books ever written. "My sister Emily loved the moors," Charlotte once wrote. "Flowers brighter than the rose bloomed in the blackest of the heath for her; out of a sullen hollow in a livid hillside her mind could make an Eden. She found in the bleak solitude many and dear delights; and not the least and best loved was liberty." Today, thousands journey to the straggling village, which lives a little too readily off its associations: summer visitors occasionally threaten to overwhelm the place entirely.

You can get to the region by taking a train to Leeds Station or a bus to Leeds's National Express Coach Station. To reach Haworth by bus or train, buy a Metro Day Rover for bus and rail, and take the Metro train from Leeds to Keighley. There are about three hourly. From Keighley, take the Keighley & Worth Valley Railway for the trip to Haworth, or Keighley and District Bus 663, 664, or 665 (one leaves every 20 minutes). From Bradford buses run every 10 minutes to Keighley.

The town's **information center** (⊠ 2–4 West La. ☎ 01535/642329) has information about accommodations, maps, and books on the Brontës, and inexpensive leaflets to help you find your way to such outlying *Wuthering Heights* sites as Ponden Hall (Thrushcross Grange) and Ponden Kirk (Penistone Crag).

Haworth's steep, cobbled **Main Street** has changed little in outward appearance since the early 19th century, but today acts as a funnel for most of the people who crowd into the various points of interest: the **Black Bull** pub, where the reprobate Branwell, the Brontës' only brother, drank himself into an early grave; the **post office** from which Charlotte, Emily, and Anne sent their manuscripts to their London publishers; and the **church,** with its gloomy graveyard (Charlotte and Emily are buried inside the church; Anne, in Scarborough).

★ The **Brontë Parsonage Museum,** in the somber Georgian house in which the sisters grew up, displays original furniture (some bought by Charlotte after the success of *Jane Eyre*), portraits, and books. The Brontës first came here in 1820, when the Reverend Patrick Brontë was appointed to the local church, but tragedy soon struck—his wife, Maria, and their two eldest children died within five years (done in, some scholars assert, by water wells tainted by seepage from the neighboring graveyard, a malady that inflicted a high toll on all Haworth at this time). The museum contains some enchanting mementos of the four surviving children, including the sisters' spidery, youthful graffiti on the nursery wall, and Charlotte's tiny wedding shoes. Branwell painted several of the portraits on display. ⊠ *Church St.* ☎ *01535/642323* ⊕ *www.bronte.org.uk* ⊠ *£4.80* ⊙ *Apr.–Sept., daily 10–5:30; Oct.–Dec., Feb., and Mar., daily 11–5; last admission 30 mins before closing.*

If you know and love the Brontës' works, you'll probably want to walk an hour or so along a field path, a lane, and a moorland track to the **Brontë Waterfall,** described in Emily's and Charlotte's poems and letters. **Top Withins,** the remains of a bleak hilltop farm 3 mi from Haworth, is often taken to be the main inspiration for Heathcliff's gloomy mansion, Wuthering Heights. Despite the bald statement on a nearby plaque, it probably isn't. There and back from Haworth is a two-hour walk. Better still is to cross the watershed to Wycollar, over the Lancashire border, or make that fine walk from Withins to the Hardcastle Crags valley. Wherever you go, you'll need sturdy shoes and protective clothing: if you've read *Wuthering Heights,* you'll have a fairly good idea of what weather can be like on the Yorkshire Moors.

Haworth is on the **Keighley & Worth Valley Railway,** a gorgeous 5-mi-long branch line along which steam engines run between Keighley (3 mi north of Haworth) and Oxenhope. Kids will like it even more on special days when there are family fairs en route. The **Museum of Rail Travel** (🎫 £1 🕐 Daily 11–4:30), at Ingrow along the line, exhibits handsome vintage train cars. ⊠ *Railway Station, Keighley* 🕾 *01535/645214; 01535/647777 24-hr information* ⊕ *www.kwvr.co.uk* 🎫 *£6 round-trip, £9 Day Rover ticket* 🕐 *Sept.–June, weekends; July–Aug., daily; call for schedules and special events.*

Where to Stay & Eat

££–£££ ✕🏠 **Weavers.** Book well in advance to secure one of these rooms, converted from a series of old cottages in a fine village location. Weavers operates mainly as a restaurant, but the pretty, chintz-filled rooms have antique French beds. Downstairs, the restaurant (closed Sunday night and Monday) serves traditional, organic Yorkshire fare, including smoked haddock soup and lamb with mint jelly, with home-baked bread. ⊠ *15 West La., BD22 8DU* 🕾 *01535/643822* 🖷 *01535/644832* ⊕ *www.weaverssmallhotel.co.uk* ➱ *3 rooms* ♿ *Restaurant, bar; no a/c* ⊟ *AE, DC, MC, V* 🕐 *Closed 1 wk at Christmas and 1 wk in summer* ⊠○⊠ *BP.*

£–££ ✕🏠 **Aitches.** This intimate 19th-century stone house is close to the Brontë Parsonage on Haworth's main street. The guest rooms are modern, with pine pieces and colorful quilts and drapes. A fixed-price meal in the elegant small restaurant (closed Sunday and Monday) might include beef fillet with Stilton crumble followed by a traditional bread-and-butter pudding and marmalade ice cream. ⊠ *11 West La., BD22 8DU* 🕾 *01535/642501* ⊕ *www.aitches.co.uk* ➱ *5 rooms* ♿ *Restaurant; no a/c, no room phones, no smoking* ⊟ *MC, V* ⊠○⊠ *BP.*

££ 🏠 **Old Registry.** The lovely themed guest rooms—Poets' Corner, Gardeners' Delight, Cherub Corner, and so on—in this creeper-covered Victorian house at the lower end of the main street are all individually decorated and equipped with CD players. One room has lavender-scented pillows, another has tapestry hangings, and there's an unusual three-poster bed in the attic. All have large bathrooms. ⊠ *2–4 Main St., BD22 8DA* 🕾🖷 *01535/646503* ⊕ *www.oldregistry.com* ➱ *8 rooms* ♿ *Some pets allowed; no a/c, no room phones, no smoking* ⊟ *MC, V.*

££ 🏠 **Old White Lion Hotel.** Next door to the church where Patrick Brontë preached stands this former coaching inn, one of the more welcoming hostelries in Haworth. Antique touches and modern conveniences mix happily in the simple rooms; public areas have wood beams and paneling. ⊠ *6 West La., BD22 8DU* 🕾 *01535/642313* 🖷 *01535/646222* ⊕ *www.oldwhitelionhotel.com* ➱ *14 rooms* ♿ *Restaurant, cable TV, bar, meeting rooms; no a/c* ⊟ *AE, DC, MC, V* ⊠○⊠ *BP.*

THE YORKSHIRE DALES

With some of the fairest scenery in England, the Yorkshire Dales stand in complete and startling contrast to the industrial towns of West Yorkshire. These meandering river valleys fall south and east from the hills known as the Pennines and, beyond Skipton, present an almost wholly rural aspect. Most, but not all, of the dales take their name from the rivers that run through them and have quintessentially English scenery: a ruined priory here, a narrow country road there, a babbling river, drystone walls made without mortar, and stone moorland hamlets (which were the settings for James Herriot's books). Some of the limestone outcroppings and caves can be explored safely even by those not used to exploring such places. Villages here fit snugly into little pockets, looking as though they, like the Pennines, have been here from eternity. In places, loveliness of setting goes hand in hand with architectural beauty, such as at Bolton Priory, the monastic ruins that once enchanted Wordsworth and Ruskin. The Yorkshire Dales contain prime walking country, and all the villages covered in this section have access to a network of paths and trails; they can also provide accommodations and hiking services. Wharfedale, one of the longest of the dales, is easily accessible from Bradford. A convenient driving route would take in Bolton Priory, the castle at Skipton, and rural Grassington, Malham, and Kettlewell, before moving farther north to see the towns of Askrigg and Hawes in Wensleydale and the glories of Swaledale. You might finish up at the market town of Richmond, where Henry VII had his family seat.

Bolton Priory

★ ❺ *12 mi north of Haworth, 18 mi north of Bradford, 24 mi northwest of Leeds.*

Some of the loveliest Wharfedale scenery comes into view around Bolton Priory, the ruins of an Augustinian priory, which sits on a grassy embankment inside a great curve of the River Wharfe itself. The priory is just a short walk or drive from the village of Bolton Abbey. Once there, you can wander through the 13th-century ruins or visit the priory church, which is still the local parish church. The duke of Devonshire owns the Bolton Abbey estate, including the ruins. Among the famous visitors enchanted by Bolton Priory were William Wordsworth (who described "Bolton's mouldering Priory" in his poem "The White Doe of Rylstone"), J. M. W. Turner, the 19th-century artist, who painted it, and John Ruskin, the Victorian art critic, who rated it the most beautiful of all the English ruins he had seen.

Close to Bolton Priory, surrounded by romantic woodland scenery, the River Wharfe plunges between a narrow chasm in the rocks (called the Strid) before reaching **Barden Tower**, a medieval hunting lodge. This lodge, where Henry, Lord Clifford, carried out his studies in alchemy in the late 15th century, is now a ruin and can be visited just as easily as Bolton Priory, in whose grounds it stands. You can also ride on the scenic 4-mi **Embsay & Bolton Abbey Steam Railway** (☎ 01756/710614; 01756/795189 recorded timetable), which has a station in Bolton Abbey. ✉ *Off B6160* ☎ *01756/718009* ⊕ *www.boltonabbey.com* ✆ *Free, parking £4* ☉ *Daily dawn–dusk.*

Where to Stay & Eat

★ **£££££** ✕▥ **Devonshire Arms.** Originally an 18th-century coaching inn, and still belonging to the dukes of Devonshire, this luxurious country-house hotel is near the River Wharfe, within easy walking distance of Bolton Abbey. Portraits of various dukes hang on the walls, and the bedrooms are tastefully decorated by the duchess of Devonshire with antiques and family memorabilia. The Burlington restaurant (no-smoking) has a fixed-price menu of superb traditional fare that uses game and fish from the estate and homegrown herbs and vegetables. The brasserie serves more modest (and modestly priced) fare. ⊠ *Bolton Abbey, Skipton, BD23 6AJ* ☎ *01756/710441* 🖷 *01756/710564* ⊕ *www.devonshirehotels.co. uk* ⇥ *39 rooms, 2 suites* ⌂ *2 restaurants, in-room data ports, tennis court, pool, health club, sauna, fishing, 2 bars, meeting rooms, some pets allowed; no a/c* ⊟ *AE, DC, MC, V* 🍴 *BP.*

Skipton

❻ *6 mi west of Bolton Abbey, 12 mi north of Haworth, 22 mi west of Harrogate.*

Skipton in Airedale, capital of the limestone district of Craven, is a typical Dales market town with as many farmers as visitors milling in the streets. There are markets Monday, Wednesday, Friday, and Saturday, and shops selling local produce predominate.

Skipton Castle, built by the Normans in 1090 and unaltered since the Civil War (17th century), is the town's most prominent attraction and one of the best preserved of all English medieval castles, remarkably complete in its appearance. After the Battle of Marston Moor during the Civil War, it remained the only Royalist stronghold in the north of England. In the central courtyard, a yew tree, planted 300 years ago by Lady Anne Clifford, still flourishes. The castle is at the top of busy High Street. ⊠ *High St.* ☎ *01756/792442* ⊕ *www.skiptoncastle.co.uk* 🎫 *£4.80* ☉ *Mar.–Sept., Mon.–Sat. 10–6, Sun. noon–6; Oct.–Feb., Mon.–Sat. 10–4, Sun. noon–4.*

Where to Eat

££–£££ ✕ **Angel Inn.** Diners at the Angel regularly clog the hidden-away hamlet of Hetton with their vehicles, such is the attraction of this locally renowned eatery. You can book in advance for the restaurant, but tables in the various cozy rooms of the bar-brasserie are available on a first-come-first-served basis, and they fill at opening time most days. Fish is a specialty; the menu may list fillet of sea bass or salmon with asparagus and hollandaise sauce. The restaurant is 5 mi north of Skipton. ⊠ *Off B6265, Hetton* ☎ *01756/730263* ⌂ *Reservations essential* ⊟ *AE, MC, V* ☉ *No dinner Sun.*

Grassington

★ ❼ *10 mi north of Skipton, 14 mi northwest of Ilkley, 25 mi west of Ripon.*

A small, stone village built around an ancient cobbled marketplace, Grassington makes a good base for exploring Upper Wharfedale. The Dales Way footpath passes through the village, and there's a good mix of guest houses, stores, pubs, and cafés. If you visit during summer, facilities become overwhelmed by day-trippers and walkers. There are plenty of local walks, however, and if you're prepared to make a day of it, you'll soon find you leave the crowds behind. The **National Park Centre** has guidebooks, maps, and bus schedules to help you enjoy a day in the Yorkshire Dales National Park. ⊠ *Colvend, Hebdon Rd.* ☎ *01756/752774* ⊕ *www.yorkshiredales.org.uk* ☉ *Apr.–Oct., daily 10–5; Nov.–Mar., Mon., Wed., Fri.–Sun. 10–4.*

Where to Stay & Eat

£–££ ✕ **Devonshire Hotel.** This traditional Dales inn makes a comfortable and refined rural dining spot, with a fine assortment of upholstered chairs in the oak-paneled and candlelit dining room. Local lamb and dishes such as smoked haddock and braised ham appear on the menu alongside stir-fries and curries. ✉ *Main St.* ☎ *01756/752525* ▭ *MC, V.*

££ ▦ **Ashfield House.** Three converted 17th-century stone cottages, once the homes of Grassington lead miners, make up this well-run small hotel off the main street. There's a cheery welcome on arrival, simple bedrooms with pine furniture and white walls, a cozy little brick-and-beam sitting room, and a walled garden. It's worth asking ahead for the deliciously hearty set dinner (£16.50). ✉ *Summers Fold, BD23 5AE* ☎ *01756/752584* ⊕ *www.ashfieldhouse.co.uk* ⇄ *7 rooms* ♿ *Dining room, Internet; no a/c, no room phones, no kids under 5, no smoking* ▭ *MC, V* ⊘ *Closed Jan.* ⦿ *BP.*

££ ▦ **Grassington Lodge** Light and airy, this Victorian house has made the most of its original features by expert and uncluttered decoration. All bedrooms have beautiful quilts; the room on the top floor has the biggest bed. A roaring log fire in the sitting room takes the edge off cold days. ✉ *8 Wood La., BD23 5LU* ☎ *01756/752518* ⊕ *www.grassingtonlodge. co.uk* ⇄ *7 rooms* ♿ *No a/c, no room phones, no kids under 12, no smoking* ▭ *No credit cards* ⊘ *Call ahead in winter* ⦿ *BP.*

Malham

★ ❽ *10 mi west of Grassington, 12 mi northwest of Skipton.*

Avid hikers descend in droves on Malham in summer to tour some of Britain's most remarkable limestone formations. The tiny hamlet has a population of about 200, yet is visited by a half million people a year. The lesson is to come before June or after August, if at all possible, to avoid the worst crowds. It's a rugged and romantic spot, whatever the weather, with intensely rural surroundings described glowingly in poems by Wordsworth and W. H. Auden, painted by Turner, and photographed by David Hockney—proof indeed of Malham's aesthetic potency. To get here from Grassington, take B6265 south 2 mi through Cracoe, then branch west onto the minor road past Hetton and Calton; Malham is also northwest of Skipton, off A65.

Maps and displays at Malham's **National Park Centre** will give you ideas of what to do locally and in Yorkshire Dales National Park. You can get a list of local B&B and pub accommodations, too; they are relatively plentiful, but highly sought after in summer. ☎ *01729/830363* ⊘ *Apr.–Oct., daily 10–5; Nov.–Mar., Fri.–Sun. 10–4.*

Sports & the Outdoors

Malham's three main destinations—Malham Cove, Gordale Scar, and Malham Tarn—can be seen on a circular walk of 8 mi that takes most people four to five hours. Those with less time should cut out the tarn: a circular walk from the village to Malham Cove and Gordale Scar can be completed in just over two hours. **Malham Cove**, a huge, 300-foot-high natural rock amphitheater, is a mile north of the village and provides the easiest local walk, although following the path *up* to the top is a brutal climb, rewarded by magnificent views. At **Gordale Scar**, a deep natural chasm between overhanging limestone cliffs, the white waters of a moorland stream plunge 300 feet. It's a mile northeast of Malham by a lovely riverside path. A walk of more than 3 mi leads north from Malham to **Malham Tarn**, an attractive lake set in windswept isolation. There's a nature reserve on the west bank and an easy-to-follow trail on the east bank.

en route
North of Malham, a dramatic moorland drive follows the minor road that skirts Malham Tarn to **Arncliffe** in Littondale. In Littondale, a superb village inn, the **Falcon** (☎ 01756/770205) revives flagging spirits and provides accommodations. In winter this road may be impassable; always check local weather forecasts. At Arncliffe, follow the signs southeast for B6160 and then turn north for Kettlewell.

Kettlewell

9 *6 mi north of Grassington, 8 mi northeast of Malham.*

A babbling river runs through the heart of Kettlewell, the main settlement in Upper Wharfedale and a fine base for a couple of days' exploration of the local hills and valleys, with their stone-flagged pubs, riverside walks, and narrow pack bridges (built for horses and donkeys carrying sacks) constructed from rubble. The Dales Way hiking path passes through the quiet, gray-stone village, and drivers will easily be able to visit Malham and Grassington from here, returning for a peaceful night away from the crowds.

Where to Stay & Eat

££ ✕⊞ **Blue Bell Inn.** Horse brasses, tankards hanging from the rafters, ornamental plates, and high-back settles decorate this 17th-century coaching inn. Guest rooms are simply furnished with colorfully striped quilts. The reasonably priced menu includes Dales lamb chops, grilled Wharfedale trout, and plenty for vegetarians. ⊠ *BD23 5QX* ☎ *01756/760230* ⊕ *www.bluebellinn.co.uk* ↪ *9 rooms* ⚭ *Restaurant, bar, no-smoking rooms; no a/c, no room phones* ▭ *MC, V* ¹⊙¹ *BP.*

££ ⊞ **Racehorses Hotel.** Traditional country hospitality is the focus of this 18th-century former coaching inn, tucked next to the river; the horse-racing memorabilia and paraphernalia will appeal to horse lovers. Narrow corridors and low ceilings abound, but the guest rooms are surprisingly light and spacious. You'll find tasty local fare in the restaurant. ⊠ *B6160, BD23 5QZ* ☎ *01756/760233* ⊕ *www.theracehorses.co.uk* ↪ *12 rooms* ⚭ *Restaurant, bar; no a/c, no room phones* ▭ *MC, V* ¹⊙¹ *BP.*

en route
From Kettlewell, it's just 4 mi north along B6160 to **Buckden,** the last village in Wharfedale. A minor road leads to the riverside hamlet of Hubberholme. Its stone chapel and ancient George Inn were favorites of Yorkshire-born author J. B. Priestley, who is buried in the churchyard. Back on B6160, you can go north through Kidstone Pass to Aysgarth in Wensleydale, where the River Ure plummets over a series of waterfalls.

Askrigg

10 *16 mi north of Kettlewell, 25 mi north of Malham.*

Askrigg would be just another typical Wensleydale village, were it not for its association with the James Herriot TV series *All Creatures Great and Small,* which was filmed in and around the village in the 1970s and 1980s. The tourist board pushes "Herriot Country" hard, but although Askrigg—dubbed "Darrowby" in the program—is a pleasing village, there's not much else to keep you here, apart from walks to a couple of local waterfalls. The **King's Arms Hotel** (⊠ Market Pl. ☎ 01969/650817), a wood-paneled, 18th-century coaching inn, was rechristened the Drover's Arms for its appearance in episodes of the Herriott TV series. The atmospheric building has nook-and-cranny rooms, good local beer, and two restaurants.

Hawes

⑪ *5 mi west of Askrigg.*

The best time to visit Hawes, reputedly the highest market town in England, is on Tuesday when farmers and locals crowd into town for the weekly market. The town is brisk and businesslike at other times, too, since Hawes retains some of Wensleydale's more traditional industries, not least its cheese making. Crumbly, white Wensleydale cheese has been made in the valley for centuries, and it is sold in local stores. Give yourself time to wander the cobbled side streets, some of which are filled with antiques shops and tearooms.

The **Wensleydale Creamery Visitor Centre,** in a working dairy farm, includes a museum that tells the story of Wensleydale cheese. A viewing gallery enables you to watch production (best seen between 10 and 3), and then you can repair to the shop to taste the various cheeses before you buy. Besides the regular Wensleydale cheese, you can try it smoked, or with ginger, or with apple pie. A restaurant is on site. ⊠ *Gayle La.* ☎ *01969/667664* ⊕ *www.wensleydale.co.uk/centre.htm* ☑ *Museum £2* ⊙ *Apr.–Oct., daily 9–5:30; Nov.–Mar., daily 9:30–4:30.*

The Yorkshire Dales National Park Information Centre in the old train station contains the **Dales Countryside Museum,** which gives a picture of Dales life in past centuries. A traditional rope-making shop here also welcomes visitors. ⊠ *Station Yard* ☎ *01969/667450* ⊕ *www.yorkshiredales.org.uk* ☑ *Museum £3* ⊙ *Daily 10–5.*

en route From Hawes, the most direct route to **Swaledale** is north by minor road over the Buttertubs Pass, a 7-mi run to Muker, a lovely village that hosts the annual Swaledale show in September. Many people regard Swaledale itself as the finest of all the Yorkshire Dales. From Muker, B6270 and A6108 run down the valley to Richmond.

Richmond

⑫ *22 mi northeast of Hawes, 25 mi northwest of Ripon.*

Richmond tucks itself into a curve above the foaming River Swale, with a network of narrow Georgian streets and terraces opening onto the country's largest cobbled marketplace. Despite appearances, it would be a mistake to date the town to the 18th century. The Normans swept in during the late 11th century, determined to subdue the local population and establish their rule in the north. This they did by building a mighty castle, around which the town grew, and throughout the Middle Ages Richmond was effectively a garrison town.

The immense keep of Norman **Richmond Castle** towers above the river, providing excellent views over the surroundings. Built around 1071 by Alan Rufus, first earl of Richmond, it was used as a prison for William the Lion of Scotland 100 years later. The castle is one of the best-preserved monuments of this era, retaining its curtain wall and chapel, and a great hall that has been partially restored to its medieval splendor; even the 14th-century graffiti remains. There's a heritage garden, and a path along the river leads to the ruins of golden-stone Easby Abbey. One historical note: when Henry Tudor (son of Edmund Tudor, earl of Richmond) became Henry VII in 1485, he began calling his palace in Shene, southwest London, Richmond (Palace), after his family seat in Richmond. The name gradually became used to describe that area of London. ☎ *01748/822493* ⊕ *www.english-heritage.org.uk* ☑ *£2.90* ⊙ *Apr.–mid-*

July and Sept., daily 10–6, mid-July–Aug. 9:30–7; Oct., daily 10–5; Nov.–Mar., daily 10–4.

The tiny Georgian **Theatre Royal**, a jewel built in 1788, retains the wooden seating from the days of the 18th-century Shakespearean actor David Garrick. The museum holds scenery dating from 1836. ⌂ *Friars Wynd* ☎ *01748/823710; 01748/823021 box office* ⊕ *www.georgiantheatre.com* ✉ *Museum £1.50* ⊙ *Museum Mar.–Dec., Mon.–Sat. 1:30–4:30; box office Mar.–Oct., Mon.–Sat. 1:30–4:30.*

Where to Stay & Eat

£££–£££ ✕ **Frenchgate Café.** Blue wicker chairs and yellow walls capture a bit of the bright Mediterranean at this bistro-style café, just below the main cobbled square. Panache and care guide the contemporary cooking; try one of the pastas, such as penne with smoked salmon, or roast rack of lamb with red wine and red currant sauce. Cappuccino, scones, and other snacks are also available. ⌂ *29 Frenchgate* ☎ *01748/824949* ▭ *AE, MC, V.*

££ ⊡ **Frenchgate Hotel.** The three-story Georgian town house on this quiet cobbled street has a secluded walled garden for summer days and a bright and welcoming interior, furnished with flair. Public rooms hark back to the 17th century, but the decorative mice (symbol of local craftsman Mousey Thompson) hidden in the woodwork are more recent. The spacious bedrooms favor prints and stripes. ⌂ *59–61 Frenchgate, DL10 7AE* ☎ *01748/822087* 🖷 *01748/823596* ⊕ *www.frenchgatehotel.com* 🛏 *11 rooms* ♨ *Restaurant, bar; no a/c* ▭ *MC, V* ⊙⃝ *BP.*

YORK

▶ It would be unthinkable to visit North Yorkshire without going first to the historic cathedral city of York, and not just because its central location makes it a practical place to start. Named "Eboracum" in Latin, York was the military capital of Roman Britain, and traces of Roman garrison buildings survive throughout the city. The Vikings also claimed York as their capital and left bountiful evidence of their tenure, and in Norman times the foundations of York Minster, the largest medieval cathedral in England, were laid. During the great industrial age, which caused so much havoc in many northern towns and cities, York was a forgotten backwater—hence the survival of so much medieval and 18th-century architecture. That's not to say that the city exists in a time vacuum: the stores that have taken over the heart of the old city can sometimes make the place seem more like an extension of London's Oxford Street than one of the great historical survivals of Europe. The Shambles, a medieval street built between 1350 and 1450, has been particularly altered by shops and boutiques.

York is 48 mi southeast of Richmond, 25 mi northeast of Leeds, and 82 mi south of Newcastle. By far the most attractive city in the region, it is one of the most popular short-stay destinations in Britain and only two hours by fast train from London on a good day.

Exploring York

After the fall of the Roman Empire in the 5th century, a Saxon town grew up over the ruins of the Roman fort at York. On Christmas Eve, AD 627, the Northumbrian king Edwin introduced Christianity to the area by being baptized in a little wooden church here. The city grew in importance during the 9th century, after the Viking conquerors of northern and eastern England made York, which they called "Jorvik," their English capital. You'll notice that many of the city's street names are suffixed with the word "-gate" (Goodramgate, Micklegate, for example). "Gate" was the Viking word for "street."

The old city center of York is a compact, dense web of narrow streets and tiny alleys, "snickleways," in which congestion is so bad that automobile traffic has been banned around the minster. It is, conversely, a fine city for walking, provided you have a map. Try to avoid visiting in July and August, when crowds choke the narrow streets and cause long lines at the popular museums. April, May, and October are far better; April is also the time to see the embankments beneath the city walls filled with the pale gold ripple of daffodils. You can get a good overview of York by strolling along these walls. For a different perspective, walk beside the River Ouse, which cuts a sizable swath through the city and in summer is full of pleasure craft.

a good walk

York's city center may be compact, but there's so much to see that you'll need an early start and plenty of stamina. You can't miss your starting point: the towers of **York Minster** 13 ⏵ are visible from virtually anywhere on the encircling **city walls** 14, so once you've got your bearings, make for Duncombe Place and the main entrance to England's largest Gothic church. After you've ogled the interior, take a few steps northward for the **Treasurer's House** 15 and its surprising interior. Next, head down either Low Petergate or Goodramgate to the famed **Shambles** 16, now a crowded shopping street. At the southern end of the Shambles, you can walk to Fossgate to visit the **Merchant Adventurers' Hall** 17, with its medieval timber-frame hall. Retrace your steps on Fossgate and turn left on Coppergate, and you're in one of York's oldest areas, where Viking finds were first discovered; the entertaining **Jorvik** 18 has all the details. From Coppergate, Castlegate runs south, passing the former church of St. Mary's and that connoisseur's delight, the elegant Georgian-era **Fairfax House** 19 before ending at the historic mound of **Clifford's Tower** 20. The **Castle Museum** 21, a collection of ephemera, costumes, and vintage machinery, marks the southernmost extent of your explorations.

From the Castle Museum, it's a 20-minute stroll back through the city center, up to the **Guildhall** 22 on St. Helen's Square—you can refuel in Betty's famous tearoom—and nearby **Stonegate** 23, another historic shopping street. Doing the walk this way, you've saved two splendid museum collections, both on the outskirts of the historic kernel, until last. From St. Helen's Square it's an easy walk up Lendal and across the main road to the archaeological exhibits of the **Yorkshire Museum** 24. Enjoy a stroll through the museum's gardens, then make your way to Lendal Bridge and cross the River Ouse onto Station Road. Taking a right on Leeman Road brings you to the **National Railway Museum** 25.

TIMING The walk itself takes about an hour, but you'll need a long day (and perhaps a second, depending on your interests) if you want to spend time at the sights. Try to avoid weekends, when the crowds can be intense.

What to See

21 **Castle Museum.** A former 18th-century debtors' prison, this museum of everyday items presents detailed exhibitions and re-creations, including a Victorian street complete with crafts shop and a working water mill, as well as notable domestic, costume, and arms and armor displays. One treasure is the Coppergate Helmet, a 1,200-year-old Anglo-Saxon helmet discovered during excavations of the city and one of only three such objects found. You can also visit the cell where Dick Turpin, the 18th-century highwayman and folk hero, spent the night before his execution. ✉ *Clifford St.* ☎ *01904/653611* ⊕ *www.yorkcastlemuseum.org. uk* ✆ *£6* ☉ *Daily 9:30–5.*

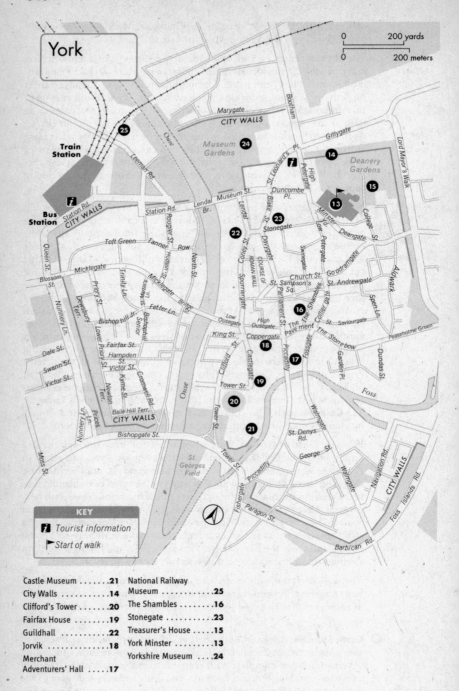

York

KEY

ℹ️ Tourist information

▸ Start of walk

Castle Museum **21**
City Walls **14**
Clifford's Tower **20**
Fairfax House **19**
Guildhall **22**
Jorvik **18**
Merchant
Adventurers' Hall **17**

National Railway
Museum **25**
The Shambles **16**
Stonegate **23**
Treasurer's House **15**
York Minster **13**
Yorkshire Museum **24**

14 **City walls.** York's almost 3 mi of ancient stone walls are among the longest and best preserved in England. A walk on the narrow paved path along the top leads you through 1,900 years of history, from the time the earthen ramparts were raised by the Romans and York's Viking kings to repel raiders, to their fortification by the Normans, to their current landscaping by the city council. The path crosses over York's distinctive fortified gates or "bars": the portcullis on Monk's Bar on Goodramgate is still in working order, and Walmgate Bar in the east is the only gate in England to have preserved its barbican. Bootham Bar in Exhibition Square was the defensive bastion for the north road, and Micklegate Bar, in the southwest corner of the city, was traditionally the monarch's entrance. To access the path and the lookout towers, find a staircase at one of the breaks in the walls. ⊕ *www.york.gov.uk/walls* ✉ *Free* ☉ *Daily dawn–dusk.*

20 **Clifford's Tower.** Dating from the early 14th century, this forbidding tower stands on the mound originally erected for the keep of York Castle. In 1190 this was the scene of one of the worst instances of anti-Semitism in medieval Europe. Of the 150 Jews who had sought sanctuary in the castle from a mob, some committed suicide and others surrendered and were massacred. ✉ *Tower St.* ☎ *01904/646940* ✉ *£2.10* ☉ *Apr.–Sept., daily 10–6; Oct., daily 10–5; Nov.–Mar., daily 10–4.*

★ **19** **Fairfax House.** One of the most elegant Georgian town houses in England is a masterpiece of rococo decoration. Now a museum of decorative arts, this often overlooked treasure was designed by Robin Carr of York and built in 1762. A distinguished collection of Georgian furniture fills the house. The marble dining room and the grand salon, all crystal chandeliers and flaming crimson silk walls, rival anything found at Castle Howard, the famous stately home northeast of York. ✉ *Castlegate* ☎ *01904/655543* ⊕ *www.fairfaxhouse.co.uk* ✉ *£4.50* ☉ *Mid-Feb.–Dec., Mon.–Thurs. and Sat. 11–5, Sun. 1:30–5; last admission 4:30; Fri., guided tours 11 and 2.*

22 **Guildhall.** The mid-15th-century guildhall, by the River Ouse, was a meeting place for the city's powerful guilds. It was also used for pageants and mystery plays (medieval dramas based on biblical stories and the lives of saints). Restoration after the damage done by World War II bombing has restored it to something approaching its erstwhile glory, although 14 Victorian stained-glass windows were lost—only one, at the west end, remains as a bright reminder. The guildhall is behind the 18th-century Mansion House. ✉ *St. Helen's Sq.* ☎ *01904/613161* ✉ *Free* ☉ *May–Oct., weekdays 9–5, Sat. 10–5, Sun. 2–5; Nov.–Apr., weekdays 9–5.*

need a break? Sink into a leather armchair in the informal **Ha!Ha! Bar and Canteen** (✉ 13–17 New St., off Davygate ☎ 01904/655868) for a tasty Mediterranean brunch and nibbles. Liquid refreshments include cappuccino as well as cocktails.

18 **Jorvik.** On an authentic Viking site, this exhibition re-creates a Viking city of the 10th century with careful attention to detail. Its time capsules whisk you through the streets to experience the sights, sounds, and smells of Viking England, and excellent displays, using high-tech wizardry, reveal the breadth of the Viking culture and social system. ✉ *Coppergate* ☎ *01904/643211; 01904/543403 advance booking* ⊕ *www.vikingjorvik.com* ✉ *£6.95* ☉ *Apr.–Oct., daily 9–5:30; Nov.–Mar., daily 10–4:30.*

17 **Merchant Adventurers' Hall.** Built between 1357 and 1368 and owned by one of the city's richest medieval guilds (its members dealt in wool and lead, which were traded far and wide), this is the largest half-timber hall in York and one of the finest in Europe. A pretty riverfront garden lies behind the hall. On most Saturdays, antiques fairs are held inside the building. ✉ *Fossgate* ☎ *01904/654818* ⊕ *www.theyorkcompany.co.uk* 🎫 *£2* ⊙ *Apr.–Sept., Mon.–Thurs. 9–5, Fri.–Sat. 9–3, Sun. noon–4; Oct.–Mar., Mon.–Thurs. 9–3:30, Fri. and Sat. 9–3.*

㉕ National Railway Museum. At this train spotters' delight, which began as a northern outpost of the Science Museum in London, Britain's national collection of locomotives forms part of the world's largest train museum. Among the exhibits are gleaming giants of the steam era, including *Mallard,* holder of the world speed record for a steam engine (126 mph). Passenger cars used by Queen Victoria are on display, as well as the only Japanese bullet train to be seen outside Japan. You can clamber aboard some of the trains, and an interactive exhibit explores working life on board a mail train. ✉ *Leeman Rd.* ☎ *01904/621261; 01904/686286 information line* ⊕ *www.nrm.org.uk* 🎫 *Free* ⊙ *Daily 10–6.*

⓰ The Shambles. Ah, that this street remained as picturesque as its name. York's best-preserved medieval street has several half-timber stores and houses with overhangs so massive you could almost reach across the street from one second-floor window to another. It's a little too cute for its own good these days, with its crafts and souvenir shops—a far cry, certainly, from the days when the Shambles was the city's meat market. Still, aim your camera at rooftop level and see if you can catch York Minster soaring over it all.

㉓ Stonegate. This narrow, pedestrian-only street of Tudor and 18th-century storefronts and courtyards retains considerable charm. It has been in daily use for almost 2,000 years, since first being paved in Roman times. A passage just off Stonegate, at 52A, leads to a 12th-century Norman stone house, one of the few to have survived in England.

⓯ Treasurer's House. A surprise awaits as you step inside this large 17th-century house, the home from 1897 to 1930 of industrialist Frank Green. With a fine eye to texture, decoration, and pattern, Green created a series of period rooms—including a medieval great hall—as a showcase for his collection of antique furniture. Delft tiles decorate the kitchen, copies of medieval stenciling cover the vibrant Red Room, and 17th-century stumpwork adorns the Tapestry Room. ✉ *Minster Yard* ☎ *01904/624247* ⊕ *www.nationaltrust.org.uk* 🎫 *£4* ⊙ *Apr.–Oct., Sat.–Thurs. 11–5; last admission 30 mins before closing.*

★ ⌐ ⓭ York Minster. Focal point of the city, this vast cathedral is the largest Gothic church in England and attracts almost as many visitors as London's Westminster Abbey. Inside, the effect created by its soaring pillars, lofty vaulted ceilings, and dazzling stained-glass windows—glowing with deep wine reds and cobalt blues, they are bested only by those in Chartres Cathedral in France—is almost too overpowering. The central towers are 184 feet high, and the church is 534 feet long, 249 feet across its transepts, and 90 feet from floor to roof. So high is the structure, it's best to come with binoculars if you wish to study the stained glass. Mere statistics, however, cannot convey the scale of the building. Its soaring columns; the ornamentation of its 14th-century nave; the east window, one of the greatest pieces of medieval glazing in the world; the north transept's **Five Sisters** windows, five tall lancets of frosted 13th-century glass; the enormous choir screen portraying somewhat whimsical images of every king of England from William the Conqueror to Henry VI; the imposing tracery of the **Rose Window** (just one of the minster's 128 stained-glass windows), commemorating the marriage of Henry VII and Elizabeth of York in 1486 (the event that ended the Wars of the Roses and began the Tudor dynasty)—all contribute to its cold, crushing splendor. Don't miss the exquisite 13th-century **Chapter House** and the **Undercroft Museum and Treasury.** After exploring the interior, you might take the 275 winding steps to the roof of the great **Central Tower** (strictly for those with a head for heights), not only for the close-up view of the cathedral's detailed carving but also for a panorama of York and the surrounding moors. ⊠ *Duncombe Pl.* ☎ *01904/557216* ⊕ *www.yorkminster.org* ☞ *Minster free, but £3.50 donation suggested; foundations (including crypt and treasury) £3.80; Central Tower £3* ☉ *Minster and Chapter House late June–early Sept., Mon.–Sat. 7 AM–8:30 PM, Sun. noon–8:30; early Sept.–late June, Mon.–Sat. 7–6, Sun. noon–6. Undercroft and Central Tower late June–early Sept., Mon.–Sat. 9:30–5:30, Sun. noon–5:30; early Sept.–late June, Mon.–Sat. 10–4:30, Sun. noon–4:30.*

㉔ **Yorkshire Museum.** The natural and archaeological history of the county, including material on the Roman, Anglo-Saxon, and Viking aspects of York, is the focus of this museum. Also on display in the solid, Doric-style building is the 15th-century Middleham Jewel, a pendant gleaming with a large sapphire. Outdoors in the botanical gardens, amid the ruins of St. Mary's Abbey, the city's cycle of medieval mystery plays is performed every four years. The museum lies just outside the walled city, through Bootham Bar, one of York's old gates. ⊠ *Museum Gardens, Museum St.* ☎ *01904/551805* ⊕ *www.yorkshiremuseum.org.uk* ☞ *£3.75* ☉ *Daily 10–5.*

Where to Eat

££–££££ ✕ **Melton's.** Once a private house, this unpretentious but excellent restaurant has local art on the walls and an open kitchen. The seasonal menus prove to be highly imaginative, a legacy of chef Michael Hjort's former stint at the Roux brothers' establishments in London, and highlight modern English and European fare such as home-cured herrings on a potato salad, and roast venison with damson plums and kale. Melton's is 10 minutes from York Minster. ⊠ *7 Scarcroft Rd.* ☎ *01904/634341* ♨ *Reservations essential* ▭ *MC, V* ☉ *Closed Sun., 3 wks at Christmas, and 1 wk in Aug. No lunch Mon.*

★ **££–£££** ✕ **19 Grape Lane.** Narrow and slightly cramped, this restaurant fills a typically leaning, timbered York building in the heart of town. The modern English food on its blackboard of specials, such as steamed trout fillets with lavender carrots, is hugely popular. ⊠ *19 Grape La.* ☎ *01904/636366* ▭ *MC, V* ☉ *Closed Sun. and Mon.*

££ ✕ **Café Concerto.** Music ephemera decorates this relaxed, intimate bistro in sight of York Minster, which prepares virtually any style of food you care to name, from Caribbean to Continental. You might choose the Cuban spiced chicken with sweet potatoes, and then savor a piece of homemade cake and a cappuccino. ⊠ *21 High Petergate* ☎ *01904/610478* ▭ *No credit cards.*

★ **£–££** ✕ **Betty's.** At the opposite end of Stonegate from the minster, this York institution since 1912 is arranged elegantly across two large floors in a beautiful art nouveau building. Best known for its teas served with mouthwatering cakes (try the "fat rascal," a bun bursting with cherries and nuts), Betty's also offers light meals and a splendid selection of exotic coffees. ⊠ *6–8 St. Helen's Sq.* ☎ *01904/659142* ▭ *MC, V.*

£ ✕ **Golden Slipper.** Although it's only a stone's throw from the busy minster, this warm and cozy place with book-lined walls resembles a country pub. Besides good homemade pies—try the pork, apple, and sage—there are baked potatoes and hot and cold sandwiches, all served until 7 PM. ⊠ *20 Goodramgate* ☎ *01904/651235* ▭ *MC, V.*

£ ✕ **Spurriergate Centre.** Churches are not just for prayers, as this decon-
secrated 15th-century church proves. Resurrected as a cafeteria by a community organization, St. Michael's is now a favorite spot for tired
travelers and mothers with strollers to refuel spiritually as well as gas-
tronomically. You may end up eating a prawn sandwich on the exact
spot where John Wesley prayed in 1768. Don't pass up the cream
scones. ✉ *Spurriergate* ☎ *01904/629393* 🕐 *Closed Sun. No dinner.*

Where to Stay

£££££ 🏨 **Middlethorpe Hall.** This splendidly restored 18th-century mansion, about
Fodor'sChoice 1½ mi from the city center, was the sometime home of the traveler and
★ diarist Lady Mary Wortley Montagu (1689–1762). Antiques, paintings, and fresh flowers fill the individually decorated rooms, some in
cottage-style accommodations around an 18th-century courtyard. The
extensive grounds include a lake and a 17th-century dovecote. The
Anglo-French menu of the wood-paneled restaurant, worth a trip even
if you're not staying here, changes seasonally but always has more than
a hint of luxury—like the hotel itself. ✉ *Bishopthorpe Rd., YO23 2GB*
☎ *01904/641241* 🖷 *01904/620176* 🌐 *www.middlethorpe.com* 🛏 *30
rooms* ♨ *Restaurant, in-room data ports, indoor pool, health club,
sauna, spa, croquet, bar, Internet, meeting rooms, free parking; no a/c,
no kids under 8* 🖃 *MC, V.*

£££–£££££ 🏨 **Dean Court Hotel.** The clergy of York Minster, just across the way, once
found accommodations at this large Victorian house. It now has traditionally furnished rooms with plenty of print fabrics, plump sofas, and
fine views overlooking the minster. The restaurant serves good English
cuisine, including a hearty Yorkshire breakfast. ✉ *Duncombe Pl., YO1
7EF* ☎ *01904/625082* 🖷 *01904/620305* 🌐 *www.deancourt-york.co.
uk* 🛏 *39 rooms* ♨ *Restaurant, coffee shop, in-room data ports, cable
TV, bar, meeting rooms, parking (fee); no a/c* 🖃 *AE, DC, MC, V* ❢⬤❢ *BP.*

£££–££££ 🏨 **Judge's Lodgings.** This Georgian mansion served as a judge's lodging, providing rooms for justices when they traveled up north from London's Inns of Court. Past the elegant gates and front yard, you mount
an imposing staircase. Beyond the lovely, somewhat shabby-genteel
lobby is the main salon—a delightful, cozy cocoon of pastels, overstuffed
chairs, and gilded mirrors. Upstairs, the furnishings continue in the
same style. ✉ *9 Lendal, YO1 2AQ* ☎ *01904/638733* 🖷 *01904/679947*
🌐 *www.judges-lodging.co.uk* 🛏 *15 rooms* ♨ *Restaurant, cable TV,
bar, meeting rooms, free parking; no a/c* 🖃 *AE, DC, MC, V* ❢⬤❢ *BP.*

£££ 🏨 **The Hazelwood.** Only 400 yards from York Minster, this tall Victorian town house stands in a peaceful cul-de-sac, away from the noise of
traffic. Service is friendly and informal, and reds and golds dominate
bedrooms furnished with rich fabrics and some handsome wood pieces.
The memorable breakfasts include black pudding, Danish pastries, and
vegetarian sausages. ✉ *24–25 Portland St., YO31 7EH* ☎ *01904/
626548* 🖷 *01904/628032* 🌐 *www.thehazelwoodyork.com* 🛏 *14 rooms*
♨ *Free parking; no a/c, no room phones, no room TVs, no kids under
8, no smoking* 🖃 *MC* ❢⬤❢ *BP.*

£–££ 🏨 **Abbey Guest House.** This terraced guest house, formerly an artisan's
house, is a 10-minute walk from the train station and town center. Although small, it's clean and friendly, with a garden by the River Ouse
and ducks waddling about outside. The bedrooms, some with four-posters,
are all individually furnished. Picnic lunches and evening meals can be
arranged on request. ✉ *14 Earlsborough Terr., Marygate, YO3 7BQ*
☎ *01904/627782* 🖷 *01904/671743* 🛏 *7 rooms, 2 with bath* ♨ *Dining room, Internet, free parking; no a/c, no room phones, no smoking*
🖃 *MC, V* ❢⬤❢ *BP.*

£–££ 🛏 **Dairy Guest House.** Victorian stained glass, pine woodwork, and in-
Fodor'sChoice tricate plaster cornices are original features of this former dairy. The bed-
  ★ rooms, done in pleasant pastels, come with books and games, and the
imaginative breakfasts can accommodate vegetarians and vegans. The
flower-filled internal courtyard is lovely. ⊠ *3 Scarcroft Rd., YO23 1ND*
☎ *01904/639367* ⊕ *www.dairyguesthouse.co.uk* ⤳ *5 rooms, 3 with
bath* ♿ *Some pets allowed; no a/c, no room phones, no smoking* ▭ *No
credit cards.*

£–££ 🛏 **Eastons.** Two Victorian houses knocked into one, this guest house successfully retains a rich period feel. Dark colors enhance the marble fireplaces, wood paneling, tiling, and antique furniture, and the big sofas
and affable hosts are equally welcoming. Breakfast is abundant, and it's
easy to find parking on the street. ⊠ *90 Bishopthorpe Rd., YO31 1JS*
☎ *01904/626646* 🖷 *01904/626165* ⤳ *10 rooms* ♿ *No a/c, no room
phones, no kids under 5, no smoking* ▭ *No credit cards* ⏹ *BP.*

Nightlife & the Arts

Nightlife

York is full of historic pubs where you can while away an hour over a
pint. The **Black Swan** (⊠ Peasholme Green ☎ 01904/686911) is the city's
oldest pub, a 16th-century local of great character. The **Judge's Lodgings** (⊠ 9 Lendal ☎ 01904/638733) has a cellar bar in which the old
vaults provide a convivial drinking hole.

Festival

York's annual **Bonfire Night** celebrations on November 5 have an added
piquancy because the notorious 16th-century conspirator Guy Fawkes
was a native of the city. It commemorates Fawkes's failure to blow up
the Houses of Parliament, and his effigy is burned atop every fire. The
tourist office has the locations of the best fires and fireworks.

The Arts

The **Early Music Festival** (☎ 01904/658338 festival office; 01904/621756
Tourist Information Centre ⊕ www.yorkearlymusic.org.uk) is held each
summer. The **Viking Festival** (⊠ Jorvik, Coppergate ☎ 01904/543402
⊕ www.vikingjorvik.com) takes place each February. The celebrations,
including a parade and long-ship regatta, end with the Jorvik Viking Combat reenactment, when Norsemen confront their Anglo-Saxon enemies.

The next quadrennial performance of the medieval **York Mystery Plays**
(☎ 01904/621756 ⊕ www.yorkmysteryplays.org) will take place in
summer 2004.

The **Theatre Royal** (⊠ St. Leonard's Pl. ☎ 01904/623568) is a lively professional theater in a lovely 18th-century building. Besides plays, it presents music, poetry reading, and art exhibitions.

Shopping

The new and secondhand bookstores around Petergate, Stonegate, and
the Shambles are excellent. The **Minster Gate Bookshop** (⊠ 8 Minster Gate
☎ 01904/621812) sells secondhand books, old maps, and prints. **Mulberry Hall** (⊠ Stonegate ☎ 01904/620736) is a sales center for all the
famous names in fine bone china and crystal. It also has a neat café. The
York Antiques Centre (⊠ 2 Lendal ☎ 01904/641445) has 25 shops selling antiques, bric-a-brac, books, and jewelry.

YORK ENVIRONS

West and north of York, a number of sights make easy, appealing day trips from the city: the spa town of Harrogate, the castle in Knaresborough, the ruins of Fountain Abbey, the market town of Ripon and nearby Newby Hall, and Thirsk, with its James Herriot connection. If you're heading northwest from York to Harrogate, you might take the less direct B1224 across Marston Moor where, in 1644, Oliver Cromwell won a decisive victory over the Royalists during the Civil War. A few miles beyond, at Wetherby, you can cut northwest along the A661 to Harrogate.

Harrogate

26 *21 mi west of York, 11 mi south of Ripon, 16 mi north of Leeds.*

During the Regency and early Victorian periods, it became fashionable for the noble and wealthy to retire to a spa to "take the waters" for relaxation. Nowhere else in Yorkshire did this trend reach such grand heights as Harrogate, an elegant town that flourished during the 19th century. When the spas no longer drew crowds, Harrogate shed its old image to become a modern business center and built a huge complex that today attracts international conventions. It has been tactfully located so as not to spoil the town's landscape of poised Regency row houses, pleasant walkways, and sweeping green spaces. Of Harrogate's parks, the most appealing is the one in the town center, known as **The Stray,** a 200-acre reach of grassland that is a riot of color in the spring. The **Valley Gardens,** southwest of the town center, include a boating lake, tennis courts, and a little café.

You can still drink the evil-smelling (and nasty-tasting) spa waters at the **Royal Pump Room Museum,** in the octagonal structure built in 1842 over the original sulfur well that brought great prosperity to the town. The museum displays all the equipment of spa days gone by, as well as some fine 19th-century china and jewelry. ⊠ *Crown Pl.* ☎ *01423/ 556188* ⊕ *www.harrogate.gov.uk* ⊡ *£2.50* ⊙ *Apr.–Oct., Mon.–Sat. 10–5, Sun. 2–5; Nov.–Mar., Mon.–Sat. 10–4, Sun. 2–4.*

In the **Turkish Baths** (1897), you can take a bath or a sauna in the exotic, tiled rooms; allow two hours or so for the full treatment. ⊠ *Parliament St.* ☎ *01423/556746* ⊕ *www.harrogate.gov.uk* ⊡ *£10 per bath and sauna session, massages additional* ⊙ *Daily; call for schedules.*

Where to Stay & Eat

£ ✕ **Betty's.** The celebrated Yorkshire tearoom began life in Harrogate in the 1920s, when Swiss restaurateur Frederic Belmont brought his Alpine specialties to England. The elegant surroundings have changed little since then, and the same scrumptious cakes and pastries, and traditional English meals, are on offer every day until 9 PM. A pianist plays nightly. ⊠ *1 Parliament St.* ☎ *01423/502746* ⊟ *MC, V.*

£££ ✕☐ **Balmoral Hotel.** Luxurious contemporary and antique furniture, patterned wallpapers, and colorful ornaments and posters fill this mock-Tudor edifice. Ten pastel-hue bedrooms have four-poster beds, all frilled and draped. The lively Villu Toots restaurant reverts to a minimalist style; the cooking is inventive and the contemporary menu eclectic, from pesto linguine to breast of squab pigeon with white pudding and spinach. It's always worth checking out the latest cocktail creation. You can also use a nearby health club. ⊠ *Franklin Mt., HG1 5EJ* ☎ *01423/508208* ⊟ *01423/530652* ⊕ *www.balmoralhotel.co.uk* ⊃ *20 rooms, 1 suite* ⧂ *Restaurant, bar, meeting rooms, some pets allowed; no a/c* ⊟ *AE, DC, MC, V* ⧄ *BP.*

Nightlife & the Arts

Harrogate's annual **International Festival** (☎ 01423/562303 ⊕ www.harrogate-festival.org.uk) of ballet, music, contemporary dance, film, comedy, street theater, and more takes place during two weeks at the end of July and beginning of August.

Knaresborough

㉗ *3 mi northeast of Harrogate, 17 mi west of York.*

A steep, rocky gorge along the River Nidd contains the photogenic old town of Knaresborough. Central attractions include its river, lively with pleasure boats, a little marketplace, and a medieval castle, now not much more than the keep where Richard II was imprisoned in 1399. **Mother Shipton's Cave**, in a park amid tree-lined riverside walks, is said to be the birthplace of the 16th-century prophetess. Events supposedly foretold by her include the defeat of the Spanish Armada and the Great Fire of London. It's just a short walk south of Knaresborough town center. ⊠ *Prophesy House, High Bridge* ☎ *01423/864600* ⊕ *www.mothershipton.co.uk* ☐ *£4.95* ⊙ *Mar.–Oct., daily 9:30–5:45; Nov., Dec., and Feb, weekends 10–4:45.*

Studley Royal & Fountains Abbey

★ **㉘** *9 mi northwest of Knaresborough, 4 mi southwest of Ripon.*

The 18th-century water garden and deer park, Studley Royal, and the ruins of medieval Fountains Abbey blend a neoclassical vision of an ordered universe with the glories of English Gothic architecture. Lakes, ponds, and spectacular water terraces adorn the gardens, and waterfalls splash around classical temples, statues, and a grotto. The surrounding deer park and woods present long vistas toward the tower of Ripon Cathedral, some 3 mi north. The majestic ruins of Fountains Abbey, with its own tower and soaring 13th-century arches, make a striking picture on the banks of the River Skell. Founded in 1132, but not completed until the early 1500s, the abbey still possesses many of its original buildings, making it one of the best places in England to learn about medieval monastic life. In this isolated valley, the Cistercian community went about its business: the "White Monks," named for the color of their habits, began a day of silence and prayer with vespers at 2:30 AM, and the lay brothers oversaw operations at the abbey's sheep farms (wool was a large and profitable business). Of the surviving buildings, the lay brothers' echoing refectory and dormitory impresses most; the Perpendicular Gothic tower was an early 16th-century addition, erected by Abbot Huby, most eminent of the abbey's leaders. Fountains Mill, with sections dating back to 1140, displays reconstructed mill machinery and has exhibits on 800 years of industrial activity on the site. The entire 822-acre complex is a World Heritage Site, and 17th-century Fountains Hall (partially built with stones from the abbey) has an exhibition and video display; you can easily spend a day here. ⊠ *Off B6265* ☎ *01765/608888* ⊕ *www.fountainsabbey.org.uk* ☐ *£4.80* ⊙ *Apr.–Sept., daily 10–7; Oct., Feb., and Mar., daily 10–5; Nov.–Jan., Sat.–Thurs. 10–4; last admission 1 hr before closing. Free guided tours of abbey and gardens Apr.–Oct., daily, usually at 11, 2:30, and 3:30.*

Ripon

29 *4 mi northeast of Fountains Abbey, 11 mi north of Harrogate, 24 mi northwest of York.*

Ripon was thriving as early as the 9th century as an important market center. A relatively small church has been designated a cathedral since the mid-19th century, which makes Ripon, with only about 15,000 inhabitants, technically a city. Market day, Thursday, is probably the best day to stop by. Successive churches here were destroyed by the Vikings and the Normans, and the current **Ripon Cathedral**, dating from the 12th and 13th centuries, is notable for its finely carved choir stalls. The Saxon crypt, now an empty series of chambers, housed sacred relics in bygone days. ⊠ *Minster Rd.* ☎ *01765/602072* ⊕ *www.riponcathedral. org.uk* ⊠ *£3 donation requested* ⊙ *Daily 8–6:30.*

Where to Stay

£££–£££££   🏨 **Swinton Park.** The Cunliffe-Lister family operates part of their ancestral castle—a stately pile rebuilt in the 18th and 19th centuries with turret and battlements—as an upscale country-house hotel. Two hundred acres of parkland near Yorkshire Dales National Park guarantee seclusion and abundant outdoor pursuits, and the plushly furnished public rooms give you room to relax. The traditionally decorated bedrooms vary widely in size and price. Masham is 8 mi north of Ripon and 35 mi north of Leeds and York. ⊠ *Off the A1, Masham, HG4 4JH* ☎ *01765/680900* 🖷 *01765/680901* ⊕ *www.swintonpark.com* ⇨ *26 rooms, 4 suites* ⟐ *Restaurant, cable TV, gym, hot tub, fishing, mountain bikes, croquet, horseback riding, meeting rooms, some pets allowed (fee); no a/c* ⊟ *AE, DC, MC, V* ❘❂❘ *BP.*

Newby Hall

☛ **30** *5 mi southeast of Ripon.*

An early 18th-century house redecorated later in the same century by Robert Adam for his patron William Weddell, Newby Hall contains some of the finest interior decorative art of its period in Western Europe. Besides an abundance of ornamental plasterwork and Chippendale furniture, there are rooms dedicated to priceless Gobelin tapestries and to proud Roman sculpture. The 25 acres of gardens are justifiably famous; a double herbaceous border, which runs down to the river, separates garden "rooms," each flowering at a different season. A miniature railroad, playground, and pedal boats amuse kids. ⊠ *Skelton-on-Ure* ☎ *01423/322583* ⊕ *www.newbyhall.co.uk* ⊠ *£7.20, gardens only £5.70* ⊙ *Apr.–Sept., Tues.–Sun. and national holidays, house noon–5, grounds 11–5:30; last admission 30 mins before closing.*

Thirsk

31 *15 mi north of Newby Hall, 23 mi north of York.*

This small market town on the western edge of the moors was a thriving place on the main east–west route from the dales to the coast. Lovely Georgian houses abound, and the cobbled medieval Market Place is handsome; Saturday and Monday are market days. Today Thirsk is best known as the place where veterinarian Alf Wight (who wrote under the name James Herriot) had his practice. The popular **World of James Herriot**, in the author's actual office, re-creates the operating room and the living spaces of the 1940s and 1950s; it also displays veterinary artifacts. Plenty of Herriot mementos add appeal. ⊠ *23 Kirkgate* ☎ *01845/*

524234 ⊕ www.worldofjamesherriot.org ⊠ £4.70 ⊙ Oct.–Mar., daily 11–4; Apr.–Sept., daily 10–6; last admission 1 hr before closing.

THE NORTH YORKSHIRE COAST

Except during the hottest summers, the North Yorkshire coast isn't the warmest place for a beach vacation. That said, there's plenty to make you glad you came, not least the good sandy beaches, rocky coves, and villages, such as Robin Hood's Bay, Whitby, and Staithes, which seem to capture imaginations at first sight. Most coastal towns still support an active fishing industry, and every harbor offers fishing and leisure trips throughout the summer. The east-coast beaches are usually fine for swimming, although you'll find the water cold. Beaches at Scarborough, Whitby, and Filey have patrolled areas: swim between the red-and-yellow flags, and don't swim when a red flag is flying. Major towns also have indoor swimming pools.

The coast is about an hour's drive away from York. Starting at Bridlington, it's a simple matter to follow the main road north to Scarborough (A165), and on to Robin Hood's Bay and Whitby (A171).

Bridlington

32 *41 mi east of York.*

A fishing port with an ancient harbor, Bridlington makes a fine introduction to the North Yorkshire coast, with its wide arc of sand that's typical of the beach resorts in the region. Boat trips through the harbor and up the coast depart frequently in summer, or you can simply join the milling crowds who promenade up and down the seafront, eating fish-and-chips, browsing at the gift shops and stalls, and frequenting the rides at the small amusement park. At **Flamborough Head** a huge bank of chalk cliffs juts out into the North Sea.

A coastal path over the cliff tops ends at **Bempton Cliffs**, one of England's finest seabird reserves, with a colony of 7,000 puffins that nest on the 400-foot-high cliffs between March and August. The reserve, off B1229, is open at all times, and displays at the nearby visitor center provide orientation. Rent binoculars for a closer view of the puffins, shags, kittiwakes, gannets, guillemots, and razorbills that make the cliffs their home. ⊠ *Visitor Centre, Cliff La., Bempton* ☎ *01262/851179* ⊕ *www.rspb.org.uk* ⊠ *Free, parking £3 Mar.–Sept.* ⊙ *Visitor center Mar.–Oct., daily 10–5; Nov., daily 9:30–4; Dec. and Feb., weekends 9:30–4.*

off the beaten path

BEVERLEY – A 20-mi drive southwest from Bridlington through the wolds and flatlands of the East Riding brings you to the unspoiled market town of Beverley, well worth exploring for its old streets, timbered houses, and Georgian terraces. Of the city's 350 buildings of architectural or historical merit, the standout is **Beverley Minster** (⊠ Minster Yard South ☎ 01482/868540 ⊕ www.beverleyminster.co.uk ⊠ £2 suggested donation ⊙ daily 9–dusk). Architecturally equal to many cathedrals, this glorious Gothic church is regarded as Yorkshire's finest, its transepts and pinnacled towers rising golden above the town.

Where to Eat

£–££ ✕ **Jerome's.** Wrought iron decorates this seafront café-restaurant, which keeps up with these multicultural times with a selection of good-value meals from around Europe. Good choices are the Greek meze (a sampler of hors d'oeuvres) and vegetarian platters. ⊠ *The Floral Pavilion, Royal Prince's Parade* ☎ *01262/671881* ⊟ *AE, DC, MC, V.*

£–££   ✗ **Seabirds.** Didn't see many seabirds on your visit to Bempton Cliffs? This village pub has a case full of them. On the menu are plenty of fish dishes, such as local crab and haddock with Mornay sauce, steaks, and imaginative vegetarian dishes. Stoke up on the Yorkshire pudding and onion gravy, but be prepared to extend your waistband. ⊠ *Tower St., Flamborough* ☎ *01262/850242* ⊟ *MC, V.*

Scarborough

③③   *17 mi north of Bridlington, 34 mi northeast of York.*

Candy floss (cotton candy) and rock candy, Victorian architecture, a sweep of cliffs above a sandy bay, and a rocky promontory capped by a ruined castle are some of the elements that make Scarborough a classic English seaside resort. A chance discovery in the early 17th century of a mineral spring on the foreshore led to the establishment of a spa, whose users not only soaked themselves in seawater but also drank it. By the late 18th century, when sea bathing came into vogue, no beaches were busier than Scarborough's, with its "bathing machines," wheeled cabins drawn by donkeys or horses into the surf and anchored there. Scarborough's initial prosperity dates from this period, as evidenced in the city's handsome Regency and early Victorian residences and hotels.

The contrast between the two faces of Scarborough makes the town all the more appealing. Its older, more genteel side in the southern half of town consists of carefully laid out crescents and squares and cliff-top walks and gardens with views across Cayton Bay. The northern side is a riot of ice cream stands, cafés, stores selling "rock" (luridly colored hard candy), crab hawkers, and bingo halls. In addition, enough survives of the huddle of streets, alleyways, and red-roof cottages around the harbor to give an idea of what the town was like before the resort days.

Paths link the harbor with the substantial ruins of **Scarborough Castle** on the promontory; dating from Norman times, it is built on the site of a Roman signal station and near a former Viking settlement. The castle has spectacular views across the North Bay, the beaches, and the shore gardens. ⊠ *Castle Rd.* ☎ *01723/372451* ⊕ *www.english-heritage. org.uk* ☑ *£2.90* ⊙ *Apr.–Sept., daily 10–6; Oct., daily 10–5; Nov.–Mar., daily 10–4.*

Scarborough's little medieval church of **St. Mary** (⊠ Castle Rd. ☎01723/ 500541) contains the grave of Anne, the youngest Brontë sister, who died in 1849. She was taken to Scarborough from Haworth in a final, desperate effort to save her life by exposing her to the sea air. The church is near the castle on the way into town.

Wood End was the vacation home of 20th-century writers Edith, Osbert, and Sacheverell Sitwell, and the west wing houses a library of their works as well as paintings. The rest of the early Victorian house, set in delightful grounds, holds the collections of the **Museum of Natural History.** ⊠ *The Crescent* ☎ *01723/367326* ☑ *£2 including Rotunda Museum* ⊙ *June–Sept., Tues.–Sun. 10–5; Oct.–May, Wed.–Sun. 11–4.*

The **Rotunda Museum,** an extraordinary circular building, was originally constructed in 1829 for William Smith of the Scarborough Philosophical Society to display his geological collection; it now contains important archaeological and local history collections. ⊠ *Vernon Rd.* ☎01723/ 374839 ☑ *£2 including Wood End* ⊙ *June–Sept., Tues.–Sun. 10–5; Oct.–May, Tues.–Sun. 11–4.*

Recognizable by its white pyramids, **Scarborough Sea Life Centre** is the best of the cheerful attractions that appeal to kids. Marine life and environmental matters are presented in an entertaining way, with different marine habitats combined under one roof. ⊠ *Scalby Mills, North Bay* ☎01723/376125 ⊕*www.sealife.co.uk* ⊠*£6.50* ⊙ *Mar.–Oct., daily 10–6; Nov.–Feb, daily 10–4; last admission 1 hr before closing.*

Where to Stay & Eat

££–£££ ✕**Lanterna Restaurant.** An unpretentious air and a high standard of cuisine make this Italian restaurant a good choice. The classic dishes are all represented, among them tender veal cooked with ham and cheese, but opt for seasonal specials using fresh vegetables and fish. ⊠ *33 Queen St.* ☎ *01723/363616* ▭ *DC, MC, V* ⊙ *Closed Sun. No lunch.*

£ ✕**The Golden Grid.** Everyone has to have fish-and-chips at least once in Scarborough, and this harborfront spot is a classic of its kind. Choose an upstairs window table and tuck into freshly fried cod or haddock, although big spenders (and those flying in the face of British seaside tradition) could also opt for grilled turbot or one of a host of other daily specials. ⊠ *4 Sandside* ☎ *01723/360922* ▭ *MC, V.*

£££–££££ ▦**The Crown.** The centerpiece of Scarborough's Regency Esplanade, this 19th-century hotel overlooks South Bay and the castle headland. Originally built to accommodate fashionable visitors to Scarborough Spa, it has been considerably refurbished; rooms are modern and done in muted colors. Rates drop for stays of two nights. ⊠ *The Esplanade, YO11 2AG* ☎ *01723/373491* 🖷 *01723/362271* ⊕ *www.scarboroughhotel.com* 🛏 *84 rooms* ♨ *2 restaurants, pool, health club, 2 bars, meeting rooms, some pets allowed; no a/c* ▭ *AE, DC, MC, V* ⚬⏐ *BP.*

£–££ ▦**Interludes.** "Theatrical" is the word to describe this Georgian town house on a steep hillside in the old town behind the harbor. Dedicated to the theme of the performing arts, the compact rooms are full of bills, posters, and the owners' theater photography. Antique and reproduction furniture, polished oak, and drapes create a traditional English look. Consider the "theatre breaks"—room and tickets for productions at the town's Stephen Joseph Theatre. ⊠ *32 Princess St., YO11 1QR* ☎ *01723/360513* ⊕ *www.interludeshotel.co.uk* 🛏 *5 rooms* ♨ *Dining room; no a/c, no room phones, no kids under 16, no smoking* ▭ *MC, V* ⚬⏐ *BP.*

Nightlife & the Arts

Scarborough has an internationally known native son in contemporary playwright Alan Ayckbourn. The **Stephen Joseph Theatre** (⊠ Westborough ☎ 01723/370541), which premieres all of his plays, incorporates two stages, a cinema, a restaurant, and a bar. Stop at the theater for a program, or contact the tourist office for box office details.

Robin Hood's Bay

★ ㉞ *15 mi northwest of Scarborough.*

Many people's favorite coastal stop is at Robin Hood's Bay, a tiny fishing village squeezed into a ravine near where a stream courses over the cliffs. Tiny, crazily scattered houses and shops fringe the perilously steep, narrow roads. The name is curious, because there is no connection with the famous English medieval outlaw. The village didn't even come into being until the late 15th century, after which it thrived in a small way as a fishing port and smuggling center. Contraband was passed up the stream bed beneath the cottages, linked to one another by secret passages, often with customs officers in hot pursuit.

It would be hard to find a **beach** anywhere in the British Isles that offers the variety and interest of the one at Robin Hood Bay. The tide rushes in quickly, so take care. Provided the tide is out, you can stroll for a couple of hours south from Robin Hood's Bay, along a rough, exposed stone shore full of rock pools, inlets, and sandy strands. A few stretches of sand are suitable for sunbathers. To the south, at the curiously named **Boggle Hole,** a ravine nestles an old water mill, now a youth hostel. Farther south is **Ravenscar,** a Victorian village that never took off and now consists of little more than a hotel, which can be reached by a hazardous but exhilarating path up the cliff. The walk back, along the cliff-top path, is less tricky but no less energetic.

Where to Stay & Eat

£–££   ✕ **Bay Hotel.** The village's most favored pub is this friendly Victorian retreat, perfectly positioned at the bottom of the village and set upon a rocky outcrop lapped by the sea. Its bar is festooned with oak and brass; in winter, a roaring fire warms all comers. Whitby scampi and chestnut and butter-bean casserole are often on the menu. ⊠ *The Dock* ☎ *01947/ 880278* ▭ *MC, V.*

££££   🏨 **Raven Hall Hotel.** This superb Georgian hotel with landscaped grounds offers unrivaled coastal views from the headland of Ravenscar, 3 mi southeast of Robin Hood's Bay. All rooms have faux-medieval beds, and you should try your utmost to secure a room with a bay view. The hotel is known for its good sports facilities; the bar marks the traditional end of the punishing, long-distance Lyke-Wake Walk, so on occasion you may share the lounge with exhausted walkers. ⊠ *Ravenscar, YO13 0ET,* ☎ *01723/870353* ⊕ *www.ravenhall.co.uk* ⟿ *53 rooms* ⌂ *Restaurant, 9-hole golf course, 2 tennis courts, indoor pool, hair salon, sauna, croquet, bar, recreation room, Internet, meeting rooms; no a/c* ▭ *AE, MC, V* ¶⊙¶ *BP.*

Sports & the Outdoors

Several superb long-distance walks start or finish in, or run through, Robin Hood's Bay. The coastal **Cleveland Way** (⊕ www.clevelandway. gov.uk) runs north (to Whitby) and south (to Scarborough) through the village. The village marks one end of the 190-mi **Coast-to-Coast Walk**; the other is at St. Bees Head on the Irish Sea. Walkers finish at the Bay Hotel, above the harbor. The trans-moor **Lyke-Wake Walk** (⊕ www. lykewakewalk.co.uk) finishes 3 mi away at Ravenscar. **Wellington Lodge** (⊠ Staintondale ☎ 01723/871234 ⊕ www.llamatreks.co.uk), 3 mi south of Ravenscar, schedules llama treks along the moors or the coast; you walk, and the llamas carry your lunch.

Whitby

35 *7 mi northwest of Robin Hood's Bay, 20 mi northeast of Pickering.*

Fodor'sChoice
★

Whitby can claim to be the most splendid town on the English coast, a scenic glory steeped in fishing and whaling lore. It's set around a harbor of great natural beauty formed by the River Esk as it comes down a long glenlike ravine cut through the moors. Above it, on either side, red-roof buildings rise tier upon tier. Fine Georgian houses line some of the central streets on the west side of the river, known as West Cliff. Across the swing bridge in the old town (part of the area known as East Cliff), cobbled Church Street is packed in summer with people exploring the alleys, enclosed courtyards, and gift shops.

On top of the cliff are the gaunt ruins of Whitby Abbey, a sight that inspired Bram Stoker when he came here to write *Dracula*. Today Whitby is a small, laid-back resort, but it was an important religious center as far back as the 7th century, when Whitby Abbey was first founded, and it later came to prominence as a whaling port. The first ships sailed from here for Greenland in the mid-18th century, captained by local men such as William Scoresby, inventor of the crow's nest, to whom Herman Melville paid tribute in his novel *Moby Dick*. At much the same time as whaling made Whitby rich, its shipbuilding made it famous: Captain James Cook (1728–79), explorer and navigator, sailed on his first ship out of the town in 1747, and all four of his subsequent discovery vessels were built in Whitby.

Climbing the 199 steps from the end of Church Street leads to the rather eccentrically designed church of **St. Mary**, with its ship's deck roof, triple-decker pulpit, and enclosed galleries. The church dates originally from the 12th century, although almost everything you see today is the (often less-than-happy) result of 19th- and 20th-century renovations. The spooky, weather-beaten churchyard, filled with the crooked old gravestones of ancient mariners, has superb views of the sea and the town itself. It was here that Bram Stoker's Dracula claimed Lucy as his victim. In the tall grass at the back, you'll find the grave of master mariner William Scoresby. ⊠ *Church La., East Cliff* ☎ *01947/603421* ✆ *Free, donation suggested* ☉ *Apr.–Oct., Mon.–Sat 10–5, Sun 1–5; Nov.–Mar., Mon.–Sat. 10–2:30, Sun. 1–2:30.*

The tumbledown ruins of **Whitby Abbey,** set high on the East Cliff, are visible from almost everywhere in town. St. Hilda founded the abbey in AD 657, and Caedmon (died circa 670), the first identifiable poet of the English language, was a monk here. An engraved cross of dubious provenance, which bears his name, stands at the top of the 199 steps near St. Mary's church. Sacked by the Vikings in the 9th century, the monastery was refounded in the 11th century and then enlarged in the 13th century, from which point these ruins date. The visitor center includes exhibits on the lives of St. Hilda and Bram Stoker, artifacts from the site, and interactive displays on the medieval abbey and monastic life. ⊠ *Abbey La., East Cliff* ☎ *01947/603568* ⊕ *www.english-heritage. org.uk* ✆ *£3.80* ☉ *Apr.–Sept., daily 10–6; Oct., daily 10–5; Nov.–Mar., daily 10–4.*

Filled with revealing exhibits relating to the man and explorer, the **Captain Cook Memorial Museum** is tucked into the period rooms of the 18th-century house belonging to shipowner John Walker, where the young James Cook lived as an apprentice from 1746 to 1749. On display are mementos of Cook's epic expeditions, including maps, diaries, and drawings, as well as some tracing the privations of his wife and family, left behind to cope with life, loss, and bereavement. Captain Cook is remembered in various places around town, most notably by his bronze statue on top of the West Cliff, near the pair of arched whalebones. ⊠ *Grape La.* ☎ *01947/601900* ⊕ *www.cookmuseumwhitby.co.uk* ✆ *£3* ☉ *Apr.–Oct., daily 9:45–5; Mar., weekends 11–3.*

> **off the beaten path**
>
> **GOATHLAND** – This pretty moorland village, 8 mi southwest of Whitby, attracts walkers and people who want to see the fictional Aidensfield of the British TV series *Heartbeat.* Its cute 1865 train station served as Hogsmeade Station for students arriving at the school of wizardry in *Harry Potter and the Sorcerer's Stone.* The 18-mi North Yorkshire Moors Railway (⊠ Pickering Station, Park St., Pickering ☎ 01751/472508 ⊕ www.northyorkshiremoorsrailway. com ☉ Late Mar.–early Nov., daily; early Nov.–Feb., some weekends and holiday periods ✆ £12 round-trip), between Grosmont and Pickering, passes through neat towns and moorland scenery. Steam-powered trains (like the one that takes Harry Potter to Hogwarts School) provide a great outing.

Where to Stay & Eat

££–£££ ✕ **Magpie Café.** Whitby is full of fish-and-chip places, but no place
FodorsChoice serves it with more style than this large, busy, old-fashioned restaurant
★ with a well-stocked menu that includes hake along with the perennial
plaice, cod, and haddock. Many regulars would argue that the Magpie's nonfish dishes (especially its meat salads) offer even better value.
The food and service are worth the wait. ⊠ *14 Pier Rd.* ☎ *01947/602058*
⚐ *Reservations not accepted* ▤ *MC, V* ⊘ *Closed Jan.*

★ **££** ✕▥ **White Horse and Griffin.** When looking for the perfect inn, you
want an old building with character, a roaring fire, and food to thrill.
This 18th-century establishment, in which Charles Dickens once slept
and railway pioneer George Stephenson lectured, fills the bill. The tidy
rooms are warmly decorated in muted colors, and downstairs the cozy
bistro-bar serves a fine, changing menu with locally caught fish and game
in season. Dinner might be grilled Dover sole or salmon Wellington, followed by lemon and orange tart or cheeses and homemade chutney.
⊠ *Church St., YO22 4BH* ☎ *01947/604857* ⊕ *www.thewhitehorse.
activehotels.com/ahh* ⚐ *12 rooms* ⚐ *Restaurant, bar, meeting rooms,
some pets allowed; no a/c, no room phones, no smoking (in bedrooms)*
▤ *MC, V* ⊙❘ *BP.*

£–££ ✕▥ **Shepherd's Purse.** This splendid little complex in the cobbled old
town consists of boutique-style guest rooms, a vegetarian restaurant that
looks as if it has been inserted into a junk shop, and dress and health-
food stores. There are two less-expensive bedrooms above the stores and
others in the galleried courtyard at the back. Although small, many rooms
have four-poster or brass bedsteads; floors are wooden, the furniture is
country style, and the top two rooms even have little balconies. ⊠ *95
Church St., YO22 4BH* ☎ *01947/820228* ⊕ *www.shepherds-purse.
co.uk* ⚐ *9 rooms, 5 with bath* ⚐ *Restaurant, meeting rooms, some pets
allowed; no a/c, no room phones* ▤ *MC, V* ⊙❘ *BP.*

£££–££££ ▥ **Dunsley Hall Hotel.** Originally built as the home of a shipping magnate, this family-run Victorian country-house hotel is set in its own
grounds, 4 mi west of Whitby. Stained- and leaded-glass windows and
plenty of wood paneling complement the rich carpets, rocking chairs,
and leather armchairs. Bedrooms are spacious and restful, the only intrusion into the peace being the occasional screech of a peacock. ⊠ *Dunsley, YO21 3TL* ☎ *01947/893437* ☎ *01947/893505* ⊕ *www.dunsleyhall.
com* ⚐ *18 rooms* ⚐ *Restaurant, putting green, tennis court, indoor pool,
croquet, bar, meeting rooms; no a/c* ▤ *AE, MC, V* ⊙❘ *BP.*

Nightlife & the Arts

The **Whitby Regatta** (⊕ www.whitbyregatta.co.uk) held in August, is a
three-day jamboree of boat races, fair rides, lifeboat rescue displays, parades, and music. Music (but also traditional dance and storytelling) predominates during **Whitby Folk Week,** usually held the week before the
late-August bank holiday, when pubs, pavements, and halls become venues
for more than 1,000 traditional folk events by performers from all over
the country.

Shopping

Whitby is known for its jet, a very hard, black form of natural carbon,
which has been used locally for more than a century to make jewelry
and ornaments. It was particularly popular as mourning memorabilia
during the Victorian era. Several shops in the old town along Church
Street and parallel to Sandgate have fine displays.

Staithes

36 *9 mi northwest of Whitby.*

There's little in the way of specific sights to see in Staithes, but over the years, many travelers have been seduced by the town's stepped alleys and courtyards. These, and the surrounding coastal cliffs, were captured on canvas by many members of the so-called Staithes School of artists, who were prominent in the earlier part of the 20th century. Tourists are a vital part of the local economy these days, and they include many in wet suits, who know Staithes to have some of Britain's best surfing.

Staithes's few houses huddle below the rocky, seagull-studded outcrop of Cowbar Nab, on either side of the beck (stream). Having survived storm and flood, they present a hoary, weather-beaten aspect, but not all were so lucky. The Cod and Lobster Inn, at the harbor, is in its third incarnation, and the drygoods shop in which James Cook had his first apprenticeship before moving to Whitby fell into the sea entirely in 1745. The house known as Cook's Cottage, near the pub, is supposedly built out of the salvaged remains of the original building.

Staithes's former Methodist Chapel has been imaginatively converted into the **Captain Cook and Staithes Heritage Centre,** which includes a life-size mid-18th-century street scene of the kind Cook would have recognized. The shop in which the young adventurer worked was re-created, alongside a fisherman's warehouse and museum displays relating to local industries and, of course, smuggling. ⊠ *High St.* ☎ *01947/841454* ⊡ *£2.50* ⊙ *Jan., weekends 10–5; Feb.–Dec., daily 10–5.*

Where to Stay & Eat

★ **££** ✕▦ **Endeavour.** The few guest rooms in this rather higgledy-piggledy old house on the main street, a well-known restaurant, are done in stripped pine and plain colors. Menus include locally caught fish and change seasonally, but dishes are often presented with Mediterranean or Asian flourishes; soups, salmon, and lobster are strong points. Have a drink in the tiny bar before you dine. The restaurant is closed Sunday–Monday and January, and you should call ahead in winter. ⊠ *1 High St., TS13 5BH* ☎ *01947/840825* ⊕ *www.endeavour-restaurant.co.uk* ⇆ *3 rooms* ⬧ *Restaurant, bar, some pets allowed; no smoking* ▭ *MC, V* ⊡ *BP.*

THE NORTH YORK MOORS

The North York Moors are a dramatic swath of high moorland starting 25 mi north of the city of York and stretching east to the coast and west to the Cleveland Hills. Once covered in forest, of which a few pockets survive, the landscape changed with the introduction of sheep at the monastic foundations of Rievaulx and Whitby in medieval times. The evidence is clear for all to see today: heather-covered hills that, in late summer and early fall, are a rich blaze of crimson and purple, and a series of isolated, medieval standing stones that once acted as signposts on the paths between the abbeys. For more than four decades, the area has been designated a national park, to protect the moors and grassy valleys that shelter brownstone villages and hamlets. Minor roads and tracks crisscross the moors in all directions, and there's no single, obvious route through the region. Perhaps the most rewarding approach is west from the coast at Whitby, along the Esk Valley to Danby, which is also accessible on the Esk Valley branch train line between Middlesbrough and Whitby. From Danby, minor roads run south over the high moors reaching Hutton-le-Hole, beyond which main roads lead to interesting towns on the moors' edge, such as Helmsley. Completing the route in this direction leaves you with an easy side trip to Castle Howard before returning to nearby York.

Danby

㊲ *15 mi west of Whitby.*

The straggling old stone village of Danby nestles in a green valley, just a short walk from the tops of the nearby moors. It's been settled since Viking times—Danby means "village where the Danes lived"—and these days it bumbles along contentedly in a semitouristed way. There's a pub, and a bakery with a tearoom, and if you bring hiking boots with you, within 10 minutes you can be above the village looking down, surrounded by nothing but isolated moorland. To get here from Whitby, take A171 west and turn south for Danby after 12 mi, after which it's a 3-mi drive over Danby Low Moor to the village.

In a converted country house on the eastern outskirts of Danby, the North York Moors National Park's **Moors Centre** has exhibitions, displays, and plenty of information. A tearoom and a garden front with picnic tables are other amenities. The summer Moorsbus operates from the center for the 30-minute journey south to Hutton-le-Hole. ⊠ *Danby Lodge* ☎ *01439/772737* ⊕ *www.northyorkmoors-npa.gov.uk* ☜ *Free* ☼ *Jan. and Feb., weekends 11–4; Mar., Nov., and Dec., daily 11–4; Apr.–Oct., daily 10–5.*

need a break? The cozy little **Stonehouse Bakery & Tea Shop** (⊠ 3 Briar Hill ☎ 01287/660006) serves excellent sandwiches on sun-dried-tomato or olive bread, herbal teas, local honey, and a fine peanut brittle. It's closed Sunday.

Where to Stay

£ ⊡ **Stonebeck Gate Farm.** There are sweeping moorland views from this homey family farm, set at the head of the dale. Florals decorate the pretty bedrooms, and downstairs are big sofas, welcoming fires, a big oak dresser, and hunting pictures. Home-baked bread and freshly laid eggs form part of the communal breakfast, and the country fare at dinner (£15) uses the farm's produce. Stonebeck Gate is 3 mi south of Danby. ⊠ *Little Fryup Dale, YO21 2NS* ☎ *01287/660363* 🖨 *01287/660363* ⊕ *www. stonebeckgatefarm.co.uk* ⇨ *3 rooms* ⚐ *Dining room, cable TV, some pets allowed; no room phones, no smoking* ⊟ *No credit cards* ⧖ *BP.*

en route From Danby take the road due west for 2 mi to Castleton, and then turn south over the top of the moors toward Hutton-le-Hole. The narrow road offers magnificent views over North York Moors National Park, especially at the old stone **Ralph Cross** (5 mi), which marks the highest point. Drive carefully: sheep-dodging is something of a necessary art in these parts.

Hutton-le-Hole

★ **㊳** *13 mi south of Danby.*

Even after seeing the varied splendors of villages throughout North York Moors National Park, it's difficult not to think that Hutton-le-Hole is the pick of the bunch. It's almost too pastoral to be true: a tiny hamlet, based around a wide village green, with sheep wandering about and a stream babbling in the background. The surroundings are equally attractive, and in summer, the local parking lots fill quickly as people arrive to take to the nearby hills for a day's walking.

The excellent 2-acre, open-air **Ryedale Folk Museum** records life in the Dales from prehistory onward through craft demonstrations and 13 historic buildings, including a medieval kiln, 16th-century cottages, a 19th-century blacksmith's shop, and an early photographer's studio. ☎ *01751/417367* 🌐 *www.ryedalefolkmuseum.co.uk* 🎫 *£3.50* ⏲ *Mid-Mar.–Oct., daily 10–5:30; last admission 1 hr before closing.*

Helmsley

39 *8 mi southwest of Hutton-le-Hole, 27 mi north of York.*

The market town of Helmsley, well known as a hiking center, is attractive enough in itself for a day trip and has a castle (partly ruined during the Civil War) and a traditional country marketplace surrounded by fine old inns, cafés, and stores. Market day is Friday.

Where to Stay

£££–££££ **Black Swan.** A splendid, relaxing base, this ivy-covered property sits on the edge of the market square. The building is a hybrid—part 16th-century coaching inn, part Georgian house. Cozy rooms overlook either the square or the fine walled garden at the back. The restaurant serves traditional British and local dishes; an open fire keeps things warm in winter. ✉ *Market Pl., YO6 5BJ* ☎ *01439/770466* 📠 *01439/770174* 🌐 *www.heritage-hotels.com* *45 rooms* *Restaurant, cable TV, croquet, bar, meeting rooms, some pets allowed; no a/c* 💳 *AE, DC, MC, V.*

Sports & the Outdoors

The town, on the southern edge of the moors, is the starting point of the **Cleveland Way** (🌐 www.nationaltrail.gov.uk), the long-distance moor-and-coastal footpath. Boots are donned at the old cross in the market square; it's 50 mi or so across the moors to the coast and then a similar distance south to Filey along the cliff tops. All told, it's 108 mi of walking, which most people aim to complete in nine days. The trail passes close to the ruins of Rievaulx Abbey, a few miles outside the town. A leaflet from the tourist information center indicates the route.

Rievaulx Abbey

★ 40 *2 mi northwest of Helmsley.*

One of the most graceful of all medieval English seats of learning, Rievaulx (pronounced ree-*voh*) Abbey occupies a dramatic setting on the River Rye. The wealth of this Cistercian foundation, which dates from 1132, came from the wool trade, and the extensive surviving ruins (as well as exhibits in the museum here) give some indication of the thriving trade with Europe in which the medieval monks engaged. Rising from the landscaped grounds are elegant Gothic arches, cloisters, and associated buildings, including the Chapter House, which retains the original shrine of the first abbot, William, by the entrance. The earl of Rutland owned Rievaulx after Henry VIII dissolved the monasteries in 1538, and he acted quickly to destroy the buildings. The abbey is a 1½-hour walk northwest from Helmsley by signposted footpath, or 2 mi by vehicle. ✉ *Off B1257* ☎ *01439/798228* 🌐 *www.english-heritage.org.uk* 🎫 *£3.80* ⏲ *Apr.–mid-July and Sept., daily 10–6; mid-July–Aug., daily 9:30–6; Oct., daily 10–5; Nov.–Mar., daily 10–4.*

> **off the beaten path**
>
> **RIEVAULX TERRACE AND TEMPLES** – If you've wandered among the ruins of Rievaulx Abbey, you might like to drive up to the Rievaulx Terraces, a long grassy walkway on the hillside above, terminating in the remains of several Tuscan- and Ionic-style classical temples. The views of the abbey from here are magnificent. ⊠ *Off B1257* ☎ *01439/ 798340* ⊕ *www.nationaltrust.org.uk* 🖃 *£3.30* 🕑 *May–Sept., daily 10:30–6; Apr., Oct., and Nov., daily 10:30–5:30; last admission 1 hr before closing.*

Castle Howard

④① *14 mi southeast of Rievaulx Abbey, 12 mi southeast of Helmsley, 15 mi*
Fodor'sChoice *northeast of York.*
★

Standing serene among the Howardian Hills to the west of Malton, Castle Howard is one of the grandest and most opulent stately homes in Britain, an imposing baroque building whose magnificent profile is punctuated by stone chimneys and a graceful central dome. Many people know it best as Brideshead, the home of the Flyte family in Evelyn Waugh's tale of aristocratic woe, *Brideshead Revisited,* because much of the 1981 TV series was filmed here. The house was designed for the Howard family (who still live here) by Sir John Vanbrugh (1664–1726). Considering its many theatrical, even flamboyant features, it seems fitting that Vanbrugh was praised more as a playwright than an architect (he also had careers as a soldier and adventurer). In 18th-century London, his plays were second in popularity only to Congreve's. Even more remarkably, this was Vanbrugh's first building design. His self-assurance knowing no bounds, he went on to create Blenheim Palace, the Versailles of England. For Castle Howard, however, Vanbrugh sought assistance, and turned to the brilliant but self-effacing Nicholas Hawksmoor (1661–1736), who at 18 had been under the tutelage of Christopher Wren. Hawksmoor encouraged adding bodies of water to the landscape, and he designed the imposing Mausoleum; many consider it a masterpiece equal to his churches in London.

The audacity of the great baroque house is startling, proclaiming the wealth and importance of the Howards and the self-assurance of Vanbrugh. It took 60 years to build (1699–1759), and it was worth every year. This was the first private residence in Britain built with a stone dome. A magnificent central hallway spanned by a hand-painted (and unfortunately, new) ceiling dwarfs all visitors, and there is no shortage of grandeur elsewhere: vast family portraits, delicate marble fireplaces, immense and fading tapestries, huge pieces of Victorian silver on polished tables, and a great many marble busts. Outside, the stately theme continues in one of the most stunning neoclassical landscapes in England; Horace Walpole, the 18th-century connoisseur, commented that a pheasant at Castle Howard lives better than most dukes elsewhere. Carefully arranged woods, lakes, bridges, and obelisks compose a scene far more like a painting than a natural English landscape. Make sure you see the Temple of the Four Winds and the Mausoleum, whose magnificence caused Walpole to comment that all who view it would wish to be buried alive. Costumed characters from the past are on hand to tell you about their contribution to the house, and hourly tours (included in the admission price) fill you in on more background and history. ⊠ *Off A64 and B1257, Coneysthorpe* ☎ *01653/648333* ⊕ *www.castlehoward. co.uk* 🖃 *£9, gardens only £6* 🕑 *House mid-Feb.–Oct., daily 11–6, last admission 4; grounds mid-Feb.–Dec., daily 10–6:30 or dusk.*

YORKSHIRE A TO Z

To research prices, get advice from other travelers, and book travel arrangements, visit www.fodors.com.

AIRPORTS

Leeds Bradford Airport, 8 mi northwest of Leeds, connects with domestic and European destinations. Manchester Airport, about 40 mi southwest of Leeds, is well served internationally.

Leeds Bradford International Airport ⊠ A658, Yeadon ☎ 0113/250-9696 ⊕ www.lbia.co.uk. **Manchester Airport** ⊠ Near Junctions 5 and 6 of M56 ☎ 0161/489-3000 ⊕ www.manairport.co.uk.

BIKE TRAVEL

Although the countryside is too hilly for extensive bicycle touring, except for experienced riders, you can rent bikes locally in several places. In York, where there are special bike paths, contact Cycleworks and pick up a cycling map from the tourist information center.

Bike Rentals Cycleworks ⊠ 14–16 Lawrence St., York ☎ 01904/626664 ⊕ www.york-cycleworks.co.uk.

BUS TRAVEL

National Express serves the region from London's Victoria Coach Station. Average travel times are 4½ hours to York, 6½ hours to Scarborough, and 7 hours to Whitby.

Each district has its own bus company; Traveline and local tourist information centers can help you discover the services. Timetable booklets for the Yorkshire Moors and Dales are widely available, and special summer services in both national parks provide useful bus connections. There are local Metro buses from Leeds and Bradford into the more remote parts of the Yorkshire Dales. Other companies are Harrogate & District for services to Ripon, Harrogate, and Leeds; Yorkshire Coastliner for Castle Howard, Scarborough, Whitby, Malton, and Leeds; and Arriva for Whitby, Scarborough, and Middlesbrough. In York, the main local bus operator is First.

CUTTING COSTS Many districts have Rover tickets; in York, the FirstWeek card (£10.50) gives a week's travel on all First bus services. With a West Yorkshire Day Rover you have a day's train and bus travel for £4.50; contact Metroline for details. The Moorsbus (information from any National Park office) runs every Sunday and bank holiday Monday from late March to the end of October, and daily from late July to the end of August. It connects Danby, Hutton-le-Hole, Helmsley, Rievaulx Abbey, Rosedale Abbey, and Pickering and costs £3 for an all-day ticket.

FARES & SCHEDULES **Arriva** ☎ 0870/608-2608 ⊕ www.arriva.co.uk. **First** ☎ 01904/622992 ⊕ www.firstgroup.com. **Harrogate & District** ☎ 01423/566061. **Metroline** ☎ 0113/245-7676 ⊕ www.wymetro.com. **National Express** ☎ 0870/580-8080 ⊕ www.nationalexpress.com. **Traveline** ☎ 0870/608-2608 ⊕ www.traveline.org.uk. **Yorkshire Coastliner** ☎ 01653/692556 ⊕ www.yorkshirecoastliner.co.uk.

CAR RENTAL

Local Agencies Avis ⊠ 81 Roseville Rd., Leeds ☎ 0113/243-9771. **Budget** ⊠ 82–84 Clifton, York ☎ 01904/644919. **Europcar** ⊠ Leeds Rd., Bradford ☎ 01274/733048. **Hertz** ⊠ 1 City Sq., Leeds ☎ 0113/242-9548 ⊠ York Train Station, Station Rd., York ☎ 01904/612586. **National Car Rental** ⊠ Nelson St., Bradford ☎ 01274/722155.

CAR TRAVEL

The M1, the principal route north from London, gets you to the region in about two hours, with longer travel times up into North Yorkshire. For York (193 mi) and the Scarborough areas, stay on M1 to Leeds (189 mi), then take A64. For the Yorkshire Dales, take M1 to Leeds, then A660 to A65 north and west to Skipton. For the North York Moors, either take B1363 north from York to Helmsley, or leave A64 at Malton and follow the trans-moor A169 that runs to Whitby. The trans-Pennine motorway, the M62, between Liverpool and Hull, crosses the bottom of this region. North of Leeds, A1 is the major north–south road, although narrow stretches, roadwork, and heavy traffic make this slow going at times.

ROAD CONDITIONS
Some of the steep, narrow roads in the countryside off the main routes are difficult drives and can be particularly perilous (or closed altogether) in winter. Main roads often closed by snowdrifts are the moorland A169 and the coast-and-moor A171. If you're driving in the dales or moors in winter, listen for the weather forecasts.

DISCOUNTS & DEALS

The Powerpass card, valid from late April through December, costs £2 and admits two adults for the price of one into 120 attractions in Yorkshire and Northumbria. Local tourist offices in the area sell the card.

The York Pass offers unlimited free entry to more than 30 attractions in or near the city (including Castle Howard), plus free transportation on City Sightseeing bus tours. You also get discounts on restaurants and theaters. Adult passes cost £25 (1 day), £31 (2 days), and £39 (3 days), and can be purchased on-line, by phone, or at the York Tourist Information Centre.

York Pass ☎ 0870/242-9988 or 01904/621756 ⊕ www.yorkpass.com.

EMERGENCIES

Ambulance, fire, police ☎ 999. **St. Mary's Hospital** ⊠ Greenhill Road, Armley, Leeds ☎ 0113/279-0121. **York District Hospital** ⊠ Wiggington Rd., York ☎ 01904/631313. **Whitby Hospital** ⊠ Spring Hill, Whitby ☎ 01947/604851.

NATIONAL PARKS

For information about local visitor centers, walks, and guided tours, contact Yorkshire Dales National Park and North York Moors National Park.

Yorkshire Dales National Park ☎ 01756/752748 head office ⊕ www.yorkshiredales. org.uk. **North York Moors National Park** ☎ 01439/770657 head office ⊕ www. northyorkmoors-npa.gov.uk.

TOURS

BUS TOURS
City Sightseeing runs frequent tours of York (£7.50), including stops at the minster, the Castle Museum, the Shambles, and Jorvik that allow you to get on and off the bus as you please. Yorktour offers walking tours of the city of York and has an excursion bus to Castle Howard, June–September, Tuesday, Friday, and Sunday, departing around noon.

City Sightseeing ☎ 01904/640896 ⊕ www.citysightseeing.co.uk. **Yorktour** ☎ 01423/360222 ⊕ www.eddiebrowntours.com.

WALKING TOURS
The York Association of Voluntary Guides arranges short walking tours around the city, which depart daily at 10:15; there are additional tours at 2:15 PM April through October, and at 6:45 PM July through August. The tours are free, but a gratuity is appreciated.

York Association of Voluntary Guides ⊠ De Grey Rooms, Exhibition Sq. ☎ 01904/640780.

TRAIN TRAVEL

Great Northeastern Railways serves the region from London's King's Cross and Euston stations. Average travel times from King's Cross are 2½ hours to Leeds and 2 hours to York. It is possible to reach the North Yorkshire coast by train; journey time from London to Scarborough (change at York) is four hours, to Whitby (change at Darlington and Middlesbrough) up to 6½ hours.

There is local service from Leeds to Skipton, and from York to Knaresborough and Harrogate and also to Scarborough (which has connections to the seaside towns of Filey and Bridlington). Whitby can be reached on the minor but attractive Esk Valley line from Middlesbrough. For train travel information in the region, call National Rail Enquiries.

CUTTING COSTS Two Regional Rover tickets for seven days' unlimited travel are available: North East and Coast and Peaks.

FARES & SCHEDULES 🚆 **Great Northeastern Railways** ☎ 0845/722–5225 booking line; 0845/748–4950 inquiries ⊕ www.gner.co.uk. **National Rail Enquiries** ☎ 0845/748–4950 ⊕ www.nationalrail.co.uk.

TRAVEL AGENCIES

🚆 Local Agent Referrals **Thomas Cook** ✉ Kirkgate, Bradford ☎ 01274/332600 ✉ 51 Boar La., Leeds ☎ 0113/214-7700 ✉ 47 Westborough, Scarborough ☎ 01723/397200 ✉ 4 Nessgate, York ☎ 01904/881400.

VISITOR INFORMATION

The Yorkshire Tourist Board has information about the area. Local tourist information centers have varied opening hours. Many offices in the North York Moors and Yorkshire Dales open only in summer.

🚆 **Yorkshire Tourist Board** ✉ 312 Tadcaster Rd., York, YO2 1GS ☎ 01904/707961 ⊕ www.ytb.org.uk. **Yorkshire's Coast & Country** ✉ Pickering Tourist Information Center, The Ropery, Pickering, YO18 8DY ☎ 01751/473791 ⊕ www.eastriding.gov.uk. **Beverley** ✉ 34 Butcher Row, HU17 0AB ☎ 01482/867430 ⊕ www.eastriding.gov.uk. **Bradford** ✉ City Hall, BD1 1HY ☎ 01274/433678 ⊕ www.visitbradford.com. **Bridlington** ✉ 25 Prince St., Humberside, YO15 2NP ☎ 01262/673474 ⊕ www.eastriding.gov.uk. **Harrogate** ✉ Royal Baths, Crescent Rd., HG1 2RR ☎ 01423/537300 ⊕ www.harrogate. gov.uk. **Haworth** ✉ 2-4 West La., BD22 8EF ☎ 01535/642329. **Helmsley** ✉ Town Hall, Market Pl., YO6 5BL ☎ 01439/770173 ⊕ www.ryedale.gov.uk. **Knaresborough** ✉ 9 Castle Courtyard, Market Pl., HG5 8AE ☎ 01423/866886. **Leeds** ✉ Leeds City Station, LS1 1PL ☎ 0113/242-5242 ⊕ www.leeds.gov.uk. **Richmond** ✉ Friary Gardens, Victoria Rd., DL10 4AJ ☎ 01748/850252 ⊕ www.yorkshiredales.org. **Scarborough** ✉ Unit 3, Pavilion House, Valley Bridge Rd., YO11 1UZ ☎ 01723/373333 ⊕ www. discoveryorkshirecoast.com. **Skipton** ✉ 35 Coach St., BD23 1LQ ☎ 01756/792809 ⊕ www.skiptononline.co.uk. **Whitby** ✉ Langbourne Rd., YO21 1YN ☎ 01947/602674. **York** ✉ De Grey Rooms, Exhibition Sq., YO1 2HB ☎ 01904/621756 ⊕ www.york-tourism. co.uk ✉ York Train Station ☎ 01904/621756.

THE NORTHEAST

DURHAM, HADRIAN'S WALL, LINDISFARNE ISLAND

FODOR'S CHOICE

Durham Cathedral, *Durham*

Hadrian's Wall

Lumley Castle Hotel, *Chester-le-Street*

Milecastle Inn, *pub near Greenhead*

HIGHLY RECOMMENDED

RESTAURANTS Jolly Fisherman, *Craster*

Seaham Hall, *Seaham*

HOTELS Da Vinci's, *Newcastle upon Tyne*

Georgian Town House, *Durham*

Seaham Hall, *Seaham*

SIGHTS Alnwick Castle, *Alnwick*

Beamish Open-Air Museum, *Beamish*

Bowes Museum, *Barnard Castle*

Cragside, *Rothbury*

Darlington Railway Centre and Museum, *Darlington*

Farne Islands

Hexham Abbey, *Hexham*

Housesteads Roman Fort, *near Bardon Mill*

Lindisfarne (Holy Island)

Updated by
Kate Hughes

A DECIDED AIR OF REMOTENESS pervades much of England's northeast corner, although one village in this region—Allendale Town, southwest of Hexham—lays claim to being the geographical center of the British Isles. For many Britons the words "the Northeast" provoke a vision of somewhat bitter, near-Siberian isolation. The truth is a revelation. For although there are wind-hammered wide-open spaces and empty roads that thread wild high moorland, the Northeast also has simple fishing towns, small villages of remarkable charm, and historic abbeys and castles that are all the more romantic for their often ruinous state. Even the remoteness can be relative. Suddenly, around the next bend of a country road, you may come across an imposing church, a tall monastery, or a gorgeous country house built by a Victorian-era millionaire. The value found in the region's shops and accommodations, the uncrowded beaches ideal for walking, and the friendliness of the people also add to the area's appeal.

Mainly composed of the two large counties of Durham and Northumberland, the Northeast includes English villages adjacent to the Scottish border area, renowned in ballads and romantic literature for feuds, raids, and battles. Hadrian's Wall, which marked the northern limit of the Roman Empire, stretches across prehistoric remains and moorland in this region. Much of it, remarkably, is still intact. Not far north of Hadrian's Wall are the 153,000-acre Kielder Forest; Kielder Water, the largest man-made lake in northern Europe; and some of the most interesting parts of Northumberland National Park. Steel, coal, railroads, and shipbuilding made prosperous towns such as Newcastle upon Tyne—now re-creating itself as a cultural center—Darlington, and Middlesbrough. Some sights reflect the area's industrial heritage, such as the Beamish Open-Air Museum and the Darlington Railway Centre and Museum.

On the region's eastern side stretches a 100-mi-long line of largely undeveloped coast, one of the least-visited and most dramatic in all Europe. Several outstanding castles perch on headlands and promontories along here, including Bamburgh, which according to legend was the Joyous Garde of Sir Lancelot du Lac. The island of Lindisfarne is a landmark of early Christendom. Fittingly, Durham Cathedral, the greatest ecclesiastical structure of the region, has memorably been described as "half church of God, half castle 'gainst the Scot." For almost 800 years, this great cathedral was the seat of bishops who raised their own armies and ruled the turbulent northern diocese as prince-bishops with quasi-royal authority.

Exploring the Northeast

Many people travel from the south to arrive at the historic cathedral city of Durham, not far east of the pretty foothill valleys of the Pennines. Farther north, Newcastle, with Gateshead, strides the region's main river, the Tyne. This reviving industrial city is making a bid for attention with new cultural facilities. Nearby, the remarkable Roman fortifications of Hadrian's Wall snake through some superb scenery to the west, and to the north lies the wilderness of Northumberland National Park. Huge castles and offshore islands such as the Farne Islands and Holy Island, also known as Lindisfarne, stud the stunning, final 40 mi of England's east coast, starting roughly an hour's drive north of Newcastle.

About the Restaurants & Hotels

You can try fine local products here, but don't wait until 9:30 to have dinner or you can have a very hard time getting a meal.

The large hotel chains do not have much of a presence in the Northeast, outside the few large cities. Rather, you can expect to find country houses converted into welcoming hotels, old coaching inns that still greet guests after 300 years, and cozy bed-and-breakfasts convenient to hiking trails. Check ahead if you're contemplating budget accommodation in winter, as many such places will be closed.

WHAT IT COSTS In pounds				
	££££££	££££	£££	££	£
RESTAURANTS	over £22	£18–£22	£13–£17	£7–£12	under £7
HOTELS	over £160	£115–£160	£80–£115	£50–£80	under £50

Restaurant prices are for a main course at dinner. Hotel prices are for two people in a standard double room in high season, including VAT, with no meals or, if indicated, CP (with Continental breakfast), BP (Breakfast Plan, with full breakfast), or MAP (Modified American Plan, with breakfast and dinner).

Timing

Although Hadrian's Wall and the coastal castles are starkly impressive in a blanket of snow, the best time to see the Northeast is in summer. This ensures that the museums—and the roads—will be open, and you'll also be able to enjoy the countryside walks that are one of the region's greatest pleasures. Rough seas and inclement weather make it extremely difficult to swim at any of the beaches except in July and August. At the end of June, Alnwick hosts its annual fair, with a costumed reenactment of a medieval fair, a market, and concerts. The Durham Regatta, England's oldest rowing event, also takes place in June. The Northumberland Traditional Music Festival takes place in venues throughout the county over two weeks in October. The Berwick Military Tattoo, a more intimate version of its Edinburgh counterpart, is at the end of August.

DURHAM, NEWCASTLE & ENVIRONS

Durham—the first major northeastern town on the main road up from London—is by far the region's most interesting historic city. Newcastle, however, along with Gateshead across the River Tyne, is the region's biggest, liveliest, and most cosmopolitan city. Most other towns in the area made their fortunes during the Industrial Revolution and have since subsided into relative decline. Several, such as Darlington, birthplace of the modern railroad, do hold interesting relics of their 19th-century heyday. The land to the west, known as County Durham, toward the Pennine Hills, is far more scenic, and a daylong drive through the valleys of Teesdale and Weardale takes you past ruined castles, industrial heritage sites, isolated moorland villages, and tumbling waterfalls.

Durham

➤ *250 mi north of London, 15 mi south of Newcastle.*

The great medieval city of Durham, seat of County Durham, is among the most dramatically sited in Britain. Despite the military advantages offered by the rocky spur on which it stands, Durham was founded surprisingly late, probably in about the year 1000, growing up around a small Saxon church erected to house the remains of St. Cuthbert. But it was the Normans, under William the Conqueror, who put Durham on the map, building the first defensive castle and beginning work on the cathedral. From here, Durham's prince-bishops, granted almost dictatorial local powers by William the Conqueror in 1072, kept a tight

Although it's possible to get a sense of the Northeast through an overnight stop en route to or from Scotland, it's worth spending four days to explore the region properly. One turn off the A1—the main north–south highway—and you'll soon learn that driving along the meandering backcountry roads is often slow business, if only because the spectacular scenery encourages long stops.

Numbers in the text correspond to numbers in the margin and on the Northeast and Durham maps.

14

If you have 2 days

Base yourself in either ⬚ **Durham** ❶–❺ ▶, with time to inspect the Norman cathedral and the castle to either side of the central Palace Green, or in smaller, quainter ⬚ **Alnwick** ㉔, with its riverside castle and cobbled square. Drive inland between the two for at least a brief glimpse of **Hadrian's Wall,** ideally at **Housesteads Roman Fort** ⑱, and wind up at the monastic settlement on **Lindisfarne** ㉚.

If you have 4 days

Having spent at least a half day exploring ⬚ **Durham** ❶–❺ ▶, set aside a full day to follow the course of **Hadrian's Wall.** An overnight stop nearby in ⬚ **Hexham** ⑮ enables you to see the excellent museums of Roman finds at **Vindolanda** ⑰ and **Housesteads Roman Fort** ⑱. Then drive northeast through the countryside to spend the evening in the little market town of ⬚ **Alnwick** ㉔ or on the coast at ⬚ **Alnmouth** ㉕. On the next morning, walk from **Craster** ㉖ to the splendidly bleak ruin of **Dunstanburgh Castle** ㉗; then visit one or two of the huge beaches to the north as you head to ⬚ **Bamburgh** ㉙ for the night. Overlooking the windswept shore, its famous castle conjures up the days of chivalry as few others do. Whether you're heading back to Durham from there, or onward to Scotland, visit the wind-battered monastic outpost at **Lindisfarne** ㉚, a short distance north.

---

rein on the county, coining their own money, raising their own taxes, and maintaining their own laws and courts; not until 1836 were these rights finally restored to the English Crown.

Together, the cathedral and castle, a World Heritage Site, stand high on a wooded peninsula almost entirely encircled by the River Wear (rhymes with "beer"). For centuries these two ancient structures have dominated Durham—now a thriving university town, the Northeast's equivalent to Oxford or Cambridge—and the surrounding countryside. Durham is more than its cathedral and castle, however. It's a great place to explore, with steep, narrow streets overlooked by perilously angled medieval houses and 18th-century town houses. In the most attractive part of the city, near the Palace Green and along the river, people go boating, anglers cast their lines, and strollers walk along the shaded paths. Between 10 and 4 on Monday through Saturday, cars are charged £2 (on top of parking charges) to enter the Palace Green area.

Architectural historians come from all over the world to admire and study the Norman masterpiece that is **Durham Cathedral,** in the heart of the city. The cathedral is an amazing vision of solidity and strength, a far cry from the airy lightness of later, Gothic cathedrals. Construction began in about 1090, and the main body was finished in about 1150. Durham

❶
Fodor's Choice
★

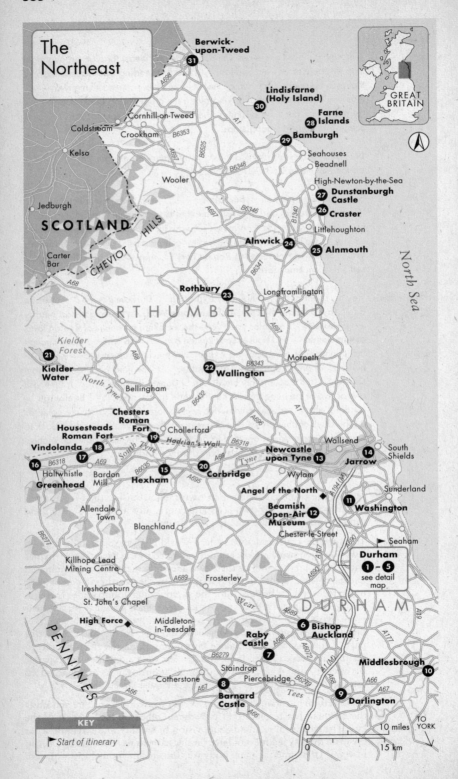

The Northeast

GREAT BRITAIN

SCOTLAND

31 Berwick-upon-Tweed

Cornhill-on-Tweed

Coldstream

Crookham

Kelso

B6353

Wooler

Jedburgh

CHEVIOT HILLS

Carter Bar

30 Lindisfarne (Holy Island)

28 Farne Islands

29 Bamburgh

Seahouses

Beadnell

High-Newton-by-the-Sea

27 Dunstanburgh Castle

26 Craster

Littlehoughton

24 Alnwick

25 Alnmouth

North Sea

23 Rothbury

Longframlington

NORTHUMBERLAND

Kielder Forest

21 Kielder Water

Bellingham

North Tyne

Morpeth

22 Wallingon

Chesters Roman Fort

Housesteads Roman Fort

19 Chollerford

Hadrian's Wall

18 Vindolanda

17

16 Haltwhistle

Greenhead

Bardon Mill

15 Hexham

20 Corbridge

Newcastle upon Tyne **13**

Wallsend

14 Jarrow

South Shields

Wylam

Angel of the North

Sunderland

11 Washington

12 Beamish Open-Air Museum

Chester-le-Street

Seaham

Durham
1 – **5**
see detail map

DURHAM

Killhope Lead Mining Centre

Ireshopeburn

St. John's Chapel

Frosterley

Wear

High Force

Middleton-in-Teesdale

6 Bishop Auckland

PENNINES

Allendale Town

Blanchland

Raby Castle

7

Middlesbrough

10

Cotherstone

Staindrop

Piercebridge

8 Barnard Castle

Tees

9 Darlington

TO YORK

KEY

▶ *Start of itinerary*

0   10 miles

0   15 km

14

Castles

Fought over for centuries by the Scots and the English, and prey to Viking raiders from across the North Sea, the Northeast was one of the most heavily fortified regions in Britain. Cities such as Durham and Newcastle—where the "new castle" is 900 years old—still hold impressive relics, and exploring the stupendous fortresses along the exposed Northumbrian coastline is among the most memorable experiences the region has to offer. Alnwick Castle, the imposing inland seat of the dukes of Northumberland, is attracting attention because of its ambitious garden renovations. Dunstanburgh Castle near Craster and Bamburgh Castle farther north on the coast are especially worth seeing.

Great Flavors

The Northeast is one of the best areas in England for fresh local produce. Look for restaurants that serve game from the Kielder Forest, local lamb from the hillsides, and fish both from the streams threading through the wild valleys and from the fishing fleets along the coast. Don't miss the simple fresh seafood sandwiches or stotties (large bread buns) served for afternoon tea. You can also sample Lindisfarne mead, a traditional, highly potent spirit produced on Holy Island and made of honey vatted with grape juice and mineral water.

Hiking & Biking

Superb walking awaits you almost wherever you go in this region, but to gain an awe-inspiring sense of history with views of stunning scenery, nothing beats a hike along the route of ancient Hadrian's Wall. The hilltop section near Housesteads Roman Fort is the best stretch for a short stroll. Long-distance footpaths include the 90-mi Teesdale Way, which follows the course of the River Tees through Barnard Castle and Middleton-in-Teesdale, finishing at Dufton in Cumbria, and St. Cuthbert's Way, an ancient inland pilgrimage route running the 63 mi from the Scottish border to Holy Island. Otherwise, the russet hills and dales of Northumberland National Park, in the northwest corner of the area, will please any serious walker. Similarly, cyclists relish the wide vistas, quiet roads, and magnificently fresh air of the Northeast, whether they attempt the 220-mi Northumbria's Cycling Kingdom loop, the 150-mi Pennine Cycleway North from Cumbria to Berwick-upon-Tweed, or a shorter route. The 81-mi Coast and Castles cycle route follows minor roads from Tynemouth to Berwick-upon-Tweed and takes in Dunstanburgh and Bamburgh castles. One spot to rent a mountain bike is Kielder Water, north of Hadrian's Wall.

---

reveals the essence of an almost entirely Norman, or Romanesque, edifice: the round arches of the nave and the deep zigzag patterns carved into them typify the heavy, gaunt style of Norman building. Yet the technology of Durham was quite revolutionary at the time. This was the first European cathedral to be given a stone, rather than a wooden, roof. When you consider the means of construction available to its builders—the stones that form the ribs of the roof had to be hoisted up by hand and set on a wooden structure, which was then knocked away—the achievement seems staggering.

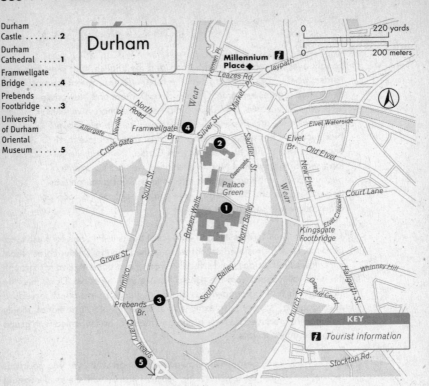

The origins of the cathedral go back to the 10th century. In 995, monks brought to this site the remains of St. Cuthbert, which had been removed from the monastery at Lindisfarne after a Viking raid in 875. Soon the wealth attracted by Cuthbert's shrine paid for the construction of a cathedral. The bishop's throne here was claimed to be the loftiest in medieval Christendom; the miter of the bishop is the only one to be encircled by a coronet, and his coat of arms is the only one to be crossed with a sword as well as a crosier. **Cuthbert's shrine** lies surrounded by columns of local marble, with the saint's remains buried below a simple slab. An unobtrusive tomb at the west end of the cathedral, in the handsome, Moorish-influenced **Galilee Chapel,** is the final resting place of the **Venerable Bede,** the 8th-century Northumbrian monk whose contemporary account of the English people made him the country's first reliable historian. He died in Jarrow in 735, and his remains were placed here in 1020.

Upon entering, note the 12th-century bronze **Sanctuary Knocker,** shaped like the head of a ferocious mythological beast, mounted on the massive northwestern entrance door. By grasping the ring clenched in the animal's mouth, medieval felons could claim sanctuary; cathedral records show that 331 criminals sought this protection between 1464 and 1524. The knocker is, in fact, a reproduction the original is kept for security reasons in the cathedral **Treasury,** along with ancient illuminated manuscripts, fragments of St. Cuthbert's oak coffin, and more church treasures well worth a look. There's also a restaurant and a bookstore. ⊠ *Palace Green* ☏ *0191/386-4266* ⊕ *www.durhamcathedral.co.uk* ✉ *£3.50 donation requested, Treasury £2, tower £2, guided tours £3.50* ☉ *Cathedral mid-June–early Sept., daily 7:30 AM–8 PM; early Sept.–mid-June, Mon.–Sat. 7:30–6:15, Sun. 7:45–5. Treasury Mon.–Sat.*

10–4:30, Sun. 2–4:30. Choral evensong service Tues.–Fri. 5:15, Sun. 3:30. Guided tours mid-Apr.–Sept., Mon.–Sat. 11 and 2:30.

2 **Durham Castle,** facing the cathedral across Palace Green, commands a strategic position above the River Wear. For almost 800 years this Norman castle was the home of successive prince-bishops, who undertook extensive renovations and repairs through the ages; from here, they ruled large tracts of northern England and kept the Scots at bay. Henry VIII first curtailed their independence, although it wasn't until the 19th century that the prince-bishops finally had their powers annulled. They abandoned the castle, turning it over to University College, one of several colleges of the University of Durham (founded 1832), the oldest in England after Oxford and Cambridge. You can visit the castle on a 45-minute guided tour. ⊠ *Palace Green* ☎ *0191/374–3800* ⊕ *www. durhamcastle.com* ☞ *£3* ☉ *Guided tours mid-Mar.–Sept., Mon.–Sat. 10–12:30 and 2–4, Sun. 10–noon and 2–4; Oct.–mid-Mar., Mon., Wed., and weekends 2–4.*

> **need a break?** Drop into the **Almshouse Café** (⊠ Palace Green ☎ 0191/386–1054), in an ancient almshouse between the cathedral and castle, for fat brownies or tasty cheesecake. These sweet treats are the perfect accompaniment to your tea or coffee.

The **River Wear** winds through Durham, curving beneath the cathedral and castle, and playing host in mid-June each year to the Durham Regatta. Britain's oldest rowing event attracts 300 racing crews. Delightful views are the reward of a short stroll along the River Wear's leafy **3** banks, especially as you cross **Prebends Footbridge,** reached from the southern end of Palace Green. J. M. W. Turner reveled in the view from here and painted a celebrated scene of Durham from the bridge. If you follow the far side of the Wear north from Prebends Footbridge, you can **4** recross the river at **Framwellgate Bridge,** which dates originally from the 12th century. Many of the elegant town houses that line the narrow lanes back up to the cathedral now house departments of the University of Durham.

5 The **University of Durham Oriental Museum** displays fine art and craft work from all parts of Asia. The collection of Chinese ceramics is particularly noted, and don't miss the nearby 18-acre Botanic Gardens. ⊠ *Elvet Hill, off South Rd. (A1050)* ☎ *0191/374–7911* ⊕ *www.dur.ac.uk/oriental. museum* ☞ *£1.50* ☉ *Weekdays 10–5, weekends noon–5.*

Where to Stay & Eat
During college vacations (late March–April, July–September, and December), very reasonably priced accommodations are available at the **University of Durham** (☎ 0191/374–3454 🖷 0191/374–3420 ⊕ www. dur.ac.uk/conference_tourism), in Durham Castle and in other buildings throughout the city.

££–£££ ✕ **Bistro 21.** Relaxed and cottagey, Durham's most fashionable restaurant lies a couple of miles northwest from the center, in a superbly restored farmhouse. The eclectic and seasonal menu lists brasserie classics and Asian favorites, as well as rich desserts. ⊠ *Aykley Heads* ☎ *0191/384–4354* 🖃 *AE, DC, MC, V* ☉ *Closed Sun.*

£ ✕ **Vennel's Café.** You'll encounter a "vennel," a local word for the very narrowest of thoroughfares, as you squeeze up the alley to this welcoming café. Order at the counter and, in good weather, sit outside in the courtyard. Soups, salads, hot dishes, and cakes are the mainstay. ⊠ *Saddler's Yard, off Saddler St.* ☎ *0191/386–0484* 🖃 *No credit cards* ☉ *No dinner.*

££ ✕▣ **Seven Stars Inn.** Warm oranges and tartans in the public areas enhance the coziness of this good-value early 18th-century coaching inn. Bedrooms are done in creamy yellows and reds and have modern pine furniture. If you're dining, tuck into such dishes as salmon on herb mash or monkfish with saffron sauce, and finish with apple crumble or sticky toffee pudding. The inn is 2 mi south of the city. ⊠ *High St. N, Shincliffe Village, DH1 2NU* ☎ *0191/384–8454* ⊕ *www.mortal-man-inns. co.uk* 🖷 *0191/386–0640* ⤹ *8 rooms* ⟡ *Restaurant, some pets allowed; no a/c* ⊟ *AE, DC, MC, V* ⫯◉⫯ *BP.*

£££ ▣ **Swallow Three Tuns.** This cheery 16th-century inn has echoes of its solid country past. Some parts retain the old oak beams and fireplaces, and a colorful modern stained-glass ceiling illuminates other rooms. The modern bedrooms are pretty and pink, with a floral motif. You can use the indoor pool and health club at the nearby Swallow Royal County Hotel. Browns restaurant serves up staples such as veal, steak, and salmon. ⊠ *New Elvet, DH1 3AQ* ☎ *0191/386–4326* 🖷 *0191/384–2093* ⊕ *www.swallowhotels.com* ⤹ *50 rooms* ⟡ *Restaurant, cable TV, piano bar, meeting rooms, some pets allowed; no a/c* ⊟ *AE, DC, MC, V* ⫯◉⫯ *BP.*

★ **££** ▣ **Georgian Town House.** Exactly as the name suggests, this friendly, family-run hotel, at the top of a cobbled street overlooking the cathedral and castle, makes the best of its Georgian exterior and details. Stylish modern furnishings, paintings, and stencils, evidence of the owner's hand, give all rooms a colorful individuality. Rooms at the back have the best view. ⊠ *10 Crossgate, DH1 4PS* ☎🖷 *0191/386–8070* ⊕ *www. thegeorgiantownhouse.co.uk* ⤹ *8 rooms* ⟡ *No-smoking rooms; no a/c* ⊟ *No credit cards* ⊘ *Closed last wk Dec.* ⫯◉⫯ *BP.*

Nightlife & the Arts

Durham's nightlife is geared to the university set. The **Coach-and-Eight** (⊠ Bridge House, Framwellgate Bridge ☎ 0191/386–3284) can get noisy with students, but outdoor seating makes it appealing. The **Hogshead** (⊠ 58 Saddler St. ☎ 0191/386–4134) pub is a true student haunt.

Durham's **Gala Theatre** (⊠ Millennium Pl. ☎ 0191/383–0100) presents plays, concerts, and opera year-round.

Sports & the Outdoors

Brown's Boat House (⊠ Elvet Bridge ☎ 0191/386–3779) rents rowboats and offers short cruises April–early November.

Shopping

Bramwells Jewellers (⊠ 24 Elvet Bridge ☎ 0191/386–8006) has its own store specialty, a pendant copy of the gold-and-silver cross of St. Cuthbert. The food and bric-a-brac stalls in **Durham Indoor Market** (⊠ Market Pl. ☎ 0191/384–6153), a Victorian arcade, are open Monday–Saturday.

Bishop Auckland

❻ *10 mi southwest of Durham.*

For 700 years, between the 12th and 19th centuries, the prince-bishops of Durham had their country residence in Auckland Castle, in the town of Bishop Auckland. When finally deprived of their powers in 1836, the bishops left Durham and made Bishop Auckland their official home. The grand episcopal palace of **Auckland Castle** that you see today dates mainly from the 16th century, although the limestone and marble chapel, with its dazzling stained-glass windows, was built in 1665 from the ruins of a 12th-century banqueting hall. Among the palace's treasures are paintings by the 17th-century Spanish artist Zurbarán of Jacob and his 12 sons. (The Church of England intends to sell these, so check ahead.) The unusual 18th-century "deer house" of adjoining Bishops Park testifies to at least one of the bishops' extracurricular interests. ⊠ *Off Market Pl.* ☎ *01388/601627* ⊕ *www.auckland-castle.co.uk* ⊠ *£4* ⊙ *Apr.–Sept., Mon. and Thurs. 12:30–5, Sun. 2–5; park daily 7 AM–sunset.*

Raby Castle

❼ *7 mi southwest of Bishop Auckland, 19 mi southwest of Durham.*

The stone battlements and turrets of moated Raby Castle, once the seat of the powerful Nevilles and currently the home of the 11th Baron Barnard, stand amid a landscaped, 200-acre deer park and ornamental gardens. Charles Neville supported Mary, Queen of Scots, in an uprising against Elizabeth I in 1569; when the uprising failed, the estate was confiscated. Dating mostly from the 14th century (using stone plundered from Barnard Castle) and renovated in the 18th and 19th centuries, the house displays art and other treasures in luxuriously furnished rooms, including an important Meissen collection. Victorian domestic ware fills the well-preserved medieval kitchens. ⊠ *A688, 1 mi north of Staindrop* ☎ *01833/660202* ⊕ *www.rabycastle.com* ⊠ *Castle, park, and gardens £6; park and gardens £4* ⊙ *Castle May and Sept., Wed. and Sun. 1–5; June–Aug., Sun.–Fri. 1–5. Park and gardens May and Sept., Wed. and Sun. 11–5:30; July–Sept., Sun.–Fri. 11–5:30.*

Barnard Castle

❽ *6 mi southwest of Raby Castle, 25 mi southwest of Durham.*

The handsome market town of Barnard Castle has sights of its own and can also serve as a base for venturing into the Teesdale valley to the northwest. Its unusual butter-market hall (known locally as Market Cross), surmounted by a fire alarm bell, marks the junction of the streets Thorngate, Newgate, and Market Place. Stores, pubs, and cafés line these thoroughfares. In 1838 Charles Dickens stayed at the **King's Head Inn** here while doing research for his novel *Nicholas Nickleby,* which deals with the abuse of children in boarding schools. The local tourist office has a free *In the Footsteps of Charles Dickens* leaflet.

The substantial ruins of **Barnard Castle,** which gave its name to the town, cling to an aerie overlooking the River Tees. Inside you can see parts of the 14th-century Great Hall and the cylindrical, 13th-century tower, built by the castle's original owners, the Anglo-Scottish Balliol family. ⊠ *Off Galgate* ☎ *01833/638212* ⊕ *www.english-heritage.org. uk* ⊠ *£2.60* ⊙ *Apr.–Sept., daily 10–6; Oct., daily 10–5; Nov.–Mar., Wed.–Sun. 10–4; call ahead in winter.*

★ The **Bowes Museum,** a vast French-inspired château a little more than a mile west of the town center, was built between 1869 and 1885 to house the outstanding art and artifacts collection of philanthropists John and Josephine Bowes. Highlights include paintings by Canaletto, El Greco, Goya, and Boucher, and one of the world's greatest collections of 18th-century French furniture. Archaeological displays chart the history of County Durham from the Ice Age to the end of the Roman period, and a gallery displays 19th-century dollhouses and models. An extraordinary 18th-century life-size, mechanical silver swan, sitting on a stream of twisted glass rods, catches and swallows a silver fish at 12:30 and 3. ⊠ *Up Newgate, follow signs from town center* ☎ *01833/690606* ⊕ *www.bowesmuseum.org.uk* ⊠ *£5* ⊙ *Daily 11–5.*

off the
beaten
path

HIGH FORCE – The Upper Teesdale Valley's elemental nature shows its most volatile aspect in the sprays of England's highest waterfall, the 72-foot High Force. From the roadside parking lot it's a 10-minute walk through woodland to the massive rocks over which the water tumbles. A precarious viewpoint puts you right above the falls, at their best in springtime, after a rain. The waterfall is 15 mi northwest of Barnard Castle. A welcome pub on the main road, the High Force (⊠ B6277 ☎ 01833/622222), serves bar meals and home-brewed beer, a boon in this isolated stretch of moorland road. ⊠ Off B6277 ☎ 01833/640209 ☜ £1; parking £1.50 ☉ Mid-Apr.–Oct., daily 9:30–5; Nov.–mid-Apr., open but unattended.

Where to Eat

£ ✕ **Market Place Teashop.** A nicely old-fashioned air pervades this 17th-century building on the main square. Uniformed waitresses serve such dishes as parsnip and bacon with Mornay sauce or one of the many vegetarian options, and afternoon tea comes with silver teapots. ⊠ 29 Market Pl. ☎ 01833/690110 ▭ MC, V ☉ Closed Sun. No dinner.

Darlington

❾ 15 mi east of Barnard Castle, 21 mi south of Durham.

Still visibly rooted in its 19th-century industrial past, the town of Darlington rocketed to fame in 1825, when George Stephenson piloted his steam-powered Locomotion along newly laid tracks the few miles to nearby Stockton, thus kick-starting the railway age. First envisaged as a means of transporting coal from the local pits to the dockside, Stephenson's invention soon attracted paying passengers, and even though it barely traveled faster than 15 mph, the Locomotion was a palpable hit. ★ ☺ The story of the coming of the railway is well told in the **Darlington Railway Centre and Museum,** in the town's original railroad station, built in 1842 and now a (signposted) 20-minute walk outside the town center. You can inspect historic engines, including Stephenson's Locomotion, as well as photographs, documents, models, and other paraphernalia associated with a 19th-century station. ⊠ North Rd. Station, Station Rd. ☎ 01325/460532 ⊕ www.drcm.org.uk ☜ £2.20 ☉ Daily 10–5.

Where to Stay & Eat

££ ✕▣ **George Hotel.** This sprawling 18th-century coaching inn, 4 mi west of Darlington in tiny Piercebridge, sits on the banks of the River Tees. Its claim to fame, however, is the longcase clock, still in place, which was the inspiration for the song "My Grandfather's Clock" by Henry Clay Work. Rooms are plain and white with dark wood furniture, and the restaurant, whose windows overlook the river, serves up traditional dishes such as black pudding and Yorkshire ham. ⊠ B6275, Piercebridge-on-Tees, Darlington, DL2 3SW ☎ 01325/374576 ☐ 01325/374577 ⊕ www.thegeorgehotel.activehotels.com ⤳ 35 rooms ♨ Restaurant, 2 bars, some pets allowed; no a/c ▭ AE, MC, V ❍I BP.

Middlesbrough

❿ 12 mi east of Darlington, 22 mi southeast of Durham.

In 1802 a mere dozen people lived in Middlesbrough, near the mouth of the River Tees. With the discovery of iron ore, it became a boom-town, with steel mills and, later, chemical industries, doing much to boost the economy, although blighting part of the town. The industrial heritage has created a few unique local attractions.

Middlesbrough's unusual **Transporter Bridge,** built in 1911, is the largest of its kind in the world, a vast structure like a giant's Erector-set model. The gantry system can carry up to 12 cars and 200 passengers across the river in two minutes, every 15 minutes. Upstream you'll find Newport Bridge, the world's largest lift span bridge, another remarkable sight, but open only if weather permits. ☎ *01642/247563* ✉ *Pedestrians 30p, cars 80p* ☉ *Mon.–Sat. 5 AM–11 PM, Sun. 2–11.*

The **Captain Cook Birthplace Museum,** in the Middlesbrough suburb of Marton, vividly explores the life and times of Captain James Cook (1728–79), the celebrated circumnavigator and explorer. You can walk through Stewart Park to the modern museum building. Interactive displays, exhibits, and films cover Cook's remarkable voyages to Australia, New Zealand, Canada, Antarctica, and Hawaii, where he met an untimely death. ✉ *Stewart Park, Marton, off A174, south of city center* ☎ *01642/311211* ✉ *£2.40* ☉ *Apr.–Oct., Tues.–Sun. 10–5:30; Nov.–Mar., Tues.–Sun. 9–4; last admission 45 mins before closing.*

Where to Eat

£–££ ✕ **Purple Onion.** A treat as idiosyncratic as its name, this restaurant lavishly decorated with assorted antiques serves a spirited modern menu. You can try creative sandwiches at lunch, and in the evening, char-grills, pastas, and seafood platters. There's jazz and blues in the cellar. ✉ *80 Corporation Rd.* ☎ *01642/222250* ▬ *MC, V* ☉ *Closed Sun., Mon.*

Washington

⑪ *34 mi northwest of Middlesbrough, 12 mi north of Durham.*

Washington, a planned "new town" divided into numbered districts, holds a link to the history of the United States. **Washington Old Hall** is the ancestral home of the first U.S. president. George Washington's direct forebears, the de Wessyngtons, lived here between 1183 and 1288. Other family members resided in the house until 1613, when the current property was rebuilt. Now owned by the National Trust, the house retains a Jacobean (17th-century) appearance, most noticeably in the fine wood paneling and the heavy furniture. Special celebrations take place on the Fourth of July. ✉ *From A1(M), 5 mi west of Sunderland, follow signs to Washington New Town, District 4, and then on to Washington Village* ☎ *0191/416–6879* ⊕ *www.nationaltrust.org.uk* ✉ *£3* ☉ *Apr.–Oct., Sun.–Wed. 11–5; last admission 4:30.*

Beamish Open-Air Museum

★ ⑫ *9 mi north of Durham, 3 mi west of Chester-le-Street.*

The historic buildings that have been brought to the more than 300-acre museum from throughout the region deserve at least half a day's attention. A streetcar takes you around the site and to the reconstructed 1920s High Street, with a dentist's operating room, a pub, and a grocery store. A stableman discusses the Clydesdale workhorses in his care, once used to draw brewery wagons. On the farm you can see such local breeds as Durham Shorthorn cattle and Teeswater sheep. Other attractions include a small manor house, a railroad station, a coal mine, and a transportation collection. In summer you can take a short ride on a steam train. The large gift store specializes in period souvenirs and local crafts. Winter visits center on the reconstructed street, and admission prices are reduced. ✉ *Off A693, between Chester-le-Street and Stanley* ☎ *0191/370–4000* ⊕ *www.beamish.org.uk* ✉ *£12 or £4 (depending on season)* ☉ *Apr.–Oct., daily 10–5; Nov.–mid-Dec. and Jan.–Mar., Tues.–Thurs. and weekends 10–4; last admission 3.*

Where to Stay & Eat

££££–£££££　✕🏨 **Lumley Castle Hotel.** This is a real Norman castle, right down to the
Fodor'sChoice　dungeons and maze of dark flagstone corridors. Antiques, silks, and deep,
★　rich fabrics furnish all the sumptuous rooms, and the bedrooms are soothing and subtly lit; those in the courtyard annex fall into the less expensive bracket. You can join in the merriment of the Friday and Saturday
night Elizabethan banquets or dine intimately in the Black Knight
Restaurant on English fare such as sea bass with roasted fennel and onions.
A full breakfast is included in the price on weekends. The hotel is just
east of town via the B1284. ✉ *Chester-le-Street, DH3 4NX* ☎ *0191/
389–1111* 🖷 *0191/387–1437* 🌐 *www.lumleycastle.com* 🛏 *60 rooms*
🍴 *Restaurant, in-room data ports, cable TV, bar, meeting rooms; no a/
c* 🖃 *AE, DC, MC, V* ❙❚❙ *BP.*

en route　　At the junction of A1(M) and A1 at Gateshead stands England's
largest sculpture, the modern, rust-color steel *Angel of the North.*
Created by Antony Gormley in 1998, it stands an impressive 65 feet
tall and has a horizontal wingspan of 175 feet. There's parking
nearby, signposted on A167.

Newcastle upon Tyne

⓲ *8 mi north of Beamish Open-Air Museum, 16 mi north of Durham.*

Durham may have the glories of its castle, cathedral, and university, but
the main and liveliest city of the Northeast is Newcastle. Settled since
Roman times, this city on the Tyne River made its fortune twice, first
by exporting coal in the Elizabethan age and then by building ships. As
a 19th-century industrial center, Newcastle had few equals in Britain,
showing off its wealth in grand Victorian buildings lining the sweeping,
central neoclassical streets. Many of these remain (particularly on Grey
Street), and after years of industrial decline, the city is striving to rein-
vent itself as a cultural and architectural center. Much of the regeneration since the early 1990s has been because of the Gateshead Quays
development on the historic quayside. Here the BALTIC Centre for
Contemporary Art and the pedestrian- and cyclist-only Millennium
Bridge—the world's first tilting bridge, which opens and shuts like an
eyelid—have risen from derelict wasteland. New housing and former
warehouses converted into lively restaurants and bars stand alongside
the surviving 17th-century houses. By the old quayside is the symbol of
the city, the celebrated **Tyne Bridge** (1929), one of seven bridges spanning the river in the city. Its elegant proportions were later reproduced
by the architects responsible for Sydney's Harbour Bridge.

Overlooking the Tyne River, the remains of the **Norman castle** recall the
city's earlier status as a defensive stronghold. This was the "new castle," originally built in 1080, that gave the city its name. ✉ *St. Nicholas
St.* ☎ *0191/232–7938* 🌐 *www.castlekeep-newcastle.org.uk* 💷 *£1.50*
🕙 *Apr.–Sept., daily 9:30–5:30; Oct.–Mar., daily 9:30–4:30; last admission 30 mins before closing.*

The finest art museum in the Northeast, the **Laing Gallery** merits at least
an hour's visit for its selection of British art. Some of the most extraordinary paintings are those by 19th-century local artist John Martin, who produced dramatic biblical landscapes. The Pre-Raphaelites are
on show, too, and the Art on Tyneside exhibition traces 400 years of
local arts, highlighting glassware, pottery, and engraving. ✉ *Higham
Pl. near John Dobson St.* ☎ *0191/232–7734* 🌐 *www.twmuseums.org.
uk* 💷 *Free* 🕙 *Mon.–Sat. 10–5, Sun. 2–5.*

need a
break? The very popular art deco **Tyneside Coffee Rooms** (⊠ 10 Pilgrim St. ☎ 0191/2619291), on the second floor above the cinema, makes an intriguing place to stop for teas, coffee, and a snack. It's closed Sunday.

The buildings of the **University of Newcastle upon Tyne** contain some of the city's best museums. The **Museum of Antiquities** (⊕ www.ncl.ac.uk/antiquities) shows finds from Hadrian's Wall, and the **Shefton Museum of Greek Art and Archaeology** (⊕ www.ncl.ac.uk/shefton-museum) of the Department of Classics contains ancient arms, decorative pottery, and figurines. ⊠ *The University* ☎ *0191/222–7849* ⊠ *Free* ⊙ *Museum of Antiquities Mon.–Sat. 10–5; Shefton Museum weekdays 10–4.*

At Life Interactive World at the **Centre for Life,** three high-tech shows and 60 exhibits bring science to life, from research on genes to the workings of the brain. There's also a virtual reality arcade and a simulation ride that lets you bungee jump without leaving your seat. ⊠ *Times Sq.* ☎ *0191/243–8210* ⊕ *www.centreforlife.co.uk* ⊠ *£6.95* ⊙ *Mon.–Sat. 10–6, Sun. 11–6; last admission 4.*

Although not all galleries will be complete until early 2004, the **Discovery Museum** remains the best place to take in the Newcastle story. Reconstructed streets and homes lead you from Roman times to the present day, and the Tyne galleries show off maritime and industrial achievements. *Turbinia* is a model of the first ship to be powered by steam turbines and, in 1897, the fastest in the world. A lively exploration of the fashion industry rounds out the exhibits. ⊠ *Blandford Sq.* ☎ *0191/232–6789* ⊕ *www.twmuseums.org.uk* ⊠ *Free* ⊙ *Mon.–Sat. 10–5, Sun. 2–5.*

The **Segedunum Roman Fort, Baths and Museum** includes the remains of the substantial Roman fort of Segedunum, built around AD 125 as an eastern extension to Hadrian's Wall; part of the original wall as well as a reproduction section; and a reconstructed Roman bath complex (check ahead for days when it's heated up). A museum with interactive displays interprets finds from the area, and an observation tower provides views of the site and the adjoining busy, modern shipbuilding area. ⊠ *Buddle St., Wallsend* ☎ *0191/295–5757* ⊕ *www.twmuseums.org.uk* ⊠ *£3.50* ⊙ *Apr.–Oct., daily 10–5; Nov.–Mar., daily 10–3:30.*

off the
beaten
path **GEORGE STEPHENSON'S BIRTHPLACE** – In 1781 the Father of the Railroads was born in this tiny stone cottage. Four families shared the house; the Stephensons lived in just one room and it's this room that is open to the public, a modest tribute to the engineer who invented the steam locomotive. You can park your car in the village by the war memorial, a 10-minute walk away. ⊠ *Wylam, 4 mi west of Newcastle, 1½ mi south of A69* ☎ *01661/853457* ⊕ *www. nationaltrust.org.uk* ⊠ *80p* ⊙ *Apr.–Oct., Thurs., weekends, and national holidays 1–5.*

Where to Stay & Eat

£££–££££ ✕ **Treacle Moon.** Well-presented contemporary dishes with a Mediterranean touch are the specialty at this modern, stylish restaurant centrally placed near the river. There's a good selection of unusual ice creams and sorbets, as well as house wines. The name comes from the poet Byron's description of his honeymoon at nearby Seaham; his words adorn the walls. ⊠ *5–7 The Side* ☎ *0191/232–5537* ⊟ *AE, DC, MC, V* ⊙ *Closed Sun. No lunch.*

£–£££ ✕ **Barluga.** What was once the city's impressive Bank of England building now holds a vibrant modern bar and restaurant decked out in reds and golds. It specializes in seafood and caviar, though you can opt for more homespun dishes such as liver with "bubble and squeak" (fried potato and cabbage) if you prefer. ⊠ *35 Grey St.* ☎ *0191/230–2306* ▱ *AE, DC, MC, V.*

★ ✕▱ **Seaham Hall.** Byron married Annabella Milbanke in this foursquare
££££–£££££ mansion in 1815; today the sumptuous, sensual contemporary interior filled with warm natural hues is a haven of luxury. Bedrooms have their own fireplaces, original artwork, large baths, and exotic flowers. At the equally elegant restaurant, indulge in dishes such as white bean and truffle soup with hot bacon toast and roast salmon with a fresh pea risotto. Make some time for the Serenity Spa. Seaham is 15 mi south of the centre of Newcastle, off the A19. ⊠ *Lord Byron's Walk, Seaham, SR7 7AG* ☎ *0191/516–1400* 🖷 *0191/516–1410* ⊕ *www.seaham-hall.com* ↰ *19 suites* ♢ *Restaurant, in-room data ports, indoor pool, gym, spa, bar, meeting rooms* ▱ *AE, DC, MC, V* ¶◐ *CP.*

£££–££££ ✕▱ **Malmaison.** Converted from an old riverside warehouse, this member of a glamorous, design-conscious chain sits right beside the pedestrian Millennium Bridge. Bedrooms, done in soft colors, are spacious, the huge beds piled high with pillows. The discreet art deco Brasserie & Bar presents French fare such as scallops with samphire and Balmoral loin of venison with chestnut crust in a room that overlooks the Tyne through arched windows. ⊠ *Quayside, NE1 3DX* ☎ *0191/245–5000* 🖷 *0191/245–4545* ⊕ *www.malmaison.com* ↰ *116 rooms* ♢ *Restaurant, in-room data ports, cable TV with movies, gym, spa, bar, meeting rooms, some pets allowed* ▱ *AE, DC, MC, V.*

££££–£££££ ▱ **Copthorne Hotel.** Close to the Tyne Bridge, this upbeat and businesslike modern hotel is right on the waterfront. Cheerful furnishings soften the grand glass atrium with polished marble floor, and bedrooms are a good size and restful. ⊠ *The Close, Quayside, NE1 3RT* ☎ *0191/222–0333* 🖷 *0191/230–1111* ⊕ *www.millennium-hotels.com* ↰ *156 rooms* ♢ *2 restaurants, in-room data ports, cable TV with movies, indoor pool, gym, sauna, some pets allowed; no a/c* ▱ *AE, DC, MC, V* ¶◐ *BP.*

★ ££ ▱ **Da Vinci's.** Italian flair prevails at this small hotel in the vibrant Jesmond district, a mile from the city center. Bedrooms are refreshingly simple and contemporary, with white walls and bed linen and blue carpets. Dine on Italian specialties in the restaurant. ⊠ *73 Osborne Rd., NE2 2AN* ☎ *0191/281–5284* 🖷 *0191/281–4103* ⊕ *www.davincis.co.uk* ↰ *16 rooms* ♢ *Restaurant, bar; no a/c* ▱ *AE, MC, V.*

Nightlife & the Arts

Nightlife centers around the Quayside. You can also head for the prettily lit, suburban Jesmond area, where lively bars and restaurants line Osborne Road. **Thirty 3i8ht** (⊠ Exchange Building, Lombard St. ☎ 0191/261–6463), a classy, contemporary café-bar, has a no-smoking area, good food, and live music. The **Offshore** (⊠ 40 Sandhill ☎ 0191/261—0921) is an old pub with a nautical theme.

The **BALTIC Centre for Contemporary Art** (⊠ Gateshead Quays ☎ 0191/477–1810), formerly a grain warehouse and now the country's largest national gallery for contemporary art outside London, schedules changing exhibitions (there's no permanent collection) and events.

The **Newcastle Opera House** (⊠ 111 Westgate Rd. ☎ 0191/232–0899) presents dance and pop and rock music, as well as opera.

The **Sage Gateshead** (⊠ Gateshead Quays ☎ 0191/443–4666), a curving modern building designed by Norman Foster, will open on the north bank of the Tyne in late 2004 as the city's principal music venue.

The **Theatre Royal** (✉ Grey St. ☎ 0191/232–2061) is the region's most established theater, with high-quality productions.

Jarrow

⑭ *4 mi east of Newcastle.*

The name "Jarrow" is to British ears linked to the "Jarrow Crusade," a protest march to London led by unemployed former workers from the town's steelworks and shipyards in the depths of the 1930s. Travelers are attracted here, however, by its much more ancient history.

Bede's World holds substantial monastic ruins, a visitor center–museum, and the church of St. Paul, all reflecting the long tradition of religion and learning that began here in AD 681, when the first Saxon church was established on the site. The Venerable Bede, deemed to be England's earliest historian, was a scholar here and in AD 731 completed his *History of the English Church and People* while ensconced at the monastery. The museum explores the development of Northumbria, using excerpts from Bede's work as well as archaeological finds and reconstructions. You can gain a sense of medieval life from the reconstructed farm buildings and the rare breeds of pigs and cattle on the 11-acre Anglo-Saxon farm. St. Paul's contains the oldest dedicatory church inscription in Britain, a carved stone inscribed in AD 685. From the southern exit traffic circle at South Tyne tunnel, take A185 to South Shields, then follow signs to St. Paul's Church and Jarrow Hall. ✉ *Church Bank* ☎ *0191/489–2106* ⊕ *www.bedesworld.co.uk* 🎫 *£4.50* ⊙ *Apr.–Oct., Mon.–Sat. 10–5:30, Sun. noon–5:30; Nov.–Mar., Mon.–Sat. 10–4:30, Sun. noon–4:30; last admission 30 mins before closing.*

HADRIAN'S WALL COUNTRY

A formidable line of Roman fortifications, Hadrian's Wall was constructed in response to repeated barbarian invasions from Scotland. The land through which the wall marches is wild and inhospitable in places, but that seems only to add to the powerful sense of history the wall evokes. Sites, museums, and information centers along the wall make it possible to learn as much as you want about the Roman era, or you can simply reflect on the evidence of vanished power.

Hadrian's Wall

Fodor'sChoice
★ *73 mi from Wallsend, north of Newcastle, to Bowness-on-Solway, beyond Carlisle.*

Dedicated to the Roman god Terminus, the massive span of Hadrian's Wall once marked the northern frontier of the Roman Empire. The most significant reminder of the Roman presence in Britain extends 73 mi from Wallsend ("Wall's End") north of Newcastle, in the east, to Bowness-on-Solway beyond Carlisle, in the west. Its completion in just four years gives a pretty good idea of Roman determination, and its construction bears all the hallmarks of Roman efficiency. The wall, now a World Heritage Site, stretches across the narrowest part of the country and follows as straight a path as possible.

For more than 250 years the Roman army used the wall to control travel and trade and to fortify Roman Britain against the barbarians to the north. At Emperor Hadrian's command, three legions of soldiers began building the wall in AD 122. Around AD 200 Emperor Severus had the wall repaired and rebuilt. During the Roman era, the wall stood 15 feet high and 9 feet thick; behind it lay the vallum, a ditch about 20 feet wide and 10 feet deep. Spaced at 5-mi intervals along the wall were 3- to 5-acre forts (such as those at Housesteads and Chesters), which could hold 500 to 1,000 soldiers. Every mile was marked by a thick-walled mile-castle (a smaller fort that housed about 30 soldiers), and between each milecastle were two smaller turrets, each lodging four men who kept watch from the tower's upper chamber.

During the Jacobite Rebellion of 1745, the English dismantled much of the Roman wall and used its stone to pave the Military Road, now B6318. The most substantial stretches of the remaining wall are between Housesteads and Birdoswald (west of Greenhead). Running through the southern edge of Northumberland National Park and along the sheer escarpment of Whin Sill, this section is also an area of dramatic natural beauty. The ancient ruins, rugged cliffs, dramatic vistas, and spreading pastures make it a good area for hiking.

Today, excavating, interpreting, repairing, displaying, and generally managing the Roman remains is a Northumbrian growth industry. At the forts, notably at Chesters, Housesteads (the best-preserved fort), Vindolanda, and at the Roman Army Museum near Greenhead, you get a good introduction to the life led by Roman soldiers on the frontier. In summer most sites sponsor talks, Roman drama, and festivals; local tourist offices, or the sites themselves, have details. It's possible to walk along sections of the wall, but this can be hard going, and it's not always possible to get off and step back onto the road (exits and entrances are few and far between). A special Hadrian's Wall Bus runs daily between Hexham and Carlisle, stopping at major sites from late May to mid-September. There is also one bus that runs daily from Wallsend to Bowness. For a memorable view, look east toward the fort of Housesteads from Cuddy's Crag, where the wall snakes up and down across the wild countryside.

Sports & the Outdoors

You can walk the entire length of the wall along the Hadrian's Wall Path, a new national trail. If you don't have time for it all, you can just walk a section or take one of the many less challenging circular routes, detailed in leaflets at tourist information offices along the way. One of the best sections is the 12-mi western stretch between Sewingshields (east of Housesteads) and Greenhead. This part is rugged country, unsuited to the inexperienced hiker. Riding schools also offer hour-long rides to full-day treks on horseback. For a full list, contact the Hexham tourist information office; advance booking in summer is essential.

Hexham

⑮ *22 mi west of Newcastle, 31 mi northwest of Durham.*

The historic market town of Hexham makes the best base for visiting Hadrian's Wall. Just a few miles from the most significant remains, it retains enough of interest in its medieval streets to warrant a stop in its own right. First settled in the 7th century, around a Benedictine monastery, Hexham later became a byword for monastic learning, famous for its book painting, sculpture, and liturgical singing.

★ Ancient **Hexham Abbey,** a place of Christian worship for more than 1,300 years, forms one side of the town's main square. Inside, you can climb the 35 worn stone "night stairs," which once led from the main part of the abbey to the canon's dormitory, to overlook the whole ensemble. Most of the current building dates from the 12th century, and much of the stone was taken from the Roman fort at Corbridge, a few miles northeast. ⊠ *Beaumont St.* ☎ *01434/602031* ⊕ *www.hexhamabbey.org.uk*

⬚ *Requested donation £2* ☉ *May–Sept., daily 9–7; Oct.–Apr., daily 9–5. No tours during services.*

Hexham's central **Market Place** has been the site since 1239 of a weekly market, held each Tuesday. Crowded stalls are set out under the long slate roof of the Shambles; other stalls take their chances with the weather, protected only by their bright awnings.

Dating from 1330, Hexham's original jail, the Manor Office across Market Place from the abbey, houses the **Border History Museum.** Photographs, models, a Border house interior, armor, and weapons tell the story of the "Middle March," the medieval administrative area governed by a warden and centered on Hexham. ⊠ *The Old Gaol, Hallgate* ☎ *01434/ 652351* ⬚ *£2* ☉ *Apr.–Oct., daily 10–4:30; Nov., Feb., and Mar., Mon., Tues., and Sat. 10–4:30.*

Where to Stay & Eat

£££–£££££ ✕▢ **Langley Castle Hotel.** Rescued by a professor from the United States in the mid-1980s, this 14th-century castle with turrets and battlements is thoroughly lavish. Bedrooms within the castle are resplendent with tapestries and hangings, and have deep window seats set in the 6-foot-thick walls; those in the Castle View annex are more modest. The baronial restaurant (fixed-price menu) showcases such dishes as sea bass in smoked salmon and duckling with scallops and wild mushrooms. The hotel is 6 mi west of Hexham. ⊠ *Langley-on-Tyne, NE47 5LU* ☎ *01434/ 688888* ▤ *01434/684019* ⊕ *www.langleycastle.com* ⬚ *18 rooms* ⚶ *Restaurant, in-room data ports, sauna, 2 bars, meeting rooms; no a/ c* ▤ *AE, DC, MC, V* ⦿| *CP.*

£££ ✕▢ **Lord Crewe Arms Hotel.** A historic hotel that once provided guest accommodations for Blanchland Abbey, this unusual place in a tiny stone village has lots of medieval and Gothic corners, including a priest's hideout and a vault-roofed crypt with its own bar. The bedrooms are solidly furnished with antique wood pieces; some have oak-beam ceilings. The elegant, sequestered restaurant produces a fixed-price menu with such dishes as wood pigeon and wild mushroom stroganoff. ⊠ *Blanchland, DH8 9SP, off B6306, about 8 mi south of Hexham* ☎ *01434/675251* ▤ *01434/675337* ⊕ *www.lordcrewehotel.com* ⬚ *19 rooms* ⚶ *Restaurant, bar, meeting rooms; no a/c* ▤ *AE, DC, MC, V* ⦿| *BP.*

£ ▢ **Dene House.** This peaceful, stone-built farmhouse on 9 acres of farmland has beamed ceilings and cozy rooms with pine and antique pieces and colorful bed quilts. Breakfasts, taken in the homey kitchen, are cooked on the Aga range save room for the homemade bread and preserves. The house is 4 mi south of Hexham; follow signs for Dye House. ⊠ *B6303, Juniper, Hexham, NE46 1SJ* ☎ *01434/673413* ⊕ *www.denehouse-hexham.co.uk* ⬚ *3 rooms* ⚶ *Some pets allowed; no room phones, no a/c* ▤ *AE, MC, V* ⦿| *BP.*

Nightlife & the Arts

One of the Northeast's most adventurous arts venues, the **Queen's Hall Arts Centre** (⊠ Beaumont St. ☎ 01434/652477) presents drama, dance, and exhibitions by local artists. It sponsors events such as the annual jazz festival (June), which sees dozens of concerts in one weekend.

Greenhead

⑯ *18 mi west of Hexham, 49 mi northwest of Durham.*

Tiny Greenhead has an informative wall site. The **Roman Army Museum,** at the garrison fort of Carvoran, near the village, makes an excellent introduction to Hadrian's Wall. Full-size models and excavations bring to life this remote outpost of the empire; authentic Roman graffiti adorn the walls of an excavated barracks. The gift store stocks, among other unusual items, Roman rulers (1 feet = 11.6 inches) and Roman cookbooks. Opposite the museum, at Walltown Crags on the Pennine Way (a long-distance hiking route), are 400 yards of the best-preserved section of the wall. For a bird's-eye view of the wall, take the 15-minute Eagle's Eye simulated helicopter ride. ⊠ *Off B6318, 1 mi northeast of Greenhead* ☎ *016977/47485* ⊕ *www.vindolanda.com* ☎ *£3.30, joint admission ticket with Vindolanda £5.60* ☉ *May–Aug., daily 10–6; Apr. and Sept., daily 10–5:30; Mar. and Oct., daily 10–5; 2nd half Feb. and 1st half Nov., daily 10–4.*

Where to Stay & Eat

£–££ ✕ **Milecastle Inn.** The snug traditional bars and restaurant of this remote
Fodor'sChoice   and peaceful 17th-century pub make an excellent place to dine. Fine local
★   meat goes into its famous pies; take your pick from rabbit, venison, wild boar, and duckling. The inn is on the north side of Haltwhistle on B6318. ⊠ *North Rd., Haltwhistle* ☎ *01434/320682* ⊟ *AE, MC, V.*

££ ⌂ **Holmhead Guest House.** This former farmhouse in open countryside is not only built *on* Hadrian's Wall but also *of* it. Stone arches, exposed beams, and antique furnishings add to the feeling of history. In addition to "the longest breakfast menu in the world," there's a set dinner (for guests only) with homegrown organic vegetables at the farmhouse table. On call is Pauline Staff, a qualified guide who can give talks and slide shows on Hadrian's Wall and the area. ⊠ *Off A69 about 18 mi west of Hexham, CA6 7HY* ☎☎ *016977/474027* ⊕ *www. bedandbreakfastonhadrianswall.co.uk* ⇆ *4 rooms* ⌂ *Dining room; no a/c, no smoking* ⊟ *MC, V* ⧖ *BP.*

Vindolanda

⓱ *8 mi east of Greenhead, 41 mi northwest of Durham.*

The great garrison fort of Vindolanda holds the remains of eight successive Roman forts and civilian settlements, which have provided much information about daily life in a military compound. Most of the visible remains date from the 2nd and 3rd centuries AD, and excavations are always under way. On view are a full-size reproduction of a section of the wall and a reconstructed temple, house, and shop. The museum displays many rare artifacts, including leather items, jewelry, glass, and writing tablets. ⊠ *Near Bardon Mill* ☎ *01434/344277* ⊕ *www. vindolanda.com* ☎ *£4.10, joint ticket with Roman Army Museum £6* ☉ *Feb., daily 10–4; May and June, daily 10–6; July and Aug., daily 10–6:30; Apr. and Sept., daily 10–5:30; Mar. and Oct., daily 10–5; Nov.–mid-Dec., weekdays 10–4; last admission 30 mins before closing; call to confirm times in winter.*

In Northumberland National Park, **Once Brewed National Park Visitor Centre,** ½ mi north of Vindolanda, provides informative displays about the central section of Hadrian's Wall and can advise about local walks. It is also a national tourist information center. ⊠ *B6318* ☎ *01434/344396* ⊕ *www.nnpa.org.uk* ☎ *Free* ☉ *Mid-Mar.–May, Sept. and Oct., daily 9:30–5; June–Aug., daily 9–5:30; Nov.–mid-Mar., weekends 10–3.*

Housesteads Roman Fort

★ **⓲** *3 mi east of Vindolanda, 38 mi northwest of Durham.*

If you have time to visit only one Hadrian's Wall site, Housesteads Roman Fort, Britain's most complete example of a Roman fort, is your best bet. It includes an interpretive center, views of long sections of the wall, the excavated 5-acre fort itself, and a museum. The steep 10-minute walk up from the parking lot by B6318 to the site rewards the effort, especially for the sight of the wall disappearing over hills and crags into the distance. The excavations reveal granaries, gateways, barracks, and the commandant's house. ⊠ *B6318, 3 mi northeast of Bardon Mill* ☎ *01434/ 344363* ⊕ *www.english-heritage.org.uk* ⊒ *£3.10* ☉ *Apr.–Sept., daily 10–6; Oct., daily 10–5; Nov.–Mar., daily 10–4.*

Chesters Roman Fort

19 *4 mi north of Hexham, 35 mi northwest of Durham.*

This cavalry fort in a wooded valley on the banks of the North Tyne River was known as Cilurnum in Roman times, when it protected the point where Hadrian's Wall crossed the river. You approach the fort directly from the parking lot, and, although the site cannot compete with Housesteads in setting, the museum here holds a fascinating collection of Roman artifacts, including statues of river and water gods, altars, milestones, iron tools, weapons, and handcuffs. The military bathhouse is the best-preserved example in Britain. ⊠ *B6318, ½ mi southwest of Chollerford* ☎ *01434/681379* ⊕ *www.english-heritage. org.uk* ⊒ *£3.10* ☉ *Apr.–Sept., daily 10–6; Oct, daily 10–5; Nov.–Mar., daily 10–4.*

Corbridge

20 *8 mi southeast of Chesters Roman Fort, 19 mi west of Newcastle, 29 mi northwest of Durham.*

A small town of honey-color stone houses and riverside walks, Corbridge is a prosperous-looking place with an abundance of welcoming pubs and attractive shops. In the churchyard of St. Andrew's Church by Market Place is the **Vicar's Pele,** built with stones taken from the Roman fort at Corbridge. This nearly 700-year-old fortified tower served as a refuge from Scottish raiders.

The ruins of the **Corbridge Roman Site,** occupied longer than any other fort on Hadrian's Wall, actually predate the wall by 40 years. The fort was strategically positioned at the junction of the east–west and north–south Roman routes—Stanegate ran west to Carlisle, Dere Street led north to Scotland and south to London. You can visit a museum rich in artifacts and rent a headset and tape to explore the remains of two giant granaries, as well as temples, houses, and garrison buildings. ⊠ *On a signposted back road ½ mi northwest of Corbridge* ☎ *01434/ 632349* ⊕ *www.english-heritage.org.uk* ⊒ *£3.10* ☉ *Apr.–Sept., daily 10–6; Oct., daily 10–5; Nov.–Mar., Wed.–Sun. 10–4.*

Where to Stay

££ 🏠 **Town Barns.** The stone-built former home of the novelist Catherine Cookson (1906–88) has three spacious rooms, approached from a double staircase and galleried landing and furnished with yew and mahogany pieces. Get set up for the day with a packed lunch and come back to a cozy fire in the evening. ⊠ *Off Trinity Terr., NE45 5HP* ☎ *01434/633345* ⇆ *3 rooms* ♦ *Some pets welcome; no a/c, no smoking* ⊟ *No credit cards* ☉ *Closed Nov.–Mar.* ⦿ *BP.*

Kielder Water

21 *24 mi northwest of Corbridge, 53 mi northwest of Durham.*

In the rugged hills on the western edge of Northumberland National Park, about 3 mi from the Scottish border, lies Kielder Water, northern Europe's largest man-made lake, surrounded by 153,000 acres of planted forest. It's a beautiful spot, crisscrossed by hiking paths, a 10-mi riding trail, and mountain-bike trails, and with a host of water-sports possibilities at **Leaplish Waterside Park**. Fishing is popular, and the upper part of the reservoir, designated a conservation area, attracts many bird-watchers. You can take a boat across to the stunning contemporary Belvedere shelter, constructed in mirrored stainless steel and warm yellow glass.

The **Tower Knowe Visitor Centre,** at the southeast corner of Kielder Water, is a springboard from which to explore not only the lake area but also the vast **Kielder Forest.** Exhibits and films illustrate the region's wildlife and natural history, and guided forest walks are offered in summer. A **cruise service** (☎ 01434/240398) operates from the center mid-April–October; the one-hour boat trip costs £5. ⊠ *Kielder Water* ☎ *01434/ 250312* ⊕ *www.kielder.org* ☉ *Mar.–May and Oct., daily 10–4; June–Sept., daily 10–5.*

Now a visitor center with exhibitions and a tearoom, 18th-century **Kielder Castle** was once a shooting lodge belonging to the duke of Northumberland. The center is at the northwest corner of Kielder Water, at the start of a 12-mi toll road that heads deep into the Kielder Forest to the north and meets A68 south of Carter Bar close to the Scottish border. Signposted footpaths provide good forest walks and there's an excellent sculpture trail. ⊠ *Kielder Water* ☎ *01434/250209* ⊕ *www. kielder.org* ☉ *Apr.–Oct., daily 10–5; Nov. and Dec., weekends 11–4.*

Sports & the Outdoors

You can rent mountain bikes at **Kielder Castle** (☎ 01434/250392). Water sports, including waterskiing, and mountain biking are the focus at **Leaplish Waterside Park** (☎ 01434/250312), open all year; you can also use the indoor pool and sauna.

Wallington

② *18 mi east of Kielder Water, 15 mi northeast of Hexham, 19 mi northwest of Newcastle.*

A striking 17th-century mansion with Victorian decoration, Wallington stands in the midst of a sparsely populated agricultural region at the village of Cambo. Besides the house, with its rococo plasterwork, Pre-Raphaelite murals, Asian porcelain, and dollhouse collection, the walled, terraced garden is a major attraction. In summer, productions of Shakespeare and concerts are held on the grounds, which include 100 acres of woodlands. The house will be closed until spring 2004 for repairs, but the garden, grounds, and other facilities will remain open. ⊠ *B6342, Cambo* ☎ *01670/774283* ⊕ *www.nationaltrust.org.uk* ☒ *Grounds and garden £4.30* ☉ *Grounds Apr.–Oct., daily 10–6; Nov.–Mar., daily 10–4. Garden Apr.–Sept., daily 10–7. For the house, call ahead.*

Rothbury

㉓ *10 mi north of Wallington (Cambo), 25 mi northeast of Hexham, 9 mi southwest of Alnwick.*

The small market town of Rothbury, in the heart of some stunning countryside, developed as a Victorian resort, attracting the gentry who roamed its hills and glades. Buildings from the era survive in the handsome center, although as with all such towns, the sheer weight of modern traffic has blunted its appeal.

The helpful staff at the **Northumberland National Park Visitor Centre** can discuss walking routes through the local Simonside Hills. It's also a national tourist information center and can advise you about accommodations and regional attractions. ✉ *Church St.* ☎ *01669/620887* ⊕ *www.nnpa.org.uk* ⊙ *Mid-Mar.–May, Sept., and Oct., daily 10–5; June–Aug., daily 10–6; Nov.–mid-Mar., weekends 10–3.*

★ The extraordinary Victorian mansion of **Cragside** was built between 1864 and 1895 by the first Lord Armstrong, an early electrical engineer. Designed by Richard Norman Shaw, a well-regarded late-Victorian architect, it epitomizes the heyday of the Victorian country house. The Tudor-style structure in a forested mountainside was the first house to be lit by hydroelectricity. Besides ingeniously devised electric lights, there are Pre-Raphaelite paintings and an elaborate mock-Renaissance marble chimneypiece. The grounds also hold an energy center with restored mid-Victorian machinery. In June rhododendrons bloom in the 660-acre park surrounding the mansion. ✉ *Off A697 and B6341, 1 mi north of Rothbury* ☎ *01669/620333* ⊕ *www.nationaltrust.org.uk* 🎫 *House and grounds £7.20, grounds only £4.80* ⊙ *House Apr.–Sept., Tues.–Sun. 1–5:30; Oct., Tues.–Sun. 1–4:30; last admission 1 hr before closing. Grounds Apr.–Oct., Tues.–Sun. 10:30–7; Nov. and Dec., Wed.–Sun. 11–4.*

Where to Stay & Eat

£££ ✕🏨 **Embleton Hall.** The 5 acres of beautiful grounds are reason enough to stay in this stone country mansion, parts of which date to 1730. Lovely antiques and paintings decorate the individually furnished guest rooms. The chintz draperies and cut-glass chandeliers in the restaurant (fixed-price menu only) make perfect accompaniments to traditional English dishes such as noisettes of lamb with mint and rosemary sauce. There are less expensive options in the bar. ✉ *A697, 5 mi east of Rothbury, Longframlington, NE65 8DT* ☎ *01665/570249* 🖷 *01665/570056* ⊕ *www.embletonhall.com* 🛏 *14 rooms* ⚭ *Restaurant, bar, meeting rooms, some pets allowed; no a/c* 🗏 *AE, DC, MC, V* ⚏ *BP.*

£–££ 🏨 **Silverton Lodge.** The Hewisons rescued the derelict village school, dated 1902, and have transformed it into a peaceful, hospitable B&B with a fireplace in the guest lounge. Coordinating fabrics furnish the attractive bedrooms, and packed lunches and dinners are available. ✉ *Silverton La., NE65 7RJ* ☎ *01669/620144* 🖷 *01669/621920* ⊕ *www. silvertonlodge.co.uk* 🛏 *4 rooms* ⚭ *Dining room, bicycles; no a/c, no smoking* 🗏 *No credit cards* ⚏ *BP.*

THE FAR NORTHEAST COAST

Before England gives way to Scotland, extraordinary medieval fortresses and monasteries line the final 40 mi of the Northeast coast, considered by many the best stretch anywhere on the North Sea. Northumbria was an enclave where the flame of learning was kept alive during Europe's "Dark Ages," most notably at Lindisfarne, the "Holy Island of saints and scholars." Castles abound, including the spectacularly sited Bamburgh and the desolate Dunstanburgh. The region also has some magnificent broad beaches. Only on rare summer days is swimming advisable, but the walking is tremendous. The 3-mi walk from Seahouses to Bamburgh gives splendid views over to the Farne Islands, and the 2-mi hike from Craster to Dunstanburgh Castle is unforgettable.

Alnwick

❷ *30 mi north of Newcastle, 46 mi north of Durham.*

Alnwick (pronounced *ann*-ick) is the best base from which to explore the dramatic coast and countryside of northern Northumberland. Its vast castle dominates the town, once a county seat, but there's more to see. A weekly open-air market (every Saturday) has been held in Alnwick's cobbled **Market Place** for more than 800 years. Note the market cross, built on the base of an older cross; the town crier once made his proclamations from here. Starting on the last Sunday in June, this site is host to the weeklong **Alnwick Fair,** a festival noteworthy for the enthusiastic participation of locals in medieval costume.

★ The grandly scaled **Alnwick Castle,** on the edge of the town center, is still the home of the dukes of Northumberland, whose family, the regal Percys, dominated the Northeast for centuries. Known as "the Windsor of the North," it has been remodeled several times since the first occupant, Henry de Percy, adapted the original Norman keep. Nowadays the castle is in favor as a set for movies such as *Robin Hood: Prince of Thieves* and the first two Harry Potter movies (in the first, the castle grounds appear as the exterior of Hogwarts School in scenes such as the Quidditch match). In contrast with the cold formidable exterior, the interior has all the opulence of the palatial home it still is. You see only six of the more than 150 rooms, but among the treasures on show are a galleried library, Meissen dinner services, ebony cabinets mounted on gilded wood, tables inlaid with intricate patterns, niches with larger-than-life-size marble statues, and Venetian-mosaic floors. The castle's gardens, undergoing a multiyear redevelopment, include a modern, 260-foot-long stepped water cascade with elaborate, computer-controlled fountain displays, as well as rose and ornamental gardens. ⊠ *Above the junction of Narrowgate and Bailiffgate* ☎ *01665/510777* ⊕ *www. alnwickcastle.com* ✍ *Castle and grounds £10, castle only £7.50, grounds only £4* ⊙ *Apr.–Oct., daily 11–5; last admission 4:15.*

Where to Stay & Eat

£££ ✕⊡ **White Swan Hotel.** The surprise feature of this comfortable modernized 18th-century coaching inn near the town square is that one lounge, the Olympic Suite, has been reconstructed from the paneling, stained glass, and mirrors of the *Olympic,* sister ship of the ill-fated *Titanic.* It's used as a function room, but guests can take a look. You can choose from the hearty dishes on the fixed-price menu in the Bondgate restaurant (dinner and Sunday lunch only); cream of barley soup and steamed plum pudding help fill you up. ⊠ *Bondgate Within, NE66 1TD* ☎ *01665/ 602109* 🖷 *01665/510400* ✍ *58 rooms* ⚫ *Restaurant, bar, meeting rooms, some pets allowed; no a/c* ▭ *AE, MC, V* ❙⊙❙ *BP.*

Shopping

The **House of Hardy** (☎ 01665/602771), just outside Alnwick (from downtown, take A1 south to just beyond the traffic circle on the left, clearly marked), is one of Britain's finest stores for country sports. It has a worldwide reputation for handcrafted fishing tackle.

Alnmouth

❷ *4 mi east of Alnwick.*

Beautifully sited on a steep spur of land between the estuary of the River Aln and the sea, Alnmouth has been a popular holiday spot since Victorian times. Beyond the cluster of seaside villas, the main street is an inviting mixture of solid 19th-century houses, pubs, and tearooms, interspersed with narrow alleyways.

Where to Stay

££ ⊡ **The Grange.** An elegant four-story 18th-century house in a walled garden overlooking the Aln estuary makes for a peaceful bed-and-breakfast stopover. Stylish modern furniture blends with antiques, and the subtly colored bedrooms are light and airy. ☒ *Northumberland St., NE66 2RJ* ☎ *01665/830401* ✑ *enquiries@thegrange-alnmouth.com* ⤺ *5 rooms, 2 with bath* ♿ *No a/c, no smoking* ▤ *MC, V* ◯ *BP.*

Craster

㉖ *7 mi north of Alnmouth.*

The tiny fishing village of Craster is known for its footpath to Dunstanburgh Castle—and for that great English breakfast delicacy, kippers: herring salted and smoked over smoldering oak shavings. You can visit the tar-blackened smokehouses and see the fish hanging in ranks, then cross the road to the pub to taste for yourself.

Where to Eat

★ **£** ✕ **Jolly Fisherman.** You can feast in this traditional pub on its famous fresh crab sandwiches or kipper paté. The splendid picture window provides views of crashing waves; on sunny days, the garden beckons. ☒ *Haven Hill* ☎ *01665/576461* ▤ *MC, V.*

Shopping

L. Robson & Sons (☒ Haven Hill ☎ 01665/576223) has been smoking fish for four generations. The smokehouse is open Monday–Saturday all year for kippers, smoked cod, and salmon.

Dunstanburgh Castle

㉗ *1 mi north of Craster, 8 mi north of Alnmouth.*

Perched romantically on a cliff 100 feet above the shore, the ruins of Dunstanburgh Castle can be reached along a windy, mile-long coastal footpath from Craster. Built in 1316 by the earl of Lancaster as a defense against the Scots, and later enlarged by John of Gaunt (the powerful duke of Lancaster who virtually ruled England in the late 14th century), the castle is known to many from the popular paintings by 19th-century artist J. M. W. Turner. Several handsome sandy bays indent the coastline immediately to the north. ☎ *01665/576231* ⊕ *www.english-heritage.org.uk* ☒ *£2.20* ◷ *Apr.–Sept., daily 10–6; Oct., daily 10–5; Nov.–Mar., Wed.–Sun. 10–4.*

Farne Islands

★ **㉘** *7 mi north of Craster, 13 mi northeast of Alnwick.*

Regular boat trips from the village of Seahouses provide access to two of the bleak, wind-tossed Farne Islands (owned by the National Trust), with their impressive colonies of seabirds, including puffins, kittiwakes, terns, shags, and guillemots. The islands also attract thriving gray-seal colonies. Inner Farne, where St. Cuthbert, the great abbot of Lindisfarne, died in AD 687, has a tiny chapel dedicated to his memory. All boat service leaves from Seahouses harbor. A 2½-hour cruise past the islands gives you a good view; during a six-hour trip (May–July) you'll make landfall. Landing fees depend on the season, because more wildlife is visible in certain months. ☎ *01665/721099 National Trust information center; 01665/720308 boat trips; 01665/720884 Seahouses Tourist Information Centre (summer only)* ⊕ *www.nationaltrust.org.uk* ☒ *Boat trips £10–£20, landing fees £3.40–£4.40 payable to the wardens* ◷ *Boat trips daily, weather permitting; call ahead in winter.*

Bamburgh

㉙ *14 mi north of Alnwick.*

Tiny Bamburgh has a splendid castle, and several beaches are a few minutes' walk away. Especially stunning when floodlighted at night, **Bamburgh Castle** dominates the coastal view for miles, set atop a great crag to the north of Seahouses and overlooking a magnificent sweep of sand backed by high dunes. Once regarded as the legendary Joyous Garde of Sir Lancelot du Lac, one of King Arthur's fabled knights, it's one of the most dramatically sited castles in Britain. The ramparts have sweeping views of Lindisfarne (Holy Island), the Farne Islands, the stormy coastline, and the Cheviot Hills inland. Much of the castle, the home of the Armstrong family since 1894, was restored during the 18th and 19th centuries, including the Victorian Great Hall, although the great Norman keep (central tower) remains intact. Exhibits include collections of armor, porcelain, jade, furniture, and paintings. ⊠ *Bamburgh, 3 mi north of Seahouses* ☎ *01668/214515* ⊕ *www.bamburghcastle.com* ⊠ *£5* ☉ *Mid-Mar.–Oct., daily 11–5; last admission 4:30.*

The **Grace Darling Museum** commemorates a local heroine as well as the Royal National Lifeboat Institute, an organization of volunteers who keep watch at the rescue stations on Britain's coasts. Grace Darling became a folk heroine in 1838, when she and her father saved the lives of nine shipwrecked sailors from the SS *Forfarshire.* ⊠ *Radcliffe Rd., opposite church near village center* ☎ *01668/214465* ⊠ *Free* ☉ *Apr.–mid-Oct., Mon.–Sat. 10–5, Sun. 10–noon and 2–5.*

Where to Stay & Eat

££££–£££££ ✕⊡ **Waren House Hotel.** Six acres of woodland surround this Georgian hotel on a quiet bay between Bamburgh and Holy Island. Public areas are furnished comfortably in period style with an assortment of ornaments, and guest rooms have individual themes. The crisply elegant restaurant has romantic views of Holy Island when the leaves are not on the trees; five-course dinners might include sautéed pigeon breast in a gin and juniper sauce, and local game or salmon. Smoking is only permitted in the library. ⊠ *Waren Mill, Belford, NE70 7EE* ☎ *01668/214581* 🖷 *01668/214484* ⊕ *www.warenhousehotel.co.uk* ➫ *8 rooms, 2 suites* ⚴ *Restaurant, some pets allowed; no a/c* ⊟ *AE, DC, MC, V* ⦿⧵ *BP.*

£££ ✕⊡ **Lord Crewe Arms.** This is a cozy stone-walled inn with oak beams, in the heart of the village close to Bamburgh Castle. It's an ideal spot for lunch while you're touring the area. Pine furnishings decorate the fairly simple guest rooms, but the food, especially the seafood, is excellent. ⊠ *Front St., NE69 7BL* ☎ *01668/214243* 🖷 *01668/214273* ⊕ *www.lordcrewe.co.uk* ➫ *18 rooms* ⚴ *Restaurant, bar, some pets allowed; no a/c, no kids under 5* ⊟ *MC, V* ☉ *Closed Jan. and weekdays in Dec.* ⦿⧵ *BP.*

Lindisfarne (Holy Island)

★ ㉚ *6 mi east of A1, north of Bamburgh, 22 mi north of Alnwick, 8 mi southeast of Berwick-upon-Tweed.*

Cradle of northern England's Christianity and home of St. Cuthbert, Lindisfarne (or Holy Island) has a religious history that dates from AD 635, when St. Aidan established a monastery here. Under its greatest abbot, the sainted Cuthbert, Lindisfarne became one of the foremost centers of learning in Christendom. The island is reached from the mainland by a long drive along a causeway that floods at high tide, so you *must* check to find out when crossing is safe. The times, which change daily, are displayed at the causeway and printed in local newspapers. Traffic can be heavy; allow at least a half hour for your return trip.

In the year 875, Vikings destroyed the Lindisfarne community; only a few monks managed to escape, carrying with them Cuthbert's bones, which they reburied in Durham. The sandstone Norman ruins of **Lindisfarne Priory**, reestablished in the 11th century by monks from Durham, remain both impressive and beautiful. A museum here displays Anglo-Saxon carvings. ⊠ *Lindisfarne* ☎ *01289/389200* ⊕ *www.english-heritage.org.uk* ⊡ *£3* ⊘ *Apr.–Sept., daily 10–6; Oct., daily 10–5; Nov.–Mar., daily 10–4.*

Reached by a walk around the coast of the island, **Lindisfarne Castle** appears to grow out of the rocky pinnacle on which it was built 400 years ago, looking for all the world like a fairy-tale illustration. In 1903 architect Sir Edwin Lutyens converted the former Tudor fort into a private home that retains the original's ancient features. Across several fields from the castle is a walled garden designed by Gertrude Jekyll. ⊠ *Lindisfarne* ☎ *01289/389244* ⊕ *www.nationaltrust.org.uk* ⊡ *£4.20* ⊘ *Apr.–Oct., Sat.–Thurs., noon–3 or longer; call ahead for exact hrs.*

Berwick-upon-Tweed

③ *10 mi northwest of Lindisfarne, 30 mi northwest of Alnwick, 77 mi north of Durham.*

Although Berwick-upon-Tweed now lies just inside the border of England, historians estimate that it has changed hands between the Scots and the English 14 times. The market on Wednesday and Saturday draws plenty of customers from both sides of the border. The town's thick 16th-century walls, among the best-preserved in Europe, completely encircle the old town; a path follows the ramparts, and the views are rewarding. The parish church, Holy Trinity, a mixture of Gothic and Renaissance styles, was built during Cromwell's Puritan Commonwealth with stone from a castle.

In the **Barracks**, built between 1717 and 1721, three accommodation wings surround a square, with the decorated gatehouse forming the fourth side. An exhibition called "By Beat of Drum" depicts the life of the common soldier from the 1660s to the 1880s. Other displays highlight the history of the local regiment, the King's Own Scottish Borderers, and that of the town itself. ⊠ *The Parade, off Church St. in town center* ☎ *01289/ 304493* ⊕ *www.english-heritage.org.uk* ⊡ *£3* ⊘ *Apr.–Sept., daily 10–6; Oct., daily 10–5; Nov.–Mar., Wed.–Sun. 10–4.*

Where to Stay & Eat

£–££ ✕ **Town House.** Delicious fresh quiches, pastries, and other snacks are your reward for seeking out this tricky-to-find spot: cross Buttermarket under the Guildhall and go through the old jail. ⊠ *Marygate* ☎ *01289/307904* ▤ *MC, V* ⊘ *Closed Thurs. afternoon, Sun. No dinner.*

££–££££ ⬚ **Coach House.** Part of a cluster of attractive, well-converted farm buildings, this friendly country guest house 10 mi southwest of Berwick-upon-Tweed includes a 17th-century cottage. The spacious bedrooms, some of which have rare chestnut beams, are done in traditional or modern style. You can relax by the fire in the lounge or try the books and games in the library at night. The breakfast menu is unending. ⊠ *A 697, Crookham, Cornhill-on-Tweed, TD12 4TD* ☎ *01890/*

820293 ⊕ *www.coachhousecrookham.com* ➪ *9 rooms, 7 with bath* ⟐ *Dining room, bar, some pets allowed; no a/c* ▤ *MC, V* ⊘ *Closed Nov.–Mar.* ⟐| *BP.*

££ ⊡ **No. 1 Sallyport.** In the heart of town, this treat of a bed-and-breakfast stands a mere 20 yards from the Elizabethan walls. The pleasantly furnished guest rooms hold pine furniture, books, paintings, and the odd antique; one has a fireplace. A private kitchen with fresh coffee adds to the pampering. Breakfast is unbeatable, with choices from salmon fishcakes to kippers with eggs to a traditional full breakfast. Evening meals can be arranged. ⊠ *1 Sallyport, TD15 1EZ* ☎☎ *01289/308827* ⊕ *www.1sallyport-bedandbreakfast.com* ➪ *3 rooms* ⟐ *Dining room, some pets allowed; no a/c* ▤ *No credit cards* ⟐| *BP.*

THE NORTHEAST A TO Z

To research prices, get advice from other travelers, and book travel arrangements, visit www.fodors.com.

AIRPORTS

Newcastle Airport, 5 mi northwest of the city center, is well served for domestic destinations and major European cities. Metro trains connect the airport to the center of Newcastle, with service approximately every 8 minutes at peak times; cost is £1.60 one-way. The airport is about 15 minutes by car from the city center.

🖪 **Newcastle Airport** ⊠ Off A696 ☎ 0191/286-0966 ⊕ www.newcastleairport.com.

BUS TRAVEL

National Express serves the region from London's Victoria Coach Station. Average travel times are 4¾ hours to Durham, 5¼ hours to Newcastle, and 8¼ hours to Berwick-upon-Tweed. Connecting services to other parts of the region leave from Durham and Newcastle. For all bus inquiries call Traveline or National Express.

A special Hadrian's Wall Bus between Housesteads and Carlisle operates all year-round (Monday–Saturday), stopping at all the major sites. Local tourist offices have timetables; a Day Rover ticket costs £5.

CUTTING COSTS The Northeast Explorer Pass (£5.50, one day) allows unlimited travel on most local services and is available from the bus driver or local bus stations.

FARES & SCHEDULES For route and fare information in Northumberland, buy the "Northumberland Public Transport Guide" (£1.60) from any tourist office.
🖪 **National Express** ☎ 0870/580-8080 ⊕ www.nationalexpress.com. **Traveline** ☎ 0870/608-2608 ⊕ www.traveline.org.uk.

CAR RENTAL

🖪 **Local Agencies Avis** ⊠ 7 George St., Newcastle upon Tyne ☎ 0191/232-5283. **Hertz** ⊠ Newcastle Airport, off A696, Newcastle upon Tyne ☎ 0191/286-6748. **Jennings Ford** ⊠ A1(M), Carrville, Durham ☎ 0191/386-1155.

CAR TRAVEL

The most direct north–south route through the Northeast is A1, linking London and Edinburgh via Newcastle (274 mi from London; five–six hours) and Berwick-upon-Tweed (338 mi from London; two hours past Newcastle). A697, which branches west off A1 north of Morpeth, is a more attractive road, leading past the 16th-century battlefield of Flodden near the Scottish border. For Hexham and Hadrian's Wall, take the A69 west of Newcastle. For the coast, leave the A1 at Alnwick and follow the minor B1340 and B1339 for Craster, Seahouses, and Bamburgh. Holy Island is reached from a minor exit off the A1. A66 and A69 run east–west through the southern and middle parts of the region, respectively.

Many country roads provide quiet and scenic, if slower, alternatives to the main routes. Part of the Cheviot Hills, which run along the Northumbrian side of the Scottish border, is now a military firing range. Don't drive here when the warning flags are flying. The military, though, has restored the Roman road, Dere Street, which crosses this region. Try also B6318, a well-maintained road that runs alongside Hadrian's Wall on the south side.

DISCOUNTS & DEALS

The Powerpass card, valid from late April through December, admits two adults for the price of one into 120 attractions in Northumbria and Yorkshire. Purchase it at tourist information centers in these areas.

EMERGENCIES

🔃 **Ambulance, fire, police** ☎ 999. **Berwick Infirmary** ⊠ Well Close ☎ 01289/307484. **University Hospital of North Durham** ⊠ North Rd., Durham ☎ 0191/333-2333. **Newcastle General Hospital** ⊠ Westgate Rd. ☎ 0191/273-8811.

TOURS

North of England Tours specializes in general tours of northern England, and can help research family trees.

🔃 **North of England Tours** ☎ 01325/308094 🖷 01325/315940 ⊕ www.northofenglandtours.co.uk.

WALKING TOURS Durham County Council Environment Department organizes a year-round program of guided walks, both in the town and countryside, which cost £2 per person. Guided walks of the region's historic towns and cities are usually available through the local tourist offices.

🔃 **Durham County Council Environment Department** ☎ 0191/383-4144.

TRAIN TRAVEL

Great Northeastern Railways serves the region from London's King's Cross Station, en route to Scotland. Average travel times are 2¾ hours to Darlington, 3 hours to Durham, 3¼ hours to Newcastle, and 3¾ hours to Berwick-upon-Tweed. From Newcastle, there is local service north to Alnmouth (for Alnwick) and to Corbridge and Hexham on the east–west line to Carlisle.

FARES & SCHEDULES 🔃 **Great Northeastern Railways** ☎ 0845/722-5225 or 0845/748-4950 ⊕ www.gner.co.uk.

TRAVEL AGENCIES

🔃 **Local Agent Referrals Thomas Cook** ⊠ 24-25 Market Pl., Durham ☎ 0191/382-6600 ⊠ 6 Northumberland St., Newcastle ☎ 0191/219-8000.

VISITOR INFORMATION

Northumbria Regional Tourist Board is open weekdays 8:30–5. Other tourist information centers are normally open Monday–Saturday 9:30–5:30, but times vary by season. The telephone for the Haltwhistle Tourist Information Centre also serves as the Hadrian's Wall Information Line.

🔃 **Northumbria Regional Tourist Board** ⊠ Aykley Heads, DH1 5UX ☎ 0191/375-3000 ⊕ www.visitnorthumbria.com. **Alnwick** ⊠ The Shambles, NE66 1TN ☎ 01665/510665 ⊕ www.alnwick.gov.uk. **Barnard Castle** ⊠ Woodleigh Flatts Rd., DL12 8AA ☎ 01833/690909 ⊕ www.teesdale.gov.uk. **Berwick-upon-Tweed** ⊠ 106 Marygate, TD15 1BN ☎ 01289/330733 ⊕ www.berwickonline.org.uk. **Bishop Auckland** ⊠ Town Hall, Market Pl., DL14 7NP ☎ 01388/604922 ⊕ www.durham.gov.uk. **Darlington** ✉ 13 Horse-market, DL1 5PW ☎ 01325/388666 ⊕ www.visitdarlington.net. **Durham** ✉ Millennium Pl., DH1 1WA ☎ 0191/384-3720 ⊕ www.durhamcity.gov.uk. **Hadrian's Wall** ⊕ www.hadrians-wall.org. **Haltwhistle** ✉ Railway Station, NE49 9HN ☎ 01434/322002. **Hexham** ✉ Wentworth Car Park, NE46 1QE ☎ 01434/652220 ⊕ hadrianswallcountry.org. **Middlesbrough** ✉ 99–101 Albert Rd., Cleveland, TS1 2PA ☎ 01642/358086 ⊕ www.middlesbrough.gov.uk. **Newcastle upon Tyne** ✉ Central Arcade, 132 Grainger St., NE1 5AF ☎ 0191/277-8000 ✉ Main Concourse, Central Station ☎ 0191/277-8000 ⊕ www.newcastle.gov.uk.

SCOTLAND
EDINBURGH TO THE HIGHLANDS

FODOR'S CHOICE

Ambassador Hotel, *Glasgow*

Cawdor Castle, *near Nairn*

Floors Castle, *Kelso*

Kalpna, *restaurant in Edinburgh*

Rogano, *restaurant in Glasgow*

The Scotsman, *hotel in Edinburgh*

HIGHLY RECOMMENDED

SIGHTS Abbotsford House, *Galashiels*

City Chambers, *Glasgow*

Craigievar Castle, *south of Alford*

Edinburgh Castle, *Edinburgh*

Fort George, *Ardersier*

Georgian House, *Edinburgh*

Glasgow School of Art, *Glasgow*

Hunterian Art Gallery, *Glasgow*

Jedburgh Abbey, *Jedburgh*

Kildrummy Castle, *Kildrummy*

Marischal College, *Aberdeen*

Melrose Abbey, *Melrose*

Museum of Transport, *Glasgow*

National Gallery of Scotland, *Edinburgh*

Palace of Holyroodhouse, *Edinburgh*

People's Palace, *museum in Glasgow*

Provost Ross's House, *Aberdeen*

Royal Museum & Museum of Scotland, *Edinburgh*

Traquair House, *near Innerleithen*

Many other great hotels and restaurants enliven this area. For other favorites, look for the black stars as you read this chapter.

Updated by
James Gracie,
Beth Ingpen,
and Shona
Main

THE IDEA OF SCOTLAND IS WORLD-EMBRACING, although this small country is no bigger than the state of Maine and contains barely a tenth of the United Kingdom's population. Scotland has produced some of the world's stormiest history, some of its most romantic heroes and heroines, much of its most admired literature, and many of its most important inventions. Its local products, customs, music, and traditional dress—from tartans and bagpipes to tweeds—travel all over the globe. Scots throughout history, especially those who emigrated to the United States, Canada, Australia, and New Zealand, have been superb propagandists for the beloved land of their ancestors. Home-based national pride has been boosted with the reestablishment in 1999, after nearly 300 years, of Scotland's own Parliament, albeit one with restricted powers. Its responsibilities include health, education, transportation, housing, economic development, agriculture, and the environment; the national government in London is still responsible for foreign policy, defense, and economic policy.

There are really two Scotlands: the Lowlands (not low at all, but chains of hills along river valleys), where populous cities such as Edinburgh and Glasgow are found; and the Highlands, which contain the highest mountains in the British Isles, the wildest lochs (lakes), and most of the islands. It is often assumed that as you travel north you proceed from Lowlands to Highlands. In fact, it is more of an east–west divide. Most travelers start out with Scotland's greatest cities, Edinburgh and Glasgow. After a while, however, those heather-clad mountain slopes and shining lochs exert their pull, as do the fast-flowing streams where salmon leap, and the great castles of baronial pride standing among the hills. There are many contrasts of landscape, building stone, and city size, and you don't have to travel too far to enjoy all of these.

Edinburgh (pronounced edin-burra) is very much a capital city, with all the inbuilt dignity that implies. The Scottish Parliament is based here and, until its new building adjacent to the Palace of Holyroodhouse is complete in late 2004, has been using the Assembly Hall of the Church of Scotland. Many elements make Edinburgh appealing: its outstanding geography (like Rome, it is built on seven hills); the Old Town district, with all the evidence of its colorful history; and the New Town, with its elegant classical buildings conceived in the surge of artistic creativity during the second half of the 18th century.

Glasgow, Scotland's largest city, suffered gravely from the industrial decline of the 1960s and '70s, but efforts at commercial and cultural renewal have restored much of the style and grandeur it possessed in the 19th century, when it was at the height of its economic power. It is once again a vibrant metropolitan center with a thriving artistic life. Glasgow is a convenient touring center, too, with excellent transportation links to the rest of the country.

The Borders area comprises the great hills, moors, wooded river valleys, and farmland that stretch south from Lothian, the region crowned by Edinburgh, to England. Everything distinctive about Scotland, such as its paper currency, architecture, opening hours of pubs and stores, food and drink, and accent, starts right at the border; you won't find the Borders a diluted version of England. Northeast of Edinburgh, on the windswept east coast of Fife, stands the ancient town of St. Andrews, filled with historic sites and known the world over as the home of golf.

Beyond the central Lowlands, the pleasures and treasures of Aberdeen and northeast Scotland, Inverness, Loch Ness (with or without its "monster" Nessie), and the Highlands await. Aberdeen is Scotland's third-

15

To take in the diversity of sights and scenery in Scotland, you need at least a week. If you have less time, you may need to choose between city and countryside: the main attractions of Edinburgh or Glasgow could be seen in two or three days, or you could visit Aberdeen and Royal Deeside. With five or six days, you will be able to base yourself at two centers, perhaps Edinburgh and Aberdeen, or Glasgow and Inverness. Alternatively, you could take day trips to St. Andrews and to the Borders from Edinburgh. To cover all the areas in this chapter, allow at least 10 days.

Numbers in the text correspond to numbers in the margin and on the Borders, Edinburgh Environs, Edinburgh, Glasgow, Aberdeen & Royal Deeside, and Inverness & Environs maps.

If you have 2–3 days

This will be long enough to see most of the major sights in one of these areas: **Edinburgh** ①–㉗, **Glasgow** ㉙–㊺, **Aberdeen** (55), or **Inverness** (65) (and Loch Ness)—assuming that you select your own choices among the museums, galleries, or stately homes. You might want to break up your three-day visit to Edinburgh or Glasgow with an overnight excursion to the Borders, staying at **Melrose** ㊼ or **Peebles** (54) to enjoy a rural change of pace; or from Edinburgh, take a day trip to check out **St. Andrews** ㉘—there's actually much more to see in this town than the legendary Royal & Ancient Course.

If you have 5 days

At least two days and nights should be spent in **Edinburgh** ①–㉗ or **Glasgow** ㉙–㊺ to allow for visits to the most important sights. (If you want to see both cities, you will need the whole five or six days.) For your remaining nights, you have three options. The first is to head south for the Borders to explore Sir Walter Scott Country. Start out (and spend the night) in **Melrose** ㊼, visiting **Abbotsford House** ㊻, Scott's View, and **Dryburgh Abbey** ㊽ as well as sights farther afield, such as the abbey at **Jedburgh** (51). For those interested in grand Scottish residences, a visit to Floors Castle is a must. After enjoying the Scottish countryside on an afternoon walk, stay overnight in **Kelso** ㊿ before heading back to the capital.

Your second option, from Edinburgh or Glasgow, is to travel to **Aberdeen** (55), arriving in the evening. The next morning, follow in the footsteps of Queen Victoria and take a trip among the castles and glens of Royal Deeside. Set out for Crathes Castle and **Banchory** (56), with its largely unchanged Victorian High Street. After lunch, follow the river upstream to Aboyne, turning due north on B9094, then left onto B9119 and finally onto A93 to reach **Ballater** (57). The next morning, visit Her Majesty's **Balmoral Castle** (58) if royal residences are high on your list. (Note that Balmoral is open only four months, in the summer.) Treat yourself to a walk in nearby Glen Muick. Head for **Braemar** (59) for your next overnight stay. The next morning, set off for some serious castle-hopping—**Corgarff Castle** (60), **Kildrummy Castle** (61), **Craigievar Castle** (63), and **Castle Fraser** (64), stopping at **Alford** (62) to visit the Grampian Transport Museum. Return to Aberdeen, either stopping overnight, or continuing south to Edinburgh or Glasgow.

Your final option, after two days in Edinburgh or Glasgow, is to travel to the Highlands and ⊞ **Inverness** ⑥⑤ for two nights, aiming to arrive in the early evening. Spend the next morning exploring the city; in the afternoon pay a call on Nessie at Drumnadrochit on the banks of **Loch Ness** ⑥⑥. Return to Inverness for the night, then the next day follow signposts to **Culloden Moor** ⑥⑦, **Fort George** ⑥⑨, **Cawdor Castle** ⑦⓪, or **Brodie Castle** ⑦① for a finale in Macbeth Country. Continue on to spend the night at ⊞ **Nairn** ⑥⑧, before traveling south to Edinburgh or Glasgow.

If you have
10 days or longer

If, having visited Edinburgh, Glasgow, the Borders, and Aberdeen and Royal Deeside (allowing two days for each), you wish to continue exploring the Highlands, turn west, after visiting one or two houses in Castle Country, at **Castle Fraser** ⑥④. Take A944 from Castle Fraser west, enjoying the valley of the River Don as far as Corgarff on A939. The A939 then climbs into the brown hills to Tomintoul, highest village in the Highlands. From there, continue west, dropping into Speyside via the A95 and A938 roads, to pick up the main A9 at Carrbridge and arrive by evening at ⊞ **Inverness** ⑥⑤. Spend your remaining time as described under the five-day option of Inverness and the surrounding area.

---

largest city, and a gateway to the splendor of Royal Deeside and the Grampian Mountains, a wealth of castles, and an unspoiled and, in places, spectacular coastline. Inverness, to the northwest, is the capital of the Highlands, with Loch Ness right on its doorstep. A map of Scotland gives a hint of the grandeur to be found here: fingers of inland lochs, craggy mountains, rugged promontories, and deep inlets. But the map does not give an inkling of the brilliant purple and emerald moorland, the forests, and the astonishingly varied wildlife: red deer, golden eagles, ospreys, seals, and dolphins. Nor can a map convey the courtesy of the soft-spoken inhabitants, and the depth of ancestral memory and clan mythology. All these delights await anyone who ventures out of the cities.

A car is essential for exploring well beyond the cities, in Scotland's wildest districts. For the short-term visitor, a bus excursion from Edinburgh or Aberdeen may give the best value. Whatever the mode of transport, try to spend a couple of days in a small Highland bed-and-breakfast, grand estate hotel, or fishing inn. Only then will you discover the spell of the Highlands, inexplicable magic that brings people back year after year.

Exploring Scotland

Edinburgh and Glasgow, Scotland's two major cities, are in the Lowlands, just 70 km (44 mi) apart by fast highway. Greatly different in style, they both divide easily into two: Edinburgh's Old and New Towns, and Glasgow's medieval-and-merchant heart and culture-rich West End. The Borders lie south of Edinburgh, with their green hillsides, river valleys, ruined abbeys, and stately homes; they can be discovered in one long day or taken in two bites, returning to Edinburgh overnight. St. Andrews, along the east coast north of Edinburgh, beckons with golf and more. The Highlands take in many rugged landscapes, only a few of which are covered in this chapter: the remote islands of the western seaboard, the silvery granite city of Aberdeen on the east coast, the Grampian Mountains and "Castle Country" of Royal Deeside lying west of Aberdeen, the northern area toward Inverness and Loch Ness, and the Northern Highlands, with Scotland's tallest mountains and greatest lochs.

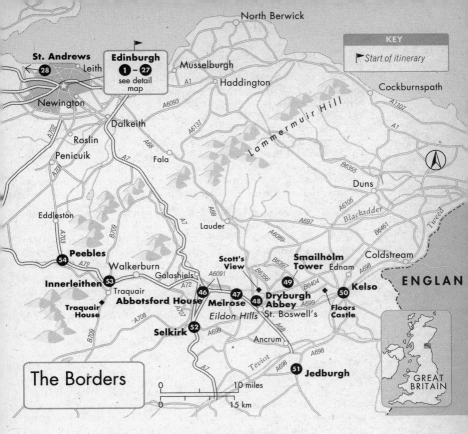

The Borders

GREAT BRITAIN

About the Restaurants & Hotels

Edinburgh and Glasgow have an increasing number of sophisticated restaurants of all kinds, as does Aberdeen; in the best, reservations are essential. Many good restaurants in the Borders and the Southwest are found within hotels rather than as independent establishments; this is also true in the Northeast.

Edinburgh, Glasgow, Aberdeen, and Inverness are splendidly served by accommodations from grand hotel suites done up in tartan fabrics to personal-touch bed-and-breakfasts. Some of the best lodgings are in lovely traditional Georgian or Victorian properties, but chic, ultramodern hotels are also finding favor. Because of the removal of much of its indigenous population by forced emigration in the 18th and 19th centuries, many parts of the Highlands became playgrounds for estate owners or Lowland industrialists, who built shooting lodges, grand mansions, and country estates. Many of these are now fine hotels or upscale B&B establishments. In rural areas, many farms also offer bed and breakfast.

WHAT IT COSTS In pounds					
	£££££	££££	£££	££	£
RESTAURANTS	over £22	£18–£22	£13–£17	£7–£12	under £7
HOTELS	over £160	£115–£160	£80–£115	£50–£80	under £50

Restaurant prices are for a main course at dinner. Hotel prices are for two people in a standard double room in high season, including VAT, with no meals or, if indicated, CP (with Continental breakfast), BP (Breakfast Plan, with full breakfast), or MAP (Modified American Plan, with breakfast and dinner).

Timing

August is the most exciting time to visit Edinburgh, largely because of the Edinburgh International Festival, when the city buzzes with cultural activity. However, this is also the busiest time, and anyone wishing to visit Edinburgh during August or the beginning of September should plan and book months in advance. Although the Borders are also busiest during summer festival time, its landscape can be fully appreciated in April and May as well. Scottish winters can be cold and wet, but the long summer evenings with sunsets as late as 10:30 from June through September are magical. The exuberant New Year celebrations known as Hogmanay draw crowds in Edinbugh and Glasgow.

Spring in the Highlands can be glorious, when snow still lies on the highest peaks. Those exuberant Highland Games, with caber tossing and hammer throwing are held during summer months: Braemar's games (September) are often held in the presence of members of the Royal Family. Autumn in Royal Deeside is very colorful. If you wish to drop in on Balmoral, the royal residence in Deeside, keep in mind that it's open April through July only. If the royals are in residence, even the grounds are closed to visitors, so call in advance. Most castles, whether in the Borders or Royal Deeside, are open April through October only; check in advance. Many accommodations and attractions in more isolated areas close during the winter months from November through March.

EDINBURGH

In a skyline of sheer drama, Edinburgh Castle watches over Scotland's capital city, and seems to frown down on Princes Street as if disapproving of its modern razzmatazz. Its ramparts still echo with gunfire when the one o'clock gun booms out each day. Nearly everywhere in the city, spectacular buildings with Doric, Ionic, and Corinthian columns add dignity to the landscape. To this largely Presbyterian gray backdrop, numerous trees and gardens provide color. The top of Calton Hill, to the east, is cluttered with neoclassical monuments, like an abandoned set for a Greek drama. Also conspicuous from Princes Street is Arthur's Seat, an 800-foot-high mountain of bright green and yellow furze rearing up behind the spires of the Old Town. This child-size mountain has steep slopes and little crags, like a miniature Highlands in the middle of the busy city. These theatrical elements give a unique identity to downtown, but head to George Street (which runs parallel to Princes Street) and look north, and you will see not an endless cityscape, but blue sea and a patchwork of fields. This is the county of Fife, beyond the wide inlet of the North Sea called the Firth of Forth; a reminder, like the misty mountains sometimes glimpsed on a clear day from Edinburgh's highest points, that the rest of Scotland lies within easy reach.

The Old Town

The brooding presence of the castle, the essence of Scotland's martial past, dominates Edinburgh. The castle is built on a crag of hard, black volcanic rock that was formed during the Ice Age when an eastbound glacier scoured around this resistant core, creating steep cliffs on three sides. On the fourth side, a "tail" of rock was left, forming a ramp from the top that gradually runs away eastward. This became the street known as the Royal Mile, the backbone of the Old Town, leading from the castle down to the Palace of Holyroodhouse. "The Mile" is made up of one thoroughfare that bears, in consecutive sequence, different names: the Esplanade, Castlehill, Lawnmarket, Parliament Square, High Street, and Canongate. Adjacent to Holyroodhouse is the site of Scot-

15

Castles

If you love castles, you've come to the right place. Scotland has just about every type of castle imaginable—from brooding medieval ruins such as Kildrummy, complete with gory tales, to magnificent Georgian and Victorian piles, full of antiques and paintings and surrounded by parkland. History-rich Edinburgh Castle is splendid and not to be missed. The northeast of Scotland inland from Aberdeen, in particular, has a huge range of castles to admire, helpfully strung together along the Castle Trail. Whether still in private ownership and full of family atmosphere, like Cawdor or Floors, or under the care of the National Trust for Scotland or of Historic Scotland, or just a jumble of stones atop a hill, Scotland's castles and fortified houses vividly demonstrate the country's splendid if unsettled past and its historically uneasy relationship with its southern neighbor.

Festivals & Events

The annual Edinburgh International Festival in August or early September fills Edinburgh with cultural events in every art form from traditional theater, big-name classical concerts, and jazz to experimental forms of dance and theater. Also held during this time is the Edinburgh Festival Fringe, the refreshingly irreverent, ever-growing, unruly child of the official festival. In the same time period, that stirring Scottish extravaganza—the Edinburgh Military Tattoo—is also performed. Tourist boards have information on the many other events that add breadth to Scotland's cultural year.

Caber tossing (the caber is a long pole) and other traditional events figure in the Highland Games, staged throughout the Highlands during summer. All tourist information centers have details. It is said that these games, a combination of music, dancing, and athletic prowess, grew out of the contests held by clan chiefs to find the strongest men for bodyguards, the fastest runners for messengers, and the best musicians and dancers to entertain guests and increase the chief's prestige.

Great Flavors

Culinary delights await: to sample genuine Scottish cuisine, look for the TASTE OF SCOTLAND sign in restaurant windows indicating the use of the best Scottish products, including marvelous salmon, beef, and venison. There is also spicy haggis, a sheep's stomach lining filled with the animal's organ meats and then simmered; it is usually served with "neeps and tatties" (mashed turnip and potato). Look for nouvelle variations on old Scottish dishes such as Cullen skink (a rich smoked-fish soup) and Loch Fyne herring. Scotland is traditionally the "land o' cakes," so be sure to enjoy the delicious buns, scones, and biscuits. In the Highlands, game and seafood are often presented with great flair; many restaurants deal directly with local boats, so freshness is guaranteed. Oatmeal, local cheeses, and even malt whisky (turning up in any course) amplify the Scottish dimension. And speaking of whisky, try a "wee dram" of a single malt, the pale, unblended spirit, when you visit the Northeast, one of Scotland's major distilling areas.

Golfing

Everyone wants to play just the big names in the British Open—St. Andrews, Turnberry, Royal Troon, and so on. This is a pity, because there are more golf courses in Scotland per capita than anywhere else in the world, and a good number are close to the major cities. The 400 or so courses include plenty of gems, from challenging coastal links to pinewood parkland delights. In the East Neuk of Fife, one of the prettiest Lowland areas of Scotland, the quiet town of St. Andrews beckons with its famous golf course, where the Royal & Ancient, the ruling body of the game worldwide, has its headquarters. Note that a round on a municipal course costs very little, whereas most clubs, apart from a few pretentious places modeled on the English fashion, demand only comparatively modest course fees.

Hiking & Walking

Walking is a superb pursuit for getting to know Scotland's varied landscape of low-lying glens and major mountains. Walks in the Edinburgh area range from city walkways along the banks of the Water of Leith, to the Pentland Hills, whose breezy but not overdemanding slopes are popular with locals on weekends. Because the Borders are essentially rural and hilly, there are a number of walking options. Peebles, within easy reach of Edinburgh, has excellent, level walking along the banks of the River Tweed, and a visit to Melrose, with its abbey, can be enhanced by a climb to the top of the Eildon Hills, for wonderful views. The Southern Upland Way, a 212-mi official long-distance footpath from Cockburnspath in the east to Portpatrick in the west, also passes through the Borders. Official footpaths in the Highlands include the West Highland Way, running 98 mi from the outskirts of Glasgow to Fort William, by Loch Lomond, Rannoch Moor, and Glen Coe, and the Great Glen Way, which runs for 70 mi from Fort William to Inverness, via the Caledonian Canal and Lochs Lochy, Oich, and Ness. Slightly gentler is the Northeast's Speyside Way, taking its name from one of Scotland's premier salmon rivers, which has excellent river valley and some moorland walking for 47 mi, from the Moray Firth coast up to the foothills of the Cairngorms. All four long-distance paths are covered in official guides available from bookshops and tourist information centers.

Shopping

Among the many traditional shopping favorites in Scotland are Shetland and Fair Isle woolens, tartan rugs and tweeds, Edinburgh crystal, and Caithness glass. Look for craft pottery and for unusual designs in Scottish jewelry, especially when they incorporate local stones. Glasgow has an excellent selection of designer clothing stores. Handmade chocolates, often with whisky or Drambuie fillings, and the traditional "petticoat tail" shortbread in tin boxes are popular. Try some of the boiled sweets in jars from particular localities, such as Jethart snails, Edinburgh rock, and similar delights.

---

land's Parliament building, under construction to a design by the late Barcelona architect Enric Miralles; until this is completed (scheduled for late 2004), the Parliament is sitting in the Assembly Hall of the Church of Scotland, overlooking the Mound (a street).

The narrow streets and passages (called "closes") leading off the Royal Mile and into the tenements or "lands" that lined the thoroughfare really *were* Edinburgh until the 18th century saw expansions to the south and north. Everybody lived here, the richer folk on the ground floors of houses, the merchant classes on the middle floors, and the poor on the top floors. Time and redevelopment have swept away some of these narrow closes and tenements, but enough survive for you to be able to imagine the original profile of Scotland's capital. Sir Walter Scott (1771–1832), Robert Louis Stevenson (1850–94), David Hume (1711–76), James Boswell (1740–95), the painter Allan Ramsay (1713–84), and many other well-known names are associated with the Old Town. But perhaps three are more famous than any others: John Knox (1513–72), Mary, Queen of Scots (1542–87), and Prince Charles Edward Stuart (1720–88).

a good
walk

A perfect place to begin a tour of the Old Town is **Edinburgh Castle** 1 ⌐. Having absorbed its attractions and taken in the city views, you can stroll down the grand promenade that is the **Royal Mile** 2. To the left of Castlehill, the Outlook Tower offers armchair views of the city with its **Camera Obscura** 3. Opposite, the **Scotch Whisky Heritage Centre** 4 offers a chance to discover Scotland's liquid gold. The six-story tenement known as **Gladstone's Land** 5, a survivor of 16th-century domestic life, is on the left as you walk down. Close by Gladstone's Land, down yet another close, is the **Writers' Museum** 6, in a 17th-century house with exhibits on Sir Walter Scott, Robert Louis Stevenson, and Robert Burns.

Farther down on the right, the Tolbooth Kirk (kirk means "church") has the tallest spire in the city, 240 feet, and is the home of the Edinburgh International Festival offices. From Lawnmarket you can start your discovery of the Old Town closes. For a shopping diversion, turn right down George IV Bridge, then right down Victoria Street, a 19th-century addition to the Old Town. Its shops sell antiques, old prints, clothing, and high-quality giftware. Down in the **Grassmarket** 7, which for centuries was an agricultural market, the shopping continues.

Walk from the Grassmarket back up Victoria Street to George IV Bridge, where you'll see the **National Library of Scotland** 8. Farther down George IV Bridge, on the right, is the **Kirk of the Greyfriars** 9. Before returning to Lawnmarket, turn left down Chambers Street, which runs from the bottom of George IV Bridge toward South Bridge. Here, the **Royal Museum** 10 displays a collection of worldwide scope. Next door, in the magnificent Benson and Forsyth–designed Museum of Scotland, you can explore Scotland's own history. Return to High Street and, near Parliament Square (site of the historic Parliament Building, not the current one), visit the **High Kirk of St. Giles** 11. Just east of St. Giles is another landmark, the **Mercat Cross** 12, which is still the site of royal proclamations. On the opposite side of High Street, below the City Chambers (the entrance is in Writers' Court), lies Mary King's Close, a street that was closed up and built over after the Plague hit the city in the 17th century.

At the North Bridge and South Bridge junction with High Street, you will find the Tron Kirk. The **Museum of Childhood** 13 is nearby on High Street. Across the street lies **John Knox House** 14, associated with Scotland's 16th-century religious reformer. Down a close nearby is the **Brass Rubbing Centre,** where you can create an unusual souvenir. Beyond this point, you would once have passed beyond the safety provided by the town walls. A plaque outside the Netherbow Arts Centre depicts the former Netherbow Port (gate). Below is the Canongate area, named for the canons who once ran the abbey at Holyrood. Here you see the handsome **Canongate Tolbooth** 15, the graveyard of Canongate Kirk, and **Huntly House** 16, a museum of local history. Facing you at the end of Canongate are the wrought-iron gates of the **Palace of Holyroodhouse** 17, residence of the Queen when she is in Scotland. Under construction to the right is the Parliament Building.

TIMING This walk contains a multitude of historical attractions, and its duration depends on your interests. Exploring the Royal Mile from the castle to the Palace of Holyroodhouse will easily take up to half a day. The Grassmarket is a good lunch spot, with its pubs and small restaurants. The Museum of Scotland building can take up to half a day.

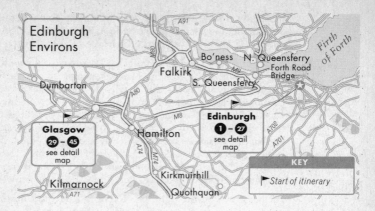

What to See

Arthur's Seat. For a grand bird's-eye view of Edinburgh, make your way up the 800 feet of the city's only minimountain, Arthur's Seat, set in the park behind the **Palace of Holyroodhouse.** It's a steep walk but well worth it for the views from here and its neighboring eminence, Salisbury Crags.

Brass Rubbing Centre. A hands-on way to explore the past, brass rubbing attracts more serious fans every year. You'll find fascinating reproduction brasses and inscribed stones, with instructions and materials supplied. ⊠ *Trinity Apse, Chalmers Close, Old Town* ☎ *0131/556–4364* ⊕ *www.cac.org.uk* ✑ *Free, £1.20–£15 for each rubbing* ⊙ *Apr.–Oct., Mon.–Sat. 10–5, Sun. (during festival only) noon–5.*

❸ Camera Obscura. Want to view Edinburgh as Victorian travelers once did? The Outlook Tower holds this optical instrument, a sort of projecting telescope that creates a bird's-eye view of the whole city illuminated onto a concave table. Holograms and modern cameras are shown in other exhibits. ⊠ *Castlehill, Old Town* ☎ *0131/226–3709* ⊕ *www. explore-edinburgh.com* ✑ *£4.50* ⊙ *Apr.–Oct., weekdays 9:30–6, weekends 10–6; Nov.–Mar., daily 10–5.*

❶❺ Canongate Tolbooth. Canongate originally was an independent "burgh," or town, which explains the presence of the Canongate Tolbooth. Nearly every city and town in Scotland once had a tolbooth. Originally signifying a customhouse where tolls were gathered, the name came to mean the town hall and, later, a prison. Today, the Canongate Tolbooth contains **The People's Story**, an exhibition on the history of the people of Edinburgh. Next door is the graveyard of **Canongate Kirk**, where some notable Scots, including Adam Smith, the economist and author of *The Wealth of Nations*, are buried. ⊠ *Canongate, Old Town* ☎ *0131/529–4057* ✑ *Free* ⊙ *Mon.–Sat. 10–5, Sun. (during festival only) 2–5.*

★ ▶ ❶ Edinburgh Castle. The crowning glory of the Scottish capital, Edinburgh Castle is popular not only because it is the symbolic heart of Scotland but also because of the views from its battlements: on a clear day the vistas, stretching to the "kingdom" of Fife, are breathtakingly lovely. Clear days are frequent now, as Edinburgh is officially smokeless and the nickname "Auld Reekie" ("Old Smokey") no longer applies.

The castle encompasses much of Scottish history. You will hear the story of how Randolph, earl of Moray, nephew of freedom-fighter Robert Bruce, scaled the heights one dark night in 1313, surprised the English guard, and recaptured the castle for the Scots. At the same time he destroyed every one of its buildings except for St. Margaret's Chapel,

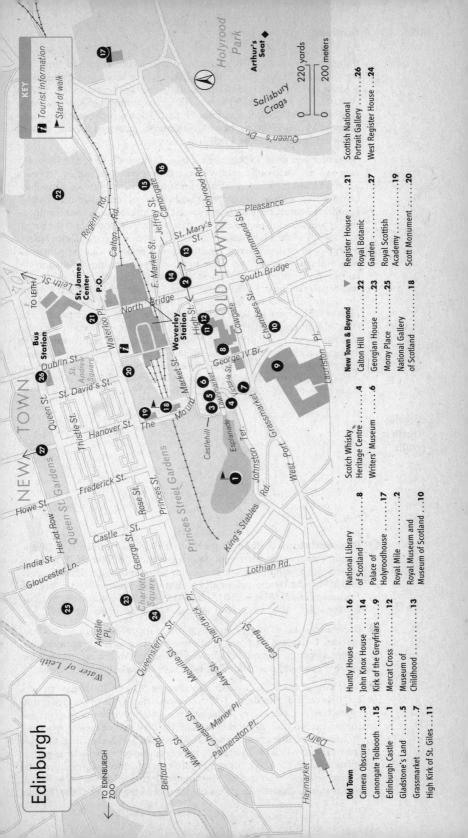

Edinburgh

KEY

i Tourist information

▶ Start of walk

TO LEITH

NEW TOWN

OLD TOWN

Holyrood Park

Arthur's Seat ◆

Salisbury Crags

Queen's Dr.

0 — 220 yards
0 — 200 meters

Leith St.
St. James Center
P.O.
Bus Station
Dublin St.
Queen St.
St. David's St.
St. Andrew Square
Hanover St.
Thistle St.
Frederick St.
Castle St.
George St.
Rose St.
Heriot Row
Howe St.
India St.
Gloucester Ln.
Charlotte Square
Queensferry St.
Ainslie Pl.
Water of Leith
Belford Rd.
Melville St.
Chester St.
Manor Pl.
Palmerston Pl.
Shandwick Pl.
Haymarket
Dalry
TO EDINBURGH ZOO

Regent Rd.
Calton Rd.
Waterloo Pl.
North Bridge
Waverley Station
The Mound
Princes Street Gardens
Castlehill
Esplanade
Johnston Ter.
King's Stables Rd.
West Port
Grassmarket
Lothian Rd.
Queen Street Gardens

E. Market St.
Jeffrey St.
Canongate
St. Mary's St.
High St.
Cowgate
George IV Br.
Victoria St.
Lawnmarket
Chambers St.
South Bridge
Drummond St.
Pleasance
Holyrood Rd.
Lauriston Pl.

Old Town

Camera Obscura 3
Canongate Tolbooth ..15
Edinburgh Castle 1
Gladstone's Land 5
Grassmarket 7
High Kirk of St. Giles ..11
Huntly House 16
John Knox House 14
Kirk of the Greyfriars ..9
Mercat Cross 12
Museum of Childhood 13
National Library of Scotland 16
Palace of Holyroodhouse 17
Royal Mile 2
Royal Museum and Museum of Scotland ..10
Scotch Whisky Heritage Centre 8
Writers' Museum 6

New Town & Beyond

Calton Hill 22
Georgian House 23
Moray Place 25
National Gallery of Scotland 18
Register House 21
Royal Botanic Garden 27
Royal Scottish Academy 19
Scott Monument ...20
Scottish National Portrait Gallery 26
West Register House ..24

dating from around 1076, so that successive Stuart kings had to rebuild the place bit by bit. Scots and Englishmen, Catholics and Protestants, soldiers and royalty have held the castle. In the 16th century Mary, Queen of Scots, chose to give birth here to the future James VI of Scotland, who was also to rule England as James I. In 1573 it was the last fortress to support Mary's claim as the rightful Catholic queen of Britain, only to be virtually destroyed by English artillery fire.

You enter across the **Esplanade,** the huge forecourt built in the 18th century as a parade ground; it now serves as the castle parking lot. It comes alive with color each August when it is used for the Tattoo, a magnificent military display, with the massed pipes and drums of the Scottish regiments beating retreat on the floodlit heights. Heading over the drawbridge and through the gatehouse, past the guards, you'll find the rough stone walls of the **Half Moon Battery,** where the one o'clock gun is fired every day in an impressively anachronistic ceremony. Climb up through a second gateway and you come to the oldest surviving building in the complex, the tiny 11th-century **St. Margaret's Chapel.** Head up farther still to enter the heart of the mighty complex, the medieval fortress. Along the dimly lit, echoing corridors you'll find the **Crown Room,** containing the "Honours of Scotland," the crown, scepter, and sword that once graced the Scottish monarch, and the Stone of Destiny, a sacred relic used in Scottish coronations. Here also is the **Great Hall,** under whose 16th-century hammer-beam roof official banquets are still held, and **Queen Mary's apartments,** where the queen gave birth to James. ☎ *0131/ 225–9846* ⊕ *www.historic-scotland.gov.uk* ✉ *£8.50* ⊙ *Apr.–Sept., daily 9:30–6: Oct.–Mar., daily 9:30–5.*

> **off the beaten path**

EDINBURGH ZOO – In Edinburgh's western suburbs, this zoo includes more than 1,000 species and has areas in which children can approach or handle animals. It's noted for its penguins and Peguin Parade, which takes place at 2:15 in summer and 12:45 in winter. However, the parade is voluntary on the part of the penguins, and it sometimes doesn't take place. ✉ *Corstorphine Rd., Corstorphine* ☎ *0131/334–9171* ⊕ *www.edinburghzoo.org.uk* ✉ *£7.50* ⊙ *Apr.–Sept., daily 9–6; Oct. and Mar., daily 9–5; Nov.–Feb., daily 9–4:30.*

❺ Gladstone's Land. A standout for those in search of authentic old Edinburgh, this six-story tenement dates from the 17th century. It includes an arcaded ground floor and intricately painted ceilings. The entire edifice is furnished in the style of a 17th-century merchant's house. ✉ *477B Lawnmarket, Old Town* ☎ *0131/226–5856* ⊕ *www.nts.org.uk* ✉ *£3.50* ⊙ *Apr.–Oct., Mon.–Sat. 10–5, Sun. 2–5; last admission at 4:30.*

❼ Grassmarket. As its name suggests, this was for centuries an agricultural market. Today, the shopping continues, but the goods are: antiques, old prints, clothing, and quality giftware. More boutiques can be found in nearby Victoria Street and West Bow. ✉ *Grassmarket, Old Town.*

⓫ High Kirk of St. Giles. Sometimes called St. Giles's Cathedral (it was briefly a cathedral in the mid-17th century), this is one of the city's principal churches, but it is more like a large parish church than a great European cathedral. The building is dominated by a stone crown, towering 161 feet above the ground; the interior is dark and forbidding. Outside the west end you'll find a life-size bronze statue of the Scot whose spirit still dominates the place, the great Protestant reformer and preacher John Knox, before whose zeal all Scotland once trembled. The most elaborate feature inside the church is the **Chapel of the Order of the Thistle,**

which refers to Scotland's highest order of chivalry and is the counterpart to England's Order of the Garter. St. Giles is about one-third of the way along the Royal Mile from Edinburgh Castle. ⊠ *High St., Old Town* ☎ *0131/225–9442* ⊕ *www.stgiles.net* ✉ *£1 suggested donation* ⊙ *May–Sept., weekdays 9–7, Sat. 9–5, Sun. 1–5; Oct.–Apr., Mon.–Sat. 9–5, Sun. 1–5.*

⑯ **Huntly House.** This attractive building houses the fascinating Museum of Edinburgh, a must for those interested in the details of Old Town life. The collection includes Scottish pottery and Edinburgh glass and silver. ⊠ *142 Canongate, Old Town* ☎ *0131/529–4143* ⊕ *www.cac.org.uk* ✉ *Free* ⊙ *Mon.–Sat. 10–5, Sun. (during festival only) 2–5.*

⑭ **John Knox House.** A typical 16th-century dwelling, this was not the home of Knox (1514–72), Scotland's fiery religious reformer, though he may have died here. It is full of mementos of his life and career. ⊠ *45 High St., Old Town* ☎ *0131/556–2647* ⊕ *www.johnknoxhouse.org.uk* ✉ *£2.25* ⊙ *July, Mon.–Sat. 10–5, Sun. noon–4; Aug., Mon.–Sat. 10–7, Sun. noon–4; Sept.–June, Mon.–Sat. 10–5; last admission ½ hr before closing.*

⑨ **Kirk of the Greyfriars.** Here, on the site of a medieval monastery, the National Covenant was signed in 1638, declaring the Presbyterian Church in Scotland independent of government control. This triggered decades of civil war. Be sure to explore the graveyard, too. Nearby, at the corner of George IV Bridge and Candlemaker Row, stands one of the most photographed sights in Scotland, the statue of **Greyfriars Bobby.** This famous Skye terrier kept vigil beside his master's grave in the churchyard for 14 years. ⊠ *Greyfriars Pl., Old Town* ☎ *0131/225–1900* ⊕*www.greyfriarskirk.com* ✉ *Free* ⊙ *Easter–Oct., weekdays 10:30–4:30, Sat. 10:30–2:30; Nov.–Easter, Thurs. 1:30–3:30.*

⑫ **Mercat Cross.** A great landmark of Old Town life, the Mercat Cross (mercat means "market") can be seen just east of the High Kirk of St. Giles. This area was a mercantile center, and in early days, it also saw executions. It is the spot where royal proclamations were—and are still—read. Most of the current cross dates from the time of Gladstone, the great Victorian prime minister and rival of Disraeli. ⊠ *High St., Old Town.*

⓰ ⑬ **Museum of Childhood.** Even adults tend to enjoy this cheerful museum— a cacophony of childhood memorabilia, vintage toys, and dolls—the first in the world to be devoted solely to the history of childhood. ⊠ *42 High St., Old Town* ☎ *0131/529–4142* ⊕ *www.cac.org.uk* ✉ *Free* ⊙ *Mon.–Sat. 10–5, Sun. (during festival only) 2–5.*

⑧ **National Library of Scotland.** This research library is a special magnet for genealogists investigating family trees. Even amateur family sleuths will find the staff helpful in their research. The library contains a superb collection of books on the history and culture of Scotland. ⊠ *George IV Bridge, Old Town* ☎ *0131/226–4531* ⊕ *www.nls.uk* ✉ *Free* ⊙ *Mon., Tues., Thurs., Fri. 9:30–8:30, Wed. 10–8:30, Sat. 9:30–1; exhibitions Mon.–Sat. 10–5; festival hrs weekdays 10–8, Sat. 10–5, Sun. 2–5.*

★ ⑰ **Palace of Holyroodhouse.** Haunt of Mary, Queen of Scots, and the setting for high drama, including at least one notorious murder, a spectacular funeral, several major fires, and centuries of the colorful lifestyles of larger-than-life, power-hungry personalities, this is now the Queen's official residence in Scotland. The doughty and impressive palace, built around a graceful central court, stands at the foot of the Royal Mile in a hilly public park. Many monarchs, including Charles II, Queen Victoria, and George V, have left their mark on its rooms. Highlights include the **Great Picture Gallery,** 150 feet long and hung with the portraits of 111 Scottish monarchs. These portraits were commissioned by Charles II, eager to demonstrate his Scottish ancestry (some of the royal figures here are fictional, and the likenesses of others imaginary).

Also here is the little chamber in which, in 1566, David Rizzio, secretary to Mary, Queen of Scots, met an unhappy end. Partly because Rizzio was hated at court for his social-climbing ways, Mary's second husband, Lord Darnley, burst into the queen's rooms with his henchmen, dragged Rizzio into an antechamber, and stabbed him more than 50 times (a bronze plaque marks the spot). Darnley himself was murdered in Edinburgh the next year, to make way for the queen's marriage to her lover, Bothwell. When Charles II assumed the British throne in 1660, he ordered Holyrood rebuilt in the architectural style of French king Louis XIV, and that is the palace that you see today. When the Royal Family is not in residence, you are free to walk around the exterior and to go inside for a conducted tour. At the entrance to the palace is the **Queen's Gallery,** which holds exhibitions of works from the Royal Collection. Behind the palace lie the open grounds of Holyrood Park, which enclose Edinburgh's own minimountain, **Arthur's Seat;** just west of the palace, Scotland's new **Parliament building** is under construction. ✉ *Abbey Strand, Holyrood* ☎ *0131/556–7371; 0131/556–1096 recorded information* ⊕ *www.royal.gov.uk* ☞ *£6.50* ☉ *Apr.–Oct., daily 9:30–5:15; Nov.–Mar., daily 9:30–3:45. Closed during royal visits.*

Parliament House. This was the seat of government until 1707, when the governments of Scotland and England were united, 104 years after the union of the two crowns. It is partially hidden by the bulk of the High Kirk of St. Giles and now houses the Supreme Law Courts of Scotland. ✉ *Parliament Sq., Old Town* ☎ *0131/225–2595* ⊕ *www.scotcourts. gov.uk* ☞ *Free* ☉ *Weekdays 10–4.*

❷ Royal Mile. The most famous thoroughfare in Edinburgh begins immediately below the Esplanade. It runs roughly west to east from the castle to the Palace of Holyroodhouse, and progressively changes its name from Castlehill to Lawnmarket, High Street, and Canongate. Strolling downhill from the castle, it's easy to imagine and re-create the former life of the city, though you will need sharp eyes to spot the numerous historic plaques and details of ornamentation.

★ ❿ Royal Museum and Museum of Scotland. In a lavish Victorian building, the **Royal Museum** displays extensive collections drawn from natural history, archaeology, the scientific and industrial past, and the history of mankind and civilization. The galleried Main Hall with its "birdcage" design is architecturally interesting in its own right. In an adjoining building, the **Museum of Scotland** concentrates on Scotland's own heritage. This state-of-the-art modern museum is full of playful models, intricate reconstructions, and paraphernalia from the ancient Picts to the latest Scottish pop stars. ✉ *Chambers St., Old Town* ☎ *0131/225–7534* ⊕ *www.nms.ac.uk* ☞ *Free, both museums* ☉ *Mon. and Wed.–Sat. 10–5, Tues. 10–8, Sun. noon–5.*

❹ Scotch Whisky Heritage Centre. Here you can learn about the mysterious process that turns malted barley and spring water into one of Scotland's most important exports. ✉ *354 Castlehill, Old Town* ☎ *0131/220–0441* ⊕ *www.whisky-heritage.co.uk* ☞ *£7.50* ☉ *May–Sept., daily 9:30–6:30, last tour 5:30; Oct.–Apr., daily 10–5, last tour 4.*

❻ Writers' Museum. This museum occupies a good example of 17th-century urban architecture known as Lady Stair's House. It evokes Scotland's literary past with exhibits on Sir Walter Scott, Robert Louis

Stevenson, and Robert Burns. ⊠ *Lady Stair's Close, off Lawnmarket, Old Town* ☎ *0131/529–4901* ⊕ *www.cac.org.uk* ✉ *Free* ☉ *Mon.–Sat. 10–5 (last admission 4:45), Sun. (during festival only) 2–5.*

The New Town & Beyond

It was not until the Scottish Enlightenment, a civilizing time of expansion in the 1700s, that the city fathers decided to break away from the Royal Mile's rocky slope and create a fresh and uncluttered Edinburgh below the castle, a little to the north. This was to become the New Town, with elegant squares, classical facades, wide streets, and harmonious proportions. In 1767 a civic competition to design this revolutionary district was won by an unknown architect, James Craig (1744–95). His plan called for a grid of three main east–west streets, balanced at either end by two grand squares. These streets survive, though some buildings that line them have been altered by later development. Princes Street is the southernmost, with Queen Street to the north and George Street as the axis, punctuated by St. Andrew and Charlotte squares. A look at the map will reveal a geometric symmetry unusual in Britain. Even Princes Street Gardens are balanced by Queen Street Gardens to the north. Princes Street was conceived as an exclusive residential address with an open vista facing the castle. It has since been altered by the demands of business and shopping, but the vista remains.

a good walk

Start your walk on the Mound, the sloping street that joins the Old and New Towns. Two impressive buildings tucked immediately east of this great linking ramp are the work of W. H. Playfair (1789–1857), an architect whose neoclassical buildings contributed greatly to Edinburgh's earning the title the "Athens of the North." The **National Gallery of Scotland** ⓲ ► has paintings from Renaissance art to postimpressionist works and one of the most impressive collections of Scottish art. The **Royal Scottish Academy** ⓳, with its columned facade overlooking Princes Street, hosts changing art exhibitions. Turn right on bustling **Princes Street**, the heart of the city. Walk east past the soaring Gothic spire of the 200-foot-high **Scott Monument** ⓴. **Register House** ㉑, farther down on the left, is an Adam-designed jewel of neoclassical architecture that marks the end of Princes Street. The monuments on **Calton Hill** ㉒ can be reached by continuing along Waterloo Place and either climbing steps to the hilltop or taking the road farther on that loops up at a more leisurely pace. On the opposite side of the road, in the Calton Old Burying Ground, is a monument to Abraham Lincoln and the Scottish-American dead of the Civil War. Cut through the St. James Centre shopping mall and find the branch of London's trendy Harvey Nichols department store and its associated fashion stores before heading west along George Street to Charlotte Square. Here you will find the handsome **Georgian House** ㉓. Also in the square, the former St. George's Church now fulfills a different role as **West Register House** ㉔, a research facility.

To explore further in the New Town, choose your own route northward, down the elegant streets centering on **Moray Place** ㉕. A neo-Gothic building on Queen Street houses the **Scottish National Portrait Gallery** ㉖. Another attraction within reach of the New Town is the much-cherished **Royal Botanic Garden** ㉗. Walk down Dundas Street, the continuation of Hanover Street, and turn left and across the bridge over the Water of Leith, Edinburgh's small-scale river. This path leads to the gardens.

TIMING   Walking from the top of the Mound along the full length of Princes Street should take no more than an hour. It is well worth allocating a few hours for Calton Hill, which provides a 360° view of Edinburgh's magnificent skyline, as far as the Firth of Forth across to Fife. The grid system in the New Town provides easy navigation for a wander downhill to the Water of Leith. The Royal Botanic Garden is a 20-minute walk from Princes Street.

What to See

off the beaten path

BRITANNIA – Moored on the waterfront at Leith, Edinburgh's port north of the city center, is the former Royal Yacht *Britannia*, launched in Scotland in 1953 and now retired to her home country. The Royal Apartments and the more functional engine room, bridge, galleys, and captain's cabin are all open to view. The land-based visitor center within the huge Ocean Terminal shopping mall has multimedia exhibits about *Britannia*'s history. ⊠ *Ocean Dr., Leith* ☎ *0131/555–5566* ⊕ *www.royalyachtbritannia.co.uk* ⊠ *£8* ⊘ *Apr.–Sept., 9:30–4:30; Oct.–Mar., 10–3:30.*

㉒ **Calton Hill.** A vantage point from which to gain panoramic views, Calton Hill also has numerous historic monuments, including the incomplete Parthenon look-alike known as Edinburgh's Disgrace, intended as a National War Memorial in 1822 (contributions fell short). You can climb the **Nelson Monument** (☎ 0131/556–2716 ⊕ www.cac.org.uk ⊠£2.50 ⊘ Apr.–Sept., Mon. 1–6, Tues.–Sat. 10–6; Oct.–Mar., Mon.–Sat. 10–3) completed in 1815, for fine views. ⊠ *Off Regent Rd., Calton.*

off the beaten path

FALKIRK WHEEL – In 2002 British Waterways opened the world's only rotating boat lift, which links two major waterways, the Forth and Clyde Canal and the Union Canal, between Edinburgh and Glasgow. Considered an engineering marvel, the wheel transports eight or more boats at a time overland from one canal to the other in about 45 minutes. The boats float into a cradlelike compartment full of water; as the wheel turns, they are transported up or down to meet the other canal. You can board tour boats at Falkirk to ride the wheel, or you can take a multiday barge cruise between Edinburgh and Glasgow. At Falkirk, allow 30 minutes before your scheduled departure time to pick up your tickets and choose your boat. Falkirk is 25 mi west of Edinburgh. ⊠ *Lime Rd., Tamfourhill* ☎ *01324/ 619888; reservations 08700/500208* ⊕ *www.thefalkirkwheel.co.uk* ⊠ *Boat trips £8, visitor center free* ⊘ *Boat trips Apr.–Oct., daily 9:30–5; Nov.–Mar., daily 10–3. Visitor center Apr.–Oct., daily 9–6:30; Nov.–Mar., daily 10–5.*

★ ㉓ **Georgian House.** Built in 1796, this house stands in Charlotte Square, the elegant urban set piece designed by Robert Adam at the west end of George Street. Graced by a palatial facade on its north side, the square is considered one of Britain's finest pieces of civic architecture. Thanks to the National Trust for Scotland, the Georgian House has been furnished in period style to show the domestic lifestyle of an affluent late-18th-century family. ⊠ *7 Charlotte Sq., New Town* ☎ *0131/225– 2160* ⊕ *www.nts.org.uk* ⊠ *£5* ⊘ *Mar., Nov., and Dec., daily 11–3; Apr.–Oct., daily 11–5.*

㉕ **Moray Place.** With imposing porticoes and a central, secluded garden, this is an especially fine example of an 1820s development. The area remains primarily residential, in contrast to the area around Princes Street. The Moray Place gardens are still for residents only.

★ ▶ ⑱ **National Gallery of Scotland.** This honey-color neoclassical building, midway between the Old and the New Towns, contains just about the best collection of old masters in Britain outside the great London museums. It is relatively small, so you can easily tour the whole collection in a couple of hours. There are superb works by Michelangelo da Car-avaggio, Titian, Diego Velázquez, El Greco, Rembrandt, J.M.W. Turner, Edgar Degas, Claude Monet, and Vincent van Gogh, among many others. Scottish painters are also well represented, chief among them the 18th-century portrait painter Sir Henry Raeburn (1756–1823). ⊠ *The Mound, Old Town* ☎ *0131/556–8921* ⊕ *www.natgalscot.ac.uk* ⊠ *Free* ⊙ *Mon.–Sat. 10–5 (extended during festival), Sun. noon–5; print room, weekdays 10–12:30 and 2–4:30, by appointment.*

Princes Street. In the humming center of Edinburgh, a ceaseless prome-nade of people patters along this street, with its mile or so of interna-tional chain stores and other retail establishments. The well-kept gardens on the other side of Princes Street act as the castle's wide green moat. The street is still a grand viewpoint for the dramatic grouping of the castle on its rocky outcrop and the long tail of Royal Mile tenements descending from it. ⊠ *New Town.*

㉑ Register House. Scotland's first custom-built archives depository was partly funded by the sale of estates forfeited by Jacobite landowners at the close of their last rebellion in Britain (1745–46). Work on the build-ing, designed by Robert Adam, Scotland's most famous neoclassical ar-chitect, started in 1774. The statue in front is of the first duke of Wellington (1769–1852). Call ahead if you wish to carry out genealogical research. ⊠ *2 Princes St., New Town* ☎ *0131/535–1314* ⊕ *www.nas. gov.uk* ⊠ *Free* ⊙ *Weekdays 9–4:45.*

need a break? Immediately west of Register House is the **Café Royal** (⊠ 17 W. Register St., New Town ☎ 0131/557–4792), serving good Scottish lagers and ales, and simple lunch items such as nachos and macaroni and cheese. The 18th-century building has plenty of character, with ornate tiles and stained-glass windows.

㉗ Royal Botanic Garden. This garden is second only to the Royal Botanic Gardens at Kew in London for the diversity of its plants and its lovely setting. The 70-acre site presents an immense display of specimens, from tropical to Nordic, including Britain's largest collection of rhodo-dendrons and azaleas and an impressive Chinese garden. You can also stop in at the café, shop, and temporary exhibition area. The garden is north of the city center, a 10-minute bus ride from Princes Street. ⊠ *In-verleith Row, Inverleith* ☎ *0131/552–7171* ⊕ *www.rbge.org.uk* ⊠ *Free, with a donation for the greenhouses* ⊙ *Nov.–Feb., daily 10–4; Mar., daily 10–6; Apr.–Sept., daily 10–7; Oct., daily 10–6. Guided tours leave from the West Gate, Apr.–Sept., daily at 11 and 2.*

⑲ Royal Scottish Academy. The William Playfair–designed academy hosts temporary art exhibitions (Monet paintings, for example), but is also worth visiting for a look at the imposing, neoclassic architecture. ⊠ *Princes St., Old Town* ☎ *0131/558–7097* ⊕ *www. royalscottishacademy.org* ⊠ *£6–£8* ⊙ *Mon.–Sat. 10–5, Sun. noon–5.*

⑳ Scott Monument. The great poems and novels (such as *Ivanhoe* and *Wa-verley*) of Sir Walter Scott (1771–1832) created a world frenzy for Scot-land; the Scots were duly grateful and put up this great Gothic memorial to him in 1844. Under its graceful spire sits Scott himself, his dog, Maida, at his feet. Behind the monument is pretty **Princes Street Gar-dens.** In the open-air theater, amid the park's trim flower beds and stately trees, brass bands and classical music ensembles occasionally per-form in the summer. ⊠ *Princes St., Old Town* ☎ *0131/529–4068* ⊕ *www.cac.org.uk* ⊠ *£2.50* ⊙ *Apr.–Sept., Mon.–Sat. 9–6, Sun. 10–6; Oct.–Mar., Mon.–Sat. 9–3, Sun. 10–3.*

26 **Scottish National Portrait Gallery.** Focusing on portraits of Scots, this museum contains a magnificent Thomas Gainsborough and portraits by the Scottish artists Allan Ramsay (1713–84) and Sir Henry Raeburn (1756–1823). Other works by contemporary artists show sitters from sports stars to world leaders. The building itself is also of great interest, with richly colored murals in the main hall. ⊠ *Queen St., New Town* ☎ *0131/624–6200* ⊕ *www.natgalscot.ac.uk* ⊠ *Free, charge for special exhibitions* ⊙ *Mon.–Wed. and Fri.–Sun. 10–5, Thurs. 10–7; extended hrs during the festival.*

24 **West Register House.** An extension of the original Register House, this research facility has records open for public examination, with helpful staff to assist you. It's best to check ahead if you wish to carry out genealogical research. ⊠ *Charlotte Sq., New Town* ☎ *0131/535–1400* ⊕ *www.nas.gov.uk* ⊠ *Free* ⊙ *Weekdays 9–4:30.*

Where to Eat

The restaurants of this sophisticated city present a mix of Scottish and ethnic cuisine. Number One in the Balmoral Hotel and La Pompadour at the Caledonian Hilton are other good choices for an elegant night out. Make reservations well in advance, especially at festival time.

★
££££–£££££ ✕ **Martins.** Don't be put off by the forbidding facade of this fine contemporary restaurant tucked away in an alley between Frederick and Castle streets. All's well inside, and the food is light and delicious. Fish and game are specialties, and the cheese board is famous. ⊠ *70 Rose St., North La., New Town* ☎ *0131/225–3106* ♨ *Reservations essential* ⊟ *AE, DC, MC, V* ⊙ *Closed Sun. and Mon. No lunch Sat.*

£££–££££ ✕ **Skippers Bistro.** Once a traditional pub, this superb seafood restaurant in the port of Leith remains cozy and cluttered, with dark wood, shining brass, and lots of pictures and ephemera. For a starter, try the creamy fish soup. Main dishes change daily but might include halibut, salmon, or monkfish in delicious sauces. Reservations are essential on weekends. ⊠ *1A Dock Pl., Leith* ☎ *0131/554–1018* ⊟ *AE, MC, V.*

££–££££ ✕ **Howie's.** This neighborhood bistro has four branches and offers good modern Scottish fare. The steaks are tender Aberdeen beef, and the Loch Fyne herring are sweet-cured to Howie's recipe. All the branches are lively, but each has a personality all its own. ⊠ *29 Waterloo Pl., East End* ☎ *0131/556–5766* ⊠ *10–14 Victoria St., Old Town* ☎ *0131/225–1721* ⊠ *208 Bruntsfield Pl., Bruntsfield* ☎ *0131/221–1777* ⊠ *4–6 Glanville Pl., New Town* ☎ *0131/313–3334* ⊟ *AE, MC, V.*

£££ ✕ **Oloroso.** In the heart of the New Town and close to the main shopping streets, this is the perfect place for a revitalizing lunch or dinner after exploring the city. Efficient service is allied to multicultural contemporary cooking that mixes influences from Europe and Asia. The bar is comfortable, and the dining room and roof terrace have stunning views across the Firth of Forth to the hills of Fife, and to the castle and city rooftops on the other side. ⊠ *33 Castle St., New Town* ☎ *0131/226–7614* ⊟ *AE, DC, MC, V.*

££ ✕ **Beehive Inn.** The Beehive snuggles in the Grassmarket, under the castle's majestic shadow. Some 400 years ago it served the passengers of coaches, and outside the pub's doors once stood the main city gallows. Bar meals and snacks are served all day, downstairs or in the beer garden. Upstairs, Rafters Restaurant opens at 6 for dinner; try the grilled salmon steaks. Don't be put off by the noisy bar; there's usually a quieter spot to be found. You can book literary lunch and supper packages downstairs in conjunction with the McEwan's Edinburgh Literary Pub Tour, which departs from here. ⊠ *18–20 Grassmarket, Old Town* ☎ *0131/225–7171* ⊟ *AE, DC, MC, V.*

££ ✕ **Britannia Spice.** This restaurant, just a few hundred yards from the berth of the former royal yacht *Britannia,* offers a long menu of meat, fish, and vegetarian dishes from India, Bangladesh, Thailand, and Nepal. Try the Thai beef or the Nepalese trout with vegetables and green chilies. This is a good place to recover from the Ocean Terminal shopping experience. ⊠ *150 Commercial St., Leith* ☎ *0131/555–2255* 🖃 *AE, DC, MC, V.*

£–££ ✕ **Bann UK.** The excellent vegetarian food at this thriving restaurant off the Royal Mile is popular with students and young people. The light, airy dining room and wooden furniture make a pleasant setting for breakfast, tapas, sandwiches, and more substantial fare. Try the enchiladas or a phyllo basket of cream cheese, herbs, and vegetables. ⊠ *5 Hunter Sq., Old Town* ☎ *0131/226–1112* 🖃 *AE, DC, MC, V.*

£–££ ✕ **Kalpna.** The unremarkable facade and low-key, print-decorated interior of this vegetarian Indian restaurant, set amid a row of shops, gives no clue to the excellence of the food. *Dam aloo Kashmiri* is a medium-spicy potato dish with a sauce made from honey, pistachios, and almonds. *Bangan mirch masala* is spicier, with eggplant and red chili peppers. The lunchtime buffet is £5; a Wednesday evening buffet, £9.95. ⊠ *2–3 St. Patrick's Sq., South Side* ☎ *0131/667–9890* 🖃 *MC, V* ☺ *No lunch Sun.*

FodorsChoice ★

Where to Stay

★ £££££ 🏨 **Balmoral Hotel.** The attention to detail in the elegant rooms and the sheer élan that has re-created the Edwardian splendor of this former grand railroad hotel make staying at the Balmoral a special introduction to Edinburgh. Here, below the impressive clock tower marking the east end of Princes Street, you get a strong sense of being at the center of city life. The hotel's main restaurant is the plush and stylish Number One, serving the best of Scottish seafood and game. ⊠ *1 Princes St., East End, EH2 2EQ* ☎ *0131/556–2414* 🖷 *0131/557–3747* ⊕ *www. roccofortehotels.com* 🛏 *188 rooms, 2 suites* ⚭ *2 restaurants, in-room data ports, indoor pool, health club, bar, meeting rooms, parking (fee)* 🖃 *AE, DC, MC, V.*

£££££ 🏨 **Channings.** Five Edwardian terraced houses have become an elegant boutique hotel in an upscale neighborhood minutes from Princes Street. Restrained colors, antiques, quiet rooms, and great views toward Fife (from the north-facing rooms) set the tone. The Brasserie offers excellent value, especially at lunchtime. ⊠ *12–16 S. Learmonth Gardens, West End, EH4 1EZ* ☎ *0131/332–3232* 🖷 *0131/332–9631* ⊕ *www.channings. co.uk* 🛏 *46 rooms* ⚭ *2 restaurants, lobby lounge, meeting rooms* 🖃 *AE, DC, MC, V* ◉❙ *BP.*

£££££ 🏨 **The Scotsman.** When the *Scotsman* newspaper moved from these premises, it left behind a magnificent turn-of-the-20th-century gray sandstone building with a marble staircase and ornate fireplaces and moldings. A chic and luxurious modern hotel has been created within the shell of the old structure. Dark wood, earthy colors, and contemporary furnishings decorate the guest rooms and public spaces. ⊠ *20 N. Bridge, Old Town EH1 1YT* ☎ *0131/556–5565* 🖷 *0131/652–3652* ⊕ *www. thescotsmanhotel.co.uk* 🛏 *56 rooms, 12 suites* ⚭ *2 restaurants, in-room data ports, cable TV, indoor pool, health club, spa, bar, Internet, business services, meeting rooms* 🖃 *AE, DC, MC, V.*

FodorsChoice ★

★ 🏨 **Caledonian Hilton Hotel.** "The Caley" recalls the days of the great railroad hotels, although its former nearby station is long gone. Its imposing Victorian decor has lost none of the original dignity and elegance. Rooms are exceptionally large and well appointed. The main restaurant, La Pompadour, with elegant plasterwork and murals, would please even Louis XV. Its classic French cuisine uses top-quality Scottish foods;

££££–£££££

try the sea bass with crispy leeks and caviar-butter sauce. ✉ *Princes St., West End, EH1 2AB* ☎ *0131/222–8888* 🖷 *0131/222–8889* ⊕ *www. hilton.com* ◔ *249 rooms* ♨ *2 restaurants, cable TV, meeting rooms, parking (fee)* ⊟ *AE, DC, MC, V* ⟦◉⟧ *BP.*

£££–££££ 🏨 **Malmaison.** A former seamen's hostel in the heart of Leith, Edinburgh's seaport, offers good value yet stylish accommodation, with king-size beds and CD players in bedrooms that reflect a chic, bold, modern style. In the public areas a dramatic black, cream, and taupe color scheme prevails. The French theme of this boutique hotel (part of a small chain) is emphasized by the art nouveau café-bar and brasserie. ✉ *1 Tower Pl., Leith EH6 7DB* ☎ *0131/468–5000* 🖷 *0131/468–5002* ⊕ *www. malmaison.com* ⬧ *60 rooms* ♨ *Restaurant, café, cable TV, bar, free parking* ⊟ *AE, DC, MC, V* ⟦◉⟧ *BP.*

££–£££ 🏨 **Ardmor House.** A 15-minute walk from Princes Street, Ardmor is a Victorian house with a relaxed but elegant contemporary style. Bedrooms have the occasional carefully chosen antique. It is gay-owned but very straight-friendly, and co-owner Robin provides advice on what to see and do in Edinburgh. ✉ *74 Pilrig St., Pilrig, EH6 5AS* 🖷🖷 *0131/554– 4944* ⊕ *www.malmaison.com* ⬧ *5 rooms* ♨ *Dining room, free parking, some pets allowed; no a/c, no smoking* ⊟ *MC, V* ⟦◉⟧ *BP.*

££–£££ 🏨 **Kew House and Apartments.** Inside this elegant house, dating from 1860, are tastefully modernized rooms with flowers, chocolates, and a complimentary decanter of sherry. The apartments, one of which is a five-minute walk from the house, have sitting rooms and full kitchens. The bar is for guests only. It's a 15-minute walk from the town center. ✉ *1 Kew Terr., New Town, EH12 5JE* ☎ *0131/313–0700* 🖷 *0131/313–0747* ⊕ *www.kewhouse.com* ⬧ *6 rooms, 2 apartments* ♨ *Dining room, bar, free parking; no a/c, no smoking* ⊟ *AE, DC, MC, V* ⟦◉⟧ *BP.*

★ ££–£££ 🏨 **Stuart House.** A Victorian terraced house with some fine plasterwork houses this classy B&B. The decoration suits the structure: bold colors, floral fabrics, and generously curtained windows combine with antique and traditional furniture to create a sense of opulence. Stuart House is a 15-minute walk from the city center. ✉ *12 E. Claremont St., Canonmills, EH7 4JP* ☎ *0131/557–9030* 🖷 *0131/557–0563* ⊕ *www. stuartguesthouse.co.uk* ⬧ *7 rooms, 2 apartments* ♨ *Some pets allowed; no a/c, no smoking* ⊟ *AE, DC, MC, V* ⟦◉⟧ *BP.*

££ 🏨 **The Conifers.** This trim B&B in a red-sandstone Victorian town house north of the New Town offers simple, traditionally decorated rooms. Framed prints of old Edinburgh scenes adorn the walls. The owner, Liz Fulton, has a wealth of knowledge about what to see and do in Edinburgh. ✉ *56 Pilrig St., Pilrig EH6 5AS* ☎ *0131/554–5162* ⊕ *www. conifersguesthouse.com* ⬧ *4 rooms, 3 with bath* ♨ *No a/c, no smoking* ⊟ *No credit cards* ⟦◉⟧ *BP.*

Nightlife & the Arts

Nightlife

COCKTAIL BARS The **Opal Lounge** (✉ 51A George St., New Town ☎ 0131/226–2275), a casual but stylish nightspot, evolves by a subtle change of mood and lighting from a restaurant to a club for drinks and dancing to soul or funk. **Tonic** (✉ 34A Castle St., off George St., New Town ☎ 0131/225– 6431) draws a mixed crowd in the 20–40 age group with lively music, snacks, and tapas. This stylish basement bar is done in pale wood and chrome, with bouncy bar stools and comfy sofas.

DISCOS/ **Club Massa** (✉ 36–39 Market St., Old Town ☎ 0131/226–4224) has
NIGHTCLUBS theme nights covering the full spectrum of musical sounds; this well-liked spot is open Wednesday through Sunday. **Po Na Na Souk Bar**

(✉ 43B Frederick St., New Town ☎ 0131/226–2224), a North African–theme dance club, is laid-back yet very slick. It often gets crowded on weekend nights. **The Venue** (✉ 15–21 Calton Rd., Old Town ☎ 0131/557–3073) blares all forms of live and DJ music.

PUBS **Deacon Brodie's Pub** (✉ 435 Lawnmarket, Old Town ☎ 0131/225–6531), named for the infamous criminal who may have inspired Robert Louis Stevenson's *Strange Case of Dr. Jekyll and Mr. Hyde,* is a good spot for a traditional pub meal or a pint. **Guildford Arms** (✉ 1 W. Register St., east end of Princes St., New Town ☎ 0131/556–4312) merits a visit for its interior alone: ornate plasterwork, cornices, friezes, and wood paneling form the backdrop for some excellent draft ales. **Milne's Bar** (✉ 35 Hanover St., New Town ☎ 0131/225–6738), with its Victorian advertisements and photos of old Edinburgh, is known as the poets' pub because of its popularity with the Edinburgh literati. Pies and baked potatoes go well with seven real ales.

The Arts

CONCERT & The **Festival Theatre** (✉ 29 Nicolson St., Old Town ☎ 0131/529–6000)
PERFORMANCE hosts performances by the Scottish Ballet and Scottish Opera. The **Play-**
HALLS **house** (✉ Greenside Pl., East End ☎ 0870/606–3424) leans toward popular artists and musicals. The **Queen's Hall** (✉ Clerk St., Old Town ☎ 0131/668–2019) is intimate in scale and hosts smaller recitals. **Usher Hall** (✉ Lothian Rd., West End ☎ 0131/228–1155) is the city's grandest venue, and international performers and orchestras, including the Royal Scottish National Orchestra, perform here.

FESTIVALS The flagship arts event in the city, the **Edinburgh International Festival** (August 15–September 4, 2004) attracts performing artists of international caliber in a great celebration of music, dance, and drama. Advance information, programs, tickets, and reservations are available from the Edinburgh Festival Centre, an impressive Victorian Gothic church renovated and renamed the Hub. ✉ *Castlehill, Old Town, EH1 2NE* ☎ *0131/473–2020 information; 0131/473–2000 tickets* 🖷 *0131/473–2003* ⊕ *www.eif.co.uk.*

The **Edinburgh Festival Fringe** (August 8–30, 2004) presents a huge assortment of theatrical and musical events, some by amateur groups (you have been warned), and it's much more of a grab bag than the official festival. The festival runs for three or four weeks in August and September during the Edinburgh International Festival. ✉ *180 High St., Old Town, EH1 1QS* ☎ *0131/226–0026* 🖷 *0131/226–0016* ⊕ *www. edfringe.com.*

The **Edinburgh International Film Festival** (August 12–23, 2004) is part of the city's summer festival logjam. Advance information, tickets, and programs are available from the Film Festival Office. ✉ *88 Lothian Rd., West End, EH3 9BZ* ☎ *0131/228–4051* 🖷 *0131/229–5501* ⊕ *www. edfilmfest.org.uk.*

The **Edinburgh Military Tattoo** (August 6–28, 2004) might not be art, but it is entertainment. It's sometimes confused with the Edinburgh International Festival itself, partly because the dates overlap. This great celebration of martial music and skills takes place on the castle esplanade, and the dramatic backdrop augments the spectacle. Dress warmly for the late-evening performances. Even if it rains, the show goes on. Tickets and information are available from Edinburgh Military Tattoo Office. ✉ *32 Market St., Old Town, EH1 1QB* ☎ *0131/225–1188 or 08707/ 555–1188* 🖷 *0131/225–8627* ⊕ *www.edintattoo.co.uk.*

The Caledonian Brewery (⊠ 42 Slateford Rd., Dalry ☎ 0131/623–8066) is one place for traditional, foot-stomping Scottish musical evenings. The brewery organizes about three *ceilidhs* (a mix of country dancing, music, and song; pronounced *kay*-lees) per month, with loads of space and plenty of beer. The well-established **Jamie's Scottish Evening** (⊠ Edinburgh Thistle Hotel, Leith St., New Town ☎ 0131/556–0111) is a popular evening of traditional entertainment.

The **Festival Theatre** (⊠ 13–29 Nicolson St., Old Town ☎ 0131/529–6000) stages operas, ballet, concerts, and occasional tours. The **King's Theatre** (⊠ 2 Leven St., Tollcross ☎ 0131/529–6000) presents comedy, musicals, and drama, as well as Christmas pantomime. The **Royal Lyceum Theatre** (⊠ Grindlay St., West End ☎ 0131/248–4848) offers contemporary and traditional drama. The **Traverse Theatre** (⊠ 10 Cambridge St., West End ☎ 0131/228–1404), specializes in staging plays by contemporary Scottish writers.

Sports & the Outdoors

Golf

Edinburgh is well endowed with courses, with 20 or so near downtown (even before the nearby East Lothian courses are considered). **Braids** (⊠ Braids Hill Rd., Braidburn ☎ 0131/447–6666), 3 mi south of the city, welcomes visitors. **Bruntsfield Links** (⊠ 32 Barnton Ave., Davidson's Mains, ☎ 0131/336–4050), 2 mi northwest of the city, permits visitors to play on weekdays by appointment. **Duddingston** (⊠ Duddingston Rd. W, Duddingston ☎ 0131/661-7688) is a scenic golf club, with a creek acting as a hazard. It's 2 mi from the Edinburgh city center; visitors can play on weekdays by appointment. The **Gullane Golf Club** (⊠ Main St., Gullane ☎ 01620/843115), about 20 mi east of Edinburgh on A198, has three exceptional courses, all 18 holes. It also has a 6-hole children's course. The excellent **Luffness New** (⊠ A198, Gullane ☎ 01620/843114) golf course is open to the public weekdays by advance booking.

Jogging

The most convenient spot downtown for joggers is **West Princes Street Gardens,** which is separated from traffic by a 30-foot embankment. It has a half-mile loop on asphalt paths. In **Holyrood Park,** stick to jogging on the road around the volcanic mountain for a 2¼-mi trip. For a real challenge, charge up to the summit of Arthur's Seat, or to the halfway point, the Cat's Nick.

Shopping

Edinburgh shops carry a cross section of Scottish specialties, such as tartans and tweeds. Antiques shops open and close rapidly, so concentrate on areas with a number of stores, such as Bruntsfield Place, Causewayside, or St. Stephen Street.

Princes Street in the New Town, despite its renown as a shopping street, may disappoint some visitors with its dull, anonymous modern architecture, average chain stores, and fast-food outlets. It is, however, one of the best spots to shop for tartans, tweeds, and knitwear, especially if your time is limited.

Edinburgh Crystal (⊠ Eastfield, Penicuik ☎ 01968/675128), south of the city, makes fine glassware stocked by many large stores in the city, but you can also visit its premises, which include shops with seconds and discontinued lines. At **Edinburgh Old Town Weaving Company** (⊠ 555 Castlehill, Old Town ☎ 0131/226–1555), you can chat with and buy from cloth and tapestry weavers as they work. **Geoffrey (Tailor) Highland**

Crafts, (✉ 59 High St., Old Town ☎ 0131/557–0256) can clothe you in full Highland dress, with kilts made in its own workshops. **Jenners** (✉ 48 Princes St., New Town ☎ 0131/225–2442) is Edinburgh's "mini-Harrods," an independent and top-quality department store.

George Street

George Waterston (✉ 52 George St., New Town ☎ 0131/225–5690) carries stationery and Scottish gifts. **Hamilton and Inches** (✉ 87 George St., New Town ☎ 0131/225–4898), established in 1866, is a silver- and gold-smith, worth visiting not only for its modern and antique gift possibilities, but also for its late-Georgian interior. **Joseph Bonnar** (✉ 72 Thistle St., Old Town ☎ 0131/226–2811), tucked behind George Street, specializes in antique jewelry. The bookstore **Waterstone's** (✉ 83 George St., New Town ☎ 0131/225–3436) carries a good selection of Scottish titles and has a café.

Victoria Street/West Bow/Grassmarket

You'll find a number of specialty stores where these three streets run together. **Bill Baber** (✉ 66 Grassmarket, Old Town ☎ 0131/225–3249) is one of the most imaginative of the many Scottish knitwear designers. **Clarksons** (✉ 87 West Bow, Old Town ☎ 0131/225–8141) sells hand-crafted jewelry, including unique Celtic designs.

Side Trip to St. Andrews

28 *42 mi northeast of Edinburgh.*

It may have a ruined cathedral, ancient castle, and the grand St. Andrews University—the oldest in Scotland—but the modern fame of St. Andrews is mainly as the home of golf. Forget that Scottish kings were crowned here, or that John Knox preached, or Reformation reformers were burned at the stake. Thousands come to St. Andrews to play at the Old Course, home of the Royal & Ancient Club, and to follow in the footsteps of Walter Hagen, Gene Sarazen, Bobby Jones, and Ben Hogan.

On the Royal & Ancient's course, golf was perhaps originally played with a piece of driftwood, a shore pebble, and a convenient rabbit hole on the sandy, coastal turf. It has been argued that golf came to Scotland from Holland, but the historical evidence points to Scotland being the cradle, if not the birthplace, of the game. Citizens of St. Andrews were playing golf on the town links (public land) as far back as the 15th century. Rich golfers, instead of gathering on the common links, formed themselves into clubs by the 18th century. Arguably, the world's first golf club was the Honourable Company of Edinburgh golfers (founded in Leith in 1744), which is now at Muirfield in East Lothian. The Society of St. Andrews Golfers, founded in 1754, became the Royal & Ancient Golf Club of St. Andrews in 1834. The **British Golf Museum** traces the history of British golf from its origins to the golfing personalities of today. ✉ *Bruce Embankment* ☎ *01334/460046* ⊕ *www.britishgolfmuseum.co.uk* 🎟 *£4* ⊙ *Apr.–mid-Oct., daily 9:30–5:30; mid-Oct.–Mar., Thurs.–Mon. 11–3; call ahead to check winter hrs.*

St. Andrew's Cathedral, near St. Rule's Tower (all that is left of an earlier cathedral), is today only a ruined fragment of what was formerly the largest church in Scotland. Work on the building began in 1160; the cathedral fell into decay in the 16th century, during the Reformation. The on-site museum helps you interpret the remains. ✉ *Off Pends Rd.* ☎ *01334/472563* ⊕ *www.historic-scotland.gov.uk* 🎟 *£2.20, cathedral and St. Andrews Castle £4* ⊙ *Apr.–Sept., daily 9:30–6:30; Oct.–Mar., daily 9:30–4:30.*

Construction of **St. Andrews Castle,** once the home of the archbishops of St. Andrews, began at the end of the 13th century. The remains include a rare example of a gruesome bottle dungeon—a windowless, bottle-shape pit. The visitor center has a good audiovisual presentation on the castle's history. ✉ *End of N. Castle St.* ☎ *01334/477196* ⊕ *www.historic-scotland.gov.uk* ✍ *£2.80, castle and St. Andrews Cathedral £4* ☉ *Apr.–Sept., daily 9:30–6:30; Oct.–Mar., daily 9:30–4:30.*

Where to Stay & Eat

££–£££ ✕ **Balaka.** At this Bangladeshi eatery with crisp white tablecloths and vases of roses, the Rouf family displays its exceptional cookery skills. Popular dishes include *Mas Bangla* (marinated Scottish salmon fried in mustard oil with garlic, spring onion, and eggplant) and chicken with green herbs, including fresh coriander from the garden. ✉ *Alexandra Pl.* ☎ *01334/474825* ▤ *AE, MC, V* ☉ *No lunch Sun.*

£££££ ✕▣ **Rufflets Country House Hotel.** Ten acres of formal and informal gardens surround this luxurious, creeper-covered hotel just outside St. Andrews. Some rooms are modern in style, whereas others lean toward the traditional. The roomy Garden Restaurant (fixed-price menu) is famous for its use of local produce to create memorable Scottish dishes such as char-grilled fillet of trout with leeks and tarragon butter sauce, or Rannoch venison with a raspberry tea syrup glaze. ✉ *Strathkinness Low Rd., KY16 9TX* ☎ *01334/472594* ▤ *01334/478703* ⊕ *www.rufflets.co.uk* ➾ *24 rooms* ⚑ *Restaurant, some in-room hot tubs, some minibars, cable TV, bar, no-smoking rooms* ▤ *AE, DC, MC, V* ¶⦿ *BP.*

££ ▣ **Aslar Guest House.** This Victorian terraced house stands close to shops, golf courses, and historic attractions such as the castle. All the rooms are large and individually decorated with striped or pattern wallpaper and quality furnishings. One room has a four-poster bed, another a fireplace. ✉ *120 North St., KY16 9AF* ☎ *01334/473460* ▤ *01334/477540* ⊕ *www.aslar.com* ➾ *5 rooms* ⚑ *No a/c, no room phones* ▤ *MC, V* ¶⦿ *BP.*

Sports

The **St. Andrews Links** (✉ Reservations Department, St. Andrews Links Trust, Pilmour House, St. Andrews, Fife KY16 9SF ☎ 01334/466666 for reservations ⊕ www.standrews.org.uk) has six superb seaside courses, all of which welcome visitors and keep waiting lists as needed. The Old Course, New Course, Jubilee, Eden, and Strathtyrum have 18 holes; the Balgove Course has 9 holes. Greens fees range from £72 to £105 for a round on the Old Course and from £7 to £50 for a round on the other courses.

GLASGOW

▶ In 1727 Daniel Defoe, author of *Robinson Crusoe*, described Glasgow as the "cleanest and beautifullest and best-built of cities," but by 1980, many would not have recognized Scotland's largest city from that description. Stretching along both banks of the River Clyde, Glasgow was known as a depressed industrial city, and in the mid-20th century, its dockland and riverside slums were infamous. Today, however, Glasgow has undergone a full-fledged urban renaissance: trendy downtown stores, a booming and diverse cultural life, stylish restaurants, and above all, a general air of confidence, have given grace and élan to Scotland's most exciting city and its major business destination. If Edinburgh is proud, age-of-elegance, and reserved, Glasgow is aggressive, industrial-revolution, and exuberant.

The city's development over the past two centuries has been unashamedly commercial, tied up with the wealth of its manufacturers and merchants, who constructed a vast number of civic buildings throughout the 19th century. Many of these have been preserved, and Glasgow claims, with some justification, to be Britain's greatest Victorian city. Among those who helped shape Glasgow's unique cityscape during its greatest period of civic expansion was the local-born architect Alexander "Greek" Thomson (1817–75). But Glasgow, always at the forefront of change, has, side by side with the overly Victorian, an architectural vision of the future in the work of Charles Rennie Mackintosh (1868–1928). The amazing Glasgow School of Art, the Willow Tearoom, and the churches and school buildings he designed for Glasgow point clearly to the clarity and simplicity of the best of 20th-century design. Glasgow is 70 km (44 mi) west of Edinburgh; the journey takes an hour by car on the fast M8/A8 road, or 50 minutes by train.

Medieval Glasgow & the Merchant City

Alongside the relatively few surviving medieval buildings in this central part of the city are some of the best examples of the architectural confidence and exuberance that so characterized the burgeoning Glasgow of the late 19th century. Today this area is experiencing a renaissance.

a good walk

George Square 29 ☞, the center of Glasgow's business district, is the natural starting point for any walking tour. It's convenient to the Buchanan Street bus and underground stations and parking lot, as well as the two main railway stations, Queen Street and Glasgow Central. After viewing the **City Chambers** 30 on the east side of the square, leave George Square by the northeast corner and head eastward along George Street. Turn left at High Street, the spine of the downtown area before Glasgow expanded westward in the 18th century; then go up the hill to **Glasgow Cathedral** 31 and the **St. Mungo Museum of Religious Life and Art** 32. Opposite the cathedral, across Castle Street, is **Provand's Lordship** 33, Glasgow's oldest house. Retrace your steps down Castle Street and High Street, continuing on to reach the Tolbooth Steeple at **Glasgow Cross** 34. Continue southeast along London Road (under the bridge) about a quarter of a mile and you'll come to the Barras (barrows, or pushcarts), Scotland's largest and most colorful market (weekends only). Turn down Greendyke Street from London Road to reach Glasgow Green, Glasgow's oldest park, by the River Clyde, with the **People's Palace** 35 museum of social history as its centerpiece.

Take the walkway west through the Green to the towering McLennan Arch, then via Saltmarket northward to Glasgow Cross. Continue westward along Trongate, where the powerful "tobacco lords" who traded with the Americas presided, then turn right into Hutcheson Street. This is Glasgow's Merchant City, with many handsome restored Georgian and Victorian buildings. At the end of the street, just south of George Square, look for **Hutchesons' Hall** 36, a visitor center and shop for the National Trust for Scotland. Turn west onto Ingram Street and left down Glassford Street to see the Trades House on the right, which has a facade built in 1791 to designs by Robert Adam. Turn right along Wilson Street to reach Virginia Street. Walk northward up Virginia Street back to Ingram Street. To the left you'll have a good view down to the elegant Royal Exchange Square and the former Royal Exchange building. Once a meeting place for merchants and traders, it is now the **Glasgow Gallery of Modern Art** 37. Royal Exchange Square leads, for pedestrians, westward to the pedestrian-zone shopping area of Buchanan Street. To the west of Buchanan Street is **The Lighthouse** 38, dedicated to the work of Charles Rennie Mackintosh. From Buchanan Street continue north across St. Vincent Street to reach Nelson Mandela Place. Here is the Scottish Stock Exchange, worthwhile for its ornate French Venetian–style exterior alone. Buchanan Galleries, a shopping mall, dominates the top of Buchanan Street beside the Glasgow Royal Concert Hall and Sauchiehall Street junction, anchored by a branch of John Lewis department store. For an art-filled finale, a short walk along Sauchiehall Street brings you to the **Willow Tearoom** 39, an art nouveau gem designed by Mackintosh; then head over one block to Renfrew Street to see Mackintosh's masterpiece, the **Glasgow School of Art** 40. A stop at the **Tenement House** 41, a few blocks to the north of Scott Street, shows the simpler side of city life.

TIMING This walk can be accomplished comfortably in a day, which will allow time to browse in Glasgow Cathedral, the People's Palace and the Glasgow Gallery of Modern Art. Aim to start after the end of the morning rush hour, say at 10, and to finish before the evening rush starts, at about 4. The Mackintosh sites—the Willow Tearoom and the Glasgow School of Art—are a coda to this walk. The Willow Tearoom closes at 4:30 PM, and the City Chambers is open only on weekdays.

What to See

★ 30 **City Chambers.** Dominating the east side of George Square, the home of the city government is a splendidly exuberant expression of Victorian confidence. Among the outstanding features of the late-19th-century interior are the vaulted ceiling of the entrance hall, the magnificent banqueting hall, the marble and alabaster staircases, and the Venetian mosaics. ✉ *George Sq., City Center* ☎ *0141/287–2000* 🌐 *www.glasgow.gov.uk* ⏲ *Weekdays 9–4:30; free guided tours weekdays at 10:30 and 2:30; may close for occasional civic functions.*

⚑ 29 **George Square.** This is the focal point of Glasgow's business district; the area just south of the square is termed the Merchant City. An impressive collection of statues of worthies such as Queen Victoria and Sir Walter Scott fills the square. On the east side of the square stands the magnificent Italian Renaissance–style **City Chambers,** and the handsome **Merchants' House** of 1874 fills the northwest corner.

31 **Glasgow Cathedral.** On a site sacred since St. Mungo (later known as St. Kentigern) founded a church here in the 6th century, the cathedral is an unusual double church, one above the other. The lower church contains the splendid crypt of St. Mungo. ✉ *Cathedral St., City Center* ☎ *0141/552–6891* 🌐 *www.glasgowcathedral.org.uk* 🎫 *Free* ⏲ *Apr.–Sept., Mon.–Sat. 9:30–6, Sun. 1–5; Oct.–Mar., Mon.–Sat. 9:30–4, Sun. 1–4 and for services.*

34 **Glasgow Cross.** This was the historic commercial center of the medieval city. The market cross, topped by a unicorn, marks the spot where merchants met, where the market was held, and where criminals were executed. Here, too, was the *tron,* or weigh beam, installed in 1491 and used to check merchants' weights. The Tolbooth Steeple dates from 1626 and served as the civic center and place where travelers entering the city paid their tolls. ✉ *Intersection of Saltmarket, Trongate, Gallowgate, and London Rd., City Center.*

need a break?

Café Cossachok (✉ 10 King St., Glasgow Cross ☎ 0141/553–0733), a colorful Russian café, serves excellent borscht and about 25 kinds of heartwarming vodka. The deep-red walls are peppered with artworks, and the low buzz of conversation keeps the place lively.

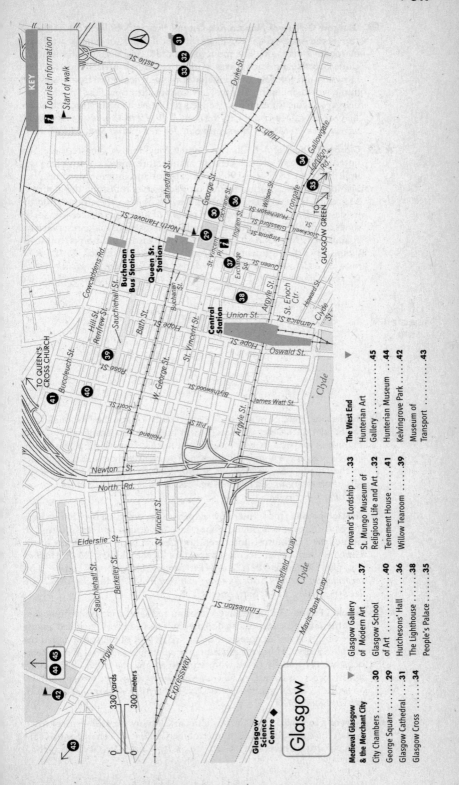

KEY

ℹ️ Tourist information

▲ Start of walk

Glasgow

Glasgow Science Centre ◆

Medieval Glasgow & the Merchant City

City Chambers **30**
George Square **29**
Glasgow Cathedral . . . **31**
Glasgow Cross **34**

Glasgow Gallery of Modern Art **37**
Glasgow School of Art **40**
Hutchesons' Hall **36**
The Lighthouse **38**
People's Palace **35**

Provand's Lordship . . . **33**
St. Mungo Museum of Religious Life and Art . . **32**
Tenement House **41**
Willow Tearoom **39**

The West End

Hunterian Art Gallery **45**
Hunterian Museum . . **44**
Kelvingrove Park **42**
Museum of Transport **43**

37 Glasgow Gallery of Modern Art. One of the city's boldest museums occupies the neoclassical Royal Exchange of 1827, originally a tobacco merchant's mansion. The modern art, craft, and design collections include Scottish figurative art, works by Scottish artists such as Peter Howson and John Bellany, and paintings and sculpture from elsewhere in the world, including Papua New Guinea, Ethiopia, and Mexico. The display scheme for each floor reflects the elements of air, fire, and water. ⊠ *Queen St., Merchant City* ☎ *0141/229–1996* ⊕ *www.glasgow.gov. uk* ⊠ *Free* ☉ *Mon.–Thurs. and Sat. 10–5, Fri. and Sun. 11–5.*

★ **40 Glasgow School of Art.** Charles Rennie Mackintosh's masterpiece, this noted monument of 20th-century architecture and decorative arts was built between 1897 and 1909. The exterior and interior, structure, furnishings, and decoration form a unified whole, reflecting the genius of Mackintosh, who was 28 years old when he won the competition for its design. Because it's a working school of art, general access is sometimes limited. Guided tours are available; it's best to make reservations. A shop sells Mackintosh gifts (prints, postcards, and books) and contemporary art by students and graduates of the art school. ⊠ *167 Renfrew St., City Center* ☎ *0141/353–4526* ⊕ *www.gsa.ac.uk* ⊠ *£5* ☉ *Tours weekdays at 11 AM and 2 PM, Sat. at 10:30 AM and 11:30 AM.*

off the
beaten
path

GLASGOW SCIENCE CENTRE – This family attraction, on the former Glasgow Garden Festival site, consists of an IMAX theater, a fun-packed Science Mall, and the Glasgow Tower, an observation point closed because of structural problems. The Science Mall focuses its state-of-the-art displays on exploration, discovery, and the environment. Leave plenty of time to make the most of it. ⊠ *50 Pacific Quay, South Side* ☎ *0141/420–5000* ⊕ *www.gsc.org.uk* ⊠ *IMAX films £5.50, Science Mall £6.50* ☉ *Daily 10–6.*

36 Hutchesons' Hall. Now a visitor center and shop for the National Trust for Scotland, this elegant neoclassical building was designed by David Hamilton in 1802. It was originally a hospice founded by two brothers, George and Thomas Hutcheson. You can see their statues in niches in the facade. ⊠ *158 Ingram St., Merchant City* ☎ *0141/552–8591* ⊕ *www.nts.org.uk* ⊠ *£2* ☉ *Mon.–Sat. 10–5 (hall may be closed for occasional functions).*

38 The Lighthouse. This former newspaper office, designed by Charles Rennie Mackintosh, is Scotland's showcase for design and architecture. It houses the Mackintosh Interpretation Centre, focusing on some of the Glasgow-born designer's most important local buildings. ⊠ *11 Mitchell La., City Center* ☎ *0141/225–8414* ⊕ *www.thelighthouse.co.uk* ⊠ *Interpretation Centre £2.50, changing exhibitions £1* ☉ *Mon. and Wed.–Sat. 10:30–5, Tues. 11–5, Sun. noon–5.*

★ **35 People's Palace.** An impressive Victorian red sandstone building houses an intriguing museum dedicated to the city's social history. Included among the exhibits is one devoted to the ordinary folk of Glasgow, called the People's Story. Behind the museum, the relatively sheltered Winter Gardens are favored by those who want to escape the often chilly winds whistling across the green. ⊠ *Glasgow Green, Glasgow Cross* ☎ *0141/ 554–0223* ⊕ *www.glasgow.gov.uk* ⊠ *Free* ☉ *Mon.–Thurs. and Sat. 10–5, Fri. and Sun. 11–5.*

33 Provand's Lordship. The oldest building in Glasgow is a 15th-century town house, built as a residence for churchmen. Mary, Queen of Scots is said to have stayed here. ⊠ *3 Castle St., City Center* ☎ *0141/553–2557*

⊕ *www.glasgow.gov.uk* ✉ *Free* ⊘ *Mon.–Thurs. and Sat. 10–5, Fri. and Sun. 11–5.*

off the beaten path

QUEEN'S CROSS CHURCH – To learn more about the innovative Glasgow-born designer Mackintosh, head for the Charles Rennie Mackintosh Society Headquarters, in a church designed by him. Although one of the leading lights in the art nouveau movement, Mackintosh died relatively unknown in 1928. You can view the church and gain further insight into Glasgow's other Mackintosh-designed buildings, which include Scotland Street School (on the South Side), the Glasgow School of Art, and reconstructed interiors in the Hunterian Art Gallery. A cab can get you here, or a bus heading toward Queen's Cross can be taken from stops along Hope Street. ✉ *870 Garscube Rd., West End* ☎ *0141/946–6600* ✉ *£2* ⊘ *Weekdays 10–5, Sun. 2–5, or by arrangement.*

㉜ St. Mungo Museum of Religious Life and Art. An outstanding collection of artifacts, including Celtic crosses and statuettes of Hindu gods, reflects the many religious groups that have settled throughout the centuries in Glasgow and the west of Scotland. The centerpiece is Salvador Dalí's magnificent painting *Christ of St. John of the Cross.* ✉ *2 Castle St., City Center* ☎ *0141/553–2557* ⊕ *www.glasgow.gov.uk* ✉ *Free* ⊘ *Mon.–Thurs. and Sat. 10–5, Fri. and Sun. 11–5.*

㊶ Tenement House. This ordinary, simple city-center apartment was occupied from 1911 to 1965 by Agnes Toward, who seems never to have thrown anything away. Her legacy is a fascinating time capsule, painstakingly preserved with her everyday furniture and belongings. The red-sandstone tenement building itself dates from 1892. ✉ *145 Buccleuch St., City Center* ☎ *0141/333–0183* ⊕ *www.nts.org.uk* ✉ *£3.50* ⊘ *Mar.–Oct., daily 2–5 (last admission 4:30).*

㊴ Willow Tearoom. Now restored to its original art deco design by Mackintosh, this tearoom is a lovely place for a break. As you sip a cup of Earl Grey, drink in all of the marvelous details, right down to the decorated tables and chairs. The tree motifs reflect the street address, as *sauchie* is an old Scots word for "willow." A block away is Mackintosh's masterpiece, the Glasgow School of Art. ✉ *217 Sauchiehall St., City Center* ☎ *0141/332–0521* ⊘ *Mon.–Sat. 9:30–4:30, Sun. noon–4:15.*

The West End

Glasgow's West End has a stellar mix of education, culture, art, and parkland. The neighborhood is dominated by the University of Glasgow, founded in 1451, making it the third-oldest university in Scotland after St. Andrews and Aberdeen, and at least 130 years ahead of the University of Edinburgh. It has thrived as a center of educational excellence, particularly in the sciences. The university buildings are set in parkland, reminding you that Glasgow has more green space per citizen than any other city in Europe.

a good walk

A good place to start is leafy **Kelvingrove Park** ㊷ ⌐, west of the M8 beltway, at the junction of Sauchiehall (pronounced *socky*-hall) and Argyle streets. The Glasgow Art Gallery and Museum here is closed for refurbishment until 2006, but the impressive red-sandstone building and its leafy surroundings still merit a visit. There are free parking facilities, and plenty of buses go to the park from downtown. Across Argyle Street next to the Kelvin Hall sports arena is the **Museum of Transport** ㊸. As you walk up the tree-lined Kelvin Way, the skyline to your left is dominated by the

Gilbert Scott building, the University of Glasgow's main edifice. Turn left up University Avenue. On either side of the road are two important galleries, both maintained by the university. On the south side of University Avenue, in the Victorian part of the university, is the **Hunterian Museum** ㊹. Even more interesting is the **Hunterian Art Gallery** ㊺, in an unremarkable 1970s building across the road.

TIMING   The distance involved is not great, but a day might not be long enough for this walk, if you want to visit the park and all three museums.

What to See

★ ㊺   **Hunterian Art Gallery.** Part of the University of Glasgow, this museum contains 18th-century Glasgow doctor William Hunter's collection of paintings (his antiquarian collection is in the Hunterian Museum nearby), together with an outstanding collection of prints and drawings by Sir Joshua Reynolds, Auguste Rodin, Rembrandt, and Jacopo Robusti Tintoretto, and a major collection of paintings by James McNeill Whistler. Also in the gallery is a reproduction of Charles Rennie Mackintosh's town house (closed 12:30–1:30), which originally stood nearby. ⊠ *Hillhead St., West End* ☎ *0141/330–5431* ⊕ *www.hunterian.gla.ac.uk* ⊡ *Free* ☉ *Mon.–Sat. 9:30–5.*

㊹   **Hunterian Museum.** The city's oldest museum (1807) and part of the University of Glasgow, the Hunterian contains part of the collections of William Hunter, an 18th-century Glasgow doctor who assembled a staggering quantity of extremely valuable material. (The doctor's art treasures are housed in the Hunterian Art Gallery nearby.) The museum displays Hunter's hoards of coins, manuscripts, scientific instruments, and archaeological artifacts in a striking Gothic building. ⊠ *Off University Ave., West End* ☎ *0141/330–4221* ⊕ *www.hunterian.gla.ac.uk* ⊡ *Free* ☉ *Mon.–Sat. 9:30–5.*

▶ ㊷   **Kelvingrove Park.** A peaceful retreat, the park takes its name from the River Kelvin, which flows through it. A castlelike red-sandstone edifice here contains the Glasgow Art Gallery and Museum, closed for renovation until 2006; the McLellan Galleries in Sauchiehall Street in the City Center and the Burrell Collection on the South Side will exhibit some of the gallery's artwork. Among the statues of prominent Glaswegians is one of Lord Kelvin (1824–1907), the Scottish mathematician and physicist who pioneered a great deal of work in electricity. The park also has a massive fountain, a duck pond, a play area, an open-air theater, and many exotic trees. ⊠ *Northwest of city center, bounded roughly by Sauchiehall St., Woodlands Rd., and Kelvin Way, West End.*

McLellan Galleries. This museum displays a superior collection of 16th- and 17th-century paintings by Dutch and Italian masters, as well as contemporary work by both Scottish and international artists, such as David Hockney and David Mach. The galleries also house a portion of the Glasgow Art Gallery and Museum's collection, including paintings by Rembrandt, Monet, and van Gogh, while the museum is closed for renovation. ⊠ *270 Sauchiehall St., City Center* ☎ *0141/331–1854* ⊡ *Free* ☉ *Mon.–Thurs. and Sat. 10–5, Fri. and Sun. 11–5.*

★ ㊸   **Museum of Transport.** Here Glasgow's history of locomotive building is dramatically displayed with full-size exhibits. The collection of Clyde-built ship models is world famous. Wallow in nostalgia at the re-created street scene from 1938, and study the many handsome Scottish automobiles, spanning the 20th century. ⊠ *Kelvin Hall, 1 Bunhouse Rd., West End* ☎ *0141/287–2720* ⊕ *www.glasgow.gov.uk* ⊡ *Free* ☉ *Mon.–Thurs. and Sat. 10–5, Fri. and Sun. 11–5.*

off the beaten path	**POLLOK PARK** – A peaceful green oasis off Paisley Road, 3 mi southwest of the city center (you can get there by taxi or car, by city bus, or by a train from Glasgow Central Station to Pollokshaws West Station), Pollok Park includes two noted sights: the Burrell Collection, one of Scotland's finest art collections, and historic Pollok House.

The artistic treasures of the Burrell Collection (⌂ 2060 Pollokshaws Rd., South Side ☎ 0141/287-2550 ⊕ www.glasgow.gov.uk ☞ Free ⊙ Mon.–Thurs. and Sat. 10–5, Fri. and Sun. 11–5) are displayed in a modern, glass-wall building so that the holdings relate to their surroundings: art and nature in perfect harmony. Inside are Chinese ceramics, bronzes, and jade as well as medieval tapestries, stained glass, and 19th-century French paintings—the magpie collection of an eccentric millionaire, Sir William Burrell. The Burrell is also hosting works from the Glasgow Art Gallery and Museum while the latter is closed for renovations.

Dating from the mid-1700s, Pollok House (⌂ Pollokshaws Rd., South Side ☎ 0141/616-6410 ⊕ www.nts.org.uk ☞ £4 Apr.–Oct., free Nov.–Mar. ⊙ Apr.–Oct., daily 10–5 and Nov.–Mar., daily 11–4) contains the Stirling Maxwell Collection of paintings, including works by El Greco, Murillo, Goya, Signorelli, and William Blake. Fine 18th- and early 19th-century furniture, silver, glass, and porcelain are also on display.

Where to Eat

Glasgow has been described as a "café society," which you will never get to know properly unless you spend time drinking coffee in as many cafés as possible. The city also has a sophisticated professional population that appreciates its many excellent restaurants.

★ **££££–£££££** ✕ **Amaryllis.** One of Glasgow's most chic restaurants, in the plush One Devonshire Gardens hotel, occupies spacious Victorian dining rooms that reinforce the splendor of the original town house. It thrives on the reputation of its owner, celebrity chef Gordon Ramsay, and a concise menu that contrasts sautéed sea bream with poached pigeon from Bresse. ⌂ 1 Devonshire Gardens, West End ☎ 0141/337-3434 ♠ Reservations essential ☰ AE, MC, V ⊙ Closed Mon. and Tues. No lunch Sat.

£££–£££££ ✕ **Rogano.** The striking black-and-gold art deco design of this restau-
FodorsChoice rant is enough to recommend it. The bonus is that the food at the
★ ground-floor main restaurant, the lively Café Rogano, and the oyster bar near the entrance is excellent. Specialties include warm salad of seared scallops with pink ginger and raspberry vinaigrette, and roast rack of lamb. Café Rogano (£–££) is cheaper and more informal than the main restaurant. ⌂ 11 Exchange Pl., City Center ☎ 0141/248-4055 ☰ AE, DC, MC, V.

★ **£££–££££** ✕ **Yes.** This stylish restaurant belies its basement location with soigné lighting, grand mirrors, and piano accompaniment. Contemporary Scottish cuisine is the specialty, and the fresh fruit sushi is exquisite. Try the Surprise Menu, an eclectic four-course selection that reflects the fresh produce available on the day. The ground-floor café-bar serves Mediterranean-Italian specialties in flashy digs. ⌂ 22 W. Nile St., City Center ☎ 0141/221-8044 ☰ AE, DC, MC, V ⊙ Closed Sun.

££–£££ ✕ **Gordon Yuill and Company.** Bright, modern surroundings reinforce this busy restaurant's fresh approach to dishes based on the best of Scottish produce. You might try the excellent seafood options, such as a steamed mussels with lemongrass starter, or the calves' liver and crispy pancetta.

Imaginative Asian-influenced vegetarian dishes round out the less expensive choices. ⊠ *257 W. Campbell St., City Center* ☎ *0141/572–4052*
△ *Reservations essential* ⊟ *AE, DC, MC, V.*

£–£££   ✕ **Mussel Inn.** Shellfish farmers own this restaurant and feed their customers incredibly fresh, succulent oysters, scallops, and mussels. The kilo
pots of mussels, beautifully steamed to order in any of a number of sauces,
are revelatory. The surroundings and staff are unpretentious yet stylish.
⊠ *61–65 Hope St., City Center* ☎ *0141/572–1405* ⊟ *AE, MC, V*
⊘ *No lunch Sun.*

Where to Stay

££££–£££££   ⬚ **One Devonshire Gardens.** A group of Victorian town houses on a sloping, tree-lined street make up this luxurious boutique hotel. Elegance is
the keynote, from the sophisticated drawing room to the sumptuous guest
rooms with their rich drapery and traditional furnishings, including four-
poster beds (in 10 rooms). The hotel restaurant is equally stylish, with
a different menu each month. Specialties include sole filled with organic
salmon and served with champagne sauce. Don't confuse the hotel
restaurant with the privately run Amaryllis restaurant on site. ⊠ *1–5
Devonshire Gardens, West End, G12 0UX* ☎ *0141/339–2001* 🖷 *0141/
337–1663* ⊕ *www.onedevonshiregardens.com* ⇆ *40 rooms* ♨ *2 restaurants, room service, cable TV, lounge, meeting room, free parking; no
a/c* ⊟ *AE, DC, MC, V* ⦿| *BP.*

★ **£££–££££**   ⬚ **Langs.** This hotel's sophisticated, ultramodern character fits perfectly
with its proximity to the Glasgow Royal Concert Hall and the Buchanan
Galleries shopping mall. The Japanese minimalist look extends from the
wooden reception bar to the platform beds in the bright bedrooms.
Mediterranean cuisine is the specialty of the Las Brisas restaurant, and
Oshi serves excellent Japanese three-course pre- and post-theater menus
for around £10. Japanese body treatments are available in the Oshi Spa.
⊠ *2 Port Dundas St., City Center, G2 3LD* ☎ *0141/333–1500* 🖷 *0141/
333–5700* ⊕ *www.langshotels.co.uk* ⇆ *70 rooms, 30 suites* ♨ *2 restaurants, cable TV, gym, spa, bar, meeting room, parking (fee); no a/c*
⊟ *AE, DC, MC, V* ⦿| *CP.*

★ **£££–££££**   ⬚ **Radisson SAS.** You can't miss this eye-catching edifice behind Central Station in Glasgow's up-and-coming financial quarter. Its glass front
makes the interior, particularly the lounge, seem as though it were part
of the street. Your room might be in Italian, Scandinavian, or Japanese
style. Both restaurants—the pop art–inspired Collage, serving Continental cuisine, and Tapaell'Ya, the tapas bar—are popular with business and artist types, as is the sleek street-level bar. ⊠ *301 Argyle St.,
City Center, G2 8DL* ☎ *0141/203–3333* 🖷 *0141/204–3344* ⊕ *www.
radissonsas.com* ⇆ *200 rooms, 4 suites* ♨ *2 restaurants, minibars, in-
door pool, gym, bar, business services, parking (fee)* ⊟ *AE, DC, V* ⦿| *CP.*

££   ⬚ **Ambassador Hotel.** Opposite the West End's peaceful Botanic Gardens
and convenient for cab, bus, and underground travel to the city center,
the Ambassador forms part of an elegant terrace of town houses on the
banks of the River Kelvin. The interior echoes the peacefulness of the
location and the Victorian ethos of the spacious former family home.
Though largely traditional, the rooms have a contemporary edge, with
rich red-and-gold fabrics and beech furniture. ⊠ *7 Kelvin Dr., West End,
G20 8QG* ☎ *0141/946–1018* 🖷 *0141/945–5377* ⊕ *www.
glasgowhotelsandapartments.co.uk* ⇆ *17 rooms* ♨ *Bar, free parking,
no-smoking rooms; no a/c* ⊟ *MC, V* ⦿| *BP.*

Fodor'sChoice
★

££   ⬚ **Kirklee Hotel.** Near the university and in the West End—a particularly quiet, leafy, and genteel district—this B&B in a cozy Edwardian
town house is replete with home-away-from-home comfort. A bay win-

dow overlooks the garden, and embroidered settees and silk-wash wallpapers adorn the Victorian morning room. Engravings and a large library are appealing touches. ✉ *11 Kensington Gate, West End, G12 9LG* ☎ *0141/334–5555* 🖷 *0141/339–3828* ✍ *kirklee@clara.net* ↩ *9 rooms* ♢ *Library; no a/c* ☰ *AE, DC, MC, V* ⦿ *BP.*

£–££ 🔲 **Travel Inn Metro.** This may be part of a chain of budget hotels, but the bright, metropolitan design and low prices appeals to savvy visitors. The rooms are larger than most in the city, with up-to-date bathrooms and coffeemakers. Rooms facing the street can be noisy at night, so ask for one that overlooks the graveyard, where noisemakers are unlikely to be found. ✉ *187 George St., Merchant City, G1 1YU* ☎ *0870/238–3320* 🖷 *0141/553–2719* ⊕ *www.travelinn.co.uk* ↩ *239 rooms* ♢ *Restaurant, bar, parking (fee), no-smoking rooms; no a/c* ☰ *AE, MC, V.*

Nightlife & the Arts

Nightlife

If you visit only one pub in Glasgow, make it the **Horseshoe Bar** (✉ 17–21 Drury St., City Center ☎ 0141/229–5711), which offers a sepia-tinted glimpse of all the friendlier Glasgow myths. Refurbishment would be a curse on its original tiling, stained glass, and deeply polished woodwork. The clientele is a complete cross section of the city's populace. The best Gaelic pub is **Uisge Beatha** (✉ 232–246 Woodlands Rd., West End ☎ 0141/564–1596), pronounced *oos*-ki *bee*-ha, which means "water of life" and is the origin of the word *whisky* (the term is a phonetic transliteration of the Gaelic word *uisge*). It serves *fraoch* (heather beer) in season and has live music on Wednesday and Sunday.

The Arts

Tickets for theatrical performances can be purchased at theater box offices or by telephone through the booking line: **Ticket Center** (☎ 0141/287–5511). **Citizens' Theatre** (✉ 119 Gorbals St., South Side ☎ 0141/429–0022), one of the most exciting theaters in Britain, stages productions of often hair-raising originality. **Cottier's Arts Theatre** (✉ 93 Hyndland St., West End ☎ 0141/357–3868) presents contemporary works in a converted church. The **King's Theatre** (✉ Bath St., City Center ☎ 0141/240–1111) focuses on light entertainment and musicals.

Glasgow Royal Concert Hall (✉ 2 Sauchiehall St., City Center ☎ 0141/353–8000) offers a calendar of classical concerts, pop concerts, jazz, and many international musical events. The Royal Scottish National Orchestra plays on many Thursdays and Saturdays throughout the year. The **Theatre Royal** (✉ Hope St., City Center ☎ 0141/332–9000) is the elegant home of Scottish Opera and Scottish Ballet.

Held in January, **Celtic Connections** (☎ 0141/353–8000 ⊕ www.celticconnections.co.uk) is Scotland's biggest Celtic music festival.

Shopping

Glasgow, preferred by many to Edinburgh as a shopping center, supplies a lot more shopping fun than its staid rival. The main shopping districts occupy a Z-shape area that runs along Sauchiehall Street from Charing Cross to the Glasgow Royal Concert Hall and Buchanan Galleries, south down Buchanan Street to St. Enoch's Square, and east along Argyle Street. Many designer boutiques and shopping malls, complete with fountains and glass-wall elevators, can be found on Buchanan Street and along adjacent streets.

The **Argyll Arcade** (✉ Buchanan and Argyle Sts., City Center) is a handsome 19th-century shopping mall with a wide selection of jewelry shops (don't miss the mosaics over the Buchanan Street entrance). The **Buchanan Galleries mall** (⊠ 220 Buchanan St., City Center ☎ 0141/333–9898) has major names such as John Lewis, Nike, and Virgin. **De Courcys** (⊠ 5–21 Cresswell La., West End), an antiques and crafts arcade, has quite a few shops to visit, and lots of goods, including paintings and jewelry, are regularly auctioned here. It's on one of the cobblestone lanes to the rear of Byres Road.

Princes Square (⊠ 48 Buchanan St., City Center ☎ 0141/204–1685) is a chic modern mall, with specialty shops on three levels and a café complex above, all under a glittering dome. You'll find many top fashion names here and also the Scottish Craft Centre for unusual, high-quality items.**Borders Books, Music and Café** (⊠ 98 Buchanan St., City Center ☎ 0141/222–7700), in a former bank, is particularly welcoming and carries many Scottish books. **MacDonald MacKay Ltd.** (⊠ 161 Hope St., City Center ☎ 0141/204–3930) makes, sells, and exports Highland dress, including kilts, and accessories for men and custom-made kilts and skirts for women. **Stockwell Bazaar** (⊠ 67–77 Glassford St., Merchant City ☎ 0141/552–5781) specializes in fine china and giftware.

The **Barras**, Glasgow's weekend market, is just north of Glasgow Green and sells just about anything, in any condition, from very old model railroads to quality jewelry at bargain prices. Haggling is compulsory. Antiques hunters might make a find, but don't be surprised if you come away empty-handed. ⊠ *London Rd., Glasgow Cross* ☎ *0141/552–4601* ☾ *Weekends 10–5.*

THE BORDERS
SIR WALTER SCOTT COUNTRY

The Borders region is the heartland of minstrelsy, ballad, and folklore, much of it arising from murky deeds of the past. This is the homeland of the tweed suit and cashmere sweater, of medieval abbeys, of the lordly River Tweed and its salmon, and of the descendants of the raiders and reivers (cattle thieves) who harried England. It's also the native soil of Sir Walter Scott, the early-19th-century poet, novelist, and creator of *Ivanhoe*, who helped transform Scotland's image from that of a land of brutal savages to one of romantic and stirring deeds and magnificent landscapes. One of the best ways to approach this district is to take as the theme of your visit the life and works of Scott. His novels are not read much nowadays, but the mystique that he created, the aura of historical romance, has outlasted his books and is much in evidence in the ruined abbeys, historical houses, and grand vistas of the Borders.

Abbotsford House

★ ㊻ *28 mi southeast of Edinburgh.*

The most visited of Scottish literary landmarks, Abbotsford House is the modest-size mansion that Sir Walter Scott made his home in the 1820s. A damp farmhouse called Clartyhole (*clarty* is Scots for "muddy" or "dirty") when the novelist bought it in 1811, it was soon transformed into what John Ruskin called "the most incongruous pile that gentlemanly modernism ever devised." The pseudo-baronial, pseudo-monastic castle chock-full of Scottish curios, Ramsay portraits, and mounted deer heads seems an appropriate domicile for a man of such an extraordinarily romantic imagination. To Abbotsford came most of the famous poets and thinkers of Scott's day, including William Wordsworth and Washington Irving. Abbotsford is still owned by Scott's descendants.

⊠ *B6360, Galashiels* ☎ *01896/752043* 🎫 *£4.20* ⊙ *June–Sept., daily 9:30–5; Mar.–May and Oct., Mon.–Sat. 9:30–5, Sun. 2–5.*

Melrose

🚳 *3 mi east of Abbotsford, 30 mi south of Edinburgh.*

Melrose is small but bustling, the perfect example of a prosperous Scottish market town, set around a square lined with 18th- and 19th-century buildings. Just off the square are the ruins of the most famous of the great Borders abbeys. All the abbeys were burned in the 1540s in a calculated act of destruction by English invaders acting on the orders of Henry VIII. Sir Walter Scott himself supervised the partial reconstruction

★ of **Melrose Abbey,** one of the most beautiful ruins in Britain. "If thou would'st view fair Melrose aright/Go visit it in the pale moonlight," says Scott in his "Lay of the Last Minstrel," and so many of his fans took the advice literally that a sleepless custodian begged him to rewrite the lines. Today the abbey is still impressive: a red-sandstone shell with slender windows in the Perpendicular Gothic style and some delicate tracery and carved capitals, carefully maintained. Among the carvings high on the roof is one of a bagpipe-playing pig. An audio tour is included in the admission price. ⊠ *Abbey St.* ☎ *01896/822562* ⊕ *www.historic-scotland.gov.uk* 🎫 *£3.50* ⊙ *Apr.–Sept., daily 9:30–6:30; Oct.–Mar., Mon.–Sat. 9:30–4:30, Sun. 2–4:30.*

The **Three Hills Heritage Centre** displays artifacts from the largest Roman settlement in Scotland, which was at nearby Newstead. Tools and weapons, a blacksmith's shop, pottery, and scale models of the fort are on display. A guided 5-mi, four-hour walk to the site takes place each Thursday afternoon (also on Tuesday in July and August). Phone for details. ⊠ *The Ormiston, Melrose Sq.* ☎ *01896/822651* ⊕ *www.trimontium.freeserve.co.uk* 🎫 *£1.50, walk £2.80* ⊙ *Apr.–Oct., weekdays 10:30–4:30, weekends 10:30–1 and 2–4:30.*

Where to Stay & Eat

£££ ✕🏨 **Burts Hotel.** This hostelry dating from the early 18th century offers period charm with modern comfort in the center of town. Bedrooms and public areas are individually decorated with reproduction antiques and floral pastels. The elegant dining room (fixed-price menu) focuses on Scottish dishes such as pheasant terrine and venison with a whisky-and-cranberry sauce. Bar food is also offered. ⊠ *Melrose Sq., TD6 9PL* ☎ *01896/822285* 🖷 *01896/822870* ⊕ *www.burtshotel.co.uk* 🛏 *20 rooms* 🅃 *Restaurant; no a/c* ▱ *AE, MC, V* ⧖ *BP.*

Dryburgh Abbey

🚳 *5 mi southeast of Melrose, 38 mi south of Edinburgh.*

The final resting place of Sir Walter Scott and his wife, and the most secluded of the Borders abbeys, Dryburgh Abbey sits on gentle parkland in a loop of the Tweed. The abbey suffered from English raids until, like Melrose, it was abandoned in 1544. The style is transitional, a mingling of rounded Romanesque and pointed Early English Gothic. The north transept, where the Haig and Scott families lie buried, is lofty and pillared, and once formed part of the abbey church. ⊠ *B6404* ☎ *01835/822381* ⊕ *www.historic-scotland.gov.uk* 🎫 *£3* ⊙ *Apr.–Sept., daily 9:30–6:30; Oct.–Mar., Mon.–Sat. 9:30–4:30, Sun. 2–4:30.*

Where to Stay & Eat

£££ ✕🏨 **Dryburgh Abbey Hotel.** Woodlands and verdant lawns surround this imposing 19th-century mansion, which stands next to the abbey ruins on a bend of the River Tweed. Guest rooms are large and sumptuous, with canopied beds and lace-trimmed curtains, and throughout the hotel you'll feel a sense of quiet and peace in keeping with the location. The restaurant specializes in traditional Scottish fare. ⊠ *Off B6404, St. Boswells, TD6 0RQ* ☎ *01835/822261* 🖷 *01835/823945* ⊕ *www. dryburgh.co.uk* ⤳ *36 rooms, 2 suites* ⚲ *Restaurant, pool, golf privileges, fishing; no a/c* ⊟ *AE, MC, V* ¶ *BP.*

en route | Combine a visit to Dryburgh Abbey with a stop at **Scott's View**, 3 mi north on B6356, which provides a magnificent panoramic view of the Tweed valley and the Eildon Hills. Legend has it that the horses pulling Scott's hearse paused automatically at Scott's View, because their master had so often halted them there.

Smailholm Tower

⑲ *5 mi east of St. Boswells, 8 mi northwest of Kelso.*

This characteristic Borders structure stands uncompromisingly on top of a barren, rocky ridge in the hills. Built solely for defense, this 16th-century peel tower offers memorable views. Sir Walter Scott's grandfather lived nearby, and the young Scott visited the tower often. The tower houses an exhibit of costumed figures and tapestries relating to Scott's Borders folk ballads. ⊠ *Off B6404, Smailholm* ☎ *0131/668–8800* ⊕ *www.historic-scotland.gov.uk* 🖷 *£2.20* ☺ *Apr.–Sept., daily 9:30–6:30.*

Kelso

⑳ *8 mi east of Smailholm Tower, 46 mi southeast of Edinburgh.*

The Tweedside roads through Kelso and Coldstream sweep with the river through parkland and game preserve and past romantic red-stone gorges. Kelso has an unusual Continental air, with fine Georgian and early-Victorian buildings surrounding a spacious, cobbled marketplace. Not much of the once grand medieval Kelso Abbey remains.

Fodor'sChoice
★

On the bank of the River Tweed, just on the outskirts of Kelso, is palatial **Floors Castle**, the largest inhabited house in Scotland and the seat of the duke of Roxburghe. Designed by William Adam in 1721 and altered by William Playfair in the 1840s, Floors is an architectural extravagance bristling with pepper-mill turrets and towers that stand on the "floors" or flat terraces of the Tweed bank opposite the barely visible ruins of Roxburghe Castle. A holly tree in the magnificent deer park marks the place where King James II was killed in 1460 by a cannon that "brak in the shooting." ⊠ *A6089* ☎ *01573/223333* 🖷 *01573/226056* ⊕ *www. floorcastle.com* 🖷 *£5.75, grounds only £3* ☺ *Apr.–Oct., daily 10–4:30; last admission at 4.*

Where to Stay & Eat

££–£££ ✕🖫 **Edenwater House.** A handsome stone house, this antique-filled former manse overlooks the river Eden, 2 mi north of Kelso. The luxurious guest rooms have views of the river and two of the Cheviot Hills. Edenwater serves some of the best food in the Borders: roast saddle of hare with foie gras and fillet of monkfish crusted with basil and coriander in a beurre blanc typify the refined but simple menu. The dining room (£30 for a three-course dinner) is open to nonresidents on Friday and Saturday. ⊠ *Off B6461, Ednam, TD5 7QL,* ☎ *01573/224070* 🖷 *01573/ 226615* ⊕ *www.edenwaterhouse.co.uk* ⤳ *4 rooms* ⚲ *Restaurant, fishing, lounge, Internet; no a/c, no room phones* ⊟ *MC, V* ☺ *Closed 1st 2 wks Jan.* ¶ *BP.*

★ **£££–££££** ⊡ **Ednam House Hotel.** People return again and again to this large, stately hotel on the banks of the Tweed, close to Kelso's grand abbey and old Market Square. The main hall, part of the original 1761 home, welcomes you with deep-seated armchairs, paintings, and an open fire. The restaurant's three windowed walls overlook the garden and river. ⊠ *Bridge St., TD5 7HT* ☎ *01573/224168* 🖷 *01573/226319* ⊕ *www.ednamhouse. com* 🛏 *32 rooms* 🛆 *Restaurant, golf privileges, fishing, horseback riding; no a/c* ☐ *MC, V* ☉ *Closed Dec. 25–early Jan.* ⊓◎⊦ *BP.*

Jedburgh

㊿ *12 mi southwest of Kelso on A698, 50 mi south of Edinburgh.*

The town of Jedburgh (-*burgh* is always pronounced *burra* in Scots), 13 mi north of the border, was for centuries the first major Scottish target of invading English armies. The large landscaped area around the town's tourist information center was once a mill but now is a stamping ground for the armies of modern visitors. The past still clings to this little town, however.

★ **Jedburgh Abbey,** the most impressive of the Borders abbeys, was nearly destroyed in 1544–45, during the destructive time known as the Rough Wooing. This was English king Henry VIII's armed attempt to persuade the Scots to unite the kingdoms by the marriage of his young son to the infant Mary, Queen of Scots; the Scots sent Mary to France instead. The **Jedburgh Abbey Visitor Centre** provides information on interpreting the ruins. ⊠ *High St.* ☎ *01835/863925* ⊕ *www.historic-scotland.gov.uk* 🎟 *£3.50* ☉ *Apr.–Sept., daily 9:30–6:30; Oct.–Mar., Mon.–Sat. 9:30–4:30, Sun. 2–4:30.*

Mary, Queen of Scots House is a fortified house characteristic of the 16th century, some say contemporaneous with Mary herself. Though historians disagree on whether or not she actually visited here, the house has many displays commemorating Mary. ⊠ *Queen St.* ☎ *01835/863331* 🎟 *£3* ☉ *Mon.–Sat. 10–4:30, Sun. 11–4:30.*

Jedburgh Castle Jail was the site of a Howard Reform Prison established in 1820. Today you can inspect prison cells, rooms arranged with period furnishings, and costumed figures. Audiovisual displays recount the history of the Royal Burgh of Jedburgh. ⊠ *Castlegate* ☎ *01835/864750* 🎟 *£1.50* ☉ *Easter–Oct., Mon.–Sat. 10–4:30, Sun. 1–4.304.*

Where to Stay & Eat

★ **£–£££** ✕ **Cross Keys.** A national treasure, this traditional pub specializes in local produce, from fish to game. A splendid array of Scottish beers—real ale, as it is known here—is served. This is the quintessential village inn, right down to the green outside the front door. ⊠ *The Green, Ancrum, 3 mi north of Jedburgh, off A68* ☎ *01835/830344* ☐ *DC, MC, V.*

£–££ ⊡ **Hundalee House.** Stunning views across to the English border at Carter Bar, and to the Cheviot Hills to the southeast, add appeal to this lodging. The tastefully furnished B&B is in a 300-year-old house with 14 acres of garden and woodland. Two bedrooms have four-posters. The house is 1 mi south of Jedburgh. ⊠ *Off A68, TD8 6PA* ☎☎ *01835/ 863011* ⊕ *www.accommodation-scotland.org* 🛏 *4 rooms* 🛆 *No a/c, no room phones* ☐ *No credit cards* ☉ *Closed Nov.–Mar.* ⊓◎⊦ *BP.*

£ ⊡ **Spinney Guest House.** Made up of unpretentiously converted and modernized farm cottages, this B&B has high standards for the price. The log cabins have kitchenettes. ⊠ *Langlee, TD8 6PB* ☎ *01835/ 863525* 🖷 *01835/864883* ⊕ *www.thespinney-jedburgh.co.uk* 🛏 *3 rooms, 3 cabins* 🛆 *Some kitchenettes, lounge; no a/c, no room phones* ☐ *MC, V* ⊓◎⊦ *BP.*

Selkirk

52 *14 mi northwest of Jedburgh, 40 mi south of Edinburgh.*

Selkirk is a hilly outpost with a smattering of antiques shops and an assortment of bakers selling the Selkirk Bannock (fruited sweet bread-cake) and other cakes. Sir Walter Scott was sheriff (judge) of Selkirkshire from 1800 until his death in 1832, and his statue stands in Market Place. To get here from Jedburgh, take A68 7 mi north to the A699 junction, turn left, and follow A699 7 mi through attractive river-valley scenery. **Sir Walter Scott's Courtroom,** where he presided, contains a display examining Scott's life, his writings, and his time as sheriff. ⊠ *Market Pl.* ☎ *01750/20096* 🕮 *Free* ⊘ *Apr.–May, Mon.–Sat. 10–4; June–Sept., Mon.–Sat. 10–4, Sun. 2–4; Oct., Mon.–Sat. 1–4.*

Halliwell's House Museum, tucked off the main square in Selkirk, was once an ironmonger's shop, now re-created downstairs. The upstairs exhibit tells the story of the town. ⊠ *Market Pl.* ☎ *01750/20096* 🕮 *Free* ⊘ *Apr., May, Sept., and Oct., Mon.–Sat. 10–5, Sun. 2–4; July and Aug., Mon.–Sat. 10–6, Sun. 2–5.*

Innerleithen

53 *15 mi northwest of Selkirk, 29 mi south of Edinburgh.*

Innerleithen, in the pretty Tweed Valley, was once famous as a spa, and is the setting of Scott's novel *St. Ronan's Well.* **Robert Smail's Printing Works** is a fully restored Victorian print shop with its original machinery in working order and a printer in residence. ⊠ *7–9 High St.* ☎ *01896/830206* 🕮 *£3.50* ⊘ *Mar.–June, Sept., and Oct., Mon.–Thurs. noon–5, Sun. 1–5; July and Aug., Thurs.–Mon. 10–6, Sun. 1–5; last admission 45 mins before closing.*

★ **Traquair House** is said to be the oldest continually occupied house (since 1107) in Scotland. Secret stairs, intricate embroidery, more than 3,000 books, a maze, and a bed used by Mary, Queen of Scots in 1566 are just a few of the discoveries. Ale is still brewed in the 18th-century brew house here, and it's worth a try. The house is 1 mi south of Innerleithen. ⊠ *B709, Traquair* ☎ *01896/830323* 🖷 *01896/830639* ⊕ *www.traquair.co.uk* 🕮 *£5.60* ⊘ *Easter–May, daily 12:30–5; June–Aug., daily 10:30–5:30; Oct., daily 11–4; last admission 30 mins before closing.*

Where to Stay

££££ 🏠 **Traquair House.** Stay in the private quarters at Traquair to experience a slice of Scottish history. The sumptuously decorated rooms are furnished with antiques and chintz-hung canopy beds. In the 18th-century Lower Drawing Room, you can enjoy a glass of the house's own ale before going to dinner. ⊠ *B709, Traquair, EH44 6PW* ☎ *01896/830323* 🖷 *01896/830639* ⊕ *www.traquair.co.uk* 🖂 *3 rooms* ⚭ *No a/c* ▤ *MC, V* ❙❙ *BP.*

Peebles

54 *7 mi west of Traquair on A72, 24 mi south of Edinburgh.*

This pleasant town on the banks of the Tweed lies in lush, green countryside, with hills deeply cleft by gorges and waterfalls. Thanks to its excellent though pricey shopping, the town gives the impression of catering primarily to country gentlefolk. Don't miss the splendid dolphins ornamenting the bridge crossing the River Tweed.

Neidpath Castle, a 15-minute walk upstream along the banks of the Tweed from Peebles, perches above a bend in the river. The castle is a medieval structure remodeled in the 17th century, with dungeons hewn from solid rock. You can return on the opposite riverbank after crossing an old railroad viaduct. ⊠ *Off A72* ☎ *01721/720333* ⊿ *£3* ⊘ *Easter wk and mid-June–early Sept., Mon.–Sat. 10:30–4:30, Sun. 12:30–4:30.*

Where to Stay & Eat

£££–£££££ ✕⊡ **Cringletie House Hotel.** A Scottish baronial mansion set amid 28 acres of gardens and woodland, Cringletie has a long tradition of pampering guests with friendly, personalized service. Public areas and guest rooms are done in British country-house style. The first-floor drawing room, with views extending up the valley, is particularly restful. Fruit and vegetables from the hotel's kitchen garden accompany refined modern Scottish fare. Afternoon tea in the conservatory is a treat. ⊠ *Edinburgh Rd., off A703, EH45 8PL* ☎ *01721/730233* ⊠ *01721/730244* ⊕ *www.cringletie.com* ⇆ *14 rooms* ⌂ *Restaurant, putting green, tennis court, fishing, croquet; no a/c* ⊟ *AE, MC, V* |⊙| *BP.*

ABERDEEN & ROYAL DEESIDE

Aberdeen, Scotland's third-largest city, is the gateway to a rural hinterland with a wealth of castles. Deeside, the valley running west from Aberdeen along which the River Dee flows, earned its "Royal" appellation when Queen Victoria and her consort, Albert, built their Scottish fantasy castle, Balmoral, here. To this day, where royalty goes, lesser aristocracy and millionaires from around the globe follow. Their yearning to possess an estate here is understandable, since birch woodland, purple moor, and blue river intermingle most tastefully.

Aberdeen

▶ ➄ *131 mi north of Edinburgh.*

Local granite quarrying produced a durable silver stone that would be used to build the Aberdonian structures of the Victorian era. The granite was used boldly, and downtown Aberdeen remains one of the United Kingdom's most distinctive urban environments, although some would say it depends on the weather. The mica chips embedded in the rock act as a million mirrors in sunshine; in rain and heavy clouds, however, their sparkle is snuffed out.

The North Sea has always been important to Aberdeen: in the 1850s, the city was famed for its fast clippers, sleek sailing ships that raced to India for cargoes of tea. In the late 1960s, the course of Aberdeen's history was unequivocally altered when oil and gas were discovered in the North Sea. Aberdeen at first seemed destined to become a soulless boomtown, but some innate local caution has helped the now-wealthy city to retain a sense of perspective.

★ **Marischal College** was founded in 1593 by the earl Marischal as a Protestant alternative to the Catholic King's College in Old Aberdeen, though the two combined to form Aberdeen University in 1860. The current facade was built in 1891, and this is still the second-largest granite building in the world; only the Escorial in Madrid is larger. The fascinating main galleries of the **Marischal Museum** hold two exhibits: the Encyclopaedia of the North East displays artifacts and photographs relating to the region's heritage; Collecting the World explores the role of local collectors on their world travels and displays Egyptian and 19th-century

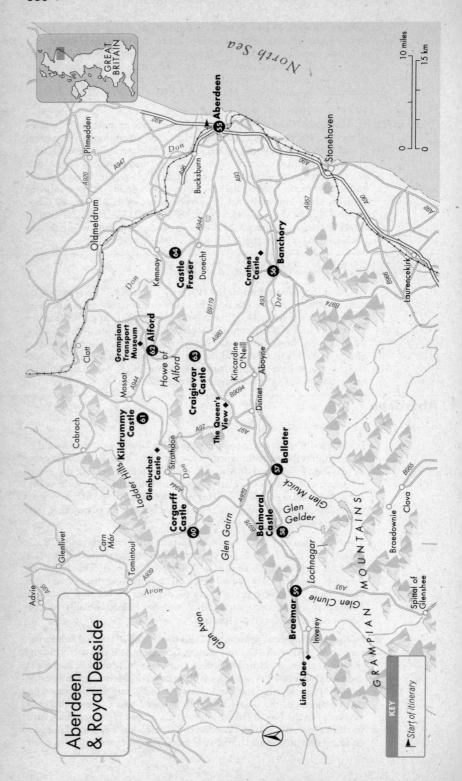

Aberdeen
& Royal Deeside

GREAT
BRITAIN

North Sea

10 miles
15 km

Aberdeen **55**

Stonehaven

Pitmedden

A920

A947

Don

Bucksburn

A96

A93

A90

A957

Oldmeldrum

A944

Castle **64**
Fraser

Dunecht

Crathes **56**
Castle

Banchory

B996

Laurencekirk

A92

B974

Kemnay

Don

B9119

A93

Dee

Clatt

Grampian
Transport
Museum

Alford **62**

Howe of
Alford

A980

Kincardine
O'Neill

Aboyne

A93

Mossat

A944

Craigievar **63**
Castle

B9094

Dinnet

Cabrach

Kildrummy **61**
Castle

A97

The Queen's
View

A97

Ballater **57**

Glen Muick

B955

Clova

Strathdon

Glenbuchat
Castle

Don

Corgarff **60**
Castle

A939

Ladder Hills

A939

Glen Gairn

A93

Balmoral **58**
Castle

B976

Glen
Gelder

Braedownie

Glenlivet

A95

Carn
Mór

Tomintoul

Avon

Lochnagar

GRAMPIAN MOUNTAINS

Advie

A95

Glen
Avon

Avon

Braemar **59**

Inverey

Glen Clunie

A93

Spittal of
Glenshee

Linn of Dee

KEY

▶ Start of itinerary

ethnographic material. ⊠ *Broad St.* ☎ *01224/274301* ⊕ *www.abdn.ac. uk* ✉ *Free* ⊗ *Museum weekdays 10–5, Sun. 2–5.*

Provost Skene's House, now a museum portraying civic life, has restored, furnished period rooms and a painted chapel. Steeply gabled and rubble-built, it dates in part from 1545. The house was originally a mayor's domestic dwelling (provost is Scottish for "mayor"). ⊠ *Guestrow off Broad St.* ☎ *01224/641086* ⊕ *www.aagm.co.uk* ✉ *Free* ⊗ *Mon.–Sat. 10–5, Sun. 1–4.*

Aberdeen Art Gallery houses a diverse collection of paintings, prints and drawings, sculpture, porcelain, costumes, and much else—from 18th-century art to contemporary works. ⊠ *Schoolhill* ☎ *01224/523700* ⊕ *www.aagm.co.uk* ✉ *Free* ⊗ *Mon.–Sat. 10–5, Sun. 2–5.*

A library, church, and nearby theater on **Rosemount Viaduct** are collectively known by all Aberdonians as Education, Salvation, and Damnation. Silvery and handsome, the **Central Library** and **St. Mark's Church** date from the last decade of the 19th century, and **His Majesty's Theatre** (1904–08) has been restored inside to its full Edwardian splendor.

★ ☾ **Provost Ross's House,** dating from 1593, with a striking modern extension, houses the excellent **Aberdeen Maritime Museum,** which tells the story of the city's involvement with the sea, from early inshore fisheries to tea clippers and the North Sea oil boom. It's a fascinating place for kids, with its ship models, paintings, and equipment associated with the fishing, local shipbuilding, and the oil and gas industries. ⊠ *Ship Row* ☎ *01224/337701* ⊕ *www.aagm.co.uk* ✉ *Free* ⊗ *Mon.–Sat. 10–5, Sun. noon–3.*

Old Aberdeen, once an independent burgh, lies to the north of the city, near the River Don. Although swallowed up by the expanding main city before the end of the 19th century, the area, which lies between **King's College** and **St. Machar's Cathedral,** still retains a certain degree of individual character and integrity. Reach it by taking a bus north from a stop near Marischal College or up King Street, off Castlegate.

King's College (⊠ High St. ⊕ www.abdn.ac.uk), founded in 1494 and now part of the University of Aberdeen, has an unmistakable flying (or crown) spire to its **chapel,** which was built around 1500. The tall oak screen that separates nave from choir and the ribbed wooden ceiling and stalls constitute the finest medieval wood carvings in Scotland.

At the **King's College Centre** you can find out more about one of Britain's oldest universities. ⊠ *College Bounds* ☎ *01224/273702* ⊕ *www.abdn. ac.uk/kcc* ⊗ *Weekdays 9:30–5, Sat. 11–4.*

Where to Stay & Eat

The Northeast is the land of Arbroath "smokies" (smoked haddock) and Cullen skink. With rich pastures supporting the famous Aberdeen-Angus beef cattle, high-quality viands are also guaranteed.

★ **££££** ✕ **Silver Darling.** This quayside restaurant is one of Aberdeen's most acclaimed. It specializes, as the name suggests (a silver darling is a herring), in fish. The cooking style is French provincial, and the grilled fish and shellfish are particularly flavorful. ⊠ *Pocra Quay, Footdee* ☎ *01224/ 576229* ⚑ *Reservations essential* ▭ *AE, DC, MC, V* ⊗ *Closed Sun. No lunch Sat.*

£–££ ✕ **Lascala Ristorante.** Blue-and-red furnishings, sparkling chandeliers, and plants everywhere set the scene for classic Italian cuisine. Veal and fish are prominent on the menu, and daily specials make the most of fresh produce. ⊠ *51 Huntly St.* ☎ *01224/626566* ▭ *AE, DC, MC, V.*

££–£££   ✕🏨 **Atholl Hotel.** One of Aberdeen's many splendid silver-granite buildings, this turreted, gabled hotel is in a leafy residential area to the west of the city center. Rooms are done in rich, dark colors; if space is more important than a view, opt for a room on the first floor. The restaurant prepares traditional fare such as lamb cutlets and roast rib of beef. ⊠ *54 Kings Gate, AB15 4YN* ☎ *01224/323505* 🖷 *01224/321555* 🌐 *www. atholl-aberdeen.com* ↩ *35 rooms* ⚫ *Restaurant, lounge, Internet; no a/c* 🖃 *AE, DC, MC, V* ⑩ *BP.*

★   🏨 **Marcliffe at Pitfodels.** This spacious country-house hotel in the West
££££–£££££   End combines old and new in the individually decorated rooms to impressive effect. Some have reproduction antique furnishings; others are more modern. The conservatory dining area focuses on international fare with a Scottish flavor. The hotel can arrange activities such as fishing. ⊠ *N. Deeside Rd., AB15 9YA* ☎ *01224/861000* 🖷 *01224/ 868860* 🌐 *www.marcliffe.com* ↩ *42 rooms* ⚫ *Restaurant, minibars, golf privileges, Internet, some pets allowed; no a/c* 🖃 *AE, DC, MC, V* ⑩ *BP.*

Nightlife & the Arts

Aberdeen Arts Centre (⊠ 33 King St. ☎ 01224/635208) presents all forms of theater, comedy shows, poetry readings, exhibitions, and other arts-based events. **His Majesty's Theatre** (⊠ Rosemount Viaduct ☎ 01224/ 637788) stages shows throughout the year. The **Lemon Tree** (⊠ 5 W. North St. ☎ 01224/642230) has an international program of dance, comedy, music (folk, jazz, rock and roll), and art exhibitions.

Shopping

Big, modern chain stores attract droves of countryfolk who come to do their major shopping here, but the city still has delightful specialty shops. At the **Aberdeen Family History Shop** (⊠ 158–164 King St. ☎ 01224/646323) you can browse through numerous publications related to local history and genealogical research. **Colin Wood** (⊠ 25 Rose St. ☎ 01224/643019) specializes in antiques, and maps and prints of Scotland. **Nova** (⊠ 20 Chapel St. ☎ 01224/641270) stocks good gifts from Scottish silver jewelry to Neal's Yard toiletries.

Banchory

⑤⑥ *19 mi west of Aberdeen.*

Banchory is an immaculate place with a pinkish tinge to its granite buildings. It's usually bustling with city strollers, out on a day trip from Aberdeen. If you visit Banchory in autumn, drive out to the **Brig o' Feuch** (pronounced fyooch, the *ch* as in loch), off the B974 south of town. In the area around this bridge, salmon leap in season, and the fall colors and foaming waters make for an attractive scene.

Crathes Castle, 3 mi east of Banchory, was once home of the Burnett family, keepers of the Forest of Drum for generations, and it retains some original family furnishings. The family acquired lands here by marriage and later built a new castle, completed in 1596. The grand gardens are noted for their calculated symmetry and clipped yew hedges. ⊠ *Off A93* ☎ *01330/844525* 🌐 *www.nts.org.uk* 🎟 *£9, castle or walled garden only £7* ⊙ *Castle Apr.–Sept., daily 10–5:30; Oct., daily 10–4:30; last admission 45 mins before closing. Tearoom and shop Apr.–Sept., daily 10–5:30; Oct., daily 10–4:30; Nov.–March., Wed.–Sun. 10–4. Garden and grounds daily 9–dusk.*

off the
beaten
path

QUEEN'S VIEW – From Banchory, follow the river upstream to Aboyne, turning north on B9094 and then left onto B9119 for 6 mi for a panoramic view (signposted), a bit north of Dinnet. This is one of the most spectacular vistas in northeast Scotland, stretching across the Howe of Cromar to Lochnagar.

Where to Stay & Eat

££££ ✕🗔 **Banchory Lodge.** With the River Dee running past at the bottom of the garden, this 17th-century house with modern additions is an ideal resting place for anglers. Rooms are individually decorated, though all have bold color schemes and tartan or floral fabrics. The restaurant (fixed-price menus) has high standards for its Scottish cuisine with French overtones; try the fillet of salmon, roasted duckling, or guinea fowl with wild berries. ⊠ *Off Bridge St., AB31 5HS* ☎ *01330/822625* 🖷 *01330/ 825019* ⊕ *www.banchorylodge.co.uk* 🖙 *22 rooms* ♻ *Restaurant, fishing, bicycles, bar, playground; no a/c* ⊟ *AE, DC, MC, V* ❙❀❙ *BP.*

Ballater

57 *25 mi west of Banchory, 43 mi west of Aberdeen.*

The quaint holiday resort of Ballater, once noted for the curative properties of its local well, has profited from the proximity of the royals at nearby Balmoral Castle. The BY ROYAL APPOINTMENT signs proudly hang from many of its shops (even monarchs need bakers and butchers). If you get a chance, take time to stroll around this neat community, which is well laid out with groups of silver-gray buildings. Note that the railway station now houses the tourist information center as well as a display on the former glories of this Great North of Scotland branch line, closed in the 1960s, along with many others in this country.

Close to the town, you can explore the eastern Highlands in **Glen Muick** (Gaelic for "pig," pronounced mick). Cross the River Dee and turn up-river on the south side; shortly after, the road, which is signposted from B976, forks into this fine Highland valley. The native red deer are common throughout the Scottish Highlands, but Glen Muick is one of the best places to see them in abundance, with herds grazing the valley floor. Beyond the lower glen, the prospect opens to reveal fine views of the battlement of cliffs edging the famed mountain called Lochnagar.

Where to Stay & Eat

£££–££££ ✕🗔 **Darroch Learg Hotel.** Standing amid tall trees on a hillside, this is everything a Victorian Scottish country-house hotel should be. Most guest rooms have a panoramic view south across Royal Deeside and are decorated with mahogany furniture and designer fabrics in rich colors. The Scottish cuisine in the conservatory restaurant (fixed-price menu) is sophisticated but also substantial, with the rich flavors of local beef, venison, and fish. Less expensive rooms are in the neighboring Oak Hall, another Victorian house. ⊠ *Braemar Rd., AB35 5UX* ☎ *013397/ 55443* 🖷 *013397/55252* ✐ *nigel@darroch-learg.demon.co.uk* 🖙 *18 rooms* ♻ *Restaurant, Internet; no a/c* ⊟ *AE, DC, MC, V* ⊗ *Closed Jan.* ❙❀❙ *BP.*

Balmoral Castle

58 *7 mi west of Ballater.*

Balmoral Castle, the Royal Family's Scottish summer residence, is a Victorian fantasy, designed, in fact, by Prince Albert himself in 1855. "It seems like a dream to be here in our dear Highland Home again," Queen Victoria wrote. "Every year my heart becomes more fixed in this dear Paradise." In truth, there are more interesting and historic buildings to explore, as the only part of the castle on view is the ballroom, with an exhibition of royal artifacts. The Carriage Hall has an exhibition of commemorative china, carriages, and a native wildlife display. Victoria loved Balmoral more for its setting than its house, so be sure to take in the pleasant gardens. Around and about Balmoral are some noted beauty spots: Cairn O'Mount, Cambus O'May, the Cairngorms from the Linn of Dee. Pony trekking is available on the Balmoral stalking-ponies around the grounds and estate. Note that if the royals are in residence, even the grounds are closed to visitors, so be sure to call in advance. A number of cottages on the Balmoral estate can be rented by the week. ⊠ *A93, Crathie* ☎ *013397/42334* ⊕ *www.balmoralcastle. com* 🖼 *£4.50* 🕙 *Apr.–July, daily 10–5; last admission at 4.*

Braemar

59 *10 mi west of Balmoral Castle, 17 mi west of Ballater.*

The village of Braemar, surrounded by the Grampian Mountains, is a good base from which to explore the mountains and woodlands of Royal Deeside. **Braemar Castle** dates from the 17th century, with defensive walls later built in the outline of a pointed star. At Braemar (the braes, or slopes, of the district of Mar), the standard, or rebel flag, was first raised at the start of the unsuccessful Jacobite rebellion of 1715. Thirty years later, during the last rebellion, Braemar Castle was strengthened and garrisoned by Hanoverian (government) troops. ⊠ *A93* ☎ *013397/ 41219* ⊕ *www.braemarcastle.co.uk* 🖼 *£3.50* 🕙 *Apr.–June, Sept., and Oct., Mon.–Thurs. and weekends 10–6; July and Aug., daily 10–6.*

Braemar is associated with the **Braemar Highland Gathering** held every September, and distinguished by the presence of members of the Royal Family, owing to the proximity of their residence at Balmoral Castle.

Seven miles west of Braemar, on an unmarked road, is the **Linn of Dee** (*linn* is a Scots word meaning "rocky narrows"), where the river's rocky gash is deep and roaring. Park beyond the bridge and walk back to admire the river and woodland, with deep, tranquil pools with salmon glinting in them.

Where to Stay & Eat

££ ✕🏨 **Invercauld Arms.** This stone Victorian hotel in the center of Braemar makes a good base for exploring Royal Deeside. The entrance lounge, with plush sofas and velvet chairs, leads to beautifully restored public rooms and to comfortable guest rooms with floral drapes and reproduction antique furniture. The restaurant serves a fixed-price dinner. Dishes might include Aberdeen Angus steak with tomato and wild-mushroom sauce or chicken with water chestnuts in oyster sauce. ⊠ *A93, AB35 5YR* ☎ *013397/41605* 🖷 *013397/41428* ⇗ *68 rooms* 🛏 *Restaurant, bar; no a/c* 🖃 *AE, DC, MC, V* 🍴 *BP.*

Sports

The **Braemar Golf Club** (⊠ Cluniebank Rd. ☎ 013397/41618) has a tricky 18-hole course laden with foaming waters. Erratic duffers, take note: the course managers have installed, near the water, poles with little nets on the end for those occasional shots that go awry.

Corgarff Castle

60 *23 mi northeast of Braemar, 14 mi northwest of Ballater.*

Eighteenth-century soldiers paved a military highway, now A939, north from Ballater to Corgarff Castle, a lonely tower house with a star-shape defensive wall, a curious reproduction of Braemar Castle. Corgarff was built as a hunting seat for the earls of Mar in the 16th century. After an eventful history that included the wife of a later laird being burned alive in a family dispute, the castle ended its career as a garrison for Hanoverian troops. ⊠ *Off A939, Cock Bridge* ☎ *0131/668–8800* ⊕ *www. historic-scotland.gov.uk* ⊡ *£3* ⊙ *Apr.–Sept., daily 9:30–6; Oct.–Mar., Sat. 9:30–4, Sun. 2–4.*

en route	On A944, the castle signposting for the **Castle Trail** leads you to a few sites. The road meanders along the River Don to the village of Strathdon, where a mound by the roadside—on the left—turns out to be a *motte*, or the base of a wooden castle, built in the late 12th century. The A944 then joins A97 (go left) and just a few minutes later a sign points to Glenbuchat Castle, a plain Z-plan tower house.

Kildrummy Castle

★ ⑥ *18 mi northeast of Corgarff Castle, 23 mi north of Ballater.*

Its age (13th century) and its ties to the mainstream medieval traditions of European castle building make this castle significant. Kildrummy shares features with Harlech and Caernarfon in Wales, as well as with Continental sites, such as Château de Coucy near Laon, France. It underwent several expansions at the hands of England's king Edward I (1239–1307); the castle was back in Scottish hands in 1306, when Edward's son besieged it. The defenders were betrayed by Osbarn the Smith, who had been promised gold by the English. They gave it to him after the castle fell, pouring it molten down his throat, or so the story goes. Kildrummy's prominence ended after the collapse of the 1715 Jacobite uprising. It had been the rebel headquarters and was consequently dismantled. ⊠ *A97, Kildrummy* ☎ *019755/71331* ⊕ *www.historic-scotland.gov.uk* ⊡ *£2.20* ⊙ *Apr.–Sept., daily 9:30–6.*

Where to Stay & Eat

★ ✗⊞ **Kildrummy Castle Hotel.** A grand, late-Victorian country house, this
££££–£££££ hotel offers a peaceful location, attentive service, and sports. Oak paneling, beautiful plasterwork, and gentle color schemes create a serene environment, enhanced by the views of Kildrummy Castle Gardens next door. The restaurant's traditional Scottish cuisine highlights local game and seafood. Fillet of beef Kildrummy Castle combines three quintessentially Scottish ingredients—beef, haggis, and Drambuie liqueur—in one dish. Golf, fishing, and horseback riding are available nearby. ⊠ *Off A944, Kildrummy, AB33 8RA* ☎ *019755/71288* ⊠ *019755/71345* ⊕ *www.kildrummycastlehotel.co.uk* ⇔ *16 rooms* ♺ *Restaurant, some pets welcome; no a/c* ⊟ *MC, V* ⊚ *BP.*

Alford

⑥ *9 mi east of Kildrummy, 28 mi west of Aberdeen.*

A plain and sturdy settlement in the Howe (Hollow) of Alford, this village on the Castle Trail gives those who have grown weary of castle-hopping a break: it has a museum instead. The **Grampian Transport Museum,** in the center of town, specializes in road-based means of locomotion and has a library and archive facility. One of its more unusual exhibits is the *Craigievar Express,* a steam-driven creation invented by the local postman to deliver mail more efficiently. ☎ *019755/62292* ⊕ *www.gtm.org.uk* ⊡ *£4.50* ⊙ *Apr.–Sept., daily 10–5; Oct., daily 10–4.*

Craigievar Castle

★ ⓺⓷ *5 mi south of Alford.*

A fine example of the Scottish baronial style, Craigievar Castle is much as the stonemasons left it in 1626, with its pepper-pot turrets and towers, the whole slender shape covered in a pink-cream pastel. It was built in relatively peaceful times by William Forbes, a merchant in trade with the Baltic Sea ports. The well-preserved interior contains fine family portraits and 17th- and 18th-century furniture. ⊠ *A980* ☎ *013398/83635* ⊕ *www.nts.org.uk* 🎫 *£9, grounds £1* ☉ *Castle Apr.–Sept., Fri.–Tues. noon–5:30; grounds daily 9:30–sunset.*

Castle Fraser

⓺⓸ *13 mi east of Craigievar Castle, 8 mi southeast of Alford.*

Massive Castle Fraser, the largest of the castles of Mar (five castles built by a family of masons named Bell), shows a variety of styles reflecting the taste of its owners from the 15th through the 19th centuries. The walled garden includes a re-creation of a 19th-century knot garden, with box hedging, gravel paths, and splendid herbaceous borders. Have lunch in the tearoom or the picnic area. ⊠ *Off A944, near Dunecht* ☎ *01330/833463* ⊕ *www.nts.org.uk* 🎫 *£7, gardens and grounds only £2* ☉ *Castle Apr.–June and Sept., Fri.–Tues. noon–5:30; July and Aug., daily 11–5:30. Gardens daily 9:30–6. Grounds daily 9:30–dusk.*

INVERNESS & LOCH NESS

Inverness, the only sizable town in northern Scotland (though it is quite small, nonetheless), is a compact place, built on both banks of the River Ness, just northeast of Loch Ness. The loch itself, 24 mi long and very deep (800 feet maximum), passes through pretty scenery. Loch Ness is the alleged home of "Nessie," world-famous monster and star of the chamber of commerce. In 1933, during a quiet news week for the local paper, the editor ran a story about a sighting of something in Loch Ness. The story lives on, and the dubious Loch Ness phenomenon keeps cameras trained on the deep waters, which tend to create mirages in still conditions. The area sees plenty of tourist traffic, drawn by the well-marketed hokum of the monster. But historic sites, castles, and mountain and lake scenery give you much more to see.

Inverness

▶ ⓺⓹ *102 mi northwest of Aberdeen, 161 mi northwest of Edinburgh.*

Inverness makes a logical touring base, with excellent roads radiating out from it to serve an extensive area. Although popularly called the capital of the Highlands, the town is far from Highland in flavor. Part of its hinterland includes the farmlands of the Moray Firth coastal strip, as well as of the Black Isle. It is open to the sea winds off the Moray Firth, and the high hills, although close at hand, are mainly hidden. Few of Inverness's buildings are of great antiquity, thanks to the competing Highland clans' habit of burning towns to the ground. Even its castle is a Victorian-era replacement on the site of a fort blown up by Bonnie Prince Charlie. Now bypassed by A9, the town positively roars with visitors in summer. Be careful in its one-way traffic system, whether you are walking or driving.

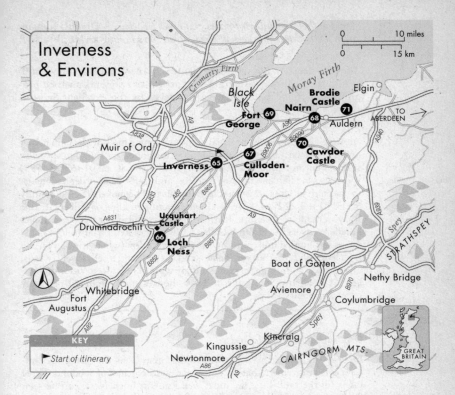

Inverness & Environs

The excellent, although small, **Inverness Museum and Art Gallery** (✉ Castle Wynd ☎ 01463/237114) covers archaeology, art, local history, and the natural environment in its lively displays.

Where to Stay & Eat

££££–£££££ ✕🏠 **Dunain Park Hotel.** You'll receive individual attention in this 18th-century mansion set amid 6 acres of wooded gardens. An open fire awaits you in the living room, a good place to sip a drink and browse through books and magazines. Antiques and traditional furnishings make the bedrooms equally cozy and attractive. The elegant restaurant serves French-influenced Scottish dishes such as Shetland salmon baked in sea salt or medallions of venison rolled in oatmeal with a claret sauce. The hotel is 2½ mi southwest of Inverness. ✉ *A82, Dunain, IV3 8JN* ☎ *01463/230512* 🖷 *01463/224532* ⊕ *www.dunainparkhotel.co.uk* ↝ *13 rooms* ♿ *Restaurant, indoor pool, sauna, badminton, Internet, some pets allowed; no a/c* 🗀 *AE, MC, V* ⦿ *BP.*

££ 🏠 **Ballifeary House Hotel.** The proprietors at this well-maintained Victorian bed-and-breakfast offer high standards of comfort and service. Rooms are individually decorated with modern furnishings, and the downstairs has reproduction antiques; there's a bar for guests. Ballifeary House is a 10-minute walk from downtown Inverness. ✉ *10 Ballifeary Rd., IV3 5PJ* ☎ *01463/235572* 🖷 *01463/717583* ⊕ *www.ballifearyhousehotel.co.uk* ↝ *5 rooms* ♿ *No a/c, no room phones, no kids under 15, no smoking* 🗀 *MC, V* ⦿ *BP.*

★ ££ 🏠 **The Lodge at Daviot Mains.** This house, done in the style of a Highland shooting lodge, provides the perfect setting for home comforts and traditional Scottish cooking (guests only). Wild salmon may appear on the menu, and you can sip fine wines with your meal. It is 5 mi south of Inverness. ✉ *A9, IV2 5ER* ☎ *01463/772215* 🖷 *01463/772099*

⊕ *www.thelodgeatdaviotmains.co.uk* ⊷ *6 rooms* ♨ *Dining room, in-room data ports, some pets allowed; no a/c, no smoking* ▭ *MC, V.* ⦿⃒*BP.*

Nightlife & the Arts

The **Eden Court** (⊠ Bishops Rd. ☎ 01463/234234), a multipurpose 800-seat theater, cinema, restaurant, and art gallery, presents a varied program year-round, including performances by the excellent Scottish Ballet.

Shopping

Although Inverness has the usual indoor shopping malls with chain names and department stores, the most interesting goods are found in specialty shops. **Duncan Chisholm & Sons** (⊠ 47–51 Castle St. ☎ 01463/234599) specializes in Highland tartans, woolens, and crafts. Mail-order and made-to-measure services are available. **Hector Russell Kiltmakers** (⊠ 4–9 Huntly St. ☎ 01463/222781) carries a huge selection of kilts, or will create one for you made to measure. It can supply by mail order overseas. **James Pringle Weavers** (⊠ Holm Woollen Mills, Dores Rd. ☎ 01463/223311) offers self-guided mill tours, a weaving exhibition (where for £3 you can try a loom and receive a certificate), and a restaurant; it sells lovely tweeds, tartans, wool clothing, crystal, and giftware. The indoor **Victorian Market** (⊠ Academy St.), built in 1870, houses more than 40 privately owned specialty shops.

Loch Ness

66 *9 mi southwest of Inverness.*

Inverness is the northern gateway to the Great Glen, the result of an ancient earth movement that dislocated the entire top half of Scotland. Three lochs fill the fault line; the most well known, Loch Ness, can be seen from the main A82 road south, though leisurely drivers may prefer the east bank road, B862 and B852, to Fort Augustus, at the loch's southern end (32 mi). The scenery around Loch Ness is pleasant without being spectacular—heather-clad mountain slopes and birch woods closer to the water. In summer you'll see quite a few boats on the lake.

Midway between Inverness and Fort Augustus on the west bank road, **Loch Ness 2000** presents the facts and the fakes, the photographs, the unexplained sonar contacts, and the sincere testimony of eyewitnesses. Loch Ness's huge volume of water has a warming effect on the local weather, making the lake conducive to mirages in still, warm conditions; these are often the circumstances in which the "monster" appears. Whether or not the *bestia aquatilis* lurks in the depths—and in 1994, the man who took one of the most convincing photos of Nessie confessed that it was a fake—plenty of camera-toting, sonar-wielding, and submarine-traveling scientists and curiosity-seekers haunt the shores. ⊠ *A82, Drumnadrochit* ☎ *01456/450573 or 01456/450218* ⊕ *www.loch-ness-scotland.com* ⊡ *£5.95* ⊙ *Easter–May, daily 9:30–5; June and Sept., daily 9–6; July and Aug., daily 9–8; Oct., daily 9:30–5:30; Nov.–Easter, daily 10–3:30; last admission 30 mins before closing.*

Two miles southeast of Drumnadrochit, right on the lakeshore, stands battered **Urquhart Castle,** which has been guarding Loch Ness since the 13th century. It was largely destroyed by the end of the 17th century, to prevent its use by Jacobite forces, but the ruins of what was one of the largest castles in Scotland are still impressive. Today swarms of bus tours pass through after investigating the Loch Ness phenomenon. Exhibits in the visitor center explore the castle's tumultuous history. ⊠ *A82* ☎ *0131/668–8800* ⊕ *www.historic-scotland.gov.uk* ⊡ *£5.50*

CLANS & TARTANS

WHATEVER THE ORIGINS of the clans—some with Norman roots, intermarried into Celtic society; some of Norse origin, the product of Viking raids on Scotland; others traceable to the monastic system; yet others possibly descended from Pictish tribes—by the 13th century the clan system was at the heart of Gaelic tribal culture. By the 15th century the clan chiefs of the Scottish Highlands were a threat even to the authority of the Stewart monarchs.

The word clann means "family" or "children" in Gaelic, and it was the custom for clan chiefs to board out their sons among nearby families, a practice that helped to bond the clan unit and create strong allegiances: the chief became "father" of the tribe and was owed loyalty by lesser chiefs and ordinary clansmen.

The clan chiefs' need for strong men-at-arms, fast-running messengers, and bards for entertainment and the preservation of clan genealogy was the probable origin of the Highland Games, still celebrated in many Highland communities each year, and which are an otherwise rather unusual mix of sports, music, and dance.

Gradually, by the 18th century, increasing knowledge of Lowland agricultural improvements, and better roads into the Highlands that improved communication of ideas and "southern" ways, began to weaken the clan system: fine clothes, French wines, and even a Lowland education became more common in chiefly households. Even before the battle of Culloden in 1746, in which Prince Charles Edward Stuart, supported by some of the clans, was defeated by George II's army, the clan system had lost its tight grip on the Highlands. After Culloden, as more modern economic influences took hold, those on the "wrong" side lost all. Many chiefs lost their lands, tartan was banned, and clan culture withered.

Tartan's own origins as a part of the clan system are disputed; the Gaelic word for striped cloth is breacan—piebald or spotted—so even the word itself is not Highland. However, it is indisputable that in the days before mass manufacture, when cloth was locally spun, woven, and dyed using plant derivatives, each neighborhood would have different dyestuffs—bilberry, iris, bramble, water lily—and therefore different colors available. In this way, particular combinations of colors and favorite patterns of the local weavers could become associated with a particular area and therefore clan, but were not in any sense a clan's "own by exclusive right."

Between 1746 and 1782 the wearing of tartan was generally prohibited. By the time the ban was lifted, many recipes for dyes and weaving patterns had been forgotten. In addition, some neighborhoods stopped making and coloring their own cloth because of the mechanization and use of chemical dyes in cloth production.

It took the influence of Sir Walter Scott, with his romantic, and fashionable, view of Highland history, to create the "modern myth" of clans and tartan. Sir Walter engineered George IV's visit to Scotland in 1822, which turned into a tartan extravaganza. The idea of one tartan or group of tartans "belonging" to one particular clan was created at this time—literally created, with new patterns and color ways dreamed up and "assigned" to particular clans. Queen Victoria and Prince Albert, with their passion for all things Scottish and for tartan in particular at Balmoral, reinforced the tartan culture later in the century, and it persists on and off to this day.

It is considered more "proper" in some circles to wear the "right" tartan, that is, that of your clan. You may be able to find a clan connection with the help of expertise such as that available at **Scotland's Clan Tartan Centre** (✉ 70–74 Bangor Rd., Leith ☎ 0131/553–5100), near Edinburgh.

Apr.–Sept., daily 9:30–6; Oct.–Mar., daily 9:30–4; last admission 45 mins before closing.

Where to Stay & Eat

★ **£££–££££**   ✕🏨 **Polmaily House.** This country house amid lovely parkland is near the northern bank of Loch Ness; sailing on the loch is even possible. Books, log fires, and a helpful staff contribute to making the hotel warmer and more personal than many grander, more expensive places, and families are sincerely welcomed. The restaurant is noted for its British cuisine, which takes advantage of fresh Highland produce. Try salmon in pastry with dill sauce, roast rack of lamb with rosemary, or cold smoked venison with melon. ⊠ *A831, Drumnadrochit, IV63 6XT* ☎ *01456/450343* 📠 *01456/450813* ⊕ *www.polmaily.co.uk* ➟ *9 rooms, 5 suites* ♿ *Restaurant, tennis court, indoor pool, boating, fishing, croquet, horseback riding, Internet, some pets allowed; no a/c* ▭ *MC, V* ⯮◎⯮ *BP.*

Culloden Moor

67 *5 mi east of Inverness.*

Culloden Moor was the scene of the last major battle fought on British soil—to this day considered one of the most infamous and tragic in all of warfare. Here, on a cold April day in 1746, the outnumbered Jacobite forces of Prince Charles Edward Stuart were destroyed by the superior firepower of George II's army. The victorious commander, the duke of Cumberland (George II's son), earned the name of "Butcher" Cumberland for the bloody reprisals carried out by his men on Highland families, Jacobite or not, caught in the vicinity. In the battle itself, the duke's army, greatly outnumbering the Scots, decimated more than 1,000 soldiers. The National Trust for Scotland has, slightly eerily, re-created the battlefield as it looked in 1746. The uneasy silence of the open moor almost drowns out the merry clatter from the visitor center's coffee shop and the tinkle of cash registers. ⊠ *B9006* ☎ *01463/790607* ⊕ *www.nts.org.uk* 🎫 *Visitor center and audiovisual display £5* ⊙ *Site, daily. Visitor center, restaurant, and shop Feb., Nov., and Dec., daily 11–4; Mar., daily 10–4; Apr.–June, Sept., and Oct., daily 9–6; July and Aug., daily 9–7; last entry 30 mins before closing.*

Nairn

68 *12 mi northeast of Culloden Moor, 17 mi northeast of Inverness, 92 mi northwest of Aberdeen.*

Once an unusual mixture of prosperous fishing port and farming community, Nairn still has a harmonious blend of old buildings in its busy ★ **69** shopping streets. The town is close to several historic sites. **Fort George,** started in 1748 and completed some 20 years later, is perhaps the best-preserved 18th-century military fortification in Europe. Because the fort is low-lying, its immense scale can be seen only from within. A visitor center and tableaux at the fort portray the 18th-century Scottish soldier's way of life, as does the **Regimental Museum of the Queen's Own Highlanders.** To reach the fort, take the B9092 north off A96 west of Nairn. ⊠ *Off B9092, Ardersier* ☎ *01667/462777* ⊕ *www.historic-scotland.gov.uk* 🎫 *Fort £5.50, museum free* ⊙ *Apr.–Sept., daily 9:30–6; Oct.–Mar., Mon.–Sat. 9:30–4, Sun. 2–4; last admission 45 mins before closing.*

70 **Cawdor Castle,** south of Nairn, is the cheerfully idiosyncratic, mellow, *Fodor's*Choice and mossy family seat of the Cawdor family, whose ancestors built it ★ as a private fortress and who continue to live here. Shakespeare's Macbeth was the Thane (or clan chief) of Cawdor, but the sense of history that exists is more than fictional. The castle's 15th-century central tower, family portraits, tapestries, and fine furniture reflect 600 years of history. The grounds include gardens and well-marked nature trails through woodlands with ancient oaks and beeches. ⊠ *Off B9090, Cawdor* ☎ *01667/404615* ⊕ *www.cawdorcastle.com* ☞ *£6.30, garden and grounds only £3.50* ⊙ *June–mid-Oct., daily 10–5.*

71 **Brodie Castle,** east of Nairn and in the care of the National Trust for Scotland, is of medieval origin, rebuilt and extended in the 17th and 19th centuries. Fine examples of late-17th-century plasterwork are preserved in the dining room and blue sitting room, and the good collection of paintings extends to works by 20th-century artists. ⊠ *Off A96* ☎ *01309/ 641371* ⊕ *www.nts.org.uk* ☞ *£5, grounds only £1 (honesty box)* ⊙ *Castle Apr., July, and Aug., daily noon–4; May, June–Sept., Sun.–Thurs. noon–4; grounds daily 9:30–sunset.*

Where to Stay & Eat

★ **££££** ✕▨ **Boath House.** Two surprises await inside this stunning 1820s mansion set on 20 acres: an Aveda health and beauty spa in the basement, and spacious rooms with 19th-century furniture, yet displaying contemporary Scottish art. The restaurant uses local produce, game in season, and seafood delivered fresh daily by the fisherfolk themselves. ⊠ *Auldearn, near Nairn, IV12 5TE* ☎ *01667/454896* ☏ *01667/455469* ⊕ *www.boath-house.com* ⇝ *5 rooms, 1 cottage.* ♿ *Restaurant, spa, Internet, some pets allowed; no a/c* ▭ *AE, MC, V* ❘⊚❘ *BP.*

Shopping

At **Auldearn Antiques** (⊠ Dalmore Manse, Lethen Rd., Auldearn ☎ 01667/ 453087) east of Nairn, it's easy to spend an hour or more wandering around the old church—filled with furniture, fireplaces, architectural antiques, and linens—and the converted farmsteads, with their tempting antique (or just old) chinaware and textiles. **Brodie Country Fare** (⊠ Brodie, east of Nairn ☎ 01309/641555) sells unusual knitwear, high-quality designer clothing and shoes, gifts, and toys, although they are *not* cheap. You'll also find a food store, a delicatessen, and an excellent, inexpensive restaurant.

SCOTLAND A TO Z

To research prices, get advice from other travelers, and book travel arrangements, visit www.fodors.com.

AIR TRAVEL

CARRIERS   Aberdeen is served by Atlantic Airways, Braathens, British Airways, British Midland, KLM UK, Coastair, EasyJet, Eastern Airways, and Wideroe. Airlines serving Edinburgh (no transatlantic flights) include Aer Lingus, Air France, Air Scotland, British Airways, British European and Scot Airways, British Midland, Eastern Airways, EasyJet, KLM, Ryanair, and Servisair. Airlines serving Glasgow for transatlantic flights are Air Canada and American Airlines (both are summer only), and Continental and Icelandair (all year). Inverness is served by British Airways (including British Regional Airways/British Airways Express), EasyJet, Eastern Airways, Highland Airways, and Servisair. Ryanair and EasyJet airlines offer unbeatable, no-frills air fares between Edinburgh, Glasgow, Glasgow Prestwick, and London's four major airports.

AIRPORTS

Aberdeen Airport serves international and domestic flights and is in Dyce, 7 mi west of the city center on the A96. Edinburgh Airport, 7 mi west of the city center, has air links with all the major airports in Britain and many in Europe; the Airport Information Centre answers questions about schedules, tickets, and reservations. Glasgow Airport offers internal Scottish and British services, European and transatlantic services, and vacation-charter traffic. Inverness Airport, locally known as Dalcross Airport, is central for internal flights covering the Highlands and islands region. There are also flights to the Highlands and islands from London (Luton), Manchester, Edinburgh, and Glasgow.

Glasgow Prestwick Airport, on the Ayrshire coast about 30 mi southwest of Glasgow, is mainly concerned with package holidays and charter flights, but is also the base for Ryanair's good-value flights, and serves as the main diversion airport in Scotland in bad weather conditions, because it usually stays clear of the worst weather. It has an excellent direct train service to Glasgow.

🛈 **Aberdeen Airport** ☎ 01224/722331 ⊕ www.baa.co.uk. **Edinburgh Airport Information Centre** ☎ 0131/333-1000 ⊕ www.baa.co.uk. **Glasgow Airport** ☎ 0141/887-1111 airport information desk ⊕ www.baa.co.uk. **Glasgow Prestwick Airport** ☎ 01292/511006 ⊕ www.gpia.co.uk. **Inverness Airport** ☎ 01667/464000 ⊕ www.hial.co.uk/inverness-airport.html.

BUS TRAVEL

Long-distance coach service operates to and from most parts of Scotland, England, and Wales. Edinburgh is approximately 8 hours by bus from London, Glasgow approximately 8½–9 hours. The main operator in Scotland is Scottish Citylink. From England and Wales, the main operator is National Express.

Lothian Buses, operating dark-red-and-white buses, is the main operator within Edinburgh. First Edinburgh provides much of the service into Edinburgh and also has day tours around and beyond the city and serves the Borders. Getting around the Inverness area and Royal Deeside is best done by car, but a number of post-bus services can help get you to the remote areas. For information contact Royal Mail. Note that if you head north of Aberdeen and Inverness, public transportation options can be limited on Sunday.

CUTTING COSTS The Lothian Buses Edinburgh Day Saver ticket (£2.50) allows unlimited one-day travel on the city's buses, and the better-value Offpeak Day Saver (£1.80) allows unlimited travel after 9:30 AM weekdays and all day on weekends; both services can be purchased in advance, or on any LRT bus (exact fare will be required on a bus). Two travel passes are available from First Edinburgh for one day, seven days, or four weeks unlimited travel in the Borders: the Reiver Rover for services within the Borders area, and the Waverley Wanderer for services within the Borders and to Edinburgh and Carlisle.

The many different bus companies in Glasgow cooperate with the Underground and ScotRail to produce the Family Day Tripper Ticket (£13), an excellent way to get around the whole area from Loch Lomond to Ayrshire. Tickets are available from Strathclyde Passenger Transport (SPT)and at main railway and bus stations.

Scottish Citylink sells an Explorer Pass providing three, five, or eight days of unlimited travel on the entire Scottish Citylink network. Aberdeen and Inverness are well served from the central belt of Scotland.

🛈 **First Edinburgh** ☎ 0131/663-9233 ⊕ www.firstgroup.com/firstedinburgh. **Lothian Buses** ☎ 0131/555-6363 ⊕ www.lothianbuses.co.uk. **National Express** ☎ 0870/580-8080 ⊕ www.nationalexpress.com. **Scottish Citylink** ✉ Buchanan Street Bus Station, Glasgow ☎ 0870/550-5050 ⊕ www.citylink.co.uk. **Strathclyde Passenger Transport** ✉ Travel Centre, St. Enoch Sq., Glasgow ☎ 0870/608-2608 ⊕ www.spt.co.uk.

Royal Mail Post Buses ✉ 7 Strothers La., Inverness ☎ 0845/774-0740 ⊕ www.royalmail.com/postbus.

CAR RENTAL

🔳 Local Agencies **Alamo National Car Rental** ✉ 76 Lancefield Quay, Glasgow ☎ 0141/204-1051. **Avis** ✉ Aberdeen Airport, Aberdeen ☎ 01224/722282 ✉ 5 Westpark Pl., Dalry Rd., Edinburgh ☎ 0131/337-6363; 0131/344-3900 airport ✉ 161 North St., Glasgow ☎ 0141/221-2827; 0141/842-7599 airport ✉ Inverness Airport, Inverness ☎ 01667/464070. **Budget** ✉ Wellshead Dr., Wellshead Industrial Estate, Dyce, Aberdeen ☎ 0800/181181 ✉ Almond Rd., Edinburgh ☎ 0800/181181 ✉ Glasgow Airport, Glasgow ☎ 0800/181181 ✉ Burns Cottage, Railway Terr., Inverness ☎ 0800/181181. **Europcar** ✉ 121 Causewayend, Aberdeen ☎ 01224/631199; 01224/770770 airport ✉ 24 E. London St., Edinburgh ☎ 0131/557-3456; 0131/333-2588 airport ✉ 38 Anderson Quay, Glasgow ☎ 0141/248-8788; 0141/887-0414 airport ✉ Friars Bridge Service Station, Telford St., Inverness ☎ 01463/235337. **Hertz** ☎ 08705/996699 central reservations ✉ Aberdeen Airport, Aberdeen ☎ 01224/722373 ✉ 10 Picardy Pl., Edinburgh ☎ 0870/846-0013; 0870/846-0009 airport ✉ 138 Hyde Park St., Glasgow ☎ 0141/248-7736 ✉ Inverness Airport, Inverness ☎ 01667/462652 ✉ Thistle Hotel, Millburn Rd., Inverness ☎ 01463/711479.

CAR TRAVEL

Downtown Edinburgh usually means Princes Street, which runs east–west. Entering from the east coast, drivers will come in on A1, with Meadowbank Stadium serving as a good landmark. From the Borders, the approach to Princes Street is by A7 and A68 through Newington. Approaching from the southwest, drivers will join the west end of Princes Street, via A701 and A702, and those coming east from Glasgow or Stirling will meet Princes Street from A8 on the approach via M90/A90. From Forth Road Bridge, Perth, and the east coast, the key road for getting downtown is Queensferry Road.

Those who come to Glasgow from England and the south of Scotland will probably approach the city from M6, M74, and A74. The city center is clearly marked from these roads. From Edinburgh M8 leads to the city center and is the highway that cuts straight across the city center; all other roads feed into it.

It is possible to travel from Edinburgh to Aberdeen on a continuous stretch of M90, a fairly scenic route that runs up Strathmore. The coastal route, A92, is a more leisurely alternative. The most scenic route is probably A93 from Perth, north to Blairgowrie and into Glen Shee. The A93 then goes over the Cairnwell Pass, the highest main road in Scotland (not recommended in winter).

The direct Edinburgh–Inverness route is M9/A9. From Glasgow to Inverness, the route is M80, then A9. If you are coming from southern Scotland, allow a comfortable 3½ hours from Glasgow or Edinburgh to Inverness via A9, and two hours to Aberdeen via A90.

A car is essential if you want to explore Scotland's wildest and most beautiful districts. Roads are always well surfaced though narrow in places. Although the area is large, road distances make it even larger: as the eagle flies, one town can be a certain distance from another, but it turns out to be three times that distance by the shortest road. Keep in mind that winter touring beyond the central Lowlands means you should check weather forecasts: minor roads are occasionally snowbound.

DISCOUNTS & DEALS

The Explorer Pass, available from any staffed Historic Scotland (HS) property, allows visits to HS properties over a 5-, 10-, or 21-day period. The Discovery Ticket issued by the National Trust for Scotland (NTS)

is available for 3, 7, or 14 days and allows access to all NTS properties. It is available from the NTS, all NTS properties, or main tourist
information centers. These tickets provide considerable savings if you
intend to visit many historic sites.

🏛 **Historic Scotland** ☎ 0131/668-8600 ⊕ www.historic-scotland.gov.uk. **National
Trust for Scotland** ☎ 0131/243-9300 ⊕ www.nts.org.uk.

EMERGENCIES

🏥 **Ambulance, fire, police** ☎ 999. **Aberdeen Royal Infirmary** ✉ Accident and Emergency Department, Foresterhill ☎ 01224/681818. **Edinburgh Royal Infirmary** ✉ Old
Dalkeith Rd., Little France ☎ 0131/536-1000. **Glasgow Royal Infirmary** ✉ Castle St.,
City Center ☎ 0141/211-4000. **Raigmore Hospital** ✉ Old Perth Rd., Inverness ☎ 01463/
704000.

TOURS

BUS TOURS Lothian Buses (⇨ Bus Travel) runs tours in and around Edinburgh departing from Waverley Bridge at regular intervals, from 9:30 to 5:30 daily.
City Sightseeing also runs tours around Edinburgh in its open-top buses
from Waverley Bridge. This company also runs tours around Glasgow
and Inverness. Prestige Tours runs luxury coach tours to most parts of
Scotland. Classique Tours has unusual vehicles: small touring coaches
dating from the 1950s and restored to immaculate condition. Specialized tours of Scotland's gardens are operated by Brightwater Holidays.

🏛 **Brightwater Holidays** ☎ 01334/657155 ⊕ www.brightwaterholidays.com. **City
Sightseeing** ☎ 0131/556-2244 ⊕ www.city-sightseeing.com. **Classique Tours** ☎ 0141/
889-4050 ⊕ www.classiquetours.co.uk. **Prestige Tours** ☎ 0141/886-1000 ⊕ www.
prestigetours.com.

CHAUFFEURED Little's Chauffeur Drive offers personally tailored chauffeur-driven tours
TOURS throughout Scotland.

🏛 **Little's Chauffeur Drive** ☎ 0141/883-2111 ⊕ www.littles.co.uk.

WALKING TOURS The Scottish Tourist Guides Association can recommend fully qualified
guides who will arrange walking or driving excursions of varying lengths.
The Cadies and Witchery Tours organizes tours of ghost-haunted Edinburgh all year. The Scottish Literary Tour Company takes you around
Edinburgh's Old and New Town, with guides invoking Scottish literary characters; it also has regional tours around Scotland.

🏛 **Cadies and Witchery Tours** ✉ 84 West Bow, Edinburgh ☎ 0131/225-6745 ⊕ www.
witcherytours.com. **Scottish Literary Tour Company** ✉ 97B West Bow, Suite 2, Edinburgh ☎ 0131/226-6657 ⊕ http://home.btconnect.com/sltc. **Scottish Tourist Guides
Association** ✉ Old Town Jail, St. John's St., Stirling, FK8 1EA ☎🖨 01786/451953
⊕ www.stga.co.uk.

TRAIN TRAVEL

Edinburgh's main train station, Waverley, is downtown, below Waverley Bridge. Travel time from Edinburgh to London by train is as little
as four hours. Glasgow has two main rail stations: Central and Queen
Street. Central is the arrival and departure point for trains from London Euston (journey time is approximately five hours), which come via
Crewe and Carlisle in England, as well as via Edinburgh from Kings Cross.
Travelers can reach Aberdeen directly from Edinburgh (three hours) and
Inverness (2½ hours). There are sleeper connections from London to Inverness, as well as reliable links from Edinburgh. There is also a direct
London–Aberdeen service that goes through Edinburgh. For those interested in train service to Aberdeen's airport, Dyce is on ScotRail's Inverness–Aberdeen route. The Borders has no rail service, and the nearest
rail station to St. Andrews is Leuchars, on the Edinburgh–Aberdeen main
line. For all inquiries, telephone National Rail Enquiries.

The Go Roundabout Glasgow discount pass allows unlimited travel on the Underground and trains around Glasgow and out to surrounding towns for one day. Trains depart Edinburgh and Glasgow for Aberdeen, Inverness, and other towns in the north. ScotRail issues discount passes as well: the Central Scotland Rover ticket covers Edinburgh, Glasgow, and the Central Belt, whereas the Highland Rover ticket is for travel in the north and west Highlands. For details, contact ScotRail.

🚉 **National Rail Enquiries** ☎ 0845/748-4950 ⊕ www.nationalrail.co.uk. **ScotRail** ☎ 0845/755-0033 ⊕ www.scotrail.co.uk.

TRAVEL AGENCIES

🚉 **Local Agent Referrals American Express** ✉ 139 Princes St., West End, Edinburgh ☎ 0131/718-2501 or 0870/600-1060 ✉ 115 Hope St., City Center, Glasgow ☎ 0141/222-1405. **Thomas Cook** ✉ 26-28 Frederick St., Edinburgh ☎ 0131/465-7700 ✉ 15-17 Gordon St., City Center, Glasgow ☎ 0141/201-7200.

VISITOR INFORMATION

Edinburgh and Scotland Information Centre is adjacent to Waverley Station in Edinburgh (follow the tourist information center TIC signs in the station and throughout the city) and can book accommodations for you. Greater Glasgow and Clyde Valley Tourist Board offers an excellent tourist information service from its headquarters near Queen Street Station in Glasgow.

Visit Scotland's Central Information Department, for telephone and written inquiries only, will answer any question on any aspect of your Scottish vacation and can supply literature by mail. It cannot make accommodation bookings, although this may change. The Scottish Tourist Board in London, open Monday–Saturday (shorter hours Saturday mid-September–May) can supply information and also has an accommodation and travel booking agency for in-person visitors only.

Within Scotland, area tourist boards run a network of more than 170 tourist information centers that offer comprehensive information and on-the-spot accommodation bookings. A number of these are listed below by town, after the national and regional tourist information offices.

🚉 **Edinburgh and Scotland Information Centre** ✉ 3 Princes St., East End, Edinburgh EH2 2QP ☎ 0131/473-3800 🖨 0131/473-3881 ⊕ www.edinburgh.org. **Greater Glasgow and Clyde Valley Tourist Board** ✉ 11 George Sq., City Center, Glasgow G2 1DY ☎ 0141/204-4400 🖨 0141/221-3524 ⊕ www.seeglasgow.com. **Scottish Tourist Board in London** ✉ 19 Cockspur St., near Trafalgar Sq. ✉ The Scotland Desk, Britain Visitor Centre, 1 Regent St., London SW1Y 4XT. **VisitScotland Central Information Department** ✉ 23 Ravelston Terr., Edinburgh EH4 3EU ☎ 0131/332-2433 🖨 0131/315-4545 ⊕ www.visitscotland.com.

Aberdeen and Grampian ✉ 27 Albyn Pl., Aberdeen ☎ 01224/288828; 01224/288825 advance reservations 🖨 01224/581367 ⊕ www.castlesandwhisky.com. **Ballater** ✉ Station Sq. ☎ 013397/55306. **Banchory** ✉ Bridge St. ☎ 01330/822000. **Inverness** ✉ Castle Wynd, IV2 3BJ ☎ 01463/234353 ⊕ www.highlandfreedom.com. **Jedburgh** ✉ Murrays Green ☎ 01835/863435. **St. Andrews** ✉ 70 Market St., KY16 9NU ☎ 01334/472021 ⊕ www.standrews.com/fife.

UNDERSTANDING
GREAT BRITAIN

THE CURTAIN RISES ON THE PERFORMING ARTS

ONE OF THE MAIN REASONS so many people want to visit Britain is its enviable reputation in the performing arts. The country is exactly what Shakespeare described, an "isle full of noises, sounds and sweet airs that give delight and hurt not." Whether it's music or drama, opera or ballet, people can enjoy themselves completely. Although government subsidies often fall short of spiraling costs, the numerous National Lottery grants have kept many a show on the road, and the performing arts scene remains surprisingly healthy. There is a fluidity about the performing arts in Britain that helps build their strength and appeal. An actor playing Lear with the Royal Shakespeare Company one day could appear in a television farce the next; an opera that has played to the small exclusive audience at Glyndebourne reappears the next week at the Albert Hall as part of the BBC's Promenade Concerts, delighting not only the 7,000 there in person, but millions more by radio. The performing arts largely transcend the social barriers that bedevil many aspects of British life to provide cultural nourishment for the widest spectrum of people.

The Theater

An evening taking in a play is a vital element of any trip to Britain. Most people head first for London's West End, the city's fabled "Theatreland." Here, you might catch Judi Dench and Vanessa Redgrave doing star turns, fabulous musical revivals such as *My Fair Lady,* more than one Andrew Lloyd Webber extravaganza, and Agatha Christie's apparently immortal *The Mousetrap,* which opened in 1955. Then there is that great mainstay, Shakespeare. At one time theater managers believed that "Shakespeare spelled ruin." Nowadays he may spell big business; witness the movie *Shakespeare in Love,* plus more filmed versions of the Bard's classics coming out of Hollywood.

Shakespeare provides a touchstone by which actors can measure themselves, and by which other people can measure them. Take *Hamlet,* for instance: occasionally a clutch of versions are staged at the same time. But that protracted procession of princes gives a fascinating lesson in the richness of talent available; indeed, Britain's actors are among the nation's very greatest treasures. However poor the play, the motive power of the performers rarely fails. In the end, all the Hamlets have something to offer that seems to shed fresh light on the weary text. Simply put, Spain has its bullfights, Italy its opera, Britain its theater.

The pinnacle of the dramatic scene consists of two great national companies, the Royal National Theatre and the Royal Shakespeare Company (generally known as the RSC). They do have separate identities, though it is not always easy to pin down the way in which they differ. The RSC is more prolific, performing at theaters in the West End and touring around the country. RSC also has three stages at Stratford-upon-Avon: the large Royal Shakespeare Theatre, the Swan, and the Other Place. The Swan, constructed on the lines of Shakespeare's Globe, is one of the most exciting acting spaces anywhere in the country. The Other Place is used for experimental staging.

The National Theatre plays in the three auditoriums in its concrete fortress on London's South Bank: the Olivier, the Lyttelton, and the Cottesloe, in descending order of size, the Olivier being huge and the Cottesloe studio-size. Of the two companies, the RSC is the more cohesive, with a very impressive volume of work and a steadily developing style, though it also suffers from serious lapses of taste and concentration in its productions. The great majority of its offerings are works of Shakespeare and the English classics, with occasional ventures into musicals. The National, on the other hand, ransacks world drama and has had notable successes with Greek classics and French tragedy, as well as mounting some of the best stagings of American musicals anywhere outside Broadway. It also attracts star performers more than the RSC, which relies largely on teamwork, and creates stars from its own ranks. Both companies suffer from financial problems, even though some of their best productions have extended runs and often grow into considerable hits.

As for the Bard of Bards, his fabled Globe Theatre, the most famous playhouse in the world, and the first venue for many of Shakespeare's greatest plays, has risen again on the South Bank of the Thames in London, not 200 yards from where the original stood. England has always held special temptations for Shakespeare fans; the reconstructed Globe has added the thrill of seeing his plays performed in the neighborhood where he lived and in virtually the same stage set.

Beyond London, provincial theaters operate in most of the cities and large towns up and down the land, and many of them have developed national and international reputations. In Scarborough, a seaside town in Yorkshire, for example, the dramatist-director Alan Ayckbourn has run for many years the Stephen Joseph Theatre, where he tries out his own plays. Most of these are transferred to London, appearing as often as not at the National Theatre. But the delight of British regional theaters lies in their great diversity and local panache. In the town of Richmond, in Yorkshire, the charming little Georgian Theatre Royal seats about 200 in rows and balconies that still reflect the 18th-century class divisions. Porthcurno, near Penzance, Cornwall, has the Minack Theatre, on a cliff top, overlooking the sea. The National Trust runs the lovely, still fully functioning, 1819 Theatre Royal in Bury St. Edmunds. There are woodland theaters, theaters in barns, and several in grand old country houses.

If you're traveling around the country, it's worth your time to find out what is on in any spot you may hit, especially in summer. In summer Britain's acting fraternity takes to the open air and strives to outdo passing planes and nearby traffic. Notable venues include York, where the famous medieval cycle of mystery plays is performed every four years in surroundings that add incalculable richness; some of the quadrangles of Oxford and Cambridge, which come alive with Oliviers-in-the-bud; and London's Regent's Park, which offers the best of the open-air theaters. There you can watch Shakespeare, after having wandered in Queen Mary's rose garden. To sit in the dusk, as Puck and

Oberon plot their magic, and the secret lights gradually create a world of fantasy, is to take part in an essentially British rite.

Opera

Dr. Samuel Johnson, who was a notable grouch, accused opera of being an exotic and irrational entertainment on the British scene. Of course opera *is* irrational. It was born in the royal and ducal courts of Europe, where expense had no meaning. London's two main companies are poles apart. The Royal Opera at Covent Garden is socially the most prestigious. This is the place for spectacles and productions to match those presented anywhere else in the world. The English National Opera (ENO) at the Coliseum, beside Trafalgar Square, has a wider appeal, with classic operas sung in English, produced by an innovative directorial team that has settled its reputation as the leader of opera fashion. Seat prices for the ENO are generally much gentler than those at the Royal Opera, and the company consists mostly of British singers. The one drawback is that the auditorium sometimes dwarfs the voices.

Apart from the two major companies in London, Britain has two other national opera companies: the Welsh National at Cardiff, and the Scottish National in Glasgow. They both embrace adventuresome artistic policies, attacking such blockbusters as Wagner's *Ring* and *The Trojans* of Berlioz. They also tour, the Welsh National especially, appearing in small towns around the country, even performing in movie houses when no other stage is available. There is also a northern England company, originally a spin-off from the English National, called Opera North, which is based in Leeds and is as venturesome as its begetter.

Opera has always been an extravagant art form, but one company managed to build its own home in 1994. Glyndebourne, in deepest Sussex, relies entirely on sponsors and its ticket sales, having no state subsidy. A visit there will cost you an arm and a leg, but you'll feel like a guest at a very superior house party.

Ballet

Ballet is a surprising art to flourish in Britain, and it does so only with a struggle. The Royal Ballet, the premier company, has instated one of its own veteran dancers, Monica Mason, in the hot seat, after the brief directorship of Australian Ross Stretton. Few other companies present the classics with such seemingly effortless style and accomplishment.

The sibling Birmingham Royal Ballet is a dynamic company to watch, with its zesty director and choreographer David Bintley. The English National Ballet (ENB) goes from strength to strength in its mission to give ballet more mass appeal. Matz Skoog, an Australian, is artistic director. You can catch the ENB performing its winter season at the London Coliseum, with summer shows at the Royal Albert Hall. Between times, it tours countrywide with its repertoire of classics.

Music
Music performance has seen a tremendous surge in popularity since 1950. In London, the three concert halls of the South Bank Centre, together with the Barbican, the Albert Hall, and the Wigmore Hall, provide the capital with venues for a rich and varied musical fare. For example, every night for six weeks in summer, the Albert Hall is host of the BBC-sponsored "Proms," the biggest series of concerts in the world, involving 10 or more orchestras and dozens of other artists. Outside London, cities with fine resident orchestras include Birmingham (home to the noted City of Birmingham Symphony Orchestra), Liverpool, Manchester, and even the seaside town of Bournemouth.

Britain's amazingly rich musical life fills every hall and theater, church and chapel throughout the land. Every week of the year you can attend performances of great choral works in concert halls, recitals of lieder in stately homes by candlelight, modern pieces on remote Scottish islands in the rich Celtic twilight of ancient buildings, and lively madrigals from boats on moonlit rivers. It's not just the Welsh who can say, in Dylan Thomas's words, "Thank God we are a musical nation."

Arts Festivals
Finally, Britain remains a land of festivals, mostly, though not exclusively, in summer. Whatever the size of the town, it will have a festival at some time. Some are of international scope, whereas others are small local wingdings. Leading the parade is the Edinburgh Festival, mid-August–early September, born in the dark days after World War II, when people needed cheering up. Today it still keeps going strong, with opera, drama, recitals, and ballet by artists from all over the world. The festival now has the added attraction of the Fringe, a concurrent event, with as many as 800 performances crammed into three weeks: small-scale productions from the classic to the bizarre.

Smaller than Edinburgh's event, but still notable, are the dozens of festivals up and down the country. In Bath the International Festival, late May–mid-June, wins praise for its music especially. In Aldeburgh, a windswept East Anglian seaside town, the Festival of Music and the Arts, mid–late June, honors the memory of Benjamin Britten, and again is mainly a music festival. In Cheltenham there are two major festivals, one musical in July, the other early–mid-October, dedicated to literature, with readings, seminars, and lectures. York holds both an early music festival in summer, and a Viking one in February. Llandrindod Wells, in Wales, goes Victorian and dresses up in late August. Worcester, Hereford, and Gloucester take turns mounting the annual Three Choirs Festival in mid-August, the oldest in the world, which has seen premieres of some notable music. Truro stages a Three Spires Festival in June in imitation. Wales has an annual feast of song and poetry late July–early August, called the Royal National Eisteddfod. At Chichester in Sussex a summer drama festival has proved so popular that the town has built a theater especially for it. At Ludlow, Shakespeare is performed in summer in the open air, with the dramatic castle as backdrop.

All these festivals have the advantage of focusing a visit to a town and helping you to meet the locals, but be sure to book well in advance, because they are extremely popular. Once the worst of the winter chill seeps out of everyone's bones, festival fever sets in. Year-round, however, Britain's performing arts offer one of the grandest and most unforgettable pageants in the world.

SPLENDID STONES & BRITISH ARCHITECTURE

N BRITAIN YOU CAN SEE structures that go back to the dawn of history, in the hauntingly mysterious circles of monoliths at Stonehenge or Avebury, for example, or the resurrected remains of Roman empire builders preserved in towns such as Cirencester. On the other hand, you can startle your eyes with the very current, very controversial designs of contemporary architects in areas such as London's Docklands. Appreciating the wealth of Britain's architectural heritage does not require a degree in art history, but knowing a few hallmarks of various styles can enhance your enjoyment of what you see. Here, then, is a primer of a millennium of architectural styles.

Norman

Duke William of Normandy brought the solid Norman style to Britain when he invaded and conquered England in 1066, although William's predecessor, King Edward (the Confessor) used the style in the building of Westminster Abbey a little earlier, in 1042. Until around 1200, it was clearly the style of choice for buildings of any importance, and William's castles and churches soon dominated the countryside. Norman towers tended to be hefty and square, arches always round-topped, and the vaulting barrel-shaped. Decoration was mostly geometrical, but within those limits, ornate. Norman motte and bailey castles had two connecting stockaded mounds, with the keep on the higher mound and other buildings on the lower mound. *Best seen in the Tower of London, St. Bartholomew's and Temple Churches, London, and in the cathedrals of St. Albans, Ely, Gloucester, Durham, and Norwich, and at Tewkesbury Abbey.*

Gothic Early English

From 1130 to 1300, pointed arches began to supplant the rounded ones, buttresses became heavier than the Norman variety, and windows lost their rounded tops to become "lancet" shaped. Buildings climbed skyward, less squat and heavy, with the soaring effect accentuated by steep roofs and spires. *Best seen in the cathedrals of York, Salisbury, Ely, Worcester, Canterbury (east end), and Westminster Abbey's chapter house.*

Decorated From the late 1100s until around 1400, elegance and ornament became fully integrated into architectural design, rather than applied to the surface of a solid, basic form. Windows filled more of the walls and were divided into sections by carved mullions. Vaulting grew increasingly complex, with ribs and ornamented bosses proliferating; spires became even more pointed; arches took on the "ogee" shape, with its unique double curve. This style was one of England's greatest gifts to world architecture. *Best seen at the cathedrals of Wells, Lincoln, Durham (east transept), and Ely (Lady Chapel and Octagon).*

Perpendicular In later Gothic architecture, the emphasis on the vertical grew even more pronounced, as shown in features such as slender pillars, huge expanses of glass, and superb fan vaulting resembling the formalized branches of frozen trees. Walls were divided by panels. One of the chief areas in which to see Perpendicular architecture is East Anglia, where towns that grew rich from the wool trade built magnificent churches in the style. Houses, too, began to reflect prevailing taste. Perpendicular Gothic lasted for well over two centuries from its advent around 1330. *Best seen at St. George's Chapel in Windsor, the cathedrals of Gloucester (cloister) and Hereford (chapter house), Henry VII's Chapel in Westminster Abbey, Bath Abbey, and King's College Chapel in Cambridge.*

Tudor

With the great period of cathedral building over, from 1500 to 1560 the nation's attention turned to the construction of spacious homes, characterized by this latest fashionable architectural style. The rapidly expanding, newly rich middle class, created by the two Tudor Henrys (VII and VIII) to challenge the power of the aristocracy, built spacious manor houses, often on the foundations of pillaged monasteries. Thus began the era of the great stately homes. Brick replaced stone as the most popular medium, with plasterwork and carved wood to carry the elaborate motifs of the age. Another way the social climbers could make their mark, and ensure their place in the next world, was by building churches. This was the age of the splendid parish churches built on fortunes made in the wool trade. Some of the most magnificent are in Suffolk, Norfolk, and the Cotswolds. *Domestic architecture is best seen at Hampton Court and St. James's Palace, London; for wool churches, Lavenham and Long Melford (though its tower is much later), both in Suffolk, and Cirencester, Chipping Campden, Northleach, and Winchcombe in the Cotswolds.*

Renaissance Elizabethan

For a short period under Elizabeth I, 1560–1600, this development of Tudor flourished as Italian influences began to seep into England, seen especially in symmetrical facades. The most notable example was Hardwick Hall in Derbyshire, built in the 1590s by Bess of Hardwick; the jingle that describes it goes "Hardwick Hall, more glass than wall." But, however grand the houses were, they were still on a human scale, warm and livable, built of a mellow amalgam of brick and stone. *Other great Elizabethan houses are Montacute in Somerset, Longleat in Wiltshire, and Burghley House in Cambridgeshire.*

Jacobean

For the first 15 years of the reign of James I (the name Jacobean is taken from the Latin word for James, Jacobus) architecture did not change noticeably. Windows were still large in proportion to the wall surfaces. Gables, in the style of the Netherlands, were popular. Carved decoration in wood and plaster (especially the geometrical patterning called "strapwork," like intertwined leather belts, also of Dutch origin) remained exuberant, now even more so. But a change was on the way. Inigo Jones (1573–1652), the first great modern British architect, attempted to synthesize the architectural heritage of England with the current Italian theories. Two of his finest remaining buildings—the Banqueting Hall, Whitehall, and the Queen's House at Greenwich—epitomize his genius, which was to introduce the Palladian style that dominated British architecture for centuries. It uses the classical Greek orders: Doric, Ionic, and Corinthian. This was grandeur. But the classical style that proved so monumentally effective under a hot Mediterranean sun was somehow transformed in Britain, domesticated and tamed. Columns and pediments decorated the facades, and huge frescoes provided acres of color to interior walls and ceilings, all in the Italian manner. These architectural elements had not yet been totally naturalized, however. There were in fact two quite distinct styles running concurrently, the comfortably domestic and the purer classical in public buildings. They were finally fused together by the talent of Christopher Wren. *Jacobean is best seen at the Bodleian Library, Oxford, Chastleton House, near Stow-on-the Wold, Audley End, Essex, and Clare College, Cambridge.*

Wren & the English Baroque

The work of Sir Christopher Wren (1632–1723) constituted an era all by itself. Not only was he naturally one of the world's greatest architects, but he was also given an unparalleled opportunity when the disastrous Great Fire of London in 1666 wiped out the center of the capital, destroying no fewer than 89 churches and 13,200 houses. Although Wren's great scheme for a modern city center was rejected, he did build 51 churches, the greatest of which was St. Paul's, completed in just 35 years. The range of Wren's designs is extremely wide, from simple classical shapes to the extravagantly dramatic baroque. He was also at home with domestic architecture, where his combinations of brick and stone produced a warm, homey effect. The influence of the Italian baroque can be seen in Sir John Vanbrugh's Blenheim Palace, where the facade echoes the piazza of St. Peter's in Rome, and at Vanbrugh's exuberant Castle Howard in Yorkshire. Nicholas Hawksmoor, Wren's pupil, designed the baroque Mausoleum at Castle Howard. The baroque had only a brief heyday in England; by 1725 the Palladian style was firmly in favor and the vast pile of Blenheim was being mocked by trendsetters. *Wren's ecclesiastical architecture is best seen at St. Paul's Cathedral (baroque with classical touches) and the other remaining London churches, his domestic style at Hampton Court Palace, Kensington Palace, the Royal Hospital in Chelsea, and the former Royal Naval College in Greenwich. English baroque is best seen at Blenheim Palace (Oxfordshire) and Castle Howard (Yorkshire).*

Palladian

This style is often referred to as Georgian, so-called from the Hanoverian kings George I through IV, although it was introduced as early as Inigo Jones's time. Classical inspiration has now been thoroughly acclimatized. Though they looked completely at home among the hills, lakes, and trees of the British countryside, Palladian buildings were derived from the Roman-inspired designs of the Italian architectural theorist Andrea Palladio (1508–80), with pillared porticoes, triangular pediments, and strictly balanced windows. In domestic architecture, this large-scale classicism was usually modified to quiet simplicity, preserving mathematical proportions of windows, doors, and the exactly calculated volume of room space, to create a feeling of balance and harmony. The occasional departures from the classical manner at this time included the over-the-top Indian-style Royal Pavilion in Brighton, built for the Prince Regent (later George IV) by John Nash. The Regency style comes under the Palladian heading, though strictly speaking it lasted only for the few years of the actual Regency (1811–20). Architects in Britain, such as Robert Adam, handled the Palladian style with more freedom than elsewhere in Europe, and America took its cue from the British. *Among the best Palladian examples are Regent's Park Terraces (London), the library at Kenwood (London), Royal Crescent and other streets in Bath, and Holkham Hall (Norfolk).*

Victorian

Elements of imaginative fantasy, already seen in the Palladian era, came to the fore during the long reign of Victoria. The country's vast profits made from the Industrial Revolution were spent lavishly. Civic building accelerated in all the major cities with town halls modeled after medieval castles or French châteaux. The Victorians plundered the past for styles, with Gothic, about which the scholarly Victorians were very knowledgeable, leading the field. The supreme examples here are the Houses of Parliament by Charles Barry and the Albert Memorial by George Gilbert Scott, both in London. (To distinguish between the Victorian variety and an earlier version, which flourished in the late 1700s, the earlier one is commonly spelled "Gothick.") But there were many other styles in the running, including the attractively named, and self-explanatory, "Wrenaissance." *Other striking examples are Truro Cathedral, Manchester Town Hall, Ironbridge, and Cragside (Northumberland).*

Edwardian

Toward the end of the Victorian era, in the late 1800s, architecture calmed down considerably, with a return to a solid sort of classicism, and even to a muted baroque. The Arts and Crafts movement, especially the work and inspiration of William Morris, produced simpler designs, returning often to medieval models. *Best seen in Buckingham Palace and the Admiralty Arch in London. Standen in East Grinstead (West Sussex) and Blackwell in Windermere (Cumbria) are notable Arts and Crafts houses.*

Modern

A furious public debate has raged in Britain for many years between traditionalists and the adherents of modernistic architecture. Britons are strongly conservative when it comes to their environment. These arguments have been highlighted and made even more bitter by the intervention of such notable figures as Prince Charles, who derides excessive modernism, and said, for instance, that the design for the Sainsbury Wing of the National Gallery in Trafalgar Square would be like "a carbuncle on a much-loved face." One reason for the strength of the British attitude is that the country suffered from much ill-conceived building development after World War II, when large areas of city centers had to be rebuilt after the devastation of German bombs. Town planners and architects encumbered the country with badly built and worse-designed tower blocks and shopping areas.

The situation created in the '50s and '60s is slowly being reversed. High-rise apartment blocks are being taken down and replaced by more user-friendly housing. Large-scale commercial areas in a number of cities are being rethought and slowly rebuilt, although so much ill-considered building was done that Britain can never be completely free of it. The emphasis has gradually moved to a type of planning, designing, and construction that pays more attention to the needs of the inhabitants of the buildings. A healthier attitude also exists toward the conservation of old buildings. As part of the postwar building splurge, houses that should have been treasured for posterity were torn down wholesale. Happily, many of those that survived the wreckers' ball are now being restored and put back to use.

Nowadays, a range of architectural styles prevail in Britain. A predominant one, favored incidentally by Prince Charles, draws largely on the past, with nostalgic echoes of the country cottage, and leans heavily on variegated brickwork and close attention to decorative detail. In urban centers can be seen the most innovative styles, which are exciting, fun, and ecologically sensitive, too—using light and heat to more thoughtful effect. These designs have turned many fatigued or declining areas into destinations to see and be seen in.

In London, the Lloyd's of London tower in the City, by Sir Richard Rogers, designer of the Pompidou Center in Paris, began the trend, but it took the millennium year to focus institutional minds on the creation of forward-looking images. The now-closed Millennium Dome, Rogers's tour de force, transformed the industrial blot of Greenwich peninsula. Sir Norman Foster's work has made equal headlines with the graceful Millennium Bridge. Foster's latest glassy masterpiece, City Hall, by Tower Bridge, has been knocked as looking like a "glass testicle" or a fencing mask, but it is one of the boldest designs to be achieved in London yet. Skyscrapers in the City of London are the exception rather than the rule, although the regenerated space of the old Docklands has allowed more room for imagination, as at Canary Wharf. Other buildings such as Barclays Bank with its jukebox dome and Swiss Re's "erotic gherkin" at 30 St. Mary Axe, the latter by Foster and looking akin to a glittering carousel pole, have begun to push height limitations.

Other centers of modern architectural excellence include Manchester, with the Imperial War Museum North by Daniel Libeskind. Since the city center was bombed in 1996, Manchester has received a brilliant face-lift. Also in the north, Gateshead Quays is the spectacularly renovated industrial area around the River Tyne and Newcastle. The tilting Millennium Bridge in Newcastle is as dramatic as London's, and the city has opened the largest arts space in Europe, the BALTIC Centre for Contemporary Art, with a vista that could rival Sydney Harbor's. Cornwall has the Eden Centre, the world's largest conservatories, massed together to make a giant glass crater covering a range of climates.

Elsewhere around the country, on a more sober scale, smaller public buildings are being built; schools and libraries, designed in a muted modernism, use traditional, natural materials, such as wood, stone, and brick. Many cultural institutions, particularly in London, have undergone innovative renovations, in part to add visitor-friendly, interactive technology. The Royal Opera House, Tate Modern and Tate Britain, the Great Court at the British Museum, the Queen's Gallery, and the Wellcome Wing at the Science Museum are among the most noteworthy projects that have embraced the new, but with a subtle emphasis on complementing the old. *Among other buildings to see are Richmond House and the Clore Building at Tate Britain (in London), the campus of Sussex University (outside Brighton), the Royal Regatta Building (Henley), the Sainsbury Centre for the Visual Arts (Norwich), the Lowry Centre (Manchester), and the Burrell Collection (Glasgow).*

BOOKS & MOVIES

Books

Many writers' names have become inextricably linked with the regions in which they set their books or plays. Hardy's Wessex, Daphne Du Maurier's Cornwall, Wordsworth's Lake District, Shakespeare's Arden, and Brontë Country are now evocative catchphrases, treasured by local tourist boards. But however hackneyed the tags may be, you *can* still get a heightened insight to an area through the eyes of authors of genius, even though they may have written a century or more ago. Here are just a few works that may provide you with an understanding of their authors' loved territory.

Thomas Hardy's *Mayor of Casterbridge, Tess of the d'Urbervilles, Far from the Madding Crowd,* and indeed almost everything he wrote is solidly based on his Wessex (Dorset) homeland. Daphne Du Maurier had a deep love of Cornwall from her childhood; *Frenchman's Creek, Jamaica Inn,* and *The King's General* all capture the county's Celtic mood. The Brontë sisters' *Wuthering Heights, Tenant of Wildfell Hall,* and *Jane Eyre* all breathe the sharp air of the moors around their Haworth home. William Wordsworth, who was born at Cockermouth in the Lake District, depicts the area's rugged beauty in many of his poems, especially the *Lyrical Ballads.*

Virginia Woolf's visits to Vita Sackville-West at her ancestral home of Knole, in Sevenoaks, resulted in the novel *Orlando.* The stately home is now a National Trust property. The country around Bateman's, near Burwash in East Sussex, the home where Rudyard Kipling lived for more than 30 years, was the inspiration for *Puck of Pook's Hill* and *Rewards and Fairies.* American writer Henry James lived at Lamb House in Rye, also in East Sussex, and after him E. F. Benson, whose delicious Lucia books are set in a thinly disguised version of the town. Both Bateman's and Lamb House are National Trust buildings.

A highly irreverent, and very funny, version of academic life, *Porterhouse Blue,* by Tom Sharpe, will guarantee that you look at Oxford and Cambridge with a totally different eye. John Fowles's *French Lieutenant's Woman,* largely set in Lyme Regis, is full of local color about Dorset.

The late James Herriot's successfully televised veterinary surgeon books, among them *All Creatures Great and Small,* give evocative accounts of life in the Yorkshire dales during much of the 20th century. For a perceptive account of life in the English countryside, try Ronald Blythe's well-regarded *Akenfield: Portrait of an English Village.*

Mysteries are almost a way of life in Britain, partly because many of the best English mystery writers set their plots in their home territory. Modern whodunits by P. D. James and Ruth Rendell convey a fine sense of place, and Ellis Peters's Brother Cadfael stories re-create life in medieval Shrewsbury with a wealth of telling detail. Colin Dexter's Inspector Morse mysteries capture the flavor of Oxford's town and gown. There are also always the villages, vicarages, and scandals of Agatha Christie's "Miss Marple" books.

The many fans of the Arthurian legends can turn to some excellent, imaginative novels that not only tell the stories but also give fine descriptions of the British countryside. Among them are *Sword at Sunset,* by Rosemary Sutcliffe, *The Once and Future King,* by T. H. White, and the four Merlin novels by Mary Stewart, *The Crystal Cave, The Hollow Hills, The Last Enchantment,* and *The Wicked Day.* Edward Rutherfurd's historical novels *Sarum, London,* and *The Forest* deal with aspects of British history with a grand sweep from the prehistoric past to the present.

An animal's close-to-the-earth viewpoint can reveal all kinds of countryside insights about Britain. *Watership Down,* by Richard Adam, was a runaway best-seller about rabbits in the early '70s, and *Wind in the Willows,* by Kenneth Grahame, gives a vivid impression of the Thames Valley almost 100 years ago, which still holds largely true today.

Those interested in writers and the surroundings that may have influenced their works should look at *A Literary Guide to London*, by Ed Glinert, and *The Oxford Literary Guide to the British Isles*, edited by Dorothy Eagle and Hilary Carnell (now out of print). One author particularly in vogue now is Jane Austen: Janeites will want to read Maggie Lane's *Jane Austen's World* and Nigel Nicolson's wonderful *World of Jane Austen*. For a vast portrait of everyone's favorite English author, weigh in with Peter Ackroyd's *Dickens*.

Some good background books on English history are *The Oxford Illustrated History of Britain*, edited by Kenneth O. Morgan, and *The Story of England*, by Christopher Hibbert. *The Isles*, a history by Norman Davies, challenges many conventionally Anglocentric assumptions. *The English: A Portrait of a People*, by Jeremy Paxman, examines the concept of Englishness in a changing world. *The London Encyclopaedia*, by Ben Weinreb and Christopher Hibbert, now out of print, is invaluable as a source of information on the capital. Simon Schama's three-volume *History of Britain*, with handsome color illustrations, were written to accompany the BBC–History Channel television series. Peter Ackroyd has written historical and contemporary fiction about London, and his illustrated nonfiction *London: A Biography*, captures the city's energy and its quirks from prehistory to the present. Jan Morris's *The Matter of Wales* (out of print) is a fine introduction to the country.

The finest book on the great stately houses of England is Nigel Nicolson's *Great Houses of Britain*, written for the National Trust (now out of print). Also spectacular are the picture books *Great Houses of Britain and Wales* and *Great Houses of Scotland*, by Hugh Montgomery-Massingberd. *The Buildings of England* and *The Buildings of Scotland*, originally by Nikolaus Pevsner, but much updated since his death, are a multivolume series, organized by county, which sets out to chronicle every building of any importance. The series contains an astonishing amount of information. In addition, Pevsner's *Best Buildings of Britain* is a grand anthology with lush photographs. For the golden era of Georgian architecture, check out John Summerson's definitive *Architecture in Britain 1530–1830*. Simon Jenkins's *England's Thousand Best Churches*, with

photographs, describes parish churches (not cathedrals) large and small. Mark Girouard has written several books that are incomparable for their detailed, behind-the-scenes perspective on art and architecture: *Life in the English Country House* focuses on the 18th century, and *The Victorian Country House* addresses the lifestyles of the rich and famous of the 19th century. For the ultimate look at that favorite subject, lovely English villages, see *The Most Beautiful Villages of England*, by James Bentley, with ravishing photographs by Hugh Palmer.

Two delightful travel books are those written by Susan Allen Toth, *England for All Seasons* and *My Love Affair with England*. Bill Bryson's *Notes from a Small Island* is perennially popular. Few of today's authors have managed to top the wit and perception of Henry James's magisterial *English Hours*. As for "the flower of cities all," *London Perceived* is a classic text by the noted literary critic V. S. Pritchett, and John Russell's *London* is a superlative text written by a particularly eloquent art historian.

Movies

From *Wuthering Heights* to *Jane Eyre*, many great classics of British literature have been rendered into great classics of film. It's surprising to learn, however, how many of them were creations of Hollywood and not the British film industry (which had its heyday from the 1940s to 1960s). From Laurence Olivier to today's Kenneth Branagh, noted directors-actors have long cross-pollinated the two centers of cinema. Any survey of British film, of course, begins with the dramas of Shakespeare: Olivier gave the world a memorable *Othello* and *Hamlet,* Orson Welles a moody *Macbeth,* Branagh gave up mod versions of *Hamlet* and *Much Ado About Nothing,* and Leonardo di Caprio graced a contemporary Miami version of *Romeo and Juliet.* Going behind the scenes, so to speak, Tom Stoppard created the Oscar winner *Shakespeare in Love.* Charles Dickens also provided the foundation for many a film favorite: David Lean's immortal *Great Expectations,* George Cukor's *David Copperfield,* and *A Christmas Carol,* with Alastair Sim as Scrooge, top this list, which continues to grow with additions such as Douglas McGrath's *Nicholas Nickleby. Pandaemonium,* about the youthful

Wordsworth and Coleridge, is fanciful but has great Lake District scenery and some insight into the poets' early work.

Harry Potter and the Sorcerer's Stone (in Britain, *Harry Potter and the Philosopher's Stone*), based on the wildly popular children's books by J. K. Rowling, was filmed in many locations, including London, Gloucester, the Cotswolds, Northumbria, and Yorkshire. The film attracted such attention that the British Tourist Authority created a Harry Potter map, "Discovering the Magic of Britain," as a guide to the film sites and places of related interest. The second movie, *Harry Potter and the Chamber of Secrets*, used many of the same settings as the first. Look for *Harry Potter and the Prisoner of Azkaban* in 2004.

Agatha Christie has provided fodder for many beloved flicks. Of the many film versions of her books, one is especially treasured: *Murder, She Said*, which starred the inimitable Margaret Rutherford. With its setting of quaint English village, the harpsichord film score, and the dotty Miss Marple as portrayed by Rutherford, this must be the most English of all the Christie films.

Lovers of opulence, spectacle, and history have many choices—in particular, Robert Bolt's version of Sir Thomas More's life and death, *A Man for All Seasons*. His *Lady Caroline Lamb*, is surely the most beautiful historical film ever made. Richard Harris made a stirring Lord Protector in *Cromwell*, and the miniseries on Queen Elizabeth I, starring Glenda Jackson, is a great BBC addition to videos. Elizabeth's adversary came to breathless life in Vanessa Redgrave's rendition of *Mary, Queen of Scots*, certainly one of her finest performances.

Musicals? Near the top of anyone's list are four films set in England—three of them in Hollywood's England—that rank among the greatest musicals of all time: Walt Disney's *Mary Poppins*, George Cukor's *My Fair Lady*, Sir Carol Reed's Oscar-winner *Oliver!*, and—yeah, yeah, yeah!—the Beatles' *A Hard Day's Night*, a British production.

If you're seeking a look at contemporary Britain, you might view *My Beautiful Laundrette*, about Asians in London, *Secrets and Lies*, about a dysfunctional London family, or *Trainspotting*, about Edinburgh's dark side. Then you might lighten up with *The Full Monty*, about six former steelworkers in Sheffield who become strippers, or one of many romantic comedies: *Notting Hill*, with Julia Roberts and Hugh Grant; Hugh Grant again in *Four Weddings and a Funeral*; Gwyneth Paltrow in *Sliding Doors*; and Renée Zellweger (and Hugh Grant, again) in *Bridget Jones's Diary*. Grant is also good in *About a Boy*, the film version of Nick Hornby's book about a cynical Londoner who learns about commitment.

Quintessentially British are some comedies of the 1950s and 1960s: Alec Guinness's *Kind Hearts and Coronets*, Peter Sellers's *The Mouse That Roared*, and Tony Richardson's Oscar-winner and cinematic style-setter, *Tom Jones*, starring Albert Finney, are some best bets. In 2001, American director Robert Altman took a biting look at the British class system in *Gosford Park*, a country-house murder mystery set in the 1930s that stars fine, mostly British actors from Jeremy Northam to Maggie Smith. A more staid, upstairs-downstairs version set in the same era is the film of the novel *The Remains of the Day*, featuring Anthony Hopkins as the stalwart butler, with Emma Thompson. Today everyone's visions of turn-of-the-last-century England have been captured by the Merchant and Ivory films, notably their *Howard's End*, which won innumerable awards. Douglas McGrath's *Emma*, starring Gwyneth Paltrow, and Ang Lee's *Sense and Sensibility*, starring Emma Thompson and Kate Winslet, are just two of the many film versions of Jane Austen's works.

CHRONOLOGY

3000 BC	First building of Stonehenge (later building 2100–1900 BC)
54 BC–AD 43	Julius Caesar's exploratory invasion of England. Romans conquer England, led by Emperor Claudius
60	Boudicca, a native British queen, razes the first Roman London (Londinium) to the ground
122–27	Emperor Hadrian completes the Roman conquest and builds a wall across the north to keep back the Scottish Picts
300–50	Height of Roman colonization, administered from such towns as Verulamium (St. Albans), Colchester, Lincoln, and York
410	Roman rule of Britain ends, after waves of invasion by Jutes, Angles, and Saxons
ca. 490	Possible period for the legendary King Arthur, who may have led resistance to Anglo-Saxon invaders; in 500 the Battle of Badon is fought
550–700	Seven Anglo-Saxon kingdoms emerge—Essex, Wessex, Sussex, Kent, Anglia, Mercia, and Northumbria—to become the core of English social and political organization for centuries
563	St. Columba, an Irish monk, founds monastery on the Scottish island of Iona; begins to convert Picts and Scots to Christianity
597	St. Augustine arrives in Canterbury to Christianize Britain
871–99	Alfred the Great, king of Wessex, unifies the English against Viking invaders, who are then confined to the northeast
1040	Edward the Confessor moves his court to Westminster and founds Westminster Abbey
1066	William, duke of Normandy, invades, defeats Harold at the Battle of Hastings, and is crowned William I at Westminster in December
1086	Domesday Book completed, a survey of all taxpayers in England, drawn up to assist administration of the realm
1167	Oxford University founded
1170	Thomas à Becket murdered in Canterbury; his shrine becomes center for international pilgrimage
1189	Richard the Lionhearted embarks on the Third Crusade
1209	Cambridge University founded
1215	King John forced to sign Magna Carta at Runnymede; it promulgates basic principles of English law: no taxation except through Parliament, trial by jury, and property guarantees
1272–1307	Edward I, a great legislator; in 1282–83 he conquers Wales and reinforces his rule with a chain of massive castles
1337–1453	Edward III claims the French throne, starting the Hundred Years War. In spite of dramatic English victories—1346 at Crécy, 1356 at Poitiers, 1415 at Agincourt—the long war of attrition ends with the French driving the English out from all but Calais, which finally fell in 1558

1348–49	The Black Death (bubonic plague) reduces the population of Britain to around 2½ million; decades of social unrest follow
1399	Henry Bolingbroke (Henry IV) deposes and murders his cousin Richard II; beginning of the rivalry between houses of York and Lancaster
1402–10	The Welsh, led by Owain Glendŵr, rebel against English rule
1455–85	The Wars of the Roses, the York-Lancaster struggle erupts in civil war
1477	William Caxton prints first book in England
1485	Henry Tudor (Henry VII) defeats Richard III at the Battle of Bosworth and founds the Tudor dynasty; he suppresses private armies, develops administrative efficiency and royal absolutism
1530s	Under Henry VIII the Reformation takes hold; he dissolves the monasteries, finally demolishes medieval England, and replaces it with a restructured society. The land goes to wealthy merchant families, creating new gentry
1555	During the reign of papal supporter Mary I (reigned 1553–58) Protestant Bishops Ridley and Latimer are burned in Oxford; in 1556 Archbishop Cranmer is burned
1558–1603	Reign of Elizabeth I, Protestantism reestablished; Drake, Raleigh, and other freebooters establish English claims in the West Indies and North America
1568	Mary, Queen of Scots, flees to England; in 1587 she is executed
1588	Spanish Armada fails to invade England
1603	James VI of Scotland becomes James I of England
1605	Guy Fawkes and friends plot to blow up Parliament
1611	King James Authorized Version of the Bible published
1620	Pilgrims sail from Plymouth on the *Mayflower* and settle in New England
1629	Charles I dissolves Parliament, decides to rule alone
1642–49	Civil War between the Royalists and Parliamentarians (Cavaliers and Roundheads); the Parliamentarians win
1649	Charles I executed; England is a republic
1653	Oliver Cromwell becomes Lord Protector, England's only dictatorship
1660	The Restoration: Charles II restored to the throne; accepts limits to royal power
1666	The Great Fire: London burns for three days; its medieval center is destroyed
1689	Accession of William III (of Orange) and his wife, Mary II, as joint monarchs; royal power limited still further
1707	Union of English and Scots parliaments under Queen Anne
1714	The German Hanoverians succeed to the throne; George I's lack of English leads to a council of ministers, the beginning of the cabinet system of government
1700s	Under the first four Georges, the Industrial Revolution develops and with it Britain's domination of world trade

1715,
1745–46 — Two Jacobite rebellions fail to restore the House of Stuart to the throne; in 1746 final defeat takes place at Culloden Moor

1756–63 — Seven Years War; Britain wins colonial supremacy from the French in Canada and India

1775–83 — Britain loses the American colonies that become the United States

1795–1815 — Britain and its allies defeat France in the Napoleonic Wars; in 1805, Nelson is killed at Trafalgar; in 1815, Battle of Waterloo is fought

1801 — Union with Ireland

1811–20 — Prince Regent rules during his father's (George III) madness, the Regency period

1825 — The Stockton to Darlington railway, the world's first passenger line with regular service, is established

1832 — The Reform Bill extends the franchise, limiting the power of the great landowners

1834 — Parliament outlaws slavery

1837–1901 — The long reign of Victoria, Britain becomes the world's richest country, and the British Empire reaches its height; railways, canals, and telegraph lines draw Britain into one vast manufacturing net

1851 — The Great Exhibition, Prince Albert's brainchild, is held in the Crystal Palace, Hyde Park

1861 — Prince Albert dies

1887 — Victoria celebrates her Golden Jubilee; in 1901 she dies, marking the end of an era

1914–18 — World War I: fighting against Germany, Britain loses a whole generation, with 750,000 men killed in trench warfare alone; enormous debts and inept diplomacy in the postwar years undermine Britain's position as a world power

1919 — Ireland declares independence from England; bloody Black-and-Tan struggle is one result

1926 — General strike in sympathy with striking coal miners

1936 — Edward VIII abdicates to marry American divorcée Wallis Simpson

1939–45 — World War II: Britain faces Hitler alone until the bombing of Pearl Harbor; London badly damaged during the Blitz, September '40–May '41; Britain's economy shattered

1945 — Labour wins a landslide victory; stays in power for six years, transforming Britain into a welfare state

1952 — Queen Elizabeth II accedes to the throne

1973 — Britain joins the European Economic Community after referendum

1975 — Britain begins to pump North Sea oil

1981 — Marriage of Prince Charles and Lady Diana Spencer

1982 — Falklands regained in war with Argentina

1987 — Conservatives under Margaret Thatcher win a third term in office

1990 — John Major takes over as prime minister, ending Margaret Thatcher's illustrious, if controversial, term in the office

1991 — The Persian Gulf War

1992   Great Britain and the European countries join to form one European Community (EC), whose name was officially changed to European Union in 1993

1994   The Channel Tunnel opens a direct rail link between Britain and Europe

1996   The Prince and Princess of Wales receive a precedent-breaking divorce

1997   "New Labour" comes to power, with Tony Blair as prime minister. Diana, Princess of Wales, dies at 36 in a car crash in Paris. She is buried at Althorp in Northamptonshire

1999   London welcomes the new century on December 31, with the gala opening of the Millennium Dome in Greenwich

2001   The Millennium Dome closes, its future uncertain. An outbreak of foot-and-mouth disease among farm animals causes some tourist sights and walking paths to close for a number of months. Prime Minister Tony Blair is elected to a second term

2002   Queen Elizabeth celebrates her Golden Jubilee. Queen Elizabeth the Queen Mother and Princess Margaret die. Euro coins and notes enter circulation as the currency of 12 European Union nations, but Britain continues to ponder adopting the euro

2003   Britain joins U.S. and coalition forces in invading Iraq

INDEX

NOTES

NOTES

NOTES

NOTES

NOTES

NOTES

NOTES

NOTES

NOTES

FODOR'S KEY TO THE GUIDES

America's guidebook leader publishes guides for every kind of traveler. Check out our many series and find your perfect match.

FODOR'S GOLD GUIDES
America's favorite travel-guide series offers the most detailed insider reviews of hotels, restaurants, and attractions in all price ranges, plus great background information, smart tips, and useful maps.

COMPASS AMERICAN GUIDES
Stunning guides from top local writers and photographers, with gorgeous photos, literary excerpts, and colorful anecdotes. A must-have for culture mavens, history buffs, and new residents.

FODOR'S CITYPACKS
Concise city coverage in a guide plus a foldout map. The right choice for urban travelers who want everything under one cover.

FODOR'S EXPLORING GUIDES
Hundreds of color photos bring your destination to life. Lively stories lend insight into the culture, history, and people.

FODOR'S TRAVEL HISTORIC AMERICA
For travelers who want to experience history firsthand, this series gives in-depth coverage of historic sights, plus nearby restaurants and hotels. Themes include the Thirteen Colonies, the Old West, and the Lewis and Clark Trail.

FODOR'S POCKET GUIDES
For travelers who need only the essentials. The best of Fodor's in pocket-size packages for just $9.95.

FODOR'S FLASHMAPS
Every resident's map guide, with 60 easy-to-follow maps of public transit, parks, museums, zip codes, and more.

FODOR'S CITYGUIDES
Sourcebooks for living in the city: thousands of in-the-know listings for restaurants, shops, sports, nightlife, and other city resources.

FODOR'S AROUND THE CITY WITH KIDS
Up to 68 great ideas for family days, recommended by resident parents. Perfect for exploring in your own backyard or on the road.

FODOR'S HOW TO GUIDES
Get tips from the pros on planning the perfect trip. Learn how to pack, fly hassle-free, plan a honeymoon or cruise, stay healthy on the road, and travel with your baby.

FODOR'S LANGUAGES FOR TRAVELERS
Practice the local language before you hit the road. Available in phrase books, cassette sets, and CD sets.

KAREN BROWN'S GUIDES
Engaging guides—many with easy-to-follow inn-to-inn itineraries—to the most charming inns and B&Bs in the U.S.A. and Europe.

BAEDEKER'S GUIDES
Comprehensive guides, trusted since 1829, packed with A–Z reviews and star ratings.

OTHER GREAT TITLES FROM FODOR'S
Baseball Vacations, The Complete Guide to the National Parks, Family Vacations, Golf Digest's Places to Play, Great American Drives of the East, Great American Drives of the West, Great American Vacations, Healthy Escapes, National Parks of the West, Skiing USA.

At bookstores everywhere.   www.fodors.com/books